I am an MCSE student, and I am currently reading the *Mastering Windows NT Server 4* book. I just had to inform you that **I think this book is absolutely fabulous! The explanations of concepts are well written and easy to understand.** Moreover, this book is full of examples and different techniques that are so helpful! In general, I am very pleased with this book because it has cleared up for me so many misconceptions and gray areas.

Linda Brokopp
Toronto, Canada

I started with NT in July of 1998 and was in total awe as to the magnitude of the O/S. Then I got your book and applied myself, and guess what? **I took the server exam on March 2 and passed!** It was adaptive and also my first time ever. **Your book was and still is a tremendous help.**

Phoebian Monu

I've read your book since the 3.5 version came out, and I usually turn to it when I need an answer. **I've found yours is about the only book that answers the tough questions** and saves me from having to call MS. Thanks, Mark.

Patrick O'Connell
IT Director
Enterprise Technology Corporation
New York, NY

For the last two years I've been an NT instructor at Computer Education Institute in Riverside and Carson. On the first day of a class, during the introduction, I tell my students that the Microsoft Press book is not enough to get them through this course. **I suggest that all of my students purchase *Mastering Windows NT Server 4,* by Mark Minasi, as it will fill in the gaps Microsoft Press missed.** It will also be the book they take with them to a job. Thus far all my students have been very pleased with your writing, and **all of them feel it was worth the investment.**

John M. McKenzie
Project Manager, MobileNetics

Just wanted to mention that **your *Mastering Windows NT Server 4* book has just traveled with me over a 3,500 meters high pass in the Himalayas.** (I've worked for 18 years in Nepal.) Took the book on the trekking tour to prepare me for fine-tuning our office network after my return.

Michael Schueber
Kathmandu, Nepal

5-Star Reviews from Amazon.com of
Mastering Windows NT Server 4

A reader from the U.S.
Excellent !!!
This is the best book in the market. It is so great that all of my students and coworkers love it, and I have learned a great deal from it. The writing style is down-to-earth, and it is written so that it is easy to understand and to laugh with the author's sense of humor. The knowledge of the author is so huge and unquestionable that I wonder whether he was part of the NT 4 developer team.

A reader from Beachwood, NJ
Worth the price
I used this book to help study for the NT Server Exam, and I passed with a 725. The book was also very good even after I passed the test, always using it to find out how to try something on both server and workstation.

A reader from Boston, MA
Fantastic!
I am a teacher, and I double as an NT administrator for a network of about 200 laptops and three NT servers. **This book gives detailed answers about a huge range of NT questions.** It covers things such as installing NT, moving my DHCP services to a different box, configuring NT to support Mac clients, working with IIS, RAS, etc. If you support a network with NT, this is $50 well spent. Subjects such as DHCP and Mac support, which only had a couple of pages in other books, are explained in detail in this one. While no book covers every topic, I think **I'll reach for this one more than any other.**

A reader from USA
This book is great!
After reading this book I feel that I have a firm grasp of what NT 4 is all about. **This is the book that I take with me at all times to use as a reference guide.** I cannot use enough superlatives to describe Mark's writing style. I am so impressed with this book that whenever I need to buy a reference book, I will see whether Mark has written one first.

A reader from Pennsylvania
I've only just begun…this is going to be a great tool!!
I've recently inherited the responsibility of running our company's NT Server. The basics are easy enough to pick up, but when I get into deeper issues, I'm more comfortable with some reference materials and real world experience to lean on. **I've only had this book for three days, and already it has helped me resolve a number of issues.** It reads smoothly with a good balance of visuals. You can crack it open at any page and glean useful information. This is one book I have bought that is going to be well used. Thanks to Mark Minasi for writing it and thanks to Amazon.com for making it so easy to find and buy.

A reader from Minneapolis, MN
The Windows NT bible

This monster pretty much covers everything you would ever want to know about NT. It is about 1,600 pages; each topic is given at least 200 pages, which means that thoroughness is not an issue. **Excellent for administrators, beginners, or intermediates; basically, anyone that uses NT in any form can use this book....*Get it!***

A reader from U.S.
Outstanding

I am an instructor and am always looking for a good reference book. **This one is fantastic.** The writing is easy to understand, making difficult concepts easy to digest.

A reader from Dubai, United Arab Emirates
This is how it should be done

The best thing about the book is the **comprehensive coverage of NT in extremely easy and readable language.** Even my dad understood everything!

A reader from Washington, D.C.
Best technical book I have ever owned!

Having recently moved into the NT world I needed a good, solid book to provide me with an in-depth description of NT networking and administration "how-tos." This book did that and more! The technical depth and good writing style make it the *best* computer book I've seen. **This book is simply a *must have* for anyone working with an NT Server.**

A reader from Chicago, Illinois
MCSE candidates—Stand up and cheer!

If you are looking for certification, then **this is the "all or nothing" book to guide your way.** It can blaze a trail through the NT nightmare into the enlightenment of understanding. Mark Minasi is able to take the complexity out of MS's manuals and bring them down to the level of real-world functionality. The tongue-in-cheek writing style really helped me understand and has helped greatly in the certification process. Thanks Mark—Great Job!

A reader from Bothell, WA
A Swiss Army knife for NT Admins

Clearly written and encyclopedic in scope, this is the first NT book I reach for when I have a problem or a new task to complete that I'm unfamiliar with. The "hot" things today are the dozens of books aimed at helping you to achieve MCSE certification. An unfortunate side-effect of the emphasis on certification study guides, self-guided curricula, cram books, etc., is that solid references that go beyond certification basics are harder than ever to find. **This book is the one that you, too, will reach for after you finally make it through the MCSE jungle and into the real world.**

Mastering™ Windows® NT® Server 4

Seventh Edition

Mark Minasi

San Francisco • Paris • Düsseldorf • Soest • London

Associate Publisher: Roger Stewart
Contracts and Licensing Manager: Kristine O'Callaghan
Acquisitions & Developmental Editor: Diane Lowery
Editors: Peter Weverka, Lee Ann Pickrell, Brenda Frink, Nancy
Conner, Bronwyn Shone Erickson
Technical Editors: Donald Fuller, Scott Warmbrand
Book Designer: Catalin Dulfu
Graphic Illustrators: Patrick Dintino, Catalin Dulfu, Tony Jonick
Electronic Publishing Specialists: Cyndy Johnsen, Kate Kaminski,
Nila Nichols
Project Team Leader: Shannon Murphy
Proofreaders: Patrick J. Peterson, David Nash
Indexer: Matthew Spence
CD Technician: Keith McNeil
CD Coordinator: Kara Schwartz
Cover Designer: Archer Design
Cover Photographer: The Image Bank

First edition copyright ©1995 SYBEX Inc.
Second edition copyright ©1996 SYBEX Inc.
Third edition copyright ©1996 SYBEX Inc.
Fourth edition copyright ©1997 SYBEX Inc.

Fifth edition copyright © 1998 SYBEX Inc.
Sixth edition copyright © 1999 SYBEX Inc.

Library of Congress Card Number: 99-69350
ISBN: 0-7821-2693-6

Manufactured in the United States of America
10 9 8 7 6 5 4 3

*This book is dedicated to the many good friends that a professional life of teaching, writing, and traveling has brought me—how else could a kid from Noo Yawk grow up to have buddies around the world? Sean, Gary, Dina, Mark (and Mark and Mark and…gosh, there's a lot of us!), Karen, Rita, Peter, Dawn, Caro, Mick, Paula, Dr. Stang, Susan, Manginelli, Patrice & Phil, Neil, Guy, the PF11ers (you know who you are…), Mary, Mike, Wayne, Christa…it seems I find myself with an embarrassment of riches. Remember those months when I sometimes didn't return phone calls as often as I should, guys? **This** is why…*

ACKNOWLEDGMENTS

HEY, DON'T TURN THE PAGE!!! This is where all the people who did the actual work on this book get credit. I mean, how would you like it if *you* helped put a book out and no one knew, hmmm? Listen, it's a really big book, it's not like you're going to get through it in one sitting, so slow down and read the acknowledgments. Please?

I wish I could truthfully say that "I wrote this book." It didn't work that way, however—very few books get written by just one person. Elizabeth Creegan, Christa Anderson, Peter Dyson, Eric Christiansen, Lisa Justice, and Kris Ashton have all helped out in one edition or another.

I did all the updates on the seventh and sixth editions (so there's no one else to blame, I guess), but the fifth edition welcomed Peter Dyson, who wrote the big new chapter on Internet Information Server, and Lisa Justice, who created the new coverage of user profiles. Peter's one of the world's great experts on IIS, and Lisa is just plain stubborn in her insistence on working with things until she understands everything about them.

Big thanks go to Elizabeth "Maeve" Creegan and Christa Anderson, the folks who wrote the initial versions of a number of chapters. When we first put together the NT 3.1 version of this book, Maeve and Christa were both research assistants in my employ, doing some of the spadework needed to get the book underway. I became very busy, and so I asked them to try their hands at writing some of the chapters in this book. They both wrote very good stuff indeed. They haven't been involved with the past three editions, but there's a fair amount of their writing still on these pages: Christa's work is still evident in Chapters 4, 8, and 16, and Maeve wrote the initial versions of (if memory serves) Chapters 6, 7, and 11, as well as the write-up on the Event Viewer in Chapter 16 and the Appendix.

Thanks also to Kris Ashton and Eric Christiansen. Kris, who knows about a million times more about Macs than I do, wrote Chapter 10. Eric did the section on kernel debuggers that now fills out the chapter on disaster recovery, the first version of the section on automating NT setups in Chapter 3, and the previous version of the Internet Information Server section.

Getting to the nitty-gritty of any product is much easier when you've got the help of people who know it inside and out and who can generously provide software and hardware for review, as well as access to experts. One such group is the Compaq-formerly-Digital-Equipment-Corp NT Wizards. Gregg Laird coordinates that particular bunch of NT *uber*-geeks and is always willing to help out. (He makes the phone calls, Nancy Gallagher does the work.) Peter Hubbard, Bill Harris, Canada Steve, Australia Steve, Ken, Gary, Anders, the one and only Steve Davis (the Bringer of Alpha Hardware) and the other Wizards (whose names escape me because it's late when I'm writing this—sorry guys!) typify the best of techiedom: people who like learning things but who *really* delight in sharing what they know. But none of the Wizards' good works could happen without the support of John Rose and others in the management suite. At this writing, it looks like Wizards is dead, and that's a sad thing. But the Compaq/Digital User's Group folks may pick up that slack, so stay tuned!

And speaking of experts, many thanks to the dozens of Microsoft people who freely shared inside information about NT—as long as I promised not to mention their names! (I *can*, however, mention Mark Hassall of Microsoft and Ann Marie Brauner of Waggener-Edstrom, so thanks very much.)

The folks at Sybex are always a pleasure to work with. Without the vision of people like Roger Stewart, Gary Masters, Rodnay Zaks, and the late lamented Rudy Langer, these books wouldn't exist. Bronwyn Erickson edited this monster and made sure that a preposition was something that I never ended a sentence with. She *also* kept participles from dangling.

Dann McDorman, Nancy Conner, Peter Weverka, Lee Ann Pickrell, and Brenda Frink edited the previous editions. Many thanks to all five of them. Thanks also to production coordinators Michael Tom, Charles Mathews, and Shannon Murphy, and desktop publishers Cyndy Johnsen, Kate Kaminiski, and Nila Nichols. And thanks to tech editor Scot Wormbrnad.

My research assistant Brenda Davidson suffered the tireless drudgery of actually *reading* this stuff and converting it into a format that the Sybex word processors could understand. (That process was made quite a bit easier by a Word template authored by Sybex's own Guy Hart-Davis and Liz Paulus.) Brenda's comments and suggestions were invaluable.

Thanks also to the folks at Microsoft for producing a high-quality product worth writing about! (And I'm talking here about *NT*, not Word. I could have gotten this done a couple of weeks early if Word didn't like crashing so much....)

CONTENTS AT A GLANCE

Appendix

TABLE OF CONTENTS

INTRODUCTION

For Those Who've Never Read a Previous Edition

Did you *plan* to become a network administrator? I sure didn't. Very few of us answered the childhood question, "What do you want to be when you grow up?" by saying, "A network administrator." Nevertheless, there are plenty of network administrators. (The money's good, right?) For me, running a network was kind of a "sink or swim" exercise, but I initially managed to keep my head above water, and now administering a network is actually a lot of fun.

And it ought to be some fun. NT Server version 3.51 and 4 (this book will help you with either version) is a terrific but not flawless network operating system. I enjoy working with NT Server even when I struggle with it in the wee hours of the morning. ("It's *my* data, you stupid operating system—give it to me, you scurrilous software!") NT was surprisingly robust and well designed from its first incarnation. However, I'm told that an F-18 fighter jet is well designed, but I wouldn't want to fly one of *those* without guidance from someone who has flown them before—hence this book. There are a number of books about NT Server, but the one you are holding in your hands has been for the past six years the bestseller. How is this book different from the rest?

When NT first arrived, I looked around for a book about running a LAN with NT. Amazingly, there was only one: John Ruley's (no longer around, alas—the book, not John). Virtually every publisher had put out a book about NT Workstation, but most had skipped NT Server altogether! The best I could do was find a few books that claimed to cover both Workstation and Server. In reality, these books were Workstation books with a few bones tossed to us Server folks. Server-centric books are scarce to this day, and most of *them* are basically old Workstation books with some Server advice thrown in or slightly-better-worded knockoffs of the Resource Kit. Books like that are certainly large and impressive, but finding answers in them is something of a treasure hunt. I didn't need a huge book. I just needed a how-to manual on NT networking. And not only did I have to run a network, I had to teach classes on NT networking, so I started assembling notes on NT networking as I learned. The result? This book.

Along the way, I'd stumble across a dialog box that solved a particular problem and think, "Why did it take me so long to find this?" Those of us who worked on this book agreed to the following rule: If we got stuck trying to get a task done and needed more than 30 seconds to figure out how to do it, we would cover the problem and give its solution in a "How Do I…" section of the book. In each "How Do I…" section, you will find click-by-click instructions for solving a particular problem.

Another problem I ran up against was the poor quality of Microsoft documentation. My intention isn't to beat up on Microsoft; in fact there is, in some areas of the documentation, a completeness that I find amazing. But Microsoft's documentation tends to be organized along the lines of "We have a program called the User Manager, and here's what all of its menu items do," when what I *needed* was "How do I create and maintain user accounts?" or "How do I build a login script?" The documentation is often silent on some very basic questions, such as these:

- How should I organize the shares on a basic file server?

- How can I build some fault-tolerance into my DHCP (Dynamic Host Configuration Protocol) servers?

- What steps do I go through to get DOS clients on my NT network?

- How do I troubleshoot a "no domain controller was available" error?

Nearly everyone comes up against these questions early when setting up an NT network, but the answers to these questions are not mentioned in the Microsoft documentation. Normally, that's not a terrible thing (hey, nobody's perfect); but in the case of NT, Microsoft charges $195 to answer questions about NT Server! (For questions about NT Workstation, you get *one* free call—kind of like when you get arrested, I suppose.) Furthermore, the Microsoft people are under a tremendous amount of time pressure when putting out documentation, and as a result some of the details in their explanations of how to do something, step-by-step explanations, just plain don't always work. That's often because they *did* work in beta versions of the software, but not in the distribution versions. Something I've tried very hard to do in this book is to check on a click-by-click and keystroke-by-keystroke basis that all of this stuff works as advertised.

This book's intent is to introduce you to NT and NT's way of doing things, show you how to set up NT so it gives you minimum trouble, teach you how to use the built-in tools to administer the network, and show you how to move to building and running big networks. With this book, you can plan, configure, install, run, and repair networks that include NT Server. And, because many of you are still running the odd 3.51 server, we cover 3.51 as well.

But that's not all I intended for this book. Today's networks don't just need simple file server capabilities; more and more networks require client-server capabilities, and NT Server actually rivals Novell NetWare in that department. Furthermore, NT Server is fairly cheap compared to Novell NetWare, which makes it even more attractive as a simple file server.

Still, most companies don't throw away their existing NetWare networks, which means that today's networks often have more than one kind of server software. There are often Novell file servers, NT Server database servers, perhaps a Unix NFS system, and the connections to the old mainframes. Additionally, everyone's jumping on the Internet bandwagon.

This multi-network world is great for users, but it's a real headache for network managers, who not only have to support all the different network operating systems but also have to support their interaction. Too many networking books are written on the assumption that the reader has one and only one kind of network. Throughout the planning of *this* book, I assumed that only the lucky few have networks composed solely of NT Server servers. (Those of you in that category should count your blessings.)

Introduction to the Seventh Edition

It's the year 2000; by the time you read this, Windows 2000 will either be shipping, or will be close to shipping. So why are we doing another edition of *Mastering Windows NT Server 4*? And—the question you're probably most wondering about—if you own an earlier version of the book, should you buy this one?

We came out with this edition for two reasons: to fix a large list of small errors, and to add two new chapters—the "premium" content. No matter how hard I try, there are always a few bugs in the text, particularly a text this size. Readers helpfully send me notes about errors that they come across, and as I reread sections I come across them. This edition fixes about 50 errors. Most are small, but as *any* are annoying, they're gone now.

The Extra Chapters

The extra chapters focus on how to get your job done more easily as an NT administrator, and help you get ready for Windows 2000. You'll find the new chapter "Using the Best Resource Kit Utilities" will make your life easier. There are a ton of great utilities packaged in the NT 4 Resource Kit, but their documentation isn't always the greatest. As a result, some real gems sit unused. Over the past two and some years, I've written a monthly column in *Windows NT Magazine* called "This Old Resource Kit." Every month, I choose a bit of hidden resource kit gold and first describe a common problem that administrators face, then demonstrate how a particular resource kit tool can solve that problem. With the kind permission of *Windows NT Magazine*, I've collected those columns, revised them, and combined them into that chapter.

You may not adopt Windows 2000 the day that it arrives, but within the next two years you'll almost certainly end up replacing old familiar NT 4 with this newer, far more powerful replacement tool. But putting Windows 2000 on your network requires a bit more work than just popping the Windows 2000 CD into a drive and running Setup. There are some fundamentally new technologies here, including Active Directory, Remote Installation Services, Plug and Play, Intellimirror, and other tools that you really need to know a bit about before putting them on your network. That's the job of the last chapter. It offers you a quick, easy-to-read overview of all of the new Windows 2000 parts and pieces. Once you understand that chapter, you'll be better equipped to start learning more about the specific parts of Windows 2000, as needed.

Who Should Buy This Edition?

Of course, I'd like for everyone who picks this up to buy it—hey, I've got a mortgage to pay like everyone else! But this book may be right for some and not for others.

As I said earlier, this book is basically the sixth edition with a number of errors corrected and the two chapters—the Resource Kit and the Windows 2000 chapters—added. If you've got the sixth edition, then use that information to decide whether or not it's worth buying.

On the other hand, if you have the fifth edition or any earlier editions, then I strongly feel that you'd benefit from this edition. See the following section—the original introduction to the sixth edition—for more details, but basically in the sixth I got a chance to overhaul a number of things (e.g., file permissions, RAS, security), add a number of new things (unattended installations, DHCP/WINS/DNS network design and disaster recovery, Windows Terminal Server, troubleshooting "No Domain Controller Found" errors and logins in general), and greatly expand others (system policies, home directories, troubleshooting, Alpha coverage), making the sixth an essential buy (in *my* opinion, anyway).

How Come It's Smaller Than the Last Edition?

It's not. It just *looks* that way.

If you put this edition next to a sixth edition on the shelf, you'll notice that the spine of this edition is a bit slimmer than the spine on the sixth. But that *doesn't* mean that the book has fewer pages. It's got to do with how books get put together.

You see, it's extremely expensive to bind a book that is physically wider than the sixth edition. "Extremely expensive" for Sybex would, not surprisingly, translate to a higher book price, and we wanted to avoid that. So the next best thing was slightly thinner paper. Compare the number of pages and you'll see—the sixth edition had about 1616 pages of content and this one has about 1700.

> **NOTE**   The following two sections "Introduction for the 'Alumni': What You'll Get from the Sixth Edition" and "What's New in the Fifth Edition" are included for readers of the fifth and fourth editions; these give overviews of the improvements you'll find over the edition you currently own.

Introduction for the "Alumni": What You'll Get from the Sixth Edition

Judging by the number of copies that this book has sold in earlier editions, an incredible percentage of NT administrators the world over have at least one copy of it. (And if you're one of those, let me say: *thank you!* Thanks. *Gracias. Merci. Spasibo. Grazie. Danke.* And any other way I can think to say it, hundreds of thousands of times over…) If you're standing in the Computer section of your bookstore and are eyeballing NT books, the chances are good that you've already *got* a copy of this book, in an earlier edition. So the logical question you're asking yourself is, "Should I get a newer edition of a book I already own, or should I buy somebody else's completely different book?" *This* Introduction is for those people: call it the "alumni page." (As I assume in this section that you *are* one of the alumni, I'll presume that it's okay to descend into Jargon Hell so that I can explain this edition's benefits quickly. For those who have *never* read a copy of this book before, I recommend that you skip this part of the Introduction, and I *promise* that if you read the book this will all be explained clearly and sequentially. Really.)

The first thing that is likely to occur to the veteran reader of *Mastering Windows NT Server* is that there are basically the same number of pages as in the fifth edition, which doesn't *seem* to bode well for those seeking lots of new information, so let me hasten to tell you that there are actually 211 more pages in this edition than in the fifth edition.

"Huh?" I hear you say, with a skeptically raised eyebrow. It's true that the fifth edition had 1,618 pages and this edition has about the same number, but there's a bit of a story there. You see, roughly 1,600 pages is just about the maximum possible number of pages in North American hardback books; the binding machines that most printers use can't hold more sheets in a book, unless they go to thinner, see-through paper. The fifth edition maxed that size out, and the sixth came up with 200+ more pages, so what to do? Option One would be to break it up into multiple volumes, but we hated that idea, so Option Two was to tighten up the text a bit. As a result, there's a little less white space in this edition, but more information!

Second, what's the occasion for this edition, on the possible eve of the arrival NT 5…oops, I mean Windows 2000? I mean, isn't *everyone* going to be using Win2K, rendering this edition pointless? I'm guessing not. Sure, I'm hard at work right now on the Win2K version of this book, but I hadn't had a chance to update this book in about a year, and I think most of us will be using NT 4 a year or two into the new millennium, at least until Service Pack 3 for Win2K. Recently, Service Pack 4 arrived and I've finally had the time to go learn *bunches* of new stuff. There was just so much of it that I begged Sybex to let me do a final edition of the NT 4 book, and they assented. (It's just flatly amazing how agreeable people can be when you're holding their firstborn over a tank full of sharks.) And if Win2K doesn't ship by mid-2000, don't be surprised if you see *another* edition of this book.

Here's what you get with this edition.

Expanded, Updated, and SP4-ed WINS, DHCP, and DNS

If you're using TCP/IP in your network (and if you're not, then you soon will be), WINS, DHCP, and DNS are three central, core, indispensable technologies. DNS has been around for a while, but DHCP and WINS are essentially two Microsoft inventions. Of the two, WINS is the one that provides the most headaches; one Microsoft insider told me that WINS generates more support calls than any other NT network technology. DHCP, WINS, and DNS were all significantly affected and improved by Service Pack 4, and that's all covered here.

Previous editions of this book haven't really done justice to understanding and solving WINS problems in a big network, and I fixed that in this edition. (Minasi's First Law of Networks: "Everything always works on small networks.") In this edition, you'll learn how to effectively design a network with more than one WINS server; believe it or not, *there's only one WINS configuration that Microsoft will support*, and they don't document that configuration—but Chapter 14 does. You'll learn why you should never put WINS on a primary domain controller, when to tombstone versus when to delete, and how the new "NBTSTAT –RR" command will make your life easier. The coverage of the extremely useful LMHOSTS file is about four times larger than the fifth edition's, and if you don't think you need LMHOSTS files in your network, please read that section in Chapter 14!

As with WINS, the DHCP writeup needed more information relevant to those of you running bigger networks, and Chapter 14 delivers that. You'll read about DHCP relay agents and the perils of putting more than 100 scopes on a DHCP server, as well as a complete review and explanation of how SP4 changes DHCP. This edition also has a complete, step-by-step explanation of how to back up and restore a DHCP database for trouble-free disaster recovery. (I'm tempted to call it "undocumented information," because while there are three different Microsoft Knowledge Base articles about how to back up and restore a DHCP server, they all suggest different things, and they're all at least a little wrong. My writeup was tested and re-tested with several machines, so I *hope* it's useful to you.)

DNS is not only important in NT 4 networks, it will be staggeringly important in Win2K networks. That's why the DNS coverage in this section includes more explanation of zones and secondary DNS servers, setting up a "caching-only" DNS server for your workgroup as well as, again, step-by-step explanations of how to back up and recover a DNS server—again, something that Microsoft's Knowledge Base partially but not completely documents. The DNS section finishes with detailed information about how Service Pack 4 changes and improves DNS.

Windows Terminal Server Coverage

The latest member of the Windows NT Server family, Windows Terminal Server, is a very neat addition. Based on a technology called *Winframe* that you may know of from a company named Citrix, Terminal Server lets you centralize your NT computing by setting up one server to be a sort of "mainframe" and then putting very cheap, simple, dumb terminals on users' desks. Despite the "dumb terminal" name, though, the users never know that they're on a dumb terminal, because it looks and behaves like a Windows NT desktop. It's got some fantastic uses both in the office *and*, I argue in Chapter 9, in the home. Terminal Server's coverage in Chapter 9 also includes a description of the insofar-as-I-can-determine undocumented command-line utilities that you can use to administer a Terminal Server, and some suggested places where Terminal Server could make sense for you.

"No Domain Controller Found" Troubleshooting

Anyone who's been running an NT network for a while is all too familiar with the irritating "No domain controller was found to validate your login" error message. The network seems to be running fine, but now and then it just refuses to do a login. What causes this, and what to do about it?

As it turns out, this is a bigger problem than just a user-can't-log-in problem. Logon failures cause broken trust relationships in big NT networks, as well, so pinpointing their cause and fixing them is essential. Sections of Chapters 12 and 17 both explain the problem and offer some very specific—and previously undocumented—solutions. They also describe a Service Pack 4 utility, SETPRFDC, that can greatly reduce the probability of broken trust relationships.

Advanced Install Scripting

I have to reinstall the NT software on my desktop constantly because of all of the experimentation that I do. But it's time consuming and boring to have to baby-sit the NT Setup program, so I learned early on how to build automated, hands-off installation scripts. But NT 4 shipped in 1996, and I find that virtually every piece of hardware in my shop has network cards, video boards, and SCSI cards that were designed *after* 1996, which means that NT Setup can't recognize them. That meant figuring out how to do unattended installs even with oddball video, network, and disk hardware—and Chapter 3 has all the details.

Of course, just setting NT up is only the first step—then you have to add your favorite applications, set up Explorer the way you want it, and apply the latest service pack. That can also be time consuming, but Chapter 3 shows you how to automate all *that*, as well. You'll find that with a bit of practice you can create an installation script for a new machine in about half an hour the first time. And once you understand how to use SYSDIFF, you can make automated installs do almost anything that you want them to. (Except load sound card drivers; grumble, grumble, grumble...)

Is it worth it? Well, I've got a batch file on my computer that will wipe out my current NT configuration, install NT, apply Service Pack 4, Word, and Powerpoint, as well as set up the Explorer the way I like it—and from the time I start up the batch file to the time that the machine's ready is *13 minutes*, start to finish. It's all in Chapter 3, along with another much-needed addition: Alpha coverage. I've been using an Alpha for the past year or so, and you'll see that reflected in Alpha discussions throughout the book.

NTFS Permissions Explained and Home Directories Fixed

One of the most important tools that an administrator can use to secure her network is the file and directory permissions available on NTFS volumes. I didn't like my old writeup on how they work and what they do, so I threw it away and re-wrote it, mostly from scratch.

And have you ever tried to make home directories work under NT? It's difficult, and in some cases it's impossible to do it Microsoft's way. But there's a free piece of code that you can find on Microsoft's Web site that makes home directories *finally* work the way they're supposed to... *if* your users run NT on their desktops. Chapter 7 covers NTFS and home directories in detail. Even if you're an NT vet, I'll bet these new and re-written sections will make NT administration just a bit easier.

And Lots More, with Thanks...

SP4 brings a profile quota manager named Proquota, but Microsoft hasn't documented it; Chapter 7 does. If you're using NT as a dial-to-the-Internet router, some free code called "Steelhead" will make life easier, and you can read about it in Chapters 14 and 18. You can fix many logon failures by load balancing domain controllers, and Chapter 11 shows you how. Ever tried to delete the C: that's been formatted as NTFS? FDISK can't do it, but Chapter 3 can show you how. Got an empty or near-empty Network Neighborhood when you dial into your company's network with Dial-Up Networking? Chapter 18's got the fix for The Case of the Empty Network Neighborhood. Promoted a BDC to PDC but it doesn't seem to recognize it? Hack the Registry to make it see things your way, in Chapter 11. Need to do an NT repair on a system without a CD-ROM? No problem, Chapter 17's got the details…

This edition does all that and a lot more. As always, one of the most important features of a new addition is that I get a chance to comb through a previous edition and try to weed out the bugs. This time, I got help from many of you, including (in no special order) Chad Dickey, Erich Paetow, Dean Giblin, Shawn Bayem, Bob Flenniken, Alan Spaeth, Reg Harbeck, Murat Yildirimoglu, and others whom I've probably forgotten (many apologies if you're one of them).

I tried very hard to put enough in this (hopefully) last edition to ensure that there was enough value added to make it worth the while of those of you who have faithfully purchased every edition back to the NT 3.5 book. I sincerely hope that you enjoy it!

And if you're *still* in the bookstore reading, take the silly thing over to the cash register, okay? This isn't a library, you know…

What's New in the Fifth Edition?

But some of you "upgraders" didn't buy the fifth edition; you own the fourth and are wondering what *else* this book has, as it contains the material in the fifth edition, as well. The fifth edition brought five (appropriately) areas of improvement.

First, we thought that the release of Internet Information Server version 4 was very significant to most NT networkers for two reasons: (1) it's a significant upgrade that's being used in a lot of enterprises and (2) the next version of NT, NT 5, will essentially make *every* NT Server a Web server. So even if you're not doing any intranetting, you should spend some time hacking around with IIS 4 just to get ready. For help with that hacking around, see Chapter 15.

Second, I've been wanting to offer this book on CD-ROM for a while, to simplify looking for things. The fifth edition included the book in CD format, and this sixth edition continues that—but we've redone it using Adobe Acrobat, a tool I like a bit better than the last system we used. If you ever find yourself saying "I *know* I saw that somewhere…" I hope you'll find the CD useful!

Third, I wanted to provide more information about user profiles and system policies. If you're trying to centralize supporting Windows 95/98 and NT users on your NT Server, then be sure to take a look at Chapters 6 and 7, where you'll find this new information.

Fourth, I went down to a Microsoft testing center one day without doing any preparation and took the two NT Server 4.0 exams ("Implementing" and "Enterprise") to see how well the book would prepare me for the exams. We had *most* of the test concepts in the book, but we were silent on a few of the exam-question areas. I've added paragraphs throughout the book to make sure that we cover it all.

Fifth, I learn new things all the time about NT, and this edition was a chance to share those things with you. There's expanded coverage of how NT security works; more advice on securing *your* network; more details on file, directory, and printer permissions; more on tuning NT Servers; a discussion on "cloning" NT installations from machine to machine; more details on NT disaster recovery (learned the *hard* way); a more "by the RFC" discussion of subnetting and non-routable addresses; amplification on putting logon scripts on backup domain controllers; a few words of caution on Windows 95's FAT32 disk format; and a whole lot more!

A Brief History of NT

Even in the early 1980s, Bill Gates knew that networking was a key to owning the computer business. So, on April 15, 1985, Microsoft released its first networking product, a tool called MS-NET, and its companion operating system, DOS 3.10. Most people knew about the new DOS and were puzzled at its apparent lack of new features. What it contained, however, were architectural changes to DOS that made it a bit friendlier to the idea of networks.

Now, Microsoft wasn't big enough at that time to create much hoopla about a new network operating system, so they let others sell it. It sold mainly in the guise of the IBM PC Network Support Program; IBM viewed it as little more than some software to go along with their PC Network LAN boards and, later, their

Token Ring cards. The server software was DOS-based, offered minimal security, and, to be honest, performed terribly. But the software had two main effects on the market.

First, the fact that IBM sold a LAN product legitimized the whole industry. IBM made it possible for others to make a living selling network products. And that led to the second effect: the growth of Novell. Once the idea of a LAN was legitimized, most companies responded by going out and getting the LAN operating system that offered the best bang for the buck. That was an easy decision: NetWare. In the early days of networking, Novell established itself as the performance leader. You could effectively serve about twice as many workstations with Novell NetWare as you could with any of the MS-NET products. So Novell prospered.

As time went on, however, Microsoft got better at building network products. 3Com, wanting to offer a product that was compatible with the IBM PC Network software, licensed MS-NET and resold it as their "3+" software. 3Com knew quite a bit about networking, however, and recognized the limitations of MS-NET. So 3Com reworked MS-NET to improve its performance, a fact that didn't escape Microsoft's attention.

From 1985 to 1988, Microsoft worked on their second generation of networking software. The software was based on their OS/2 version 1 operating system. (Remember, Microsoft was the main driving force behind OS/2 from 1985 through early 1990. Steve Ballmer, Microsoft's number two guy, promised publicly in 1988 that Microsoft would "go the distance with OS/2." Hey, the world changes and you've got to change with it, right?) Seeing the good work that 3Com did with MS-NET, Microsoft worked as a partner with 3Com to build the next generation of LAN software. Called Microsoft LAN Manager, this network server software was built atop the more powerful OS/2 operating system. As with the earlier MS-NET, Microsoft's intention was never to directly market LAN Manager. Instead, they envisioned IBM, 3Com, Compaq, and others selling it.

IBM did indeed sell LAN Manager (they still do in the guise of OS/2 LAN Server). 3Com sold LAN Manager for years as 3+Open but found little profit in it and got out of the software business. In late 1990, Compaq announced that they would not sell LAN Manager because it was too complex a product for their dealers to explain, sell, and support. Microsoft decided then that if LAN Manager was to be sold, they'd have to do the selling, so they announced on the very same day as the Compaq withdrawal that they would begin selling LAN Manager directly.

LAN Manager in its first incarnation still wasn't half the product that Novell NetWare was, but it was getting there. LAN Manager 2 greatly closed the gap, and in fact, on some benchmarks LAN Manager outpaced Novell NetWare. Additionally, LAN Manager included administrative and security features that brought it even closer to Novell NetWare in the minds of many network managers. Slowly, LAN Manager gained about a 20-percent share of the network market.

When Microsoft designed LAN Manager, however, they designed it for the 286 chip (more accurately, I should say again that LAN Manager was built atop OS/2 1.*x*, and OS/2 1.*x* was built for the 286 chip). LAN Manager's inherent 286 nature hampered its performance and sales. In contrast, Novell designed their premier products (NetWare 3 and 4) to use the full capabilities of the 386 and later processors. Microsoft's breakup with IBM delayed the release of a 386-based product and, in a sense, Microsoft never released the 386-based product.

Instead of continuing to climb the ladder of Intel processor capabilities, Microsoft decided to build a processor-independent operating system that would sit in roughly the same market position as Unix. It could then be implemented for the 386 and later chips, and it also could run well on other processors, such as the PowerPC, Alpha, and MIPS chips. Microsoft called this new operating system NT, for *new* technology. Not only would NT serve as a workstation operating system, it would also arrive in a network server version to be called *LAN Manager NT*. No products ever shipped with that name, but the wallpaper that NT Server displays when no one is logged onto it is called LANMANNT.BMP to this day.

In August of 1993, Microsoft released LAN Manager NT with the name *NT Advanced Server*. In a shameless marketing move, they referred to it as version 3.1 in order to match the version numbers of the Windows desktop products. This first version of NT Advanced Server performed quite well. However, it was memory-hungry, it lacked Novell connectivity, and it had only the most basic TCP/IP connectivity.

September of 1994 brought a new version and a new name: Microsoft Windows NT Server version 3.5, dropping "Advanced" from the name. Version 3.5 was mainly a "polish" of 3.1; it was less memory-hungry, it included Novell and TCP/IP connectivity right in the box, and it included Windows for Workgroups versions of the administrative tools so network administrators could work from a Workgroup machine rather than an NT machine. Where many vendors would spend 13 months adding silly bells and whistles, NT 3.5 showed that the Microsoft folks had spent most of their time fine-tuning the operating system, trimming its memory requirements, and speeding it up.

In October of 1995 came NT version 3.51, which mainly brought support for PCMCIA cards (a real boon for us traveling instructor types), file compression, and a raft of bug fixes.

NT version 4, 1996's edition of NT, has a new face and a bunch of new features, but no really radical networking changes. If you are a network administrator under NT version 3.51, you'll find 4 a snap to learn. The *big* changes will come with the version of NT called Windows 2000 Server, which will probably appear in mid-February 2000, just about the same time this book will come out.

What's in This Book

If you're reading this, then you made it past that huge table of contents. Here's the 25-cent tour of what's inside this book.

The book starts in Part I with an overview of NT's strengths, as well as a look at the features new to version 4. Then I take you through Chapter 2, "Microsoft Enterprise Concepts," where I introduce you to the overall Microsoft approach to networking so that you understand what a workgroup and a domain are, among other things.

In Part II, we roll up our sleeves and install NT Server. I show you the step-by-step method that works best for me and produces the least problems in the long run. Following that, you'll want to set up your disk drives for maximum performance and fault-tolerance, and Chapter 4 shows you how to do that. Part II finishes off with a chapter on the NT Registry, the place where NT keeps all of its internal configuration information. All network administrators end up twiddling the Registry, and this chapter shows you how.

Part III shows you how to run an NT network—it's the "administration" unit, so to speak. Chapter 6 shows you how to create user accounts. Working with passwords, groups, profiles, logon hours, auditing—it's all there. Following that is a complementary chapter on creating file shares on an NT network. You learn the differences between share-level permissions and file and directory permissions, how file ownership works, and how to create home directories. Chapters 6 and 7 conclude with an explanation of how to write top-quality logon scripts. Chapter 8 follows that with a discussion of sharing printers. Chapters 9 and 10 show you how to attach client PCs (Chapter 9) and Macintoshes (Chapter 10) to an NT network. You see how to put the client software on the machine, how to attach it to a domain, and how to log in, change passwords, browse the network, and attach to shares.

In Chapter 11, you see how to manage single domains. You see how to create directory replication, something that *looks* scary but isn't bad when someone takes you through it step-by-step. In this chapter, I also explain the nuts and bolts of how to design a domain. How many users should you have in the domain? How many backup domain controllers do you need? It's all there.

In Part IV, we talk about managing NT Server in an enterprise network. Chapter 12 shows you how to run an "enterprise" network, a network of some size and perhaps with more than one network architecture all under one roof. In Chapter 12, you see how to design and manage multi-domain networks. Chapter 13 covers Novell integration. NT networks with NetWare servers will adopt one of the "three D's"—détente, deception, or dismissal. Put more simply, you either continue to run two networks in parallel (détente), run some software to fool your system into thinking that the NT servers are NetWare servers or vice versa (deception), or look for advice on how to smoothly move from NetWare to NT (dismissal).

You can't spell *Internet* without *NT*, so that's the topic of the largest chapter in this book, Chapter 14. If, like others, your firm has been swept up in the tide of Internet fever, you may be a bit confused about IP addresses, CIDR blocks, subnet masks, and static routing. That's covered in the first part of the chapter, a tutorial on the Internet's TCP/IP protocol. Then we move along to an in-depth discussion of implementing TCP/IP on your NT network, including the Dynamic Host Configuration Protocol (DHCP) and the Windows Internet Naming Service (WINS). There's also a big section on name resolution, where you learn about both WINS and the Domain Naming Service (DNS): what they do, how they're similar, and how they're different.

Chapter 15 is a soup-to-nuts discussion of the Internet Information Server 4, Microsoft's Web server software. While I can't get a concrete statistic, I keep hearing that over fifty percent of the Internet Web servers, and some much larger percentage of *intranet* Web servers, run NT. My guess would be that most of them run IIS; hence this chapter. Not only is IIS one of the fastest Web servers around, it can also host (with the new version 4) a news server, Active Server Pages, a "chat server," and more.

Chapter 16 discusses tuning and monitoring an NT network, with the essential guide to the Performance Monitor. I'll show you just a few counters that you can monitor to keep track of your network's health. But if the network *does* take ill, then you'll turn to Chapter 17 and see how to recover from disaster. Ever wondered how to read an NT "blue screen?" It's there. And Chapter 18 wraps things up with an explanation of Remote Access Services, including a cookbook that'll show you how to use RAS to route two separate offices over a WAN!

As you read earlier, Chapter 19 gives you an overview of Resource Kit utilities, and Chapter 20 introduces the Windows 2000 Server.

Finally, the appendix shows you how to use the command prompt to "NET results."

Conventions Used in This Book

In this book, things can be quite complex, so I've followed some conventions to make them clearer and easier to understand.

*x*86 versus RISC

The term "*x*86," which is used in this book and in similar books, refers to any machine that uses a processor in the Intel line, including the 8086, 8088, 80188, 80186, 80286, 80386DX, 80386SL, 80386SX, 80486DX, 80486SX, 80486SL, 80486DX2, Intel DX4, the Pentium, and Pentium Pro processors.

When I am referring to client machines, I could be referring to any of these processors. When I am referring to an NT Server or NT Workstation system, then it must be one of the 386, 486, Pentium, or Pentium Pro families of chips.

RISC is short for, as you probably know, Reduced Instruction Set Chip. As I write this, NT is available for the Compaq Alpha processor, but there will be no new support for that processor unfortunately. Once it supported the MIPS R4000 RISC processor and the IBM/Motorola/Apple Power PC chip, but that's no more. (Ironically enough, I found that my Casio Windows CE palm-sized PC uses an R4000. I haven't liked CE much and pretty much stick with my PalmPilot. But I wonder if I can get NT 3.1 to run on the Casio?)

All RISC systems must follow a standard called the Advanced RISC Computer (ARC) standard. For that reason, I generically refer to these three RISC families as "RISC," even though internally they are quite different. That's the good thing about NT: as an architecture-independent operating system, it masks hardware differences.

Our Assumption: The System Is on the C: Drive

If you're running NT Server on an *x86*-based machine, I've assumed that you've installed your operating system in C:\WINNT. That would mean that you have a C:\WINNT\SYSTEM directory, which I'll refer to as the *system* directory, and a C:\WINNT\SYSTEM32 directory, which I'll refer to as the *system32* directory. (Actually, things don't get all that different if the system is on another drive.)

The Text Icons

As you read through the text, you'll see icons and sidebars used in different ways. I include them to point out items of particular interest.

Notes, Tips, and Warnings

Tips, Notes, and Warnings are "aside" information. Often I enclose information I stumbled on when researching NT in Notes, Tips, and Warnings.

NOTE	This is a Note. Notes offer definitions, advice, and the like.

TIP	This is a Tip. Tips tell you shortcuts and highlight information that is worth knowing well.

WARNING	This is a Warning. When you see one of these, prick up your ears.

"How Do I" Sidebars

NT's big. I mean, really big. As such, quite a number of procedures aren't hard to do or even hard to learn, but they do take time. As I mentioned earlier, I decided when writing this book that any step-by-step procedure that took me more than 30 seconds to figure out would take you more than 30 seconds, too, and those procedures have been pulled out of the text and put in sidebars for easy reference.

How Do I Read a Sidebar?

This is a sidebar. All sidebars begin with the words "How Do I…" You will find a complete list of "How Do I" sidebars (along with the numbers of the pages where they are found) after the Index of this book.

Enterprise Networking

ENTERPRISE
NETWORKING

Much of what NT makes sense for, and one of my main objectives in writing this book, is enterprise networking. An *enterprise network* is one that is built with heterogeneous pieces. Issues that are specific to connecting NT networks to other NT networks, connecting NT networks to wide-area networks (WANs), and connecting NT networks to other local area networks are marked by the Enterprise Networking icon you see here.

NT Server

As I mentioned earlier, I set out originally to write a book for people who would work mainly with NT Server, rather than with NT. There were books aimed at NT users in general, but no books aimed at NT Server users, at least not until I finished writing this one. But I found to my surprise that most of the power of NT Server was shared by the basic NT Workstation product, so this book is of value to users of the NT Workstation product after all. For that reason, I attempted to make clear which parts of the text were only relevant to NT Server with the icon you see here.

How Can I Use This Book to Study for MCSE Exams?

A fair amount of the e-mail that I get asks for advice on studying for a Microsoft Certified Systems Engineer (MCSE) certification. Can someone use this book to study? Judging from my mail, the answer is "Yes." I've gotten dozens of letters from people who say they have successfully used this book to study for their NT Server and TCP/IP tests.

To get your MCSE, you must pass six tests. They are all computer-administered multiple-choice exams (I saw one fill-in-the-blank question, but that was an anomaly). There are four core tests and two elective tests, as follows:

Exam	Title	MCSE	MCSE + Internet
70-058	Networking Essentials	Required	Required
70-067	Windows NT Server 4.0	Required	Required
70-068	Windows NT Server 4.0 in the Enterprise	Required	Required
70-073	Windows NT Workstation 4.0 *or*	Required	Required
70-064	Windows 95 *or*		
70-098	Windows 98		
70-059	Internetworking with TCP/IP on Windows NT 4.0	Elective	Required
70-077	Internet Information Server 3.0 and Index Server 1.1 *or*	Elective	Required
70-087	Internet Information Server 4.0		
70-079	Internet Explorer Administration Kit	Elective	Required
70-076	Exchange Server 5.0 *or*	Elective	Elective
70-081	Exchange Server 5.5		
70-026	System Administration for SQL Server 7.0 *or*	Elective	Elective
70-028	Administering Microsoft SQL Server 7.0		
70-088	Proxy Server 2.0	Elective	Elective
70-085	SNA Server 4.0	Elective	Elective
70-018	Systems Management Server 1.2 *or*	Elective	Elective
70-086	Systems Management Server 2.0		

NOTE   For a more detailed description of the Microsoft certification programs, go to www.microsoft.com/train_cert.

Here are a few other books that you could pick up for help with reviewing:

- Review for the Network Essentials test with *Mastering Local Area Networks* by Christa Anderson, available from Sybex.

- Review for the Windows 3.1 test with *Troubleshooting Windows*, which I wrote and Sybex published.

- I'm told that my book *The Expert Guide to Windows 95* is a good study guide for the Windows 95 test, although truthfully I've never taken that test, so I can't say that I had the test in mind when I wrote it.

- Review for the two NT Server tests by reading this book.

- Review for the TCP/IP exam by reading Chapters 14 and 15 of this book. (Three tests in one book; what a bargain, eh?)

- Choose another topic—SMS, SQL Server, Exchange, Microsoft Mail—and get one of the many review guides for it. Many are available from Sybex's Network Press imprint; and of the networking books I've thumbed through, Sybex's seem the most complete and readable.

You can register to take an exam by calling (800) 755-EXAM; they'll tell you where there's a testing center near you. Exams cost $100. Don't just go in cold and take an exam; get ready by pretesting for it first. On Microsoft's Web site you can download sample tests; run through them once before paying money to take the test. And find a third-party "quizzer" product to help you study for some of the less obvious parts of the tests. I like the series of quizzes from Net-Com Image, a series called the Beachfront Quizzer. At only $60/test, it's a good deal. You can find them at www.bfq.com or (888) 992-3131.

I'm As Close As Your (E-) Mailbox

NT is an enormous system. I've worked with it as long as anyone has, but I don't know it all, not by a long shot. Got a tip that you'd like me to share with the rest of the world? Send it to me, and I'll acknowledge your help in the next edition of this book. Got a question that I didn't answer? Mail it to me, and I'll do my best to get an answer. Found a (*gasp!*) error? You can find me at help@minasi.com. When I'm out of the country (which is two months a year), I don't pick up my e-mail, so if I don't get back to you immediately, don't be offended because I'll respond as soon as I can. (And please don't send me mail with receipts; our mail server automatically deletes them. Hey, it's kind of rude, you know what I mean?)

Thanks for reading, and I hope you find this book to be the ultimate NT Server guide!

PART

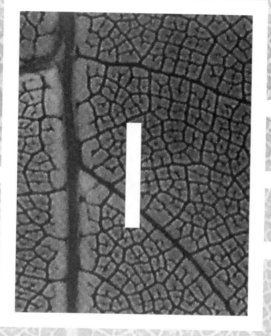

I

Getting Acquainted

NT Server Overview

- Looking at NT Server 4's capabilities

- NT Server 4's enterprise networking features

- New features in NT Server 4 and Service Pack 4

Pretty much all of the big companies and government offices were already networked by mid-1993, back when the first version of NT arrived. Since network administrators—and most people in general—aren't fond of change, the product must have been good (or especially well marketed) to have been brought to market that late and to have still succeeded.

One analysis says that by the end of the decade, 60 percent of the desktop servers in the world will be running NT. A statistic from early 1996 claimed that one-half of World Wide Web servers are running NT; a Microsoft employee claimed at a 1998 presentation that the number's up to 70 percent. I personally have been amazed at how quickly some of my large Fortune 500 clients have just wiped NetWare off their servers' hard disks and replaced it with NT Server.

If you're a NetWare, VINES, or LAN Server administrator and you've looked around and said to yourself, "What's going *on*?" or you've decided to finally take the plunge and learn a major network operating system, then you'll want an overview of NT's strengths.

In many ways, NT Server is a big departure from previous PC-based server products. Those currently managing a LAN Server, Novell NetWare, or LAN Manager will have to understand the ways that NT Server departs from its LAN Manager past in order to get the most from NT Server.

NT Server Capabilities

Whether it is to be used as a workstation operating system or a server operating system, the NT operating system itself has some quite attractive features. Let's take a look at some of the features that make NT Server stand out from the competition.

Architecture Independence

Most operating systems are designed from first conception with a particular target processor in mind. Operating system designers get caught up in things like the following:

Word size   How many bits does the CPU work with on each operation? CPUs once handled only 8 bits at a time, and then 16-bit processors appeared, 32-bit processors appeared, and now there are 64-bit and even 128-bit processors.

Page size   What's the size of the "quantum" of memory that a processor works with? On an Intel Pentium/Pentium II/Xeon chip, it's impossible for the processor to allocate less than 4K of RAM to any given application. For example, if an application wants 2K, then it gets 4K, and if it wants 5K, then it gets 8K. This is called the *page size* of the processor. On a DEC Alpha CPU, the page size is 8K, so the smallest memory allocation is 8K. That means that whether an application wants 2K or 5K, it gets 8K on an Alpha. While this seems like a small thing, it's just the kind of minutiae that operating system designers get caught up in. They embed that 4K or 8K value throughout the operating system code, making the prospect of porting the operating system's code to another processor sound impossible. NT avoided that problem, as you'll see.

Big-endian or little-endian   How are bytes organized in memory? Here is another example of the kind of minutiae that can make an operating system end up extremely processor-dependent. RAM in most desktop computers is organized in 8-bit groups called bytes. (I *knew* you knew that, but I defined it just in case someone out there doesn't.) But most modern CPUs store data in 32-bit groups. You can write 32 bits as four bytes. Reading those four bytes left to right, let's call them byte one, two, three, and four. Now, here's the question: When the processor stores that one word—that four bytes—in what order should it store it in memory? Some, including NT, store the left-most byte first and move to the right, so the order in which the bytes appear is one, two, three, and four. Other processors store the bytes in reverse order: four, three, two, one. The first approach is called a *little-endian* storage approach; the second is called *big-endian*.

Tons of other things are processor-specific, but those are three good examples. What I want you to understand is the trap that operating system designers can fall into, a trap of building their operating systems to be very specific to a particular processor. When hardware vendors come out with new chips, these are of course faster than most (or no one would pay them any mind), but they also often include some interesting oddball feature, like on-chip support for multimedia or the like. Operating-systems designers asked to develop an OS for this new chip are usually intrigued by the new feature and incorporate it into the OS, figuring that as long as this cool new feature comes free with the chip, why not make the OS more powerful with the feature? Sometimes the powerful-but-gimmicky features of a processor become integral parts of operating systems, while essential features that the processor doesn't support go by the wayside. For example, look at the pervasive 16-bit nature of many Intel-based operating systems, a nature directly attributable to the 8088 and 80286 processors. The first member of the Intel processor family that PC compatibles were built around, the 8086, first appeared in 1977. Eight years went by before a 32-bit Intel x86 processor appeared (x86 refers to the family of PC-compatible processors: the 8086, 8088, 80188, 80186, 80286, 80386, 80486, and Pentium chips). Even though that 32-bit processor has been available since 1985, it took nearly 10 years for 32-bit operating systems to be generally accepted.

When Microsoft designed NT, it initially did *not* specifically implement it on an x86 chip. Microsoft wanted to build something that was independent of any processor's architecture. They were aware that Microsoft programmers knew the x86 architecture intimately and that the intimate knowledge would inevitably work its way into the design of NT. So, to combat that problem, Microsoft first implemented NT on a RISC chip, the MIPS R4000. Since then, NT has been ported to the x86 series (the 80486, Pentium, and Pentium Pro/II/Xeon/Celeron chips), the PowerPC CPUs, and the Alpha chips.

The parts of NT that are machine-specific are all segregated into a relatively small piece of NT (compared to the total size of the operating system). This small piece is made up of the Hardware Abstraction Layer (HAL), the kernel, and the network and device drivers. Implementing NT on a new processor type, therefore, mainly involves just writing a new HAL, processor, and network subsystem.

What does this mean to a network manager? Well, many LANs have used Intel x86-based servers for years. As the needs of the LANs grew, so (fortunately) did the power of the x86 family of Intel processor chips. These chips steadily grew faster and more powerful. When the average network had about 15 users, 286-based servers were around. When people started putting a hundred users on a server, 486s could be purchased.

Unfortunately, however, since 1991 x86 processors haven't really grown in power as quickly as they did previously. RISC machines that are reasonably priced and that offer pretty high-speed processing have begun to appear. That's why the architecture-independent nature of NT Server is so attractive. The next time you need a bigger server, you needn't buy a PC-compatible machine, with all that PC-compatibility baggage weighing the machine down. Instead, you can buy a simple, fast, streamlined machine designed simply to act as a LAN server and potentially provide decent service to hundreds of users.

While that all sounds good, is NT truly architecture independent? As of summer 1999, no. Compaq and Microsoft have terminated any new Alpha support, so now it's an all-Intel world for NT. That's a terrible shame—I've always loved my Alpha—but it's true. No Windows 2000 support for Alpha, and no new fixes for NT past Service Pack 6.

Multiple Processor Support

I just said that CPUs weren't getting faster quite as quickly as they once did. There's more than one way to make a faster computer, however: you can use a faster processor *or* you can just use *more* processors.

Compaq's Systempro was the first well known PC-compatible computer to include multiple processors; its modern equivalent would be the Compaq Pro-liants. Nowadays, *everybody* offers a dual-Pentium or dual-Pentium Pro system, even the "Jeff and Akbar's House of Clones" guys, and dual Pentium II implementations are appearing, as well. That's also true for the RISC world. Where multiprocessor machines once cost over $100,000, you can now put together a pretty decent multiprocessor PC for about $10,000.

NT in its basic form was designed to support up to 32 processors in a PC. NT Server can also split up its tasks among 32 processors. For some reason, however, Microsoft chose to cripple the basic versions of NT Workstation and NT Server, shipping Hardware Abstraction Layers (HALs) that only support two and four processors, respectively. If you want to use more than two processors on an NT workstation or four processors on an NT server, then you'll have to bug your hardware vendor for an improved HAL that supports more than those numbers of processors. (All you need is a HAL—no new kernel, drivers, or network subsystem is necessary to use multiple processors.) In any case, servers can have up to 32 processors in them, with the right HAL. The Enterprise Edition of NT Server ships with a HAL that can handle eight processors.

Among multiprocessing systems, a computer is said to be a *symmetric* or *asymmetric* multiprocessor. An asymmetric multiprocessor has more than one processor, but each processor has a different, specifically defined job. The early Systempros were asymmetric systems. A symmetric multiprocessing system, in contrast, has processors that can take over for one another without skipping a beat. Each processor has complete access to all hardware, bus, and memory actions. NT Workstation and NT Server must have symmetric processor systems in order to use multiprocessor capabilities.

Having said that NT can support up to 32 processors, though, how *well* does it support them? It depends. Many NT applications are simply incapable of utilizing more than one processor. Exchange 4 and 5 could not use more than two processors, so adding a third or fourth processor to an Exchange server was pointless. Depending on whom you ask, SQL Server maxes out at four or eight processors. So while NT *theoretically* supports over 30 processors, the reality is that most systems won't benefit from more than eight or, more likely, more than four processors. Additionally, I've been told that *x*86 processors just simply don't work well in large groups, making a 10-processor *x*86 machine a bit of an expensive folly. One of Windows 2000 Server's goals is to redesign NT's internals to allow it to use more processors better.

Multithreaded Multitasking

Whether you have just one processor or more than one processor in your system, NT supports multitasking. The multitasking is true multitasking in that it is preemptive, time-sliced, priority-driven multitasking. (All that is explained in Chapter 16, on server tuning.)

Multitasking usually means that a single computer can run several different programs. Each program, however, usually is only single-tasking within itself. Consider, for example, how a word processor is built. It picks up keystrokes; then it does something with them, and then it goes on to the next keystroke. Apply that to a *graphical* word processor, and you can see that problems can result.

Suppose you press the Page Down key, so the word processor retrieves a page of text either from memory buffers or from the disk and then displays the text. That can take a bit of time, particularly if the page contains a few graphics, each of which must be retrieved and rendered in a fashion consonant with the abilities of the particular graphics board that you're using. But now suppose you're on page 30 and you want to move to page 33. You just press Page Down three times, and the three Page Down keystrokes go into the keyboard buffer of the word-processing program. Now, because the word-processing program is single-threaded—that is, because it does just one thing at a time, and in a particular order—it will see the first Page Down key, and it will then retrieve and render the entire page 31. Only after it's through doing that does it look again in the keyboard buffer, see another Page Down, and goes through the whole process again for page 32 and then for page 33.

One way to avoid this kind of time-wasting "tunnel vision" is to build the word processor as a group of smaller programs, all of which run simultaneously. There could be a kind of "boss" program that reads the keystrokes, calling the "render the page" routine. That program could interrupt the "render the page" routine when a new keystroke comes in, keeping it from wasting time displaying pages that would be over-written on the screen immediately.

NT lets developers create such a program, called a *multithreaded* program. Each of the small independent subprograms is called a *thread*, hence the term multi-threaded. Whether the developers actually *use* that capability is quite another story; some major NT applications are multithreaded, and some aren't. On a single-processor system, being single-threaded isn't terrible. On a multiprocessor system, being single-threaded is a crime—it wastes that extra processor, because each thread can live on one and only one processor at a time. A single processor can handle multiple threads, of course, but a single thread can't span multiple processors.

How can you find out if your application is multithreaded? Run it on a multi-processor NT system and give it something pretty time-consuming to do; then run the Performance Monitor and monitor how much of each CPU is taken up by the application. If one processor is 99-percent utilized and the other one is 11-percent utilized, then it's pretty clear that the application is single-threaded. Again, see Chapter 16 for more on the Performance Monitor and on tuning.

Multithreading is essential for server-based programs like database servers, which must be able to respond to multiple requests for information from many client sources.

Massive Memory Space

NT programs don't have to worry about running up against some kind of 640K or 16MB barrier. The NT architecture can support RAM of up to 4096MB (four *gigabytes*). (Now, where did I put those one-gig SIMMs...?) Some programs, like Oracle for NT, can actually use more RAM than that—*if* you're running NT on an Alpha. Hey, I guess there're still good reasons to buy an Alpha...

I should mention, by the way, that it's not a good idea to put more than 16MB on an ISA (Industry Standard Architecture) bus machine. If your servers are to have more than 16MB, get a PC based on the Extended Industry Standard Architecture (EISA) or Peripheral Component Interconnect (PCI) bus. Or you could get a RISC machine, where there is no 16MB boundary.

Now, that last paragraph generated a lot of reader letters in previous editions, so let's elaborate on it. Machines with old ISA buses (and most modern PCs still come with ISA bus slots in combination with PCI bus slots) have a problem because the ISA bus can only address 16MB of memory. Virtually all NT Server machines have at least that much memory, and usually more, which presents a problem to the ISA bus. The bus "overhears" all addressing references, no matter whether they're intended for a piece of hardware in an ISA slot, for a PCI slot, or are on the system motherboard. As the ISA bus can only work with 16MB of memory addressing space, any references to memory above 16MB just "wrap around," so that accessing a memory location like 17MB looks like accessing address 17-1 or 1MB to the ISA bus. If there were a memory board in an ISA slot with address 1MB, then the ISA bus would mistakenly send the message to that board.

Normally that's not a big problem, as people don't usually put memory in ISA slots. But some boards that might end up in ISA slots have a small amount of memory and some ISA boards access memory directly in the form of something called *bus mastering*. If you had a bus master board in an ISA slot, it could conceivably lose or damage data because of the confusion about memory addresses. Now, motherboard designers know that, so they placed extra circuitry to check for these problems and to avert them. But using that circuitry slows down PCs a bit, with the result that many PCs actually run slower with more than 16MB of RAM than they do with less memory. It's another argument for buying RISC-based servers, I guess.

Centralized User Profiles

Each Windows or DOS program seems to need its own configuration file or files, leading to a disk littered with a lot of files with the extensions INI, CNF, and the like. NT centralizes program initialization information with a database of program setup information called the *Registry* and part of that database, a user-specific part, is called a *user profile*. NT even allows you to store an NT workstation's profile on a server, making it possible to centrally control the equivalent of CONFIG.SYS and AUTOEXEC.BAT (and Windows.INI) files for a workstation from a central server. Thank heaven for support folks.

If your work takes you from workstation to workstation, then you may feel a bit like a Bedouin, with no home but the great wide world itself. Nomadic computing means that when you log on to a new workstation, you have to spend time arranging the look of that workstation to your particular tastes. (And, of course, the person who *usually* uses the workstation may not appreciate your "improvements.")

NT improves upon that with the notion of a *profile*. A user profile contains information like

- Background colors
- Wallpaper
- Screen saver preferences
- Program manager groups
- Persistent network connections
- Start menu items

Under NT, you can create a profile *for an NT workstation* (this is no good for a regular Windows or Windows 9*x* workstation) and then you can tell NT to cause that profile to follow you around. Windows 95 has profiles as well, but unfortunately Windows NT and 95 profiles are incompatible, so you end up with at least one of each. Additionally, you'll read later on that you can use a tool called *system policies* to configure and control a user's Desktop, and that those policies can also roam the network as a profile does.

Furthermore, with Service Pack 4 you can now control the *size* of a user's profile. By forcing users to only store data in folders on their Desktops, you can control how many megabytes (well, kilobytes, actually) of space a user can take up with his files. (You'll learn more about this in Chapter 7, and there *is* a catch—the users must be running NT on their desktops, as well.)

As a support person, you'll like the fact that you can use a profile to restrict the kinds of things a user can do. You can even make a profile mandatory, moving us one step closer to central control of desktop PCs. The only catch? Again, NT profiles are different from Windows 95 profiles, so the profiles you set up for your NT clients won't work for 95 clients, and vice versa.

Enhanced Metafile Printing

If you have both NT workstations and servers, then you'll find a really neat approach to network printing. When you print to a network server, the entire print job goes out to the *server* to print, leaving the workstation with little to do in the printing process. That means that the workstation is available much more quickly after you tell it to print something. Additionally, print drivers sit only on the server, so when a new print driver comes out, you needn't put it on every workstation—just the servers. A terrific feature if you're using NT workstations.

Enterprise Networking Features

ENTERPRISE NETWORKING

On top of NT Server's basic operating system features, however, is a wide array of networking capabilities, many of particular value to builders of multi-operating system *enterprise* networks. Enterprise networks are those networks built of large numbers of machines and servers. Enterprise networks have some special needs; here's how NT meets those needs.

Internet and TCP/IP Compatibility

Whether your company intends to get onto the Internet or not, most networks speak the language of the Internet, a protocol called Transmission Control Protocol/ Internet Protocol (TCP/IP). Many companies build TCP/IP-based networks and never connect them to the Internet for security reasons. Such networks are called *private IP networks*, or, more recently, *intranets*. In any case, TCP/IP is the way to go for many networks. NT supports most of the protocols of the Internet, so it's possible to build your own enterprise intranet based on Windows NT.

Event and Account Logging

When I got started in the computer business, I worked on a mainframe-based system. Like all users on that system, I had an account that kept track of a balance of "pseudomoney." Whenever I "logged on to" my mainframe, the account would be debited a bit for every minute that I was on, a bit more for each byte of shared disk storage that I used, and some more for each program run on that mainframe.

The other mainframe users and I called these accounts "funny money" because after running a program, you'd get a printout detailing the charges that you engendered by running the program—so much for each page printed, so much for the disk space used, and so on. Although it would have a dollar total, no money changed hands. The whole purpose of "funny money" accounts was to impress upon the mainframe's users that the mainframe was a limited resource and shared computer resources should not be wasted.

LANs are getting to be more and more like mainframes. They serve hundreds of users in many companies, they're a shared resource, and they cost a lot of money to keep up and running. Eventually, companies will assign "funny money" accounts to LAN users as a means of keeping track of who is putting the greatest strain on the system. While this may sound a trifle authoritarian, it's not. Users depend on LANs more and more, and if just a few users make it difficult for others to get *their* jobs done, then there must be a way for network administrators to figure out who's killing the network.

That's what event logging and auditing are all about. Under NT Server, you can keep track of who prints on what printer at what time, who uses what files at what time and for how long, and who's logged on to which server. NT Server provides a great deal of power for keeping track of what's happening on your network.

Remote Access Services

There's always been a need for information workers to be able to take their work home. Once, workers brought a briefcase stuffed with papers home. Then mainframe users dragged home a thermal paper terminal called the "Silent 700." More recently, people with PCs at home dialed up to the company LAN via a program like Carbon Copy or PC Anywhere, or perhaps via a more expensive solution like the Shiva NetModem. It's not just office workers who need remote access, either; members of roving sales forces may only physically touch their home bases once a month or so, but they need to exchange data with that home base regularly.

NT Server has a remote access capability built right into it. The remote access software shipped with NT is the *server* end of the software; the client end—the piece that goes on the workstation—is included in the NT Workstation software and Windows version 3.11 and later. Microsoft also offers remote access client software for DOS and earlier versions of Windows; those files can be found in the \CLIENTS\RAS directory of the installation CD-ROM disk. Windows 95 and 98

[Handwritten annotations at top: PPP LINK Slow speed communication / All 3 lines connect to / on modem the internet connection / to look like a single connection]

[Handwritten annotation at left margin: PPTP use internet as a router to speak to your office network for a virtual private network]

call their RAS support software "Dial-Up Networking," and in fact it's also the case for NT that the client side of RAS is called DUN: Dial-Up Networking.

Also included in RAS are two powerful TCP/IP protocols: Point to Point Tunneling Protocol (PPTP) and Multilink PPP. The first allows you to use the entire Internet as a "router," so to speak, to communicate with your office network using encryption to allow you to safely create a "virtual private network" over the Internet. Multilink PPP lets you take several slower-speed communication links and blend them into just one link. For example, you could have three phone lines that each have 28.8Kbps modems. All connect to the same Internet service provider, and together those connections would look like one single connection running at 86.4Kbps. (Of course, that only works if the ISP supports Multilink PPP. Many don't, simply because they don't want the increased strain on their network.)

Domain and Workgroup-Based Administration Features

NT Server includes programs that make it simple to control security on a number of servers.

If your company has just one server, then these features won't be very attractive. But if your firm has a number of servers, then you'll soon find that administering groups of servers can be a real pain in the neck. For example, suppose you want to add a user to the Finance department. There are four servers in Finance. That means you've got to log on to each one individually and create the same user account on each one; ditto if you have to delete a user account. With the domain management capabilities of NT Server, you can make those changes to a whole group of servers with just a few mouse-clicks.

As NT Server is a modern LAN operating system, it goes without saying that you can assign security access rights all the way down to the user and file level; you can say that user X can only read file Y, but user Z can read and write file Y. You can also set files to an "execute-only" privilege level, making it possible for someone to run a program on the server, but *im*possible to copy the program from the server. About the only thing that you can't do with the security features of NT Server is to link them to security programs in the mainframe world, like ACF/2 and RACF, unfortunately. But once Microsoft buys IBM, they'll probably get around to solving that problem. (Just kidding…)

Fault Tolerance and RAID Support

NT SERVER

Part of security involves keeping people from data that they're not supposed to have access to, but an equally big part of security's function includes keeping safe the data that people have entrusted to the network. To that end, NT Server incorporates a number of features that support fault tolerance:

- The database of domain security information resides on a single server called the *domain controller*, but other servers can act as backup domain controllers in the domain, ready to step in as domain controller whenever the primary goes offline.

- NT Server supports multiple network cards in a server, so a network card failure doesn't necessarily bring down a server.

- *Directory replication* makes it possible to designate a directory on a particular server and then create a backup server whose job it is to match, on a minute-by-minute basis, the contents of that directory. That makes sure that essential things like logon scripts are available from several sources, making logons quicker.

- *Hotfixes* are a feature on any NT Server whose disk has been formatted under the NTFS file system. NTFS constantly monitors the disk areas that it is using, and if it finds that one has become damaged, then it takes the bad area out of service and moves the data on that area to another, safer area automatically.

- RAID (*Redundant Array of Inexpensive Disks*) is a six-level method for combining several disk drives into what appears to the system to be a single disk drive. RAID improves upon a single-drive answer in that it offers better speed and data redundancy.

  - Level 0, or *disk striping*, improves speed only. It creates what appears to be one disk out of several separate physical disk drives. Areas that appear to be a cylinder or a track on a logical disk drive are actually spread across two or more physical disk drives. The benefit is realized when accessing data; when reading a block of data, the read operation can actually become several simultaneous separate disk reads of several physical disks.

NT SUPPORT ONLY 3 0, 1, 5

- Level 1 is a straightforward *disk mirroring* system. You get two disk drives and tell NT to make one a mirror image of the other. It's fast and fault-tolerant.

- Levels 2, 3, and 4 are not supported by NT Server.

- Level 5 is very much like level 0, in that data is striped across several separate physical drives. It differs, however, in that it adds redundant information called "parity" that allows damaged data to be reconstructed.

[handwritten margin note: MOST COMMONLY USE REPAIRS ITSELF]

[handwritten note: MIN 3 disk MAX 32 disk]

The different levels of RAID do not get better as they rise in numbers; they're just different options. The interesting part about NT's RAID support, however, is that it happens in *software*, not hardware. You needn't buy a specialized RAID box to get the benefits of RAID—all you have to do is just buy a bunch of SCSI drives and use the NT Disk Administrator program to RAID-ize them. (You need not use SCSI drives, but they are easier to connect. SCSI drives also support sector remapping, which is another fault-tolerant feature that other drives may not support.)

You can accomplish further fault tolerance by pairing NT servers into a *cluster*, two machines that keep an eye on one another; if one crashes, the other picks up its failed friend's work in mid-stream, offering users more reliable system response. To do all that, you'll need to run Microsoft Cluster Server, the main feature of a version of NT Server called "NT 4.0 Enterprise Edition."

Reasonable Price for Server and Client Software

Pricing server products is a difficult thing. On the one hand, network server software equals mainframe operating systems in complexity, so software vendors want to realize the same kind of return that they would from mainframe software. That's not possible, however, because no one would pay mainframe software prices for software running on a server with eight workstations. But a *hundred* workstations…?

Server software must be reasonably priced for small LANs. But the very same software runs on large LANs, so how does a LAN software vendor justify charging more money for the very same software, based solely on the number of people using it? Nevertheless, major vendors *do* charge more for server software, depending on the number of users; NetWare can cost from hundreds of dollars to tens of thousands of dollars, depending on the number of users on a server.

NT is priced in two parts. Basically, you buy the server for $700, and you buy a "client license" for each user at $40 apiece. Those are, of course, list prices, so your mileage will vary, but basically you can estimate how much it will cost you to set up an NT Server network by taking the number of servers you'll need and multiplying by $700, and then taking the number of workstations—desktops, laptops, and home machines—who will access the network and multiplying by $40. There is particularly bad news for people who already own NT Server 3.51 and intend to upgrade to 4. Microsoft requires that you upgrade each client license at $25 apiece!

There are some specific "gotchas" that you have to know about, but they're covered in Chapter 3, on setting up NT Server.

NDIS Protocol Support

Getting network boards to work with network operating systems has never been a simple thing. Even more difficult has been supporting multiple protocols on a single network card, and most unpleasant of all has been getting multiple protocols to work on multiple network cards.

Novell attacks this problem with its Open Data-Link Interface (ODI) standard. Microsoft's answer is the Network Driver Interface Specification (NDIS). Each has its own plusses and minuses, but NDIS 3 and later has a terrific feature in its ability to load client software in extended memory, which is quite a plus for those running memory-hungry DOS software.

One of NT's problems over its brief lifetime has been getting decent driver support. Buy a high-performance Ethernet card and there will certainly be a Novell NetWare driver in the box for that card. But there may or may not be an NT driver. Microsoft wants this problem to go away forever, and their plan for doing that is to integrate the driver model for Windows 98 and Windows NT. The widespread nature of Windows 95 means that it will be easy to find a Windows 95 driver for a given board, and that, no doubt, will be true for Windows 98, as well. The original idea Microsoft presented was that if you had a 98 driver, then you automatically had an NT driver. More recently, however, Microsoft has revealed that 98 drivers and NT drivers are only *source code* compatible, meaning that 98 drivers and NT drivers *aren't* identical, but that it's very easy for a vendor who's successfully created a 98 driver to quickly produce an NT driver. That's still good news, but not good as the "98 and NT drivers are compatible" story, sadly.

Protocol Compatibility with Forebears

Obviously, NT Server communicates with its forebears. In particular, LAN Manager 2.2 servers can act as members of NT Server's domains and can assist in some, but not all, domain control functions.

NetWare Support

Knowing that much of its audience needs to be able to interface with existing Novell NetWare servers, NT Server contains some capabilities to communicate with Novell products. The connectivity isn't perfect, however. You can't unify the domain administration for your Novell NetWare network with the administration for NT Server.

NT includes the network protocol used in NetWare networks, a protocol called IPX/SPX; NT calls it NWLink. NWLink is actually the default network protocol that the NT setup program suggests when you install NT.

With NT's Client and Gateway Services for NetWare, you can extend Novell services to parts of your network that don't even run Novell software. That's a sneaky way to bend Novell's maximum number of users on each server, but it's a little *too* good: NT makes it tough to carry over Novell security to NT users. (In any case, you can learn all about it in Chapter 13.) And two new tools, File and Print Services for NetWare and Directory Services Manager for NetWare, allow you to smooth the path from NetWare to NT.

NetBEUI, TCP/IP, and DLC Options

Over the years, a number of network/transport/session protocols have become significant in the networking industry. There is a great variety of these protocols for two reasons. First, some are just products of large computer companies that want to build their own proprietary protocols and give themselves a competitive advantage. Second, different protocols are built to serve different needs.

NetBEUI was originally built by IBM to quickly zip data around small LANs. It's a really "quick and dirty" protocol in that it's not easy to move NetBEUI data over wide area networks (WANs). You'll hear people beat up on NetBEUI for its simplicity, but make no mistake: for a single-segment network, it is *the* fastest transport protocol available.

TCP/IP is a kind of *de facto* standard for building networks composed of many different vendors' products. TCP/IP has until recently not been very popular in the role of LAN protocol, but it *can* serve quite well in that role, and recent improvements to TCP/IP have made it even more attractive on LANs. It is possible to replace NetBEUI with TCP/IP in NT Server, and in fact for a network of any size, I highly recommend it.

DLC (Data Link Control), also known as IEEE 802.2, is not a complete protocol, so it can't serve in the role of LAN or WAN protocol. But DLC can provide connectivity to many mainframe gateway products and to some printers that attach directly to the network, such as any Hewlett-Packard LaserJet with a JetDirect print server (network interface) card.

Macintosh Connectivity

Getting Macs and PCs to communicate has always been a bit of a headache. But NT Server makes it very simple. I connected a Mac to my NT Server within 15 minutes, and it worked the first time.

Under NT Server, you need only create a directory on your server, designate it as a Mac-accessible volume, and start up the Mac Server subsystem.

NT Server has all the ingredients necessary to make it successful as an enterprise network server in many organizations. In the next chapter, we'll look at the network concepts that you have to understand in order to work in the Microsoft networking world.

What's New in Version 4?

Everything you've read about so far has existed in NT since version 3.1. Microsoft has spent a fair amount of money selling version 4, although most of the marketing money has gone into selling NT Workstation 4. What's new in NT Server 4?

Some of the big news in NT is built into NT Server 4 and comes right in the box. Other news appears in the form of new and separate products, only some of which I cover in this book. Still more comes from four "Service Packs": extensive collections of both bug fixes and new features.

New GUI

A new GUI is the "big news" in NT Server 4, although truthfully it's not that important for network administrators; after all, who cares what user interface is on the server? Having said that, however, it's worth noting that adding the Windows 95 user interface to NT Server 4 will make it just a bit easier to teach new network administrators how to do their jobs, because many of those people will have already worked with Windows 95.

Little Change in Administration Tools

Besides the change in the user interface, veteran users of NT Server will see (thankfully!) very little change in the basic tools that they've come to know and love. The User Manager for Domains, the Print Manager, the Server Manager, Performance Monitor, NT Backup, DHCP Manager, and the WINS Manager are basically unchanged—and that's good. Someone already using NT Server version 3.51 will find the transition to version 4 simple.

Internet Information Server

Although the phenomenon was virtually unknown just a few years ago, nowadays there probably isn't a single company in America without a "home page," a marketing presentation of some kind on the World Wide Web. You ain't nobody unless your company has a Web page. (Ours is at www.minasi.com.) Setting up your own Web page, however, requires a connection to the Internet and a computer of some type running a Web server.

Web server programs used to cost a fair amount of money, and one company, Netscape, has Wall Street believing that it will make tons of money selling them. Now, Microsoft is *scared* of Netscape (Microsoft President Steve Ballmer said a few years ago that Microsoft wants to "crush" Netscape), so Microsoft is giving away a Web server, which they call their Internet Information Server. Included in that is an improved FTP server (an FTP server was always included with NT, but this one has a few more bells and whistles) and a Gopher server.

New Communications Protocol Support

As mentioned earlier, version 4 has the multilink PPP and PPTP protocols, both new to NT. The Remote Access Server (RAS) now has *autodial* capabilities whereby you can tell your computer that you are linked to another computer over a phone line. That's not new; RAS has been around all along. What *is* new is that now you can create all sorts of connections to other computers via RAS, and the computer will act as if those virtual connections actually exist, even though it hasn't dialed up the connection yet. Then, when you try to actually use one of those connections, the system automatically dials the other computer to enable the connection.

NT 4 also includes the Telephony Application Program Interface (TAPI), a nice feature that unified communications programming under Windows 95 and will no doubt benefit NT, as well. You see, in older operating systems, each communication program had to load its own modem-specific drivers; if you ran four different communications programs on your computer, you ended up telling four different programs what kind of modem you had, which was cumbersome. Under NT 4, you'll be able to buy communications applications that are "TAPI-enabled," meaning that they'll interrogate your system for modem information rather than interrogating *you*.

Network Administration Tools

Windows 95 had a powerful administrative tool in the form of the System Policy Editor (SPE). The SPE didn't work in NT, not until NT 4. With the SPE, you can control a particular user's machine so completely that it's possible to say that a given user can only run Word and Excel on her machine. For the control freaks out there, this is a blessing. For the rest of us, it's a new tool to master, and you can start doing that by reading Chapter 6.

RIP Routing and DNS Server Support

With every release of NT, Microsoft makes it clearer and clearer that their network direction is TCP/IP and the Internet. Up to now, most of the computers running the Internet were UNIX machines, mainly because most of the Internet tools are available for free on UNIX. But that's a part of the world that Microsoft wants to own, so each new version of NT includes some new essential Internet tool. In addition to the Web server, NT Server 4 includes a Domain Name Service (DNS) server and support for both the RIP (Routing Internet Protocol) and OSPF (Open Shortest Path First) standards. If you've never heard of them, trust me, they're pretty essential—and, again, you can learn more about them in Part IV.

(To get the OSPF support, you've got to download a service called Routing and Remote Access Service (RRAS) from Microsoft.)

The DNS server in version 4 comes with a graphical front end and helpful Wizards that you can use to quickly set up a DNS server.

Network Monitor

In the years that I've worked with PC networks (since 1985), one of the most desirable, sought-after, and *expensive* tools for network troubleshooting has always been the network sniffer. Put simply, a *sniffer* turns your network cable figuratively into a "piece of glass," meaning that you can see everything that goes on in it. A full-blown network sniffer records every piece of data that goes back and forth on the network—a troubleshooter's dream and a security officer's nightmare. At one point, one network sniffer product was going for $18,000.

Microsoft has shipped a sniffer application called the Network Monitor as part of the Server Management System (SMS) for the past few years, but SMS is expensive and it really should have been part of NT Server from the start. In NT Server version 4, Microsoft fixes that by including a slightly dumbed-down version of the Network Monitor in NT Server.

Why "dumbed-down?" Because the full-blown version of Network Monitor tracks and records all data going on the network, and the version shipping with Server Management System still does that. The version of Network Monitor that ships with NT Server, in contrast, will only record network frames that either originate with or are destined for the particular server on which it is running. So, if you want to use Network Monitor to examine traffic from your server to machine X, and from machine X to your server, then you'll love the version that ships with NT Server; on the other hand, if you want use Network Monitor to examine traffic moving between machine X and machine Y, then you can't do that from your server (assuming that your server is neither machine X nor Y). Still, it's a neat tool, and you can learn more about it in Chapter 16, "Tuning and Monitoring Your NT Server Network."

Windows Terminal Server: NT as Mainframe

For years, support people have wished for the power and flexibility of a desktop operating system like Windows, OS/2, or NT, but with the ease of central control that a mainframe offers. One firm, Citrix, has offered this for years as a product called Winframe. Originally offered in an OS/2 flavor and later moved to NT, Winframe let you put a special version of NT on a central PC and then attach dumb terminals to the central machine. Users who were logged into the dumb terminals would not even *know* that they weren't sitting at a PC, because they could run Windows programs. The trick was that most of the processing was being done by the large central PC; all their local computers did was display some graphics and transmit mouse clicks and keystrokes over the network to the central Winframe server. Most user problems arose not on the local terminal, but instead on the central Winframe server, making most support tasks easier—the servers are usually physically close to the support people.

Microsoft customers asked for this kind of power, and so Microsoft licensed the Winframe technology and put it on NT 4, selling it as Windows Terminal Server. WTS will attach to dumb terminals (*winterms*) or PCs running the Windows Terminal Client software that makes them into winterms. Got a few 25MHz 386 systems with 8MB of RAM running Windows for Workgroups? Put the Windows Terminal Client on it and *presto!* You have an old system now running NT workstation. You'll read more about WTS later in the book.

Smarter, More Flexible Routing

While you can currently build a complete top-to-bottom intranet using only NT, a few pieces weren't as filled out as would have been nice. For example, there was no way to use NT machines to connect two geographically separated networks with modems or ISDN or the like, unless you connected the two networks and *left* them connected.

But if you add the Routing and Remote Access Service add-on to NT 4, you'll be able to tell those two NT "router" machines to only connect with each other when necessary, allowing potential communications savings.

Service Pack 4 Enhancements

In late October 1998, Microsoft shipped the fourth service pack for NT 4. Not only does it include a pile of bug fixes, it actually adds a few completely new features.

Improvements to WINS and DHCP

Two keystone technologies for anyone building an NT network using the TCP/IP (Internet) protocol are the Windows Internet Naming Service (WINS) and the Dynamic Host Configuration Protocol (DHCP). (Both systems are described in Chapter 14.) Under Service Pack 4, it's easy to remove an entry from the WINS name database by just pointing and clicking in the WINS Manager, something you couldn't do before. Conversely, WINS sometimes forgets about important machines like servers, leading to immense network headaches. When WINS forgets about a server, the only way to smack WINS on the head and tell it about the server is to *reboot* the server—not a good answer for many shops. A new command, NBTSTAT –RR, lets you re-register (RR) a machine with WINS without rebooting the machine.

DHCP helps out people who need to merge two different groups of IP addresses (*scopes*) into a single, larger "superscope." DHCP also runs into trouble now and then when you replace an area's old existing DHCP server with a newer one; SP4 fixes this. Further, DHCP servers under NT don't work very well when you give them a lot of scopes—ranges of network addresses—to use and can in fact go completely deaf due to an odd bug, a bug that SP4 fixes. There are a few other fixes to WINS and DHCP as well, covered in Chapter 14.

The Security Configuration Editor

Run an NT network for a while, and you'll soon be inundated with dozens of things that you should do to make—and keep—your network secure. How can you keep track of all this? SP4 offers help in the form of the Security Configuration Editor. Put simply, it's a template, a kind of on-line guide to building a secure network. But it does more, as well; once you've established your security policies, it will then go out and audit your systems to see if the policies are being followed.

Many Security Fixes

NT must have achieved the level of popularity that Microsoft hoped for—you can tell because the hackers have targeted it. It seems that barely a week goes by without word of yet another NT security hole, and Microsoft's fix for it. Getting all of these fixes—*hotfixes* is the term for them—and installing them on your server can be time consuming. Service Pack 4 offers all of the fixes up through mid-October 1998 in a single installation. Additionally, Microsoft somewhat modified the way in which authentications—logons—occur so as to reduce the risk of someone gaining access to a network.

User Profile Quotas

As mentioned earlier, Service Pack 4 allows you to set a maximum size for user profiles. Unfortunately, the users must be running NT Workstation on their desktops for this to work. Fortunately, this profile-management system came free with SP4, so it's hard to do too much complaining about it...

Fewer Bugs and Odds and Ends

Well, it shouldn't be a surprise that SP4 stomps bugs. But the interesting story is that in the process of building Windows 2000, Microsoft claims they've found about 50 bugs so bad that they caused *blue screens*: complete system crashes. Of course, they fixed those bugs in Windows 2000, but—here's the good news—they incorporated those fixes into NT's SP4, as well.

Microsoft also took a few Resource Kit tools and moved them from the RK "ghetto" (that is, Microsoft doesn't support them) to "official" status. In particular, there's a tool that helps analyze memory dumps and a tool to assist in tracking down memory leaks.

For those who use NetShow and Media Player, there're updates to make them faster. Folks building virtual private networks with PPTP will find a faster, more secure version of PPTP with SP4. If you *do* install this new version, however, you'll have to poke around Microsoft's Web site looking for updates for the Windows 95 and Windows 98 PPTP clients.

Year 2000 Fixes

And what would a set of bug fixes be in the closing years of the millennium without some Y2K fixes? In general, NT doesn't have many Year 2000 problems, but there are a few, and a separate file of bug fixes released at the same time as SP4 (and twice its size, oddly) reputes to fix those problems.

Beyond NT Version 4: What You Can Expect

Microsoft isn't done with NT, not by a long shot. The year 2000 will see the release of another version of NT named *Windows 2000 Server* with the following features:

- Windows 2000 Server will make it possible to build very large networks around a user and resource database called *Active Directory*.

- Windows 2000 Server will include Plug and Play, thankfully.

- That Plug and Play capability will allow you to make a lot of changes to your NT machine's configuration without having to reboot, unlike NT 4—in fact, under Windows 2000 Server, you can repartition and format a drive *over a network*—you needn't even be sitting at the computer to wipe and re-build a drive.

- Supporting NT—oops, gotta get used to saying "Windows 2000"—will get easier as Microsoft offers a group of tools to simplify getting an operating system on a new machine and then deploying applications on existing machines. The tools, called *Computer Configuration Management* (CCM), are part of a larger drive called *Zero Administration Windows* or ZAW.

- Part of every network is something called *name resolution*, which converts friendly English-like names like MarksPC to low-level network addresses like 199.34.57.66. Most of the world uses something called the Domain Naming Service (DNS), but Microsoft for its own reasons uses a home-grown name resolver called the Windows Internet Naming Service. With Windows 2000 Server, Microsoft surrenders and moves over to DNS.

- Network and user naming structures will also follow the LDAP (Lightweight Directory Access Protocol) Standard. Applications accessing user information and seeking authentication will use both LDAP and another old Internet standard, Kerberos.

- Under Windows 2000 Server, it will be possible to gather together groups of files from different hard disks, directories, and even different machines, but to put them all together to look like one unified drive or directory. This new system, called the *Distributed File System*, will be a cornerstone of Windows 2000 Server.

Service Pack 5 Update Overview

Service Pack 5 brings 246 bug fixes to NT. In comparison, SP4 fixed 249 bugs, SP3 squashed 181, SP2 patched 142 defects, and SP1 only handled nine bugs. There aren't a lot of "showstoppers" here, but there are a number of bugs that may have bedeviled you late one evening while trying to get NT to do something that you were *sure* it did…. Before applying it, however, be aware that SP5 "breaks" many power management drivers, so if you're running NT on a laptop, check with your laptop vendor to see if you've got new APM (Advanced Power Management) drivers. Apparently a bug created by SP4 caused the disk to write a time stamp every five minutes, which caused some systems to report that they hadn't been shut down properly and also got in the way of power management software. Unfortunately, in order to fix this, Microsoft ended up restructuring how power management drivers work under NT 4, hence the possible need for a driver upgrade.

Among the irritants soothed by SP5 is an obscure bug that strikes the User Manager for Domains program, the tool that creates user accounts. If a user is a member of more than 1,000 global groups, User Manager crashes. SP5 also fixed a Policy Editor bug that caused an "access violation" when trying to restrict user access to particular programs. It eliminates a bug in Dfs, the Distributed File System, when NetWare servers are part of the Dfs tree, and crushes another Dfs-related bug, which keeps NT from showing you any of the Dfs servers that you're connected to in My Computer. XCOPY /D is *supposed* to only copy files created on today, but until Service Pack 5, it defined a day in Greenwich Time, not your local time. Folks in England wouldn't have noticed the problem, but it could be vexing to people on the West Coast of the U.S., where they're eight hours different from GMT.

In a particularly troublesome bug, the SYSDIFF utility used to quickly reproduce configurations from one desktop to another will "forget" any Registry value larger than about two billion (which is not as unusual as it might sound) unless you apply Service Pack 5.

As with the past few service packs, SP5 eliminates a number of sources of memory leaks—large file uploads, File and Print Services for NetWare, some kinds of RAS connections, some NTFS accesses, the SNMP agent, certain AVI file accesses, and Active Server Page scripts using the Response.CacheControl method all could leak memory and SP5 plugs those holes.

SP5 has squashed some troublesome bugs found in a few basic TCP-/IP-based intranet functions. The DHCP server, an essential infrastructure tool that hands out IP addresses to machines started rejecting pre-assigned—"reserved"—addresses if those addresses were for a distant network; additionally, SP4 was intended to fix a problem that got in the way of a single DHCP server serving a large number of networks. It fixed *that* problem, but created another that, once again, made it tough for a DHCP server to support a large number of networks. Running the DHCP administration tool would sometimes crash not only the administration tool, but the entire DHCP server service. Another intranet tool, the Routing Internet Protocol (RIP v2), did not communicate information properly to other RIP systems. Further, when you delete a given IP address from a computer, any routing information associated with that IP address should be deleted as well—but it wasn't. More intranet bugs appeared in the Domain Naming Service, or DNS, the catalog relating names like `www.minasi.com` to corresponding net-work address. The DNS client on NT workstations and servers had a problem; if you did a query on a location with multiple IP addresses, as in the case of `www.microsoft.com`, then the client would attempt to communicate with each server in turn. But if the client got an error message from the *first* server, then it would stop looking, which isn't how things are supposed to work—it should keep trying all of the others. In another DNS problem, NT DNS servers would sometime refuse to respond to requests from Unix machines. SP5 fixes all that.

SP5 also fixes a number of small but annoying hardware-specific problems (e.g., NT didn't recognize Iomega Clik! drives) and user interface bugs. In one example, folders left on the Desktop don't retain their settings when you log out, or, in another, the WINS manager (the administrative tool for a DNS-like system that keeps track of computer names on a network) sometimes ends up with some messages overwriting others. And speaking of WINS, setting WINS replication to happen every day doesn't *exactly* cause it to replicate every day. If you told it to replicate every day at 1 A.M. and it took until 2 A.M., then the next day WINS wouldn't start replicating at 1 A.M.—it'd start at 2 A.M. The day after, it'd start later and then later the following day, and so on. Service Pack 4's fixes to the WINS manager caused it to delete some "static" mappings, which are names that an administrator inserts (rather than the majority of the names, which WINS dis-covers automatically). SP5 fixes that.

And it's a small point, but in general Microsoft has pledged not to add any new functionality with service packs—but they've apparently changed their mind, as they added "automatic router discovery" to their TCP/IP internetworking soft-ware. Router discovery is a great way to make your network more reliable; it allows your workstation to discover changes in the network and adapt automatically.

Service Pack 6 Enhancements

Anyone doubting that NT 4 is a "mature" operating system has only to look at the fixes offered in Service Pack 6. There are 288 of them, and yet most are fairly minor: small fixes, fixes to previous fixes, and even a handful of fixes to the program that installs the service packs themselves!

Of the items fixed in Service Pack 6, there are several that stand out for network admins. The first concerns removable hard disks, like Jaz drives. If you format a Jaz cartridge as NTFS, write some data to it, eject the cartridge, and insert another Jaz cartridge formatted as NTFS, you'll blue-screen the system, or rather you *would* before SP6. Those building truly large servers might notice another NTFS-related issue: once the number of files on an NTFS drive exceeds four million, the drive becomes corrupted. A busy print server on NT 4 can sometimes end up acknowledging receiving a print job, but then disregard the print job unless you apply SP6.

SP6 fixes a few "new system" problems. Now and then people tell me that when Disk Administrator writes its "signature" file to a newly installed disk, the signature file ends up making the system non-bootable. According to Microsoft, that's because NT's Setup program can't always properly recognize large disk partitions that have been pre-created by OEMs like Compaq or Dell and as a result ends up putting NT on what *Setup* thinks is the first partition. Once NT's up and running, it sees the large partition and interprets the drives in a different way than Setup. When the Disk Administrator writes out the state of the disks as it sees it (the "signature" file), NT's boot routine uses that information to configure the boot process and, as the disk's self-identification is now different from how NT was originally set up to boot, NT *can't* boot. SP6 fixes that. Another problem with new machines appears when you install NT and create a domain account during setup, then log on as the local administrator the first time and install a service pack. In the process of installing the service pack, the NT machine's machine account on the domain gets corrupted, so no one can log onto a domain account from that machine until the machine account is rebuilt. SP6 helps you avoid that problem.

Two service pack-delivered features had troubles that SP6 fixed as well—the Security Configuration Editor had a few bugs, and TCP/IP's dead gateway detection had a bug, and all of them are fixed now.

I hope that by now I've sparked some interest in learning how to use NT Server in networks great and small. Before going any further, however, we have to get some very important basic networking concepts out of the way—and I don't mean the "Ethernet versus token ring" stuff; I mean learning the particular terms that Microsoft uses when discussing networking. We do that in Chapter 2.

Microsoft Enterprise Concepts

- ■ Working with a primitive Microsoft network

- ■ Understanding browsers and workgroups

- ■ Understanding centralized security

- ■ The users and machines that make up a Microsoft network

- ■ Working with network software

The first thing you've got to understand when you want to become an expert in any network is how the networking company *thinks*. Just as would-be Novell administrators must learn how the Novell Directory Services system works, or beginner Banyan administrators must learn what StreetTalk is, so also must new Microsoft network administrators learn all of the Microsoft networking lingo. It's something that you have to do even if you're an expert at some other network already, because every company that writes networking software has a different networking paradigm. (And you know what they say about paradigms—shift happens.) For example, Novell's networks have always been strongly oriented toward workstation/server architecture. In contrast, Microsoft's networks grew out of a peer-to-peer network approach, and they still have a bit of that flavor today.

So that's the goal of this chapter, to learn the basic concepts that you need in order to plan and manage a Microsoft network. I'll start out by building the simplest network possible. From there I'll be able to clarify why certain basic things about Microsoft networks are as they are. If you're already comfortable with concepts like Universal Naming Convention names, domains, workgroups, browse lists, and how NetBEUI is different from NetBIOS, then skip along to the next chapter. If not, stay with me a few pages, and in no time you'll become fluent in "speaking Microsoft."

Setting the Stage: A Primitive Microsoft Network

Basically, all networks allow you to share files and printers, and most of them nowadays let you build and use client-server systems as well. Another thing that all networks have in common is that they soon get large and hard to manage if they're successful. How their creators choose to solve management problems is mainly what makes different brands of network software different, so let's start out with a simple circa 1985 Microsoft network, kind of a Mesozoic network. (I suppose on a network like that, you'd "Jurassic Park" the drive heads... sorry, couldn't resist.)

Back in April of 1985, Microsoft shipped their first networking product, a tool called MS-NET. You couldn't buy MS-NET directly from Microsoft under that name, because Microsoft only sold it through other vendors, most prominently IBM. IBM sold it as the "IBM PC Network Program." Basically, it was just a bunch of programs that you'd load on a DOS PC to allow the PC to share its files with other PCs. It's still sold today, although in a considerably more jazzed-up form, as Artisoft's LANtastic package. Imagine an office with just two PCs, as you see in Figure 2.1.

FIGURE 2.1:

A simple Microsoft network

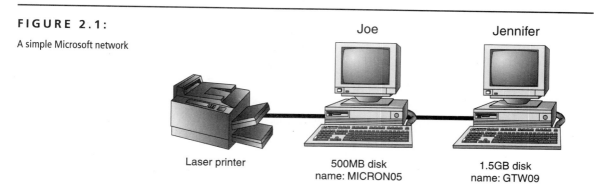

	Joe	Jennifer
Laser printer	500MB disk name: MICRON05	1.5GB disk name: GTW09

Now, in our simple office, Jennifer's got more storage capacity on her machine than Joe has on his, but Joe's got the office laser printer attached to *his* PC. (It's there because he's bigger than she, and, as he could carry it to his desk, he got it, rapscallion that he is.) Each PC has an inventory control number, like MICRON05 or GTW09; that will be important soon.

Both Jennifer and Joe work on the office accounting system, so they need to share the accounting files—either that or they have to pass floppies around. Since Jennifer's got more disk space, they put the accounting files on her machine. So, the network problems that they have to solve are to

- Share Joe's printer with Jennifer
- Share Jennifer's disk with Joe

Let's see how they solve their problem with a simplified Microsoft network. With this network, Jennifer just puts her hard disk on the network so that Joe can use it, and Joe puts his printer on the network so that Jennifer can use it.

Assigning Network Names

The first step in setting up a Microsoft network is to name the PCs, both servers and workstations. Then, you have to give a name to each user—Joe and Jennifer work fine for this network. We may as well name the PCs with their inventory numbers, so Jennifer's machine is named GTW09 and Joe's machine is named MICRON05. This leads me to a tip…

TIP   PCs may get reassigned, so it's a bad idea to name machines after their users. Calling Joe's PC "JOESPC" could cause confusion if it's reassigned to someone else later.

NOTE   Each PC's machine name can be no longer than 15 characters. Upper and lower case do not matter. You can have blanks in a machine's name, but I wouldn't recommend it because blanks will crash some setup programs.

In Microsoft networking there are machine names, user names, share names, and passwords—and they all have different rules about how long they can be and whether case matters or not.

Sharing File Directories on the Network

The first network task Jennifer and Joe set themselves to is getting Jennifer's hard disk onto the network so Joe can get to it. The two basic steps are (1) Jennifer must tell the network software on her computer that it's okay to offer her disk to the world in general, and (2) Joe must tell the network software on his computer that it should go out and exploit Jennifer's newly offered network resource.

Now, despite her obviously giving nature, Jennifer doesn't want Joe to get access to *everything* on the network, just some files that they share in her directory of accounting data, a directory called C:\ACCNTING. She wants to tell the network software, "Take the \ACCNTING subdirectory on my C: drive and offer it to anyone who wants it. Call it ACCT.'"

Understanding Share Names

ACCT is then called, in Microsoft enterprise networking terminology, the *share name* of the C:\ACCNTING directory on Jennifer's machine. It's the name that others will use to access the directory over the network. Jennifer *could* have called it ACCNTING, just like the directory name, but I gave it a different name just to underscore that it's not necessary to give a directory share the same name as its directory name. And since a share name is a new kind of name in Microsoft networking, let's take a second to mention the rules for creating share names.

IN THEORY

NOTE
Share names can have up to 81 characters, although DOS redirectors don't like names with more than eight characters. Also, Windows 95 cannot handle printer share names with more than 12 characters. Case does not matter. You can use blanks, but it's not recommended.

So let's see, machine names can be 15 characters long and share names can be up to 81 characters long...

Offering the Share on the Network

In a simple Microsoft network, the command that Jennifer would issue (after loading the network software, of course) would be

```
net share acct=c:\accnting
```

Now the network software running in Jennifer's machine (GTW09) knows that if anyone asks for a shared named ACCT, it should go ahead and share it.

NOTE
That particular NET SHARE command works with certain types of Microsoft network products (NT server and workstation, Windows for Workgroups, the Workgroups Add-On for MS-DOS, and LAN Manager) but not with all (Windows 95, for example). Be prepared for the fact that network commands in all Microsoft networking products are similar, but not always exactly the same.

Accessing a Shared Directory over the Network

Now Joe wants to use ACCT. Joe is, of course, running DOS, and DOS is pretty dumb when it comes to networks. DOS thinks that all data is stored on devices with names like A:, B:, C:, and so on. Now, the network software running on Joe's machine is built with the understanding that it's running on the network-challenged DOS, and so it fools DOS into letting Joe use network shares by giving network shares names like hard disks—names like D:, E:, and the like.

Joe then says to the networking software on his PC, "Attach me to the ACCT share on Jennifer's machine." Joe doesn't know whether ACCT is all of Jennifer's drive or just part of it. Joe's networking software then says something like, "You're now attached to ACCT on Jennifer's machine. It will appear to you as local drive D:."

The actual command that Joe would issue would look like this:

```
net use d: \\gtw09\acct
```

All those backslashes need some explaining, as they're very important. Better read on.

Introducing UNCs

Notice the \\GTW09\ACCT term; it's called a *universal naming convention* name, or a *UNC* name. You'll use UNCs again and again in NT networking, so let's pick that term apart. Also pay attention to this NET USE command; even though it's been around for a long time, it is still extremely useful even in modern Microsoft networking. It is one command-line networking command that you'll find in all Microsoft networking products (as far as I know).

First, the two backslashes are a warning that the name following is a *machine* name, and the backslash after that refers to the *share name* ACCT, rather than the directory name. Because Jennifer's machine, which owns the share, is named GTW09, and the share is named ACCT, the UNC for that share is \\GTW09\ACCT. Upper- and lowercase don't matter when you're working with UNCs, by the way.

Again, Joe doesn't really *have* a D: on his machine; he's just got network software that takes read and write requests for a mythical (logical) "drive D:" and reformulates those requests into network communication to Jennifer's machine.

Sharing a Printer on the Network

Joe now has access to Jennifer's disk and can clog it up with whatever garbage he likes. (Oddly enough, in Microsoft networking there is no notion of "disk quotas," the limitations on how much a user can dump into a share. There's no way for Jennifer to say, "Joe can use this share, but he can't put more than 10 megabytes of files in it." This weakness extends even to the most recent version of NT Server.) In return, however, Joe promised Jennifer that he'd let her use his printer over the network. So he must tell the network software on his PC to share the printer. Back in the MS-NET days, the command looked like

```
net share joeshp=LPT1:
```

This says, "Share the printer attached to LPT1:, giving it the share name of JOESHP."

NOTE
I said a couple of lines ago, "Back in the MS-NET days..." because that syntax doesn't work with NT, so don't try it. It seems to only work in Windows for Workgroups, LAN Manager, and the Workgroups Add-on for MS-DOS. As I said before, the NET commands vary from Microsoft product to Microsoft product. (I once asked a Microsoft person via e-mail why the "net share" command didn't work for printers, and he responded, "Uh, it's because, huh huh huh, we just don't, uh uh uh." I asked what the extra "huh" and "uh" sounds were and was told that it was a reference to Beavis and Butthead. Very funny to some, I suppose, although "Gates and Ballmer" might have been more amusing.)

Jennifer then tells her networking software to attach JOESHP, on Joe's machine, to her LPT1: port, with the command

```
net use lpt1: \\micron05\joeshp
```

Picking that command apart, Jennifer has told her PC to look on a machine named MICRON05 for a share called JOESHP and to attach it to her LPT1:. From now on, whenever Jennifer tells an application program to print to a LaserJet on LPT1:, the network software will intercept the printed output and direct it over the network to Joe's machine. The networking software on Joe's machine will then print the information on Joe's printer.

By the way, remember when I said not to use blanks in names? Here's an example why. If Joe's machine were named Micron no. 5, Jennifer would have to put the UNC in quotes, like this:

```
net use lpt1: "\\micron no. 5\joeshp"
```

And it's more than just an annoyance; several Microsoft setup utilities don't work properly when you ask them to set up over a network from a machine with a blank in its name.

Problems with the Primitive Network

Now, this is a nice network so far, as long as it never gets much bigger. But if it *does* get bigger, then there can be problems like these three:

- How did we know that Joe's LaserJet was called JoesHP, or that Jennifer's drive was called ACCT?

- What if Jennifer wants Joe to have access to *some* of the files in the shared directory, but not *all* of them?

- Once the network gets bigger—as other people want to join it—it will have to communicate with other networks. As different networks use different *languages*, or, more correctly, *protocols*, how can our one network manage multiple kinds of networks with their multiple languages/protocols?

In short, the problem posed by the first question was solved by a Microsoft notion called a workgroup, the second problem is solved by another Microsoft notion called a domain, and the third problem is solved with Microsoft's layered structure of networking software. Those three topics will take up the rest of the chapter.

Who's Out There: Browsers and Workgroups

Years ago, I actually used an IBM PC Network program on a network like Jennifer and Joe's. As you saw with Joe and Jennifer, you hooked up to a drive on a server by saying to the PC Network program, for example, "Attach me to drive E: on the machine named AVOCADO." Nice and simple, but it had a major flaw: How did you find out in the first place that the server was named AVOCADO and that the drive that it was offering was called E:? The answer is, *you just had to know the name of the resource before you could use that resource.* There was no "scan the network to find out what's available" feature to the network. (An IBM guy once explained to me that this was a "security feature." Now, why didn't *I* think of that?)

I wanted a kind of "net scan" command, something that would shout to the other systems, "Hey! Whaddya got?" As it turns out, that's not very simple. The whole process of offering services on a network is part of what's known generically as *name services*, or *directory services*, and they're not easy to offer.

Solving the Directory Service Problem

How would you make a workstation know about every service on the network? There are several approaches.

Static Service Lists

The simplest approach would be to put a file with some kind of services database on every workstation, a kind of "yellow pages" of system capabilities. For example, you might have an ASCII file on every PC that says, "There is a file server on machine BIGPC with a shared disk called BIGDISK, and the computer named PSRV has a shared printer called HP5SI."

This has the advantage of being very fast and very simple to understand. To add a new resource, just modify the service list file.

It has the *disadvantage*, however, of being static. Any changes to the system, and some poor fool (that would be *you*, the network administrator) has to go around to all the workstations and update the file. If there were two hundred workstations on your network, then you'd have to actually travel to all two hundred and copy that static service list file to each workstation's hard disk. Even worse, this method wouldn't take into account the services that were temporarily unavailable, such as a downed server.

This method sounds too primitive to use, but it's not completely useless. In NetWare 3.*x*, you identify yourself to your desired server via information in NET.CFG. That's a hard-wired server name, and would require a fair amount of editing on every workstation if you wanted to rename an important server—which is why, I suppose, you don't rename servers often in a NetWare world, and it's probably why Novell handles it differently in NetWare 4.

Periodic Advertising

Another approach is an occasional broadcast. Every 30 to 60 seconds (depending on how the network administrator sets it up), each resource on NetWare 3.11 tells the rest of the network about itself by shouting, "I'm here!" Novell calls this the Service Advertising Protocol (SAP). This is another good idea and it works great in many cases.

It's not the perfect answer, however. Its problem is that broadcasts can clog up a network if that network has a fair number of servers, all advertising. (Imagine if every store in the U.S. were to remind you that it exists *every minute or so*—you'd spend so much time responding to advertising that you'd get nothing else done, and your mailbox would be full.) Periodic advertising works on small to medium-sized LANs, but on larger networks it is unworkable due to the sheer number of broadcasts flooding the net.

Furthermore, those advertisements probably wouldn't be able to travel around an enterprise network due to *routers*. Most networks of any size are divided up into *segments*, and the segments are connected with devices called routers. In general, routers carry messages from one segment to another, when necessary; they're smart enough to avoid retransmitting messages unnecessarily. That's good because it means that routers cut down on network congestion.

The problem that routers pose to periodic advertisements is that routers do not in general retransmit broadcasts; a SAP broadcast in one segment generally isn't heard on any other segment. I say "generally" because you can configure most routers to retransmit broadcasts, but you usually don't want to do that because it defeats the congestion-reducing aspect of routers. Anyway, the result of periodic advertising on most networks would be that a server's advertisements would only be visible to workstations within its local segment.

Larger networks, then, need some other method of spreading the news about services.

Name Servers

ENTERPRISE NETWORKING

Yet another approach, and the one used by most enterprise network products, is to assign the task of keeping track of network services to one or more computers called *name servers*. Servers identify themselves to these name servers, and the name servers keep a list of the servers that they know of, as well as the shares offered by each of those servers. Each segment gets its own name server, and the name servers know of one another and compare notes about what's available. Because the name servers talk to one another in one-to-one directed communications rather than broadcasts, routers are no longer an obstacle to making an entire large network aware of a given server's services.

A machine that's acting as a name server usually isn't dedicated to that task; usually it's also a file server. Particular machines become name servers when a network administrator installs name server software on them. Setting up name servers is a bit more work for a network administrator, which is about the only downside of a name server.

Microsoft's Answer: Browse Services

Microsoft decided (perhaps rightly) that name servers were hard to set up, but that something like a name server was essential, so Microsoft networking uses a kind of name server system where you, the network administrator, don't have to do *anything*; the name servers set themselves up automatically.

Microsoft doesn't have a "name service" per se; the Microsoft name for name services is "browse services." What most of the network world would call name servers Microsoft calls *browse masters* or *master browsers*. A search of the April 1996 TechNet CD shows 53 occurrences of "master browser" and 41 occurrences of "browse master," so I guess either name is correct. What's different about the concept of Microsoft browse servers is that no one computer is fixed as the browse master. Instead, when your computer logs on to your network, it finds a browse master by broadcasting a request for a browse master and saying, "Are there any browse masters out there?" The first browse master to hear the workstation (there can be multiple browse masters, as you'll see) responds to the workstation by saying, "Just direct all your name service requests to me."

When a server starts up, it does the same thing. It broadcasts, "Are there any browse masters out there?" and when it finds one, it says to it, "I am a server with the following shares. Please add me to your list of servers." The list of servers that a browse master maintains is called the *browse list*, not surprisingly.

By now, you may be wondering, "How come I've never seen one of these browse lists?" You have. If you ever work with earlier versions of NT or with Windows for Workgroups, then you would see Figure 2.2 when you opened up the File Manager and clicked Disk ➤ Connect Network Drive.

From Windows 95 or Windows NT 4, you can see a browse list by opening up the Network Neighborhood folder, as in Figure 2.3.

From DOS, you can see a browse list by typing

```
net view or net view \\machinename
```

You see a screen like the one in Figure 2.4.

Each figure shows you the list of servers available: Aldebaran, Astro, and Artemis. Other servers—Daffy and MWM66—appear only in some of the browse lists because a few minutes passed between taking the screen shots, and a few "test" servers went up or down in those few minutes. In all three cases, the workstations that these screens were taken from got their browse lists from a local browse master.

FIGURE 2.2:

Sample browse list from
Windows for Workgroups
or Windows NT version 3.x

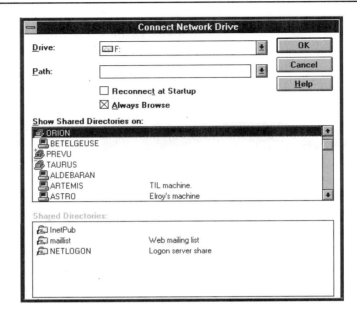

FIGURE 2.3:

Sample browse list from Windows NT 4 or Windows 95/98

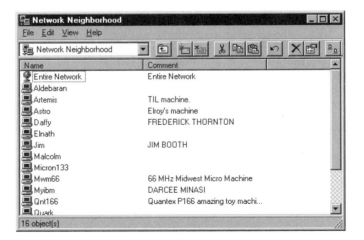

You can drill down further into these browse lists, as well. In Windows 95/98 or Windows NT 4, you can double-click on any one of those servers and see the list of shares that the servers offer; that, too, is information from the browse list. In

Windows for Workgroups or Windows NT 3.*x*, you'd just click once on a server, and the list of its shares would appear in the bottom pane of the dialog box. From DOS, you'd get the list of servers by typing **net view**, as you've already seen, and then you get the list of shares for any given server by typing **net view** *server-name*, where *servername* is the name of the server you want to see the shares of.

FIGURE 2.4:

Sample browse list from DOS

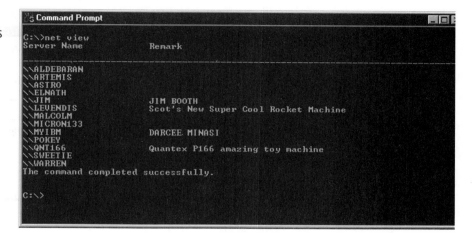

```
Command Prompt
C:\>net view
Server Name                       Remark
-----------------------------------------------------------------------------
\\ALDEBARAN
\\ARTEMIS
\\ASTRO
\\ELNATH
\\JIM                             JIM BOOTH
\\LEVENDIS                        Scot's New Super Cool Rocket Machine
\\MALCOLM
\\MICRON133
\\MYIBM                           DARCEE MINASI
\\POKEY
\\QNT166                          Quantex P166 amazing toy machine
\\SWEETIE
\\WARREN
The command completed successfully.

C:\>
```

When Browse Lists Get Too Large: Workgroups to the Rescue

As I've described them so far, browse lists seem pretty convenient. But in the little test network that I used for the previous screen shots, you saw only a few servers. Hell, *everything* works fine on *small* networks.

Now let's talk about *your* network. Sit down at a corporate network of any size and you see dozens, hundreds, or *thousands* of servers. Scrolling down through a 500-server browse list would be a bit time-consuming—to say nothing of how much work the browse master would have to do to keep it up to date! The problem to solve is, then, managing the size of the browse list. There are two ways to do that:

- Reduce the number of servers in your enterprise

- Divide up the enterprise-wide browse list into a number of smaller browse lists called *workgroups*

Disable Peer-to-Peer Sharing on Workstations

The first answer is actually a bit off the main topic, but let me digress for a moment and talk about it before returning to the main item: workgroups. When I say, "Reduce the number of servers," I'm talking about an unfortunate side-effect of running Windows for Workgroups, Windows 95, and Windows NT workstations—they all have the capability to become peer-to-peer servers. The browse masters don't distinguish between industrial-strength servers running NT Server and low-octane peer-to-peer servers, so you could end up with a browse list that's *supposed* to only list your servers, but *actually* lists all of your servers and workstations. In general, I think peer-to-peer networking is a bad idea. If a piece of data is important enough to be used by two employees, then it's a company asset that should be backed up regularly and so should go on a managed file server, not a desktop machine that's probably backed up once a decade. My recommendation is this: disable the peer-to-peer sharing option on your Windows for Workgroups, Windows 95, and Windows NT workstations. How you do this depends on the operating system of the workstation(s) in question. Directory shares in NT Server and NT Workstation computers are discussed in Chapter 7. In Windows 9*x*, go to Control Panel ➤ Network ➤ File and Print Sharing and make sure both options, to share files and printers, are unchecked. In Windows for Workgroups, make sure the sharing control in Network Setup is set *not* to enable file or printer sharing (see the section "Doing the Network Setup Work" in Chapter 9).

Not only will your network have less traffic—every workstation will no longer have delusions of serverdom, so they won't be chattering at the browse master all of the time—but not loading the server part of the workstation's operating system saves RAM on the workstation.

Divide the Browse List Up into Workgroups to Keep It Manageable

The other approach to keeping a browse list to a manageable size is to subdivide it in some way. That's a reasonable thing to suggest if you realize that, no matter how large an organization *seems* to be, it's usually composed of lots of smaller groups, such as Manufacturing, Sales, Marketing, Accounting, Finance, Personnel, Senior Management, and so on. Each of those groups can be called *workgroups* and you can pretty much chop up your enterprise into workgroups in any way you like (but a rule of thumb says that a workgroup should be a group of people for whom 95 percent of the data generated by that group stays within that group).

From a more network-technical point of view, the minimum definition of a workgroup is just *a group of workstations that share a browse list*. (That's my definition, not Microsoft's.) The idea is that when someone in Accounting opens up her browse list, you want her to see just the Accounting servers, not the Manufacturing servers, as she's got no use for the Manufacturing servers. (Besides, there's a good chance that she doesn't have permission to access the Manufacturing servers anyway—but I'll get to workgroups and security in a little bit.) How do you join a workgroup? See the sidebar "How Do I Join a Workgroup?"

How Do I Join a Workgroup?

Generally, all you need to do is to tell the networking software on your workstations and servers that they're members of a given workgroup. There isn't any "security" in being part of a workgroup—you pretty much just declare yourself a member and you are a member. (As a matter of fact, if you misspell the name of the workgroup, you end up accidentally founding a whole new workgroup all by yourself, which I'm sure was not your intention!)

Specifically, you designate which workgroup you're a member of in one of the following ways:

- **From a DOS or Windows for Workgroups workstation**   In the [network] section of the SYSTEM.INI file you'll find a WORKGROUP= parameter. (You'll have a SYSTEM.INI even if you're just running DOS because the network client software creates one.) You can also set the workgroup from the MS-DOS Network Client Setup program, or in the Windows for Workgroups' Network applet of the Control Panel.

- **From Windows 95/98**   Open the Control Panel and double-click on the Network Icon. In the property sheet that you see, click the Identification tab. You see the place to fill in the workgroup name.

- **On Windows NT 3.x**   Open the Control Panel and double-click the Network applet. You'll see a button labeled Domain or Workgroup. (NT has a kind of confusing way of blurring workgroups and domains, which I'll make clearer later in this chapter.) Click that button, and you can change the workgroup you're a member of. Again, NT complicates choosing a workgroup somewhat, so read the rest of this chapter if you want to change an NT workgroup.

- **On Windows NT 4**   Open the Control Panel and double-click on the Network applet. Like Windows 95, Windows NT 4 has a property sheet with an Identification tab. Click on Change to change the workgroup. Again, with NT you may see no references to workgroups at all; instead you see references to domains. Read on to understand the differences.

NOTE   Workgroup names are like machine names, and can be up to 15 characters long.

So, to review what we've seen so far:

- Network browse lists allow a user at a workstation to see all of the servers on the network, and from there to see all of the shares on a given server.

- Browse lists can get fairly long, so you can partition your entire network into *workgroups*, which are just groups of people that share a browse list.

- When you request a browse list, you don't get the entire list of servers in your enterprise network, you only get the list of servers within your workgroup.

- Each workgroup has one or more servers that act as gatherers of browse information. They're called browse masters or master browsers, and they're picked automatically.

- Machines that are only workstations and don't act as servers even in a peer-to-peer capacity do not appear on browse lists.

As the question of what machines go on a browse list and what machines don't is important to the length of a browse list, let me list the kinds of machines that can act as servers in a Microsoft enterprise network:

- Windows 3.*x* (with the Workgroup Add-On for MS-DOS clients)
- DOS (with Workgroup Add-On for MS-DOS clients)
- Windows for Workgroups
- Windows 95
- NT Workstation
- NT Server

As it's an unusual product, let me just explain that the Workgroup Add-On for MS-DOS is a separate Microsoft product that lets you use a DOS machine as a peer-to-peer server. Again, I recommend that you disable file and print sharing on all of these machines except, of course, for the machines dedicated to the task of being servers, all of which are probably running NT Server.

And once you're in a workgroup, you'll no doubt want to see your browse list; "How Do I View a Browse List?" tells you the specifics.

How Do I View a Browse List?

Microsoft has built different browse programs into its various network client software.

- **From DOS**   Type **net view**. That shows you the list of servers. You can view the shares on a given server by typing **net view *servername*. To see the browse list for a workgroup other than your own, type **net view /workgroup:*workgroupname***.

- **From Windows for Workgroups or Windows NT 3.*x***   Open up the File Manager, click Drive, and then click Connect Network Drive. You'll see a window with two panes. The browse list for your workgroup and a list of the other workgroups on the network appears as the list of possible servers in the top pane and, when you click on a server, that server's shares appear in the bottom pane. To see the browse list for a workgroup other than your own, double-click on the name of the workgroup in the top pane.

- **From Windows 95/98 or Windows NT 4**   Open up the Network Neighborhood folder. You'll see the servers in your workgroup represented as PC icons in a folder. Double-click on one of the servers, and a folder will open up showing you the shares. To see the browse list for a workgroup other than your own, double-click on the Entire Network icon and you'll see a list of workgroups. On Windows NT 4, click on Entire Network and then Microsoft Network, and then you'll get a list of the other workgroups.

Security in a Workgroup

When it comes to security and workgroups, I'm tempted to shorten this entire section down to a few words: "There isn't any." But it's a bit more complex than that… .

I made a passing reference to security a few paragraphs back when I suggested that not only would an Accounting user not want to see the servers in Manufacturing, but also that The Powers That Be in the Manufacturing network might not *want* the Accounting user to see the servers in Manufacturing. Security is important—it's essential—in every network, even Jennifer and Joe's network. For example, suppose after a while Joe finds that he doesn't want everyone in the world using his laser printer. He has discovered that every time someone prints a document on his machine, his computer slows down as a result because, after all, the very act of being a print server takes up a fair amount of Joe's CPU time. He wants *some* people to be able to use the printer, but not *most* people. What should he do? There are two possible answers in a workgroup:

- He could hide his laser printer, sharing it but keeping it off the browse list.

- He could put a password on his laser printer.

Hiding Shares in Microsoft Networks

Joe can share his printer but hide it from the browse list by putting a dollar sign ($) at the end of its name. For example, if in sharing his printer he didn't name it "joeshp," but rather "joeshp$," then *the printer share would not show up on the browse list*. Someone could still get to it, but she'd have to know the name of the printer, as she couldn't get it off the browse list if she forgot. Other than that, you attach to a hidden share in the usual way—Jennifer would now type net use **lpt1: \\micron05\joeshp$** rather than **net use lpt1: \\micron05\joeshp**, as she did before.

NOTE   Here's an example of why knowing the command-line version of the networking commands (rather than only knowing how to get to the network via the graphical user interface) is essential—the NET USE command is one way to attach to a hidden share from Windows 95/98 or NT Workstation 4 machine. (Other ways are via Disk ➤ Connect to Network Drive in NT 3.*x* or Tools ➤ Map to Network Drive in the Explorer under NT 4.)

And if for some reason you want to keep an entire computer off the browse list, you can do that, as well. Go to the computer and open up a command prompt, type **net config server /hidden:yes**, and reboot the machine. This puts the PC in "run silent, run deep" mode, and it no longer shows up on the browse list. You can still NET VIEW and NET USE to it, as with hidden shares.

Password-Protecting Shares in Microsoft Networks

A little investigation showed me that hidden shares *are* indeed reported by the browser, after all! When a workstation PC asks the local browse master for a browse list, the browse master actually ships out the entire list of shares to the PC, including the hidden shares. It is the software on the workstation PC—the NET VIEW, File Manager, or Network Neighborhood software—that filters out the shares suffixed with a dollar sign. So a programmer *could* write a version of Network Neighborhood that showed all of the shares, "hidden" or no!

Clearly, hiding a share and trying to keep the existence of joeshp$ a secret is not exactly great security, but it's a sort of minimum way to keep other people off your printer or directory share. The other way to secure a share is by putting a password on it. Exactly *how* you do that depends on what kind of server you're using. Some Microsoft networking systems let you create user-specific passwords, and others only offer you the ability to put a single share on a password, which is then the password for *all* users.

Let's first look at the server products that only let you put a single password on a share. (This includes the Workgroup Add-on for MS-DOS, Windows for Workgroups, and, optionally, Windows 95/98.) The problem with putting a single password on a share is that it's the *same* password for *all* of the share's users. (Remember that *share* generically means *shared printer* or *shared disk directory*.) If you wanted to exclude one current user, you could only do it by first changing the password, then finding every one of the other printer's users and telling them the password.

How NT Improves upon Workgroup Security

Now let's see how NT handles security in a workgroup. When you set up a Windows NT computer, the setup program asks you if you want to use workgroup-level security or "domain"-level security. I'll discuss domain-level security later in this chapter and setting up in the next chapter, but for the moment let's look at how NT brings its own twist to the *workgroup* security that you've met so far.

As you've already read, you can still hide a share under NT by suffixing a dollar sign on the end of its name; that's no different from any other Microsoft networking product. What *is* different about workgroup security under NT is that NT lets you separate security information *by user*, rather than only letting you set a single password on a share for all of that share's users. This is one way in which NT is fundamentally different from Windows for Workgroups and Windows 95/98. On DOS, Windows, and Windows 95, those earlier operating systems don't maintain separate user accounts. Having such fine-grained control of security is really neat, but it's got a cost—someone's got to actually create all those user accounts.

Workgroup Security in Windows For example, suppose you've got a small network, so small that you've decided to use a Windows 95/98 machine as your "server" (can't you just see the sneer when I write that?). Suppose in a fit of originality you call it SERVER and create a disk share called DISKSHARE. You then have a bunch of workstations running DOS with some network software added to it, like Windows for Workgroups or Windows 95/98. You hire a new employee named Gertrude who sits down at a workstation, starts up the network software, and does a **net use e: \\server\diskshare**, which of course attaches her to the Windows 95/98 machine that acts as the "server." SERVER asks her for DISKSHARE's password, which is (for example) "swordfish," and since Gertrude and the rest of the office know that the password is "swordfish," she types in **swordfish** and she's in.

Workgroup Security in NT Notice that you never had to "introduce" a user named Gertrude to the server. Anyone who knows the password "swordfish" can attach to the server. *That's* where NT is different, even with a workgroup. Now suppose we rerun the above scenario, but this time, instead of using a Windows 95 machine as the server, let's use an NT Workstation machine with workgroup-level security.

You create the shares as before, but you do not put passwords on the shares. Instead, you must first use a program called the User Manager to create a user account for each person who will access the shares on this server. These user accounts are stored in a file called SAM, located in \winnt\system32\config. (You'll learn more about SAM later.) Then, you go to the shares and explicitly name the people who can access which shares. Now if you want to access an NT machine on a workgroup, you must have been properly introduced—so Gertrude isn't going *anywhere* until you (1) create a Gertrude account on the NT Workstation machine and (2) add Gertrude to the list of approved users for DISKSHARE. Gertrude then must use her name and password to get onto the NT machine, even if she's communicating with the server from a DOS or Windows workstation.

NOTE Now that I've introduced user names, I should tell you that user names can be up to 20 characters long. According to Microsoft, passwords can in theory be up to 128 characters long, but the program that you use to create user accounts—the User Manager, which you'll meet in a later chapter—only lets you type in 14 characters. To summarize: machine names and workgroup names can be up to 15 characters long, share names up to 12 characters long, user names up to 20 characters long, and passwords up to 14 characters long. Bizarre, eh?

All this talk of user accounts and user-specific abilities sounds a bit more strict, doesn't it? That's because NT has "Security" as its middle name, so to speak. It also sounds like there's not much more you could want in terms of security, right? Well, not exactly, which is why understanding domains is fundamental to understanding how to build a good NT-based network. And although I've been keeping you waiting about domains for a while now, I've got to cover *one* more thing before we get to domains.

Keeping One Workgroup from Peeking into Another's Shares

Before moving on to domains, let's cover an important aspect of NT networking that many people consider a real security breach, but that you can't do anything about. It applies to *all* Microsoft enterprise networks, whether built with workgroups or domains.

Let's return to our accountant who normally only sees the ACCOUNTING browse list. There is another workgroup on the same enterprise network called MANUFACTURING, and let's suppose that the manager of the MANUFACTURING workgroup doesn't want those accountants seeing *anything* about manufacturing's network. Now, suppose our accountant is bored one day, and wants to see if she can peek into some manufacturing files. To do that, she has to do the following:

1. Find out the workgroup name of the manufacturing department.

2. Find out the names of the servers in that workgroup.

3. Retrieve a list of shares on those servers.

4. Actually access one of the shares.

How hard is it to do that? The first two steps are pretty easy; the last two can be a bit more difficult. Retrieving the names of the workgroups on your network is easy, as the browse lists show you not only your workgroup, but also the names of the other workgroups. Remember, the name servers (browse masters) all talk to one another. The only browse program that I know of that does not show other workgroups is the one built into the DOS redirector; the NET VIEW command only shows you your workgroup, and I haven't been able to figure out how to make it show me the names of the other workgroups.

Second, once she knows that the name of the other workgroup is MANUFAC-TURING, then all she has to do is to ask for its browse list. In the graphical browse lists that are part of NT, Windows for Workgroups, and Windows 95, it's just a matter of clicking. On DOS, again, if she figured out a way to get the workgroup name and typed **net view /workgroup:***workgroupname*, she would get the list of servers in that workgroup.

NOTE   Note one deficiency of browse lists: there's no easy way to find out which of the "servers" that you see are truly servers, and which are just workstations that have the ability to do peer-to-peer networking.

Now that she's got the list of servers, she drills down to the share list for each server. Ah, but here our intruder may run into some trouble. Double-click on an NT machine (workstation or server) and the NT machine will say to the intruder's workstation, "Who wants to know what shares I've got?" The intruder's workstation then automatically and invisibly replies with the user's name and password. The NT machine then checks that against the list of names and passwords that it knows. If there's a match, then she gets the browse list. If not, then she either gets a message like "System error 5 has occurred; access is denied" or simply "Access is denied," or she gets a dialog box that says something like (I'm being vague because every operating system handles it differently) "Incorrect password or unknown username," with the chance to type in a new user name and password.

Here is the question, then. We have an unrecognized individual who requests that the master browser show her the list of shares on a server. Does she get the list? The extremely specific, 100-percent complete answer is pretty lengthy, but the basic conditions are

- If the server is a Windows for Workgroups machine, it always gives out the list of its shares to anyone.

- If the server is a Windows 95/98 machine that employs share-level password authentication for its shares, then it always gives out the share list.

- If the server is a Windows 95/98 machine that employs user-level password authentication, then it only gives out its share list if the server that it gets its user names from recognizes the user.

- If the server is a Windows NT machine and its Guest account is enabled, then it always gives out its share list.

- If the server is a Windows NT machine and you're logged into your workstation with a user name and password that match a known user name and password on the Windows NT machine, even if you're currently a member of a different workgroup (or domain), then you get the share list.

Finally, if the intruder from Accounting tries to actually access a share, she will only be successful if she's got the permissions to access that share.

To review the facts about browsing and security:

- Anyone who's physically attached to your network can find out the names of your workgroups (and domains, actually).

- Anyone who's physically attached to your network can retrieve the list of servers on any workgroup.

- Someone who's physically attached to your network may or may not be able to see the list of shares on a given server. Basically, Windows for Workgroups and Windows 95/98 "servers" give out their share list to anyone, but Windows NT machines must know you before they do that.

I know I had to be a bit fuzzy on some of this, but it will make more sense when we get to domains, the next topic in this chapter.

Domains: Centralized Security

You've already seen that you could set up a network with an NT Server machine and a workgroup. You'd just install NT Server on a computer, declare it a member of workgroup XYZ, and create a user account for each user. Then you'd create directory and printer shares on that server, and designate which users can access what shares. So far, so good. What do domains do for us, then?

Well, not a heck of a lot ... until you want to add another server.

Multiple Servers Means Multiple User Accounts

You see, you've got to build each user on each NT server or workstation. (Remember that there's no such thing as a user account for DOS, Windows for Workgroups, or Windows 95/98.) Those user accounts are stored in a database called the Security Accounts Manager, or SAM. (For Novell administrators, this is like the NetWare 3.*x* Bindery.) Each NT machine, whether workstation or server, has a SAM on its hard disk. Just to make this clear, suppose you had users named John, Mary, Sue, Paul, and Ignatz in your workgroup, two NT Servers named S1 and S2, and an NT Workstation named W1. (There's DOS, Windows for Workgroups, and

Windows 95/98 workstations here also, but they don't matter for this example, as they don't keep user accounts—they don't have a SAM.) Suppose also that there are shares on S1, S2, and W1 that everyone will need to get to. To set up *this* network as a workgroup named XYZ, there are a few more steps:

1. Install NT Server on S1 and S2, and NT Workstation on W1. Make sure they all describe themselves as being members of workgroup XYZ.

2. While installing S1, S2, and W1, NT automatically creates an Administrator account for each machine which, as you'd expect, has powers and abilities far beyond those of normal users. Each Administrator account is only an Administrator account recognized at its particular computer, so you'll end up with three distinct accounts, one on each machine. That also means that you may have chosen to give them all different passwords, so you need to somehow keep track of those passwords.

3. Go to S1, log on as Administrator using the Administrator password for S1, and create users John, Mary, Sue, Paul, and Ignatz.

4. Go to S2, log on as S2's Administrator using the Administrator password for S2, and create users John, Mary, Sue, Paul, and Ignatz—and, of course, *these* user accounts are totally separate and distinct from the ones you just created on S1, so you could end up with different passwords.

5. Go to W1, log on as W1's Administrator using the Administrator password for W1, and create users John, Mary, Sue, Paul, and Ignatz—and, of course, *these* user accounts are totally separate and distinct from the ones you just created on S1 and S2, so you could end up with different passwords.

In other words, you must rebuild the SAM for each NT machine in your workgroup!

Multiple User Accounts Means Multiple Logins

Now suppose John fires up his Windows 95 workstation first thing in the morning and grabs his e-mail, which is sitting on S2. When he first tries to attach to the directory that holds the e-mail, S2 stops and says, "Should I let this guy get to my directory?" It then asks John for a user name and password. He complies, and all is well. Then, a little later, John needs something from S1. This is the first time today that S1 has seen John, and so S1 challenges him for a user name and password. John's an organized kind of guy, so he's got the user name and password that he uses for S1 right at his fingertips. He'll have to do the same thing if ever he tries to get data from W1—he'll need another user name and password.

Local Password Files

Microsoft network client software simplifies this process a bit with files called *password lists*. They're distinguished by the extension PWL. Every time you type in a user name and/or password at the request of a server, your local workstation software remembers it for you, and stores it in this PWL file. Then, all you have to do is identify yourself to your workstation once in the morning, and from there the workstation software automatically responds to any user name or password challenges that a server makes. But PWL files don't follow you around the network, so you have to repeat the process every time you log on to a new workstation. In addition, some people don't like the idea of having all of their passwords stored on their local hard disk, even if they *are* encrypted. Worse yet, in the mid-'90s, some Windows 95 users figured out how to crack PWL files, so many companies forbid their use.

One Answer: Multiple User Accounts, One Password

For security's sake, then, it's best to tell your workstation software not to create PWL files, which means we're back to typing in a slew of passwords and user names each and every day. Is there an easier way? Well, yes, kind of. If the network administrator sets it up so that John has the same user name and password on all three servers, then the first time each day that John types in his name and password, that information is cached by his workstation and, the next time he tries to connect to a server, the workstation offers that user name and password to that second (or third or whatever) server. If all of the servers that John uses all see him as a user named "John" with password "hassenpfeffer," then he need only log on to one server explicitly, and all subsequent logons that day will be automatic.

This *kind of* works, but it surely means that password-changing day will be a busy one for John—and for every other user, for that matter. And that's just with three servers; this scheme would be unworkable with more than that.

Let's see, now… So far, with just three servers and five users, you could have up to 18 different passwords, and each user must remember at least three passwords.

The main problem here seems to be that there are a lot of SAMs to keep track of. Domains improve upon this by designating one computer's SAM as the "central" SAM. Other NT machines still have SAMs, but they are small ones that essentially only say, "Go check with central SAM." This isn't that unusual of an idea. We've met print servers, file servers, and name servers. Why not a *security* server? That's the whole idea of a domain. A domain is basically a "super workgroup," a workgroup with centralized control of security. For comparison's sake, Figure 2.5 shows a simple workgroup.

FIGURE 2.5:

Workgroup security relationships

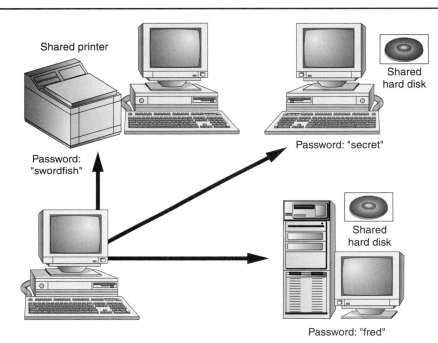

Shared printer

Password: "swordfish"

Password: "secret"

Shared hard disk

Shared hard disk

Password: "fred"

Just to keep things simple, I've diagrammed a workgroup with several servers, each of which some imaginary user uses the password "swordfish," "fred," or "secret" to access. You or your workstation must remember a whole bunch of passwords.

Domains: One Account, One Password, Many Servers

In a domain, in contrast, you need only remember one password—the password for your domain account, the one maintained on the "central SAM," as you see in Figure 2.6.

FIGURE 2.6:

Domain security relationships

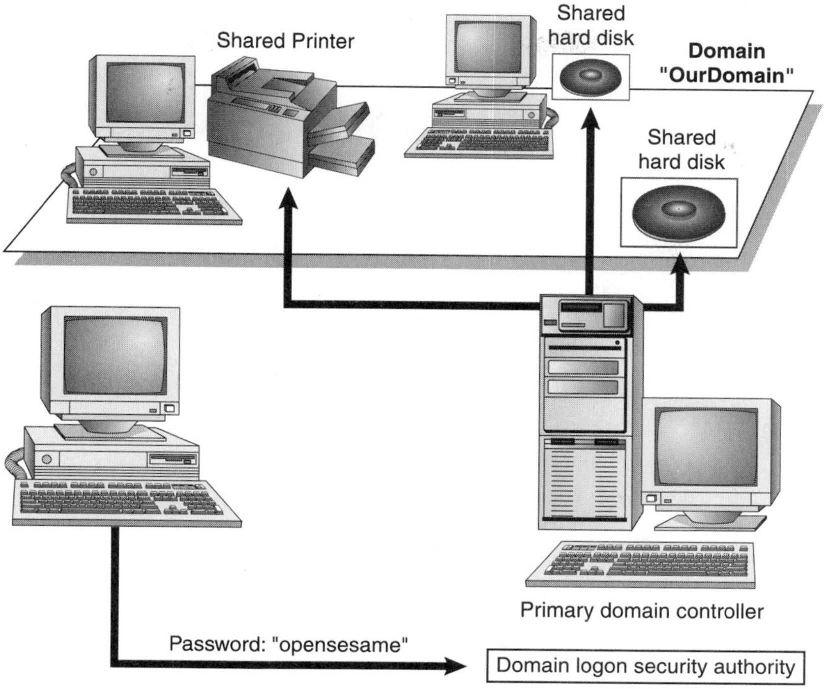

(Figure labels: Shared Printer; Shared hard disk; Domain "OurDomain"; Shared hard disk; Primary domain controller; Password: "opensesame"; Domain logon security authority)

Domains Need Domain Controllers

Domains are groups of NT machines—DOS, Windows for Workgroups, and Windows 95/98 machines can't join a domain—whose owners don't want to have to worry about maintaining a SAM database of users on their machine. As maintaining dozens of identical or similar SAMs would be a *lot* of work for some poor administrator (that would be *you*), NT allows a group of machines to *centralize* a shared SAM database on a single machine. Then, whenever one of these NT machines needs to log a user on, the NT machine doesn't look to its own SAM—it instead looks up the user's account on the machine with the central SAM database.

That machine with the central Security Accounts Manager database is called the *primary domain controller*, or PDC. Its SAM contains the user names, passwords, which groups each user belongs to, and what *rights* a user has—rights

(handwritten margin notes: USER NAME / PASSWORDS / user privilege / group application)

mean whether the user is an administrator, a normal user, or something in-between. The PDC's main job is to log people onto the domain.

The PDC can get a bit congested first thing in the morning, so it can have helpers in the form of *backup domain controllers*, or BDCs. BDCs hold identical images of the domain's SAM and can log in users just like a PDC. Part of the process of design-ing a domain involves figuring out how many BDCs you'll need and where to put them; you'll learn more about that in Chapter 12.

As I've said before, all NT machines—workstations and servers—have local SAMs. When an NT machine "joins a domain," it adds a few entries to its SAM that essentially say, "If you're looking for a user account and you can't find it in this SAM, check in the SAM on the PDC."

You decide whether or not a machine is a domain controller when you run the NT Setup program. Only NT Server machines can be domain controllers.

A Simple Domain Login Example

NT domain security can sound a bit complex at first, but understanding how it works is central to tracking down login problems. The following example is quite detailed for an early chapter, but it will give you a good idea of how NT logins work.

Suppose a user named "Amy" normally accesses data from an NT server named "S1." S1 is an NT server that is *not* a domain controller. (Recently, Microsoft has begun referring to non-domain controller servers as "member servers," a term that I first heard back in the LAN Manager days and which seems to be creeping back into the networking lexicon.) Suppose also that both S1 and Amy are members of a domain named "KINGDOM"—that is, the S1 machine is a member of KINGDOM, and Amy has a user account on KINGDOM, which just means that her user account is contained in the SAM on the primary domain controller and backup domain controllers for KINGDOM. The domain needs a domain controller, so we'll call that machine "DC1." (DC1 can be either a primary or backup domain controller for purposes of this example.) Suppose also that Amy works on an NT workstation named "W1."

On a typical day, Amy comes into the office, sits down at her W1 workstation and logs in with the user name Amy and password swordfish. Then she opens up Network Neighborhood, where she finds server S1. She then just double-clicks on

S1 and gets access to its shares. But what's going on under the hood? For our purposes, there are two big events going on here:

- Amy logs onto her workstation W1 as "Amy from domain KINGDOM," which causes the workstation to communicate with a domain controller DC1 to verify that she is indeed Amy.

- When Amy tries to access S1 by opening up its icon, S1 communicates with DC1 to verify that Amy is indeed Amy.

Let's first look at the workstation login.

Logging On to an NT Workstation from a Domain Account Amy sits down at W1 and presses Ctrl+Alt+Del to bring up the NT login screen. It asks for her name, password, and domain. She fills in **Amy, swordfish**, and **KINGDOM**, respectively.

Now, W1 isn't going to let just *anybody* log onto it. Anyone with an account on W1's local SAM could log in; that's one way to get onto W1. Alternatively, W1 has joined the KINGDOM domain. What does that really mean? It means that W1 is willing to accept authentication from any of the domain controllers in KINGDOM.

That's why NT machines ask you to fill in your name, password, and domain. The "domain" box is sort of misleading—it doesn't actually mean "what domain are you a member of," it means "what SAM should I look in to verify your name and password?" Thus, if Amy says that she's "Amy from W1," then W1 will expect to find Amy's user account locally, on W1's own local SAM file. As Amy told W1 to log her on from an account on KINGDOM, however, W1 knows not to look to its local SAM.

Instead, W1 will have to ask a domain controller for KINGDOM to verify that Amy is Amy, in other words, to check her password. So now W1's got Amy's name and password. What does it do with that? Well, believe it or not, the first thing that W1 does is to forget Amy's password.

Well, actually, that's the *second* thing. The first thing the machine does is to take Amy's password and run it through a *one-way hash function*, a mathematical operation that's easy to do but hard to undo. NT takes whatever string of characters that you choose as a password, treats that string of characters like one very large binary number, and performs the "hash" function on that number.

Here's a simple example of a hash function: take a number and divide it by 273. Keep the remainder, throw away the quotient. That's an easy operation to do, but very hard to undo: merely telling you that my original number had a remainder of 151 doesn't tell you much.

NT hash functions solve this problem: how do you store passwords in memory or on disk without compromising them? The answer is, you don't. Instead, when a user chooses a password, NT just hashes it and saves the hashed result (which is called the *OWF password*, or "One-Way hashed Function password"). A domain controller doesn't contain a list of passwords, it contains a list of OWF passwords. *That's* why it's impossible for a domain administrator to see a user's password, no matter how clever the domain administrator is—the passwords just aren't there. And by the way, hash functions are a lot more complex than simple division and remainder; one such function is called MD5, but it would take too long to explain how it works here.

Now that W1 has converted Amy's password to OWF format, it needs to find a domain controller to verify the password's correctness. W1 does this with a broadcast, saying in effect, "Hey! Can anyone hear me who is a domain controller for KINGDOM?" DC1 responds, saying, "Yes, I'm a domain controller."

"Terrific," W1 responds. "Can you verify that a user named Amy has a domain account?"

Well, now, DC1 needs Amy's password to answer that question, but there's no way we're going to send Amy's password over the wire, even *if* it's a hashed password. So how do we prove to DC1 that Amy really knows the correct password? With what's known as a *challenge*. The logon server (DC1, in this case) says to W1 something like, "Okay, take the OWF version of Amy's password; again, treat it like a big number. Multiply it by 725, take the cosine of that value, square it, and then take the logarithm of the result. What is the third digit to the right of the decimal point?" The workstation does that and sends the result (suppose it's 7) to the logon server DC1. DC1 then does the same set of operations to the OWF password for Amy and also gets 7. DC1 then knows that it is indeed Amy sitting at W1. That number "725" will vary from challenge to challenge; that way, anyone listening on the wire won't get useful information. The next time DC1 issues a challenge, it'll be based on a different number, and so the results will be different, as well. DC1 then packages up what it knows about Amy (whether she's an administrator or just a user, what her description is, and the like) and sends it off to W1.

W1 then takes this information about Amy and uses it to build a *security access token* for Amy, a security access token that's only good on W1. That security access token is specific to a particular machine, as a given domain account might have more or less power on different machines. For example, even though Amy is a regular old user from the domain controllers' points of view, she might have been granted Administrator status on workstation W1. Then, once W1 was convinced that Amy was indeed Amy, then the security access token that W1 built for Amy would include the information that she was an administrator, at least from W1's point of view.

Attaching to a Member Server from an NT Workstation Now Amy's logged on to her workstation as "Amy from domain KINGDOM." In NT security parlance, we'd say that she is logged in as KINGDOM\Amy. She opens up Network Neighborhood, finds member server S1, and double-clicks on S1 to view S1's shares. She sees that one share is named DATA, and that's the one that she wants. Once again, she double-clicks on DATA to access that share. There's just a brief pause, and she's in. What happens during that pause?

The server S1 sees a user, KINGDOM\Amy, attempting to access a local share named DATA. Suppose that the security settings on S1 allow DATA to be read by anyone who's got a user account in the KINGDOM domain—a pretty loose security setting, but it still requires that Amy prove that she's a member of KINGDOM.

S1 then says to W1, "Who is this user?" W1 replies that she is "Amy from KINGDOM." S1 is, correctly, skeptical, and actually requires that Amy log into itself, S1. But it all happens invisibly: here's how.

S1 replies to W1, "Okay, if she's 'Amy from KINGDOM,' then what's her password?" Of course, S1 can't really ask the question this way; instead, S1 does a challenge like the one DC1 did. S1 says something like, "Divide Amy's password by 41, then take the cube root of it and give me the fifth digit to the right of the decimal point." Suppose W1 does that calculation and replies, "That digit is 3." Sounds like the initial domain logon, but it isn't, because *S1 cannot verify that 3 is the correct answer.* After all, S1 is just a member server, and *it* doesn't carry a copy of the whole domain SAM around with it. So S1 does what's called an *impersonation*. It calls up a domain controller (again, it broadcasts to find one in the first place) and says, in effect, "Listen, I've got this user who claims to be Amy with an account on your SAM. I told her to divide Amy's password by 41, then take the cube root of it and give me the fifth digit to the right of the decimal point; she told me the result is 3. Is that right?" DC1 says, "Yes, that is right," and tells S1 what it knows about Amy—that she's a member of the domain's group of users, her description, and the like. Then, just as W1 did, S1 takes this information that it has about Amy and uses it to create a security access token for Amy on S1. *Now S1 can use the security access token that it has constructed for Amy and ask, "Is Amy one of the people allowed to use the DATA share?"* Amy is a member of KINGDOM's group of regular old users, and that group is granted access to DATA, so Amy is granted access.

That seemed like a lot of work. Does S1 have to go through that every time Amy wants to access DATA? No. Once Amy's credentials are established for DATA, she—or rather, her workstation, as Amy didn't see any of this—doesn't have to worry about security. And if Amy tries to access another share on S1, then S1 can just examine the security access token that it has assembled for Amy; that will contain enough information for S1 to decide whether or not she's authorized to access that share, so S1 needn't revisit DC1 to check up on her.

A Simple Domain Setup

Let's compare how to set up domain XYZ to the earlier description of how to set up workgroup XYZ:

1. When you install the NT Server machines, choose one to be a domain controller. Only NT Server machines can be domain controllers, and you have to make an NT Server machine a domain controller when you first install the NT Server software (you can't make a machine a domain controller later on without completely reinstalling the NT Server software). Suppose you choose to make S1 the domain controller. Because the first domain controller in every domain is by definition the primary domain controller, S1 is the domain controller. The primary domain controller designates the name of the domain, and that's where you'd say that the name of the domain is XYZ.

NOTE   You can choose to make each NT server a domain controller. If you do that, you have to designate the second domain controller a backup domain controller because only one machine per domain can be a primary domain controller. You probably wouldn't make every server a domain controller, however, as DCs must spend a bit of their CPU power keeping up to date with the PDC. Instead, you would probably make most servers into regular old member servers.

---

2. S1 will still be a file and print server, as it was before; the duty of the domain controller probably won't eat up too much CPU time in this small network. S2 and W1 get installed as before, *except* that they will get a chance to *either* join a workgroup *or* a domain. They should opt to join the domain named XYZ.

3. Domains automatically offer all of the browsing services that workgroups offer, so the dumber workstations—the DOS, Windows for Workgroups, and Windows 95 workstations—should all declare that they are members of the *workgroup* XYZ. Why workgroup rather than domain? Because these operating systems aren't built to exploit the centralized security features of a domain. The only real benefit that they get from joining "workgroup" XYZ is that they will be able to use the browse lists generated by the servers in both domain XYZ and workgroup XYZ; the NT servers will show up on their browse lists.

4. On S1, create user accounts for John, Mary, Sue, Paul, and Ignatz. This is the only time you'll have to create user accounts for them.

Then suppose Mary starts up her workstation, a Windows for Workgroups machine. At some point in the day she ends up doing something that attracts the attention of S1, the primary domain controller. That something could be either trying to access a share on S1, S2, or W1, or trying to explicitly log on to the XYZ domain. *Note* that merely requesting the browse list for workgroup XYZ will not attract the domain's attention, nor will asking for the share list of one of the non-NT machines (unless it's a 95/98 machine using user-level security access). Trying to retrieve the share list of S1, S2, or W1—one of the machines that are members of the domain—will also count as "attracting the domain's attention." Mary will have to be recognized by the domain before she'll get that share list. "Recognized by the domain" means, again, either that she should have explicitly logged onto the domain by now, or, if she hasn't, then the domain will probably ask her for a password. ("Probably" because the exact behavior depends on which operating system her workstation is using. Some just reject the request; others display a dialog box that requests a password.)

A domain, then, is just a collection of NT machines that share a *security server*, or primary domain controller. The PDC keeps the database of users and user permissions, and any NT machine that has joined the domain may avail itself of the PDC's database of user permissions. If a large number of servers are on a network, then a network administrator may "deputize" some or all of those servers to be *backup domain controllers* (BDCs), machines that can respond to authentication requests. The PDC replicates its user database to the BDCs at a particular interval (five minutes by default, but you can change it).

What complicates a domain a bit is that it also acts as a workgroup. In my XYZ example, remember that only the NT machines could join the XYZ domain and share in the centralized security services, but *any* machine could join the XYZ *workgroup*, which automatically includes the XYZ domain members in itself.

The notion of a domain is the foundation upon which Microsoft enterprise networks are built. You'll learn more details about domain management in Chapters 11 and 12.

Network Citizens: Users and Machines

I've discussed the first and second problems that I posed—how we keep track of available network resources automatically and how we manage security—and I'll get to the third question in a few pages. First, however, let me digress a bit about the things that make up a Microsoft enterprise network: *users* and *machines*.

Users in a Microsoft Enterprise Network

A user is just a person who uses the network. Each user has a *user account*, a small database record of information about that user. At minimum, a user account includes information like this:

- User name
- User password
- Use restrictions or, more formally, user permissions and rights

The actual meaning of *user account* here is a bit nebulous if your network consists only of simple workgroups; user account is a more important piece of information for a user in a domain.

The user account is part of the SAM (Security Account Manager) file in your primary domain controller's SYSTEM32\CONFIG directory. That file is part of the *Registry*, which you'll learn more about in Chapter 5. Basically, the Registry is a central database of information about the network system itself, its applications, and its users.

User Rights and Permissions

Every network has its own terminology that it uses to describe how it protects its data from its users. In the NT Server world, we talk of rights and permissions.

A *right* is the ability to do a particular thing, like back up data on the file server (this poses a huge security risk because whoever is doing the backups could also abscond with them) or log on to the server, whether via the network (not much of a security risk) or locally at the server (a much greater risk). Rights are the difference between administrators and users.

A *permission* is simply a grant of access to a printer, a directory, a file, or some other network resource. There are different levels of access—Read-only, Execute-only, Read/Write, and so on—and they can be applied on a file-by-file, user-by-user basis.

User Groups

Of course, setting specific permissions for specific users can be tedious and time-consuming. That's why NT Server offers *groups*. Groups let you assign common rights and permissions to collections of users.

Examples of groups of users include:

- Administrators, who have a lot of control over a particular NT machine

- Users, who have areas over which they have a lot of control, but no control over the administration of the network

- "Enterprise" administrators (Domain Admins): administrators with control over all NT machines in a given domain

Those are by no means the only possible groups—they're just examples. For example, suppose you had a single server shared by two departments: the biology researchers and the chemical researchers. Each user has her own area. Meanwhile, the biology researchers have a common area that they want other biologists to be able to access, but that they don't want anyone else to be able to get to. The chemical researchers, likewise, have a common area of their own that they want to keep biologists from getting into.

Instead of just making all of the researchers "users," you can create a group called Biology and another called Chemistry. You'd start off by copying the user rights and permissions from the generic Users group into the two new groups, then you could give the Biology group access to the shared biology area and *deny* them access to the shared chemistry area. The Chemistry group, similarly, could be granted access to their area and denied access to the biology area.

User Characteristics

We'll mainly be concerned in this book with the *networking* implications of NT, but it's worthwhile taking a quick look at how NT handles users who physically log on to an NT workstation or NT Server.

If you use Windows, then you're accustomed to being able to set your machine's colors, wallpaper, video drivers, and the like. With NT workstations in a domain, however, the notion of "my machine" fades a bit, as the security information on you is, you recall, kept on a central repository.

Settings on NT machines are either user-specific or machine-specific. The user-specific settings include:

- Colors
- Wallpaper
- Mouse settings
- Cursors
- Personal groups
- Persistent network connections

This user-specific configuration information is stored in a file named NTUSER.DAT, which is usually located in a directory named WINNT\PRO-FILES*username*.

User names are one of the most important characteristics that the network keeps track of for a user. A user name can be up to 20 characters long. Passwords can actually be 128 characters long, sort of. According to Microsoft Knowledge Base Article Q109927, an NT password can be up to 128 characters long, but the User Manager only accepts passwords of up to 14 characters.

Machine Types: Redirectors, Receivers, Messengers, and Servers

In the Microsoft networking world, a server or a workstation can exhibit four kinds of capabilities: redirector, receiver, messenger, or server. These capabilities can appear in combinations. Following is a discussion of each of these network roles.

Redirector

The *redirector* capability allows software running on your workstation to intercept (redirect) requests for data from network drive letters and printer ports and convert them into network I/O requests. You need a unique user name and machine on the network. A machine running redirector software can request data from a server—that is, it can *initiate* a communication with a server. However, it cannot receive or act upon a *request* from a server. A server can't, so to speak, tap a redirector on the shoulder and hand it a message. You might say that a redirector can talk, but it can't listen.

Receiver

The *receiver* has redirector capabilities, but it can also receive messages forwarded from a computer set up as a messenger. It's an old and basically obsolete type of network citizen, but you see a reference to it now and then.

Messenger

The *messenger* module sends and receives messages from administrators or from the Alerter service. Messages like print job notification or imminent server shutdown are examples of messages that require the messenger service. While it sounds a bit circular-defining, the main value of supporting the messenger service is that you can then receive SMB messenger-type blocks from other networked machines. Messenger service is supported via broadcast datagrams. Messenger service uses your user name and your workstation name in the NetBIOS name table, with a hex 03 appended to the end of each name. Messenger service will also support forwarding messages from one workstation to another. In that case, the name has a hex 05 appended to its NetBIOS name and that name type is called a *type 5 name.*

Server

Server refers to service that allows a device to accept requests from another computer's redirector. It supports remote procedure calls (RPCs), file and print sharing, and named pipes.

Machine Characteristics

You saw earlier that some characteristics of an NT machine are user-specific, and some are machine-specific. The machine-specific characteristics include the following:

- Initial logon bitmap
- Shared groups
- Network settings, including persistent connections
- Drivers, including video, sound, tape, SCSI, network card, and mouse drivers
- The "services" settings in the Control Panel
- The "system" settings in the Control Panel
- Printer settings

Again, machine names can be up to 15 characters in length. Before going on, let's summarize legal lengths of names and passwords.

Name/Password	Length
User names	Up to 20 characters
Passwords	Up to 128 characters in theory, but 14 characters in practice
Share names	Up to 12 characters (8 if you want DOS workstations to recognize them)
Machine, domain, and workgroup names	Up to 15 characters

Inter-Domain Security: Trust Relationships

The users in a domain control how they share information via the user rights and permissions of that domain. Again, that information is maintained for that domain by the primary domain controller and its backup domain controllers in the domain security database.

But suppose you need information in *another* domain? How do you access the resources of that domain?

Inter-Domain Relationships without Trusts

Well, obviously, one way to get to another domain's resources is to become a user on that domain. Figure 2.7 shows an example of that.

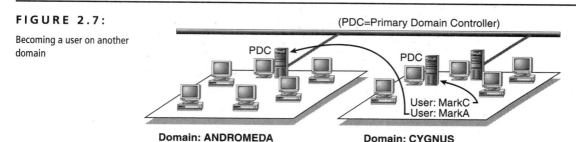

Domain: ANDROMEDA   **Domain: CYGNUS**

In the figure, you see two domains: one named Andromeda and the other named Cygnus. Both domains are on the same Ethernet. In fact, from the Ethernet's point of view, there aren't two domains here, just one big Ethernet segment with a whole bunch of machines on it. The question of which domain a particular workstation is in is a *software* question, not a hardware question.

What all that means is that there's no reason why my workstation can't be a part of two domains and use two identities. In the figure, my user ID is MarkC for the Cygnus network, and MarkA for the Andromeda network. What this really means is that there is an entry in the Cygnus security database (SAM) recognizing someone named MarkC with certain rights and permissions, and there's an entry in the Andromeda SAM recognizing someone named MarkA with certain rights and permissions.

More specifically, suppose I log on as MarkC. Now, Cygnus knows MarkC, but Andromeda does not. That means that Andromeda's primary domain controller wouldn't log MarkC on to the Andromeda domain at all, but the Cygnus primary domain controller would accept MarkC's logon.

This underscores an important point: when you log on to a Microsoft enterprise network, you've got to specify which domain you're logging on to. You specify that with your startup parameters. Once I log on as MarkC, I cannot access the resources of Andromeda, but I *can* access the resources of Cygnus.

In the same way, I can use my MarkA account to access resources in Andromeda, but not Cygnus. (By the way, the choice of names MarkA and MarkC are purely arbitrary; I could have had user names Orca and Delphinus for all it would matter. I just picked MarkA and MarkC to make it easier to remember what each user name did.)

What's wrong with this scenario? Two things. First, it involves administration headaches. If there are five domains in your company, consider what you'd have to do in order to maintain accounts on the five domains. You'd have to physically travel all over the company to each domain, log on to a workstation on that domain as an administrator, and make whatever changes were required—and you'd have to do it for each domain, *every time* you needed to change a password, user right, or the like. This would, as you'd imagine, get old quickly.

The second problem is that you can't simultaneously access resources from more than one domain. Each account, like MarkA or MarkC, could only access one domain's resources, so to get to the resources of Andromeda while in domain Cygnus, you would have to log off the MarkC account and log back in on the MarkA account. Again, no fun for someone trying to run a network.

One way around this would be for Mark to have an account on Cygnus and one on Andromeda, both named "Mark" with an identical password. But managing *that* is no joy, either, as it means password-changing day gets a bit cumbersome.

Trust Relationships

It would be really convenient to be able to essentially be a part of more than one domain. You can accomplish that with *trust relationships*.

One domain can choose to "trust" another in that it allows users from the trusted domain to access resources in the trusting domain. If Andromeda trusts Cygnus, then Cygnus users can access Andromeda resources, as you see in Figure 2.8.

FIGURE 2.8:

A trust relationship

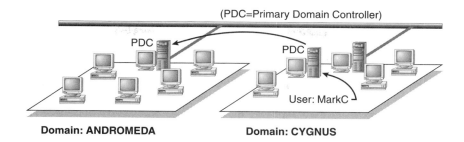

(PDC=Primary Domain Controller)

PDC

PDC

User: MarkC

Domain: ANDROMEDA　　　　**Domain: CYGNUS**

With a trust relationship, the only account that I need is the MarkC account. Because Andromeda trusts Cygnus, the primary domain controller for Andromeda extends the normal user rights and permissions to any "visitor" who has been vouched for by the primary domain controller for Cygnus (that is, any normal user on the Cygnus domain).

Notice in this example that Cygnus members can access the Andromeda resources, *but the reverse is not true.* If I were a member of the *Andromeda* domain, I would only be able to access Andromeda resources. Just because Andromeda trusts Cygnus, that does not imply that Cygnus trusts Andromeda. Each trust relationship is a one-way relationship. That's not to say that you *couldn't* also build a Cygnus-to-Andromeda trust link, but it would require an extra, explicit step.

Network Software: Drivers, Protocols, and Redirectors

The last "basic" that you really have to master in order to be comfortable with NT networking is Microsoft enterprise network software components.

Understanding Network Software Parts

Not too many years ago, one company would assemble an entire soup-to-nuts package of networking software. Not only would you buy the network boards and cables from them, but you'd also get a single large piece of software that served as one-stop shopping for everything that the network accomplished.

Why Are There Different Parts to Networking Software?

As it turns out, that was a major problem. Why? Well, it's probably best illustrated with an example. Suppose that there is a networking company named Ajax Network Solutions. Ajax sells a hardware/software network solution. Suppose also that it's pretty popular and that Ajax is the market leader with 50 percent of the network market. They're falling prey to that killer of market leaders: complacency. (Note: in the text that follows, you may *think* that I'm parodying a network vendor; I'm not. A lack of responsiveness to the needs of users is something that all network vendors are guilty of, some to a greater degree than others. So no, I'm not picking on Novell, or Microsoft, or Banyan, or IBM, or DEC, or any other company.)

Way back in the Cretaceous period of networking, say around 1987, Ajax realized that people wanted to hook their PCs together and share files. Ajax also figured that people would only run DOS, since it didn't look like OS/2 was going anywhere, and NT was just an idea that Dave Cutler was still mulling around. So the Ajax guys ("guys" because this is 1987, recall, when the only female in the business was Esther Dyson) got the Acme Ethernet Board Company to sell tons of Ethernet cards to Ajax for a good price, and then Ajax put its name on the boards. Once they had boards, the Ajax folks wrote a DOS TSR that was about 60K in size. It installed on a DOS system as a device driver, and only worked with the Ajax network cards. But hey, it worked, and you could share files and printers over a network among DOS workstations. Pretty cool, the industry thought, and started buying the stuff.

Almost a year goes by, and Ajax has taken the PC world by storm. Everybody's buying their networking kits. Everybody loves the Ajax package. Soon, however, computer experts are noting that the Ajax network cards cost $200 apiece, and that another firm, 2Com, makes pretty good Ethernet cards for a mere $180. Ajax claims, however, that the 2Com cards are not Ajax cards, haven't been tested for compatibility, and, worst of all, the Ajax software can't control the 2Com cards, so while the Ajax management regrets that their boards cost $200, the true reason for the higher price is that quality costs money, and the Ajax boards guarantee quality. Everyone buys this explanation, as Ajax is the *Wunderkind* of the industry and has the trust of their customers.

Shortly thereafter, however, someone notices the similarities between Ethernet cards sold by the Acme Ethernet Board Company and Ajax. Noticing also that the boards are $170 and that they work fine with the Ajax software, Ajax finds sales of their Ethernet cards quickly declining. Pretty soon, they don't sell many

Ethernet cards, and so they really don't care *whose* Ethernet cards you buy, just as long as you keep buying Ajax software. The problem with supporting other Ethernet cards, however, is that the piece of the network software that communicates with the network board must be modified a bit for each new brand of network card. For every single board that Ajax supports, they must modify their network software. Clearly that's no fun, and will mean a larger network program as well, but the customers are demanding support for more boards. Ajax finds out which network card models are the 20 or so most popular on the market. About a year later, they release separate versions of their network software that supports those boards.

By the time they've done that, however, more network boards have come out that are cheaper and faster. Ajax is still behind the 8-ball. But that's nothing compared to the fact that people are now demanding support of mainframe protocols like SNA and DECnet. So Ajax returns to the drawing board. Now, they're smart people, and putting SNA and DECnet support into their software isn't that hard. It does, however, make their software significantly bigger, and their DOS TSR is now up to 160K. Most people don't care about the mainframe protocols and complain about the new bloated TSR, so Ajax is forced to offer separate versions of their software, categorized by the boards supported and the protocols included.

By 1993, there are too many new network cards to keep track of, and Ajax is falling hopelessly behind. They can't realistically provide support for thousands of software versions, so they've got to triage all but the most popular boards. About 30 percent of the users are now demanding new network services like e-mail, and 40 percent want to connect their networks to the Internet, which means a new network protocol and a bunch of new network services. The marketing directory calculates that if they support 40 network cards, six protocols, and 15 different network services—the bare minimum they must have in order to survive, surveys show—Ajax will have to support 40 times 6 times 15, or 3600, different versions of their network software! Further, Ajax was spending more and more of its time just treading water, while its competition just sailed by it. By 1996, Ajax was a minor player in the network market, and in 1997 a competitor bought it and closed it.

What went wrong?

Put simply, too many things are part of the job of "networking" to think that they can all be lumped together into one piece of software. Things change for pricing reasons (new, better, cheaper network cards) and reasons of technological advancement (the Internet, new protocols). The best answer is a flexible, modular answer.

Now, in actual fact, networking people knew that answer way back in the early '80s when they sat down to create a standard that would act both as a model for networks and as a kind of "reference" network that companies could implement. It was called the Open Systems Interconnection (OSI) model, and it was developed by the International Standards Organization (ISO). Thus, it was called the *ISO OSI 7-layer model.* It's also one of those really terrific examples of the evil that a committee can do with a good idea, as I have yet to meet someone who thinks it's a great idea. When people try to explain networks, they often use the OSI model, but I find it to be of limited value. Instead, it seems that most network products use a kind of *three*-layer model, which I'll present here.

A Simple Network Problem

I'll underscore the functions of a network with a simple example involving a fairly dumb workstation (not surprisingly, it will run DOS) and a dedicated file server. It could be an NT server, but it could just as easily be a NetWare server, a VINES server, or a LAN Server machine.

Looking at networks from a high-level point of view, LANs have this basic job: let the application programs (WordPerfect, Lotus 1-2-3, Quicken, or whatever) on the workstations utilize the network hardware to get at data on the network. Figure 2.9 shows this.

FIGURE 2.9:

How applications exploit network hardware to access data

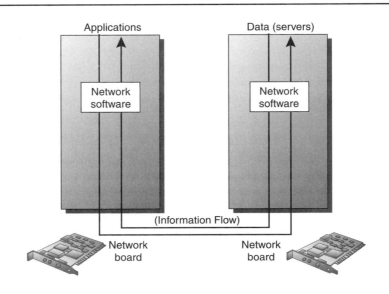

Put in concrete terms, there are a number of things that this network must accomplish. First, on the workstation side, the workstation is running DOS, which, as I've already observed, is network-dumb. The workstation needs to get to a file called LETTER.DOC, which is in a directory named DOCUMENT, located on a server called SERVER01 in a share called BIGSHARE. In one sense all the workstation has to say is, "Go get me \\server01\bigshare\document\letter.doc." The problem is that, among other things, DOS and most DOS programs know nothing of UNCs. So the first problem to solve is the DOS and DOS applications' ignorance of networks. Other kinds of compatibility problems that the network must face include the following:

File name length   Although most servers allow long file names, not all client operating systems do. For example, most DOS and Windows applications still can't handle file names longer than eight characters.

Multiple networks   Your network may need to talk to more than one kind of server, and perhaps may need to have a wide area network portion that communicates with a mainframe network, the Internet, or some other value-added network service.

Differing hardwares   As described in the Ajax example, new network boards appear all the time, and the network must be able to support them quickly.

Third-party solution provider   If Ajax had had a well-documented way for third parties to add network applications, then it could have relied on the hundreds of independent software vendors to offer an e-mail package, rather than derailing itself from the process of making its central networking package fast, bug-free, and secure.

My simple three-layer network consists of three layers and two interfaces:

- The bottom layer is the *board driver*, which controls the network board.

- The middle layer is the *transport protocol*, the rules of communication in the network.

- The top layer is the *network service* itself, like the e-mail package or a network fax application.

- In between the board driver and the transport protocol is the *network binding interface*, which assures that a board driver written by one vendor will communicate with a transport protocol written by another vendor.

- In between the transport protocol and the network services layer is the *network application program interface,* which is a published, standard, well-defined interface that network applications can sit atop, making it possible for someone to write a network application that isn't specific to a particular network.

The Bottom Layer: The Board Driver

For the application to use data, messages go across network boards and through the network software that runs in both the client and the server machine. The first, and easiest, piece of software to understand is the network board driver, as you see in Figure 2.10.

FIGURE 2.10:

A network board driver

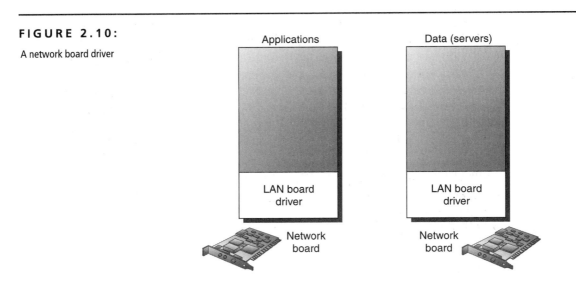

Drivers decouple the network board from the network operating system. For example, suppose you have a token ring–based network. When you first create your network, you may start off by buying boards from IBM, but you don't want to be locked into IBM, or any other vendor for that matter. And you wonder whether or not a competitor's token ring boards, like the Madge or 3Com token ring boards, will continue to work with your NT Server-based network. For that matter, token-ring cards offer another reason why separate drivers makes sense. If your networking software were tied to a network board, then there would probably only be support for Ethernet cards, as they're more popular than token-ring cards. But separating the specifics of the network card into a modular driver eliminates that problem.

Looking specifically at NT, we can see that NT needs an ability to incorporate any kind of network card into its networking system, whether that card is an Ethernet, token ring, ARCnet, FDDI (Fiber Digital Distributed Interface), or other board, and it's got to be able to incorporate boards from virtually *any* vendor.

The board driver must know things like which IRQ a LAN board is set for and which I/O address it uses. For some boards, it must also know which RAM base address it uses.

The Top Layer: Network Services

I'll jump to the top because in general it's easier for people to understand network services than to understand protocols, since we *use* network services.

A *network service* is any application that leverages the network to provide some capability. For example, in my company we use a network fax application that, as you'd guess, lets us share a fax machine over the network. It is just a simple program that we load on each workstation. The effect of that program is, however, that when you want to print a document at your workstation and you choose from a list of printers, a new printer called "network fax" appears. You print to that "printer" and the network fax application invisibly converts that command into a command to grab the document, shoots it across the network to the fax server, and tells the fax server to dial somewhere and fax the document.

E-mail is another example. E-mail wouldn't exist if it weren't for networks. You type a message to Sally and click Send, and it's sent. The e-mail program, an example of a network service, takes the message and sends it to a machine on your network that acts as the "post office" for your network's e-mail system.

But the most common network application is one that most people aren't even aware exists. It goes by several names, *shell*, *redirector*, and *client* being the most common. A redirector fools applications into thinking that the application gets data from a local drive, rather than from the network.

For example, let's return to the dumb DOS workstation in my example, and let's run ancient WordPerfect 5.1 on it. Now consider the case of WordPerfect reading a document from a network drive. From WordPerfect's point of view, there *is* no network. Instead, it knows that one or more disk drives are available, with names consisting of a letter and a colon, as in A:, B:, C:, and so on. Word-Perfect 5.1 was not built to accommodate storage devices that don't have names like A: or D:. Therefore, a layer of software must be placed just below WordPerfect, a layer of software whose job it is to present a letter-and-colon face to Word-Perfect when supplying data stored on the network. WordPerfect thinks that it is addressing local drives, but its requests for information from drives with names like D: must be *redirected* to network requests, like "Get the data from directory WPFILES on the server named SEYMOUR." The redirector software does that, as you see in Figure 2.11.

FIGURE 2.11:

Using the redirector software

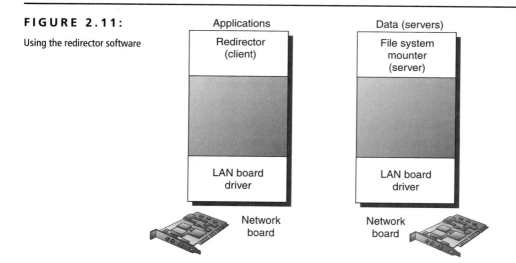

But the redirector doesn't do all of the work, just as the e-mail package or the network fax application doesn't do all of the work. Most network services are part of a two-part team; one part of the team is called the *server* application, and that part goes on the server. The other part is called the *client* application, and it sits on a user's workstation.

The redirector is only half of a client-server team of software. The redirector is the piece that goes on the client or workstation, and the *file system mounter* is the piece that goes on the server. There are several file system mounters in the network world—the best-known are Novell's NetWare File System, UNIX's Network File System (NFS), and Microsoft's file system mounter, which they usually just call the "server." The redirector on the client and the file system mounter on the server must match for the client to use the server's resources.

In the Internet world, servers may run an NFS server; workstations must run NFS client software. In the Novell world, servers run a program called NFS.NLM to support the Novell File System mounter, and workstations run a client program called NET3, NET4, NETX, or the like in order to communicate with the Novell server. Banyan users run a program called REDIRALL to access shared volumes on their servers.

The Internet also provides me with a number of other network applications as examples. Web browsers and servers, FTP client and server programs, and Telnet clients and servers are examples of applications that only exist because of a network. Your firm may well be using client-server applications that they designed themselves.

The Middle Layer: Network Protocols

Third in the trio of network software components is the network protocol. In general, a *protocol* is just a set of rules that have been standardized for the sake of compatibility. For example, when I call you on the phone, we've got a protocol that says, "When you hear the phone ring and you pick it up, then *you* should talk first, not me." There's no good reason for why it happens this way—it's just the common agreement in our culture as to how to conduct a phone communication.

I left this middle piece for last, as it's the most abstract of the three network software components. You might think of it this way: the board driver keeps the LAN board happy, the redirector keeps the applications happy, and the *transport protocol* glues the two of them together by establishing the rules of the road for network communications. You can see the result of adding the transport protocol to our network software system in Figure 2.12.

Just as we couldn't use the phone without some agreements about how to use it, NT needs a common communication language so that all of the machines on an NT network can talk to one another without confusion. NT also needs to be able to speak the networking languages used by *other* kinds of networks, so it needs to be something of a polyglot. Networking protocols—"protocol" is a somewhat more accurate term than "language" here—differ widely because they were each originally designed to do different things, and because network protocols were never designed to be compatible with other kinds of networks.

There are a number of transport protocols, unfortunately. Every vendor has its own favorite protocol. On the following pages is a quick overview of the ones you'll run across.

FIGURE 2.12:

Adding the transport protocol to the network software system

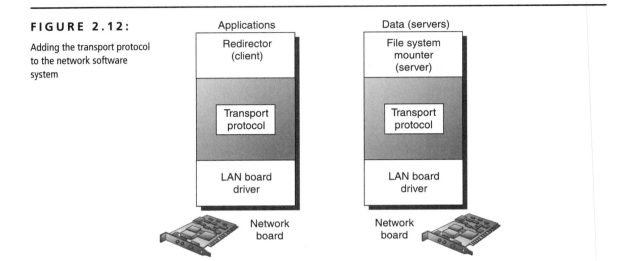

NetBIOS/NetBEUI

Back when IBM first started marketing its PC Network, it needed a basic network protocol stack. IBM had no intention of building large networks, just small work-groups of a few dozen computers or fewer.

Out of that need grew the Network Basic Input/Output System (NetBIOS). NetBIOS is just 18 commands that can create, maintain, and use connections between PCs on a network. IBM soon extended NetBIOS with the NetBIOS Extended User Interface (NetBEUI), which was basically a refined set of Net-BIOS commands. Over time, however, the names NetBEUI and NetBIOS have taken on different meanings.

- NetBEUI refers to the actual transport protocol; it has been implemented in many ways by different vendors, to the point where it's in some ways the fastest transport protocol around for small networks.

- NetBIOS refers to the actual set of programming commands that the system can use to manipulate the network. The technical term for it is an Application Program Interface (API).

NetBEUI is the closest thing to a "native" protocol for NT. Unless you tell your system to use another protocol, NetBEUI is one of the protocols that the NT Setup program installs by default (IPX/SPX is the other). NetBEUI should be your protocol of choice for small networks, however, as it's the fastest one around.

TCP/IP (Transmission Control Protocol/Internet Protocol)

The famous "infobahn," the information superhighway, is built atop a protocol created by the U.S. government over the years—a protocol stack called the *TCP suite.* The TCP suite is an efficient, easy-to-extend protocol whose main strength has been in *wide* area networking, gluing together dissimilar networks and bringing together similar networks that are separated by distance and low-speed connections. It's one of the best-supported, well-designed internetworking protocols around today.

**ENTERPRISE
NETWORKING**

Traditionally, however, microcomputer networks haven't used TCP/IP as a *local* area network protocol. But that's not true any more. In fact, if you're building an NT network of any size, I strongly recommend building it on TCP/IP; that's why the TCP/IP chapter is so long.

DLC (Data Link Control)

Data Link Control is related to an international standard protocol called IEEE 802.2. You'll see it used for two main reasons.

First, many token ring shops use DLC to allow their PC workstations to talk to mainframe gateways. If you use token ring and your CONFIG.SYS contains three device drivers whose names start with DXM, then you're using DLC drivers. Not all gateways require DLC, but many do.

The second common use is to communicate with network printers. The most common example is if you've got a laser printer on the network that is attached *directly* to the network via a JetDirect print server (network interface) card, then you can use DLC to control that printer.

IPX/SPX (Internetwork Packet Exchange/Sequenced Packet Exchange)

The most popular local area network type in the world is Novell NetWare. When the Novell folks were building NetWare, they decided to build their own protocol, rather than use an existing protocol. (It's actually based on a Xerox protocol called Xerox Networking Services, or XNS.)

IPX/SPX support came late to NT, but it's here in NT 4 as part of the NetWare Compatible Services.

Multiple Transport Stacks

It should be obvious by now that, first of all, there is no single best network protocol, and second, you may want to run all four of the protocols described here. You can.

One of the values of the NT networking model is that it supports *multiple* transport protocols, as you see in Figure 2.13. In the figure, you can see that the client machine has four transport protocols loaded, and the server has one protocol loaded. This could happen if the client machine connected to more than one server. For example, the IPX stack might talk to a Novell server, the DLC stack might allow the workstation to talk to a mainframe gateway, and the TCP/IP stack might talk to an Internet mail router.

FIGURE 2.13:

Running multiple transport protocols

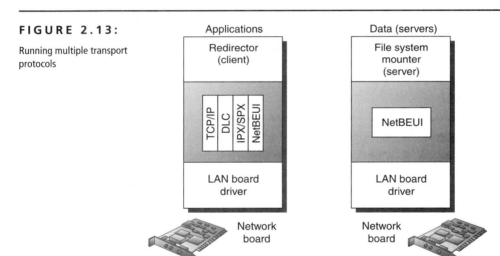

Network Binding Interfaces

But to make all of this *work*, we need a way to attach the network boards to the transport stacks—to *bind* the network transport layer to the LAN board's driver. (The definition of "binding" is to create a software connection between, to essentially "marry," a network card driver and a network transport protocol.) That leads to the need for an important standard interface: the interface between a

LAN board driver and a transport stack. There are two competitors for the title of "world standard binding interface," Microsoft's NDIS and Novell's ODI.

Network Driver Interface Specification (NDIS)

Microsoft's standard provides the Network Driver Interface Specification (NDIS) as its interface between a network card driver and a protocol stack.

NDIS-compliant drivers are easy to find for most network boards, so availability is a strong plus for NDIS. Furthermore, there are NDIS-compatible versions of the NetBEUI, TCP/IP, DLC, and SPX/IPX protocol stacks. NDIS 3 drivers are particularly attractive in the DOS/Windows world because they load up in extended memory, away from the precious lower 640K. NDIS 3.1 drivers added support for "hot plug and play," which, unfortunately, NT still doesn't support. NDIS 4.*x* drivers will appear with versions of NT 4.*x* and Windows and will let Microsoft unify the drivers for NT and Windows, which will be a great thing for us NT users. *Everyone* supports Windows, right?

Open Data-Link Interface (ODI)

Novell's answer to the binding problem is a different standard, one named the Open Data-Link Interface (ODI). ODI drivers do not, unfortunately, load high, but they are the easiest drivers to obtain. If a board has any drivers at all, they will be DOS ODI drivers.

Packet Drivers

Some PC-based UNIX implementations use TCP/IP but don't write their own drivers. These usually rely upon a driver called *packet drivers* and are sometimes called the *Clarkson drivers* after Clarkson Tech, where they were invented.

Network Application Interfaces (APIs)

As you've already read, most applications are unaware of the network or networks that they use. But some, like e-mail or groupware programs, must be cognizant of the network, and exist only *because* of the network. They need to be able to "plug in" and communicate with other programs running on other machines in the network.

Programmers build network-aware programs to be tailored to sets of commands that a network offers to applications programs. Those sets of commands are called APIs, or application program interfaces.

Think of an API as being something like the controls you use when driving a car. Your car's steering wheel, accelerator, and other controls form the interface that you see, and you learn to use them in order to operate the car. You might have no idea while you're driving what's under your car's hood—you just push down the accelerator and the car goes faster.

These controls consist of just a few "primitive" commands: brake the car, accelerate the car, shift the car's transmission, and so on. There is no command "back the car out of the driveway," and yet you can still back a car out of a driveway by just assembling a number of the primitive commands into the actual action of backing a car out of a driveway. Once you learn how to drive one car, you can instantly use another. In other words, you are "designed for the car driver controls API." In the same way, if you buy a network fax application that was designed for a network API named NetBIOS, you should be able to run that network fax application on any network at all, so long as the network supports the NetBIOS API.

In contrast, consider how private pilots learn to fly. They have two pedals on the floor of their plane, but the left pedal turns them left and the right pedal turns them right. Taking someone who can fly a plane and plunking him down in a car without any other training wouldn't work too well. In the same way, if an application is built for *one* network API, then it won't work on another. But if you built a car whose controls acted like an airplane's, airplane pilots could drive the car without any trouble. For example, NetBIOS is an API that first appeared on Microsoft networks, but Novell included it in their network. As a result, many applications designed for Microsoft networks work fine on a Novell network.

You'll probably come across three APIs in the NT enterprise world:

NetBIOS   A simple set of 18 commands implemented on an NT network. It is Microsoft's "native" network API.

TCP/IP Sockets   The preferred API for working over the Internet. Sockets are commonly implemented on PCs—and on NT—under a standard called WinSock. If you bought Netscape Navigator and you want to run it, then your network must offer the WinSock network API. Now, NT only implements WinSock on its TCP/IP protocol, not on IPX or NetBEUI. Consequently, if you loaded Navigator on an NT (or a Windows 3.1 or DOS or Windows 95) workstation that didn't have TCP/IP loaded, then it couldn't work. (Recently, WinSock has been slightly redesigned and can also run atop IPX.)

Novell Sockets   Novell's API.

Getting comfortable with NT networking requires learning a new language, but it's not an impossible language to learn. In this chapter, you've gotten the background that you need to "speak NT." Next, you'll see how to *install* NT.

PART

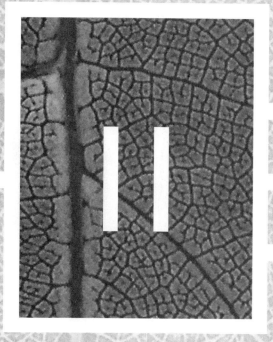

II

Setting Up
NT Server

Installing NT and NT Server

■ Getting the hardware ready

■ Getting the data ready

■ Running the installation program

■ Using an uninterruptible power supply

■ Performing unattended installations

■ Using the Sysdiff utility

■ Advanced unattended install tricks

Installing NT Server is simple… *if* you do your homework beforehand. This chapter provides a step-by-step plan for getting a server up and running. It is also of value if you are installing NT on a workstation.

In this chapter, I'll discuss

- Getting ready to install

- The options for installing

- The confusing parts of the installation program

- How to automate NT Server rollouts, including doing unattended installs on "problem" machines

Preparing the Hardware

Despite the fact that NT is a big, complex operating system, you have a pretty good chance of getting it installed right the first time *if* you first make sure that you're free of hardware problems. If not, NT can be kind of picky—but that's a good thing, at least in contrast to DOS. Under DOS, you can have some pretty glaring hardware problems, but DOS runs nonetheless. The reason why DOS works—or *appears* to work—on a machine with major hardware problems is simple: DOS isn't really an operating system. It doesn't monitor the hardware, so it never really gets a chance to notice a hardware failure or conflict. DOS basically leaves the problems of hardware control to device drivers and applications programs. When a hardware problem arises, it arises while an application program is running, and it is the *DOS application program* that must detect, diagnose, and recover from the hardware failure. Or at least that's the ideal situation.

The reality is, of course, that most DOS programs just crash when hardware problems happen. I just implied that DOS program designers should plan for these problems and attempt to avert them in their code, but the fact of the matter is that the DOS application designers shouldn't *have* to worry about this kind of thing—the operating system should. And, to a certain extent, Windows shares this lack of awareness. It often doesn't complain about a faulty piece of hardware until you try to *use* that hardware—and that's not the best time.

Under DOS, a memory failure usually doesn't show up until you actually try to *use* that memory. Disk failures cause the "Abort, Retry, Fail?" error message, with no real recovery. Interrupt conflicts become mysterious freeze-ups. In contrast, NT is so picky about the hardware that you run it on that some have commented that the best memory diagnostic program around is NT itself.

You can't afford crashes on your NT server (or workstation, for that matter). For that reason, my strong advice to you is to *test your hardware thoroughly before installing NT*.

Having said that, I've got to admit that it's pretty hard to build any kind of hardware diagnostic program under NT, because a hardware diagnostic must be able to directly access the hardware in order to test it, and one of NT's stated design goals is to make it *impossible* for an application to get to the hardware. Furthermore, most diagnostics require that they be the only thing running in the system, and NT is built out of literally dozens of mini-programs called *threads*.

For that reason, I recommend that you run your system through a gamut of specialized DOS-based diagnostics before proceeding with the NT installation. I'll discuss them in more detail a bit later in this chapter.

Getting Ready to Install

First of all, make sure that you have the right hardware for an NT installation. Check the latest Windows NT Hardware Compatibility List for any hardware you are thinking of buying (you can find it at http://www.microsoft.com/ntserver/hcl/hclintro.htm, among other places). If it's not on the list, check with the manufacturer to be sure it will work with Windows NT. You see, a piece of hardware may well be NT-compatible but not be on the HCL. Microsoft manages the HCL, and they charge hardware vendors tens of thousands of dollars to test hardware before Microsoft will put that hardware on the HCL. On the one hand, this seems like a pretty good deal for us, the consumers, because somebody big tests compatibility. But on the other hand, the fact that Microsoft controls the HCL—which is the "hardware certification" program—as well as the MCSE certification program—the "expert certification" program—means that Microsoft has a kind of scary incentive to keep turning out upgrades whether we need them or not. Personally, I'd rather see an independent group like the Association for Computer Machinery (ACM) or the Data Processing Management Association (DPMA) put in charge of certification because there would be less of a "fox guarding the hen house" air to it.

In any case, here are a few things to consider when choosing hardware. But the sad fact is that if you don't buy your hardware off the HCL, you won't be able to get support of any kind from Microsoft and other places. Worse yet, if you try to use Microsoft's support, they will *first* take your money ($245/question), listen to the question, ask you if your hardware is HCL-compliant and, if it isn't, they'll just say, "Oh, well, we can't help you," and hang up. And no, you don't get a refund.

CPU

In the *x*86 world, you can run NT on a 486 or better, but I strongly recommend that you purchase Pentium Pro/Pentium II/Xeon machines or better. Do not buy the MMX chip, as NT cannot exploit any of its features and so you'll just be paying a fair amount for useless hardware. Avoid the Celeron, as its lack of cache memory cripples it speed-wise. Don't buy PowerPC or MIPS or Alpha machines, as NT no longer supports them.

RAM

I strongly recommend no fewer than 64MB to run NT Workstation and 96MB to run NT Server (unless it's a demonstration machine, which can run with considerably less memory). An interesting benchmark published in an issue of *Windows NT Magazine* in the spring of 1997 showed that NT 3.51 machines are often faster than the same computers running NT 4 *when the computers have 32MB of RAM*; but when those same machines were upgraded to 64MB RAM, the NT 4 machines were faster. Moral of the story: NT is RAM-hungry, and newer versions are hungrier than old ones. If you plan to run some other BackOffice application like Exchange or SQL Server, then plan for even *more* RAM.

NT Server needs more RAM if you ask it to do more things. If you're going to load RAS or TCP/IP, you need more memory. NT Server also needs more memory if it will serve more people.

NOTE   Chapter 16, "Tuning and Monitoring Your NT Server Network," has more information on this.

Video

You need at least a VGA video board in order to load NT Server. (This surprised me when I first loaded it, because I was used to being able to put low-quality video on a server; after all, nobody's going to use it as a workstation, so who cares what kind of video it has?) It's chic to buy the fastest turbo-charged PCI video accelerator board for systems nowadays, but there's no point to doing that for an NT Server installation; a cheap VGA board is fine and, indeed, is *recommended*.

With NT 4 came a change in NT architecture, a change intended to speed up the performance of NT Workstation. The change did, indeed, make NT Workstation faster—but at the price (in my opinion) of reduced system robustness. It's a long story, but the basics of it are this: parts of NT are housed in one of two places, either the *kernel mode* or the *user mode*.

Kernel mode programs can, in general, run faster than user mode programs, but they do it at the price of reduced security. When a kernel mode module in NT crashes, it's likely to take the entire operating system with it. One of the things that has made NT so stable is the fact that it stores relatively few things in kernel mode (well, relatively few things compared to *other* operating systems). The video drivers and printer drivers are two examples of modules that lived in user mode under NT 3.*x*. That means that if you were to install a particularly buggy printer driver under NT 3.51, then the worst that would happen would be that you couldn't print—everything else would work fine.

Under NT 4, however, print and video drivers are moved into kernel mode. Again, that speeds up video performance noticeably; run the 3-D Pinball game from Windows 95's Plus Pack on NT Workstation 3.51 and its performance is glacial. Run it on NT 4, however, and it flies. Most definitely, this is an improvement…

If you run video games on your servers, that is.

This architecture shift was clearly done to make NT Workstation more competitive. I can't say I like it much, however. If you've been in the PC business for any time, you know what a pain it can be to procure up-to-date, properly debugged video drivers. Owners of ATI or Diamond video cards jokingly refer to themselves as the "driver of the week club." Since its introduction in 1993, NT has distinguished itself from other PC operating systems in that it is slow, expensive, and doesn't boast much native software—but it's stable. Rock solid. Microsoft's move of the video and print drivers into kernel mode threatens that, in my opinion at least. Which brings me back to my recommendation: *use the VGA driver on servers.* You're not doing anything fancy on the server, and the NT VGA driver is one of the best, most bug-free pieces of software that Microsoft offers. It was written by Michael Abrash, probably the guy on the planet who understands the VGA better than anyone. It runs in kernel mode, so a crash in the VGA driver can kill your system, but the chances of that happening are considerably reduced if you stay with Mike's driver.

If you're running an NT *workstation,* in contrast, by all means invest in better video. The Matrox-based boards are probably the best way to go, and by the time you read this there should be a good set of drivers for them.

As video accelerators go, the S3-based systems are definitely not the fastest boards around. As I've said, you could look to an ATI or Matrox video system, but, on the other hand, think twice before straying from S3-based systems. S3 boards are the ones that will always get the most solid, debugged drivers among the video accelerator bunch, and they likely get the *earliest* drivers when beta versions of new software arrive. The S3 systems also tend to be cheaper than the other accelerators. Be careful with Diamond systems; some use S3 chips, but some are based on the "ARK" chip set, and as I write this there are no NT drivers for this chip set, which would mean spending a lot of money for a board that just runs the VGA driver. Please don't write to me and ask me what board to buy. I get a lot of that kind of mail, and I really can't help you there. Just be sure to follow a simple rule: if it's not on the Hardware Compatibility List, don't buy it.

CD-ROM

You definitely want a CD-ROM for the server, if you're loading NT Server. As you'll read later in this book, you can't get to a number of pieces of software in the NT package from the floppies because they're only on the CD-ROM. Additionally, one NT floppy installation will convince you that CD-ROM installations are the way to go.

What about CD-ROMs on workstations? I'd still think about getting at least a cheap quad-spin CD-ROM. Software has gotten so huge that even *games* are shipping on CD-ROMs. Terrific, inexpensive databases are available on CD-ROM; for example, you can buy 12 months' worth of *PC Magazine* on CD-ROM for about $20! Think of the time saved with just one literature search, and the CD-ROM drive starts to look like a bargain. NT troubleshooters will want to subscribe to Microsoft's TechNet service, a complete set of all Microsoft literature on supporting their applications and environments. There's a fantastic trove of goodies there, but you can't get to them if you don't have a CD-ROM. It runs about $300 for a year's subscription and gets you much faster access to Microsoft's database of bugs and workarounds (the Knowledge Base).

If you decide to buy a CD-ROM, I recommend a SCSI-based CD rather than one of the EIDE-based CD-ROMs. NT has always supported SCSI better than IDE or EIDE. The older CD-ROMs that are attached to a proprietary interface card are generally not supported by NT, and I've never gotten one of those CD-ROMs that attach via the parallel port to work on an NT install.

A last, somewhat esoteric but important point about CD-ROMs under NT: not only must they be SCSI-based, they must also support the SCSI-II interface, since NT requires that a feature called *SCSI parity* be enabled in order for the installation to go well.

Tape Drive

It is essential that any enterprise server have a tape backup unit. I use a 4mm DAT tape with a Sony SCSI-II compatible drive, and it suits the backup job just fine. The tape subsystem should be SCSI-based.

Hard Disk

If you want to support large drive sizes *and* asynchronous read/write, then you'd do well to choose some kind of SCSI-based hard disk. NT supports SCSI host adapters very well, so you can choose from a large number of adapters. (It would be a good idea to consult the Hardware Compatibility List, available from Microsoft, before buying a SCSI host adapter.)

- Any machine that is running NT Server should have a lot of PCI slots. When buying machines, I'd avoid any other kind of bus slots, even ISA or EISA. Why? Well, first, boards in PCI slots are of course faster, as PCI runs at 33MHz, faster than the 8MHz you find in EISA and ISA. Second, PCI boards are designed to be automatically configured; they're much more Plug and Play friendly. NT is not yet Plug and Play compliant, but it will be with the next version, Windows 2000 Server, which is due out some time around mid-1999, and you want your hardware to be as Windows 2000 ready as possible. Further, it is generally easier to write a reliable NT driver for PCI hardware than for older ISA boards.

- It is a good idea to stay with a big name SCSI vendor, like Adaptec. Their 2940 adapter is probably the most popular PCI-based SCSI host adapter among NT users, and its 32-bit EISA cousin, the 2742T, is a mite pricey—about $300—but quite a performer, and serves as two SCSI controllers on a single board. I strongly recommend that you avoid the somewhat cheaper Ultrastor controllers. My experience with Ultrastor has been that they're slow to deliver drivers, they're difficult to get in touch with for technical support, and they tend to completely abandon any controller that isn't their latest and greatest. I'm not saying that Adaptec makes the best SCSI boards, just that installing NT on a machine with an Adaptec board in it will be easier, simply because Adaptec drivers are always easier to find.

- One of my Micron servers shipped with the BusLogic FlashPoint host adapter. It's powerful, but the drivers for it are always a bit hard to find. I hope that will change eventually.

- Another reason to buy SCSI-based storage systems is fault tolerance: disk mirroring and RAID pretty much *require* SCSI disk subsystems in order to work. You can create a mirrored set of non-SCSI drives, but the drives may not have sector-remapping capability (which is an important part of any fault-tolerance scheme), so I would not recommend it.

Oh, and by the way, if the machine that you're installing NT Server (or Workstation) on currently has Windows 95 or Windows 98 on it, then you might want to use that operating system's FDISK program to completely delete any existing disk partitions before installing NT. (Remember that this destroys all data on those partitions, so back up before proceeding.) Why do this? Because later versions of Windows 95 and all versions of Windows 98 include the capability to format a drive as something they call *FAT32 format*. It's great for Windows users, but death on NT, as NT cannot recognize or use drives formatted in FAT32 format.

TIP   Actually, if you really need FAT32 compatibility, there's a terrific utility by from Mark Rossinovich and Bruce Cogswell that enables NT to use FAT32 drives. You can find it at http://www.sysinternals.com/fat32.htm. The utility costs $39. I have it and like it quite a bit.

Mice and Serial Ports

This is pretty straightforward, but one word of advice: get PS/2 type or InPort mice. You need a port for your mouse, a serial port to which attach to your Uninterruptible Power Supply (UPS), and a serial port for a modem to support the Remote Access Services (RAS). If the mouse is a serial mouse, the system requires three serial ports, which gets problematic because you can't really have more than two serial ports on most PC-compatible systems.

Once you have the hardware together, you have to test it.

Testing Memory

An awful lot of people think that the short ten-second memory test that their systems go through every time the system is turned on actually *does* something. (Now, if you believed *that*, you probably think that those buttons next to the "Don't Walk" signs on the street corners actually do something.) The quick power-on RAM test is just a quick "Are you there?" kind of memory inventory.

The problem with this approach is that many memory errors are not absolute errors that essentially "sit still" and let you find them. Some memory errors appear because of addressing logic problems: change a bit at address X, and bits change at address Y. Others occur because the memory modules have a trifle different access speed from other memory modules in the system. A third group of errors can appear from differences in electrical characteristics between memories on a motherboard and memories on a high-speed expansion card.

In any case, thorough memory testing is a step that shouldn't be skipped. To that end, here are a few suggestions:

- Use either Checkit from Touchstone software, or QAPlus from DiagSoft. They're the only two programs I've ever looked at that can find those pesky odd errors.

- Run these tests in their "slow" mode. By default, they run a quick test, but you don't want a quick test—you want all of the tests, like "walking bit," "checkerboard," "address line," and whatever your package supports.

- Run the tests from DOS, and do *not* load a memory manager before you do.

- If you're using an ARC (Advanced RISC Computer) machine, ask your vendor for a recommendation on a stringent memory tester.

Don't be surprised if a memory test takes up to eight hours; that's possible on a 32+MB system.

For maximum memory reliability, buy Pentium II-based systems with 72-bit SDRAM, then enable ECC in the system's BIOS. ECC uses hardware to detect and *correct* RAM failures.

Testing Disks

You'll find that NT relies heavily upon *paging* data out to disk. *Paging* is a process wherein disk space is used as a stand-in for memory space. Whenever data is paged from RAM to disk, the operating system assumes that the data will remain safe and sound out on the disk. When NT reloads the data from disk to RAM, it doesn't even check to see that the data is undamaged. Therefore, you need a 100-percent reliable disk to support NT.

As with memory, disks often show problems only under certain circumstances. It would be nice if you could just write out a simple bit of data like the word *testing* all over the disk, then go back and read the disk to be sure that the word *testing* was still on it, but a test like that would only find the grossest of disk errors. DOS's SCANDISK is a tester of this variety, useful only in the most disk-damaged situations.

Instead, you need a *pattern tester* for your disk drive. There is one that I can recommend: SpinRite 4 from Gibson Research. SpinRite is a high-quality disk tester.

Now, there are two disadvantages to disk testing: the time involved, and the fact that all the good ones are DOS-based. It can literally take *days* to do a thorough test on a disk. Running SpinRite on a 1700MB disk took *three days,* but when it was done, SpinRite had found some errors on the disk that hadn't been found by the manufacturer, the low-level format program, or the DOS FORMAT program.

The DOS heritage of these programs means that the only disk system that they recognize is the FAT file system, *arrgh*! That implies that when you get a new server, you should put DOS on it temporarily, format its disk to a FAT format, install NT Server, and convert the FAT format to NTFS format.

Here's a case where those of you installing an NT workstation system will have it better, as you'll probably stay with the FAT file system for an NT workstation.

You may be scowling right now because of the work that I'm setting out for you; *don't*. Believe me, I've seen a number of client network problems boil down to flaky memory or flaky disks. You really only need to test RAM once, when you first install it. Disks really should be tested once a year.

Preparing the Data

If this is a brand-new server, there's really nothing to do in the way of backup.

If you're converting your server from another operating system to NT Server, then you first have to protect the data on your server's disk. Here are a few strategies.

Backing Up to Another Machine

If you have another computer around with enough mass storage to hold your server's data, you could run some kind of peer-to-peer LAN (like the built-in networking capabilities of Windows 95/98 or Windows for Workgroups), share that machine's drive, and then just copy the whole drive over with an XCOPY /S command. Then, once NT Server is up, you can connect the NT Server machine easily to the Windows for Workgroups machine, and XCOPY back.

Temporarily Installing the Tape to Another Machine

Suppose you're currently using a lower-level, FAT-based server system like LAN-tastic or Windows for Workgroups, and you're going to change over to NT Server. You run a DOS-based tape backup program, put the tape drive away, and install NT Server. In the process, you format your server to the New Technology File System (NTFS). Then try to restore the data to the server.

And that's when the problem becomes evident.

You see, just about every backup program saves data in a different way. Say you have some program—let's call it SB, for Simple Backup—that shipped with the tape drive. It's a DOS-based program, so it ran fine when you were backing up the disk, but *now it won't run under NT*. Why? Two reasons. First, it probably directly controls the tape drive, and NT absolutely forbids DOS programs (or NT applications programs, for that matter) to directly manipulate hardware; try to run the program, and it would crash. Second, the tape restore program *might* work by directly writing data to the disk, and that would not only be intercepted by NT, it would fail even if NT didn't stop the restore program—after all, this disk is now formatted in NTFS, not FAT.

Or perhaps you could buy a piece of big-name software like Backup Exec or ArcServe for Novell (presuming you're moving the server from Novell to NT). Can you back it up with the Novell version and then restore with the NT version? In my experience, you can't do it. I guess the security models of NetWare and NT are too different to allow a simple crossover.

What about going at it the other way? Just boot the server from a DOS floppy and run the restore program. That'll work, won't it? Unfortunately, no, it won't work. Remember, the disk is now formatted under NTFS, so a DOS program couldn't recognize the C: drive anyway.

Well, NT comes with a tape backup program. Won't it read my DOS backups? No. Emphatically, *no*. The NT backup program uses its own Microsoft Backup Format to write tapes, a format that, so far as I know, is unique in the industry. (Question: "How many Microsoft programmers does it take to change a light bulb?" Answer: "None; they just declare darkness a Microsoft standard.")

So what's the answer? One approach is to just take the tape drive out of the server, install it in another computer, use Windows 95/98 or Windows for Workgroups or something like it to share the hard disk of the soon-to-be NT Server machine, and then do the backup over the peer-to-peer network onto the tape. Then set up the server, reconnect it to the Windows for Workgroups machine, and restore from the Windows for Workgroups machine. Cumbersome, but it'll work.

Setting Up the Server for FAT, Restore, and Convert

This last approach takes a bit more time, but it is simpler, and truthfully it's the one that I've used. The best way to restore your backups may be to restore your backups to a FAT volume and then convert the volume to NTFS. Read the "How Do I" sidebar to find out how.

How Do I Convert a FAT Volume to an NTFS Volume?

To convert a FAT volume to an NTFS volume:

1. Do the backup under DOS, a FAT-based backup.

2. Install NT Server, but don't reformat the disk to NTFS.

3. Reboot under DOS, from a floppy.

4. Run the tape restore program and restore the files.

5. Boot the server, and run the FAT-to-NTFS conversion program CONVERT.EXE to make the server's disk NTFS (CONVERT *drive:* /FS:NTFS).

After you've done the conversion, run NTBACKUP *immediately* and get a first backup of the new disk format.

One of the morals of the story: backups look different on different operating systems. I found that out a few years ago when using a portable Bernoulli box.

My Bernoulli box was a 90MB cartridge storage device (they have them in 150MB and larger now, but the one I worked with was a 90) whose most interesting feature was that it could be hooked up to a parallel port via a converter built by the Iomega people, makers of the Bernoulli box. The Bernoulli box really uses a SCSI interface, but the Iomega parallel port converter faked the box out into thinking that the parallel port was a SCSI port.

Anyway, you could do backups easily, if not quickly, via the parallel port with the Bernoulli box. A few of my systems, however, already have SCSI ports built right into them, so I tried hooking the Bernoulli right into the SCSI port. It worked, but not with the Iomega software; I ended up using a generic SCSI removable cartridge hard disk formatting software. I was able to back up, and back up much more quickly than via the parallel port, but the resulting cartridges couldn't be read when the Bernoulli was attached via the parallel port. So be careful when backing up!

Making Backups If You're Converting from LAN Manager

One more thought: Microsoft distributed SyTOS, a tape backup program, with its LAN Manager 2.2 product. The version of SyTOS that came with LAN Manager won't run under NT, but the NTBACKUP program *can* read SyTOS-formatted tapes, *if you get the LAN Manager upgrade version of NT Server, that is*. Even better, the Upgrade is less than half the list price of NT Server.

Further, the LAN Manager Upgrade package has a utility to convert from the HPFS and HPFS386 formats used by LAN Manager to NTFS *in situ*, so you may never need those backups at all.

Setting Up the LAN Card

Next, get your network card set up properly. If you're just installing the network card now, be careful that the things you do right now don't get you in trouble later. Now is the time to be sure that

- Your system doesn't have any interrupt (IRQ) or input/output (I/O) address conflicts.

- You've written down any settings that you've made to the system.

- The card works in a stand-alone mode.

The first step is to find acceptable interrupts and input/output addresses.

Setting an Interrupt

Interrupts are how your LAN card tells the CPU that the CPU must pay attention to the LAN card, *now!* Why does the LAN card have the right to bug the CPU like that? Well, mainly because the LAN card has only a limited amount of buffer space, and if the CPU doesn't come get this data quickly, then *more* data will come into the LAN card, knocking the current data right out of the LAN card's buffers and off to data heaven.

Your system can support up to 16 different devices interrupting your CPU. Each one of those interrupts is more properly called a *hardware interrupt* or an *IRQ (interrupt request) level*. In general, you can only have one hardware device on a given IRQ level. I say "in general" because it is *possible* to share IRQs on a machine with a Micro Channel, EISA, or PCI bus architecture. EISAs and PCIs, however, usually coexist with older, ISA bus slots, making interrupt sharing impractical in most cases.

You can see common IRQ settings in Table 3.1.

TABLE 3.1: Common IRQ Settings

IRQ Level	Common Usage	Comments
0	Timer	Hard-wired on motherboard; impossible to change.
1	Keyboard	Hard-wired on motherboard; impossible to change.
2	Cascade from IRQ 9	May or may not be available, depending on how the motherboard is designed; best to avoid if possible; some old VGAs may use this for "autoswitching"; disable the feature, if present.
3	COM2 or COM4	
4	COM1 or COM3	

Continued on next page

TABLE 3.1 CONTINUED: Common IRQ Settings

IRQ Level	Common Usage	Comments
5	LPT2	Most of us don't use a second parallel port, and so can use this for something else. It is safe to use this if you have a "virtual" LPT2, as in the case of a network connection.
6	Floppy disk controller	
7	LPT1	
8	Real-time clock	Hard-wired on motherboard; impossible to change.
9	Cascade to IRQ 2	Wired directly to IRQ 2, so this does not exist as a separate interrupt. Sometimes when you set a board to IRQ 2, you have to tell the software that you set it to IRQ 9 to make it work.
10	Unused	
11	Unused	
12	PS/2, InPort mouse	
13	Math coprocessor	Used to signal detected errors in coprocessor.
14	Hard disk controller	
15	Unused	

Part of setting up a LAN board involves setting an IRQ level. You set a board's IRQ either by moving a switch or jumper on the card, in the case of older cards, or by running a setup program, in the case of most modern LAN boards. For example, in the case of the Intel EtherExpress LAN boards, you run a program called SoftSet, which is shipped with the EtherExpress board. It examines your system and attempts to find a good IRQ address (and I/O address, for that matter) for your system. It then suggests these settings, and you can either accept them or reject them. If you reject the settings, then you can directly enter the ones that you desire.

These software setup programs are a great improvement over the LAN boards of just a few years ago, which required interminable DIP switch flipping and jumper-setting. The process that I described for the Intel board is similar to what I've seen on the SMC Elite cards, the GVC NE2000-based boards, and the 3Com 3C509 cards.

But let's get down to work. Which interrupt is the right one to choose?

A lot of people buy themselves grief by putting their network cards on IRQ 2. Don't do it. IRQ 2 was available back on the 8-bit PC/XT type designs, but it serves a valuable role in modern PCs.

The PC/XT systems had a single interrupt controller, an Intel 8259 chip. The 8259 could support up to eight interrupt levels, and the original PC/XT systems hardwired channels 0 and 1 to the system timer (a clock circuit that goes "tick" every 18.2 microseconds) and the 8042 keyboard controller.

The system was wired with those interrupts because IBM wanted to make sure that the keyboard and the timer had high priorities. You see, with an 8259, when two interrupts occur at the same time, the one with the lower number gets priority.

Interrupts 3 and 4 went to COM2 and COM1, respectively; the idea was that COM2 would support a modem and COM1 would support a printer, and so the modem would have slightly higher priority.

TIP   To this day, it's usually a good idea to use COM2 for higher-speed communications.

Interrupts 5, 6, and 7 were assigned to the hard disk controller, the floppy disk controller, and the parallel port.

In 1984, the first 16-bit PC compatible system was released—the IBM AT. The proliferation of add-in devices on the market made it clear that eight interrupt levels just weren't enough. So IBM decided to add another 8259. The problem was that just slapping the extra 8259 onto the motherboard might present some backward compatibility problems, so IBM decided to kind of slip the extra 8259 in "via the back door," as you can see in Figure 3.1.

The way IBM did it was to take the new IRQs 8 through 15 and route them through IRQ 9, then connect IRQ 9 to IRQ 2. Result: whenever IRQ 8 through 15 is triggered, IRQ 9 goes off, which makes IRQ 2 look like *it* went off. The PC's BIOS then knows that whenever IRQ 2 appears, that *really* means to check the second 8259 to find out which IRQ *really* triggered. By the way, they also freed up IRQ 5; it's no longer needed by your AT or later hard disk controller.

These IRQ changes imply a few things:

• Don't use IRQ 2, as it's already got a job: it's the gateway to IRQs 8–15.

- If you *do* use IRQ 2, then you may have to tell the NT software that your network card is set to IRQ 9. IRQ 9 and IRQ 2 are electronically equal under this system, because they're tied together.

FIGURE 3.1:

Extra 8259 on the IBM AT

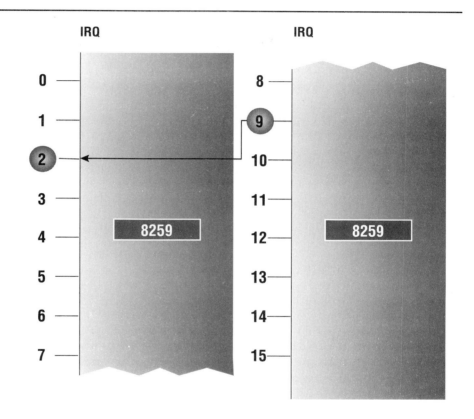

- Because interrupts 8–15 slide into the architecture via IRQ 2, they essentially "inherit" IRQ 2's priority level. That means that IRQs 8–15 are of higher priority than IRQs 3–7.

- Don't use IRQ 9, because it has a cascade responsibility.

- Safe IRQs are 5, 10, 11, and 15; avoid the others. You probably need these IRQs for the following hardware:

  - Sound card: if it's an 8-bit card, then your only option is IRQ 5 for the sound card

- LAN board, as we've already discussed

- SCSI host adapter (although an Adaptec 2742 can actually forgo interrupts, needing only a DMA channel)

TIP   Whatever you set your boards to, *write it down!* You'll need the information later. I tape an envelope to the side of my computers. Each time I install a board (or modify an existing board), I get a new piece of paper and write down all the configuration information on the board. For example, I might write, "Intel EtherExpress 16 card installed 10 July 1994 by Mark Minasi; no EPROM on board; shared memory disabled; IRQ 10 used; I/O address 310 set."

Setting an I/O Address

IRQs are a mite scarce, so they're the things that you worry about most of the time. But LAN boards also require that you set their *input/output* address, or I/O address (it's sometimes called the *port address*). I/O addresses are generally three-digit numbers, and for LAN cards they're typically a range starting at either 300 hex or 310 hex.

A LAN board's input/output address is the electrical "location" of the LAN board from the CPU's point of view. When the CPU wants to send data to a LAN card, it doesn't issue an instruction that says, "Send this data to the EtherExpress board," because the computer's hardware has no idea what an EtherExpress board *is*. Instead, every device—keyboard, video adapter, parallel port, whatever—gets a numerical address between 0 and 1023 called its *input/output address*. The value is usually expressed in hex, so it ends up being the range 000–3FF in hex. (A discussion of hexadecimal is beyond the scope of this book, but many other sources cover hex.) Just as the postal deliverer would be confused if there were two houses at 25 Main Street, a PC system can't function properly if there is more than one device at a given I/O address. Hence, part of your installation job is to ensure that you don't set the LAN card to the same I/O address as some other board.

In general, I/O addresses won't give you too much trouble, but once in a while… On one of my systems, I had a video accelerator that used I/O addresses around 300 hex. My newly installed board, which also was set to 300 hex, didn't work. My clue to the problem was that the video display showed some very odd colors when first booting up. I checked the video accelerator's settings, and *voilà!* the problem became apparent. I then changed the Ethernet card's address and the problem went away.

In any case, the I/O address is another thing that you have to be sure to write down in that envelope attached to your computer. For those of you working for larger companies, an envelope taped to the side of a computer isn't a practical answer, of course, but why not build a small database of PC information? Keep it on your system and key it to an ID number that you can affix to a PC either by engraving it on the side of the case or with hard-to-remove stickers.

Stand-Alone Card Tests

Now that the card is installed, it's a good idea to test the card and the LAN cable before going any further. The four kinds of tests that you do on most networks include:

- An on-board diagnostic
- A local loopback test
- A "network live" loopback test
- A sender/responder test

These three tests are usually encapsulated in a diagnostics diskette that you get with the LAN board. The first is a simple test of the circuitry on the board. Many of the modern boards have a "reset and check out" feature on their chips, so this program just wakes that feature up. If the chips check out OK, then this step is successfully completed.

That first test can be a useful check of whether or not you've set the IRQ to a conflicting level, or perhaps placed any on-board RAM overlapping other RAM.

The second test is one wherein you put a loopback connector (exactly what a loopback connector *is* varies with LAN variety) on your network board. The loopback connector causes any outgoing transmissions from the LAN board to be "looped back" to the LAN board. The loopback test then sends some data out from the LAN card and listens for the same data to be received by the LAN card. If that data *isn't* received by the LAN card, then there's something wrong with the transmitter or the receiver logic of the network card.

Notice that for the first two tests, you haven't even connected your system to the network yet. In the third test, you do the loopback test again, but this time while connected to the network. The board should pass again.

The final test involves two computers, a sender and a responder. The responder's job is to echo back anything that it receives. For example, if Paul's machine is the responder and Jeff's is the sender, then any messages that Jeff's machine sends to Paul's machine should cause Paul's machine to send the same message back to Jeff's machine.

To make a computer a responder (and any computer can be a responder; you needn't use a server) you have to run a program that makes it into a responder. But that's where the problem arises. The responder software is packaged on the same disk as the diagnostic software that comes with the network board and, unfortunately, the responder software usually only runs on network boards made by the company that wrote the diagnostic software. So, for example, if you have an Ethernet that is a mixture of 3Com, SMC, and Intel LAN boards, and you want to test a computer with a new 3Com Ethernet board, you have to search for another computer that has a 3Com board so that you can run the responder software on that computer. (I was recently impressed to see that some 3Com boards now come with board diagnostics that run under *NT*, not DOS. Quite a nice touch; I hope other vendors follow suit!)

Once you're certain that the hardware is all installed, you're ready to start installing NT or NT Server.

A Word about PCI Systems

Most modern servers are based on the Pentium Pro/II/Xeon CPUs. Built around the Intel chip sets, these computers usually have a few PCI slots and a few ISA slots.

Their power is terrific, but they have one major problem: hardware configuration. You see, PCI systems are pretty much all designed with a single assumption in mind, that they will run a plug-and-play operating system like Windows 95/98. But, unfortunately, NT *isn't* a plug-and-play operating system, making setting up PCI systems a bit tougher.

The problem arises when you try to set the resources—IRQs, DMAs, I/O addresses, and the like—on a PCI board. Most of them don't have jumpers or DIP switches, nor do they have software setup programs. How, then, does a PCI network card figure out which IRQ to use? Well, it depends on the manufacturer of the computer. The only company who really knows how to design a PCI-based system correctly is Compaq (which is why they're so expensive); there's a neat built-in configuration program that lets you set up a PCI board as if it were an EISA or MCA board. For most vendors, however, it works like this: a board in the first PCI slot gets IRQ 9, the second PCI slot gets IRQ 10, and so on. Of course, this can be a real problem if you already have an ISA board in your system that uses one of those IRQs. There's no way for the PCI board to know that the conflict exists. How, then, to set up a PCI/ISA hybrid system?

Three possibilities come to mind. First, buy PCI systems without any ISA boards, if possible; the PCI components will keep from conflicting with one another. Second, try installing all of the PCI boards and find out what resources they are using. Then, once you know what DMA channels, memory addresses, and IRQs are being used by the PCI cards, install the ISA boards with those already-taken resources in mind. Essentially, I'm telling you to install the PCI cards and let them settle down, then set up the ISA cards to tiptoe around them. A sad approach, yes, but probably the best one we've got until Windows 2000 Server, when NT is supposed to be plug-and-play compliant. Third, more and more systems' BIOSes let you control which IRQ goes with which slot. Some even let you tell the BIOS, "I've already given IRQ 9 to an ISA card, so don't use that one." Look for this feature when buying hardware.

Answer These Questions Before Running NT Setup

One last thing before you start the Setup program: figure out what this computer will do in the network and make sure you have the answers to the questions that Setup will ask. You already have some hardware information written down:

- What kind of network card you have

- What IRQ and I/O addresses it is set to

- What kind of disk adapter you have

- How you want to partition the drive

- Optionally, make and configuration information for a sound card (presuming you have a sound card on your server for some strange reason)

But consider these next questions before you start running Setup.

What Kind of Server Will This Be?

An NT Server machine can assume one of three roles in the network:

- A primary domain controller in a brand-new domain

- A backup domain controller in an existing domain

- An ordinary file and/or application server

NOTE   This decision is important because *once you've made it, you can't change it*—at least not without doing a completely fresh installation.

Only install an NT Server machine as a primary domain controller if you are creating a new domain. Since no machines around are members of this domain, by definition—you don't have a domain without a primary domain controller—there are no security considerations. But in the process of creating the primary domain controller, NT will also create an account that is the Administrator account for the entire domain, so you have to pay attention there. NT will prompt you for an administrative password if you create a new domain (that is, if you install a primary domain controller). You can make up any password that you want, but *please* be sure to write it down! If you don't, then you have to start all over again because you can't retrieve a forgotten password, and, without the domain administrator's password, you can't even log on to the primary domain controller that you just installed.

If you're going to install a backup domain controller, an existing primary domain controller must already be set up, and the machine that you're installing must be on the network with that machine. Setup will reject an attempt to install a backup domain controller if it can't see the primary domain controller. In that case, you will again be asked for an administrative password, but this time you're not making one up; rather, you must supply the name and password of an existing domain administrator account. Don't install backup domain controllers willy-nilly throughout your network. In fact, Microsoft reckons that you only need one backup domain controller per 2,000 users. You can read more about domain design in Chapters 11 and 12.

If you opt to just install an NT Server machine with no domain responsibilities, then you will be asked again to think up a new password for an administrative account on the server that you are installing, but it's an administrative account solely for that server, not for the entire domain. You will also be asked if you want to join a workgroup or a domain. This is a little misleading.

Every domain contains a workgroup. Remember that a number of types of machines can join a workgroup but not a domain. For example, suppose I create domain US out of two NT machines and two Windows for Workgroups machines. The NT machines can join the domain; the Windows for Workgroups machines cannot. But the two NT machines automatically constitute a *workgroup* named US as well, and the Windows for Workgroups machines can join that workgroup.

What does the following question mean: "Do you want to join a domain or a workgroup?" If you join the workgroup, you see all of the servers on the workgroup, but you can't make use of the central user account's database on the domain controllers. Everyone who wants to access data on your workgroup server must have a personal account on that server, independent of their account on the domain. In contrast, joining the domain means essentially that you don't have to bother creating user accounts on the server, because the server just uses the user accounts on the domain controllers' SAM database.

If you want to join a domain or workgroup, make sure you know how it's spelled. To join a domain, you need the name and password of a domain user account that has administrative privileges. You can't just join a domain all by yourself; an administrator from that domain must approve it. Alternatively, an administrator can create a *machine account* beforehand using the Server Manager (see Chapter 11).

What Will This Be Named?

Before running the installation program, think about what to name the server. As I said in a previous chapter, don't name it after people. Use a name that will be of value to you in supporting the network, like an inventory number or the like. Similarly, you'll be prompted for a name, organization name, and product ID number. Make sure in particular that you can lay your hands on the ID number.

And if your network runs on the TCP/IP protocol, then you may have to gather this information for your new installation:

- IP address

- Subnet mask

- Default gateway address or addresses

- DNS server address or addresses

- WINS server address or addresses

- LMHOSTS file

- Internet domain name

All of this is explained in Chapter 14, on TCP/IP.

How Will This Server Be Licensed?

Like all software vendors, Microsoft has a real problem trying to figure out how to price its products. Economic theory says that, in a correctly competitive market, a price will (in the short term) drift toward the short-run marginal cost of the product. In other words, if the software industry were properly competitive, NT Server would cost what Microsoft paid to produce the floppies, CD, box, and manual—probably a wholesale price of about $20, with normal profit margins included.

Of course, that isn't how Microsoft prices its server product because, first of all, the server market is *not* properly competitive, not by a long shot, and second, the software business is one in which many of the costs are invested up front, on programmers and computing equipment. And that's the problem.

You see, we consumers of Microsoft products are allowed to know so little about how Microsoft (a publicly traded company, remember) runs its development efforts that we have no idea whether $700 for NT Server is a bargain or a boondoggle. And, judging from how Microsoft changes its pricing structure, they have no idea either.

The latest approach, which has existed all the way back to version 3.51, goes something like this. First, as you know, you must buy the NT Server software itself; it lists for $700 when last I checked. But you don't have the right to use that software unless you (or anyone else who wants to use it) own a *client license*. A client license is just a piece of paper—no ID codes, no passwords, just the "honor" system—saying that Microsoft allows you to use the software. Client licenses list for $40.

Let's stop and be clear about what a client license is. Again, it's just a piece of paper. It doesn't give you the right to put NT Server on any machine you like; you paid the $700 for the right to put NT Server on *one* machine. But if 100 users want to access that server, you have to buy a client access license for each one of them. Then, on top of that, you *still* must buy them all copies of Windows 95, NT Workstation, Windows for Workgroups, or the like. Ignoring the client operating system costs, the network software costs $700 plus 100 licenses at $40 apiece, or $4700.

But now suppose you put a machine in the waiting area of your building running some kind of information kiosk software. Someone comes in off the street and runs the program, which happens to access the server over the network for information. Now you have 101 people on the network.

And hey, it's a wired world. Suppose you put that server on the Internet and put a Web page on it. Some random surfer checks out your Web page, which technically means you have 102 people on your network, including the guy at the information kiosk.

So in addition to your 100 employees, how many licenses do you need? For the folks who visit your Web site, none. For the information kiosk, you'll need a license. But some unknown number of people view the information kiosk in a given year—must you buy a license for each of them, or can you just buy one license that you apply generically to whoever's at the kiosk at the moment?

Microsoft allows you to make a choice about how to use those $40 client licenses. They call the options *per seat* and *per server*. For each server, you must decide whether to treat client licenses as per seat or per server.

"Per server" is also known as a *concurrent* license. Buying a license for a per-server machine means that one person can access that server at a time. For example, if you had 100 employees that worked in two shifts, 50 in the day and 50 at night, then you'd never have more than 50 people on the network at any time, so you could install the server as "per server" and buy 50 licenses. If you bought another server, you would need another 50 licenses, and so on for each new server.

"Per seat" is not oriented to the number of network connections, as is per server, but instead to the number of enterprise network users. If you set up your servers as per-seat servers, then all you need to do is buy one license for each user. That license allows that user to access any and all servers on your network. If your enterprise has 100 servers in it, one client license gives one user the right to access all of the servers in the enterprise. In the case of the company with the one server and two employee shifts, you'd have to buy 100 licenses, however, as the per-seat arrangement requires you to buy one license for each user.

Think about it for a bit, and you'll see that for anyone with two servers or more, per seat is the way to go, save for the information kiosk scenario.

Armed with hardware, software, and network knowledge, we're ready to start installing NT Server.

Starting the NT Install Program

Briefly, there are two ways to kick off the NT installation program, both of which have their pros and cons:

- Put the NT Server CD-ROM into your drive, take the three setup floppies out of the NT box, insert the NT Setup diskette into drive A:, and reboot.

- Run the WINNT or WINNT32 program from the I386 directory on the CD-ROM.

Both techniques are discussed below.

Installing from the Setup Floppies

Look in the NT box, and you see floppies labeled "Windows NT Setup boot disk," "NT disk 2," and "NT disk 3." These floppies don't contain all of NT; they contain enough software to kick off the installation process so that the NT installation CD can take over.

This is the preferred method in many cases. But it won't work if you have a CD-ROM that is accessible from DOS but not from NT, like the CD-ROMs on the old Creative Labs Multimedia kits. The NT Setup program just can't recognize the CD-ROM and stops working. That's when WINNT or WINNT32 is useful.

Installing with WINNT and WINNT32

In the case of Intel users, all the files that you need to install NT are in the folder on the CD named I386. You can install NT just as long as you can get access of some kind to this directory—over the network, on the hard disk, or even from a CD-ROM that can only be accessed by DOS.

There's no real trick to this. Just make sure that all of I386—including its sub-directories—are on a CD, hard disk directory, or network drive. Log on to that I386 directory and either type WINNT if you're upgrading from DOS or Windows, or WINNT32 if you're upgrading from a previous version of NT. If you're using Windows 95, I recommend that you reboot Windows 95 in "safe mode command prompt" and use WINNT because WINNT32 seems not to work under Windows 95.

WINNT and WINNT32 have a couple of disadvantages. First, they require you to format three floppies before you start it up. You can often avoid that by using the /b option (WINNT/b or WINNT32/b), which skips the floppies. You need the floppies, however, if you either want to specify a nonstandard disk controller driver or you want to do an NT repair from WINNT.

NOTE   It's much harder to do an NT repair on a computer without a CD-ROM drive. You can do WINNT or WINNT32 installs, but by default the repair process fails if NT can't find a CD-ROM drive. You *can* make an NT repair work without a CD, but you've got to mess around with some of the NT setup files to make it work—you'll see how in Chapter 17.

The second disadvantage is time. Before taking you to the initial setup screens that you would see if you were installing from the three floppies and the CD-ROM, you have to sit through about 45 minutes of file copying. You can shorten that a bit by using WINNT32 and choosing to make the setup floppies, but uncheck the Create local source option in the dialog box that appears.

Installing NT on an Alpha

For those of you running NT on an Alpha, you'll start the setup a bit differently. In addition to the NT Server CD-ROM, you'll probably also need a floppy disk containing the HAL file for your system—just about every Alpha seems to need a different HAL. Check with your hardware vendor to see if you need other drivers, as well—for example, my Alpha system requires extra files for a HAL, graphics drivers, and a driver for the EIDE host adapter in the system.

Just put the CD-ROM into the drive and restart the system. When you get the option to enter the Setup routine, do so—on my system, you see the option to press F2 at a point in the boot sequence. That will kick off a menu that includes the option to Install Windows NT. Choose it, and the NT install process will start, taking you immediately to the blue Windows NT Setup screen. From that point on, it's the same as installing NT on an Intel system.

Running the NT Install Program

Next, you start the Setup program. My examples assume that you're installing from the CD-ROM. Floppy installations are nearly the same but are more tedious.

Starting with the Floppies

Pop the "Setup Boot Disk" into drive A: and reboot. NT then runs NTDETECT .COM, which figures out what kind of hardware you have on your system. You see a message that says, "Windows NT Setup/Setup is inspecting your computer's hardware configuration."

Next, you see the following on a blue screen with white letters:

```
Windows NT Setup
```

And on the bottom of the screen:

```
Setup is loading files (Windows NT Executive)...
```

NT next loads the Hardware Abstraction Layer, after which you are prompted to insert Setup Disk number 2 and press Enter. You see some messages on the bottom of the screen about what's loading, including

- "NT config data"
- Fonts
- Locale-specific data
- Windows NT setup

- PCMCIA support

- SCSI port driver

- Video driver

- Floppy disk driver

- Keyboard driver

- FAT file system

Setup then turns the screen to 50-line mode. It announces how much system memory you have in megabytes and says that the NT kernel, as well as a "build number," is loading. For example, NT version 3.51 was build 1057.

Welcome to Setup

The screen shifts back to normal mode and the Welcome to Setup message appears. It offers these choices:

- To learn more, press F1

- To set up Windows NT now, press Enter

- To repair a damaged installation, press R

- To quit, press F3

Press Enter, insert Setup Disk #3, and press Enter again. Setup goes into device detection.

Scanning for SCSI Adapters

Setup auto-detects any SCSI adapters in your system. Your adapter should be auto-detected properly (I've installed systems with four different SCSI adapters, and they all installed correctly). If the adapter wasn't recognized, you have a chance to punch it in directly, or if it's not on NT's built-in list of adapters, you can tell NT to use a device support disk.

If your adapter is on the NT compatibility list and wasn't recognized, I recommend *not* hand-configuring the SCSI adapter by pressing S. Instead, I recommend that you exit Setup (press F3) and go back and recheck that the SCSI adapter is installed correctly. In the SCSI host adapter scanning process, you have to insert the third (and final, if you're doing a CD-ROM installation) diskette. If you *do* have to insert a manufacturer's extra driver, you have to swap disk 3 and the driver disk a couple of times before going any further; just follow the prompts.

Upgrade or Fresh Install?

Next, you often see this message:

```
Setup has found Windows NT on your hard disk in the directory shown
below. To upgrade, press Enter. To cancel upgrade and install a fresh
copy of Windows NT, press N.
```

This is an important choice. If you choose to upgrade an existing copy of NT rather than do a fresh install, you will preserve all of your user accounts—the data in your SAM—as well as all directory share information that existed before this upgrade. If you are upgrading a primary domain controller, you probably want to upgrade. If you want to clean out old user accounts and start all over, a fresh install is probably the right choice.

What Do You Have and Where Does It Go?

NT Setup then tells you what it thinks you have in terms of

- Basic PC type
- Video system
- Keyboard
- Country layout for keyboard
- Mouse

The list is usually correct, except for the video. The NT Setup program seems to set just about every video board to basic VGA, and there's a good reason for it. The NT designers reasoned that if you choose a super VGA type, you may choose wrong, and if you choose wrong, the system won't be bootable and you will have to reinstall from the ground up. In contrast, VGA drivers work on just about any video board around. They may not exploit the full resolution or color depth of most boards, but they *do* work. So, once the system is up and running with the

VGA drivers, you can install the super VGA drivers. If, after installing the new drivers, your system doesn't work, you can always load the Last Known Good Configuration, as you'll see in Chapter 17.

Actually, even if you *do* mess up when picking a video type, NT resolves the problem by including an option on the Operating System Picker called NT 4 [VGA mode]. No matter how badly you've bollixed up the video, you can always reboot and choose the VGA option. Then, once you've booted, you can adjust your video driver to something more appropriate.

When you're satisfied that the list matches your configuration, highlight "The above list matches my computer," and press Enter.

At this point, if you're installing the NT Workstation operating system and you intend to coexist with DOS, or if you're installing an NT Server on top of an existing DOS machine, you may see a message that tells you that you are using the Delete Sentry or Delete Tracking features of Undelete under DOS. NT does not recognize that feature (it doesn't have either Delete Sentry or Delete Tracking), and so NT may end up reporting different amounts of free space than DOS does.

In English, this means that NT may think that you don't have as much free space on your disk as DOS reported before you got started. Unless you're going to reformat the partition, this may make it impossible for NT to install on your system. If that's the case, reboot under DOS, disable the Delete Sentry system, and destroy the \SENTRY directory. (This defeats the Delete Sentry feature, but that may be necessary in order to get NT to load.)

Choosing an NT Partition

Next, NT Setup shows you the partitions on your system and asks which one you want to install NT on. You can delete partitions with this option, but, as always, be aware that you're permanently destroying data if you do that. (You *did* back up before you started doing this, didn't you?)

TIP

If you're converting a server from Novell NetWare, you must delete the existing NetWare partition before proceeding. Again, that will destroy data on your partition, so don't do it unless you've backed up to a backup format that can be restored under NT, as discussed earlier in this chapter.

Picking Your Drive

Select the partition that you want to install NT on and press Enter. You next choose how you want to format the partition, if you want to format it at all. Your choices are

- Wipe the disk, formatting to a FAT system up to 4098MB

- Wipe the disk, formatting to an NTFS system up to 4098MB

- Convert an existing FAT system to NTFS

- Leave current file system and data alone

- Convert an existing HPFS/HPFS386 system to NTFS (LAN Manager upgrade of NT Server only)

FAT or NTFS Disk Partitioning Options?

Of the FAT or NTFS disk partitioning options, which should you use?

On an NT server, you should use NTFS partitions on the data drives unless you have a very good reason not to. But let's look at the details.

The File Allocation Table file system has only one advantage, but it's a compelling one: it's the file system that DOS uses. If you're moving from a FAT-based workstation (which is likely) or a FAT-based server (which is unlikely), you may want to be able to boot from a DOS floppy and read the hard disk. That's possible if you leave the disk in a FAT format. Moving to NTFS makes it impossible to boot from a DOS floppy and still be able to read the hard disk (a security feature of NTFS). That's why I like to keep a 200–500MB bootable FAT partition on my servers; it makes working on a nonbooting server easier, since I can use my DOS-based data recovery tools. Again, however, the drives that contain the data shared on the network are always NTFS on my servers.

The main features that NTFS offers include

- Directories that are automatically sorted.

- Support of upper- and lowercase letters in names.

- Support of Unicode in file names.

- Allows permissions to be set on directories and files.

- Multiple "forks" in files—subfiles that essentially "branch off" from a file (the closest analogy would be to the data fork and resource fork in the Macintosh file system).

- Faster access to large (over .5MB) sequential access files.

- Faster access to all random access files.

- Long names are automatically converted to the 8+3 naming convention when accessed by a DOS workstation.

- Macintosh compatibility (you cannot share volumes with Mac clients on an NT network unless the host disk partition has been formatted to NTFS).

- NTFS uses the disk space more sparingly than does FAT. Under FAT, the minimum size that a file *actually* uses on a disk is 2048 bytes, and as disk partitions get larger, that minimum size also gets larger: on the 1700MB disk I use on my server, that minimum size would be *32,768* bytes! Under NTFS, that same hard disk—and any hard disk, in fact—supports files so that no file actually takes more than 512 bytes of space.

I'll discuss all of this in more detail later in Chapter 4, but as I've said earlier, it's just plain crazy to use NT Server with any disk format other than NTFS. Without NTFS, you lose most of the security options, a good bit of performance, and some of the disk space currently wasted by the FAT file system for its clusters. The FAT and HPFS conversion routines both have worked without a hitch for me, so long as enough free space is on the hard disk (make sure there's about 118MB free before proceeding).

For an NT workstation, you may want to stay with the FAT file system so that you can dual-boot to DOS, because DOS can't read or write a disk partition formatted to the NTFS format.

CHKDSK in Disguise

NT Setup runs a special version of CHKDSK to make sure that the file system is clean. This test is *not* a disk media test like the old Novell COMPSURF, so—as I've said earlier in this chapter—the onus is on you to make sure that you have a reliable disk before beginning the installation process. This CHKDSK-like program runs if you're not formatting the partition. If you're formatting, you see a message to that effect, and the Setup program will format the hard disk. Then, unbelievably, Setup will run the CHKDSK program on your just-formatted disk (*grrr...*).

Which Directory Do I Put It On?

Choose the directory that you'll install the NT files to. The recommended directory, \WINNT, is fine. Next you see the message, "Setup will now examine your hard disk(s) for corruption." Press Enter to run CHKDSK.

When CHKDSK is done NT Setup copies a bunch of files, just enough to boot the system, to your hard disk. If you're installing from floppies, you get a minor workout. These files are mainly just enough to get the graphical portion of Setup running, although a number of help files get installed in the process, including help files for things that aren't necessary until the system's up and running (Mail, Schedule+, and so on).

Even with a quad-spin CD-ROM, this takes about ten minutes, so be patient until you get a message like the following:

```
This portion of Setup has completed successfully.
If there is a floppy disk inserted in drive A:, remove it.
Press ENTER to restart your computer.
When your computer restarts, Setup will continue.
```

Pop out the Installation disk and reboot the computer. It then boots a kind of mini-NT into a graphical Setup program.

TIP   If you told the Setup program to use NTFS, you'll be confused when Setup reboots. A message says "Check in file system on C:... the type of the file system is FAT." Don't worry about it; you won't see NT say that you have an NTFS volume until you're done with the installation.

Entering Graphical Setup

As the system reboots, you first see NTDETECT's announcement; NTDETECT runs every time you boot NT. You then get a black screen with white letters that tell you to press the spacebar now to return to the "Last Known Good" menu. That's really not relevant here, as you don't yet *have* a Last Known Good menu. (Why you don't is explained in "Common Installation Problems" at the end of this chapter.) Then the screen turns blue because the NT kernel has loaded, and the graphical portion loads.

The first thing you see is the End User Licensing Agreement, kind of a "Microsoft loyalty oath." You're required to click I Agree, because if you don't, you can't go further. (Interestingly enough, much of the license is in French. I don't speak French. Does that render me legally unable to use NT, I wonder?) Once you've done that, NT builds the Setup Wizard.

Who Are You?

As with many products these days, you personalize your copy of NT or NT Server by entering your name and company name. Enter those and click the Continue button; you are asked to verify what you entered and click Continue again. (Be sure to put the correct product number in your server. If you must make one up or leave it blank, remember that your server won't be able to communicate with any other NT Server machine with the same product number.)

The Per-Server or Per-Seat Licensing Option?

Next, your licensing choices appear. In the dialog box, you are presented with two licensing options; per-server and per-seat. As I've explained, the implications of these two options are:

Per-seat Per-*seat* licensing means that you need a license for every *work-station* (not <u>user</u>) that will ever log onto the domain. Per-seat is the kind of licensing that first appeared back in NT 3.5. Per-seat licensing has a few advantages. First, it's easy to understand; you count the number of people that log on to the domain and you have the number of licenses that you need. Second, you don't have to worry about the number of servers in the domain. Whether you have one server in the domain or six, per-seat licensing requires that you have one license for each workstation that logs in to the domain. But don't forget to count the laptops and home machines when you're buying licenses!

Per-server Per-*server* licensing means that you need a license for every simultaneous NT Server connection. If user Ignatz logs on to server RAMSES, that uses up one license. If she then logs on to server ISIS to get to the printer (without leaving her user directory on RAMSES), that uses up another license. If Ignatz connects to six servers, she uses up six licenses.

Think about your needs before choosing a licensing method. You get one shot at changing the licensing style from per-server to per-seat (by using the Licensing icon in the Control Panel). After that, or if you originally specified per-seat licensing, you have to reinstall to legally change it.

NOTE   Oh, and if you *do* choose per-server licensing, be sure to specify at least one client license, or the file server and print server services will refuse to start up.

Choosing a Computer Name

NT next prompts you for a computer name. Recall that it cannot exceed 15 characters in length, and while you can use blank spaces, it's best to avoid them.

Domain Controller or Server

Recall from the last chapter that an NT domain differs from a workgroup in that a domain has a master security database, and that security database is used to approve or reject requests for data or other resources on the network. In a simple NT network, all of the burden of security verification is shouldered by an NT Server machine acting as the primary domain controller. The workload of verifying requests can be shared, however, among a number of NT servers by making them backup domain controllers.

NT Server machines do not *have* to be domain controllers, however; they can simply act as servers. The Setup dialog box labeled "Windows NT Server Security Role" lets you choose which part this server will play in your domain—primary domain controller (which implies a new domain), backup domain controller (which implies an existing domain), or server.

The first NT server that you install in a domain *must* be a primary domain controller. The second should be a backup domain controller, because it's just about impossible to reinstall a primary domain controller, if you need to, without a backup domain controller to stand in for the primary while you're reinstalling the primary. Designate other servers as just "Server."

You can't change a machine's status from server to domain controller without reinstalling NT Server.

You are prompted to create an administrative password if you're installing a primary domain controller or a server. Again, if it's a primary domain controller, then you are creating an administrative account for the entire domain. If it's for a server, then that administrative account only controls that one server.

Creating the Emergency Repair Disk

I have mentioned the important Emergency Repair Disk (ERD) before. This part of the installation asks if you want to create one. Later on, Setup will prompt you to create it. Just put a floppy that you don't mind zapping into the A: drive and Setup will format it and create an Emergency Repair Disk. This isn't a *bootable* disk. The Emergency Repair Disk is just a disk that contains the data necessary to reconstruct a configuration if your NT system is no longer able to boot.

The formatting part of the program seems to run the drive pretty hard. You may find that the format process gets a bit noisy after about 75 percent, but don't worry about it. If the floppy is bad, you get a chance to insert a different floppy.

TIP

If you don't create an ERD right now, you can always make one later. Just click Start ➤ Run, type in **RDISK/S**, and press Enter. The RDISK utility will, among other things, let you create or update an ERD at any time.

Selecting Components

Here you get the list of things you can add to your system, like Microsoft Exchange. Choose whichever pieces are appropriate for your installation. Then NT will move to Phase 2, Network Setup.

Beginning Network Setup

NT then says

Windows NT needs to know how this computer should participate in a network.

The options are

- Do not connect this computer to a network at this time.

- This computer will participate on a network:

    - Wired to the network

    - Remote access to the network

If it's to be a domain controller, you must be on the network. Therefore, choose "This computer will participate in a network/Wired to the network."

Next, choose if you would like to install Microsoft Internet Server (for Windows NT Server OS only).

Setting Up Network Cards

Next, you have to set up your network card. One of NT's really nifty features is an "auto-detect" system that is right most of the time. You see a dialog box labeled "Network Adapter Card Detection." Click Continue and, the vast majority of the time, NT figures out which network card you have without any trouble.

On the other hand, if Setup can't detect your network card, or, in rare instances, if it locks up when it tries to detect your network card, then rerun Setup, choose "Do Not Detect," and directly choose the network card. If the driver for the card isn't on the NT setup disks, you're probably out of luck. There is not a huge market for NT LAN card drivers, so you probably won't find them on the driver disk that came with your LAN card (that may change with time, however). As I suggested a few pages back, it's a good idea to buy one of the top 20 or so LAN cards, since it's easy to find drivers for those cards. And if you want to be pretty *sure* that your NT drivers are good, consider this: much of Microsoft uses the Intel EtherExpress 16 LAN boards. Guess which drivers are likely to be the most stable under NT?

Once Setup has detected your LAN card, click Continue to set up the card. One thing that Setup is *not* good at is figuring out things like which IRQ, I/O address, and RAM addresses your card uses, but that isn't a problem if you took my advice earlier in this chapter and documented those things. Enter those values and click Continue. NT moves on to the main installation process.

Next, you select the protocols that you use on the server. NetBEUI is available and a good idea for small networks, and IPX/SPX is checked by default, but don't install IPX/SPX unless you need it for Novell. I recommend using TCP/IP because

- Most medium to large networks use it nowadays.

- If you intend to connect to the Internet or run your own intranet, then TCP/IP's a good idea because it *is* the protocol upon which intranets and the Internet are built.

- It looks like much of Windows 2000 Server will require TCP/IP to run.

Then Setup prompts you to see if you want to install services. The ones it installs by default are

- RPC Configuration
- NetBIOS interface
- Workstation
- Server

Optionally, you can also install

- Microsoft Internet Information Server 2
- DHCP Relay Agent
- Gateway (And Client) Services for NetWare
- Microsoft DHCP Server
- Microsoft DNS Server
- Microsoft TCP/IP Printing
- Network Monitor Agent
- Network Monitor Tools and Agent
- Remote Access Service
- Remote Boot Service
- RIP for Internet Protocol
- RIP for NwLink IPX/SPX compatible transport
- RPC support for Banyan
- SAP Agent
- Services for Macintosh
- Simple TCP/IP Services
- SNMP Service
- Windows Internet Name Service

You will meet most of those services in this book.

If you chose the TCP/IP protocol, you are prompted to see if you want to use the DHCP protocol to assign TCP/IP addresses. For many systems, you say yes; but read Chapter 14 for the details of TCP/IP setup.

NT now installs the networking components you selected.

Domain/Workgroup Follow-Up

Next, NT asks more questions about the security role that your computer plays. I don't like the arrangement of these dialog boxes because they really should follow the earlier question about whether the machine is to be a primary domain controller, backup domain controller, or server.

If you're just installing an NT Server machine in an existing domain, you see a dialog box called Domain/Workgroup Settings. You have the choice of joining an existing workgroup or becoming a member of an existing domain.

Remember that NT is massively security-conscious. As a result, not just any NT workstation or server can be part of an NT domain; instead, it has to be *granted* access to the domain by the primary domain controller. That happens one of two ways:

- An administrator of the domain creates a machine account with the Server Manager (covered in Chapter 11) before installing the new server.

- The Setup program gives an administrator the option to create a machine account right here in the Domain/Workgroup Settings dialog box.

This can be a bit confusing (at least, it threw *me* when I first started working with NT), so let's look at what's going on in more detail. Most kinds of workstations can just jump right onto an NT domain without any kind of prior notice. For example, DOS, Windows, OS/2, and Windows for Workgroups machines can just "appear" on an NT domain without the permission of the NT primary domain controller, *except* for the fact that whoever is logging on to the NT domain must be a user with a valid network account created by the User Manager for Domains (see Chapter 6).

In contrast, an NT domain won't even *talk* to an NT workstation or server to which it has not been "properly introduced." Now, in general, you introduce a machine to a domain by first logging on to the domain as an administrator, then running the Server Manager. In the Server Manager, you can tell the domain to expect to hear from a new machine called, say, Ignatz. Then, when you're installing your next NT machine—workstation or server—you just name that machine Ignatz. The domain says, "Oh, *you're* Ignatz! We've been expecting you!" and all is well.

The problem with that approach, of course, is that nine times out of ten you end up forgetting to run the Server Manager before installing NT, which forces you to abort an NT installation in midstream or to run around looking for an already-working NT machine from which to run the Server Manager. For that reason, Microsoft decided to make your life easier and just put a tiny piece of the Server Manager in the Setup program. If you are installing NT *and* if you are an administrator (which you must verify by entering the user name for your administrative account and password), you can create the machine account right then and there in the Setup program.

In the Create Computer Account in Domain part of the dialog box, you're prompted for a Username and a Password. It kind of looks like you're being asked to create a new user in this dialog box, but you're not; this is the username and password of your administrative account, the administrative account that you use to create the new *machine* account on the NT domain.

Once that's all plugged in, click OK.

If you are upgrading a machine, your domain controller may become confused about why a machine that it already knows is all of a sudden a different operating system version. If that happens, you may have to rebuild your machine's account, and you need to know a trick to do that. Wait until the server is set up and running, then go to Network in the Control Panel and choose Identification. Click Change Name and you get the chance to change from a domain to a workgroup. Change to a workgroup of any name. Then close the Control Panel. It prompts you to reboot, but you needn't do that. Reopen Network in the Control Panel and again choose Identification and press Change. Now choose to join your old domain, but also check the box labeled "Create Computer Account in [fill in blank] domain." Punch in the name and password of a domain administrator, and your domain will build a new machine account for your server.

Video Test Screen

Finally, NT offers to test your video driver. Go ahead and set up whatever color depth and resolution you like, but recall that I advise you to use the VGA driver on server machines.

NT then finishes up and tells you to reboot.

Now, it may have to go through another boot or two if you are converting from FAT to NTFS, but by then you have finished getting the basic operating system on your server.

Applying the Service Pack

You've got the basic operating system set up, but you're not done yet. *Now* you get to install the service packs. Come to think of it, however, you might *first* try to get a display driver on your system, which leads to this warning:

WARNING   If you have an AGP type video card—and trust me, you probably do if you've purchased the hardware since 1997—then don't bother trying to install the video driver. It won't work until you install Service Pack 3 or later.

Make sure you get the right service pack. The generally-available service packs on the Web typically contain files that replace existing files, and one file in particular—SCHANNEL.DLL—contains code that encrypts Web transactions. Due to government regulations, Microsoft is forced to put the SCHANNEL.DLL, which only supports the low-level 40-bit or 56-bit encryption, on the service packs distributed over the Web. You can order service packs with the full 128-bit encryption either in the form of CDs or you can go through an identification process that will allow you to download the 128-bit version of the service pack right from the Web. Check out Microsoft's Web site for details.

Get the Latest Drivers

Putting the latest service pack onto a system is always a kind of scary proposition. Two different service packs (SP3 of NT 3.51 and SP2 of NT 4) have completely destroyed previously working NT installations, so I'm always a bit wary of new fixes. But one thing that I've seen that seems to make service pack installs easier: get on the Web and pull down the most up-to-date drivers for the hardware in your system (you can be 100 percent sure that most of the drivers on the circa-1996 NT distribution disk aren't the latest), and install them. *Then* apply the service pack.

Installing the Service Pack

Unfortunately, every service pack installs a bit differently, but here's the overview for most of them. First, your service pack will be packaged in one of two ways. The first way is as a single large EXE with a name like SP5I386.EXE (as in the case of Service Pack 5). That's typically how you'll download it from the Internet or how it's packaged on some CD-ROMs. The other way is as a pre-expanded set of files. Alternatively, you can pre-expand a service pack by invoking it with the "/x" switch; typing "SP5I386 /X" would create the directory of files with UPDATE.EXE.

If your service pack came as a single EXE, then invoke it by just typing its name at a command prompt or double-click it from the Explorer. If the service pack was pre-expanded, then look for a program named UPDATE.EXE—that's normally how you start the program that installs the service packs. Either way, you'll be prompted whether or not you want the service pack to be able to uninstall itself, a feature that's existed since (if memory serves) Service Pack 3. I don't generally use the option myself, as I've found that I can't rely on the uninstall feature. Applying service packs can sometimes render a working system unusable, but uninstalls usually aren't much help, as a system that can't boot can't uninstall.

Re-Installing a Service Pack

It's a pain, but every time you install new system software onto your computer, you've got to re-install the service pack. One thing that you can do to save a little time, however, is to learn how to invoke the service packs to run hands-off, so that they don't make you wait around and answer their prompts and then tell them to reboot. If you have your service pack expanded, you can tell SP5 to run unattended by running UPDATE.EXE with four of its command line switches: the –u switch says to run in unattended mode; the –q switch says to run in quiet mode. The difference is that quiet mode doesn't show anything—no dialog box copying files or the like. It's kind of eerie; unless you run Task Manager, you have no clue that the service pack is being applied. The –n switch says not to back up files for an uninstall, which as you've already read is my preference, and -f forces any programs that are running to shut down. Put them all together and you get "update –u –q –n –f."

After the Installation, What Next?

But you're not done yet, not by a good bit. Network installations vary from location to location, but at this point some tasks usually remain. The following list describes those tasks. If an item is followed by a chapter subject, then you can read about it there; otherwise, I'll cover it in the remainder of this chapter.

- Finish setting up Windows apps on a workstation
- Create users (Chapter 6)
- Set the policy for the Guest account (Chapter 6)
- Make whatever modifications are necessary to user rights (Chapter 6)
- Install, interface, and configure a UPS
- Install optional modules, like Mac support, TCP/IP, DLC, or Remote Access Services (Chapters 10, 14, and 18, respectively)
- Tuning (Chapter 16)
- Install fault-tolerant features (Chapter 4)
- Create a directory structure and share it (Chapter 7)
- Install tape drivers
- Set up scheduled events (Chapter 11)
- Install extra printer drivers (Chapter 8)
- Share printers (Chapter 8)
- Set default printer (Chapter 8)
- Establish links to and from trusted domains (Chapter 12)

While I'd like to cover every detail of a complete installation in this chapter, I felt that some of the larger issues should stay in their own chapters. In the next few sections, we'll take a look at some of the simpler setups you'll do to move your server install further along.

Migrating Windows Applications

For some reason, even though Setup promises to migrate your Windows applications over to your NT setup, it doesn't do it—and version 4 is particularly bad at it. That means that you have to sort of lead it by the nose. This part of the chapter explains how.

Not Every Windows Program Will Run

Understand right off that not every Windows program will run. In particular, say goodbye to your programs like

- Undelete
- Many DOS-based fax programs
- System utility

Those will, in general, not work under NT.

Moving the Fonts

Even though the Event Log shows that the Registry was updated with font information, NT seems unaware of your old Windows fonts. Fixing that is a snap.

1. Open the Control Panel.
2. Open the Fonts applet. You see a dialog box like the one in Figure 3.2.
3. Choose File ➤ Install New Font, as shown in the figure. Now you see a dialog box like the one in Figure 3.3.

FIGURE 3.2:

Fonts dialog box

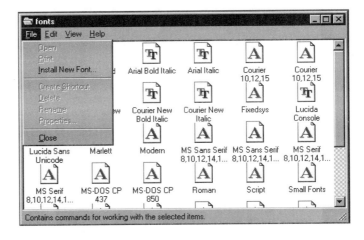

FIGURE 3.3:

Adding fonts

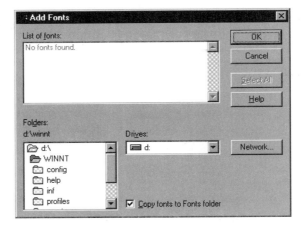

4. Uncheck the Copy fonts to Fonts folder check box at the bottom of the dialog box. No sense in having two copies of a font on your already-overworked hard disk.

5. Click the C:\windows\system directory. After a minute or two of disk activity, your fonts appear.

6. Select them all (just click on the top one, then scroll down to the bottom font, press the Shift key, and click the bottom item), or click the Select All button and click OK. You soon see a dialog box like the one in Figure 3.4.

FIGURE 3.4:

Control Panel asking about
an already recognized font

The dialog box is just telling you that you asked for a font that is already recognized by the system. That's OK.

7. Click OK and keep going. You see a bunch of these dialog boxes, but just keep clicking OK until you're done.

8. After the last "Remove this font and reinstall" dialog box, just click Close on the Fonts dialog box, and close up the Control Panel. Your fonts are now restored.

In short, read the "How Do I" sidebar for a quick summation.

How Do I Get My Old Windows Fonts Back?

To get your old Windows fonts back:

1. Open the Control Panel.

2. Open the Fonts applet and Choose File ➤ Install New Font.

3. Uncheck the Copy fonts to Fonts folder check box and select the C:\windows\ system directory.

4. After a minute or two of disk activity, you see your fonts appear. Select them all (just click on the top one, then scroll down to the bottom font, press the Shift key, and click the bottom item) or click the Select All button and click OK. You see dialog boxes that tell you that a copy of this font is already on the system, but just click OK and keep going.

After the last "Remove this font and reinstall" dialog box, click Close on the Fonts dialog box, and close up the Control Panel. Your fonts are now restored.

Getting Your Apps Back

For some reason, migrated Windows apps don't get migrated properly. The result: you probably experience problems getting your Windows apps to run on an NT workstation. My suggestions for fixing this are

- Make sure that the application's directories are on the right path.

- You may have to copy the application's INI files to the C:\WINNT directory, or whatever directory you've put NT in.

- In many cases, you simply have to reinstall the application.

Believe me, reinstalling seems to be the best method. I know, it's bad news, but there doesn't seem any way around it. Funny thing: install OS/2.*x* on a system and it effortlessly moves your Windows applications over to its desktop. Odd that IBM can do with *its* operating system what Microsoft can't do with *its own*.

Choosing and Installing an Uninterruptible Power Supply

One of the most important parts of server security is *power* security. Once backup power supplies were tremendously expensive, but that's not true any more. You can buy a cheap, basic *standby power supply* (SPS) for around $200. Better yet, that cheap SPS can alert NT as to when the power's going down. But let's take a moment and look at what kinds of power protection devices you should invest in.

The Problem with Electrical Outlets

Power coming in from outlets is of a high quality, but it's not reliable enough to trust your server to it. For example, on my sites (two commercially zoned buildings), we experience about three or four outages per year. They're not *long* outages—usually just a minute or two—but that's quite enough to shut down the servers and sometimes damage data.

Power problems come in three main types:

Surges and spikes   Transient noise appearing on the power line that can permanently damage electronic components.

Voltage variation   The power coming out of the wall is supposed to be 120 volts in North America, 240 volts in the UK and Ireland, and 220 throughout continental Europe. (EC members will note how delicately I sidestepped the "Is the UK part of Europe?" question.) Usually too *little* voltage is the problem, but sometimes you get too much voltage. In any case, neither is desirable.

Outages   Whether they last for a second or a day, a power outage crashes servers, which can spell disaster for application servers.

You've heard of surge protectors, and perhaps some of you *use* them.

But I recommend avoiding them because they are really only rated to catch one surge. After that, they're not reliable. (Honest, it's true—surprising, though, isn't it?) Worse yet, there's no way to find out if that surge has *already happened*! Furthermore, surge protectors are of no value whatsoever in low voltage or outage situations.

What, then, is the best answer for power protection? Some combination of a *power conditioner* and a battery-backed power supply.

Power Conditioners for Protecting Data

Between a surge protector and a backup power supply is a device called a *power conditioner*. A power conditioner does all the things that a surge protector does—it filters and isolates line noise—and it does more besides. Rather than relying on the non-reusable components found in surge protectors, a power conditioner uses the inductance of its transformer to filter out line noise. Additionally, most power conditioners boost low voltage so that machines can continue to work through brownouts.

Which power conditioner is right for you? The one that I use is Tripplite's LC1800. I've seen it in mail-order ads for as little as $200, and I've used mine for many years.

The LC1800 even shows incoming voltage via some LEDs on its front panel. *Do not* plug your laser printer into a power conditioner, as most power conditioners are only rated for a few amps; laser printers, in contrast, draw up to 15 amps. If you *do* want to use a power conditioner for a laser printer, make sure that the power conditioner is one of the more expensive models that provide sufficient amperage to keep the laser going.

Backup Power Supplies

In addition to protection from short power irregularities, you may need backup power. I have lived in a number of places in the northeastern U.S. where summer lightning storms kill the power for just a second—enough to erase memory and make the digital clocks blink. Total loss of power can only be remedied with battery-based systems. Such systems are in the $200 to $1200 range and up. There are two types of backup power systems, *standby power supplies* (SPSes) and *uninterruptible power supplies* (UPSes). Figure 3.5 illustrates the differences between them.

FIGURE 3.5:

How UPSes and SPSes work

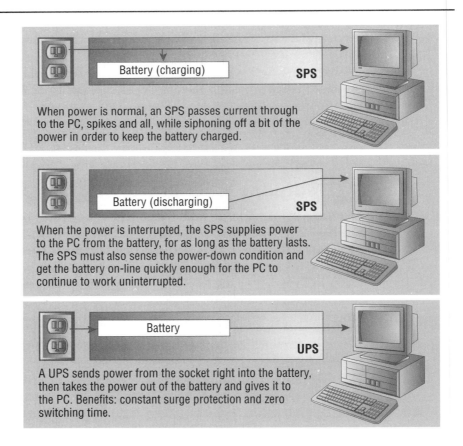

When power is normal, an SPS passes current through to the PC, spikes and all, while siphoning off a bit of the power in order to keep the battery charged.

When the power is interrupted, the SPS supplies power to the PC from the battery, for as long as the battery lasts. The SPS must also sense the power-down condition and get the battery on-line quickly enough for the PC to continue to work uninterrupted.

A UPS sends power from the socket right into the battery, then takes the power out of the battery and gives it to the PC. Benefits: constant surge protection and zero switching time.

Standby Power Supplies

SPSes charge their batteries while watching the current level. If the power drops, the SPS activates itself and supplies power until its batteries run down.

The key difference between a good SPS and a not-so-good SPS appears when the power goes out. When that happens, the SPS must quickly figure out that power's going down and must start supplying power from the battery just as quickly. A fast power switch must occur here, and it's important to find out what that switching time *is* for whatever model SPS you are thinking of buying. The speed is rated in milliseconds (ms); 4ms or under is fine. Eight ms—the speed of some SPSes—is, in my experience, not fast enough.

Uninterruptible Power Supplies

UPSes, the other kind of battery backup device, is a superior design, but you pay for that superiority. A UPS constantly runs power from the line current to a battery, then from the battery to the PC. This is superior to an SPS because no switching time is involved. Also, surges affect the battery charging mechanism, not the computer. A UPS also serves in the role of a surge suppressor and a voltage regulator.

A UPS or SPS must convert DC current from a battery to AC for the computer. AC is supposed to look like a sine wave, but cheaper UPS and SPS models produce square waves. The difference between the two is shown in Figure 3.6. Square waves are bad because they include high frequency harmonics which can appear as EMI or RFI to the computer. Also, some peripherals (printers in particular) can't handle square wave AC. So, when examining UPSes, ask whether they use square wave or sine wave. Some produce a pseudo-sine wave. It has the "stairstep" look of a square wave, but fewer harmonic problems.

Ordinarily, the purpose of a UPS is to allow enough time to save whatever you're doing and shut down gracefully. If you are in an area where the power may disappear for hours and may do so regularly, look for a UPS to which you can attach external batteries so that you can run the PC for longer periods.

Remember that a sine-wave UPS is the only way to really eliminate most power problems. The reason *everyone* doesn't have one is cost.

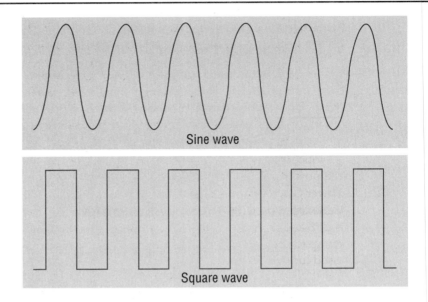

Sine wave

Square wave

A decent compromise can be found in a fast (4ms) square-wave SPS. I know I said square waves are bad for your peripherals, but how often will the SPS actually do anything? Not very often. Remember that an SPS only supplies power when the line voltage drops out, which isn't a common occurrence. The brief minute or two each month of square-wave power that your peripherals end up getting won't kill them. And you save a pile over a UPS by using an SPS.

On the other hand, a UPS is *always* online, and so must produce sine-wave output. But UPSes have the benefit of providing surge protection by breaking down and reassembling the power, and SPSes *do not* provide this protection. You must still worry about surge protection when you buy an SPS, but not if you buy a UPS. So make the choice that your budget allows.

Whether you buy an SPS or UPS, be sure to look for a backup power supply with a serial port. *Serial port?* Yes, a serial port. NT and NT Server can monitor a signal from a serial-port-equipped UPS/SPS. When power fails, the operating system is informed by the backup power supply of that occurrence, and the operating system does a graceful shutdown in the battery time remaining. Table 3.2 summarizes what we've seen about power problems and solutions.

TABLE 3.2:   Power Problems and Solutions

Protection Method	Remedies Surges?	Remedies Low Voltage?	Remedies Outages?
Power Conditioner	yes	yes	no
SPS	no	no	yes
UPS	yes	yes	yes

Notice that a combination of a power conditioner and an SPS would provide all the power protection that you need. Recognizing that, a firm called American Power Conversion has made a device that combines an SPS with a power conditioner. Called their Smart-UPS (OK, so even *they* don't understand the difference between a UPS and an SPS), they offer 400-watt models (the mail-order price is about $350) on up to 1800-watt models. I use Smart-UPS 400s in my office and have had very good luck with them. (Of course, they have the serial port connection.)

Interfacing the UPS/SPS

NT in both its server and workstation configuration is designed to be able to control and act on information from a UPS/SPS. NT expects two kinds of signals *from* the UPS/SPS (*power failed* and *battery low*), and can give one signal *back* to the UPS/SPS (*remote UPS shutdown*).

Power failed   This signal goes from the UPS/SPS to the NT machine. When this signal is activated by the UPS/SPS, it means that input power has failed and that the NT machine is now running on battery power.

Battery low   Some UPS/SPS systems can only signal that the power has failed, leaving NT to guess how much battery life is left on the UPS/SPS. Others can signal that about two minutes of battery life is left. If you have such a UPS/SPS, then NT can recognize the battery low signal.

Remote UPS shutdown   If your power backup device is an SPS rather than a UPS, it may sometimes be desirable to temporarily disable the battery. NT does this if it senses extremely erratic signals from the power failed or battery about to fail signal. If that happens, NT instructs the SPS to shut down its *inverter*, a part of the SPS circuitry, so that all the SPS does is charge the battery and provide power from the mains. This is a signal *from the PC* to the SPS.

If you have a UPS/SPS with a serial port, you should get a cable built for that UPS/SPS from its manufacturer. The manufacturer can also probably guide you in how to set the UPS service settings.

TIP

If your UPS/SPS manufacturer does not sell a cable for interfacing with NT Server, buy the cable for Microsoft LAN Manager. The interfacing is the same, except that the third parameter is not referred to as "remote UPS shutdown" in LAN Manager documentation, but rather as "Inverter shutdown."

Configuring a UPS

To configure your UPS, get the correctly wired cable from the UPS/SPS manufacturer and hook it up to a serial port on the server and to the back of the UPS/SPS. Then, in NT, start up the Control Panel and choose UPS. You see a screen like the one in Figure 3.7.

FIGURE 3.7:

Configuring the UPS

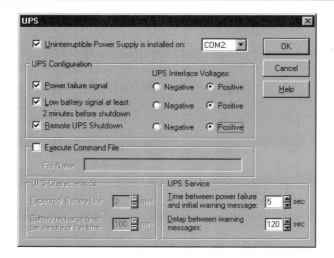

This is a setup screen for an SPS that supports all three features. Notice that, next to Power failure signal, Low battery, and Remote UPS Shutdown options, there are radio buttons called Negative and Positive. These radio buttons refer to the kind of signal from the UPS/SPS. No real standard exists for using a serial port to interface a UPS/SPS with a PC, and there are 25 different control lines on a serial port. Furthermore, each one of those 25 lines can either display negative voltages or positive voltages. The purpose of these radio buttons is to inform NT of what a signal means. You see, on one UPS, a negative signal might mean, "We're losin' power, Captain! Better evacuate while we still can!" *or* it might mean, "All is well." Where do you get this information? Well, the best source is, again, the manufacturer. Failing that, however, you can just try the combinations until the system works. Or you can do what I ended up doing: working with a breakout box.

Breakout Boxes

Interpreting serial port signals involves a bit of experience with a data communications test device called a *breakout box*. If you don't know what they are or how to use them, I'm afraid that explaining that is a bit beyond the scope of this book. There are, however, many good sources on the subject, including a book by me called *The Complete PC Upgrade and Maintenance Guide* (Sybex). This discussion assumes that you've worked a bit with serial ports, but even if you're not an expert, you may find it useful anyway.

Serial ports have either a 9-pin or 25-pin connector. Every UPS/SPS system that I've ever worked on used the 9-pin, so I'll assume that we're working on one of those. Most breakout boxes are equipped with 25-pin connectors, so get one of the 25-to-9 converters and plug the breakout box into the port on the back of the UPS.

Turn the UPS on. On the breakout box, you see LEDs up to 25 different signal lines (depending on how well-designed the breakout box is), but you should notice the ones labeled as follows:

- CD or DCD (carrier detect)
- CTS (clear to send)
- DSR (data set ready)
- DTR (data terminal ready)
- RTS (request to send)
- RX (receive data)
- TX (send data)

NT expects three signals on these lines:

- Power failed must appear to the PC on its CTS line.

- Low battery must appear to the PC on its DCD line.

- Remote UPS shutdown signals are provided from the PC on its DTR line.

Breakout boxes display the status of a serial port's 25 lines with LEDs. Some breakout boxes' LEDs glow whether the line is positive or negative; those breakout boxes aren't of any help to you. The LEDs on better-designed breakout boxes glow either red or green depending on whether the line is positive or negative; that's the kind of breakout box that you want.

With the breakout box connected, unplug the UPS/SPS. You see one of the LEDs change color. That line is the Power Failed line; it should connect to the CTS line on the PC serial interface. Leave the UPS/SPS unplugged until it runs out of power. A bit before the batteries run down all the way, you see another one of the LEDs change color. That's the Low Battery connection; that line should connect with the DCD line on the PC serial interface. You may not see any LED change color before the UPS/SPS fails. If so, that means that your UPS/SPS does not support the Low Battery signal. There really is no reliable way to detect which line to use for the Remote UPS shutdown.

Before you start playing around with a UPS and a breakout box, however, let me stress that this is a time-consuming project, inasmuch as your hard work won't really pay off until you take the information that you've gained and construct a cable to connect your PC and your UPS/SPS.

What Does the UPS Service Do When Power Fails?

When the Power Failure signal is asserted to the PC, the NT machine sends a broadcast to all users like the one in Figure 3.8.

FIGURE 3.8:

NT broadcast concerning power failure

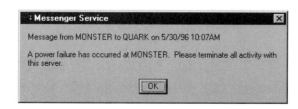

Messenger Service

Message from MONSTER to QUARK on 5/30/96 10:07AM

A power failure has occurred at MONSTER. Please terminate all activity with this server.

OK

Your workstation only gets this message if you've enabled the Messenger service or run the WinPopup program or an equivalent. This message gets rebroadcast every *x* seconds, where *x* is set in the UPS dialog box that you saw a page or two back. You can also specify a delay between the power failure signal and the first message, although I'm not sure why you would want to do this. After all, the sooner people know that there was a power failure at the server, the sooner they can save their work to another drive or shut down their application. At this point, however, the Server service is paused and new users cannot attach to the server.

If power is restored before the batteries fail, the UPS service sends out an "all clear" message like the one in Figure 3.9.

FIGURE 3.9:

NT's power restoration message

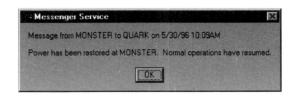

Two fields are relevant if your UPS/SPS does not support the Battery Low signal:

- Battery recharge time
- Expected battery life

Both of these fields are basically "guesses" of how much time is left before the system fails. Use the manufacturer's suggested values, but be darn sure to test them, which brings me to…

Testing the UPS Service

Whether you have a UPS/SPS that supports Low Battery or not, you should do a scheduled test of the UPS/SPS. How do you do it? Simple. First, be sure to run the test after hours. Second, send a network broadcast to everyone warning them that the server is going down because of a planned power outage, and that they should log off *immediately*!

The "How Do I" sidebar explains how to notify everyone of the imminent server shutdown.

How Do I Send a Broadcast Message to the Entire Network?

To send a broadcast message to an entire network:

1.   Start the Server Manager.

2.   Click on the primary domain controller.

3.   From the menu, select Computer ➤ Send Message.

4.   Fill in the message and click OK.

Make sure that you're on a workstation, either Windows with WinPopup, or an NT workstation. Then go to the UPS/SPS and pull out its power plug. Let it run until the server loses power altogether.

Then check the following:

- Did your workstation get a message about the power failure?

- Did you get a message every two minutes, or however far apart you set the messages?

- Did you get a final "The UPS service is about to perform final shutdown" message?

- How long was the server able to run with the UPS?

If necessary, go back and adjust the UPS service software if you don't have a Low Battery support or if your guesses were wrong about how much time you had on the battery.

Setting up the UPS is a bit of a pain, but once it is done, write down what you did so that you can redo it quickly if you ever reinstall.

Installing Tape Drivers

Most servers have a backup device of some kind, usually a tape drive, but it is smarter to use a SCSI tape drive because that is supported by the most backup software.

While the beauty of SCSI is supposed to be that it is "plug-and-play," you still need a driver for your tape drive. Therefore, it wouldn't be a bad idea to look at the current Hardware Compatibility List that Microsoft publishes before purchasing a tape drive (there is a copy in the NT Server box, but it's also on CompuServe, TechNet, and a number of other sources).

I use a Tandberg model 4100 and have had very good luck with it. The product is packaged by Colorado Memory Systems as a "PowerTape." As with many tape drives, however, Colorado falsifies the tape's capacity by claiming that it is a 2GB tape drive when actually it is a 1.2GB tape drive. However, with the data-compression software included with the tape, you can store 2GB of data. I say that it's falsification for these reasons:

- Not all data *can* be compressed.

- The compression and backup software that gives this "2GB" tape its supposed 2GB capacity is *DOS* software that doesn't run under NT or OS/2.

It's a good idea to look closely when buying a tape drive, as this blatant lying about tape capacities seems to be business as usual in the tape business. For example, every single tape on the market that advertises itself as a 250MB tape drive is actually a 120MB drive that assumes a 2-to-1 compression ratio. I mean, optimism has its *place*, but… And even worse, the NT Backup program doesn't compress.

You install the tape drive just as you would any SCSI device. When you power up your system, your SCSI BIOS will probably list the SCSI devices that it finds on the SCSI bus. The tape drive should show up. Now, if the tape drive *doesn't* appear on the list, you've probably installed the tape drive incorrectly. Go back and get the physical installation straightened out before going any further.

Then, once the drive is recognized on the SCSI bus, you have to install an NT driver for it. Here's how to do it:

1. Open Control Panel, then double-click on Tape Devices.

2. Click on the Drivers tab and you see a dialog box like the one in Figure 3.10.

FIGURE 3.10:

Tape Devices setup
dialog box

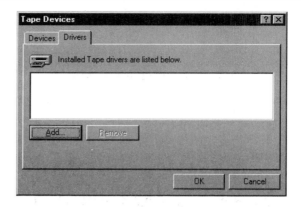

Don't panic when you don't see your tape drive in the box; that's normal.

3. Click Add and you see a dialog box like the one in Figure 3.11.

FIGURE 3.11:

Select Tape Driver dialog box

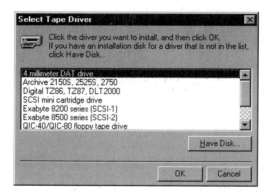

4. Browse through the model numbers to see if you can find a tape drive that matches yours. If you can't find an exact match, try something close to it. Again, using my Tandberg as an example, when I turn my system on I see the following report from my SCSI BIOS:

```
SCSI ID #0 - FUJITSU M2652S-512  -Drive C: (80h)
SCSI ID #1 - MAXTOR 7290-SCSI   -Drive D: (81h)
SCSI ID #2 - TANDBERG TDC 4100
SCSI ID #3 - MAXTOR 7290-SCSI   -Drive 82h
SCSI ID #5 - NEC  CD-ROM DRIVE:841
```

I see from my device number 2 that I've got a Tandberg 4100, which unfortunately does not match any option. The closest option is the Tandberg 3660, 3820, 4120, 4220 option. I tried that option for my 4100 and it worked. Later, Microsoft agreed in a Knowledge Base article that the 4100 would work with the other Tandberg drivers.

Once you have the driver set up, you have to restart your server. After restart, you can use the NTBACKUP program.

The "How Do I" sidebar gives a brief rundown on installing an NT Server tape driver.

How Do I Install an NT Server Tape Driver?

To install an NT Server tape driver:

1. Open Control Panel, then double-click on Tape Devices.

2. Click on the Drivers tab.

3. Don't panic when you don't see your tape drive in the box; that's normal. For some reason, Microsoft did not include auto-detect on tape drives. You're pretty much on your own here. Click Add.

4. Browse through the model numbers to see if you can find a tape drive that matches yours. If you can't find an exact match, try something close to it.

Once the driver is set up, you have to restart your server. After you restart, you can use the NTBACKUP program.

The License Manager

OK, you've installed all of these clients and they're merrily accessing the servers in your domain. Ah, but have you *licensed* all those users? If so, how have you organized it so that you can keep track of new and outdated users?

Licensing can be a pain to administer, and the bigger the network the harder it becomes. To help you do it, NT Server comes with a tool called the License Manager. This tool can monitor licensing not just on the local machine but on NT servers in other domains with which the domain you're starting from has a trust relationship. With the License Manager, you can monitor the entire network without trotting from server to server.

When you install NT Server, its icon automatically goes into the Administrative Tools group. Click it and you see a dialog box like the one in Figure 3.12.

FIGURE 3.12:

Opening screen of License Manager

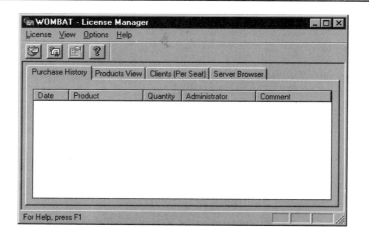

Microsoft went to a lot of work to create some very good Help files for the License Manager, so there's not much to be said that the Help files don't say already. Just to review, however, following are the basics of the License Manager and how you can use it to inventory software licenses. This isn't all there is to this tool, but these essentials will get you started.

Purchase History

Click on the Purchase History tab and you see a record of all the software licenses that you've purchased and entered into this database. (If you don't enter them, this database can't help you—it only knows what you tell it.) You also enter new per-seat licenses and change the domain to administer here.

Products View

From the Products View tab, you can view product information either for the entire network or a selected domain. Select the Per Seat or Per Server mode as needed to get information about

- Which products are licensed properly (and which are not)
- Which products are at their license limit

From here, you can also add and delete per-seat licenses or view the properties of a particular license.

Clients (per Seat)

Click on the Clients (Per Seat) tab to access information about clients who have accessed a particular product (such as NTS) throughout the domain or entire network. From here, you can see the number of licenses already used, those still available, and the dates on which all the licenses were last accessed.

Server Browser

From the Server Browser tab, you can access other domains to see their licensing information, add and delete per-server client licenses for servers and products, and add new per-seat licenses for the entire enterprise.

Basic Unattended Installations

If you've made it this far, you've probably done a few NT installations by hand, sitting at the machine baby-sitting the Setup program. As you've no doubt discovered, it's a bit tedious.

There's an alternative—unattended installations. With an unattended install, you pre-answer all of Setup's questions in a file, then feed that file to NT Setup. Between eight and 40 minutes later (depending on your hardware and what you asked your system to do), you've got a system with a brand-new copy of NT on it.

But it gets better. Once Setup is done, your job isn't, right? You've got to apply the latest Service Pack. And I find many of NT's defaults tremendously irritating—why does the Recycle Bin ask me if I'm sure when a few clicks will recover a "deleted" file, anyway? If you know what you're doing, you can get an unattended install to *also* apply Service Packs and preset program settings, and I'll show you how in this section. Finally, you will find in more and more cases that the hardware in your PC just plain didn't exist in summer 1996, when NT 4 arrived, meaning that the NT 4 CD-ROM does not contain drivers for that hardware. Adding newer drivers during installs is a pain as it's just one more thing that you've got to baby-sit—but I'll show you how to automate *that* as well.

Automated Install Overview

The great thing about unattended NT installs is that you can do so much and yet almost no one knows about it—there's a lot of hidden gold there.

Automated Install Mechanics

There is potentially quite a lot to setting up a successful automated install, but here're the basics.

1. Build the *answer file*, the ASCII file that pre-answers all of Setup's questions. It's got to be formatted in a special way, but that's not terribly hard, as Microsoft includes a program with NT called Setup Manager that lets you check boxes to indicate setup preferences, then writes out an answer file in the correct format. Now, Setup Manager is good, but it's not great. Its main value is that it does most of the initial grunt work in setting up the answer file. Then, as the answer file is an ASCII file, you can use Notepad to add whatever special settings you might require.

2. Connect the machine that you want to put NT on—call it the target machine—to a copy of the I386 directory somehow. In most cases, you'll have I386 sitting on a network share. Boot up the target machine using some kind of network client software and attach to the network share including I386.

3. Use WINNT or WINNT32 to start the unattended installation process. It's similar to the WINNT/WINNT32 Setup that you've already read about, but with a few changes. You must specify where the answer file is and where the I386 files are. So, for example, suppose you had the I386 files on a server named INSRV on a share called INSFILES. Suppose also that you had an

answer file for your particular PC called COMPAQPC.INF, and that file was located in the same I386 directory. You'd first attach to that share with a command like **net use X: \\insrv\insfiles**. Then you'd start the install process by typing **winnt /b /u:x:\compaqpc.inf /s:x:**—the /u: tells the Setup process where to find the answer files, the /b says not to prompt you to create floppies, and the /s: tells it where to find the I386 setup files. From that point on, you're pretty much sitting around waiting for the setup to finish. (Although if you've arranged the unattended install right, why wait? Go do something fun while NT installs.)

Under the Hood with WINNT and WINNT32

But what's WINNT or WINNT32 doing? The WINNT or WINNT32 program then copies all of the files that it guesses that it will need to a local hard disk. This may seem a bit dumb if you're installing from C:\I386, and after watching the PC copy files from C:\I386 to C:\$WIN_NT$.~LS and C:\$WIN_NT$.~BT for 45 minutes, you may find yourself muttering, "It's already on the bloody C: drive, you idiot, why are you wasting my time copying..."—but there's a reason for all that copying, kind of.

> **TIP** Be sure to run SMARTDRV before starting WINNT; it cuts the copying time tremendously.

First of all, as WINNT/WINNT32 copies the files, it also expands them from their compressed state. Second, WINNT/WINNT32 is really intended to support an install off a *network* share point rather than a local hard disk (although I've often found it useful to do WINNT/WINNT32 installs from a local hard disk). The idea is that you start up a brand-new computer with a basic copy of DOS and a network client, attach to an I386 share point, and run WINNT. When WINNT starts up, it's attached to the networked I386, certainly, but once Setup reboots the system—as it must—then the network connection's broken, and Setup would lose access to the files.

Now, I've always thought that if I installed from a local I386, it would be nice to be able to say to WINNT, "You'll have constant access to the files, relax and don't bother copying them"—but I guess the Microsoft folks felt it wasn't important to a big enough crowd. In any case, WINNT/WINNT32 create two directories: one named WIN_NT.~BT and one named WIN_NT.~LS.

WIN_NT.~BT contains a bit over three megabytes of files needed to get the Setup program started—the ~BT is short for *boot*. A normal NT Setup starts off with three floppies before it starts copying files from the CD-ROM; WIN_NT .~BT contains those files. NT Setup always puts this directory on drive C:.

WIN_NT.~LS contains all of the other files, the vast majority of the files in I386. By default it goes on drive C: or, if drive C: doesn't have enough room for it (the whole directory takes just under 87MB of disk space), then WINNT/WINNT32 puts it on the first drive that *does* have space. Alternatively, you can instruct NT Setup to place NT on another drive with the /t option. For example, suppose you wanted to install NT from C:\I386 with an unattended install script C:\UAT.INF but wanted NT installed to D:\WINNT. The command to start the unattended install would be

```
winnt[32] /s:c:\i386 /u:c:\uat.inf /t:d: /b
```

The /t:d: tells WINNT or WINNT32 to put both the WIN_NT.~LS directory and NT itself on the D: drive. The /b option means, "Don't require me to create boot floppies."

A basic NT Setup has two parts—a text-based part and a graphical part. A WINNT/WINNT32 setup precedes those two parts with its own copying part, which creates WIN_NT.~BT and WIN_NT.~LS. The text-based part of Setup draws mainly from the files in WIN_NT.~BT and the graphical part of Setup draws mainly from the files in WIN_NT.~LS.

More Things You Can Do in an Unattended Install

That's the overview and mechanics of a basic automated install. You can do a few other, very valuable things by creating a directory called OEM inside your I386 directory: \I386\OEM. Once you've got one of those, you can tell NT Setup to do things like:

- Include drivers that are not on the NT CD-ROM, drivers for new hardware or updated drivers for older hardware

- Include a set of batch-style commands that Setup will execute after installing NT, commands such as "Automatically install Service Pack 4 once you're done putting NT on this system"

- Create any arbitrary directory structure on the target PC's hard disk

But that's not all. Using a built-in tool called Sysdiff, you can take a group of dissimilar applications (like a word processor and a scheduler program), applications with complex setup programs, and just reduce them to a file, then tell Setup to apply that file to your NT machines. This can be quite useful both for servers *and* workstations!

There's a lot to the subject of unattended installs. First, this section will cover basic unattended installs, installs that are so simple that Setup Manager can do 99 percent of the work. Then, once you're comfortable with that, we'll introduce the things that you can do with the OEM directory. From there we'll look at installing non-standard network card, video, and SCSI drivers. Then we'll see how to use a file called CMDLINES.TXT to direct NT Setup to automatically do tasks *after* the formal NT setup has occurred. But before we get to that, there's one more set of introductory comments…

The Bad News: What Unattended Installs *Can't* Do

While it's great that NT can do unattended installations, there are few things that you can't accomplish with an unattended installation. So, before you go promise the boss that you'll be able to write answer files for 2,000 machines and get NT on them in a week, consider the following limitations.

You Cannot Overwrite an Existing NT Installation

The unattended install procedure was *really* designed to make it easier for computer manufacturers to preinstall NT on machines—machines with generally empty hard disks. If you have, for example, a copy of NT installed in C:\WINNT on your hard disk, an unattended install will not overwrite it; rather, it will put *another* installation on your hard disk, in a directory called C:\WINNT.0. If you do it again, you'll get *another* copy of NT on your hard disk labeled C:\WINNT.1, and so on.

Can this be worked around? Well, sure—you could always kick off the WINNT from a batch file and precede the WINNT command with a command to delete the C:\WINNT directory, but it's more work and, as you'll see in the next point, it doesn't even solve the whole problem.

There's No Way to Say "Yes to All" or "No to All" When Overwrite Messages Appear

Consider the following scenario. You install NT Server on a system. Along the way, NT installs Hyperterminal and Internet Explorer. Unlike the other applications that NT installs, however, the files for Hyperterminal and IE aren't installed in C:\WINNT—they're installed in C:\Program Files. Next, you install Service Pack 4, which includes new files for Hyperterminal and Internet Explorer; so far, so good. But then try to do an unattended installation of NT, placing NT in another directory, like C:\NT2 or something like that.

The install goes OK until near the very end, when the application files—including the ones for Hyperterminal and IE—get copied. Remember, Hyperterminal and IE don't go in C:\NT2, they go into C:\Program Files. NT Setup notices that there is *already* a copy of IE in C:\Program Files—*and the copy is newer than the one that NT Setup is trying to write*. (Recall that this is because the files currently on the disk are from Service Pack 4, and the ones that NT Setup is using are from back in 1996.) NT Setup's designed to err on the side of caution, and so it stops dead in the middle of your "unattended" installation and says that you're trying to copy some old files on top of some new files, and are you sure that you want to do that?

There's nothing you can do about this. The best answer I have come up with is, again, to start the process with a batch file that erases any Hyperterminal or Internet Explorer files from C:\Program Files before starting the WINNT process.

You Cannot Automatically Install Sound Drivers and Tape Drivers

There's no provision in the automated install support for sound drivers or tape backup device drivers, unfortunately. There *may* be a way around it using Sysdiff, and I'll describe it later, but it doesn't always work.

Some Drivers Cannot Support Automatic Install

I literally spent a week trying to make NT install a driver for Creative Labs' Graphics Blaster 3D card before finally giving up. The odd thing is that if you "hand feed" the driver to NT—that is, if you get NT up and running and then install the driver by hand—then it works fine. Unfortunately some drivers don't have the support they need for unattended installs.

It Is Not Possible to Do Unattended Installs of Some Services

Some NT software ships as standard, run-of-the-mill programs, but others are designed as services. You will probably find that most services don't lend themselves well to automated installs.

Building Basic Scripted Installs

If the unattended install "bad news" wasn't so bad that you feel that you won't have any use for unattended (or, as they're also known, *scripted*) installs, then let's get started.

In this first section, I'll show you how to build an unattended installation for a very simple, "vanilla" system. Once you're comfortable with a simple unattended install, we'll move on to the more complex—and powerful—options.

You can't do a scripted install without a "script"—an answer file. Where do you get such a file from? There are two ways to create the answer or batch file to run an unintended installation. You can either create a text file with a program like Notepad or use a tool supplied with NT called the Setup Manager, which in turn uses dialog boxes to obtain the same information. In general, my strategy is to let the Setup Manager do most of the work for me, building the basic script/answer file, then I use Notepad to make whatever changes I need that the Setup Manager can't handle well.

However, the Setup Manager requires a machine with NT 4 already installed to use it, making it sort of useless if you don't have an NT machine around and, besides, I want you to have some understanding of all of the commands in an answer file. So I'll discuss the Setup Manager process later in this chapter.

As with all computer endeavors, it's important to make your answer file error free; if the file contains lines with mistakes or misspellings, Setup ignores those lines and your installation may remain incomplete or fail altogether.

The answer file is composed of sections. Each section of the file needs a section head and any installation information pertinent to that section. The section head must appear in any answer file even if the section contains no other information. A missing section head causes Setup to pause for user input. For new installations, all of the parameters must be specified in the answer file because Setup does not have existing information to use. I have noted the parameters needed to perform upgrades in the description which follows each parameter listed below.

Answer File Conventions

You must follow some basic conventions when creating or editing your answer file:

- Surround section headings with brackets ([]): for example, **[Unattended]**. You must include all section headings, even if they do not contain any information, unless otherwise noted in the following section descriptions.

- User-defined keys, values, and headings that are surrounded with arrows (< >) can be replaced by anything you wish as long as it conforms to the rules under that heading, key, or value. For example, *<path>* indicates that the user must enter the name of a directory path, like

    ```
    C:\I386
    ```

- Precede each line of a comment with a semicolon (;). Everything after a semicolon is ignored.

- Do not change *key names*. A key name is the term used to identify an installation option. It is easily identified as the first word on the left side of every item below a section heading. For example, the following line will always be used in an NT Server unattended installation answer file. The key name on this line would be JoinDomain.

    ```
    JoinDomain = <DomainName>
    ```

- Leave a space before and after equal signs. For example:

    ```
    keyname = value
    ```

- Use double quotes ("") to indicate an empty value.

- Parameters surrounded by brackets ([]) are optional.

- If a comma is included, this means that additional parameters may be listed on the same line. For example

    ```
    ComputerType = IBM PS/2 or other Micro Channel-based PC, Retail
    ```

- If I have indicated that additional drivers, sections, parameters, and so on, may be listed, but no commas are present, then the key name and its parameters must be repeated on another line to add those additional options. For example, if you knew you had an Adaptec SCSI adapter card on your system, but you weren't sure which type, you can always specify more than one in the [MassStorageDrivers] section:

    ```
    "Adaptec AHA-154X/AHA-164X SCSI Host Adapter" = RETAIL
    "Adaptec AHA-174X EISA SCSI Host Adapter" = RETAIL
    ```

- Type all entries *exactly* as they appear in the description below, except for those options that have user-defined keys, values, and parameters. Quotation marks are not optional. If you see them used in the text here, they should also be used in your answer file.

- Italicized entries are choices that the user can make for each parameter. For example: OEMPreinstall = *yes* | *no* means that

  ```
  OEMPreinstall = yes
  ```
and
  ```
  OEMPreinstall = no
  ```

are valid text lines.

Answer File Parameters

You can construct your own answer file using the parameters I'll describe in the following sections. An example of a simple working answer file is included at the end of the Setup Manager section later in the chapter.

I should warn you that what you're going to see in roughly the next 30 pages is a bit dry—sorry, there's no way to liven up INF files—and you may just want to skip ahead to the section on how to simply use the Setup Manager tool to create unattended installation scripts and come back to this part for reference when necessary.

[Unattended]   This header tells Setup that the installation is unattended. A bit redundant, I know, but if the header isn't included, the file will be ignored and you'll have to install NT manually. This header must be the first one in the file; all other headers can be in any order.

The following parameters can exist in this section:

- OEMPreinstall = *yes* | *no*

  A value of *no* means that this is a regular unattended installation. In a regular unattended installation, you don't have to input much information, but some user input is still required, such as rebooting the computer after each phase of installation.

  If the value is *yes*, NT Setup behaves differently in a few ways. For one thing, setting OEMPreinstall to *yes* makes NT Setup ready to use the OEM directory mentioned earlier. OEM is a powerful unattended install feature and you'll often find use for it. The other thing that works differently when you set OEMPREINSTALL = YES is that you now have access to two new commands, commands that tell NT Setup not to stop and ask your permission when rebooting. Those two commands follow.

NoWaitAfterTextMode = 0 | 1   A value of *0* indicates that the setup program will stop after preinstallation, the text-based part of Setup.

     A value of 1 means that Setup will reboot the system into GUI mode when the preinstallation is complete. If this command is missing, the default of 0 is used.

NoWaitAfterGuiMode = 0 | 1   A value of *0* indicates that the setup program will stop after installation is complete.

     A value of *1* means that Setup will reboot the system when the installation is complete. If this command is missing, the default of 0 will be used.

- OEMSkipEula = *Yes* | *No*

  An important command, and one that Setup Manager won't install for you. During a normal setup, you'll see an End-User License Agreement screen—even if you've told NT that you want to do an unattended install, it thinks that you want to stop and read the software license agreement. (Yup, right after I've finished reading the ingredients on this shoe polish can.) Since you'll be performing an unattended setup, of course you wouldn't want Setup to stop for this. This key will cause Setup to automatically agree with the license agreement so that you can continue setup uninterrupted.

    - *Yes* causes Setup to skip the agreement.

    - *No* (the default) will stop the installation and prompt you to agree or disagree with the statement.

- FileSystem = *ConvertNTFS* | *LeaveAlone*

  Specifies how the NT partition will be formatted.

- ExtendOEMPartition = *0 | 1*

    Used to install NT on a disk bigger than 2GB. Setup extends the partition containing the temporary NT files into any unpartitioned space that follows it on the disk. This disk must be a primary partition no larger than 1024 cylinders. If writing occurs beyond the 1024th cylinder, the installation will crash.

    A value of *0* indicates that no extension will take place.

    A value of *1* means that you want the partition extended; in which case, the FileSystem shown above must also be set to *ConvertNTFS*.

- ConfirmHardware = *yes | no*

    The ConfirmHardware key determines whether users must confirm that the hardware and mass storage devices detected by Setup are correct. *A mass storage device* is anything that is controlled by a SCSI mini port driver. For example, all CD-ROM drives, SCSI adapters, and hard drive controllers—except Atdisk, abiodisk, and standard floppy disks—are mass storage devices.

    Yes indicates that the user must confirm that the storage devices detected by Setup are correct.

    No lets Setup use the hardware it detects.

- NtUpgrade = *manual | yes | no | single*

    The NtUpgrade key determines whether a previous installation of Windows NT Server should be upgraded. *Manual* indicates that users will specify the path of a previous installation of NT Server that will be upgraded.

    Yes tells Setup to upgrade the previous installation of NT Server. If it detects multiple installations, it will upgrade the first one. On *x*86-based systems, the first NT installation is the first one listed in the [Operating Systems] section of BOOT.INI. On Alpha, MIPS, and PowerPC systems, the first installation is the first one listed in the Startup environment. If NtUpgrade = Yes, the rest of the settings in the answer file will be ignored.

    No tells Setup to install a new copy of NT Server.

    Single means to upgrade only if a single previous installation of NT is detected. If Setup detects multiple installations, it pauses for a user to indicate which installation to upgrade.

- Win31UpGrade = *yes* | *no*

  The Win31Upgrade key determines whether previous installations of Windows for Workgroups or Windows 3.1 should be upgraded if detected on your system.

  Yes indicates that a Windows installation should be upgraded.

  No indicates that the previous Windows installation should not be upgraded.

- OverwriteOEMFilesOnUpgrade = *yes* | *no*

  Indicates whether OEM-supplied files having the same name as NT system files should be overwritten during an unattended upgrade.

  Yes, the default, means that the OEM-supplied files will be overwritten.

  No means you don't want the files overwritten.

- TargetPath = *Manual* | * | *<path>*

  Determines in which directory NT Server 4 will be installed.

  Enter *Manual* and the user will be prompted to enter the path where the files will be installed.

  A * indicates that Setup will automatically generate a unique directory name and install the files there. That path name will be \WINNT.*x*, where *x* is 0, 1, etc., depending on how many installations are present. *Do not* put a drive letter in the path name—use **\winnt**, not **e:\winnt**. To install NT on an alternative drive, use the /t: parameter on WINNT or WINNT32. As described earlier in this chapter, just invoke WINNT or WINNT32 like **WINNT[32] /t:F: [other options]** and NT will install to drive F:.

  <path> is a user-defined installation directory. For example:

  ```
  TargetPath = \NTWS40
  ```

- ComputerType = *<HAL description>* [,*RETAIL* |,*OEM*]

  Determines the type of Hardware Abstraction Layer (HAL) to be installed during Setup. If this key is absent, Setup will try to detect the computer type and install the corresponding HAL. This key is valid only when OEMPreinstall = Yes.

<HAL description> indicates the HAL to be installed. This string must match one of the strings in the [Computer] section of TXTSETUP.SIF (retail HAL) or TXTSETUP.OEM (OEM HAL). For example, if you have an IBM PS/2, you would then use the description gleaned from this line in TXTSETUP.SIF:

```
mca_up = "IBM PS/2 or other Micro Channel-based PC",files.none
```

<HAL description>, in this case, would be

```
IBM PS/2 or other Micro Channel-based PC.
```

RETAIL means that the HAL is supplied as part of the Windows NT installation.

OEM means that the HAL is supplied by OEM. If the driver listed above were OEM-supplied, the driver name must also be listed in the [OEM-BootFiles] section of the answer file. ([OEMBootFiles] is described later.) Here's an example of this line:

```
ComputerType = IBM PS/2 or other Micro Channel-based PC, Retail
```

• KeyboardLayout = *<layout description>*

Determines the type of keyboard layout. If this key is missing, Setup will detect the layout and install the type it found.

<layout description> needs to match one of the strings on the right side in the ["Keyboard Layout"] section of TXTSETUP.SIF or TXTSETUP.OEM. For example, the ["Keyboard Layout"] section of TXTSETUP.SIF contains the following line:

```
STANDARD = "XT, AT, or Enhanced Keyboard (83-104
keys)",files.i8042,i8042prt
```

You would therefore enter the line:

```
KeyboardLayout = XT, AT, or Enhanced Keyboard (83-104 keys)
```

[MassStorageDrivers] You'll only use this section if you're trying to install a system with a SCSI or EIDE host adapter driver that's not shipped on the regular CD. If this section is missing or empty, Setup will attempt to detect the mass storage devices on the computer and install the appropriate drivers.

• *<MassStorageDriverDescription>* = *RETAIL | OEM*

The value for *<MassStorageDriverDescription>* must match one of the values in the [SCSI] section of the TXTSETUP.SIF file (for a retail driver) or

TXTSETUP.OEM (for an OEM driver). For example, if you want to install an Adaptec 2940 driver, you would enter the description found in the [SCSI] section of TXTSETUP.SIF, which looks like the following:

```
aic78xx = "Adaptec AHA-294X/AHA-394X/AIC-78XX SCSI Controller"
```

More than one *<MassStorageDriverDescription>* can be listed in this section.

RETAIL implies that the driver is supplied as part of the NT Server installation.

OEM indicates that the driver is OEM-supplied. If the driver listed above were OEM-supplied, the driver must also be listed in the [OEMBootFiles] section of the answer file. ([OEMBootFiles] is discussed later.) An example would be

```
Adaptec AHA-294X/AHA-394X/AIC-78XX SCSI Controller = Retail
```

NOTE You can read more about doing this later in the chapter.

[DisplayDrivers] This is a list of the display drivers to be loaded and installed during Setup. Like the [Mass Storage Devices] section, it will be ignored unless OemPreinstall = Yes (discussed earlier). If this section does not exist or is empty, Setup will automatically detect the display devices and install drivers for them.

- *<DisplayDriverInformation> = RETAIL | OEM*

  Indicates the driver to be installed. *<DisplayDriverInformation>* is replaced by a string that matches those in the right side of the [Display] section of TXTSETUP.SIF (for retail drivers) or TXTSETUP.OEM (for OEM drivers). More than one driver can be listed in this section. For example, if you want to install a Cirrus GD5422/24 v1.41 driver instead of automatically detecting a display driver, you would use the description from the following line in the [Display] section of TXTSETUP.OEM supplied by the manufacturer:

  ```
  CL640x480x4x60 = "GD5422/24 v1.41 640x480", 16 colors 60Hz cir-
  rus1m
  ```

  RETAIL implies that the driver is supplied as part of the NT Server installation.

OEM indicates that the driver is OEM-supplied. An example:

```
GD5422/24 v1.41 640x480, 16 colors 60Hz = OEM
```

If the driver given above were OEM-supplied, the driver must also be listed in the [OEMBootFiles] section of the answer file (discussed later).

NOTE   After I said all that, however, you can probably pretty safely ignore this section; you'll never use it. That's because there are actually *two* ways to have NT automatically install a display driver, and *this* way is by far the more difficult. The easier way is with the [Display] section, which you'll read about later in this chapter.

[KeyboardDrivers]   The following is a list of the keyboard drivers to be installed during Setup; however, it will be ignored unless OemPreinstall = Yes (discussed earlier). If this section does not exist or is empty, Setup will automatically detect the keyboard devices and install drivers for them.

- *<KeyboardDriverInformation>* = *RETAIL* | *OEM*

    Tells Setup which keyboard driver to install. *<KeyboardDriverInformation>* is a string that matches those in the right side of the [Keyboard] section of TXTSETUP.SIF (for retail drivers) or TXTSETUP.OEM (for OEM drivers). For example, the [Keyboard] section in TXTSETUP.SIF contains the following line:

    ```
    STANDARD = "XT, AT, or Enhanced Keyboard (83-104
    keys)",files.i8042,i8042prt
    ```

    <KeyboardDriverInformation> would then be replaced with

    ```
     XT, AT, or Enhanced Keyboard (83-104 keys)
    ```

More than one driver can be listed in this section. *RETAIL* means that the driver is supplied as part of the NT Server installation.

OEM means that the driver is OEM-supplied. In which case, the driver must be listed in the [OEMBootFiles] section of the answer file.

[PointingDeviceDrivers]   Setup will install the pointing device drivers you list in this section. The section is ignored unless OemPreinstall = Yes (discussed earlier). If this section does not exist or is empty, Setup will automatically detect the mouse, or other pointing devices, and install drivers for them.

- *<PointingDeviceDriverInformation> = RETAIL | OEM*

  Indicates the mouse or other pointing device driver to be installed. *<PointingDeviceDriverInformation>* is a string that matches those in the right side of the [Mouse] section of TXTSETUP.SIF (for retail drivers) or TXTSETUP.OEM (for OEM drivers). More than one driver can be listed in this section. For example, say that you want to install a Logitech serial mouse driver. In the [Mouse] section, you'll find the following line:

  ```
  lgser = "Logitech Serial Mouse",files.sermouse,sermouse
  ```

  You'd then replace *<PointingDeviceDriverInformation>* with "Logitech Serial Mouse" as the description. For example:

  ```
  "Logitech Serial Mouse" = RETAIL
  ```

  RETAIL implies that the driver is supplied as part of the NT Server installation.

  OEM indicates that the driver is OEM-supplied. If the driver given in the example above were OEM-supplied, the driver must also be listed in the [OEMBootFiles] section of the answer file.

[OEMBootFiles] This section contains a list of OEM-supplied boot files. It will be ignored unless OEMPreinstall = Yes (see earlier section) and unless the files are also located in the OEM\Textmode directory of the OEM's share directory.

- TXTSETUP.OEM

  This file contains descriptions of all OEM-supplied drivers needed. It also includes instructions on how to install drivers that are listed. This file must be listed for this section to work.

- *<HALFileName>*

  Maps to the HAL description that you created in the ComputerType key. The same filename listed in the description found in TXTSETUP.SIF or TXTSETUP.OEM must be listed here. For example, you may recall that the line containing the HAL description that we found in TXTSETUP.SIF looked like this:

  ```
  mca_up = "IBM PS/2 or other Micro Channel-based PC",files.none
  ```

This time, however, we want to use the filename that in the above example is FILES.NONE. Basically, this filename indicates that the driver is built into NT. If this filename exists in the line found in TXTSETUP.SIF, you wouldn't need to add a HAL file name to this section. Only with OEM-supplied drivers would you have an actual filename to enter here. The *<HALFileName>* entry would then be

```
files.none
```

- *<SCSIDriverFileName>*

    Maps to the mass storage driver description that you listed in the [MassStorageDriver] section of the answer file. More than one *<SCSIDriverFileName>* can be listed. Using the example detailed in the [MassStorageDrivers] section, let's say that we're installing an Adaptec 2940 SCSI card. Instead of using the description, however, we want the filename. In the example we used before, the line in the [SCSI] section looks like this:

    ```
    aic78xx = "Adaptec AHA-294X/AHA-394X/AIC-78XX SCSI Controller"
    ```

    This time, we'll use the left side of this description. The filename we'll use in this case is AIC78XX.SYS. The SYS extension indicates that this is a driver file.

Just to make things clearer, based on the examples given above the [OEMBootFiles] section should look like the following. You'll notice that only file names are actually listed.

```
[OEMBootFiles]
TXTSETUP.OEM
MCA.SYS
AIC78XX.SYS
```

NOTE   There's more detail on this later in this chapter.

[GuiUnattended]   The following keys are used by Setup during the GUI portion of the unattended installation.

- OEMSkipWelcome = *0 | 1*

    A *0* means that the Welcome to Windows NT screen that you see at the first logon appears.

    Using *1* skips that welcoming screen. The default is *1*.

- OEMBlankAdminPassword = *0* | *1*

  A *0* indicates that the user will be required to enter a password for the Administrator ID.

  A *1* indicates that this screen will be skipped and the password for the administrator will be left blank.

- TimeZone = *<time zone>*

  If this key is empty, the user can define a time zone. *<time zone>* is used to specify one of the options in the following list; for example:

  ```
  TimeZone = (GMT-04:00) Eastern Time (US & Canada)
  ```

Time Zone	Geographic Location
GMT (Greenwich Mean Time)	Dublin, Edinburgh, London
GMT+01:00	Lisbon, Warsaw
GMT+02:00	Eastern Europe
GMT+03:00	Moscow, St. Petersburg
GMT+04:00	Abu Dhabi, Kazan, Muscat, Tbilisi, Volgograd
GMT+04:30	Kabul

Time Zone	Geographic Location
GMT+05:00	Islamabad, Ekaterinburg, Karachi, Tashkent
GMT+05:30	Bombay, Calcutta, Colombo, Madras, New Delhi
GMT+06:00	Alma Ata, Dhaka
GMT+07:00	Bangkok, Jakarta, Hanoi
GMT+08:00	Hong Kong, Perth, Singapore, Taipei
GMT+09:00	Tokyo, Osaka, Sapporo, Seoul, Yakutsk (and you thought Yakutsk only existed on the *Risk* game board)

GMT+09:30	Adelaide
GMT+10:00	Brisbane, Melbourne, Sydney
GMT+11:00	Magadan, New Caledonia, Solomon Islands
GMT+12:00	Fiji, Kamchatka, Marshall Islands
GMT-01:00	Azores, Cape Verdi Islands
GMT-02:00	Mid-Atlantic
GMT-03:00	Rio de Janeiro
GMT-04:00	Atlantic Time (Canada)
GMT-05:00	Eastern Time (U.S. & Canada)
GMT-06:00	Central Time (U.S. & Canada)
GMT-07:00	Mountain Time (U.S. & Canada)
GMT-08:00	Pacific Time (U.S. & Canada), Tijuana
GMT-09:00	Alaska
GMT-10:00	Hawaii
GMT-11:00	Midway Island, Samoa

- DetachedProgram = <*DetachedProgramString*>

  Indicates the path of a custom program that will run concurrently with Setup.

  - Arguments = <*ArgumentsString*>

  Lists any arguments or parameters here that are required by the DetachedProgram.

- AdvServerType = *SERVERNT* | *LANMANNT* | *LANSECNT*

  SERVERNT indicates that the server will not participate as a domain controller.

  LANMANNT makes the computer a Primary Domain Controller (PDC).

  LANSECNT makes the computer a Backup Domain Controller (BDC).

[OEM_Ads] This section will allow you to specify a background display, your company logo, and a banner to be displayed at the top of the screen during the GUI portion of the unattended installation. If you choose to use a logo or background file other than the default, you must make sure OEMPreinstall = Yes as described in the [Unattended] section.

- Banner = *"text"*

    You can include any text you wish in your banner as long as it includes the phrase *Windows NT*. Insert an asterisk (*) at the point where you wish to start an additional line for your banner. If this line is empty, missing, or does not contain the *Windows NT* string, the default is to display *Windows NT Server Setup* instead. For example, here's a sample banner that I have used:

    ```
    Banner = "Mastering Windows NT Server 4.0*Mark Minasi © 1996"
    ```

    OK, that's a bit of self-promotion, but you get the idea.

- Background = *filename [,n]*

    Two keys, Background = and Logo =, allow you to modify the look of the graphical portion of Setup. Normally the graphical part of Setup uses a dark blue bitmap as its background. With Background and Logo, you can change that look. The Background command lets you specify the name of a bitmap that fills the background of the screen. Logo lets you lay *another* bitmap on top of that background bitmap, but in the upper right-hand corner.

    So, for example, let's say you've got a simple bitmap of an ocean (we'll suppose you're tired of clouds). The ocean bitmap is a nice background, but you want your company logo to appear during Setup, as well. Setup will tuck your presumably smaller logo bitmap up in the upper right-hand corner of the screen—the same place that a postage stamp appears on a letter.

    I'll explain the syntax of the Background and Logo commands, then give a simple example.

    This key specifies that you wish to use a unique background bitmap file in place of the standard Microsoft graphic. If your bitmap file is referenced by a dynamic link library (DLL), you'll need to specify the name of the DLL along with the resource ID. For example, say your bitmap file was named BCKGRND.DLL and had a resource ID of 5, you'd enter this line:

    ```
    Background [TECH] = bckgrnd.dll, 5
    ```

Otherwise, if you have a bitmap file that isn't referenced by a DLL, you can still indicate a file to be used as a background graphic. Instead of specifying the DLL, you can indicate the bitmap to be displayed. For instance, if you have a bitmap named BCKGRND.BMP, you would add this line to your answer file:

```
Background = bckgrnd.bmp
```

NOTE   In either case, the DLL or bitmap file must be located in the OEM/Oemfiles directory of the distribution share point. If this key isn't specified, the default Microsoft background will be displayed.

- Logo = *filename [,n]*

    If you have a bitmap file containing your company logo, you can specify that with this key. If your bitmap file is referenced by a dynamic link library (DLL), you'll need to specify the name of the DLL along with the resource ID. For example, say your bitmap file was named LOGO.DLL and had a resource ID of 4, you'd then enter this line:

    ```
    Logo = logo.dll, 4
    ```

    If, as is more likely, you have a bitmap that isn't referenced by a DLL, however, you can still display your logo. Instead of specifying the DLL, you can indicate the bitmap to be displayed. For instance, if you have a bitmap named LOGO.BMP, you would add this line to your answer file:

    ```
    Logo = logo.bmp
    ```

    In either case, the DLL or bitmap file must be located in the OEM/ Oemfiles directory of the distribution share point. If this key isn't specified, no logo will be displayed at all.

Here's a simple example you can try out, assuming you can get your hands on a couple of bitmaps. Suppose you have a background bitmap named OCEAN.BMP, and a logo for your company, Acme Industries, in a file named ACME.BMP. OCEAN.BMP should be 640 × 480 pixels in size; ACME.BMP should run around 100 × 100 pixels. First, copy all of the files from the \I386 directory on the NT CD-ROM to a directory on your local hard disk—call it C:\I386 for this example. Then create a directory named OEM *inside* C:\I386—C:\I386\OEM. Copy OCEAN .BMP and ACME.BMP to that directory. Then create text file named TEST.INF in the root of the C: drive. C:\TEST.INF should look like this:

```
[unattended]
oempreinstall = yes
```

```
[OEM_Ads]
banner = "Acme installs Windows NT"
background = ocean.bmp
logo = acme.bmp
```

Then kick off the installation by typing **c:\i386\winnt /s:c:\i386 /u:c:\test.inf** (use WINNT32 if you're running from NT). While the entire installation won't be unattended, you'll see the effects of setting a banner, background bitmap, and logo bitmap. (OK, it's a bit silly, but it's fun to play around with if you're doing a bunch of installs.)

[UserData] This section specifies who will use the computer. None of the information in this section is optional, except for OrgName.

- FullName = *"Your Full Name"*

    Type the user's name in this line. If the FullName key is empty, the user will be prompted to enter a name after installation.

- OrgName = *"Your Organization Name"*

    Fill in the organization's name. If the OrgName key is empty, the user will be prompted to enter an organization name after installation.

- ComputerName = *COMPUTER_NAME*

    Fill in the computer's name. If the ComputerName key is empty, the user will be prompted to enter a computer name after installation.

- ProductId = *"123-4567890"*

    This specifies the Microsoft product identification number. The product ID specified takes precedence over any other product ID specified in the INITIAL.INF file. The product ID must be specified in order to perform an unattended upgrade.

[LicenseFilePrintData] This section specifies the licensing mode and the number of licenses that have been purchased for the server.

- AutoMode = *PerServer / PerSeat*

    Specifying *PerServer* indicates that the licenses purchased for the server will allow a limited number of connections to the server. You must also use the AutoUsers key defined next.

PerSeat specifies that each computer that accesses the server will have its own license. If this key is empty or missing, Setup will pause to ask the user to decide which license mode to use.

- AutoUsers = *<decimal number>*

  This key is only valid when AutoMode = *PerServer*. The *<decimal number>* specifies the number of licensed computers that can be logged on to the server at one time. If this key is empty or missing, Setup will pause to ask the user for the number of licensed connections allowed.

[Display] This is the easier of the two ways to automatically install a display driver with NT, and so it's the preferred method. But rather than try to explain part of it here, I'll cover it a bit later in a separate section.

[Modem] Remote Access Service (RAS) uses this section to install a modem. DeviceType must equal Modem in the *<PortSectionName>* of the [Network] section.

- InstallModem = *<ModemParameterSection>*

  Defines the section where the parameters to install modems are located (see [*<ModemParameterSection>*]). This key must exist if you want to install a modem.

[*<ModemParameterSection>*] This section lists the parameters needed to install a modem on a specific COM port. The heading name was defined in the [Modem] section and must be the same as the name you chose for it there. If this section is empty, RAS will attempt to detect your modem.

- *<COMPortNumber>* = "*<ModemDescription>*" [,*<Manufacturer>*,*<Provider>*]

  <COMPortNumber> indicates the COM port on which a modem will be installed. This number must match the ports configured by the RAS installation.

  <ModemDescription> matches the modem description in the [Strings] section of a MDMxxxxx.INF file that corresponds to the modem. For example, if you have a U.S. Robotics Sportster 28.8 modem, you'd then look up the modem's description in MDMUSRSP.INF (the driver file for all U.S. Robotics Sportster modems). There, you'll find the following line in the [Strings] section of the file:

```
Modem20 = "Sportster 28800"
```

<ModemDescription> would then be *Sportster 28800*. *<Manufacturer>* and *<Provider>* identify the manufacturer of the modem and provider of the driver and are used when the modem description is not unique. For example, if you wish to indicate the manufacturer and supplier of this modem in addition to the modem description, you'd enter the following line:

```
COM2 = "Sportster 28800", "U. S. Robotics", "Microsoft"
```

[Network] If you don't include this section head, Setup will not install networking.

- Attend = *Yes* | *No*

    Using this key, regardless of whether Attend is set at *Yes* or *No*, will force the user to manually configure your network—however, this can be a good idea. With an unattended installation, if you're installing NT on dozens of machines, you may get the same problem when installing NT on each and every computer if Setup can't detect the network card. Also, if a network card is configured incorrectly, it may cause problems with other computers on the network. Another reason to install networking manually is that you won't be able to install many less popular network adapter cards in an unattended installation because Setup doesn't have the ability to detect many cards as of this writing. If you wish to perform a true unattended installation (no user input required), however, don't use this key.

NOTE   If you *do* have a computer with an odd NIC and want to do an unattended install, I'll show you how to do that later in this chapter.

- JoinWorkgroup = *<WorkgroupName>*

    If the computer is joining a workgroup, you name the workgroup here. For example, let's say that you want this server to join the Marketing workgroup. You'd enter this line:

    ```
    JoinWorkgroup = Marketing
    ```

    If you use the JoinWorkgroup key, make sure you don't include the Join-Domain or InstallDC keys in the answer file. Workgroup members cannot also be members of domains or domain controllers.

- JoinDomain = *<DomainName>*

  If the computer is joining a domain, type in the domain's name here. For instance, say that I'm installing a stand-alone server as a member of the ORION domain. I'd then add this line to my answer file:

  ```
  JoinDomain = ORION
  ```

  Don't use this key in combination with the JoinWorkgroup or InstallDC keys because computers that are members of a domain can't also be members of a workgroup or be domain controllers.

- CreateComputerAccount = *<AdministratorName>*, *<AdministratorPassword>*

  If the computer you are installing is not listed in a domain controller's Server Manager, you'll want to use this key when adding the computer to the domain or installing it as a BDC. You'll have to indicate a user name with administrative permissions and that user's password in order for the computer name to be added to the list.

- InstallDC = *<DomainName>*

  Use this key when installing a PDC or BDC. Make sure the AdvServer-Type key, which I described earlier in the [GUIUnattended] section, has been set appropriately. To illustrate, if I'm installing a domain controller, I'd add this line to the answer file, which indicates the domain that the PDC or BDC will control:

  ```
  InstallDC = ALDEBARAN
  ```

  You may not use this key in conjunction with the JoinDomain or Join-Workgroup keys. The reason is simple: a computer can't be a domain controller and be a member of a workgroup or domain at the same time.

- DetectAdapters = *<DetectAdaptersSection>* | *""*

  Setup will install the first network card it detects if the value of this key equals "". For example, if you want to have Setup automatically detect your network adapter card, you'd enter the following line:

  ```
  DetectAdapters = ""
  ```

  If you want a specific network card or cards detected, give *<DetectAdapters-Section>* a name of your choosing, then go to the *<DetectAdaptersSection>* heading (below) to detail the detection process. To have Setup detect specific networked adapter card(s), you would add this line to your answer file:

  ```
  DetectAdapters = DetectAdaptersSection
  ```

DetectAdaptersSection, in the above example, is the name of the section where you'll indicate which card(s) you have installed on your machine. Setup would then try to detect only those card(s) listed.

- InstallAdapters = *<InstallAdaptersSection>*

  Either this key or the DetectAdapters key must exist if you want to install a network card. Instead of detecting a network card here, you name a network card driver you want installed, regardless of whether Setup detects it on your system. For example, if you chose not to let Setup detect your network adapter card, you could enter this line:

  ```
  InstallAdapters = InstallAdaptersSection
  ```

  Setup will look in *InstallAdaptersSection* for the specific adapters you want to install. If you know which card(s) you have installed on your system, you can use the InstallAdapters key to install the driver without having the computer detect them with DetectAdapters.

- InstallProtocols = *<ProtocolsSection>*

  Points to the *<ProtocolsSection>* section listed below. The name you give *<ProtocolsSection>* must be the same as the name you give the *<Protocols-Section>* section header. For instance, if you want to install a network protocol, such as TCP/IP, NETBEUI, or NWLink, you must add a line that looks like this:

  ```
  InstallProtocols = ProtocolsSection
  ```

  This says that any network protocols to be installed can be found under the ProtocolsSection header of the answer file.

- InstallServices = *<ServicesSection>*

  Again, this line points to the *<ServicesSection>* section listed later. You can fill in any name for this section, as long as it matches the name you give the *<ServicesSection>* header. For example, if you're going to install any services, you must add this line to your answer file:

  ```
  InstallServices = ServicesSection
  ```

  Services to be installed are found under the ServicesSection header. Now, you've got to have an InstallServices key, but if you're not installing any special services, then you need not actually *create* a ServicesSection section. For example, the above line, InstallServices = ServicesSection, seems to imply that there's a section named [ServicesSection] somewhere, but if you're not installing any services other than the default ones (the file/print server, redirector, and so on), then you needn't create a [ServicesSection] section at all.

- InstallInternetServer = *<InternetInformationServerParameters>*

  Points to the *<InternetInformationServerParameter>* header (discussed later) which contains the parameters for installing the Internet Information Server. IIS is installed by default when installing Windows NT Server. Use this key when you want to customize your IIS installation. For example, if you want to only install the WWW service and the FTP service but not the Gopher service, you can specify that in the answer file. Otherwise, Setup will automatically install all Internet services on your server.

[*<DetectAdaptersSection>*] This section is defined by the DetectAdapters key that was mentioned in the last section. The heading name is defined in the [Network] section. If you have an unusual NIC, then you'll see later that you'll want to bypass this section altogether and just hardwire your particular NIC type into your NT install script.

- DetectCount = *<number of detection attempts>*

  Determines the number of attempts to make to detect a network card.

- LimitTo = *<NetcardInfOption>* [, *<NetcardInfOption>*...]

  Indicates a list of options to limit the network card detection. These options can be found in the [Options] section of the network adapter card's OEMNADxx.INF file. You may have to do some searching to find the right file, since these INF files are not clearly named. For example, the 3Com Etherlink III network card driver is named OEMNADE3.INF. The only entry in the [Options] section of this file is ELNK3ISA50. Therefore:

  ```
  LimitTo = ELNK3ISA50
  ```

  - *<NetcardInfOption>* = *<NetcardParameterSection>*

  Points to the section containing the parameters of the network card specified in the LimitTo parameter. You can name the *<NetcardParameterSection>* anything, as long as the name of the *<NetcardParameterSection>* is the same as the *<NetcardParameterSection>* heading (discussed later).

[<*InstallAdaptersSection*>] This section head name was defined in the [Network] section.

- *<NetcardInfOption>* = *<NetcardParameterSection>*

    The *<NetcardInfOption>* parameter was defined in the [DetectAdapters] section of the answer file (in the previous section). The *<NetcardParameterSection>* is user-defined.

[<*NetcardParameterSection*>] This section lists the parameters for a specific network adapter card. This card should also be listed in either the *<DetectAdapters>* section or the *<InstallAdapters>* section of the answer file. The section head name must be the same as you defined it in either the *<DetectAdaptersSection>* or the *<InstallAdaptersSection>* you are going to use. Not every card uses the same parameters, but these are the two main ones:

- InterruptNumber = *<Interrupt>*

    The *interrupt* number is a number between 0 and 15. The network card must be the only hardware device that uses the address. Basically, the address you'll want to use is 5, 10, 11, or 15. Avoid the others. See the section on installing a LAN card earlier in this chapter for a more detailed explanation.

- IOBaseAddress = *<InputOutputBaseAddress>*

    Like the interrupt number, the I/O base address must not be used by any other hardware device. These addresses generally start at 300 or 310 hex. Again, see "Setting Up the LAN Card" earlier in this chapter for more details.

[<*ProtocolsSection*>] This section lists the parameters for network protocols. This card should also be listed in either the *<DetectAdapters>* section or the *<InstallAdapters>* section of the answer file and the section head name is defined in those sections discussed previously.

- NBF = *<NetBeuiParameters>*

    Implies that NetBEUI should be installed. The [*<NetBeuiParameters>*] section must also exist to successfully install NetBEUI, though it will remain empty. Apparently because TCP/IP needs parameters, somebody at Microsoft figured NetBEUI would need them, too. So we have to follow the form of putting a NetBEUI Parameter head in, as illogical as it is.

- NWLNKIPX = *<IPXParameters>*

  Points to the [*<IPXParameters>*] section (discussed in a moment) which defines the parameters for IPX protocols installation. Again, like Net-BEUI, no one needs parameters for it, but the form has to be the same for some unknown reason.

- TCPIP = *<TCPIPParameters>*

  Points to the TCP/IP protocol header. The [*<TCPIPParameters>*] section (discussed in a moment) must exist to perform a successful installation of TCP/IP.

- DLC = *<DLCParameters>*

  Points to the DLC protocol header. The [*<DLCParameters>*] section (discussed in a moment) must exist to perform a successful installation of DLC.

- RASPPTP = *<RaspptpParameters>*

  Points to the RasPPTP protocol header. The [*<RASPPTPParameters>*] section (discussed in a moment) must exist to perform a successful installation of RASPPTP.

- STREAMS = *<StreamsParameters>*

  Points to the Streams protocol header. The [*<StreamsParameters>*] section (discussed in a moment) must exist to perform a successful installation of Streams.

- ATALK = *<AtalkParameters>*

  Points to the AppleTalk protocol header. The [*<AtalkParameters>*] section (discussed in a moment) must exist to perform a successful installation of AppleTalk.

[*<NetBEUIParameters>*] If you're installing NetBEUI, you have to have this heading, even though NetBEUI doesn't require any parameters. You are forced to indicate that you want NetBEUI to be installed by specifying a parameters section, and because you've already told Setup to look for a parameters section, you must include the section in the answer file.

[*<IPXParameters>*] Again, to install IPX, you need this heading, even though there are no IPX parameters.

[<*TCPIPParameters*>] This section lists the parameters required to install TCP/IP. Remember to keep the heading the same as you named it in the *<ProtocolSection>*.

- DHCP = *Yes | No*

    Use this key to tell Setup if you want to use DHCP to set your computer's IP address.

    If DHCP = *Yes*, no other keys need to be specified.

    If DHCP = *No*, then all of the keys listed in this section must be entered in this section.

- ScopeID = *<scope ID>*

    If you are using a network that uses NetBIOS over TCP/IP, use this key to specify the scope.

The rest of the keys in this section are self explanatory.

- IPAddress = *<IP address>*
- Subnet = *<subnet address>*
- Gateway = *<gateway address>*
- DNSServer = *<IP addresses>*

You can identify up to 3 DNS servers.

- WINSPrimary = *<IP address>*
- WINSSecondary = *<IP address>*
- DNSName = *<DNS domain name>*

[<*DLCParameters*>] Just like NetBEUI and IPX, you'll need to include this heading in the answer file even though there are no parameters to install the DLC protocol.

[<*RASPPTPParameters*>] You must include this heading if you want to install RASPPTP even though it does not have any parameters.

[<*StreamsParameters*>] This section is required for Setup to install the STREAMS protocol, although it has no parameters.

[<AtalkParameters>] You'll need to include this section in order to install the AppleTalk protocol. At the time of this writing the parameters for setting the default zone and adapter aren't known, however. These settings must be set once the installation has been completed. This protocol is used mainly for printing. Apple printers are typically used by high-end publishing companies and need this protocol to print.

[<ServicesSection>] This section sets up pointers to the following sections, which list the parameters required to install SNMP, RAS, and NetWare services. This section header name was defined in the [Network] section, discussed previously.

- SNMP = <SNMPParameters>

  Points to the section containing Simple Network Management Protocol (SNMP) parameters. You can name <SNMPParameters> anything as long as the section head it points to has the same name.

- RAS = <RASParameters>

  Points to the section containing RAS parameters. Again, you can name <RASParameters> anything as long as the section head it points to has the same name.

- NWWKSTA = <NetWareClientParameters>

  Points to the section containing NetWare client parameters, as long as the heading name is the same as what you name this.

- INETSTP = <InternetInformationServerSection>

  Points to the section containing Internet server parameters, as long as the heading name is the same as what you name this.

[<NetWareClientParameters>] This section specifies NetWare client parameters. The name of this section head was defined previously in [<ServicesSection>].

- DefaultLocation = <server location>

  Indicates the default login server for the NetWare client.

- DefaultScriptOptions = 0 | 1 | 3

  Indicates the default action to be performed with scripts.

  A value of 0 means no scripts will run.

A value of *1* means that only NetWare 3.*x* scripts will run.

A value of *3* means that either NetWare 3.*x* or NetWare 4.*x* scripts will run.

[**<SNMPParameters>**]   This section lists parameters needed to install SNMP. The name of this section head was defined in [*<ServicesSection>*] (earlier).

- Accept_CommunityName = *<community name>* [, *<community name>*, *<community name>*]

    Use this key to identify up to three community names that the SNMP service computer accepts traps from. A community name can be considered a password between the SNMP management computers and the clients running SNMP. All SNMP messages must contain a community name. The default community name for this service is *public*. You can also indicate additional community names by using this key. For example:

    ```
    Accept_CommunityName = TechTeachCommunity
    ```

    This example would add a community name, *TechTeachCommunity*, to the default community, *Public*. Community names have no relationship to domain names. *Community names* are shared passwords among groups of computers on the network and should be selected or changed as you would any password. Usually, community names are given to computers in physical proximity to one another.

- Send_Authentication = *Yes* | *No*

    Specifies whether an authentication trap should be sent when an unauthorized community or host requests information.

- Any_Host = *Yes* | *No*

    Use this key to indicate whether the SNMP service computer should accept packets from any host computer. If *No*, you can specify host names to accept in the Limit_Host line.

- Limit_Host = *<host name>* [, *<host name>*, *<host name>*]

    Up to three host names can be indicated. This key can only be used when Any_Host = No.

- Community_Name = *<community name>*

    Indicates the community name for the computer.

- Traps = *ComputerName* | *<IP addresses>* | *<IPX addresses>*

  Indicates that traps should be sent to up to three IP or IPX addresses. Traps are identified by a computer name, IP address, or IPX address of the computers on the network where the traps are to be sent. Traps can only be sent to computers running the SNMP service.

- Contact_Name = *<name>*

  Indicates the name of the SNMP service administrator.

- Location = *<computer location>*

  Indicates the physical location of the computer.

- Service = *Physical, Applications, Datalink, Internet, End-to-End*

  Indicates the type of SNMP service to be installed. Any combination of the above services can be listed as long as the elements are separated by commas.

[*<RASParameters>*] This section lists the parameters needed to install the RAS service. The name of this section head was defined previously in [*<ServicesSection>*].

- PortSections = *<PortName1>*, *<PortName2>*, *<PortName3>*...

  Points to the parameters for a given port listed in a separate heading below. If you're using more than one port, you should keep each port's parameters in its own separate section.

- DialoutProtocols = *TCPIP* | *IPX* | *NETBEUI* | *ALL*

  Indicates the network protocols that RAS uses when dialing out.

  ALL means to install all three protocols. The default for this key is *ALL*.

The following parameters are for RAS Server installations only:

- DialinProtocols = *TCPIP* | *IPX* | *NETBEUI* | *ALL*

  Indicates the network protocols that RAS uses when dialing in.

  ALL means to install all three protocols. The default for this key is *ALL*.

- NetBEUIClientAccess = *Network* | *ThisComputer*

  Default is *Network*.

- TCPIPClientAccess = *Network* | *ThisComputer*

  Default is *Network.*

- UseDHCP = *Yes* | *No*

  Default is *Yes.*

  If *No,* then you need to include the following two keys:

  1. StaticAddressBegin = *<IP address>*

  2. StaticAddressEnd = *<IP address>*

- ExcludeAddress = *<IPAddress1–IPAddress2>*

  Use this key if you are manually assigning a range of IP addresses. Static-AddressBegin and StaticAddressEnd must also be listed in this section to use ExcludeAddress.

- ClientCanRequestIPAdress = *Yes* | *No*

  Default is *No.* If you use *No,* include the following key:

  - IpxClientAccess = *Network* | *ThisComputer*

  Default is *Network.*

- AutomaticNetworkNumbers = *Yes* | *No*

  Default is *Yes.*

- NetworkNumberFrom = *<IPX net number>*

  Valid numbers range from 1 to 0xFFFFFFFE. You must use this key if AutomaticNetworkNumbers = *No.*

- AssignSameNetworkNumber = *Yes* | *No*

  Default is *Yes.*

- ClientsCanRequestIpxNodeNumber = *Yes* | *No*

  The default is *No.*

Here is an example of how the *<RASParameters>* section might look for a computer using TCP/IP with DHCP:

```
[RasParameters]
PortSections = COMPort1
```

```
DialoutProtocols = TCP/IP
DialinProtocols = TCP/IP
TcpipClientAccess = Network
UseDHCP = yes
ClientCanRequestIPAddress = no
```

[<*PortSectionNames*>]   This section lists the parameters for the COM port you will use for RAS. The name of this section head was defined previously in [<*RASParameters*>].

- PortName = *COM1 | COM2 | COM3–COM25*

  Indicates the port to be configured for this port section.

- DeviceType = *Modem*

  Tells Setup which device type RAS will install. As of this writing, the only available option is *Modem*. If this key is used, then the InstallModem key must also be included in the [Modem] section of the answer file.

- DeviceName = *<device name>*

  Include here the name of the device being installed.

- PortUsage = *DialIn | DialOut | DialInOut*

  Indicates the dialing properties for the port named in the PortName key.

For example, here is how the [<*PortSectionNames*>] section might look for a single modem with dial-in and dial-out properties:

```
[COMPort1]
PortName = COM1
DeviceType = Modem
DeviceName = "USR Sportster 28800"
PortUsage = DialInOut
```

[<*InternetInformationServerSection*>]   The parameters contained in this section are for installing the Internet Information Server. The value of *1* means that the component will be installed. A value of *0* means that the component will not be installed. The name of this section head was defined previously in the [Network] section.

- InstallNETSTP = *0 | 1*

  The default of 1 means that Internet Services will be installed.

- InstallADMIN = *0 | 1*

  Tells Setup if the Internet Service Manager should be installed.

- InstallFTP = *0 | 1*

  Tells Setup if the FTP service will be installed.

- FTPRoot = *<FtpRootDirectory>*

  Points to the root directory for the FTP service.

- InstallWWW = *0 | 1*

  Tells Setup if the World Wide Web service should be installed.

- WWWRoot = *<WWWRootDirectory>*

  Points to the virtual root directory of the World Wide Web service.

- InstallMOSAIC = *0 | 1*

  Tells Setup if the Internet Explorer browser should be installed.

- InstallGOPHER = *0 | 1*

  Tells Setup if the Gopher service should be installed.

- GopherRoot = *<GopherRootDirectory>*

  Points to the virtual root directory for the Gopher service.

- InstallDir = *<InternetServicesInstallDirectory>*

  Points to the directory where all of the components of Internet Services will be installed.

- InstallW3SAMP = *0 | 1*

  Tells Setup if the World Wide Web sample files should be installed.

- InstallHTMLA = *0 | 1*

  Indicates if the HTML form of the Internet Service Manager will be installed.

- InstallDNS = *0 | 1*

  Indicates whether the Domain Name Service (DNS) will be installed.

- InstallGATEWAY = *0 | 1*

  Tells Setup if the Gateway service will be installed.

- UseGateway = *0 | 1*

  Indicates whether a gateway is to be used.

- GatewaysList = *\\gateway1 [, \\gateway2]*

  Lists the gateways to be used. Use this key only when UseGateway = 1.

- GuestAccountName = *<name>*

  Indicates the anonymous user name used for World Wide Web, FTP, and Gopher services.

- GuestAccountPassword = *<PasswordString>*

  Indicates the password used by the Guest account. If you do not define a password, IIS will create a random string for the Guest account. Of course, you always have the option of setting a new password using the User Manager for Domains once you log on. You must make sure, however, that the password in the User Manager for Domains matches the password set in the Internet Information Service Manager.

Running Setup Manager

Of course, no one (or almost no one) would sit down and build an unattended installation script by hand when there's a perfectly good tool to do it for you. NT comes with just such a tool: the *Setup Manager*. It can't do *everything*, but I strongly recommend that you use Setup Manager to build your basic installation script. Then, as the script is an ASCII file, you can use a program like Notepad to modify the script. For example, Setup Manager will not insert the OEMSkip-EULA command—you must insert that by hand.

The Setup Manager, SETUPMGR.EXE, can be found in the \SUPPORT\ DEPTOOLS*<platform>* directory on your NT Server 4 CD, where *<platform>* is I386 (for Intel-based computers), Alpha, MIPS, or PPC.

Now, despite all of the install = script sections that you just read about in the previous section, "Answer File Parameters," you don't need to use each and every possible section; in fact, you can get NT installed on many systems with a pretty simple script, which I'll present a bit later. In many cases, all you have to fill in are the following, which Setup Manager can do for you:

1. General Setup

   - User Information dialog box.

- General dialog box.

- Computer Role dialog box: If the computer is to be a member of an existing domain, make sure the domain name is valid.

- Install Directory dialog box.

- Display Settings dialog box: Make sure that the "Automatically use the above settings" box is checked.

- Time Zone dialog box.

2. Networking Setup

- General dialog box: Click the Unattended Network Installation radio button and the "Automatically detect and install first adapter" radio button, or if you know which card you want to have detected or installed, you'll need to specify those by clicking either of the Specify radio buttons.

- Adapters dialog box: If you chose to specify an adapter to be installed or detected, you'll need to add a network card to the list here. Also, if there are any parameters for that card that need to be set, you'll have to specify those, as well.

- Protocols dialog box: If you're using TCP/IP and DHCP, you'll only need to add TCP/IP without any parameters. If you would like to specify an IP address, check with your network administrator first and add the address by clicking the Parameters button.

3. Advanced Setup

- General dialog box: Check the After Text Mode, After GUI Mode, Skip Welcome Wizard page, and Skip Administrator Password Wizard page check boxes.

Anyway, let's get back to actually *using* Setup Manager. Start it up and you'll see the dialog box shown in Figure 3.13.

You'll see that there are three buttons: General Setup, Networking Setup, and Advanced Setup. For General Setup, you specify user information, the role the computer plays on the network, the directory to install NT on, and the display settings. Networking Setup allows you to do a manual or unattended network installation. Here, you specify adapters, protocols, services, and modems to be installed. You can also make your computer an Internet server. Advanced Setup enables you to specify which OEM-supplied drivers are to be installed, which file system you would like to use, and whether you want the computer to automatically reboot after each installation phase.

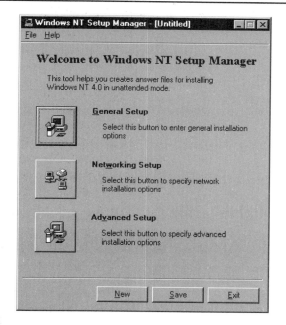

General Setup

Click on the General Setup Button, and you'll see Figure 3.14.

User Information On the User Information tab, Setup Manager is asking for general information. The username and organization name are self-explanatory. The computer name must be a name that is unique to the domain. The product ID can be found in the certificate of authenticity provided with your Windows NT CD.

General Click on the General tab, and you'll see the dialog box shown in Figure 3.15.

FIGURE 3.14:

User Information tab

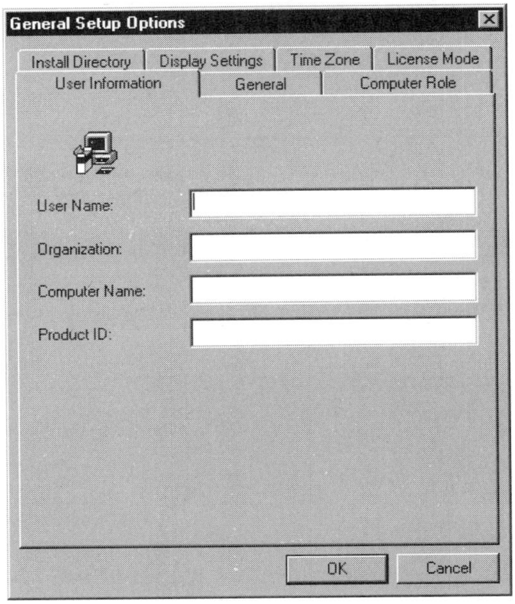

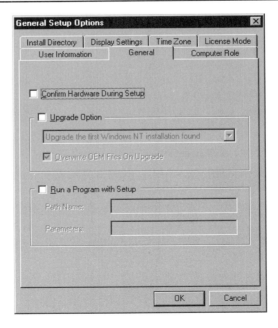

FIGURE 3.15:

General tab

If you're sure that your computer's hardware settings are configured properly, then check the Confirm Hardware During Setup box. If you want to upgrade your current NT installation, check the Upgrade Option box. You'll then be able to choose the following options from the pull-down list:

- Prompt user for Windows NT installation to upgrade
- Upgrade the current single Windows NT installation
- Upgrade the first Windows NT installation found
- Upgrade Windows 3.1 or Windows for Workgroups

Check the Overwrite OEM Files On Upgrade box to overwrite any existing OEM files. If you want to run a program at the same time that Setup is running, check the Run a Program with Setup box, and then provide the path and file name of the program and its parameters.

Computer Role Click on the Computer Role tab and you'll see Figure 3.16.

Here you determine how you want your computer to participate on your network:

- As a member of a workstation in a workgroup
- As a member of a workstation in a domain
- As a stand-alone server in a workgroup
- As a stand-alone server in a domain
- As a Primary Domain Controller (PDC)
- As a Backup Domain Controller (BDC)

At first, the choice to make the computer a workstation seems odd for a server, but you can use the Setup Manager program to install workstations, as well.

Install Directory Next, click on the Install Directory tab. You'll see the dialog box shown in Figure 3.17.

FIGURE 3.16:

Computer Role tab

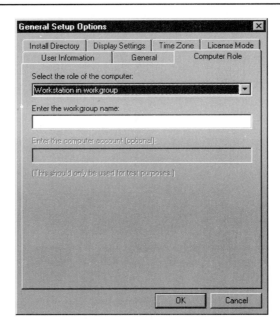

FIGURE 3.17:

Install Directory tab

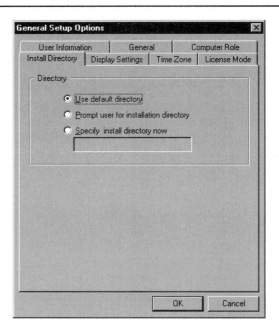

Here, you tell Setup where you want Windows NT Server to be installed on your hard drive. You have three options:

Use default directory   Setup will automatically create a unique NT system directory on the same drive from which Setup was run and install the files there. Setup will name the directory WINNT if no other installations are present. If other installations are present, Setup will name the directory WINNT.*x*, where *x* is a single-digit number starting with 0. The first directory is named WINNT.0; the second would be named WINNT.1; the third WINNT.2; and so on.

Prompt user for installation directory   Setup will halt and ask the user to provide a directory where the files will be installed. This is a good option if the user's computer has more than one hard disk and you're not sure where the available space will be.

Specify install directory now   If you know where you'd like to install the files, click this button and enter the path.

Display Settings   Click on the Display Settings tab to configure your monitor. You'll see the dialog box shown in Figure 3.18.

Here, you can tell Setup to configure the display settings. If you're not sure which settings you want, check "Configure the graphics device at logon" and the user can test the display settings later.

To configure the display, you need to set the following parameters (the defaults for these settings have already been set for you). The documentation for your graphics device should include this information.

- Bits Per Pixel

- Horizontal Resolution

- Vertical Resolution

- Refresh Rate

- Flags

Check the "Automatically use the above settings" check box if you don't want to confirm that the setting are correct during the installation. If the screen looks odd to you later, you can always change the settings.

FIGURE 3.18:

Display Settings tab

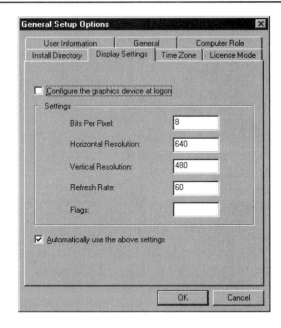

Time Zone Click the Time Zone tab to select the time zone from the pull-down menu and click OK to return to the Setup Manager screen.

License Mode Click the License Mode tab to choose a license type. NT Server uses two license modes, as shown in Figure 3.19.

Per Server The server holds all the licenses for all concurrent connections. For example, if you purchase 50 licenses for Windows NT, then you are entitled to have a maximum of 50 simultaneous connections at one time.

Per Seat The number of connections you may have are unlimited, but each computer connected to your server running NT must have its own license.

Click on the radio button of the license mode you wish to use. When done, click OK several times to get back to the opening Setup Manager screen (Figure 3.13).

Setting the license mode

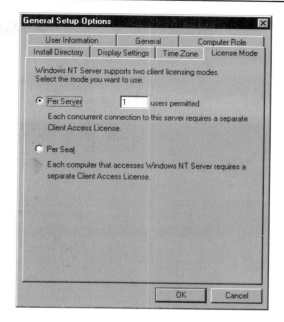

Networking Setup

From the opening Setup Manager screen, click on the Networking button to configure your computer for the network.

General Options First, you'll see the dialog box in Figure 3.20.

Checking the Manual Network Installation radio button will cause Setup to halt during the installation so you can manually configure the network settings.

Click on the "Automatically detect and install first adapter" radio button to allow Setup to automatically detect your network adapter. The most common network adapter cards are detected, so you shouldn't have a problem. However, if Setup can't find your network card, you can always install it after you log on. If you know which card you want to install, you can specify that here, as well. Instead of clicking the "Automatically detect and install first adapter button," click the radio buttons labeled either "Specify adapter to be installed or detected" or "Specify adapter to be detected."

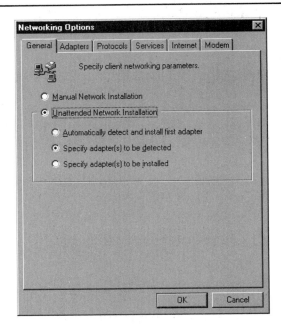

Adapters If you chose to have a specific adapter card installed or detected, click on the Adapters tab to see the dialog box in Figure 3.21. If you checked the "Automatically detect and install first adapter" button, you won't be able to view this dialog box.

Usually Setup will only need to make one attempt to detect your card. You can, however, change the Detect Count number to whatever number you choose. To add an adapter, click the Add button for a list of adapters to choose from. Click the appropriate adapter for your computer and click OK. You can see the adapter you chose in the List of Adapters box. You'll then want to click the Parameters button to set your network card's parameters. If your card has parameters that need to be set, you'll see the dialog box shown in Figure 3.22.

Typically, you'd not have to include a network bus number, but check with your network administrator.

FIGURE 3.21:

Specify adapters to be
installed or detected

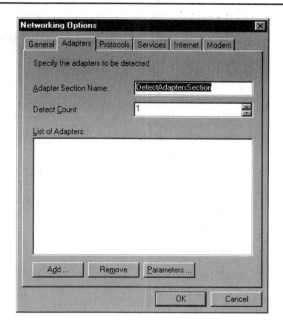

FIGURE 3.21:

Specify adapters to be
installed or detected

Protocols Click on the Protocols tab, shown in Figure 3.23 to indicate which
network protocols you want to use.

FIGURE 3.22:

Adapter Parameters
dialog box

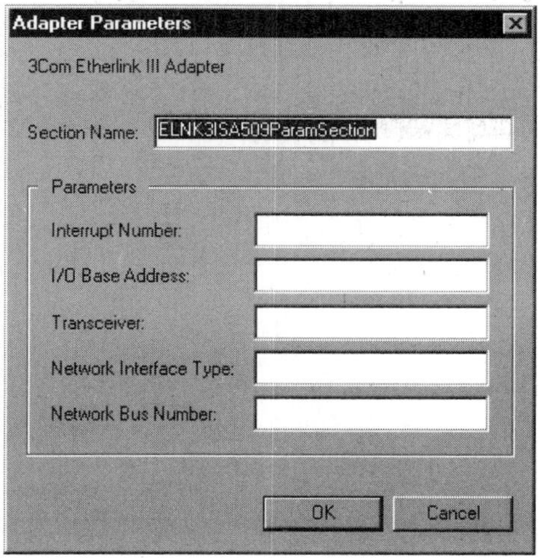

FIGURE 3.23:

Specify protocols to be installed

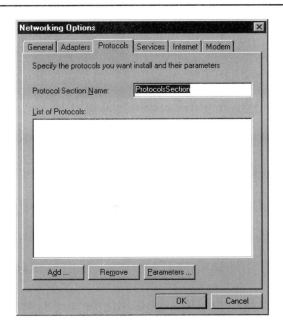

Click on the Add button at the bottom of the screen to add a network protocol. Choose TCP/IP, NetBEUI, or IPX from the list provided and click OK. You'll now see a protocol listed in the List of Protocols box. If you chose TCP/IP, click on the Parameters button. Here, you'll be able to choose between setting your computer's IP address and using your network's DHCP server to assign an address. Choose the appropriate one for your system and click OK to return to the Protocols dialog box.

Services Click on the Services tab, shown in Figure 3.24.

Click on the Add button at the bottom of the screen and select from the list of services that appears: SNMP, Client Service for NetWare, and Remote Access Service (RAS).

FIGURE 3.24:

Services tab

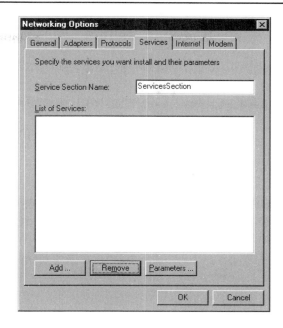

Highlight Client Service for NetWare if you chose to install this service. Click on the Parameters button and enter the default server location. Then choose which type of script you want to run. You'll be given the choice of not running a script, running NetWare 3.*x* level scripts only or running NetWare 3.*x* or 4.*x* level scripts. Click OK to return to the Services dialog box.

If you chose to install RAS, configuring it requires a few more steps than for NetWare. Highlight Remote Access Service in the list and click on the Parameters button. The General tab contains only the section name for the answer file. Click on the Ports tab and you'll see Figure 3.25.

You need to type in a Port Section Name that will be used to specify which port your modem will use. Click on the Add button to add the highlighted name, and then click on the Parameters button and you'll see Figure 3.26.

FIGURE 3.25:

Ports tab

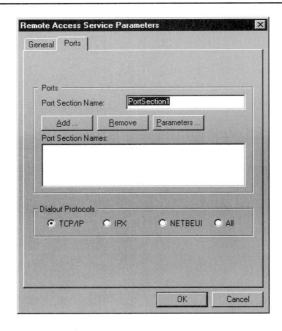

FIGURE 3.26:

Port Parameters dialog box

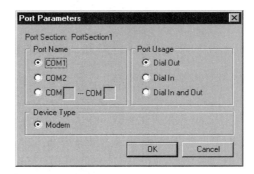

Here, you specify which port you want your modem to connect to and indicate how you want the port to be used. If you wish to use a COM port higher than COM2, you can specify that in the box on the last line. You can also choose to use the COM port for dialing in, dialing out, or both. Click OK several times to return to the Services dialog box.

Modem If you indicated that you wanted to install RAS and configured the port you're going to use, click on the Modem tab, shown in Figure 3.27, to configure your modem.

FIGURE 3.27:

Modem tab

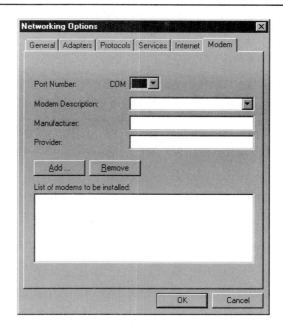

Select the COM port you want to connect to your modem. Next, provide a description of the modem. This description must match the modem description in the [Strings] section of a MDMxxxxx.INF file of the modem you are installing. The INF files are on the NT Server CD. Each INF file contains all of the available NT-compatible modems made by a specific manufacturer. For example, if you have an internal AT&T Dataport 14.4 modem, you would find it listed in MDMATT.INF in the [Strings] section. It looks like this:

```
Modem3 ="AT&T DataPort 14.4-Fax Internal"
```

Therefore, the modem description would be *AT&T DataPort 14.4-Fax Internal*.

You can also specify the manufacturer and provider of the modem in case the modem description is not unique. Click on the Add button to identify which modem you are installing. Select a modem from the list provided and click OK.

You'll now see the modem listed on the screen. Click OK to return to the Networking Options screen.

Internet If you chose to have your computer participate as a server, you'll see an additional tab. Click on the Internet tab and you'll see the dialog box shown in Figure 3.28.

FIGURE 3.28:

Internet tab

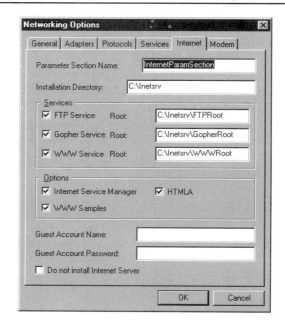

You can install the following Internet services and applications:

- File Transfer Protocol (FTP)
- World Wide Web (WWW)
- Gopher
- Internet Service Manager

You can create a new Parameter Section Name if you wish. You can also install the Internet directory where you wish. Then, check the boxes next to the applications you want. For the administrator's use, you can also establish an e-mail address and directory to store log files and such, and you can type in a guest account name for anonymous user logons. If you do not define a password, Setup will create a random string for the guest account. Click OK and the Network portion of the unattended installation is complete. Keep clicking OK until you get back to the opening Setup Manager screen (Figure 3.13).

Advanced Setup

Click on the Advanced Setup button on the opening Setup Manager screen to see the general options shown in Figure 3.29.

FIGURE 3.29:

General tab in the Advanced Options dialog box

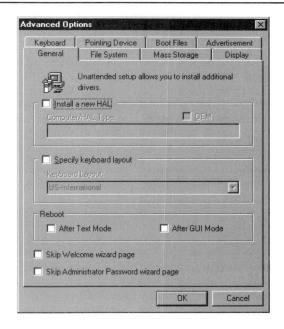

In this series of dialog boxes, you can install a new HAL and specify a keyboard layout. If the HAL box is not checked, Setup will attempt to detect the type of computer and install its appropriate retail HAL. If you want to specify which HAL to install, check the "Install a new HAL" check box and enter the description in the box below. This description must match one of the strings in the [Computer] section of TXTSETUP.SIF (if using a retail HAL) or TXTSETUP.OEM (if using an OEM HAL). These files are on the NT 4 CD. For instance, if you have a PC with a C-step I486, you would then need to look up the [Computer] section of TXTSETUP.OEM and find the following line:

```
486c_up = "Standard PC with C-Step I486",files.none
```

In this case, you would therefore enter **Standard PC with C-Step I486** as the description. Make sure that it matches the description in TXTSETUP.SIF exactly or else it will be ignored and Setup will attempt to automatically detect your machine's computer type. Check the OEM box if the HAL being installed is OEM-supplied.

Check the "Specify keyboard layout" box and provide a description of the keyboard layout. This description must match one of the right-hand strings in the ["Keyboard Layout"] section of TXTSETUP.SIF. For example, our French Canadian friends may want to use a layout that uses a combination of French and English. The following line in the ["Keyboard Layout"] section of TXTSETUP.SIF shows that, indeed, there is a layout to suit their needs:

```
00010C0C = "Canadian French (Multilingual)"
```

The string *Canadian French (Multilingual)* is the keyboard layout description. This string must match the one located in the TXTSETUP file *exactly*, or Setup will ignore the entry and attempt to detect the keyboard automatically.

Also, you will want to check the After Text Mode and After GUI Mode boxes. These boxes will enable Setup to automatically reboot your computer after each phase of installation. Checking the "Skip Welcome Wizard page" box enables Setup to skip past the Welcome to Windows NT Setup screen in the GUI mode portion of the unattended installation. Likewise, checking the "Skip Administrator Password Wizard page" box enables Setup to skip past the Administrator Password dialog box by creating a blank administrator password instead of requiring you to enter a password for the Administrator ID.

File System Next, click on the File System tab, shown in Figure 3.30.

At this point, you're given the opportunity to use the file system that currently exists (which is typically FAT) or to convert the file system to NTFS (if you haven't already done so). Select the appropriate file system for your computer.

If you have a hard drive greater than 2GB, you must check the Extend OEM partition box. Setup will then extend the partition where the temporary source files are located into any unpartitioned space that physically follows it on the disk.

FIGURE 3.30:

File System tab

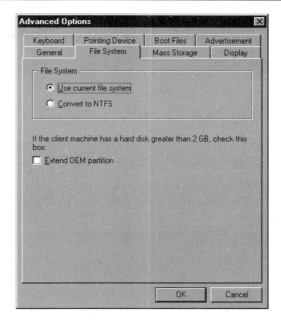

> **WARNING**   For an unattended installation to work, the temporary files *must* be located on a primary partition and limited to 1024 cylinders. The installation will fail if data is written beyond the 1024th cylinder. The reason is that the initial part of Setup isn't running NT yet (it's not yet installed, right?); it's running a version of DOS. DOS relies upon a system's BIOS to access its drives, and for historical reasons BIOSes cannot access drives with more than 1024 cylinders.

Mass Storage   Click the Mass Storage tab, shown in Figure 3.31, to specify the mass storage drivers to be installed.

FIGURE 3.31:

Mass Storage tab

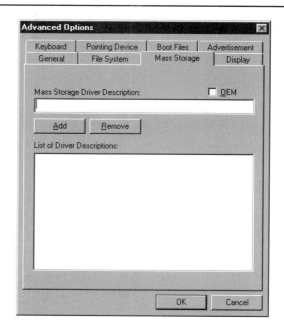

If this screen is left blank, Setup will attempt to detect any mass storage devices and install the appropriate drivers. To add a driver, enter a description that identifies the driver to be installed. This description must match one of the strings defined on the right-hand side of the [SCSI] section of TXTSETUP.SIF or TXTSETUP .OEM. For example, if you wanted to add a BusLogic FlashPoint SCSI adapter, you'd find the following entry in the [SCSI] section of TXTSETUP.SIF:

```
flashpnt = "BusLogic FlashPoint"
```

You would then enter **BusLogic FlashPoint** as the description. Click the Add button to add the description to the list. You can provide multiple driver descriptions. Click OEM for the drivers that are OEM-supplied. (Again, I'll explain in more detail how to install unusual SCSI drivers a bit later.)

Display Click on the Display tab, shown in Figure 3.32, to specify which display driver should be installed.

FIGURE 3.32:

Display tab

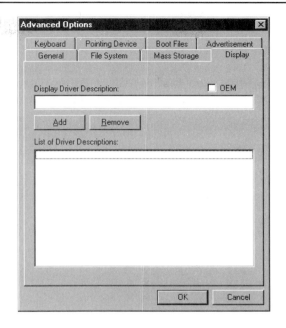

If you do not enter any descriptions on this screen, Setup will attempt to detect your machine's display devices and install the corresponding retail drivers. To add a driver, enter a description that identifies the driver to be installed. This description must match one of the strings defined on the right-hand side of the [Display] section of TXTSETUP.SIF or TXTSETUP.OEM. For instance, if you have a display driver that is incompatible with Windows NT 4, you have the option of installing the standard VGA driver. To do this, you would find the following entry in the [Display] section of TXTSETUP.SIF:

```
forcevga = "Standard VGA (640x480, 16 colors)",files.none
```

You would then enter **Standard VGA (640x480, 16 colors)** as the description. Click the Add button to add the description to the list. You can provide multiple driver descriptions if you like. Click OEM if the driver you are installing is OEM-supplied.

As I said earlier, you probably will never use this method of installing a display board; you'll see a bit later how to force NT to do an unattended install of a particular display board.

Keyboard Click on the Keyboard tab, shown in Figure 3.33, to tell Setup which keyboard to install.

FIGURE 3.33:

Keyboard tab

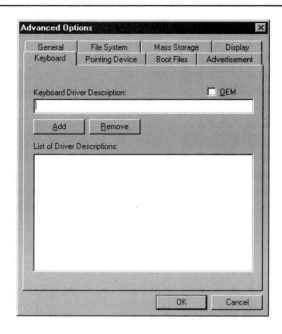

Like the display driver, if you wish to install your own driver, you'll need to provide a description of the keyboard driver. If you leave this screen blank, Setup will attempt to detect the keyboard device and install the corresponding driver. Enter the driver description in the space provided and click Add. This description must match a string defined on the right-hand side of the [Keyboard] section of TXTSETUP.SIF or TXTSETUP.OEM. For example, the [Keyboard] section contains the following line:

```
STANDARD = "XT, AT, or Enhanced Keyboard (83-104
keys)",files.i8042,i8042prt
```

Type in **XT, AT, or Enhanced Keyboard (83-104 keys)** for the keyboard driver description. Because this is the only keyboard description in TXTSETUP.SIF, you'd only need to enter a description if you had an OEM-supplied driver. Click the OEM box if the driver is OEM-supplied. You can add multiple driver descriptions.

Pointing Device Click on the Pointing Device tab to specify any pointing devices you want to install.

Figure 3.34 shows the Pointing Device tab, which is similar to the Display and Keyboard tabs. Here, you'll enter a description of the pointing device, which must match a string defined on the right-hand side of the [Mouse] section of TXTSETUP.SIF or TXTSETUP.OEM. And, like the others, multiple descriptions may be listed. For example, say that you want to install a Logitech serial mouse. In the [Mouse] section, you'll find the following line:

```
lgser = "Logitech Serial Mouse",files.sermouse,sermouse
```

You'd enter **Logitech Serial Mouse** as the description.

FIGURE 3.34:

Pointing Device tab

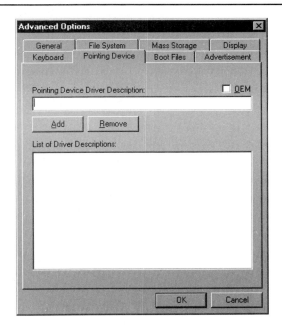

Boot Files Click on the Boot Files tab, shown in Figure 3.35, to specify OEM-supplied boot files.

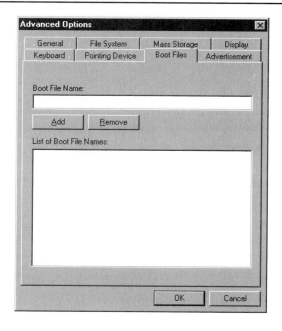

If you're installing OEM-supplied boot files, one of the files that absolutely *must* be included in this section is TXTSETUP.OEM. This file contains descriptions of all of the OEM-supplied drivers that will be installed. It also includes instructions on how to install the drivers listed here.

If you decide to install a different HAL, you may list that file here, which then maps to a HAL description that you have defined in the Computer Type/HAL description found at the beginning of the Advance Options.

Also, you may want to specify a SCSI-driver file name. This file name will map to the driver description you specified in the Mass Storage dialog box mentioned previously. Multiple SCSI-driver file names may be listed.

Advertisement The Advertisement tab, shown in Figure 3.36, makes modifications to the Setup interface.

In the Banner text box, enter the appropriate text. A *banner* is a string displayed in the upper left-hand corner of the computer screen. The string must contain the phrase *Windows NT* or else it will be ignored. You can separate the text into more than one line by using the asterisk (*) character.

FIGURE 3.36:

Advertisement tab

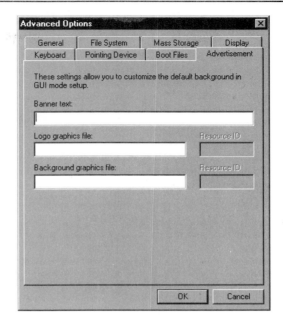

By specifying a file name, you can display a logo and/or background image on the screen. If only one field is entered on this line, it is assumed that the file is a BMP file located in the OEM\Oemfiles directory of the distribution share point. However, if two fields are specified, the first field is the name of a DLL file and the second is a base 10 number that represents the resource ID of the bitmap in the DLL. The DLL that you specify must be located in the OEM\Oemfiles directory, as well.

A Sample Answer File for a Basic Install

Whew, we've gone a fairly long time without an example, so let's look at a simple basic answer file, about the most basic that will work correctly to install a server. Here is an install script that will probably work on a system if

- Your system only has hardware that NT can auto-detect and whose drivers are on the NT CD-ROM.

- You're using TCP/IP with DHCP.

- The server you are installing is a simple member server and you have used Server Manager to create a machine account for it before running this installation.

The answer file looks like this:

```
[Unattended]
OEMPreinstall = yes
OEMSkipEula = yes
NoWaitAfterTextMode = 1
NoWaitAfterGUIMode = 1
[UserData]
FullName = "Mark Minasi"
ComputerName = "MINTAKA"
ProductId = "123-4567890"
[GuiUnattended]
OEMSkipWelcome = 1
OEMBlankAdminPassword = 1
TimeZone = "(GMT-05:00) Eastern Time (US & Canada)"
AdvServerType = servernt
[LicenseFilePrintData]
AutoMode = PerSeat
[Display]
ConfigureAtLogon = 0
BitsPerPel = 8
XResolution = 640
YResolution = 480
VRefresh = 1
AutoConfirm = 1
[Network]
DetectAdapters = ""
InstallProtocols = ProtocolsSection
InstallServices = ServicesSection
JoinDomain = ORION
[ProtocolsSection]
TC = TCParamSection
[TCParamSection]
DHCP = yes
```

Let's examine this a section at a time. The first section is the "[Unattended]" section:

```
[Unattended]
OEMPreinstall = yes
```

```
OEMSkipEula = yes
NoWaitAfterTextMode = 1
NoWaitAfterGUIMode = 1
```

Basically, this section tells Setup to skip the End-User License Agreement screen during installation and automatically reboot the system after each installation phase. The next section, [UserData], is pretty self-explanatory.

```
[UserData]
FullName = "Mark Minasi"
ComputerName = ALDEBARAN
ProductId = "123-4567890"
```

You've got to have those three lines or NT can't do an unattended install.

The next section, [GuiUnattended], can also be kept pretty short:

```
[GuiUnattended]
OEMSkipWelcome = 1
OEMBlankAdminPassword = 1
TimeZone = "(GMT-05:00) Eastern Time (US & Canada)"
AdvServerType = LANMANNT
```

Here, I've told Setup to skip the Welcome to NT Setup screen at the beginning of GUI mode, create a blank password for the Administrator ID, set the computer's time zone to eastern standard time, and install the computer as a member server.

```
[LicenseFilePrintData]
AutoMode = PerSeat
```

This section is only used when installing a server. In this case, I've set the license type to "per seat," as most NT Servers are probably configured.

```
[Display]
ConfigureAtLogon = 0
BitsPerPel = 4
XResolution = 640
YResolution = 480
VRefresh = 1
AutoConfirm = 1
```

The display section above configures a basic VGA with a 640 × 480 screen, 16 colors, and hardware default refresh rate. The ConfigureAtLogon and

AutoConfirm settings tell Setup not to wait for my confirmation, but to just set the video board as indicated and then keep going.

```
[Network]
DetectAdapters = ""
InstallProtocols = ProtocolsSection
InstallServices = ServicesSection
JoinDomain = ORION
```

This section will cause Setup to automatically detect a network adapter card and to point to other sections that deal with protocol and services installation. It's important to note that this will only work if your network card is among the ones supported by NT 4's original CD-ROM. This also causes the computer to join the ORION domain. That will only work if you've pre-created a machine account for the computer. If not, you can add this line:

```
CreateComputerAccount = administrator,hispassword
```

That command tells NT Setup to create a computer account right then and there. The two parameters *administrator* and *hispassword* are, respectively, the name and password of a domain administrator. The problem with this approach is, of course, that you probably won't be excited about the idea of putting an administrative name and password into a text file that anyone can see. Of course, you needn't use an administrative account—the account need only be a member of the Server Operators group—but it's still never a great idea to leave passwords lying around.

The last two sections take care of the protocol details:

```
[ProtocolsSection]
TC = TCParamSection
[TCParamSection]
DHCP = yes
```

Those sections just say to use DHCP to configure TCP/IP.

Running the Unattended Installation

Now that you have an answer file, let's use it. To run Setup in unattended mode for new installations, use the WINNT or WINNT32 command with the /u parameter and specify the location of the answer file. The WINNT32 command will only work with 32-bit operating systems, such as Windows NT 4 or OS/2. And yes, Windows 95/98 is *supposed* to be a 32-bit operating system, but WINNT32 doesn't see it that way. If you're installing NT on a system with Windows 95/98 on it, do this:

1. Reboot the system to the command prompt—reboot and when you see the "Loading Windows" message, press F8 and choose "command prompt."

2. Type **SMARTDRV**. It'll speed up the process immensely, so much you won't believe it.

3. Lock the C: drive so that NT can rewrite your boot record. Type **lock C:**, and press Enter. It'll ask if you're sure; tell it that you are. Then do your install with WINNT rather than WINNT32.

The unattended setup command syntax is as follows:

```
WINNT /u:<answer_filename> /s:<sourcepath> /t:<destination>
```

or

```
WINNT32 /u:<answer_filename> /s:<sourcepath> /t:<destination>
```

where

-   /u indicates unattended Setup mode.

-   *<answer_filename>* is the location of the answer file.

-   /s indicates that the installation files are located on a drive other than the CD-ROM. This parameter is optional.

-   *<sourcepath>* is the path to the distribution files.

-   /t indicates two things. First it tells WINNT/WINNT32 to put most of its temporary files to a drive other than C:. (Some temporary files will *always* go on C:, about three megabytes' worth—there's nothing you can do about that.) Second, /t tells WINNT/WINNT32 to install NT itself to that drive. So, for example, "winnt /t:e:…" would put a bunch of temporary files on E:, and it would also install NT on E:, probably directory E:\WINNT. This parameter is optional.

-   *<destination>* indicates the path to the directory where Windows NT Server files will be installed.

Start up WINNT or WINNT32 and you can then just walk away. In a while you'll have a fresh copy of NT installed on your system. Of course, what you've seen so far will only work on a computer with a fairly vanilla set of hardware. What about the rest of the machines out there? We'll take that up next.

Using a Batch File for Installations

If you're like me, you use these installation scripts on machines that you need to periodically wipe clean and reinstall, either test machines or machines whose hard disks have gotten clogged up with things you installed and then un-installed. For that reason, you might find that your unattended install comes to a screeching halt the second time, displaying a dialog box about HyperTerminal and asking if you want to overwrite a newer file with an older file.

What's happening here is this: first, you installed NT 4, then you installed some service pack. In the process of installing the service pack, you got all new files, including HyperTerminal and Internet Explorer. Now you want to install a new copy of NT, which will overwrite a bunch of newer service pack–vintage files with some older 1996 NT 4 files. Setup, like all programs, asks whenever it looks like you're going to overwrite newer files with older files.

Now, this isn't a problem for most files, as you can't do an unattended installation on top of an existing one; Setup will simply stop. That's why you put **target-path = *** in your script, so that Setup will be smart enough to put NT into a directory called WINNT.0 unless there's one by that name, in which case it'll put NT into a directory called WINNT.1, and so on.

Ah, but here's the rub: HyperTerminal and Internet Explorer *aren't* in the WINNT directory structure—they're in the Program Files directories, *which are shared by all Windows NT and Windows 9x installations on a disk*! So suppose you want to keep two copies of NT on your disk, a version with no service packs and one with Service Pack 4. Setup's very good about segregating the two different builds of NT on a disk, *except* for the couple of things in Program Files. (If you in fact *do* need to put more than one copy of NT on a computer, I suggest you put them on different logical drives, which will lead to different Program Files directories on the different logical drives.) This can be particularly frustrating if you have a desktop machine dual-booting Windows 98 and Windows NT 4—their Internet Explorer 4 files overwrite each other.

What, then, to do to make your hands-off installation completely hands-off? Use DELTREE.EXE, a command-line utility shipped with DOS 6 and Windows 9x (but not NT, sadly) to wipe out the \Program Files\Windows NT and \Program Files\Plus! directories. For example, I have an installation script that creates a BDC for me, stored in a file called INTBDC.INF. The batch file that kicks off the installation is just three lines:

```
deltree /y c:\progra~1\window~1
deltree /y c:\progra~1\plus!
c:\i386\winnt32 /b /s:c:\i386 /u:c:\intbdc.inf
```

Two major ingredients to a truly hands-off automated install, then, are the 128-bit version of whatever service pack you're using, and a few DELTREEs in the startup batch file.

Creating Install Scripts for Unusual Hardware

Microsoft shipped NT 4 to their CD copiers in mid-July 1996—over two years ago. At that time, no one had AGP video boards, many popular SCSI host adapters didn't even exist, and popular network adapters like 3Com's PCI-based XL adapters were just appearing. The result is that NT Setup can't automatically detect many NICs, video boards, and mass storage controllers, making automated installs more difficult.

Fortunately, there *is* a way to tell NT Setup to use NIC, video, or SCSI drivers that weren't shipped with the original version of NT 4, as you'll see in this section.

TIP

If the remaining part of this chapter is of interest to you—and I hope that it is—then let me suggest that you first jump ahead to Chapter 5 and read about the Registry; you'll need some knowledge of what it is and how to work with it to get everything that you can from the remaining part of this chapter.

Installing New Network Interface Card Drivers

I tend to buy 3Com network interface cards and Adaptec SCSI host adapters for my systems. That's not necessarily because I think those vendors make particularly good boards—although in general their products *are* good—but because I know it'll be easy to find drivers for those products. About a year ago I bought a new clone system and told the dealer who assembled it to put a 3Com PCI Ethernet card in the system. I expected that he'd put a 3C590 in the system—I'd had lots of experience with the 3C590s and liked them—and so I was surprised to find that I instead had a 3C900 XL card. This board wasn't very common in mid-1996, so its drivers didn't ship with NT. NT Setup is good at detecting hardware, but it can't detect what it doesn't know about.

How to automate adding the 3C900 drivers? By using the OEM Preinstall feature of NT Setup. (It's another chance to use the OEM directory I mentioned earlier.) To make a "strange" NIC work, you'll need these ingredients:

- An installation script that's complete save for the instructions to set up the new NIC

- The installation files for the NIC from the NIC's vendor— usually a floppy called the "drivers disk"

You'll start off getting this new NIC to work by getting a functioning copy of NT on a computer in which the new NIC has been installed. You'll need this computer to gather configuration information about the new NIC. Using the NIC's installation files, load the drivers for the NIC on NT.

Once you have a machine with the new NIC's drivers working, you'll use that machine to determine the *internal product name* of the network card. For example, the 3C900 driver's internal name is El90x. Find that out by starting up REGEDIT or REGEDT32 (if you haven't ever done that, you might take a look ahead at the Registry chapter first). Once you're in the Registry, look in HKEY_LOCAL_MACHINE\ SOFTWARE\Microsoft\Windows NT\CurrentVersion\NetworkCards\1. You'll see a value entry ProductName; its value is the internal product name.

Next, you'll have to put the installation drivers where NT Setup can find them. Create a directory in \I386 (the I386 that you intend to install NT from) named OEM and, under that, OEM\C\DRIVERS. So, for example, if you chose to put I386 on a machine's C: drive, you'd have directories named C:\I386\$OEM$ and C:\I386\$OEM$\C\DRIVERS. Take the installation files for the network card and put them in C:\I386\$OEM$\C\DRIVERS.

What we're doing here is exploiting a built-in feature of \I386\$OEM$. If you create a directory in \I386\$OEM$ called C, then WINNT/WINNT32 will copy anything in that directory to the C: drive of the computer that you're installing NT on. For that matter, if you create a directory named D in I386\$OEM$, then WINNT/WINNT32 will copy anything in \I386\$OEM$\D to the local D: drive of the machine that is receiving a new copy of NT. So by creating a directory called \I386\$OEM$\C\DRIVERS, I'm instructing WINNT/WINNT32 to create a directory called C:\DRIVERS on this new machine that I'm installing NT on. That way, I'm sure that the drivers are on a local drive where they will be easy to find, and I know *exactly* where they are. In the case of the 3Com card, I just created the \I386\$OEM$\C\DRIVERS directory and then used XCOPY /S to copy the whole 3Com Drivers floppy to the \I386\$OEM$\C\DRIVERS directory. (The /s option ensures that the floppy's directory structure gets reproduced accurately within \I386\$OEM$\C\DRIVERS.)

Now that you know the product name, you can set up your install script to force NT Setup to use its drivers. In the [Network] section, add these lines:

```
[Network]
InstallAdapters = Adapterslist
...other commands...
[Adapterslist]
productname = NICparms, c:\drivers\
[NICparms]
```

By putting the InstallAdapters command into your install script, you've told NT Setup *not* to try detecting your adapter, but instead to use the particular adapter that you want it to use. Of course, your existing install script will probably already have sections named [Network], [Adapterslist], and [adapterparameters]; these will replace those sections, although your [Network] section probably has lines that refer to protocols and services to load—keep those lines. For example, if I modified the very basic script that I presented a while back for installing a member server so that it could install using the 3C900 XL drivers, the script would now look like the following (the modified lines are in bold):

```
[Unattended]
OEMPreinstall = yes
OEMSkipEula = yes
NoWaitAfterTextMode = 1
NoWaitAfterGUIMode = 1
[UserData]
FullName = "Mark Minasi"
ComputerName = "MINTAKA"
ProductId = "123-4567890"
[GuiUnattended]
OEMSkipWelcome = 1
OEMBlankAdminPassword = 1
TimeZone = "(GMT-05:00) Eastern Time (US & Canada)"
AdvServerType = servernt
[LicenseFilePrintData]
AutoMode = PerSeat
[Display]
ConfigureAtLogon = 0
BitsPerPel = 8
```

```
XResolution = 640
YResolution = 480
VRefresh = 1
AutoConfirm = 1
[Network]
InstallAdapters = Adapterslist
InstallProtocols = ProtocolsSection
InstallServices = ServicesSection
JoinDomain = ORION
[AdaptersList]
El90x = NICParms, c:\drivers
[NICParms]
[ProtocolsSection]
TC = TCParamSection
[TCParamSection]
DHCP = yes
```

I haven't said anything so far about the [NICParms] section, but you've probably noticed that I left it empty. Its purpose is to give you a place to put board-specific configuration information like I/O address, IRQ, or media type. It's empty in the above example, and it will *probably* be empty in your case, because the 3C900 is, like most modern PCI boards, self-configuring.

But if you're configuring an ISA or many PCMCIA NICs, you may have to specify parameters—but the *names* of the parameters vary from board to board, so how do you know what to specify for a given board? You go back to the Registry and do a little digging. Recall the Registry key where you found ProductName in step one? In that same key, you'll find another entry labeled ServiceName, which is usually just the ProductName with a 1 appended to it—in the example of the computer with the 3C900 XL board, it's El90x1. That ServiceName is then the name of the key in HKEY_LOCAL_MACHINE\System\CurrentControlSet\Services that will control the NIC, and that key will contain within *it* a key named Parameters.

For example, I have an older computer with a 3Com ISA Ethernet card in it. As the ISA card is not self-configuring, I've got to somehow tell NT Setup that the board is set to I/O address 300 and IRQ 10. I find that the computer's NIC has a ProductName of Elnk3. Looking further, I find that the ServiceName of the installed NIC is, not surprisingly, Elnk31—just the ProductName with a 1 appended—and so see that there is a key named HKEY_LOCAL_MACHINE\System\CurrentControlSet\Services\Elnk31\Parameters. That key contains value entries InterruptNumber = 0xA and IoBaseAddress = 0x300. I would then specify the [adapterparameters] and [Adapterslist] sections like so:

```
[Adapterslist]
Elnk3 = adapterparameters, c:\drivers
[adapterparameters]
IoBaseAddress = 768
InterruptNumber = 10
```

Here, the ProductName was Elnk3 and the ServiceName was Elnk31. Notice the 768 value for the I/O address and 10 for the interrupt; while the Registry displayed the values in hex, NT Setup scripts need their numeric values in decimal.

This is extremely powerful and quite useful, but if you try this, I've got two words of caution:

- First (and you'll see me saying this again), *make sure you have the latest drivers*. Don't just work with the floppy disk that came with the NIC, get on the Web and download the latest driver disk.

- Second, be aware that unfortunately this procedure won't work for all NICs. All third-party drivers need a support file called OEMSET.INF. It's basically a computer program written in a special language designed by Microsoft specifically for the purpose of helping Setup get a driver settled in. Here's where it turns out to be a problem: in order for NT Setup to do an unattended installation with a particular driver, that driver's OEMSET.INF program must include a specific section intended for unattended installations. Some don't have it, and others *do* have support for unattended installations, or try to—but their programs aren't written right.

Installing New Video Drivers

That's NICs; what about video boards?

NT's automated install process has evolved over the versions, as Microsoft tries to make it a bit easier. Of SCSI, NIC, and display drivers, the automated install process for displays is the easiest. (And we can all be thankful that Microsoft is using that method as its template for automated installs in Windows 2000 Server.) Before getting into the guts of writing installation scripts for display boards, however, let me make a few very important points.

Many video boards nowadays use the higher-speed Advanced Graphics Processor (AGP) type bus slot. And NT 4 has a bit of a problem: it simply cannot install a video driver for an AGP board unless you've installed Service Pack 3. Gotta do it, period. Further, some regular old PCI video cards run into trouble under NT if they're installed in PCI slot 0. Whether or not your video card is in slot 0 can be a little challenging, as some motherboards put slot 0 closest to the edge of the motherboard and others put slot 0 farthest from the edge. The motherboard's documentation *may* say which it is, but in any case you can fix the slot 0 problem also with Service Pack 3.

The problem with this is, of course, that you can't directly install Service Pack 3, you've got to first install NT and then apply Service Pack 3. Insurmountable problem? Not at all; you can't install Service Pack 3 directly, but you *can* install the HAL from Service Pack 3 directly, and it's really just the HAL that needs updating. Here's how.

First, take a look at your I386 installation directory. In that directory, you'll find all of the HALs that NT supplies, files with names like HAL.DL_, HALAST.DL_, HALMCA.DLL, HALMPS.DLL, and HALNCR.DLL.

NOTE   The names that end with an underscore are already compressed—some HALs ship compressed and some ship uncompressed for some reason.

Most systems use the basic HAL.DLL, but yours may be different. In any case, we're going to copy all of the HALs from Service Pack 3 to your I386 directory, so you needn't worry about which HAL is right for your system.

Next, expand the files from Service Pack 3 to a directory. Just put NT4SP3_I.EXE into a directory, open up a command window and type NT4SP3_I.EXE /X, and all the files from Service Pack 3 will be extracted into that directory. Copy all of the files whose names begin with HAL from the Service Pack 3 directory to your I386 directory.

Now when NT installs, it'll automatically install a Service Pack 3 HAL and your AGP or slot 0 PCI video card's drivers will load without trouble. You're now ready to set up your video drivers for a hands-off installation.

NT video drivers comprise three files: an INF file, a SYS file, and a DLL file. The INF file is just a text file that tells NT how to install the other two files. Typically the SYS file goes into \WINNT\SYSTEM32\DRIVERS and the DLL file goes into

\WINNT\SYSTEM32; again, the INF file includes instructions on where to put the files, but those are their normal homes. Don't be confused by the fact that many video cards come with tons and tons of other utility files—in every case I've seen, you can set up a video card for an unattended install with just an INF, SYS, and DLL file. Got those? Then here are the steps to follow.

Return to the \I386\$OEM$ directory and create a DISPLAY directory under it, creating \I386\$OEM$\DISPLAY. Put the three files (INF, SYS, and DLL) into the \I386\$OEM$\DISPLAY directory.

Second, edit your installation script file. It should have a section named "[Display]"; if it doesn't, add one. It should look something like the following:

```
installdriver = 1
ConfigureAtLogon = 0
autoconfirm = 1
inffile = "VIDEOBOARD.INF"
infoption = "Descriptive Name of Video Board"
bitsperpel = 8
xresolution = 640
yresolution = 480
vgacompatible = 0
vrefresh = 60
```

We've already met many of these commands; I've bolded the new ones. You'll probably have to modify those lines, so let's look at them individually. Installdriver = 1, ConfigureAtLogon = 0, and Autoconfirm = 1 all tell NT Setup to do the installation automatically, and not to stop and ask you for information. As with all lines in an installation script file, case doesn't matter, but spaces do; be sure to leave a space on either side of the equals sign.

As you know, the bitsperpel, xresolution, yresolution, vgacompatible, and vrefresh values describe the default video mode. The tricky part is that it's fairly important that you get these right, as video drivers can be kind of finicky. For example, the Chips and Technologies video chip in my Digital Ultra HiNote II will only work with an unattended setup if I set the display to 800×600, 65,536 colors. Typical values for bitsperpel are 8 (256 colors), 16 (65,536 colors) or 24 (16,777,216 colors). You can get most video boards to work fine even if you leave out the vrefresh and vgacompatible values.

But how to know the proper values for xresolution, yresolution, and bitsperpel? There are three possible strategies. One is to simply do a normal attended installation of NT, install the video driver, reboot, and see what resolution it comes up in the first time. Second, call the vendor to find out. Now that we've had a little laugh, there's also the third method: guess. Ninety percent of the boards seem to be happy starting up in $640 \times 480 \times 256$ color (8 bitsperpel) mode. For other boards, sadly, you've just got to experiment—and if you must do that, you might as well do an attended installation to gather the proper values. (This assumes that you're doing unattended installs of more than one computer with this video board, of course.)

TIP   And remember that vrefresh = 1 is worth trying, as it just tells the video board to use whatever vertical refresh rate is the hardware default.

The inffile parameter should name the INF file that you put into the I386\ OEM\Display. The infoption tries to use an English-like, colloquial description of a display board. But where to find this colloquial description? You *can* decipher the INF file, but there's another way. Put the three files on a floppy and walk over to a working NT machine. Open the Control Panel, choose Display, and click the Settings tab. Click the Display Type button and a dialog box will appear which tells you what drivers are currently loaded for your display board. Click Change and Have Disk, insert the floppy and click OK. A Change Display dialog will appear and, in a field labeled Display, you'll see the descriptive name for this driver. Put that value in infoption—and your installation script will be ready to go. (Cancel out of the dialog box on the already-functioning NT machine, by the way.) For example, I recently put a no-name video board based on the S3 Virge chip into a system; the vanilla installation script looked like this (again, new stuff in bold):

```
[Unattended]
OEMPreinstall = yes
OEMSkipEula = yes
NoWaitAfterTextMode = 1
NoWaitAfterGUIMode = 1
[UserData]
FullName = "Mark Minasi"
ComputerName = "MINTAKA"
ProductId = "123-4567890"
[GuiUnattended]
OEMSkipWelcome = 1
OEMBlankAdminPassword = 1
TimeZone = "(GMT-05:00) Eastern Time (US & Canada)"
```

```
AdvServerType = servernt
[LicenseFilePrintData]
AutoMode = PerSeat
[Network]
InstallAdapters = Adapterslist
InstallProtocols = ProtocolsSection
InstallServices = ServicesSection
JoinDomain = ORION
[AdaptersList]
E190x = NICParms, c:\drivers
[NICParms]
[ProtocolsSection]
TC = TCParamSection
[TCParamSection]
DHCP = yes
[Display]
ConfigureAtLogon = 0
AutoConfirm = 1
infFile = "s3.inf"
InfOption = "S3 Incorporated Display Driver v2.00.17"
InstallDriver = 1
BitsPerPel = 8
XResolution = 640
YResolution = 480
Vrefresh = 60
```

So, in sum: add the DISPLAY directory, copy the three files into there, and make the modifications to UNATTEND.TXT, and you'll probably have no trouble with an unattended video installation. Again, however, let me make a couple of points.

First, before you embark on this (and I know I've already said this), GET THE LATEST DRIVERS. I don't have space to copy that 100 times, so just imagine that I did. I know in my heart that newer drivers often solve problems, but I sometimes forget it and this has cost me *days* as I struggle with some troublesome driver, only to recall that *I haven't even looked on the Web for a newer driver—I just trusted the floppy that came in the box*. One thousand lashes for the balding fool… This is a true story; while researching this section of the book I spent seven days trying in vain to find the magic words that would make a no-name S3 Virge video board's drivers install correctly. After the penny dropped that I hadn't looked for new drivers, five minutes' surfing got me a new set of drivers that I could install unattended without trouble.

Second, understand that there are some video boards that this will never work on. I bought a Creative Laboratories Graphics Blaster 3D and hand-installed the drivers that came with the board—no problem. But try an *unattended* install? Forget it. I never could make it work. I'm told by Microsoft folks that this has to do with how the initialization code is written in a driver, and it makes sense. So understand that not *every* unattended problem can be solved, and remember that sometimes discretion is the better part of valor.

Installing New Mass Storage Controller Drivers

Of NICs, display, and new SCSI drivers, I saved the best (that is, the most complex) for last. You load new *mass storage controller*—let's call them SCSI for short—drivers using a method called the TXTSETUP.OEM method.

As you know by now, NT Setup has two main phases: the text setup part and the GUI setup part. The text setup part basically runs under DOS or a DOS-like loader. That's why when you put NT on a system and tell Setup to make drive C: NTFS, Setup goes through the whole process on a FAT drive and then, as its final act, it converts the FAT drive to NTFS—the DOS-like part of the text setup doesn't know how to work with NTFS.

While much of NT Setup is in the graphical part—clearly Microsoft would eventually like to make the whole thing graphical one day, look at the Windows 98 Setup program for comparison—certain basic, low-level things require a bit of bootstrapping, so to speak. The kind of mouse or video board or printer that your computer has can wait for a bit, but an NT Setup program must know how to read and write a hard disk fairly soon in the process. Thus, installing disk adapter drivers happens in the text part of setup. As you read earlier, in general NT drivers are usually accompanied by a file called OEMSETUP.INF which instructs NT where and how to load the drivers. And OEMSETUP.INF files are usually sufficient for doing unattended installs of most drivers, as the vast majority of the unattended installation process answers questions raised by the *graphical* part of Setup. Loading drivers called for by the text part, however, requires not only an OEMSETUP.INF but also another file: TXTSETUP.OEM.

Suppose you've got a SCSI host adapter (or some kind of whiz-bang EIDE host adapter, for that matter), drivers that are newer than the ones on the 1996 NT 4 CD, or suppose you've got drivers for an adapter that just plain didn't exist back in 1996. (I originally wrote "back in '96," but changed it to "1996" so that this book would be Y2K compliant.) You want to set up an unattended install for a machine with those drivers and/or new hardware. How to do it? First, some ingredients. You'll need

- An OEMSETUP.INF for the board
- A TXTSETUP.OEM for the board
- A driver file

The OEMSETUP.INF and TXTMODE.OEM files are ASCII text files written by the vendor. (In other words, if you can't get them from the vendor, you're out of luck.) The driver file is a program and it will usually have an extension of SYS. You typically get all three files from the vendor of the drive host adapter. So, for example, suppose you go out and buy a brand new BitSlalom host adapter from BitSlalom Scientifics. ("Bits Just Slide Off Your Drive At Olympic Speeds!") There're floppies with drivers in the box, but don't bother even looking at them, because remember one of the main rules of hardware installation:

> *No matter how recently you buy a new board, there will be drivers on the Web site that are newer than the ones that came with the board.*

I know I sound like a broken record about this, but it's important; trust me. So you surf on over to www.bs.com and sure enough, there's a ZIP or self-extracting EXE file containing drivers for NT 4. Download it and open it up, and you get three files: OEMSETUP.INF, TXTSETUP.OEM, and BSNT.SYS. Now that you've got those three files, set up your system for automated install.

Step one: again, you will modify OEM. *Inside* that directory, create a directory called Textmode. Following the example that I've made so far, then, I'd have a directory \I386\OEM\Textmode.

Step two: put copies of the OEMSETUP.INF, TXTMODE.OEM, and driver (BSNT.SYS) files into that Textmode directory.

Step three: modify your unattended setup script file to add a section named [OEMBootFiles]. In the [OEMBootFiles] section, just list the names of the three files in the Textmode directory. In my example, the [OEMBootFiles] section would look like this:

```
[OEMBootFiles]
OEMSETUP.INF
TXTMODE.OEM
BSNT.SYS
```

Step four: modify the unattended setup script file again, this time to add a section called [MassStorageDevices]. It will have a line (or lines, if you've got more than one type of host adapter) describing the host adapter. The line looks like

```
"Some descriptive text in quotes" = "OEM"
```

The quotes really *do* go in there, and "OEM" is just a magic word you've always got to use. For example, for the BitSlalom, it might look like

```
[MassStorageDevices]
"BitSlalom PCI Wide SCSI Adapter" = "OEM"
```

But where do you get that magic name, like "BitSlalom PCI Wide SCSI Adapter?" It's a string that must match up with a string inside TXTSETUP.OEM. To see *where* that string is, let's take a look inside a TXTSETUP.OEM. Here's the one for BitSlalom:

```
[Disks]
disk1 = "BitSlalom Scientifics NT Drivers Disk", \drvdisk, \

[Defaults]
scsi = bscsi

[scsi]
bscsi =   " BitSlalom PCI Wide SCSI Adapter"

[Files.scsi.bscsi]
driver = disk1, bsnt.sys, bsnt
inf    = disk1, oemsetup.inf

[Config.bsnt]
value = "", tag, REG_DWORD, 1
```

Take a peek through that, and you can see two things in quotes: "BitSlalom Scientifics NT Drivers Disk" and "BitSlalom PCI Wide SCSI Adapter." The first one is in the [Disks] section, and it describes the drivers disk. The purpose of it is that if you tell the system to install the BitSlalom driver and it can't find the drivers for the adapter, you'll see a dialog box that says something like "Insert the following disk: / BitSlalom Scientifics NT Drivers Disk / Press OK when ready." The only other descriptive string that you're likely to see is the descriptive name for your driver. Once in a great while you'll see several descriptive strings in addition to the string describing the disk; that would happen if your hardware vendor wrote one TXTSETUP.OEM for multiple SCSI boards. In that case, just read the descriptions, and it'll be obvious which one applies to your SCSI board. Another way to find the descriptive name is to hand-install the driver from the Control Panel—click the Have Disk button, insert the drivers disk and click OK, and then a descriptive name will appear.

You may have to modify TXTSETUP.OEM itself in one way. Look at a line from the [Disks] section of one real-life SCSI adapter:

```
d2 = "Adaptec 7800 Family Manager Set v2.11 for Windows NT 4.0",
\disk1, \winnt\4_0
```

The last parameter on that line, \winnt\4_0, refers to the fact that the actual Adaptec drivers floppy has a \winnt directory on it, and a directory named 4_0 beneath *that*. The driver files OEMSETUP.INF and AIC7800.SYS (the Adaptec driver's name) can be found in A:\winnt\4_0—that's why the directory reference appears at the end of the line. But I've advised you to just take the TXTSETUP .OEM, OEMSETUP.INF, and whatever the particular SYS file's name is and put them all in the \I386\OEM\Textmode directory. If you leave the end of the [Disks] line as winnt\4_0, then NT Setup will look for the drivers in \I386\ OEM\Textmode\winnt\4_0. But what if you change the [Disks] line so that it looks like this:

```
d2 = "Adaptec 7800 Family Manager Set v2.11 for Windows NT 4.0",
\disk1, \
```

Then NT Setup will look in \I386\OEM\Textmode.

Summarizing then—to do an automated install on a SCSI driver, you should first locate the TXTSETUP.OEM, OEMSETUP.INF, and specific SYS driver file for the SCSI board. Then add an [OEMBootFiles] section to your installation script naming those three files. Create a OEM\Textmode directory and copy the three files to that directory. Modify the TXTSETUP.OEM's [Disks] section to remove any references to a directory structure below OEM\Textmode. Then find the descriptive name for your SCSI board and create a [MassStorageDevices] section referring to it. Yes, it's a bit more complex than loading a display driver was, but Microsoft's working on making this process much easier for Windows 2000 Server, if that's any consolation…

Pre-choosing a Mass Storage Driver

One problem with forcing NT to use some driver, like a new Adaptec driver or the mythical Bitslalom driver, is that once you tell NT, "Hey, I'm going to help you and choose a driver," NT gets stupid and refuses to do any auto-detection. That's a pain because in many cases your CD-ROM is attached to the standard EIDE host adapter built into 99.99 percent of the motherboards these days.

For that reason, you may find yourself needing to tell NT to not only load some oddball driver, but also to load the EIDE driver. To do that, add the following line to the [MassStorageDrivers] section:

```
"IDE CD-ROM (ATAPI 1.2)/PCI IDE Controller" = "RETAIL"
```

You may even want to use this feature even if you *don't* have an oddball SCSI adapter. For example, I've got a system like many with the Adaptec 2940 SCSI host adapter and the standard EIDE adapter as well; my [MassStorageDrivers] section looks like this:

[MassStorageDrivers]

```
"IDE CD-ROM (ATAPI 1.2)/PCI IDE Controller" = "RETAIL"
"Adaptec AHA-294X/AHA-394X/AIC-78XX SCSI Controller" = "RETAIL"
```

In a situation like this, you needn't have a TXTSETUP.OEM file; the RETAIL is the signal to NT to just shut up and use the supplied driver.

At that point, you'll be able to do a hands-off install of any mass storage controller that you like. Cool, eh?

Just a reminder: while NT will install NIC drivers, video drivers, and SCSI drivers hands-off, I have not found a way to do this with sound cards. A Microsoft person once told me that there's a way, but he didn't know exactly how, and he claimed it was on Microsoft's Web site somewhere. I've not found it, but I mention this in case you have the time and determination to try to find it. Another reason to look forward to Windows 2000 Server…

Getting to I386: A Network Boot Disk

By now, you've got I386 sitting on a server somewhere. On that same server you've probably also got an installation script file, in fact the *perfect* script file. You've got a brand-new machine that you want to put NT on and you're pretty much ready, except for one thing: how do you get the new machine attached to the I386 share on the network in the first place?

The key is to create a simple boot floppy with just enough DOS on it to start up and just enough network client code to get the machine attached to the network. How do you create such a floppy? With a bootable floppy and a program supplied with NT Server called the *Network Client Administrator*. In this section, I'll describe how to use Network Client Administrator to build floppies that can jump-start your installations.

NOTE   I should note that you'll need to have at least one machine running NT Server from which you can create a network client boot disk. Only NT Server contains the Network Client Administrator—the tool you'll need to install the network client on your bootable floppy disk. If you don't have NT Server running on any machines yet, you'll have to install it and then create your bootable installation floppy.

Creating the Boot Disk

Begin making your boot disk by creating a bootable DOS disk. You can create this disk in either DOS or Windows 95 (sorry, NT users, NT doesn't format disks properly to do this), running SYS A: at the command prompt. Then clear a bit of space off the floppy by un-hiding and deleting DRVSPACE.BIN or DBLSPACE.BIN—you won't need them and there's only barely enough space on a floppy to create an all-in-one boot disk.

Once you've got a bootable floppy, you can add files to it to make it network-ready. Go to an NT Server machine and log on as an administrator. In the Start Menu, click Administrative Tools ➤ Network Client Administrator (see Figure 3.37). Click the Make Network Installation Startup Disk radio button and click Continue. The next dialog box will ask you where the shared directory containing the Network Client installation files is located (see Figure 3.38). Here, you're given four choices: use an already existing directory on the machine containing the network client information, create a share of the source files on your NT Server CD, create a shared source directory on your hard disk, or use an existing shared directory. Your choice depends on two things:

- If you have a CLIENTS folder already existing on your server, select either Use Existing Path if the folder exists locally or Use Existing Shared Directory if the CLIENTS folder exists elsewhere on the network. If the folder does exist elsewhere but isn't shared, share the folder before selecting this option.

- If a CLIENTS folder doesn't exist, you have your choice of using the files residing on your NT Server CD or creating a shared source directory on your server. If you choose to use the CD files, create the share name and NT will automatically create the share for the folder. If you don't want others to have access to your CD-ROM, you can always create a shared folder on your server. Determine the path where you'll install the files and provide NT with a share name.

FIGURE 3.37:

Network Client Administrator

FIGURE 3.38:

Location of shared client directory

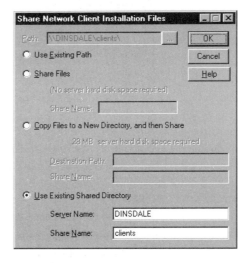

Click OK and NT will either use the existing CLIENTS folder or create a new one, depending on the option you've chosen.

Next comes the tricky part: selecting your network card (Figure 3.39). This is the part where you'll wish you had put the same card on every machine. For some reason, Microsoft neglected to provide an automatic detection routine in its setup program. This means that you're going to need to know what type of card resides on each machine. Also, if you're going to be using this disk on machines using different network cards, you're going to have to make a disk for each individual card.

FIGURE 3.39:

Selecting a network card

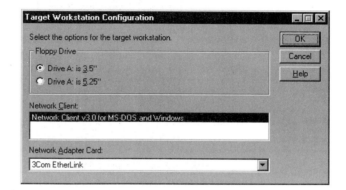

NOTE

One more thing: the list of network cards is rather small. This doesn't mean that the list is reserved to just the most popular cards. I have a 3Com Etherlink III PCI Bus-Master that I was testing this out on and, wouldn't you know it, it wasn't on the list. Of course, practically every other 3Com card was. Fortunately, there's a way to work around this problem. I'll talk about that when I'm finished telling you how to create the boot disk. If your card isn't listed, pick any one from the list and we'll soon make your card work.

Once you've selected your network card, click OK and you'll see the dialog box shown in Figure 3.40. In order for your computer to run the network client and connect to the network, it must have a name, just like any other workstation or server. We'll call ours Clyde. If the machine already has a name on the network, use that one. Since we're only using the network client disk to obtain a network connection to start installing NT, the computer name is moot. It'll be easier to use an existing name than to have to go to the server and create 20 new computer names just to allow them to connect to your network, especially when you'll only use the client once.

FIGURE 3.40:

Network logon settings

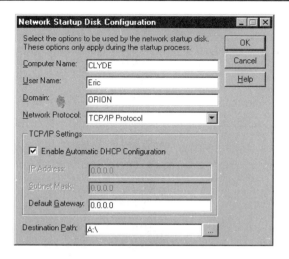

You must also provide NT with a username with administrative privileges, the domain name, and the network protocol. The only protocols listed in the dialog box will be the one(s) in use by the server that you're creating the boot disk on. For example, if you have a server that's only running TCP/IP, then TCP/IP will be the only protocol listed. If you want the network clients to access the network via NetBEUI, for instance, then you'll have to add NetBEUI to your protocol list using the Network applet in the Control Panel.

If you're running TCP/IP, you can check the DHCP configuration box in order to let your DHCP server configure your network client's IP address. Otherwise, you must provide Setup with a static IP address, Subnet Mask, and Default Gateway in order to access the network. If you're not running TCP/IP, this section will be grayed out.

Click OK and you'll see a confirmation screen summarizing everything we've discussed. Click OK if you're sure that the settings are correct and Setup will create your boot disk. If you're not sure, click Cancel and you can go back to the previous screen to make your changes.

Using Unsupported Network Cards with the Network Client Administrator

Unfortunately, NT 4 shipped in mid-1996 and most network cards that you'd buy today didn't even *exist* then, rendering the chances that NCA supports your network card pretty small. So what do you do if you want to prepare a boot floppy for a computer containing a NIC that isn't supported by the NCA? Never fear—you can work around this problem by editing a couple of files on your boot disk.

Before we start our file manipulation, you'll need to put a copy of your NDIS driver on the boot disk. The driver will have a name such as *FILENAME*.DOS, where FILENAME is hopefully easy to associate with the name of your network card.

Next, edit the NET\PROTOCOL.INI file, and change the old driver name to the same name as your driver. For example, let's say we're trying to use my 3Com PCI Bus-Master card. Since there isn't one listed, we'll pick a plain-vanilla 3Com Etherlink card. As I said before, it really doesn't matter which one you pick. The 3Com Etherlink PROTOCOL.INI has a number of entries with the filename ELNK$. However, the filename of our 3Com PCI Bus-Master driver is EL59X$ (the dollar sign is put at the end to denote that it's a filename). Using a text editor, you should be able to do a cut-and-paste or search-and-replace to make this change easily.

Save the PROTOCOL.INI file and open SYSTEM.INI. In the [network drivers] section, you'll see a line that says netcard=elnk.dos. Change the filename to EL59X.DOS and save the file.

You still have to make a few more changes. If you're installing NT on a machine with 16MB or less of RAM installed, then you'll have to add this line to A:\CONFIG.SYS (without this line, your machine will run out of memory when it tries to start the network client):

```
device=a:\net\himem.sys
```

Also, in order for your NT installation to start automatically, we'll have to add a line or two to your AUTOEXEC.BAT file. I say "two" because it depends on whether you created your DOS boot disk in DOS or Windows 95.

1. Open the A:\AUTOEXEC.BAT file and replace the last line in the file with this line:

   ```
   Net use z: \\SERVERNAME\I386
   ```

   where *SERVERNAME* is the name of the machine where the NT installation source files are kept.

2. Then, make these the last two lines in the file:

   ```
   z:
   WINNT /u:filename.txt /s:sourcepath /t:temp
   ```

where *FILENAME*.TXT is the path and filename of your unattended batch file, *sourcepath* is the location of the \I386 folder that you specified in the AUTOEXEC.BAT file and *temp* is the partition on which the temporary installation files will be located (for more information, see the section on installing NT).

If you created your DOS boot disk using Windows 95, there's one more thing you're going to have to do. Make this the first line in A:\AUTOEXEC.BAT:

```
Lock c:
```

Without this line, the boot will come to a crashing halt. If you put this line in even though you've created the boot disk using DOS, you'll see an error when booting, but don't worry about it; that's only because DOS doesn't recognize the LOCK command.

OK, *now* you're done. Pop the disk into your machine and reboot it. Here's a summary of what will happen:

- Your machine will boot into DOS (or 95, again depending on which operating system you used to create the system disk).

- If you inserted the LOCK command in AUTOEXEC.BAT, you'll be notified that in order to continue, you'll have to permit direct disk access to occur. Press Y to continue.

- The Network Client will connect to the network.

- You'll be asked to provide a user ID and password (OK, so maybe you won't be able to just "walk away," but you can at least get away from the machine with the least amount of effort).

- The client will map a drive to your network's I386 directory and start the unattended installation.

WARNING   Once the installation has started, take the disk out of the floppy drive. If you leave it in, the computer will run the network client all over again and start the installation from the beginning after it reboots the first time. Once you've started the installation, there's no need for the disk any more. This will allow you to start the installation on a number of machines using a small number of disks.

And that's it! In 30–40 minutes, you'll have yourself a brand-new NT installation.

Extending the Power of Setup: CMDLINES.TXT and Sysdiff

Installing NT hands-off is cool. But the truth is that a simple operating system installation is only the start of your job. Most NT installations require a bunch of small tweaks (like telling the Recycle Bin not to ask for confirmation every time you dump a file) and large additions like entire applications. There are many good third-party tools to assist you in doing post-installation configuration of NT, but why spend that money when you have CMDLINES.TXT, REGEDIT, and Sysdiff, all free in the box with NT?

Using CMDLINES.TXT and REGEDIT

If you're like me, you find it irritating to have to tell every new NT installation that you *don't* want My Computer to open window upon window, but instead to do all of your browsing in one window. And what *is* the point of the Recycle Bin asking if you really want to recycle a file, anyway? Given that I can open up the Recycle Bin and recover a file, why annoy me with a confirmation dialog box? And while we're at it, I *want* to see hidden files, I want to see the file extensions, turn off the Autorun feature of CD-ROMs, get rid of that stupid "Tip of the Day" screen, and put the entire file path in the title bar! And while we're at it, let's install Service Pack 3 or 4 automatically. Sound like a lot of work? It isn't.

The key to making this all work is a file named CMDLINES.TXT, one of the less documented features of the NT Setup program. Simplified, it works like this: once Setup is almost completely finished, it looks for CMDLINES.TXT, which is basically a batch file. Setup then executes those commands just as if it were regular old NT rather than Setup running the commands. More specifically, you've got to do a few things to make CMDLINES.TXT work.

First, as far as I can tell, Setup only notices CMDLINES.TXT if you are using an installation script with the OEMPREINSTALL option enabled.

Second, as you've already seen is the case when you enable OemPreinstall, you must have a directory named OEM in your \I386 directory. Suppose for the purposes of this section that I've got a server named SHAREMACH which offers a share from which NT can be installed called (unimaginatively) \\SHAREMACH\ I386. This way, I install NT on a new machine by booting DOS and the MS-DOS Network Client on the new machine, then attach to \\SHAREMACH\I386, and install from over the network. As a matter of fact, I needn't even map to \\SHAREMACH\I386, I can just start an NT install like so:

```
Winnt /s:\\sharemach\i386 /u:simple.inf
```

What's OEM doing this time? It's where CMDLINES.TXT must go—in \\sharemach\i386\oem\cmdlines.txt, in this example.

Third, CMDLINES.TXT isn't just a straightforward batch file, it looks like this:

```
[Commands]
"first command"
"second command", and so on...
```

CMDLINES.TXT is an ASCII file, and its first line should be [Commands]. Each command you want executed should follow, and each command *must be surrounded by double quotes*. If NT Setup finds oempreinstall = yes, a OEM directory, and a properly formatted CMDLINES.TXT file, then your commands will be executed.

Now let's make the Registry fixes. (I apologize that I'm discussing Registry fixes before the Registry chapter, but it can't be helped—my guess is that you won't go back and read this section in earnest until you're doing some heavy-duty NT configuration, and by that time you will not only have read the Registry chapter, you'll be quite experienced in working in the Registry.) We'll need a command-line tool that can modify an NT Registry. Most people don't know it, but the built-in Registry editor REGEDIT has command-line options that make it plenty powerful for automated Registry changes.

Suppose, for example, that I want to disable Autorun on my CD-ROM drive. I can do that by modifying the Autorun value entry, which is in HKEY_LOCAL_MACHINE\System\CurrentControlSet\Services\CDROM. Autorun is a REG_DWORD parameter; set it to 0, and CD-ROMs don't autorun when you insert them any more. But I don't *want* to hand-edit the Registry—and that's where REGEDIT comes to the rescue. Just create a four-line ASCII file (call it CDFIX.REG) with these contents:

```
REGEDIT4

[HKEY_LOCAL_MACHINE\SYSTEM\CurrentControlSet\Services\Cdrom]
"AutoRun"=dword:00000000
```

Note the blank line between REGEDIT4 and [HKEY...; you need that.

Now open up a command line and tell REGEDIT to apply this change by typing **regedit /s cdfix.reg**; the /s means, "Be silent, REGEDIT!"—and so you won't get a message. But reboot your NT machine and you'll find that Autorun is now disabled. Notice how what I could call the REGEDIT "command language" works: the first line is REGEDIT4, then a blank line, then you indicate what key you want to work with, in brackets, and then the value entry. You can put a whole bunch of changes into a single file. I've collected my favorite changes—the ones I cited earlier—in the following lines:

```
REGEDIT4

[HKEY_CURRENT_USER\Software\Microsoft\Windows\CurrentVersion\Explorer]
"ShellState"=hex:10,00,00,00,07,00,00,00,00,00,00,00,00,00,00,00

[HKEY_CURRENT_USER\Software\Microsoft\Windows\CurrentVersion\Explorer\C
abinetState]
"Settings"=hex:0c,00,01,00,0b,01,00,00,60,00,00,00

[HKEY_CURRENT_USER\Software\Microsoft\Windows\CurrentVersion\Explorer\S
treams\4]
"ViewView"=hex:1c,00,a4,77,04,00,00,00,00,00,00,00,00,00,1c,00,03,00,00
,00,01,\
  00,00,00,03,00,00,00

[HKEY_CURRENT_USER\Software\Microsoft\Notepad]
"fWrap"=dword:00000001

[HKEY_CURRENT_USER\Software\Microsoft\Windows\CurrentVersion\Explorer\T
ips]
"DisplayInitialTipWindow"=dword:00000000
"Show"=hex:00,00,00,00
"Next"=hex:03,00

[HKEY_LOCAL_MACHINE\SYSTEM\CurrentControlSet\Services\Cdrom]
"AutoRun"=dword:00000000
```

Let's see how to make this work with CMDLINES.TXT.

First, collect all of those REGEDIT changes into an ASCII file; let's call it FIXNT.REG. Copy that file to the OEM directory. Next, help out Setup by copying REGEDIT.EXE itself to OEM. Then create a CMDLINES.TXT (which *also* goes in OEM) with these contents:

```
[Commands]
".\regedit /s .\fixnt.reg"
```

Note the ".\" references; they're there so that I can be completely sure that Setup can find both REGEDIT and FIXNT.REG. ".\" is simply a way of pointing to the current directory. By default, all of the files in OEM on the distribution share get copied to the target PC's local hard disk in a directory called C:\$WIN_NT$.~LS\$OEM$, but hard-wiring the entire directory name into the command lines may be self-defeating if you find that you've got to tell Setup to put its temporary files on a directory other than C:; that's why the relative ".\" references make better sense.

Now what about automatically applying Service Pack 3? I keep Service Pack 3 on another share: \\SHARMACH\SP3. According to Microsoft's Knowledge Base, you can run SP3 unattended simply by invoking the command Update –U –Z. So I write the following batch file, SPINST.CMD:

```
net use y: \\sharmach\sp3 /persistent:no /user:mydomain\instguy sword-
fish
ren %systemroot%\system32\schannel.dll sc1.dll
y:
update –u –z
del %systemroot%\system32\schannel.dll
ren %systemroot\system32\sc1.dll schannel.dll
net use y: /delete
```

Let's examine this batch file line by line.

First, why did I write a batch file instead of putting these lines in CMDLINES .TXT? Because CMDLINES.TXT is a bit of a pain to work with, truthfully—it doesn't work well with commands that are internal to CMD.EXE, the NT command processor. Second, all of those quotation marks and ".\"s get old after a while.

Anyway, to examine the batch file: first, it attaches to the network share that contains the Service Pack files. The /user: parameter gets authorization to access the share. Instguy is the username for a user in a domain named Mydomain whose password is swordfish. Yes, that's right, you've got a password in a batch file; I can't figure a way around it. The best thing I can offer is to ensure that instguy has no power whatsoever save for Read access to the SP3 share.

TIP

Note you can simplify things a bit with an alternate strategy: just copy all of the Service Pack 3 files to \I386\OEM; then all you need are the commands that handle schannel.dll. I originally took the "put the service pack on a share" approach thinking I'd save copying time, but the more I do this, the more I come to think that it's just smarter to put the service pack files in OEM.

Next, note that I'm re-naming SCHANNEL.DLL; if I don't do that, then the SP3 install stops dead and won't go further until I confirm that no, I *don't* want it to overwrite my 128-bit security with SP3's lame old 40-bit security.

TIP

Actually, the best way to handle this is to get the version of the Service Pack that includes the 128-bit security. You can order that directly from Microsoft. You can *also* download it from the Web, but only if you're sitting at a machine that is (1) in Canada or the US and (2) has a registered DNS name. The current URL for the 128-bit version is http://mssecure.www.conxion.com/cgi-bin/ntitar.pl, although that may change and you might have to do a bit of surfing to find it. You can also call (800) 370-8758 or fax (716) 873-0906 to order the CD rather than download-ing the files. Microsoft re-arranges their phones and Web site pretty regularly, so if this URL or phone numbers no longer work as you read this, please don't e-mail me, as I don't keep close enough track of where Microsoft keeps things to be able to help.

Despite the fact that –U is supposed to be the "unattended" option, there is apparently no way to *truly* say, "When I say unattended, I *mean* unattended!" So by first renaming SCHANNEL.DLL to something else, SP3 can install *its* SCHAN-NEL.DLL without complaint, as it's not overwriting anything. (The other way around this is to get the version of SP3 or SP4 with the 128-bit security, as noted above.)

The next couple of lines start off the Service Pack 3 installation. I then delete the newer 40-bit SCHANNEL.DLL and restore the original file with no muss and no fuss, removing the need for an SP3 prompt and keeping this whole process hands-off.

CMDLINES.TXT now looks like this:

```
[Commands]
".\regedit /s .\fixnt.reg"
".\spinst.cmd"
```

What about automatically installing Service Pack 4? Service Pack 4 comes all bundled up as a file called SP4I386.EXE, a 32MB-sized whopper that is probably the best argument for buying a cable modem that I've come across recently. You must first extract it into its separate files before you can do an automated install with it; to do that, just type **SP4I386 –X**. It will then prompt you, asking where to put the files. Your best bet is to tell SP4 to just unpack itself into the \I386\OEM

directory that you're doing your automated installs from. Then, assuming you've got the 128-bit version of SP4, SPINST.CMD can look like the following:

```
update\update.exe -U -Z -O -N
```

And by the way, case doesn't matter in this command or in the options.

Thus, CMDLINES.TXT and REGEDIT united can let you do a fair amount of heavy-duty reconfiguration, completely automated. But how did I know what parts of the Registry to change in order to do things like shut up the Recycle Bin? Again, with REGEDIT. REGEDIT has an export option that's quite useful. With it, I can dump an ASCII file describing the Registry at any point. Here's how I did it:

1. I dumped an ASCII export of the Registry before telling the Recycle Bin not to ask for confirmations. (REGEDIT will export if you click Registry ➤ Export Registry File.)

2. I told the Recycle Bin not to ask for confirmations.

3. Once more I used REGEDIT to export the Registry to a large ASCII file.

4. Finally, I used the command-line command FC (file compare) to compare the old and new exported ASCII files. FC showed just the differences.

You can alternatively track before-and-after changes with Sysdiff, explained in the next section.

Adding Applications Using the Sysdiff Utility

Being able to do REGEDIT tweaks is useful, but what about propagating bigger changes? In many cases I don't want to just put NT on a computer, I also want to put an application like Office on that computer. (That's more likely if I'm installing an NT Workstation, of course.) Installing Office or, for that matter, most modern applications is as complex as installing the operating system itself. It involves a complex setup program that requires as much baby-sitting as NT Setup did. And that's true not only for Workstation applications—putting SQL Server on an NT Server machine is no simpler.

Overview

It would be great to somehow simplify the process of getting applications onto a computer. But sometimes you don't want to install an entire application; instead, you may want to just replace a single file on a large number of computers, or perhaps to try out some change on one computer and, if it works out fine, to duplicate that change to other computers easily.

NT ships with a free tool to do that, called *Sysdiff*. Sysdiff is a utility that lets you quickly encapsulate (and reproduce) a set of changes to a computer. Suppose you wanted to install an application (say it's called BugWord) to 100 computers. Here's how Sysdiff could help:

- You start with a computer that does not have BugWord on it.

- Run Sysdiff on that computer. Sysdiff essentially takes a snapshot of the computer "before BugWord."

- Install BugWord on the computer.

- Run Sysdiff again on the computer, directing it to note the differences.

- Sysdiff runs, creating a large file of the differences.

The resulting Sysdiff *difference file* contains not only any Registry changes, but also the actual contents of any files that it finds on that system that weren't there before—that is, the BugWord application files. So, for example, if BugWord took up 10MB of file space on a computer once installed, then the resulting Sysdiff difference file would be 10MB or more in size. Sysdiff will then apply that difference file to any computer that you like.

Big deal, you might be thinking, so instead of running the BugWord setup program I run Sysdiff and the difference file instead—where are the savings? Actually, the results are amazing: where it might have taken 20 minutes for that 10MB program to load on the initial computer, applying a Sysdiff difference file takes only *seconds*. And the result is that the new computer now has a working copy of the 10MB application, just as if you'd stood over the computer baby-sitting the BugWord setup program. And, of course, the whole process is easily automated—you can apply the difference file to the new NT Server or Workstation installation by using a command in the OEM/Cmdlines.txt file.

Because the difference file contains all the binary files, initialization settings, and Registry settings for the applications, it can be a rather large file, and therefore installing the whole works at once can take awhile. There is another way, however; you can create an INF file from the difference file, which only contains the Registry and initialization settings. The command that creates the INF will also create a directory tree within the OEM directory containing all the files in the difference file. These files, copied along with the other files required by Setup, are in place when the INF is called into play by the OEM/Cmdlines.txt file during installation.

You'll find SYSDIFF.EXE and its configuration file, SYSDIFF.INF, on your NT Server CD in the \Support\Deptools\<system> directory, where <system> is I386 (for Intel-based computers), Alpha (for Alpha-based computers), MIPS (for MIPS-based computers), or PPC (for PowerPC computers).

NOTE
Microsoft has revised Sysdiff a few times, so it's a *very* good idea to look in ftp://ftp.microsoft.com/bussys/winnt/winnt-public/fixes/usa/nt40/utilities/ Sysdiff-fix for the latest version of Sysdiff—I found that the version of Sysdiff on the NT 4 CD-ROM tended to crash in mid-operation, leaving nothing but a Dr. Watson screen.

A Sysdiff Example

Let's walk through an example of using Sysdiff first to create a difference file for Microsoft Word and then to apply that difference file in an unattended installation.

1. Copy SYSDIFF.EXE and SYSDIFF.INF to the NT root directory on a computer currently running Windows NT Server (we'll call this the reference computer). This computer should be the same CPU type as the destination computer(s) on which you're installing NT and applying the difference file. You'll then take a snapshot of the reference computer. The syntax for this command is as follows:

   ```
   sysdiff /snap [/log:LogFile] SnapshotFile
   ```

   where *LogFile* is the name of an optional log file; *SnapshotFile* is the name of the file that will contain the snapshot of the reference computer. For example, I'll create a snapshot file called "snap" using the following command line:

   ```
   sysdiff /snap /log:snaplog snap
   ```

2. Install the applications on the reference computer that you want to have on the server you are installing. For example, I'll install Microsoft Word on my C: drive in the \MSoffice directory.

that by opening up My Computer and modifying your folder options, but what did that change in the Registry? Sysdiff can tell you. Just run a snapshot of your system with Sysdiff, then open My Computer and tell it that you only want to see one window at a time, then run Sysdiff and create a difference file. Then run a /dump on the difference file and the Registry change will be right there on the file—very neat.

Now that you have this file DifferenceFile, how do you apply it to another NT machine? Just copy SYSDIFF.EXE, SYSDIFF.INF, and DifferenceFile to the new NT machine and tell Sysdiff to apply the changes like so:

```
Sysdiff /apply /m differencefile
```

You'll instantly have Word on the new machine.

> **NOTE** Sysdiff /apply can *only* apply a difference file to a PC if that PC has NT installed on the same drive letter and directory as the original reference PC.

Distributing and Using Difference Files

Now that I've got a file named DifferenceFile that lets me quickly put Word on a system, how can I use it to make automated installs easier?

Well, the first thing to do is to rename the thing to an eight-letter name—the early part of NT Setup isn't too smart when it comes to long filenames. Let's rename it as APPLYWRD.

Second, copy SYSDIFF.EXE, SYSDIFF.INF, and APPLYWRD to the \I386\OEM directory.

Third, add this command to the CMDLINES.TXT file (assuming that there already *is* a CMDLINES.TXT file; if not, then make one as described a few pages back):

```
".\sysdiff /apply /m .\applywrd"
```

> **NOTE** Remember that CMDLINES.TXT needs those quotes or this won't work.

An Even Better Way to Distribute Difference Files

Putting a Sysdiff /apply into a CMDLINES.TXT is *one* way to automatically install applications—but Sysdiff's got another way, an even more automatic one.

I've got a Sysdiff difference file called APPLYWRD; recall that earlier I said that I put the I386 files on a share called \\SHAREMACH\I386. I can tell Sysdiff to set up \\SHAREMACH\I386 so that whenever you do an OEM installation (that is, whenever you set OEMPreinstall = yes), NT Setup will also apply the APPLY-WRD file—meaning that whenever you install NT, you get Word, as well. Open up a command prompt and just type

```
Sysdiff /inf /m /u applywrd \\sharemach\I386
```

Sysdiff then creates directories inside \\SHAREMACH\I386 with the Word distribution files, and *also* modifies CMDLINES.TXT to include a command to make NT Setup automatically invoke Sysdiff to complete Word's installation.

To use Sysdiff's /inf option, you've got to first create a difference file, and you've got to have an installation distribution point somewhere, like \\SHAREMACH\I386. Then invoke Sysdiff like so:

```
Sysdiff /inf /m /u name_of_difference_file
location_of_installation_distribution_files.
```

The rest is automatic—one of those terrific little-known features of NT.

Cool OEM Tricks

CMDLINES.TXT, REGEDIT, and SYSDIFF are cool tools, but sometimes all you want to do is simply copy a file. As it turns out, NT Setup lets you do that *extremely* easily, with OEM.

I've already told you that you can create directories I386\$OEM$\C, I386\ OEM\D, and so on, that you can create directory structures within them, and that you can put files in those directories. When WINNT or WINNT32 run, they see those directory structures and replicate them on the target PC's hard disk— put a directory I386\$OEM$\C\WORDFILE on the distribution share point, and you'll have a C:\WORDFILE on the target PC. Additionally, any files that were in I386\$OEM$\C\WORDFILE would be copied to C:\WORDFILE. You can use this to distribute documents or any other file that you consider to be part of a new PC's basic needs.

OEM lets you place things into the NT directory, as well, using the OEM\$$ construct. Anything that WINNT/WINNT32 finds in OEM\$$ it will direct Setup to place in the \WINNT directory of the target PC once Setup completes. So, for example, suppose you wanted to put a driver called SOMEDISP.SYS into NT's drivers directory, \WINNT\SYSTEM32\DRIVERS. Just create a directory I386\$OEM$\$$\System32\Drivers and put a copy of SOMEDISP.SYS into that directory. The result will be that whenever someone installs NT to a computer from that particular I386, he will have a copy of SOMEDISP.SYS in his NT drivers directory.

Putting It All Together

I've told you about a lot of tools to automate an install; let's quickly review what you can do.

1.   Build an automated installation script. If you have widely varying hardware then you may have to build more than one.

2.   Build a installation share point directory on a server somewhere with not only I386 but all of the drivers that you'll need to install systems with hardware that appeared after NT 4's release.

3.   Use Sysdiff to create difference files for whatever applications you might need, and create REGEDIT files for short modifications like the Explorer configurations discussed earlier, for example, telling Recycle Bin not to confirm deletes.

4.   Create a CMDLINES.TXT on the share point's OEM directory. In that file, include the commands to apply Sysdiff difference files and to apply the latest service pack.

5.   Use the Network Client Administrator to build bootable floppies. You'll need one floppy for each type of network card in your system.

Armed with these tools, you can take the formerly ugly task of building a new system with NT and applications and make it hands-free.

Cloning an NT Installation

Wouldn't it be nice if you only had to install NT once and could then distribute it on your network? Sounds like a great idea. Of course, this idea is one of those things that are too good to be true. In a sense, it is possible with NT under the right circumstances, but it can also be a big pain in the you-know-what.

Originally it was said that all that was needed in order to clone a machine was to install NT up through the text portion of Setup. Then, you would be able to copy the temporary directory created by Setup to another machine, which would continue the installation in GUI mode just as though the text portion of Setup had already occurred on the new machine.

As simple as that? It couldn't be. And, wouldn't you know it, it isn't. This technique will work only if the partition where NT is being installed was originally formatted in NT. OK, this is great if you're doing an upgrade or are reinstalling NT on the new machine, but what do you do if your machine is running DOS or Windows 95?

One thing you can do is to take the hard drive out of the new machine (or, if you have an external hard drive, just disconnect it) and connect it to a machine running NT. Then, format the hard drive while running NT and copy the temporary installation files onto it. Once that's done, you can put the hard drive back on the new machine and turn it on. The new machine will now start installing NT from the GUI mode.

If you have to install NT on a lot of machines, this may or may not be an easier way of installing NT, depending on your point of view. On the one hand, you won't have to sit down at each machine to install NT. However, the convenience of skipping past half of what can be a tedious install is balanced by the time it takes to remove a hard drive from a machine, format it, and reconnect it, all before you even get to start the installation. Unless your partition is already NT-formatted, I'd stay away from cloning an entire NT installation. It's just too time-consuming. Try doing an unattended installation instead.

What about simply putting NT on a system and then using a tool like Ghost from Symantec or Drive Image Pro from PowerQuest, programs that let you essentially photocopy a drive on one computer to a drive on another? These are good tools, but you'll then end up with multiple NT workstations (or, worse yet, servers) with identical SIDs. That can be a problem: here's why.

Suppose I take my NT workstation and clone it to your machine. You rename your machine, of course—can't have two machines on the network with the same name, NT won't allow it—and now your machine is called \\MYPC. We now have identically configured machines. Now suppose that I create an account named "Mark" on my machine and give it administrative privileges—I'm master of my own machine. Similarly, you create an account on your system named (modestly) "Deity," and give that account administrative powers over your machine.

Here's where things get weird. Because my Mark account and your Deity account were each the first user accounts created on the machines, *and* because both machines started from identical SID databases, *both accounts have identical SIDs*. When checking security, NT doesn't really look at account names; it looks at SIDs. So suppose I'm logged on to my computer as Mark and you're logged onto yours as Deity. I decide to be unprincipled, sneaky, and nosy and try to connect to your C: drive with the command **net use * \\mypc\C$**. Now, only a person that \\MYPC recognizes as an administrator should be able to do this. But recall that my SID is identical to Deity's. Your PC just thinks that it's *you* requesting data over the net, and lets me in. Not good news, eh?

There is a fix for this, however. The latest versions of DriveImage Pro and Ghost have *SID scramblers* that force a cloned machine to reset its SIDs to something new, solving the identical SID problem.

If you have a relatively small number of types of PCs, then cloning is not a bad idea. Just install an NT machine and get it the way you like it, then copy the drive image to a server somewhere. If you've got to rebuild the computer quickly, just boot to the network and use Ghost or DriveImage Pro to restore the disk image. The process is fairly quick—I've used Ghost to restore a system in under 20 minutes. Of course, if you're proficient with installation scripts, you can accomplish an automated install in just about the same time.

Before leaving this topic, let's take a look at a few examples. When researching this part of the book, I built unattended install scripts for several PCs. In each case, I'll explain

- What is unusual or problematic about the PC
- How I modified I386 and in particular I386\OEM
- What the unattended installation script contained

Example Machine 1: A Generic Clone

The first computer that I built an automated script for was a generic Pentium II machine with a relatively new ATX motherboard which included two Universal Serial Bus connectors and an infrared interface (not that NT could use either of them). It included a PCI video board built around the S3 Virge chip, an Adaptec 2940 SCSI host adapter, and the 3Com 3C900 XL Ethernet card that I've referred to earlier. I wanted to install this as a member server on an existing domain named TAURUS. The SCSI board is the industry standard and it existed in 1996, so it'll pose no problem, but the display card is newer than NT 4, as is the NIC.

In addition to installing NT Server on the system, I wanted to apply Service Pack 3 and make the Explorer modifications that I've referred to before—stop the Recycle Bin confirm, put the entire path on the title bar of a directory window, show all files, wrap lines in the Notepad, get rid of the "helpful" tips every time you log on, disable Autorun on CD-ROMs.

Preparing the I386 Installation Directory

First I copied the I386 directory from an NT CD-ROM to the clone's local hard disk. (I did that rather than installing from an I386 on the network solely because it's faster to pull it from a local hard disk than over the network—although if you've got a private gigabit Ethernet, then who knows? Perhaps the network would be faster!)

Then I created the OEM directory inside I386. Inside OEM I placed three files:

- **MRD.BMP**: A replacement background, a 640 × 480 bitmap I created

- **TOP.BMP**: A small 210 × 144 pixel-sized bitmap with my company's logo. Both bitmaps were just there to test the OEM_Ads section.

- **FIX.REG**: A text file with my desired Registry fixes.

- **REGEDIT.EXE**: A program needed to apply the Registry fixes.

- **DELTREE.EXE**: A program needed to delete entire directories.

- **CMDLINES.TXT**: Commands to tell Setup to apply the Registry fixes, run Service Pack 3, and delete some directories that I didn't need any more.

I put two directories inside OEM:

- **\I386\OEM\Display**: This contains S3.INF, S3MINI.SYS, and S3VIRGE .DLL: the three driver files for my video board. (Of course, my computer came with those files but I found more recent ones on the Web.)

- **\I386\$OEM$\C\3C**: This contains the 3Com drivers floppy. I created the \I386\$OEM$\C\3C directory and then popped the 3Com drivers floppy (and I naturally had the most recent set of drivers, as I'd just pulled them off the Web) into the A: drive and typed XCOPY A: C:\I386\$OEM$\C\3C /S. Recall that this will cause WINNT/WINNT32 to create a C:\3C directory on the target PC and copy the driver files there.

Then I copied all of the Service Pack 3 files over to \I386\OEM. That will make it easy to let CMDLINES.TXT apply Service Pack 3, and it's an alternative approach to the one that I outlined earlier in this chapter. Either method works, but this one's a bit simpler.

The CMDLINES.TXT File

The CMDLINES.TXT file looks like this:

```
[Commands]
".\cmdlines.bat"
```

That just says to run a batch file named CMDLINES.BAT, and *that* file looks like this:

```
deltree /y c:\3c
ren %systemroot%\system32\schannel.dll sc1.dll
update.exe -U -Z -N
del %systemroot%\system32\schannel.dll
ren %systemroot\system32\sc1.dll schannel.dll
regedit /s .\fix.reg
```

The first line just deletes the directory that had the 3Com files. The second applies the Service Pack, and the third makes the Registry changes. The renames and deletes accommodate the 128-bit Web browser DLL, as described earlier in this chapter.

The Installation Script

The automated install script I called INTELEC.INF (the name is a reference to the clone vendor's name), and it looks like the following:

```
[Unattended]
OemPreinstall = yes
NoWaitAfterTextMode = 1
NoWaitAfterGUIMode = 1
FileSystem = LeaveAlone
ExtendOEMPartition = 0
ConfirmHardware = no
NtUpgrade = no
Win31Upgrade = no
OverwriteOemFilesOnUpgrade = yes
OEMSkipEULA = Yes
targetpath = *

[OEM_Ads]
Banner = "Mark's copy of Windows NT now setting up"
Logo = top.bmp
Background = mrd.bmp

[UserData]
FullName = "Mark Minasi"
OrgName = "MR&D"
ComputerName = INTELLECT
ProductId = "111-1111111"

[GuiUnattended]
OemSkipWelcome = 1
OEMBlankAdminPassword = 1
TimeZone = "(GMT-05:00) Eastern Time (US & Canada)"
AdvServerType = SERVERNT

[LicenseFilePrintData]
AutoMode = PerSeat

[Display]
ConfigureAtLogon = 0
AutoConfirm = 1
infFile="s3.inf"
```

```
InfOption="S3 Incorporated Display Driver v2.00.17"
InstallDriver = 1
BitsPerPel = 8
XResolution = 640
YResolution = 480
Vrefresh = 60

[Network]
InstallAdapters = Adapterslist
InstallProtocols = ProtocolsSection
InstallServices = ServicesSection
DoNotInstallInternetServer = Yes
Joindomain = taurus
CreateComputerAccount = administrator,swordfish

[Adapterslist]
E190x = adapterparameters, c:\3c\

[adapterparameters]

[ProtocolsSection]
NBF = NBFParamSection
TC = TCParamSection

[NBFParamSection]

[TCParamSection]
DHCP = No
IPAddress = 207.97.52.51
Subnet = 255.255.255.0
Gateway = 207.97.52.1
DNSServer = 207.97.52.3
WINSPrimary = 207.97.52.2
DNSName = intellect.minasi.com

[ServicesSection]
```

I've covered most of this elsewhere in the book, but here are a few notes. I created this script by starting off with Setup Manager and letting it build an initial script, then I modified it—that's why you see some extraneous lines in there like ConfirmHardware = no; I certainly didn't want to have to confirm hardware, but then again there's no real reason for the command, as it appears that unattended installs work fine without the command, as well.

By setting the AdvServerType to SERVERNT, I'm telling the system to install as a member server. Creating a computer account for the new machine requires an administrator account on the domain, hence the "CreateComputerAccount = administrator,swordfish" line. The administrator account here, recall, does not refer to a *local* administrator account, but to an account recognized as an administrative account on *a domain controller*. "Swordfish" is the password on that account. (And no, my domain administrator account doesn't *really* use "swordfish" as the password, I just needed to put something in here.)

The only other thing that you haven't seen before is the fully populated TCP/IP parameters section. I wanted to assign a static IP address to this machine, and those are the commands to do it.

Obviously, this took me some time to get working. Was it worth it? Absolutely. This machine is a test machine that I use to try out software and configuration techniques and I need to reset it to a basic state between experiments. Believe it or not, if I start off this unattended installation, then WINNT32 can do the complete install, Service Pack 3 and all, in under *eight minutes*. Not bad at all, eh?

The Registry Fix Script

I presented this earlier, but I can apply the fixes that I like with this REGEDIT script:

```
REGEDIT4

[HKEY_CURRENT_USER\Software\Microsoft\Windows\CurrentVersion\Explorer]
"ShellState"=hex:10,00,00,00,07,00,00,00,00,00,00,00,00,00,00,00

[HKEY_CURRENT_USER\Software\Microsoft\Windows\CurrentVersion\Explorer\C
abinetState]
"Settings"=hex:0c,00,01,00,0b,01,00,00,60,00,00,00

[HKEY_CURRENT_USER\Software\Microsoft\Windows\CurrentVersion\Explorer\S
treams\4]
"ViewView"=hex:1c,00,a4,77,04,00,00,00,00,00,00,00,00,00,1c,00,03,00,00
,00,01,\
  00,00,00,03,00,00,00

[HKEY_CURRENT_USER\Software\Microsoft\Notepad]
"fWrap"=dword:00000001
```

```
[HKEY_CURRENT_USER\Software\Microsoft\Windows\CurrentVersion\Explorer\T
ips]
"DisplayInitialTipWindow"=dword:00000000
"Show"=hex:00,00,00,00
"Next"=hex:03,00


[HKEY_LOCAL_MACHINE\SYSTEM\CurrentControlSet\Services\Cdrom]
"AutoRun"=dword:00000000
```

Example Machine 2: Compaq Presario 4860

This second machine is another Pentium II, a 333MHz system with 128MB of RAM. Compaq built an ATI 3D Rage Pro onto the motherboard using the higher-speed AGP bus interface. Disk interface was just generic EIDE; network card once again a 3Com 3C900 XL. Again, I wanted to apply Service Pack 3, create a member server, and apply my desired Registry fixes.

The main difference with this computer was the display adapter, as you can imagine. The install script is essentially the same as the clone's, save for the [Display] section, which looks like this:

```
[Display]
ConfigureAtLogon = 0
AutoConfirm = 1
BitsPerPel = 8
XResolution = 640
YResolution = 480
VRefresh = 60
InstallDriver = 1
inffile = "ati.inf"
infoption = "ATI Technologies Inc. 3D RAGE PRO"
```

The \I386\OEM\Display section contains different files, as well—ATI.INF, ATI.SYS, ATI.DLL, ATIMCD.DLL, and ATIMCDR3.DLL. (Why five files instead of three? I don't know, but installing the drivers by hand caused them all to be copied, so I included them in the Display directory.)

Finally, recall that because NT 4 can't handle AGP drivers, I needed to take the HAL.DLL file from Service Pack 3 and use it to overwrite the HAL.DLL in the original I386 directory. After that, NT installed to this system without a problem.

Example Machine 3: Digital Hinote 2000 Laptop

I've got a laptop that I use for presentations and classes about NT, a Digital (now Compaq) Ultra Hinote 2000. In addition to being fairly fast (266MHz), it accommodates a lot of RAM—or at least 144MB of RAM *seems* like a lot of RAM as I write this in September, 1998—and has a built-in 100/10 Ethernet card and modem as well as a beautiful 14.5" screen. Disk and CD-ROM access are plain-vanilla EIDE.

You have, by now, figured out what the challenges will be for this computer—again, video and NIC. For this last example, however, let me take you along with me step by step as I develop the unattended installation script.

The laptop comes with Windows 95 pre-installed, which is kind of convenient—the Windows 95 Device Manager lets me peek at the display and NIC and see what hardware vendor they're built around. It turns out that the network card/modem is a modified Xircom CEM56, although sadly only Digital provides drivers—the basic Xircom CEM56 drivers don't work. Fortunately, Digital has drivers for their flavor of the CEM56 on their Web site. *Unfortunately*, the Xircom board is basically a PCMCIA board, so I may not be able to get away with an empty parameters section; it'll be safest to at least specify the I/O addresses and IRQ level.

But 95's Device Manager has the great strength of making it easy to find out what I/O addresses, IRQs, and the like boards are using, so I note that the board is using I/O 2E8–2EF (not surprising, that's the I/O range for COM2, no doubt the modem's using that part), I/O 110–11F (that's probably what the NIC is using), IRQ 3 (again, logical, as it's associated with COM2), and memory ranges D0000–D1FFF and D2000–D2FFF. I copy the drivers into a directory called D:\CEM56. I'm not going to bother with storing them into OEM\C\XIRCOM or something like that because I may as well have the drivers resident right on the laptop's hard disk at all times. That way, if I run into a configuration problem on the road, the drivers are right there where I can find them.

The display is a Chips and Technologies 65554 video system, more good news as my experiences with doing unattended installs on systems with chips from Chips & Tech have been uniformly good. Digital has new drivers for the video, as well, and they're pretty much what we expect—three files named OEMSETUP .INF, CHIPS.SYS, and CHIPS.DLL.

I copy the I386 directory on the NT 4 CD-ROM to a new directory on my laptop called D:\I386—this is not a case where originality is a virtue—and then create a directory D:\I386\$OEM$. Just for fun, I copy my bitmaps to the D:\I386\$OEM$ directory, as well as REGEDIT.EXE, and FIX.REG. (I'm not going to need DELTREE because I won't be creating and deleting any directories in the setup process.) I'll need to build a CMDLINES.TXT in a bit, but I'll leave that for now.

Service Pack 3 files go into D:\I386\$OEM$ next. Service Pack 3 ships as one big executable called NT4SP3_I.EXE, but I need all of its files extracted for Setup's sake. I do that by opening up a command prompt and typing **NT4SP3_I /X** after copying NT4SP3_I.EXE to D:\I386\$OEM$. Time to write a batch file and call it from CMDLINES.TXT. The batch file (call it CMDLINES.BAT) looks like this:

```
ren %systemroot%\system32\schannel.dll sc1.dll
update -u -z
del %systemroot%system32\schannel.dll
ren %systemroot%\system32\sc1.dll schannel.dll
regedit /s .\fix.reg
```

The CMDLINES.TXT file looks like this:

```
[Commands]
".\cmdlines.bat"
```

The two rename and one delete commands, you may recall, get around the 128-bit Internet Explorer DLL problem. Note that I didn't bother with the %systemroot% stuff, as I know that I want NT on drive E:. The update command applies the Service Pack and the regedit command applies the Registry fixes, as you've seen before.

TIP

And by the way, when you try out a CMDLINES.BAT for the first time, it's not a bad idea to put an extra line in—*pause*. The pause command does what you'd expect it to: it stops the process and waits for you to press a key. It's useful because if you typed something wrong, the syntax error may flash by so quickly that you miss it. Using pause the first time you try out an install script lets you make sure that everything's working as it should.

Next, I need a place for the display drivers. I copy OEMSETUP.INF, CHIPS.DLL, and CHIPS.SYS to a new directory named D:\I386\OEM\DISPLAY. Time to start working on the install script, so I start from the one I used for the Presario. The first obvious thing that I've got to do is to change the computer name from Presario to HN2000, the name I'll use for the laptop. Then, as the computer will often be far from my home domain of TAURUS, I'll have the computer—a member server—just join a *workgroup* named TAURUS. Otherwise, the computer will spend a few minutes every time I reboot it looking in vain for a domain controller for TAURUS.

To automate the network card install, I need to modify these lines in the Presario script:

```
[Adapterslist]
E190x = adapterparameters, c:\3c\

[adapterparameters]
```

I look in HKEY_LOCAL_MACHINE\Software\Microsoft\Windows NT\CurrentVersion\NetworkCards\1 and find that the Xircom Ethernet/Modem circuit's ProductName is CEM56. Recall that I put the drivers in D:\CEM56, so I'll reflect that change when modifying the Presario script for the Hinote 2000. But what about parameters? A look in HKEY_LOCAL_MACHINE\System\CurrentControlSet\Services\CEM561\Parameters shows that there are a *lot* of them, but usually the I/O address and IRQ information are sufficient. As there are two functions on the card—network card and modem—there are two I/O address ranges and an IRQ level:

```
InterruptNumber = 11
IOBaseAddress = 744
IOBaseAddress_1 = 800
```

Recall that these values are in decimal, as that's how NT Setup wants to see them. Address 744 is 2E8 hex, one of the COM port addresses, and address 800 is 320 hex; it's likely used by the Ethernet circuit.

```
[Adapterslist]
CEM56 = adapterparameters, d:\cem56

[adapterparameters]
```

The [Display] section needs some changes, as well, to reflect that fact that there's no ATI board in the laptop. As copied from the Presario, the [Display] section looks like this:

```
ConfigureAtLogon = 0
AutoConfirm = 1
BitsPerPel = 8
XResolution = 640
YResolution = 480
```

```
VRefresh = 60
InstallDriver = 1
inffile = "ati.inf"
infoption = "ATI Technologies Inc. 3D RAGE PRO"
```

I need to know three things:

- The name of the INF file

- The internal name of the display board

- The initial display resolution that this driver is "comfortable" with

The first part's easy, as I already know the file is named OEMSETUP.INF. Looking inside OEMSETUP.INF, I see a descriptive string that starts "Chips Video Accelerator (64300...", and so I just copy the line from OEMSETUP.INF and paste it into HN2000.INF, the name I'm using for the Hinote install script. But how to find out what default resolution the Chips chipset prefers to start from? About the only way I've ever found (besides guessing) is to just install NT once on a system with the chipset and then hand-install the video driver, reboot, and note what resolution comes up.

I do a quick install of NT on the laptop, a no-frills install that gets me to the Desktop in basic VGA 640×480 16 color mode. Right-click on the Desktop and choose Properties, then click the Settings tab. Click the Display Type button in the lower right-hand corner and then click Change in the dialog box that appears. Yet another dialog appears (hmmm, it's starting to look like guessing isn't such a bad idea after all); choose the Have Disk option. Yet *another* dialog box asks where to find the display drivers and I tell it D:\I386\OEM\Display and click OK. A dialog box (yes, another one) offers me the choice of "Chips Video Accelerator (64300/10...," the same string that I just found in OEMSETUP.INF. I click OK, it asks me if I'm sure, I tell it that I am, and as is usual for NT, I've got to close up all the dialog boxes and reboot to see the changes take effect.

After the reboot, the Display control panel pops up to tell me that a new display driver has been loaded and that I should find a resolution that I like. That's not important, though. What *is* important is that the screen is in 640×480 resolution, 256 colors, and 60Hz vertical refresh. *Now* I can update the [Display] section:

```
[Display]
ConfigureAtLogon = 0
AutoConfirm = 1
infFile = "OEMSETUP.INF"
```

```
InfOption="Chips Video Accelerator(64300/10 65535/40/45/48/50/54/55)"
InstallDriver = 1
BitsPerPel = 8
XResolution = 640
YResolution = 480
Vrefresh = 60
```

The only thing left to do before I can try the automated install is to craft the WINNT/WINNT32 command. I want to install NT over on my E: drive, the source files are in D:\I386, and the script file is D:\HN2000.INF, so the command looks like this:

```
D:\i386\Winnt32 /s:d:\i386 /t:e: /u:d:\hn2000.inf
```

I make life just a bit easier by saving that one line into a file named REINSTALLNT .BAT, and double-click it to try it the first time...

What happened? Something I didn't expect. The first time I did the automated install, it worked fine. So I tried it again. The second time, however, Setup stopped and double-checked whether I wanted to overwrite Hyperterminal. Hmmm... what's going on here? The problem is that Hyperterminal (and a few other files) are stored not in \WINNT, but instead in E:\Program Files. Deleting an old \WINNT or overwriting an installation doesn't get rid of the old Hyperterminal files. Then, when I try to do another install, the original NT 4 Hyperterminal files are older than the newer Hyperterminal files deposited by Service Pack 3. NT doesn't like copying older files atop newer ones, so it stops and asks.

The best answer to that seems to be to modify the batch file that contains the WINNT32 command, deleting E:\Program Files\Windows NT. The command to do that is

```
Del /s /q /f  "e:\program files\windows nt"
```

One more thing—the video works at 640 × 480, but can we get it to immediately go to 1024 × 768, its highest resolution? Those Chips guys apparently did a good job, because the answer is yes, the unattended install still works fine if I specify higher resolution in the [Display] section. (As I've said before, this won't work on many video boards.)

With those changes made, I can do a hands-off install in just *12 minutes*. It's even faster than attaching to a network share and pulling down a Ghost image—and it works when I'm on the road, as well.

Here are the files that I used to make this work. First, the install script, HN2000.INF, which I've stored in the root of D:

```
[Unattended]
OemPreinstall = yes
NoWaitAfterTextMode = 1
NoWaitAfterGUIMode = 1
FileSystem = LeaveAlone
ExtendOEMPartition = 0
ConfirmHardware = no
NtUpgrade = no
Win31Upgrade = no
OverwriteOemFilesOnUpgrade = yes
OEMSkipEULA = Yes

[OEM_Ads]
Banner = "Mark's copy of Windows NT now setting up"
Logo = top.bmp
Background = mrd.bmp

[UserData]
FullName = "Mark Minasi"
OrgName = "MR&D"
ComputerName = HN2000
ProductId = "111-1111111"

[GuiUnattended]
OemSkipWelcome = 1
OEMBlankAdminPassword = 1
TimeZone = "(GMT-05:00) Eastern Time (US & Canada)"
AdvServerType = SERVERNT

[LicenseFilePrintData]
AutoMode = PerSeat

[Display]
ConfigureAtLogon = 0
AutoConfirm = 1
infFile = "OEMSETUP.INF"
InfOption="Chips Video Accelerator(64300/10 65535/40/45/48/50/54/55)"
InstallDriver = 1
BitsPerPel = 24
```

```
XResolution = 1024
YResolution = 768
Vrefresh = 60


[Network]
InstallAdapters = Adapterslist
InstallProtocols = ProtocolsSection
InstallServices = ServicesSection
DoNotInstallInternetServer = Yes
Joinworkgroup = ursamaj

[Adapterslist]
CEM56 = adapterparameters, d:\CEM56

[adapterparameters]
InterruptNumber = 11
IOBaseAddress = 744
IOBaseAddress_1 = 800

[ProtocolsSection]
NBF = NBFParamSection
TC = TCParamSection

[NBFParamSection]

[TCParamSection]
DHCP = No
IPAddress = 206.246.253.101
Subnet = 255.255.255.0
Gateway = 206.246.253.1
DNSServer = 206.246.253.200
WINSPrimary = 206.246.253.200
DNSName = hn2000.minasi.com

[ServicesSection]
```

Then the CMDLINES.BAT file, stored in D:\I386\OEM:

```
ren %systemroot%\system32\schannel.dll sc1.dll
update -u -z -n
del %systemroot%\system32\schannel.dll
ren %systemroot%\system32\sc1.dll schannel.dll
regedit /s fix1.reg
```

CMDLINES.TXT is also in D:\I386\OEM:

```
[Commands]
".\cmdlines.bat"
```

Finally, the batch file to start the process:

```
del /f /s /q "e:\program files\windows nt"
d:\i386\winnt32 /s:d:\i386 /t:e: /u:d:\hn2000.inf
```

This whole process took a bit of time, about two hours including testing time, but it's well worth it.

The Rollback Utility

Included on your NT Server CD is a utility named ROLLBACK.EXE. Microsoft designed this utility to allow computer manufacturers to preinstall Windows NT 4 and for users to configure their computers according to the desired role of the computer. Basically, this utility will remove all Registry configurations from your system and return you to the end of the text mode portion of Setup, thereby undoing everything you've installed or configured on your NT server.

WARNING Once you've run ROLLBACK.EXE, there's no turning back. A repair disk can't even help you as there's no system to restore—the Registry and SETUP.LOG file no longer exist. There is also no warning that you're about to destroy your system. The only way to fix your system once you've run ROLLBACK.EXE is to restore the entire system from a tape backup. To be safe, you may want to keep this utility off of your computer altogether.

Unless you want to change your server to a PDC or BDC, you're better off not using this utility. If you don't like the way your system is set up and you're not going to change the computer's role, go to the Control Panel and change the settings individually instead. It's much easier to take the time to change what you don't like instead of having to reinstall all of your applications and reconfigure everything (including user account information, network adapters, display settings, and so on).

Common Installation Problems

Most installations of NT Server (or NT Workstation, for that matter) are pretty trouble-free. But here's a look at some of the more common problems and questions that *do* arise.

Lockups on Install

NT ties to the hardware on your system with a program called, appropriately, NTDETECT.COM. Sometimes NTDETECT gets confused, however, and all you're left with is a message that NTDETECT version 4 is running—forever. What to do? You can troubleshoot hardware detection with a "debug" version of NTDETECT.COM.

Located in the \SUPPORT directory of NT CD-ROM disc, the file is called NTDETECT.CHK. Just DISKCOPY the NT Setup installation disk (the one you boot from to start off NT installation), erase the original NTDETECT.COM from the copied disk, and replace it with NTDETECT.CHK. (Then, rename NTDETECT .CHK to NTDETECT.COM, of course.) You then get a blow-by-blow description of what NTDETECT sees as it examines your hardware.

Incorrect Hardware

If you can't get *anywhere*, did you make sure that you have "regulation" NT hardware? Check back in this chapter to ensure that you have the right hardware and that it's configured correctly. Use the debugging version of NTDETECT.COM to find out where Setup is hanging up. Remember that interrupt conflicts that never gave you trouble under DOS stick out like a sore thumb under NT!

Image Can't Be Relocated, No Fixup Information

NT requires that 600K of memory be free in the low 1MB of RAM space. While most computers have 640K of conventional memory, a few either have only 500K of conventional memory, or—in the case of some high-performance server computers like the Compaq System Pro XL—have no conventional memory at all. Now, if you *do* have an XL, you can run its EISA configuration program and set the memory on the motherboard from "linear" to "640K Compaq compatible." That will solve the problem on that machine.

How Do I Remote Boot NT?

Most PC operating systems support remote boot. NT, however, does not, at least not now.

Crash on First Reboot

You run NT Setup and everything's fine through the text portion. It reboots to enter the GUI portion of Setup and crashes. The most common reason? A boot sector virus. Run a virus scanner before installing NT.

"Boot Couldn't Find NTLDR. Please Insert Another Disk."

One of the essential files to boot NT, a file that you can't hope to start up without, is the NT loader program NTLDR. It *must* appear in the root directory, and that's where you can get in trouble.

You see, on hard disks formatted with the FAT file system, you are limited to 512 files in the root directory. That's an unusual number of files to see in a root, but some people do have that many files in their root.

It's particularly easy to accumulate files in the root if you've had disk problems and you ran CHKDSK/F under DOS or OS/2 before installing NT. The result is potentially hundreds of files with names like FILE0000.CHK. Having 512 of them means that you can't put any more files on your root, including NTLDR.

You see this problem crop up if your system is unable to perform the reboot that happens about one third of the way through the installation process.

The fix is simple: clean out some files from your root directory and do the installation again. If you don't want to do the whole installation, read the "How Do I" sidebar.

TIP   If you're expanding NTLDR from floppies, it is called NTLDR._ on floppy disk 2.

How Do I Fix the System After It Can't Find NTLDR?

To fix a system after it can't find NTLDR:

1. Boot the system with a DOS bootable floppy (assuming you have a DOS partition. If you have an NTFS partition instead, use the Emergency Repair Boot disk mentioned in "How Do I Create A Generic Boot Floppy?")

2. Eliminate unnecessary files in the root directory.

3. In the \I386 directory of the NT Setup CD-ROM (or disk 2 of the Setup floppies—not the CD-ROM Installation disk), you see NTLDR._. It is the compressed version of NTLDR. (I understand why Microsoft compressed the files on the floppies; but why the CD-ROM version? There's plenty of space on that CD-ROM disk.)

4. Expand the file onto your root directory by using the EXPAND program from MS-DOS 6.0, Windows 3.1, or Windows for Workgroups. For example, if the NTLDR._ file were on the CD-ROM and the CD-ROM is drive D:, then the command would look like this:

   ```
   expand d:\i386\ntldr._ c:\ntldr.
   ```

You should be able to continue with Setup now.

Where Do I Load ANSI.SYS?

Problem: I've got DOS programs that require ANSI.SYS, but I can't get them to run under NT.

There is a file in your SYSTEM32 directory called CONFIG.NT that tells NT how to run DOS 5 sessions. Add this line to CONFIG.NT:

```
device=c:\winnt\system32\ansi.sys
```

Alternatively, you can say

```
device=%systemroot%\system32\ansi.sys
```

Then start up a command-line session by starting the COMMAND.COM that comes with DOS 5 (gotta search around for that one...).

While it *is* a pain having to find a copy of DOS 5.0's COMMAND.COM, it *is* pretty neat that you can change this CONFIG.NT file and see its effects without having to reboot.

Must My RISC Computer Be FAT-Based?

The FAT file system has its problems, but it's your *only option* if you're using a RISC-based system, at least for your boot partition.

The answer is to create a small FAT partition that contains your boot files, and format most of the hard disk as NTFS, so that you can keep the data files secure on the NTFS partition. Microsoft claims that you can actually make this boot partition only about 1MB in size, and the only files that *must* be on that partition are HAL.DLL and OSLOADER.EXE.

Another problem that some RISC machines (MIPS machines, in this case) may show is that the MIPS machines must have an R4000 chip that is version 2 or later.

Reinstalling NT Server

Once you get NT Server up and running, you probably never have to reinstall it. But, if you *do…*

Recall that an NT domain keeps track of the particular machines in the domain that run NT or NT Server as part of the security that is so integral to the design of NT. A side effect of this security is that you can't simply reinstall NT on a workstation, server, or domain controller, and expect it to work. NT reasons something like this: "Well, you *say* that you're a machine named PSERVER01, and I know a machine named PSERVER01, but how do I know that *you're* that computer?"

NT internally creates passwords that you never see. These passwords are used by the primary domain controller to verify that a machine is, indeed, who it says it is. As a result, if you reinstall NT or NT Server on a machine that's already running NT or NT Server and you give the machine the same name that it was previously using, you get a message that looks like this: "No domain controller was available to validate your logon."

That means that there is a *very* specific way to reinstall NT or NT Server on a computer. It's just three steps:

1. Shut down the computer that you're going to reinstall NT or NT Server on.

2. Log on to your domain as an administrator, run the Server Manager, and delete the to be reinstalled computer from the domain.

3. Re-install NT on the computer, specifying that you are not *upgrading* but rather are *replacing* the NT software on the machine. During the reinstallation process, you are given the chance to create a new machine account on the domain. Take that opportunity and you'll be back up and running.

Don't ignore this! In the course of writing this book, I reinstalled NT Server a number of times. I thought that I understood how the system worked fairly well—but I *didn't* understand the reinstallation procedure. Worse yet, I only had one domain controller on my network for quite some time. That's why it surprised me when the following happened.

One of my networks had been based on Windows for Workgroups prior to using NT Server. As I was previously using Windows for Workgroups, I didn't have a domain, I had a workgroup—a workgroup somewhat facetiously named "us." In my other office, we had a workgroup named "NextGeneration." When I first installed NT Server, I frankly expected to spend several days on it. After all, I've installed a pile of networks. I've installed IBM PC LAN, LAN Manager 1.*x* and 2.*x*, Novell 2.15, 3.11, LANtastic, PC-Office, PC-Net, and a number of others (if you've never heard of some of those, don't worry about it because no one else has, either). And when I installed networks, I learned the hard way that you have to set aside a day or two *at least* the first time that you install a server.

That's why installing NT Server the first time was such a pleasure. The whole installation took me about two hours, including all the ancillary stuff. Of course, to do it I just converted my workgroup "us" to a new domain named "us."

By the next time I installed NT Server—*re*installed it on that same server machine—we had an ISDN bridge in place between the LANs in the two buildings. Since the workgroup in the other building ("NextGeneration") would interact with our workgroup, "us" seemed like a silly name. Casting around for domain names, I picked a constellation name, figuring that many constellations are easy to spell (well, OK, except for Sagittarius, Cassiopeia, and Ophiuchi). The idea was, if necessary, to name machines in the domain after stars in the constellation.

So this time I installed NT Server with a new domain name, Orion (a nice, easy-to-spell name). Knowing that all the workstations would run into trouble because they were set up to log on to a domain named "us," I went to all the workstations in the office and reset their logon domain to "Orion." I was able to do this because, as you probably surmised, I did the work after hours, just as *you* probably have to do just about *all* the work on *your* server after hours.

The *next* time I reinstalled NT Server, however, I was merely reinstalling the primary domain controller for Orion, so when I installed the server software (after hours, again), I just typed in **Orion** as the domain name. I didn't go to the workstations and make any changes, as it didn't seem that I'd changed anything.

Hoo boy. *Big* mistake.

The DOS and Windows for Workgroups workstations were quite happy, logging on and emitting no complaints. But two things were quite wrong:

- The NT workstations all complained that "a domain controller could not be found." They refused to let me get to any server resources.

- The domains that we previously trusted, and that trusted us, wouldn't talk to us any more.

After a little thought, the answer dawned on me: *I had created a completely new domain*. A new domain named "Orion," to be sure, but a new domain nonetheless. I mean, suppose you're a foreign domain that trusts another domain named Orion? Some domain named Orion says, "Here I am," but the foreign domain's got to ask itself, "Yeah, this guy *says* he's Orion, but how do I know?"

NT uses not merely *names* like Orion to identify objects, but also internal security ID numbers (or SIDs, as Microsoft calls them). When you reinstall a primary domain controller, you create new security IDs, even if you use an old name.

Each domain needs a primary domain controller. Primary domain controllers *must* be computers running NT Server. But in my domain—as in many domains in the real world—there is only one NT Server, so when you take the server down and reinstall it, you kind of create a vacuum. When the server's running again, it says, "I'm the primary domain controller of Orion," and the NT machines on the network say, "OK, but you're not the primary domain controller of the Orion that *we* know."

What's the answer? Two possibilities:

- If you only have one NT Server in your domain, then do the following. First, make sure you have an Emergency Repair Disk for that machine. Re-install NT Server on the computer—a fresh installation—and then run Setup again with the intention of doing a "repair." The repair routine will prompt you for an Emergency Repair Disk. Give it the original one, and the repair routine will restore the old Registry with the old Security IDs. Then your PDC is back in business.

- That first answer sounds like a bit of work, and it is. A better answer requires that you have a backup domain controller in your domain. Just promote the backup domain controller to primary domain controller, demote the one that you're going to reinstall, then reinstall the machine as a backup domain controller, and promote it to primary domain controller, which will in passing demote the other domain controller.

Creating an NT Boot Disk

Those of you who've had to support DOS in the past (and those who haven't, spare us the condescending grins, OK?) know that an essential support tool is the boot floppy.

A boot floppy is just a floppy diskette that contains a minimum operating system. You used it to get a faulty system started. Is it possible, then, to create a boot disk for NT Server? Not completely. NT Server is so large that there isn't a prayer of getting it running simply from a floppy.

Sometimes, however, an important boot file can get lost and keep NT from booting. For example, I recently added two SCSI hard drives to my server. Either some sort of power glitch occurred, or NT doesn't like you adding drives, or.... I'm not sure what caused it, but when I turned the system on and tried to boot, I got this message:

```
error 08: error opening NTDETECT.COM
```

Now, NTDETECT.COM is the first program that NT loads, and this error message indicated that NT couldn't load it, so the server would not boot. As it turned out, the only file damaged on the server was NTDETECT.COM, so it would have been nice to have a floppy around that contained NTDETECT.COM to get the server started in the boot process. After that, the hard disk could take over.

One good answer—and the one that I eventually used—was the Emergency Boot Floppy. But each Emergency Boot Floppy is specific to a particular NT machine, and this bootable NT floppy is generic.

Given that bit of information, the "How Do I" sidebar explains how to create a generic NT boot floppy.

How Do I Create a Generic NT Boot Floppy?

To create a generic NT boot floppy:

1. Format a floppy under either NT Explorer or from a command line under NT. *Do not use a DOS-formatted floppy, or this won't work.* A DOS-formatted floppy looks for the DOS boot files IO.SYS and MSDOS.SYS; an NT-formatted floppy looks for the NT boot file NTLDR. (From Explorer, just right-click on the drive, and then Format.)

2. You're going to copy a bunch of files from the root directory of your server to the floppy in the A: drive. The files are hidden, however, so you have to tell the Explorer to show you hidden files. To do that, click View, then By File Type, and then check the Show All Files radio button.

3. Looking in your server's root directory, copy the following files from the server's root to the floppy disk:

   - NTLDR

   - NTDETECT.COM

   - BOOT.INI

   - NTBOOTDD.SYS (if your server boots from a SCSI hard disk and the hard disk does not support the INT 13 interface; if not, you probably don't have this file in the root and you don't need to copy it)

When you are finished, you have a floppy that can essentially "jump start" your system.

As John Ruley at *Windows* magazine has pointed out, this doesn't constitute a complete NT boot disk—but it's enough to get NT running in some situations.

Setting up NT Server right is essential if you want a trouble-free network from the beginning. And you can take another step toward keeping your network trouble-free by setting up fault-tolerant disk systems, which just happens to be the subject of the next chapter.

C H A P T E R

F O U R

4

RAID for Speedier, Safer Disks

- Understanding Disk Administrator terminology

- Using SLED

- Managing space with volume sets

- Using simple disk striping

- Mirroring disks

- Using disk striping with parity

Disk
Administrator

Disks on servers are different from disks on workstations.

Server disks must be faster, more reliable, and larger than their workstation-based cousins. How do you achieve those goals of speed, reliability, and size? Well, there's always the simple answer: spend more money for a drive with more of those three characteristics. But the past few years have yielded another solution: a group of mediocre drives can band together and, acting in concert, can provide speed, capacity, and high fault tolerance. The process of doing that is called *redundant array of inexpensive drives* (RAID). Until recently, putting a RAID on your server required buying an expensive RAID system (the drives are inexpensive, but the entire RAID subsystem isn't, unfortunately). However, NT changes that with the Disk Administrator. With the Disk Administrator, you can take a bunch of hard disks and "roll your own" RAID system.

The Disk Administrator offers a lot of options, and this chapter explains what your organization and protection options are and how you can use the Disk Administrator to best arrange your data for your particular situation.

While you'll set up the initial disk partitioning when you install NT Server, you can use the Disk Administrator (it is found in the Administrative Tools program group) to make changes to your disk setup after you've installed NT. With the Disk Administrator, you can

- Create and delete partitions on a hard disk and make logical drives.

- Get status information concerning these items:

  - The disk partition sizes

  - The amount of free space left on a disk for making partitions

  - Volume labels, their drive-letter assignment, file system type, and size

- Alter drive letter assignments.

- Create, delete, and repair mirror sets.

- Create and delete stripe sets and regenerate missing or failed members of stripe sets with parity.

Don't recognize some of these terms? Hang on, they're defined in the next section.

Disk Administrator Terminology

Before we get into the discussion of how you can use the Disk Administrator to arrange and protect your data, you need to know some of the terms that we'll be tossing around. These terms will be explained further in due course, but this section introduces them.

SLED

An acronym for *single large expensive drive*, SLED is a way of arranging your data on one very large, very (I hope) reliable drive. SLED is currently the most popular method of arranging data for two reasons:

- It's simple. You only have to buy one disk and store your data on it.
- Dedicated RAID hardware has been expensive in the past.

RAID

"Apply a shot of RAID, and all those nasty data problems will be gone!" No, it's not really a household product. RAID, which stands for redundant array of inexpensive drives, is a method of protecting your data by combining smaller, less expensive drives in such a way that your data redundancy and therefore security (fault tolerance) is increased. There are six kinds of RAID implementation, each of which works in a different way and has different applications. NT Server can handle levels 0, 1, and 5, also known as striping without parity, disk mirroring, and striping with parity, respectively. We'll talk about exactly what those levels are later in this chapter.

Free Space

This sounds like an obvious term. "Free space on a disk is just space that's free, right?" It's not. *Free space* is space on the disk that is *not part of a partition.* That means that it's not committed to be a simple logical drive, a volume set, mirror set, or stripe set. You can convert free space to anything else. In the Disk Administrator, it is indicated with diagonal striping.

Notice here that free space refers to *uncommitted* space, space that is not part of any drive letter. Free space does not refer to unused areas within established drives.

Physical Drives versus Logical Partitions

Physical drives are not usually important in the Disk Administrator, but getting the difference between physical drives and logical drives or partitions clear is worthwhile. A *physical drive* is that contraption of plastic and metal that you inserted in your server's case or have stacked up next to it. Numbers such as 0, 1, 2, 3… which you cannot change are assigned to physical drives. You cannot change the size of a physical drive. In order to use it, you must do a *low-level* format or a *physical* format, two synonymous terms for a software preparation that all hard drives must undergo before an operating system can use them. There is no way in NT to do that, because formatting is usually handled by directly executing a program on the disk drive controller. Note that IDE drives usually can't be low-level formatted. Consult the documentation on your disk controller to see how to do a low-level format on your drive. The size to which it is low-level formatted is the size that it will always be.

Note, by the way, that if you're putting a number of hard disks on a PC, the PC may only recognize two of those drives when it boots up. Don't worry about that; what you're seeing is a limitation of the DOS-based BIOS on the SCSI host adapter. Once you've booted NT, it will be able to see however many drives you've attached to your system. Similarly, DOS and BIOS have a lot of trouble seeing more than 1GB on a hard disk, so you may be told by the installation program that you've only got 1GB on your hard disk, even if you have a larger disk. The installation program is misinformed because it's still relying on your PC's BIOS, which can't usually see more than 1GB. Once NT is up and running, however, it will see all of your hard disk.

In contrast to a physical drive, a *partition* is a volume set, logical drive, primary partition, or anything else in the Disk Administrator that is assigned a drive *letter*. You can change drive letter assignments and adjust the sizes of logical partitions, as they have no physical presence. A logical partition can be part or all of a physical drive, or even (in the case of volume sets, mirror sets, and stripe sets) extend across more than one physical drive.

Partitions

A *partition* is a portion of a hard disk that is set up to act like a separate physical hard disk, rather like splitting a single physical hard disk into several logical drives. Partitions are referred to as either *primary* or *extended* partitions.

Primary Partitions

A *primary partition* is a portion of a physical hard disk marked as bootable by an operating system (like Windows NT). Under DOS, you can only have one primary partition. Under NT or Windows 95, you can have multiple partitions on a drive, and one at a time is marked "active," meaning you can boot from it. Primary partitions cannot be broken down into sub-partitions; there can only be up to four partitions per disk. You might partition your hard disk so one primary partition is running Windows NT and another is running OS/2. In the Disk Administrator, a primary partition is indicated with a dark purple stripe across the top. The exact colors vary depending on your video card's capabilities. The legend at the bottom of the screen tells you the status of your drives. They also can be changed according to the user's preference.

Extended Partitions

An *extended partition* is created from free space on the disk. Extended partitions can be broken down into smaller logical drives. You can only have one extended partition per hard disk, but you don't have to have a primary partition to have an extended one. In the Disk Administrator display, an extended partition is striped and labeled just like free space. The only way that you can tell a free space area from an extended partition is by clicking on the area. In the status bar, you'll see a description of exactly what the selected area is. Once you've established an extended partition, you can convert it to a logical drive.

Logical Drive

A *logical drive* is a partition on one disk that behaves like an entity unto itself. You can divide an extended partition into as many logical drives as you like, with only two limitations:

- NT Server only supports 24 fixed-disk drive letters (25 if you don't have a second floppy drive).

- There is a minimum size for each logical partition. This shouldn't be much of a limitation, however, because the minimum size is 2MB. That's not much bigger than a floppy disk's capacity.

> **NOTE**   The logical drive that the NT operating system itself is installed on cannot be larger than 4GB. Data can go on logical drives of any size.

Logical drives are indicated in the Disk Manager display with a royal-blue stripe. (I'm sorry this book's not in color and I can't show stripe colors. You'll have to take my word for it.)

Volume Set

A *volume set* is a drive or portion of a drive that has been combined with space on the same or another physical drive to make one large volume. You can assign a drive letter to a volume set and format it like a logical drive, but a volume set can extend across two or more physical disks, while a logical drive is restricted to one physical disk.

Why use a volume set rather than a logical drive? The ability to extend across more than one disk is the answer. Since volume sets are not limited to one physical disk, you can make a quite large volume set out of a bunch of tiny little pieces of free space. Therefore, you can use your disk space as efficiently as possible. It's much easier to figure out how to fit 30MB of data into a 35MB volume set than it is to fit it into two 10MB logical drives and one 15MB logical drive. What if you need to resize a volume set? You can make a volume set larger by *extending* it if more free space becomes available, but you cannot make it smaller unless you delete it and create a new one.

That's worth repeating: you can enlarge a volume set without damaging the data on it, but you cannot *reduce* a volume set without destroying it and rebuilding it altogether.

> **NOTE**   You cannot extend a FAT-formatted volume set.

Volume sets do not protect your data; they only give you more efficient use of your available drive space. If something happens to one of the hard disks used in a volume set, that volume set is dead. Since the more hard disks you have, the more likely it is that one will fail at any given time, be sure to back up volume sets regularly.

In Disk Administrator, yellow stripes indicate volume sets.

Mirror Set

Disk mirroring helps protect your data by storing a copy of all your data on an identically sized area of free space on another disk. The original and the copy together are called a *mirror set*. If anything happens to your original data, you still have an identical copy on the other half of the mirror set. Mirror sets are not very space-efficient because every piece of data that you record has an identical twin on the other half of the mirror set. You need exactly twice as much storage space as you have data. The Disk Administrator displays mirror sets with a magenta stripe across the top.

Stripe Set

For data protection, or to decrease your disks' read time, you can select areas of free space on your disks (three or more if you want parity, two or more if not) and combine them into a *stripe set*. Data stored in a stripe set is written in chunks of a certain size, called *stripes*. A stripe set is assigned a drive letter and, once it has been formatted, behaves as a drive.

Once the stripe set is established, every time you write to the drive letter that represents the set, your data is written in stripes across all the members of the stripe set. In other words, not all your data ends up in one place. Even if there's room for an entire file in one of the areas in the set, the data won't all be written there. If you've established a stripe set *with parity*, then parity information is written to the disks along with the data. Parity information on the stripe set is always stored separately from the data to which it corresponds. That way, if something happens to the disk with the original data, the parity information will still be all right and the data can be reconstructed from the parity information. Obviously, a stripe set without parity cannot be reconstructed if the disk with the original data on it fails, since the data only exists in one place in the stripe set.

The Hazards of Striping without Parity

And there's the rub: since the stripe set, although spread out over a number of disks, acts as one drive, all the parts of the stripe set must be working for any of the data to be accessible. If one member of a stripe set without parity information becomes inaccessible for whatever reason, all the data in the stripe set is lost.

You can see, therefore, how striping without parity actually increases your failure risk. While it's true that the more disks you have, the less likely it is that *all* of them will fail at the same time, the flip side of this is that the more disks you have, the more likely it is that *one* of them will fail at any given time. In a situation in which one disk failure brings down the entire system, having more disks actually increases your vulnerability to hardware failures. As with volume sets, you must back up nonparity stripe sets regularly.

With or without parity, all stripe sets are shown in light green in the Disk Administrator. You can tell what kind of stripe set a particular one is by clicking on it and looking at the status bar below the color legend.

Before Using the Disk Administrator...

The Disk Administrator is very easy to use and can be fun to play around with. (When experimenting with it for this chapter, my assistant Christa spent a couple of hours creating and deleting logical partitions and cackling, "The power is mine, all mine!") This is fine, as long as you keep a couple of things in mind:

- You can make any change you like in the Disk Administrator, adding, adjusting, or deleting partitions, and the changes will not take effect until you save them.

- Once you *do* save them, the changes will take effect as soon as you shut down the system and restart.

- If you save a change, the system will want to shut down and reboot when you exit the Disk Administrator. If you're not in a position where you can reboot, press Ctrl+Esc to switch to the Start Programs menu.

- If you add a new physical disk to your system, it should automatically show up in the Disk Administrator after you reboot. If it doesn't, then something is wrong with the installation.

- Deleting a partition of any kind will destroy any data saved there.

- If you intend to experiment with a partition or drive on which you have data, back it up before doing anything else.

Keeping It All Together with SLED

Even if it's partitioned into smaller logical drives, most of us use a single large expensive disk (SLED) as the arrangement for our data storage. Why SLED? Essentially, SLED is so popular because it's easy. You buy a large disk from a trusted manufacturer, slap it in, save your data there, perform regular backups, and you're good to go. Using SLED is like buying all your stock in one giant company with an excellent track record. It's dependable, but if it goes, you're sunk—time to haul out the backups. (Pity that you can't haul out the backup *money* when it comes to stock losses.)

Using Logical Drives to Divide Up Information

Even if you rely on the SLED model for your data storage, you may want to divide that single large physical drive into smaller logical ones. You could, for example, keep all the accounting information on logical drive C, the engineering information on logical drive D, the personnel information on logical drive E, and so on.

Creating an Extended Partition

To create a logical drive, you must first take free space and convert it to an extended partition. Open the Disk Administrator, so that you see the screen in Figure 4.1.

FIGURE 4.1:

Disk Administrator window

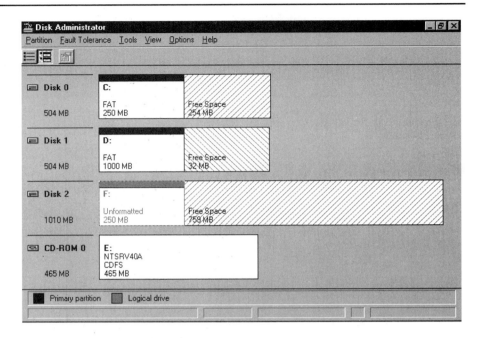

Notice that my example screen shows three drives on my server. Drive 1 is taken up almost entirely with a large FAT partition where I put my data. Drives 0 and 2 have 254MB and 759MB, respectively, of free space that I will use for my examples. Click on the free space, and then choose Create Extended Partition from the Partition drop-down menu. When you have done so, you'll see a dialog box like the one in Figure 4.2. It asks how big you want to make the extended partition.

FIGURE 4.2:

The Create Extended Partition dialog box

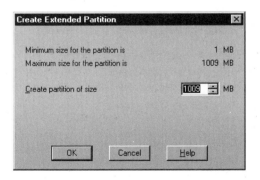

Select the size that you want (you don't have to use up all the free space available) and click OK.

Converting the Extended Partition to a Logical Drive

Once you've created the extended partition, you're ready to create a logical drive. To do so, click on the area of the extended partition to select it, and then select Create from the Partition drop-down menu. You see a dialog box that looks like Figure 4.3.

FIGURE 4.3:

The Create Logical Drive dialog box

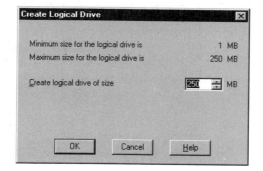

Type in the size of the logical drive that you want to create, or press Enter to select the default option and take all the available space. Once you've pressed OK, your logical drive is set up.

When you exit from the Disk Administrator, you see a dialog box like Figure 4.4. Click Yes to save. The Disk Administrator confirms that it made the changes with the dialog box shown in Figure 4.5.

FIGURE 4.4:

Confirm configuration changes dialog box

FIGURE 4.5:

A dialog box confirming your
configuration

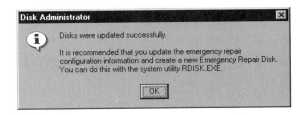

When you quit the Disk Administrator, you see a dialog box like the one in Figure 4.6. It advises you that the changes you have made require restarting your computer. Click OK and the system will shut down and restart automatically.

FIGURE 4.6:

The dialog box asking you to
restart your computer

TIP   If you don't want to shut down now, you can press Ctrl+Esc to switch to the Start Programs menu. However, the changes have still been made, and, once you shut down and restart the system, the repartitioning will take effect.

Formatting the New Drive

Before you can store data on the new drive, you've got to format it. With version 4 come the My Computer and Explorer folders. Open either folder and right-click the logical drive. You'll see an available option to format a drive.

To format, you must first create a partition or logical drive; you can't format free space. Click on the partition to be formatted to select it, and then choose Commit Changes Now from the Partition menu. When the partition information has been stored, keep the partition highlighted and choose Format from the Tools menu.

In the Format dialog box, choose the file system that you want to use on the partition. If you format NTFS, you can even change the cluster size—but don't do that. The default works fine for most uses. For best security, make all of your partitions NTFS. The only exception to this is that it may be a good idea to keep the boot partition FAT, so you can boot from a DOS system floppy if necessary; and any partitions that you need to be available if you boot from DOS must use the FAT system as well. (DOS doesn't recognize NTFS partitions.) Please note: that's "if you boot from DOS." DOS machines connected to the server can access data in an NTFS partition without any problem.

If you're formatting a partition or logical drive, you can check Quick Format to tell NT Server not to scan the disk for bad sectors. If the section you're formatting is a fault-tolerant volume such as a mirror set or stripe set with parity, then this is not an option.

Click OK to start the format. A dialog box will appear and ask you to confirm the format; click OK again and the format operation will begin. A dialog box will show you the process of the format. Be warned: although the dialog box has a Cancel button, canceling the format won't necessarily restore the partition to its original condition.

If you're addicted to the command prompt, you can still use it to format disks. To do so, open an MS-DOS prompt and type

```
format driveletter: /fs:filesystem
```

where *driveletter* is, of course, the drive letter of the logical drive, and *filesystem* is either FAT or NTFS. (You could format drives in HPFS in version 3.1, but not in any version since then.) For example, to format a newly created drive E: as NTFS, you would type **format e: /fs:ntfs**.

If you open Windows Explorer and try to access the new drive letter before you format it, you get a nastygram like the one in Figure 4.7.

FIGURE 4.7:

An "Is Not Accessible" error message

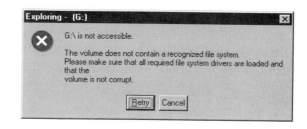

How Do I Create a Logical Drive?

Take the following steps to create a logical drive:

1. Open the Disk Administrator and select an area of free space.

2. From the Partition menu, select Create Extended and choose the size of the extended partition that you want to make.

3. Having selected the extended partition that you just made, select Create from the Partition menu and choose the size of the logical drive that you want to make.

4. You see the new logical drive in royal blue. Open the Partition menu and choose Commit Changes Now for the changes to take effect.

5. Format the drive to NTFS or FAT by using the Format option on the Tools menu.

You can now use the logical drive letter as you would any other.

Use the Most Recent Drivers!

If you experience strange problems with the Disk Administrator, make sure that you've got the most recent drivers. For example, if your NT Server has an EIDE (Enhanced Integrated Drive Electronics) drive controller for which you're using the DOS drivers, you may notice problems with the Disk Administrator. First of all, when you open the Disk Administrator and then exit, the system demands that you reboot even if you didn't do anything. Second, the EIDE hard disk won't hold a partition no matter what you try. What's going on?

It appears that the two sides of the problem have their root in the same difficulty: the EIDE disk won't hold a partition, so every time you run the Disk Administrator, it perceives changes whether you personally made them or not. There is a happy end to the story, however. When we called the EIDE controller manufacturer and had them send us the NT drivers, the problems went away. Other Disk Administrator problems may also be caused by obsolete driver software.

Deleting a Logical Drive

Deleting a logical drive will destroy all the data on it, so back up before you do anything drastic. The next "How Do I" sidebar explains how to delete a logical drive.

How Do I Delete a Logical Drive?

To delete a logical drive:

1. Select the drive in the Disk Administrator and choose Delete from the Partition drop-down menu.

2. A message like this one appears:

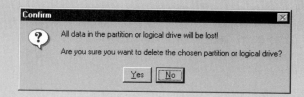

3. Yes is the default. Once you've confirmed, the logical partition will be deleted and will become an empty extended partition. If you want to convert the extended partition to free space, you must delete it as well.

When you exit the Disk Administrator, you are prompted to confirm your changes. Once you've confirmed, click OK to restart the system or press Ctrl+Esc to go to the Start Programs menu.

Getting Rid of a System Drive: Wiping NT Off Your Computer

Once it's on your system, NT can be a bit difficult to get rid of in some ways. NT will not allow you to delete the logical drive that the operating system is on, which can be a bit of a pain. I found this out the hard way.

I had a laptop computer that I used for class demonstrations, a machine that I sometimes ran Windows 95 on and sometimes ran NT Server on. I'd partitioned its hard disk into drives C:, D:, and E:. C: lived by itself on the primary partition. D: and E: were both on an extended DOS partition. I needed an NTFS partition for demonstration purposes, and so I made the E: drive an NTFS drive. I did that so that both NT and Windows would see drives C: and D: identically. Recall that Windows 95 cannot understand NTFS drives. If I had made drive D: an NTFS drive, then NT would have lettered the drives as C: (primary partition, FAT), D: (extended partition, first logical drive, NTFS), and E: (extended partition, second logical drive, FAT), but Windows would have lettered the drives as C:—again, primary partition, same as NT and D:—*but* what Windows would call D: would be the *second* logical drive in the extended partition, as again Windows doesn't have a clue about NTFS drives and so would skip the first logical drive in the extended partition. The result would be that what NT called drive E: would be called drive D: by Windows.

Now, that's not the end of the world, but it *can* raise a bit of havoc if you're trying to install and configure applications so that they'll run under both Windows and NT. That's why I put the NTFS drive last, on E:. But it caused me a bit of trouble, as you'll see.

At one point, I wanted to wipe drive E: completely off the computer and rebuild both NT and drive E: from scratch. But it seemed that I was completely unable to get rid of drive E:! First I tried to eliminate E: with the FDISK program that comes with Windows 95, but the program was blind to the NTFS partition, never offering drive E: for deletion. Hmmm, I thought, time to boot NT and use Disk Administrator, but no go there, either—Disk Administrator specifically forbade me from deleting the drive that comprises the system.

The tool that I *would* have turned to normally would be the amazingly useful and indispensable *Partition Magic* from PowerQuest software, but I didn't have my copy around (the hazards of computing on the road). What to do? Then I remembered—NT Setup could help me!

Early on during the text mode part of NT Setup, you're presented with a list of drives on the system and you're asked which drive to place NT on. The message goes something like this:

"The list below shows existing partitions and spaces available for creating new partitions…"

And then, a bit further down, it says:

"... To delete the highlighted partition, press D."

Highlight the NTFS drive that you want to eliminate and press **D**. NT Setup will respond:

"You have asked Setup to remove the partition..." and it will display information about the partition. It will then say, "To delete this partition, press L..." Quite a nice touch, that—too often we're all too trigger-happy with the Enter key or the Y key. Finding L requires engaging the ol' gray matter and has saved my bacon on a couple of occasions. Anyway, once you press L, you return to the screen asking what drive to put NT on, except now where you once saw drive E: (or whatever drive you're attempting to annihilate), you'll instead see "Unpartitioned space." You might think that you can just press F3 and exit Setup, confident that you've zapped the NTFS drive, but you haven't; you'll need another step before you can go any further.

Highlight the "Unpartitioned space" and press **C** to tell NT to create and format the erstwhile NTFS drive. Another screen will pop up, asking you how large to make the new drive, and you'll probably just press Enter to accept that amount (although if you want to chop up the unused space further, you'll enter some smaller amount).

That will once more take you to the Setup screen, asking which drive to put NT on. Once more, highlight the place where the NTFS drive was—it'll now say "New (Unformatted)"—and press Enter. The next screen will give you the chance to either format the partition as FAT—which is probably the right thing to do if your goal here is to simply wipe NT off the computer—or NTFS, which is of course the right thing to do if you only seek to clean off the drive. Select the format that you want and press Enter. You'll then see a message that says, "Please wait while Setup formats the partition," followed again by specific information about the partition.

Once Setup is done formatting, it asks what to name the directory where it will install NT, offering the default "\WINNT." If you press F3 twice at this point, your system will reboot, and you'll find that your reluctant-to-leave NTFS houseguest has vacated the premises.

Using Space Efficiently with Volume Sets

Even if you're a SLED aficionado, you may one day be faced with space restrictions that force you to get another drive. In that event, you'll want to use the space on that new drive as efficiently as possible.

Volume Sets to Get the Most Out of Existing Disks

How can you use disk space efficiently? Well, keeping the drives separate from each other clearly isn't the way. Unused space is more efficient if combined because, even if you have a total of 40MB of unused data space on the two drives, you can't fit one 35MB chunk of data in it if 25MB of unused space is on one disk and 15MB is on the other. If you want to get as much data squeezed onto your disks as possible, therefore, you can combine the two (or more) disks into a volume set, as seen in Figure 4.8.

FIGURE 4.8:

How a volume set works

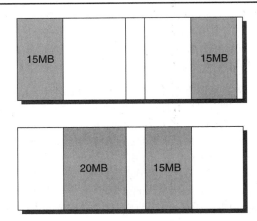

In this figure, 65MB of free space is available, but no more than 20MB of this space is contiguous. To get the most efficient use of this space, you could combine it together in a volume set, so all of the data is considered in one large chunk. Once this free space has been made into a volume set, you could store a 65MB chunk of data in it, even though the largest contiguous space is only 20MB in size.

Cautions about Volume Sets

Don't forget that volume sets have one big drawback: they can span more than one physical disk and are dependent on all of those disks to function. If one disk turns belly-up and dies, the rest of your volume set is inaccessible. If you try to read or write to a dead volume set, you get several messages like the ones in Figure 4.9 and Figure 4.10

System Process—Lost Delayed-Write Data message box

Another System Process—Lost Delayed-Write Data message

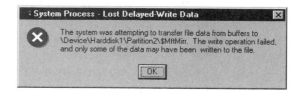

Here's a case where the user interface folks were out to lunch. At this point it would have been easier and clearer to just put up a dialog box that said, "One of your drives isn't working. You can no longer access data on drive X." This is just another reason why frequent backups are essential.

> **TIP**
>
> If you accidentally switch off an externally mounted drive that's part of a volume set and get messages like those in Figures 4.9 and 4.10 when you try to write to or read from that drive, just reboot. The volume set will recover without any problems.

Creating a Volume Set

To create a volume set, back up any data on your disks, make sure that there is free space on them, and follow these steps:

1. Open the Disk Administrator in the Administrative Tools program group.

2.   Select one or more areas of free space on your hard disk(s) by clicking on the first one and then Ctrl+clicking on the others to select them all at once—just like selecting more than one file at a time in Windows Explorer. This is demonstrated in Figure 4.11.

FIGURE 4.11:

Selecting free space on a hard drive

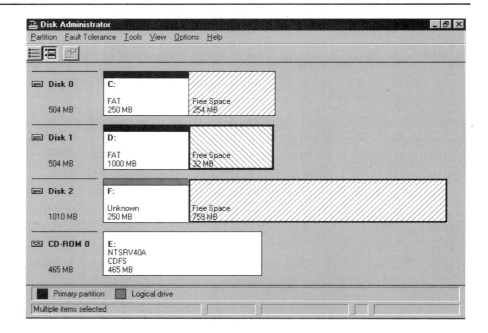

3.   Go to the Partition menu and choose Create Volume Set. When you've done this, you'll see a dialog box that displays the minimum and maximum sizes for the volume set, as in Figure 4.12.

FIGURE 4.12:

The Create Volume Set dialog box

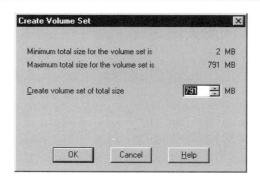

4. In the box, type the size of the volume set that you want to create. Obviously, the size must be somewhere between the minimum and the maximum sizes available: here, 2MB and 791MB, respectively. When you've got the proper size entered, click OK. You'll return to the Disk Administrator display and see the members of the volume set in yellow. In Figure 4.13, drive G: is the volume set.

FIGURE 4.13:

The volume set dialog box

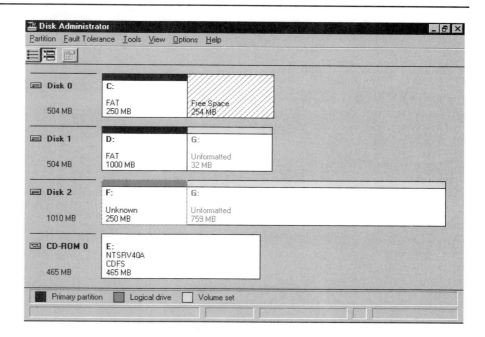

Figure 4.13 shows a volume set on two disks that already have primary partitions. If there is still free space left on the disks, it could be used for something else. When creating a volume set, you don't have to use all the available space. If you select a size smaller than the maximum, the Disk Administrator divides the size you choose roughly equally across all the partitions that you selected to be part of the volume set, so that all the partitions in the volume set are approximately the same size (so far as possible).

When you exit the Disk Administrator, you are prompted to save your changes and shut down the system, as discussed in earlier sections. Shut down, restart, and the volume set will be created.

Formatting the Volume Set

After you've restarted the system, format the disk either from the Tools menu or from the command line with the following command:

```
format x: /fs:filesystem
```

where *x* is the appropriate drive letter and *filesystem* is the type of file system (NTFS or FAT) to which you want to format that drive. Formatting may take a while, depending on the size of the set you've created. Read the "How Do I" sidebar to review how to create a volume set.

How Do I Create a Volume Set?

To create a volume set, do the following:

1. Open the Disk Administrator and select all the areas of free space that you want to be in the set.

2. From the Partition menu, choose Create Volume Set.

3. Choose the size of the set that you want and click OK. You can choose any size as long as it is within the maximum and minimum parameters.

4. Exit the Disk Administrator. You are prompted to reboot the system.

When you return to the Disk Administrator, the new volume set appears in yellow. It has a drive letter but won't yet be formatted.

5. To finish, you have to format the new logical drive, using either the command prompt or the Format command on the Tools menu. To format from the command prompt, open a DOS window and type

```
format driveletter: /fs:filesystem
```

where *driveletter* is, of course, the drive letter of the logical drive, and *filesystem* is either FAT or NTFS. For example, to format a newly created drive E: as NTFS, type

```
format e: /fs:ntfs
```

Deleting a Volume Set

Ultimately, you may want to reorganize the data on your disks, or you might start having problems with one of your disks and need to replace it. If one of these situations is the case, you need to delete the volume set. See the sidebar, "How Do I Delete a Volume Set?"

TIP

Deleting the volume set will permanently delete all the information that was in it, so back up any data in the set before deleting it. The next "How Do I" sidebar explains how to delete a volume set.

How Do I Delete a Volume Set?

To delete a volume set:

1. Go to the Disk Administrator.

2. Click on the volume set that you want to delete to select it. It will become outlined in black.

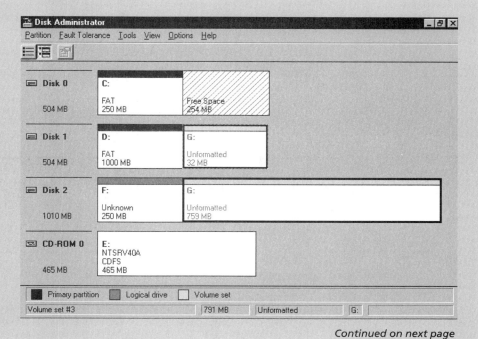

Continued on next page

3. From the Partition menu, select Delete.

A message box like the one following tells you that all data in the set will be lost. The message box asks you to confirm the action before continuing.

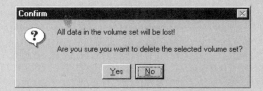

4. Click Yes to continue.

Once the set is deleted, the area used in the volume set reverts to free space.

Enlarging a Volume Set

If it turns out that your volume set is smaller than you need it to be, it's not necessary to delete it and re-create it from scratch. Instead, you can *extend* it by adding areas of free space to its volume. The instructions in the "How Do I Extend a Volume Set?" sidebar also apply to extending existing primary partitions to make their area bigger. (Once you extend them, however, they show up in the Disk Administrator color-coded as volume sets.)

You cannot use the instructions in the "How Do I" sidebar to make volume sets *smaller*. To do that, you must delete the volume set and create it again.

How Do I Extend a Volume Set?

To extend a volume set:

1. From the Disk Administrator, select an existing volume set or primary partition that has been formatted (one that is not part of a mirror set or stripe set) and one or more areas of free space. The volume set *must* have been previously formatted to extend it.

Continued on next page

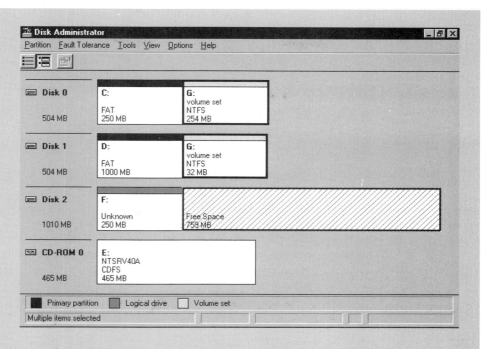

2. Go to the Partition menu and select Extend Volume Set. As you did when you created the volume set, you see a dialog box showing the minimum and maximum sizes for the volume set.

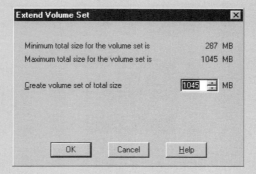

3. Enter the size of the volume set that you want and click OK.

The volume set is now the larger size that you specified, and all the area in it will have the same drive letter. The free space that you added is automatically formatted to the same file system as the rest of the volume set.

These limitations apply to extending volume sets:

- Again, you cannot use this procedure to make a volume set smaller. To do that, you need to delete the volume set and create a new one.

- You cannot extend the volume set for the partition with the system files on it. The Disk Administrator will not let you add free space to this partition.

- You cannot combine two volume sets, nor add a logical drive to a volume set.

- You cannot extend a FAT-formatted drive, only an NTFS one.

Simple Disk Striping

Another way to get more bang for your disk-buying buck is with disk striping without parity, also known as RAID level 0. When you create a stripe set from free space on your disks, each member of the stripe set is divided into stripes. Then, when you write data to the stripe set, the data is distributed over the stripes. A file could have its beginning recorded onto stripe 1 of member 1, more data recorded onto stripe 2 of member 2, and the rest on stripe 3 of member 3, for example. If you're saving data to a stripe set, a file is never stored on only one member, even if there is room on that member for the entire file. Conceptually, striping looks something Figure 4.14.

FIGURE 4.14:

Stripe set without parity

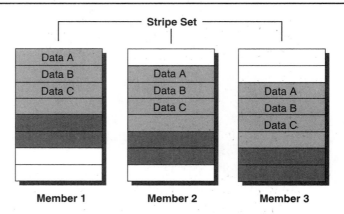

Different data files are represented here with different shades of gray. As you can see, an entire data file is never all put onto one member of the striped set. This improves read time, since, if Data A is called for, the disk controllers on all three members of the set can read the data. With a SLED data arrangement, only one of the members could read the data.

If you take free space on your disks and combine it into one stripe set with its own drive letter, the seek-and-write time to that drive will be improved, since the system can read and write to more than one disk at a time. To do striping without parity information included, you need at least two, but not more than 32, disks. You can create a stripe set and format it to NTFS; FAT won't work.

Creating a Stripe Set

Creating a stripe set without parity is quite simple. Just follow the steps in the "How Do I" sidebar.

How Do I Create a Stripe Set without Parity?

To create a stripe set without parity:

1. In the Disk Administrator, select two or more areas of free space on 2 to 32 hard disks (without parity, you need a minimum of only 2 disks, not 3). To do this, click on the free space on the hard disk and then Ctrl+click on the others as though you were selecting more than one file in Windows Explorer.

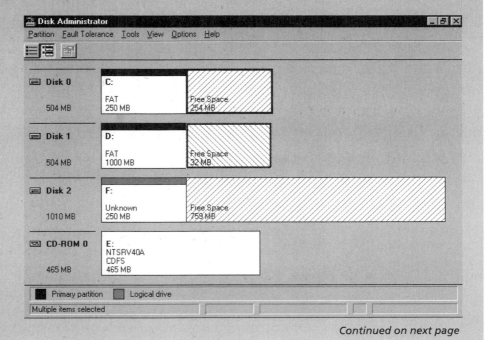

Continued on next page

2. From the Partition drop-down menu, choose Create Stripe Set. You see a dialog box that displays the minimum and maximum stripe sizes.

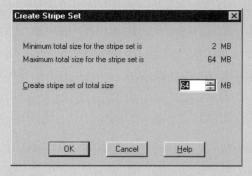

3. Choose the size of stripe set that you want, and click OK.

The Disk Administrator will now divide the total size of the stripe set that you selected equally among the available disks, and then assign a single drive letter to this set. If you selected a size that could not be divided equally among the number of disks involved in the stripe set, the Disk Administrator rounds to the nearest number. When you exit, the system reboots to implement the change, unless you press Ctrl+Esc.

The stripe set is now created but not formatted, as you can see from this picture:

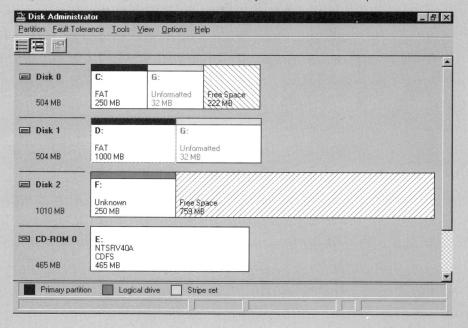

Continued on next page

To format the stripe set, either choose Format on the Tools menu or open a command prompt and type

```
format driveletter: /fs:filesystem
```

where *driveletter* is, of course, the drive letter of the logical drive, and *filesystem* is either FAT or NTFS. For example, to format a newly created drive G: as NTFS, you would type

```
format g: /fs:ntfs
```

When you're done, the stripe set will show up like this:

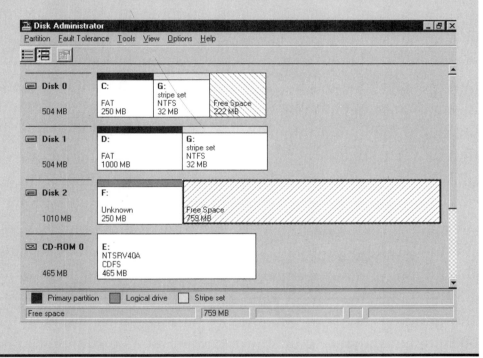

Deleting a Stripe Set

If anything happens to any member disk of your nonparity stripe set, all the data in the set is lost. Not only can't you get the data back (except through backups), but the disks that are part of the stripe set are unusable until you delete the stripe set and establish a new one. If the disk is dead, you have to delete the stripe set and start over. How to do that is explained in the sidebar.

How Do I Delete a Stripe Set?

To delete a stripe set:

1. In the Disk Administrator, select the stripe that you want to delete, as you see in the next graphic.

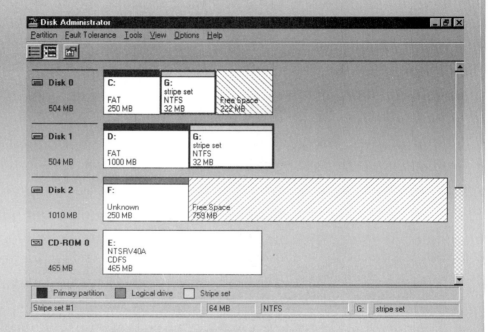

2. From the Partition drop-down menu, select Delete.

You see a message advising you that this action deletes all the data. The box asks you to confirm that you want to delete.

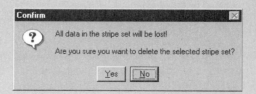

3. Click the Yes button in this message box.

Protecting Your Data

Using your disk space efficiently and improving data throughput are important, but they don't do anything to protect your data's integrity. If you want to do that, NT Server offers you two methods: disk mirroring and disk striping.

Disk Mirroring

If you have more than one disk, you can *mirror* a partition on one disk either FAT or NTFS onto free space on another. By doing so, you keep an exact copy of one partition on another disk. Once you have established this relationship between the two disk areas, called a *mirror set* (mirror sets are explained earlier in this chapter), every time that you write data to disk a duplicate of that data is written to the free space on the other half of the mirror set. Disk mirroring is equivalent to RAID level 1.

TIP   You can even mirror the c:drive, which is one nice way to make your system a bit more fault-tolerant.

How well does disk mirroring perform? Data must be written to both drives in the mirror set, but it suffers no performance lag because each disk can do its own writing *if duplexed* (see next paragraph); otherwise, writer will be a bit slower with mirroring. In addition, mirrored drives are fast when it comes to reads, as data can be pulled from both halves of the mirror set at once.

Mirroring and Duplexing

If you've ever heard or read anything about disk mirroring, you've probably also heard a term called disk *duplexing*. Disk duplexing is much the same as disk mirroring, except that duplexing generally refers to mirroring information on disks that each have their own disk controller, so that the data is not vulnerable to controller failures. When NT Server talks about disk mirroring, it is referring to both duplexing and mirroring, as Figure 4.15 demonstrates.

FIGURE 4.15:

Disk mirroring versus disk duplexing

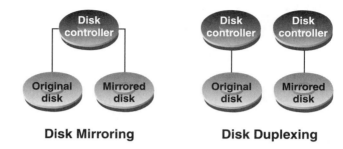

Disk Mirroring   **Disk Duplexing**

Establishing a Mirror Set

You can mirror a drive's data without affecting that drive's accessibility while you do it. See the sidebar to find out how.

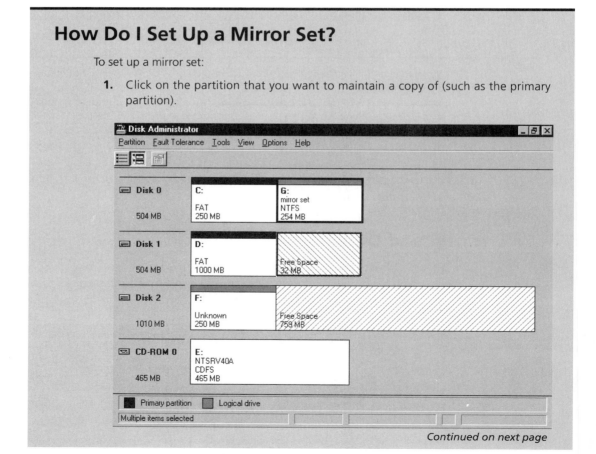

How Do I Set Up a Mirror Set?

To set up a mirror set:

1. Click on the partition that you want to maintain a copy of (such as the primary partition).

Continued on next page

2. By pressing Ctrl and clicking at the same time, choose the free space on another disk that you want to make the other half of the set.

This area must be the same size as, or greater than, the partition or drive that you are mirroring. If you select an area of free space that is too small, the system will complain, "The free space you have chosen is not large enough to mirror the partition you have chosen."

3. From the Fault Tolerance drop-down menu, select Establish Mirror.

Once you've done this, you have established the mirror set. The Disk Administrator now establishes an equal-sized partition in the free space to be the mirror. It also assigns the drive letter to the mirror set. Now, whenever you save a file to that drive letter, two copies of the file will really be saved.

4. Format the new logical drive. You do that either with the Format command in the Tools menu or by opening a command prompt and typing

```
format driveletter: /fs:filesystem
```

If you are mirroring a drive with data already on it, you won't need to format it. You'll need to commit changes and restart. NT will boot up more slowly as it is writing a copy of the data in the background to the new mirror "partner." This partner will have the same File System as the original.

5. *Driveletter* is, of course, the drive letter of the logical drive, and *filesystem* is either FAT or NTFS. For example, to format a newly created drive E: as NTFS, you would type

```
format e: /fs:ntfs
```

Breaking a Mirror Set

If something unrecoverable—like hardware damage—happens to half of the mirror set, you need to break the mirror set to get to the good data that you've backed up. It will be pretty apparent when something's gone wrong. You'll see a message like the one in Figure 4.16 when you try to write to the mirrored drives if one of the disks isn't working. Kind of looks more like a fortune-cookie fortune than a system message, doesn't it? You can still use the drive, but the benefits of mirroring will be suspended.

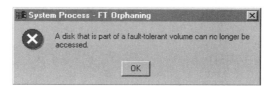

How Do I Break a Mirror Set?

To break a mirror set:

1. Open the Disk Administrator and select the mirror set that you want to break. When you open the Disk Administrator, you see a message like this that tells you something is different:

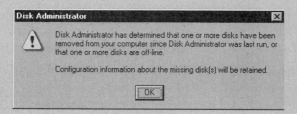

2. From the Fault Tolerance menu, select Break Mirror. You then see a message like this one:

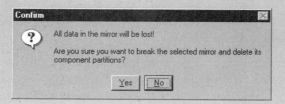

3. Click Yes to break the mirror set.

Breaking a mirror set does not affect the information inside it. Still, as always before doing anything drastic with the drive that holds your data, it's a good idea to back up first.

If you break a mirror set when nothing's wrong with it, each half becomes a primary partition with its own drive letter. The original partition keeps its original drive letter, while the backup partition gets the next available one.

Recovering Data from a Mirror Set

Once you've broken the mirror set so that you can get to the good data, the good half of the mirror set is assigned the drive letter that belonged to the now-defunct mirror set. The half that crashed is now called an *orphan* and is, in effect, set aside by the fault-tolerance driver so that no one will attempt to write to that part of the disk. When you reboot, the dead disk disappears, as in Figure 4.17.

FIGURE 4.17:

Recovering data from a mirror set

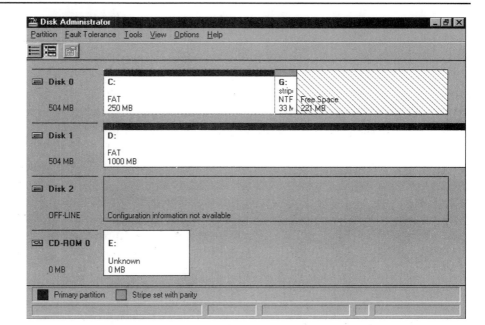

At this point, you take the good half of the old mirror set and establish a new relationship with another partition, as was discussed earlier in "Establishing a Mirror Set." When you restart the computer, the data from the good partition is copied to its new partner. While the regeneration process is going on, the type on the new half of the mirror set shows in red, but it doesn't take long to regenerate mirrored material. The process takes place in the background anyway, so you don't have to wait for it to finish to use the computer.

To review how to repair a broken mirror set, read the sidebar.

How Do I Repair a Broken Mirror Set?

To repair a broken mirror set:

1. Open the Disk Administrator and select the good half of the mirror set and an area of free space the same size or larger than the area to be mirrored.

2. Choose Establish Mirror from the Fault Tolerance menu.

The new mirror set will be displayed in magenta.

Mirroring Considerations

As you're deciding whether or not to protect your data by mirroring it, keep these things in mind:

- Mirroring to drives run from the same drive controller does not protect your data from drive controller failure. If any kind of controller failure occurs, you won't be able to get to the backup copy of your data unless you are mirroring to a disk run from a separate controller.

- For higher disk-read performance and greater fault tolerance, use a separate disk controller for each half of a mirror set.

- Disk mirroring effectively cuts your available disk space in half. Don't forget that as you figure out how much drive space you've got on the server.

- Disk mirroring has a low initial cost, since you must purchase only one extra drive to achieve fault tolerance, but a higher long-term cost due to the amount of room your redundant information takes up.

- Disk mirroring will slow down writes, as the data must be written in two places every time, but will speed up reads, as the I/O controller has two places to read information from. For multiuser environments (like the network you're using NT Server for), it gets the best performance of all the RAID levels.

Disk Striping with Parity

In addition to disk mirroring, NT Server gives you the option of using level 5 RAID, also known as *disk striping with parity*. Disk striping with parity differs from regular disk striping in the following ways:

- Although data lost from a stripe set without parity is unrecoverable, data from a parity stripe set can usually be recovered. ("Usually" because if someone puts a bullet through every one of your disks, all the parity information in the world won't help you.) If more than one disk of the 3 to 32 hard disk drives fails, you will not be able to recover your data.

- Regular disk striping improves data read and write speeds. Striping with parity slows down writes but improves access speed.

How Disk Striping Works

Every time you write data to disk, the data is written across all the striped disks in the array, just as it is with regular disk striping (RAID level 0). In addition, however, parity information for your data is also written to disk, always on a separate disk from the one where the data it corresponds to is written. That way, if anything happens to one of the disks in the array, the data on that disk can be reconstructed from the parity information on the other disks.

Level 5 RAID differs from level 4, which also uses parity information to protect data, in that the parity information in level 5 RAID is distributed across all the disks in the array. In level 4, a specific disk is dedicated to parity information. This makes level 5 RAID faster than 4, as it can perform more than one write operation at a time. This is shown in Figure 4.18.

If you think about it, writing parity information every time that you save a document could turn into quite a space-and-time waster. Take, for example, the document I'm creating for this book. If I've protected my data with level 5 RAID, and parity information is stored to disk every time that this file is saved, does that mean that there is parity information for every incarnation of this document from the time I began writing? If so, how can all the parity information and data fit on the disks?

FIGURE 4.18:

Disk striping with parity information

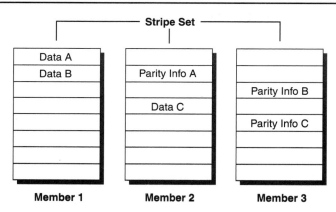

As you can see, no single member of the stripe set keeps all the original data or all the parity information. Instead the data and parity information are distributed throughout the stripe set, so if one member disk fails, the information can be reconstructed from the other members of the stripe set.

The answer is, of course, that it doesn't, and this is what produces the performance degradation that's unavoidable in striped disk writes. Every time a document is saved to disk, its parity information must be updated to reflect its current status; otherwise, you would have to keep backup parity information for every version of the document that you ever saved.

Updating the Parity Information

There are two ways to update the parity information. First, since the parity information is the XOR (exclusive OR) of the data, the system could recalculate the XOR each time data is written to disk. This would require accessing each disk in the stripe set, however, because the data is distributed across the disks in the array, and that takes time.

What is an *XOR?* On a very *simplistic* level, the XOR, or *exclusive OR arithmetic,* is a function that takes two one-bit inputs and produces a single-bit output. The result is 1 if the two inputs are different, or 0 if the two inputs are the same. More specifically:

0 XOR 0 = 0

1 XOR 0 = 1

0 XOR 1 = 1

1 XOR 1 = 0

When you're XORing two numbers with more than one bit, just match the bits up and XOR them individually. For example, 1101010 XOR 0101000 equals 1000010. The result you get from this function is the parity information, from which the original data can be recalculated.

A more efficient way of recalculating the parity information, and the one that NT Server uses, is to read the old data to be overwritten and XOR it with the new data to determine the differences. This process produces a *bit mask* that has a 1 in the position of every bit that has been changed. This bit mask can then be XORed with the old parity information to see where *its* differences lie, and from this the new parity information can be calculated. This seems convoluted, but this second process only requires two reads and two XOR computations, rather than one of each for every drive in the array.

Establishing a Stripe Set with Parity

To create a stripe set with parity, follow these steps:

1. In the Disk Administrator, select three or more areas of free space on from 3 to 32 hard disks (the exact number is determined by your hardware configuration; NT Server can handle up to 32 separate physical disks but your hardware setup may not be able to). To select the free space areas, click on the free space on the first hard disk and then Ctrl+click on the others in the same way that you select more than one file in Explorer.

As you can see in Figure 4.19, the areas of free space that you select don't have to be equal in size because the Disk Administrator distributes available space evenly and adjusts the size of the stripe set as necessary.

FIGURE 4.19:

Choosing free space for a stripe set with parity

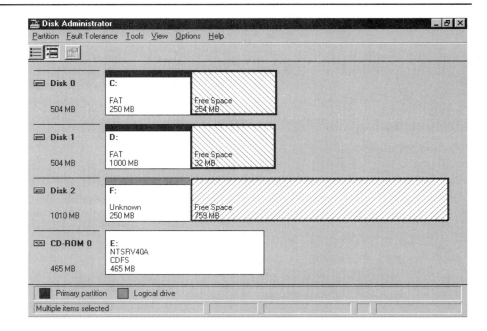

2. From the Fault Tolerance menu, choose Create Stripe Set With Parity. You see a dialog box like the one in Figure 4.20 that displays the minimum and maximum sizes for the stripe set with parity.

FIGURE 4.20:

The Create Stripe Set With Parity dialog box

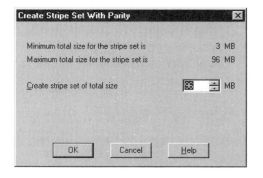

3. Choose the size stripe you want and click OK.

The Disk Administrator will now equally divide the total size of the stripe you selected among the available disks. Then it will assign a single drive letter to this set, as you see in Figure 4.21. In this case, the stripe set has been assigned letter G.

FIGURE 4.21:

The Disk Administrator after creating a stripe set with parity

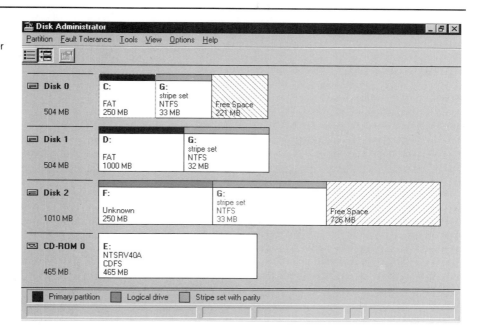

If you selected a size that could not be divided equally among the number of disks involved in the stripe set, the Disk Administrator rounds down the size to the nearest number evenly divisible by the number of disks in the stripe set.

After you've created the stripe set and try to exit the Disk Administrator, you see the usual dialog box that tells you the changes that you have made require you to restart your system. Click OK to begin shutdown.

When you restart, rebooting takes a little longer than normal. When you reach the blue screen that tells you what file system each of the drives on your system is using, the system informs you that it cannot determine the file system type of the stripe set's drive letter—not that it is RAW, as you've seen before, but that it can't determine it. This may look worrisome, but it's just due to the fact that the system has to initialize the stripe set. Wait for the drive activity on the stripe set drives to subside, and then format the new partition. If you don't format first, you get an error message like the one in Figure 4.22, but once you have formatted, everything should be ready to go.

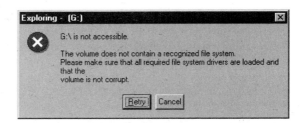

To recap, the next sidebar explains how to stripe with parity.

How Do I Create a Stripe Set with Parity?

To create a stripe set with parity:

1. Open the Disk Administrator and select areas of free space on at least three physical disks.

2. Pull down the Fault Tolerance menu and select Create Stripe Set With Parity.

3. Fill in the size that you want the stripe set to be and click OK.

The system will reboot upon your confirmation, and the stripe set will be initialized. As always, you've got to format it from the command line before you can use the drive.

Retrieving Data from a Failed Stripe Set

If an unrecoverable error to part of a striped set with parity occurs, you can regenerate the information stored there from the parity information stored on the rest of the set. You can even do this if one of the member disks has been low-level formatted.

How do you know when something's wrong? If you attempt to write to a stripe set and see an error message like the one in Figure 4.23, it's a bad sign.

FIGURE 4.23:

Error message while writing a stripe set

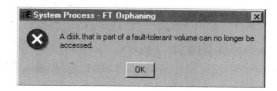

To recover the data, put a new disk in place and reboot so the system can see the new disk. Next, go to the Disk Administrator and select the stripe set that you want to fix and a new piece of free space that is at least equal in size to the other members of the set. Choose Regenerate from the Fault Tolerance menu, quit the Disk Administrator, and restart the computer.

When you restart the computer, the fault-tolerance driver collects the information from the stripes on the other member disks and then re-creates it onto the new member of the stripe set. If you open the Disk Administrator while it is doing this, you'll see that the text on the part being regenerated is displayed in red. Although the regeneration process may take a while, you can still use the server. You don't need to keep the Disk Administrator open because the restoration process works in the background and you can access the information in the stripe set.

Once the stripe set is fixed, you need to assign it a new drive letter and restart the computer. The failed portion of the original stripe set is set aside as unusable and is called an *orphan*. In the Disk Administrator, the failed disk looks like Figure 4.24.

TIP

When you're regenerating an NTFS stripe set with parity, make sure that you have a new disk in the system. When a disk goes bad and you're trying to regenerate its data onto a new one, NT Server does not gray out the Regenerate option even if you don't have a new disk in yet to put the data on. Instead, it tells you that the stripe set with that number has been recovered, but when you reboot and check the Disk Administrator, you see that the stripe set is still listed as "Recoverable."

FIGURE 4.24:

Failed disk in the Disk Administrator

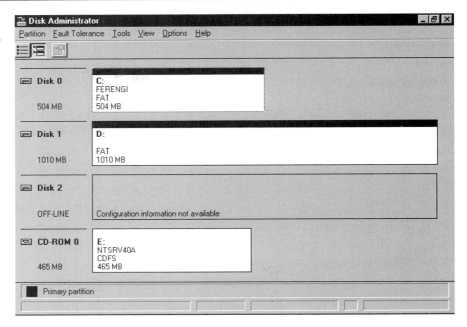

The next sidebar reviews how to regenerate a failed stripe set.

How Do I Regenerate a Failed Stripe Set?

To regenerate a failed stripe set:

1. Put a new disk in place and reboot the system.

2. After you've logged on, go to the Disk Administrator and select both the stripe set that you need to fix and an area of free space at least equal in size to the other members of the set.

3. Choose Regenerate from the Fault Tolerance menu.

The system shuts down and the regeneration process takes place in the background after it restarts. The regeneration process doesn't affect your ability to use the computer or access the information being regenerated.

Deleting a Stripe Set

Deleting a stripe set is quite simple. It is explained in the next "How Do I" sidebar.

How Do I Delete a Stripe Set?

To delete a stripe set:

1. In the Disk Administrator, select the stripe that you want to delete.

2. From the Partition drop-down menu, select Delete. You see a message that advises you that this action will delete all the data and asks you to confirm that you want to do this.

3. Click the Yes button in this dialog box.

Don't forget that deleting a stripe set destroys the data in it—even the parity information.

Things to Remember about Disk Striping with Parity

Keep these things in mind when it comes to disk striping with parity:

- It must be NTFS; FAT won't work.

- When you first set up the stripe set and reboot, the rebooting process takes longer than normal because the system must initialize the stripe set before it can be used.

- Striping with parity has a greater initial cost than disk mirroring does (it requires a minimum of three disks, rather than two). Nevertheless, it allows you to get more use out of your disk space.

- Although you can access the information in a stripe set even after one of the members has failed, you should regenerate the set as quickly as possible. NT Server striping cannot cope with more than one error in the set, so you're sunk if anything happens to the unregenerated stripe set.

- Striping with parity places greater demands on your system than disk mirroring, so you may get better performance from your system if you add 2MB of RAM to the system minimum of 16MB.

- If you have fewer than three physical hard disks on your server, you cannot make stripe sets with parity. The option in the Fault Tolerance menu will be grayed out.

Working with NTFS

NTFS is the filing system especially designed for use with Windows NT and NT Server. It is significantly different from the FAT system that you're used to if you've been working with DOS:

- NTFS supports filenames up to 256 characters long (including spaces and periods), with multiple extensions; FAT supports 8-character filenames with 3-character extensions, except under Windows 95, 98, or NT.

- NTFS is designed for system security (that is, setting file permissions); FAT is not. (You can, however, restrict network access to directories even when using FAT.) To learn how file permissions work, see Chapter 7.

- DOS is not equipped to read the stripe sets, volume sets, and mirror sets, so any of these partitions will be invisible to anyone trying to read them if you boot the server under DOS or Windows 9x.

- NTFS keeps a log of activities, in order to be able to restore the disk after a power failure or other interruption.

In short, Table 4.1 gives you an at-a-glance comparison of NTFS and FAT.

TABLE 4.1: Comparing NTFS and FAT

	NTFS	FAT
Filename length	256 characters	8+3 characters (except under Windows 9x, NT)
File attributes	Extended	Limited
Associated operating system	NT *and* NT Server	DOS
Organization	Tree structure	Centrally located menu
Software RAID support?	Yes	No

NTFS Naming Conventions

NTFS filenames can be up to 256 characters long with the extension, including spaces and separating periods. You can use any upper- or lowercase character in an NTFS filename except the following characters, which have special significance to NT:

> ? " / \ < > * | :

Even though NTFS supports long filenames, it maintains its compatibility with DOS by automatically generating a conventional FAT filename for every file. The process doesn't work in reverse, however, so don't save a file when working with an application that doesn't support long filenames. If you do, the application that doesn't like long names will save the file to the FAT name and erase all memory of the NTFS filename. The data won't be erased, however; only the descriptive filename is affected.

When converting a long filename to the short-name FAT format, NT Server does the following:

- Removes spaces

- Removes periods, all except the last one that is followed by a character—this period is assumed to herald the beginning of the file extension

- Removes any characters not allowed in DOS names and converts them to underscores

- Converts the name to six characters, with a tilde (~) and a number attached to the end

- Truncates the extension to three characters

Given how NT Server converts NTFS filenames to FAT conventions, you may want to keep that in mind when using long filenames, so that your filenames make sense in both FAT and NTFS. For example, you could name a file PRSNLLET-Personal letters file.SAM, so that the shortened name would be PRSNLL~1.SAM.

File Forking and Extended Attributes

Two of the things that make NTFS extra easy to work with are its ability to use file forking and extended attributes.

The term *file forking* has been used primarily in the Mac world, so don't be surprised if it sounds unfamiliar. Essentially, file forking is an association, so that if one file gets opened, another one associated with the first gets opened, too. Ami Pro, a Windows word processor, saves files with a SAM extension. Due to file association, if you open a SAM file from the File Manager, a copy of the Ami Pro program opens to support it. Under true file forking, each Ami Pro document would contain a small program that would tell NT to start up Ami Pro. That would allow an Ami Pro document to have *any* extension, instead of requiring the SAM extension.

Like file forking, *extended attributes* is a concept that sounds much trickier than it is. If you're familiar with DOS, you're familiar with file attributes. You can attach an attribute to a file to say that it's been modified since the last backup, that it should be read-only, or that it should be a hidden or system file. You do this by setting the *archive bit* on the file to whatever you like.

FAT's attributes are limited, however. You can say that a file should be read-only, but you can't identify it as the last CONFIG.SYS that you got to work properly on your machine. NTFS, on the other hand, allows you to tack extended attributes onto filenames to get a more complete description of what a file is for. Essentially, in combination with its ability to handle 256-character filenames, NTFS's extended attributes give your system a somewhat more Mac-like feel. You're no longer dependent on FAT's 8+3 naming conventions or limited attributes.

Long Names on Floppies

NT's support of NTFS sort of slops over into floppies. You can't format a floppy to NTFS format. If you try, you get an error message that says, "Cannot lock current drive." However, you *can* create files with long names on a floppy.

NT keeps two names for floppy files, the long name that you originally assigned and a truncated 8+3 name. DOS sees the shorter 8+3 name, however, making it possible for you to work with files that have long names under NT but short names under DOS.

Final Thoughts about Drives and NT Server

Let's wrap up with a few pieces of advice concerning hardware or software RAID, viruses, and FAT partitions.

Hardware or Software RAID?

You've seen here that you can hang a bunch of drives on your computer and that you can weave them into RAID sets and mirror sets. That all sounds good from a fault-tolerance point of view, since the probability that you'll actually lose any of your data is considerably reduced. Consider what you'll do when drive damage does occur, though.

You've got a mission-critical system up and running and one of the four drives in a stripe set with parity goes to its maker. Your next move is to bring the server down, replace the bad drive with a new good one, and then reintegrate that new one into the stripe set in order to recover the data.

Sounds good, until you really think about it. First of all, you've got to bring down this mission-critical server for several *hours* while you take out the old drive, install a new drive, and put the stripe set back together. In contrast, you could buy a *hardware* RAID system, a box containing several drives that act as one and that look to the NT system as just one drive. An external RAID box costs a bit more, but a hardware-based RAID system can rebuild itself faster than can NT's software. And, best of all, most hardware-based RAID systems allow you to "hot-swap" the bad drive—that is, to replace the bad drive without bringing down the server. So if your application is *truly* mission-critical, think about investing in RAID hardware. Of course, if you can't afford it, NT's solution isn't bad either.

Double-Check for Viruses

Around my company, we occasionally come across a computer that just won't take NT. You try to install it, and you get past the text part just fine. Then the NT install program reboots—and you get nothing but blue screens.

There are two likely causes for this. The first is that you've got a disk adapter whose NT driver is buggy. I've seen it on no-name SCSI and EIDE host adapters. But a surprising number of times, the cause is a boot sector virus like Form, Stoned, Anti-EXE, Anti-CMOS, NYB, Michelangelo, Stealth-B, or Joshi. So before you try to install NT (or *any* operating system, for that matter), turn the computer off, cold-boot it with a write-protected DOS floppy containing an up-to-date virus checker, and scan the computer's disks. Even if they're all formatted as NTFS, the virus checker can still scan the boot record, which is operating system-independent and is the home of the aforementioned viruses. In one case, we had a computer with a virus that wouldn't go away until we discovered that there was also a virus on the bootable floppy that we had to run in order to set up the EISA boards in our machine (*Arghh...*).

Leave a FAT Partition

Some people get positively antsy about the very *notion* that you should put anything but an NTFS partition on your server. I disagree.

You'll probably end up reinstalling NT a time or two on your system. And it's easiest to do that if the contents of the NT setup directory—I386 for most people—are right there on a local hard disk, rather than a CD-ROM. So make sure you've got about 500MB of FAT partition on your system and I386 on that.

On that partition, I put I386 and the operating system. User data, mailbox directories, home directories, and the like—files I want to secure—go on the other, NTFS-formatted drives.

Understanding the Registry Database

- Understanding Registry terminology

- How to work with the Registry

- Finding Registry keys

- Working with hives

- Modifying a remote Registry

- Backing up and restoring a Registry

Is there anybody out there who had to support Windows 3.1? Okay, then here's a quiz: Where did Windows keep its color settings? Let's see, it could be SYSTEM.INI or WIN.INI. But wait, that kind of stuff is set by the Control Panel, and there's a CONTROL.INI. Or maybe it's in AUTOEXEC.BAT?

NT tries to improve upon this configuration mess with something called the *Registry*. (Microsoft always capitalizes it—"the Registry"—so I will, too, but it always seems a bit overdone, don't you think?) The Registry is terrific in that it's one big database that contains all of the NT configuration information. Everything's there, from color settings to users' passwords. (In case you're wondering, you can't directly access the part with the passwords.) Even better, the Registry uses a fault-tolerant approach to writing data to ensure that the Registry remains intact even if there's a power failure in the middle of a Registry update.

So you've just *got* to like NT's Registry. Except, of course, for the *annoying* parts about the Registry, including its cryptic organization and excessively complex structure. But read on and see what you think.

What Is the Registry?

The Registry is a hierarchical database of settings, much like INI files, that describe your user account, the hardware of the server machine, and your applications. Knowing how to work with the Registry is an important key to being able to tune and control NT servers and NT workstations.

Now, editing the Registry is likely the part that you *won't* like about NT. The Registry is not documented in the pile of manuals that came with NT Server, but many Microsoft help files and bug-fix reports refer to it. You're just supposed to *understand* phrases like this one:

You can…force a computer to be a Browse Master by opening HKEY_LOCAL_ MACHINE\SYSTEM\CurrentControlSet\Services\Browser\Parameters, and creating an IsDomainMasterBrowser value, defining it as type REG_SZ, and specifying the text TRUE for the value of the string.

Sentences like those are a major reason for this chapter. You will come across phrases like that in Microsoft literature, magazine articles, and even parts of this book. Much of that information contains useful advice that will make you a better network administrator if you understand how to carry it out. My goal for this chapter, then, is to give you a feel for the Registry, how to edit it, and when to leave it alone.

Registry Terminology

What did that stuff with all the backslashes mean? To get a first insight, let's look at the Registry. You can see it by running the program REGEDT32.EXE (it's in the C:\winnt\SYSTEM32 directory) or by accessing it through WINMSD.EXE (click File and Run and a list of programs to run appears, one of which is "Registry Editor [Please use caution]"). Run it and click on the HKEY_LOCAL_MACHINE window. You'll see a screen like the one in Figure 5.1.

FIGURE 5.1:

Registry Editor dialog box

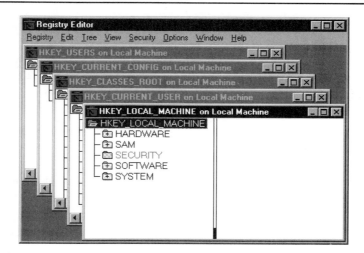

NOTE	NT 4 now has another Registry Editor called REGEDIT. It has a few features that REGEDT32 lacks.

The terms to know in order to understand the Registry are *subtree*, *key*, *value*, *data type*, and *hive*.

WARNING   It's easy to accidentally blast important data with the Registry Editor, so it might be a good idea at this point to put the Editor in *read-only* mode by clicking on Options, then on Read Only Mode. You can always reverse the read-only state whenever necessary in the same way. It is truly simple to render a server completely un-usable with a few unthinking Registry edits, so be careful, please.

Subtrees

If you ever supported Windows 3.1, you know that there were two essential INI files: WIN.INI and SYSTEM.INI. Roughly speaking, WIN.INI contained settings specific to a user and SYSTEM.INI contained settings specific to the machine. NT's Registry is divided up, as well.

The Registry stores all information about a computer and its users by dividing them up into five subtrees:

Subtree	Description
HKEY_LOCAL_MACHINE	Contains information about the hardware currently installed in the machine and about programs and systems running on the machine. You do most of your work in this subtree.
HKEY_CLASSES_ROOT	Holds the file associations, information that tells the system "whenever the user double-clicks on a file with the extension BMP in the File Manager, start up PBRUSH.EXE to view this file." It also contains the OLE registration database, the old REG.DAT from Windows 3.*x*. This is actually a redundant subtree, as all its information is found in the HKEY_LOCAL_MACHINE subtree.
HKEY_USERS	Contains two user profiles, a DEFAULT profile used to tell NT which set screen colors, wallpaper, screen saver, and the like to use when no one is logged in, and a profile with a name like S-228372162..., which is the profile of a user already known to the system. The long number starting with the *S* is the Security ID of the user. (The other user profiles are stored elsewhere, as you'll see later, either on the network or on the local \winnt\profiles directory.)
HKEY_CURRENT_USER	Contains the user profile for the person currently logged on to the NT Server machine.
HKEY_CURRENT_CONFIG	Contains configuration information for the particular hardware configuration you booted up with.

Some Registry entries are specific to a machine (HKEY_LOCAL_MACHINE, HKEY_CLASSES_ROOT, HKEY_CURRENT_CONFIG), and some are specific to a user (HKEY_USERS, HKEY_CURRENT_USER, and other Registry files that are in the \WINNT\PROFILES directories). That's important, and it's a great strength of the Registry's structure. The entries relevant to a particular machine should, of course, physically reside on that machine. But what about the settings relevant to a user: the background colors you like, the programs you want to see in your Start menu, the sounds you want on the system? These shouldn't be tied to any one computer, they should be able to move around the network with that user. Indeed, they can. NT supports the idea that "roving users" can have their personal settings follow them around the network via *roaming profiles*, which you will learn more about in Chapter 7.

Registry Keys

In Figure 5.1, you saw the Registry Editor display five cascaded windows, one for each subtree. HKEY_LOCAL_MACHINE was on top; you can see the other four subtrees' windows too. HKEY_CURRENT_USER's window has a right and left pane to it. The pane on the left looks kind of like a screen from the Explorer or the old Windows 3.1 File Manager.

In the File Manager, those folders represented subdirectories. Here, however, they separate information into sections, kind of in the same way that old Windows INI files had sections whose names were surrounded by square brackets, names like [386enh], [network], [boot], and the like. Referring back to the HKEY_LOCAL_MACHINE picture shown in Figure 5.1, let's compare this to an INI file. If this were an INI file, the name of its sections would be [hardware], [sam], [security], [software], and [system]. Each of those folders or sections are actually called *keys* in the Registry.

But here's where the analogy to INI files fails: you can have keys within keys, called *subkeys* (and sub-subkeys, and sub-sub-subkeys, and so on). Let's open the SYSTEM key. It contains subkeys named Clone, ControlSet001, ControlSet002, CurrentControlSet, Select, and Setup, and CurrentControlSet is further sub-keyed into Control and Services.

NOTE   If you use REGEDIT, it will show you where you are in the Registry at the bottom of the window.

Notice, by the way, that key called CurrentControlSet. It's very important. Almost every time you modify your system's configuration, you do it with a sub-key within the CurrentControlSet subkey.

Key Naming Conventions

The tree of keys gets pretty big as you drill down through the many layers. CurrentControlSet, for example, has dozens of subkeys, each of which can have subkeys. Identifying a given subkey is important, so Microsoft has adopted a naming convention that looks just like directory trees. Current-ControlSet's fully specified name would be, then, HKEY_LOCAL_MACHINE\ SYSTEM\CurrentControlSet. In this book, however, I'll just call it Current-ControlSet to keep key names from getting too long to fit on a single line.

Value Entries, Names, Values, and Data Types

If I drill down through CurrentControlSet, I find subkey Services, and within Services, there are many subkeys. In Figure 5.2, you can see some of the subkeys of CurrentControlSet\Services.

FIGURE 5.2:

Subkeys of
CurrentControlSet\
Services

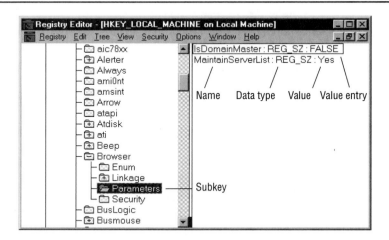

One of those keys, Browser, contains subkeys named Enum, Linkage, Parameters, and Security. Once we get to Parameters, however, you can see that it's the end of the line—no subkeys from there. Just to quickly review Registry navigation, the key that we're looking at now is in HKEY_LOCAL_MACHINE\SYSTEM\ CurrentControlSet\Services\Browser\Parameters.

In the right-hand pane, you see two lines:

```
IsDomainMaster : REG_SZ : False
MaintainServerList : REG_SZ : Yes
```

This is how the Registry says what would be, in the old INI-type files, something like this:

```
IsDomainMaster=Yes
MaintainServerList=Yes
```

Each line like IsDomainMaster:REG_SZ:False is called a *value entry*. The three parts are called *name*, *data type*, and *value*, respectively. In this example, IsDomain-Master is the *name*, REG_SZ is the *data type*, and False is the *value*.

Microsoft notes that each value entry cannot exceed about 1MB in size. It's hard to imagine one that size, but it's worth mentioning.

What is that REG_SZ stuff? It's an identifier to the Registry of what *kind* of data to expect: numbers, messages, yes/no values, and the like. There are five data types in the Registry Editor (although others could be defined later):

Data Type	Description
REG_BINARY	Raw binary data. Data of this type usually doesn't make sense when you look at it with the Registry Editor. Binary data shows up in hardware setup information. If there is an alternative way to enter this data other than via the Registry Editor— and I'll discuss that in a page or two—then do it that way. Editing binary data can get you in trouble if you don't know what you're doing. The data is usually represented in hex for simplicity's sake.
REG_DWORD	Another binary data type, but it is 4 bytes long.
REG_EXPAND_SZ	A character string of variable size. It's often information understandable by humans, like path statements or messages. It is "expandable" in that it may contain information that will change at run time, like %username%—a system batch variable that will be of different sizes for different people's names.
REG_MULTI_SZ	Another string type, but it allows you to enter a number of parameters on this one value entry. The parameters are separated by binary zeroes (nulls).
REG_SZ	A simple string.

Those who first met a Registry with Windows 95 will notice a few differences here. Windows 95 has six subtrees, but only three data types—*string*, which is like REG_SZ, REG_MULTI_SZ and REG_EXPAND_SZ; *dword*, which is like REG_DWORD; and *binary*, which is like REG_BINARY.

And if you're wondering how on earth you'll figure out what data type to assign to a new Registry value, don't worry about it; if you read somewhere to use a particular new value entry, you'll be told what data type to use.

Working with the Registry: An Example

Now, I know you want to get in there and try it out despite the warnings, so here's an innocuous example. Remember it's only innocuous if you *follow* the example to the letter; otherwise, it will soon be time to get out your installation disks.

That's not just boilerplate. Don't get mad at *me* if you blow up your server because you didn't pay attention. Actually, you *may* be able to avoid a reinstallation if the thing that you modified was in the CurrentControlSet key; NT knows that you often mess around in there, and so it keeps a spare. In that case, you can reboot the server and wait for the message that says, "Press spacebar now to restore Last Known Good menu." That's NT-ese for "press the spacebar and I'll restore the last control set that booted well for you." Again, that doesn't restore the entire Registry, however; it just restores the control set. Fortunately, the current control set is a *lot* of the Registry. It doesn't include user-specific settings, however, like "what color should the screen be?" Thus, if you were to set all of your screen colors to black, rendering the screen black on black (and therefore less than readable), rebooting and choosing "Last Known Good" wouldn't help you.

In any case, let's try something out, something relatively harmless. Let's change the name of the company that you gave NT when you installed it. For example, my firm changed its name back in 1995 from Mark Minasi and Company to TechTeach International, but all of the Help➤About dialog boxes still say that I work for Mark Minasi and Company. Fortunately, the Registry Editor lets me change company names without re-installing:

1. Open the Registry Editor. From the Start menu, choose Run.

2. In the command line, type **REGEDT32** and press Enter.

3. Click Window and choose HKEY_Local_Machine. Maximize that window and you see a screen somewhat like the one in Figure 5.3.

FIGURE 5.3:

Registry Editor-HKEY_ LOCAL_MACHINE on Local Machine dialog box

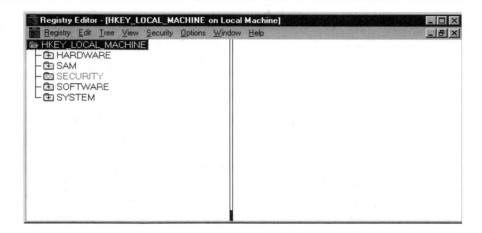

4. We're going to modify the value entry in HKEY_LOCAL_MACHINE\ Software\Microsoft\Windows NT\CurrentVersion. Double-click on the Software key, then double-click the Microsoft key, then double-click the Windows NT key, and finally double-click the CurrentVersion key. You see a screen like the one in Figure 5.4.

FIGURE 5.4:

CurrentVersion-Registered- Organization

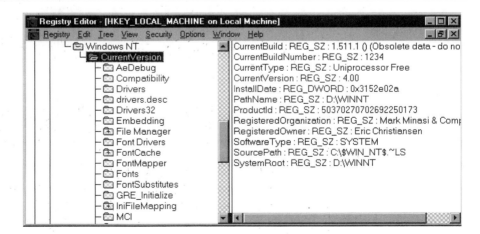

On the left pane, you still see the Registry structure. On the right, you see the value entry RegisteredOrganization.

5. Double-click on RegisteredOrganization, and you see a screen like the one in Figure 5.5.

FIGURE 5.5:

The String Editor dialog box

6. Highlight the old value and replace it with TechTeach International. Click OK, and close up the Registry Editor.

Now click Help➤About for any program—even the Registry Editor will do—and you'll see that your organization is now TechTeach International.

> **NOTE** Click all you like, you will not find a Save button or an Undo button. When you edit the Registry, it's immediate and it's forever. So, once again, be *careful* when you mess with the Registry.

How Do You Find Registry Keys?

How did I know to go to HKEY_LOCAL_MACHINE\Software\Microsoft\ Windows NT\CurrentVersion in order to change my organization name? I found it by poking around the Registry.

If you have the *Windows NT Resource Kit* from Microsoft—and if you don't, then *get it!*—you'll find 150 pages detailing each and every key. (That, by the way, is why there isn't a complete key guide in this book. First of all, there wasn't anything that I could add to what's in the *Resource Kit*; second, Microsoft has already published the Kit; and third, 150 pages directly lifted from someone else's publication is a pretty serious copyright violation. I don't think it's possible to paraphrase 150 pages of reference material.) Additionally, the Registry keys are documented in an online help file. Unfortunately, some keys aren't documented anywhere except in bits and pieces on Microsoft TechNet or the like, and I'll mention *those* in this book.

In my opinion, the Registry Editor has a glaring weakness: no effective search routine. Suppose you knew that there was something called "RegisteredOrganization" but you had no idea where it lives in the Registry? You'd be out of luck. Regedit32 includes a View ➢ Find Key, but it only searches the names of *keys*, not value entries. In contrast, the newer REGEDIT.EXE *can* search keys, values, and names. I could then search for "Registered Organization."

Even More Cautions about Editing the Registry

If you're just learning about the Registry, you're probably eager to wade right in and modify a value entry. Before you do, however, let me just talk a bit about using caution when you manipulate the Registry. (I know I've mentioned it before, but it's important, so I'm mentioning it again.)

The vast majority of Registry items correspond to some setting in the Control Panel, Server Manager, User Manager for Domains, or the like. For example, you just saw where we could change the RegisteredOrganization directly via the Registry Editor. I only picked that example, however, because it was fairly illustrative and simple to understand. In general, *don't use the Registry to modify a value that can be modified otherwise*.

For example, suppose I choose to set a background color on my screen to medium gray. That color is represented as a triplet of numbers: 128 128 128. How did I know what those color values meant? Because they're the same as Windows 3.*x* color values. Color values in Windows are expressed as number triplets. Each number is an integer between 0 and 255. If I input a value greater than 255, the Registry Editor would neither know nor care that I was punching in an illegal color value. Now, in the case of colors, that probably wouldn't crash the system. In the case of *other* items, however, the system could easily be rendered unusable. For example, I'm running NT Server on a system with just a single 486 processor, so the Registry reflects that, noting in one of the Hardware keys that NT is running a "uniprocessor" mode. Altering that to a multiprocessor mode wouldn't be a very good idea.

Why, then, am I bothering to tell you about the Registry Editor? Three reasons.

First, there are settings—important ones—that can only be altered via the Registry Editor, so there's no getting around the fact that an NT expert has to be proficient in the Editor.

Second, you can use the Registry Editor to change system value entries on *remote* computers. To use a very simple example: I'm at location A and I want to change the background color on the server at location B, and to do that I have to physically travel to location B in order to run the Control Panel on the NT machine at that location. Instead of doing that, however, I can just start up the Registry Editor, choose Registry ➤ Select Computer, and edit the Registry of the remote computer. (This assumes that you are running NT Server and you have the security access to change the Registry of the remote computer—that is, you're a member of the Administrators group on that computer.)

Third, a program comes with the *Resource Kit* called REGINI.EXE that allows you to write scripts to modify Registries. Such a tool is quite powerful; in theory, you could write a REGINI script to completely reconfigure an NT setup. Again, however, before you start messing with that program, *please* be sure that you have become proficient with the Registry. I've explained the various kinds of mischief that you can cause working by hand with the Registry Editor. Imagine what kinds of *automated* disasters you could start at 450MHz with a bad REGINI script!

Where the Registry Lives: Hives

The Registry is mostly contained in a set of files called the *hives*. ("Mostly" because some of it is built automatically every time you boot up your system. For example, devices on a SCSI chain aren't known until you boot.) Hives are binary files, so there's no way to look at them without a special editor of some kind, like the Registry Editor. Hives are, however, an easy way to load or back up a sizable part of the Registry.

Most, although not all, of the Registry is stored in hive files. They're not hidden, system, or read-only, but are always open, so you're kind of limited in what you can do with them.

A Look at the Hive Files

The machine-specific hive files are in the \WINNT\SYSTEM32\CONFIG directory. The user-specific hive files are in the \WINNT\PROFILES directories. You can see the hive files that correspond to parts of the subtree listed in Table 5.1.

TABLE 5.1: Hive Files

Subtree/Key	File Name
HKEY_LOCAL_MACHINE\SAM	SAM (primary) and SAM.LOG (backup)
HKEY_LOCAL_MACHINE\SECURITY	SECURITY (primary) and SECURITY.LOG (backup)
HKEY_LOCAL_MACHINE\SOFTWARE	SOFTWARE (primary) and SOFTWARE.LOG (backup)
HKEY_LOCAL_MACHINE\SYSTEM	SYSTEM (primary) and SYSTEM.ALT (backup)
HKEY_USERS\DEFAULT	DEFAULT (primary) and DEFAULT.LOG (backup)
HKEY_USERS\Security ID	NTUSER.DAT
HKEY_CURRENT_USER	NTUSER.DAT
HKEY_CLASSES_ROOT	(Created from current control set at boot time)

Table 5.1 needs a few notes to clarify it. First, about the HKEY_CLASSES_ROOT subtree: it is copied from KEY_LOCAL_MACHINE\SOFTWARE\Classes at boot time. The file exists for use by 16-bit Windows applications. While you're logged on to NT, however, the two keys are linked; if you make a change to one, then the change is reflected in the other.

The user profiles now live in \winnt\profiles*username*, where each user gets a directory named *username*. For example, I've got a user account named "mark," so there's a directory named d:\winnt\profiles\mark on my computer. If I look in it, I find the files ntuser.dat and ntuser.dat.log.

To summarize, then, the core of the Registry is the four *S*'s:

- SAM
- SECURITY
- SYSTEM
- SOFTWARE

SAM contains the user database; SECURITY complements SAM by containing information like whether a server is a member server or a domain controller, what the name of its domain is, and the like. SYSTEM contains configuration information like "what drivers and system programs does this computer use, which should be loaded on bootup, and how are their parameters set?" SOFT-WARE tends to contain more overall configuration information about the larger software modules in the system, configuration information that does *not* vary from user to user. And then every user has an NTUSER.DAT with her specific application preferences in it.

One question remains about the hive files, however. Why do all the files have a paired file with the extension LOG? Read on.

Fault Tolerance in the Registry

Notice that every hive file has another file with the same name but the extension LOG. That's really useful, because NT Server, and NT workstations for that matter, uses it to protect the Registry during updates.

Whenever a hive file is to be changed, the change is first written into its LOG file. The LOG file isn't actually a backup file; it's more a journal of changes to the primary file. Once the description of the change to the hive file is complete, the journal file is written to disk. When I say "written to disk," I *mean* written to disk. Often, a disk write ends up hanging around in the disk cache for a while, but this write is "flushed" to disk. Then the system makes the changes to the hive file based on the information in the journal file. If the system crashes during the hive write operation, there is enough information in the journal file to "roll back" the hive to its previous position.

The exception to this procedure comes with the SYSTEM hive. The SYSTEM hive is really important because it contains the CurrentControlSet. For that reason, the backup file for SYSTEM, SYSTEM.ALT, is a complete backup of SYSTEM. If one file is damaged, the system can use the other to boot.

Notice that HKEY_LOCAL_MACHINE\HARDWARE does not have a hive. That's because the key is rebuilt each time you boot, so that NT can adapt itself to changes in computer hardware. The program NTDETECT.COM, which runs at boot time, gathers the information that NT needs to create HKEY_LOCAL_MACHINE\HARDWARE.

Confused about where all the keys come from? You'll find a recap in Table 5.2. It's similar to the table a few pages back, but it's more specific about how the keys are built at boot time.

TABLE 5.2:   Construction of Keys at Boot Time

Key	How Constructed at Boot Time
HKEY_LOCAL_MACHINE:	
HARDWARE	NTDETECT.COM
SAM	SAM hive file
SECURITY	SECURITY hive file
SOFTWARE	SOFTWARE hive file
SYSTEM	SYSTEM hive file
HKEY_CLASSES_ROOT	SYSTEM hive file, Classes subkey
HKEY_USERS_DEFAULT	DEFAULT hive file
HKEY_USERS\Sxxx	Particular user's NTUSER.DAT file
HKEY_CURRENT_USER	Particular user's NTUSER.DAT file

Remote Registry Modification

You can modify another computer's Registry, perhaps to repair it or to do some simple kind of remote maintenance, by loading that computer's hive. You do that with the Registry Editor by using the Load Hive or Unload Hive commands.

You can only load or unload the hives for HKEY_USERS and HKEY_LOCAL_ MACHINE. The Load Hive option only appears if you've selected one of those two subtrees. Unload Hive is only available if you've selected a subkey of one of those two subtrees.

Why, specifically, would you load a hive or a remote Registry?

First of all, you might load a hive in order to get to a user's profile. Suppose a user has set up all of the colors as black on black and made understanding the screen impossible. You could load the hive that corresponds to that user, modify it, and then unload it.

Second, you can use the remote feature to view basically *anything* on a remote system. Suppose you want to do something as simple as changing screen colors. You'd do that on a local system by running the Control Panel, but the Control Panel won't work for remote systems. Answer: Load the Registry remotely.

You could load and save hive files to a floppy disk, walk the floppy over to a malfunctioning machine, and load the hive onto the machine's hard disk, potentially repairing a system problem. This isn't possible if you're using NTFS, unless you have multiple copies of NT on your system, something most of us don't have. But if you've got an NT workstation running a FAT file system, then you can always boot from DOS, replace the hive files under DOS, and then reboot under NT.

When you boot under NT, you see the reference to a "known good menu." That's because NT keeps track not only of the current control set, but also the *previous* control set. That way, if you mess up your system, you can always roll back to the previous configuration. Those control sets are kept in the same key as the CurrentControlSet. Within HKEY_LOCAL_MACHINE\SYSTEM\Select\Current, \Default, \Failed, and \LastKnownGood are numbers indicating which of the two kept control sets are failed, current, good, and the like.

There is yet another way to control Registries remotely, through something called System Policies, which are covered in the next chapter.

Backing Up and Restoring a Registry

By now, it should be pretty clear that the Registry is an important piece of information and should be protected. It protects itself pretty well with its LOG files, but how can you back it up?

Unfortunately, the fact that Registry hive files are always open makes it tough to back up the Registry, since most backup utilities are stymied by open files. The NTBackup program that comes with NT works well, but it only backs up to tape.

Nevertheless, if you use NTBackup—and it's pretty good, particularly for its price—then you should tell it to back up your Registry every night.

Outside of NTBackup are a couple of other protection possibilities. A program named RDISK creates emergency repair disks. By typing **RDISK/S**, you'll back up your Registry in the directory \WINNT\REPAIR. The program even lets you save it to floppy. And the *Resource Kit* includes two useful utilities: the REGBACK.EXE program allows you to back up a Registry file; the REGREST.EXE restores it.

REGEDIT versus REGEDT32

Since NT 4.0 arrived, we've had a choice of Registry editors. NT always shipped with REGEDT32, but Windows 95 included REGEDIT and Microsoft decided to offer it for NT, as well. (There's even a third Registry editor called the System Policy Editor, which you'll meet in Chapter 7, but we'll leave that discussion for later.) Are there good reasons to use one or the other?

REGEDT32 has a couple of features that REGEDIT lacks. For one thing, you can set the size of the display font that REGEDIT uses. That may not sound exciting, but I get a lot of use out it when teaching classes. It seems like more and more Microsoft administration tools use *really* tiny fonts, making on-line demonstrations difficult in a room holding more than about 20 people. REGEDT32's greater strength, however, is its ability to set security on Registry keys. As with everything else in NT, each key in the Registry has a *security descriptor* or *ACL* (Access Control List), a description of who is and who isn't allowed to modify that key. Sometimes Microsoft will discover a "hole" in NT security caused by some incorrect security setting, and you must use REGEDT32 to seal that security hole—REGEDIT can't do the trick here.

For most other work, I use REGEDIT. First of all, I like the fact that the status bar at the bottom of its window always tells me the complete path to my current position in the Registry. The ability to search for any string is convenient, as well. For example, one time I'd gotten my system so confused that it kept asking for a particular program every time I booted up. Clearly the command to start this program was somewhere in the Registry—but where? A quick search solved the problem, showing me where in the Registry the problem lay, making it easy for me to undo the problem. Perhaps the best capability, however, is in REGEDIT's built-in Registry modification language. Look back to Chapter 3 for details on that; it's a convenient way to record favorite software settings in an ASCII file and then play them back onto a new system whenever you want.

No one *wants* to play around in the Registry, but in real life most network administrators will find a bit of Registry spelunking to be the only answer to many problems. Knowing how the Registry is organized and what tools are available to modify it will prove valuable to all NT fixers.

PART

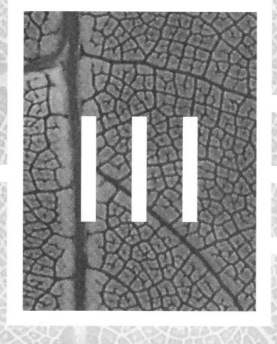

III

NT Server
Administration

CHAPTER

SIX

6

Managing and Creating User Accounts

■ Working with the User Manager for Domains

■ Creating new user accounts

■ Working with user accounts

■ Working with groups

■ Managing security policies

■ Using the System Policy Editors

User Manager
for Domains

I have introduced NT Server and some of its components. Now let's tackle the job of actually being an NT Server administrator. As an administrator, you have to

- Create accounts for network users and define what those users can do
- Create shared areas on server disks and define who can access those shares
- Create shared printers and define access to them
- Set up desktop computers to connect with the servers

Those are the goals of the next few chapters. The first goal, setting up user accounts, is the primary object of this chapter. The tool you use to set up user accounts is called the *User Manager for Domains*.

Introducing the User Manager for Domains

In Windows NT Server, the User Manager for Domains is the primary administrative tool for managing user accounts, groups, and security policies for domains and computers on the network. User Manager for Domains only runs on NT server machines, and even then by default only on domain controllers. Run User Manager on another machine, such as a regular old NT workstation or an NT server that is not a domain controller, and you get a cut-down version called simply the User Manager rather than the User Manager for Domains. You can run User Manager for Domains on those machines (heck, there are even versions for Windows for Workgroups and Windows 95/98), but you've got to load them from the NT CD-ROM in the \CLIENTS\SRVTOOLS directory.

User Manager for Domains versus User Manager

What does it mean to be the User Manager *for Domains*? Well, recall from Chapter 2 that NT machines of all stripes flatly refuse to share data with anyone that they don't recognize; in a simple nondomain network, every single server would have to be introduced to every single user. NT workstations create and manage user accounts with a program called simply *User Manager*. The job of the User Manager on machine XYZ is to create user accounts that are only relevant and useful on machine XYZ. If a user on machine ABC wanted to get access to data on machine XYZ, the owner of machine XYZ would have to create an account for the ABC owner on the XYZ machine with the User Manager on machine XYZ.

That would lead to a situation wherein a company with 20 servers (and therefore 20 copies of User Manager running) and 100 users would have to keep track of 2,000 accounts, making for an administrative nightmare. To simplify things, NT provides for a kind of "account sharing" called a *domain*. One NT machine, the Primary Domain Controller (PDC), holds a shared database of all users known to the machines that have all agreed to constitute a domain. That way, if user John needs access to all 20 servers in the domain, all you've got to do is to build a single domain-wide account for John—and build a domain-wide account with the User Manager for *Domains*. Put simply, the User Manager is the program that manipulates a machine's SAM—the user database. The main difference for the User Manager for *Domains* is that it manipulates the SAM on the primary domain controller.

User Accounts Sit on the PDC

User accounts contain information like the username, the password, and a description. All of that data sits in a file called SAM in the primary domain controller's \winnt\system32\config directory. SAM, which is short for *Security Access Manager*, lives in the PDC's Registry, in an area that's grayed out if you try to peek into it.

NOTE   Backing up the Registry of your PDC is an important part of disaster prevention, because it contains all of your user accounts. If you ever have to rebuild a PDC from scratch, then you can restore your user accounts by restoring the Registry. Recall that the command RDISK/S backs up your Registry to \WINNT\REPAIR. While there are other Registry backup tools—and you should use them—a simple RDISK/S now and then is a good bit of insurance.

Whenever you run the User Manager for Domains, you're directly manipulating that part of the Registry on the PDC. No matter what machine you run the User Manager for Domains from, your changes get stored in the PDC's Registry. If your system cannot get a real-time connection to the PDC, you will be unable to modify user accounts. The connection must, again, be to a PDC—BDCs aren't good enough.

User Manager for Domains Functions

User Manager for Domains provides the network administrator with the means to

- Create, modify, and delete user accounts in the domain
- Define a user's desktop environment and network connections
- Assign logon scripts to user accounts
- Manage groups and group membership within the accounts in a domain
- Manage trust relationships between different domains in the network
- Manage a domain's security policies

If you are logged on as an administrator and you start up the User Manager for Domains, all of its features are available to you. If you log on as a member of the Account Operators group, you won't be able to use some of the User Manager for Domain's capabilities; you can manage most user accounts, but you cannot implement any of the security policies. If you log on as a mere mortal—"user," I believe, is the common term—you can only look at usernames with the User Manager for Domains; the User Manager for Domains won't let you make any changes to those accounts. Which reminds me...

NOTE   Most changes that you make to a user's account will not show up until the next time she logs on. That means, if she is in the middle of a network session, any changes you've made won't take effect until she logs off and then back on.

A Look around the User Manager for Domains

When you open User Manager for Domains, you see a screen like Figure 6.1. In that screen, you can see a list of all of the accounts in the domain, followed by a list of the groups defined in the domain. The user and group information displayed initially is that for the domain where your user account is located (your home domain), and the name of the domain appears in the title bar; in this case, it's ORION.

To view users and groups from other trusted domains (trust relationships are discussed in detail in Chapter 12), use the Select Domain command under the User menu. In the resulting dialog box, seen in Figure 6.2, select or type in the name of the domain whose accounts you wish to view.

FIGURE 6.1:

User Manager for Domains

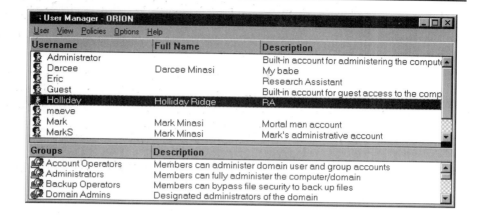

FIGURE 6.2:

Select Domain dialog box

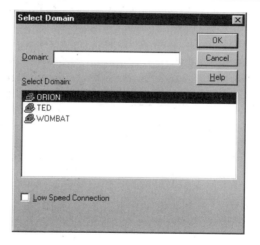

You can also use this command to view the accounts on individual computers that maintain their own security databases (that is, workstations running Windows NT). To do this, type in the computer name preceded by two backslashes (*computer-name*) in place of the domain name. At that point, the User Manager for Domains looks more like the regular old User Manager that comes with NT Workstation. Oh, by the way, if the computer that you choose is a domain controller, the domain information is displayed instead. If you want to, you can open multiple instances of User Manager for Domains, each with a different domain's data.

If the domain or computer you choose happens to communicate with your computer through a connection that has relatively low transmission rates, select Low Speed Connection on the Options menu (or in the Select Domain dialog box). This option disables the producing and displaying of lists of user accounts and groups in the User Manager for Domains window (which can take a long time across a low-speed link). Although the option is disabled, you can still create or manage user accounts and local groups by using these commands: New User, New Local Group, Copy, Delete, Rename, or Properties. Under the Low Speed Connection option, global groups can't be created or copied, but global group membership can still be managed, somewhat indirectly, by managing the group memberships of individual users. Global and local groups are explained in detail in Chapter 12.

Lists of users and groups can be sorted by either username or by full name with the options on the View menu. Bear in mind that View menu commands are unavailable if the low-speed connection is selected. Any changes made to any account or group while in User Manager for Domains are automatically updated in the view. Other changes, such as an administrator adding an account in your domain from a different, trusted domain, are updated at fixed intervals. If necessary, use the Refresh command to get the latest information for the domain.

To view and manage the properties of a displayed user account or group, simply double-click on the name of the account or group (alternatively, you can select the entry and then choose Properties on the User menu). You see the User Properties dialog box in Figure 6.3.

I'll explain what the Groups, Hours, Logon To, and Account buttons do in this chapter. The Profile button is easier to understand once you've learned how to create file shares, so I'll tackle the Profile button in the next chapter.

Sometimes you want to make a change to several user accounts at the same time—to change logon hours, for example. All you have to do in that case is choose a number of users (Ctrl+click on the ones you want to work with) and then choose Users ➤ Properties.

In NT Server, a user account contains information such as the username, password, group membership, and rights and privileges the user has for accessing resources on the network. These details are explained in Table 6.1.

FIGURE 6.3:

User Properties dialog box

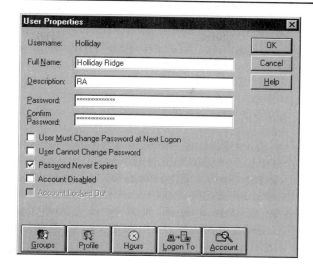

TABLE 6.1:   Information in a User Account

Part of User Account	Description
Account type	The particular type of user account; that is, a local or global account.
Expiration date	A future date when the user account automatically becomes disabled.
Full name	The user's full name.
Home directory	A directory on the server that is private to the user; the user controls access to this directory.
Logon hours	The hours during which the user is allowed to log on to and access network services.
Logon script	A batch or executable file that runs automatically when the user logs on.
Logon workstations	The computer names of the NT workstations that the user is allowed to work from (by default, the user can work from any workstation).
Password	The user's secret password for logging on to his or her account.
Profile	A file containing a record of the user's Desktop environment (program groups, network connections, screen colors, and settings that determine what aspects of the environment the user can change) on NT workstations.
Username	A unique name the user types when logging on. One suggestion is to use a combination of first and last names, such as JaneD for Jane Doherty.

Security Identifiers

User accounts, when first created, are automatically assigned a *security identifier* (SID). A SID is a unique number that identifies an account in the NT Server security system. SIDs are never reused; when an account is deleted, its SID is deleted with it. SIDs look like

S-1-5-21-D1-D2-D3-RID

where *S-1-5* is just a standard prefix (well, if you *must* know, the 1 is a version number, which hasn't changed since NT 3.1; the 5 means that the SID was assigned by NT; 21 is also an NT prefix and D1, D2, and D3 are just 32-bit numbers that are specific to a domain). Once you create a domain, D1 through D3 are set, and all SIDs in that domain henceforth have the same three values. The *RID* stands for Relative ID. The RID is the unique part of any given SID.

Each new account always has a unique RID number, even if the user name and other information is the same as an old account. This way, the new account will not have any of the previous rights and permissions of the old account, and security is preserved. (I know, you're wondering, "What if I run out of RIDs?" Well, there are 4 billion of them, so you're not likely to run out. If you *did* end up running so many people through your system that you ran out, would the system start reusing RIDs? I have no idea.)

Prebuilt Accounts: Administrator and Guest

If you're creating a new domain, you'll notice that two accounts called Administrator and Guest are built already. The Administrator account is, as you've guessed, an account with complete power over a domain. You can't delete it, but you can rename it.

WARNING　One of the first things to do after you've set up an NT machine is to rename the Administrator account. As you'll see later, it's dangerous and so it shouldn't be easy for people to figure out the new name of the Administrator account.

You assigned the password for the domain's Administrator account when you installed NT Server on the machine that became the Primary Domain Controller for the domain. Don't lose that password, as there's no way to get it back! (Well, you can always rebuild the domain from scratch with the installation diskettes, but it's no fun.)

The other account is the Guest account. *Guest* means "anyone that the domain doesn't recognize." By default, this account is disabled, and it should *stay* that way. If you've ever worked with a different network, like a Unix or NetWare network, then you're probably familiar with the idea of a guest account—*but NT's works differently, so pay attention!* With most other operating systems, you can get access to the operating system by logging on with the user name Guest and a blank password. That Guest account is usually pretty restricted in the things it can do. That's true with NT, as well, although remember that the Everyone group includes the guests.

Here's the part that *isn't* like other operating systems. Suppose someone tries to log on to an NT network that has the Guest account enabled. She logs on as melanie_wilson with the password "happy." Now, suppose further that this domain doesn't *have* a melanie_wilson account, so it rejects her logon. On a DOS, Windows for Workgroups, or Windows 95 workstation, Melanie can still do work, because none of those operating systems require you to log on to a domain in order to get access to the local workstation. On an NT workstation, she might log on to an account on the local machine. Now she's working at a computer and tries to access a domain resource. And guess what?

She gets in.

Even though an explicit domain login requires that you use a username of Guest, you needn't explicitly log on to a domain to use guest privileges. If your network is attached to my network and your Guest account is enabled, then I can browse through your network and attach to resources that the Guest can access. I needn't log on as Guest; the mere fact that there *is* an enabled Guest account pretty much says to NT, "Leave the back door open, okay?" So be careful when enabling the Guest account.

Creating a New User Account

Creating new user accounts in NT Server is fairly easy. Under the User menu, choose the New User option. You'll see the dialog box shown in Figure 6.4.

FIGURE 6.4:

The New User dialog box

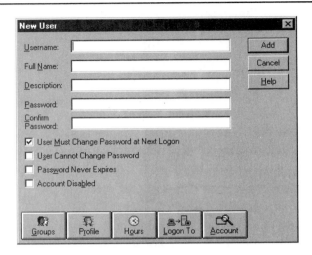

To begin, type in a unique user name in the Username box (as suggested in Table 6.1, one option is a combination of the user's first and last names). The user name can have up to 20 characters, either upper- or lowercase, and can't include the following characters:

" / \ [ ] ; : | = , + * ? < >

Blanks are okay, but I'd avoid them, because they make it necessary to surround usernames with quotes when executing commands.

In the Full Name and Description boxes, type in the user's full name and a short description of the user or of the user account. Both of these entries are optional, but recommended. Establish a standard for entering full names (last name first, for example), because the viewing options in User Manager for Domains allow you to sort user accounts by the user's full name instead of the username.

Next, type a password in both the Password and Confirm Password boxes. Passwords are case-sensitive, and their attributes are determined under the Account Policy, which I'll cover a bit later in the section about managing security. After you've entered and confirmed a password, select or clear the check boxes that determine whether or not the user can or must change the password at the next logon. If you don't want anyone using the new account just yet, check the

Account Disabled box. All of the options in this series of check boxes are described in Table 6.2.

TABLE 6.2:   Password and Account Options for Creating a New User Account

Option	Default	Description
User Must Change Password at Next Logon	Yes	Forces the user to change the password the next time that he or she logs on; this value is set to No afterwards.
User Cannot Change Password	No	If Yes, prevents the user from changing the account's password. This is useful for shared accounts.
Password Never Expires	No	If Yes, the user account ignores the password expiration policy, and the password for the account never expires. This is useful for accounts that represent services (such as the Replicator account) and accounts for which you want a permanent password (such as the Guest account).
Account Disabled	No	If Yes, the account is disabled and no one can log on to it until it is enabled (it is not, however, removed from the database). This is useful for accounts that are used as templates.

At the bottom of the New User dialog box are five buttons: Groups, Profile, Hours, Logon To, and Account. With these buttons, you define the properties of the user account. You'll learn about them in detail in the next sections, save for Profile, which I cover in the next chapter.

Assigning Groups

Selecting the Groups button allows you to specify which groups the new user account will have membership in. NT Server has a number of useful predefined groups, and I'll explain them in more detail a bit later in this chapter in "Managing Groups." (For a more complete description of groups—in particular, local groups versus global groups—look at Chapter 12, on multi-domain planning and management.) Group membership is shown in the Group Memberships dialog box, seen in Figure 6.5.

FIGURE 6.5:

Group Memberships
dialog box

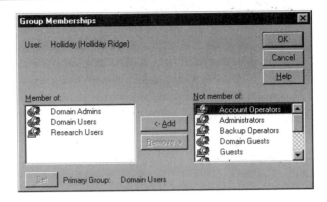

You can click on the Groups button to open this dialog box. The dialog box displays which groups the user is or isn't a member of. Note the icons next to the group names:

- An icon representing a white woman and a black man in front of a globe indicates a global group.

- A computer terminal behind the two faces indicates a local group.

I can't help but observe that the icon for single user accounts is neither white nor black, but *gray*. Perhaps these users are dead? Could this be a George Romero operating system—the User Manager of the Living Dead? (Sorry, couldn't resist.)

Again, sorry to appear to be ducking the explanations of global and local groups, but the whole discussion of global and local groups is completely incomprehensible until you understand how to manage multiple domains under NT; hence locals and globals are covered in Chapter 12. To quickly summarize the differences, however, global groups are groups that can be made accessible to the entire network, while local groups are local to the domain in which they are defined.

To give new group memberships to the user account, select those groups from the Not Member of box, then choose the Add button or drag the group icon(s) to the Member of box. To remove membership in any group from the user account, select the desired groups from the Member of box and click on the Remove button or drag the icon(s) to the Not member of box.

User accounts must be a member of at least one group, referred to as the *primary group*, which is used when the user logs on to NT Services for Macintosh or runs POSIX applications. Primary groups must be global groups, and you can't remove a user from that user's primary group. To remove a user from that user's primary group, you have to first move the user to a different primary group. To do this, select a global group out of the Member of box, then click the Set button beneath the Member of frame. When you're finished configuring the group membership, click OK.

Permissible Logon Hours

By selecting the Hours button in the New User dialog box (see Figure 6.4), you can specify the days and hours during which a particular user can access the network. Similarly, choosing the Logon To button lets you limit which workstations a user can log on from. Push the Hours button from the Properties dialog box of any user or group of users, and you see a dialog box like Figure 6.6.

FIGURE 6.6:

The Logon Hours dialog box

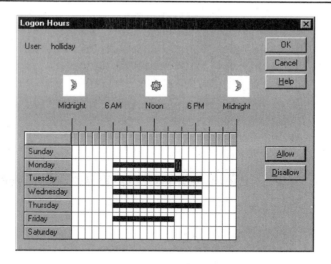

By default, a user can connect to the network all hours of all days of the week. If for some reason you don't want a user to get access to the network all hours of the day, you can restrict logon hours with this dialog box.

To administer the hours during which the user account is allowed to access the network, select the hours by dragging the cursor over a particular block of hours. Conversely, you can select all the hours of a certain day by clicking on that day's button, or you can choose certain hours across all seven days by clicking the button on top of an hour's column. Then click either the Allow or Disallow button to grant or deny access to the network at those selected hours. Filled boxes indicate the hours when the user is authorized to connect to the network; empty ones indicate the time when access is denied. When done, click OK.

As its title implies, you must understand that this dialog box controls *logon* hours. Suppose you've restricted someone so that she can only log on between 9 A.M. and 5 P.M. and she tries to log on at 8:59. She won't get on, and she will see a message like this (on an NT workstation):

```
Your account has time restrictions that prevent you from logging on at
this time. Please try again later.
```

Or, if she's at a Windows 95 workstation, she'll see this:

```
You are not allowed to log on at this time.
```

From a DOS workstation, the message is a bit more garrulous:

```
Error 2241: You do not have the necessary access rights to log on at
this time. To change access rights, contact your network administrator
about changing the logon hours listed in your account.
```

Of course, if our imaginary user tries to log on a few minutes later, after 9 A.M., she gets in without a hitch. But what happens toward the *end* of the logon hours? What happens, for example, when 5:01 P.M. rolls around? Does the system dump her off?

No, not by default. A bit later in this chapter, you'll see a dialog box labeled Account Policy. (If you want to look ahead to it, turn to Figure 6.18 or go to the User Manager for Domains and click Policies ➤ Account.) Account Policy is a big dialog box, and it would be easy to miss one small check box at the bottom labeled "Forcibly disconnect remote users from server when logon hours expire."

That's not a very clear statement in the Account Policies dialog box, is it? To me at least, a "remote user" is someone who's dialing into the network; but to NT, it just means anyone who's accessing the server via the network, rather than sitting right down at the server itself. By default, the box isn't checked. If you check it, the user gets this message five minutes before the end of the logon hours:

```
Your logon time at [domain name] ends at [end time]. Please clean up
and log off.
```

Three minutes after that, the message gets a bit more nasty:

```
WARNING: You have until [end time] to log off. If you have not logged
off at this time, your session will be disconnected, and any open files
or devices you have open may lose data.
```

Finally, at the appointed hour, you're history:

```
Your logon time at [domain name] has ended.
```

To get those messages, you must be running a message receiver like WinPopup (for Windows for Workgroups or Windows 95) or the Messenger service on a Windows NT workstation. You get logged off even if you're not running a message receiver.

Once a user has been booted off, whatever network resources she was using just seem to vanish. Looking at a network drive named F:, for example, will likely generate this error message or one like it: "No files found on directory F:." Trying to browse in a domain server may lead to an error message like this: "[server-name] is not accessible. You are not allowed to log on at this time."

Remember that changes to a user's account don't take effect until the next time he logs on, so changing someone's logon hours today probably won't have any effect until tomorrow.

This talk of enforced logoff hours leads to a common question: "How can I boot everyone off the server at 2 A.M. so that the scheduled backup can occur?" That's simple. Just write a batch file with these commands:

```
Net pause server
Net send * The server is going down in 5 minutes for maintenance.
Sleep 300
Net stop server
```

The pause command keeps anyone new from logging on. The send command sends a message to everyone running the messenger service and a network pop-up. The sleep command tells NT to just wait for 300 seconds (five minutes). SLEEP.EXE isn't shipped with NT, but it is on the CD-ROM that comes with the NT *Resource Kit*, and I highly recommend installing the SLEEP program. The stop command shuts down the server, disconnecting everyone.

Controlling Where Users Can Log On

When you select the Logon To button in the New User dialog box (see Figure 6.4), you get the Logon Workstations dialog box shown in Figure 6.7. This dialog box allows you to restrict which workstations the user can log on from. Now, I know you're wondering, "Why does the button say 'Logon To' when it means 'Logon From?'" As to that question, all I can do is quote a Microsoft employee: "Well, yes, it should be 'Logon From,' but...well...a programmer built the dialog box, you know what I mean?" (For obvious reasons, the Microsoft employee asked to remain anonymous.) As with the logon times, the default is No Restrictions; a user is allowed to log on at any workstation on the network.

FIGURE 6.7:

Logon Workstations
dialog box

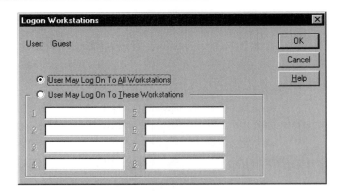

If you want to restrict the user's choice of workstations where he or she can log on to the network, select the User May Log On To These Workstations button and type in the computer names (without preceding backslashes) of the allowed workstations. Up to eight workstations can be specified. For example, if the machines that I regularly log on to are called SDG90 and LAPDOG, then I just punch in those names, again with no preceding backslashes.

This feature works for all workstation types.

Account Duration and Type

When creating or managing a user account, you can set the account to expire after a certain time period. If you have a summer intern or other temporary personnel, you don't want them to be able to log on to the network beyond the time that they're authorized. Setting an account to expire will avoid this problem. Click the Account button in the New User dialog box to display the Account Information dialog box shown in Figure 6.8.

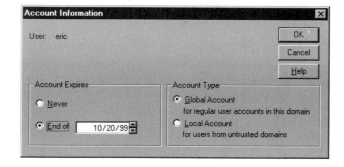

An account with an expiration date becomes disabled (not deleted) at the end of the day specified in the Account Expires box. If the user happens to be logged on, the session is not terminated, but no new connections can be made, and once the user logs off, he or she can't log back on.

In addition to setting an account expiration date, you can also set whether the user account in question is a *global account* or *local account* (don't confuse these with global and local *groups*).

Global accounts, the default setting, are normal user accounts in the user's home domain. These accounts can be used not only in the home domain, but also in any domain that has a trust relationship with the home domain. (More on trust relationships shortly.)

Local user accounts, on the other hand, are accounts provided in a particular domain for a user whose global user account is not in a trusted domain (that is, an untrusted NT Server domain or a LAN Manager 2.*x* domain). A local account can't be used to log on interactively at an NT workstation or an NT Server server. Like other accounts, however, a local account can access NT and NT Server computers over the network, can be placed in local and global groups, and can be assigned rights and permissions. If a user from an untrusted domain (either NT Server or LAN Manager 2.*x*) needs access to other NT Server domains, that user needs to have a local account on each of those other domains, since local accounts from one domain (the user's home domain) can't be used in other trusting domains.

Now, by default, all user accounts are global—you've got to click a radio button, as you can see in the dialog box in Figure 6.8, to make a user account a local account. The main difference between a local account and a global account is that you can never get an external domain to recognize a local account. When would you use a local user account, then? "I wouldn't," replied a Microsoft employee, when I asked. "It really doesn't have much use right now," he continued, implying, I suppose, that it had some meaning once but no longer does.

When you've finished selecting the desired account options, choose Add, choose Close, and then choose OK. Then, choose OK in the New User dialog box to create the new user account with the properties you've just specified. The new account will now appear in the list of users on the current domain shown in the User Manager for Domains window.

How Do I Create a User Account in a Domain?

Open User Manager for Domains. Under the User menu, select New User. In the New User dialog box, do the following:

1. Type in a username and the user's full name.

2. Type in a description of the user or account (optional).

3. Type in a password in the Password and Confirm Password boxes. Select the password's characteristics from the options presented. Choose whether or not the account will be disabled.

4. Using the Groups, Profile, Hours, Logon To, and Account buttons, do the following: set the user's group membership; user profile, logon script, and/or home directory; hours that the network will be available to the user; from which workstations the user is allowed to log on; and account characteristics (expiration date and account type).

5. When you're done configuring the account using the options in step 4, choose Add.

Managing User Accounts

Once a user account has been created, you can look at and modify its properties either by double-clicking on that account or by highlighting the account and choosing Properties from the User menu. You'll see the User Properties dialog box, as shown in Figure 6.9.

FIGURE 6.9:

User Properties dialog box

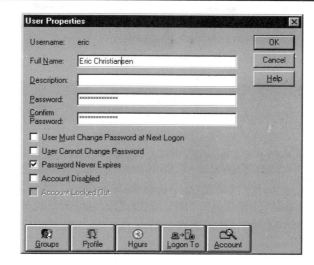

Anyone logged on as an administrator or as a member of the Account Operators local group (more on groups shortly) can then reconfigure the account's properties, following the same procedure used for creating a new user account.

Template for each department

Copying Accounts

Instead of creating each user account on your network individually, you can also copy existing user accounts. The primary advantage of creating user accounts this way is that all of the original user account's properties (including group memberships) are copied over to the new user account, thus speeding up administrative chores. If you have a large network, you might want to create one or more template accounts that contain specific properties shared by groups of users. For greater security, keep the template accounts disabled so that no one can actually log on to them.

To copy an existing user account, select the account from the list of user accounts in the User Manager for Domains window, then choose Copy from the User menu. You see the Copy dialog box shown in Figure 6.10.

FIGURE 6.10:

Copying an existing user account

password
SID
Certain options

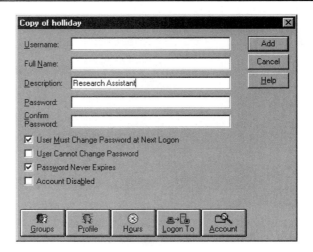

The copy retains all of the information from the original, except for the username, full name, and password, which you must provide. Configure the new account, making changes to names and properties as needed, and then choose Add. When done, select Close.

Note that the original user's rights, as defined by the User Rights command under the Policy menu, are not copied from one user account to another. If the newly copied accounts must have certain rights, you must grant them separately. Granting rights to a group and putting accounts in that group is the best way to manage rights for multiple users.

All user accounts, including the built-in ones, can be renamed by choosing the Rename command in the User menu. Renamed accounts retain their original security identifier (SID), and thereby keep all of their original properties, rights, and permissions.

Managing Properties for More Than One Account

You can manage several user account properties for more than one account at once. To do this, first select two or more user accounts. You can select a number of accounts either individually with the mouse from the currently displayed list of users, or (if there are a significant number of user accounts) you can select all members of a particular group within the domain with the Select Users command in the User menu. You see the Select Users dialog box shown in the Figure 6.11.

FIGURE 6.11:

Select Users dialog box

You'll notice that the Select Users command is actually more of a "Select Group" command; by choosing a group on the domain, you are selecting all of the users who are members of that group. The Select Users option is cumulative; if you first select Administrators and then select Backup Operators, all members who are either in the Administrators group or the Backup Operators group are selected (the Deselect button lets you take groups off of the selected list). Note that when you choose a group using the Select Users command, only members from the local domain are chosen. For example, if you select a local group (which can contain both users from the home domain as well as users from other, trusted domains), any changes that are made won't affect members from the trusted domains.

After you've selected the user accounts, choose Properties from the User menu. Figure 6.12 is the screen you see next.

FIGURE 6.12:

Modifying the properties of a group of user accounts

As with a single user account, you can select any of the buttons at the bottom of the dialog box to make certain modifications to all of the selected accounts.

For example, let's say you want to modify the group membership for the selected user accounts. By choosing the Groups button, you can see the group memberships that each of the selected accounts have in common in the All Are Members Of box. You can see this box in Figure 6.13.

FIGURE 6.13:

Modifying the group membership of selected users

You Can NOT Recreate A SID

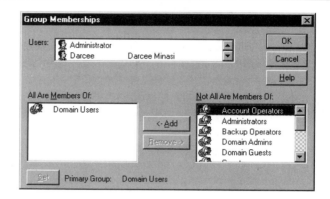

You can then add or remove group membership from the selection of users by highlighting the groups and choosing the Add or Remove button.

How Do I Make Sure That Selected Users Are *Not* Members of a Particular Group in a Domain?

To make sure, do the following:

1. Select the users in the User Manager for Domains window.

2. From the User menu, choose Properties.

3. In the User Properties dialog box, choose Groups. Add the particular group from the Not All Are Members Of box to the Members Of box.

4. Choose OK to save the change.

5. In the User Properties dialog box, choose Groups again.

6. Select the group in the All Are Members Of box and choose Remove.

Deleting User Accounts

There are three ways to rescind a user's ability to log on to the network with his or her account: by disabling the account, by restricting the access hours, and by deleting the account.

As mentioned earlier, a disabled account continues to exist on the server, but no one can access it. Even so, it (and with it, its properties) can be copied, it appears on lists of user accounts, and it can be restored to enabled status at any time. A deleted account, on the other hand, is completely removed from the system, vanishes from user account lists, and cannot be recovered or restored.

A new user account can be created with the same name and properties as a deleted account, but it will receive a different, unique security identifier (SID). Because internal processes in NT refer to a user account's SID rather than its username, none of the rights or permissions granted to the deleted user account will transfer to any new account that has the same name as the old.

As a measure against inadvertent, hasty, and perhaps regretted deletions of user accounts, you might choose to first disable unused accounts, then periodically remove those disabled accounts. Incidentally, NT Server prevents the deletion of the built-in Administrator and Guest accounts.

To delete one or more user accounts, select the account or accounts from the list in the opening window of User Manager for Domains. Then, under the User menu, choose Delete. Confirmation boxes appear to remind you of your choice and ask if you want to continue. Select OK to proceed.

Managing Groups

NT SERVER In NT Server, a user group is a set of users who have identical network rights. Placing your domain's user accounts in groups not only simplifies general (as well as security) management, but also makes it easier and faster to grant multiple users access to a network resource. Additionally, to give a right or permission to all of the users in a single group, all you have to do is grant that permission or right to the group.

NT uses two kinds of groups: local groups and global groups. I'll talk more about them in Chapter 12, but for the curious here's a quick overview of what these two groups do.

Local groups are the basic kind of user group in NT. Every NT machine, whether workstation or server, contains a local group called Users and another called Administrators. (There are others also, but these two are fundamental and simple to understand.) Any person with an account in the Users group is, well, a user. He can do anything that users can do on this machine. Any person with an account in Administrators has full administrative powers.

Local groups are called *local* because they are local to a given NT machine. One machine's Administrators group cannot be connected to another machine's Administrators group. A given user might be included in machine X's Administrators group but might only be in machine Y's Users group; in that case, when that user sits down and logs into machine X, then X will treat him as an administrator—but if he sits down and logs into machine Y, then Y will only treat him as a regular old user.

This arrangement makes managing a large number of machines difficult. Suppose you had 200 NT Workstation machines to administer in your department, and you just hired Lynn, a new administrator. From what I've said, you'd have to walk around to all 200 machines, log in as an administrator on that machine, create a Lynn account, and put it in each machine's local Administrators group. Not much fun—and that's why there are *global* groups.

Global groups can be created only on a domain controller; workstations and member servers can't contain them. But global groups are different from local groups in that they can be essentially "seen" from one machine to another—it's possible for a local group of machine X to contain global groups from machine Y.

Where that becomes useful is in managing domains. You can create a global group on your domain controller and fill it with accounts of users who should have administrative rights all over the domain. Then you can put that global group in the *local* Administrators group on each NT workstation and server machine. Result: when you hire Lynn, all you've got to do is put her in the global Administrators group. As that group is a member of every local Administrators group, she is instantly recognized as an administrator on every machine in the domain.

By the way, that's done automatically in the NT world. Remember that every machine has local groups named Users and Administrators? Well, each domain controller *also* has pre-built *global* groups named Domain Users and Domain Admins. By default, when an NT machine joins a domain, that NT machine's local Users group gets the domain's Domain Users group inserted into it, and that NT machine's Administrators group gets the domain's Domain Admins group inserted into it.

Again, we'll examine this in closer detail in Chapter 12. But for now, understand that there are two kinds of groups, local and global. Every machine has local groups; only domain controllers can have global groups. And it's possible to include a global group inside a local group.

Creating and Deleting Groups

To create a new local group, select New Local Group under the User menu. You see the dialog box shown in Figure 6.14.

FIGURE 6.14:

New Local Group dialog box

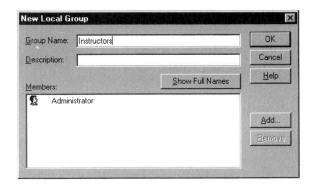

Type in the name of the local group you wish to create (in this example, I'm creating a group called Instructors). Include a description of the group, if you want.

Select the Add button to add members to the group. You will see the Add Users and Groups dialog box in Figure 6.15.

FIGURE 6.15:

Adding accounts to the new local group

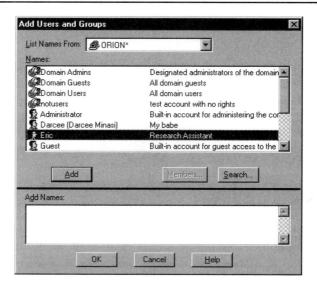

In the Add Users and Groups dialog box, select a name or global group from the desired domain list, and click the Add button to place the group in the Add Names list (remember, a local group can contain both users and global groups from trusted domains as well as from the local domain). Alternately, you can type the user names into the Add Names list; make sure you separate the names with a semicolon. When you've collected all of the names in the Add Names list, click OK.

The names you've chosen will appear in the Members box of the New Local Group dialog box. (To see their full names, click the Show Full Names button.) To remove a name from the list, just highlight it and click on the Remove button. When your new local group's membership is to your satisfaction, click OK. The new group will now appear in the User Manager for Domains list of groups.

Creating a Global Group

Creating a new global group is just as easy. Under the User menu, choose New Global Group. In the New Global Group dialog box, as seen in Figure 6.16, type in a name and description for the new group. In this example, the new global group is called Research Assistants.

FIGURE 6.16:

New Global Group dialog box

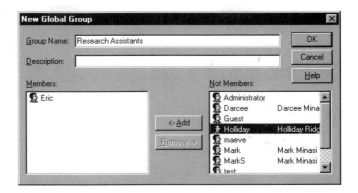

A global group can only contain user accounts from the domain where it is created, so the Not Members box will contain only those accounts on the current domain. To give any user on the list group membership, select one of the entries in the Not Members list and click on the Add button. When finished, choose OK; the new global group will be visible in the User Manager for Domains group list.

You can change any user's or group's membership in another group by displaying that group's Properties (in the User Manager for Domains window, either select the group and choose Properties from the User menu, or double-click on that group). The dialog boxes for Group Properties are identical to those for New Groups, and you can add and remove members using the same procedures described above.

Deleting groups is accomplished by selecting the group in the User Manager for Domains window and choosing Delete (in the User menu). The same cautions about deleting user accounts also apply to deleting groups, since groups also have their own unique security identifiers (SIDs). Before allowing you to delete a group, NT Server prompts you with a reminder message, as in Figure 6.17. Deleting a group removes only that group from NT Server; all user accounts and groups within the deleted group are unaffected.

FIGURE 6.17:

Warning message for deleting a group

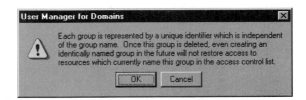

Examining the Predefined Groups

A number of predefined groups, both local and global, are built into NT Server to aid network administration and management. The local groups are described in the following pages.

Administrators

Not surprisingly, Administrators is the most powerful group. Members of the Administrators local group have more control over the domain than any other users, and they are granted all of the rights necessary to manage the overall configuration of the domain and the domain's servers. Incidentally, users in the Administrators group do not automatically have access to every file in the domain. If the file's permissions do not grant access to Administrators, then the members of the Administrator's group cannot access the file. If it becomes necessary, however, an administrator can take ownership of such a file and thus have access to it. If he or she does, the event is recorded in the security log (provided that auditing of files has been activated) and the administrator does not have the ability to give ownership back to the original owner (or to anyone else for that matter).

Within the Administrators group is a built-in Administrator user account that cannot be deleted. By default, the Domain Admins global group is also a member of the Administrators group, but it can be removed.

Given that it's possible for the Administrator account to be disabled, it might be wise to create a backup administrator account to be used in case of emergency.

Server Operators

The Server Operators local group has all of the rights needed to manage the domain's servers. Members of the Server Operations group can create, manage, and delete printer shares at servers; create, manage, and delete network shares at servers; back up and restore files on servers; format a server's fixed disk; lock and unlock servers; unlock files; and change the system time. In addition, Server Operators can log on to the network from the domain's servers as well as shut down the servers.

Account Operators

Members of the Account Operators local group are allowed to use User Manager for Domains to create user accounts and groups for the domain, and to modify or delete most of the domain's user accounts and groups.

An Account Operator cannot modify or delete the following groups: Administrators, Domain Admins, Account Operators, Backup Operators, Print Operators, and Server Operators. Likewise, members of this group cannot modify or delete user accounts of administrators. They cannot administer the security policies, but they can use the Server Manager to add computers to a domain, log on at servers, and shut down servers.

Print Operators

Members of this group can create, manage, and delete printer shares for an NT Server server. Additionally, they can log on at and shut down servers.

Backup Operators

The Backup Operators local group provides its members the rights necessary to back up directories and files from a server and to restore directories and files to a server. Like the Print Operators, they can also log on at and shut down servers.

Everyone

Everyone is not actually a group, and it doesn't appear in the User Management list, but you can assign rights and permissions to it. Anyone who has a user account in the domain, including all local and remote users, is automatically a member of the Everyone local group. Not only are members of this group allowed to connect over the network to a domain's servers, but they are also granted the advanced right to change directories and travel through a directory tree that they may not have permissions on. Members of the Everyone group also have the right to lock the server, but won't be able to unless they've been granted the right to log on locally at the server.

Users

Members of the group simply called Users have minimal rights at servers running NT Server. They are granted the right to create and manage local groups, but unless they have access to the User Manager for Domains tool (such as by being allowed to log on locally at the server), they can't perform this task. Members of the Users group do possess certain rights at their local NT workstations.

Guests

This is NT Server's built-in local group for occasional or one-time users to log on. Members of this group are granted very limited abilities. Guests have no rights at NT Server servers, but they do possess certain rights at their own individual workstations. The built-in Guest user account is automatically a member of the Guests group.

Replicator

This local group, different from the others, supports directory replication functions. The only member of a domain's Replicator local group should be a single domain user account, which is used to log on to the Replicator services of the domain controller and to the other servers in the domain. User accounts of actual users should *not* be added to this group at all. (Wondering what you'd use the Replicator group for? It's instrumental to directory replication, which is discussed in Chapter 11.)

Table 6.3 summarizes the user rights (more on user rights in the next section) and special abilities granted to NT Server's predefined local groups.

TABLE 6.3: Rights/Special Abilities Granted to Predefined Local Groups

User Rights	Members Can Also
Group: Administrators	
Log on locally	Create and manage user accounts
Access this computer from the network	Create and manage global groups
Take ownership of files	Assign user rights
Manage auditing and security log	Lock the server
Change the system time	Override the server's lock
Shut down the system	Format the server's hard disk
Force shutdown from a remote system	Create common groups

Continued on next page

TABLE 6.3 CONTINUED: Rights/Special Abilities Granted to Predefined Local Groups

User Rights	Members Can Also
Group: Administrators	
Back up files and directories	Keep a local profile
	Share and stop sharing directories
	Share and stop sharing printers
Group: Server Operators	
Log on locally	Lock the server
Change the system time	Override server's lock
Shut down the system	Format the server's hard disk
Force shutdown from a remote system	Create common groups
Back up files and directories	Keep a local profile
Restore files and directories	Share and stop sharing directories
	Share and stop sharing printers
Group: Account Operators[1]	
Log on locally	Create and manage user accounts, global groups, and local groups
Shut down the system	Keep a local profile

1 They cannot, however, modify administrator accounts, the Domain Admins global group, or the local group's Administrators, Server Operators, Account Operators, Print Operators, and Backup Operators.

User Rights	Members Can Also
Group: Print Operators	
Log on locally	Keep a local profile
Shut down the system	Share and stop sharing printers

Continued on next page

TABLE 6.3 CONTINUED: Rights/Special Abilities Granted to Predefined Local Groups

User Rights	Members Can Also
Group: Backup Operators	
Log on locally	Keep a local profile
Shut down the system	
Back up files and directories	
Restore files and directories	
Group: Everyone	
Access this computer from the network	Lock the server[2]

2 In order to actually do this, the member of the group must have the right to log on locally at the server.

Group: Users	
(None)	Create and manage local groups[3]

3 In order to actually do this, the user must either have the right to log on locally at the server, or must have access to the User Manager for Domains tool.

Group: Guests	
(None)	(None)

NT SERVER   NT Server has only three built-in global groups: Domain Admins, Domain Users, and Domain Guests. These will only appear on NT Servers that are acting as domain controllers. In fact, it's *only* possible to create global groups on domain controllers.

Group	What It Does
Domain Admins	By placing a user account into this global group, you provide administrative-level abilities to that user. Members of Domain Admins can administer the home domain, the workstations of the domain, and any other trusted domains that have added the Domain Admins global group to their own Administrators local group. By default, the built-in Domain Admins global group is a member of both the domain's Administrators local group and the Administrators local groups for every NT workstation in the domain. The built-in Administrator user account for the domain is automatically a member of the Domain Admins global group.
Domain Users	Members of the Domain Users global group have normal user access to, and abilities for, both the domain itself and for any NT workstation in the domain. This group contains all domain user accounts, and is by default a member of the Users local groups for both the domain and for every Windows NT workstation on the domain.
Domain Guests	This group allows guest accounts to access resources across domain boundaries, if they've been allowed that by the domain administrators.

Built-In Special Groups

In addition to the built-in local and global groups, a few special groups appear now and again when viewing certain lists of groups:

INTERACTIVE   Anyone using the computer locally

NETWORK   All users connected over the network to a computer

SYSTEM   The operating system

CREATOR OWNER   The creator and/or owner of subdirectories, files, and print jobs

Incidentally, the INTERACTIVE and NETWORK groups combined form the EVERYONE local group.

Managing Security Policies

The User Manager for Domains is part of a quartet of programs that provide network security options in NT Server. While the Explorer/My Computer team and the Printer Folder control specific access to files, directories, and printers, User Manager for Domains gives the administrator the ability to assign system-wide rights and to determine what the auditing policies of the network will be.

In User Manager for Domains, an administrator can manage the following security policies:

- Account, which controls the characteristics of passwords for all user accounts

- User Rights, which determines which user or group is assigned particular system rights

- Audit, in which the kinds of security events to be logged are defined

- Trust Relationships, which establishes how other domains on the network interact with the local domain

Password Characteristics

Under the Account policy, you can set and adjust the password characteristics for all user accounts in the domain. From the Policies menu, choose Account. You see the Account Policy dialog box in the Figure 6.18.

Make your selections for the following options:

Maximum Password Age This option sets the time period in which a password can be used before the system requires the user to pick a new one.

Minimum Password Age The value set here is the time that a password has to be used before the user is allowed to change it again. If you allow changes to the password to be made immediately, make sure you choose Do Not Keep Password History in the Password Uniqueness box.

Minimum Password Length This option defines the smallest number of characters that a user's password can contain.

Password Uniqueness   Here you can specify the number of new passwords that must be used before a user can employ an old password. If you choose a value here, you must specify a password age value under Minimum Password Age.

Account lockout   This option prevents anyone from logging on to the account after a certain number of failed attempts:

Lockout after *x* bad logon attempts   This value defines how many times the user can attempt to log on.

Reset count after *x* minutes   This setting defines the time in which the count of bad logon attempts will start over. For example, suppose you have a reset count of two minutes and three logon attempts. If you mistype twice, by waiting two minutes after the second attempt, you'll have three tries again.

Lockout Duration   This setting determines whether the administrator must unlock the account manually or can let the user try again after a certain period.

FIGURE 6.18:

Account Policy dialog box

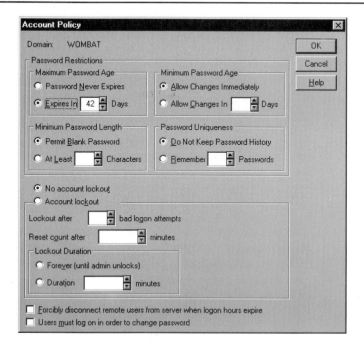

TIP   By default, you can never lock out the built-in Administrator account, no matter how many failed logon attempts are made. However, the *NT Resource Kit* contains a program named PASSPROP which can render the default Administrator account vulnerable to lockout. Just run PASSPROP from the command line at any domain controller like so: **passprop /adminlockout**, and then reboot.

The "Forcibly disconnect remote users from server when logon hours expire" option is tied in to the available logon hours you specified when you created the user account. If this option is selected, the user is disconnected from all connections to any of the domain's servers once the logon hours expire.

Not selecting this option enables the user to stay connected once the logon hours expire, but no new connections will be permitted. Checking "User must log on in order to change password" makes it impossible for the user to change her password after it's expired.

User Rights and Object Permissions

User access to network resources—files, directories, devices—in NT Server is controlled in two ways: by assigning *rights* to a user that grant or deny access to certain objects (for example, the ability to log on to a server), and by assigning *permissions* to objects that specify who is allowed to use objects and under what conditions (for example, granting read access for a directory to a particular user).

Consider the groups Users and Administrators. What makes administrators different from users? Well, administrators can log on right at the server; users can't. Administrators can create users and back up files; users can't. Administrators are different from users in that they have rights that users don't have. The central thing to remember here is that the very thing that separates one group in NT from another mostly has to do with the rights the groups have. You control who gets which rights via the User Manager for Domains.

Rights generally authorize a user to perform certain system tasks. For example, the average user can't just sit down at an NT server and log on right at the server. The question, "Can I log on locally at a server?" is an example of a right. "Can I back up data and restore data?" "Can I modify printer options on a shared printer?" These are also user rights. User rights can be assigned separately to a single user, but for reasons of security organization, it is better to put the user into a group and define which rights are granted to the group. You manage user rights in User Manager for Domains.

Permissions, on the other hand, apply to specific objects such as files, directories, and printers. "Can I change files in the LOTUS directory on the BIGMACHINE server?" is an example of a permission. Permissions are set by the creator or owner of an object. Permissions regulate which users can have access to the object and in what fashion.

TIP

You can only set permissions on particular files on an NTFS volume. Directory and file permissions are administered in My Computer and the Explorer, or from the command line; printer permissions are regulated in the Printers folder.

As a rule, user rights take precedence over object permissions. For example, let's look at a user who is a member of the built-in Backup Operators group. By virtue of his or her membership in that group, the user has the right to back up the servers in the user's domain. This requires the ability to see and read all directories and files on the servers, including those whose creators and owners have specifically denied Read permission to members of the Backup Operators group; thus the right to perform backups overrides the permissions set on the files and directories.

There are two types of user rights: regular user rights and advanced user rights. NT Server's built-in groups have certain rights already assigned to them; you can also create new groups and assign a custom set of user rights to those groups. As I've said before, security management is much easier when all user rights are assigned through groups instead of being granted to individual users.

To look at or change the rights granted to a user or group, select the domain where the particular user or group resides (if they are not in the local domain), then choose User Rights from the Policies menu. You see the User Rights Policy dialog box, as shown in Figure 6.19.

FIGURE 6.19:

User Rights Policy dialog box

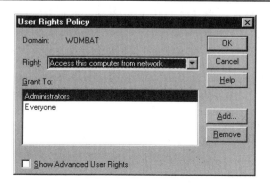

Check the arrow box next to the currently displayed user right to see the entire list of regular user rights. By clicking one of the rights, you can see the groups and users who currently have been granted that particular right. In the figure, you can see that the right "Access this computer from network" has been granted to the Administrators and Everyone group.

The regular rights used in NT Server are

Access this computer from network   Allows a user to connect over the network to a computer.

Add workstations to domain   Makes machines domain members.

Back up files and directories   Allows a user to back up files and directories. As mentioned earlier, this right supersedes file and directory permissions.

Change the system time   Grants a user the right to set the time for the internal clock of a computer.

Force shutdown from a remote system   Note that, although presented as an option, this right is not currently implemented by NT Server.

Load and unload device drivers   Lets a user add or remove drivers from the system.

Log on locally   Allows a user to log on locally at the server computer itself.

Manage auditing and security log   Gives a user the right to specify what types of events and resource access are to be audited. Also allows viewing and clearing the security log.

Restore files and directories   Allows a user to restore files and directories. This right supersedes file and directory permissions.

Shut down the system   Grants a user the right to shut down Windows NT.

Take ownership of files or other object   Lets a user take ownership of files, directories, and other objects that are owned by other users.

NOTE   Ownership is explained in Chapter 7.

The advanced rights in NT Server are summarized in the Table 6.4. These rights are added to the rights list when you click the Show Advanced User Rights option located at the bottom of the User Rights Policy dialog box.

TABLE 6.4:   Advanced User Rights

Advanced User Right	Allows Users To
Act as part of the operating system	Act as a trusted part of the operating system; some subsystems have this privilege granted to them.
Bypass traverse checking	Traverse a directory tree even if the user has no other rights to access that directory; denies access to users in POSIX applications. See Chapter 7 for more information.
Create a pagefile	Create a pagefile.
Create a token object	Create access tokens. Only the Local Security Authority can have this privilege.
Create permanent shared objects	Create special permanent objects used in NT.
Debug programs	Debug applications.
Generate security audits	Generate audit-log entries.
Increase quotas	Increase object quotas (each object has a quota assigned to it).
Increase scheduling priority	Boost the scheduling priority of a process.
Load and unload device drivers	Load and unload drivers for devices on the network.
Lock pages in memory	Lock pages in memory to prevent them from being paged out into backing store (such as PAGEFILE.SYS).
Log on as a batch job	Log on to the system as a batch queue facility.
Log on as a service	Perform security services (the user that performs replication logs on as a service).
Modify firmware environment values	Modify system environment variables (not user environment variables).
Profile single process	Use Windows NT profiling capabilities to observe a process.
Profile system performance	Use Windows NT profiling capabilities to observe the system.
Receive unsolicited device input	Read unsolicited data from a terminal device.
Replace a process level token	Modify a process's access token.

Most of the advanced rights are useful only to programmers who are writing applications to run on Windows NT, and most are not granted to a group or user. However, two of the advanced rights—Bypass traverse checking and Log on as a service—might be useful to some domain administrators. Bypass traverse checking is granted by default to the Everyone group in NT Server. And notice the Increase object quotas right. Hey, sounds like it's possible to control how much disk space a user takes up. A "disk quota?" Nope. It's a right that's existed in NT since version 3.1, and one small notation in the documentation says that the quota feature "is not in use yet." Oh well. Maybe in Windows 2000 Server…

In general, I find that the only user right that I ever end up granting is to log on to the server locally; now and then, a user needs that ability. Additionally, the Internet mail package that I use to route my company's Internet mail requires that I allow users the right to "log on as a batch job."

Security Event Auditing

NT Server maintains three event logs to which entries are added in the background—the System log, the Applications log, and the Security log. You can set up security auditing of a number of events on NT Server in User Manager for Domains to help track user access to various parts of the system. To enable security auditing, pull down the Policies menu and select Audit. You see the dialog box in Figure 6.20.

FIGURE 6.20:

Audit Policy dialog box

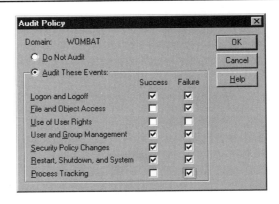

As you can see, the Audit Policy dialog box gives you the option to activate auditing, followed by a list of the types of security events you can audit. The default setting is Do Not Audit; with this option selected, all of the Audit These Events options are grayed out. If you choose to activate auditing, the information about that event is stored as an entry in the computer's Security log. This log, along with the System and Application logs, can then be viewed with the Event Viewer.

Table 6.5 describes the auditing options you can select.

T A B L E 6 . 5 :   Security Auditing Options

Events to Audit	Description
File and Object Access	Tracks access to a directory or file that has been selected for auditing under File Manager; tracks print jobs sent to printers that have been set for auditing under the Printers folder
Logon and Logoff	Tracks user logons and logoffs, as well as the creating and breaking of connections to servers
Process Tracking	Records detailed tracking information for program activation, some types of handle duplication, indirect object accesses, and process exit
Restart, Shutdown, and System	Tracks when the computer is shut down or restarted; tracks the filling up of the audit log and the discarding of audit entries if the audit log is already full
Security Policy Changes	Tracks changes made to the User Rights, Audit, or Trust Relationship policies
Use of User Rights	Notes when users make use of a user right (except those associated with logons and logoffs)
User and Group Management	Tracks changes in user accounts or groups (creations, changes, deletions); notes if user accounts are renamed, disabled, or enabled; tracks setting or changing passwords

It's important to keep in mind that all of the event logs are limited in size. The default size for each of the logs is 512K, and the default overwrite settings allow events older than seven days to be discarded from the logs as needed. When managing the auditing policy in User Manager for Domains, choose your events to audit carefully. You may find that you get what you ask for, sometimes in great abundance. For example, auditing successful File and Object Accesses can generate a tremendous number of security log entries. A reasonably simple process, such as opening an application, opening a single file within that application, editing and saving that file, and exiting the application, can produce more than 60 log events. A couple of users on a system can generate 200 log entries in less than two minutes. Auditing successful Process Tracking events can produce similar results.

If your network requires you to monitor events that closely, make sure you choose the appropriate log size and overwrite settings. You can change these settings for the Security log (and for the other two logs, for that matter) in the Event Viewer.

Summary: Managing User Accounts

That's not all that the User Manager for Domains can do. I haven't covered trust relationships and local and global groups, but, again, I *will* cover those things in Chapter 12.

Notice that the User Manager does more than just manage users; it is, in some way, the Security Manager for NT—but just a *part* of the Security Manager role. Before leaving the User Manager for Domains, let's review what it does. It lets you

- Create, destroy, and modify network user accounts
- Assign and remove user rights
- Create, destroy, and modify groups
- Control which users go in which groups
- Assign and remove rights to and from groups
- Create and destroy trust relationships

That's a lot of what you need to create and manage user accounts, but you will find another set of tools useful in that line—user profiles and the System Policy Editors. We'll take those up next, in order.

User Profiles: How They Work and How to Make Them Work for You

A user profile is a set of configuration settings that make up a user's Desktop, including color scheme, screen saver, shortcuts and program groups. These settings may be configured by a user who wishes to personalize her Desktop, by a system administrator responsible for configuring Desktops, or by a combination of the two. In other words, a user may create shortcuts and select a screen saver, while an administrator may configure special program groups for the user's Desktop. However, the two are not mutually exclusive. By default, every user on an NT machine (except members of the Guests group) keeps a local profile directory that NT names after the user ID. Guests are not allowed to keep local profiles.

Working with User Profiles

User profiles can be implemented in several different ways, according to the needs of your organization. In situations where a network-based solution is not feasible or not desirable, there are still several options to keep in mind.

Local Profiles   Users keep only local profiles and create and configure these profiles themselves.

Preconfigure the Default User Profile   Users keep only local profiles, but an Administrator preconfigures the Default User profile to set up a customized template for new local users.

Preconfigure Local Profiles   Users keep only local profiles, but an Administrator preconfigures all or part of the local user profiles.

Network-based solutions include the following:

Roaming Profiles   Add a user profile path to the user's account information to automatically create and maintain a copy of the user profile in a network location (the user can configure her own profile).

Preconfigured Roaming Profile   Add a user profile path to the user's account information and copy a preconfigured profile to the network location specified (the user can make changes to her profile).

Network Default User Profile   Create a Default User profile and copy it to the NETLOGON share of the authenticating domain controller(s). This will hand out default profiles to all new users (users can make changes to their profiles). This option can be used in conjunction with roaming or local profiles.

Mandatory Profiles   Add a user profile path to the user account, copy a preconfigured profile to that path and use special file and directory name extensions to specify that this is a mandatory profile. The user must use the profile and cannot make any changes. A mandatory profile can be shared by a group of users.

Anatomy of a User Profile

A local user profile is created automatically by the system the first time a user logs onto an NT machine. This profile directory is located in %SYSTEMROOT%\ PROFILES. Figure 6.21 shows the contents of the \PROFILES directory. This directory contains a profile for every user who logs on to the NT machine (in this case, user Lisa and the user administrator), as well as a directory called \All Users and one called \Default User. The \All Users directory stores common program groups (programs available to all users on a specific machine) and shortcuts that will appear on every user's Desktop on that machine. For example, Administrative Tools is stored in the \All Users folder, so the programs listed in this group will be made available to anyone logging on to the machine. The Default User folder exists because NT uses this as a template for creating individual profiles for new users. Figure 6.22 shows the contents of an individual user profile directory, C:\WINNT\PROFILES\LISA.

FIGURE 6.21:

Profiles directory

FIGURE 6.22:

Individual profile directory

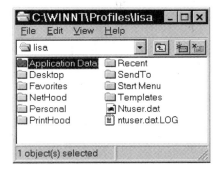

Each user's profile contains several folders with links to various Desktop items plus the NTUSER.DAT file, which contains configuration settings from the Registry. NTUSER.DAT.LOG is a transaction log file that exists to protect *NTUSER .DAT* while changes are being flushed to disk. There is no NTUSER.DAT.LOG for the Default User profile because it is a template. The other folders store information on the contents of the user's Desktop and Start menu items, including shortcuts and program groups. Remember that a user's profile also includes the common program groups and shortcuts indicated in the All Users folder. Table 6.6 describes the various folders in a user profile.

TABLE 6.6:   Folders in a User Profile

Folder	Explanation
Application Data	A place for applications to store user-specific information.
Desktop	Any file, folder, or shortcut in this folder will appear directly on the user's Desktop.
Favorites	Shortcuts to favorite Web sites and bookmarks can be stored here.
NetHood *	Shortcuts placed here will appear in Network Neighborhood.
Personal	Sort of a mini home directory; many applications save things here by default.
PrintHood *	Shortcuts placed here will appear in the Printers folder.
Recent *	NT automatically puts shortcuts to recently used files here. Linked to Documents in the Start menu.
SendTo	Place shortcuts to apps, printers, and folders here to quickly copy an item to a predefined place (3? Floppy), open a file within a specific application (Notepad) or even to print a file.
Start Menu	Contains personal program groups and shortcuts to program items.
Templates *	Contains shortcuts to templates created by applications, such as PowerPoint and Word.

* These folders are hidden by default.

In addition to the folders, a user profile includes numerous user-definable settings for Windows NT Explorer (View all files, Display full path in the title bar, and Show large icons), the Taskbar (Auto hide, Show small icons in Start menu, and Show clock), Control Panel (command prompt, mouse, and display preferences), and Accessories (Calculator, Clock, and Notepad). Network Printer, Drive

Connections, and Windows NT Help bookmarks are also saved in the user profile. Virtually any application written for Windows NT can remember user-specific settings. These settings, not directly linked to Desktop items, are contained in the NTUSER.DAT file. NTUSER.DAT is the Registry part of a user profile. It corresponds to the HKEY_CURRENT_USER subtree in the Registry Editor (REGEDT32.EXE), shown in Figure 6.23.

FIGURE 6.23:

The HKEY_CURRENT_USER Subtree

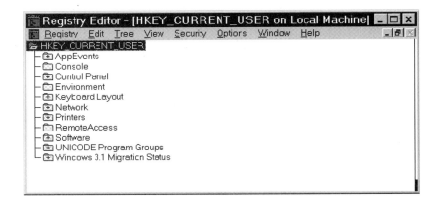

Configuring Your Own User Profile

Before you configure user profiles on your network, you will need to master techniques for configuring your own profile. You can then use these skills to configure profiles for other users.

The NTUSER.DAT file for the user currently logged on may be edited using a Registry editing tool such as REGEDT32.EXE or REGEDIT.EXE, although these tools are not particularly intuitive (an understatement if I have ever heard one). Chapter 5 describes how to edit the Registry and cites several sources of information on Registry entries. The System Policy Editor (POLEDIT.EXE, covered in the upcoming section on system policies) that comes with Windows NT Server is more user-friendly and can be used to directly edit a number of selected settings in the local Registry.

System Policy Editor is a "selective" Registry editor and is easier to use as it does not require any knowledge of Registry syntax or structure. While this application offers several options that are not available in the graphical interface, very little would be of interest to normal users setting up their own profiles, even assuming that they have access to the application (it can only be found on an NT Server installation or on the NT Server CD). Even though the System Policy Editor can be used to edit the machine's local Registry, as shown in Figure 6.24, most of the Local User options focus on restricting a user's Desktop. Joe User probably would not do that to himself. However, this little piece of information will come in handy when *you* want to restrict other users' Desktops.

FIGURE 6.24:

Using the Systems Policy Editor to change the local Registry

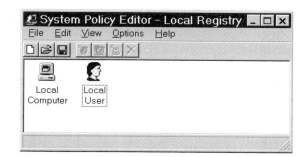

Actually, the best way to configure the NTUSER.DAT part of your profile is simply to configure your Desktop. By using the applets in the graphical interface to change your color scheme, map network drives, and connect to printers, you are making changes to NTUSER.DAT. Use a Registry editor only when you want to make a change that is not offered in the Control Panel. For example, under NT 3.51, the only way to change the Icon Title font, size, and style was in the Registry, under HKEY_CURRENT_USER\CONTROL PANEL\DESKTOP. In NT 4, however, these and other formerly unavailable options can be adjusted using the Appearance Tab in Control Panel ➢ Display.

WARNING   As I've warned you before, you're just asking for trouble if you start playing with your machine's Registry for no good reason. Don't edit the Registry if you can make the changes using the Control Panel.

To configure the Taskbar, program items and shortcuts in your profile folder, right-click on the Taskbar and choose Properties. The Taskbar Options tab (Figure 6.25) allows you to adjust a couple of things in the Taskbar. Toggle the check boxes to see how your display will change. The Start Menu Programs tab (Figure 6.26) allows you to add and remove shortcuts and folders from the Start menu. The Add and Remove buttons are the easiest way to go, but Advanced gives you more flexibility. The Advanced button takes you directly to your Start Menu folder in NT Explorer (Figure 6.27). Add a folder to create a program group and add a program. Folders and shortcuts may be added in NT Explorer or by double-clicking My Computer on your Desktop. Either way, changes to the folders in your profile directory show up right away on your Desktop.

FIGURE 6.25:

Specifying Taskbar Options in Taskbar Properties dialog box

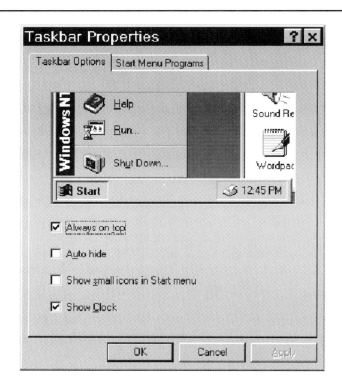

TIP

You can create shortcuts and drag them right onto your Start menu button to create a shortcut at the top of the Start menu. The shortcuts to the command prompt and to PowerPoint Viewer shown in Figure 6.27 were created in this way. You can also create a folder in this location with shortcuts to several program items. Microsoft calls these "custom program groups."

FIGURE 6.26:

Customizing the Start
Menu in Taskbar Properties
dialog box

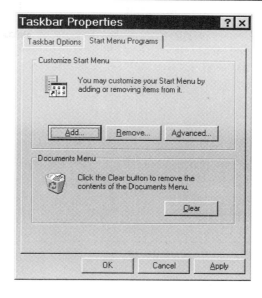

FIGURE 6.27:

The Start Menu in NT
Explorer

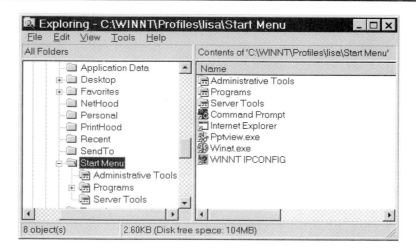

| **TIP** | Add a few shortcuts to the SendTo folder in your profile. If SendTo contains short-cuts to your home directory, word processing or spreadsheet applications, and printers, you can right-click on a file to copy it to your home directory, open it in Word, or even print it! |

Birth of a Profile

The next step in mastering user profiles is to understand how NT creates a user profile and how a user obtains one. In short, when a user (we'll call him "Sneezy") logs on for the first time (and therefore does not yet have a local profile), a new profile folder is created for that user. The Default User profile information is copied to that new directory. This information, along with the shortcuts and program items found in the All Users folder, is then loaded to create Sneezy's Desktop. The new profile now exists in a folder named after the user in the same path as the Default User profile directory, %SYSTEMROOT%\PROFILES*SNEEZY*. After NT creates the local profile, any user-specific changes made by Sneezy, such as Desktop color schemes, shortcuts, persistent network connections, or personal program groups, will be saved to Sneezy's profile. (For information about ownership and permissions, see Chapter 7.)

NOTE   Only users who are members of the local Administrators group may make changes to the All Users folder.

By the way, if that profile is created on an NTFS partition, Sneezy will be the *owner* of the profile because he created it. Permissions will be set to allow him to modify his own profile. SYSTEM and Administrators will also have full access to the profile. Figure 6.28 shows permissions of the profile created for the user SNEEZY on the NT Workstation \\SWEETIE.

FIGURE 6.28:

Permissions of a user's profile

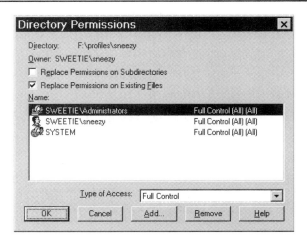

Roaming Profile Basics

A network administrator might choose to specify a path on the network to store a user profile. A profile is a "roaming profile" (rather than a local profile) when either User Manager for Domains or User Manager indicates a profile path, even if that path is local. In the simplest of scenarios, the administrator has simply created a share on the server, set appropriate permissions on the share (and directories), and indicated in User Manager for Domains that a copy of the user's profile should be stored there. NT will keep a local copy on Sneezy's workstation, but now the profile will follow Sneezy around. When he has to go downstairs and log on to the domain from Grumpy's NT workstation, NT will download the copy of his profile from the server. Sneezy also has made a "backup" of his local profile stored in a network location in case of disaster.

To specify a roaming profile path for a user on your NT network, complete these two easy steps:

1. Create a shared directory. I like to create a share and name it "profiles" or "PROFILES$" (to hide it from the Browse List). Set share level permissions to Change or Full Control to allow all users storing profiles to alter their profiles. (Read about creating user directories and directory shares, as well as setting share-level permissions, in Chapter 7.) You do not have to create profile directories for the users. Like a home directory, NT will create the profile directory for the user and set appropriate permissions.

2. Open User Manager for Domains and specify the path for the user profile directory as shown in Figure 6.29. The figure shows the user's roaming profile located in \\ALDEBARAN\PROFILES\LISA. Use %USERNAME% (Figure 6.30) in place of the username if you are specifying roaming profiles for more than one user account. You may also specify the user profile path as the user's home directory, as shown in Figure 6.31.

FIGURE 6.29:

Profiles dialog box in User Manager for Domains

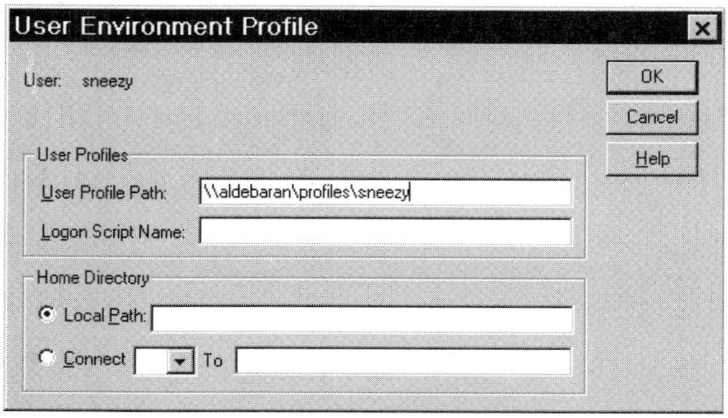

FIGURE 6.30:

Assign user profiles to
multiple users

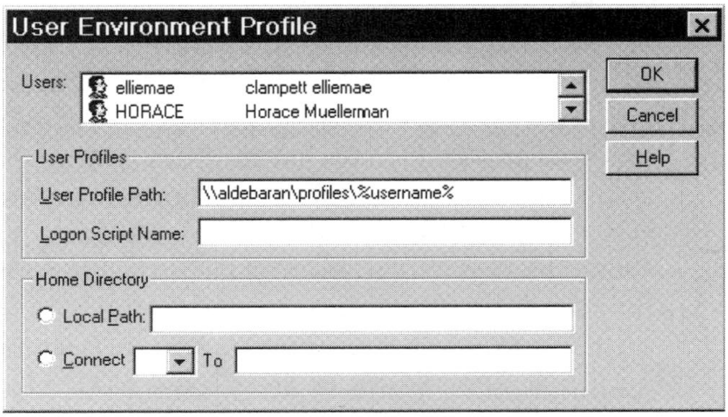

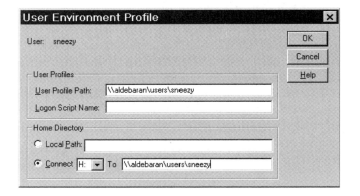

The next time that Sneezy logs on, NT will see that there is a network path specified for the home directory. Now, if you have been following our story, you'll know that Sneezy already has a local profile stored on his NT workstation. This appears to pose a problem, however—there is no profile on the server yet, and one does exist on the local machine. So, NT simply loads the local profile and creates a directory on the server to store the roaming profile. When Sneezy logs off, NT will copy the local profile directory to the network path. In other words, NT used the preexisting local profile to create the roaming profile directory on the server. From now on, whenever Sneezy logs on, NT will check to make sure that the profiles still match (using a time stamp) and will load the most recent version.

FIGURE 6.31:

Profile path as home directory path

NT will save any changes Sneezy makes to both profiles: the local copy and, when Sneezy logs off, Sneezy's profile directory on the server. OK, why all this rigmarole about saving the user profile to the local path and to the server? By default, NT will always keep a local profile folder to ensure that the user can access his profile if the network profile is unavailable. This is also useful with slow network connections.

NOTE   If the profile directory on the server is unavailable for some reason when Sneezy logs on (because the server is down, for instance), NT will simply let you know this and load the local copy. In that case, NT will not attempt to copy changes to the server when you log off. The next time Sneezy logs on, NT will display another dialog box saying, "Your local profile is more recent than your server profile." Sneezy can then choose which profile to load.

What if newcomer Dopey also has a roaming profile path specified in User Manager for Domains and he logs on his NT machine for the first time? Like Sneezy, Dopey doesn't have a profile directory on the server at all. Unlike Sneezy, he has no local profile on the workstation. In this case, NT will use the information in Default User to create his local profile and will also create a profile directory in the network path. Just as with Sneezy, when Dopey logs off, NT will copy his local profile, including any changes, into the newly created directory.

Table 6.7 illustrates the order for loading a user profile, given the two scenarios we've discussed.

TABLE 6.7:   Loading a User Profile When the Roaming Profile Is Not Yet Created

Situation	What NT Does
A local profile exists	NT loads the local profile and creates a roaming profile directory on the server. Changes to the local profile are updated automatically. When the user logs off, the contents of the local profile directory are copied to the server profile directory.
No local profile exists	NT uses a Default User profile to create a local profile. Local profile is updated dynamically. A roaming profile directory is created on server. When the user logs off, NT copies the contents of the local profile directory to the server.

NOTE   While it is possible to specify a "roaming" profile for a local account on an NT workstation in User Manager, it's not really useful unless you are preconfiguring mandatory profiles for the local machine. Also, do not expect consistent roaming profile behavior if the user is logging on locally and has a "roaming" profile path specified on the local machine.

Preconfiguring User Profiles

Whether you want to create a preconfigured roaming profile or preconfigure the Default User profile, the principles are the same. It is a good strategy to create a bogus account to which you log on to configure the profile. This way you won't have to change your own profile and go through the hassle of cleaning it up. Use the Taskbar, Explorer, and the Control Panel applets to configure the Desktop, program items, and Start menu to your satisfaction, then log off. Log back on to that machine using a local administrator account.

Now you can copy the contents of the newly created profile over the existing contents of the Default User profile on the local machine. You can also copy that profile folder to a server location to implement a preconfigured roaming profile. You can even change the name and assign appropriate permissions during the process if you use the System applet to perform the copy rather than Explorer or another file management utility. Although a copy from Explorer would work in some scenarios, you would still have to set the directory permissions separately. Also, in certain other procedures regarding user profiles, NT needs to know that we are dealing with *profiles* here, not just files and directories. Get into the habit of using the System Applet when dealing with user profiles.

Figure 6.32 shows the User Profiles tab in the System Applet. Select the profile you have configured (Sneezy, in my case) and choose Copy To. Specify the path for the copy as shown in Figure 6.33, and remember to change the Permitted to Use information or only the bogus user (Sneezy) will be able to load it.

FIGURE 6.32:

The User Profiles tab in the System Applet

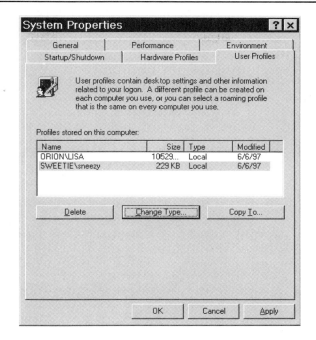

FIGURE 6.33:

Copy profile over Default User

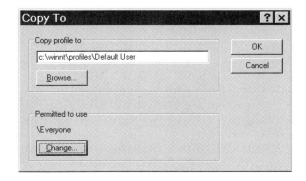

How Do I Create and Copy a Preconfigured User Profile?

That's a good question. Fortunately, it's as easy as this:

1. On an NT workstation, create a new user account using User Manager. We'll call ours "Sneezy." Sneezy doesn't need any particular user rights or group memberships.

2. Log off and log back on to the workstation as Sneezy. NT will create a user profile for Sneezy using the default.

3. Customize Sneezy's Desktop. Create any Desktop shortcuts and put those shortcuts into the Start menu. Set up persistent network connections. Using Windows NT Explorer or by right-clicking on the Taskbar and choosing Properties, you can add new program groups or shortcuts to the Start menu folders. By default, any user can change his or her profile.

4. When the profile is exactly the way you want it, log off. The system will now save the changes in the user's profile directory (\\%SYSTEMROOT%\PROFILES\SNEEZY). Actually, they are flushed to disk as you make changes to the profile.

5. Log back on the workstation as a local administrator. Right-click on My Computer and choose Properties to get the System Applet (also accessed through Control Panel ➢ System). Choose the User Profiles tab. You should see at least a user profile for your administrator account and for Sneezy; if no one else has ever logged on to the workstation, that's all you will see.

6. Use the mouse to highlight the template profile, then choose Copy To. Browse to the location of the directory, or type in the path. This may be a local path or a UNC path. NT will create the profile directory where you specify as long as you have permissions to write to that path. Be sure to give the Everyone group (or the appropriate users or groups) permission to use the profile; Sneezy is the only user that has access right now. Choose OK to start the copy process. Figures 6.32 and 6.33 above show the dialog boxes you will be using in this step.

7. Log off. You're done!

The Path's the Thing

This procedure can be used for several functions, depending on the path you specify. On the local level, you may specify the path as C:\WINNT\PROFILES\ DEFAULT USER to preconfigure profiles for all new users on the NT Workstation who do not have a roaming profile stored on a server. It's also possible to copy the customized profile to other NT workstations, if you have administrative rights on them. Take advantage of the fact that the system root directory on all of the workstations is shared as ADMIN$. Use the path \\MACHINENAME\ ADMIN$\PROFILES\DEFAULT USER to preconfigure the Default User profile on other NT workstations.

You can easily overwrite existing user profiles by typing in %SYSTEMROOT%\ PROFILES*USERNAME*, or the appropriate UNC path, but again, don't forget to set permissions. You also need permission to overwrite the user's existing profile.

Set up preconfigured roaming profiles by copying the profile to the same UNC path you specified in User Manager for Domains. In other words, copy the profile to the path *MACHINENAME*\PROFILES\SNEEZY and also use that path as the user profile path for the user.

Preconfigured local profiles may be set up this way, but you must specify a path in the user's local account information (use the User Manager to do this). Do not try to put the directory into the %SYSTEMROOT%\PROFILES directory: NT has no way of linking that profile with the new user, so the machine will just create a new directory (for example, SNEEZY001).

Interestingly enough, you can copy the profile to the NETLOGON share on the Domain Controller to set up a domain-wide Default User profile. You see, if a user is logging on to an NT domain, the machine first checks in the NETLOGON share (by default, %SYSTEMROOT%\SYSTEM32\REPL\IMPORT\SCRIPTS) of the authenticating domain controller to see if there is a Default Users directory there. Only if no Default User directory is found in the NETLOGON directory does the machine use the local Default User information. If a Default User directory exists in this network path (where login scripts and system policies are also stored), all new domain users will use this as the domain-wide Default User template instead of using the local Default User directory. The path should be specified as \\MACHINENAME\ADMIN$\SYSTEM32\REPL\IMPORT\SCRIPTS\ DEFAULT USER. Alternatively, you can save it directly to the NETLOGON share (\\MACHINENAME\NETLOGON\DEFAULT USER) if you modify the default share permissions to allow Administrators at least Read and Write permission (by default, Everyone has Read permission only). Be sure to name the directory "Default User" and grant permission to Everyone (or another appropriate group) to use the profile.

NOTE One thing about a domain-wide Default User Profile: the Default User Profile must exist in the NETLOGON share of every domain controller. You must copy the profile to each NETLOGON share. You can use the Directory Replicator Service discussed in Chapter 11 to simplify this task.

For any of the above, users can still modify their own profiles once they are created. A variation of this procedure is used to set up mandatory profiles; it will be discussed later.

Editing the NTUSER.DAT Hive File

You can change many user profile settings by editing the contents of the folders or by configuring the Desktop. However, if you want to place restrictions on the preconfigured Default User or roaming profile to protect the system from inexperienced users, you will need to edit the hive file (NTUSER.DAT) of the template profile. To do this, you will need a Registry-editing tool.

WARNING As always, *do not edit the Registry unless you really know what you're doing*. Editing the Registry can have disastrous consequences: you could ruin your system configuration and have to reinstall your whole operating system. Be careful!

NOTE Unfortunately, you cannot log on as a user named "default user" and make changes directly to the Default User profile. If you try it, NT will get really confused. If you create a user DEFAULT USER and set the profile path in User Manager as %SYSTEMROOT%\PROFILES\DEFAULT USER, of course NT will use the Default User directory to create the profile. NT will also create a DEFAULT USER.000 profile directory for the user, and changes made to the profile while logged on as DEFAULT USER will not be saved to the Default User directory. In fact, they won't be saved to DEFAULT USER.000, either. You might even find that changes the user makes do not even apply on the Desktop!

Using REGEDT32.EXE

To edit user profiles using REGEDT32.EXE, open HKEY_USERS as shown in Figure 6.34. Usually HKEY_USERS only contains two keys: .DEFAULT and the SID of the user currently logged on. The key .DEFAULT is not the Default User hive file, as you might think. That is located in %SYSTEMROOT%\PROFILES\ DEFAULT USER\NTUSER.DAT. The hive file represented in Figure 6.34 is loaded from C:\WINNT\SYSTEM32\CONFIG\.DEFAULT and is known as the *system default profile*. Microsoft describes it as the profile in effect when nobody is logged on. This seems to be a dangling chromosome from NT 3.51 profiles, when each profile was its own hive file in the %SYSTEMROOT%\SYSTEM32\CONFIG directory, as shown in Figure 6.35.

FIGURE 6.34:

HKEY_USERS Subkey

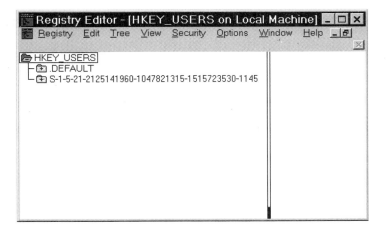

FIGURE 6.35:

Profiles in NT 3.51

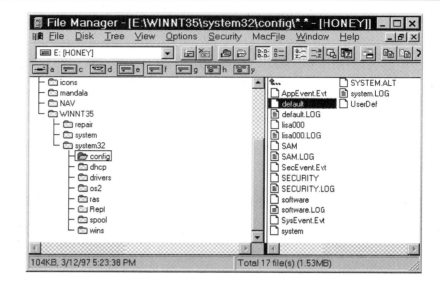

The System and Default User profiles are independent of each other. That is, changing the color scheme in the Registry for the .DEFAULT hive will not affect the Default User Profile hive in %SYSTEMROOT\PROFILES. Otherwise, when I set the System Default to use some neat (I mean practical and informative) bitmap wallpaper, any user who logged on without a profile already established will also get stuck with my wallpaper.

> **NOTE** Have you ever wanted to change that default Windows bitmap you see on the screen when nobody is logged on? Well, that bitmap is the wallpaper for the SYSTEM profile. Since SYSTEM is a user (or at least an entity) under NT, it makes sense that SYSTEM should have a profile, right? The SYSTEM default profile is the profile in effect when no one is logged on (you see the Ctrl+Alt+Del login dialog box). Simply use a Registry editor such as REGEDT32.EXE or REGEDIT.EXE to specify different wallpaper. The entry is found in HKEY_USERS\.DEFAULT\CONTROL PANEL\DESKTOP. Edit the Value Entry for Wallpaper, specifying the full path of the bitmap that tickles your fancy as the value of the string. You will be editing the hive file %SYSTEMROOT%\SYSTEM32\CONFIG\DEFAULT. Screensavers in effect when no one is logged on can be specified in the same way.

You can use REGEDT32 to edit a user profile other than the system default and the profile that is actively loaded. Load the hive file, using the Load Hive option from the Registry menu (Figure 6.36). This may be the NTUSER.DAT file from the Default User profile directory or any NTUSER.DAT file; you can browse for it (Figure 6.37). NT will prompt you for a temporary key name (Figure 6.38) and will then load the hive into the Registry Editor as shown in Figure 6.39. Make changes to the Registry settings of the Default User profile. To finish up, select the loaded hive and choose Unload Hive from the Registry Menu to save changes and clear the hive from the Registry Editor.

FIGURE 6.36:

Loading hive in REGEDIT.EXE

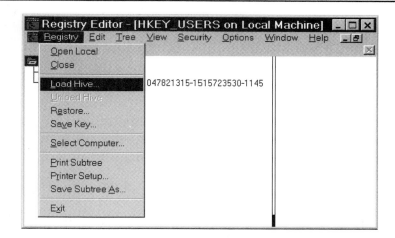

FIGURE 6.37:

Browse to find hive file

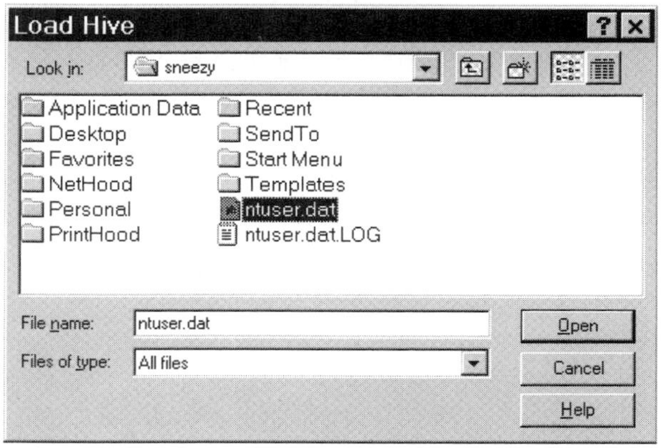

FIGURE 6.38:

Assign temporary key name

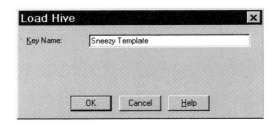

FIGURE 6.39:

Hive is loaded

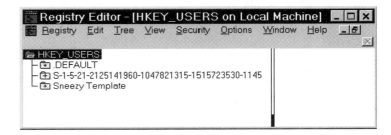

So which changes do you make once the hive is loaded? Ahh, that is the real question. You might configure all profiles to wait for login scripts to execute before starting the user's shell. That way, any drive mappings or environmental variables specified in the login script will take precedence over those in the user's profile. This entry is called "RunLogonScriptSynch" (run login scripts synchronously) and is found in HKEY_USERS*KEYNAME*\SOFTWARE\MICROSOFT\WINDOWS NT\CURRENTVERSION\WINLOGON (Figure 6.40). Although I could suggest a couple of others, the fact is that REGEDT32.EXE and REGEDIT.EXE are not all that user-friendly. Without spending copious amounts of our time reading Registry documentation (which is not always helpful) and experimenting, we do not know what is possible. We need a GUI Registry editor. At this point, the System Policy Editor steps back onto the scene.

FIGURE 6.40:

The RunLogonScript-
Sync entry

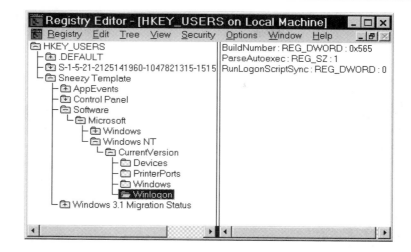

System Policy Editor to the Rescue

Instead of trying to hack everything out in REGEDT32.EXE, you can use the System
Policy Editor to place restrictions directly on the profile. (I know we haven't covered the System Policy Editor yet, but we will soon; forgive me for jumping the
gun, but this won't take long.) Run the System Policy Editor (POLEDIT.EXE) while
logged on as the template user SNEEZY. In this scenario, you will be using the Policy Editor as a user-friendly Registry editor, instead of as a tool to impose system
policies on your network. Choose File ≻ Open Registry ≻ Local User, as shown in
Figures 6.41 and 6.42. Now you can actually read about your options in English
(Figure 6.43). Apply your restrictions. You'll notice that you can take away the Run,
Find and Settings in the Start menu, as well as many other potentially dangerous
"built-in" options on the Desktop. You'd better be careful, though: changes will
apply immediately to the open profile you are configuring, so you might want to
make that the last thing you do when configuring the profile. Also, don't touch
Local Machine, or you will be making changes to your other local hive files (like
the System hive). These restrictions are written to the Registry. You can now go

back and view them by looking under HKEY_CURRENT_USER\SOFTWARE\ MICROSOFT\WINDOWS\CURRENTVERSION\POLICIES\EXPLORER (Figure 6.44). When you finish, close POLEDIT.EXE, log off, log back on as an administrator, and follow the steps outlined above to copy the profile, restrictions and all, to the Default User or Roaming Profile path.

FIGURE 6.41:

Open local Registry

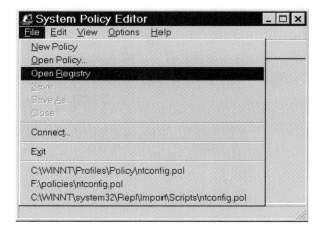

FIGURE 6.42:

Local User/Local Registry

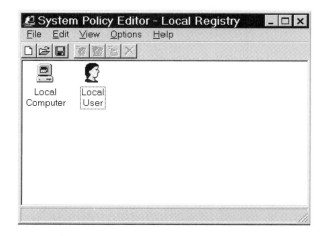

FIGURE 6.43:

Local User Properties in
POLEDIT.EXE

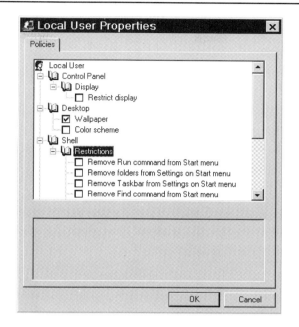

FIGURE 6.44:

REGEDIT32 policies subkey

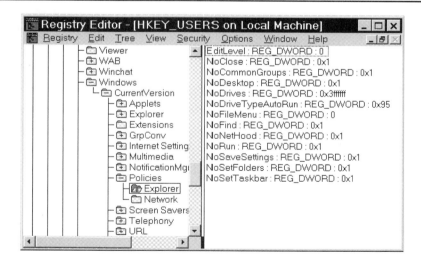

If you are configuring a domain-wide Default Profile, log on to the domain as a new user; you will get the preconfigured default profile and any restrictions you built in. This will be a good opportunity to inspect your work and look for any loopholes or problems. Remember to create your own profile or an administrator profile before doing this stuff, or it will apply to you as well.

A Note about System Policy Editor's Day Job: Another way to apply restrictions is the more traditional method of using System Policy Editor, as you're going to learn in a few pages. Use POLEDIT.EXE to create a new policy, placing restrictions on DEFAULT USER and/or specific groups, users, or computers. Save that policy as NTCONFIG.POL, placing it in the NETLOGON share on all your Domain Controllers. What is the difference between the two methods? In the first scenario, restrictions are "built in" to the Default User profile. Unless you specify a mandatory profile, and depending on how you restricted Default User, users may be able change their Desktop and Registry settings once they get their own profile. A savvy user could theoretically edit the Registry directly (unless you disabled Registry-editing tools for the Default User profile) and remove your restrictions. However, if NTCONFIG.POL exists in the NETLOGON share, NT will find the policy and reapply it every time a user logs on. Also, if NTCONFIG.POL specifies restrictions to be placed only on Default User, these would apply only the first time a user logs on and gets a new profile template.

The Bad News about Preconfigured Default Profiles

The problem with a "powerless, preconfigured" Default User profile becomes apparent when a new administrator or some such person logs on for the first time (oops). In this case you would need to keep a stash of unrestricted profiles in reserve somewhere (preconfigure them or make a copy of an untouched Default User profile). Users who should not get these powerless preconfigured profiles must have unrestricted profiles specifically assigned to them. Furthermore, these profiles will have to exist in the network path specified in User Manager or User Manager for Domains before the user ever logs on. If she has already logged on and received the altered Default User Profile, you have to delete that user's profile from the local machine and from the server to remedy the situation. In other words, the user will need to start over with a new profile and will lose any changes made to customize her Desktop.

Problems with Preconfigured and Roaming Profiles

As you create profiles for users, or simply allow them to have roaming profiles, keep in mind that a user profile includes settings on screen placement, window sizes, and color schemes. The display adapters and monitors on the workstations should be taken into consideration. If Sneezy has SVGA and sets up his Desktop accordingly, he may have an unpleasant surprise when he logs on to Grumpy's machine equipped with only VGA (no wonder he's grumpy). When preconfiguring a profile for a user, sit at a computer that has the same video capabilities as the user's primary workstation. If you are configuring a Default User profile or one that will be used by multiple users, those workstations must have the same video capabilities. Alternatively, use the lowest common denominators to ensure that the settings will work on all platforms.

Video problems are not all of it. If you are installing applications on the Desktop, always use default installation directories so that shortcuts created will resolve more smoothly. Also, keep in mind that NT will first attempt to resolve the *absolute* path for the shortcut. Failing that, NT will try the relative path. In other words, if you created a shortcut to Notepad on \\WOMBAT, saved that as a roaming profile, then sat down and logged on at \\POLECAT, the shortcut would first try to resolve to \\WOMBAT\WINNT\SYSTEM32\NOTEPAD.EXE. If the user cannot connect to \\WOMBAT, the system will try the relative path, %Systemroot%\SYSTEM32\NOTEPAD.EXE. It's a good thing that shortcuts are somewhat dynamic. When creating shortcuts, use expandable variables (like %WINDIR%, %SYSTEMROOT%) whenever possible. Luckily, shortcuts work just fine when they point to a shared directory on the server, as long as they are created properly and permissions are appropriate.

Also, take into consideration that when users on your network regularly move from one NT machine to another, every machine they use will store a copy of their local profile. These will eventually add up and take up a chunk of disk space. Local profiles may be deleted periodically by an administrator, using the Delete Option in the User Profiles tab of the System Applet. You may also use System Policy Editor to delete cached copies of roaming profiles when the user logs off, as shown in Figure 6.45. This is a machine-specific setting, so the easiest way to implement it is with an NTCONFIG.POL file in the NETLOGON share. However, you can edit the workstations' Registries remotely. You will need to add an entry to HKEY_LOCAL_MACHINE\SOFTWARE\MICROSOFT\WINDOWSNT\CURRENTVERSION\WINLOGON. The name of the value entry should be DeleteRoamingCache, with a datatype REG_DWORD, and a value of 1 (it should read, "DeleteRoamingCache:REG_DWORD:1").

Finally, accessing roaming profiles across a WAN link is not recommended. Whenever possible, load profiles from a server locally. Besides eating up network bandwidth (when the profile is sucked off the server at login and copied back to the server at logoff), timeout intervals for slow connections will cause numerous problems in synchronizing the local and server copies of the profiles.

NOTE   DELPROF.EXE, a command-line utility included in the *NT Workstation* and *NT Server Resource Kits*, allows administrators to delete user profiles on a local or remote computer running any version of Windows NT through 4.0 but not Windows 95. Of particular interest is its ability to delete profiles that have been inactive *x* number of days.

"Cached" Profiles: A Tip

It doesn't precisely fit in here, but talk of mandatory profiles reminded me of a peculiar behavior of NT, one that may bedevil you if you're extremely security-conscious.

Suppose I've given you an NT workstation named \\PC027, but I've not created a local account for you. Instead, I've given you a domain account on the SONGBIRDS domain and told you to log in from that. Thus, every morning you sit down at your workstation and tell your machine that you want to log in from a SONGBIRDS account, not a PC027 account—you want your workstation's Local Security Authority to look not in your workstation's SAM but instead to use NETLOGON to communicate with one of the domain controllers in SONGBIRDS, and then to ask one of those controllers to look up your user account in the domain SAM.

Sounds good—but what about those times when you get that dratted "no domain controller found" error message? If your workstation's NETLOGON can't find a domain controller, it seems that there's no way for your local LSA to establish your credentials. That seems to mean also that if there's no domain controller around, then you can't get on your workstation, doesn't it?

Or does it?

The first time this happened to me, I was somewhat taken aback to see that my NT workstation logged me in *anyway*, using "cached credentials." The idea is that if you got in all right *yesterday* we'll give you the benefit of the doubt *today*, even if the local LSA *can't* find a domain controller. Cool, eh? Well, yes, it might be cool for many, but the more security-conscious among us might be quite unhappy about the idea that if a network administrator modifies or deletes your account on Tuesday, by Wednesday your workstation might not know about it.

Fortunately, there's a Registry setting that you can use to make a workstation require a domain logon. Just go to HKEY_LOCAL_MACHINE\Software\Microsoft\Windows NT\CurrentVersion\Winlogon and create a value entry called CachedLogonsCount of type REG_DWORD and set its value to 0. Make this change on every NT workstation that you want to require strict logins. And if making all of those Registry changes sounds like a lot of work, then stay tuned—a little later I'll show you how to use a tool called *system policies*, a neat way to let you remotely (and automatically) control Registries.

Furthermore, you might consider that this whole issue of cached credentials becomes much less of a problem if you can just stamp out those annoying and random "no domain controller found" error messages—and you can read how later in Chapter 17, under "Troubleshooting Login Failures."

Mandatory Profiles

So far in this discussion, all of the types of user profiles allowed users to make changes to customize their own profile (assuming you did not set up System Policy Editor to discard changed settings at logoff). Another option for controlling user profiles is to assign a *mandatory profile* to the user or to a group of users.

A mandatory profile is a read-only profile that the user must use. Mandatory profiles are a tad more work, since the profile must exist ahead of time and it must exist in the path you point to, or the user cannot log on. Remember, with roaming profiles, we could just let NT copy the profile to the network path, unless we wanted Sneezy to use a profile we created for him.

Mandatory profiles are a type of roaming profile, in that you must specify a profile path in the user's account information. To create a mandatory profile directory, name it with the extension .MAN (for example, \\ALDEBARAN\PROFILES\SNEEZY.MAN). This tells NT that the profile is mandatory and that the user will not be able to log on if the profile is unavailable. In that case, the user will see a dialog box that says

```
Unable to log you on because your mandatory profile is not available.
Please contact your administrator.
```

Also, rename the NTUSER.DAT file to NTUSER.MAN so that the user cannot save changes to the profile. Once the local profile is created on the workstation, the locally created copy of the profile will also be read-only. This does not set permissions on the profile per se; it works on FAT or NTFS. Nor does changing the name to NTUSER.MAN set the read-only attribute on the file. It's just a special extension for the profile that tells NT not to save changes at logoff (changes will apply while the user is logged on but will be lost when the user logs off). This feature is useful if you want to assign one profile to a group of users and you do not want these users to be able to save changes. In other words, everybody shares a copy of the same profile, and it is protected against users' "personal touches."

NOTE   Strangely enough, if the mandatory directory does exist in the specified path, but permissions on the directory do not grant at least read access to the user, that user will be able to log on, using a default profile. The user encounters the following message (this is actually a problem in the USERENV.DLL and is corrected in Service Pack 3): "You do not have permission to access your central profile located at *SERVERNAME\SHARENAME\USERNAME*.MAN. The operating system is attempting to log you on with your local profile."

The following are your options for setting up mandatory profiles.

Use a read-only profile   Simply rename the file NTUSER.DAT to *NTUSER.MAN* before you assign the profile to the user or users. Keep in mind that when a user first logs on, NT does not know that this user's profile is a mandatory profile, since the directory name is *USER*NAME, not USERNAME.MAN. If the profile is unavailable, the system will load a local or default profile. However, once the system loads the mandatory profile from the profile path, the System applet on the workstation shows the profile as MANDATORY. The user or users will not be able to save changes to the Desktop. At this point, if the network profile becomes unavailable, the system will load the local profile; but because NT now considers it a mandatory profile, changes will not be saved. Incidentally, renaming the NTUSER.DAT file to *NTUSER.MAN* can be done as an afterthought, as well. In other words, if a user formally has a local and configurable profile, you can go to the C:\WINNT\PROFILES\USERNAME directory and rename the hive file. It will be read-only from that point on.

Force the user to load a particular profile   If you specify the directory path on the server as DIRECTORYNAME.MAN but do not rename the hive file to NTUSER.MAN, the operating system will not see it as a mandatory profile. If the hive file is not named NTUSER.MAN, the workstation will classify it merely as a roaming profile. At login, however, the user will not be able to log on if the profile directory does not exist in the specified path. Users can make changes to their Desktops, however, since it's not a real mandatory profile to NT.

Create a read-only profile that must be used   Specify the directory name as DIRECTORYNAME.MAN and rename the NTUSER.DAT file to *NTUSER.MAN*. This is ideal if you want to force users to load a profile off the network and you want to prevent them from making any changes.

How Do I Configure a Mandatory Profile?

Mandatory profiles are created in much the same way as preconfigured profiles. Mandatory profiles can be assigned to individual users or to groups. In the example below we show how to create and assign a shared mandatory profile to everyone in a particular group (Research Users).

1.   Create a user, log on as that user, and set up the Desktop.

Continued on next page

2. Apply any restrictions you want at that time using the System Policy Editor as described earlier. Log off.

3. Log back on to the machine as an administrator.

4. Use the System applet (you can find it under Control Panel ≻ System ≻ User Profiles) to select the profile and copy it to a shared directory on the network, naming it SOMETHING.MAN. Remember to set permissions to allow your user (or a group) at least Read and Execute access to the profile and its contents. In Figure 6.46, we name the directory RESEARCHUSERS.MAN and assign permissions to the group Research Users.

5. Use Explorer or your favorite file management tool to rename the NTUSER.DAT file to NTUSER.MAN.

6. In User Manager for Domains, select the user or group of users, choose Properties from the User menu, then the Profile Button. Fill in the profile directory path, pointing to your mandatory profile directory. In Figure 6.47, we have selected all of the members of the Research Users Group and are assigning their profile path as \\ALDEBARAN\PROFILES\RESEARCHUSERS.MAN.

7. You are now ready to have users log on and receive their mandatory profiles.

You can see what profiles are saved on a local machine, and what type they are, in the System Applet, the same place you go to copy profiles. Figure 6.48 shows all three types on a machine.

FIGURE 6.46:

Copying a profile to USERS.MAN

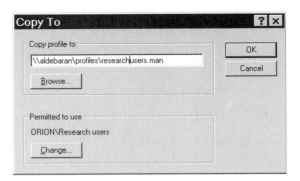

FIGURE 6.47:

Assigning a mandatory
profile path

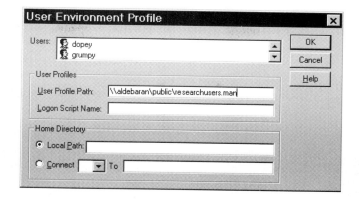

FIGURE 6.48:

Local, roaming, and
mandatory profiles

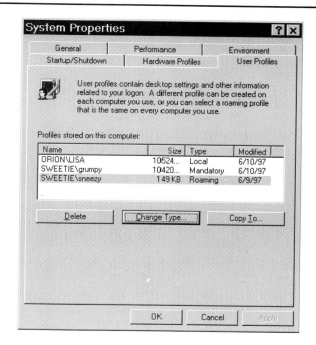

Setting Up a Group Template Profile

As you can see, it's relatively easy to assign "shared" profiles to users and groups. However, anytime two or more users are pulling their profiles from the same profile directory, it should be a mandatory profile. Otherwise, changes made by each user to the group profile directory on the server will be saved. Happy and Grumpy will have to deal with Sneezy's eggplant color scheme or Ninja Turtles icons.

How much more trouble is it to preconfigure and assign profiles based on, say, group membership, which will then be under the control of the individual user? This would not be a mandatory profile but just a point of departure for the user. Actually, it's a lot more trouble. Sure, you can make profile templates for groups, but how do you assign them and still let users customize the Desktop according to their own preferences or needs?

Assigning User-Configurable Profiles to Groups

If you use the standard preconfigured user profile procedure, follow these steps:

First, make group template profiles by creating three GROUPS (CLEAVERS, ADAMS, and CLAMPETTS). Then create three bogus group member accounts, naming them, for instance, *Clampetts template*, *Adams template*, and *Cleavers template* (you were getting pretty tired of the Seven Dwarves stuff, weren't you?). Log on and off as each bogus user, and then configure the group profiles.

Before you add Ward or June user to the Cleavers group, open the System Applet and copy the Cleavers group template profile to a shared profile directory, renaming it after the new user you are about to create. Then create the user, specifying his profile path as *MACHINENAME**PROFILESHARENAME**USERNAME*, where *PROFILESHARENAME* is the directory where you copied the profile. This is not overly complicated, but you will have to remember to copy a new profile to the shared directory and assign the profile to that specific user each time you create a new account.

Using System Policy Editor to Assign and Control User Profiles

To create a centrally configured group template profile while still allowing users to change their color schemes, mouse orientation, and so forth, use the System Policy Editor.

Create your user, "Cleaver template," and log on as that user. Configure the Desktop, program groups, and so on, thus creating a template profile, "Cleavers template." Log off and log back on as an administrator. Copy the template profile to a shared directory on an NT server (you actually do not have to copy the NTUSER.DAT file). This need not be done with the System Applet, but you still must assign permissions so that users can have at least Read and Execute access to the folders. So far, this is very much like the other procedures for preconfigured profiles. From this point on, everything changes.

The next step is to create a global group for the Cleavers (Domain Cleavers?) in User Manager for Domains. The members of this group will use the folders in the shared directory to make up part of their profile.

Now, open the System Policy Editor. Choose New Policy (or Open Policy if you already have one) from the File menu. Choose Add Group from the Edit menu as shown in Figure 6.49. Add the global group, Domain Cleavers in this case. Open the Group policy by double-clicking on the Group icon. Now choose Windows NT Shell and expand Custom Folders, shown in Figure 6.50. You will see that by default the path for Start Menu Programs is %USERPROFILE%\ START MENU\PROGRAMS. Replace the default path with a network path; for example, \\ALDEBARAN\PROFILES\CLEAVERS TEMPLATE\START MENU\PROGRAMS, shown in Figure 6.51. This indicates the folders you want the Domain Cleavers members to use. You can also assign a network path for their Desktop icons, Start Up folder—even a customized Network Neighborhood. Just be sure to also select Hide Start Menu subfolders (see Figure 6.52), or the Cleavers will get both the template folders and their regular Start menu folders.

FIGURE 6.49:

Adding a global group policy

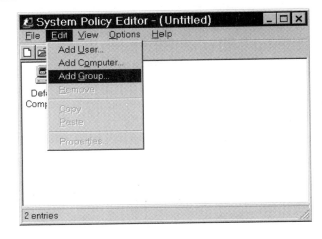

FIGURE 6.50:

Default path for custom folders

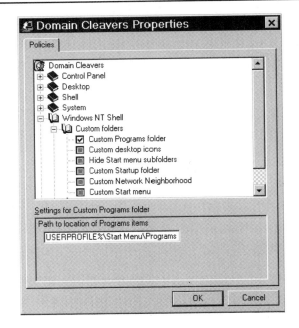

FIGURE 6.51:

Specify path for custom folders

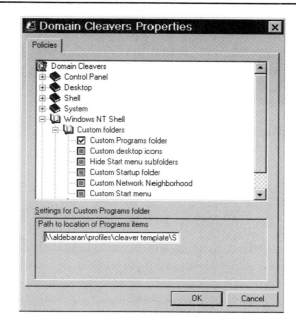

FIGURE 6.52:

Hide other Start menu folders

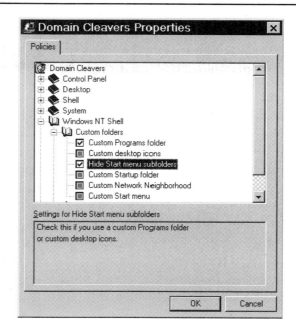

Make any other changes or restrictions you want to apply to the Domain Cleavers group members, repeat as needed for Domain Adams and Domain Clampetts, then save that policy as NTCONFIG.POL in the NETLOGON share (%SYSTEM-ROOT\SYSTEM32\REPL\IMPORT\SCRIPTS) on the authenticating domain controller(s). Now you are ready to create users, put them into the Cleavers group, and assign roaming profiles for NT to create at the time of first login. NT will see that there is no profile in the network path specified and will create one, using the Default User profile directory (possibly a Network Default Profile) and the policy that exists in the NETLOGON share. If you have specified a network path for custom folders, these will be built into the new user's profile at the time of first login. The good news is that you should now be able to centrally administer the users' Desktops by just changing the template on the server. As long as the policy exists, the NT workstation will get those custom folders from the network directory (policies are reapplied every time a user logs on). Also, users can still change their color schemes, mouse orientation, and other options (unless you have used POLEDIT.EXE to restrict *those* as well) because that information is in their very own NTUSER.DAT file.

WARNING If your template for program groups or other folders is stored on an NTFS partition, you must be very attentive to the permissions set on the template folders. You will need to grant permissions to the user group or groups (Read and Execute permissions should be sufficient) and remember to replace permissions on sub-directories. (Again, see Chapter 7 for details on setting permissions.) Poor user Wally logged on and got an empty Desktop because he did not have access to the folders NTCONFIG.POL was making him use!

Also, use a variation of this strategy to assign common program groups, normally pulled from the All Users folder on the user's local workstation. These machine-specific settings can be changed using the System Policy Editor. First configure the All Users folder on some workstation, then copy it to a network path and set appropriate permissions. Then open System Policy Editor, choose Open Policy to edit your existing NTCONFIG.POL file, then choose Default Computer (remember, this will apply to *all* computers). Next, open Default Computer and select Windows NT Shell, Custom Shared Folders. Replace the default path, %SYSTEMROOT%\PROFILES\ALL USERS\START MENU\PROGRAMS, with the network path of the shared All Users directory, such as \\ALDEBARAN\PROFILES\ALL USERS\START MENU\PROGRAMS (see Figure 6.53). Like the settings for Domain Cleavers, you have the option to specify a network path for the Start Up folder, Desktop shortcuts, Start menu programs, or the entire Start menu, depending on which of these boxes you select. Unfortunately, you can only select Default Computer or select the computers by machine name individually.

FIGURE 6.53:

Network path for All Users

How Does NT Choose between Local, Roaming, and Mandatory Profiles?

In all of this discussion about locally cached profiles, roaming profiles stored on a server, and mandatory profiles, it's important to understand the order in which NT looks for a profile and how the system chooses among the three. Plus, there are a couple of considerations that have not been explained yet. To make this simple, let's view the scenarios from two perspectives: a user that has never logged on to that NT workstation before (Morticia) and a user that has logged on to the machine already (Gomez).

Morticia logs on to her newly assigned NT 4 workstation. Assume that there is no profile path specified for Morticia in her account information. She will only have a local profile. NT must create a profile for her from a Default User directory. If Morticia is logging on to an NT Server domain, the operating system will first look in the NETLOGON share for a Default User profile (it has to look there anyway for the login script, why not just kill two birds with one stone?). No Default User directory in the NETLOGON share? Oh well, the system will just have to use the Default User info from the local machine.

If there is a profile path specified for her account, however, the system will look in that path for the profile directory. If it exists, NT will load it and use it to make a local copy. This may be a roaming or a mandatory profile. If no profile exists in the path and the path was indicated as mandatory, \\SERVERNAME\SHARE-NAME\USERNAME.MAN, for example, the user will not be allowed to log on at all! If there is no profile in the specified path and a roaming profile is specified (\\SERVERNAME\SHARENAME\USERNAME), NT will make one. Again, for an NT Server domain login, the system first checks in NETLOGON. If no Default User directory is found there, the system creates Morticia's profile from the local Default User directory.

So far, so good. Now let's tackle Gomez, who has been using his NT 4 workstation for a few weeks already. If no profile is specified in his account information, nothing changes for Gomez. He continues to use his locally stored profile.

If by chance you decided to implement roaming profiles one evening or weekend and Gomez comes in the next morning and logs on, NT has to check a few things. First, if a profile path exists in the account info, NT must first check to see if Gomez has changed his roaming profile type back to local. Aha! You see, Gomez might get tired of waiting for his roaming profile to load off the server and may decide to tell his workstation not to bother, to just use the local copy all the time. He does this by opening the System Applet, User Profiles Tab, selecting his own profile, and choosing Change Type. Gomez then sees the dialog box shown in Figure 6.54. Gomez could not do this if the profile was mandatory, and of course one cannot change a local profile to a roaming profile unless you are changing it *back* to a roaming profile.

FIGURE 6.54:

Changing a user profile from roaming to local

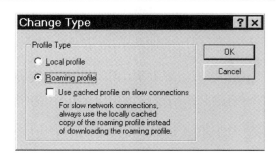

Any user may change an unrestricted roaming profile back to local and may also choose the option to automatically "use cached profile on slow connections." If Gomez checks that box, he's saying to NT, "If there is a slow network connection, just go ahead and load my local copy and don't bother me." What qualifies as a slow connection? That depends on an interval set in the Registry, called SlowLinkTimeout. The default interval is 2 seconds. Generally, if the 2-second interval is exceeded, then Gomez will see a dialog box stating that a slow network connection has been detected, asking whether to load the local or the roaming profile. By default, Gomez has 30 seconds to choose (that value is determined by a Registry entry called ProfileDlgTimeout), after which time the system will load the local profile. But if Gomez chooses to "Use cached profile on slow connections," NT will automatically load the local profile without asking Gomez. Hmmm.

The Registry entries affecting detection of slow network connections are found in HKEY_LOCAL_MACHINE\SOFTWARE\MICROSOFT\WINDOWS NT\ CURRENTVERSION\WINLOGON. All of the following values may be set using the System Policy Editor:

SlowLinkDetectEnabled   Has a data type of REG_DWORD and possible values of 0 (disabled) or 1(enabled). Slow link detection is enabled by default and the system is told to be aware of slow network connections.

SlowLinkTimeOut   Has a datatype of REG_DWORD and a default value of 2000 (2 seconds expressed in milliseconds). Possible values are 0–120,000 (up to 2 minutes). When this threshold is exceeded and SlowLinkDetectEnabled is set to 1, users can log in by using a local profile instead of the roaming profile.

ProfileDlgTimeOut   Has a datatype of REG_DWORD and a default value of 30 (expressed in seconds). This value determines how long a user has to choose between a local or server-based profile when the value of SlowLinkTimeOut is exceeded.

Assuming that there is not a slow network connection and assuming Gomez has not changed his roaming profile back to a local profile (he hasn't had a chance yet, right?), the system will check to see whether (1) the profile is mandatory or (2) the profile on the server is more current.

If (1) or (2) is true, the system will load the server copy. If neither is true, then Gomez gets a pesky dialog box. You see, if (2) is not true, then the profile on the server is not more current than the local copy. This implies that there was a problem in synchronizing the profiles the last time Gomez logged off. So NT will announce that the local profile is more recent than the network profile and will ask if Gomez wants to load the local instead.

Whew! That was a bit complex, so maybe the following flow charts will help. Figures 6.55 and 6.56 describe Morticia (new user to the workstation, local profile and roaming profile) and Figure 6.57 follows Gomez (an existing user with locally stored profile). Finally, we've thrown in Figure 6.58 to show how a user's profile is saved at logoff.

FIGURE 6.55:

How a new user gets a local profile

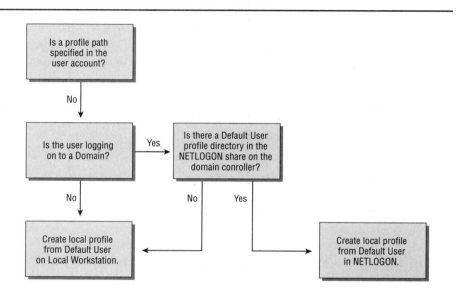

Which Type of Profile Is Right for My Network?

Now that you are an NT profile guru, you'll need to decide what kind of profiles to implement on your NT Server/NT Workstation network. Even if you do nothing, you are still making a choice to just let users keep local profiles. For that reason, the following paragraphs summarize the pros and cons of the different types of profiles:

Local profiles only   Local profiles may be the best choice in a mixed client environment or where users don't need to roam. Windows 95 profiles are not interchangeable with NT Workstation profiles, though the Desktop is similar, so users moving from one client OS to another need

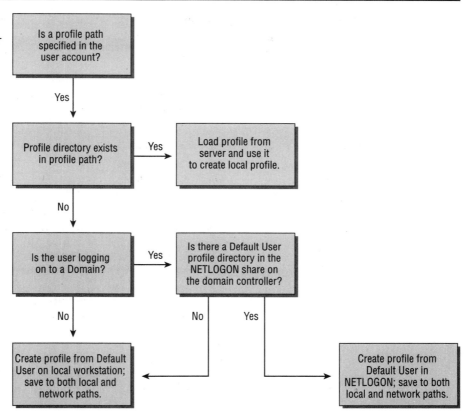

FIGURE 6.56:

How a new user gets a roaming profile

either local profiles only or two roaming profiles. (Do you feel a migraine coming on?) This option has the lowest administrative overhead and offers the fewest options for preconfiguring profiles and controlling Desktops. However, you can still use System Policy Editor to configure Desktops and impose restrictive policies without implementing roaming profiles.

Roaming profiles   A roaming profile has two major benefits: mobility and fault-tolerance. Not only can users move from desktop to desktop and have their preferred settings follow, but users also have a "backup" of their profile stored on the server. If you have to reinstall the Workstation, the user doesn't necessarily have to reconfigure the Desktop. Plus, you can let NT create the profile for you, as long as there are no special settings to hand out to users. This is also the option to use if you want profiles to be

FIGURE 6.57:

How a user with a local profile gets a roaming profile

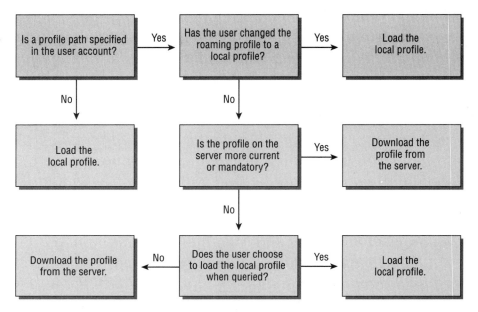

centrally located and controlled. The downside is that roaming profiles
may follow you to another machine but may not work flawlessly once they
are downloaded. Shortcuts to applications that exist only on the user's
"home workstation," and different video adapters and monitors are only
two of the possible problems users may encounter. Also, roaming profiles
shooting across your Ethernet every time a user logs on or off will generate
more traffic and slow down user logons. If it's a consideration at 10Mbps,
consider the problems if you have an ISDN connection at 64Kbps. Finally,
remember that NT will store a local copy of the profile for every user that
logs on to a given NT machine. If users roam and roam and roam, they
leave copies behind, taking up hard drive space as well as presenting a
security issue (my Desktop may have a few items on it I don't want to
leave behind). To address this problem, set up the machines to delete
cached copies of roaming profiles.

Mandatory Profiles   Mandatory profiles, because they are also roaming
profiles, have the benefit of being mobile and fault-tolerant. They can also
be centrally located and controlled, like roaming profiles. Plus, mandatory
profiles are the only way you can force a user to load a particular profile.
Because it is read-only, users can share a profile; you keep fewer profiles
stored on the server instead of one for every single user. While mandatory

FIGURE 6.58:

How user profiles are saved at logoff

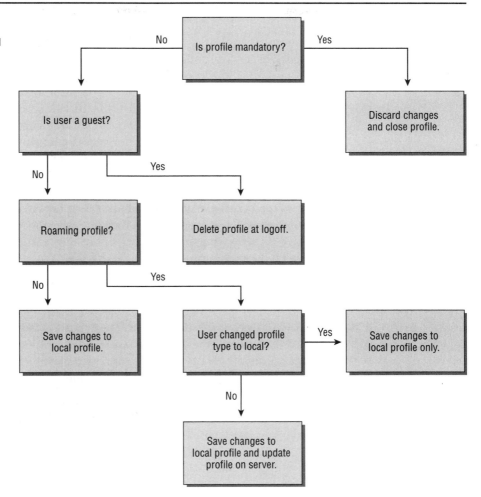

profiles offer more control than roaming profiles, they also require more setup on your part. You must manually create a mandatory profile and place it in a network path: NT can't create a mandatory profile for you. Finally, if a user attempts to log on and the mandatory profile is unavailable, NT will not allow the user to log on. This prevents a malicious user from logging on with the Default User profile and running amok, but it can also be seen as a drawback if you are not the Control Master of the Universe, but just a nice network administrator trying to do shared network profiles.

Network Default User Profile One of the best things about a domain-wide Default User profile is that it may be implemented in conjunction with roaming profiles. This offers a great way to preconfigure all new user profiles; and although it does not help you hand out special program groups to, say, the accounting department, it can be used as a point of departure. You can use the System Policy Editor to hand out custom Start menu items to group members. However, if you place heinous restrictions on the Default User profile in the NETLOGON share, you'll have to create and assign a special roaming profile to folks who shouldn't get the restrictions (like new MIS employees). Also, the Default User directory has to exist in the NETLOGON share of every domain controller on the domain. Otherwise, if your user is validated by a Backup Domain Controller that does not have the network Default User directory in NETLOGON, the NT workstation will use its own local Default User directory.

Implementing User Profiles: An Example

Let's see what we've learned by looking at a sample situation and determining the best way to use profiles.

Suppose you manage several computer labs at a university, and each lab has 35–100 NT 4.0 NT workstations. Up to 10,000 students at the university, who all have accounts on the university-wide system, visit various labs using various machines. A few students cause problems in the network. Some of these students are malicious, while some are just inexperienced.

If you stand by and do nothing, users will leave profiles behind when they log off. You'll have to periodically delete profiles. If you allow users to have access to all possible tools on the Desktop, administrative overhead increases as you troubleshoot problems and reinstall the OS on the workstations.

Solution #1: Preconfigure a Domain-Wide Default User Profile You may have to create more than one if user accounts are in multiple domains. Restrict profiles as necessary, assign roaming profiles, and delete cached copies of roaming profiles using System Policy Editor or the *Resource Kit* utility, DELPROF.EXE.

This is a good solution, but it poses one big problem. Even if users have restrictions placed on the profile, with roaming profiles for every user the network servers will hold thousands of copies of the very same profile. Not only that, but savvy users may be able to change their own Registry settings and break free of restrictions.

Actually, there is a very simple solution to the profile detritus problem. Rather than going to the trouble of setting up a policy to delete cached copies of roaming profiles, editing the Registry of every machine, or running DELPROF.EXE at regular intervals, you can make every user a Guest at the local machines in the lab. Although this approach has several other implications that might make it unfeasible for your situation, it would take care of profile buildup. Members of the Guests group are not allowed to keep local profiles unless they are also members of the Users group.

Solution #2: Create a Shared Mandatory Profile A better solution is to create a restricted profile directory, name it USERS.MAN, rename the hive file to NTUSER.MAN, and assign this as a shared mandatory profile to all users. You'll also need to delete cached copies of roaming profiles. This way, even if a user manages to edit the Registry settings to take off the restrictions, changes will be discarded at logoff. You also save space on the network servers.

There is one possible problem with this solution: if many students try to download the mandatory profile at exactly the same time, they may experience sharing violations. Service Pack 2 fixes this problem.

Distributing User Profiles

You may also want to keep several copies of the mandatory profile (for example, one in each lab) for load balancing. There is a way to distribute user profiles across domain controllers using the undocumented environment variable %LOGONSERVER%: create a share of the same name on each domain controller, put the mandatory profiles into each of the shared directories, then indicate the profile path in User Manager for Domains as something like \\%LOGONSERVER%\PROFILES\USERS.MAN. To prevent major profile synchronization problems, don't use this variable with regular roaming profiles, use it only with mandatory profiles.

What if you don't want to store profiles on the domain controllers, or what if not every lab has one? If the students logged on at the same lab every time, there wouldn't be any problem. You could just point to the local server for that lab in the user account's information. Unfortunately, you can't count on each student using the same lab every time.

You can tell the workstation where to look for the profile by creating a new environmental variable on each of the NT workstations. The new environmental variable will be %SERVERNAME% and will point to the local lab server keeping the mandatory profile.

How Do I Make Users Load Profiles from Local Servers?

Use the System Applet Environment Tab to set a System Variable pointing to the local server, as shown in Figure 6.59. Fill in the information as shown. In this case the local lab server will be LAB01FSUNC. (Do not include % signs or \\ as part of the variable.) Choose the Set button and OK. Although the new variable will be set, you will need to restart NT before these settings take effect, since NT reads the system variables at startup.

Once you have defined the %SERVERNAME% variable on each of the NT workstations (REGINI.EXE, a *Resource Kit* utility, can be pretty handy for that type of thing), created a share of the same name on each server, and copied the mandatory profiles to those shared directories, you must indicate the profile path in User Manager for Domains as \\%SERVERNAME%\PROFILES\USERS.MAN.

FIGURE 6.59:

Make a System Variable point to local server

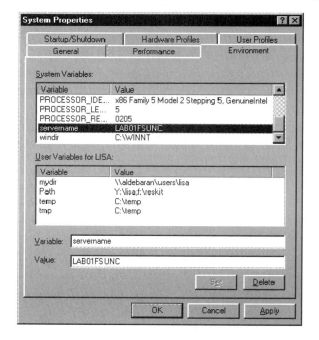

Windows NT 3.51, NT 4, and Windows 95 Profiles

As you can see, there's a lot that can be done with user profiles in an NT Server/ NT Workstation environment. However, you probably won't be managing a network of just NT 4 clients, so to round out our discussion, here is a quick rundown of the differences between NT 3.51, NT 4 and Windows 95 user profiles. The important thing to keep in mind is that Windows 95, NT 3.51, and NT 4 profiles are not cross-platform. In other words, a user who requires a roaming profile and customarily sits at several types of clients would need a Windows 95 profile and an NT profile for each version.

NT 3.51 Profiles

In NT 3.51, each user profile is a single hive file (found in %SYSTEMROOT%\ SYSTEM32\CONFIG) and profiles are stored with the rest of the Registry hive files (see Figure 6.60). Instead of a bunch of folders and a hive file, everything is included in the one file, for example, LISA000.

FIGURE 6.60:

NT 3.51 user profile

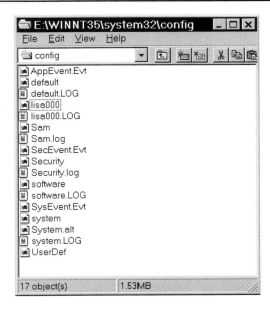

NT 3.51 supports per-user profiles (equivalent to roaming profiles) and mandatory profiles. The profile path for an NT 3.51 personal profile would be specified as \\SERVERNAME\SHARENAME\USERNAME.USR in the User Manager for Domains and, for a mandatory profile, \\SERVERNAME\ SHARENAME\FILENAME.MAN.

Because there was no System Policy Editor under NT 3.51, options for restricting profiles were limited. NT 3.51 did provide a tool called User Profile Editor (UPEDIT.EXE), shown in Figure 6.61, which allowed you to log on as your bogus user, configure the Desktop, and save a configured profile with a skimpy set of restrictions to the current, user, or system default. This was also the tool used to save the profile to a specified path when implementing per-user or mandatory profiles.

FIGURE 6.61:

User Profile Editor

NT 4 profiles have taken on the Windows 95 profile structure, so NT 3.51 profiles will be converted to NT 4.0 profiles when upgrading from 3.51 to NT 4. NT 3.51 per-user profiles formerly named USERNAME.USR, for example, will be converted to a directory called *USERNAME.PDS*. Mandatory profiles named USER.MAN will be converted to a directory called *USER.PDM*. If a user is in a mixed environment, she will have a separate profile for each version, and they will not be synchronized (changes made to one won't show up in the other) if changes are made after the initial migration.

Windows 95 Profiles

In Windows 95, individual profiles are not created by default but must be enabled in Control Panel ➤ Passwords. If roaming profiles are enabled on the Windows 95 machine, they will be stored automatically in the user's home directory and will then operate in the same way as the NT Workstation profiles. You need not specify a profile path for the user in User Manager for Domains.

Individual mandatory profiles can be used in Windows 95, but shared mandatory profiles cannot. For this reason, the administrator must create a profile for each user and copy it to that user's home directory.

The structure of a Windows 95 user profile contains differences from an NT user profile. Instead of an NTUSER.DAT file, Windows 95 has a USER.DAT file. Instead of NTUSER.DAT.LOG, Windows 95 uses a file called USER.DA0. These two files are not exact equivalents. Windows 95 uses USER.DA0 as a "backup," writing a copy of USER.DAT to USER.DA0 every time the user logs off. NT 4 uses NTUSER.DAT.LOG as a transaction log file, to protect the hive file while it is being updated. To create a read-only mandatory profile, rename the USER.DAT file to USER.MAN. NT 4 and Windows 95 use the same folder structure, except that the Application Data folder does not exist in Windows 95.

Additional differences in Windows 95 profiles include the following:

- Not all Desktop items will roam, only LNK (shortcuts) and PIF (program information) files.

- Common program groups aren't supported in Windows 95.

- Windows 95 can't use a centrally stored Default User profile.

For more information on Windows 95 profiles, consult the *Expert Guide to Windows 95* or the *Windows 95 Resource Kit*.

System Policies: Central Registry Control

Over the years, Microsoft has accomplished many things in some areas but hasn't been too successful in others. NT has superbly implemented multitasking, a large memory model (when was the last time you worried about whether or not something would fit into 640K?), and a vastly improved user interface. Put simply, users have just *got* to love many of the things that NT offers.

Support people, on the other hand, haven't got so much to like. In the typical modern corporation, each corporate support person must ride herd on hundreds or sometimes thousands of PC desktops, solving problems, installing upgrades, and giving advice. But modern PC operating systems don't offer much help to those support folks. Want to remotely control a PC over a network? Remotely install a new piece of software? Can't do any of that with the tools that come in the box with NT. What happens when you've got NT half-installed and the Setup program goes into the weeds? You have a completely useless computer—half installed is no better than newborn as far as NT (or just about any other PC operating system, for that matter) goes.

All that's supposed to change with Windows 2000 Server and its associated Zero Administration Windows. But you don't have to wait until Windows 2000 Server for support relief—there are two tools built into NT 4 that make it a bit easier to support and control hundreds of workstations from a single point. The first is *user profiles*, which you read about earlier in this chapter. The other tool is *system policies*.

So what's a system policy and why do you care? That's the topic of the next few dozen pages, but first let's look at the overview. System policies are essentially *central control of users' Registries*.

Why Would You Want to Control Registries?

As you know, virtually *everything* that has anything to do with controlling an NT machine (and a Windows 95 machine, for that matter) is in the Registry. But I'll bet you didn't know all of the things that you can control with the Registry; certainly some of these surprised *me*. Here are a few examples:

- The contents of the folders that a user sees when she clicks the Start button
- Which icons and controls appear on the Desktop

- Whether or not a user can directly access the drives on her computer

- Which programs she can use on her computer

The basic idea is this: you can use Registry entries to lock down a Windows NT workstation or Windows 95 desktop, thereby offering users a consistent and simplified user interface and making the support task simpler. Cool!

Using System Policies

Well, cool except for the fact that to change these important Registry entries on a bunch of machines, it seems like you'd have to walk around to each computer in the building, sit down at the computer, and run REGEDT32 or REGEDIT to modify that machine's Registry. Don't worry: there's an answer to that. There's an automatic feature built right into Windows NT and Windows 95 machines that can make remote Registry modification much easier. Whenever a user logs onto a domain from a Windows NT or Windows 95 machine, the machine looks on the domain's PDC for a file called a *system policy* file. The system policy file basically consists of a bunch of instructions, like "Make sure that HKEY_LOCAL_ MACHINE\System\CurrentControlSet\Services\Browser\Parameters has a key named MaintainServerList, and be sure to set it to No." This system policy can centrally control *any* Registry entry except for those of type REG_MULTI_SZ, and this isn't a big restriction, as there aren't that many REG_MULTI_SZ entries.

Central Registry control through system policies is a neat feature, but there are a few problems with it.

- First, a user must be logging into a domain for the user's system to look for the system policy file.

- Second, you can't have one common system policy file for both the Windows NT and Windows 95 machines; you have to build one set of policies for Windows NT desktops and another for Windows 95 desktops.

- Third, the policy file gets automatically read from only the PDC, not the BDC, which may pose problems for some large networks. You *can* change that, but it involves some machine-by-machine modifications and that's what we're trying to avoid in the first place.

- Fourth, because these system policies are just changes to the Registry and because different Registry entries get read at different times, it can be a little confusing to try to figure out whether a system policy actually took effect—it may take an extra reboot to see the change in action.

The system policy files are created for Windows NT and Windows 95 with programs named the System Policy Editor for Windows NT and the System Policy Editor for Windows 95. Both System Policy Editors are actually user-configurable Registry editors. But unlike REGEDT32 and REGEDIT, they do not show all of the Registry: you essentially "program" them to work with the small subset of Registry entries that you care about, using files called "templates." Fortunately, you don't usually need to do any of that "programming" as Microsoft includes some pre-built templates that will serve most people's needs.

Using the Registry to Restrict a Desktop: A Basic Example

But before I get into the specifics of system policies, and in particular the administrative tool that you use to create system policies (something called the System Policy Editor, not surprisingly), let's try out one of those Registry changes that I mentioned.

Two important things to understand about system policies are that first, they're just remote-controlled Registry changes, and second, a lot of the Registry changes that we'll find useful for central control of desktops are Registry entries that restrict the user shell program EXPLORER.EXE. EXPLORER.EXE—what's that? Well, you probably know that all of the programs that you run on a PC are just specially designed files with the extension .EXE or, on some older programs, .COM. (There are no NT programs that use .COM, but there are some old DOS programs that do.) You probably also know that the Registry just contains program-specific settings; for example, the Word for Windows section of the Registry contains settings that are only obeyed by Word—put a Registry parameter intended for the Computer Browser service into the Word section, and it'll be ignored.

If I asked you what Windows program you ran most often, you might tell me Word, your Web browser, or perhaps your e-mail program. But there's a Windows program that you use much more—the *shell program* EXPLORER.EXE. Explorer is the program that puts the Desktop on your screen; it starts automatically when you log on to a Windows NT computer. Explorer is the program that knows, when you double-click on an icon, to go out and start the program associated with that icon. Explorer puts the Start button on the Desktop and controls what possible actions you can take when you push Start. It's also the program that displays the time in the "system tray" area of the Taskbar.

So, again, what's the value of controlling Explorer? Well, as you'll see, Explorer is normally the program that you use to start *other* programs: Word, Internet Explorer, Solitaire, or whatever. Being able to control which programs a user can run adds up to some real power.

One of the things that Explorer shows you is the Network Neighborhood folder. Let's see how to modify Explorer's Registry settings to make Network Neighborhood disappear.

The Network Neighborhood icon that appears on Windows 95 and Windows NT desktops can be more trouble than it's worth. As you know, NetHood (as it's known internally to NT) is the user interface for the network browser, which allows someone to view the servers and shares on a network. It's nice, but in many cases it's also superfluous, as the network's administrators probably create pre-mapped drives for users. Network Neighborhood can, then, end up being an invitation to waste time browsing the local network. You can keep NetHood from appearing on a Desktop by adding an entry to USER\Software\Microsoft\Windows\CurrentVersion\Policies\Explorer, where "USER" is the user-specific part of a Registry. The new value (the entry is almost certainly not there by default) is NoNetHood, of type REG_DWORD. Set it to 1, and the next time that user logs on she won't see the Network Neighborhood icon. You can demonstrate it on your own account (I'll show you how to undo it, don't worry) like so:

1. Open up REGEDIT.

2. Open up HKEY_CURRENT_USER\Software\Microsoft\Windows\CurrentVersion\Policies\Explorer.

3. With the cursor on the Explorer folder, right-click and choose New ➢ DWORD Value. The screen will look the one shown in Figure 6.62.

4. Click Edit ➢ Rename, change New Value #1 to NoNetHood, double-click on NoNetHood, and then change the value from 0 to 1.

5. Exit REGEDIT.

6. Log off and log back on using the same username.

You'll see that the Network Neighborhood icon isn't present any more.

FIGURE 6.62:

Setting a new value in Registry Editor

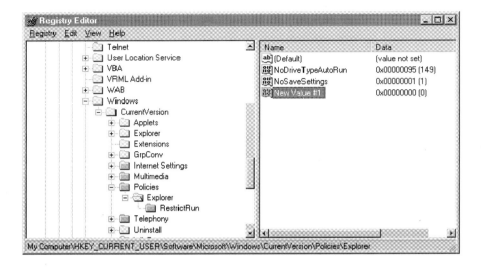

NOTE   To make NetHood appear again, return to REGEDIT and change the 1 value to 0, exit REGEDIT and again log off and log back on.

Following the steps above imposed the restriction on *your* account. But suppose several people share a particular NT machine, either workstation or server; can you modify how the machine treats them? Sure; it's just a bit more work.

By default, REGEDT32 and REGEDIT only load the Registry for the user who's currently logged on and the Registry for the "System Default" user, the settings that are in effect when no one's logged in. (For example, if you set the Desktop background color to red for the "default" user, then the screen background will be red when no one's logged in at the computer.) But if you've got a number of people who use a given computer, then that computer will retain Registry settings for those people; you just need to grab those settings in order to modify them.

Unfortunately, you can't tell REGEDIT to load the Registry settings for another user. However, you *can* tell REGEDT32 to load another user's Registry settings. I sometimes use a user account called TESTUSER on my machine; as a result, there are Registry settings for TESTUSER, and I'll demonstrate how to load them.

NOTE   You'll need to be working on a computer with an account named TESTUSER in order to follow along. TESTUSER must have logged on to and off of this computer at least once for TESTUSER's Registry entries to be sitting on the computer.

1. Run REGEDT32; again, REGEDIT won't work here.

2. Open the HKEY_USERS subtree and click the HKEY_USERS key.

3. Click Registry ➤ Load Hive, and you'll get a dialog box labeled Load Hive, which looks like a normal File ➤ Open dialog box.

4. Navigate over to whichever directory and drive hold your operating system. In my case, it's E:\WINNT, but it'll be different for you. Within that directory is a directory named PROFILES. You'll see a dialog box like the one shown in Figure 6.63.

FIGURE 6.63:

Viewing user profiles using the Load Hive dialog box

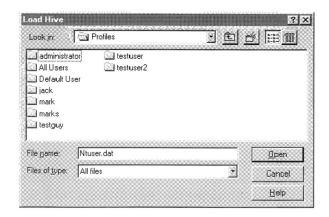

There's a directory for every person who's ever logged on to this computer—administrator, jack, mark, marks, testguy, and TESTUSER—as well as a couple of extra directories labeled All Users and Default User (you'll see in the next chapter what those two do).

5. Open up the TESTUSER folder; you'll see the dialog shown in Figure 6.64.

6. Choose the file NTUSER.DAT because it contains the user-specific Registry entries for this user. REGEDT32 then needs to know what to call this new hive, as shown in Figure 6.65.

FIGURE 6.64:

Viewing user Registry entries in the Load Hive dialog box

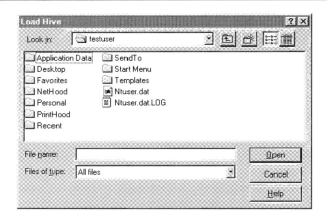

FIGURE 6.65:

Naming a user's hive

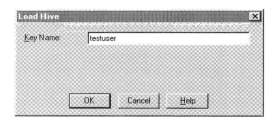

7. Name it *TESTUSER*. Click OK and REGEDT32 will look like Figure 6.66.

8. Now you can edit the Registry entries for TESTUSER just as I did for my own entries—just navigate down to HKEY_USERS\TESTUSER\Software\Microsoft\Windows\CurrentVersion\Policies\Explorer and add NoNetHood as before.

9. Once you're done modifying TESTUSER's settings, click the TESTUSER key and choose Registry ➤ Unload Hive.

The next time TESTUSER logs on, he won't see a Network Neighborhood folder.

FIGURE 6.66:

Registering user entries

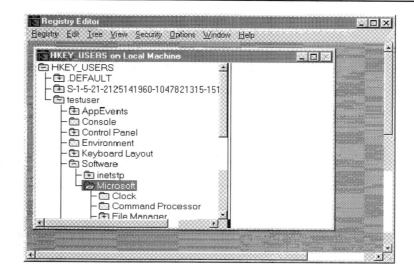

Desktop Control Policy Entries

There are about two dozen settings like NoNetHood that you can use to restrict the NT (or 95) Desktop located in various places in the Registry. I'll discuss them according to their location. But before going any further, this important warning:

WARNING	My experiments show that many of these Registry entries have no effect whatsoever unless you're running Service Pack 2 or later on your NT Workstation machine.

And this note:

NOTE	If you have worked with Windows 95 systems policies, then read this section carefully because NT includes some *extra* policies that Windows 95 doesn't have.

Explorer Policies

The first bunch is located near NoNetHood, in a user's HKEY_CURRENT_USER\
Software\Microsoft\Windows\CurrentVersion\Policies\Explorer. Each entry is
of type REG_DWORD. You activate these settings with a value of 1 and de-activate
them with a value of 0 unless otherwise stated.

NoClose   Removes the Shut Down option from the Start button if set to 1.
The user can still shut down using the Security Dialog (Ctrl+Alt+Del).

NoCommonGroups   Removes the common groups from the Start ➤ Programs menu if set to 1. Recall that "common groups" are the program
icons that everyone who logs onto this computer sees. If you've never
noticed them before, click Start ➤ Programs, and you'll see one or more
lines separating some of the program groups; the bottom bunch shows the
common groups. If you don't want particular users seeing those common
groups, use this Registry entry.

NoFileMenu   Removes the File menu from NT Explorer. Removing it
largely de-fangs NT Explorer, as it's one less tool a user can employ to create, move, copy, or delete files.

NoTrayContextMenu   Removes the little pop-up menu (the official term
is the *context menu*) that you get when you right-click the Taskbar.

NoViewContextMenu   Removes *all* the pop-up (oops, I mean *context*)
menus that appear in the Explorer user interface. This keeps menus from
appearing if you right-click the Desktop, My Computer, the Taskbar, or
any other object on the Desktop.

NoNetConnectDisconnect   Removes the option to connect and disconnect to/from network resources using Network Neighborhood and My
Computer. You might not have even known that you can do this, but if you
right-click My Computer or Network Neighborhood, two of the options
you'll get on the context menu (hey, that "context menu" stuff kind of slips
off the tongue after a while, doesn't it?) will raise dialog boxes to control
network connections; forget that possibility, and you're leaving a hole in
your Desktop.

DisableLinkTracking   Does *something*—it's in the Registry—but I can't
figure out quite what, and of course it's not documented like the other user
interface-oriented Registry entries.

ApprovedShellEx   Will, if set to 1, tell the shell to show items on the Desktop or in program menus only if they have recognized file extensions, like .EXE, .LNK, .TXT, or the like. As far as I can see, it's of no use; after all, if you put an object in one of those places that *doesn't* have an extension that NT recognizes, then you can't do anything with it anyway.

NoDesktop   Removes everything from the Desktop when set to 1. You don't see Internet Explorer, Briefcase, or any user-supplied icons. This can be very useful if you're just going to pare a user's options down to just a couple of applications. So far as I know, it's the only way to get rid of the My Computer folder, which is pretty useless anyway when you've removed all the drives from it (see the NoDrives setting, covered a bit later).

NoFind   Will, if enabled (set to 1) remove the Find option from the Start menu.

NoNetHood   Has already been described. There are two related settings that you might find useful if you *are* using the Network Neighborhood: NoEntireNetwork and NoWorkgroupContents, both of which are in a different Registry key, HKEY_LOCAL_USER\Software\Microsoft\Windows\CurrentVersion\Policies\Network. NoEntireNetwork removes the "Entire Network" entry from the Network Neighborhood, and NoWorkgroup-Contents hides machines, just the "Entire Network" entry. To see the machines in your workgroup, you'd actually have to click Entire Network, then Microsoft Windows Network, then your workgroup's name. It's not clear to me why this is useful, but it's available.

NoRun   Removes the Run option from the Start menu.

NoSaveSettings   Will, in theory, ignore any user changes to the Desktop—colors, icons, open windows, and the like—and on Windows 95 machines, it works fine. Unfortunately, under NT it doesn't work at all, and a call to Microsoft support got an official acknowledgment of that fact. Maybe Service Pack 23?

NoSetFolders   Has a name that doesn't offer much of a clue about what it does. If set to 1, the Settings folder (the one that normally contains the Control Panel and the Printers folder) does not appear on the Start menu.

NoSetTaskbar   Removes the ability to set options for the Taskbar if set to 1. That's the dialog box that lets you set AutoHide and the like for the Taskbar.

NoStartMenuSubFolders Is associated with custom program folders. You'll read in a page or two how you can control exactly what the user sees when she clicks Start ➤ Programs. But if you *do* use a custom program folder, then you must set NoStartMenuSubFolders to 1, or NT will not only display your nice hand-crafted program folders, it'll *also* show the standard ones, which you probably didn't want to happen if you created your own program folders.

NoDrives Allows you to hide one or more drives from the My Computer folder. How it works is a bit esoteric, so don't worry if you've got to read this a couple of times. The REG_DWORD value is a 32-bit number that isn't just 0 or 1. Rather, this uses the rightmost 26 bits of the 32-bit number (see, I told you it was esoteric) to describe whether or not to show a given drive. The rightmost bit in the number controls whether or not you see drive A:. Set it to 0 and you see A:, set it to 1 and you don't. The next bit to the left controls B: in the same way.

- Thus, suppose you wanted to only hide the C: drive. The C: drive is the third drive, so you'd set the third bit over from the right to 1, and the others to 0. The correct value for NoDrives would then be 00000000000000000000000000000100 in binary, which is 4 in decimal. (Use the Calculator if you hate converting between binary and decimal.)

- Another example: suppose you wanted to hide the floppy drives from My Computer. They're drives A: and B:, first and second, so set only the two rightmmost bits to 1, a value of 00000000000000000000000000000011, or, in decimal, 3.

- In most cases, you'll want to hide *all* drives, so the value for NoDrives should be 00000011111111111111111111 to hide all 26 drive letters. That's 03FFFFFF in hex or 67,108,863 in decimal. This removes all drives *from My Computer and the Explorer*—not the old Windows 3.*x* File Manager, which still ships with NT as WINFILE.EXE.

Now that you know how you can set Explorer policies to lock down what a user sees when running Explorer, let's look at how you can set them to restrict the programs the user runs.

Restricting What Programs a User Can Run with Explorer Policies

RestrictRun is another mildly complex Registry setting; it's incredibly powerful. You can use it to say to the Windows interface, "Do not run any programs unless they are on the following list." For example, you could say, "The only programs that this user can run are Word and Internet Explorer." RestrictRun is another 1 or 0 Registry setting: 0 says, "Don't restrict which programs this user can run," and 1 says, "Only allow this user to run the programs listed in HKEY_CURRENT_USER\Software\Microsoft\CurrentVersion\Windows\Policies\Explorer\RestrictRun." *That* key is just a list of applications that can run, and it consists of as many value entries as you like, all of type REG_SZ, and one application to a value. The name of the first entry must be, simply, 1, and again should contain the file name of the acceptable program. The second would be named 2, and so on. It's probably easiest to see an example, as in Figure 6.67. In that example, I've allowed this user to run (respectively) the Calculator, Internet Explorer, Word, and Command Prompt.

FIGURE 6.67:

Using RestrictRun to limit user application

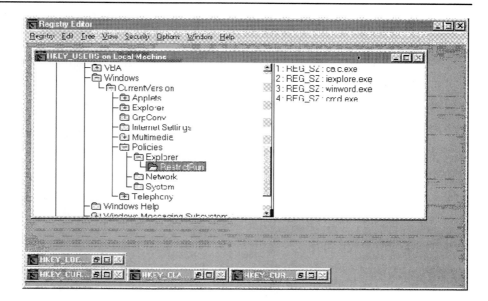

I've said RestrictRun is a powerful way to control what runs on a Desktop, but it's not perfect.

As you read a few pages back, one of the main reasons to control Explorer, the Windows user interface, is so you can control which programs run on a given computer. Whether you start a program by clicking on an icon on the Desktop, by clicking Start ≻ Programs, or by opening up My Computer and clicking on an icon from one of the drives, the program is launched by Explorer. Suppose you use RestrictRun to tell Explorer, "Allow user Max to run only WINWORD.EXE, EXCEL.EXE, CMD.EXE (the command prompt), and IEXPLORE.EXE (Internet Explorer). Reject attempts to run any other programs." Suppose then that Max decides that he wants to run FreeCell. He opens up My Computer and looks around for FREECELL.EXE, the actual FreeCell program. He double-clicks on it and gets a message, "This operation has been canceled because of restrictions in effect on this computer. Please contact your system administrator." Same message when he tries to run FreeCell from Start ≻ Programs ≻ Accessories ≻ Games ≻ Freecell. If he tries to run it from the NT Explorer, he won't even get started: the NT Explorer isn't on the approved list, so it won't run either. Is Max FreeCell-less?

No, and that's one of the weaknesses of the policies approach. It only controls the behavior of the Explorer. Max *could* open up a command prompt, type **freecell**, and FreeCell would start up! Why? Because Explorer didn't start Free-Cell; CMD.EXE, the command prompt, did. In most cases, the launching pad for applications is Explorer; but in this case, CMD.EXE started FreeCell. So to really lock down a Desktop—to control absolutely what applications get run on a given computer—you'd need restrictions on CMD.EXE. Unfortunately, that's not an option. As a result, it's probably not a good idea to include CMD.EXE on the "approved" programs list, if you intend to restrict what programs can run on a user's Desktop.

Are there any other program loopholes? Other ways to launch programs? Yes, unfortunately: someone who knows what she's doing can write a three-line Word macro that will launch a program from inside Word; and, again, there are no ways to restrict what programs launch from inside Word. I'm sure other programs have macro languages as powerful.

How about browsing the hard disks? Any ways to do that on a locked-down Desktop? Believe it or not, Internet Explorer is a lockdown hole big enough to drive a truck through. Go to the URL line, type **C:**, and you'll get a complete view of your C: drive, complete with icons for your viewing and clicking pleasure.

You won't be able to run any restricted EXEs from IE, but you can certainly view, copy, and delete files. So, in the final analysis, be aware that RestrictRun is a *nice* feature, but not an airtight one.

Keeping People from Getting to the Display Applet in the Control Panel

In HKEY_CURRENT_USER\Software\Microsoft\Windows\CurrentVersion\ Policies\System, there's a setting, NoDispCPL, that will keep Windows NT from allowing a user to access the Display part of the Control Panel. When set to 1, this setting keeps a user from changing the screen by either right-clicking the Desktop or opening the Control Panel.

This could be particularly useful in a classroom setting, where you don't want users wasting time playing with colors and background bitmaps.

Keeping People from Using the Registry Editing Tools

After restricting the Explorer, you don't want people using the Registry editors to undo your work. You can do that by adding an entry in HKEY_CURRENT_USER\ Software\Microsoft\Windows\CurrentVersion\Policies\System for a particular user. The entry's name is DisableRegistryTools: and, if set to 1, it will keep the user from running either REGEDIT or REGEDT32. Be aware though, that it will *not* keep that user from running POLEDIT, the System Policy Editor that we'll work with in a few pages. POLEDIT can modify the Registry, so either keep it off the approved list of programs (assuming you're using RestrictRun) or just make sure that it's not anywhere that a user can easily get to.

Getting Rid of the "Welcome" Tips

I know this is a matter of taste, but I find that Welcome screen with the helpful tip *really* annoying. Yes, you can check the box that says, "Don't show me these any more," but I create and use a lot of accounts for testing purposes and so I'm forever clicking the darn box. Instead, however, you can use a Registry entry, which we'll control over the network, to keep the silly box from appearing in the first place. In HKEY_CURRENT_USER\Software\Microsoft\Windows\CurrentVersion\Explorer\Tips, just create a key named Show of type REG_DWORD and set it to 0. Set it to 1 and the dumb tips appear.

On the other hand, you might want to be *sure* that people read the tips. You might do that because you can redefine the tips, as they live in the Registry in HKEY_LOCAL_MACHINE\Software\Microsoft\Windows\CurrentVersion\ Explorer\Tips. There is a value entry for each tip; they're all of type REG_SZ, and the value entry names are just numbers: 1, 2, and so on. You *could* use the central Registry control that we're leading up to in order to essentially "download" a bunch of tips to everyone's machine. They'd see those tips whenever they logged on to their system.

Controlling the Start Programs Folders

Part of creating a custom Desktop for a user includes controlling the programs that he can run. Once you've gone to all the trouble of keeping him from running all but a few programs, you'll have to give him the way to *get* to those few programs.

Most of the items that you see on the Start menu are just folders pointed to by various Registry entries. Look in any user's Software\Microsoft\Windows\ CurrentVersion\Explorer\User Shell Folders, and you'll see the values AppData, Desktop, Favorites, Fonts, NetHood, Personal, PrintHood, Programs, Recent, SendTo, Start Menu, Startup, and Templates. They contain the locations of directories that contain user-specific information. For instance, Startup contains the location of a folder that contains shortcuts to the programs that you want that user to automatically run when he logs in.

Where the Menus Come From

The folder that we're most interested in at the moment is Programs. How can a disk directory correspond to menu items? Take a look at Figure 6.68, a full screen shot of a Windows NT Desktop with some menus and sub-menus opened.

Note that the Programs menu has four sub-menus: Accessories, Startup, Administrative Tools (Common), and another Startup. You can tell from the folder-and-PC icons for the Administrative Tools (Common) and lower Startup folders that they are common folders. In a fully controlled Desktop, they probably wouldn't appear, as you'd use the NoCommonGroups Registry entry to keep them out of the picture anyway, so let's just focus on the Programs menu without the common folders. In addition to the Accessories and upper Startup sub-menus, there are icons for Books Online, Command Prompt, Microsoft Access, Microsoft

Binder, Microsoft Excel, Microsoft PowerPoint, Microsoft Schedule+, Microsoft Word, and Windows NT Explorer. I've also opened the Accessories sub-menu, which contains a number of items and two of what might be called "sub-sub-menus," Hyperterminal and Multimedia.

FIGURE 6.68:

Screen with opened menus and sub-menus

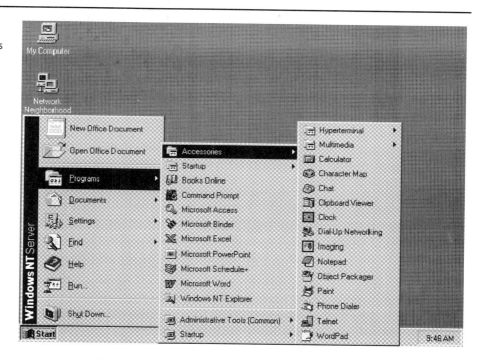

To look under the hood and see how this is actually accomplished, I go to the Profiles directory of my Windows NT installation. I'm currently logged on as MarkS, and I've installed NT Server in a directory called \TORUSMM; so if I look in \TORUSMM\PROFILES\MARKS, I will see a number of folders, and one of them will be named Start Menu. Looking in that, I find a folder named Programs, which has shortcuts for each icon that appears on the menu. There is also a folder named Accessories in the Programs folder, and opening that shows me, again, shortcuts corresponding to each icon in the Accessories menu. You can see the Programs and Accessories folders in Figure 6.69. In this figure, you see two open directories. The top one shows the shortcuts that appear when user MarkS clicks Start and Programs, the bottom one when that user clicks Start ➤ Programs ➤ Accessories.

FIGURE 6.69:

Two open applications directories

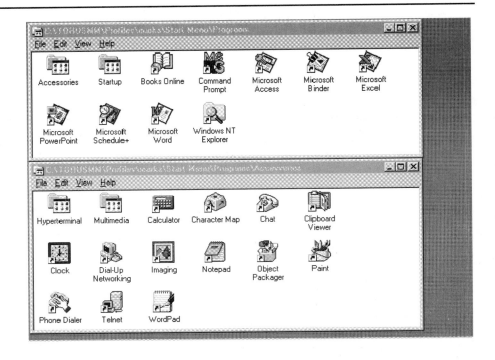

How can all of this help *you*? Well, again, suppose you've got a set of approved applications that you want to restrict users to. Just create a folder on the network that contains shortcuts to those applications. Then modify each user's Registry so that Software\Microsoft\Windows\CurrentVersion\Explorer\User Shell Folders\Programs points to the UNC of that folder. When the user logs in, his only program icons will then be the ones that you've placed in this centrally located folder.

A Sample Custom Programs Folder

You can try this out by creating a "throwaway" user account and giving it a very limited menu of programs. I'm going to tell you to place all of the relevant files on the local system so you don't even need a network to try this out: even a copy of Windows NT Workstation would work fine. I'll assume for the example that you've installed NT in the default location, C:\WINNT.

1. Create a folder named PROGS on the root of C:, C:\PROGS.

2. In C:\PROGS, create shortcuts for Internet Explorer, the Calculator, and Notepad. (You can do this either by right-clicking in the folder, choosing New ➤ Shortcut, and following the Wizard or just by locating IEXPLORE.EXE, CALC.EXE, and NOTEPAD.EXE and dragging them into the C:\PROGS folder. The shell will automatically create shortcuts rather than copy the files.)

3. Create a bogus user account; BOGUS would be a perfectly good name.

4. Log on and off once as BOGUS so that NT will create a directory for the BOGUS user account in the Profiles directory. Log back on with an account with administrator level of privilege.

5. Start up REGEDT32 and load the Registry for user BOGUS. Put the cursor on the top of HKEY_USERS, click Registry ➤ Load Hive, navigate to C:\WINNT\Profiles\Bogus, select file NTUSER.DAT, and give it a name when prompted—again, "bogus" works just fine.

6. In BOGUS, open Software\Microsoft\Windows\CurrentVersion\Explorer\User Shell Folders and look at the current contents of the "Programs" entry. It's probably currently C:\WINNT\Profiles\Bogus\Programs; change it to C:\PROGS.

7. While you're there, go to Bogus\Software\Microsoft\Windows\Current-Version\Policies\Explorer and add a new value, NoStartMenuSubFolders; type REG_DWORD, and set it to 1. In the same key, add NoCommon-Groups, again REG_DWORD, set to 1.

8. Click the top of the Bogus tree, and unload it with Registry ➤ Unload Hive.

9. Confirm that you do want to unload the hive. Exit REGEDT32.

10. Log on as BOGUS. Click Start ➤ Programs. See the difference? On my computer, when I click Start ➤ Programs, my screen looks like Figure 6.70.

If you're interested, let's take this a bit further and *really* lock down this Desktop. In addition to the NoCommonGroups and NoStartMenuSubFolders settings, add NoDesktop, NoFind, NoRun, NoSetFolders, NoTrayContextMenu, and NoViewContextMenu (remember that they all go in Software\Microsoft\Windows\CurrentVersion\Policies\Explorer) and set them all to 1. The result is a *very* simplified Desktop perfect for someone who just needs to run a few programs and doesn't want to be bothered with the other NT 4/Windows 95 Desktop clutter.

FIGURE 6.70:

Limiting the Programs folder

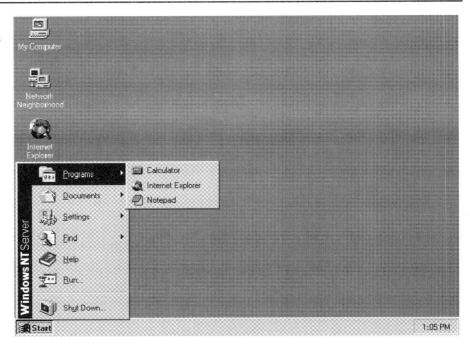

Again, this simple example was pretty labor-intensive, and I'll show you very soon how to network this kind of control. But there's an important point to be made here: eventually I'll have to network the folder that I called PROGS so that I can deliver the same set of program icons to everyone. But NT shortcuts refer to particular locations, so how can one set of program shortcuts serve an entire network? For example, my Calculator icon has embedded in it the fact that the Calculator program's full path is C:\TORUSMM\SYSTEM32\CALC.EXE as that's where I've got the Calculator on my system. If I networked the PROGS folder and distributed it to a user whose Calculator wasn't in C:\TORUSMM\SYSTEM32, she wouldn't be able to access the Calculator. How, then, do you create a set of common program folders that are networkable?

One way is to network the apps; point the shortcuts not to drive letters like C:\TORUSMM\SYSTEM32 but to UNCs like \\APPSERVER\ENGINEERING\. This won't work for complex applications like Office 95, as Office 95 *must* install some files to the local hard disk before running. (Office 97 is a bit better behaved but still poses some problems.) The other possible approach is to standardize the locations of applications on each workstation's hard disk. If one machine loads Word in C:\MSOFFICE, make sure that they *all* do. It's a bit of a pain, but it's necessary to make networked program groups work—and you'll see in the next chapter that it's useful for networked user profiles, as well.

> **NOTE**
>
> Remember, if you intend to distribute program menu folders to multiple users, you *must* be sure that all of the users have the applications that are in those folders in the same directories: if Word is in C:\MSOFFICE\WINWORD on one computer, make sure it's in C:\MSOFFICE\WINWORD in *all* of those users' computers. Otherwise, Word will show up as an option on the program menu, but clicking it won't do anything.

You can also control what a user sees in the *common* program folders, if you allow those folders; there is a key in HKEY_LOCAL_MACHINE that lets you designate a location for common folders. Look in any of the "machine" icons in the System Policy Editor.

Distributing Registry Changes over a Network with NTCONFIG.POL

Just that little demonstration of controlling a program menu illustrated how powerful a few Registry changes can be—imagine if you were to take what we did a step further and use RestrictRun to let that computer run only Internet Explorer, Calculator, and Notepad. Then, not only would the user see only those three but they would be the only things that would run. I'm simplifying the matter a trifle, of course, if you recall the discussion of all the loopholes in the user interface. But with a few more changes you could pretty quickly bolt down a user's Desktop. (As I mentioned a page or two back, in addition to RestrictRun, I'd use NoDesktop, NoFind, NoRun, NoSetFolders, NoTrayContextMenu, and NoViewContextMenu.)

This sounds like a lot of work, and indeed it would be if you had to go out to every user's machine and hand-edit his Registry. So, as I mentioned in the beginning of this section, NT has this cool built-in way to order changes to Registries automatically over the network. (It'll actually also allow you to control Windows 95 Registries as well with a little extra work, as you'll see.)

The trick is this: when an NT workstation (or a Windows 95 computer, for that matter) logs on to an NT domain, the networking client software is designed to look on the Primary Domain Controller's NETLOGON share—the place where you normally keep login batch scripts—for the system policy file that I mentioned earlier. More specifically, the system policy file is a binary file called either NTCONFIG.POL (the file that NT machines look for) or CONFIG.POL (the file that Windows 95 machines look for).

It's logical at this point to wonder why there are different files for NT policies versus Windows 95 policies. It's because Windows 95 stores character data using ASCII (the American Standard Code for Information Interchange, a 35-year-old, English-centric method for storing characters), while NT, surprisingly, does *not* use ASCII; rather, it uses a more flexible character set called Unicode. NT's use of Unicode is one reason that it works so well in international environments. Microsoft's decision to *not* use Unicode in Windows 95 was unfortunate, but it's one of the dozens of reasons to use NT instead. (One Microsoft person—an *NT* developer, mind you, not a 95 developer—wryly commented that to me that it was a sad example of what he called "MESE thinking." MESE is pronounced *meezie*, and he explained that it stood for "Make 'Em Speak English.")

Bottom line is this: you'll have to build all your policies twice, once for the Windows 95 machines and once for the Windows NT machines. And when I say the files use ASCII or Unicode, I don't mean that these are simple text files—they're not—but that the portion of the file that *is* text is either stored as ASCII or Unicode. The other reason you end up with two different policy files is that Windows NT and Windows 95 Registry entries are *similar* but not identical—Windows 95 has some Registry entries that Windows NT doesn't, and vice versa.

Again, the POL file is largely binary, neither ASCII nor Unicode, so you can't just create one with Notepad. As you'll see in a minute, you've got to use a particular tool called the System Policy Editor to create a POL file.

Again, this notion of modifying Registries remotely with the POL files is called *system policies*. Thus, if you created a central POL file that removed Network Neighborhood from a user's Desktop, then it's just a Registry change. But because it was effected via the POL files, you'd say that you'd imposed a system policy.

These POL files essentially contain commands that your system uses to modify its Registry. So, before going any further, let me summarize some specifics of how the POL files work:

- The files must be created by one of the System Policy Editors.

- POL files will affect only the behavior of Windows 95, Windows NT 4, or NT Server 4 machines. They won't work with NT 3.*x* or Windows 3.*x* machines.

- They must reside on the NETLOGON share of the Primary Domain Controller, Backup Domain Controllers are of no help here. (Recall that NETLOGON is in \WINNT\SYSTEM32\REPL\IMPORT\SCRIPTS, although you may alternatively keep yours in \winnt\system32\export\scripts, as you'll read in the Chapter 11 discussion of directory replication.)

This is a "pull" technology in the sense that the PDC never forces the POL files, or their effects, on the workstations. Rather, a workstation *requests* a file as a side effect to a domain logon, which brings me to the next point:

- This approach works *only* if you're doing a domain logon. You've got to specifically configure a Windows 95 workstation to do a domain logon (Control Panel ➢ Networking ➢ Client for Microsoft Networks ➢ Properties), and in the same way you've got to be logging onto a domain account from an NT machine for the NT system policies to take effect.

- These changes are Registry changes, so they won't always take effect until after the user's rebooted.

Using NTCONFIG.POL to Modify a User's Registry

The first example I gave of a Registry change was to eliminate the Network Neighborhood from TESTUSER's Desktop. Let's do that again, but this time let's do it with the System Policy Editor.

Before, I walked over to the computer that I usually use, fired up a Registry editor, and directly edited HKEY_CURRENT_USER\Software\Microsoft\Windows\CurrentVersion\Policies\Explorer, logged off and then logged back on. *Now*, I'm going to use the System Policy Editor (the NT version, as my desktop operating system is NT) to create a CONFIG.POL with instructions to remove Network Neighborhood, and I'll save that CONFIG.POL on my domain's PDC. If you want to follow along, you'll need a user account named TESTUSER.

First, I'll need the NT System Policy Editor. The NT System Policy Editor ships with NT Server, and it appears in Start ➢ Administrative Tools (Common). If you're using NT Workstation, then you'll get the System Policy Editor with the other administration tools in the \CLIENTS\SRVTOOLS directory of the NT Server CD-ROM. Start up System Policy Editor, and you'll see a blank screen. Select File ➢ New Policy, and you'll see something like Figure 6.71.

FIGURE 6.71:

Creating policies in Systems
Policy Editor

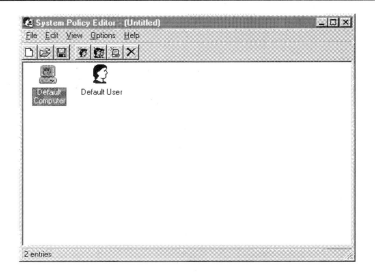

There's an icon of a PC, and an icon of a gray-colored guy (there's that dead user again) with a dopey-looking haircut or, come to think of it, that might be a gray-colored icon of a *woman* with a dopey-looking haircut; hmmm, many's the time I wish for insider information at Microsoft. In any case, why the two icons? Well, recall that Registry entries tend to be either machine-specific, like the things in HKEY_LOCAL_MACHINE (SAM, SECURITY, SYSTEM, SOFTWARE), or user-specific, like the things in the \WINNT\PROFILES directory (NTUSER.DAT .LOG). You modify machine Registry entries through PC icons, and you modify user-specific Registry entries through user icons.

WARNING   The icons that appear automatically, the Default Computer and Default User icons, are *extremely powerful* and *extremely dangerous*.

Any policies that you impose through Default Computer or Default User apply to every machine or every person, even domain controllers and administrators. Do something like hide the Desktop of the Default User and set Default User to a very restricted set of program folders, and *no one* will be able to undo that from an NT workstation; it's very possible that poorly set policies on Default User or Computer would make you have to rebuild your entire domain.

WARNING   Any changes that you make to Default User will automatically be copied to *all specific user policies*. (Ditto machines.) This makes it extremely difficult to create a diverse set of policies, as the dumb Default User keeps over-writing what you've done. My advice: don't do anything with Default User or Machine unless you've got a really good reason.

In fact, you can delete Default User and Default Machine, and I usually do. If you ever want them back, just re-create a user named "Default User" or a machine named "Default Machine."

So, because I want to affect only *my* Desktop, I'll tell System Policy Editor to create a policy for just user TESTUSER. I know that I'm modifying a user icon rather than a machine icon because I know that the entry that I want to modify is in the user part of the Registry rather than the machine part.

Choose Edit ➤ Add User, and you'll see a dialog box allowing you to either type in a user name (like ORION\TESTUSER in my case, as that's the name of my master domain) or to browse a list of users. I browse over to my ORION domain, where TESTUSER lives, and choose TESTUSER. My screen now looks like the one shown in Figure 6.72.

FIGURE 6.72:

Adding a new user

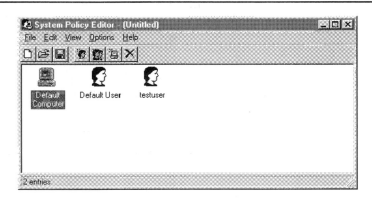

Now double-click TESTUSER, and you'll see a dialog box, as shown in Figure 6.73.

FIGURE 6.73:

The User Properties
dialog box

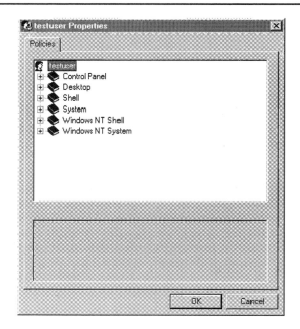

Hey, *this* looks quite a bit different from the Registry editing tools! System Policy Editor is organized completely differently than REGEDT32 and REGEDIT are. As I mentioned earlier, System Policy Editor doesn't contain all of the thousands of Registry entries, just a small subset that it has been directed to offer to you. (I will explain later how you can control which Registry entries show up.) Open up the Shell book (click on the plus sign), and you'll see another book, labeled "Restrictions;" open that up, and you'll see a screen like Figure 6.74.

See the entry labeled Hide Network Neighborhood? Click it, and it'll show up as a checked box. A checked box means, "Set the value to 1." Click it again, and you'll see that it is now a cleared box. A cleared box means, "Set the value to 0." Click it again, and it becomes gray, as it originally was. A gray box means, "There's no system policy about this, so leave it alone." Finally, click it yet again, and it will appear checked: recall that we want the value of NoNetHood to be 1 so that the Network Neighborhood will not appear. Then click OK to clear the TESTUSER Properties dialog.

FIGURE 6.74:

User Properties Restrictions

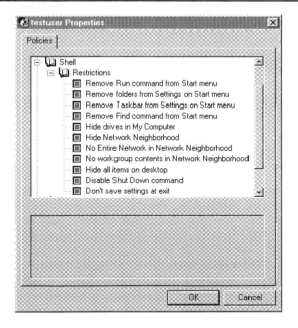

Next, tell System Policy Editor to save the policy file so that it'll take effect. Click File ➤ Save As and navigate over to the NETLOGON share of your domain's Primary Domain Controller. If you are sitting at the PDC, then recall that it is in \WINNT\SYSTEM32\REPL\IMPORT\SCRIPTS (or perhaps in \WINNT\SYSTEM32\REPL\EXPORT\SCRIPTS if you are doing directory replication). If you're going to access the PDC's NETLOGON share over the network, then remember beforehand to give yourself the share permissions to save files in NETLOGON—by default, NETLOGON only has share permissions of Everyone/Read. Save it as file NTCONFIG.POL.

Next, I log off and log onto the domain using the TESTUSER account. (Again, TESTUSER must log onto an *NT* machine to see the effect of the policy change; there's no Windows 95 policy file, and so if I logged onto the domain with a Windows 95 computer as TESTUSER, I'd still see the Network Neighborhood.) The result: no Network Neighborhood. (How did checking Hide Network Neighborhood cause a change in the Policies key of the Registry? Through template files, which I'll explain later.) But first, let's see how to undo a policy.

Undoing the System Policy

Now suppose I want to restore the Network Neighborhood to TESTUSER, or, better, what if TESTUSER tries to *take* it back. Can he just edit his Registry to restore NetHood? Actually, TESTUSER can't change the NoNetHood entry; by default, regular old user accounts only have Read permission on entries in the HKEY_ CURRENT_USERS\Software\Microsoft\CurrentVersion\Windows\Policies key. But suppose he *could* change his Registry? Would that let him get NetHood back? No. The next time he logged on, his system would read NTCONFIG.POL, see the order to remove NetHood, and he'd be back where he started.

Suppose, however, that while he can't modify his own local Registry, he talks some administrator into erasing NTCONFIG.POL. Then what happens? As it turns out, nothing. In the same way, what if an administrator decides to change the Hide Network Neighborhood policy from checked to gray—what happens? Again, nothing; our user still doesn't have a Network Neighborhood.

The sequence of events for central Registry control goes like this: assume there's an NTCONFIG.POL on the PDC, and the file has a no-NetHood policy in it. Over on TESTUSER's desk, TESTUSER turns on his computer. The computer powers up and reads its local Registry, the part relevant to the machine only. The PC doesn't know who's going to log on to it. Next, TESTUSER logs onto the domain using his account. When TESTUSER's workstation PC contacts the domain's PDC, the PDC's NTCONFIG.POL file essentially tells TESTUSER's workstation, "Change the value of HKEY_CURRENT_USERS\Software\Microsoft\Current-Version\Windows\Policies\Explorer's NoNetHood to 1 and then log this TEST-USER guy in." The local user-specific Registry information for TESTUSER gets changed accordingly, and so as Explorer starts up, it leaves out NetHood.

Now suppose someone erases NTCONFIG.POL on the PDC. TESTUSER logs off and then back on. Will that get NetHood back?

No. Remember that the NoNetHood=1 setting is in his *local Registry on the workstation's hard disk*. He must either modify that Registry (which he can't do, as he has only Read access to the Policies key) or ask an administrator to use a system policy to return the Network Neighborhood to his Desktop. (If it sounds like I'm beating a dead horse, trust me, I'm not; many people find system policies confusing if they don't take the time to think through what NT is doing on the Desktop.)

So TESTUSER comes to you, his friendly administrator, and asks that NetHood be returned to him. How do you do it? Start up the System Policy Editor, load the policy file—it's conveniently located on the Most Recently Used list at the bottom of the File menu—and open up TESTUSER back to the Shell/Restrictions screen.

Recall that the check box had not two, but three states: checked, which meant, "Force TESTUSER not to have NetHood"; unchecked, which meant, "Force TEST-USER to *have* NetHood"; and gray, which meant, "Do not modify this part of TESTUSER's Registry." If you were to simply say, "We don't care anymore what users do with their NetHoods" and gray the box, where would that leave TEST-USER? He still wouldn't have a Network Neighborhood, as gray means, "Don't change anything," and the current state of his Registry says to not show Net-Hood. To restore NetHood would require a three-step process:

1. First, clear the box. Don't check it or leave it gray.

2. Then ask TESTUSER to log on. He should now have NetHood back.

3. The current system policies now *force* TESTUSER to have NetHood, but you want the policy to be silent. Once TESTUSER's logged off, go back and edit NTCONFIG.POL to make the box gray.

NetHood is now restored.

NOTE   It's not intuitive (until someone explains it), but it's important to understand the above steps. Remember, to release people from a policy, it's not sufficient to simply gray the policy's box. You must first re-enable whatever the policy disabled, *then* gray the box.

Changing a Policy about a Machine

In most cases, you'll use the System Policy Editor and the POL files to control user settings. But what about machine settings? Are they ever useful? Personally, I can think of two things I'd like to set about a machine, both of which are discussed in later chapters: HKLM\System\CurrentControlSet\Services\Browser\Parameters\MaintainServerList=No, which removes a machine from contention to be the master browser and HKLM\System\CurrentControlSet\Services\NetBT\Parameters\EnableProxy=1, which allows a machine to be a WINS proxy agent. (Browsers are covered in greater detail in the "Tuning" chapter, and WINS proxy agents in the "TCP/IP" chapter. Without going into detail here, you can reduce your network's chatter by telling 99 percent of your machines to stay out of the race to be browser (hence the first Registry change), and you can assist your computers to find one another by designating one computer on each network segment to be a WINS proxy agent (hence the second Registry change), but *don't* make more than one computer per segment into a proxy agent, or you'll be making things worse.)

Neither of those useful possibilities is handled by the System Policy Editor by default, however, so let's look at a couple of less useful ones that are built in: the logon legal notice caption and whether or not to update the "access time" information in the file system. You can set your systems up so that they will display a legal notice banner when someone tries to log on to them, a message along the lines of "You'll be prosecuted if you try to hack this computer." It's a Registry entry, HKLM\System\CurrentControlSet\Software\Microsoft\Windows NT\ CurrentVersion\Winlogon, and two REG_SZ entries: LegalNoticeCaption and LegalNoticeText. The caption is the text that goes on the title bar of the warning dialog box, and the text is the text inside the dialog box. Anyway, open up a machine icon in the System Policy Editor, open up the Windows NT System book, and open up the Logon book, and you'll see a dialog like the one shown in Figure 6.75.

FIGURE 6.75:

Default Computer Properties

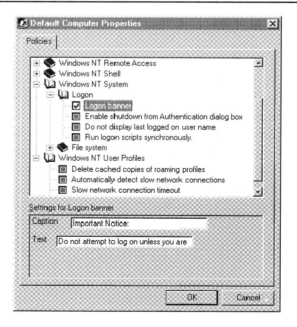

This option isn't enabled by default, so I checked it to allow you to see the caption and text fields. You can put any text that you like into the fields; if you want to try it out, check the box and type in the text of your choice.

The other possible change effected in System Policy Editor is whether or not to update a field in NTFS called "access time." Not only does NTFS keep track of when you created a file, it also remembers when you last modified it and when you last accessed it. That's useful, but constantly recording when a file was last looked at can slow the computer down a bit. So there's a Registry entry that says, "Don't bother keeping track of when the file was last accessed."

Anyway, while neither the legal caption setting nor the "Don't keep track of the last access time" setting is earth shattering, they're good, simple examples of when you make a change in NTCONFIG.POL versus when the change takes effect.

Suppose you make this policy change for some specific machine, say a machine named PPRO200, the name of one of my NT machines. When does the change take effect? Well, the policy file only gets read when a user logs in. Suppose I log in at PPRO200. In the process of logging me onto the domain, PPRO200 reads NTCONFIG.POL and receives the commands to incorporate the legal caption and not to record access times. The relevant questions here are

- When will I first see the legal notice?
- When will the system stop logging access times?

The legal notice change is a modification to a Registry entry for Winlogon, the program that runs whenever you press Ctrl+Alt+Del to log on to a system. How often, then, does Winlogon check its Registry for changes? Every time someone logs on. As a result, you'll see the legal notice caption the next time you log onto that machine.

The access-time information is part of the Registry entries for NTFS, however. When do *they* get examined by NTFS? Only at system boot time. You could log on 50 times and not see the "Don't keep track of access times" change take place. Reason: you must reboot the computer for these changes to take effect. Moral of the story: system policies can drive you crazy because when you make a bunch of changes (like the two I just made), and you see some of them take effect almost immediately and some may take a day or two. That is, you may not have the occasion to reboot for that long, and so you won't see your changes until then. So before you start tearing your hair out, stop and analyze the matter: What change *did* the System Policy Editor make to the Registry? Should I reboot before the change will take effect? And, here's one of my favorite dumb things to do when playing with system policies—did you remember to *save* the updated NTCONFIG.POL?

Which Domain to Save the Policy To?

We won't take up the question of managing multiple-domain NT networks until Chapter 12, but let's consider the following question. I log in as MarkA, my administrative account, which is a member of a domain named ORION. But my workstation, PPRO200, is a member of domain TAURUS. Now, I want to save a policy that affects my *machine*, which again is a member of domain TAURUS, not me. So the $64,000 question is: should I create (or modify) the NTCONFIG.POL on the ORION PDC, or the one on the TAURUS PDC?

My analysis says to put it on the user's domain, not the machine's domain. Examining the powerup and logon sequences with a network monitor, I see that the machine upon powerup certainly communicates with a domain controller so that the NT machine can essentially "log on to" its domain, but it never looks for NTCONFIG.POL. It's only when a user logs in that NTCONFIG.POL gets read. Therefore, oddly enough, even though your machines may be members of one domain (often called the *resource domain*, discussed in detail in Chapter 12) and your user accounts are members of another domain (often called the *master domain*, also discussed in Chapter 12), *all* policies, user and machine, should go on the PDC of the user's ("master") domain.

Battling Policies: Default User versus Groups, Groups versus Users

You may have noticed when browsing to add a new user name that not only can you create policies for particular users, you can also create policies for particular domain-wide groups. (They're called *global groups* and they're discussed in Chapter 12, and for now you needn't worry about what a global group is—but the two global groups you'll probably end up using are a built-in group called "Domain Users" that contains all the regular users and another group called "Domain Admins" that contains all the people who have domain-wide administrative powers.)

How can you use group-based policies to your advantage? My colleague Clayton Johnson, another contributor to *Windows NT Magazine*, has suggested that you could create new global groups—Beginning Users, Intermediate Users, and Advanced Users—and then you could create different program folders for them. When someone starts working for your firm, you make her a Beginning User, perhaps with access to nothing more than simple e-mail and some on-line tutorials. Intermediate and Advanced Users would then have access to appropriately more functions. The power of this is, again, the centralizing power of system policies: just put a user into the Beginning Users group, and upon her next reboot she'll see whatever policies and program menus you've assigned to beginners, without your having to create a specific policy for her.

That's a cool idea—thanks, Clayton, for thinking of it, and thanks, Microsoft, for system policies—but what about a conflict in policies? For example, let's return to user TESTUSER. Suppose also that I've put him into both the group Domain Admins and the group Domain Users. Further, I decide that I want to create policies that are group-wide for the Domain Admins and Domain Users groups. Adding the groups is easy: just click Edit ➤ Add Group and browse to find the group or groups that you want to add. I now have a System Policy Editor that looks Figure 6.76.

FIGURE 6.76:

Adding groups using System
Policy Editor

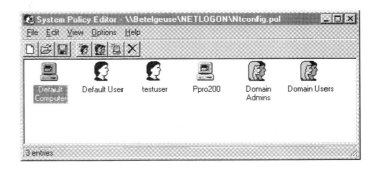

It's now possible for me to say, "Everyone in Default User's Desktop background color will be *red*, everyone in the Domain Users group will have a green background, everyone in Domain Admins will have blue backgrounds, and TESTUSER in particular will have a yellow background." TESTUSER logs in. Who wins?

The hierarchy of policies is as follows:

- If there's a policy that is specific to a particular user account, it predominates over any group or Default User settings.

- If there *aren't* any policies specific to the user who's logging in, then any relevant group policies predominate over any Default User settings.

- Of course, if there are no user-specific settings and no group settings relevant to a user who's logging in, but there are Default User settings, then the Default User settings will take effect.

As TESTUSER has a specific policy, his background will be yellow.

Summarizing, then, user-specific settings beat group settings, which beat Default User settings. Sounds good, *except* for group-versus-group conflicts! Suppose that I've added a policy that specifically removes the Network Neighborhood from the Desktops of all Domain Users and specifically *adds* it to the Desktops of all Domain Admins. (Suppose also that I had never created a user-specific policy about that for TESTUSER.) So TESTUSER's a member of Domain Admins, which gets NetHood, but TESTUSER's also a member of Domain Users, which *doesn't* get NetHood. Who wins?

I guessed Domain Admins, but I was wrong. As it turns out, System Policy Editor just remembers which groups it heard of *first* and gives them priority. You can control that, however, by clicking on a group and choosing Options ➤ Group Priority; you'll see a dialog box like Figure 6.77.

FIGURE 6.77:

Group Priority dialog box

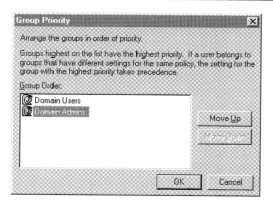

I just choose Domain Admins and click Move Up, and Domain Admins takes its rightful place in the grand scheme of things or, rather, in the grand scheme of policies.

Using Templates to Create New Policies

Let's return to a question I posed a few pages back: why does clicking Remove Network Neighborhood from Desktop cause a change in HKEY_CURRENT_USERS\Software\Microsoft\CurrentVersion\Windows\Policies\Explorer? Because of *policy templates*. Rather than simply presenting a somewhat raw and sometimes cryptic set of Registry entries, the System Policy Editor uses a simple kind of programming language that allows the System Policy Editor's user to see a somewhat more friendly, explanatory interface. The files containing the programming commands are called *templates*.

Introducing the Template Language

As I said, templates are intended to make the System Policy Editor look friendlier, but "friendly" isn't the word I'd use for the programming language itself. Here's the code that you'd use to tell the System Policy Editor to produce a check box for Remove Network Neighborhood from Desktop that will create an entry in HKEY_CURRENT_USERS\Software\Microsoft\CurrentVersion\Windows\Policies\Explorer. System Policy Editor will call the entry NoNetHood and will set it to either 0 or 1:

```
CLASS USER
CATEGORY "Shell"
  CATEGORY "Restrictions"
    KEYNAME Software\Microsoft\Windows\CurrentVersion\Policies\Explorer
      POLICY "Hide Network Neighborhood"
        VALUENAME "NoNetHood"
      END POLICY
  END CATEGORY      ; End of Restrictions category
END CATEGORY      ; End of Shell category
```

See, I *told* you it was ugly. Put these lines into an ASCII file and load them into the System Policy Editor (I'll show you how in a moment), and you'll see *just* the NetHood adjustment, as shown in Figure 6.78.

FIGURE 6.78:

Changing User Properties in
System Policy Editor

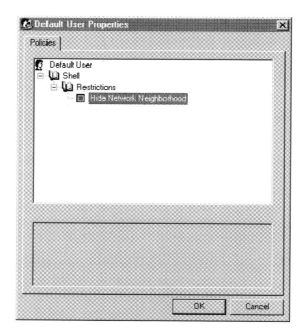

Here's how the template program works. First, recall that policies are either relevant to a machine or to a user; the first line, CLASS USER, defines which it is—the alternative is CLASS MACHINE. The next two commands are CATEGORY; they define the books that you see. As you can have books inside books, each CATEGORY command is paired with an END CATEGORY command. Anything that appears on a line after a semicolon is ignored—it's a comment for *your* use, not the System Policy Editor's—and so I've added comments to clarify which END CATEGORY goes with which CATEGORY command. Note that CATEGORY really doesn't have anything to do with which Registry entries you're modifying; it's just there to allow you to define the user interface. As you've probably guessed, the labels in quotes after the CATEGORY command ("Shell" and "Restrictions," in the two examples you see here) are the labels that should appear in the System Policy Editor.

The next four lines, KEYNAME, POLICY, VALUENAME, and END POLICY, all go together. KEYNAME and VALUENAME together define the actual Registry entry to work with. KEYNAME, as you'd guess, defines the particular Registry key that we're working with. VALUENAME is the name of the particular Registry entry. The POLICY/END POLICY pair just does some more System Policy Editor user-interface stuff, defining the Hide Network Neighborhood label.

Creating and Using a New Template

If you want to try this out, then do the following steps:

1. Using Notepad, create a file with the nine lines shown earlier.

2. Save the file in your \WINNT\INF directory as TEST.ADM. Check that Notepad hasn't helpfully named it TEST.ADM.TXT; I sometimes have to open up My Computer and rename the file myself.

3. Start System Policy Editor.

4. Click Options ➤ Policy Template, and you'll probably see a dialog box like Figure 6.79.

FIGURE 6.79:

Adding a policy template

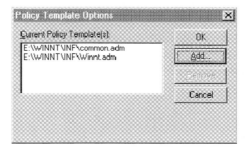

5. For all files listed in the Current Policy Template(s), click the template file and then click Remove.

6. Once you've cleared out all of the existing template files, click Add and choose TEST.ADM. (System Policy Editor template files use the extension ADM.)

7. Click OK.

8. Click File ➤ New Policy and open Default User.

You'll see the System Policy Editor showing just the Network Neighborhood policy, as in the screen shot a couple of pages back. To restore your System Policy Editor back to where it was, close the policy (File ➤ Close), open the Templates dialog box (Options ➤ Policy Template), and add WINNT.ADM and COMMON.ADM back; again, you'll find them in \WINNT\INF.

The Existing Template Files

You probably noticed that there are three ADM files: WINNT.ADM, WINDOWS .ADM, and COMMON.ADM. Why three files? Because you'll probably want to create POL files for both NT Desktops and Windows 95 Desktops, but the Windows NT and Windows 95 Registries aren't exactly the same. Microsoft thought about what Registry entries an administrator would find useful to control as policies, and so they built these three templates to save you the trouble of having to build a template. Both the Windows NT and Windows 95 System Policy Editors use the same format for their templates, however, so you can load COMMON.ADM into either System Policy Editor.

COMMON.ADM contains the Registry entries that are common to both Windows NT and Windows 95. WINNT.ADM contains Registry entries that don't exist in Windows 95, and WINDOWS.ADM contains Registry entries that exist in Windows 95 but not in Windows NT. Remember, however, that you *cannot* use the NT System Policy Editor to create a policy file that Windows 95 machines can understand or respond to. So, then, to summarize how you'd use the System Policy Editors and the templates to control Registries on machines in a domain:

- Windows NT computers will respond to a file that is named NTCONFIG.POL.

- Windows 95 computers will respond to a file called CONFIG.POL.

- You must create NTCONFIG.POL using the NT version of System Policy Editor, which ships with NT Server. Load the WINNT.ADM and COMMON .ADM templates, as well as any templates you've defined, to help you create an NTCONFIG.POL. NTCONFIG.POL must be stored on the NETLOGON share on the Primary Domain Controller of your users' domain.

- You must create CONFIG.POL using the Windows 95 version of the System Policy Editor, which you can install from the Windows 95 CD-ROM; you'll find it in ADMIN\APPTOOLS\POLEDIT. (Not all Windows 95 CDs contain this file, but most do. If yours doesn't have it, then you'll definitely find it in the *Windows 95 Resource Kit*.) Load the WINDOWS.ADM and COMMON .ADM templates, as well as any templates you've defined, to help you create a CONFIG.POL. CONFIG.POL must also be stored on the NETLOGON share on the PDC of your users' domain. Windows 95 will ignore policies unless the user explicitly logs onto the domain.

- And remember that policy files get read when *users* log in, not when machines start up, so put the policy files into the NETLOGON share of the *users'* domain's PDC.

Building a Template to Enable a WINS Proxy

I've demonstrated how the template language allows us to control the NoNet-Hood Registry parameter, but in truth that's not all that useful, as Microsoft has already *done* that work for us. How about a more useful example?

If your network is based on the TCP/IP protocol (and if it's not, start using TCP/IP—Windows Server 2000 will require it), and if you have a mix of computer types, then some of the computers on your network may have trouble finding others on the network. You can help them out by installing a *WINS proxy server* on each network segment. There's more explanation in Chapter 14, so I won't go into detail about this here, save to mention a few important points: first, again, it's a good idea to designate one machine per segment as a WINS proxy server. It doesn't take much CPU power, so virtually any machine can serve in the role. Second, under Windows 3.*x* and Windows NT 3.*x*, it was easy to make a machine a WINS proxy server through the Control Panel, but this is no longer the case. Windows 95 and Windows NT 4 machines can act as proxy servers if instructed to via their Registries, but there's no way through the user interface to adjust the Registry entry that controls it, the EnableProxy entry, which goes in HKEY_LOCAL_MACHINE\System\CurrentControlSet\Services\NetBT\ Parameters. It's of type REG_DWORD; if its value is 0, which is the default, then the machine isn't a proxy server; if it's 1, then it's a proxy server.

Anyway, suppose I want PPRO200 to be my WINS proxy server for its segment. Again, I could walk over to the machine and modify its Registry, but let's create a system policy. The template would look like the following:

```
CLASS MACHINE
CATEGORY "WINS proxy"
KEYNAME System\CurrentControlSet\Services\NetBT\Parameters
```

```
      POLICY "Make this computer a WINS proxy server"
        VALUENAME "EnableProxy"
      END POLICY
   END CATEGORY
```

All I did there was basically copy what I did before for NoNetHood, and then change these items:

- It's a machine entry, so it goes under CLASS MACHINE rather than CLASS USER.

- I didn't use a category inside a category; I just created a single-level category called "WINS proxy."

- The name of the key that I wanted to control is HKEY_LOCAL_MACHINE\ System\CurrentControlSet\Services\NetBT\Parameters, but as I've already said it's a machine entry, I didn't need the HKEY_LOCAL_ MACHINE; the result is on the KEYNAME line.

I then loaded this template and applied the policy to a machine on my network called PPRO200. The next time someone logged in and the machine had been rebooted, the machine became a WINS proxy agent.

Programming More Complex Entries

Thus far, we've seen REG_DWORD entries whose values are only 0 or 1. But how do you set up the System Policy Editor to offer you one of several options? For example, in Chapter 16 ("Tuning and Monitoring Your NT Server Network") you'll read that you can reduce network chatter by introducing a setting to all of your NT Workstation machines: Just modify entry MaintainServerList in HKLM\ System\CurrentControlSet\Services\Browser\Parameters, setting it to No. The result is that when your domain is holding network elections to determine who will be the master browser, the workstations won't take part in the election, lessening the number of candidates and thus reducing network chatter. (Again, don't worry so much about the details; I'm just using this as an example. There's much more information on this later in the book.)

Setting up a MaintainServerList policy will be a bit more complex than the policies we've looked at so far, so we'll have to delve further into the template programming language. I can't document every possible command in the template language here, but if you need to do something fancy with System Policy Editor, look to the existing ADM files for examples. As far as I know, the only time that Microsoft has documented this was in the *Windows 95 Resource Kit*; I can't find it in the *NT Workstation* or *NT Server Resource Kit*.

Offering a Limited Number of Values In addition to No, MaintainServerList can also accept values of Auto or Yes. Auto, the default value for workstations, means, "I'm willing to be the master browser if necessary." Yes means, "Not only am I willing to be a browser, but I'd like my machine to be a preferred candidate to be a browser." Yes gives a small edge to that machine during the election. As you've probably guessed, MaintainServerList is of type REG_SZ. Previously, I set up a check box with System Policy Editor, which System Policy Editor translates into (1) use REG_DWORD and (2) if checked, store a value of 1 and if unchecked, store a value of 0. MaintainServerList is a bit different—first, it uses REG_SZ values; and, second, it should respond to only a few particular values (Yes, No, and Auto). How do you get System Policy Editor to offer only three options?

If you want System Policy Editor to offer anything but the most basic check boxes, you've got to create what it calls a *part*. A part allows you to define in some detail what kinds of values a user can give to a System Policy Editor item. Here's how you'd set up MaintainServerList:

```
CLASS MACHINE
CATEGORY "Browser Elections"
  KEYNAME System\CurrentControlSet\Services\Browser\Parameters
  POLICY "Can this machine act as the master browser?"
    PART "Possible options:" DROPDOWNLIST REQUIRED
      VALUENAME "MaintainServerList"
      ITEMLIST
        NAME "Do not ever act as a browser" VALUE NO
        NAME "Prefer PC selected as a browser" VALUE YES
        NAME "Willing to be a browser if necessary" VALUE AUTO
      END ITEMLIST
    END PART
  END POLICY
END CATEGORY
```

Much of this looks familiar: the CLASS, CATEGORY, KEYNAME, POLICY, and VALUENAME commands. But notice that between POLICY and VALUENAME comes PART. PART defines the user-interface component that the System Policy

Editor should use to offer options to a user: CHECKBOX for a simple check box, NUMERIC for a single value that should be a number, EDITTEXT for a single value that should be textual information, COMBOBOX for a single value with suggested possible values, or DROPDOWNLIST for a single value with only a few possible legal values. The REQUIRED keyword means, "Don't accept this policy unless the user picks a value, and don't take null or blank as an option."

Once you've chosen DROPDOWNLIST, you must specify the list of possible legal values; that's what the ITEMLIST/END ITEMLIST group does. Each NAME line lets you specify labels that the user will see, like "Do not ever act as a browser," along with the corresponding value to store in the Registry. Create a template like that, and the System Policy Editor will look like the one shown in Figure 6.80.

FIGURE 6.80:

Using parts to offer a limited number of values

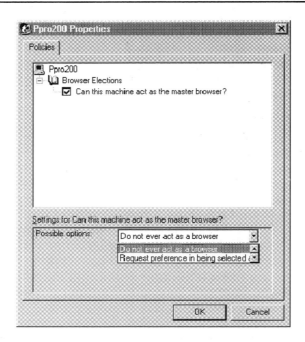

What if those labels need to correspond to numeric values? Suppose the possible legal values of MaintainServerList were 1, 0, and 1 rather than No, Yes, and

Auto. How would you tell System Policy Editor to save those values? With just one extra parameter on VALUE, VALUE NUMERIC. The ITEMLIST would then look like this:

```
ITEMLIST
  NAME "Do not ever act as a browser" VALUE NUMERIC -1
  NAME "Prefer PC selected as a browser" VALUE NUMERIC 0
  NAME "Willing to be a browser if necessary" VALUE NUMERIC 1
END ITEMLIST
```

Allowing Numeric Inputs Sometimes you'll need to create a policy that affects a numeric Registry entry that ranges from some minimum to some maximum. Use a NUMERIC part for that; they look like

```
PART label NUMERIC DEFAULT value MIN value MAX value SPIN value
REQUIRED
```

Here, DEFAULT, MIN, and MAX specify the default value, the minimum allowable value, and the maximum allowable value. REQUIRED again means that the user must specify a value, or the System Policy Editor should not store the policy. SPIN tells System Policy Editor what increments to use for the numeric spinner; you can use the default value of 1, or you can disable the spinner with a value of 0.

For example, you can tell a PDC how often to update its BDCs with an entry in HKLM\System\CurrentControlSet\System\Netlogon\Parameters named "Pulse." Pulse says how often in seconds to communicate with BDCs; the minimum allowed value is 60 (one minute) and the maximum is 172,800 (48 hours; that's what the documentation says, but I can't say that I've tested it). You could create a policy to allow administrators to easily modify Pulse like so:

```
CLASS MACHINE
CATEGORY "PDC-BDC updates"
  KEYNAME System\CurrentControlSet\Services\Netlogon\Parameters
  POLICY "Frequency of user data updates"
    PART "Time interval in seconds:" NUMERIC
    MIN 60 MAX 172800 DEFAULT 600
      VALUENAME "Pulse"
    END PART
  END POLICY
END CATEGORY
```

This *ought* to work, but it doesn't, due to a bug in the System Policy Editor: it can't handle an integer larger than 32767. If that number looks odd, it shouldn't: it's the largest integer (well, okay, the largest *signed* integer, an integer that can take either a positive or negative value) that can fit into 16 bits. Unfortunately, most Registry numeric values have 32 bits to play with, so whoever programmed the System Policy Editor to only handle 16 bits was seriously derelict in his or her job. The bottom line is that if you want to create a policy with a numeric value, it'll work best if you keep the value under 32767. So if you want to do the above example, change 172800 to 32767, and it'll work. Once you do that, the System Policy Editor looks like Figure 6.81.

FIGURE 6.81:

Using parts to allow numeric inputs

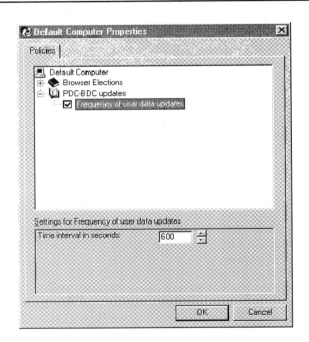

One other bug you'll run into is that the System Policy Editor won't let you punch in a value larger than 9999. In the Pulse example above, you could specify MIN 60 MAX 32767 DEFAULT 60, but you'd actually have to lean on the spinner buttons (those are the little buttons with the upward-facing and downward-facing triangles) to get to 32767. By my calculations, on a Pentium Pro 200 that takes about 35 minutes. Hmmm, perhaps a DROPDOWNLISTBOX would be a better answer here...

Sometimes you'll just want your users to punch in a numeric value, and don't want to show them the spinners; in that case, add the parameter SPIN 0, which makes the spinners disappear. Alternatively, you may want to keep the spinners, but have them increment by, say, 100 with each click; you can do that with the parameter SPIN 100. That would modify the PART statement above to look like

```
PART "Time interval in seconds:" NUMERIC MIN 60 MAX 32767 DEFAULT 600
SPIN 100
```

Allowing Free-Form Text Input We've seen check boxes, text input restricted to a few options, and numeric input, but how can you create a policy that allows the user to type in any old text that she likes? For example, you've probably noticed that if you click Help ➤ About on any screen, you get the name and organization name that someone typed in when he or she installed NT on the computer. Can you change that: can you force the organization name to be consistent across all computers? Sure. It's in a Registry key HKLM\ Software\Microsoft\Windows NT\CurrentVersion, with entry name RegisteredOrganization. It's a REG_SZ, and you can type in any old thing, no maximum length that I know of save for the practical one of length. So let's build a policy that makes sure that every PC in the company uses "Acme Technologies" as the organization name.

The part type we'll need is a simple one, EDITTEXT. It can have the REQUIRED and DEFAULT parameters, as well as a MAXLEN parameter. So, for example, if we wanted to set the maximum length of the RegisteredOrganization to 80 characters, we'd build a template like the following:

```
CLASS MACHINE
CATEGORY "General Information"
  KEYNAME "Software\Microsoft\Windows NT\CurrentVersion"
  POLICY "Setup info"
    PART "Organization name:" EDITTEXT MAXLEN 80
      VALUENAME "RegisteredOrganization"
    END PART
  END POLICY
END CATEGORY
```

Straightforward by now, but notice that I had to use quotes in the KEYNAME line; that's because there was a space in the key's name. You can see what it looks like in Figure 6.82.

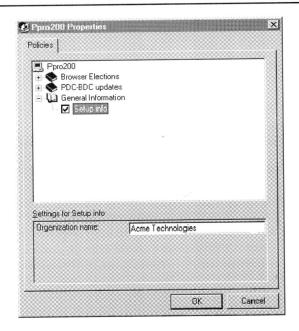

I hope you've learned three things here: First, you can create a wide array of
templates to allow you to control the Registry entries of systems all throughout
your network. Second, the language is a bit obtuse, but not impossible to master.
Third, you'll have to be ready to do a fair amount of experimentation, as the System
Policy Editor and templates are a bit buggy. But before you get *too* heady a
rush at the prospect of controlling everything from your desktop, recall that system
policies *cannot* modify any Registry entries of type REG_MULTI_SZ.

Another Example: Assigning Mapped Drives with Policies

Here's another great application of system policies, and it illustrates how you can
start from a Registry entry and use system policies to propagate user configurations.

Suppose you want a given user upon logon to see a drive V: connected to
\\BIGSERVE\COOLDATA—how would you accomplish this? Of course, you
can use logon batch scripts to assign this drive; just add this line to the logon
batch script:

```
Net use v: \\bigserve\cooldata
```

But a little poking around in the Registry shows that once you've mapped a drive, it appears in your user profile. Under HKEY_CURRENT_USER, you'll find a key called Network, which contains a key for each drive letter. The keys are named *F* for the mapped F: drive, *V* for the mapped V: drive, and so on. Thus, if I'd mapped my V: drive to \\bigserve\cooldata, I'd find (after logging off and then on) a key HKEY_CURRENT_USER\Network\V. It contains these value entries:

- **ConnectionType**: A numeric value equal to 1

- **ProviderName**: A string equal to "Microsoft Windows Network"

- **ProviderType**: A hex value 20000

- **RemotePath**: A string containing the UNC (\\bigserve\cooldata)

- **UserName**: Another string with my name (ORION\MarkM)

NOTE   A bit of experimentation shows that UserName works just as well with a blank value. That's probably because when the user tries to use the V: drive and NT's security system asks, "Who are you?" the user's workstation simply replies with the user's name. One could imagine a case when you'd want to attach under another name, but not often.

Let's see how to make this a policy. The first question is, does this go in USER or MACHINE? Simple—we found the Registry entry in HKEY_CURRENT_USER, so it's CLASS USER. We'll have a key Network\V, as that's the name of the key with the drive mapping information.

This template item will have five value entries in it, four of which we don't want to have to fill in—ConnectionType, ProviderName, ProviderType, and UserName—as we already know what values they're supposed to take. Rather than hard-wiring RemotePath to \\bigserve\cooldata, let's allow an administrator to tailor this to her needs. So it would be neat if we could build a template that essentially says, "If you enter a UNC for the V: drive, then I'll automatically also fill in these four other value entries." You can, with a thing called *ActionListOn*. It's best explained in the template itself, which follows.

```
CLASS USER
Category "Map Drive V:"
    Policy "Map drives"
```

```
        KeyName "Network\V"
                ActionListon
                        VALUENAME ConnectionType      VALUE NUMERIC 1
                        VALUENAME ProviderName        VALUE "Microsoft
 Windows Network"
                        VALUENAME ProviderType        VALUE NUMERIC 131072
                        VALUENAME UserName            VALUE ""
                End ActionListon
                Part "Drive V:" EditText
                        VALUENAME RemotePath
                End Part
        Part "Enter the UNC path." TEXT END PART
        END Policy
 End Category
```

The one thing here that may be a bit odd-looking is the numeric value 131072; where did that come from? Again, recall that the original value for ProviderType was 20000, but that was a hex value, and policies want decimal. A few mouse clicks in Calculator convert 20000 hex to 131072 decimal.

Notice how the ActionListOn part works. Between ActionListOn and End ActionListOn, I just specify some value entries and their desired values. When the associated part—the EditText part—is used, the items in the ActionListOn group just "wake up."

Home-Grown Zero Admin Windows: Locking Down a Desktop

Let me just wrap up this section on locking down a Desktop with Registry entries and system policies with a set of policies that you can use today to greatly simplify both the user interface that your users see and your support task. Microsoft has been working on some very powerful tools that will allow you to centrally control Windows Desktops, a project they call Zero Administration Windows, but you needn't wait for that. You can do some pretty amazing things right now.

Open up the System Policy Editor using the standard WINNT.ADM and COMMON.ADM templates; you don't need to build any custom templates. Then enact the following policies, all of which are user policies rather than machine policies.

In Shell/Restrictions   Remove Run command from Start menu, remove folders from Settings on Start menu, remove Taskbar from Settings on Start menu, remove Find command from Start menu, hide drives in My Computer, hide Network Neighborhood, and hide all items on Desktop.

System/Restrictions   Run only allowed Windows applications (and name them, of course).

Windows NT Shell/Custom Folders   Create a folder, as you learned earlier in this section, containing shortcuts to the programs that you want the users to be able to access.

Windows NT Shell/Restrictions   Remove File menu from Explorer (if you've allowed Explorer in the first place), remove common program groups from Start menu, disable context menus for the taskbar, and disable Explorer's default context menu.

Windows NT System   It's just personal taste, but I disable the "Show welcome tips at logon" setting.

Remember that you've got to come up with a completely standard set of locations for program files across the enterprise, or your users won't be able to get to their applications. And a final piece of advice: make these policies specific to a group, not to Default User, or you'll have a domain that you can't do any administration from!

CHAPTER
SEVEN

7

Creating and Managing Directory Shares

- Creating shared directories

- Setting share-level permissions and access control lists

- Setting file and directory permissions

- Owning a file in NT

- Managing the Profiles dialog box

[handwritten margin notes: "directories/files, printers, applications" and "Level of permissions, directory, file, share"]

Once you've created some users, you need to give them a reason to use the network. People get three main services from a network: shared directories and files, shared printers, and shared applications. In this chapter, you will see how to handle the first of those services—shared directories and files.

You share files with the My Computer folder, the Explorer, or the command line. In this chapter, I'll focus on using the My Computer folder and the Explorer's graphical user interface (GUI) to share data; the appendix shows you how to do it from a command line with the NET SHARE command. And, if you're an NT 3.51 administrator, you can do all of the same things that version 4 users can do, save that 3.51 doesn't have an Explorer or My Computer; in 3.51, you use File Manager to share directories and control directory and file access over the network.

Sharing data under NT gets a little confusing because NT offers several levels of control over who can access a given set of files. It offers *share-level* permissions, *directory-level* permissions, and *file-level* permissions. You have to understand those levels of control, and we'll cover them in this chapter. Then, once you understand how data shares work, I will backtrack a bit and explain user profiles and home directories, a subject that kind of fits with the previous chapter's discussion of user accounts, but doesn't make sense until you understand the different levels of permissions. Finally, when you're comfortable with home directories, it will make sense to explain file "ownership" and file access auditing.

Creating a Shared Directory

Most servers on networks function as repositories for files and directories that must be accessible to the network's users. Files and directories on a server running NT Server must first be *shared* before network users can access them. Merely setting up a server won't do anything, because the server will just announce itself by saying, "Hi, I'm a server, but I'm not sharing anything."

To share a directory, you must be logged on as a member of the Administrators or Server Operators group. Creating a share is easiest if you're physically logged in at the server itself (that's how I'll describe most of the examples in this chapter), but you can also create new server shares remotely with a program called the Server Manager, as I'll show you a little later.

NT can only share *directories*, not files; it's not possible to pick just one file and say to an NT Server, "Share this on the network as SFILE," or something like that. You have to specify an entire directory when sharing.

The Server service must be running on an NT Server before you can share a directory on that server. Of course, it's usually started by default on NT Server machines, but I've seen NT machines occasionally start without the Server service started. I'm not sure why it happens, but it seems that if you install NT on a system with fewer than 16MB of RAM, the Server service does *not* start by default. (Of course, in truth this won't matter, as you really should have at least 16MB on an NT Server, and 32MB is an even better minimum.) If you *do* find that you have to start up the Server service, you can start the Server service by using the Services option in Control Panel. (In Control Panel, click on Services, then on Server, and, finally, click the Start button.) Or you can open up a command line and type **net start server**.

Open up the Explorer and you'll see what is probably a familiar view of your computer. An Explorer view of NT Server is shown in Figure 7.1.

FIGURE 7.1:

Explorer view of NT Server

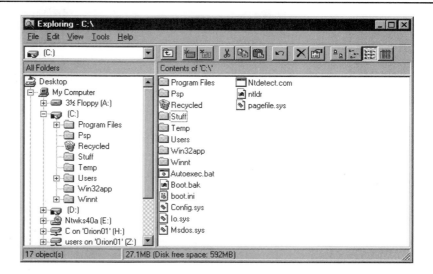

In the figure, you can see a directory named STUFF in drive C:. (The same thing works with the My Computer folder.) I can share that by right-clicking on the STUFF folder, which produces a drop-down menu like the one in Figure 7.2.

Notice the Sharing option. Click it and you get a Properties dialog box like the one in Figure 7.3. When this dialog box first appears, the Not Shared radio button is selected and everything is grayed out (which would make for a rather dull book illustration). I clicked Shared As to enable the sharing options that are shown in Figure 7.3.

FIGURE 7.2:

Object menu for the STUFF directory

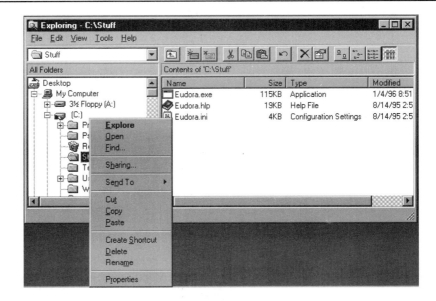

FIGURE 7.3:

Sharing tab of the Properties dialog box

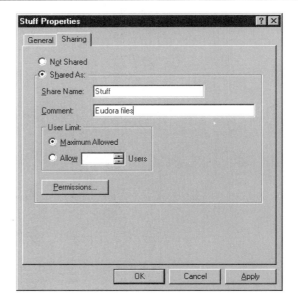

Handling Share Names

You already learned about share names in Chapter 2; they can be up to 12 characters long. However, you may want to keep to 8 characters instead, because the DOS redirector doesn't like names with more than 8 characters. (If all of your clients are Windows for Workgroups, Windows 9*x*, or Windows NT, then names with more than 8 characters are fine.) You *can* use blanks in a share name, but I strongly suggest that you don't, because you will have to surround the name with quotation marks every time you want to use it.

By default, the share name is the same as the last part of the directory name. For example, if you shared a directory called C:\TRAVEL\TICKETS\1STCLASS, then the offered share name would be 1STCLASS. You can change a share name, but the default is usually good enough.

Hiding Shares

I mentioned this in Chapter 2, but just in case you've forgotten, you can create a directory share that won't show up on the browse list by ending the share name with a dollar sign ($). For example, if I shared a directory named C:\TRAVEL\TICKETS\1STCLASS on a server, then, as the previous paragraph explains, the suggested share name would be 1STCLASS. If I named it 1STCLASS$ instead, then anyone browsing that server would not see that hidden share. Someone could still attach to the share, but they would have to do it from the command line (**net use x: \\server\1stclass$**) or from the Explorer (Tools ➤ Map Network Drive).

Using the Comment Field

In a big network with hundreds of shares, it may not be immediately obvious that OB12A36, for example, is the share that contains the retirement information. That's why the Comment field is useful. When someone browses in a server and sees that server's list of shares, the text you put in the Comment field shows up as well, and the user can read the brief description to find out what the share is all about. It's a good habit to get into, as well, because in Windows 2000 you'll "publish" this share information to a central directory of server information called the *Active Directory*. People will then use that information to search for specific pieces of data on the network.

Restricting Access to Shares

Sometimes you want to restrict the number of people who can access a network share. Most likely you'll find the options useful for satisfying the need of some software license. For example, suppose you put a program in a directory and tell people to run the program from that directory. If you only purchased 10 concurrent licenses for the software, you could tell NT Server not to allow more than 10 people to access the directory simultaneously.

Restricting user access to a share is done with the User Limit spinner box. Just designate the maximum number of users who can simultaneously access the share or choose the Unlimited option. If you try to attach to a share that has exceeded its allowable number of users, you get an error message. The error message that is shown on a client workstation varies from operating system to operating system. For example, from a DOS workstation you see this message:

```
Error 71: This request is not accepted by the network. The server may
have run out of resources necessary to process your request. Try the
request again. If the error persists, contact your network administra-
tor. For more information, type NET HELP 71 at the command prompt.
```

Windows 95 workstations are more terse:

```
An extended error has occurred
```

Windows for Workgroups workstations also keep it brief and uninformative:

```
This request is not accepted by the network
```

And NT clients are a bit more chatty and descriptive:

```
No more connections can be made to this remote computer at this time
because there are already as many connections as the computer allows.
```

Now, before you start relying on this feature, let me tell you about a problem that I saw in NT Server 3.1 and 3.5: the user maximum seemed not to work. I would create a share, give it a maximum number of users of 1, fire up 20 Windows for Workgroups machines, and watch all 20 get onto the share. My experience with version 4 leads me to believe that NT Server 4 *does* enforce the user maximum, but test it before you build a security system around this feature.

The last button in the Create New Share dialog box is Permissions. It's important, but before I get to it, let me bring up one more topic: sharing directories on remote servers.

Sharing Directories on Remote Servers

If you're not physically logged on to a server, you can't use the Explorer or My Computer to share volumes on that computer. If you want to use Explorer to create a share named BIGFILES on server AJAX, for example, you have to go over to AJAX, sit down, and log on. But if AJAX isn't located nearby—perhaps you can only get to it over a long-distance link (or you're feeling lazy)—then you can still create new shares with another tool: the Server Manager.

Running Server Manager

You'll find the Server Manager in an NT computer's Start menu under Programs, then Administrative Tools—that is, *assuming* that you're sitting at a machine running NT *Server*. If not, you have to install Server Manager from either the NT *Resource Kit* CD-ROM or find it in the CLIENTS\SRVTOOLS directory of the original NT Server CD-ROM. Earlier versions of NT Server included a version of Server Manager that ran atop Windows for Workgroups, but NT Server 4 only includes versions of Server Manager that run on Windows *9x* and Windows NT. The opening screen looks something like Figure 7.4.

FIGURE 7.4:

Server Manager opening screen

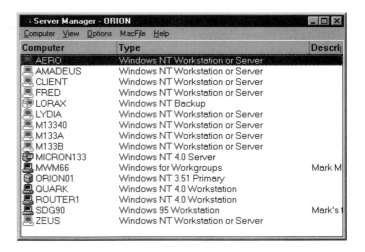

Here, Server Manager shows me the machines that can potentially share data in this workgroup. The gray computers are not currently active, but Server Manager knows of them because it has met them before.

TIP   Once in a while, Server Manager fails to notice an active computer. If you think a computer *ought* to be enabled but it's grayed out, try this trick: on a command line at a command prompt type net use *machinename*\IPC$ where *machinename* is the name of the machine that's grayed out. It doesn't always work, but it's one way to sometimes "kick Server Manager in the pants" and wake it up. (In actual fact, what you're waking up is called the Remote Procedure Call Locator, but that's a story for another day.)

Click on a server (click *once*—don't double-click!), and then choose Shared Directories in the Computer menu. You see a dialog like the one in Figure 7.5. The Shared Directories dialog box shows the shares that the server currently offers.

FIGURE 7.5:

Shared Directories dialog box

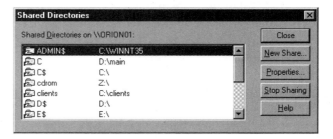

Understanding the Administrative Shares

In Figure 7.5, notice all of the hidden shares: ADMIN$, C$, D$ and E$. Why did I put *those* on this server?

I didn't.

When you run the Server service on an NT Workstation or NT Server machine, NT automatically shares the following:

* Every hard disk partition and CD-ROM drive *at their roots* (that's C$, D$, and E$).

* The directory that the NT programs are in (ADMIN$).

- The directory that contains the logon scripts (NETLOGON), which is shared if it's a domain controller. Microsoft calls them the "administrative shares." (This Netlogon share only appears on domain controllers—it won't appear on a member server or a workstation.)

By now, you must be sweating. "Arghh!" I cried, the first time I realized this. "*Anyone* can just NET USE to get to the root drive of my server! What will I do?" As it turns out, only administrators can gain access to these shares—whew! Oh, and by the way, if you try to unshare these shares, they just get re-created automatically the next time you boot the NT machine.

Creating a New Share on a Remote Machine

Anyway, back to the task at hand. Suppose machine ORION01 is in Milwaukee, and I'm in Dallas. How do I get ORION01 to share a directory named, for example, FACTS? From the Shared Directories dialog box (see Figure 7.5), just click New Share and a dialog box like Figure 7.6 will appear.

FIGURE 7.6:

Remotely creating a new share

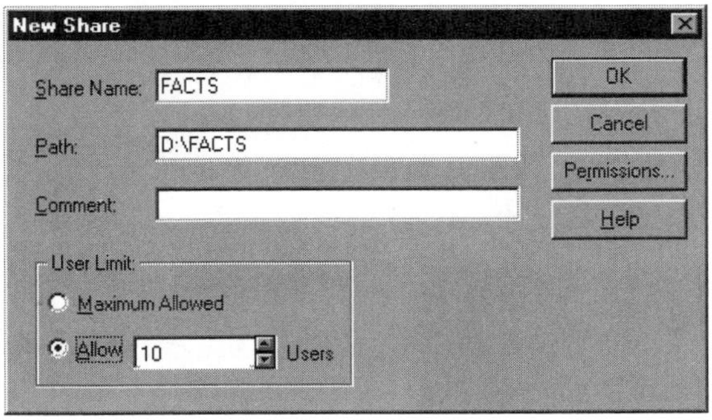

The items in this dialog box are pretty self-explanatory. Just type in the name of the new share in the Share Name field, the path (like D:\FACTS) in the Path field, a comment if you want, and, optionally, the maximum number of users. Notice what is, to me at least, a pretty major flaw in this dialog box: no Browse button.

Once you fill in the share information, the Permissions button is enabled. Which brings me to share-level permissions, my next topic.

Share-Level Permissions and Access Control Lists

Whether sharing from a local machine (remember, here "local" means the machine you're physically logged on at) or a remote machine, the last button that you have to work with is Permissions. Click it, and you see a dialog box like Figure 7.7.

FIGURE 7.7:

Access Through Share Permissions dialog box

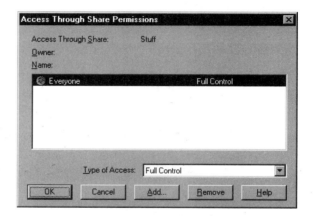

NT uses the word *permissions* to describe the type of access that a particular user has for a particular network resource. For example, if I can read and write files in \\SERVER01\WPFILES, but I can only read files in \\SERVER01\CLIENTSW, then I'd say that my permissions for the first share were "change" and my permissions for the second share were "read-only." NT lets you get as specific as you like when it comes to who can do what. For example, although I can only read files in \\SERVER01\CLIENTSW, some other user, perhaps an administrator, could have permissions to both read and write those files. As you do more with NT, you'll see that NT can also assign permissions for printer shares and network applications.

Although there is only one item in the dialog box in Figure 7.7, you can add any number of entries, as you'll see presently. The entire list of permissions for a share is called its *Access Control List* (ACL).

Everyone Includes, Well, *Everyone*

The permission list that you see in Figure 7.7 shows a small picture of a globe, the word *Everyone*, and the word *Full Control*. Those permissions—the group Everyone has Full Control—are the default permissions for any share you create in NT. "Everyone" is a group, like the user groups that you learned about in the previous chapter—but it's a special group. "Everyone" means all users on the domain *and* any trusted domains. I know we haven't discussed trust relationships yet, but briefly, a trust relationship is a kind of "treaty" or "trade agreement" between two domains. If you had two domains named RED and BLUE, and RED and BLUE trusted each other, and you created a share that the group Everyone could access, then all of the users in RED and BLUE would be able to access that share. (More on trust relationships in Chapter 12.)

WARNING   Be careful what shares you give the group Everyone access to. In my two-domain example, suppose RED is run by very security-conscious people who take the excellent step of disabling the Guest account, and BLUE is run by slobs who keep the Guest account enabled. Since a RED share available to Everyone is available to everyone in the BLUE domain, and since BLUE has the Guest account enabled—in other words, as long as BLUE is essentially open to the whole world—the RED Everyone shares are available to the whole world.

Share-Level Access Types

Notice that the Everyone group has access which is *Full Control*. There are four levels of share access, as you can see in Table 7.1.

TABLE 7.1:   Share Permissions

Share Permission	Level of Access
No Access (None)	Prevents any access to the shared directory, its subdirectories, and its files.
Read	Allows viewing file names and subdirectory names, changing to the shared directory's subdirectories, and viewing data in files and running application files.
Change	Allows viewing file names and subdirectory names, changing to the shared directories' subdirectories, viewing data in files and running applications files, adding files and subdirectories to the shared directory, changing data in files, and deleting subdirectories and files.
Full Control (All)	Allows viewing file names and subdirectory names, changing to the shared directories' subdirectories, viewing data in files and running applications files, adding files and subdirectories to the shared directory, changing data in files, deleting subdirectories and files, changing permission (NTFS files and directories only), and taking ownership (NTFS files and directories only).

If you look at Table 7.1, you'll probably wonder what the difference is between Change and Full Control. I *will* explain it, but before my explanations make much sense, I have to first explain the concepts of *file and directory permissions*, which I'm going to get to in a few pages, and *file ownership*, which I'll cover much later in this chapter. Put simply, however, the difference between Change and Full Control is that someone with Full Control can change file and directory permissions and the ownership of a file. Oh, by the way, this is only relevant on a share formatted as NTFS, since you've got to have NTFS for it to be possible to set file and directory permissions or file ownership. On a shared network volume formatted as FAT or NTFS, there is literally no difference between Full Control and Change.

Multiple Groups Accumulate Permissions

It's possible, as you'll see in a page or two, to add a number of other users or groups to this share. You might have one group in your network called Accountants, and another called Managers, and they might have different permission levels. For example, the Accountants might only be able to read the files, and the Managers might have *Change* access, which is just NT-ese for *Read* and *Write* access. What about the manager of the Accounting department, who is in both the Managers and the Accountants group? Does he have Read or Change access?

In general, your permissions to a network resource *add up*, so if you have Read access from one group and Change from another group, then you end up with Read *and* Change access. However, because Change access completely *includes* all of the things that you can do with Read access, there's no practical difference between having Read and Change access and having only Change access.

Using "No Access" to Keep the Guests Out

There *is* one exception: No Access. If one of your groups gives you No Access, that trumps all the others. If you're a member of a hundred groups that give you Full Control and a member of just one that gives you No Access, it doesn't matter, because you can't access the share at all.

Where would you use this? Well, one place I've found it useful is in domains that must leave their Guest account enabled. There were more reasons to keep the Guest account enabled back in the NT 3.1 days than there are under NT 4, but there may still be occasions in which you would enable the Guest account. The problem with enabling the Guest account is that the Everyone group, which is normally such a useful and succinct way to grant general network-wide access, becomes useless: granting Everyone access on a network with an enabled Guest account is tantamount to offering access to everybody on the planet.

Ah, but No Access gives us a workaround. Just explicitly add the Domain Guests account, and grant them No Access. Guests are, of course, members of Everyone, and so get Full Control; but they're also Guests, and so get No Access. No Access always wins, so the guests are locked out.

Adding to the ACL

Suppose I want to add a different group to a list of permissions or an access control list (ACL) for the STUFF directory. Click Add and you see a dialog box like the one in Figure 7.8.

FIGURE 7.8:

Adding users or groups to an NT share

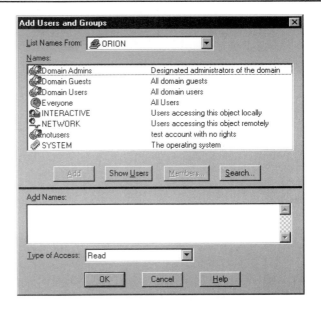

You may recognize some of these groups—Domain Admins, Domain Users, Domain Guests, and Everyone. The Notusers group is just something I created while experimenting. INTERACTIVE, NETWORK, and SYSTEM are also built-in groups. And if you're trying this out while sitting at a machine that not only shares files but also acts as a domain controller, you'll see groups named Administrators, Users, and Guests.

Adding a Group to an ACL

Suppose I want to grant Full Control of my STUFF share to Domain Admins. (This is superfluous in this particular example, as the Everyone group already has Full Control and obviously all Domain Admins users are part of Everyone, but I'm just looking for an example.) From the previous dialog box, click Domain Admins, and the Add button. Then, in the bottom pane of the window, you'll see something like *Domain Admins* and a drop-down list box labeled *Type of Access*. By default, the box contains Read, but you can pull it down and choose any one of the four access types.

Adding a Single User to an ACL

Notice that the list only contains the names of groups. What if I want to add one user to a permissions list? I might do that if I didn't trust one particular person and wanted to grant him No Access, or if he were a member of a group with Read access and I wanted to give him Change access.

It's simple to add a user to a permissions list: just click the Show Users button. The top pane of the dialog box then includes the names of particular users. Just click the user's name in the top pane and specify the access level in the bottom pane.

Controlling Permissions from the Command Line

Sometimes in class I get asked about changing ACLs with a command-line command. You may occasionally need to control permissions in a batch file, where it is not so easy to start up the User Manager for Domains and tell the batch file to click its way through the GUI. That's where the Change ACLs or CACLS.EXE program comes in handy. But to use it, you have to be using NTFS, as CACLS doesn't work on share-level permissions; it works on *file and directory* level permissions, which I'll get to very soon.

Changing Permissions on an Existing Share

In my STUFF example so far, I've been modifying permissions on a new share. How do you do it on an existing share?

Well, first of all, you can identify an existing share by opening the Explorer or My Computer folders and examining the folder icons for each directory. Most directory icons look like a manila folder; shared directories look like a folder with a hand below it. Right-click the folder, choose Sharing, and you see the same Properties dialog box as the one I showed you when I first shared STUFF (see Figure 7.3). Again, just click the Permissions button and you can make ACL changes to your heart's content.

File and Directory Permissions

Share-level permissions predate NT and have been around Microsoft networking for years. But NT brought to Microsoft networking a whole new level of security. As you probably know, one of Microsoft's goals in designing NT was to enable you to make the data on your stand-alone workstation as secure from intruders as the data on your network. It's actually possible to set up an NT workstation so that multiple people can share a computer, yet be unable to access each other's data. If Joe and Jane share an NT Workstation machine—perhaps Joe works the day shift and Jane the night shift—then it's possible to create a directory called Joe and make Jane unable to access that data for love or money, and likewise Jane can have a directory that only she can get to. Again, no networking is involved in this scenario—just one computer being shared by two people.

This is a really great feature of NT. In my experience prior to NT with operating systems of all kinds, if you could gain physical access to a computer, you could get to its data. Before NT, the only way to secure data with any confidence was to put the data on a server and put the server behind a locked door. With NTFS, there was no need for physical security.

But *can* you simply put data on an NTFS drive and then walk away, secure in the knowledge that someone can't come around with a DOS boot disk and peek at your secured data? Well, actually, no, not any more. There's a free utility called NTFSDOS, available from www.sysinternals.com, that will allow DOS to access NTFS drives. So I suppose the old advice still holds: physically secure your server if you want its data to be secure.

This ability to attach security information to areas of a disk under NT is called *file and directory permissions*. Notice that NT lets you put file and directory permissions on disk areas even if you've not shared those disk areas. As shared directories are protected by share-level permissions and *all* directories are protected by file and directory permissions, file and directory permissions are, then, an extra layer of "fine-tuned" security for network shares.

There *is* one detail about using file and directory permissions, however, and it is important enough to put in a note.

NOTE   You must format a disk volume to NTFS in order to use file and directory permissions.

Thus far, I've described security enforced by the *file server* software. In contrast, file and directory permissions are security enforced by the local *file system*, which must be in NTFS for this to work. Recall the security example in Chapter 2 about the LSA, SAT, SRM, and SDs. NTFS allows you to have *two* sets of SDs on a directory share: the server SDs (share permissions) and the file system SDs. Both SDs must be satisfied or a user will not be able to access a file over the network.

When File and Directory Permissions Conflict

Before going further, let me get a small point out of the way. Because NTFS lets you put permissions on files and permissions on directories, *and* as files exist inside directories, conflicts *could* arise. Suppose a file named README.TXT sat in a directory called TEXTFILES, and suppose further that you had NTFS directory permissions granting you Read access to the TEXTFILES directory—but the NTFS file permissions for the README.TXT file did *not* include Read permissions. Reading the file would be fine from the directory's point of view, but not from the file's point of view. Who wins?

In general, the file wins. This makes sense, as you should be able to create general rules (directory permissions) with particular exceptions to those rules (file permissions). But we'll see later that there is one very bizarre exception to the "file permissions override directory permissions" rule—the rules governing whether or not you can *delete* a file. Believe it or not, if the directory says that you can delete a file, but the file says you *can't* delete it, the file's opinion on the matter is ignored—and you can delete the file.

The File and Directory Permission Types

Recall that you have only four options for permissions on shares: Read, Change, Full Control, and No Access. On directory permissions—and note that there *is* a difference between file and directory permissions, as you'll see—you've got more options:

- No Access
- List

- Read

- Add

- Add & Read

- Change

- Full Control

- Special Directory Access

- Special File Access

You probably won't *often* use file permissions, but they allow you to fine-tune your permissions down to the finest grain—files themselves. You get five options with file permissions:

- No Access

- Read

- Change

- Full Control

- Special Access

Table 7.2 briefly describes the file and directory permission types.

TABLE 7.2:   File and Directory Permission Types

Permission	Result When Applied to Directory/File
No Access	*To a directory*: User is not allowed to view or modify directory or directory permissions.
	To a file: User is not allowed to view or modify file or file permissions.
Read	*To a directory*: Allows display of filenames within the directory and their attributes; permissions and owner of the directory; also allows user to navigate the directory structure, moving down through subdirectories.
	To a file: Allows display of the file's data, attributes, permissions, and owner; if the file is a program, allows user to execute the program.

Continued on next page

TABLE 7.2 CONTINUED: File and Directory Permission Types

Permission	Result When Applied to Directory/File
Add	*To a directory*: Allows user to put files into a directory, either by copying them from the command line, dragging and dropping in Explorer, or the like, but that user cannot access files put in that directory, nor can she view the contents of the directory. User also cannot modify permissions in the directory. Add permission is somewhat like a public mailbox—you can drop a letter into the box, but once it's in there you can't get to it or see what else is in there.
	To a file: This permission has no meaning for a file. Setting a directory to Add does not modify the permissions of the files in that directory.
Add & Read	*To a directory*: User can read files in a directory, navigate the directory structure, and execute any programs in the directory, but can't modify permissions in the directory. User can copy files into the directory, but cannot *modify* or delete those files. This leads to the odd circumstance that you can right-click the directory and create a new file, say a Word document, but you can't save it after you've edited it—not even to a different filename.
	To a file: Making a directory Add & Read modifies the files in the directory to Read level permission, as described above.
List	*To a directory*: User can see what files are in the directory and can view those files and the file and directory permissions, as well as navigate the directory structure. User can execute any programs in the directory.
	To a file: This permission has no meaning for a file. Setting a directory to List permissions will not modify the permissions of the files inside the directory.
Change	*To a directory*: User can create new files and directories, modify files, delete them, execute them if they're programs, navigate the directory structure. About the only thing the user can't do is modify file and directory permissions.
	To a file: User can view, modify, or delete file. If it's a program, user can execute the program. User cannot modify file permissions.
Full Control	*To a directory*: User can view, create, modify, delete, and navigate directory. User can also change directory permissions and take ownership of directory.
	To a file: User can view, create, modify, delete, and (if it's a program) execute file. User can also change file permissions and take ownership of file.
Special Access (File or Directory)	*To a directory or file*: Special access lets you create access permissions other than the pre-built permissions described above, using the *atomic permissions* (described later).

Rolling Your Own Permissions: Special File/Directory Access

That's a fair range of options, but you may need your own special permission. You can get that extra control by choosing to set a directory's permissions to "special directory permissions," or a file's to "special file permissions."

In its heart of hearts, NT does not really have file and directory permissions like Change, Full Control, or Add & Read. In actual fact, NT has a set of six basic, very low-level permissions that I think of as its "atomic" permissions. You can assign any combination of these atomic permissions to a file or directory, but Microsoft has saved you that trouble by building commonly used combinations like Change (a combination of four atomic permissions), Full Control (all six atomic permissions combined), and Add & Read (three atomics combined). And if the basic six are "atomic" permissions, the combinations must be "molecular" permissions, right? (Well, it seems that way to me, but then I *enjoyed* science classes in school...)

The atomic permissions are Read, Write, Execute, Take Ownership, Delete, and Change Permissions. I'm going to explain what those six do in a minute, but let me quickly provide an example of how atomics combine to form a molecular permission; take, for example, the Add permission.

The Add permission is really just a combination of the Write and Execute atomic permissions, where the Write atomic directory permission lets you write new files (but not modify existing files) and the Execute atomic directory permission lets you navigate subdirectories; without it, you're not allowed to do any work inside a directory (again, a more detailed explanation is coming up). Earlier, I described the Add permission is being like a physical mailbox—something you could drop things into but could not retrieve. The Write permission allows you to write a new file to the directory *once you get inside the directory*—but you've got to be able to get into the directory. Execute lets you do that.

Oh, and note one confusing thing about atomic and molecular permissions—there are *two* permissions named Read: an atomic one and a molecular one. The atomic Read permission does what you expect it to do: it lets you read things. But for some dumb reason, Microsoft built a molecular permission named Read and an atomic permission named Read—*but they don't do the same thing*. Molecular Read comprises atomic Read *plus* atomic Execute. Molecular Read should have been named Read *Only*, as that's its effect: any directory that you have molecular Read permissions for lets you examine its contents, but not modify them.

Read Permission

The atomic Read permission does pretty much what you expect it to do—it allows you to examine an object, to look inside it. If it's a directory, that means that you can see the names of the files and directories inside it. If it's a file, Read permission means that you can look at the file's contents. For either files or directories, it means that you can examine attributes, permissions, and ownership (something I'll explain in a few sections). Every atomic permission has a one-letter abbreviation used in several NT utilities to describe the permissions set on an object. Read's is *R*.

Read permission can be a bit difficult to understand in the context of directories because, again, Read permission means only that you can see the names of the items in the directory, be they files or other directories. Thus, for example, if E:\DIR1 contains DIR2 (E:\DIR1\DIR2), and you have Read access to E:\DIR1 but No Access to E:\DIR1\DIR2, you can open up the DIR1 folder and see that a folder called DIR2 lives inside E:\DIR1—but that's as far as it goes. You could examine DIR1's attributes, owner, permissions, and list of contents, but if you try to open DIR2, examine its attributes, permissions, or owner, you'll get a variation on the message "access denied." This is true whether you try to navigate these directories via the Explorer, or simply by opening up a command line and typing **cd e:\dir1\dir2**; both will net you the "access denied" message.

Execute Permission (Directory Version)

Having just read that, consider the following. Drive E: contains directory E:\DIR1, DIR1 contains DIR2 (E:\DIR1\DIR2), DIR2 contains DIR3 (E:\DIR1\DIR2\DIR3), and DIR3 contains DIR4 (E:\DIR1\DIR2\DIR3\DIR4). This is illustrated in

Figure 7.9. Assume that I set the directory permissions (files are irrelevant for this discussion) to atomic Read—*not* molecular Read—for E:\DIR1, E:\DIR1\DIR2, and E:\DIR1\DIR2\DIR3, and that I set directory permissions to Change for E:\DIR1\DIR2\DIR3\DIR4. It seems that this simple permission will lead to your being able to examine the contents of DIR4, right? Wrong.

FIGURE 7.9:

Sample four-level directory structure

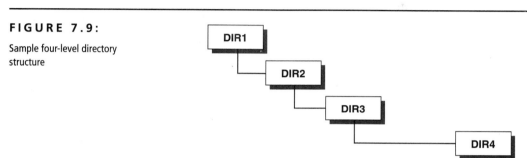

Read permission lets you *look* at files and directories. But all you can do with a directory is look at it—you can't enter it. To examine DIR4, you must essentially traverse the directory tree from E:\ down to E:\DIR1\DIR2\DIR3, and "traversing the directory tree" is a separate permission. I don't know why, but Microsoft called this "traversing the directory tree" permission by the name Execute permission. (Execute's abbreviation, by the way, is X.) Thus, either trying to navigate down to DIR4 with Explorer or opening a command line and typing **cd \dir1\dir2\dir3\dir4** will result in an error message if DIR1, DIR2, and DIR3's directory permissions are simply atomic Read.

In contrast, if you set the directory permissions for E:\DIR1, E:\DIR1\DIR2, and E:\DIR1\DIR2\DIR3 to X, then you *can* get to E:\DIR1\DIR2\DIR3\DIR4. Just open up a command prompt and type **cd \dir1\dir2\dir3\dir4**; from that point on, you're in DIR4 and you can do anything that you like in that directory.

Note, however, that if you try to do this from Explorer by first opening up E:\DIR1 and finding E:\DIR1\DIR2 inside, then opening E:\DIR1\DIR2 and finding E:\DIR1\DIR2\DIR3 inside, and so on, then you'll fail. That's because Explorer would have the permission to *enter* E:\DIR1, certainly (because of the X permission), but Explorer also *shows* you what's in E:\DIR1. To do that, Explorer would need the atomic Read permission. The command line's strength was that in changing your default directory all the way down to DIR4, a CD command need not stop and look around, and so it doesn't need R permission. Of course, once you're *there*, you need R permission to look around DIR4, but in this example we've already set DIR4's permissions to Change.

Now, before you run off to your computer to *try* this, don't bother. If you've installed NT to be pretty much a default configuration, then your user will have no trouble moving all around the directory structure with no more access than Read permissions. Why? Read on.

Blurring Read and Execute: The "Bypass Traverse Checking" Advanced Right

You may recall the discussion in the previous chapter on user rights. One of those user rights was an advanced user right named *Bypass Traverse Checking.* It's really not explained well in any of the Microsoft documents or Help files that I've seen. Here's my definition of Bypass Traverse Checking: if you possess the Bypass Traverse Checking right, then having Read access to a directory will essentially allow you both Read and Execute access to the directory.

By default, this right is given to Everyone, which explains why countless NT administrators have torn their hair out experimenting with NT, trying to understand the difference between Read and Execute directory permissions. Since by default Everyone has the Bypass Traverse Checking right, then anyone who has Read access to a directory structure can also traverse the directory, a right that they would only have if they had Execute access.

Thus, if you tried to repeat the DIR1\DIR2\DIR3\DIR4 experiment that I outlined above and set DIR1, DIR2, and DIR3's directory permissions to simply atomic Read, then trying to navigate down to DIR4 with Explorer would *not* fail, as the atomic Read directory permission would essentially act like the Read *and* Execute directory permissions.

Why'd they call this permission "Execute" rather than "Traverse" or the like, anyway? My guess goes something like this. The Execute *file* permission has been around since the early LAN Manager days, and it's a simple permission to understand: if a file is a program file, like a file ending in COM or EXE, and you have Execute permission, then you can execute that program. When Microsoft built the NT security system, most atomic permissions made sense from a file *and* directory perspective—Read, Write, Delete—but Execute had no real meaning for directories. At the same time, they had this notion of traveling up and down the directory tree, and they needed a permission to control it. Execute wasn't doing anything directory-wise anyway, so why not? (Because it's *confusing*, that's why not!)

Execute Permission (File Version)

Now that we've covered the directory side of the Execute permission, let's consider the Execute permission for files. As you've read, it specifies whether or not you can run a particular program file. But how to use it? Two scenarios suggest themselves: in one, you want people to take program files from a server, but not to run them on the server, and in the other, you *don't* want people to copy program files—instead you want to force them to run a program from the server.

In the first case, you can use the Execute file permission to build a program "distribution point." Suppose you have a program on a shared directory and you want users to copy it to their local hard disks and run it there. You tell them how to connect to the share and copy the files locally, but some people are lazy and decide to run it directly from the server, causing extra disk action on the server and perhaps significantly slowing it down. Set the directory permissions to Read and Execute, but then set the *file* permissions to just Read. People will be able to navigate to the directory and read the files, but not run them.

Alternatively, you may want people to be able to run a program from your server, but you don't want them copying the program to their floppy or ZIP drives and walking out the door with it. In that case, put the program in a shared directory, set the directory permissions to RX, and the program file's file permissions to just X. (Note that these last two paragraphs illustrate two good examples of when you can use file permissions to override directory permissions in order to solve a particular problem.)

Write Permission

You won't be surprised when I tell you that the Write (abbreviated *W*) permission lets you write files. If you only have Write permission, however, you will only be able to *create* files, and not modify them. To be able to modify files, you'll need Delete permission (well, and of course you'll need the ability to Read them in the first place, or you won't get very far).

Why Delete? Because of the way that most programs modify files. Suppose you read a file named SCHEDULE.DOC into Word, change it, and write it back out—let's see how Word does it, in slow motion.

First, Word writes the new file out under a new name, some temporary name like $WORDTMP.$$ or something like that. Then, once the file is successfully written, Word deletes the old SCHEDULE.DOC file. Finally, it renames the new file from $WORDTMP.$$ to SCHEDULE.DOC. It looks to you and me like Word just modified a file, but what it actually did was to create a new file, delete an old file, and rename the new file. Thus, without Delete permission, Word would not be able to complete its Save operation. In my experience, you cannot rename a file or directory without Delete permission. (That may mean that telling the Explorer to rename actually causes a deleted directory entry, but I don't know that for a fact.)

You can see this with a simple example. Create a directory with Write and Read permissions. Open it up in Explorer and right-click inside the folder. You'll get the option to create a new document (among other options), which will show up with the name New Text Document.TXT. Try to rename it, or try to change it with Notepad—no go.

Delete Permission

It seems that many of the atomic permissions' actual abilities run counter to what you'd think they'd do, given their names. (You'd think that Write permission would be sufficient to allow you to re-write a file, right?) Delete is one of those permissions. The official Microsoft definition of Delete runs something like this: "If you have the Delete permission on a directory or file, then you can delete that directory or file; if you don't have Delete permission, then you can't."

Ah, but then you try it. Suppose I create a folder called STUFF and give you the Delete atomic permission, and then add a file called DONTERASE.TXT in that directory. As I don't want it erased, I specifically remove your Delete atomic permission. You try to delete the file—and you can, despite the file's NTFS permissions forbidding you from deleting it.

You may recall that I mentioned this a few pages back. It's just an oddity of the way that NTFS file and directory permissions work out when they conflict. Basically, what it means is this: the Delete atomic permission is useful on directories but useless on files. Delete's abbreviation is *D*.

Change Permissions and Take Ownership

These two are simple. Change Permissions, abbreviated *P*, does what it sounds like (for once)—if you have Change Permissions permission on an object, you can change its permissions. Take Ownership, abbreviated *O*, is a permission that is also somewhat self-explanatory; if you've got the permission, then you can take ownership of an object. But what's "ownership?" I'll explain that later in this chapter.

Reexamining the Built-In Permissions

Now that I've explained the six atomic permissions, let's go back and take another look at the nine molecular permissions to see how they're built.

Read Molecular Read sets both directories and files to RX: Read and Execute. By now, it should be clear what the point of that is. Read lets you examine a directory's or file's contents; Execute lets you navigate the directory structure.

List Set a user's permissions to List, and you'll see (RX) (Not Specified) next to her name on the permission list. What that means is that the *directory* permissions have been set to RX, which is Read and Execute—the ability to see a directory and to traverse its directory structure. There's nothing said about the *file* permissions, so setting a directory to List doesn't cause NT to modify the permissions on any existing files. That's a good thing, as you'll use the List permission to grant someone the ability to browse a directory or directories—you wouldn't want NT rearranging a lot of file permissions just because you gave someone the ability to peek at a directory. And, of course, there's no Write or Delete atomics included in List, so you haven't a prayer of changing any of the files that you can see.

Add Add is composed of (WX) (Not Specified). The W lets the user write new things to a directory. The X lets the user open up the directory enough to put those new things in the directory. The lack of an R means that the user can't see what's in that directory, and the lack of D means that the user can't modify something that's in the directory, hence the mailbox analogy I've used earlier. The "Not Specified" means don't mess with the file permissions, as with List.

Add & Read   Add & Read uses permissions (RWX) (RX), meaning that Add & Read is the Add permission with the addition of the directory permission R, enabling the user to not only traverse the tree and add files, but also to examine what's in the directories. The lack of a D means that once she's dropped a file in the directory, it's still stuck there. She can also examine and execute any files that she comes across in the directory.

Change   Change, a commonly used molecular permission, is (RXWD)(RXWD), identical permissions for files and directories. A user can traverse the directory structure, add and examine files, and modify or delete any files.

No Access   No Access isn't really a permission, it is the *lack* of permissions. If I specify a user name or group in an object's permissions list and then grant that person or group no permissions, I am telling NT that they should have no access at all to that object.

Full Control   Full Control is (RXWDOP)(RXWDOP), complete permission to an object. There is no greater access to an object.

File and Directory Permissions versus Share Permissions: Who Wins?

As I've mentioned, one very important thing to understand about file and directory permissions is the fact that they work whether you're networked or not. When you access share-level permissions on the Sharing tab of the Properties dialog box and share or unshare a directory, file and directory permissions show up in a separate tab labeled Security. To see this tab, right-click any file or directory *on an NTFS volume* from the My Computer or Explorer window. You see a window like the one in Figure 7.10.

FIGURE 7.10:

Security tab on STUFF
directory

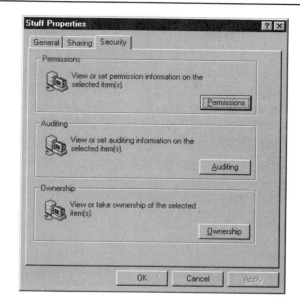

Recall that even though I shared STUFF, it would have a Security tab whether it was shared or not. Notice the Permissions, Auditing, and Ownership buttons. Click Permissions and you see a dialog box like the one in Figure 7.11.

FIGURE 7.11:

Directory Permissions
dialog box

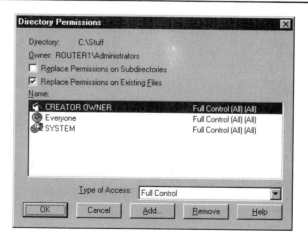

You may recall that the share-level permissions on STUFF was just Everyone/ Full Control. That's quite a bit different from *this* dialog box. Why is that? It's an important question, and understanding the answer will drive home an important point about file and directory permissions.

The STUFF folder had file and directory permissions specified on it *before* I shared it. Merely sharing it and creating a list of share permissions *does not affect the file and directory permissions at all.* Just to provide an extreme example, suppose STUFF had file and directory permissions that only allowed a user named Meredith to access it. Then suppose STUFF was shared with share permissions only allowing share access to another user named Martin. Once I shared STUFF, no change would appear on the file and directory permissions for STUFF. The share-level permissions would think it's okay for Martin to access the file, but the file and directory permissions would only let Meredith in.

In this case, what would happen? Could Martin access STUFF? Could Meredith? Could both or neither access STUFF? The answer is, neither could access STUFF over the network. When Meredith tried to attach to the share, the share-level permissions would keep her out. When Martin tried to attach to the share, the share-level permissions would give him the thumbs-up, but the file system's permissions would nix the connection.

Now, Meredith could physically walk over to the computer that STUFF sits on, log on to it, and access the directory, because she wouldn't tickle the network software and so she wouldn't be denied access. Summarized, here is the basic rule of data access on a network share that's been formatted as NTFS: to access some data on the network, you must have both share-level *and* file and directory permissions for that data.

Making Home Directories Work

It may seem that the combination of share-level permissions and file and directory permissions is overkill, but it has its uses. Sure, it would have been nice to just integrate them into one unified set of permissions, but there wasn't any easy way to add file and directory permissions to the old FAT file system. Share-level permissions presented one way to tack security atop a FAT-based file system. Share-level permissions let the network server software check a program's credentials before getting any access to the non-secure FAT file system, but Microsoft wanted to build more fine-tuning into the security, and so file and directory permissions were born.

But back to the question, "Where would you use this stuff?" There's no more perfect application than on a domain controller in the home directories.

What Is a Home Directory?

A *home directory* is a directory on the network that is yours and yours alone; no one else can access the data in those directories, save perhaps the administrator. Home directories are often stored on a domain controller, but they needn't be—they only need to be in a share on the network. The home directory is usually the place where users stash personal documents on the network.

The data structure for a home directory is often a root named USERS and subdirectories named after their owners. For example, there would be a USERS\MEREDITH, USERS\MARTIN, USERS\IGNATZ, and so on.

There are two steps to creating and using home directories:

- First, of course, you must create the directories on some server and allow users access to them.

- Second, you've got to tell the user's machines to connect to those shares.

And on top of all this is the fact that you as an administrator don't want to have to do any more work than is necessary.

Warning: Home Directory Limitations

Speaking of doing a lot of work, before going on I should parenthetically note that home directory support on NT has traditionally been pretty spotty, and even with the latest service packs it's *still* not great. Just so I don't get your hopes up unnecessarily, let me offer a few caveats:

- If you've got DOS, Windows 3.*x*, or Windows 9*x* clients, you're going to have to do some work to make this work right. It's possible to give these folks home directories, but it's not easy.

- If you've got NT clients, then you can make home directories work as you expect them to, but you'll first have to download a file from Microsoft that will add something called *distributed file system* support, and you'll have to put that file on all of your NT systems. Once you've done that, supplying home directories is a breeze—although, again, it's only a breeze if your users have NT on their desktops.

This amazes people coming from the NetWare world, as building home directories for each user is simplicity itself. Unfortunately, however, home directories have been something of an afterthought in the NT world.

One Approach to Home Directories: Securing Home Directories with Share-Level Permissions

Suppose you had a thousand users and you needed to create a home directory for each one. How would you do it? Well, one way to do that would be to create a thousand subdirectories of the USERS directory. (A USERS directory was created when you installed NT 3.*x*, but it appears that NT 4 doesn't create one, so feel free to create one on whatever server will hold the home directories.) Then, you'd go individually to each directory, share it, and change its permissions so that only its owner could access it.

Now, that's a *lot* of work, but it's possible. It's not a good idea, either, but it's possible. Just imagine—a thousand users would mean a thousand shares, which would mean one heckuva big browse list! Nevertheless, the difficulty of making home directories available to DOS and Windows users has impelled many to choose the "one user, one share" course of action. They typically hide those shares, but it's even more effort. *Enterprise Administrator*, from Mission Critical Systems, does all of this automatically, so if you want to pursue this approach, then you might look into EA, but of course it's an added cost.

Another Approach to Securing Home Directories: File and Directory Permissions

There is an easier way, fortunately, one that exploits file and directory permissions:

1. Put the USERS directory on an NTFS volume. Remember that you must be using NTFS, or you will never see the Security tab.

2. Share the USERS directory, giving Full Control to the Everyone group. (Share-level permissions, remember.)

3. Set the *directory* permissions in the users directory to Read and Execute for Everyone and Full Control for Administrators. Set *file* permissions to None for Everyone and Full Control for Administrators. You're doing this to keep users from creating new directories and files in the root of the USERS share.

4. For each user, click on that user's directory and choose the Security tab (from the Explorer or My Computer, right-click the directory and choose Properties to see the Security tab).

5. Click Permissions and you see the Directory Permissions dialog box for that directory (see Figure 7.11).

6. Click the Remove button to remove all entries from the dialog box.

7. Click the Add button to add the user. You see a dialog box like the one in Figure 7.12.

FIGURE 7.12:

Adding users to file and directory permissions

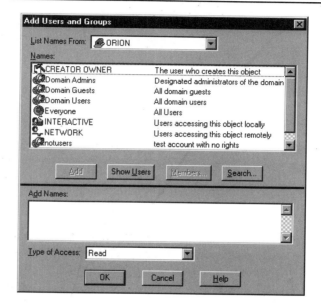

8. Click the Show Users button to display the names of individual users.

9. Choose the correct user, click Add, and choose Full Control in the Type of Access list box.

10. Click OK three times and you'll be back to the NT Desktop.

Now you have a share—the USERS share—with user directories in it, such as USERS\JOHN, USERS\SUE, USERS\MARY, and the like. Everyone can access the top level of the USERS share, but each user can only get to his or her specific subdirectory.

I know it sounds odd, but think of it this way: imagine the USERS share is a large hotel and each directory and file is a guest room. Share-level permission for USERS—the fact that the permissions for USER are Full Control for Everyone—just gets you into the lobby. Without a guest room key—file and directory permissions are the guest-room keys in my analogy—someone can't get very far; into the lobby, but no further, save for his or her home directory. One security system guards the front door (the server subsystem and its security) and another security system guards the guest rooms (the NTFS file subsystem and *its* security). You have to get past *both* of them to get to a guest room (your home directory).

Now suppose we return to user Meredith. I give her No Access share-level permissions to the share Users, but Full Control file and directory permissions on her home directory USERS\MEREDITH. She could do anything she wanted to her home directory… if she could get to it.

Essentially, Meredith *has* a guest room key but can't get in the front door. She has no share-level permissions, so she can't attach to the share in the first place. (She'd see a message like "USERS is not accessible. Access is denied.") If she *could* get access to the share, she'd have full control of USERS. The guest room security folks like her fine, but the front-door guard doesn't let her by. The only way for her to access the USERS data is to sit right down at the machine that USERS physically resides on, log on, and access USERS\MEREDITH.

An Even Easier Way to Create Home Directories

But it was some work putting that together, wasn't it? We need an easier way and, fortunately, there is an easier way. It's in the User Manager in the Profiles dialog box (I said in the last chapter that I'd get to it in this chapter). Open the User Manager for Domains, double-click on a user, click the Profiles button, and you see a dialog box like the one in Figure 7.13.

FIGURE 7.13:

Dialog box controlling user home directories, profiles, and logon scripts

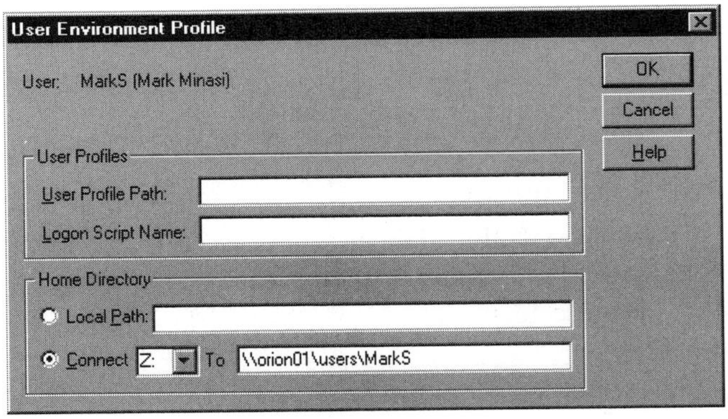

Notice the bottom field in the dialog box. It says, "Connect Z: To \\orion01\ users\MarkS." This dialog box is one of the most confusing in all of NT, and this field is no different. If you create a new user or highlight an existing user in the User Manager for Domains, then click Profiles and fill in a location in the To field, NT does several things:

- It remembers that whenever the user MarkS issues a command that involves Mark's home directory, then NT should use the MarkS directory which is in the USERS share on the server ORION01.

- *If* the directory \\orion01\users\MarkS does not yet exist, then NT creates the directory *and* sets its file and directory permissions so that only MarkS can access it.

- *If* the directory \\orion01\users\MarkS *does* exist, then NT does nothing to the directory, save to remember that it is MarkS's home directory.

Notice a couple of things here. First, the value in the To field *must* be a universal naming convention (UNC). You cannot fill it with something like C:\USERS\ MARKS, because, recall, this is a domain-wide account. If you were allowed to tell NT to put a user's one and only home directory on C:\USERS\MARKS, then NT would have to wonder, "*Which* C:?" There are a lot of machines in the domain, and they all have a C:. That's why you need a UNC.

Second, you're probably going to try this out on your network's domain controller, and it is likely to fail. Microsoft tells you in the NT manual to do something like this: fill in a UNC in the To field of the "Profile" dialog box to have NT automatically create the home directory. But it ain't so, and it will fail because *NT does not share the USERS directory by default*. (As NT 4 no longer seems to *create* a USERS directory in the first place, this seems reasonable, although it confused me a bit under NT 3.*x*.) As USERS isn't shared, no UNC can refer to USERS, so the attempt fails.

Third (this *still* sounds like a lot of work), how can I get NT to create home directories for dozens of users all in one operation? Follow these steps:

1. In the User Manager for Domains, highlight the users for which you want User Manager for Domains to create home directories. You can select users at random by holding down the Ctrl key and left-clicking on the names for which you want to create home directories.

2. Choose User ➤ Properties. You see a list of the users you selected, and the Groups, Profile, Hours, Logon To, and Account buttons. The User Manager for Domains is functioning just as it always does, except it's simultaneously working on multiple users.

3. Click Profile.

4. Now, in the bottom field where it said "To \\orion01\users\marks" before, you want to put in a kind of "wildcard" value that will work for any user. There is such a thing, the %username% built-in variable. Just fill in the To field with *servername***USERS****%user-name&**, where *servername* is the name of whatever server holds the home directories. The disk grinds for a moment or two, and in a trice NT has created a pile of home directories.

By the way, if you're wondering what the *other* fields in the Profiles dialog of the User Manager for Domains are good for, hang on for a page or two, because I'll get to them.

Attaching NT Users to Home Directories

Now that you've gotten all of those home directories built, how do you get the users connected to them? Recall that I've been saying that home directories aren't as easy under NT as they should be—here's where you'll see the truth of this.

If your users are running NT on their desktops, then it's relatively simple. You first should have Service Pack 3 on the computer where the USERS share resides, and second, you should install the Distributed File System (Dfs), a free NT upgrade from Microsoft.

You'll find the Dfs upgrade program on Microsoft's Web site. Microsoft has an irritating way of re-arranging their Web site periodically, so this URL may no longer work by the time you read this, but I've most recently found Dfs at www.microsoft.com/windows/downloads/contents/other/ntsdistrfile/default .asp. If it's not there, search the Microsoft Web site for "Distributed File System." (Please *don't* e-mail me asking for the current URL; I don't keep track of where Microsoft puts things, and I won't be able to help. Unfortunately, all I'd do is suggest that you search for "Distributed File System.") There's both an Alpha and an Intel version of the Dfs program; the Intel file is called dfs_v41_i386.exe.

Once you've downloaded the Intel version of the file, you need to install it:

1. Copy the file to the server that you host USERS on.

2. Then, run the program. It will copy some files into a new directory: \winnt\system32\dfs.

3. Install the Dfs service. Start the Control Panel and open up the Networking applet. Click on the Services tab and click the Add button.

4. Click the Have Disk button and fill in the location of the newly copied Dfs files—C:\WINNT\SYSTEM32\DFS, D:\WINNT\SYSTEM32\DFS, or wherever they went. Then click OK.

5. You'll see a dialog box labeled Select OEM Option with just one option—Distributed File System. Click OK.

6. A dialog box will then appear labeled Configure Dfs containing a check box labeled Host a Dfs on share; check the box.

7. Once you check the box, you'll get a drop-down single-selection list box showing the current shares on that server. One of them will be USERS; click USERS and click OK to clear the Configure Dfs dialog box.

8. Click Close to close the Network applet. You'll have to reboot for Dfs to start up.

Once you've installed the Dfs code on the server, you're done. From now on, whenever you log on to your domain account from an NT workstation, you'll automatically be connected to your home directory.

Attaching Non-NT Users to Home Directories

The reason that you had to go find and install Dfs on the server containing your home directories is because NT can't do something called a *deep net use*. NetWare people know of this, but they call it by another name—*map root*.

Suppose we've got a server named HOMES and it's got a share named USERS on it; as you know, the UNC for that is \\HOMES\USERS. But you've got a user named Dana, and her home directory is in the Dana directory of \\HOMES\USERS. You can try simply connecting her to the home directory by adding a line to her logon batch script like this:

```
net use h: \\homes\users
```

But this is of no real value, as Dana's dumped into the middle of the Users directory rather than users\dana. Not very user friendly. It would be *much* better if we could instead put this line in the logon script:

```
net use h: \\homes\users\dana
```

This notion of mapping a drive letter to a directory *inside* a share is called a "deep" net use. You can do such a net use—but only if the server is using Dfs and if your workstation is running a Dfs client. That's why it works in NT, as NT 4 has included the Dfs client since its release in August 1996 (which is why you didn't have to add anything to your NT workstations); the Dfs server-side code didn't appear until later (which is why you had to download some extra code from Microsoft). Now, Microsoft *does* make a Dfs client for Windows 95, and Dfs support is built right into Windows 98, *but* they neglected to include the deep net use support. (This is to nudge corporate America to throw away Windows and use NT instead, I guess.)

The result? You've got a bunch of work to do. One approach might be to first connect to the Users directory, then do a SUBST to create a mapped drive letter to a directory inside USERS, something like the following:

```
net use x: \\homes\users
subst h: x:\dana
```

Sadly, SUBST is on to us—you'll get "you cannot SUBST a network drive" if you try. The best bet is to do a CD to the user's directory, like this:

```
net use h: \\homes\users
h:
cd h:\dana
```

The problem is that it's very time consuming, as you'll have to hand-modify every user's logon batch script. One thing that you can do to make it a bit simpler in some cases is to use the /home parameter of net use—that connects to a user's home directory, like so:

```
net use h: /home
h:
cd h:\dana
```

The /home tells the client machine to ask the domain controller where to find a home directory. Unfortunately, I've found that this *doesn't* work on Windows 98 clients—grumble, grumble, grumble...

Take Note: Administrators Can't Normally Access Home Directories

Suppose you've just created a user directory for someone named James. You've created USERS\JAMES, cleaned out all permissions, and inserted James as the only person with any right to access USERS\JAMES. But you're an administrator, so you can still get in, right?

Try it. Open a command prompt and type **dir c:\users\james**. You'll be told that the directory is empty, even if it isn't. Try to access it from the Explorer or My Computer and you'll be flatly refused entry: "C:\USERS\JAMES is not accessible."

This *really* upsets some administrators, but it's the NT default, and I don't think it's all that bad. I mean, this *is* supposed to be a secure network, right? And besides, an administrator can usually add him- or herself to the ACL for a file or directory— or an administrator can seize control of an object by taking ownership of the object, as I'll describe soon. But before I cover ownership, let me get past a few other issues: changing file and directory permissions from the command line, understanding the default file and directory permissions on a newly installed NT Server, and auditing file access.

Controlling File and Directory Permissions from the Command Line

You've seen that you can control file and directory permissions from the GUI, but sometimes you want to make permission changes from the command line. The tool for that is CACLS. CACLS only works on NTFS volumes, and it doesn't let you change share-level permissions, only file and directory permissions.

Its syntax looks like this:

```
CACLS filename [/T] [/E] [/C] [/G username:permission] [/R username
[...]][/P username:permission [...]] [/D username [...]]
```

where each option works as follows:

- If you only specify a filename, you see the current ACL for the file or files (wildcards are acceptable). For example, you might see a response like "letter.txt Everyone: (OI) (CI) F," which means that the Everyone group has Full Control.

- /T says that whatever changes you make to a directory should also be applied to all files in the directory and all subdirectories of that directory.

- /C means to continue on access denied errors. If you make a change to a group of files, there may be files in that group whose ACLs you don't have the right to change. This says to keep on going and do whatever can be done.

- /G *username:permission* grants specified user access rights. Permission can be R (Read), C (Change), or F (Full Control). For example, "cacls letter.txt /g MarkS:F" would give Full Control to user MarkS. But note that this will remove any existing permissions to access letter.txt; if, for example, the Everyone group had Full Control before this command, Everyone would no longer have access after this. If that's not what you want—if you want to *add* items to the list of approved users, rather than wipe out the list altogether and start over—use the /E parameter.

- /E adds the ACL entry to the existing ACLs rather than deleting existing ACLs. In the previous example, "cacls letter.txt /e /g MarkS:F" would have added MarkS to the list of approved users of letter.txt, and Everyone would still be on the list of approved users.

- /R *username* revokes specified user's access rights (only valid with /E).

- /P *username:permission* replaces specified user's access rights. As before, the valid values for *permission* are N (No Access), R (Read), C (Change), and F (Full Control). Note that this will act like option G in that not only will you change the user's permission, you will also zap any existing users. For example, if letter.txt has MarkS with Full Control and Everyone with Full Control, and you do "cacls letter.txt /P MarkS:C," you'll demote MarkS from Full Control to Change as well as remove Everyone from the list altogether! Note the difference between /G and /P: /G adds a new user to the list and /P just modifies an existing user on a list.

- /D *username* denies specified user access.

You may find this useful when creating large directories and setting their permissions automatically. For example, to add Domain Admins to each home directory, giving that group Full Control, type **CACLS C:\USERS /T /E /G "DomainAdmins" :F**. Along the same lines, the *Resource Kit* includes a program called *SCOPY*. SCOPY is a large-scale file-copying program very much like XCOPY, but with the added benefit that it not only copies the files, but copies the security information (the ACLs) of the files, as well.

Default Directory Permissions for NT Server Directories

Before you leave the topic of permissions, you may find Table 7.3 useful. It is a compilation of all of the default directory permissions of NT Server (and NT) directories. Subdirectories and files created in these directories will inherit the directory permissions unless you set their permissions to something else. Although several of the system directories seem to give the Everyone group Change permission, many of these directories are not accessible over the network unless you are a member of the Administrators or Server Operators groups (see the earlier section on share permissions and administrative shares).

TABLE 7.3:   Default Directory Permissions in NT Server

Directory	Groups (Permissions)
\ (root directories of all NTFS volumes)	Administrators (Full Control)
	Server Operators (Change)
	Everyone (Change)
	CREATOR OWNER (Full Control)
\SYSTEM32	Administrators (Full Control)
	Server Operators (Change)
	Everyone (Change)
	CREATOR OWNER (Full Control)
\SYSTEM32\CONFIG	Administrators (Full Control)
	Everyone (List)
	CREATOR OWNER (Full Control)
\SYSTEM32\DRIVERS	Administrators (Full Control)
	Server Operators (Full Control)
	Everyone (Read)
	CREATOR OWNER (Full Control)

Continued on next page

TABLE 7.3 CONTINUED: Default Directory Permissions in NT Server

Directory	Groups (Permissions)
\SYSTEM32\SPOOL	Administrators (Full Control)
	Server Operators (Full Control)
	Print Operators (Full Control)
	Everyone (Read)
	CREATOR OWNER (Full Control)
\SYSTEM32\REPL	Administrators (Full Control)
	Server Operators (Full Control)
	Everyone (Read)
	CREATOR OWNER (Full Control)
\SYSTEM32\REPL\IMPORT	Administrators (Full Control)
	Server Operators (Change)
	Everyone (Read)
	CREATOR OWNER (Full Control)
	Replicator (Change)
	NETWORK*
\SYSTEM32\REPL\EXPORT	Administrators (Full Control)
	Server Operators (Change)
	CREATOR OWNER (Full Control)
	Replicator (Read)
\USERS	Administrators (Change)
	Account Operators (Change)
	Everyone (List)
\USERS\DEFAULT	Everyone (RWX)
	CREATOR OWNER (Full Control)

Continued on next page

TABLE 7.3 CONTINUED: Default Directory Permissions in NT Server

Directory	Groups (Permissions)
\WIN32\APP	Administrators (Full Control)
	Server Operators (Full Control)
	Everyone (Read)
	CREATOR OWNER (Full Control)
\TEMP	Administrators (Full Control)
	Server Operators (Change)
	Everyone (Change)
	CREATOR OWNER (Full Control)

* No Access, except for Administrators, Server Operators, and Everyone. This is the only case where No Access does not override previously granted permissions.

Permissions on Newly Moved, Copied, and Created Files

Suppose you have a file in one directory with a particular set of file permissions and you copy it to *another* directory, which has a *different* set of permissions. Does the copied file have the permissions of the old directory or the new directory? What if you move a file? Copy a file? Move or copy a file from a FAT drive to an NTFS drive?

According to the NT documentation, the general rule for permissions is this: when you copy or create a file to a directory, the newly created file or copy takes on the permissions of the directory that it's in. If you *move* a file, then it takes its permissions with it. (That's basically right, except that it seems to be impossible to move a file from one logical drive to another without losing its permissions, but let's focus first on the basic principles and then take up the exception.)

For example, suppose on an NTFS volume I have directory DIR1 with file and directory permissions Everyone/Full Control, and directory DIR2 with file and directory permissions Everyone/Change. Also, I've got a file called FILE1 in DIR1; its permissions will be Everyone/Full Control unless they've been explicitly changed. I copy FILE1 to DIR2. DIR2\FILE1 will have permissions Everyone/Change. Next, I move FILE1 from DIR1 to DIR2. FILE1's permissions will *remain*

Everyone/Full Control. Finally, I create a new file FILE2 in DIR2. Its permissions will be Everyone/Change. Of course, both DIR1 and DIR2 must be directories on an NTFS volume, as FAT volumes don't maintain permissions.

But suppose I move a file from a FAT volume to an NTFS volume? Then NTFS treats the move like a file creation; the file moved from the FAT volume gets the permissions of the directory to which it was moved.

As I mentioned above, the exception seems to be moving files from one volume to another. If I move a file from D:\DIR1 to E:\DIR2, whether with the Explorer or from the command line, the file that is now in E:\DIR2 seems always to take on the permissions of the E:\DIR2 directory, in contradiction to Microsoft documentation. (Again, this assumes that both D: and E: are NTFS volumes.)

By the way, whether you move, copy, or create a file, you assume something called the *ownership* of that file—but more on that in a few pages.

Monitoring Access to Files and Directories

In any network, the administrator needs at times to monitor user activity, not just to assess network performance, but for security reasons. NT Server provides administrators the opportunity to audit events that occur on the network. It maintains three different types of logs in which to record information: the Applications log, the System log, and the Security log, as you've seen if you've ever looked in the Event Viewer.

In order to record, retrieve, and store log entries of events, the administrator must activate auditing on the server. Not surprisingly, file and directory auditing is activated within the Security menu, either the Security menu from the NT 3.*x* File Manager or the Security tab in the Windows Explorer ➤ My Computer in NT 4.

Auditing for File and Object Access

With NT Server, an administrator can specify which groups or users, as well as which actions, should be audited for any particular directory or file. The information is collected and stored in the Security log and can be viewed in the Event Viewer.

For directories and files to be audited, *you must first* set the security audit policy in User Manager for Domains to allow the auditing of file and object access. To do this, open User Manager for Domains and, from the Policies menu, choose Audit. You see the dialog box shown in Figure 7.14.

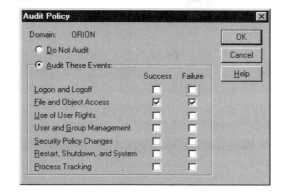

One of the auditing options available in the list is File and Object Access; make sure you select it. As you can see from the dialog box, you can audit both successful and failed accesses.

Auditing Directory and File Access

After activating file and object access auditing, you have to choose which files and/or directories, as well as which groups or users who might use the files and directories, you specifically want audited.

To do this, highlight the desired directory or file in the Windows Explorer window. Then, from the Security menu, choose Auditing. If you've selected a file for auditing, you see the dialog box in Figure 7.15.

You can choose a specific set of events to audit for each different group or user in the Name list. In this example, everyone's access to the file UPDATE.TXT is subject to auditing; however, only failed attempts to read, write, execute, and delete (as well as a successful deletion of the file) are actually recorded in the Security log. To add users and groups to those whose access to the file is being audited, click the Add button and specify the new users and groups in the resulting dialog box. Remove a user or group by clicking on it in the current Name list and selecting Remove.

If you are setting up auditing for a directory, there are two additional options to consider, Replace Auditing on Subdirectories and Replace Auditing on Existing Files. Figure 7.16 shows these two options in the Directory Auditing dialog box.

FIGURE 7.15:

Setting up file auditing

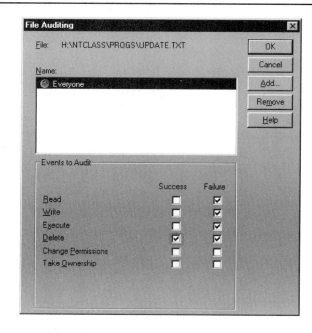

FIGURE 7.16:

Setting up directory auditing

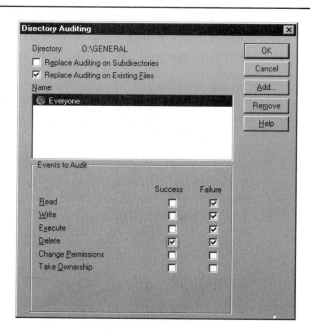

The default replace option is Replace Auditing on Existing Files. When this option is selected, changes made to auditing apply to the directory and the files within that directory only, not to any subdirectories in the directory. To apply auditing changes to the directory and its files as well as existing subdirectories within the directory and their files, check both boxes. Clearing both boxes applies the changes in auditing to the directory only, not to any of the files or subdirectories contained within it. Selecting only Replace Auditing on Subdirectories applies audit changes to the directory and subdirectories only, not to existing files in either.

As with file auditing, you can set auditing for each group or user in the list by selecting the name of a group or user in the Names list and specifying which events will be audited for that group or user.

To remove file auditing for a group or user, select that group or user and select Remove. To add groups or users to the audit, use the Add option. When you are satisfied with the auditing options, choose OK. The results appear in the Event Viewer. The Viewer isn't the clearest thing in the world, but it gives you the rough information you need to track a security violation—provided auditing is enabled. On the other hand, auditing costs in terms of CPU time and disk space; if you turn on all file audits, you will fill up your event log in no time at all.

Creating a Drop Box

Have you been looking for a way to allow your users to view and submit paperless memos or other documents online? Try creating a *drop box*—a repository folder where users can save data and documents and read other files without allowing users to change or delete the items of the folder.

Creating a drop box is as simple as changing the permissions of a folder. Just create the folder in a public area on your server's hard drive where you want your repository to be. Right-click on the folder and select Properties. Select the Security tab and click Permissions. Remove everything except the Everyone group from the dialog box and change its permissions to Add & Read. If you want to have control over the folder and its contents, give Full Control to Domain Administrators but restrict everyone else to Add & Read. Don't share the folder—if you do, the permissions of the folder and its files will be changed to those of the share. Instead, create a shortcut to the folder.

Users will now be able to save documents to this directory and read everything inside the folder, but they won't be able to make changes to the content.

File Ownership in NT

All this talk of file permissions leads to an interesting question (well, interesting to *me*, but then I don't get out much). What happens if I use the GUI or CACLS to remove every entry in the ACLs? No one has access to the file, rendering it sort of useless. *Now* what do we do?

We find the file's owner.

You see, even when an ACL list has been completely cleaned out, there is in fact an extra, invisible entry. A directory or file's "owner" always has full control. Who is the owner of a file? By default, it's the person who created it. It's also possible to take ownership of a file if you have the permission to do so.

The Definition of "Ownership"

Now, having worked with NT since its inception, I don't mind telling you that the whole idea of a directory or file's "owner" seemed a bit confusing until I finally figured out the definition of a file or directory's owner. Here's my definition (and from this point on, let me shorten "file or directory" to "object"): an object's owner is a user who can *always* modify that object's permissions, no matter what entries are in the object's ACL.

Ordinarily, it is only an administrator who can control things like an object's permissions. But you want users to be able to control things in their own area, their own home directory, without having to involve you at every turn. For instance, suppose I have a directory in my home directory that I want to give another user access to. Rather than having to seek out an administrator and ask the administrator to extend access permissions to that other user, I as the owner can change the permissions directly. Ownership is a way for NT to allow you to make users into mini-administrators, rulers of their small fiefdoms.

You can see who owns an object by right-clicking on the object and choosing Properties. You then see a dialog box with several tabs, one of which is Security. Click the Security tab and you see an Ownership button. Click that, and you see who owns the object, as in Figure 7.17.

FIGURE 7.17:

Viewing the owner of a file or directory

Experimenting with Ownership

If the implications of ownership aren't clear yet, let me walk you through a little exercise you can do to experiment with ownership. To do this experiment, you will need

- An account with administrative powers

- An account with normal user powers

- A PC running NT workstation

- A home directory for the normal user account

Like many administrators, I have two accounts: a Mark account that has only the powers of normal mortals, and a MarkS account that has administrative powers (the *S* is for "Supervisor"). You need the NT workstation machine because it has the versions of Explorer and My Computer that include the Security tab. (Actually, you can also get those from Windows 95 if you load the NT Server Tools for Windows 95, which are on the NT Server CD-ROM in the CLIENTS\ SRVTOOL directory.) The home directory should be a regulation home directory with file and directory permissions set only to the normal user account—"Mark" in my case—and no one else.

To start off, who owns Mark's, the normal user's, home directory? Well, an administrator created it, so the Administrators group owns it. If I look in the USERS directory on my primary domain controller, where my user home directories are, I will see that indeed Administrators owns the USERS\MARK directory.

So I'm now logged on as Mark, the mere mortal, and am attached to my home directory. I create a file in that home directory. If I check the security settings on the file, I'll see that Mark owns the file. If I create a directory in my home directory, then I'll own that, too. Check the file and directory permissions and you'll see that they've inherited the file and directory permissions of the directory they were created in, and so only Mark has access to them. Now I'll create a directory called SECRET, where I'll store things I don't want anyone else to see.

What I've accomplished so far is to see that when I create a file, I own that file. Now let's see what that does to an imaginary snoopy administrator who wants to poke around my private files.

Assuming the role of that snoopy administrator, I log off and log back on as MarkS, the administrator. It doesn't matter what machine I log on to, because the USERS share has share-level permissions of Everyone/Full Control. I attach to USERS and see that, not surprisingly, there is a directory called MARK, which is the user Mark's home directory. I try to look in \USERS\MARK and I'm denied access because only Mark has access to this directory. Hmmm… What *can* an administrator do? Well, I could just add myself to the list of people with access to Mark's home directory, heh heh… I access the Permissions dialog box, and sure enough, only Mark has access. I add MarkS and I now have access to Mark's directory.

Snooping in Mark's home directory, I see that folder named SECRET. Hey, that sounds interesting; let's take a look. I double-click the SECRET folder and get that snotty "Access denied" message because Mark is the only one with access to that folder. Well, we've gotten past *that* before, right? I just click the button to see the permissions for the Secret folder… and get "Access denied."

Huh?

Well, the SECRET folder is owned by Mark. The only permissions for the SECRET folder are Mark's. The MarkS account is never mentioned in the ACL for SECRET. So MarkS can't get in.

How did MarkS get into \USERS\MARK in the *first* place? After all, MarkS had no permissions for *that*, either. Yet he was able to access and change the permissions for \USERS\MARK.

The answer? MarkS is an administrator. Administrators own \USERS\MARK because they created it—they create *all* home directories. So, as MarkS was an owner, MarkS can always change the permissions on \USERS\MARK—remember, that's the definition of an owner. But *Mark* created SECRET, not *MarkS*, so Mark is the owner. Moreover, in addition to being the owner, Mark is the only person on the ACL, so MarkS has no access to Mark's SECRET directory.

Sound scary for administrators? Fear not, there's a way to seize control; read on.

Taking Ownership

Look back at Figure 7.17, and you will see a button in the Owner dialog box labeled Take Ownership. Snoopy MarkS can't force himself onto the ACL for \USERS\MARK\SECRET, but he *can* become the owner and, once he's the owner, *then* he can add himself to the ACL.

Logged on as MarkS, I attempt to bring up the Ownership dialog box. The system sees that I'm not the owner and that I don't have any access to the object. It shows the dialog box you see in Figure 7.18.

FIGURE 7.18:

Attempting to seize ownership

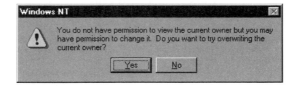

If I click Yes, I will be told that the system couldn't retrieve the ownership information, but other than that the next dialog box looks like the one in Figure 7.17. If I click Take Ownership, then I become the owner. Can I then see what's in SECRET? No, because I'm still not on the ACL. Keep this basic truth in mind: owners of files can't necessarily access those files.

> **NOTE** Owners of files can't necessarily access those files. All owners of files can do is to change the permissions on those files.

Okay then, how do I get to SECRET? Well, since I'm an owner, I can change permissions. So I'll add myself to the ACL and *then* gain access to SECRET.

Now, why was MarkS able to do that? Because of a user right that administrators all have—"Take ownership of files and other objects." By default, administrators have that right. I suppose if you were a more user-oriented than administrator-oriented company, you could remove the Administrators group from that right. If you did that, there would be *no* way for an administrator to poke around a user's area.

Further, a user can always shore up her security just a bit by taking control of her home directory from the Administrators. Recall that each user has Full Control of her home directory, and Full Control includes the ability to take ownership of an object.

And if you're concerned about the fact that an administrator can take control at any time—where's the security in that?—then consider that the administrator must *take* ownership in order to add herself to the object's ACL. In doing that, she leaves fingerprints behind. If I log on one day and find that I'm no longer the owner of something that I owned yesterday, then I know that an administrator has been snooping. And if file auditing is in place, then I can even find out who the snoop was.

Let's summarize what we've seen so far about permissions and ownership:

- By default, new files and new subdirectories inherit permissions from the directory in which they are created.

- A user who creates a file or directory is the owner of that file or directory, and the owner can control access to the file or directory by changing the permissions on it (NT machines only).

- When you change the permissions on an existing directory, you can choose whether or not those changes apply to all files and subdirectories within the directory.

- Users and groups can be denied access to a file or directory simply by not granting the user or group any permissions for it. You don't have to assign No Access to every user or group that you want to keep out of a file or directory.

- Permissions are cumulative, except for No Access. No Access overrides all other permissions a user might have by virtue of his or her group membership.

Controlling the Rest of the Profile Dialog Box

In the last chapter, I promised I'd finish up explaining the rest of the Profile dialog box in the User Manager for Domains. I couldn't explain all of it then because it doesn't make much sense until you understand all of the file permissions stuff. Just in case you've forgotten, the Profile dialog box in the User Manager for Domain looks like Figure 7.19.

FIGURE 7.19:

Profile dialog box in User
Manger for Domains

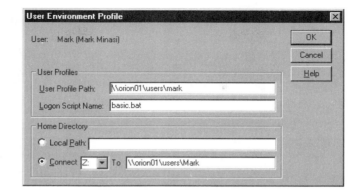

Three user factors are controlled from this dialog box:

- The location of an *NT* user profile, which is only relevant for people who use NT Workstation or NT Server machines as their personal workstations.

- The name of a logon batch script, which can be useful for someone running a client of virtually any sort save a Macintosh.

- The desired home directory, which is mainly a command that, like the user profile, is only of interest and use to people who use NT machines as workstations, and which has a side effect that you've already met, of reducing some of the donkey work for the administrator creating home directories.

One of the reasons I left all of this for later, as you can probably see, is the number of ifs, ands, and buts concerning these features.

Logon Batch Scripts

Most networks have the ability to kick off a set of commands whenever a user attaches to the network; NT's are called *logon scripts.* A logon script is simply a batch file (with the BAT or CMD filename extension) or an executable program (EXE extension). Logon scripts are set to run automatically whenever a user logs on, and the same script can be assigned to one or many user accounts. Unlike user profiles, logon scripts work on computers running on NT, Windows 9*x*, Windows for Workgroups, and MS-DOS. Logon scripts are used to configure users' working environments by making network connections and starting applications.

Applications of Logon Scripts

Logon scripts aren't as versatile as user profiles, but they are useful in the following situations:

- The network contains users using MS-DOS workstations (user profiles only work on NT workstations).

- You want to manage only part of the users' environments (for example, network connections) without managing or controlling the entire environment.

- You have an NT network using only personal (not mandatory) profiles, and want to create common network connections for multiple users without having to individually modify each profile.

- You have LAN Manager 2.*x* running on your network and you want to keep the logon scripts you made for that system.

Logon scripts are also easier to create and maintain than user profiles; depending on your network situation, they might be the better choice.

Where to Place a Logon Script

Whenever a user logs on, the server authenticating the logon looks for the logon script by following the server's logon script path (the default path is WINNT\ SYSTEM32\REPL\IMPORT\SCRIPTS, or WINNT\SYSTEM32\REPL\EXPORT\ SCRIPTS if you are setting up directory replication as explained in Chapter 11). If you place your logon script there, you only have to type in the name of the script itself in the logon script path name box. If the logon script happens to be located in a subdirectory of the logon script path, include that relative path when you type in the name. The entire logon script path can be changed in Server Manager, under Directory Replication. Consult Chapter 11, on server management, for the procedure.

If your domain has more than one NT Server machine (configured as a PDC or BDC), any one of them may authorize a user's logon attempt, so copies of logon scripts for every user in the domain should exist on each of the servers in the domain. Using the Directory Replicator service is the best way to ensure this.

Creating a Logon Script

To create a logon script, simply create a batch file. This file can contain any valid batch commands. For example, you could have a batch file that contains the following two lines:

```
@echo off
net time \\orion01 /set /yes
```

This logon script synchronizes each workstation's clock with that of the primary server in the domain (which, in this case, is the computer \\orion01). As far as I'm concerned, all logon scripts should start with the time synchronization command NET TIME; that way, all of the workstations' times are in sync with the server's. (Of course, before you make everyone fall in line with the server, it would be a good idea to find one of those shareware programs that lets your server dial a time source somewhere and ensure that its time is exactly right. Such a program is in the NT *Resource Kit*.)

Not to belabor the point, but here's another reason to synchronize network time. We had a workstation whose calendar was several months behind; it thought it was March when we were actually in June. Oddly enough, any file saved to the server by that workstation was time-stamped March rather than June! I say "oddly" because when a workstation saves data to a server, it just says to the server, "Time-stamp this with this time and date," and the server blindly obeys. The only possible reason I could imagine for this would be that Microsoft wanted to support people who would have networks that span time zones. But even then, time zones shouldn't be so problematic, because Windows 9x and Windows NT workstations all know what time zone they're in, and some little kludge could certainly have been worked up for the DOS and Windows for Workgroups workstations! (I guess the guy who did the time-stamp is also the one who's responsible for the missing disk quota feature.) If you log on to a Windows NT workstation as a regular user rather than an administrator or power user, you get an error message (error 1340) if you try to set the time on the workstation, because for some reason regular old users aren't allowed to set time. I just change the user right "Change the system time" and extend it to all users, in particular the Domain Users group in my domain.

By the way, if **net time \\orion01 /set /yes** seems like a lot of typing, you can shorten it. Read the following tip…

TIP

You can tell an NT machine to be the "official" time source of the domain by going to the HKEY_LOCAL_MACHINE\System\Current Control Set\Services\LAN MAN SERVER\Parameters. Add a new key TimeSource of the type REG_DWORD and set it to 1. After you reboot the machine, you can enter the command **net time /set /yes** to have the PC *find* the time source. You must have at least one time server per domain.

Besides the NET TIME command, here's another one you'll find useful:

```
net use h: /home
```

Once you've created home directories for your DOS, Windows for Workgroups, and Windows 9*x* users, you'll be a bit disappointed at what you see of those directories when you log on… *nothing*! Merely having a defined home directory doesn't do anything for those machines; they still need a NET USE command to attach to the directories. That's the benefit of the /home option: the command above says to your DOS, Windows for Workgroups, or Windows 9*x* workstation, "Go interrogate the primary domain controller about where my home directory is, then attach me to it as drive H:." (Of course, you needn't use H:.)

NOTE

Even though you use the NET USE command as I suggested, you will find that your user will now see not his home directory but instead the root directory of *all* of the home directories! This is caused by a flaw in the network redirector software that you'll find in all Microsoft products. The best that NET USE can do is to point the user to the top of the home directory share. To do more specific, or "deep," NET USE commands, you will need an upcoming NT technology, the *distributed file system* or dfs, which will first appear in Windows 2000 Server. For now, either you can take your chances with the Dfs beta that you can download from Microsoft's Web site, or you can write more complex logon batch files.

Other than those two commands, you can put messages in logon scripts, run antivirus programs, or do a number of other things, depending on your network's needs. But keep your logon scripts short if your network uses Windows and Windows for Workgroups machines. When a Windows 3.*x* user who has been assigned a logon script logs on, the machine starts a virtual DOS session in which to execute the script. The virtual DOS session typically lasts only about 30 seconds and isn't configurable. If the script takes longer than that, it will quit and the user will get a system integrity violation error. This is especially a problem for remote users working over slow links (for example, using RAS or a TCP/IP gateway over async modem lines).

At worst, you can disable script operation for users with the following procedure:

1. In Control Panel, choose the Network icon.

2. Choose the Networks button.

3. In the Other Networks In Use box, select Microsoft LAN Manager.

4. Choose the Settings option.

5. Clear the Logon to LAN Manager Domain check box.

Using the Logon Script Variables

You can use several wildcards as you write a logon script. They are listed in Table 7.4 (these script variables only work for people with NT workstations).

TABLE 7.4:   Logon Script Variables

Parameter	Description
%HOMEDRIVE%	A user's local workstation drive letter connected to the user's home directory
%HOMEPATH%	The full path name of the user's home directory
%HOMESHARE%	The share name containing the user's home directory
%OS%	The operating system of the user's workstation
%PROCESSOR%	The processor type (such as 80486) of the user's workstation
%USERDOMAIN%	The domain containing the user's account
%USERNAME%	The user name of the user

If you are typing up a logon script for multiple users who, for example, are not all in the same domain, you can type %USERDOMAIN% instead of an actual domain name in a command, and the system will automatically insert the specific user's domain when it executes the logon script.

In addition to the logon scripts, these wildcards can also be used in other situations, such as when specifying application path names in Program Manager, or when assigning user profiles and home directories to a number of users at once. On NTFS volumes, you can use the wildcards regardless of name length.

Controlling the Home Directory Setting

The last group in the Profile dialog box (see Figure 7.19) is labeled Home directory, but it includes two seemingly unrelated items offered in the form of radio buttons:

- Local Path

- Connect *driveletter* To

Since this is a set of radio buttons, the choices are mutually exclusive and collectively exhaustive (gosh, I love that phrase). In English, you've got to choose one or t'other. Just what is this all about?

Well, first of all, it is vitally important to understand what the radio buttons mean on DOS, Windows for Workgroups, and Windows 9x workstations. In fact, it's so important that I'm going to put it in a tip.

TIP　　Choosing between the two radio buttons in the Home Directory group is almost totally meaningless on DOS, Windows for Workgroups, and Windows 9x workstations. It is only relevant if you use an NT Workstation or NT Server machine as your workstation.

The last group shouldn't be labeled "Home Directory"; it should be labeled "default directory." If you're at a computer running NT and you open a command prompt, what shows up at the command line? C:\>? D:\USERS\IGNATZ? It's controlled by this group in the Profiles field.

Local Path versus Connect...

What the choice between Local Path and Connect really means is, "When a program asks NT for a default directory, do you want that program directed to a network-based personal directory, which will coincidentally act in all other ways like a home directory, or do you want NT to direct the program to a local drive like C:, D:, or the like?"

The consequences of someone's choosing Connect *driveletter* to *UNC* will be that, over time, more and more of her data will end up in her personal directory on some server, rather than her local hard disk. When she installs a new program, it will usually offer to install itself on the personal network area, rather than the local hard disk. In contrast, choosing *local directory* and pointing to some drive letter will mean that things tend to happen on the local hard disk. I'm saying "tend to" because there's nothing keeping that user from overriding the defaults and storing any program or any data anywhere she wants (assuming she has the permissions). Most of us, however, take the defaults and go.

If you *do* choose the Connect radio button, you have to put a UNC into the last field; drive letters won't work. If you want to hard-wire a drive letter in there, select the Local Path option.

Reconciling Home Directories with Non-NT Workstations

Reconciling home directories with non-NT workstations can be tremendously confusing if you chose the Connect option to create a home directory for a DOS user. That's why it's vitally important to understand that the Home Directory group in the Profiles dialog box performs a double duty, and in some ways those duties have nothing to do with each other.

For a DOS, Windows for Workgroups, or Windows 9x workstation, it is convenient to make the domain (that is, the SAM account's user database, which lives on the primary domain controller) aware of a designated home directory for a particular user. It's useful because

- Windows 9x workstations automatically keep Windows 9x user profiles there, provided you are running the right network client software.

- When you execute a "NET USE *driveletter* /home," your workstation asks the primary domain controller where its home directory is.

That's about all you get in terms of benefits from having a home directory on an NT domain if you're not running an NT machine of some kind as your workstation, but the benefits are significant. NT's home directory function offers only one other benefit and you've already met it—it will create and set permissions for home directories for users automatically. (Remember that if the user's home directory already exists, NT won't change the permissions.)

What is even more confusing is the design of the home directory group. I could enter **Connect X:** to **\\orion01\users\mark**, and, assuming that Mark doesn't use an NT machine as his workstation, he sees nothing in the way of a home directory when he boots up. Even more bizarre, when he executes **NET USE h: /home**, he ends up with a home directory mapped to drive *H:* rather than X:! Nowhere does the dialog box say, "When you designate a drive letter in the 'Connect...' field, NT will ignore it." And yet that's exactly what happens, unless you use NT or NT Server machines as workstations. Oh, and one more thing, before I end this chapter...

How Do You Set Disk Quotas in NT?

I've mentioned disk quotas elsewhere in the book, but it's important enough to mention it here as well, because someone may flip through the table of contents and look for the answer here. The *question* is, "How can I restrict how much data my users can put in their home directories?" After all, home directories are on a shared volume, and one jerk who uploads his entire 1.3GB of data from his laptop onto his home directory on the server may well fill the disk and make everyone else unable to save data to their home directories. What can we do to prevent that?

Quotas *Really* Arrive in the Next Version

Well, Cairo—oops, I meant NT 5, oh darn, what I *really* meant was Windows 2000 Server, there, now I've got it right—will include a disk quota manager of some kind. But what about NT 4 users? Well, there are a couple of third-party tools around, but they don't supply review copies to journalists, which kinda makes you wonder...

This is one of the great frustrations about NT. Novell administrators have been able to set disk limitations on their users for *years*—nearly 10 years, in fact. Unix admins have similar powers. Perhaps most frustrating, NT's precursor, LAN Manager, could enforce disk quotas, making a move from LAN Manager to NT a slight "downgrade" rather than an upgrade! (And while I'm complaining, let's mention another thing that Novellians can do that we can't—control simultaneous logins. There is no way under NT to forbid more than one person to log in using the same account name and password. As a result, there are shops all over where everyone logs in using the default Administrator password, because the person who set up NT said, "It would be easier that way." Furthermore, the next version of NT will continue to support simultaneous logins. A Microsoft person I once asked about it said flatly, "We don't know how to solve that problem.")

But until Then, There's Proquota (and It's Free)

There's some good news, although not *great* news, if you're using Service Pack 4: a program called *Proquota*. It's not exactly a disk quota, but it does something a bit like it, with two big limitations:

- It allows you to set a maximum size on a user's *profile*, rather than a more sweeping maximum size on all files for a user, but that can still be useful, as we'll see.

- The program is of use only if the users run NT as their desktop operating system; Proquota does nothing at all to control how much data a Windows for Workgroups, Windows 95, or Windows 98 user saves on NT servers.

That last limitation is a big one, and it may render Proquota useless for many of you. If not, however, here's how to set up and use Proquota.

How Proquota Works

Proquota is a client-side, rather than a server-side, tool. A program, PROQUOTA .EXE, runs on each user's workstation. PROQUOTA.EXE constantly monitors the size of the user's profile, checking that profile's size against a maximum size (in kilobytes) stored in the user's Registry. If the profile ever exceeds that maximum allowable size, Proquota nags the user about it, popping dialog boxes up on the user's desktop until Proquota sees that the profile's down to the size it should be. Furthermore, Proquota won't let that user log off until she deletes enough files to get her profile down to its proper size.

Proquota can't really give you iron-fisted control of your network. All of the Proquota restrictions are enforced by PROQUOTA.EXE, which is just a program running under NT. Any user with a bit of knowledge can just start up the Task Manager, click the Processes tab, choose PROQUOTA.EXE, and click End Process. Task Manager will then remove PROQUOTA.EXE, and all annoying messages will disappear. Now, most users won't *know* that, but it's still a bit of a weakness.

Setting Up Proquota

Assuming that you're using only NT on the desktop and can live with Proquota's disadvantages (and it's worth noting that while Proquota's got disadvantages, it's hard to complain too much, as it *is* free), how to set it up?

Step One is to install Service Pack 4 on all user workstations. As near as I can tell, you actually don't have to put SP4 on the servers, but in my experience SP4's worth the install. On the other hand, I *have* heard of cases where putting SP4 on a server blew up the server, so use the normal cautions when installing any new software on an important machine.

Step Two is to tell NT to use Proquota and how much space to allow each user. As I noted before, you store each user's maximum profile space quotas in that user's NTUSER.DAT Registry hive. But what's the best way to propagate changes to a user's Registry settings?

Well, hopefully you answered "with system policies," as that's how it's done. Among the many files modified by Service Pack 4 is WINNT.ADM, one of the policy template files shipped with NT. Start up the System Policy Editor and open up a user policy; the resulting properties will look like Figure 7.20.

Note the new section: Windows NT User Profiles. Open it and you'll see a screen like the one in Figure 7.21.

FIGURE 7.20:

User Policies screen under
Service Pack 4

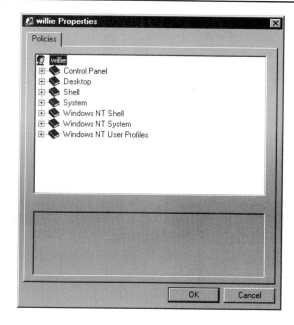

FIGURE 7.21:

Policies controlling
profile size

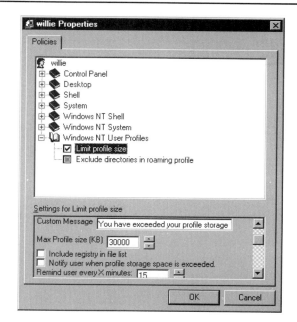

It includes two new check boxes: Limit profile size and Exclude directories in roaming profile. I have checked the former to display the panel in the bottom part of the dialog box; those are the controls you'll use to rein in profiles. Taken in order, here's what the controls do:

Limit profile size   You must check this box, or Proquota won't load at all.

Custom Message   This option allows you to tailor the message the user sees when he exceeds his alloted profile space. Once Proquota detects that the user's over his limit, it pops up a message box containing the text specified in this Custom Message field. Go with the default one, or get creative, as in Figure 7.22.

FIGURE 7.22:

Example of the dialog box a user might see after exceeding allowed profile disk space

NOTE   An over-quota user will also see a red circle with a cross in it appearing in the user's system tray, next to the time of day. When the user has space remaining in her profile, a small "profile" icon reports to her how much of that space remains.

Include Registry in file list   This says whether or not to count the size of the Registry file NTUSER.DAT when calculating the total number of bytes in a user's files. Users' Registry hives aren't normally that large, but I suppose if you're getting really picky it could be important.

Notify user when profile storage space is exceeded   This tells Proquota to put up the dialog boxes referred to by the Custom Message entry. If this isn't checked, then Proquota only checks to see if a user's profile's too big when she tries to log off. (As far as I can tell, there's no way to disable the profile size check at logoff.) This is just an on/off check box.

Remind user every *X* minutes   This means not only will we tell her that she's over her limit, we'll *nag* her about it. In this field, you specify a numeric value which is the number of minutes between nags.

If you *do* try to log off with a profile that's too large, you get a dialog box showing you how far over the line you are, as well as a list of the files in your profile, making it a bit easier to decide what you need to delete in order to log off. You see a sample dialog in Figure 7.23.

FIGURE 7.23:

Proquota dialog when a user tries to log off with too many files in a profile

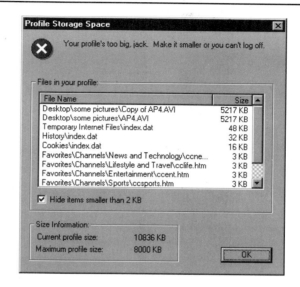

For some reason, this dialog shows you the files, but that's it. I'd expected that I could right-click them or something to delete right from this dialog, but no such luck. To delete files to get a profile down to the right size, do the deletions as you usually do, either from the command line or in the GUI.

Making This Useful

"All right, then," I hear you thinking, "This is nice, but what good does it do me?" Well, you can essentially make this a disk quota management system by only allowing users to save files within their profiles. In other words, don't provide any home directory save for some directory that is perhaps *inside* the user's desktop. If you install Internet Explorer 4 with Active Desktop on the users' machines, then they'll get a folder on their Desktop named "My Documents." Tell them to save their data there. That way, it'll roam with them when they go to other desktops, and the sum total of bytes in the files in My Documents will count against the profile quota. (I'm talking about storing profiles on central servers here: *roaming profiles*.)

There's one more thing to be concerned about when you do that. Suppose you have a roaming profile and log on to a machine that you've never logged on to before. NT by default makes a local copy of the entire roaming profile to whatever computer you're sitting at. Imagine if your profile contained 20MB of other user data—that would make logons a bit slower, eh? Okay, so nothing's perfect...

Proquota Registry Values

As you've seen, Proquota requires two pieces—the PROQUOTA.EXE program, which runs on each NT desktop, and some settings in the Registry, which give Proquota its marching orders. But what are those Registry entries? The following text summarizes them. All of these entries are stored in NTUSER.DAT, in HKEY_CURRENT_USER\Software\Microsoft\Windows\CurrentVersion\Policies\System.

EnableProfileQuota, type REG_DWORD, determines whether or not to run PROQUOTA.EXE at all, whether or not to track profile space. A value of 0 means "don't track profile space"; 1 means to track it.

MaxProfileSize, type REG_DWORD, tells how much space to allow the user. Entry is a numerical value equal to the number of kilobytes of allowed space; thus, to allow 4MB of profile space, set this to 4000 or 4096. (4096K is the *correct* value for four megabytes—a megabyte is 1,048,576 bytes, but in the past few years marketing people in the employ of hard disk manufacturers have attempted to redefine a megabyte to 1,000,000 bytes; that way, their drives appear to be larger than they actually are. Thus, if you're a hard drive marketer, use the former number; other people, the latter.)

WarnUser tells Proquota whether to nag the user when her profile space is exhausted. It's of type REG_DWORD, and if it's set to 1 then the nagging messages appear; if it's set to 0, no messages, save for the mandatory one that appears when she tries to log off with too much stuff in her profile.

ProfileQuotaMessage is a REG_SZ entry that you can use to tailor the nagging message to your personal taste.

WarnUserTimeout tells Proquota how *often* to nag the user. It's a REG_DWORD and you enter the number of minutes for Proquota to wait between messages. If WarnUser is set to 0, then this is irrelevant, as Proquota doesn't pop up messages in that case.

IncludeRegInProQuota tells Proquota whether to include the size of the Registry file in its profile size calculations. It's REG_DWORD: set to 1 to include the Registry, 0 to not include it.

Well, by now, you have some users, and they have places to put data. But things aren't really true until they're on paper, so we need some printers, and that's where the next chapter comes in.

Managing Printing Services with NT Server

- Looking at NT-specific print sharing features

- Adding a printer

- Customizing printer setup

- Working with a shared printer

- Printer security

- Creating separator pages

- Troubleshooting shared printing problems

Printers are essential in any office where computers are used. I mean, you really don't believe that something is true until you see it on paper, right? (If you don't believe me, wouldn't you feel a little unsure about a notice that you got a raise—delivered via e-mail?) Printers convert all those little electronic bits in your computer into hard copy.

But printers cost money, and, worse yet, they take up space. Laying equipment and toner costs aside, most offices wouldn't have enough office space to give a laser printer to every employee even if they *wanted* to.

Of course, one solution to the printer management and support problem is a network; hence this chapter. In this chapter, you'll learn about

- Creating and fine-tuning network printer queues

- Optimizing the printing process

- Controlling access to the printer

- Troubleshooting printing problems

NT Server uses some special vocabulary when discussing printers:

Network-interface printers   Whereas other printers connect to the network through a print server that is hooked into the network, network-interface printers are directly connected to the cabling without requiring an intermediary. These printing devices have built-in network cards.

Print server   The computer to which the printer is connected and on which the drivers are stored.

Printer   The *logical* printer as perceived by NT Server and NT. As you'll see during this chapter, the ratio of printers to printing devices is not necessarily one to one—you can have one printer and one printing device, one printer and multiple printing devices, or multiple printers and one printing device, or some combination of any of the above. We'll talk about the situations in which you might find each of these arrangements useful.

Printing device   The physical printer, that largish box with the display panel from which you pick up documents.

> **Queue**   This is a group of documents waiting to be printed. In OS/2, the queue is the primary interface between the application and the printing devices, but in NT Server and NT the printer takes its place.

NT-Specific Print Sharing Features

The unique printer sharing features that NT Server has can make the process of connecting to a networked print device easier than it is with other operating systems.

NT Workstations Don't Need Printer Drivers

If you're running an NT workstation with your NT Server, not needing printer drivers is likely one of your favorite features, as it makes the connection process a lot easier. When you're connecting the workstation to a printer on the server, you don't have to specify what kind of printer you want to connect to or tell the system where to find the drivers, as you do when connecting a Windows workstation to a networked printing device. Instead, you need only go to the Printers folder or Add New Printer Wizard (depending on which version of NT you are running, 3.*x* or 4.*x*), look to see what printers are shared on the network, and double-click on the one that you want. Once you've done that, you're connected.

TIP   If you're using Windows 95, by the way, you can also put printer drivers on a central location, removing the need to place them on Windows 95 workstations.

Direct Support of Printers with Network Interfaces

To use a network interface print device (that's one that connects directly to the network, rather than requiring parallel or serial connection to a print server, remember), you need only load the Data Link Control protocol onto the print server (unless you have a TCP/IP-based network interface print device). Although network interface print devices can connect directly to the network without an intervening print server, those network interface print devices still work best with a connection to a computer acting in the role of print server because they have only one incoming data path. With only one path, once the

[handwritten note: INTERFACE PRINT DEVICES WORK BETTER WITH COMPUTER ACTING AS A PRINT SERVER]

printer had received one print job, it would not be able to queue any others until that job was done. More paths mean more efficient use of printing time, as queuing means that you don't have to keep checking to see if the printer's done or worry about someone beating you to the printer.

Network interface printers can be useful because, although they still usually connect to a print server through the network media, they can be physically distant from it because they don't get jobs through the parallel or serial port. The network connection can also speed up the process of downloading documents to the printer, since a network connection is faster than a parallel or serial port. The speed difference isn't great, though, because the printer still has to access the drivers from the print server.

Totally Integrated Printer Support in One Program

The Printers folder in Control Panel takes care of all printer maintenance. To connect to, create, fine-tune, or manage a printer, you need only open the Printers folder.

Who Can Be a Print Server?

Like many networks today, your network's workstations and servers are likely to be pretty heterogeneous when it comes to operating systems. Print servers don't necessarily have to be your main file server, or even NT Server machines, but there are limitations on who can share a printer with the rest of the network.

Machines running the following operating systems can be print servers:

- Windows for Workgroups
- Windows 95
- Windows 98
- Windows NT
- Windows NT Server
- LAN Manager
- MS-DOS and Windows 3.1 (when running the MS-DOS Workgroup Add On)

Adding a Printer

The process of adding a printer to NT Server 4 has changed significantly from NT 3.51. Although the process is different, the functions have remained similar. With this incarnation of NT, Print Manager is no longer a part of the program. All of the functions previously found in Print Manager are now located in the Printers folder.

The Printers folder can be found by going to the Control Panel by way of the Start menu. For those of you familiar with NT 3.51 and before, the process of setting up a printer to be shared over the network was called "creating" it. Now you simply go to the Printer window and click on the Add Printer icon. The Printer Wizard walks you through the process of setting up a printer. The properties of the printer, giving permissions for groups to use the computer, and all other functions and settings for printers can be found in the Printers folder—more specifically, in the Properties dialog box in the File menu.

To add a printer, double-click on the Add Printer icon in the Printers folder. You see the opening dialog box of the Add Printer Wizard, as shown in Figure 8.1.

FIGURE 8.1:

Opening screen of the Add Printer Wizard

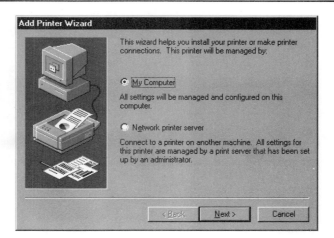

Choose Network printer server to connect your machine to a printer managed by another machine in your domain. Choose My Computer to set up a printer for your server to manage.

You need to set up your own printer (as opposed to connecting to one) if you are

- Physically installing a printer on a computer
- Physically installing a printer that connects directly to the network
- Defining a printer that prints directly to a file (no hard copy)
- Associating multiple printers with diverse properties for the same printing device

Click on My Computer and choose next. The Printer Wizard asks which port the printer is connected to, as shown in Figure 8.2. If you don't see your port listed, click on Add Port to see additional choices.

FIGURE 8.2:

Choosing a port for the printer

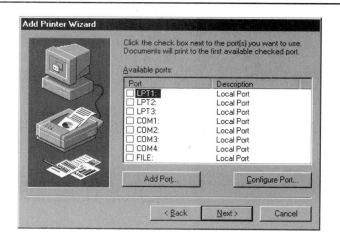

Click on Next when you are done to get to the next dialog box, which is shown in Figure 8.3. You are asked to tell the Printer Wizard who the manufacturer of the printer is. Click on the manufacturer on the left of the screen. On the right is a list of printers that they make. Choose the printer. If you wish to use the manufacturer's printer driver, click on Have Disk and follow the prompts. If you wish to use NT's printer driver, just click Next. If the driver you selected is already present, the Wizard asks if you want to replace it, as shown in Figure 8.4.

FIGURE 8.3:

Telling the Wizard which manufacturer and model your printer is

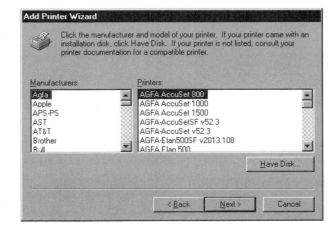

FIGURE 8.4:

Printer driver replacement dialog box

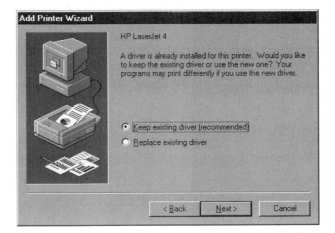

The Printer Wizard now asks you to name the printer, as you can see in Figure 8.5. The name can be up to 32 characters, including spaces. Click Next to continue with the installation.

FIGURE 8.5:

Entering a name for the printer

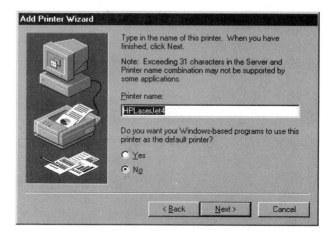

Now you have to say whether the printer is to be shared with others, as shown in Figure 8.6. If you share it, you have to give it a share name. The share name does not have to be the same as the printer name, but it might be easier to manage the printers if your printer names and share names are the same. A share name can be up to 12 characters long, including spaces. Notice also the list of operating systems in Figure 8.6. NT stores drivers for a printer on the print server, which means Windows NT and Windows 95 clients need not install them locally. Select all the operating systems that you use in this dialog box (see Figure 8.6) before moving to the next screen.

FIGURE 8.6:

Sharing the printer

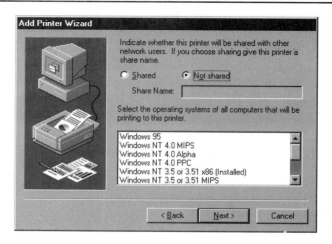

By telling the printer that machines from other operating systems—NT 4 for Alpha, NT 3.51, NT 3.51—will be using this printer, you are telling your printer to locate and copy the printer drivers needed for those operating systems. The computer will then ask you to supply those drivers. That means that you should either have the original CD-ROMs around and handy (now, where *did* I put my NT 3.5 CDs?) or have kept the \Alpha and \I386 directories from those operating systems somewhere on a server.

If you choose Windows 95, things get even more complex. For some reason, NT is unable to read the so-called "cabinet files," compressed files that Microsoft ships Windows 95 in. If you simply tell the Printer Wizard to go looking on the Windows 95 CD, it'll tell you that it *can't* find the files, as it's not able to look inside a CAB file. What to do, then? You *could* install the printer drivers on a Windows 95 workstation, share the \WINDOWS directory of the workstation, and then point the Printer Wizard there—the files will already be uncompressed. Or create a directory on your server and uncompress *all* of the CAB files. Do it this way:

1. Create a directory on some server and copy all of the CAB files from your Windows 95 CD to that directory.

2. Open up a command line and navigate to that directory. Type **extract.exe /e precopy2.cab *.*** to unpack the files in the first CAB file.

3. Do the same thing for the other CAB files. You'll end up with just under 300MB of files.

Now you can share this directory and refer to it when newly created print servers need Windows 95 print drivers.

WARNING   If you want MS-DOS machines to be able to use this printer, you need to make sure that the printer name conforms to DOS's 8+3 naming convention.

You can set the user permissions in the Properties dialog box after you finish adding the printer. However, if you intend to share the printer, tell the Printer Wizard now which operating systems will be used to print from this printer and be sure to have on hand the driver files for each operating system you choose. Printer Wizard will tell you which ones it needs in a dialog box like the one shown in Figure 8.7.

FIGURE 8.7:

Telling the Printer Wizard driver files are needed

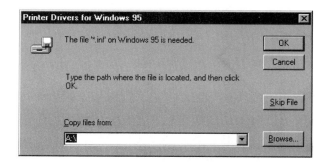

Click Next when you have finished. You are advised to print out a test page. That is all there is to it—your printer is ready to be used by one and all. Except, of course, that you may not want everyone and her brother to use the printer. That is where the user permissions come in handy. We'll talk about them later in this chapter.

> **TIP**
>
> RISC and x86 machines use different printer drivers, so you need to install both kinds if you have both kinds of machines on your network.

Adding a Second Printer for the Same Print Device

It's often desirable for you to have two (or more) names for the same print device on the network. Having different people access the same device from different names allows you to assign different printing priorities to different users, assign different hours that the printer is available for printing, make one printer for network use and another for local use, and so forth. Having two or more names allows you to fine-tune the network users' access to the printer.

The process of adding a second printer for the same print device is identical to that of adding the first one. Select Add Printer from the Printers folder and follow the Printer Wizard's instructions. Make sure to do the following:

1. Select a new name for the printer.

2. Choose the same driver for the printer that the other printer on this print device uses, and make sure that all other settings are as they should be. You don't have to share all printers on the network, even if they're attached to the same printing device.

If you shared the new printer with the network, it will now be available for connection.

How Do I Set Up a Printer the First Time for Network Use?

The first time that you're setting up a printer on the network, you need to add it. To do this, go to the Add Printer option in the Printers folder and fill in the appropriate information, including the type of printer, its share name, and whether or not it will be shared with the network.

You can give one physical printer more than one share name and assign each name to a different group, perhaps with different print privileges. Just repeat the creation process, but assign the printer a different name.

Customizing a Printer's Setup

Once you've done the basic work of adding a printer, you can further customize it. You don't have to customize your printer at the same time that you set it up if you don't want to—you can always adjust the settings at a later date with the Properties option on the Printer menu.

Using the Printer Properties Dialog Box

Highlight the printer you want and click on the Properties button in the Printers folder. You see a screen that looks like Figure 8.8. From here, you can do many things, including the following:

- List the hours that this printer will print. If you restrict the printing hours, jobs will still spool to the printer during the off-times, but will not print until the hour indicated.

- Choose a separator page file to print before each print job. Separator pages are discussed in detail later in this chapter, under "Separator Pages for Sorting Documents."

- Choose the ports that you want to print to for printer pooling (more on this below).

- Select the print processor.

FIGURE 8.8:

Printer Properties opening
dialog box

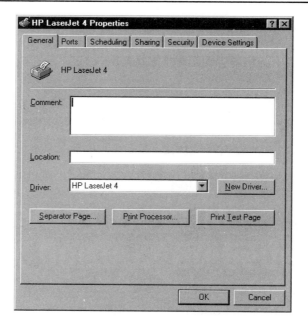

- Determine the printer's priority, if the printer goes by more than one name on the network. For example, if you have the same printer shared under the name HP4-22 and HP4, and you assign a higher priority to the printer name HP4-22, then print jobs sent to that printer name are printed first. The default priority is 1, which is the lowest priority. You can set the priority from 1 to 99.

Printer Pooling

Just because you send a print job to a particular print name doesn't mean that your print job has to print at one particular printing device. To save time for print jobs, you can use the Properties dialog box to pool several *identical* printers into one logical one. If you do this, the first available printing device will do the job when you send it to that printer name. This is called *printer pooling*, and it is illustrated in Figure 8.9. Printer pooling will not work unless the pooled printers are physically identical—the same make and model and the same amount of memory.

FIGURE 8.9:

Printer pooling

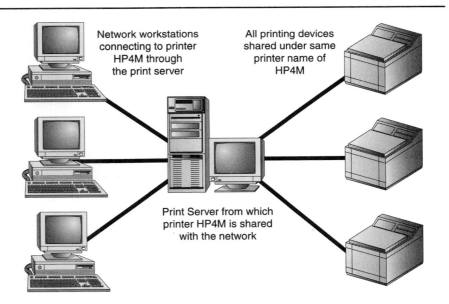

Network workstations connecting to printer HP4M through the print server

All printing devices shared under same printer name of HP4M

Print Server from which printer HP4M is shared with the network

If you have more than one identical printer, you can share them under the same printer name to facilitate speedy printing. This type of sharing is called *printer pooling*. To the network, it will look as though there is only one printer to connect to, but print jobs will automatically go to whatever pooled printer is available first.

How Do I Set Up More Than One Printer under the Same Name?

To have more than one printer handle print jobs sent to the same print name, you must set up printer pooling. To do this, go to the Properties item in the File menu and click on the Ports button. Select the ports that correspond to the ports where you've plugged in the other printers. If the ports you need aren't on the list, you can add them by clicking on the Add Port button. Then, make sure the Enable Printer Spooling box is checked.

On an NT Server machine, you only need one copy of the driver for the type of printer you're pooling, unlike Windows for Workgroups, which requires one copy of the driver for each printer.

Printing Directly to Ports

By default, documents for printing spool to the printer before they are printed. When a document is spooled, it is sent to the print server's hard disk, which in turn sends it to the printer in an effort to save time and let the user get back to what she was doing as soon as possible. This is called *background printing*.

If you like, however, you can use the scheduling dialog box to send print jobs directly to the port that a printer is connected to. But if you do this, you won't be able to use your application until the print job is done.

How Do I Print Directly to Ports?

To send print jobs directly to the port to which the printer is connected rather than spooling normally, go to the Properties item in the File menu of the Printers folder and click on the Scheduling button.

Setting the Printer Timeout Number

If the printer you are setting up is connected to a parallel port, you can specify the time lapse before the print server decides that the printer is not responding and notifies you (as the user) of an error. Setting the Transmission Retry number higher or lower adjusts the amount of time that the Print Server will wait for a printer to prepare itself to accept data.

This setting affects not only the printer that you've selected, but also any other local printers that use the same printer driver. Clicking on the Configure Port button in the Ports tab of the Printer Properties dialog box nets you a small dialog box that looks like Figure 8.10. To adjust the time-out, just click on the arrows on the right side of the box or type in a number by hand. As you can see, the time is measured in seconds.

FIGURE 8.10:

Configure Port dialog box

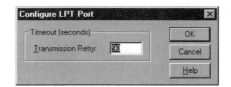

How Do I Set Printer Timeouts?

To set the number of seconds between the time that you send a print job to the printer and the time that, if the printer doesn't see the job, it tells you that there is a transmission error, choose the Properties item in the Printer menu, click on the Ports tab, and choose Configure Port in the dialog box; then type in the number of seconds that you want for the timeout.

Connecting to a Shared Printer

How you connect a workstation to a printer that is hooked up to a server running NT Server depends on the operating system that the workstation is using. Windows and Windows for Workgroups machines can connect from the graphical interface, but OS/2 and MS-DOS machines must make connections from the command line. Easiest of all are the Windows NT machines—they don't even require locally loaded printer drivers!

Printing from MS-DOS

All DOS workstations, whether they are running Windows or not, require locally installed printer drivers to share printers on an NT Server network. From a DOS workstation that is not running Windows or Windows for Workgroups, install the MS-DOS printer driver file for the laser printer and make sure that it is accessible to all your applications. Depending on how your disk is set up, you might have to copy the file to all your application directories.

To set up a printing port from MS-DOS, go to the command prompt and type **net use lpt1:** *server**sharename*. For *server* and *sharename*, substitute the name of the print server and the name by which the printer is known on the network. Substitute another port name if LPT1 is already in use.

If you want the connection to be made automatically every time that you log on to the network, add the **/persistent:yes** switch to the end of the command. Just typing **/persistent** won't do anything, but if you leave off the persistency switch altogether, it will default to whatever you selected the last time that you used the NET USE command.

For example, suppose you have an MS-DOS workstation that does not have a locally attached printer on any of its parallel ports. Since some older DOS programs don't really give you the chance to select an output port, you'd like the network printer HP4, which is attached to the server BIGSERVER, to intercept any output for LPT1 and print it on HP4. Suppose also that you want this network printer attached every time that you log on to the network. The command for that would be

```
net use lpt1: \\bigserver\hp4 /persistent:yes
```

TIP

If the print server is using NTFS, workstations may not be able to print from MS-DOS if they only have Read and Execute privileges. The print jobs spool to the print queue, but never print. To resolve this problem, give all users who print from DOS applications or the command prompt full access to the printer.

DOS workstations, whether or not they're running Windows over DOS, use the locally installed printer driver rather than the one stored on the server. Therefore, if you get an updated version of a printer driver, you need to install it at each DOS/Windows workstation individually.

Printing from Windows and Windows for Workgroups

Connecting to an NT Server shared printer from Windows for Workgroups is just like connecting to the same printer on a WfW server. To connect, go first to the Control Panel and select the Printers icon. You see a screen that looks like Figure 8.11. This screen shows you the printer connections that you currently have. To connect an existing printer to a new port, click on the Connect button. You see a screen that looks like Figure 8.12.

FIGURE 8.11:

Connecting to an NT Server printer from Windows for Workgroups (screen 1)

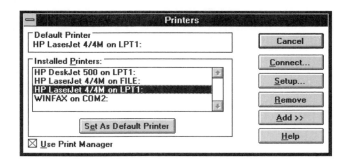

FIGURE 8.12:

Connecting to an NT Server printer from Windows for Workgroups (screen 2)

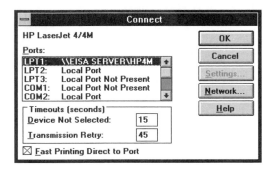

If, however, you want to connect to a new printer, click on the Network button in this dialog box. Do so, and then you see a screen like Figure 8.13. It shows you which printers are available for connection. Click on the printer you want, and when its name appears in the Path box, click OK. Return to the previous screen, where you can ensure that the printer is connected to the port that you want.

FIGURE 8.13:

Connecting to an NT Server printer from Windows for Workgroups (screen 3)

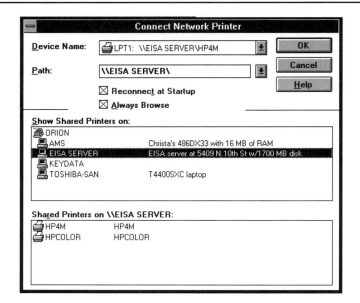

That's how you connect to a networked printer *if* the drivers for that printer are already loaded. If they're not loaded, you need to use the Add button in the first screen (see Figure 8.11) to add the printer driver to the system. Click on the Add button and you see the list of printers shown in Figure 8.14.

Select the printer that you want (for example, the HP LaserJet III), and then click on the Install button. You see a screen like the one in Figure 8.15. You can use the Browse button or type in the proper path if the driver is somewhere on the network; otherwise, you need to insert the appropriate disk. Once you've installed the correct driver, you're ready to connect to the printer.

FIGURE 8.14:

Adding a printer driver to the system (step 1)

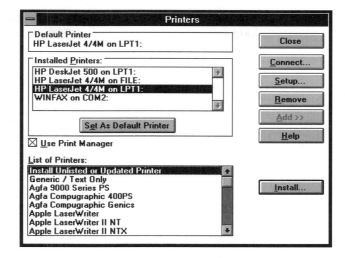

FIGURE 8.15:

Adding a printer driver to the system (step 2)

Printing from OS/2

Connecting to an NT Server printer from OS/2 is much like doing it from DOS. To set up a printing port, go to the command prompt (reached from the System folder) and type **net use lpt1:** *server**sharename*. For *server* and *sharename*, substitute the name of the print server and the name by which the printer is known on the network. Substitute another port name if LPT1 is already in use. If you want the connection to be persistent, add the **/persistent:yes** switch to the end of the command.

When connecting to networking printers, OS/2, like DOS and Windows, uses local printer drivers rather than drivers stored on the print server. Thus, you need to load the printer drivers locally for the printers you connect to, and if you update the drivers, you need to install the new ones at each workstation.

Printing from Windows NT

If you're using Windows NT, connecting to a shared printer is so easy you'll be tempted to believe that you didn't do it right until you try to print and it works. Since NT workstations can access the printer drivers located on the print server, you don't need to load them locally. How this works is illustrated in Figure 8.16.

FIGURE 8.16:

Locally loaded printer drivers versus centrally loaded printer drivers

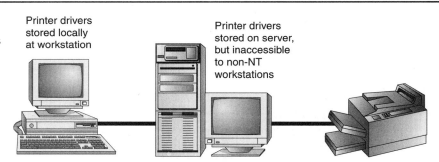

Windows for Workgroups accessing printer through NT Server print server

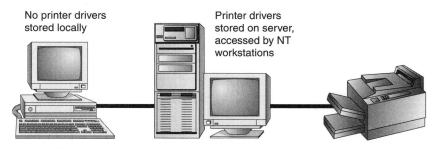

NT workstation accessing printer through NT Server print server

Therefore, rather than define the proper port, find the drivers, or do anything else, all that you need do is go to the Control Panel, select the Printers icon, and double-click on Add Printer. When you do, you see the first Add Printer Wizard screen shown in Figure 8.17.

FIGURE 8.17:

First screen in the process of connecting to a shared printer

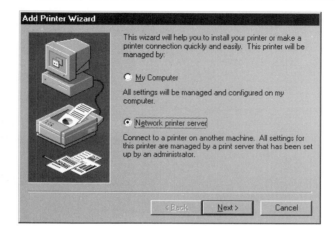

When you've reached this screen, choose the Network Printer Server option button, and then click the Next button. A screen like Figure 8.18 appears. It shows you the available printers that you can connect to. As you can see from the figure, two printers are currently available on this network.

FIGURE 8.18:

Display of available printers on the network

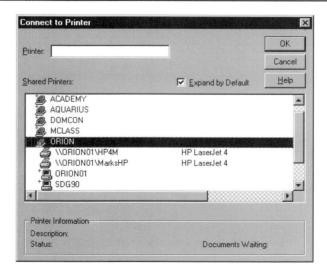

To connect to both HP4M and MarksHP, the printers shown in Figure 8.18, you have to connect one printer at a time. Double-click on HP4M to select it, or click once and then click OK. Once that's done, that's it—you don't have to load drivers or tell the system the kind of printer that you want to connect to. To connect to MarksHP, just repeat the process.

NT workstations use the printer drivers stored on the print server, so if you install a newer version of a driver on the print server, the NT workstations will use it automatically. You don't need to tweak the workstation connection.

How Do I Connect a Workstation to a Shared Printer?

The process of connecting a workstation to a networked printer varies with the type of operating system that the workstation is using. To connect DOS and OS/2 machines, use the NET USE command from the command prompt (see the previous section for details). For Windows and Windows for Workgroups, you can use the Print Manager. For Windows NT machines, use the Print Wizard. Printer drivers for each kind of printer must be loaded locally on all kinds of workstations except Windows NT. An NT print server can also offer drivers to Windows 95 clients if they are added via the Sharing tab.

Controlling and Monitoring Access to the Printer

Just because you've networked a printer doesn't necessarily mean that you want everyone on its domain to be able to access it. Maybe it's the color printer with the expensive ink that only the graphics people need to use, or perhaps you want to reduce the risk of security breaches by limiting the people who can print out company secrets. Either way, you want to control access to the printer just as you would to any other network device.

By default, only Administrators, Print Operators, and Server Operators have full access to the printer. Only those with full access can pause or resume a printer or set its permissions. Those who just have print access can only administer their own documents.

Setting Printer Permissions

As you'll recall from elsewhere in this book, you secure an NT Server network by setting user rights for what people can *do* on the network, and setting user permissions for what people can *use.* Just as you can with other devices on the network, you can restrict printer use by setting its permissions.

To set or change printer permissions, first go to the Printers folder, and select the icon for the printer you want. Next, go to the Properties dialog box in the File menu, choose the Security tab, and select Permissions. You see a dialog box that looks like Figure 8.19.

FIGURE 8.19:

Printer Permissions
dialog box

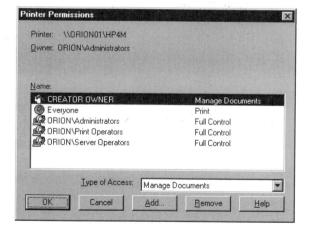

The Printer Permissions dialog box lists the groups for whom some kind of printer access has been set up. From here, you can change the kinds of access that each user group has. The kinds of access are as follows:

Access	What It Means
No Access	No member of that user group can do anything with the printer, including print.
Print	Members of that user group can print documents as well as pause, resume, restart, and delete *their own* documents.
Manage Documents	Members can control document settings as well as pause, resume, restart, and delete documents that are lined up for printing.
Full Access	Members can do anything with the printer: print; control document settings; pause, resume, and delete documents and printers; change the printing order of documents; and change printer properties and permissions.

To change a group's type of access, click on the group to highlight it, and then choose the new access type from the Type of Access box in the lower-right corner of the dialog box. Make sure that you leave one group with Full Access, or you won't be able to change printer permissions in the future.

To add a user group or user to the printer permissions list, click on the Add button. You see a dialog box that looks like Figure 8.20.

FIGURE 8.20:

Adding users and groups to printer permissions list

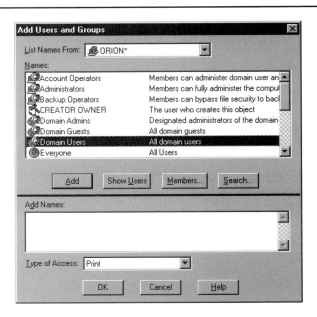

To add a group to the printer permissions list, highlight the kind of permission that you want to give that group, click on the group you want, click Add, and click OK. To add only a particular person to the printer permissions list, you have two options:

- You can select a group that the user belongs to and click on Members. This gives you a list of all the users who belong to the group. Highlight the user who you want.

TIP

Clicking on Members to show the members of the Users group does not get you a list of users; use the Show Users button to do that. If you try to see the members of the Domain Users group, you'll only get a message informing you that the composition of that group is identical to that of the Users group.

- Click on the Show Users button and scroll down the user groups list until you see the entry for Users. Below this entry is a list of every user on the system. Double-click on the name, just as you would when selecting a user group.

Once you've selected the group or user, the name should appear in the Add Names box in the bottom half of the screen. When you're done adding groups or users, click OK.

To remove a group or user from the printer permissions list, go to the Printer Permissions dialog box (see Figure 8.19), highlight the name of the user or group, and then click Remove.

TIP

If a user is a member of more than one group with different printer permissions, the system always grants the highest-level permission. For example, if Jane is a member of one group with Print privileges and one with Full Access privileges, she always has Full Access privileges. The only time that print permissions are *not* cumulative is when one of the groups that a user belongs to has No Access to the printer. In that case, that permission level overrides all higher levels and the user has no access to the printer, regardless of the access level of other user groups she belongs to.

How Do I Set Printer Permissions?

To control which groups or individuals have access to a networked printer and the kind of access that they have, go to the Security tab in the Properties dialog box and choose Permissions. Select existing groups and change the kind of printer access that they have, or click on Add and select new groups to configure. To select individual members of a group, click on the Users button to display membership.

For users in more than one group with different printer permissions, permissions are cumulative except for No Access. If any group of which that user is a member is forbidden access to the printer, that overrides all other permissions.

Creator-Owner of *What*?

Did you notice that you can set permission levels on creator-owners in the Security tab? I did, and it got me thinking: creator-owner of *what*? Someone must create a printer in the first place. (Recall that *printer* in NT-ese means a logical printing object, not the actual mirrors, lasers, toner, and paper. The actual physical, mechanical printer is called a *printer device*.) You can create as many printers as you like from a single printer device; and if you created a printer, then you're the printer's owner.

If you attach to a printer and print something on that printer, you create a print job on that printer, and you are the *owner* of that print job. So when you set permissions for creator-owner, which is it—the printer or the print job? As it turns out, it's the print job.

Experimenting with Printer Permissions

While I'm on the topic of permissions and print jobs, here's an oddity that I discovered about print jobs and security. When logged in as my normal account, I've got Print permissions. Print permissions, you may recall, let me not only print, but also delete, pause, restart, or resume *any print job that I created*; in other words, I can mess around somewhat with any print jobs that I created, but I can't touch other people's print jobs. People with the next level of permissions, Manage Documents, *can* go meddle in other people's documents.

If you'd like to see this in action, log on as an administrator and pause a printer. (Just open the Printers folder, locate the printer, right-click it, and choose Pause.) Then log onto the system as a regular user and print something to that printer. Since the printer is paused, the print job will go into the printer's queue, and you'll be able to view it even if you're just a regular user by opening up that printer's folder.

Then log off and log back on as another regular user. Print something else to that printer. Open up the printer folder and you'll see both jobs, and the folder will look something like the one shown in Figure 8.21.

FIGURE 8.21:

Jobs in paused printer queue

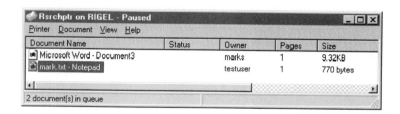

In the figure, you see one document created by a user named "marks" and another by a user named "testuser." While logged on as TESTUSER, I can right-click the MARK.TXT document, choose Properties, and get a dialog box like the one shown in Figure 8.22.

Figure 8.22 shows the *job settings* for this print job. In particular, there are three items here that could be useful to change. First is the Notify: field. Suppose you printed a job for someone and had to leave the office, but that person wanted to know when the job was done. You could bring up this dialog box and fill in the person's name, and she'd then be informed when the print job was done. Adjusting the Priority slider would affect how quickly a job gets printed on a busy printer—"busy" because raising a job's priority on a printer with no waiting documents doesn't affect printing speed at all. And you could use the Schedule buttons to restrict when the job printed.

If either user MARKS or TESTUSER tries to do that, however, he or she will be rebuffed, as they cannot change the print settings even for their own jobs. Again, they can delete, pause, restart, or resume their own jobs, but they can't fiddle with the job properties in the dialog box above. Remember the levels of printer access? People with No Access, Print, and Manage Documents levels of permission cannot change print job settings; only people with Full Control can.

FIGURE 8.22:

Job settings for a printer job

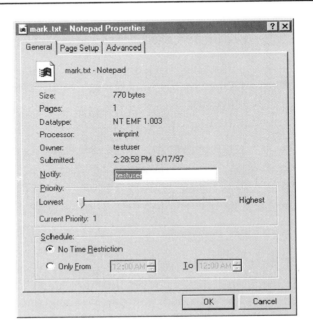

Let's get back to what MARKS and TESTUSER can do. Logged in as TEST-USER, I can right-click my job and pause it, which in this case is a kind of "double pause": Not only is the entire printer paused, but also my job is paused; if the administrator un-pauses ("resumes") the printer (you must be a member of Administrators, Server Operators, or Print Operators to pause and resume an entire printer), then my job still will not print until I resume the job. On the other hand, if I try to pause MARKS's document, I'll see in the printer window's status line "access denied."

TIP

I ran into something else that is counter-intuitive (to me, anyway) in NT's printer handling: you cannot open up a printer and re-arrange the print jobs through the GUI, save by fiddling with their print priorities; you can't, for example, drag and drop them within a printer folder.

Hiding a Printer

You can conceal the fact that a printer even exists, but still share it with the network for a chosen few to access. To do this, attach a dollar sign ($) to the end of the printer share name. This way, the printer name does not show up on the list of networked printers, but if the user types in the name by hand, she is able to connect to the printer.

How Do I Hide a Shared Printer?

To share a printer with the network but keep it from showing up when people browse the network for printers, tack a dollar sign to the end of its name. That way, users have to type the printer's name in the printer name box—it doesn't show up on the list of printers shared with the network.

Setting Print Job Priorities

As discussed earlier, you can set printer priorities from the Scheduling tab of the Properties dialog box (see Figure 8.8). This way, if you want to share your printer with the network but don't want everyone else's print jobs crowding out your own, you can give it two names: a name you use that has a high priority, and a name with a low priority that is used by everyone else who connects to the printer. To further hone print priorities for different user groups, you can give the printer three or more names, each with its own priority attached, and then assign each group that needs access to the printer a name by which to connect. How this works is illustrated in Figure 8.23.

When you're setting the printer priorities in the Scheduling tab of the Properties dialog box, don't forget that higher numbers (up to 99) have a higher priority than lower ones. The default value is 1.

FIGURE 8.23:

Setting print priorities with different printer names

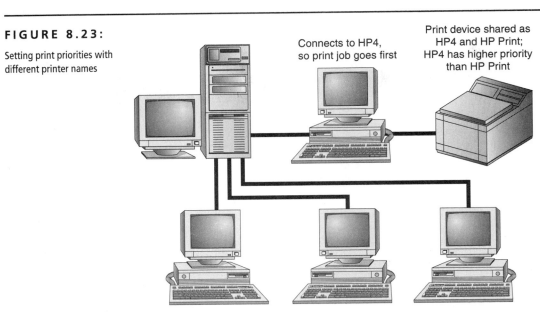

Connects to HP4, so print job goes first

Print device shared as HP4 and HP Print; HP4 has higher priority than HP Print

Connect to HP Print, so all print jobs have lower priority than HP4 jobs

How Do I Set User Print Priorities?

You can give the print jobs of one person or group priority over those of another person or group. To do this, create another printer for the same print device. Click on the Scheduling tab in the Properties dialog box, and you see a dialog box in which you can set printer priorities. Set the number to 1—or any number up to 99, which has the highest priority—since the default is 1.

Setting Printing Hours

As discussed in "Using the Printer Properties Dialog Box" earlier in this chapter, you can set the hours during which a printer produces output. To adjust print times, just click on the ↑ or ↓ arrow of the Available From and To boxes, or type in the times that you want the printer to be available. If a print job is sent to a printer during its "off hours," it doesn't disappear but sits there until the printer is authorized to print again.

While you can set user logon hours and printer hours, you can't set printing hours for a particular user or group that are different from those of the others who have access to that printer. For example, you can't restrict users to a particular printer between 9 and 5 if Administrators can access it at any time, unless you adjust the users' logon times and configure their accounts so that the system kicks them off when their time is up. What you *can* do is set up two printer names, one with one time window when it's open for use, and the other with another one. Those who connect to the printer name with the limited hours will only be able to use the printer during those hours. How this works is described in the Figure 8.24.

FIGURE 8.24:

Restricting printing hours for a user group

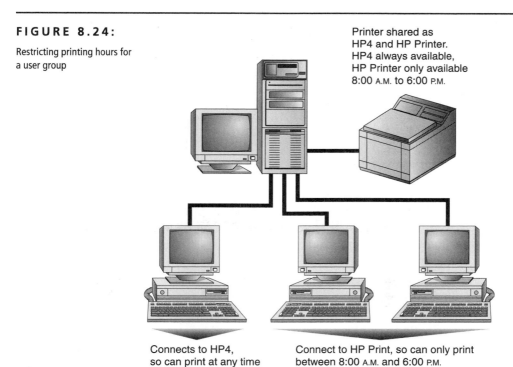

Printer shared as HP4 and HP Printer. HP4 always available, HP Printer only available 8:00 A.M. to 6:00 P.M.

Connects to HP4, so can print at any time

Connect to HP Print, so can only print between 8:00 A.M. and 6:00 P.M.

Receiving Status Messages

One of the auditing functions that you use most often is some kind of messenger service that tells you what's happened to print jobs after you've sent them to the server. Printer status messages can tell you when

- The print job is done

- The printer is out of paper or off-line

- The printer is jammed

- A print job has been deleted

How Do I Set Varying Printing Hours for Different Groups?

Although you can't make a printer accessible to one group for one set of hours and to another group for a different set, you can still customize printer access hours for different sets of users. Simply add more than one printer (remember, printers are logical entities, distinct from the physical printing devices), set the hours for each printer as you require, and then tell each group which printer to connect to.

Arranging to receive printer status messages is done a little differently, depending on what operating system the workstation in question is using:

NT *and* **NT Server**   Begin the messenger service (it's on by default, so you probably don't have to do anything).

Windows for Workgroups *and* **Windows 95**   Run WINPOPUP.EXE in the Windows directory.

DOS *and* **Windows**   Load the messenger service through NET POPUP.

NetWare   Begin the CAPTURE program and run the messenger service.

Logging and Auditing Printer Usage

In order to keep an eye on a printer's usage, it's a good idea to audit it. To set up auditing, first go to the User Manager and enable file and object access auditing. Once you've done that, you can set up printer auditing for individuals and groups.

To configure printer auditing, go to the Printer Properties dialog box and select the Auditing option in the Security tab. When you do, you see the dialog box in Figure 8.25.

FIGURE 8.25:

Printer Auditing opening screen

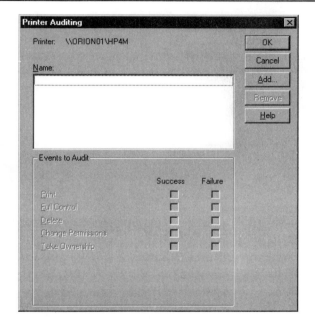

Why are all the auditing options grayed out? Before you can audit printer activity, you have to select a group or user to audit. To do this, click on the Add button. You see a screen like Figure 8.26. To select a group for auditing, double-click on it or click once and then click on Add. When you've selected a user or group, it should show up in the Add Names box in the bottom half of the screen. When you've chosen all the groups that you want to audit, click OK to return to the Printer Auditing screen. It now looks something like Figure 8.27.

FIGURE 8.26:

Add Users and Groups dialog
box for printer auditing

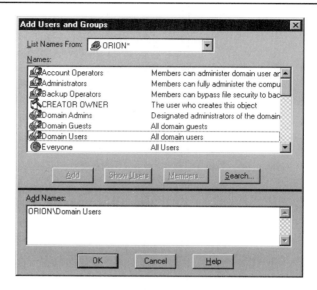

FIGURE 8.27:

Auditing screen with groups
chosen for auditing

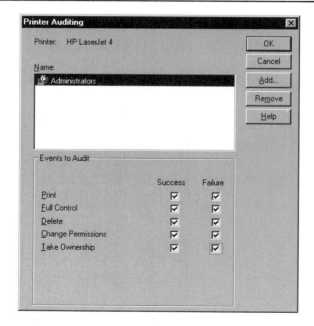

For each group or user that you've chosen to audit, you can select different items to keep track of by checking in the appropriate check boxes. When you highlight a group in the Name box here, you see the auditing items that you selected for that particular user or group. No defaults are attached to auditing a particular group, so you have to set them all by hand. To view the audit information, use the Event Viewer in the Administrative Tools program group.

How Do I Set Up Event Auditing for the Printer?

To keep track of printer events, go to the Auditing item in the Printer Properties Security tab. By default, no groups are selected for auditing, so you must select a group. Click on the Add button and a list of possible groups to audit appears. Select a group, click on the Add button so that the group name appears in the lower box, and then click OK. Once you've selected a group for auditing, you can choose the events that you wish to audit from the list. For each group that you audit, you can set up a special auditing schedule.

Separator Pages for Sorting Documents

Separator pages are extra pages that are printed before the main document. They can be used to identify the owner of the print job, record the print time and date, print a message to users of the printer, and record the job number. Separator pages are useful mainly for keeping documents sent to the printer separate from each other. If a number of people are using the same networked printer, you probably want to use separator pages to help them keep their documents sorted. Several separator page files are included with NT Server, and you can also create your own by using Notepad.

Creating a Separator Page

To make your own separator page file, begin a new document in Notepad. On the first line, type a single character and then press Enter. This character will now be the *escape character* that tells the system that you're performing a function, not entering text. You should use a character that you don't anticipate needing for anything else, such as a dollar sign ($) or pound sign (#). Here, I've used a dollar sign as the escape character.

Now that you've established your escape code, you can customize your separator page with the following variables:

Variable	What It Does
BS	Prints text in single-width block characters until $U is encountered.
$D	Prints the date the job was printed. The representation of the date is the same as the Date Format in the International section in Control Panel.
$E	Ejects a page from the printer. Use this code to start a new separator page or to end the separator page file. If you get an extra blank separator page when you print, remove this code from your separator page file.
$Fpathname	Prints the contents of the file specified by path, starting on an empty line. The contents of this file are copied directly to the printer without any processing.
$Hnn	Sets a printer-specific control sequence, where nn is a hexadecimal ASCII code sent directly to the printer. To determine the specific numbers, see your printer manual.
$I	Prints the job number.
$Lxxxx	Prints all the characters (xxxx) following it until another escape code is encountered. You can use this code to enter text exhorting people to not waste paper on unnecessary print jobs, to have a nice day, to save the planet, or to do anything else that you like.
$N	Prints the user name of the person that submitted the job.
$n	Skips n number of lines (from 0 through 9). Skipping 0 lines moves printing to the next line.
$T	Prints the time the job was printed. The representation of the time is the same as the Time Format set in the International section in Control Panel.
$U	Turns off block character printing.
$Wnn	Sets the width of the separator page. The default width is 80; the maximum width is 256. Any printable characters beyond this width are truncated.

As an example, consider the following Notepad separator page file:

```
$
$N
$D
$L TEST SEPARATOR. DON'T USE THESE; SAVE THE PLANET.
$T
$E
```

It nets you this output:

```
Mark 4/11/1997 TEST SEPARATOR. DON'T USE THESE; SAVE THE PLANET.
9:21:22 AM
```

Notice that, even though I pressed Enter after each entry, the output is all on one line. This is because I didn't use the $n character to tell the separator page to skip lines between entries.

How Do I Create a Separator Page?

If you don't want to use any of the default separator pages included with NT Server, you can create your own with Notepad. Begin a new document, and, on the first line, type a single character to be the escape character (the system's indicator that the next character is a code). Choose an escape character that you won't need for anything else in the file. On the following lines, use the escape character and the variables described above to make a custom separator page.

Choosing a Separator Page

To specify a particular separator page, choose the General tab in the Properties dialog box and then click the Separator Page button. You see a dialog box that looks like Figure 8.28.

FIGURE 8.28:

Separator Page dialog box

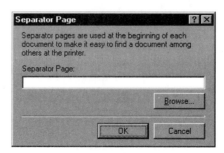

If no separator file is listed, you can select one by typing in the name of the file you want to use or by browsing for the correct file by clicking on the Browse button. Once you've selected a separator file, the page with that information prints out before every print job.

To stop using a separator page, just go to the Separator Page dialog box and delete the entry in the text box. There is no <None> setting in a drop-down list as there is in some menus. It's a pity that the separator page selection isn't set up like that, but I suppose it's because custom separator pages wouldn't necessarily be in the WINNT35\SYSTEM32 directory where all the defaults are.

When specifying a separator page, you can type a filename (if you're already in the proper path to find the file) or the filename and path (if you're in another path). You must, however, use a file that is *physically* located on the computer that controls the printer for which you're specifying the separator page. Why can't you use any file that's accessible from the network? The answer is that the computer that controls the printer stores separator page information in its Registry, and so it needs to have that information available locally. If you tell the printer to use a separator file that is not located on its hard disk or one that is not in the path that you've indicated, you get an error message that says, "Could not set printer: The specified separator file is invalid."

Solving Common Shared Printing Problems

While printing under NT is usually trouble-free, you may run into a few problems. The remainder of this chapter describes some of the most common problems and tells you how to solve them.

Connection Problems

Connection problems appear before you can even use the printer.

Can't Connect to Printer

When connecting to a printer in the Printer Wizard, you may get an error message that says, "Could not connect to the printer: The remote procedure call failed and did not execute." This isn't really your fault. This problem usually occurs after you've set up and then deleted multiple printers, logging off and on in between removes and setups. Essentially, the Registry gets confused. If you see this message, click OK in the dialog box with the error message, and then log off and then back on again. When you get back on, you should be able to connect to the printer.

Can't Create Printer

When you go to the Printer icon to remove a printer or create a new one, that option—Create Printer or Remove Printer—may be grayed out, indicating that it's inactive. If you see this, check to make sure that you're logged on as a member of a group with privileges to create or remove printers; only Administrators and Power Users have this privilege.

No Default Printer

If you try to set up a printer from several layers deep in dialog boxes and then select Help while you're still working on the setup, you may get a message that says, "No default printer. Use Printer Wizard to install and select default printer." You may get this message even though a default printer is already installed. To avoid this bug, set up printers before trying to use Help.

Deleted Port

While it is possible to delete a port in the Printer Properties dialog box, be warned that it's a lot easier to delete a port than it is to retrieve it. If you blow away a port, you need to use the Registry Editor to replace it.

To retrieve a printer port:

1. Start the Registry Editor (REGEDT32.EXE) and go to the following subkey in the HKEY_LOCAL_MACHINE on Local Machine hive:

    ```
    Software\Microsoft\Windows NT\CurrentVersion\Ports
    ```

2. From the Edit menu, choose Add Value.

3. In the Value Name box, type the printer port that you deleted (for example, COM1: or LPT1:). Keep the default value in the Data box (REG_SZ) and click on OK.

4. In the String box, type the appropriate settings that correspond to the port that you typed in the Value Name box. For example, you would type **9600,*n*,8,1** for any COM ports.

Table 8.1 tells you exactly what the value in each section should be for each port. If you're doing this fix, here is a list of the appropriate settings for each port.

TABLE 8.1: Port Settings

Port Name	Data Type	String Value
COM1	REG SZ	9600,*n*,8,1
COM2	REG SZ	9600,*n*,8,1
COM3	REG SZ	9600,*n*,8,1
COM4	REG SZ	9600,*n*,8,1
FILE	REG SZ	empty
LPT1	REG SZ	empty
LPT2	REG SZ	empty
LPT3	REG SZ	empty

5. Exit the Registry Editor. Log off and then log back on, and the port should be back.

WARNING   Be *extremely careful* when using the Registry Editor! It's possible to completely screw up your NT Server installation with it. In fact, you could screw it up enough that you have to reinstall the operating system to fix the problem.

Basic Troubleshooting Tips

The previous sections don't cover every possible printing problem and solution, but are instead meant to give you an idea of what *could* go wrong and how to fix it. If your problem isn't dealt with above, this section should give you an idea of how to attack it.

Software

If your print job isn't coming out quite like you expected it to (or not at all), make sure that the printer is set up correctly. Have you specified an existing printer port? What about the printer driver? Did you install the right driver for your printer? If so, you may want to try deleting and reinstalling the printer driver. (Remove the printer from the system and re-create it.)

The problem could also be in the application. Can you print to another printer? Can you print to that printer from another application? If it's a DOS application, copy the driver file to the application's directory and then try to print again.

Hardware

It's perfectly possible for something to go wrong with the printer itself, or the cabling, especially if you can't print from DOS. Once you've checked the printer itself to make sure that it is on-line, plugged in, and has paper, check the connection. Will the printer work when attached to another parallel or serial port? You could have a network problem. Try printing the file directly from the print server and see if that works. If nothing else works, try removing extraneous cards from the print server to see if there is a hardware conflict.

Miscellaneous Printing Problems

At one point, Microsoft claimed that printing problems were what they got the most trouble calls about. Here are a few common problems and, where they exist, solutions.

PrintScreen Doesn't Work from DOS Box

When running a DOS text-mode utility in a command window, you'd like to just press PrtSC to capture a screen. Unfortunately, that doesn't work in NT—you'll see the first four lines printed and that's it.

A better approach is to try to copy the screen to the Clipboard with the Alt+Prtsc key sequence, then paste it into Notepad and print it from there.

You Need to Set Up a Network Printer with IP

See Chapter 14 for instructions on how to connect printers directly to your network using the IP protocol rather than the DLC protocol.

Color Printing under NT Doesn't Look As Good As under Windows 9x

Frustrating but true. Printing bitmaps and other images with my Epson Color 800 made me scratch my head and go over to Epson's Web site looking for new NT drivers. I found some, but to no avail. Then I ran into an NT printing expert at a Microsoft conference and asked him for suggestions.

His response was to immediately look sheepish, which is a bad sign. He told me that NT's color printing model just doesn't do the same job that Windows' does. In other words, then, this is a "just live with it" sort of problem. I understand that more expensive printers—color lasers and the like—do just fine, so if you're thinking of investing five grand in one of those you'll probably be happy with the results. Come to think of it, however, maybe it'd be best to try the printer first under both Windows and NT...

Printing a Document Causes a "KMODE EXCEPTION"

You try to print a document and your system bluescreens with an error like

```
STOP:  0x0000001e (0xc0000094, 0xfe7533ca, 0xc0000094,
0x00000010)Kmode_Exception_Not_Handled. RASDD.DLL
```

Go back into the document and look around for some small text—one-point text, to be exact. Text that small causes NT to divide by zero, a generally bad thing for software to do.

The answer? Apply Service Pack 3 or greater.

The Last Page of a Document Does Not Print

You print a document and everything comes out... except the last page. This usually happens because the program neglects to send an "end of page" or "form feed" command at the end of the print job.

There are two possible answers. First, on the server side, you can set the default datatype value to RAW [FFAuto] or [RAW FF Appended]. Alternatively, you can just tell the application to send a form feed at the end of its print jobs.

You Get an Extra Blank Page at the End of a Document

The reverse problem to the previous one. Either tell the apps to *stop* putting form feeds at the end of their jobs, or set the default datatype to simply RAW [FF Auto]. If that still doesn't work, try simply RAW.

Postscript Jobs Only Print One Page

If you're printing a Postscript document and you've told the printer to reverse the order of the pages, you'll sometimes end up with just the first page. The answer is to enable *page independence* for that print server.

In the Printers folder, locate the Postscript printer that you're trying to print on. Right-click it and choose Document Defaults. You'll see an Advanced Tab; choose it.

Now double-click on Document Options and, when that opens, double-click on the Postscript Options. Next, click on Page Independence, and make its setting equal to Yes. Click OK until you're free, then either restart the server or the Spooler service.

You Cannot Print to a Local Printer from DOS or CMD.EXE

This is more of a problem that you'll see from NT Workstation, but it's worth mentioning. When you try to print from a text-mode program or from a DOS program, your system must write a spool file to WINNT\SYSTEM32\SPOOL\PRINTERS. But if \WINNT is on an NTFS volume and you don't have Change permissions, then the file doesn't get written. There also isn't an error message of any kind, sadly—you just get no printed output. Check the permissions on the directory.

Keeping Track of Printing Errors

Being able to choose whether to be notified when someone prints on a remote machine is a new and handy feature of the Print Server Properties dialog box. Those of you familiar with NT 3.51 or before probably remember that you had to go into the Registry in order to turn off the printer notification message, the message that shows up on your server every time someone on a remote machine prints a document. With NT Server 4, it is much easier.

In the Printers folder, pull down the File menu, choose Print Server Properties, and click on the Advanced tab. This tab offers several options. A check in the last check box, "Notify when remote documents are printed," gives you the same print notification message with which you may already be familiar.

But turning off the notification does not mean compromising security, because you can keep a log file to record the status of spooled print jobs. A log file is a combined file for all the printers attached to your print server. Notice in this same dialog box that you can tell the print server to log the following events:

- Error events
- Warning events
- Information events

Just type in a filename and path where it asks for a spool folder. A default file is already listed for you.

You can also tell the server to take a more active role by beeping at you if a spooler event fails. To do that, click the "Beep on errors of remote documents" check box.

Two other tabs appear in the Print Server Properties dialog box. The Ports tab is a recap of the Ports tab in the Printer Properties dialog box, and the Forms tab allows you to define margin sizes. These forms are stored on the print server itself, so all printers can access them.

By now, you've got a server set up, some users, a few shares, and a printer or two. Even though all network administrators know that it's a lot easier to run a network if it doesn't have any users, let's throw caution to the wind and get a few users' PCs hooked up to the network. We do that in the next chapter.

9

Connecting PCs to NT Networks and Running Windows Terminal Server

- Connecting a DOS workstation

- Connecting Windows workstations

- Connecting Windows 95/98 workstations

- Configuring and using Windows Terminal Server

Once a server is up and running, the next thing you want to do is to set up some workstations to access that server. I'll assume that you already know how to install an Ethernet or token-ring card in your system. What I'm concerned with in this chapter is installing the software to support all of the different workstations that you are likely to find out there: DOS, DOS and Windows 3.*x*, Windows for Workgroups, and Windows 95 or 98 workstations.

Setting up workstations is not difficult, and you could, in truth, probably figure most of it out yourself—you will find no rocket science in this chapter. What you will find is a walk-through of setting up each kind of workstation. My examples assume that

- I'm attaching to a workgroup and a domain called ORION.
- The user's name is MarkM.
- The initial password is hi.
- The workstations will connect with Ethernet.

The logical place to start is with DOS.

Connecting a DOS Workstation to NT

DOS is the worst of the bunch to attach to NT because DOS has no intrinsic knowledge of networking. You must add a few programs to your DOS work-station's AUTOEXEC.BAT and CONFIG.SYS in order to add networking capabilities to DOS.

To Use or Not to Use the Network Client Administrator

NT comes with a program called the Network Client Administrator (NCA) that is *supposed* to make this easier, but I recommend against using it. NCA is intended to simplify the process of getting network code onto a PC, and in some ways it accomplishes that. Basically, you tell the NCA what kind of network card you have, what protocol you want to use, what user name to use, and the like. Then you shove an already-formatted floppy into drive A, and the NCA adds files to the floppy. You then take that single floppy over to the workstation and boot from the floppy. Enough code is on the floppy to get the PC to the NT Server, and from there to kick off a batch file that installs the Microsoft Network Client 3 for DOS. Under NT 3.*x*, you could alternatively install Windows for Workgroups from the NT CD-ROM, but that's changed with NT 4. Now you can only install the DOS client software or Windows 95.

Anyway, I recommend against using the Network Client Administrator for several reasons:

- It's not *that* convenient. It's annoying to have a DOS-formatted floppy on hand before the process starts, and there is no reason why Microsoft couldn't have built the NCA to produce DOS-formatted floppies for the convenience of its network administrators.

- While the NCA simplifies the network client setup process, it's not complete by any means. All you tell the NCA is, "I have a 3Com 3C509 card," not, "I have a 3Com 3C509 card set to I/O address 210 and IRQ 11." The NCA requires you to go through the whole process of creating the floppy, after which you have to use the Notepad or something like it to edit a file called PROTOCOL.INI, which is in A:\NET.

- If the NCA includes the drivers for your card, you're in good shape. But if not, then the NCA is of virtually no help. Over the years I have used a number of Ethernet cards from Standard Microsystems Corporation (SMC), and I've found them to be fast, well-designed cards. But for some reason, Microsoft chose not to include all of them in the NCA's list of known boards. This made installing SMC cards so cumbersome with the NCA that I stopped using the NCA, and not only that, but I don't buy many SMC cards any more.

I did manage to find one way to make the NCA useful, however: unattended installations (see the section on unattended installations in Chapter 3). Once you make the Network Client boot disk, add a few more commands to the AUTOEXEC.BAT, and you'll be able to pop your disk in and walk away. Come back 30–40 minutes later, and you'll have a brand-new NT installation.

The Microsoft Network Client 3 for MS-DOS

Instead of using the Network Client Administrator, my recommendation is that you create two disks called the Microsoft Network Client 3 Installation Disks 1 and 2. Doing that is simple. You can create these two disks by looking in a directory called CLIENTS on the NT Server CD-ROM. In CLIENTS, there is a directory called MSCLIENT, and under that two directories named Disk1 and Disk2. Just copy all of the Disk1 directory onto one diskette and all of the DISK2 directory onto another diskette—each will fit on a 1.44MB floppy. Label both disks and carry them around with you on network calls.

Installing Microsoft Network Client 3

After you've created the disks, just walk over to the DOS machine, put the first disk into the A: drive, change to that drive, and type **setup**.

Setup will show you the familiar blue screen with white letters that announces you are about to install the Microsoft Network Client 3 for MS-DOS. The first question the screen asks is where to put the network software. C:\NET is the default, and that's as good a place as any. Next, you identify your network card. If you have a card that's not on this list, you will be happy to know that this program is much more forgiving than the Network Client Administrator. You just pick "Network adapter not shown on list." Soon you are prompted for a disk with the network drivers. You received those drivers with the network card.

Now, you are *never* going to find a diskette labeled "Drivers for Microsoft Network Client 3.0 for MS-DOS." Instead, look for a diskette labeled "NDIS 3.0 driver." Some boards don't call them NDIS 3; they call them "Windows for Workgroups version 3.11 drivers." It's the same in any case.

Next the setup program offers to use more memory for greater speed. Go ahead and experiment with this. I've found that sometimes the Network Client can't load at all with TCP/IP if I give it the extra buffers, so I press C to skip the extra buffers. Then the setup program asks for a user name; fill that in.

After that, the setup program presents you with a sort of overall setup configuration screen labeled "Setup for Microsoft Network Client v3.0 for MS-DOS," with three main sections:

- Change names
- Change setup options
- Change network configuration

You first tackle "Change names." It lets you modify

- The default user name
- The PC's machine name

- The name of the workgroup that the PC will be a member of
- The name of the domain (if any) that the PC's user will log on to

Fill all of these in. I usually give my workgroups and domains the same name, and I recommend that you do, also. When you're finished in that section, you get to "Change setup options." It lets you

- Change redir options
- Change startup options
- Change logon validation
- Change net popup key

You don't need to do anything with any of these options except Change logon validation. By default, it doesn't log you on to the domain. Change that option to "logon to domain."

The third and final section of the setup process is called "Change network configuration." It's divided into two parts, network board and network protocols. First you pick a network board and then you either remove the board, add a new board, or change settings on the board. You almost certainly have to pick "change settings" and set the I/O address and/or the hardware interrupt (IRQ) setting of the network board.

About all you do in the Protocol part is choose a protocol. If it's TCP/IP, then you go through the usual TCP/IP exercise of specifying IP address, subnet masks, and the like, unless you are using DHCP servers, in which case you need only choose "Use DHCP to obtain IP address." If you have no idea what I'm talking about here, hang on until Chapter 14; it will make a lot more sense then.

Once I've set it all the way I like, I choose "The listed options are correct." Network Client Setup then copies some files to my system, modifies AUTOEXEC .BAT and CONFIG.SYS, and prompts me to reboot. I reboot and then log on to the server.

Dealing with Passwords

Suppose I've created a new user account named MarkM with the password "hi." Now, remember, the server requires that I change the password immediately, as this is a new account. Believe it or not, changing my domain password isn't intuitive on the DOS network client. That's unfortunate, because the first contact that any user has with the network is that first logon, which requires the user to figure out how to change a password. So let's see how…

When I reboot the DOS client, I see the system start up and say:

```
Type your user name, or press ENTER if it is MARKM:
```

Since I'm MarkM, I press Enter.

The PC then says:

```
Type your password:
```

Now, believe it or not, the password I am being asked for *isn't* the NT user password "hi" that I just created. Instead, this is a kind of convenience that the Client for Microsoft Networks offers me. You see, you may end up having to use a number of passwords on the network—passwords for things that you may use on the network but aren't covered by the domain. The Client for Microsoft Networks keeps track of all of those passwords for you, so you only need to enter them once. After you've entered them, the Client for Microsoft Networks supplies them automatically.

These passwords are kept in an encrypted file called a *password list file*. You can recognize them because they have the extension PWL. What `Type your password:` really says is, "I want to create a password file, and I'll need a password to lock the password file." A *really* annoying part about this is that the Client for Microsoft Networks requires this password, even if it doesn't keep a password list. For some benighted reason, Microsoft seems to be trying to ensure a level of security by requiring this password *in addition to* the domain password. People have figured out ways to crack the password list files, so I recommend that you don't create one.

In any case, I need something to shut this thing up, so I enter the password **hello** and press Enter. The computer then responds:

```
There is no password-list file for user MARKM.
Do you want to create one? (Y/N) [N]:
```

Only *then* does it ask me for my password to get onto my domain:

```
Please enter your password for the domain ORION:
```

Now, I enter **hi** and get this message:

```
Error 2242: The password of this user has expired.
```

It's almost comical: after all that work, I get the error message that the password has expired.

I said "almost" comical; I do wish Microsoft would make this a bit more logical. They *did* make this first-time logon much easier with later operating systems, as you'll see a bit later in this chapter. In a sense, however, this is actually a *good* message. It tells you that the domain recognized your password, even though it has expired. If you had punched in the wrong password, you would have seen some other error message.

Now you have to change your password so that you can get onto the domain, but it looks like you've got to log on before you can change your password, right? No, actually not; there's a command for that called NET PASSWORD.

Ah, but which password does NET PASSWORD work on, the bogus local password or the domain password? By default, it works on the bogus local password, but there's an option to change the domain password. By specifying the option /domain:, you can change the domain password. You can do it all in one line, like so:

```
net password /domain:orion markm hi hello
```

That's a long line, so let's take it apart. The net password you understand. The /domain:orion says, "The password I'm changing is the password for the Orion domain, not my local password list. Markm hi hello is, respectively, my user name, my old password, and my new password."

When I press Enter after I type the command line, I see this useful message:

```
Error 7210: There is no entry for the specified user in the [Password
Lists] section of the SYSTEM.INI file.
```

Yes, it's annoying, but just ignore it. The domain password has been changed just fine. Now I can log on for real, like so (I've included my responses in italics):

```
net logon markm
Type your password: hello
Please enter your password for the domain ORION: hello
The server \\ORION01 successfully logged you on as MARKM.
Your privilege level on this domain is USER.
The command completed successfully.
```

Notice that I had to type the local workstation password first to make the local network software happy, then the domain password. If, by the way, you create a password list, you will never again be prompted for the domain password because your workstation will remember it and fill it in for you automatically.

Connecting to Directories and Print Shares

Now that I'm on the server, there are three basic things to do:

- Browse the network
- Connect to a directory share
- Connect to a print share

Browsing is simple. I just type **net view** and I see something like this:

```
Servers available in workgroup ORION.
Server Name     Remark

\\MICRON133
\\ORION01
The command completed successfully.
```

I want to see what's in the ORION01 server, to find out what shares it has, so I type **net view \\orion01**. That produces this:

```
Shared resources at \\ORION01
Sharename    Type         Comment

C        Disk     Main share on ORION01
cdrom      Disk     CD-ROM drive on ORION01
clients    Disk
HP4M       Print  HP LaserJet 4M on LPT1:
NETLOGON   Disk    Logon server share
PUBLIC     Disk    Public directory
USERS      Disk
The command completed successfully.
```

I'm looking for some files on the PUBLIC share, so I connect to that. I attach to it as my E: drive by typing **net use e: \\orion01\public**. Because you'll use this command a lot, let's pick it apart. First, NET USE is the command that says to go find a particular network resource and connect it to a local drive letter. The drive letter I'll use is E:.

If you plan to use drive letters above E:, then you have to add a LASTDRIVE command to CONFIG.SYS. By default, DOS only sets aside enough space for five drive letters. If you want network drives F:, G:, and H:, add the line **LASTDRIVE=H** to your CONFIG.SYS. I usually just add the command LASTDRIVE=Z to my CONFIG.SYS files as a matter of course, but if you're running old Novell software, that may not be a good idea. Check with whoever runs the rest of your network before you change the LASTDRIVE statement on all of your computers.

The last part of the command line, \\orion01\public in our case, is the Universal Naming Convention reference to the shared directory. Remember how they're built up? Two backslashes and the server name—that's \\Orion01—and then one backslash and the share name, making \\orion01\public. You can use lowercase or uppercase, it doesn't matter. You get a confirmation that it worked with this message:

```
The command completed successfully.
```

The next time I start up the network client on this system, it will automatically restore this E: drive. If I want to break the connection, I type the following:

```
NET USE E: /delete
```

I can do the same thing to tell my system to use a network printer. As you know, the printer ports on PCs are called LPT1, LPT2, and LPT3. Even though no printer is on this workstation, I'll tell the network software to direct any requests to print to LPT1 to another printer instead, the network printer HP4M. Again, doing that requires a NET USE command:

```
NET USE LPT1: \\ORION01\HP4M
```

The only difference is that I told the network to map to LPT1, not a drive letter, and to use the share HP4M on server ORION01.

You can log off with a net logoff command, and if you ever want to see your current connections, type **net use** all by itself.

Attaching Windows Workstations to NT Networks

Many of you are using one of three kinds of Windows on your workstations: Windows 3.1, Windows for Workgroups 3.11, or Windows 9x. If you're using Windows 3.1, you already know how to attach to your NT network. All you have to do is load the Microsoft Network Client and start Windows 3.1 on top of it. If you're using Windows for Workgroups, it's even easier.

Part of the process of installing Workgroups is identifying your network card to the Workgroups setup program. Once the Windows for Workgroups setup program is done, you're pretty much connected, except you still have to identify yourself to the domain. I will soon show you how to do that.

Now, if you didn't choose any of the network options when you set up Windows for Workgroups or you have to do some changes to a Windows for Workgroups machine, knowing where all the network setup stuff is can be useful, so let's go through all of it.

Setting up the network portion of Windows for Workgroups happens in two different places, unfortunately. The problem has been fixed in Windows 95 and Windows NT, but fiddling around with network setup in Windows for Workgroups requires doing some work in Network Setup. To find Network Setup, either go to the Main group in the Program Manager, start up Windows Setup, and click Options ➤ Change Network Settings, or go to the Network group and start up the program Network Setup. The rest of the network configuration happens in the Control Panel in the Network applet.

Doing the Network Setup Work

To start out configuring a Windows for Workgroups workstation to access a domain, go to the Network Setup program. Its opening screen looks like Figure 9.1.

FIGURE 9.1:

Network Setup screen

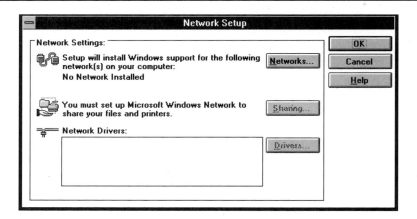

There are three sections to this window. Up top, you choose the redirector or client software that you want your workstation to use. In the middle, you enable or disable the file and print sharing feature of Windows for Workgroups. In the bottom part of the screen, you load network board drivers and protocols, and control settings for board drivers and protocols.

I start off by telling my workstation to load the client for Microsoft networks. To do that, click Networks. You see the dialog box in Figure 9.2.

FIGURE 9.2:

Choosing a network redirector

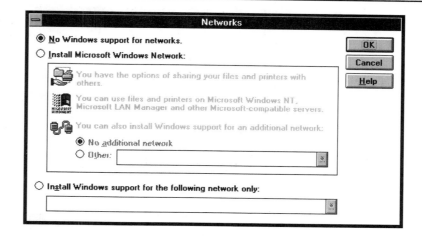

Click on Install Microsoft Windows Network and click OK. You go back to the Network Setup dialog box. Redirectors are no good without some data, which they get from protocols, which protocols in turn get from boards. To add a board, click the Drivers button. You see the dialog box in Figure 9.3.

FIGURE 9.3:

Adapter and protocol control window

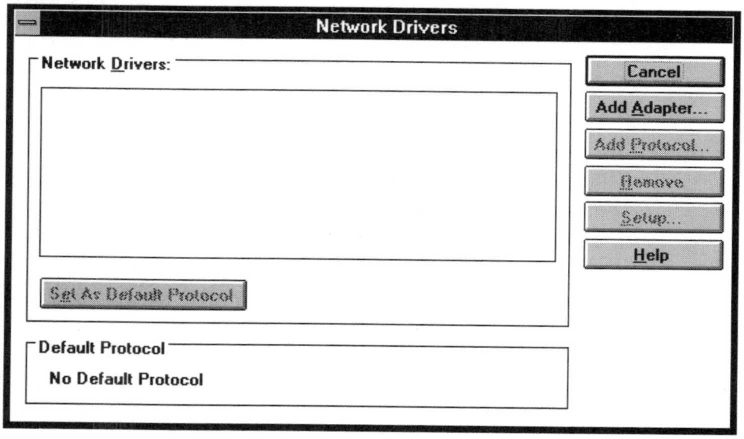

Click on the Add Adapter button and choose either a particular adapter or let Windows for Workgroups automatically detect your adapter. If you know what adapter is in your system, I strongly recommend specifying it rather than having Windows for Workgroups automatically detect it. Automatic detection can sometimes crash the system.

Once you've picked an adapter, your adapter wants you to make hardware settings such as the I/O address, IRQ, memory addresses, whether it's 10baseT or 10base2, and things like that. Fill in the information. When you're done, the dialog box will look something like the one in Figure 9.4.

FIGURE 9.4:

The Network Setup dialog with the board filled in

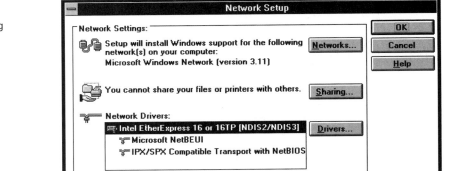

Notice that it automatically includes the IPX and NetBEUI protocols. Now, in my network I don't make much use of IPX, so I get rid of it by clicking on it and then clicking Remove. It asks if I'm sure, and I confirm that I am.

You can choose to make a protocol the "default" protocol, but in the final analysis it doesn't mean anything. One more problem before I go on: my Intel EtherExpress is set to IRQ 5, but the program never gave me the chance to set that. So I click on the Intel EtherExpress line and the Setup button. That lets me alter the IRQ setting. Note that this is specific to network cards; you may or may not have to do this on your system.

Click Close and you're back at the Network Setup screen. As you've seen, there's a button that controls whether the workstation shares its files with other PCs or not. By now, you know that my advice is not to do that. Click OK in the Network Setup screen, and you see the Microsoft Windows Network Names dialog box in Figure 9.5.

FIGURE 9.5:

Prompting for network
names

FIGURE 9.5:

Prompting for network
names

Microsoft Windows Network Names

These names identify you and your computer
to others on the Microsoft Windows
Network.

OK

Help

User Name: MarkMina

Workgroup: WORKGROUP

Computer Name: MarkMina

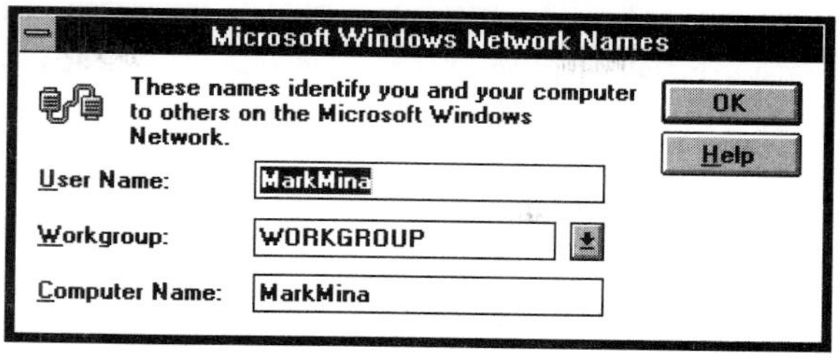

The defaults are all wrong, so I fill in the correct values and click OK. The Network Setup program then copies the files and asks to reboot.

Setting and Changing Domain Passwords

Do that and type **win** to start up Windows for Workgroups. A dialog box labeled Welcome to Windows for Workgroups prompts you for a name and password. As before, it's not the real domain password, but we'll get to that. You are prompted whether or not to create a password-list file. Again, it's your call whether to do it or not. Just to be different, I let it create a password list file this time around. It will ask you to type in the password again.

TIP

It's a pretty good idea to make your local password the same as your domain password. That's because when you try to access a domain, the domain interrogates your Windows for Workgroups workstation for a password, and, if you haven't yet told Windows for Workgroups your domain password (more on this later), Windows for Workgroups automatically responds with your local password.

You are then logged on to Windows for Workgroups, but not yet to your domain. In the case of my example, the domain isn't yet aware of MarkM. Before trying to access domain resources, I recommend that you set up your Windows for Workgroups workstation to explicitly log on to the domain. To do that, open the Control Panel and double-click the Network applet. It is illustrated in Figure 9.6.

This is an important dialog box. As you can see, you can use it to change the default logon user name or the workgroup. To log on to a domain, however, click the Startup button. You'll see a dialog box like the one in Figure 9.7.

FIGURE 9.6:

Control Panel Network applet

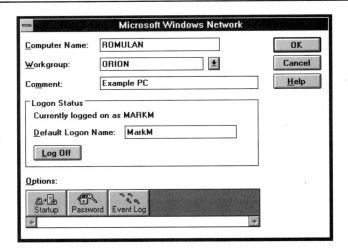

FIGURE 9.7:

Startup Settings dialog box

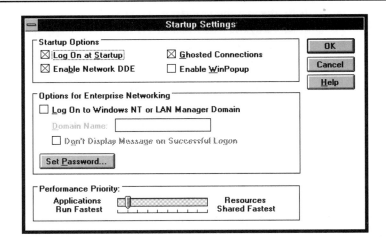

The center group is called Options for Enterprise Networking. Click the check box labeled Log On to Windows NT or LAN Manager Domain and enter the domain's name. Now, in my case I have to change the password for MarkM, as it's a new account, so I need a way to change my domain's password. I can do that by clicking the Set Password button. I see the dialog box in Figure 9.8.

This dialog box lets me, first of all, inform my Windows for Workgroups workstation what my domain password is so it can automatically supply the password when it logs me on to the domain. This dialog box also gives me a simple vehicle for changing my domain password. When I'm done, I click OK to return to the dialog box labeled Microsoft Windows Network (see Figure 9.6).

FIGURE 9.8:

Setting and changing a domain password from Windows for Workgroups

Change Domain Password

Change Password for User:	MARKM	OK
Change Password on:	ORION	Cancel
		Help
Old Password:		
New Password:		
Confirm New Password:		

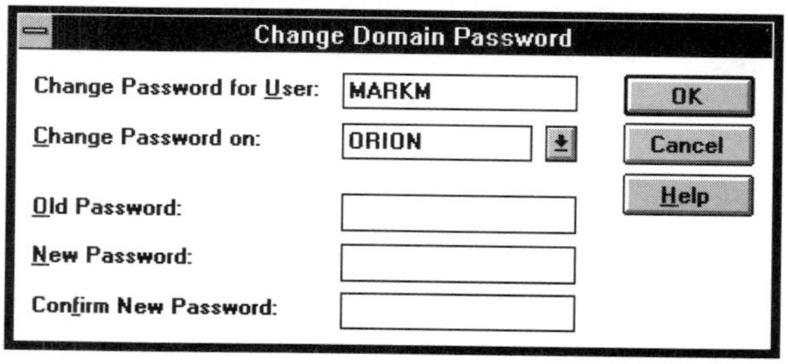

You're pretty much set now, but if you click OK, the system will want to reboot before you can get on to the domain. That's not necessary, however. To log on to the domain then and there without rebooting, just click the Log Off button. Once you've done that, its label changes to Log On; click it. Windows for Workgroups prompts you for your *Windows for Workgroups* password. Fill that in, and then you should get the dialog box shown in Figure 9.9.

FIGURE 9.9:

Domain Welcome dialog box

Windows for Workgroups

You were successfully logged on to ORION as MARKM by \\ORION01 with USER privilege.

OK

Attaching to Network Resources

Now that you're on the network, you can attach to a network resource. First, what's out there? You can see that by starting up the Windows for Workgroups File Manager and clicking Disk ➢ Connect Network Drive. You see a dialog box like the one in Figure 9.10.

This is the Windows for Workgroups version of a browse list. You can see in the figure that I have three workgroups named ACADEMY, ORION, and TED, and that ORION includes servers named MICRON133 and ORION01 at the moment. If you click on a server, as I have clicked on ORION01, you see the shares available on that server. Click OK and you're connected. If the share is a hidden one, then, of course, you can't see it on the browse list. But you can directly punch in a UNC such as **\\server01\myshare$** in the Path field.

FIGURE 9.10:

Windows for Workgroups
directory share browse list

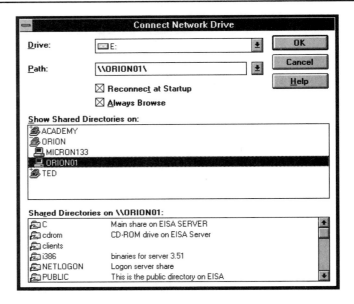

To attach to a shared printer, go to the Main group of the Program Manager and start up the Print Manager. Then click Printer ➤ Connect Network Printer. You see a dialog box almost identical to the directory browse list. Choose a networked printer and Print Manager loads the appropriate print driver.

Just to reiterate, you can't change your domain password by clicking Control Panel, then Network, then Password because that changes the local Windows for Workgroups password. I've already explained it, but just as a reminder you can change the domain password by opening the Control Panel, opening Network, clicking Startup, and clicking Set Password (which refers to the domain password).

Before I leave the topic of Windows for Workgroups, let me make a very important point: when Microsoft came out with NT, they improved the networking part of Windows for Workgroups a bit. On the CD-ROM, in the Clients\wfw\Update directory, you see a few files, fewer than ten. If you already have Windows for Workgroups on a computer, then attach it to the NT server and get those files. Copy them to both your Windows and your Windows\System directories, and reboot. Doing so will speed up your networking and at the same time will make your NT connection go a bit more smoothly, because there are some bug fixes in the revised code.

Attaching Windows 95 and 98 Workstations to NT Networks

Many of you have moved from Windows 3.*x* or Workgroups to the newer Windows 95 or 98. In actual fact, Windows 95/98 is really just Windows for Workgroups with a pretty face, but finding your way around network controls if you only know Windows for Workgroups can be a little tricky. And if you're concerned that Windows 98 changes things yet again, don't worry—there's basically no difference between the way that Windows 95 and Windows 98 network with NT, save for some improvements to the Dial-Up Networking Client. Again, let me start off by assuming that your workstation knows nothing so far about networking (after all, it's easy enough to get it to that state) and then work from there.

Configuring the Workstation

In Windows 95/98, click Start, Control Panel, and Networking. You see a screen like the one in Figure 9.11.

FIGURE 9.11:

Networking page in Control
Panel for Windows 95/98

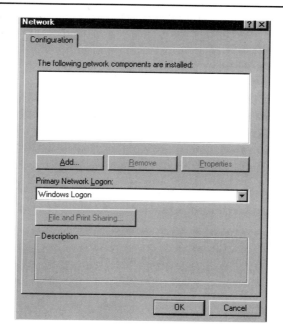

As before, this needs a redirector/client, at least one protocol, and at least one board driver. You can add any of those things by clicking the Add button. You then see the dialog box shown in Figure 9.12.

FIGURE 9.12:

Choosing a redirector, protocol, or board type

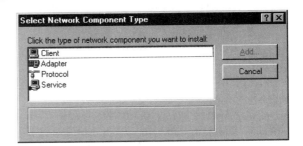

I load a redirector or, as it's more commonly called these days, a *network client*. I click Client and I see the dialog box in Figure 9.13.

FIGURE 9.13:

Picking a Microsoft-written network redirector/client

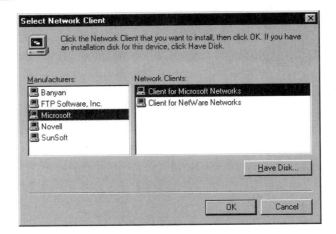

Microsoft ships both an NT-compatible and a NetWare-compatible client. To talk to NT networks, I choose the Client for Microsoft Networks and click OK. Now, recall that a client (redirector) sits on top of a protocol, and a protocol sits on top of a board driver. That means that just loading a client without a protocol and board would sort of leave the client software hanging in empty space, so to speak. Therefore, the Control Panel asks also for a board driver, as you see in Figure 9.14.

FIGURE 9.14:

Prompting for a network
card type

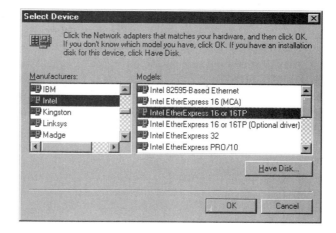

When I choose a board, the Control Panel automatically loads the NetBEUI and
IPX protocols, as did Windows for Workgroups. You can see that in Figure 9.15.

FIGURE 9.15:

New state of the Network
applet of the Control Panel

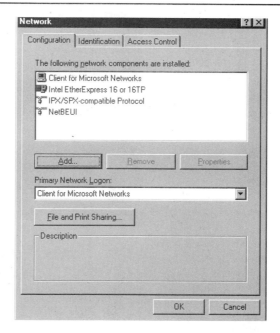

I've already said I don't use IPX, so I highlight it and click Remove; that may or may not make sense for your network. Then I have to double-click on the network card icon to set its I/O address, IRQ, and the like. Again, this will vary from network board to network board. Click the Advanced and Resources tabs to see what you can set for your particular network board, and click Close when you're done.

Attaching to the Network

You then go back to the Network applet. Click the Identification tab to continue. You see a screen similar to the one in Figure 9.16.

FIGURE 9.16:

Identification tab of Network applet

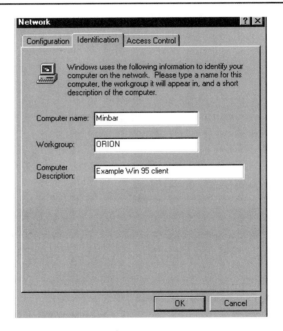

In the figure, I've filled in a machine name, a workgroup, and a description. But what about the domain? Where do I specify a domain? Return to the Configuration tab and double-click on the Client for Microsoft Networks. You see a dialog box like the one in Figure 9.17.

To log onto a domain, just check the box labeled Log on to Windows NT domain and fill in the domain's name. Click OK to return to the Network applet and OK again to tell the Control Panel that you're finished. It will load some files and reboot.

FIGURE 9.17:

Setting the domain settings

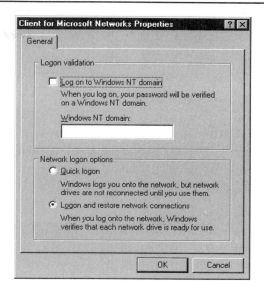

Once your computer has rebooted, you'll see a new logon dialog box, one with three fields: username, password, and domain.

Remember how much trouble it was to change the domain password the first time around on Windows for Workgroups? Well, in contrast, you're going to love Windows 95/98 because it produces a nice dialog box that tells you that it's recognized your domain password, but that the password has expired, and would you change it please? It even provides fields in which to type the new password. Much improved!

Once you're in, you can browse your network with the Network Neighborhood (I imagine calling the folder "browse network" would have been too complex). Open up Network Neighborhood and you see a screen similar to Figure 9.18.

FIGURE 9.18:

Browsing a network with Windows 95/98

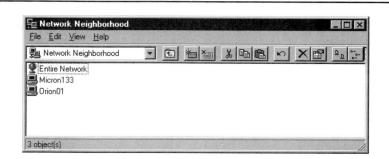

Open a server and you can see what it offers. In Figure 9.19, you can see the shares that ORION01 offers.

FIGURE 9.19:

Listing a server's shares

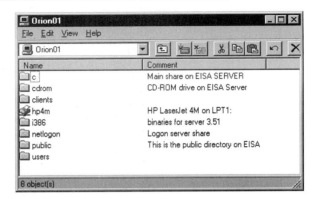

Actually, I cheated and clicked View ➤ Details so that you could see the comments, but that's a basic browse. You can map to a share by right-clicking on it, choosing Map Network Drive, and clicking OK. In the same way, you can attach to a shared printer. Look at Figure 9.19 and you can see that the Network Neighborhood shows not only the directory shares, but the printer shares, as well.

To attach to a network printer, click Start, Settings, and Printers. You see an option to create a new printer. Click on that and you start a Wizard that leads you through the process. First, the Wizard asks if you'll be adding a local or network printer, and you choose network. Click Next, and it asks where to find the printer. In response, you can either punch a UNC right in or browse the network. It also asks if you print from DOS programs; what it's really asking is whether or not it should map a printer interface name, like LPT1 or COM2, to the network printer. You have to point it to the drivers (they're on the installation CD-ROM or floppies), after which you are prompted to print a test page. Printing a test page is a good idea, so do it.

Supporting "Thin" Clients with Windows Terminal Server

Thus far in this chapter, we've seen how to set up the traditional (well, if "since 1985" is the same as "traditional") type of local area network client—a DOS,

Windows, or (in the next chapter) Mac system connected to a server for file and print sharing services. But this tradition has turned out to be expensive to implement and to support, as Windows on every user's desktop means many complex machines to support.

Years ago, before Windows 3.0 even appeared and it seemed to some that OS/2 would be the dominant desktop operating system, Citrix Systems developed an alternative to putting a copy of OS/2 on every desktop—a multi-user version of OS/2. Founded by some of the original OS/2 developers, Citrix built a version of OS/2 wherein instead of buying a whole bunch of powerful machines that run OS/2, you instead buy a few *very* powerful machines and run Citrix OS/2. Then you buy low-power machines for every desktop, machines that are really not much more than dumb terminals. All of the computing gets done on the few powerful centralized machines; all the terminals do is supply keystrokes and mouse input and display graphical output.

Winframe: Multi-User NT

Following the market's move from OS/2 to NT, Citrix developed a centralized version of NT called *Winframe*. Again, a special version of NT runs on a central machine or machines, and users use low-power terminals. It's somewhat like an old-style mainframe in that everything takes place at a single machine or a small group of machines, making support much simpler for a central support group. The "mainframes" can also be better protected behind walls and locked doors, backed up from one location, and even rebooted without too much trouble. Support folks can do a lot of support without wearing out shoe leather.

On the other hand, Winframe *wasn't* like a mainframe in that mainframes tend to only support text-only, two-color applications, and keyboards only—no mice. A user sitting at a terminal attached to a Winframe system, in contrast, would have very little way to know that she was at a dumb terminal rather than a standard Windows NT system; she could run basically any program that Windows NT could run—*unmodified*. No need to buy a special version of Word, Netscape Navigator, or WordPerfect: just put a standard app on the central Winframe machine and away you go.

Microsoft Gets in the Act: Windows Terminal Server

Microsoft licensed the Winframe technology from Citrix and incorporated it into Windows NT 4.0 in mid-1998, resulting in the *Windows Terminal Server version 4.0*. (Who but Microsoft could call a first version "version 4.0?" I wonder if I could sell more books if I called this the "Silver 25th Edition"…) Good performance, convenience of support and setup, and a variety of potential terminal types make this a product that you should look at seriously. It's not without its costs, however, as you'll see.

Windows Terminal Server will run on just about any machine that NT Server will run on, but you'll probably want *lots* more memory and potentially more CPUs, as well.

TIP   Plan to add about 32MB of RAM for each user that you'll put on a server, and plan for about five to ten users per CPU, depending on the applications you're running.

Windows Terminal Options and Applications

One of the beauties of Terminal Server is the potential savings on desktop hardware, or so I've said. But how much *does* a dumb terminal—the WTS phrase is a *windows terminal* or *winterm*—cost? Maybe *nothing*. Got an old Windows for Workgroups machine running on a 386 with 8MB of RAM? Then all you've got to do is run a program called the Windows Terminal Client, which ships free with WTS, on that machine, and you've got a winterm that will provide all the performance that you'll need to run big spreadsheets, complex documents, and animation-ridden desktop presentations, as all the memory and RAM requirements are felt elsewhere, on the Terminal Server machine. Much of the advertising hype about the WTS talks of *thin clients*, meaning desktop terminals that are both simple to set up and cheap to buy—but the ultimate thin client is a machine that you already own and, in the case of the example 386, that's completely paid for and depreciated.

There's a 32-bit version of Windows Terminal Client included with WTS, as well, so you can make winterms out of your Windows 95/98 or NT workstation machines. You may wonder, why bother making a winterm out of an NT workstation—why not run applications straight on the NT machine? Several reasons. For some firms, the cost of support is considered to be so great that the cost of NT-ready hardware is irrelevant. As a result, they put an NT machine with a very vanilla configuration on every desktop: a configuration that can be re-created in minutes with Ghost, SysPrep, or some other quick-configuration tool. No user data or applications reside on the user's desktop, save basic NT and the Windows Terminal Client. Then, if a user reports a problem that can't be fixed from the central WTS server, all the support person has to do is to go over to the user's machine, wipe its hard disk, and pull down the basic system "image" onto the hard disk, restoring the troubled workstation to a pristine state both quickly and simply—no in-depth troubleshooting required, unless the problem's a hardware-based one.

Other firms set up standard NT or 95/98 desktops with local copies of standard applications like Office 97, but want to strongly control a particular application, perhaps a very expensive or specialized application. They put that application on the WTS machine, and then users fire up Windows Terminal Client whenever they need to run that application. It's very simple for a WTS administrator to control how many people are simultaneously logged onto a WTS server, which, in passing, controls how many access an application.

Alternatively, if you don't already own machines that can act as winterms, you can *buy* one. Several firms now sell machines that are not PCs, not smart or powerful enough to be PCs, but are smart enough to be winterms. And they're *cheap*, as low as $350 for a winterm without a monitor, and small—they take up less space than PCs do.

NOTE   If I sound effusive about WTS, I am—I've been running it since its beta days. My house is wired for Ethernet and I've got a small Wyse winterm on an adjustable arm bolted to the wall in my kitchen, a place that I'd never previously considered a good spot for a PC. It's incredibly convenient for looking something up on the Web, checking my e-mail, and the like. One of these days someone will build a winterm about the size of a Toshiba Libretto (which, if you've never seen one, is the size of a VHS videocassette) with a wireless connection, and I'll be a very happy man.

Protocols: Two Languages for Communicating between Winterms and WTS

There are three parts to setting up a WTS system:

- The WTS server
- The winterms
- The language that they use to speak

You have two choices for this server-to-client language (the *protocol*), and it's an important choice that, like so many things in life, lets you trade price for quality.

Remote Desktop Protocol

The first protocol option is called the *Remote Desktop Protocol* or RDP. (During development Microsoft called it T.Share, so you may see some documentation and help files refer to it by that name.) RDP ships free with WTS, and it's a pretty good option if your winterms are connected to their WTS servers with high-speed connections—1Mbps and faster.

RDP's problem is that it's not very discriminating in the things that it transfers. Suppose you're sitting at a winterm and you do something to your Desktop that doesn't affect it much—such as moving an icon over on the Desktop an inch or so. Your winterm doesn't understand that you've only made a minor change— whether large or small, the terminal depends upon the WTS machine for its screens. And despite that fact that your move-the-icon action has only modified a few hundred of the hundreds of thousands of pixels on your Desktop, RDP takes the "shotgun" approach and just re-transmits the entire Desktop, every single pixel, to your winterm. A little math will show that you're going to need some significant bandwidth in order for the server to keep the terminal's responses feeling snappy to the user. Over local connections, then, RDP's a good answer. RDP *does* have a optional setting whereby you say to it, "Do some compression and save some bandwidth, OK?" and it certainly offers some improvement, but it's still not acceptable for 56K and slower connections—a dual-channel 128Kbps ISDN connection would be fine with compressed RDP.

The RDP protocol is very geared to supporting dumb terminals, so much that any Windows Terminal Clients that you run cannot access your local hard disks; when your machine is in a terminal client window, your C: drive is the C: drive of the Terminal Server, not your machine's, the floppy is the Terminal Server's floppy, and so on.

You may want to offer a client the ability to log onto a Terminal Server, but only to use one program. You can do that both with RDP and MetaFrame, saying, for example, that when user Jane logs on she doesn't see an entire Windows Desktop, just Internet Explorer, Word, or whatever.

MetaFrame/Independent Client Architecture (ICA)

The Citrix folks have had almost 10 years to tune and perfect their server-to-terminal protocol—and they've used that time wisely. They've developed a protocol that they once called the Independent Client Architecture (ICA) protocol, but now they call *MetaFrame*. MetaFrame is extremely parsimonious with your server-to-terminal bandwidth; it's so good, in fact, that you can actually get good performance on a winterm that is connected to a WTS server *over a 56K dial-up connection*. (I didn't believe this until I tried it, but it's true.) MetaFrame doesn't send entire screens to winterms, but instead sends the *changes*, a considerably smaller amount of data.

MetaFrame offers you more flexibility, as well, giving you the option to connect to your system's local hard disks. Within a MetaFrame desktop a user can access his own disks by doing a NET USE.

Support people in a MetaFrame-using environment will like *shadowing*. With shadowing, you run a Windows Terminal Client and "eavesdrop" on another person's winterm session. (Provided you have the proper security level, of course.) You can even enter keystrokes and mouse clicks, making it a sort of three-way session between the Windows Terminal Server and two users both employing the same application and data. Sounds like a terrific remote support tool!

Why not use MetaFrame always, then? It's not cheap. Microsoft doesn't give it away—you've got to buy it from Citrix. Citrix licenses it for about $200 per desktop: a pretty steep price to pay when you consider that the entire Windows NT Workstation operating system costs about that. (On the other hand, rumor has it that they had to give the Winframe software to Microsoft essentially at gunpoint, so I guess they've got to make money *somewhere*.) Additionally, for some reason Citrix has made the serious strategic error of not offering a version of MetaFrame for the Alpha chip—and there's no better machine to put WTS on than an Alpha with its raw CPU power.

And Speaking of Cost...

Even if you *don't* buy MetaFrame, get ready for a bit of sticker shock. What does WTS cost? Well, the server cost is basically the same as regular old NT Server. But when you go to add the clients, things get a bit more expensive. You'll need to buy an NT Workstation license for every machine that runs as a winterm, regardless of whatever other operating systems are on the client.

So, for example, if you ran the Windows Terminal Client on a Windows 98 machine, you'd not only have paid for the Windows 98 license, you now also have to fork over a couple of hundred bucks for an NT Workstation license. Additionally, any software that you run from a Terminal Server requires extra licenses. Even if you *had* a copy of Office on that Windows 98 system already, you can't run the copy of Office on the Terminal Server without paying for an extra Office license. You can see that while the benefits are potentially lower desktop hardware costs and support costs, the price you'll pay for those benefits are higher server costs—Terminal Servers should be fairly muscular machines—and quite a lot of software license costs.

Setting Up Terminal Server

As I mentioned before, Terminal Server is a separate product from NT Server, rather than an add-on to an existing NT Server. (That *won't* be true for Windows 2000 Server—in the next version, Terminal Server will be offered as a built-in option.) Once you've acquired it, however, running Setup for Terminal Server is almost identical to running Setup on NT Server 4, save for a few things. Here are some tips on installing Terminal Server.

The initial text part of Setup is virtually identical to standard NT Server, save that it offers the default directory name \WTSRV rather than the more familiar \WINNT. The changes only become apparent once Setup does all of its file copying and reboots to its graphical phase. The first thing you'll notice is the background wallpaper: instead of the deep blue bitmap with the picture of the phone and other desk items, an abstract graphic announces that you're running Setup for Windows Terminal Server.

After the screen asking you to tell what licensing mode you'll be using for the server—per seat or per server, recall?—a new screen appears labeled Terminal Server Desktops. It asks, "Please specify the number of Windows Terminal Server desktops that will be connected to this server." As I said in the last section, you've got to buy NT Workstation licenses for each person connected to a Terminal Server. There's a spinner box on this screen where you fill in the number of licenses that you've purchased. But don't worry too much about getting this number right, because Terminal Server automatically installs an administrative tool called Terminal Server License Manager, which you can use to increase or decrease the number.

Windows Terminal Server has Service Pack 3 built right into it, so you'll notice a second round of file copying as Setup installs the newer SP3 files. You'll also be asked if you want to install Internet Explorer 4; I'd recommend that you do install it, as many of Microsoft's new patches and free enhancements won't install on a machine until the machine has IE4 on it. I've found IE4 useful because, as I mentioned earlier, I run Terminal Server on an Alpha and the main uses that I put my winterm to are browsing the Web and checking e-mail. My firm's small enough that I just use Internet-based e-mail for our office mail, so all I need for a mail client is a simple Internet e-mail client—and Outlook Express not only works admirably for my modest needs, it's also the only Internet e-mail client that I've found for the Alpha that works.

Member server or domain controller? Most terminal servers should probably be member servers, as they need all the memory that they can get and domain controllers must devote some RAM to retaining a copy of the domain's SAM in that RAM. (You can read more about this in the second half of Chapter 11.) You need not create a whole new domain for your WTS clients, as a Terminal Server machine can read a standard SAM from a domain controller as easily as any member server can.

After what looks like the finish of a normal NT setup, Terminal Server Setup will reboot and do a *third* phase, running Active Setup if you've installed IE4. Along the way you may get a message that tells you that Terminal Server is going to copy files but has found a newer file. Terminal Server Setup then asks, "Should I overwrite this newer file with its older file," offering Yes (overwrite file), No (don't overwrite this one), and No to all (don't bother me again, and don't overwrite any files). Normally I'd say No to all—newer files are always better than older files, right?—but in this case the answer is an unqualified Yes.

If you see this message, what's probably happening is this. You've installed Windows 98 on the machine for whatever reason, or perhaps the machine came from the manufacturer with Windows 98 already on it. The Internet Explorer 4 files that come with Windows 98 are a bit different and newer than the ones that come with Windows Terminal Server. In this case, newer files are *not* better—if you leave the Windows 98 files in place, the IE 4 features will not work under Windows Terminal Server. Too bad there isn't a "Yes to all" option!

Alternatively, it's probably not a bad idea to simply wipe a machine's hard drive clean before installing Terminal Server. It would be a real shame if some leftover free program that just came with the computer, such as Quicken or the like, were discovered by a WTS user, leading to all kinds of potential license violation problems.

Once WTS starts up for the first time, you'll see a fairly standard-looking NT Desktop, save for a different bitmap and background color—the default is black rather than teal. The Administrative Tools group will look as it always does, save for four new programs:

- **Terminal Server Administration**   This is the big kahuna of WTS admin tools. You'll do most of your admin work from this and the User Manager, which, as you'll see, is changed a bit under Terminal Server. Lets you see who's connected at the moment, log people off, and the like.

- **Terminal Server Client Creator**   This is a program that puts the Windows Terminal Client program on three floppies so it's easy to walk over to a machine and install the client program. Now, given that you've got to be networked in the first place to run Windows Terminal Client, why not put these files on the Terminal Server instead, as a simple file share? No reason not to, so you probably won't be needing those floppies—or the Terminal Server Client Creator—very much.

- **Terminal Server Connection Configuration** This configures the RDP protocol on a Terminal Server. Lets you control the encryption between client and server, allow or disable shadowing (assuming you're using MetaFrame), and set security on WTS sessions.

- **Terminal Server License Manager** As mentioned before, this allows you to inform Terminal Server when you add (or possibly subtract) client licenses.

Setting Up a Windows Terminal Client

If you're using a winterm to connect to a Terminal Server, then you'll typically configure it through some built-in GUI specific to that particular winterm's vendor.

> **TIP**
>
> If you *are* planning to buy a winterm, bear in mind that some winterms can only support MetaFrame or, as they'll probably call it if they were sold before mid-1998, ICA. As the server portion of MetaFrame does not come free with Windows Terminal Server, an ICA-only terminal would not be of much value to you if you haven't decided to make the separate MetaFrame purchase—and remember that an ICA-only winterm will never be able to communicate with an Alpha server.

If, on the other hand, you just want to make a Windows or NT desktop able to act as a winterm, you'll just need to install the Windows Terminal Client on that desktop. One way to do that is to just walk the WTS installation CD around and run its AUTORUN/AUTOPLAY program, choosing option Win32 Client Setup. Alternatively, just copy the \clients\tsclient\win32\i386\net directory from the WTS CD-ROM to a network share and run the Setup program from there. If you're installing on Windows for Workgroups, run the 16-bit version from \clients\tsclient\win16\i386\net. Finally, you can also create three floppies using the Terminal Server Client Creator and then walk those floppies over to the target desktop.

Once you start Setup for the Terminal Client, you'll see an initial screen like the one shown in Figure 9.20.

Its main job, as you can see, is to remind you of the dire penalties for violating copyright laws. Once you've been properly warned, you click Continue, and see the screen shown in Figure 9.21.

Here's a familiar screen. (Although why it can't simply pull this information from the Registry and give me the chance to change it later, rather than making me answer the question explicitly, is beyond me.) Click OK, and you'll be reminded again of the dire penalties for copyright violation, as shown in Figure 9.22.

FIGURE 9.20:

Starting Setup for Terminal Client

FIGURE 9.21:

Enter Name and Organization

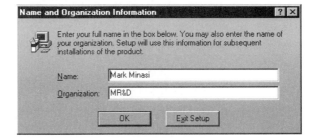

FIGURE 9.22:

Second copyright warning

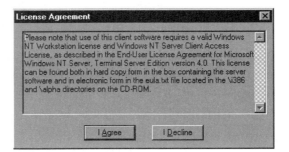

This particular Setup program is beginning to look less like a setup program and more like an on-line tutorial—a mandatory one. Click I Agree for yet another unnecessary screen, as you see in Figure 9.23.

FIGURE 9.23:

Start installation

For heaven's sake, Microsoft, why not just install the silly thing and let me uninstall if I decide I don't want it? Anyway, once that's done, and you click the button, then a *useful* screen—or least a mildly useful screen—appears, as you see in Figure 9.24.

FIGURE 9.24:

Setting initial settings for all users

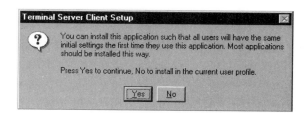

Remember user profiles? You may decide that you want every WTS user to have a different initial profile. On the other hand, you may just say, "Hey, I've got lots of control over WTS users, no reason to get too user-specific." My guess is that you will find that giving every user the same basic profile will work out just fine—if you need to fine-tune one particular user account, then go ahead and do that one later. I'd just click Yes and continue. At that point, the user will have a new program group labeled Terminal Server Client with three programs:

- Client Connection Manager
- Terminal Server Client
- Uninstall

Client Connection Manager is basically just a Wizard that walks you through the process of creating a pre-built client connection. It's just as easy, however, to activate Terminal Server Client; when you do, you'll see a screen like Figure 9.25.

FIGURE 9.25:

Starting up Terminal Server Client

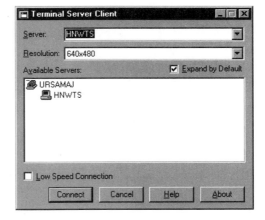

The initial screen shows you all of the Terminal Servers that it knows about, prompting you to pick one and to choose a screen resolution. You can also choose Low Speed Connection, but this is RDP we're playing with, not ICA—the Low Speed Connection implies that you can make 128Kbps connections acceptable, not 28.8Kbps connections. Still, if you're bandwidth-limited and don't mind squandering some of the server and clients' CPU power on compressing and expanding data, use Low Speed Connection. The display resolutions that you're offered will depend on the resolution used by the Terminal Server itself—if it only displays 800 × 600, you'll be offered 640 × 480 and 800 × 600, but if the Terminal Server runs at 1024 × 768, you'll get the option of 1024 × 768, as well. Choose which server and resolution you want and click Connect, and you'll see something like Figure 9.26.

FIGURE 9.26:

Terminal Server logon screen

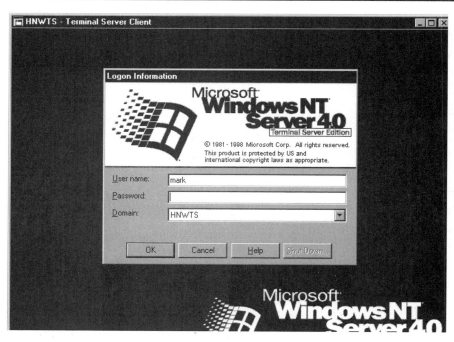

This works just as the normal logon works—fill in your name, password, and domain to tell the system which SAM to look you up in, and click OK. You'll see a window containing an entire Desktop. Click the Start button and you'll see something like Figure 9.27.

When you want to stop a Terminal Server session, you've got two options—Disconnect and Logoff. Logoff tells the Terminal Server to just shut down whatever programs you're using, just as if you were to shut down a Windows NT Desktop. The Terminal Server gets to reclaim whatever memory it has dedicated to your session. Disconnect, however, is a different—and kind of neat—story. Suppose you start some big task going, perhaps a big print job. It'll take a while and it's time to go off to lunch, but you don't want to leave your terminal logged on while you're away from your desk. Just disconnect, and the job keeps running! You can then log back on later and check on the task's process—you can even log on from a different terminal.

Getting back to Terminal Server client sessions, once you've got one running, the Desktop inside the Terminal Server Client window acts like a normal NT Desktop. Remember, however, the one thing that can be a bit confusing while running a Terminal Server client session on a Windows or NT machine: the drive letters. While working inside a Windows Terminal Client window, the drive letters refer to drives on the Terminal Server, not the local machine, and in fact when your machine is running Windows Terminal Client, it is flatly impossible to access the machine's local hard or floppy disks, as I mentioned earlier in this chapter.

FIGURE 9.27:

Terminal Server Client showing security and disconnect buttons

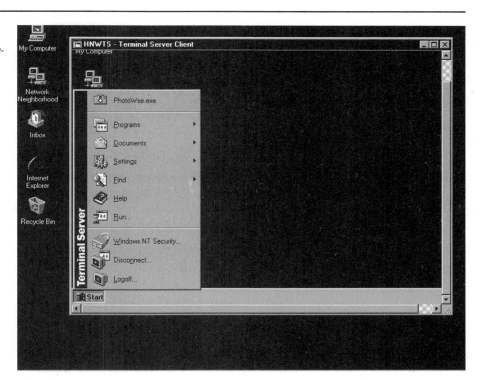

| TIP | And speaking of logoffs and disconnects, here's a tip for Terminal Server administrators. In *general*, Terminal Server's user interface is the same as standard NT's, *except* when it comes to saying "goodbye." When I walked over to a Terminal Server and logged on as an administrator, I was a little confused when I wanted to shut down the server—the Shutdown option just plain didn't appear, just a Logoff option. I couldn't figure out how to shut down Terminal Server so I could turn the PC off, until I remembered the NT Security dialog box. You access the NT Security dialog box by pressing the Ctrl+Alt+Del key combination. The dialog has, among other things, a button labeled Shutdown—*that's* how you shut down a Terminal Server! |

Controlling User Access

Terminal Server gives you a fair amount of control over what a user can and can't do. In particular, you can

- Specify a maximum time length for any Terminal Server session
- Restrict a user to a single program
- Prohibit particular users from using Terminal Server
- Prohibit particular users from using particular applications

In addition, all of the user-administration tools that you already know about work with Terminal Server. So, for example, you can use the Hours button in User Manager to restrict the times that a user can log on, or you can use system policies to create a clean Desktop and/or a very limited Start Programs menu.

Run the User Manager for Domains from a Windows Terminal Server machine, select Properties for a user's account and you'll notice that in addition to the usual Groups, Profile, Hours, and other buttons, User Manager now has a new button labeled Config. Click it, and you'll see a screen like the one in Figure 9.28.

FIGURE 9.28:

Terminal Server User Configuration

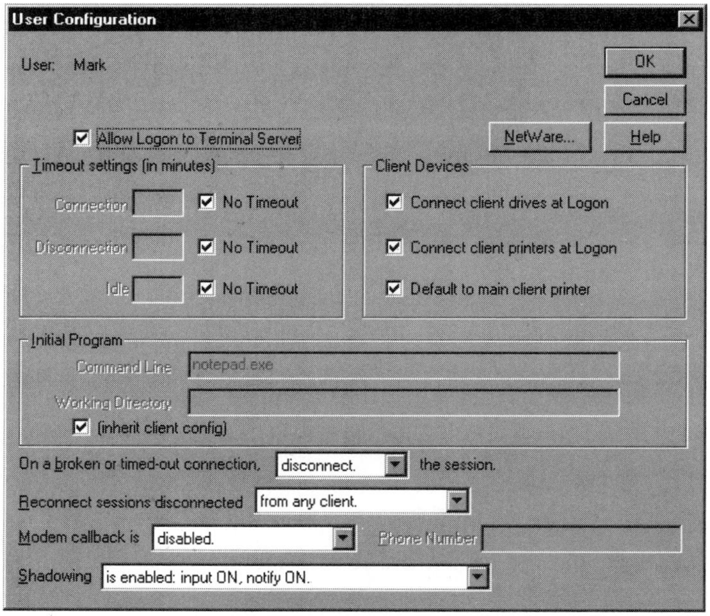

This dialog is adapted from Citrix's WinFrame product, which explains why most of it is useless unless you're running MetaFrame. But some is of value to RDP users, as well.

Allow Logon to Terminal Server   Lets you control which users can and cannot connect to this terminal server. (To control access to some other terminal server, just click User ➤ Select Domain, and type in the machine name of the other terminal server. Of course, you must have an administrative account on that server in order to be able to do this kind of administration.)

Timeout Settings (in Minutes)   Lets you control how the server should react if a user's terminal session is inactive (or active) for a long period of time. Connection specifies the maximum length of a Terminal Server session. You might want to keep users from staying on Terminal Server for more than, say, three hours; in that case, put **180** in this text field and users will be logged off or disconnected after three hours. You control whether the user is logged off or disconnected in the later field that says, "On a broken or timed-out connection, disconnect/reset the connection." You choose disconnect or reset (which means to log off the user) with a single-selection drop-down list box.

TIP   It could become quite a problem if a large number of users habitually did not log off, but instead disconnected, as that would chew up a lot of memory on the Terminal Server; further, those disconnected sessions could leave a lot of files open, making system backup problematic. You can reduce the number of disconnected sessions by specifying a timeout, as this dialog box allows. The third timeout tells WTS what to do if a user just walks away from a terminal without logging off.

Initial Program   Lets you specify the program certain users can access. Un-check the setting "(Inherit client config)" and you can specify that when the user logs on, she only gets a particular program—Internet Explorer, Word, or whatever—and that's all she'll see in her Windows Terminal Client session. When she exits the program, she logs off her session. The remaining items in this dialog box—client devices, shadowing, and modem callbacks—only apply to MetaFrame users.

MetaFrame administrators get a nice program called the Application Registry that lets them control which users can run what programs. But what about RDP users? There's no Application Registry, but you *can* use the NTFS execute permission to control whether a particular user can run a given application. (Of course, this implies that you've got to store the apps on an NTFS drive.)

Monitoring Terminal Server

Once things are up and running, you'll want to keep an eye on your terminal servers—how many users are attached, what are they doing, and the like. The main tool for that is the Terminal Server Administration program, located in Administrative Tools. Open it up and you'll see a screen like Figure 9.29.

FIGURE 9.29:

Starting Terminal Server Administration

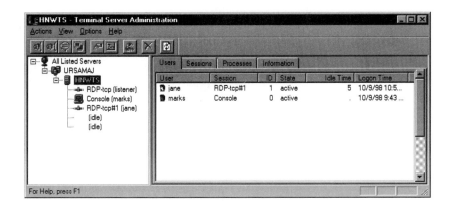

The TSA shows that I've got a WTS server in domain URSAMAJ named HNWTS. Under HNWTS you see several RDP-TCP connections, which indicates that the network protocol that I'm using is TCP and the client-to-server protocol I'm using is RDP rather than ICA. In the right-hand panel you see that I've got two users connected: Jane and Marks. Jane is attached over the LAN to the Terminal Server, but Marks is logged in right at the console, sitting at HNWTS. You can't see it, but Marks's icon is green and Jane's is white, no doubt reflecting that Marks is connected at the console. (Or it means "administrators are from Mars, users are from Venus"?)

Another look will show that the right hand panel actually has four tabs on it:

- Users
- Sessions
- Processes
- Information

We're looking at the Users tab now; click Sessions and you'll see something like Figure 9.30.

FIGURE 9.30:

Sessions tab in Terminal
Server Administration

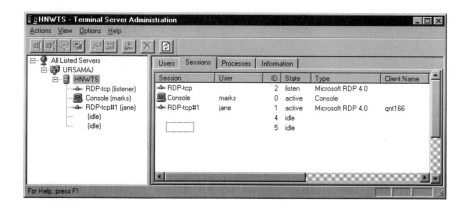

This screen answers a question that you might have had in mind—namely, how do I know where Jane is connecting from? I can see from the right-hand side of the panel that she's logged in from a machine named QNT166. QNT166 is a machine running Windows Terminal Client, but even a dumb winterm will have a machine name. Notice that in addition to the two sessions we've seen, TSA shows two idle sessions. Before you ask me why TSA shows them, I have no idea—it's not like there are only five available sessions on this system. Some things just didn't translate well from Winframe, I guess!

By nature we administrator types are snoopy and would like to know what the users are running; you can do that by clicking the Processes tab, but before you do, you'll probably find Processes most useful if you filter out some of the process list by clicking View ➤ Show System Processes. That will disable displaying system processes—I recommend it because quite frankly there's not much you can do with the information, usually, and it just clutters up the screen. If I click the Processes tab and then click on Jane in the left-hand side panel, I get a screen like the one shown in Figure 9.31.

Two of the programs—Explorer and loadwc—load automatically; they are the user interface itself (Explorer) and support for the Windows Terminal Client (loadwc). WordPad and Paint are two applications that she's running at the moment. Of course, the next question I'd wonder about is, what is she *doing* with WordPad and Paint? To find *that* out, I'd have to shadow her session—but I need MetaFrame to do that, sadly.

FIGURE 9.31:

Displaying current processes

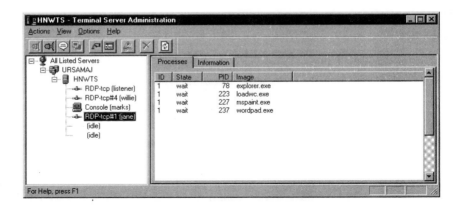

Getting Common Administrative Tasks Done with WTS

After that tour of TSA, let's wrap up this chapter with some of the most common administrative tasks and how to accomplish them. Some are pretty basic to anyone who's read this far, but if you need to refer to this a few months down the road, you might find this "quick reference" section handy. It also covers the basically undocumented command-line utilities that come with Terminal Server.

How Do I Check to See If a Particular User Is Already Logged On to Terminal Server?

Start the Terminal Server Administration program: tsadmin.exe. In the right-hand pane, click User to sort the user names in lexical order. ("Lexical order" basically means "alphabetical order," but it's strictly speaking more correct, as "alphabetical" doesn't include numbers and symbols and "lexical" does. Besides, think how technical the term will sound the next time you use it around the boss or spouse.) Just look down the list and you'll see the user.

From the command line, type

```
query user username
```

And you'll either get the answer, "No user exists for *username*" (an obtuse way of saying, "That person's not logged on"), or you'll get a bunch of information about the user, including the user's session name, like rdp-TCP#21, as well as the user's *session ID*, a number. Hang on to that number, you'll need it for other command-line utilities.

How Do I Log a Particular User Off a Terminal Server? Start the Terminal Server Administration program: tsadmin.exe. In the left-hand pane, click the icon representing the Terminal Server that the user is logged on to. In the right-hand pane, right-click the user's icon and choose either "logoff" or "disconnect."

From the command line, either type

```
reset session_number
```

or

```
disconn session_number
```

Reset logs off; disconn disconnects.

How Do I Ask a Terminal Server User to Log Off? Politely. (Sorry, couldn't resist.) When you right-click a user's name in TSA, you can send messages. Alternatively, there is a command-line tool named MSG.EXE that will send messages and even await responses. It looks like

```
msg username/sessionname/sessionnumber message
```

Thus, you could send a message to Jane:

```
msg jane Jane, we're bringing the server down. Would you please log
off?
```

Or even better, you can ask Jane to acknowledge the message with an OK:

```
msg jane /w Jane, we're bringing the server down. Would you please log
off?
```

The /w informs you when Jane clicks OK. It waits 60 seconds by default, but you can specify a different time length with the /time: parameter:

```
msg jane /w /time:120 Jane, we're bringing the server down. Would you
please log off?
```

And you can pester *all* of a server's users with *:

```
msg * Everyone off the server NOW, please.
```

How Do I Log All Users Off a Terminal Server? From the Terminal Server Administration program, select all of the users, right-click and choose "logoff" or "disconnect." You can also Ctrl+click any disjoint set of users and log them off.

How Do I Keep Any New Users from Logging On to a Terminal Server, "Pausing" It? Although there is a service called "Terminal Server," you cannot pause it. That's frustrating because being able to pause the file server service—keeping anyone new from logging on but not dumping current users off—is quite convenient. Running the License Manager for Terminal Server and dropping the number seems not to do much either—so it's fortunate that there's a command-line tool to do it. Just open a command line at the Terminal Server and type

```
change logon /disable
```

Existing logons will be unaffected, but new ones will be rejected.

How Do I Get RDP to Run on Slow Communications Links? RDP will never be *great* on slow links, but you can request compression from the client side—no way of enforcing server-side control, sadly—by choosing Low Speed Connection in the initial screen of the Windows Terminal Client. Dedicated winterms may or may not include this option in their configuration screens; I can't tell you exactly how to modify a winterm's configuration because they're all a bit different.

How Do I Monitor the Effectiveness of RDP Compression? Once you've gone to the trouble to use compression, was it worth it? After a user's been working for a while, go over to the Terminal Server that he's attached to and start the Terminal Server Administration program, tsadmin.exe. Find the user's connection in the left-hand side panel—it'll look like rdp-TCP#9 (mike). Right-click on the connection and choose Status. In the dialog box that appears, you'll see a compression ratio reported.

How Do I Create a New Terminal Server User? There's no special task here. Just create an NT user in the normal way, with the User Manager. It's probably best to create the user on a domain controller, but you may want instead to create the user in the Terminal Server's local SAM. Either way, be sure to tell the user what domain to use when logging in.

How Do I Configure Terminal Server to Accept Logins from Pure Winterms versus PCs Running Windows Terminal Client? You don't have to. WTS works the same, whether talking to a dedicated RDP client like a winterm or a PC running Windows Terminal Client.

How Do I Restrict a User from Using a Program? Use NTFS permissions on the program file.

How Do I "Eavesdrop" on a User's Session to See What He/She Is Doing? It's called "shadowing," and you can't do it unless you're using ICA.

How Do I Control Where the User's Temp Files Go? A utility named *flattemp*. Flattemp /disable gives each user a different temp directory; /enable gives everyone the same temp directory. Why would you care? It's a potential security hole.

How Do I Give a User a Smaller Menu with Just a Few Items on It? Use system policies as you've done before.

How Do I Give a User a Different Profile and Home Directory When Interacting with Terminal Server than When the User Is Logged On as a File/Print Server Client? Click the Profiles button in the User Manager, and you'll see that the dialog box has changed once you've installed Terminal Server. You have the option to fill in a different home directory and profile location.

Microsoft's inclusion of Citrix technology in Windows Terminal Server has created a very useful tool. Give it a try, and you may find that it'll make your job easier.

How Can I Remotely Reboot a Terminal Server? The shutdown command lets you remotely shut down and reboot a terminal server. The basic syntax is

```
shutdown /server:servername /reboot
```

or

```
shutdown /server:servername /powerdown
```

to either reboot a server or just turn it off. You can tell it to notify users and then terminate their sessions *x* seconds after notifying them by adding a parameter after shutdown like so:

```
shutdown 120 /server:\\mytermsrv /reboot
```

This would wait 120 seconds after notifying users.

How Can I Find Whether a Given User Is on a Terminal Server? Quser finds out who's on the system: quser all by itself lists people on a server; quser *username* yields info about whether or not a particular user is on the system, in the process telling you their session number. You can also run it backwards—quser *sessionnumber* will yield the name of the person on a particular session. It only gives info about the server you are working on, unless you add the /server:*servername* parameter.

How Can I Find Out What Sessions Are Running on a Terminal Server? Qwinsta tells you about connections to a server, not only active sessions but idle sessions as well. Just type **qwinsta** for a list of sessions active and idle. You can add the /server:*servername* to query a particular server.

How Can I Find Out Who's Using a Given Application, and Perhaps Stop the Application? The qprocess command reports what processes are running on a terminal server at any moment. Main uses:

- qprocess *username* shows what programs that user is using. Also works with session number. Example: "qprocess Larry" shows what programs Larry is using.

- qprocess *programname* shows which users are using a particular application. Example: "qprocess wordpad" shows who's using WordPad.

Kill a process with "kill." In its simplest form, it looks like

    kill *processID*

or

    kill *processname*

NOTE You can get the process ID from qprocess.

If you just use a process's name, then leave off the ".exe" on the end, as in "kill wordpad." In that case, WTS will just kill any WordPad instances in the current session—your session, in other words. To tell WTS to seek out and terminate *all* such processes, use the /a option—"kill wordpad /a" will stop WordPad on all user sessions. Adding the /v option makes kill a more chatty executioner, identifying particular instances of WordPad before zapping them. To kill WordPad on a session other than your own, find the session ID and use the /ID: option like so:

    kill wordpad /ID:*sessionnumber*

As with other commands, add the /server: option if you're doing this on a server other than the one you're logged on to.

How Can I Locate Machines Running Terminal Server? The qappsrv command shows the names of the Terminal Servers in this domain; qappsrv /domain:*domainname* reports on other domains. Adding the /address gets the MAC address of the server. There *is* a Network address field, but it comes up blank for me, rather than displaying the IP address as I'd expected.

And that's about it for setting up an NT Server and DOS, Windows, and Windows 95/98 clients. Now you can get your *PC*-based workstations onto your NT network. But what about your Macs? That's the topic of the next chapter.

CHAPTER

TEN

10

Making the Mac Connection

- Using Services for Macintosh

- Preparing the server

- Launching Services for Macintosh

- Connecting the Mac to NT

- Printing in Services for Macintosh

- Transferring data using NT Server

ENTERPRISE NETWORKING

Attaching a Macintosh computer to a PC-based network has never been easier than with NT Server. All the software you need to support Mac clients, called Services for Macintosh, is included right in the box for NT Server. There's nothing else to buy.

The ability to support Macintosh clients is significant, since Apple represents a sizable proportion of corporate networked computers. Users of Mac computers are beginning to demand access to the same shared services that PC users enjoy. In fact, Mac users and PC users often work together on shared projects and *require* access to shared information and resources. Bridging requirements are growing, and until now, Mac to DOS connections have been less than easy.

At the same time, supporting Mac clients is a challenge. Perhaps the biggest challenge lies in working with the filing systems of both Mac and DOS-based computers. The Macintosh file system is significantly different from the DOS file system, and any DOS-based server must be able to accommodate these differences. NT Server uses NTFS to provide what looks to a Mac like native file space, while making the same space available to NT, DOS, Windows, and OS/2 clients.

The Features and Benefits of Services for Macintosh

The following list summarizes some of the other features and benefits of Services for Macintosh.

Feature	Benefit
A file server that is fully compliant with AppleShare Filing Protocol	Mac users access the NT server in the usual way. They may not know that the server is not a Macintosh computer.
Support of Macintosh file name attributes, such as resource forks and data forks (stored as a single NT file), 32-character file names, icons, and access privileges	Mac users don't have to change their filenames or learn a new file naming convention, although this may be desirable if files are to be shared with PC users.

Continued on next page

Feature	Benefit
Native support for AppleTalk protocols	A protocol converter (gateway) is not required.
PostScript emulation for non-PostScript printers	Allows Mac users to access PC printers without converting documents.
Access to LaserWriter printers by Windows, NT, DOS, and OS/2 clients	Allows PC users to access Mac printers without converting documents.
255 simultaneous connections to an NT server, using approximately 15K per session	Relatively low overhead for a large number of potential users.
Support for LocalTalk, Ethernet, Token Ring, and FDDI	Macintosh computers can use any Data Link mechanism to connect to the network.
Extension mapping for PC data files	Enables PC files to be recognized by Mac-based applications, for those apps which are not cross-platform.

Mac Connection in a Nutshell

In this chapter, I'll cover all of the things that you have to do to get Macs to talk to your NT Server. First, you have to get the server ready for Mac support. That means you have to load some NT software that enables NT to create Mac-accessible volumes. Then you create the folders that will hold Mac data.

Next you have to load the NT network software on each Mac workstation. Now, Microsoft could have enclosed a Mac-readable diskette with the drivers to allow a Mac to get onto an NT network, but instead they adopted (in my opinion) a more elegant plan. You see, all Macs have networking capabilities built right into their operating systems. That networking capability isn't really compatible with NT, however, because it doesn't enforce the kind of security that NT requires. So NT lets the Mac into the domain solely as a guest who can access one file and one file only—the Macintosh NT client software. Your Mac logs on to the NT Server machine, grabs the NT client software, reboots with the new client drivers, and it is then able to conduct itself as an NT-compatible workstation. Very easy, and very clean. Following are the details.

Preparing the Server to Support Your Mac

All of the software to support Services for Macintosh is included in every box of NT Server, although it is not enabled by default. Before installing the components to support Mac clients, you must prepare the NT server as described below.

The Physical Connection

AppleTalk is Apple's built-in networking system. LocalTalk is the physical component of AppleTalk—the port, software driver, and cable used to connect Macs. AppleTalk is not a high-performance network like Ethernet; in fact, it's quite a bit slower, at one-fortieth the speed of the average Ethernet.

Macintosh computers can be connected together via a number of data link mechanisms. LocalTalk is the most inexpensive method because just about everything needed to connect this type of network is included with every Mac computer. If the Macs are connected on a LocalTalk network, a LocalTalk card is needed for the server. A router that knows AppleTalk must exist somewhere on the network; NT Server itself can act as a router, if necessary.

Macintosh computers can also be connected together via Ethernet, Token Ring, or FDDI. In this case, just connect the existing PC network to the Mac network—no additional hardware or routing is needed on the NT server.

Unfortunately, NT Server does not support RAS for Mac clients. Remote or dial-in access is not available.

Preparing the NT Server Hard Disk

Two requirements need to be met before Services for Macintosh can be installed on the server drive:

- Services for Macintosh requires an additional 2MB of space on the server drive.

- Folders for Mac clients must exist on an NTFS partition of the server hard disk or on a CD-ROM drive. You need an NTFS partition to load Services for Macintosh.

Getting Services for Macintosh Up and Running

Installation of Services for Macintosh is straightforward, except for a few diversions along the way. These diversions are not very well documented. After a few false starts, here is what seems to be the best procedure for the installation:

1. Install the Services for Macintosh module. This activates the software required for Mac file sharing, print sharing, and application extension mapping. The installation adds some additional tools to your Control Panel, as well as additional selections to your Server Manager and File Manager menus.

2. Set attributes for all the Mac-accessible volumes that you create on the server. Here you can create a logon message and set security and connection limitations.

3. Prepare the Microsoft UAM Volume for use by Mac clients. This volume is created during the installation and contains software for Mac clients that enables user authentication (a fancy word for encrypted passwords). You can connect Mac users at this point and enable user authentication, or you can continue with the process and create Mac-accessible volumes, as described here.

4. Create Mac-accessible volumes. These are folders of the NTFS partition to which Mac users have access. Mac users won't have access to any other folders or partitions on the server.

Each step is discussed in this section.

Installing Services for Macintosh

Search through the *Installation Guide* in the NT Server box and you will find a chapter called "Services for Macintosh." Just follow the book for this part of the installation. Here's a recap of the procedure, in case you can't find the book:

1. Open Control Panel, double-click Network, and open the Services tab. You see the Network Settings screen shown in Figure 10.1.

FIGURE 10.1:

Network Services dialog box

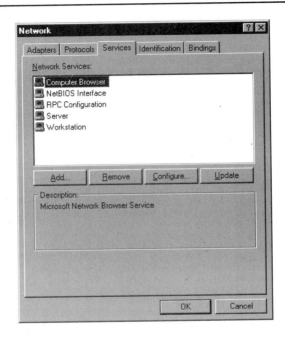

2. Click the Add button. You see a dialog box like the one in Figure 10.2. It says something like "Building Network Service Option List." Scroll down the list until you find Services for Macintosh. Select that and click OK.

FIGURE 10.2:

Adding Services for Macintosh

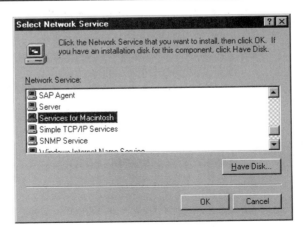

3. Enter the path where the NT Server software is located (this is probably the drive that contains the CD that NT Server was originally installed from, or the I386 directory on the hard disk).

The files to support Mac services are copied to the server drive. Click the Close button and protocol binding will occur. In Figure 10.3, you see the Microsoft AppleTalk Protocol Properties dialog box (now open), where you can set up AppleTalk routing for the network.

FIGURE 10.3:

AppleTalk Protocol Properties

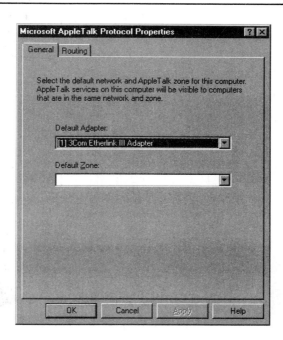

Before you set up routing on the NT Server, there are a few things you should know about routing AppleTalk:

- Using the NT Server as an AppleTalk router enables the entire AppleTalk protocol stack. Many network administrators feel that the AppleTalk protocol is extremely "chatty"; a significant amount of network traffic and system overhead is associated with AppleTalk. If you are serious about routing AppleTalk traffic, think about using a hardware router and not NT Server.

- An AppleTalk network is divided into *segments*. Each segment, generally a length of cable connected to one of the router's ports (or network adapters, in this case), carries one or more *network IDs*. A LocalTalk segment has a single ID number, whereas an Ethernet, Token Ring, or FDDI segment can each have several network IDs.

- Each network ID supports up to 256 AppleTalk devices. For example, if a length of network cable connects to one NT Server adapter, and that cable has 500 machines connected to it, that segment requires two network IDs (generally configured as a *range* of network IDs for the segment).

- Each network segment can be divided into *zones*. A zone is a logical grouping of machines, generally a group that shares the same purpose. (You might think of an AppleTalk zone as being similar to a Microsoft workgroup.) A LocalTalk segment is a single zone, while Ethernet, Token Ring, and FDDI segments can contain multiple zones. If zones are defined, then each machine on the network, including the NT Server, must be in a default zone.

Let's take an example. Say I have a network with a LocalTalk segment and an Ethernet segment, and I want to use NT Server as a router. The Ethernet segment is connected to a 3Com Etherlink III adapter in the server; I'll configure this adapter for the example.

I want the Ethernet segment to be divided into three logical zones—one for Accounting, one for Graphics, and one for Human Resources. The Ethernet segment has 100 Macintosh devices connected to it.

From the Microsoft AppleTalk Protocol Properties screen, click on the Routing tab. You see a screen similar to Figure 10.4. If an AppleTalk router already exists on this network segment, network IDs and defined zones are detected and displayed (at which point you probably don't need to configure another router).

Click Enable Routing only if you are using this NT Server as an additional router on the network, and network IDs and zone names already exist. Click both Enable Routing and the "Use this router to seed the network" check box if you don't have another router.

If you use this router to seed the network, you need to provide a range of network IDs for that segment. I use the range From 10 To 10, which is adequate to support up to 256 devices. (These network numbers are somewhat arbitrary, although they do correspond to my overall network numbering plan.) If I had more than 256 devices, I would create a larger range. A segment of 500 machines, for example, needs two numbers in the range. I might use the range From 10 To 11, or the numbers From 100 To 101. The numbers themselves don't matter—it's the *number of numbers* that is important. Just think of it this way: for each 256 devices on a segment, you need one number.

FIGURE 10.4:

The Routing tab of the AppleTalk Protocol Properties dialog box

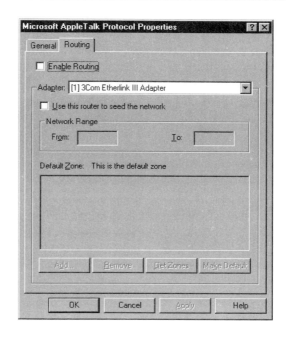

Next I add zone names. To add a zone name, click the Add button. You see a dialog box similar to Figure 10.5.

FIGURE 10.5:

Add Zone dialog box

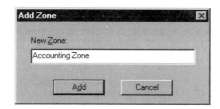

Enter the zone name and click Add. Add other zone names by using the same procedure. When all the zone names are added, I'm finished configuring the router, and the Routing tab looks like Figure 10.6.

FIGURE 10.6:

AppleTalk Routing completed configuration

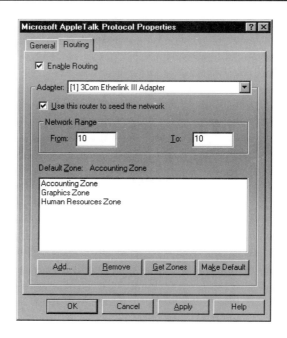

Click OK. The installation is now complete. Click OK in the dialog box that tells you the changes will take effect when you restart AppleTalk. You will need to reboot the NT server for the changes to take effect, (a dialog box prompts you to reboot). Choose Yes and your machine restarts.

Setting Attributes for Mac-Accessible Volumes

The next step is to set up access attributes for all of the Macintosh volumes that you'll create. Go to Control Panel (it is open when you restart) and select MacFile. You see the MacFile Properties dialog box, as shown in Figure 10.7. Click on the Attributes button. You see the MacFile Attributes dialog box shown in Figure 10.8.

FIGURE 10.7:

MacFile Properties dialog box

FIGURE 10.8:

The MacFile Attributes
dialog box

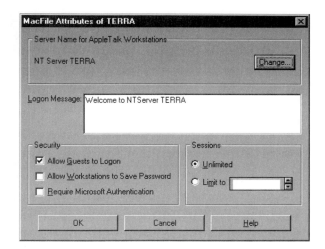

There's really nothing to change or set in the MacFile Attributes dialog box, unless you want to create a logon message or change the name of the NT server (the name that you use here is the name that appears in the Mac user's Chooser). This does not change the name of the NT server. You will need to reboot the server before Mac clients see the changed name.

At some point, you should come back to this section and check the Require Microsoft Authentication box (it may already be checked on your system—if so, just leave it). This check box enables additional security for Mac clients. Click the OK button when done. Then click the Close button and exit Control Panel.

Setting Up Microsoft Authentication

Any time after restarting the server (this step could be done before the previous step), go to Windows NT Explorer. You see that the Microsoft UAM Volume was added to the NTFS partition, as shown in Figure 10.9. This volume contains the software needed to enable Microsoft Authentication for the Mac clients. Microsoft Authentication enables password encryption for Mac clients. The Mac operating system only supports *clear text* passwords, which can be intercepted by a sniffer device. Clear text passwords violate NT Server's C2 level security.

FIGURE 10.9:

The Microsoft UAM Volume, now visible in Windows NT Explorer

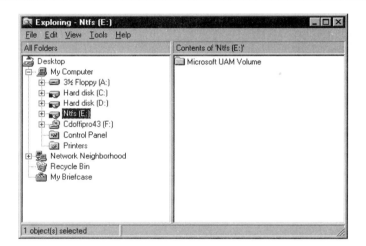

Don't try to get to the volume from the Mac yet. Highlight the volume, select your computer, and go to Server Manager's MacFile menu (it magically appeared when you rebooted with Mac services). On the MacFile menu, highlight the Mac volume, and click the Volume button. You see a dialog box with the volume highlighted, as in Figure 10.10. Click on the button labeled Properties. You see the Properties of dialog box shown in Figure 10.11.

FIGURE 10.10:

Configuring the Mac-accessible volume

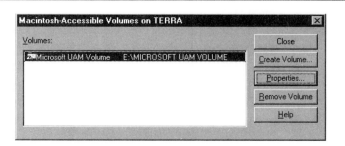

FIGURE 10.11:

Properties of the Mac-
Accessible Volume dialog box

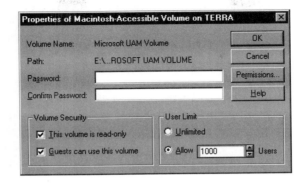

You needn't change this dialog box at all. I bring it to your attention so that you know where to go to control permissions on the volume. (Don't change permissions on *this* volume, as it doesn't contain anything except the Microsoft Authentication software. But other Mac-accessible volumes may require permissions.)

Creating Mac-Accessible Volumes

The final step in the server setup process involves setting up shared folders for Mac clients (called the "Mac-accessible volumes"). This is done in much the same way that shared folders are set up for PC clients. Only permissions are handled differently.

TIP	Mac-accessible volumes can be CD-ROMs. Just mark the volume read-only.

First, create a new folder on the NTFS partition. Then, share the folder and follow these steps:

1. From Server Manager, select your computer, select MacFile, Volumes, and select Create Volume.

2. Enter the volume name (usually the name of the folder you created).

3. Enter the full path name for the folder, as seen in the example in Figure 10.12.

FIGURE 10.12:

Creating a new Mac-accessible volume

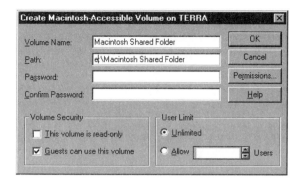

4. Set volume security and user limits, if required.

5. Click the Permissions button. You see a screen similar to the one in Figure 10.13.

FIGURE 10.13:

Directory Permissions dialog box

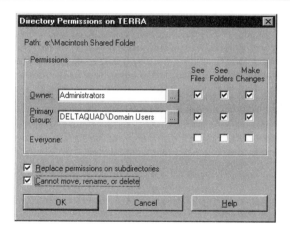

You've probably seen a screen like this before, except the permissions look a little different. Table 10.1 explains what these permissions mean.

TABLE 10.1: Mac versus NT Server Permissions

Mac Permission	NT Server Equivalent
See Files Allows the owner, Primary group, or Everyone to see and open the files that are contained within this folder.	Read
See Folders Allows the owner, Primary group, or Everyone to see and open any folders contained within this folder.	Read
Make Changes Allows the owner, Primary group, or Everyone to add or delete files and folders, and save changes to files in this folder.	Write, Delete
Replace permission on subdirectories Copies the permissions you just set to all folders within this volume or folder. (This is the same as "Make all enclosed folders like this one" on Mac file servers.)	Same
Cannot move, rename, or delete Prevents the volume or folder from being moved, renamed, or deleted by Mac users.	Same

There's one other main difference between this screen and the others you've seen. With NT Server, permissions for a user or group override those for "Everyone." This is a major difference between NT Server and Macintosh file servers, where permissions for "Everyone" override permissions for an individual or group.

Create additional volumes if you wish, or exit Server Manager. That's all that needs to be done on the NT server.

Setting Up the Mac for NT Connection

NT Server is an *AFP-compliant* server, which means NT Server directly supports the AppleShare Filing Protocols (AFP) required by Macintosh clients. There's nothing to do from the Mac except log on to the NT server in exactly the same way you logged on to a Macintosh server. NT Server's Mac-accessible volumes and shared printers are directly available through the Apple Chooser. To access them, either click AppleShare for the file server(s) or LaserWriter for the printer(s).

Mac clients that connect to NT require System 6.0.7 or higher. NT Server fully supports System 7.x clients. Power Macintosh computers can be clients to an NT server.

No additional software is required for the Mac, although it is advisable to enable Microsoft authentication to maintain NT Server's C2 security. The software for this is included with NT Server and needs to be installed at each Mac workstation.

First Time Logon

Before Mac users log on to an NT server as a registered user, they have to log on as a guest and fetch the software to enable Microsoft Authentication. Here's how that's done:

1. From the Mac's Apple menu, select Chooser.

2. Click AppleShare. A list of available servers appears, as shown in Figure 10.14.

FIGURE 10.14:

Selecting the NT server in the Chooser

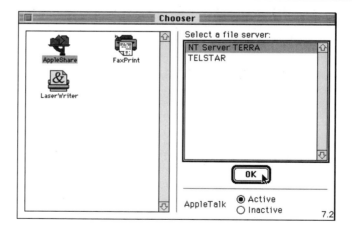

3. From the list, select the NT server, and then click OK.

TIP	Any server that is configured with Services for Macintosh will appear in the Chooser's list of servers, no matter what domain(s) it is in. Mac users don't see domain names or workgroup names—they only see server names.

As shown in Figure 10.15, you get the option to log on as a guest or a registered user.

FIGURE 10.15:

Logging on to the NT server

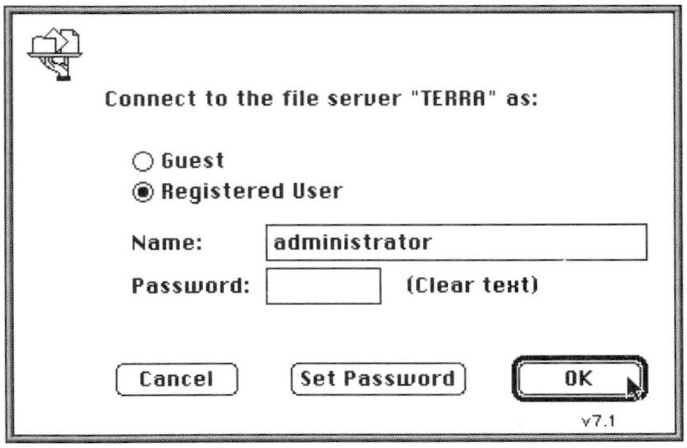

4. Log on as a guest or a registered user, since it doesn't matter which you log on as the first time, except that a registered user must have an account on the NT server. You might log on as Administrator if the Mac users' accounts haven't been created yet.

Notice that the first time you log on, the Mac doesn't know anything about NT. It looks just like another Macintosh server. Later, when the Microsoft encryption module is installed on the Mac client, this screen will change.

5. Enter your name and password, and click OK.

6. You see the list of shared volumes, as shown in Figure 10.16. The first time around you may see only one: the Microsoft UAM Volume. Click on that, and then click OK.

FIGURE 10.16:

Selecting the volume

If a logon message was enabled from MacFile Attributes, you see a screen similar to the one in Figure 10.17.

FIGURE 10.17:

Logon message from the NT server

7. Click OK, and then close the Chooser. An icon for Microsoft UAM Volume appears on the Mac desktop, as shown in Figure 10.18.

FIGURE 10.18:

Microsoft UAM icon

8. Open the Microsoft UAM Volume. It contains a folder called AppleShare Folder, as seen in Figure 10.19. Drag that folder into your System folder. If this Mac was a client of an earlier version of NT Server, there is already an AppleShare Folder in the System Folder. This version of the Microsoft UAM

software will overwrite the older version. Don't worry—it's fully backward-compatible with previous versions of NT Server. Mac clients can access any NT server on the network, regardless of the version.

FIGURE 10.19:

The AppleShare Folder

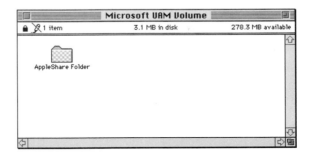

9.   Restart the Mac. From now on, when you log on to a server, your password will be encrypted for additional security.

TIP   Before dragging the AppleShare Folder into your System Folder, check to see if there is already a folder with that name. If so, take the contents from this folder and drag them into your existing AppleShare Folder.

Next Time Logon

The next time you log on from the Mac, select the NT server through the Chooser as usual. You get a dialog box asking you to select a logon method, as in Figure 10.20. Choose Microsoft Authentication and click OK.

FIGURE 10.20:

Selecting a logon method

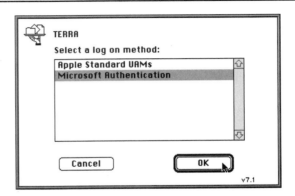

Then you see a logon screen similar to Figure 10.21, in which you can enter your user name and password. This dialog box looks slightly different from the dialog box that you would see if this were a Mac-based server, because you installed Microsoft authentication support in the previous step.

FIGURE 10.21:

Logon dialog box after
Microsoft authentication
support is installed

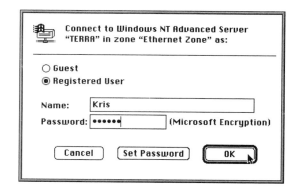

Click Registered User, enter your user name and password, and click OK. Select from the list of available Mac-accessible volumes. If a volume name is grayed out, it means that you are already logged on to that volume or you don't have the correct privileges to access it.

Services for Macintosh Printer Support

Services for Macintosh provides printer support in two different ways: Mac users can use non-PostScript printers connected to an NT Server network, and PC users can use Mac printers connected to an AppleTalk network.

Mac clients access non-PostScript printers via PostScript emulation. This emulation is provided as part of Services for Macintosh and is invisible to Mac users. They don't need to change anything about their documents or change the way they access the printer. Mac clients work through the Chooser, as usual.

Mac printers may be made available to PCs by using NT Server's Printers folder (and the associated print spooler) along with "capturing" the Mac printers. *Capturing* means to create a print spool or print queue on a print server.

Macintosh printers (we're talking about laser printers here) are usually connected to AppleTalk networks and are network-ready devices. When a Mac user sends a print job to a Mac printer, the Macintosh computer spools the print job to the user's local hard disk and prints it in the background. This often slows response time for the Mac.

Capturing a Mac printer causes a print spool to be created; print jobs are sent to the server and stored in a print queue.

Avoiding "LaserPrep Wars"

LaserPrep is a part of the Mac's built-in laser printer driver. The LaserPrep driver is downloaded to the printer at the beginning of any printer session. If multiple users share the same printer, the first LaserPrep driver is retained in the printer's memory and does not need to be downloaded each time. This saves time when printing.

There are many different versions of LaserPrep, and a network administrator is often faced with the task of making sure that all versions of this driver are the same for every Mac on a network. If all versions are not the same, users complain of slow printing, as the LaserPrep driver is downloaded at the beginning of each print job and the printer resets itself.

By capturing the printer, LaserPrep wars are avoided. NT sends its own Laser-Prep code with each print job—this takes a little time, but not as much as keeping the driver resident in the printer and replacing it each time.

Installing Services for Macintosh Printing

Installing print services for Mac clients is described in detail in the NT Server documentation, and summarized here for reference.

Start the Print Manager by clicking the Start button, choosing Programs, choosing Accessories, and choosing Print Manager. Then select Printer ➤ Create Printer. You see a dialog box like the one in Figure 10.22.

FIGURE 10.22:

The Create Printer dialog box

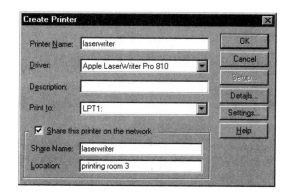

Type in a name for the printer, select a driver from the available list, and provide a description and location for the printer if you like. If the printer is a networked Macintosh printer, select Other from the Print to menu. If you select Other, you get a dialog box like the one in Figure 10.23. It lists possible print destinations. Select AppleTalk Printing Devices. Click OK. From the Available AppleTalk Printing Devices dialog box, double-click a zone (if zones were created) and then a printing device. Then click OK and click Share This Printer on the Network. The Share Name is shortened if it's too long for DOS system users to see. The Macintosh users will see the name in the Printer Name box. If you like you can fill in the Location box. Click OK. The printer is now available to PC users as usual and appears in Print Manager.

FIGURE 10.23:

Print Destinations dialog box

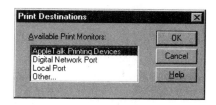

For Mac users, you need to create a user account. Start Control Panel ➤ Services, select Print Server for Macintosh, and click the Startup button. A dialog box like the one in Figure 10.24 appears.

FIGURE 10.24:

Print server for Macintosh
services

Under the Log On As section, click System Account (the default) to enable all Mac users to access the printer. Click This Account and enter a user name (no groups) to enable only a single Mac user to access the printer. Click OK and then Close to exit Control Panel.

Macs should now have print access. They'll access the printer as usual, through the Chooser.

Transferring Data between Macs and PCs with NT Server

Now that you have the data from the Mac to the NT server, what can you do with it? Well, that depends...

If all you want to do is use the NT server as a place to *store* files, then there's nothing else to do except copy them from the Mac local hard drive to the NT shared volume. But before getting into that, it's good to understand a few things about the Mac file system. Then you can consider the problems of file formats, extensions, filtering, and document translation.

Forks, Forks Everywhere—and Nothing to Eat

Mac files are created as two distinct pieces—a *data fork* and a *resource fork*. The data fork contains the data for the file, while the resource fork contains information needed by the application that created the file, such as fonts, formatting information, and the like. A data file has a big data fork and a small resource fork, while an application program has a large resource fork and a small data fork.

PC-based file systems don't understand forks, since PC files are stored as one distinct entity (albeit that entity may be in fragments on the disk, which is not the same thing). Forks are okay with NT, though. NT stores the data fork and the resource fork together on the server in a single file.

Those Pesky Filenames

First, the rules for naming files on DOS, Mac, and NT. Then, let's see what happens to the file names when files are moved around.

File Type	Naming Convention
DOS	8-character file name followed by an optional period and a 3-character extension. DOS file names can't contain spaces and shouldn't contain any special characters. This is the FAT convention.
Mac	32 characters, and can include any character on the keyboard with the exception of the colon (:) character. The colon is used to distinguish levels of folders; kind of like a backslash distinguishes levels of directories in DOS or NT.
NT	256 characters, and can include upper- and lowercase characters, spaces, and some special characters. This is the NTFS convention. It is available only to users of Windows NT workstations (and the server, of course).

Now, using those rules, let's see what happens when you move files around:

- A file created using the FAT convention (8+3) displays as created to NTFS users and Mac users.

- A file created using the 32-character Mac limit displays as created to NTFS users. DOS users see the name truncated to 8+3 format. This can have some very unusual (not to mention unwanted) results.

- A file created using the NTFS 256-character limit displays as created to Mac users if it is 32 characters or less. Otherwise, it is truncated to the 8+3 format.

- Mac users should use 8+3 filenames if they are going to *share* the files with DOS users. While this may seem limiting to Mac users, it avoids a lot of confusion down the line.

To Which Application Does the Data File Belong?

The DOS world has something of a convention when it comes to naming files. Many applications attach a particular extension to their data files—SAM to Ami Pro documents, WK3 to Lotus 1-2-3 worksheets, DBF to dBASE databases, and so forth. Users can generally change these extensions if they like, although most don't because application programs are written to display data files using their default extensions.

Mac files don't follow these rules; they have their own. Every Mac file that's created is assigned a *type* and *creator* code, which defines which application created it. The type and creator code are embedded in the file's resource fork, and enable the file to be displayed on the Mac desktop with an icon that is unique and recognizable for each application program. This type and creator code enables Mac users to double-click documents to launch their associated applications.

When a Mac file is placed on the NT server, the Mac user loses the ability to determine what type of file it is. Worse yet, any PC file that the Mac user copies to her Mac doesn't have a type and creator code; and the PC file appears as a blank document.

The first problem, determining the type of file, is easy to overcome if Mac users name files using the same conventions that DOS users employ, a three-character extension that indicates the file type. The second problem, that of making the Mac understand a PC file type, is overcome by using something called extension mapping.

Extension Mapping

Extension mapping is a process that ensures that users see the correct icon on their computers for a file stored on the computer running Windows NT Server. For example, Macintosh users will see a Macintosh-style icon for a Microsoft Excel file, and Windows users will see the Windows-style icon for the same Microsoft Excel file.

Extension mapping is a good idea in theory, but it doesn't ensure that a data file is compatible with a particular application. The data file may need to be *translated*.

NT Server's Services for Macintosh is already set up for extension mapping when it comes to some of the more popular application programs. A listing of available extension maps can be found in the Services for Macintosh help file. Additional maps can be created using NT Server's File Manager Associations.

To add additional associations, open the File Manager and select MacFile. From the MacFile menu, select Associate. You see a screen similar to Figure 10.25.

FIGURE 10.25:

Associate dialog box

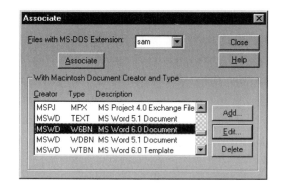

Add the MS-DOS file extension you want to be associated with a Mac application in the appropriate field, and then select from the list the Macintosh application you want to be associated with files containing that extension.

If a Mac application program's name isn't included on the list, you can add it, but you need to know its creator code and the type codes for the documents it supports. If you don't know this information, you can generally find it in the application program's documentation, or you can get it by calling the manufacturer of the application program.

Let's say you want to add the Mac application Teach Text to the list:

1. Open the File Manager. (From the Start menu, choose Run, and then enter the word **winfile**. There doesn't seem to be any other way to do this.)

2. Select MacFile.

3. From the MacFile menu, select Associate.

4. Click the Add button. You see the screen in Figure 10.26.

FIGURE 10.26:

Add Document Type
dialog box

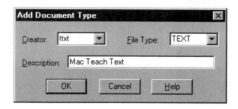

5. Type in the four-letter creator code and the four-character type code for the application you want to add.

6. In the Description field, type in the name of the Mac application program. The name will be added to the list that you used in the previous step.

7. Click OK when you're done.

TIP

Type and creator codes are four-character codes that are assigned to application programs by Apple. They are not made up by programmers or by users. Be careful when adding type and creator codes. If you don't know an application's codes, check the documentation, call the program's manufacturer, or call Apple.

About File Filters and Translations

Many application programs have built-in *file filters,* the programs that convert one kind of data file to another. Perhaps the best example of this is a program like Microsoft Excel. Excel can read data files created from Lotus 1-2-3 and several other spreadsheet programs and convert them to Excel format. Other programs have optional filters that must be installed. Word processors and graphics programs, for example, often support a number of file formats.

Be careful when using filters. Just because a program has a translator built into it doesn't mean everything translates properly.

If a particular application program doesn't have built-in translators or doesn't include them as options, several third-party programs are available to do the job. Conversions Plus and Mac-In-DOS are two that come to mind. For the Mac, try MacLink Plus, Access PC, or PC Exchange.

Using Cross-Platform Applications

Just about the cleanest way to get applications to understand data files in a shared environment is to use *cross-platform applications*. These applications include both a PC version and a Mac version, and the data files are fully transportable across the two platforms.

Examples of cross-platform applications include

- cc:Mail
- FileMaker Pro
- First Class Mail
- Lotus 1-2-3
- Microsoft Word, Excel, PowerPoint, and Mail
- PageMaker
- Quark Xpress
- QuickMail
- WordPerfect

Be careful with cross-platform applications. Just because an application is cross-platform doesn't necessarily mean that documents convert entirely correctly. Also, if a document contains embedded graphics (as is the case with PageMaker), the graphics need to be removed from the original, converted separately, and reinserted in the cross-platform document.

Bad Dates

A word of caution about dates: Mac and DOS files are date-stamped differently. At Microsoft, time started on January 1, 1980. At Apple, time began on January 1, 1904. All file dates are internally converted to a Julian dating system, which calls day 1 whatever the first day was for the particular company and numbers each day from there.

The difference in date-stamping methods causes enormous problems when using data files that contain date functions. Suppose you have a spreadsheet with a formula such as (*today*)+30. If this is a Mac file, *today* means something completely different when the file is used by a PC application.

The Downside (and You Knew There'd Be One)

While all of this Mac connectivity stuff sounds good, there are a few limitations to what Mac clients can do in the NT world:

- Dial-Up Networking doesn't support AppleTalk, since AppleTalk doesn't send NetBIOS packets.

- MS-Mail is supported, but Mac client support is not provided unless you buy it separately (buy the upgrade kit—Mac clients aren't compatible with Workgroup mail).

- Mac clients do not execute logon scripts and can't take advantage of user profiles.

- Mac clients can't participate in inter-domain trust relationships or see resources from other NT Server domains, unless Services for Macintosh has been enabled in those domains and they are on the *same* network.

CHAPTER

ELEVEN

11

Managing a Single Domain

- Understanding Server Manager's capabilities

- Managing server properties

- Managing services

- How to schedule events

- Managing directory replication

- Working with domain controllers

- Managing PDC-BDC communications

Server
Manager

In earlier networks, you had to administer servers by physically walking over to a server, sitting down, and working right at it. Modern network operating systems are built with the understanding that you manage multi-server networks and that often you manage networks from many different locations. To help you out in that job, NT includes a number of tools, but the most important is the Server Manager. It is the focus of most of this chapter. But there's another important topic in managing multiple servers—domain controllers. How many domain controllers you need, how to use them in fault-tolerant roles, and how to manage them is covered in the last part of this chapter.

Server Manager's Capabilities

Before getting to the business of domain design, let's first get familiar with another administrative tool, the *Server Manage*r.

When users successfully connect to the server, they each begin a *session* with that server. Server Manager monitors session activity and keeps track of all resources and which users on the network are accessing those resources. Server Manager displays statistics showing current usage levels on both servers and NT workstations.

Server Manager Functions

With Server Manager, you can view and track

- All users who are currently running sessions on a selected computer
- The resources open during each session
- How long a resource has been open by a user
- How long a session has been idle
- Current information on the number of open file locks, resources, and printers in use

You can also

- Control directory shares on remote servers, removing existing shares or creating new shares

- Add or remove NT machines from the domain

- Shift domain controllers from the role of backup domain controller (BDC) to that of primary domain controller (PDC) and back again

- Send messages to users

- Receive alerts—in other words, messages from the system—at designated computers

- Configure directory replication

You can use the Server Manager to get minute-by-minute server statistics. By familiarizing yourself with the statistics that are generated during normal operation, you will be in a better position to spot abnormal activity. For example, when there's a slowdown in throughput, you might see that a number of users are trying to download data at the same time. Further investigation into share usage might reveal that the problem is concentrated in a particular spot—an overused resource, perhaps.

Not Everyone Is Allowed to Use Server Manager

Server Manager's statistics can only be generated for NT workstations and servers running NT Server or LAN Manager 2.*x*. You can't monitor or modify attributes of a server with Server Manager unless you are a member of either the Administrators or the Account Operators group. Members of the Account Operators group can use Server Manager, but only to add computers to a domain.

Gathering Cumulative Server Data

Server Manager displays present usage levels and session information; it does not collect statistics over a period of time. To see a computer's cumulative usage statistics since startup, enter the command **net statistics server** at the command prompt, or configure the Performance Monitor to collect statistics.

Who's Who in the Domain

As shown in Figure 11.1, the Server Manager window displays a list of all of the computers that are members of the logon domain, plus computers that the Computer Browser service reports as being active in the domain. This list includes NT servers, NT workstations running the Server service, and LAN Manager 2.*x* servers. Computers running Windows for Workgroups 3.11 and Windows 95 appear in the list, but they can't be remotely administered through Server Manager.

FIGURE 11.1:

Server Manager window

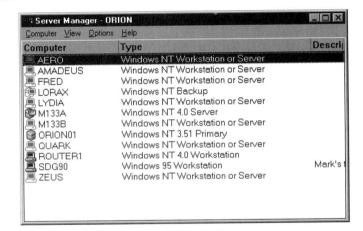

Icons identify the three categories of computers in the Server Manager list:

- *Primary domain controllers*, which maintain the domain's security base and authenticate network logons.

- *Backup domain controllers and NT servers*, NT Server machines that are *not* the primary domain controller. These computers *may* be backup domain controllers, in which case they receive copies of the domain's security base and also authenticate logons, but there's no way to tell from the icon if they're simply servers or servers that also act as backup domain controllers.

- *Workstations*, which are any other listed computer (NT workstations, Windows 95, Windows for Workgroups, DOS machines).

The icons may or may not be dimmed, depending on whether the computer is accessible by the network. If an icon is dimmed on a machine but you know that the machine is active, you can try to force Server Manager to see it by typing

```
net use \\servername\IPC$
```

This may not work if you're using the TCP/IP protocol and WINS (see Chapter 14 for information about TCP/IP and WINS). The icon for a computer is dim, and remains dim, if the computer has been hidden from the browser ("Hiding a Server from the Browser," later in this chapter, explains how to hide a computer from the browser). In other cases, the computer may only "un-dim" if you force it to do something: for example, if you turn on or turn off a service remotely.

Commands in the View menu allow you to filter the list to show all computers or only the servers, workstations, Macintosh computers, or domain members. Press the F5 key to refresh the display.

This aspect of the Server Manager is sort of like the User Manager, in that the listing of machines that you see in the window is simply a listing of the machine accounts that the Server Manager knows about. Recall that in NT, not only users have accounts—machines have accounts, as well. An interesting side-effect of this is that while machines have passwords just like users do, machines change their passwords every seven days. Why would you care about this? Well, if you have a domain that extends over a large geographical area, with WAN links, then you might notice an otherwise inexplicable increase in WAN traffic every week or so, as the PDC updates the BDCs with the new machine passwords.

TIP

While I don't recommend it, you *can* tell NT not to change passwords every seven days with a change to HKEY_LOCAL_MACHINE\System\CurrentControlSet\Services\Netlogon\Parameters: create a key called RefusePasswordChange of type REG_DWORD, and set it to 1.

To administer the servers of a different domain or workgroup, choose the Select Domain command from the Computer menu. If the domain or workgroup happens to communicate with your server over a slow link, make sure you choose the Low Speed Connection option.

Server Properties

The properties of any server on the Server Manager list, whether local or remote (provided that remote administration is supported), can be accessed by using these techniques:

- Selecting the computer on the list and choosing Properties from the Computer menu

- Selecting the computer and hitting Enter

- Double-clicking on the selected computer's name in the list

Once you select the server, you see the Properties for dialog box, as in Figure 11.2.

FIGURE 11.2:

The Properties for dialog box

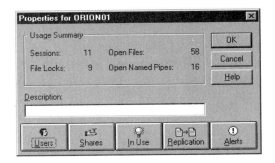

You can also access this dialog box from the Control Panel of the machine for which you want the information. The big value of the Server Manager, however, is that you can access this dialog box for any server on the network, right from your workstation. In contrast, the Control Panel can only show this dialog box for whatever computer you're currently sitting at.

The Usage Summary box displays

- The total number of users who have established sessions—in other words, who have remotely connected to the server

- The total number of shared resources currently open on the server

- The total number of file locks held by open resources on the server

- The total number of named pipes currently open on the server

Beneath the Usage Summary box is a box that contains the server's optional description. If you want to add or change a server's description, just type the new information in the box.

At the bottom of the dialog box are five buttons:

Button	What It Does
Users	Lets you view all users connected to the server, as well as the resources opened by a specific user, and disconnect one or all of the connected users.
Shares	Displays the server's shared resources and those users connected over the network to a selected resource. One or all of the connected users can also be disconnected here.
In Use	Shows the open shared resources on the server and provides the capability to close one or all of the resources.
Replication	Lets you manage directory replication for the server and determine the path for user logon scripts.
Alerts	Allows you to view and manage the list of users and computers that are notified when administrative alerts occur at the server.

Hiding a Server from the Browser

You can't do this with the Server Manager, but it's worth knowing anyway: if you have a workstation or server that is running the Server service and you want to keep it off the browse list for some reason, just modify its Registry.

Look in HKEY_LOCAL_MACHINE\System\CurrentControlSet\Services\LanManServer\Parameters. There should be a value "Hidden" that is, by default, equal to 0; it's of type REG_DWORD. Set it equal to 1 and reboot, and the server will not appear on the browse list. (Alternatively, you can open up a command line and type **NET CONFIG SERVER/HIDDEN:YES**.) You can still get to it by using NET USE or NET VIEW command, but you have to know the name in order to see it.

User Sessions

To look at and manage user sessions on the server, click on the Users button in the Properties for dialog box. The resulting User Sessions on dialog box, as seen in Figure 11.3, lists all users remotely connected to the server and what resources they are using.

FIGURE 11.3:

User Sessions on dialog box

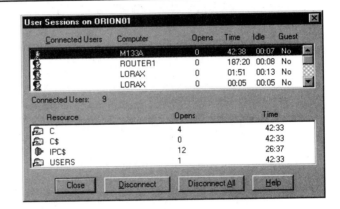

The Connected Users box lists each connected user, the name of the computer the user is on, the number of resources opened by the user, the time since the session was established, the length of time since the user last initiated an action, and whether or not the user is logged on as a guest. Right below the list is a summary of the total number of users remotely connected to the server.

The bottom box displays the resources in use by the currently highlighted user. To view those of a different user, simply click on that user in the Connected Users list. Resources in use are graphically identified by the icons shown in Table 11.1.

TABLE 11.1: Resource Icons

Icon	What It Is
	A shared directory
	A remote procedure call
	A shared printer
	A communication-device queue (LAN Manager 2.*x* servers only)
	An unrecognized resource

Next to the icon is the name of the resource, the number of times the selected user opened the resource, and the time elapsed since the resource was first opened. Incidentally, a connection to a printer sometimes shows up as a connection to a named pipe instead.

How Do I Disconnect Users from a Server or Share?

To disconnect a single user from the server, select the user name from the Connected Users list, then choose the Disconnect button. Selecting the Disconnect All Users disconnects everyone from the server. When administering a remote server, your own user account shows up as a user connected to the IPC$ resource, which will not be disconnected.

This isn't a "hard" disconnect; if a user tries to use something on a disconnected resource, then NT automatically reconnects him or her. To keep someone off a share, first modify the share's permissions to give that person No Access (or, more drastically, delete or disable his account) and *then* disconnect him with the Disconnect button in the Server Manager, as discussed above.

You should inform users before disconnecting them—use Send Message on the Computer menu to relay your intentions to the connected users.

How Can You Kick People off a Server?

People used to managing a NetWare network are used to being able to kick people off a server fairly easily; with just a command or two, NetWare administrators can remove any user or group of users, instantly terminating their access to a server.

With NT, things work a bit differently. Play around with the Server Manager, and you'll see buttons labeled Disconnect and Disconnect All; these sound like they'll do the trick, but if you click a button to disconnect a user, you'll probably find that nothing at all changes as a result. Sound odd? Read on.

Recall from Chapter 2 how security works in an NT domain: a group of servers called "domain controllers" stores the security information about the users in the domain. A server (or, to use Microsoft's phrase, a *member server*) looks to these domain controllers for authentication information. More specifically, when a user tries to access data on a member server's shares, the member server interrogates the user (well, actually it interrogates the user's workstation) for user name and password information. Armed with that information, the member server communicates with a domain controller and tries to authenticate the user. Once the member server knows that the user is indeed who she says she is, the member server constructs a *Security Access Token*, or SAT. That token is the member server's information about which groups that user belongs to; the member server will look on that token whenever that user wants to open access to a new share.

For example, suppose user Jack wants to access a share named "Data" on some server. Suppose also that Data has share permissions of Full Control for the local Users group. In order for Jack to access the Data share, then, Jack must be a member of the Users group on this server. That information is stored on Jack's token, assuming that the server already has a token for Jack—if not, of course, the server will go talk to a domain controller. The server will only examine the token when it first needs to establish Jack's connection to a share; it doesn't have to check Jack's credentials every single time he examines a byte on the share.

But here's where it gets interesting: assume that Jack establishes a connection with the share first thing in the morning and uses the share throughout the day. From what I just said, you'd think that the only instance where the server would have to authenticate Jack would be once in the morning; it would seem that when Jack first tried to use the share, the server would authenticate him through the domain controller, which would have the side-effect of causing the server to create a local Security Access Token for Jack. The server would use that token to authenticate Jack on the Data share, and there would be no need for further authentication. But there's another factor at work here: the auto-disconnect feature of NT. By default, if you are attached to a share and do not access that share for 10 minutes, the share's server will disconnect you.

Now you may be thinking, "I've been on lots of servers and lots of shares and been away from them for more than 10 minutes many times, but I've never had to re-connect to a share." Well, actually you *have*, but you just never knew it. After 10 minutes go by and the server disconnects you, it will automatically reconnect you if you try to access the share again, quite nicely and invisibly. If, while performing that reconnection, the server finds that it has a token for you already in its memory, then the server can reconnect you without having to go talk to the domain controller again. If, on the other hand, all of your connections have been broken or timed out, then the server *forgets* your token; in *that* case, the server will, of course, have no choice but to communicate with the domain controller.

That was a long windup to explaining what you must do to disconnect an unwanted user from a server. If all you do is to highlight the user and share and click the Disconnect or Disconnect All buttons, then the user won't even know that you did anything; the next time he tries to access one of the shares that you disconnected him from, the server will merely re-authenticate him. How, then, can you boot people off of a server?

There are two ways. You can kick *everyone* off the server by stopping the server service: just type **NET STOP SERVER**, and everyone will be booted unceremoniously off the server and all of its shares. This is pretty drastic, and you should think twice before doing it. Alternatively, you can remove a particular user from a share or set of shares in two steps: first, set his permission level on those shares to No Access; and second, disconnect him from the shares in question. Then, when he tries to reuse the share or shares, the server will be forced to reexamine his security access; when it sees the No Access, he'll be kept from the share.

Controlling Automatic Disconnection

On the topic of maintaining connections between servers and users, let me mention a few things that aren't controlled by the Server Manager, but that are important.

NT can monitor how long a user has been using a connection; for example, a connection to a share. If the share has been unused for 10 minutes, NT automatically disconnects the user from the share. It's not a very harsh disconnection, despite its sound, because if the user tries to do anything on the share, then NT automatically and invisibly reconnects the user.

Why, then, does NT bother? Well, each user connection takes up server memory, and disconnected users don't take up any memory. That's the good part, but the bad part is that the "invisible" reconnection may take an extra second or two, which can be annoying. You can control these "soft disconnects" with a command: NET CONFIG.

The command net config server /autodisconnect:*value* sets the disconnect period to a value other than 15 minutes; the value is in minutes. Using a value of -1 says not to disconnect at all. You can see which of your connections are disconnected by typing **net use** at the command line; under Status, you will either see "OK" or "Disconnected." You can see an example of that in Figure 11.4.

FIGURE 11.4:

OK and Disconnected shares in NET USE

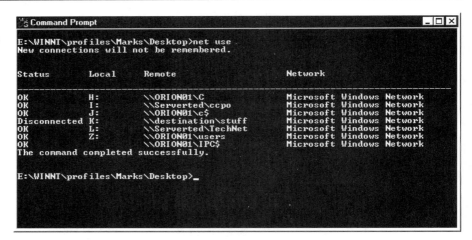

Available Shares

By choosing the Shares button in the Properties for dialog box (see Figure 11.2), you can view the Shared Resources on dialog box, as shown in Figure 11.5. The dialog box lists both the shared resources available on the currently selected server and the users connected to those resources. Shared directories can be managed in either Server Manager or in Explorer, while shared printers are managed in the Printers folder.

FIGURE 11.5:

Shared Resources on
dialog box

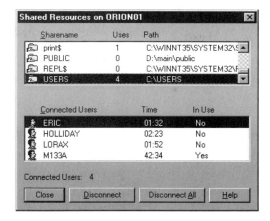

The top box lists all of the shared resources on the selected computer. For each share, the share name, the number of uses, and its path are given. Once again, icons next to the share name show whether the resource is a directory, named pipe, printer, communication-device queue (LAN Manager 2.*x* servers only), or an unrecognized resource (see Table 11.1).

When you click on one of the shared resources in the list, you see a list of the users connected to that resource (and the time elapsed since the connection was made) in the bottom box. For example, in the preceding figure, a user named Eric is connected to the shared directory C:\USERS. Although he has been connected for an hour and a half, the shared directory is currently not in use.

As with User Sessions, you can disconnect one or all users from all shared resources on the server by selecting a user in the Connected Users box and choosing the Disconnect button, or by simply choosing the Disconnect All button. Remember to warn users before disconnecting them from server resources.

Managing Shared Directories in Server Manager

In Server Manager, just as in File Manager, you can

- View shared directories

- Share an unshared directory

- Manage the properties of a shared directory

- Set permissions for a shared directory

- Stop sharing a directory

However, in Server Manager you can create new shares and administer shared directories not only on the local server, but on remote servers in the domain, as well.

To view any server's list of shared directories, select the server in the Server Manager window, then choose Shared Directories from the Computer menu. You see the Shared Directories dialog box, as in Figure 11.6.

FIGURE 11.6:

Shared directories on a selected computer

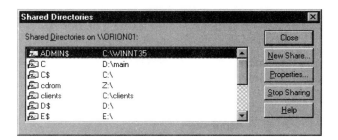

The list shows the share names and paths of the shared directories. It includes directories shared by users and administrators, as well as some or all of the following special shares created by the system:

Resource	What It Does
driveletter$	The root directory of a storage device on the server (can be accessed remotely only by members of the Administrators, Server Operators, and Backup Operators groups).
ADMIN$	The resource used by the system during remote administration of a server. It is always the directory where Windows NT is installed.
IPC$	This resource shares the named pipes essential for communication between programs. It is used when a computer is being remotely administered, or when viewing a computer's shared resources.
NETLOGON	The resource used by the Net Logon service for processing domain logon requests; Netlogon is the service that keeps BDCs and PDCs in synchronization, and it only runs on domain controllers.
PRINT$	The resource that supports shared printers.
REPL$	Required for export replication, this resource is created by the system when a server running NT Server is configured as a replication export server.

In general, these system shares should not be removed or modified.

To modify the properties of a shared directory in the list, select the directory and click the Properties button. Share access permissions can be set by choosing the Permissions button in the Share Properties dialog box. To stop sharing one of the directories in the list, select the directory and choose the Stop Sharing button. The directory itself is not removed, but it can no longer be accessed by network users. To share an unshared directory on the server, choose the New Share button and type in the sharename, path, and other properties, including share permissions.

These procedures are covered in Chapter 7. Note that you can modify share permissions on a remote computer with Server Manager, but you can't modify directory or file permissions on a remote computer with Server Manager. For that, you just use File Manager if you're on a 3.*x* machine or the Security tab if you're on a 4.*x* machine. You'll find that the Security menu works just as it always does, assuming that you're logged on as an administrator.

Active Resources

By choosing the In Use button in the Properties for dialog box (see Figure 11.2), you can see how many resources are currently open on the server, as well as a list of those resources, as Figure 11.7 demonstrates. Once again, the resources are graphically distinguished by icons. Table 11.2 tells what the icons mean.

FIGURE 11.7:

Open Resources dialog box

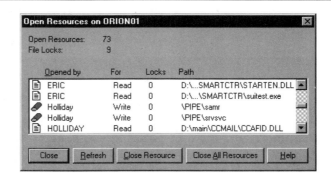

TABLE 11.2: Resource Icons

Icon	What It Is
	A file
	A named pipe (a type of connection between computers)
	A print job in a print spooler
	A communication-device queue (LAN Manager 2.x servers only)
	An unrecognized resource

Following the icon is the name of the user who opened the resource, the permission granted when the resource was opened (read, write, execute, and so on), and the path of the resource. Print jobs are sometimes represented in this list as open named pipes.

Close an open resource by selecting that resource from the list and then clicking the Close Resource button. If you want to close all open resources, hit the Close All Resources button. Make sure you notify the connected users of your intent before you carry it out. To exit, choose Close, then choose OK in the Properties for dialog box.

Open Resources can be useful, as well, for performing a common function, covered in the following "How Do I…"

How Do I Identify Who's on a Server and Shut Down the Server Gracefully?

You'll often find yourself in a position where you need to bring down a server but need first to notify whoever's on that server. But how to find out who's on the machine?

Continued on next page

Open Server Manager and double-click on the server, but don't look at the Users button—it doesn't say much about who's active on the network. Open Resources is the better measure. You'll see explicitly who's using what resource. You can then call or use NET SEND to communicate (for example, NET SEND Larry "Get off server MX002 now, please") with those folks. The Server Manager option to send a message to everyone attached to the server is nice (I'll cover it in a page or two), but remember that the Windows 95/98 people will only receive those messages if they're running WINPOPUP.EXE, a program that comes with Windows, but which doesn't load by default.

Sending Alerts to a Workstation

When system errors or important events relating to the server or its resources occur, NT Server generates *alerts*. In Server Manager you can specify which users and computers receive these alerts.

You can, alternatively, set up a DOS client with the Microsoft Network Client 3.0 for DOS, a slightly more complex operation that you can accomplish with the Network Client Administrator under NT Server. When you install the Network Client for DOS, you get the option to either "run the Network Client" or "run the Network Client and Load Pop-up." If you load the pop-up, you have the messenger service.

TIP

In order to generate an alert, a server must be running the Alerter and Messenger services. On computers that must receive alerts, the Messenger service must be up and running. If the destination computer happens to be turned off, the message eventually times out. In practical terms, this means that the workstation must either be running NT, OS/2, Windows for Workgroups, or Windows 95/98—all four of which ship with Messenger support—or you'll have to load a DOS or Windows-based Messenger driver. The Workgroup Connection client software from Microsoft, which allows a DOS workstation to connect to an NT network, only requires one diskette, and so that's what I usually recommend to carry around for quick-and-dirty network installs. The Workgroup Connection, however, does not include the messenger service, and so no DOS machine set up with the Workgroup Connection would be able to receive alerts.

To specify the recipient of administrative alerts

1. Double-click on the server in the Server Manager window to retrieve its Properties for dialog box.

2. In the Properties for box, choose the Alerts button. You see the Alerts on dialog box, as in Figure 11.8.

FIGURE 11.8:

Alerts on dialog box

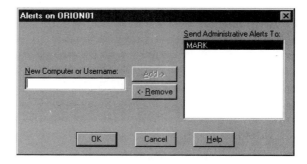

3. To add a user or computer to the list of computers that are receiving alerts, type in the username or computer name in the New Computer or Username box, then choose Add.

4. To remove a user or computer from the list of those set to receive alerts, select the username or computer name in the Send Administrative Alerts To dialog box, then choose Remove.

The Server and Alerter services both need to be restarted in order for the changes to take effect.

Sending Messages to Users

Prior to administering a server, especially if you have to put certain services or resources on hold while working, you can send a message to users currently connected to the server. To send a message

1. Choose the server from the list in the Server Manager window.

2. From the Computer menu, choose Send Message. You see the Send message dialog box shown in Figure 11.9.

FIGURE 11.9:

Send Message dialog box

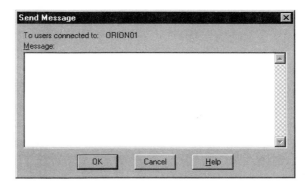

3. Type in the message you want relayed to users.

4. Choose OK.

The message is sent to all users currently connected to the selected server, provided that those workstations using NT and NT Server are running the Messenger service and other workstations (such as those running Windows for Workgroups) are using a message utility, such as WinPopup. *Remember* that users don't run WinPopup by default, so unless you've configured their logon scripts to run WinPopup, don't assume that they'll *get* those messages!

TIP

If you have an AppleTalk segment on your NT Server network, don't forget to send messages to Macintosh users before taking the server down. From the MacFile menu, choose Send Message.

TIP

To send a message to just one user, open a command window and type **net send** ***name message***, where *name* is the user name or machine name to send the message to, and *message* is the text of the message you're going to send. For example, to say "hello" to a user named Sally, you would type **net send Sally hello**.

Adding Computers to a Domain

Members of the Administrators, Domain Admins, and Account Operators groups can grant computers membership in a domain (note that it's the *computers*, not their users, that are acknowledged as members of the domain). It makes sense to add an NT machine to a domain because domain members can share access to the common database of user accounts (the Security Access Manager or SAM database), so that the network administrator doesn't have to go out and build an account on every single NT workstation for every single possible network user.

Adding a computer to a domain is a two-step process. First, the machine account for the computer must be created in the domain. Then, the computer must actually join the domain—a separate step, performed at the computer itself during installation of NT or afterwards in its Control Panel.

Adding Domain Controllers to Domains

NT SERVER You can add a new domain controller to a domain at either of two times:

- During the installation of the NT Server (domain controllers *must* be running NT Server), you're asked if you want to act as a domain controller or a server; choose "domain controller."

- Before installing a new machine, you can tell Server Manager to expect a new domain controller like so:

    1. From the Computer menu, choose Add to Domain. You see the Add Computer To Domain dialog box, as in Figure 11.10.

FIGURE 11.10:

Add Computer To Domain dialog box

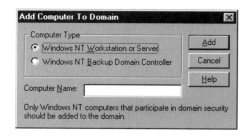

2. Under Computer Type, choose the option Windows NT Backup Domain Controller.

3. Type in the name of the computer (to a maximum of 15 characters), and then choose Add.

This action creates the machine account in the domain's security database for a computer of the specified name. The computer, however, doesn't become a member of the domain until it actively joins it.

Non-Domain Controller Machines (NT Workstations and Servers)

For any other NT machine, domain membership can be granted during the installation of NT on the machine, but only if it's done by an administrator. Once NT has been installed, however, domain membership can be granted in two fashions:

- On the NT workstation itself, by an administrator using the Network option of that workstation's Control Panel.

- Through Server Manager, in which the administrator or account operator adds a machine account for the computer to the domain's security database, then instructs the computer's user to join the domain under that account (using the Network option in Control Panel).

To create a machine account for an NT machine using Server Manager, choose Add to Domain from the Computer menu, select Windows NT Workstation or Server in the Computer Type box, type in the computer name, and choose Add. You can add a number of computers at once. Choose Close when you are finished.

Then, to add the workstation to the domain, log on to that computer. In its Control Panel, choose Network. You see the Network Settings dialog box. Choose the Identification Tab and then select the Change button next to the domain (or workgroup). You see the Domain/Workgroup Settings dialog box, as in Figure 11.11. In the Member of box, select the Domain button and type in the name of the domain that the workstation must join.

FIGURE 11.11:

Changing the domain
membership

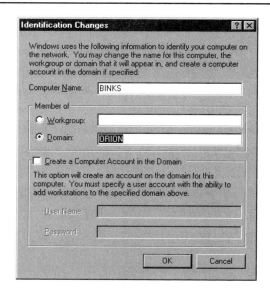

NT machines that are members of a domain don't actually get a copy of the domain's user database and don't help out verifying login requests, but they still get the benefits of the domain's centralized user and groups database.

LAN Manager 2.x Servers

LAN Manager 2.x servers are the only servers outside of NT Servers that can be granted membership in a domain. LAN Manager servers can function as supplementary servers in NT Server domains as long as the domain controller is an NT Server. A LAN Manager server can be designated as a domain controller only in a domain where all of the domain's servers are running LAN Manager 2.x.

As with other NT Servers, LAN Manager servers receive and keep copies of the domain's security database, but they can only validate logon attempts by workstations running Windows for Workgroups or LAN Manager 2.x workstation software (they can't validate logon attempts by NT users).

Because they don't support all of the types of information contained in NT Server accounts, LAN Manager 2.x servers don't recognize local groups or trust relationships, and are unable to use the users and global groups that are defined in other NT Server domains. Even so, resources in these domains can be accessed by NT Workstation users, provided that the user has a second account in the LAN Manager domain, or the LAN Manager domain permits guest logons. All in all, LAN Manager servers should be treated as just servers, not domain controllers under NT.

Managing Services

In addition to providing domain membership and shared resource management capabilities, Server Manager also lets you configure the services available on each of your servers. You can start, stop, pause, continue, and provide startup values to specific services. Each of the services in Server Manager are duplicated under the Services option in Control Panel, but unlike Control Panel (which manages services for the local computer only), Server Manager allows you to manage services for remote servers as well as the local computer.

The default services in NT Server are:

Default Service	What It Does
Alerter	Notifies selected users and computers of administrative alerts that occur on the server. Used by the Server and other services; requires the Messenger service.
Clipbook Server	Supports the Clipbook Viewer application; allows pages to be seen by remote Clipbooks.
Computer Browser	Maintains a current list of computers and furnishes the list to applications when requested; provides the computer lists shown in the main Server Manager window and in the Select Computer and Select Domain dialog boxes.
Directory Replicator	Replicates directories and their contents between computers.
Event Log	Records system, application, and security events in the event logs.
License Logging	Keeps track of used and available licenses.
Messenger	Sends out and receives messages sent by administrators and the Alerter service.
Net Logon	Performs authentications of account logons in NT Server. Keeps the domain's security database synchronized between the domain controller and other servers running NT Server in the domain.

Continued on next page

Default Service	What It Does
Network DDE	Provides network transport and security for DDE (Dynamic Data Exchange) conversations.
Network DDE DSDM	The DSDM (DDE Share Database Manager) service manages the shared DDE conversations; it is used by the Network DDE service.
Remote Procedure Call (RPC) Locator	Manages the RPC name service database and allows distributed applications to use the RPC name service.
Remote Procedure Call (RPC) Service	This is the RPC subsystem for Windows NT.
Schedule	Permits the use of the AT command to schedule commands and programs to run on a computer at a specific time and date. For some odd reason, this is not started by default, and so one of the things that you end up doing early on is to set this service to start up automatically.
Server	Provides Remote Procedure Call (RPC) support and allows file, print, and named pipe sharing.
UPS	Manages a UPS (uninterruptible power supply) connected to the server. Should be used in conjunction with Alerter, Messenger, and Event Log services to ensure that events related to the UPS service (such as a power failure) are recorded in the System log and that designated users are notified.
Workstation	Allows network connections and communications.

Additional services appear in the list based on your network configuration. For example, if you installed a Macintosh segment of the network, you may see File Server for Macintosh and Print Server for Macintosh listed as services.

To view and manage the services using Server Manager, select the desired server from the main window, open the Computer menu, and select the Services command. You see the Services on dialog box shown in Figure 11.12. If the entry in the Status column for a particular service is blank, that indicates that the service has been stopped. You should really only manipulate non-automatic services through this dialog box.

FIGURE 11.12:

Services on dialog box

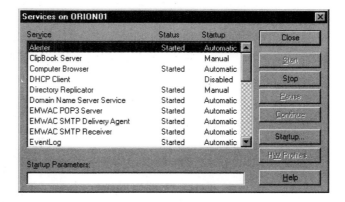

Starting and Stopping Services

You can start, stop, pause, or continue any of the services for a particular computer by following these steps:

1. Select a computer in the Server Manager window.

2. Choose Services from the Computer menu.

3. In the Services on dialog box, select the service in the Services window.

4. Click the Start, Stop, Pause, or Continue button.

If you need to pass startup parameters to a service, simply type them in the Startup Parameters box at the bottom before choosing the Start button.

Stopping the Server service disconnects all remote users. You should follow this procedure for stopping the Server service:

1. Pause the Server service first; users are thus prevented from establishing any new connections.

2.   With the Send Message command, tell connected users that they will be disconnected after a specific time period.

3.   After the specific time period expires, stop the Server services.

When the Server service is stopped, you can't administer it remotely; you must restart it locally.

Configuring Service Startup

Members of the domain's Administrators local groups can choose whether or not a service is started automatically, manually, or is initially disabled. To do this, select the service in the Services box and choose the Startup button. You see the Schedule Service on dialog box, as in Figure 11.13.

FIGURE 11.13:

Schedule Service on
dialog box

Under Startup Type, you can choose these options:

Automatic   Starts the service each time the system starts

Manual   Allows the service to be started by a user or by a dependent service

Disabled   Prevents the service from being started

TIP   Incidentally, the Server service won't start automatically unless the server has at least 12MB of memory.

Beneath the Startup Type, you can choose which account the service will log on as. Most services log on using the system account. However, a service such as the Schedule service may need more access than that given by the system account, which only provides Guest access. In such a case, you can create a special user account with the required access for the service to log on as. User accounts that are used to log on as a service must have the Password Never Expires option selected.

For the service to log on using the system account, simply select the System Account button. To specify a different account, choose the This Account button and use the browse button (...) to find and select the user account.

When you've acquired the proper account, type in its password in the Password and Confirm Password boxes. Then choose OK to return to the Services dialog box. When you've finished configuring the services, choose Close.

Scheduling Events

When the Schedule service is activated, you can execute programs or commands on the server (or a remote server) to run at a predetermined time. Scheduling these events uses the network command AT. If you've purchased and installed the NT Server *Resource Kit*, you can also use WinAT, which is a graphical interface for the AT command.

Note that the Schedule service, by default, logs on under the system account, the same account used by most services. Under these circumstances, the AT command can only access those resources that allow Guest access, which may not provide enough access for the desired activity. To gain greater access to network resources when using the AT command, you need to create a special user account, give it the appropriate access (if you're scheduling automatic backups, you might want to put the account in the Backup Operators group), then configure the Schedule service to log on using that special account. Make sure you select the Password Never Expires option when you create the account.

Setting Up a Scheduled Event

To set up a scheduled event (a "job") using the AT command, open the Command Prompt and type in the command, using the following syntax:

```
at [\\computername] time [/every:date[,...] | /next:date[,...] ]
/interactive command
```

where

- *computername* is the computer you are scheduling the event to run on. Leaving it out schedules the event on the local computer.

- The scheduler uses 24-hour time. For 11 A.M., type **11:00**; and for 2:30 P.M., type **14:30**.

- Any legal command, program, or batch file can be used in the *command* field.

- For the /every: and /next: options, you can either type in the days of the week (Sunday, Monday, etc.), or the number corresponding to the day of the month. Don't leave a space between the colon and the date. (You can abbreviate a day of the week in the /every: and /next: options to M, T, W, Th, F, S, or Su.)

- Interactive allows the program to raise dialog boxes, perhaps to report errors or to request user intervention (for example, to change a tape).

TIP   It's an especially good idea to use the /interactive option, particularly when testing out an AT command. Without /interactive, you'll never see any error messages that the program generates.

For example, to copy a file at 11:00 A.M. of the current day on a computer named Procyon (a one-time event), you would type

```
at \\procyon 11:00 "copy c:\users\ellenh\summary.txt c:\users\miked"
```

To run a program named cleanup.exe on the local computer at 5:00 P.M. on the 7th, 14th, and 21st of every month, you would type

```
at 17:00 /every:7,14,21 "cleanup"
```

You can use AT for other things, as well. Suppose you're working at an NT workstation or server, it's 9 A.M., and you need to remember to make a phone call at 10 A.M. Suppose also that you are working on a machine named WKSTATN. Just type

```
at 10:00 net send WKSTATN Don't forget that phone call!
```

To run a batch file named sayhi.bat on a computer named Rigel at 9:00 A.M. next Thursday, you would type

```
at \\rigel 9:00 /next:Thursday "sayhi"
```

To view any of the jobs currently scheduled at the local computer, type **at**, then press the Enter key (to see the scheduled jobs on another domain server, type **at** *computername*).

Each job is listed with its own ID number. To delete any of the scheduled jobs displayed, type

```
at \\computername [id number] /delete
```

If you wanted to remove a scheduled job (with the ID number 22) from the local computer, the command would be

```
at 22 /delete
```

Using WinAT to Schedule Events

WinAT is simply a graphical interface for the AT command that comes with the NT Server *Resource Kit*. But truthfully, there's no "simply" about it; it's a blessing to work with it instead of the command-line AT command. Opening the WinAT window displays the currently scheduled jobs on the local computer, as shown in Figure 11.14.

FIGURE 11.14:

The WinAT window

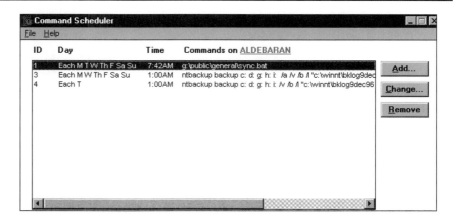

You can view the jobs at a remote server by pulling down the File menu and choosing Computer. To add a new scheduled job, select the Add button. You see the Add Command dialog box, as in Figure 11.15.

FIGURE 11.15:

Add Command dialog box

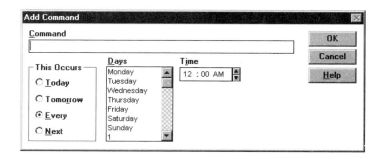

Type in the desired command in the Command box, and choose the Today, Tomorrow, Every, or Next button. Then, select the days and time the command needs to be run from the Days and Time boxes. When finished, select OK. The new job appears in the list of scheduled jobs in the main window.

If you need to change an existing job, select that job in the main window and click the Change button. You see the Change Command dialog box. Make the necessary changes, then choose OK. To remove a job on the list, simply highlight it and select Remove.

How Do I Set Up a Prescheduled Job at the Local Server?

In this example, we're going to schedule an incremental backup to take place every morning at 3:00 A.M. Type the following command (in an unbroken line):

```
at 3:00 /every:M,T,W,Th,F ntbackup backup c: /a /v /t incremental
/d "Daily backup"
```

The NTBackup command option /a appends data to the tape; otherwise, you overwrite the tape's previous backups. The /v option verifies the backup, and the /t followed by *incremental* tells NTBackup to only back things up with the archive bit set, and to reset the archive bit once the backup is done. In the label, two sets of quotes are interpreted as a single set of quotes. Truthfully, keeping track of all of those quotes gets to be a pain, and I strongly recommend that you load the WinAT program that comes with the *Resource Kit*; it makes setting up prescheduled jobs much easier.

Directory Replication

Directory replication is exactly what it sounds like: the duplication of a master set of directories from a server (called an *export server*) to other NT servers or workstations (called *import computers*). The most common application for this is to export login scripts from a primary domain controller to backup domain controllers; in that case, the PDC is the export server and the BDC the import server.

NOTE   This is the main reason to read this section—to ensure that the Netlogon directory on the PDC is properly replicated to the Netlogon directories of the BDCs. If you don't do that, the logon scripts, profiles, and the like don't get to the BDCs, and the result is that if users are verified by the PDC they get their profiles, logon scripts, and so on, but if they're logged on by a BDC they *don't* get that stuff. As there's no real way to control who logs you on—the question of which DC logs you on can be largely random for some networks—this can lead to some pretty puzzling behavior.

Now, at the outset, let me warn you that directory replication is a bit more complicated than it ought to be, but stick with me. At the end of this section I have some step-by-step recipes for making directory replication work.

Machines Replicate, Not Users

Just like members of a domain, the exporters and importers are not users, but machines (server ORION01 exports to workstation AMS, not the domain administrator to user Christa). These duplicate directories are not static copies, but rather remain dynamically linked to the master copy of the directory stored on the export server. If changes or additions are made to that directory, they are automatically reflected in the duplicates on the import computers.

Uses for Directory Replication

Why would you want to duplicate directories? There are two reasons why having constantly updated, identical copies of directories in more than one place can be a good idea. First of all, replicated directories can help you balance workloads. For example, if a number of workstations need to access a certain directory, you can export that directory to another server and direct some of the workstations to access it from there, rather than from the master copy. This way, you avoid bottlenecks at the server.

The *main* application of directory replication, however, is to make sure that all of the backup domain controllers (BDCs) have up-to-date copies of the login batch scripts for all users. That way, when a BDC logs you in instead of the PDC, the BDC can supply the login batch script, and the PDC needn't be burdened with having to always supply login batch scripts.

As a matter of fact, directory replication is almost set up by default to propagate login batch scripts from a PDC to its BDCs, and I'll show you in a bit how to do that.

Who Can Import? Who Can Export?

Potential exporters on an NT Server network are limited; only NT Server machines can export directories to the rest of the network. Importers are less limited, as NT Server, OS/2 LAN Manager, and Windows NT Workstation machines can all import directories from the export servers. The only restriction placed on export computers is that the directories or files exported must match the naming conventions of the file system of the volume set to which they are imported. For example, if the volume to which the files are exported is formatted to NTFS, the export directory must be set for NTFS. See Figure 11.16 for a demonstration.

FIGURE 11.16:

Exporting either to domain names or to individual import computers

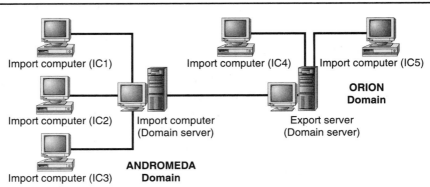

Import computer (IC1)

Import computer (IC4)

Import computer (IC5)

Import computer (IC2)

Import computer (Domain server)

Import computer (IC3)

Export server (Domain server)

ORION Domain

ANDROMEDA Domain

ORION's domain server is the export server in this figure. ORION can export either to domain ANDROMEDA and domain ORION, or to the individuals (IC1, IC2, IC5, etc.), or perhaps to one entire domain and to individuals in the other one.

You don't have to name particular computer names when exporting and importing; it's possible to just point to a domain. For example, suppose a machine named WOLF359 says, "I'm exporting to domain LOCALGRP," and the domain LOCAL-GRP contains machines named ACENTAUR, BCENTAUR, PCENTAUR, SIRIUS, TCETI, EERIDANI, and our exporter, WOLF359. Suppose also that the Directory Replicator service is only active in SIRIUS, TCETI, and WOLF359, and that each of them has specified that it wants to import not from a particular machine but from domain LOCALGRP. The result is that the exported files from WOLF359 appear in the import directories of SIRIUS, TCETI, and WOLF359. Notice that WOLF359 is exporting *to itself* (it can do that, and it's quite useful, as you will learn a bit later).

The only time that you might have problems exporting to a domain is when some of the domain's import computers are located across a WAN (wide area network) bridge from the export server. In that case, when setting up the list of computers to export to from the export server, you should specify the individual importers by name, and when importing from another domain across the WAN bridge, specify the name of the export server to import from, rather than the domain name. This is illustrated in Figure 11.17.

FIGURE 11.17:

Exporting across a WAN bridge

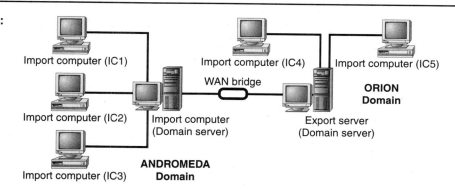

ORION's domain server is the export server in this figure. Because it is exporting to computers across a WAN bridge, it must refer to all import computers individually by name (even those in its own domain), rather than exporting to the entire domain and letting the domain server distribute the exported directories.

Setting Up the Directory Replicator Service

Before any machine can either send (export) or receive (import) files, its Directory Replicator service must be active. That's very similar to starting any NT service: you can monkey around with it with the Services applet in the Control Panel, but where most services just start up as belonging to the "System," the Directory Replicator service requires you to create a bogus user, give that user some powers, and tell NT that the *bogus user* is starting the Directory Replicator service, rather than the System.

Before you can configure an NT Server computer to be an export server, you need to set up a special user account that is part of the Backup Operators group. The Directory Replicator service uses this account to log on, so you need to make sure that

- The account's password never expires
- The account is accessible 24 hours per day, seven days per week
- The account is assigned to the Backup Operators group

User accounts are set up under User Manager for Domains (consult Chapter 6 to see how). Don't try to name this account "Replicator"; the system won't let you because there is already a user group by that name. In my examples, I've created a user named REP.

Once you've set up this user account, go back to the Server Manager. You now have to configure the Directory Replicator service to start up automatically and to log on using that separate account for each computer in the domain that will participate in replication. To do this, select the computer in the Server Manager window, and then, from the Computer menu, choose Services. You see the Services on dialog box (see Figure 11.12). Select the Directory Replicator service and then click the Startup button. You see the Directory Replicator Service on dialog box, as shown in Figure 11.18.

FIGURE 11.18:

Configuring startup for the
Directory Replicator service

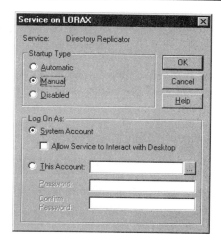

Select the service to begin automatically, select the This Account radio button,
and then click the (...) button to select the account that you set up for the Directory Replicator service to use. You see a screen that looks like Figure 11.19.

FIGURE 11.19:

Selecting an account for
Replicator service to use

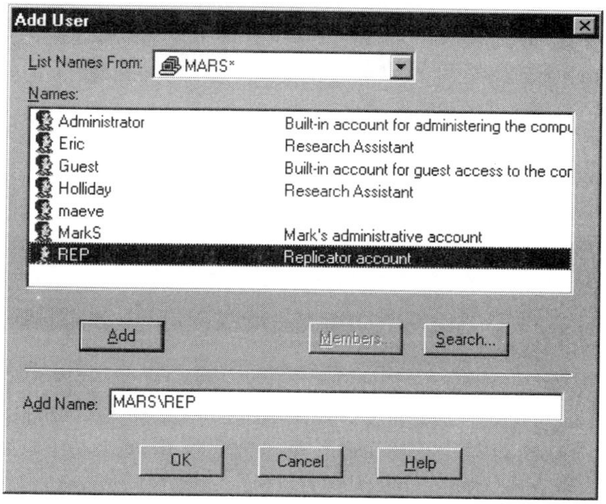

Double-click on the name of the account that you want to use (I called mine REP) and, when the name of the account shows up in the Add Name text box, click OK. You find yourself back in the directory Replicator Service screen, but now it has the name of the account that you want to use.

Type in the password that you assigned to the account and click OK. NT Server shows you a confirmation screen that looks like Figure 11.20. If you like, you can go ahead and manually start the service now, since it won't automatically begin until you've logged off and logged back on again.

FIGURE 11.20:

Confirmation of startup configuration

NOTE   Note that what you just did you must do for every computer that will either export or import directories!

Configuring the Export Server

Once you've set up the Replicator service properly, you're ready to set up the export server for export. As mentioned before, export servers do the following:

- Contain the master set of directories that will be duplicated during replication
- Maintain the list of computers to which the subdirectories are imported
- Are able to export to domain names as well as to individual computers in the domain

 **NT SERVER** Any NT Server computer can become an export server—but *only* NT Server computers can, not NT workstations.

Now for the directories to export. When NT Server or NT Workstation is installed on a machine, the default export and import paths C:\winnt\SYSTEM32\REPL\ EXPORT and C:\winnt\SYSTEM32\REPL\IMPORT are automatically created. (If NT Workstation or NT Server is installed in a different location than C:\WINNT, these default paths are adjusted accordingly.) Any directories created within the export path are automatically exported, and they and their contents are subsequently placed in the default import path.

NOTE

> Only directories inside the export directory will be exported! If you put a *file* in \WINNT\SYSTEM32\REPL\EXPORT, it will not be exported. But a *directory* under \WINNT\SYSTEM32\REPL\EXPORT will be exported, once directory replication is under way.

Unless you've changed your default directories, you will create the directories that you intend to export within C:\winnt\SYSTEM32\REPL\EXPORT. You don't need to put all the files in the directory yet, since any changes that you make to the directory will be dynamically reflected on the import computers once the replication service is going.

Once you've created your directories, you must configure directory replication so as to tell your system whether it will export, import, or do both. You configure directory replication in Control Panel (if you're seated at the machine you want to configure) or in Server Manager. Server Manager, however, lets you configure directory replication remotely for more than one machine at a time.

To set up replication

1. Do one of the following:

    - In Control Panel, select the Server option; or

    - In Server Manager, select the computer, then choose Properties from the Computer menu (or simply double-click on the computer in the Server Manager window).

2. Choose Replication from the buttons on the bottom of the window. You see a screen that looks like Figure 11.21.

FIGURE 11.21:

Initial screen for directory replication

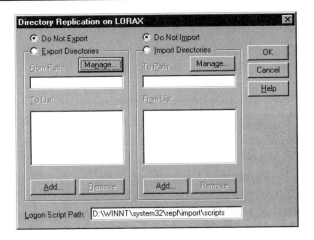

3. Select the Export Directories radio button and type the name of the path from which you want to export (you can leave it unchanged if you choose to use the default export path).

4. Click on the Add button in the southwest corner of the dialog box, double-click on the domain you want, and select a computer to export to from the list. Your list looks like the one in Figure 11.22.

FIGURE 11.22:

List of computers to add to the Export To List

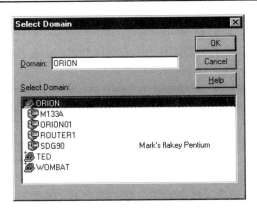

The To List box contains the list of computers that your export directories will be copied to. By default, the list is blank and the local domain automatically receives the exported subdirectories. However, once an entry is made to this list, the local domain is no longer exported to, and must be explicitly added to the list if you want it to receive exported subdirectories.

TIP

If all you want to do is to have your PDC replicate logon scripts to your BDCs, then do *not* enter anything in the To List box. Just tell each of the BDCs to import, tell the PDC to import *and* export, and place your domain's login scripts in \WINNT\SYSTEM32\REPL\EXPORT\SCRIPTS (note the EXPORT, not the usual IMPORT) on the PDC.

This is what I meant a few pages back when I noted that WOLF359 could export to itself and that it was a good thing. Suppose WOLF359 is the PDC for a domain. You want to place the login scripts in one place and have them automatically end up where they are needed—that is, in every \WINNT\SYSTEM32\ REPL\IMPORT\SCRIPTS directory. By putting logon scripts into the PDC's \WINNT\SYSTEM32\REPL\EXPORT\SCRIPTS directory (rather than the normal \WINNT\SYSTEM32\REPL\IMPORT\SCRIPTS directory), you'll ensure that the BDCs all get copies of the login batch scripts. That's easy to see, as \SCRIPTS is then a directory of \WINNT\SYSTEM32\REPL\EXPORT, and any directory in \WINNT\SYSTEM32\REPL\EXPORT on a directory export server (the PDC, again, in this case) gets replicated to the corresponding \WINNT\ SYSTEM32\REPL\IMPORT directory on the import servers.

But how will the *PDC* get the login batch scripts, as they must be in the \WINNT\ SYSTEM32\REPL\IMPORT\SCRIPTS directory to be useful? Answer: Have the PDC export to itself—make it both an export server and an import server. Now you can place the login batch scripts in one directory, set up the PDC to replicate to the domain, and the scripts will end up where they should.

By the way, permissions for an export directory grant Full Control to members of the Replicator local group. If you change these permissions, files are copied to the import computers with incorrect permissions and an "access denied" error is written in the event log.

If you need to be more specific as to which subdirectories need to be exported, you can choose the Manage button in the Directory Replication dialog box (see Figure 11.21) to manage locks, stabilization, and subtree replication for the subdirectories exported from the server. You see the Manage Exported Directories dialog box in Figure 11.23. It shows the current locks, stabilization status, and subtree replication status for the subdirectories that are to be exported.

FIGURE 11.23:

Managing the export
directories

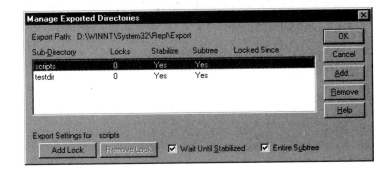

Locks prevent a particular subdirectory from being exported. Subdirectories can have more than one lock applied to them; exportation will occur only if this column contains a zero. If a subdirectory has been locked, the date and time of the oldest lock is displayed in the Locked Since column. To add a lock to a subdirectory, select it from the list and choose the Add Lock button. To take away a lock, choose the Remove Lock button.

If you choose the Stabilize option by selecting the Wait Until Stabilized check box at the bottom, files in the selected export subdirectory will wait two minutes or more after any changes are made before being exported (this helps eliminate partial replication). Otherwise, files are exported immediately. The default is to *not* wait until stabilized.

Selecting the Entire Subtree check box allows all subdirectories and their contents (including additional subdirectories) within the selected subdirectory to be exported. If this option is cleared, only first-level subdirectories are exported. Unless you decide to change it, NT Server exports the entire subtree of the directory.

Configuring the Import Computers

Import computers, you recall, are specific servers and computers in the same or other domains that receive a duplicate set of directories from the export server. They maintain a list of export servers from which subdirectories are imported and can import from domain names as well as from individual export servers. Alternatively, you can choose not to specify any export servers to expect data from, and the import machines will by default collect any files intended for their domain in general.

Both NT Server and NT machines can become import computers, but you have to set them up for the service first, just as you did for the export servers. Likewise, you can configure import servers locally using Control Panel, or you can do so remotely with Server Manager. The procedure is the same, except you choose import options rather than export options in the dialog boxes:

1. Use Administrative powers to create a new user account for the Replication service to use on the import computer, just as you did on the export server.

2. If you're working locally at the workstation, go to the Services icon in the Control Panel and configure the Directory Replicator Service to begin automatically, just as you did on the export server. (If the computer can be remotely administered, you can do this at the server using Server Manager).

3. Using the Server option in the local computer's Control Panel, or by displaying the computer's properties remotely in Server Manager, choose the Replication button and follow the same procedure as for exporting directories, but choose the import directories options instead.

How Often Does the System Replicate?

By default, the export server replicates to its import servers every five minutes. The export server doesn't want to waste bandwidth replicating files that change constantly, however, so a file must have been unchanged for two minutes before the Replicator service propagates it. Those "five-minute" and "two-minute" intervals can both be adjusted with Registry entries:

- HKEY_LOCAL_MACHINE\SYSTEM\CurrentControlSet\Services\ Replicator\Parameters can contain a value named *Interval* that takes values from 1 to 60 minutes. It is type REG_DWORD, and controls how often to replicate to import servers.

- The same key can hold another value, GuardTime, that says how long a file should be stable before it can be replicated. Again, it's REG_DWORD, value in minutes; it must be one-half of *Interval* or less.

Summary: Creating an Import/Export Pair

You have to worry about an awful lot of things when making an import/export pair work. Here's a step-by-step recipe to make a server named SOURCE replicate to a server named DESTINATION. First, some ingredients (this *is* a recipe, right?):

- You have to be logged on as an administrator to make this work.

- SOURCE must be an NT Server.

- DESTINATION can be any kind of NT machine.

- This works best if Source and Destination are members of the same domain.

To make an import/export pair

1. With User Manager for Domains, create a user named REP. Give it any password you like, but set "Password never expires," and don't force the user to change the password next time it logs on ("it" because it's not a real human, just a bogus account to make NT happy). Also, don't restrict the logon hours.

2. Click Groups, and add REP to the Backup Operators group. Save the user account, and close User Manager for Domains.

3. Start up Server Manager. Select the SOURCE machine. You see a main Server Manager screen like the one in Figure 11.24.

FIGURE 11.24:

Initial Server Manager screen showing SOURCE and DESTINATION

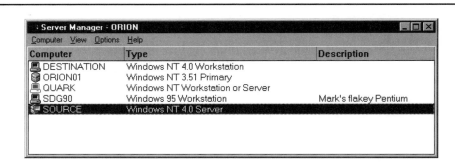

4. Choose Services on the Computer menu. You see a screen like the one in Figure 11.25.

FIGURE 11.25:

List of services on SOURCE

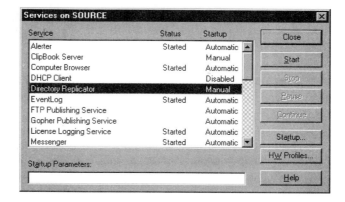

5. Choose Directory Replicator service and click the Startup button. You see something like Figure 11.26.

FIGURE 11.26:

Controlling startup of Replicator service on SOURCE

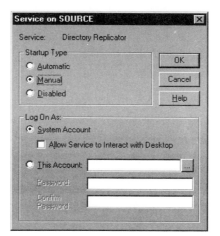

6. Under Startup Type, click the Automatic radio button.

7. Under Log On As, click the This Account radio button.

8. Click the ellipsis (…) button and you see a screen like Figure 11.27. This dialog box lists the users of the domain.

FIGURE 11.27:

Choosing a replicator user
account

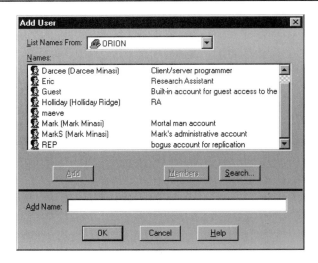

9. Choose REP, click Add, and then click OK to return to the previous Service
on SOURCE dialog box. REP's name is filled in, as you can see in Figure 11.28.

FIGURE 11.28:

Service control box after
filling in necessary
information

10. You have to prove to NT that you have the right to plunk REP into this dialog box. In other words, you have to prove that you know REP's password. I

set it to blank, so I'll just fill in blanks in the Password and Confirm Password boxes and click OK. As this is the first time I've done this, I get the confirming message box shown in Figure 11.29.

FIGURE 11.29:

Confirming that REP is in the Replicator group

Server Manager

The account ORION\REP has been granted the Log On As A Service right and added to the Replicator local group.

OK

11. Click OK to clear that dialog box and you get back to Service on SOURCE dialog box. Notice that it says "Service" and not "Services." Click Close.

12. You are now be back at the main Server Manager screen, with SOURCE still selected. Click Computer, then Properties, and then Replication. You see a dialog box like the one in Figure 11.30.

FIGURE 11.30:

Setting up replication on the export computer SOURCE

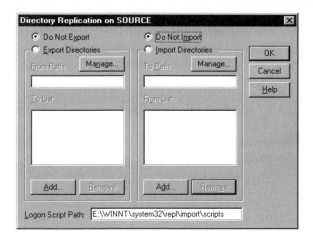

Directory Replication on SOURCE

- Do Not Export
- Export Directories
  - From Path: Manage...
  - To List:

- Do Not Import
- Import Directories
  - To Path: Manage...
  - From List:

OK
Cancel
Help

Add...   Remove   Add...   Remove

Logon Script Path: E:\WINNT\system32\repl\import\scripts

13. Click the Export Directories radio button. Click Add and choose a computer to export to. First you are asked for a domain; it's ORION for my example, so I choose that, and then I see a list of machines in ORION. The list is shown in Figure 11.31.

FIGURE 11.31:

Choosing a machine to
export to

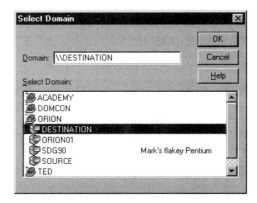

14. Once you've highlighted the target machine, click OK. Notice that the export directory is by default \WINNT\SYSTEM32\REPL\EXPORT. You can change that if you want to with the Manage button, but I'm leaving it alone for this example. My target machine is called DESTINATION, so I picked that. Click OK in the Directory replication on Source dialog box to return to the main window of Server Manager. You see a message telling you that the replication service is starting.

15. By now, you should be back in the main window of the Server Manager. Now it's time to set up the receiving import computer, DESTINATION. Choose DESTINATION and click Computer, then Services on the menu.

16. You will do the same thing to DESTINATION to make sure that it can receive the files. Click the Directory Replication services, click Startup, choose Automatic in Startup type, put This Account in Log on as, fill in REP's name and password, go to services, tell it to start automatically, fill in the name of REP, punch in REP's password, and click Properties for DESTINATION and Replication.

So far, what you're doing is a carbon copy of what you did with SOURCE, so I'll spare you the screen shots. But now take a look at the directory replication on DESTINATION dialog box shown in Figure 11.32. This is only half the dialog box that SOURCE had. Why? Well, recall that DESTINATION is, for this example at least, an NT Workstation machine. Therefore, it does not have the ability to export.

FIGURE 11.32:

Directory replication on a
non-server machine

17. Choose the Import Directories radio button, click Add, and fill in the name of SOURCE. Click OK, and you again see that the system starts up the Directory Replicator service.

18. Put a file into whatever directory you specified for SOURCE to export, and wait five minutes. It should show up in the import directory on DESTINATION; there's no need to reboot.

NOTE   Remember that only subdirectories in the \WINNT\SYSTEM32\REPL\EXPORT directory will replicate, not files in the export directory itself. To make a file replicate, make sure it's in a subdirectory inside the export directory.

Summary: Setting Up Your PDC to Replicate Login Scripts to the BDCs

But I've said before that the main reason you'll set up replication is to keep the NETLOGON directories of your domain controllers in sync, so here's a more specific summary. This shows you specifically how to set up your PDC and BDCs to keep the login scripts on the PDC replicated out to the BDCs. I assume that you want to keep the login scripts in their normal place: \WINNT\SYSTEM32\ REPL\IMPORT\SCRIPTS.

1. Set up each PDC and BDC's Directory Replicator service. Follow the steps in the previous section to see how to do this. Again, you have to go through the process for each domain controller.

2. Place the domain's login scripts on the PDC in \WINNT\SYSTEM32\ REPL\EXPORT\SCRIPTS. Make any future changes to this directory, not the \WINNT\SYSTEM32\REPL*IMPORT*\SCRIPTS directory.

3. Get the Directory Replication control dialog box for the PDC either by double-clicking on the PDC in the Server Manager and then clicking Replication, or by opening up the Control Panel on the PDC, double-clicking on the Server applet, and clicking the Replication button.

4. Click the Export Directories and Import Directories radio buttons. *Ensure that there isn't anything in the To List or From List fields.* If there is, remove it. Click OK to close the box.

5. For each BDC, open up its Directory Replication control dialog box and click the Import Directories radio button. *Again, make sure nothing is in the From List field.*

6. Stop and then start the Directory Replication service on the domain controllers and wait at least five minutes. You will find that the batch scripts now sit in the \WINNT\SYSTEM32\REPL\IMPORT\SCRIPTS directories on the PDC and the BDCs.

Changing the Logon Script Path

At the bottom of the Directory Replication dialog box is an edit field that contains the logon script path. It is shown in Figure 11.33.

FIGURE 11.33:

Directory Replication on dialog box

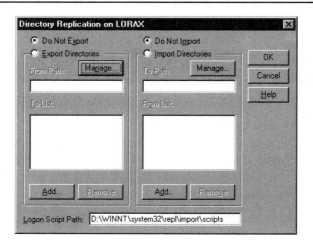

Logon scripts are batch files that can be assigned to specific user accounts so that when a user logs on, the script executes. They are assigned as part of a user's profile (see Chapter 7 for more information). When a user logs on, the system looks for the logon script by combining the script's file name (in the user account data) with the logon script path, which is specified in the Directory Replication on dialog box.

In NT Server, replication is configured so that servers export logon scripts from the directory C:\winnt35\SYSTEM32\REPL\EXPORT\SCRIPTS and import them to the directory C:\winnt35\SYSTEM32\REPL\IMPORT\SCRIPTS on the import computer. The path for importing logon scripts must be entered in the Logon Script Path box for the domain controller as well as each server that participates in logon authentication for the domain.

How Do I Set the Logon Script Path for a Server?

To configure the logon script path for the selected server, type in a local path in the Logon Scripts Path box of the Directory Replication dialog box (the default, C:\WINNT\SYSTEM32\REPL\IMPORT\SCRIPTS, usually suffices). Entries are required in this edit field, so don't enter a blank space.

Troubleshooting Directory Replication

Setting up the replication service properly can be a bit tricky. If you run into problems, these are some things that you might want to check:

- Have you made the replication service's account a member of the Backup Operators group, or given it the rights accorded to that group?

- Has the Directory Replicator service been started on both the import and export computers?

- Are the import and export computers in the same domain? If not, are the username and password the same in both domains? Do the domains trust each other?

- For NTFS partitions, have the permissions for the export directory and its contents been altered? Does the Replicator local group have at least Change privileges to these directories?

- Does an account have a file open (on import or export) all the time? This would appear as a sharing violation in the event log.

- When importing or exporting from an NTFS directory, does either directory have filenames that differ only in case? The export computer may choose one file while the import computer chooses the other; this can set replication out of sync.

- Are some files with extended attributes (EAs) being replicated from an HPFS volume to an NT Server? NT doesn't support EAs that are written in non-contiguous parts of the disk (OS/2 sometimes does).

- Are the clocks of the import and export machines synchronized? If they are too far off, the server cannot export properly to the import computer.

- Did you wait long enough? It make take five minutes before replication kicks off.

If you are using OS/2 LAN Manager, be aware that LAN Manager only allows one set of credentials (that is, a user name and password) to be used at a time. If someone is logged on locally to one user ID and the Replicator is trying to use another, replication is delayed until that user logs off.

Errors in the replicator service are entered into the applications log. You can view these entries by opening the Event Viewer in the Administrative Tools group and choosing Application from the Log menu. Make sure you check the logs on both the import and export computers.

Finally, make sure you start the Alerter service and configure alerts so that you can receive messages about the success or failure of directory replication in your system.

Managing Domain Controllers

All domains have a primary domain controller (PDC) that keeps a database of users and groups for the entire domain: the SAM (Security Accounts Manager) database I've referred to before. It is part of the Registry on a PDC.

For the sake of fault tolerance, NT allows a network to have more than one domain controller. The first domain controller in a domain must be, by definition, a PDC; subsequently installed domain controllers are all BDCs. All that domain controllers really do is keep track of which users can access what objects (files, directories, printers). The job of domain controller may be low-intensity enough that your domain controllers can serve "double duty" as file servers, name servers, and the like.

While the first PDC is born to the throne, so to speak, it is possible to "promote" a BDC to a PDC and demote the old PDC in the process.

The Server Manager assists with some of these duties. It lets you

- Promote and demote primary domain controllers
- Synchronize backup domain controllers with the primary domain controller

One thing you *can't* do with the Server Manager is create new backup domain controllers. Unfortunately, the only way to make an NT Server machine into a domain controller is to install that machine as a domain controller. You make that decision when you run NT's Setup program, and it's one you can't change without reinstalling from scratch.

I'll cover all of those issues in this section, but I'll also take up more complex questions, to wit: How many domain controllers should I have in my domain? How many users can I have in my domain? How large will the SAM be? How can I fine-tune the communication between the PDC and the BDCs to minimize unnecessary network traffic?

Promoting a Primary Domain Controller with Server Manager

Let's start off with a simple question: How do I make a BDC into the PDC?

Recall that every domain must have a primary domain controller. The PDC keeps the master copy of the domain's account and security database, which is automatically updated whenever changes are made. Copies of this database are also automatically received by all other servers in the domain. Every five minutes, the other servers query the domain controller, asking if changes in the database have occurred. If any changes were made within those five minutes, the domain controller sends the changes (not the entire database) to the other servers. (That "five minutes" value can be adjusted, as I'll explain shortly.)

You establish which machine is a domain's PDC when you create the domain, and you officially create a domain by installing a PDC for the domain. Other domain controllers are also anointed when you run Setup to create them. Inside Server Manager, though, you can change a domain controller from a PDC to a BDC or vice versa.

To designate one of the domain's BDCs as the PDC, select that computer in the Server Manager window, and choose the Promote to Primary Domain Controller command on the Computer menu. The old PDC will automatically revert to server status unless it's unavailable to the network—for example, if it's turned off. If that is the case, you have to manually demote it (in the Computer menu, the Promote to Primary Domain Controller command changes to the Demote To Backup Domain Controller command). If you don't demote it and the old domain controller returns to service, it won't run the Net Logon service or participate in user logon authentication; but I'll get to that in the section "What Happens When a PDC Fails?" later in this chapter.

Why would you promote a BDC to a PDC, by the way? Probably because you're about to take down the PDC and you want to make sure that the domain continues to run in a smooth, uninterrupted fashion.

When Promotion Doesn't Work...

Sometimes you'll try to promote a BDC to PDC and the process doesn't quite complete. The PDC hangs and you've got to reboot. Upon reboot, it seems either that neither PC or both PCs are PDCs. Here's how to muck around in the Registry and force a BDC to PDC or vice versa. You've got to use REGEDT32 for this—REGEDIT can't do it.

The change is in HKEY_LOCAL_MACHINE\Security, but you don't have access to its keys initially. So choose that key and then choose Security ➤ Permissions and ensure that Administrators have Full Control on this key and all subkeys. (This is why you need REGEDT32.) Then navigate to HKEY_LOCAL_MACHINE\Security\Policy\PolSrvRo and change the *<no name>* value entry from 03000000 to 02000000—in this case, 3 indicates a PDC and 2 indicates a BDC. Restart the system and all should be well.

Synchronization: Keeping a Uniform Security Database

Server Manager can help out in another place as well: making sure that all the BDCs are in sync with the PDC.

Synchronizing a domain's servers forces the replication of the domain's security database from the PDC to all of the BDCs in the domain. NT Server synchronizes the BDCs automatically, but in the unlikely event that one BDC's copy of the SAM database becomes out of sync with the rest of the domain, you can perform the synchronization manually.

To synchronize the domain account database (the SAM, recall) on a BDC with the SAM on the primary domain controller, select that BDC from the Server Manager list and, on the Computer menu, choose Synchronize with Primary Domain Controller. If you need to synchronize *all* of the BDCs with the PDC in one command, choose the PDC from the Server Manager list. Then, from the Computer menu, choose Synchronize Entire Domain. You see the message in Figure 11.34.

FIGURE 11.34:

The synchronization confirmation message

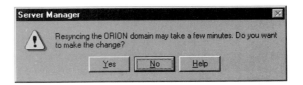

As the message implies, a manual synchronization can take a significant length of time to complete if the security database is large. (If you're wondering, "*How large?*" stay tuned for the upcoming section "Estimating the Size of the SAM.")

For a LAN Manager 2.*x* server, the Synchronize with Domain Controller command re-establishes the computer account password on both the LAN Manager server and the domain controller.

Controlling Synchronization

I mentioned earlier that the PDC replicates its SAM database out to the BDCs every five minutes. That can be adjusted with a number of parameters in the Registry. All are value entries that go in HKEY_LOCAL_MACHINE\System\CurrentControlSet\Services\Netlogon\Parameters.

How Often to Replicate? First, you can control how often the PDC replicates to the BDC with the *Pulse* value. It is of type REG_DWORD, and it is in seconds. The lowest value you can set is 60 (one minute) and the largest value is 3600 (one hour). You might want to increase the value from its default of 300 if your BDCs are connected to the PDC via slower WAN links.

Just Say Hello Now and Then In general, PDCs don't try to replicate to BDCs if there hasn't been any change since the last update. But every once in a while, they go tap the BDCs on the shoulder just to make sure they're still out there. How often they do that is controlled by a value called *PulseMaximum*, another REG_DWORD, that is calibrated in seconds. The minimum value is 60 seconds; the maximum is 86,400 seconds (one day). In general, I wouldn't mess with it.

Tell Me Everything You Know By default, the PDC doesn't replicate the entire database out to the BDCs; it just sends the changes. But, if you want (and I can't think of a reason why you would want to), you can tell the PDC to replicate the whole silly SAM database every time it replicates by setting a value called *Update* to Yes. The Update value is of type REG_SZ.

Don't Hog the WAN Because the replication conversation between a PDC and a BDC over a WAN link can consume a fair amount of the bandwidth of that WAN link, Microsoft has included a parameter that it claims will let you control how the PDC-BDC conversation uses the WAN link. By default, every transfer of SAM data can be a block of data up to 128KB. That large a data block would tie up a 64Kbps line for 16 seconds without overhead and probably 30 seconds *with* overhead, a significant length of time. You can, instead, tell your BDC to accept PDC data in smaller chunks with the *ReplicationGovernor* value.

ReplicationGovernor is of type REG_DWORD and it ranges from 0 to 100. The 0 to 100 is a percentage of the basic 128K byte block that NT usually uses in its PDC-BDC conversations. Set it to 50, and you get a transfer block that is 50 percent of 128K bytes, or 64K bytes. Set it lower, and the DCs will never hog your WAN link for an extended length of time. Set it *too* low, however, and the DCs will spend all day transferring tiny, incomplete pieces of data, and by the time they get done, it will be time to start all over again! Of course, setting this to 0 means that blocks of 0 bytes get used, which means that the BDC *never* gets replicated. This parameter goes on the Registry of the *BDC*, not the PDC.

The Microsoft explanation of this parameter is a little confusing. Microsoft says that it defines "both the size of the data transferred on each call to the PDC and the frequency of those calls." It kind of implies (well, to me anyway) that setting the ReplicationGovernor parameter to 50 will halve the size of the replication blocks *and* the frequency with which the BDC/PDC conversation occurs, both of which sound like good methods of reducing WAN traffic. In actual fact, setting the parameter to 50 means that each block *will* be smaller—64K bytes rather than 128K bytes—but, as a result, the *number* of blocks will double, meaning that the PDC and BDC will have to talk more often albeit for shorter times. So, yes, the Microsoft documentation is correct, as this defines both the *size* of the data transferred on each call to the PDC (it gets smaller) and the frequency of these calls (they get *more* frequent). When I say "frequent," however, I don't mean more calls *per minute*, just more calls in total. Setting ReplicationGovernor to 50 will also tell Netlogon to space out the calls a bit, leaving bandwidth for other programs.

What Happens When a PDC Fails?

PDCs replicate the SAM database to the BDCs every five minutes. (That value can be changed, as I'll show you later in this section.) The BDCs can authenticate login requests, requests for object access, and the like. Therefore, the BDCs have a complete, up-to-date version of the SAM that they can refer to. What BDCs *can't* do, however, is *change* the SAM. If the PDC is down, then the BDCs can log people on to the domain, but people can't change their passwords. If the PDC is down and an administrator tries to make a change to a user's account, she sees the message in Figure 11.35.

FIGURE 11.35:

User Manager cannot save changes to the SAM if the PDC is down.

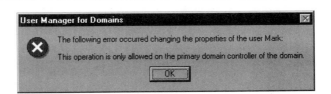

The SAM does not contain share permissions, nor does it contain file and directory permissions for any computer. That means that if the PDC is down, you cannot do the following:

- Change your password
- Change a user's name, account settings, logon hours, or "logon to" list

- Change a user's rights

- Create, destroy, or modify global groups

- Create, destroy, or modify any local groups that are local to the domain

If the PDC is down, you still can do the following:

- Create, destroy, or modify directory shares

- Change, destroy, or modify file and directory permissions

- Access print and directory shares for which you have permission

You can control permissions without a functioning PDC because permissions don't live in the SAM hive; rather, they're in the SECURITY hive, which is machine-specific. (In general, so is the SAM—most machines have their own distinct SAM—but that's not true for BDCs. BDCs don't really have a SAM of their own, just a read-only copy of the SAM on the PDC.)

Anyway, back to the original question: What happens when the PDC dies? Assume that some fool reaches over and disconnects the PDC from the UPS. (You *do* have your domain controllers on UPSes, don't you?) What does that look like?

Well, obviously, any shares on the PDC won't be available any longer, unless by the time you're reading this Microsoft has released the Wolfpack modifications to NT that will allow two PCs to be a "cluster" that acts like one PC. Yes, the services on the PDC won't be available any more. Here is what else will happen:

- Domain logins will still happen, assuming you have at least one BDC—and I *am* assuming that you have at least one BDC.

- Existing sessions will remain in place, but…

- No machine will act as the PDC.

All of the BDCs will have an identical copy of the domain's SAM, but none of them will be able to make any changes to that SAM, as you read a few paragraphs back. Firing up the Server Manager will get an error message that warns you that it couldn't find a primary domain controller, but that it will run anyway. Then, even though it can't find the PDC any more, it still shows up in the Server Manager list, but as a BDC, as you can see in Figure 11.36.

FIGURE 11.36:

Server Manager screen with
PDC not active

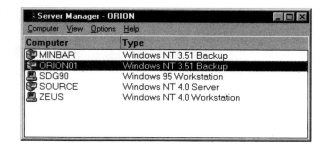

Now, in this actual domain, ORION01 is the PDC, but it is the *downed* PDC. This brings up an important point:

NOTE   When the PDC fails, the BDCs do not automatically become PDCs. BDCs remain BDCs until you promote one of their number to PDC.

So let's anoint a new PDC. I click on the BDC named MINBAR (try it on ORION01, which isn't turned on, and you get, "The network path was not found," as in Figure 11.37).

FIGURE 11.37:

We can't find a PDC, but
we'll have a coronation
anyway.

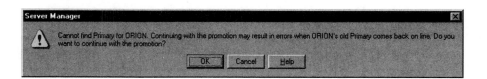

I click Computer and Promote to Primary Domain Controller. Once I do that, Server Manager looks normal, and MINBAR now has the Borg-like cube icon that indicates that it's a PDC. But suppose I bring ORION01 back now? Well, then Server Manager looks like Figure 11.38.

FIGURE 11.38:

Gadzooks! The PDC and a pretender!

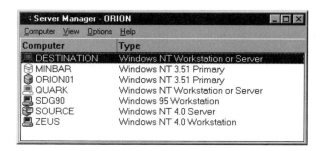

MINBAR seems now to have gone to "stealth" mode. It is still a cube, so it thinks it is the PDC, but it is a colorless cube. ORION01 also thinks that it is the real deal, so someone has to sort this out. I click on MINBAR and Computer, and I get the menu that you see in Figure 11.39.

FIGURE 11.39:

Server Manager offers to demote the impostor.

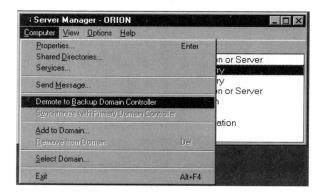

When there are two apparent PDCs is the only time you ever see Demote to Backup Domain Controller on the menu.

To summarize: when a PDC fails, the BDCs don't automatically slide into the PDC role. Promote one of them, and when the old PDC returns, it continues to claim that it is the one true PDC, as does the erstwhile BDC. You have to resolve the conflict with the Server Manager and demote one of the upstarts.

How Many BDCs Do You Need?

As you learned in earlier chapters, the primary domain controller can handle logon validations, but it's a good idea to have another domain controller as a backup.

Benefits of BDCs

You want the backup for several reasons:

- A BDC can handle login requests, improving user response time. If there are more DCs around to validate login requests, users can log on quicker first thing in the morning—that's pretty good PR for you network types, right?

- If the primary domain controller goes down, a backup domain controller can be promoted to primary domain controller and the domain will continue to function.

- It is a major pain in the neck to reinstall NT Server on the primary domain controller if you have no backup domain controllers, as I explained in Chapter 3.

In a domain with both NT Servers and LAN Manager 2.*x* servers, don't rely solely on LAN Manager servers as your only backups. LAN Manager servers can neither validate logon requests from NT workstations nor be promoted to the domain controller of an NT Server domain.

All right then. I imagine by now you're sold on the idea of BDCs. Suppose you're going to design a domain with a few dozen servers and a few hundred users. How many of those servers should be DCs?

Network Traffic: One BDC Disadvantage

Well, on the plus side, the more BDCs, the quicker logons can be, and, to a much lesser extent, the more reliable the domain is (a disaster would have to kill *all* of the BDCs and the PDC to zap a domain). On the minus side, BDCs are *servers*, which aren't cheap, and they have other things to do.

TIP
If your network is large enough to dedicate a single machine to the role of domain controller (either PDC or BDC), then you can speed up logons by going to that machine's Control Panel ➤ Network applet, clicking on Services, and double-clicking on the Server service to configure it. By default, it will allocate memory to maximize throughput for file sharing. Instead, click the radio button labeled Maximize throughput for network applications. You see, the file server module uses *lots* of RAM, which forces the part of NT that does logins to live in a limited amount of memory. But if you choose to maximize memory for network applications, the login module gets more RAM and can run more quickly—up to three times more quickly by some people's measurements.

Additionally, as I'm going to explain in the upcoming section "Estimating the Size of the SAM," the entire SAM must fit into the physical memory of each of the domain controllers. If your domain's accounts database were, say, 10MB in size, you would have to add 10MB of RAM to each machine that was a domain controller simply because it wanted to be a domain controller; that means making lots of machines into BDCs in addition to their duties as file servers, which is just plain a waste of RAM chips.

Recommended Numbers of BDCs in One Location

Microsoft says they've done studies with big networks and have found that the negatives of BDCs outweigh their positives—that is to say, the network chatter that BDCs cause isn't outweighed by their usefulness as login servers. Their general advice is this:

NOTE
Microsoft's BDC rule of thumb: one BDC for every 2,000 users.

That seems a good rule, except for the 8 A.M. problem: everyone wants to log in at the same time—when they come in, around 8 A.M. Microsoft estimates that a PDC built on a 66MHz 486DX2 with 32MB of RAM can do seven to ten logins per minute. Now suppose our 2,000 users all come in and try to log on. At ten logons per minute, with two domain controllers (the PDC and the first BDC), that would be 100 minutes, or right around morning coffee break (9:40 A.M.) before everyone gets logged in!

What can we do about that?

Well, first, we could make the adjustment to the Server service by configuring throughput for network applications rather than file servers. Microsoft says that increases throughput by a factor of up to three, so we'll be generous and say that the login time would decrease to 100/3, or 33 minutes—significantly better, but it still means people are sitting around for a half hour waiting for the logon to finish.

A 133MHz Pentium can handle many NT operations three times faster than a 486DX2-66 can, so using a Pentium gets it down to 11 minutes, which is much better. And putting more than 32MB of RAM on the DCs would speed things up even more. Which leads me to Minasi's corollary to the Microsoft rule of thumb:

NOTE   One BDC for every 2,000 users is fine, as long as they are dedicated machines that don't do anything else, are at least 133MHz Pentiums, have 64MB of RAM, and are tuned for network applications.

BDCs in Remote Areas

There is another reason to add BDCs: remote locations. Suppose you had a home office in Cincinnati with 1,500 users, a branch office in Dayton with 20 users, and an office in Cleveland with 100 users. Suppose that you're connected to the two branch offices via a 64Kbps leased line. Should you put a BDC in Dayton and one in Cleveland?

On the one hand, it's a certainty that at least one server of some kind is in each branch office. Using servers in the central office in Cincinnati would be ludicrous. It would be silly to make over a dozen people wait around for data served up from a 64Kbps line, so it's imperative to have at least one file server locally in each office. And, since there's going to be a file server in each office, why not make it a backup domain controller, as well? The benefits would include:

- On days that the leased line was down, people could still log on to the domain, because the local BDC could log them on.

- People's domain logins would be quicker, as the local BDC would log them in, rather than requiring that all of the login verification information be shuttled to and from on the slower 64Kbps WAN link.

But it's not all wine and roses. There's a downside to having a local BDC:

- Remember that the PDC in Cincinnati must replicate the domain SAM to the BDCs in Dayton and Cleveland. In the worst case, that could mean transferring 1.5MB of data (I'll show you how I did that calculation in the next section) over that 64Kbps line. One and a half megabytes over a 64Kbps line would take a minimum of about three minutes, a fairly long time to take up the WAN link. You *can* tune that with the Registry parameters that I described a few pages back, but 1.5MB is still a lot of data.

- Is it so very bad to do logins over the LAN? A typical domain login transfers about 2K bytes of data. On a 64Kbps connection, that's only a quarter of a second transfer time. Users may not even notice the difference between logins over the WAN and logins to a local BDC.

The bottom line is this: if you have a large number of user accounts, replication can take a long time, and that can chew up WAN bandwidth. In contrast, if you only have a few users out in the branch offices, the time they waste waiting for logins over the WAN may be negligible. So don't assume that it's always a good idea to put a BDC at every remote location.

Load Balancing Domain Controllers

Logons can both keep a domain controller busy *and* slow down a network if not handled right. But suppose our Dayton/Cleveland firm's Cincinnati office had 5,000 users and a dozen domain controllers. Five thousand people need to use a DC on a regular basis to validate a login; does that imply that NT will automatically shift the login work around evenly among the domain controllers? In other words, could it be that some people end up waiting unnecessarily long for one DC to authenticate them while others authenticate quickly on a lightly loaded domain controller?

Yes, unfortunately. There is no formal mechanism in NT whereby a group of domain controllers passes around login requests so as to load-balance the login task. But you can make a few adjustments to smooth things out as much as possible.

First, make sure that your domain controllers devote a maximum amount of memory to being domain controllers rather than file servers. By default, NT allocates a staggering percentage of the system's RAM to the file and print server function. That makes for good performance in a file server, but it doesn't make any sense on an NT machine that's not doing any file/print server work and is mostly validating logins. You can tell NT to recover all that memory, so that the domain controller functions can use it, like so:

1. Open up Control Panel.

2. Within Control Panel, open the Network applet.

3. Click the Services tab in the Network applet.

4. You'll see the loaded network services, including Server. Double-click Server, or click Server and then the Properties button.

5. A dialog box will appear with four radio buttons in a group labeled Optimization; by default, the selected radio button will be Maximize Throughput for File Sharing. Change that to Maximize Throughput for Network Applications. Click OK.

6. You'll get a dialog box telling you that your changes will not take effect until you click OK to reboot the system (wow, *that* was a big surprise, eh?); click OK.

This is a small thing, but I've seen benchmark results showing that domain controllers can perform logins *four times faster* after this change, making it well worth a few minutes' time.

Other than improving domain controller performance, what *can* you do to even out the load amongst domain controllers? Not as much as would be nice. If you've got an NT workstation on your desk rather than a Windows workstation, then the NT workstation actually logs onto the domain before it logs you on. The "hard work" of logging in, then, is accomplished by the workstation before you even type in your name, password, and domain.

Exactly how an NT system finds a domain controller varies according to network configuration, but assuming that your network uses TCP/IP as its main protocol, workstation PCs find domain controllers by doing these steps:

1. First, the workstation PC requests a list of domain controllers from the local WINS server. I haven't explained WINS yet—it's in Chapter 14—but basically the WINS server's job is to keep a list of all of the computers' names and network addresses, kind of a "super browse list." All domain controllers in a domain identify themselves with a special name—the domain's

name, followed by a hexadecimal 1C value. The workstation asks WINS for its list of these 1C machines, the domain controllers.

2.   While it's waiting for that, the workstation PC broadcasts a request for a domain controller, *any* domain controller, to identify itself. It *always* does this broadcast regardless of whether or not there's WINS in your network. The broadcast basically says, "Hey, if there's a domain controller within earshot, will you please log me on?"

3.   While awaiting a response from a local DC (assuming one ever arrives), the workstation PC gets the list of domain controllers from WINS. The workstation PC then sends each of them a separate invitation to log it in, saying in effect, "I understand you're a DC in my domain. Will you log me on to the domain?"

4.   Eventually (one hopes) one of the DCs responds, and the workstation logs o on to the domain.

This sounds like it ought to work just fine, but sometimes your DCs don't respond quickly enough, partly because of all of the network traffic generated by all the query requests. That's why it's sometimes useful to know that there is a way to *force* a workstation to log onto its domain using a particular domain controller. This technique only works if you're using TCP/IP. I know we haven't covered TCP/IP yet, but I'll just do this briefly here and if it's not clear now then it will be after you read Chapter 14.

To force an NT workstation to log on to a domain using a particular domain controller, you use a file called LMHOSTS. It's an ASCII file and it goes in the \winnt\system32\drivers\etc directory of the NT workstation.

Each machine on a TCP/IP network has an *IP address*, a set of four numbers separated by periods, like 221.109.4.13. You'll need to know the IP address of the domain controller that you want to force the workstation to use. You'll also need to know the name of your workstation's domain (not a very hard thing to know, granted, but you'll need it to make this work).

Now create a plain ASCII text file. It'll have one line: the IP address of the domain controller, followed by the name of the domain *in quotes* with spaces added *to the end of the domain name* so that the domain name takes up 15 characters, followed by \0x1C, followed by #PRE. Complex, eh? It works much better with a couple of examples.

Suppose I want to force my workstation to log on to a domain controller at IP address 100.100.17.31. The domain's name is SONGBIRDS, which is nine characters long. I'll need to pad the name with six blanks to the right, so the LMHOSTS entry looks like this:

```
100.100.17.31 "SONGBIRDS      \0x1C" #PRE
```

That one-line file (it needn't be only one line, your network may have other uses for LMHOSTS so there may be other lines, as well) gets saved to \winnt\ system32\drivers\etc. *on your workstation.* (Don't put that LMHOSTS file on the domain controller.) Reboot and your workstation will zero in on the DC at 100.100.17.31.

One more example: suppose a domain controller with IP address 205.44.179.33 is in domain TROPICAL. You want a workstation to use that domain controller when logging in. What should be in the LMHOSTS file for the workstation? TROPICAL is eight characters long, so we'll need to pad seven blanks to the right:

```
205.44.179.33 "TROPICAL       \0x1C" #PRE
```

NOTE   Don't forget the quotes around the domain name!

And be aware that there's a downside to this technique: if that particular domain controller isn't running, then the workstations that are hard-wired to it can't get onto the domain. You may wonder, "What happens if you have more than one entry in LMHOSTS for the same domain, entries for different domain controllers in the same domain?" Oddly enough, if you've got LMHOSTS entries for more than one domain controller, your workstation can only use the *last* entry that it finds. If there are four entries for SONGBIRDS domain controllers, the workstation will only try to use the last one; it's blind to the others.

But what about if your users have Windows desktops rather than NT desktops—can you compel a Windows machine to use a particular domain controller? No, unfortunately not.

Estimating the Size of the SAM

Part of the previous analysis involved estimating how large the SAM was for my mythical Ohio-based company. You need to be able to estimate your SAM for several reasons:

- The entire SAM database must sit in the RAM of your primary domain controller (and backup domain controllers) at all times. If the SAM is too large, your PDC spends too much time paging data into and out of disk.

- The size of the SAM becomes important on replication times and network bandwidth considerations, as you just read.

- You can use this to determine how many domains you should break your network into.

You may be skeptical at this point. How big can a SAM *be*, anyway? Well, it depends, but Table 11.3 shows how to compute the size of the SAM on your domain.

TABLE 11.3: Size of Components in SAM

For Each One of These...	The SAM Grows By...
User account	1024 bytes (1K)
Computer (machine) account	512 bytes (1/2K)
Global group	12 bytes/user + 512 bytes
Local group	36 bytes/user + 512 bytes

Now, suppose you had (just to make the calculation easy) 100 users, 10 machine accounts, five global groups, and five local groups. Assume also that every user is in every group. (There are 100 users but only 10 machine accounts because, recall, only NT machines need machine accounts. Windows 3.*x*, Windows 95, and MS-DOS machines don't need machine accounts.) The total size of the SAM would then be

- 102,400 bytes for the user accounts

- 5,120 bytes for the machine accounts

- 1200+512, or 1,712, bytes per global group, with five groups for a total of 8,560 bytes in global groups

- 3600+512, or 4,112, bytes per local group, with five groups for a total of 20,560 bytes in local groups

The total is 136,640 bytes.

That's not a very large SAM, and its impact on the design of the domain controllers is minimal because the SAM takes up less than 200K of RAM. Now go back and do the math for a domain with 10,000 users, 1,000 machine accounts, and a reasonable number of local and global groups, and it's easy to see that the SAM can grow to megabytes and megabytes in size.

Many wonder how many people can be put in a single domain. The answer is, simply, it depends on how large a SAM you can afford for your PDC (and BDCs) to manage. Microsoft says that a SAM shouldn't exceed 40MB in size, but it's hard to imagine even that. Microsoft itself admits that reading a 40MB SAM increases the length of time required to boot a PDC by 15 minutes! (Good thing I don't reboot my PDC very often...)

Anyway, the answer to the "How many people can be put in a domain?" question is this: compute how large the SAM would be if you put your whole company on one domain. Figure out roughly how large you think a SAM should be (a matter of some guesswork, of course) and divide the one number by the other. For example, suppose you'd like your SAMs to all be under 10MB in size (a nice, reasonable maximum as far as I'm concerned). You compute that the 22,000 employees and sundry machines and groups in your firm results in a SAM that is 26MB in size. Divide that by 10, round up, and you see that you need three domains. Or you can go with one very large domain, but you had better be ready to buy some powerful domain controllers—the fastest Alphas money can buy and all the RAM they can stand!

Controlling PDC-BDC Communications

If you'll have BDCs connected to a PDC over a wide area network link, then you may find that the SAM replication traffic can be pretty heavy, perhaps to the point of finding it takes a significant percentage of the WAN bandwidth. If that's the case, then you'll find it useful to understand in some detail how the PDC-BDC conversations work. There are a few Registry settings you can use to control those conversations, which will tune NT's use of your precious WAN connections.

The PDC-BDC conversation is handled by a service called the *Netlogon* service. Netlogon has a number of jobs: it handles user logons to a domain; it handles communications between domain controllers across trusted domain boundaries, as well as handling chatter between PDCs and BDCs in a domain. In this section, we'll take a closer look at that last job (the "latter chatter," you might say). All of the Registry parameters that I'll describe here are in HKEY_LOCAL_MACHINE\System\CurrentControlSet\Services\Netlogon\Parameters.

Once a BDC starts up for the day, it must find a PDC. It does that by looking for a computer with a special name. Under Microsoft networking, computers can have a number of names associated with them, all stored in the computer's RAM in an area called the *NetBIOS Name Table*. A primary domain controller will include in its name table a name composed of the name of the domain, with a hexadecimal 1B added to its end. More specifically, the name that a primary domain controller declares for itself is the domain's name padded with blanks to make it 15 characters long with the hex 1B added to the end. For example, if I'm a BDC in a domain named MANUFACTURING, then I'll look for a computer whose NetBIOS Name Table includes the name MANUFACTURING <1B>—note I padded the name with two blanks because the word *manufacturing* is 13 characters long.

Once the BDC and PDC have been introduced, the PDC and BDC communicate on a regular basis to ensure that the BDC has the latest information in its local copy of the SAM database. It works roughly like this: the PDC knows how up-to-date each BDC is. Every few minutes, the PDC will choose a bunch of BDCs to update and invite them to initiate a SAM update session with the PDC. The PDC doesn't choose *all* of them because there could be in theory *thousands* of BDCs needing updates—yes, it's unlikely, but it's possible—and that many conversations would probably bring the network down. Each BDC receiving this invitation to update can then start up a SAM update session with the PDC. (A BDC might not respond to the invitation, perhaps if it were too busy doing something else at the moment.) Note that each BDC starts up its own session with the PDC—recall that the PDC only *invites* the BDC to start an update session. Because each BDC can theoretically have different abilities to absorb the updated SAM data, NT does SAM replication this way.

So in each update session it's the *BDC*, not the *PDC*, that sets the parameters for the session. In particular, when the BDC starts the session with the PDC, the BDC says how much data the PDC should send; for example, if the PDC has a megabyte of changes to give the BDC, the BDC might well ask the PDC to send those changes 32K at a time—if that BDC were connected to the PDC via a relatively slow WAN link. That's roughly how the domain SAM's database gets replicated; now let's look in a bit more detail, so I can introduce the Registry entries that let you fine-tune the process.

First, when a PDC and BDC get introduced, the PDC figures out how out-of-date the BDC's SAM is. If the BDC is *really* out of sync, the PDC won't try to send just the changes; it'll give up and just say to the BDC, "Here, let me send you the whole SAM database." You can control whether the PDC sends just the changes or the whole database with a Registry parameter named *ChangeLogSize*. It is of type REG_DWORD, and it contains the amount of data in bytes that is the critical value in answering the question "Should the PDC just send the BDC the updated records, or should the PDC just flush the SAM on the BDC and send the whole SAM database?" ChangeLogSize's default value is 65,536 (64K), which is also the minimum allowable value (which is equal to about 2,000 differences between the PDC and the BDC). So, if you've got ChangeLogSize set to the default value, and a PDC must send 100K of changes to a BDC, then the PDC will just re-send the entire SAM to the BDC. If, on the other hand, there are only, say, 50K of changes—less than 64K—then the PDC will send only the updates to the BDC. You can set this value as high as four megabytes (4,194,304KB).

Then every few minutes, the PDC examines what it knows about its BDCs and chooses a number of them to update. It invites these BDCs to begin the SAM replication process by sending them a message called a *pulse*. In general, the PDC will only pulse BDCs that are out of sync; if nothing new has happened in awhile, the PDC will generally have nothing to say to a BDC. There are a few Registry parameters that control the PDC's pulsing behavior:

- Pulse determines how often the PDC chooses a list of BDCs to update. The value is in seconds and can range from 60 (one minute) to 172,800 (48 hours). By default, it is 300, or five minutes, and the data type is REG_DWORD.

- PulseMaximum is why I said, "The PDC will *generally* have nothing to say." Whether the BDC needs an update or not, the PDC will pulse it now and then just to see if it's alive. This value is also in seconds and can range from 60 (one minute) to 172,800 (48 hours). It is also data type REG_DWORD. The default is 7,200, or two hours.

- PulseConcurrency controls how many BDCs the PDC tries to initiate update conversations with. Again, if the PDC has a thousand machines to update, it won't try to do it all at once, choosing instead to just have a few conversations at a time. This REG_DWORD value can take any value from 1 to 500. The default is 20.

Now, suppose you set PulseConcurrency to some small number like two, and also suppose that the PDC is unlucky and chooses to update two BDCs who are both offline for some reason. The PDC sends out the invitations (pulses), but no one responds. What happens now—is the PDC just stuck waiting for the two dead BDCs to come back to life while all the other BDCs just soldier along with their out-of-date SAMs? No, due to another Registry value named *PulseTimeout1*.

The REG_DWORD parameter, PulseTimeout1, specifies a length of time in seconds that the PDC must wait for the BDC before giving up and skipping it. In my previous example, the PDC would wait for a few seconds—five, by default—and then decide that those BDCs weren't going to respond and move along to other BDCs. The range of possible values for PulseTimeout1 is from 1 to 120 seconds.

By default, a BDC will respond to a pulse by requesting the first 128K bytes' worth of SAM updates. As soon as it gets those updates, it'll request the next 128K, and so on, until it's done. In general, that's a perfectly good idea, but it *could* have some negative side effects. While not immediately obvious, it's theoretically possible that the sheer volume of SAM updates could be so great that it would completely fill the WAN connection between the PDC and BDC. Choking the WAN is certainly one way to keep the BDC up to date, but from the point of view of *other* users of the WAN connection, it may not be desirable. NT lets you tune that with yet another Registry entry (it goes in the same place as the others that I've described here), the ReplicationGovernor Registry parameter. It is of type REG_DWORD and can take a value from 0 to 100. The value is a percentage—a percentage of *what*, I'll get to in a minute. Its default value is 100.

ReplicationGovernor reduces the volume of the BDC-PDC conversation in two ways. First, it lowers the size of the blocks requested from the PDC. By default, the BDC requests 128K byte blocks. The percentage value in ReplicationGovernor lets you reduce that 128K. For example, if you set ReplicationGovernor to 75 on a given BDC, that BDC will request not 128K byte blocks but instead 96K byte blocks (96 is 75 percent of 128).

The second way that ReplicationGovernor reduces the volume of the BDC-PDC conversation is by reducing *how often* the BDC requests blocks. Assuming that the SAM update is big, then the BDC will have to request several blocks. But once the BDC has received one block, how quickly should it request the next block? By default, immediately. If you've set ReplicationGovernor to some value below 100, however, that'll cause Netlogon to wait a bit between requesting blocks. Despite the fact that there are about a dozen TechNet articles referring to Replication-Governor, none of them explains in detail what this means, so forgive me for being vague. The closest is one article that says if ReplicationGovernor were set to 50, Netlogon would have a block request outstanding on the network only 50 percent of the time. In any case, the lower the ReplicationGovernor is, the smaller the amount of data that gets sent from PDC to BDC, and the less frequently the BDC asks for the information. Clearly, setting ReplicationGovernor too low could theoretically cause the flow of data from PDC to BDC to be less than the rate of change of the SAM at the PDC, making the BDC get more and more behind.

If you are managing a domain with remote BDCs connected at low speeds with the PDC, then you may find that tuning the PDC-BDC SAM replication process can make your network run more smoothly. Remember that there are two parts to the communication: first the pulse, which is initiated by the PDC, and then the update conversation itself, which each BDC controls. The Pulse, PulseConcurrency, PulseMaximum, ChangeLogSize, and PulseTimeout1 values each only make sense on, and should only be adjusted by, the PDC. The only parameter that controls the BDC's part of the conversation is ReplicationGovernor, and, again, should be adjusted on the BDC, not the PDC.

But I see that we're starting to talk about really big, multi-domain networks. It was my intention to start this book out by showing you how to run a small NT network. Once you had those basic tools, I intended to show you how to scale up from there. This is the end of that "basic" section; from here on in, we'll see how to extend NT to an entire enterprise, starting with multiple-domain networks—and that starts in the next chapter.

PART

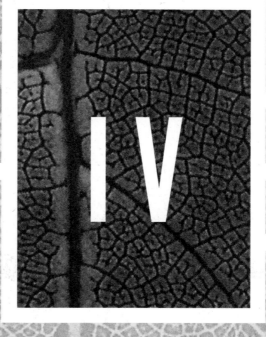

IV

Managing NT Server in an Enterprise Network

Cross-Domain Management in NT Networks

- Reasons for building multi-domain networks

- Creating trust relationships

- Extending file permissions

- Understanding local and global groups

- Working with resource domains

- Working from foreign domains

- How to structure your enterprise

By now, you've learned about the basic administrative tools in the NT Server world:

- The User Manager for Domains lets you manage users, groups, user rights, and trust relationships with other domains.

- Windows Explorer and My Computer (or File Manager, if you're using NT version 3.*x*) let you control user permissions on files and directories.

- The Printers folder (or Print Manager, if you are using NT 3.*x*) lets you control user permissions on printers and printer pools.

- The Server Manager lets you control user permissions on files and directories of other shares on machines in your domain and in other domains, as well as how domain controllers interact.

But so far I've pretty much restricted the discussion to a single-domain network. For many of us, however, that's not how the world is. Instead, any given NT domain is just a part in a larger enterprise network that includes other NT domains, some Novell servers, and perhaps a connection to a TCP/IP-based network like a corporate intranet or perhaps *the* Internet. Those three things—multi-domain NT enterprise networks, coexistence with NetWare, and TCP/IP/Internet support—are the focus of the next three chapters.

In this chapter, I want to focus on two large issues: how to manage a multiple-domain network as easily as possible, and how to *design* a multi-domain NT network. These are two very different ideas. The first is very "nuts and bolts" and the second more of a "big-picture" concept.

Why Build Multi-Domain Networks?

Well, if you can avoid it, then do so. NT 3.*x* and 4.*x* just aren't designed to let you manage multiple domains very well.

Domains are the cornerstone of Microsoft's powerful security system in NT, but they were built more with the idea of keeping outsiders out than they were with the idea of making it easy for enterprise network managers to run enterprise networks. Microsoft's own network managers say that keeping Microsoft's domains all linked up with one another is a nightmare.

As a result, you really should minimize the number of domains in your network, at least if keeping your network administration task to a minimum is one of your goals. I'm not saying that last thing facetiously; impregnable security may be your network's number one target, and if that's the case, then by all means separate functional units into domains, fill the moats, and lower the portcullises to be extremely secure.

In the long run, controlling multi-domain networks will get easier, particularly when Microsoft releases Active Directory Services with Windows 2000 Server, the next major version of NT, which will probably appear in mid-1999. Windows 2000 Server changes how you can use domains in a number of ways. First, it'll be possible to build large domains, domains of *millions* of users, rather than thousands as is currently the case. Second, you can build "trees" of similarly organized domains, or "forests" of domains.

That's all neat stuff, but I wouldn't deliberately build a large NT network that was *currently* difficult to manage, assuming that it would soon become simple to manage because of an imminent NT release—in other words, don't set yourself up for a fall if Windows 2000 Server ships after mid-1999. At one time, most of us in the industry expected to see Windows 2000 Server in *1997*, so it could well end up considerably later than 1999. Or it could be that Windows 2000 Server does indeed ship in mid-1999 but is too unreliable for real-world use, requiring us all to wait for Windows 2000's Service Pack 3 before the new NT becomes usable. As has been true for many computer companies over the years, Microsoft products are usually better *before* they're announced than after they're announced, if you know what I mean...

Why, then, *would* you build multi-domain networks? Several reasons.

- Multiple domains might allow you to mirror the structure of your organization. Similarly, politics in the organization might force multiple domains.

- The communications needs within a domain might make wide-area networking impractical or expensive, forcing you to build separate domains in separate geographical areas.

- You might have too many user and machine accounts, leading to an unwieldy Security Accounts Manager (SAM) database.

- Finally, it might be that you've been handed a *fait accompli*.

Domains Might Mirror Organizational Structures and Politics

In some cases, you or your clients will be happier with multiple domains. It may well be that the Manufacturing division has its own support people and its own networking infrastructure, so it really doesn't want to share much in the way of resources with Sales, which has its own network group. The VP of Manufacturing and the VP of Sales may look the company's IS/IT manager in the eye and say, "Keep your corporate network boys out of our system." In cases like that, the IS/IT department probably serves an advisory or consulting role only, offering recommended server platforms, disaster recovery systems, and the like.

Eventually, however, the various user departments will find places where some synergy should occur, and then they'll ask you for help in bringing *glasnost* to the network. That's when understanding what you've learned in this chapter will come in handy.

Domains Might Follow Geographic Boundaries

One undeniable fact of life within domains and workgroups is that they do a lot of chattering among themselves. Maintaining the browser means that every server must announce itself every 12 minutes. All session-oriented activities require that each side of the session say to the other side every now and then, "I'm still here." Such messages are called *keep alive* messages, and they range from one every 30 seconds to one every hour, as you see in Table 12.1.

TABLE 12.1: Regular Communications on NT Networks

Message Type	Protocol/Transport	Default Interval
PDC-BDC message replication	Any	Every 5 minutes
Master browser to backup browser replication	Any	Every 15 minutes
Server announcement to master browser	Any	1 minute, then 2 minutes, then 4 minutes, then 8 minutes, then 12 minutes, then every 12 minutes thereafter
NetBIOS keep alive message	TCP/IP	Every 60 minutes
NetBIOS keep alive message	IPX, NetBEUI	Every 30 seconds

Notice that some of this chatter goes on twice a minute. All that overhead might take up too much of your WAN connections' bandwidth. If that is the case, it probably makes sense to draw domain boundaries to mirror geographical ones.

You Might Have Too Many Accounts for One Domain

The most compelling reason for building more than one domain is simply that the domains get too large because too many accounts are in the domain. Recall from the last chapter that a few things, all of them related to the size of the domain's SAM database, limit domain size.

The formula for determining the exact size of a domain was explained in the previous chapter, but to summarize here, a SAM's size is roughly equal to per user plus 0.5 KBps per machine account. As you make domain size calculations, remember that you don't need a machine account for each machine; rather, you only need a machine account for each NT workstation or server that is a member of the domain. Of course, as time goes on, NT workstations will probably be a larger and larger part of your network because, at least in my opinion, it's clear that the NT Workstation will ultimately be the desktop operating system of choice.

The size of the SAM is vital because the entire SAM must remain resident in the memory of your domain controllers at all times ("the SAM lives in the RAM... "). A huge SAM, therefore, could require some serious RAM on your primary and backup domain controllers. If a large company with 200,000 employees wanted to create one large domain, the SAM would be at *least* 200MB in size. It would require at least 200MB of physical RAM on every domain controller—clearly not an acceptable situation in today's hardware market.

Additionally, every domain controller must read and parse the SAM database every time it boots. According to Microsoft, a 40MB SAM adds 15 minutes to boot-up time on a PDC built on a 66MHz 486.

The bottom line is this: I can't tell you what to restrict your maximum SAM size to because I don't know how patient and cheap you are. If you want to buy 33MHz 486 machines with 16MB of RAM for domain controllers, you will find that a hundred users creates a strain on the machine. An Alpha with four processors, a 300MHz clock, and 512MB of RAM could very well be able to handle 10,000 users. Given the speed of modern Intel and Alpha-based systems, I wouldn't want to exceed about 10MB on a SAM; Microsoft used to agree with me, but in 1996 they revised their recommendation to 40MB.

To really get the best answer to the question, "How large a SAM should we have?" try loading one of your typical domain controllers up with 1,000 user accounts. Then time how long it takes to boot and how long it takes to log on one user. Then create 1,000 more accounts and do it again, and then create 1,000 more accounts and time bootup and logon a third time. Those three data points will give you a rough idea of how large the SAM can be. Then, once you know the maximum acceptable SAM size, compute the size of a SAM for your whole company by using the formula in the previous chapter. Divide the one by the other, and you get the number of domains.

For example, suppose I've decided that a 5MB SAM is the biggest I want. Suppose also that my firm has 10,000 users and 1,000 NT machines. That makes the total SAM size about 10MB + 0.5MB, or 10.5MB. (I left the accounts out of the calculation for the sake of speed.) Divide 10.5 by 5 and you get a little over two. If you want to give your domains room to grow, then round up and plan for three domains. If you prefer fewer domains (less management) and don't mind a big loss in network response time, plan for two slightly bulging domains.

"It Just Growed That Way"

Many times, you'll face a multi-domain network that got that way simply because no one was paying attention. You may want to just leave it alone, but on the other hand, a look at this chapter may convince you to try to at least reduce the number of domains on the list.

Note: There Is No Easy Way to Merge Existing Domains

Before you start laying out a multi-domain system with the thought that you can always go back and modify it later, read this. Suppose someone *does* hand you an organization with 200 domains that you're supposed to combine into a mere dozen. What tools let you easily combine two or more domains into one? It's surprising—and important—but the answer is "there aren't any." The only way to combine two domains is to take one domain and re-type all of its user accounts into the second domain. No fun, eh?

Here's the closest you can get to an automatic tool: the NT Resource Kit includes a program called ADDUSERS.EXE, which will dump out a SAM's list of users to an ASCII file. ADDUSERS.EXE can *also* read an ASCII file of user names and create those user accounts in another SAM. What you could do, then, would be to use ADDUSERS to dump out a list of users from domain A and then use ADDUSERS to create user accounts in domain B.

So what's wrong with ADDUSERS? Well, for one thing, it doesn't dump user passwords, so you'll have to tell all of the domain A users to be prepared to create new passwords. For another, it can't handle the situation wherein domain B already has an account named Bill and you try to create *another* account named Bill. For a free program, it's good, but not great, and again the basic point I want you to get is this: it's hard to smoosh domains together. Don't create one unless you're sure you need it.

Multi-Domain Management Tasks

I've said that running multi-domain networks is tougher than running single-domain networks. But, specifically, *how* is it different? As I've said, you use the same administrative tools (User Manager, Server Manager, Explorer, and the like), but with a few twists. The particular tasks that you probably most want to perform across domains include (in roughly increasing order of complexity):

- Permitting one domain to communicate with another, a concept called *trust relationships*

- Permitting one domain's users to physically log on at computers in another domain

- Permitting one domain's users to access directories and files on machines in another domain

- Permitting one domain's users to print on printers in another domain

- Making users of one domain users of another domain as well

- Doing all this with a minimum of administrative work

In this chapter, you'll see how to do all of those things. And, in the process, you'll see me spend a hefty portion of this chapter explaining a somewhat thorny concept: *local groups* versus *global groups*.

A Simple Multi-Domain Model

I find when teaching my classes about NT that cross-domain stuff makes people's heads hurt. ("Now, let's see, domain Personnel trusts domain Finance, but Finance doesn't trust Personnel, so…") In order to make this easier to follow, I've structured much of this chapter around a simple multiple-domain example—my network. My network consists of two domains: ORION, which mainly contains user accounts, and TAURUS, which contains the shared directories, printers, and applications servers.

Master Domains and Resource Domains

My network of ORION and TAURUS domains is a common multi-domain model, as you'll learn at the end of this chapter. ORION mainly consists of a primary domain controller named BETELGEUSE whose main job is to verify people's logins. It contains *user* accounts, but not too many *machine* accounts; our NT Workstation machines are members of TAURUS. Domains that mainly contain user accounts are called *master domains*. TAURUS, in contrast, is a domain that contains very few user accounts, other than the obligatory Administrator and Guest accounts, but it holds all of the shared resources. The main machines on TAURUS are named ALDEBARAN and ELNATH; they are the primary and backup domain controllers, respectively. A domain with shared resources and very few user accounts is called a *resource domain*.

Design Goals for ORION and TAURUS

The main task facing an ORION/TAURUS administrator is this: The users are members of ORION. The resources, all the shared items, are in TAURUS. How can we set up these domains so that the ORION users can get to TAURUS resources with the least trouble for the users and the administrators?

Getting Acquainted: Trust Relationships

The first step in getting ORION and TAURUS to work together is getting them talking.

Because high-quality security was one of the most important design principles of NT Server, communication between domains is tightly controlled. Domains can't even *acknowledge* each other unless they are properly introduced, so to speak. That's done with *trust relationships*.

Furthermore, someone from the ORION domain can't even *sit down* at a machine that is a member of the TAURUS domain unless TAURUS trusts ORION. *That's* how paranoid NT security is: it doesn't even want you working at a workstation unless the workstation is in your domain. (Please note that I'm referring to NT workstations and servers; you don't have to be a member of a given domain to log on to a Windows 9*x*, Windows 3.*x*, or Windows for Workgroups workstation.)

For some reason, trust relationships are controlled with the User Manager for Domains. I guess there's no Domain Security Manager. (Perhaps there should be one.)

What Is a Trust Relationship?

Domains are the basic unit of an NT Server network structure, as you know. But domains by default cannot communicate with one another. It takes a conscious act to make it possible for two domains to communicate. The first step in domain-to-domain communication is to establish a trust relationship.

People get confused when I explain trust relationships in class because they want to know, "When I create a trust relationship, what did I cause to happen? What *is* a trust relationship?" It's important to understand that creating a trust relationship doesn't *do* all that much; it's just the first step in a larger set of actions.

Perhaps it's easier to explain what's going on when there *isn't* a trust relationship. Before TAURUS trusts ORION

- It is impossible for a TAURUS administrator to extend permissions (for shares, files, directories, or printers) to an ORION user.

- An ORION user or even an ORION administrator can't just sit down at an NT workstation that's a member of TAURUS, even if all the ORION user wants to do is to connect to a resource on the ORION domain. They would not be able to connect to a resource on the Taurus domain either, because they have no account there.

Again, just creating the trust relationship doesn't do much, but from a technical point of view, these are the effects of making TAURUS trust ORION:

- ORION users can sit down and log on to NT workstations—but they won't be able to access TAURUS resources unless they are given permissions to TAURUS resources by a TAURUS administrator.

- The definition of the Everyone group in TAURUS now is "all of the TAURUS users and guests and all of the ORION users and guests."

That's not much, is it? Here's what is important about trusts: trust relationships open the lines of communications between domains, making it possible for administrators in the *trusting* domain to extend permissions and rights to users in the *trusted* domain. In some ways, a trust relationship is like a treaty between two sovereign nations: once the two of them decide to allow trade between their countries, they agree to a treaty between themselves. The treaty doesn't really do anything—no money changes hands (at least, no money's *supposed* to change hands)—but the treaty makes it possible for businesses on either side of the border to do business with one another. Without the treaty, vendor/client relationships can't take place.

Like a treaty between nations, wherein the leader of each nation must initiate the treaty, so must an *administrator* from each domain initiate a trust relationship between two domains. Not surprisingly, you've got to be an administrator to create and maintain trust relationships.

A trust relationship is a link between two domains. It allows one domain (the trust*ing* domain) to recognize all global user accounts and global user groups from another (the trust*ed* domain).

Trust relationships can be one-way or two-way. *A two-way trust relationship* is just a pair of one-way trust relationships, where each domain trusts the other. When established correctly, trust relationships allow each user to have only one user account in the network (defined in the user's home domain) yet have access to network resources in other domains.

For example, Figure 12.1 shows a network containing two domains whose names are TAURUS and ORION.

FIGURE 12.1:

The domains TAURUS and ORION

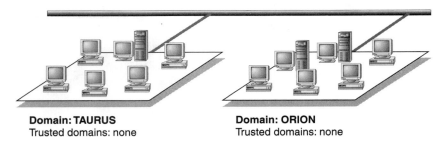

Domain: TAURUS
Trusted domains: none

Domain: ORION
Trusted domains: none

Two independent domains on the network

If TAURUS establishes a trust relationship with ORION, then all user accounts in ORION (the trusted domain) can be used in TAURUS. Now a trust relationship is established, as shown in Figure 12.2.

FIGURE 12.2:

A trust relationship with ORION

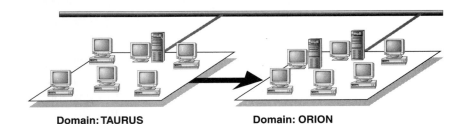

Domain: TAURUS   **Domain: ORION**

Domain TAURUS establishes a trust relationship with ORION.

With the trust relationship established, ORION users can log on at TAURUS's workstations, and user accounts created in ORION can be placed in TAURUS's local groups (I *am* going to explain what local groups are, I promise) and be given permissions and rights within the TAURUS domain, even though they don't have accounts there. This does *not* mean that TAURUS users can log on at ORION workstations or use ORION servers or printers. However, since TAURUS trusts ORION, *ORION* gets many benefits, as explained in Figure 12.3.

FIGURE 12.3:

The benefits of a trust relationship

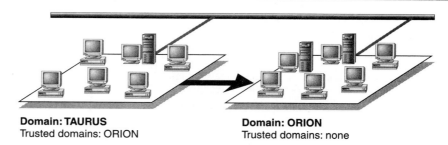

Domain: TAURUS
Trusted domains: ORION

Domain: ORION
Trusted domains: none

TAURUS trusts ORION.

All ORION users can log on at TAURUS workstations.
ORION user accounts and global groups can be placed in TAURUS local groups.
ORION users can be given rights and permissions in the TAURUS domain.

Unless the ORION domain in turn establishes a trust relationship with TAURUS, accounts in the TAURUS domain can't be used in ORION. In other words, TAURUS may trust ORION, but that doesn't make ORION automatically trust TAURUS.

Trust between different domains is likewise not *transitive* (in the algebraic sense) or transferred. For example, if TAURUS trusts ORION, and ORION trusts a domain named ANDROMEDA, then TAURUS does not automatically trust ANDROMEDA, as shown Figure 12.4. If the TAURUS network administrator wanted to be able to use ANDROMEDA's accounts in the TAURUS domain, she would have to set TAURUS to trust ANDROMEDA.

FIGURE 12.4:

Trust is not transferred through trusted domains.

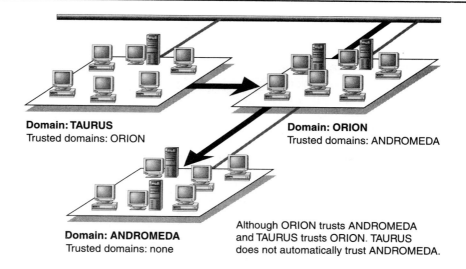

Domain: TAURUS
Trusted domains: ORION

Domain: ORION
Trusted domains: ANDROMEDA

Domain: ANDROMEDA
Trusted domains: none

Although ORION trusts ANDROMEDA and TAURUS trusts ORION. TAURUS does not automatically trust ANDROMEDA.

Bear in mind that trust relationships can only be established between NT Server domains. The Trust Relationships command isn't available when administering LAN Manager 2.*x* domains or NT workstations.

Avoiding Trust Relationships: A Note

Besides all of this trust relationship stuff, there is another way to get access to resources to multiple domains. It's a bit kludgy and hard to manage, but I'll mention it for the sake of completeness.

If TAURUS and ORION aren't speaking—if they don't have a trust relationship—but I must access both TAURUS and ORION resources, then I can just create a Mark user account on both TAURUS and ORION.

The tricky part (that is, the hard-to-manage part) concerns passwords. In general, to make this work, you have to keep the passwords on the two domain accounts exactly the same. By doing that, I can access both TAURUS and ORION resources. What is actually happening under the hood is that I first log on to ORION, and of course I supply a user name and password to do that. Then, the first time I try to access a TAURUS resource, TAURUS tries to authenticate my Mark user account. The TAURUS PDC asks my workstation for my password, and my workstation just tells the TAURUS PDC the same password that I used for ORION. If the passwords match, I can attach to TAURUS resources. If they *don't* match, then TAURUS asks my workstation to prompt me for a password, and at that time I can type in my TAURUS password if it's different from the ORION password.

Unfortunately, however, not all client software knows how to ask for that TAURUS password. For example, a DOS client doesn't give you the chance to enter the TAURUS password. It just says to TAURUS, "I don't know how to ask for the password," and so the attempted TAURUS access fails. *That's* why the whole thing runs best with identical passwords on all domains for which you are a member. However, identical passwords make password-changing day a bit more complex.

Establishing Trust Relationships

Establishing a trust relationship with another domain is a two-step process that is performed in two domains. First, your domain must permit a second domain to trust it, and then the second domain must be set to trust your domain. This shouldn't be a surprise; after all (he said with a grin), trust is a two-way street, right?

That sounds a little odd, so let me rephrase it: if domain TAURUS wants to trust domain ORION, then domain ORION must *allow* domain TAURUS to trust it before TAURUS can trust ORION. And after all that is done, it is only TAURUS that trusts ORION; ORION doesn't trust TAURUS at all! Remember, if you want a symmetrical trust relationship—TAURUS trusts ORION and ORION trusts TAURUS—then you have to establish two separate trust relationships, one in each direction.

The two steps—ORION allowing TAURUS to trust it, and TAURUS actually trusting ORION—can be performed in any order, but if you "permit the trust, then trust," the new trust relationship takes effect immediately. You can reverse the order of the two steps and still establish the trust relationship, but you won't receive confirmation that the trust was established. What's more, the process can be delayed up to 15 minutes. Let's see how to make TAURUS trust ORION.

Step 1: Permitting the TAURUS Domain to Trust ORION

Permitting TAURUS to trust ORION is done at ORION. But before we do it, let's look at the domains TAURUS and ORION again. If you want the outside domain TAURUS to trust your domain ORION, you must first *permit* TAURUS to trust ORION. To do this

1. Log on to the ORION domain as an ORION administrator.

2. Open User Manager for Domains in the ORION domain.

3. From the Policies menu, choose Trust Relationships. You see the Trust Relationships dialog box shown in Figure 12.5.

FIGURE 12.5:

Trust Relationships dialog box

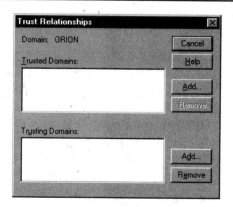

The Trust Relationships dialog box shows the domains that ORION is currently permitted to trust, as well as those that are already trusted. In this case, there are none.

4. Select the Add button next to the Trusting Domains box.

5. Type in the name of the domain you want to permit to trust, the TAURUS domain in our sample case.

6. Type a password in both the Initial Password and Confirm Password boxes, as in Figure 12.6. Passwords are case-sensitive and can be blank. By the way, the password is optional, and is really only relevant in the brief period between when ORION permits TAURUS to trust it and when TAURUS actually gets around to trusting ORION.

FIGURE 12.6:

Add Trusting Domain
dialog box

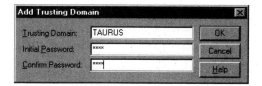

7. Choose OK. TAURUS, the added domain, now appears in the Trusting Domains section in the Trust Relationships dialog box.

8. Double-click the Close button in the top-right corner to close the Trust Relationship dialog box.

You've basically given one domain (TAURUS) permission to trust your domain (ORION), but the trust relationship isn't complete until the other domain actually takes the action of trusting your domain.

Step 2: Trusting ORION (Performed at TAURUS)

Now that you've permitted TAURUS to trust ORION, you must give the password you entered in the Trust Relationships dialog box to the administrator of the TAURUS domain. He or she should then do the following:

1. Log on to the TAURUS domain as an administrator.

2. Open User Manager for Domains for the TAURUS domain.

3. From the Policies menu, choose Trust Relationships.

4. Select the Add button next to the Trusted Domains list. The Add Trusted Domain dialog box appears, as in Figure 12.7.

FIGURE 12.7:

The Add Trusted Domain dialog box

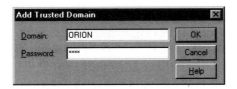

5. In the Domain and Password boxes, the TAURUS administrator should type in ORION and the password you provided and choose OK. (If you didn't use a password, then don't put anything in the password field.)

The added domain name, ORION, should now appear in the Trusted Domains list of the Trust Relationships dialog box—TAURUS now trusts ORION.

6. To exit from the Trust Relationships dialog box, double-click the Close button in the upper-right corner.

Once a domain is trusted, its users can access the domain that trusts it. Note the following about trust relationships:

- The trusted domain shows up as an option in the logon box on an NT Workstation, which means that users from the trusted domain can log on at workstations in the domain that trusts it.

- When you're logged onto an NT machine and you try to browse an untrusted domain, you *can* see the list of servers on that domain. But if you try to view the shares on one of the domain's servers, you are refused. Even if there *is* trust, you've got to have an account on the domain to get the browse list.

- Network connections can be made to shared directories on the trusting domain's servers.

Terminating a Trust Relationship

Just like establishing a trust relationship, terminating a trust relationship is also a two-step process done in two different domains. First, one domain has to stop trusting another domain, then the other domain has to take away the permission of the first domain to trust it.

To stop trusting another domain, open User Manager for Domains and choose Trust Relationships from the Policies menu. Highlight the name of the domain in the Trusted Domains box that will no longer trust your domain, then choose Remove. The explicit message shown in Figure 12.8 appears to remind you about the two-step process. Choose Yes, then close the Trust Relationships dialog box.

FIGURE 12.8:

Removing a domain from the Trusted Domains list

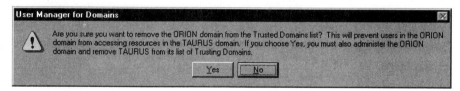

Now, still following our TAURUS trusts ORION example, the administrator in ORION has to stop permitting the TAURUS domain to trust it. This is done by opening User Manager for Domains in ORION, selecting Trust Relationships under the Policies menu, highlighting TAURUS in the Trusting Domains box, and once again selecting Remove. When finished, close the Trust Relationships dialog box.

Keep in mind that both of these steps must be performed to properly terminate the trust relationship between domains. Let's summarize this whole process with a "How Do I?"

How Do I Get One Domain to Trust Another?

Let's say that you have a domain named TRUSTING and you want it to trust the main administrative domain (named TRUSTED) so that its administrator can manage TRUST-ING's accounts.

TRUSTED's administrator must complete the following steps:

1. In the User Manager for Domains, open the Policies menu and choose Trust Relationships.

2. Choose the Add button next to the Trusting Domains list.

3. Type TRUSTING in the Add box, and then type in a password (it can be a blank password). Choose OK.

TRUSTING is now *permitted* to trust TRUSTED, but the trust relationship isn't complete until TRUSTING actually takes the action of trusting TRUSTED. To do this, TRUSTING's administrator must:

4. Open User Manager for Domains in the TRUSTING domain and choose Trust Relationships on the Policies menu.

5. Next to the Trusted Domains box, choose Add.

6. In the Add Trusted Domain box, type in TRUSTED and the password provided by TRUSTED's administrator.

This establishes the trust relationship between the two domains—TRUSTING now trusts TRUSTED.

When you trust another domain, you are giving it the potential to control your domain. Users from TRUSTED can log on at TRUSTING's workstations, and TRUSTING's local groups can now contain TRUSTED's global groups.

Saving a Little Time by Establishing Both Sides Simultaneously

In this discussion, though, I've ignored the fact that in a master/resource domain, it's often true that the same people are administrators for both domains. Suppose you're physically located at a machine on a master domain, and must establish a trust relationship with a resource domain that is physically many miles away, but is connected over a network of some kind. Is there a way to avoid having to travel to be able to sit at the servers on the resource domain? No, but there's a bit of a sneaky trick you can use.

Suppose I'm an ORION administrator sitting at an ORION machine. I've just allowed TAURUS to trust ORION. But how do I get to a TAURUS machine to log in as a TAURUS administrator and tell TAURUS to trust ORION? I'll need the password of the TAURUS administrator account. Then I do this:

1. From the ORION machine, I open up a command line.

2. I then type

    ```
    net use \\tauruspdc\IPC$ /user:TAURUS\administrator
    ```

    and press Enter. I then replace *tauruspdc* with the name of the TAURUS primary domain controller.

3. I'll be prompted for a password. I type in the password of the TAURUS administrator.

4. Now, still using the User Manager for Domains, I click User ➤ Select Domain.

5. The TAURUS domain won't show up on the list, but I type it in anyway.

6. As the system has already recognized me as a TAURUS administrator, my request to shift the focus of User Manager for Domains from the ORION domain to the TAURUS domain is approved.

7. I can now click Policies ➤ Trust Relationships and direct TAURUS to trust ORION.

That'll save you a little shoe leather (and maybe an airline ticket).

Extending File Permissions across Domains

Now that the two domains have some trust, let's put it to use. As I told you before, my network includes two domains: ORION and TAURUS. I'm a member of ORION, which is to say, I have a user account on ORION. How could I get access to files on machines in TAURUS? For example, suppose there's a share on one of the TAURUS servers named STUFF. How do I get to it?

Reprise: Everyone Means, Well, *Everyone*

Well, first of all, I may *already* have access to STUFF in TAURUS. As you've seen, whenever you create a directory share, it automatically gets the share permissions Everyone/Full Control. (As far as I know, there's no way to change that default set of share permissions.) Unless the TAURUS administrator customized the share permissions in some way, the Everyone group can get to the share.

As long as STUFF is shared to Everyone, my Mark account from ORION can get to TAURUS's STUFF share, because the TAURUS Everyone group includes all users *from all trusted domains*. Since TAURUS trusts ORION, all ORION users are part of TAURUS's Everyone group. (Remember that since ORION doesn't trust TAURUS, the TAURUS users—there are only two, TAURUS\Administrator and TAURUS\Guest—are *not* part of ORION's Everyone group. Go ahead, re-read that sentence a couple of times; this trust relationships stuff *does* get confusing.)

Adding a User from a Foreign Domain to Share Permissions

But suppose STUFF has a different set of share-level permissions, perhaps to TAURUS's group of regular old users, a group called *Domain Users*. The reason it has the name Domain Users will get clearer when I explain local groups versus global groups a little later in this chapter.

Basically, a TAURUS administrator can grant an ORION user access to a TAURUS resource via share permissions, just as you saw in Chapter 7, which covered directory shares; there's just an extra step to the process, the step of asking for the list of users and groups not from TAURUS, but from ORION.

Suppose a TAURUS administrator wants to extend file permissions for a share named STUFF to the ORION user group named Domain Users. She starts off by displaying the permissions dialog box for the STUFF share, as you see in Figure 12.9.

FIGURE 12.9:

Access Through Share Permissions dialog box for STUFF

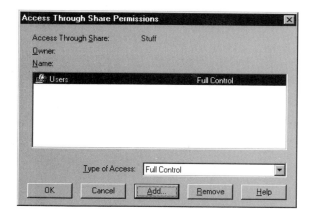

So far, so good—there's nothing here we haven't seen before. Currently, people in the Users group for TAURUS can access this share.

Now, let me see who the TAURUS administrator can add to this permission list. As you learned before, she just clicks Add and she'll see a dialog box like the one in Figure 12.10. Notice something that's been in these dialog boxes all along, but that I haven't drawn attention to—the List Names From drop-down list box.

FIGURE 12.10:

Adding a user to STUFF's share list

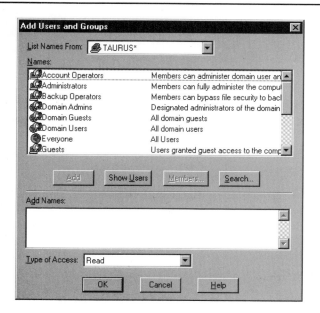

Now, List Names From is an important list box. From now on, whenever you see that, you should have a Pavlovian response (well, I guess you can skip the salivating part) along the lines of, "Hey, a cross-domain tool!" Not all NT dialog boxes include that list box, so noticing it is important.

Anyway, after the TAURUS administrator clicks on the List Names From drop-down list, she sees ORION as one of her options, so she clicks that, waits a few seconds, and then sees the dialog box shown in Figure 12.11.

FIGURE 12.11:

Share permissions dialog box after choosing the ORION domain

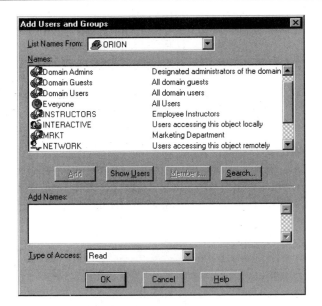

This dialog box looks a lot like the previous one, but now she's looking at the ORION users, as you can see by the presence of new groups named INSTRUC-TORS and MRKT. Notice that ORION, like TAURUS, has a group called Domain Users. Now she adds the Domain Users group—which is, recall, the ORION\ Domain Users group—to the share, and gives it Full Control. Now the permissions dialog box looks like Figure 12.12.

FIGURE 12.12:

FIGURE 12.12:

Adding ORION's Domain
Users group to share
permissions

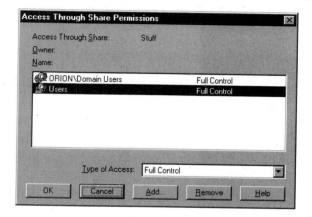

You'd use the same procedure to just add one person to a share list on TAURUS. Again, notice the notation describing the Domain Users account—ORION\Domain Users. That keeps TAURUS from becoming confused with a group in the *TAURUS* domain named *Domain Users*. (All domains have a Domain Users group by default.)

Now, that was a change in the share-level permissions for STUFF. Recall that you can get to that dialog box in one of two ways:

- Physically log on to the server that contains STUFF, open My Computer, open Explorer (or if you're using NT 3.*x*, open File Manager), and bring up the dialog box.

- Start up Server Manager, click on the server that holds STUFF, click Computer ➢ Shared Directories, choose Stuff, click Properties, and then click Permissions, just as I discussed in Chapter 7.

If the volume in question is an NTFS volume, you may have to worry about file and directory permissions. Use the same procedures to set file and directory permissions across domains that you learned already, except take the extra step of clicking List Names From. Yes, it's in the file and directory permissions dialog box, as well. Choose the foreign domain.

Cross-Domain Groups: Local and Global Groups

That was a fair amount of work just to get one group to be able to access one share. Let's look at an individual user for a moment. What if an ORION user like Mark needed to access a lot of TAURUS things to the point where he needed to access things to the same degree that a normal TAURUS user does?

Unfortunately, there's really no way to accomplish that, at least not simply. The object of this section (and be warned, it's a big one) is basically to explain *why* that's the case, and what you *can* do to extend permissions over domain boundaries.

If you need the short version, however, here it is: if there are ten servers in TAURUS holding 20 shares in total, and if I want Mark from ORION to be able to access all 20 shares, I have to add him to each share, one by one. (In earlier editions of this book, I claimed that there was an easy way to do that, but I'm afraid I was wrong. The method I described only worked if every one of your servers was also a domain controller, which isn't a very good solution.)

Adding Users from One Domain to Another Domain's Domain Users Group

Let's see, though. The name of the Users group that's prevalent throughout the TAURUS domain is the group called Domain Users. (It's the domain-wide Users group, hence the name.) Can I add the Mark account from ORION to TAURUS's Domain Users group?

To try doing that, a TAURUS administrator would start up the User Manager for Domains and double-click the Domain Users group. That leads to the dialog box shown in Figure 12.13.

Hmmm... notice the painful lack of a List Names From drop-down list. (Notice also that there aren't too many user accounts here. Remember, TAURUS is a resource domain, so that's to be expected.) No, there's no way to add ORION\ Mark to TAURUS\Domain Users. But why not?

FIGURE 12.13:

Adding users to TAURUS's Domain Users group

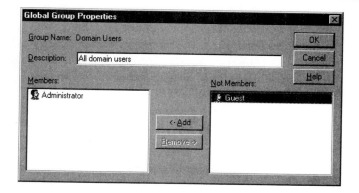

The brief but cryptic answer to that question is, "Domain Users is a *global group*, and global groups cannot contain users from other domains." The longer but clearer answer takes up the following bunch of pages.

Now, I *can* make this all make sense, but before I can do this, I have to give you some background on local groups and global groups.

Local Groups and Global Groups in NT Domains

While NT's got some really good, well thought-out networking features, some of those features *aren't* so stellar, and local and global groups are two such benighted features. You see, the whole matter of local and global groups has as its basis an old and, by now, unfortunately familiar assumption: this feature really makes the most sense if you're using NT workstation*s*.

Thus far in this book, we've run across stumbling blocks like this (the User Profiles dialog box in the User Manager for Domains is one example) and in general I've been able to say to you, "This is a feature that's really only relevant for people using NT workstations, so if you're using Windows 9*x* or Windows for Workgroups workstations, don't worry about it."

Local and global groups, however, are quite a different story. Even though they have their roots in networks composed entirely of NT machines, their effects apply to all NT users, and they apply particularly to people trying to design NT domains with workstations of *any* kind.

To explain local and global groups, I need a very simple domain, simpler than ORION or TAURUS. I need a simple network composed only of four NT machines, each one a different kind of NT machine:

- A primary domain controller called PDC

- A backup domain controller called BDC

- An NT server that is *not* a domain controller called SERVER (you needn't name machines like this, of course; this is just an example with unoriginal machine names)

- An NT workstation named WS

I'll show you what you must do to make sure that any user can get to any share in this network. I'll start with a simple workgroup, and then I'll show you how making these four computers into a domain changes things.

Letting a User on One Machine Access a Share on Another without Domains

Suppose these four machines live together in a workgroup (we'll make it a domain later) called MYDOMAIN. I want a user named Jim, who is logged in at WS, to be able to access a share on SERVER. Suppose also that this share is open to the Users group on SERVER. What must I do to get Jim access to SERVER's share?

Recall that NT workstations keep local user accounts—accounts of their own—in their "personal" SAM database in the file \winnt\system32\config\sam. Those accounts are created with the trimmed-down version of the User Manager that comes with NT Workstation. NT servers that are *not* domain controllers also keep a local SAM.

The WS machine knows Jim because he has a local user account on it, but the SERVER machine doesn't know him. If I want Jim to be able to have any kind of communication with SERVER, I have to build a user account for Jim on the SERVER machine. More specifically, I have to create a SERVER\Jim account that sits in the SERVER\Users group—the normal default user's group for SERVER. Notice that previously in this chapter, I used NT's notation, so that ORION\Mark meant "the Mark account on the domain ORION." Since you can have local machine accounts on NT workstations and NT servers, the notation holds: SERVER\Jim means "the user account named Jim in the SERVER machine."

Once I've created a user account for Jim on the SERVER machine, Jim sits down at WS and logs in, indicating that he wants to log in as *Jim* on machine WS. WS then searches its local Users group and finds the WS\Jim account. Assuming Jim remembers his password, WS lets him in. Then, when WS\Jim tries to access a share on SERVER, SERVER says to itself, "Who's this WS\Jim guy? Hey, I know a SERVER\Jim; I wonder if it's the same guy?" SERVER asks the WS workstation for Jim's password. If the password for the Jim account on the WS machine is the same as the password for the Jim account on the SERVER machine, SERVER lets Jim get to the share. But if the passwords are *different*, SERVER asks WS to ask Jim for a password, and Jim punches in the password for his account on the SERVER machine. Jim is not simultaneously logged onto WS and SERVER, with two different accounts; he is logged on with one account and two different passwords.

Then, because SERVER\Jim is a member of SERVER\Users, and SERVER\Users has access to the share on SERVER, Jim can have access. Simple, right? Yeah, sure; that's why there are domains.

Using a Single Domain Account across a Domain

Let's re-examine how domains improve things. Rather than having to go and create a Jim account on each of my four machines (PDC, BDC, SERVER, and WS), I just go to my PDC machine and create a Jim account for the domain—an account MYDOMAIN\Jim. Now, that does *not* go into a group called MYDOMAIN\Users, at least not directly. It goes into a group called MYDOMAIN\Domain Users instead. Why Domain Users instead of Users? Stay tuned; we have come to the crux of this local versus global discussion.

Here is how domains make things easier for people using NT workstations: to log on to an NT workstation, you must be a member of the Users group of that workstation. As I've said, building a given user on hundreds of workstations would be a pain. Therefore, when an NT workstation (or server, for that matter) joins a domain, the workstation's Users group automatically gets a new member—the Domain Users group of the workstation's new domain. For example, when WS joined MYDOMAIN, the group MYDOMAIN\Domain Users was inserted into the WS\Users group. The net effect is twofold:

- Anyone who is a member of MYDOMAIN can sit down at WS—or any other workstation that has joined MYDOMAIN—and log in.

- Because SERVER has also joined MYDOMAIN, the SERVER\Users group must now contain MYDOMAIN\Domain Users. Since MYDOMAIN\Jim is in MYDOMAIN\Domain Users and MYDOMAIN\Users is in SERVER\Users, Jim can access shares on SERVER that are intended only for people in SERVER's Users group.

Notice something a trifle new to the discussion: NT allowed us to put a *group* into the Users group.

The Users Group versus the Domain Users Group

The "magic" here is that you need only put a new user account in a domain user group. Why? Because NT has placed one group (MYDOMAIN\Domain Users) into another group (every machine's Users group). Since the Domain User group was previously placed in all of the local Users groups, the new user is automatically recognized by all machines in the domain.

But one thing is confusing: why does NT put the Domain Users group from the domain into the local Users groups of all the domain's servers and workstations? Why not just have a Users group for the domain—MYDOMAIN\Users—and put it into the Users groups of the domain's machines? Why bother with a different group name?

NT's Problem: No Circular Groups

The reason? Laziness on the part of the NT designers. Suppose you could put the Users group from machine A into the Users group for machine B, which in turn put its Users group into the Users group for machine C. Then, every time machine C's security module needed to verify if someone was in C\Users, it would have to interrogate machine B about *its* users, and machine B in turn would have to interrogate machine A. This might take time.

Worse, what if you then, in a fit of forgetfulness, put the Users group from machine C into the Users group from machine A? You'd have a loop, kind of like a spreadsheet with a circular reference. This sounded like it would complicate NT too much, so the NT designers came up with a rule: "We'll let people put one group into another group, but we won't let them take it any further—no groups inside groups inside groups!" (By the way, apparently Microsoft figured out how to handle this, because Windows 2000 Server lets you put groups inside groups inside groups, as many layers deep as you like.)

Local and Global Groups Defined

To prevent "circular groups," the designers of NT created two types of groups, local and global:

- Local groups can contain user accounts, of course, but they also can contain global groups.

- Global groups can contain user accounts, but that's it; they can't contain other groups.

Right about now, most of us start getting confused: "Hey, wait, if it's *global*, how come I can't put anything in it?" I had a lot of trouble remembering what global and local groups do, too, until I realized that I had a problem keeping that information in my brain because the words *global* and *local* mean something to me in English. If it helps, call local groups "group type number 1" and global groups "group type number 2." Group type number 1's can contain group type number 2's, but 1's can't contain 1's, 2's can't contain 2's, and 2's can't contain 1's. Just kind of chant to yourself, "Globals go into locals, globals go into locals, globals go into locals…" In no time, the difference between global and local groups will become second nature.

By creating two types of groups, Microsoft guaranteed that you couldn't go further than putting one group inside another. Put a global group inside a local group and you have one level of "nesting" in groups. But you can't go further than that, because you can't put a local group in another group.

Using Local and Globals inside a Domain

Here's how Domain Users relates to Users: the Users group that every NT machine has is a local group. The Domain Users group that every domain has is a global group. Since globals go into locals, the domain's Domain Users group can fit nicely into each machine's (local) Users group. Because of the way Domain Users relate to Users, you can't take the Users group from one machine, like WS, and put it into the Users group of SERVER because WS\Users is a local group and SERVER\Users is a local group, and you can't put locals in locals.

Just to be difficult, let's take this a bit further. Could I create a group called Users2 on WS, but make it a *global* group, and then put WS\Users2 into SERVER\Users?

No, I couldn't, for an important reason: only domains can have global groups. Since MYDOMAIN is a domain, it's possible to create MYDOMAIN\Domain Users; it's not possible to create a global group on WS, like WS\Domain Users.

Let's summarize what I've said so far by taking a look at Figure 12.14.

FIGURE 12.14:

Local and global user accounts in a domain

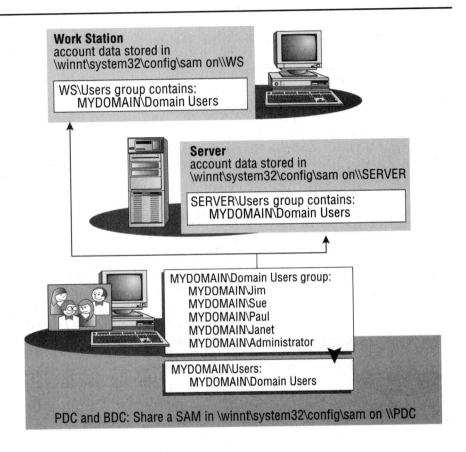

Work Station
account data stored in
\winnt\system32\config\sam on\\WS

WS\Users group contains:
    MYDOMAIN\Domain Users

Server
account data stored in
\winnt\system32\config\sam on\\SERVER

SERVER\Users group contains:
    MYDOMAIN\Domain Users

MYDOMAIN\Domain Users group:
    MYDOMAIN\Jim
    MYDOMAIN\Sue
    MYDOMAIN\Paul
    MYDOMAIN\Janet
    MYDOMAIN\Administrator

MYDOMAIN\Users:
    MYDOMAIN\Domain Users

PDC and BDC: Share a SAM in \winnt\system32\config\sam on \\PDC

In a well-designed domain, most of the user accounts reside in the domain-wide group Domain Users. In my example, I've created accounts named Jim, Sue, Paul, and Janet (notice that the domain's Administrator account is automatically placed in the domain's Domain Users group). The Administrator account is placed into the local Users groups of each of the NT machines in the domain; that happens automatically when a machine joins the domain. Each computer's database of user and group accounts lives in a file called SAM in \WINNT\SYSTEM32\CONFIG directory of each computer. The domain's SAM lives on the PDC, and any BDCs really don't *have* SAMs, save for the read-only replicated copy they get from the PDC.

Notice that this implies that domain controller machines don't have local groups of their own—there is no PDC\Users or BDC\Users. Both just get ORION\Users, TAURUS\Users, or whatever the domain's name is.

Not only are there global and local users' groups, there are also local and global administrator and guest groups in a default NT setup. It's very important to understand how to use them. With that in mind, take a look at Figure 12.15. It's similar to Figure 12.14, but it now shows the relationships of the Administrator accounts and Administrator Groups (global) in a domain.

FIGURE 12.15:

Local and global Administrator accounts in a domain

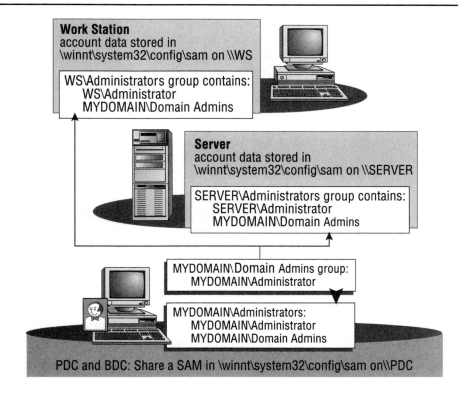

Work Station
account data stored in
\winnt\system32\config\sam on \\WS

WS\Administrators group contains:
  WS\Administrator
  MYDOMAIN\Domain Admins

Server
account data stored in
\winnt\system32\config\sam on \\SERVER

SERVER\Administrators group contains:
  SERVER\Administrator
  MYDOMAIN\Domain Admins

MYDOMAIN\Domain Admins group:
  MYDOMAIN\Administrator

MYDOMAIN\Administrators:
  MYDOMAIN\Administrator
  MYDOMAIN\Domain Admins

PDC and BDC: Share a SAM in \winnt\system32\config\sam on\\PDC

Let's see why this information is useful. Suppose you went to the PDC and created an account for yourself called Super that is supposed to be a domain-wide administrator account. Because you want Super to be an administrator, you put Super in the Administrators group on PDC. What does this accomplish? Do you now have a domain-wide administrator?

Well, you just put Super into the Administrators group on the primary domain controller, right? That must make Super a domain-wide administrator—but it doesn't.

Stop and think for a minute: is Super now a member of the PDC\Administrators or MYDOMAIN\Administrators group? It's something of a trick question. As I've already said, domain controller machines don't have local groups, so PDC\Administrators does not exist (and neither does BDC\Administrators).

In contrast, if you want to create an account that controls SERVER (an NT server machine that is *not* a domain controller), you can log on to SERVER by using SERVER's local Administrator account (on the Domain pull-down menu, choose SERVER, not the Domain name). You did remember to make a note of SERVER\Administrator's password when you installed SERVER, didn't you? Start up User Manager on SERVER (remember that, since SERVER isn't a domain controller, the User Manager program isn't User Manager for Domains, and has somewhat less functionality than User Manager for Domains) and add a new user to the Administrators group on SERVER. You can even add a domain account like MYDOMAIN\Super rather than a local SERVER account. Now that you have created an account that controls SERVER, anyone logging on to SERVER who uses the domain user account MYDOMAIN\Super can act as administrator on SERVER.

But, again, domain controllers—PDC and BDC, in my example—are different. There *is* no PDC\Administrators or BDC\Administrators group. Instead, there is a group called MYDOMAIN\Administrators that is shared by PDC and BDC and would be shared by any other domain controllers, if MYDOMAIN had any more. To administer and control the PDC or BDC machines, you must instead be a member of a group called MYDOMAIN\Administrators.

If you don't yet see why I find this a bit jarring, consider this: having a domain-wide global account like Domain Users is useful and makes sense because that Domain Users group is automatically inserted into all of the local Users groups on the domain. In the same way, you'll find another useful global group called Domain Admins that is automatically installed inside the local Administrators group of each NT machine in the domain. But you cannot place the MYDOMAIN\ Users group into another machine's Users group, nor can you place the MY-DOMAIN\Administrators group into another machine's Administrators group, because that would require placing a local group into a local group, and NT won't let you do that. So, on the one hand we have these local groups named MYDOMAIN\Users and MYDOMAIN\Administrators, but the groups aren't even *visible* to any machines save the domain controllers, which makes them seem less than "domain-ish."

Anyway, the bottom line is this: if you were to create a domain user account called Super that was supposed to be able to act as an administrator on any machine in the domain, then placing that account in the Administrators group of the domain would be a mistake. Super would be able to act as an administrator only on domain controllers—PDC and BDC, in my example. The Super account would have been automatically included in the MYDOMAIN\Domain Users group, and so SERVER and WS would recognize the domain account and allow someone to log on to them using the Super account, but SERVER and WS would only extend user-level privileges to Super, not administrative privileges.

"You might be a big guy when you're working the domain controllers," SERVER and WS effectively say, "but you're just a user as far as we're concerned." If you were instead to put Super into the Domain Admins group, *then* the Super account could control all of the machines in the domain, as the MYDOMAIN\Domain Admins group is automatically placed in the local Administrators group of each machine, including the MYDOMAIN\Administrators group itself.

Let me stop at this point and underscore what it means for an NT machine to "join a domain." Put simply, it means

- Your NT machine now has a machine account on the domain's SAM. In fact, some NT system messages refer to a *trust relationship* between your machine and your domain controller.

- Your local Users group now contains the Domain Users group of the domain.

- Your local Administrators group now contains the Domain Admins group of the domain.

- Your local Guests group now contains the Domain Guests group of the domain.

- It's possible to simultaneously log in to a domain while logging in to your local machine.

That's pretty much all there is to "joining a domain." As the Domain Admins group gets placed in your NT machine's Administrators group, anyone in the Domain Admins group can walk around the domain and exercise administrative power. As Domain Users gets placed in your NT machine's Users group, anyone in the domain can sit down and log in at an NT workstation that has joined the domain. Those settings are, of course, the defaults, and you could choose to remove Domain Admins and/or Domain Users. Your machine would still be a member of the domain, but you'd restrict a bit what the other people in the domain could do with the machine.

Let's wrap up this discussion about how to use local and global groups in a domain. Basically, to create a group that can be seen and exported all over your domain, make it a global group, and place that global group in whatever local groups you require.

Using Global Groups across Domains

Having read the lengthy discussion of how you would use local and global groups in a *single* domain, how does that apply across domains? As it turns out, very simply.

Global groups are not only "global" in the sense that they can be placed in a local group of an NT machine; they can also be placed into a local group of any NT machine—workstation, server, or domain controller—in another domain (a *trusted* domain).

Let's use that data to answer the question I posed much earlier: "How do I give ORION users access just like TAURUS users?"

First, recall that many shares on a domain are shared to the group Everyone. The simple action of TAURUS trusting ORION put all of the ORION users into TAURUS's Everyone group. ORION users are thus automatically granted TAURUS-like access to anything shared to Everyone in the TAURUS domain.

Second, if you've had to make restrictions on a share's permissions, you've had to add permitted users or groups one by one. Most commonly, you add the Domain Users group from your domain to the share-level permission list of any share on an NT server or workstation in your domain. It would be great if you could say, "Well, since the TAURUS\Domain Users group has access to a whole bunch of shares, and I want the ORION folks to get to that too, I'll just put the ORION\ Domain Users group into the TAURUS\Domain Users group." But you know you can't do it. So what's the trick? Unfortunately, there isn't one. You just have to go to each share and add the ORION\Domain Users group by hand. But perhaps there's a way to automate the process a trifle…

One approach is to leverage the power of file and directory permissions. I'd like to tell you that a command-line utility lets you control share-level permissions, and that you can construct batch files to add a new domain's Domain Users group all in one fell swoop, but there isn't such a utility. But here's an idea. Recall that if a disk share is on a volume formatted as NTFS, then you have to satisfy two levels of security to get in: the original share-level permissions and then the file- and directory-level permissions.

Now, file and directory permissions *do* have a command-line utility called CACLS, which I discussed back in Chapter 7. So you might try this:

1. Make sure all of your disk shares are in NTFS.

2. Share them with share-level permission of Full Control to the group Everyone.

3. Do the "real" permissions with file and directory permissions.

This way, it's simple to add a new domain's groups with a batch file using CACLS. Not a great answer, but it will have to do until the release of Windows 2000 Server.

Another approach uses only share-level permissions. Suppose you want to create a share on TAURUS that you want just about everyone on ORION to be able to get to. Suppose the name of the TAURUS server containing the share is called ELNATH, and the share is called STUFF. Try this:

1. Include in the ELNATH server's Users group the group ORION\Domain Users.

2. Now the ELNATH\Users group contains the TAURUS users (not that there are many of them) and the ORION users. Any shares generally available on ELNATH should be shared to ELNATH\Users; that way, both TAURUS and ORION users can access the share.

3. If there are more master domains, then add their Domain Users groups to the local ELNATH\Users group.

More generally, the advice goes like so: place the Domain Users group of the master domain into the local Users groups of every server in the resource domain. Then share things on the resource servers to their local Users groups.

Of course, that makes sense if you want to create shares that are generally available. If you want to restrict access to a share, then you should get more specific than Domain Users.

Granting User Rights and Printer Permissions across Domains

Thus far, I've discussed granting file permissions, which is probably of more concern to you more often than are user rights or even printer permissions.

By now, you've seen that the Add button that appears in many dialog boxes opens up the door, when clicked, to other domains. By using those dialog boxes, you can assign user rights and printer permissions to users from other domains, just as you've seen how to assign file permissions to "alien" users.

Setting Up NT Workstations in a Resource Domain

I've said that in our network we have a master domain named ORION that contains users and a resource domain named TAURUS that contains machines. Many of our users are running NT Workstation as their desktop operating system, and of course those machines are members of TAURUS, not ORION. Here are the steps that you complete to make sure that it works well:

1. Log onto the NT workstation using its local Administrator account. Every workstation has one, and you've got to use it or some other account that is in the Administrators group local to that workstation.

2. Make sure an administrator in the resource domain (TAURUS, in the example I've been using) has created a machine account for you in the resource domain.

3. In the Control Panel, select Network and then Change. Fill in the name of the new domain and click OK. If your new machine account is in place, you'll get a message like "Welcome to the TAURUS domain."

4. The system will want you to restart at that point, but don't. Instead, go into the User Manager and look in the Users and Administrators groups. They will contain the Domain Users and Domain Admins groups from the resource domain. That's not much help to you, however, because there's basically nobody there—the accounts are in the master domain. So add the Domain Users group from your master domain to the local Users group, and add the Domain Admins group from your master domain to the local Administrators group.

Then you can reboot and you'll be set up to work without trouble from your NT workstation.

Logging On from Foreign Domains

Many companies adopt a model wherein user departments are organized into domains, and the MIS group has its own domain from which all other domains are managed. In that model, the trust relationships look like Figure 12.16.

FIGURE 12.16:

Special trust relationship model

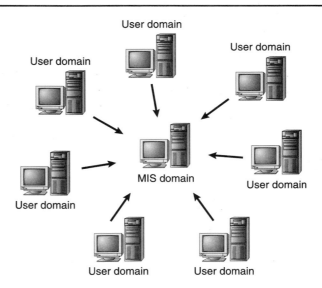

In that model, all the user departments trust the MIS domain, but the MIS domain doesn't trust any of them. A LAN administrator, who is probably a member of the MIS domain, may find him- or herself at a server in *any* domain, wanting to log on to that server and do some kind of maintenance. How should the accounts be arranged so that this LAN administrator can log on to any server?

Well, logging on to a server requires two things: a recognized account on a trusted domain and the right to log on to a server as a user (ordinary users can't just sit down to the server and start working). As you've seen, it doesn't make sense to give this central administrator an account on every single domain. Besides, that makes for some cumbersome administrative nightmares.

The LAN administrator in this example can get onto any machine via a two-step process.

First, make sure that the MIS domain's Domain Admins group is in every user department domain's Administrators group, and on the local Administrators group of *every server and NT workstation in that domain*. Yes, it's a pain, but hopefully by now it's clear that it's the only way to exert comprehensive control over all of the enterprise's domains. This assures that all MIS administrators are granted Administrator status when they sit down and log on to any domain controller, and it also gives the MIS administrators the User right to log on at a server.

Here's an oddity that you may come across. Suppose you were a normal user in the MIS domain, not an administrator. Could you sit down to a Windows for Workgroups machine in a user department's domain and get to your machine? You could, because you can specify from Windows for Workgroups which domain you wish to log on to. Suppose you're at the desk of a member of the Personnel domain, and you go to log on to the MIS domain. You log on okay, but then you notice that the machine that you've logged on to has persistent connections that hook it up to some resources in the Personnel domain. After a moment, it dawns on you: *I shouldn't be able to get to Personnel resources*. And yet you can. What's going on?

The Guest account, that's what's going on. If the Guest account doesn't have a password, and if you haven't restricted its access to domain resources, then someone who logs on, whom the domain doesn't recognize, gets logged on to the local domain's resources as a Guest. This is true even if the user logging on is from a trusted domain. If the Guest account has been disabled, you are prompted for a password before you can go any further, because the Windows for Workgroups machine wants to finish establishing persistent connections.

The thing that separates NT from many other network systems, including earlier Microsoft offerings, is its enterprise-wide structure. By using global groups, by having a good knowledge of cross-domain techniques, you can build a network that is easy to administer, even from miles away.

Enterprise Designs: Single- and Multiple-Domain Models

Let's finish up with a few approaches to domains. Here are some ideas about how to structure your enterprise. There are four basic ways to build an enterprise with NT domains: single domain, master/resource domain, multiple master/resource, and complete trust.

Single-Domain Enterprise Model

For networks with few users that don't need to be logically divided for effective management, one single, large domain may suffice.

Benefits: Simpler to manage.

Drawbacks: Your enterprise may be too big, or links to remote sites may make it ineffective to use a single domain.

Complete Trust Model

Once you've built a bunch of domains, you will probably find that at least one person in any given domain X always needs access to a server in domain Y. Person X hasn't a prayer of getting to a server in domain Y unless Y trusts X, so you're forced to create, and manage, a trust relationship between Y and X. It's extremely likely that at least one person in one domain always needs to get to another given domain, so you end up creating all possible trust relationships.

Benefits: It's certainly flexible for users.

Drawbacks: You've got to be kidding if you think you can keep track of it all. Suppose you have 30 domains. You create a new one. You now have to create 30 trust relationships between the new domain and each existing domain, and 30 trust relationships going in the reverse direction—and each trust relationship requires the cooperation of an administrator from each side of the relationship. And every time you rebuild a domain that's had a disaster, you have 60 *more* things to remember to do.

Master Domain Model

The master domain model came about when Microsoft realized that they couldn't fit all of Microsoft into one domain and when they realized that managing a complete trust enterprise would be an abhorrent task. So they came up with an enterprise model that is built of a single master domain, a domain that contains all of the user accounts for the enterprise, and resource domains that only contain machine accounts for servers and NT workstations.

To understand how the enterprise model works, suppose you and I are the network planners for our firm, Ajax Industries, and our firm is located in three places—an office in the U.S., one in Europe, and one in Australia. We could define four domains, which I'll call AJAX, US, EUROPE, and OZ. They work as follows:

- AJAX contains a user account for each Ajax employee. It also contains user groups. It is referred to as the *master domain*.

- US is a domain without any user accounts in it (save for Administrator and Guest, which can't be removed). It contains the machine accounts for all of the servers in Ajax's U.S. offices. We set up US to *trust* AJAX. Recall that this means that AJAX members—that is, the employees in our firm—can sit down at NT workstations and log on even though the machines are members of the US domain and the employees are members of the AJAX domain. It also means that it is possible to give access to servers in the US domain to AJAX members. As US really only contains network resources—file servers, print servers, applications servers—it is called a *resource domain*.

- Likewise, EUROPE is a resource domain. It does for Ajax's European offices what the US domain does for the American offices. EUROPE trusts AJAX.

- Finally, OZ is another resource domain, for the Australian offices.

Summarized in a few words, you build a master domain-type enterprise as follows.

First, create a domain and put all user accounts into it. That's the master domain.

Then, create domains out in the branch offices called resource domains, and in them place only machine accounts for NT workstations and servers. Your file servers, print servers, and applications servers (SQL Server, SMS) would be in the resource domains.

Next, create trust relationships between the resource domains and the master domain. In my Ajax Industries example, US would trust AJAX, EUROPE would trust AJAX, and OZ would trust AJAX. US, EUROPE, and OZ wouldn't have to trust each other.

In each resource domain's shares, include the Domain Users group from the master domain. For example, if there's a file share in OZ, then include in its permissions AJAX\Domain Users. Of course, you may want to get more specific than simply the entire user community. If that's the case, then create a global group—it must be global!—in the AJAX domain and place *that* in the permission list for the OZ share.

In each server's Administrators group, place the accounts or groups from the master domain that you want to be able to administer that server. For example, if Ajax Industries had decided that it needs a set of company-wide network administrators, then it could put those users into the AJAX\Domain Admins group, and then put the AJAX\Domain Admins group into the local Administrators group *of every single server in OZ, US, and EUROPE*. (Yes, it's a pain, but it's the only way to do it.)

Just to speed up logins, you might place backup domain controllers from the master domain onto the same networks as the resource domains. As a user from AJAX trying to access a resource in US must be authenticated by a domain controller from AJAX, placing an AJAX controller nearby means faster logins.

I've been using a master/resource model throughout this chapter: ORION is the master domain, and TAURUS is the resource domain.

Multiple Master Domain Enterprise Model

If the organization is too large to fit all the user accounts into one domain, you end up with the *multiple* master domain model. It works just like the master domain model, except you replace one master domain with a number of master domains. Then you build complete trust among the master domains, and build trust relationships between each of the resource domains and the master domains.

For example, if you had two master domains named M1 and M2, and three resource domains named R1, R2, and R3, you would first create the M1-M2 and M2-M1 trusts; both masters must trust each other. (If you had three master domains, you'd end up with six trust relationships, as four master domains would require 12 trust relationships, and so on; for n master domains, you'd end up with n $(n-1)$ trust relationships.) Then you would create a trust from each resource to each master, like so: R1-M1, R1-M2, R2-M1, R2-M2, R3-M1, and R3-M2. No trusts are necessary between resource domains. None are required from master domains to resource domains, either.

Fixing Broken Trusts

Does this look like a mess? It is. But it gets worse, believe me. You see, in order for each domain to communicate with each of the ones that it trusts or that trust it, each domain controller—both backup and primary—must build and maintain a link to one other domain controller in each trusted or trusting relationship. Yes, it's as complex as it sounds, and yes, it happens automatically, and no, there's not much you can do about it.

For a variety of reasons, these links from domain controller to domain controller can fail unexpectedly; the most common reason is that one DC can no longer locate its partner DC in another domain. The result is that networks with a lot of trust relationships seem to experience a lot of broken links in those trust relationships.

How Trusts Break

How to fix those broken links? Well, basically what happens is that some controller from domain A picks a "buddy" from domain B, they establish a communications link, and any trust-relationship communication—the domain controller in A verifying that Jack is indeed a user in domain B, for example—goes over that link. But if the server in A goes looking for the server in B and the B server doesn't respond quickly enough, then the A server isn't smart enough to just go make a new friend. (This can happen for a number of reasons, any of which would make the B server unfind-able for some probably-brief period of time.) Instead, it loses the ability to participate in A-to-B authentication conversations. You can fix things by *forcing* the A server to go find another buddy.

One way to do that is to reboot the A server, as rebooting will compel it to go find a currently active buddy in domain B. In fact, many firms have addressed this kind of problem (and others) by simply re-booting the domain controllers daily or once every few days. This isn't a really good answer—important machines like DCs ought to be able to stay up and running for months at a time without reboots—but it *is* an answer.

Using NETDOM to Reestablish Trust

But not the only one.

Supplement Two to the NT Server Resource Kit brings NETDOM.EXE. It's got a lot of uses, but perhaps its greatest strength is in maintaining trust relationships. NETDOM will let you build new trust relationships *from the command line*, as well as "reset" or refresh existing trusts, which has the side effect of forcing DCs to find new buddies.

Let's see how building or refreshing a trust relationship with NETDOM differs from the method I showed you earlier in this chapter, employing the User Manager for Domains. As before, you need two accounts, one from the trusted domain (let's call it TRUSTED) and one from the trusting domain (let's call it TRUSTING). As you'll see, NETDOM gives you the ability to include the admin name and password for your account on the TRUSTING domain, but *not* for the TRUSTED domain. I'm not quite sure why this is so, but it is. As always, though, you can establish credentials with the TRUSTED domain beforehand with the old NET USE...IPC$ trick:

```
NET USE \\nameofPDCinTRUSTEDdomain\IPC$ /user:TRUSTED\adminusername
```

NETDOM can get a bit confused if the TRUSTED account name is the same as the TRUSTING account name *but they have different passwords*, so either use account names that appear only in one domain or use accounts with identical names and passwords in both domains. Assume for this example that the name of the administrator account on TRUSTING is "administrator" and its password is "swordfish." NETDOM works best if you're logged in as a domain administrator on the trusted domain, as that removes the need to the NET USE to the IPC$ share. Assuming that you're logged on as a TRUSTED administrator, you'd make TRUSTING trust TRUSTED like so:

```
NETDOM /domain:trusting /user:trusting\administrator
/password:swordfish master trusted /trust
```

That's a long line—let's see what's going on there. NETDOM can do a lot of things and so has a fairly complex set of command-line options, but that last line basically boils down to this:

NETDOM info about the trusting domain MASTER name of trusted domain /TRUST

Again, this won't just *create* new trust relationships; it will *rebuild* trust relationships. Next time you come to work in the morning and find several domain controllers complaining about being unable to establish a link with some trusted domain, don't reboot them—try NETDOM.

Using SETPRFDC to Reestablish Trust

Yet another tool that you may find useful is SETPRFDC, "Set Preferred DC," a tool that first appeared in Service Pack 4. Recall that each NT system has a connection with a domain controller; an NT workstation in domain BONYFISH might have been originally authenticated by a domain controller named TROUT. But TROUT might be across the ocean from the workstation due to a fluke (reader, I hope you appreciate that I'm trying *really* hard not to use any bad puns here, but the temptation is positively diabolical) of logon—perhaps when the workstation was first powered up today, the local domain controllers were all busy and the only one that responded quickly was TROUT. It's nice that TROUT handled the logon, but the bad news is that TROUT will handle all authentications for the rest of the day. Worse yet, what if this *isn't* a workstation we're talking about, but a *domain controller*? DCs must establish sessions with DCs from trusted domains. Suppose BONYFISH has a trust relationship with another domain named BONE-LESSFISH. BONYFISH has a domain controller named SUNFISH (it runs the Unix interoperability software as well—darn, I see I succumbed). As SUNFISH must sometimes handle authentication across the trust relationship, it needs to find a "buddy" DC from BONELESSFISH. It finds this buddy by essentially doing a logon to BONELESSFISH; if it gets lucky, it finds domain controller WHITESHARK, which is just down the hall. If it gets unlucky, it ends up talking to MONKFISH across the Atlantic—and skating across the pond for each authentication clogs the intercontinental bandwidth!

You can nudge a DC (or any other machine) to "prefer" a particular set of domain controllers with SETPRFDC. It looks like this:

```
SETPRFDC name_of_domain DC1,DC2,DC3,DC4…
```

You run this from the command line (or just use AT to have it run automatically periodically) and, like NETDOM, it breaks and rebuilds communications links with DCs. For example, suppose you've got an NT workstation in BONYFISH and you want your workstation to do its authentications through a machine named BARRACUDA; just type

```
SETPRFDC BONYFISH BARRACUDA
```

and it will respond (assuming all works properly) with

```
Successfully set DC to "\\BARRACUDA".
```

Finally, why would you use the AT command to reset these connections? If an NT workstation can't get a response quickly enough from its "preferred" DC, it'll drift around looking for another. In very large enterprises, this can lead to a situation wherein people working in the central headquarters—a place with a busy network—slowly (and unknowingly) migrate out to connections with domain controllers in smaller branch offices over slow WAN connections. The unnecessary authentication traffic clogs the WAN connections, and then the branch office starts wondering why they're getting such terrible response time from the main office. So SETPRFDC can help keep your DC usage local.

Oh, and one other tip—if you're using TCP/IP—and if you're not, you should be—then you should avoid at all costs using static IP addresses, opting instead for DHCP reservations. I'll explain this in more detail in Chapter 14, but I wanted to mention it here.

When you're finished getting your NT domains to talk to each other, it's time to include the NetWare servers. That's the topic of the next chapter.

CHAPTER
THIRTEEN

13

Novell NetWare in an NT Server Environment

- Understanding how NT and NetWare interact

- How to use NWLink without the Gateway Service

- How to run NetWare and NT Server in parallel

- Using the Microsoft Gateway Service

- Setting up the NetWare Gateway Service

- Providing access to Print Gateway services

- Migrating from Novell to Windows NT

Novell NetWare commands somewhere between 60 and 70 percent of the PC-based server market, between its three offerings in versions 2.2, 3.12, and 4.*x*. For that reason, many NT networks incorporate some kind of NetWare connectivity. Similarly, many NetWare networks out there find themselves having to deal with NT Server and NT workstations, as networks these days just aren't homogeneous.

In this chapter, you'll learn how to integrate NT- and NetWare-based networks, so that you can enjoy the best of both worlds. There are several options for integrating the two networks, but the best one (in my opinion) is the Client and Gateway Services for NetWare that ships with NT Server.

How NT and NetWare Interact

There are three main ways in which NT networks and NetWare networks interact. They are described here.

NT Workstations on Novell NetWare   First, a Novell NetWare network may incorporate NT machines solely as workstations. This is fairly simple, as it requires no work on the server side at all. All you need to do is obtain NT NetWare client software from Novell to accomplish this. Another way to access the Novell servers directly from NT is to use the Client Service for NetWare, which is provided with NT Workstation.

Both versions of this solution are really only relevant to NT *workstations*, however. Users of an NT Server network would not be able to access resources on the Novell network with this solution.

NT Server in a Novell NetWare Network   If your current network is a Novell NetWare–based one, then your workstations all run NetWare client software. If you add an NT Server machine to an existing Novell NetWare network, you have to load *dual* network client software on the workstations. Here are some things to consider with this solution:

- It requires dual network client software, which can be hard to manage and requires more memory.

- It *does* provide for access to both Novell NetWare and NT Server resources, but security and programming interfaces are not integrated.

- Remote access and backup processes could not be shared under this system.

- It involves no special software installation on the *servers*, and so may be attractive to some network administrators. In a sense, because it's the older one, it even may be a slightly more reliable solution.

This second option is, unfortunately, the one that most of us use. But many could benefit from the third option, Novell NetWare in an NT Server Network.

Novell NetWare in an NT Server Network   Starting with NT 3.5, a third solution—the Gateway Service—was available. With the Gateway Service, all NetWare resources become NT Server resources. Yes, you read that right: all access to NetWare resources occurs through the NT servers. Aspects of this solution include

- You need only run one set of network software, the NDIS and NetBIOS software, on the client in order to access the NetWare servers.

- Backup and remote access services can be integrated.

- Security can be integrated.

- As a side bonus, Novell NetWare server/user limitations can be bypassed.

It's quite an attractive solution, but how does it work? I'll cover that in most of the remainder of the chapter, but first let's take a quick look at Novell's answer.

NetWare Client Software for NT

The NetWare Client for NT (NCNT) software was released by Novell in late June of 1994. It has the following features:

- It replaces the NDIS-based network stack on an NT workstation with an ODI-based stack.

- The Open Data-link Interface (ODI) standard is the Novell analog to NDIS, which is troublesome, because there are likely to be fewer NT-compatible ODI drivers around.

- The NT services that require NDIS get NDIS-like service from ODI via an on-the-fly translation program called ODINSUP.

Overall, it's an answer more appropriate for a few lone NT workstations in a NetWare environment than it is for an NT Server-based environment.

Using NWLink without the Gateway Service

Using NWLink without the Gateway Service is not really a NetWare connectivity solution, but one thing that ships with NT is NWLink, a transport protocol that is IPX/SPX-compatible. (IPX/SPX stands for *internetworking packet exchange/sequenced packet exchange*.) NWLink is another STREAMS and TDI-integrated transport protocol, a plug-and-play option like TCP/IP. You could, if you wanted, install it in place of (or in addition to) NetBEUI or TCP/IP as your domain's transport protocol.

Why would you do that? Well, NWLink supports the "sockets" application program interface (API). Since some NetWare-based applications servers, or NetWare Loadable Modules (NLMs), use sockets to communicate with client computers, your NT machines could act as clients in a NetWare-based client/server environment. NWLink is relatively useless all by itself, however, because it does not include a NetWare-compatible redirector. In English, that means that you could not access NetWare file servers or shared printers solely with NWLink.

NWLink mimics Novell's IPX/SPX stack, but many Novell users also load a Novell version of NetBIOS. To maintain compatibility with that NetBIOS, Microsoft also ships NWBLink, a transport stack that runs alongside NWLink and provides NetBIOS support much like that provided by Novell. (Novell's NetBIOS is a bit different from the Microsoft version, as you probably figured out if you ever tried to install something on your Novell network that required NetBIOS.)

If you're installing this product on an Ethernet, you may run up against a common situation that appears under Novell with Ethernets: frame type. In the Ethernet world, you can configure your network to work with either the IEEE 802.3

(CSMA/CD) or IEEE 802.2 (Logical Link Control) frame formats. If you are communicating with a NetWare 2.2 or 3.11 server, the frame format is usually 802.3. NetWare 4.*x* servers generally use frame type 802.2.

Running NetWare and NT Server in Parallel

The idea here is simple: your office contains both NT servers and a NetWare server or servers. The NT servers talk NetBIOS/NetBEUI and perhaps TCP/IP, and the Novell servers talk IPX/SPX. Getting the two server families (NetWare and NT) to talk to one another is a mite tricky, goes the reasoning, *so don't bother*. Instead, load both IPX/SPX and NetBIOS/NetBEUI stacks on your workstations.

Many of you have probably already chosen this solution if you're running Windows for Workgroups. Windows for Workgroups ships with an IPX/SPX stack that runs in combination with NetBIOS/NetBEUI and makes it possible to carry on conversations with both servers. Here are some features of the NetWare and NT Server in parallel solution:

- Simplicity, kind of, in that you needn't install any software on the servers. You needn't put NWLink on your NT machines, nor some kind of odd NLM on your NetWare servers.

- Lack of drivers. To date, Windows for Workgroups does not ship with a NetWare redirector. The IPX/SPX protocol is in place, but the redirector is not, so you have to run the redirector that came with Windows for Workgroups version 3.1. Microsoft gives you no warning of this until you're part way through the installation of Windows for Workgroups version 3.11. (Nice touch, boys and girls!) In addition, the combination of 3.11 and the old 3.1 driver is a bit wobbly.

- Lack of drivers II. If you're running NetWare 4.*x* servers, then there's just no way that you can make the old Windows for Workgroups 3.1 NetWare drivers work reliably. You have to download a bunch of drivers from Novell. They seem to work fairly well when it comes to talking to the NetWare servers, but they tend to eliminate some of the benefits of Workgroups. Besides, they cut off your connections to NT Server machines periodically.

- Memory management becomes a problem in that you're loading a *lot* of stuff on the workstation.

- Because you're still running two different server environments, they don't share anything. You have to create separate user accounts on the NT side of the house from the NetWare side. Remote access services aren't shared, so twice as many modems are required. Backup services aren't shared, which means you have to keep track of twice as many tapes.

Windows 95 greatly simplifies matters because Microsoft has written complete protocol stacks and client software for both NT and Novell networks. Use all Microsoft client software and you'll only have to deal with one vendor.

Configuring NT to Run in Parallel

On your NT workstation, running NT Workstation and NetWare in parallel is a straightforward procedure. You will need to enable the Client Service for NetWare:

1. Open My Computer, open Control Panel, and then open the Network Icon.

2. Select the Services property page.

3. Click the Add button. You see the Select Network Service dialog box shown in Figure 13.1.

FIGURE 13.1:

Select Network Service dialog box

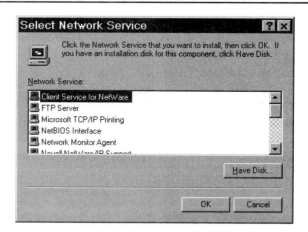

4. Select Client Service for NetWare by double-clicking on it.

5.   Tell Windows NT Setup the path to the NT 4 files.

6.   Click OK.

NT copies the appropriate drivers to your system and makes changes to your Registry that enable the Client Service for NetWare to load the next time your start your system. Close the Network Dialog box and your bindings will be reconfigured. Once you reboot the system, NT attempts to log on to Novell for the first time. With the client software provided by Microsoft, you can either log on to a Novell 3.*x* Bindery by clicking on the Preferred Server radio button shown in the dialog box in Figure 13.2, or you can log on to a 4.*x* NetWare Directory Service Tree by clicking on the Default Tree and Context radio button. If you are going to log on to an NDS tree, do not provide the parameter codes before each option (that is, omit the o= and the cn=). Enter the name of the Tree and its context. Figure 13.2 gives an example.

FIGURE 13.2:

Select Preferred Server for NetWare dialog box

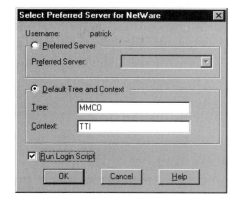

On NT Server, the service and the client service are combined when you install the gateway services. All the steps that you took above still apply. The only difference is that you select the Gateway (and Client) Service for NetWare option instead of the Client Service for NetWare option. The last two dialog boxes are identical, although you have the additional option of configuring the Gateway Service, which is discussed in the next section.

NOTE   At the writing of this book, Novell provides a beta copy of their 32-bit drivers for NT on their Web site (www.novell.com). The drivers work in 3.51 but crash the system when installed on NT 4. Stay tuned to Novell for updated NT 4 drivers.

Microsoft Gateway Service

The Microsoft Gateway Service could become a good candidate for "the" NT-to-NetWare answer.

In mid-June 1994, Microsoft released the first version of its complete NetWare-to-NT solution. It comes in two parts: the NetWare Client Service and the NetWare Gateway Service. You'll be most interested in the Gateway Service.

The Client Service is a complete NT-based, 32-bit NetWare redirector. It allows you to sit at an NT machine and use all the resources of your NetWare network, just as you've been able to do for years from DOS workstations. The Client Service is just software like TCP/IP or NWLink that you install via the Add Software option on the Control Panel. No changes are required on the NetWare servers except, of course, the NT user must have a valid account. You must load NWLink before the Client Service can function. Fear not, because when you select the Client service, NWLink installs automatically.

Where things get really strange is when you install the Gateway Service, which is only available for NT Server. After you install it, *any workstation that is connected to your NT Server machine can also see the NetWare drives.*

NOTE   When you install the Gateway Service, you install the Client Service automatically. You cannot load one without the other on the NT Server platform.

Pretty spooky, but the NT Server machine becomes a gateway to the NetWare services. All the NetWare server sees is the one logical connection between NetWare and the NT machine, so actually dozens of people can use a single NetWare connection!

The characteristics of the Gateway Service are

- It allows shared remote access services.

- It allows shared backup services.

- Accounts become integrated because the NT Server machine is the "front end" to the NetWare network, and so the NT Server machine handles logon validation and permissions as if they were just other resources in the NT domain. However, all of the users who access a NetWare server through the gateway must share identical access rights to Novell server. This situation is ideal for accessing a common post office or public directory that resides on the NetWare server. It would not be a viable option for home directories to be located on the NetWare server, since each user should have explicit and separate security permissions to their own home directory.

- An NT Server machine must serve as the gateway.

- This works on 3.*x* servers and only works with 4.*x* servers that are running bindery emulation; there's no support for NetWare directory services so far.

The Gateway Service answer is the newest one to the "How do I integrate NetWare and NT?" question, and it could be the best one.

Installing the NetWare Gateway

When you install the NetWare Gateway Service, you also install NWLink. As with all NT network software modules, you install the Gateway Service by starting up the Control Panel and clicking on the Networks icon.

Select the Services tab, click the Add button, and you see options for other add-ons to NT (see Figure 13.3). Choose Gateway (and Client) Services for NetWare and click Continue. You then have to provide the path where NT can find the setup files (the CD-ROM for most of us), and once again click Continue.

FIGURE 13.3:

Selecting the Gateway Service

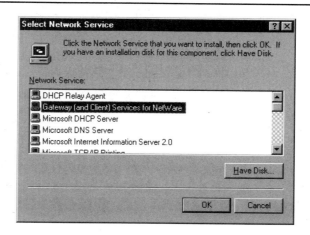

If you have RAS running, you receive the following setup message: "Setup has discovered that you have Remote Access Services installed. Do you want to configure RAS to support NWLink protocol?" If you want to configure remote access for using the IPX protocol, click OK. Click Cancel if you don't want to install the IPX protocol for use with RAS.

Creating the User

As the server boots, move over to a NetWare-attached workstation and run SYSCON, NWADMIN, or its equivalent. You have to get the NetWare servers ready for the NT client by following these steps:

1. Create a user whose name is the same as the user who will log on to the NT machine. In my example, I'm hooking up an NT Server machine to NetWare, so the username that I use to log onto the NT Server machine is "Administrator." Create a *Novell* user named Administrator.

2. Create a NetWare group called NTGATEWAY.

3. Put your user—called Administrator in my example—into that NTGATEWAY group.

4. Set the password of Administrator to the same value as the password of the NT user named "Administrator." (This isn't necessary for the simple Client Services setup, but it will prove essential for the Gateway Services later.)

Now, back to the NT side of the setup.

TIP

If you are going to run the Gateway Service (in contrast to the Client Service), be aware that if you log on to the machine running the Gateway Service, then you may be unable to access the Novell drives unless you supply the gateway name and password. For example, I've been using a user named Administrator for my examples. If I logged onto EISA66, the NT machine that's running the Gateway Service, and used the name "Mark," I would get a password verification the first time that I tried to use the Novell drives locally. All I'd have to do would be to supply the user name "Administrator" and the password for that account.

The Gateway Service Setup, Part 2

When the server comes back up, the client part of the service will attempt to log on to the NetWare server. It will prompt you for a preferred NetWare server if you are logging on to a 3.x server, or a preferred context if you are logging on to a 4.x server. If you are just going to use the Gateway service, don't pick one yet; choose Cancel for now, and when it asks you if you want to continue, tell it Yes. Start up the Control Panel and you see a new icon labeled GSNW. Click on GSNW, and you see the Gateway Service for NetWare dialog box, as shown in Figure 13.4.

FIGURE 13.4:

Gateway (and Client) Service
for NetWare 3.x dialog box

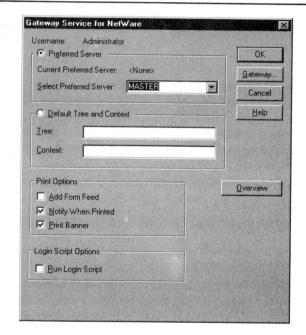

The important areas here are Preferred Server and Default Tree and Context (depending on which version of NetWare you are connecting to). Your system should be able to list the available NetWare servers without any trouble. I haven't chosen one yet, but the server that I want to log on to is called Master, so I chose that server. Your server no doubt has a different name.

Note that the dialog box says, "Username: Administrator" at the top. That's the name that the *Novell* network sees. Click OK and close the Control Panel. (You can also do this by starting up the File Manager and then choosing Connect Network Drive.)

To browse the NetWare network, double-click Network Neighborhood, double-click Entire Network, and double-click NetWare or Compatible Network, as in Figure 13.5. NetWare servers and NDS trees become visible.

FIGURE 13.5:

Connect Gateway Service for NetWare 4.*x* dialog box

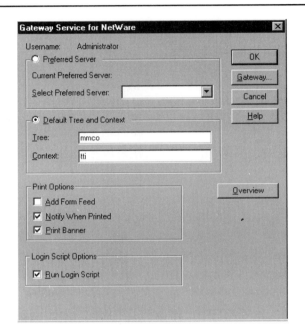

Notice that there is now a reference to NetWare Network in the Shared Directories box. This and only this NT machine can see the Novell servers; none of the clients of the NT machine can see the Novell resources. This is the *client* part of the NetWare connectivity software. To activate gateway services, go back to the GSNW icon in the Control Panel and click the Gateway button. You see a dialog box like Figure 13.6.

FIGURE 13.6:

Configure Gateway
dialog box

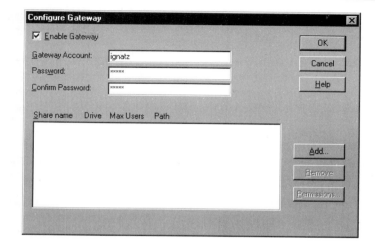

Notice that the buttons in the lower right-hand corner of the dialog box on your screen are grayed out. Don't worry, they will be enabled in a minute. Get this going with the following steps:

1. Enable the gateway by checking the Enable Gateway check box.

2. In Gateway Account, enter the username that you've created on your Novell network. In my example it's Ignatz. You could, if you wanted, create a special account just to be the gateway's name.

3. Enter the password. It should be both the NT password and the Novell password.

You're ready to start making NetWare volumes available for sharing. Now, you're used to using the File Manager to share drives, but you share NetWare volumes right here in the Configure Gateway dialog box. (Not very obvious, but after all this is relatively new software.) The Add button will be enabled by now. Click it and you see a dialog box like the Figure 13.7.

FIGURE 13.7:

New Share dialog box

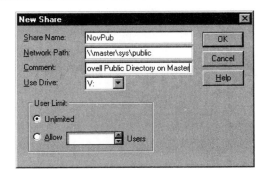

To make NetWare volumes available for sharing, follow these steps:

1. In the Share Name box, enter the share name that you want a workstation to see, as you do with normal NT shared directories.

2. In the Network Path box, enter the name of the Novell volume. Its name should be a UNC-type name, just as you've used so far: *machinename*\ *volumename*. For example, on my network the NetWare 4.*x* server's name is MASTER, and its volume is SYS. The UNC name is, therefore, \\MASTER\SYS.

3. Add a comment if you like, and assign a drive letter to it.

4. Click OK to get out of the New Share dialog box.

5. Click OK in the Configure Gateway dialog box.

Testing the Gateway

Now it's time to go see if the gateway works. Just go to any client machine and try to attach to the share name. For example, in the case of my network, I go to a DOS workstation and type

```
net use * \\EISA66\NovPub
```

Notice that EISA66 is the machine name of the NT server, rather than "master," the machine name of the Novell server. If I were connecting from inside Windows for Workgroups, I could, as usual, just use the Network Neighborhood to connect (File ➤ Map Network Drive. . .).

Security for Novell Volumes: The Bad News

Volumes shared through the gateway are subject to permissions *not* made via My Computer, as you're accustomed to, but rather through the GSNW icon in the Control Panel. The Configure Gateway dialog box includes a button labeled Permissions that you use to control access to the Novell volume.

What this means is that the Gateway Service only provides *share-level* permissions. You can share a particular Novell volume on the NT network, but all Gateway Service users on the NT network will have identical permissions for the data on the Novell volume. If you try to set file or directory permissions with My Computer, you see the following message: "This is an invalid device name."

The downside should be obvious. It's customary to give all users on a network their own "private" directory that only they can access. That's impossible here. The only alternative would be to create different shares and give them different drive letters. For example, you saw how I shared the volume SYS, which was on the server MASTER. Within MASTER\SYS was a subdirectory called MARK. I could add a new share called \\MASTER\SYS\MARK and give only myself access to it. That would give me my own home directory, but that Novell share would get a drive letter on my NT gateway server—and there are only 26 letters in the alphabet.

In case that's not clear, here's an example. Before NT existed, suppose I had a NetWare 3.12 server with 50 users on it. Each of the 50 users had his or her own private "home" directory, and I would have owned a 50-user license for NetWare 3.12. Could I use the NT/Novell Gateway Service to get around that 50-user limit?

At first glance, it might seem possible to buy a five-user license for NetWare 3.12, install the NT Gateway Service, and then hook up the 50 users as NT users. They would all then have access to the NetWare volumes via the Gateway. But that wouldn't work, as my NT server probably has four drives already (A through D, including a CD-ROM), so I can only create a maximum of 22 new NetWare shares, drives E through Z. That means that I couldn't serve more than 22 users with home drives on the NetWare server.

(In case you're wondering, I'm told that it *is* legal to put those 22 users onto Novell via NT because the Novell licenses are not per *user* but per *connection*. Novell sees just one connection, so it's legal. In fact, I imagine that the legality question will boil down to which of the two companies can afford better lawyers.)

The Gateway Service seems to best fit the case wherein I want to share a directory both on the Novell and the NT sides of the house. However, I don't want to have to load IPX/SPX and a NetWare redirector on all of the machines on the NT side just to get to this particular directory on this NetWare volume.

Providing Print Gateway Services

The Gateway Service not only allows NT clients access to NetWare volumes, it also provides access to NetWare print queues. The printer gateway software is activated at the same time as the volume gateway software, but you have to complete one step before the clients can get to the printer: you have to connect your NT Server machine to the Novell printer queues.

Just as you provide access to NetWare drives via a bogus drive on your NT server, so also can you provide access to NetWare print queues by claiming that your NT servers are physically connected to printers that are actually the NetWare printers. That sounds complex, but it's not. Here's how to do it:

1. On the NT Server machine, start up the Add Printer Wizard (My Computer ➤ Printers ➤ Add Printer).

2. Choose Network Printer server, then click the Next button. The Connect to Printer dialog box appears.

3. Click on NetWare Network to open up that network, and you see your NetWare servers. Open them up, and you see the NetWare print queues, as shown in Figure 13.8.

FIGURE 13.8:

Connect to Printer dialog box

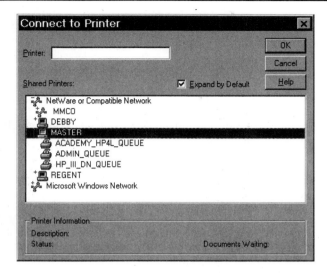

4. Choose a printer. You'll probably get a dialog box that says that a printer driver is not available for the printer you chose. This message just means, "There is no Windows printer driver on that Novell machine." It's not terribly important, as your DOS and Windows clients use their own local drivers, anyway.

5. Click OK.

6. You are asked what kind of printer is on the Novell print queue. The driver of the printer you choose will then be grabbed off the NT installation CD-ROM. The Novell printer will then appear on the Print Manager as if it were a locally attached printer. You can view its queue, delete documents, and so on.

    Before the rest of your NT network can see the printer, however, you have to share it, just as you always do, by way of the Printer Properties dialog box.

7. Click the Start button, click Settings, and then click Printers.

8. Right-click the printer you want to share and click Properties from the shortcut menu.

9. Click the Sharing tab and then click Shared.

10. Type a share name, and it will be available to all NT clients.

How Do I Share a Novell Printer with an NT Network?

To share a Novell printer with an NT network:

1. On the NT Server machine, start up the Print Manager.

2. Choose Printer and then Connect to Printer. The Connect to Printer dialog box appears.

3. Click on the NetWare Network option to open up that network. You see your NetWare servers. Open them up and you see the NetWare print queues.

4. Choose a printer.

5. Even though you probably get a nastygram telling you that there is no Windows printer driver on that Novell machine, it's not terribly important because your DOS and Windows clients use their own local drivers, anyway. Click OK.

6. You are asked what kind of printer is on the Novell print queue, and that printer's driver is then taken off the NT installation CD-ROM. The Novell printer appears on the Print Manager just as if it were a locally attached printer. You can view its queue, delete documents, and so on.

Before the rest of your NT network can see the printer, you have to share it from the Printer Properties dialog box.

7. From the Print Manager, choose a printer, and then click Printer and Printer Properties. Check the "Share this printer on the network" box.

The printer is now available to all NT clients.

Novell Commands Available from NT

At the NT server, you can open up a command line and run a number of Novell commands, including the ones in Table 13.1.

TABLE 13.1: Novell Commands at NT Command Line

chkvol	help	rconsole	settts
colorpal	listdir	remove	slist
dspace	map	revoke	syscon
flag	ncopy	rights	tlist
flagdir	ndir	security	userlist
fconsole	pconsole	send	volinfo
filer	psc	session	whoami
grant	pstat	setpass	

You can also run NetWare-aware applications (some of them, anyway) with some support programs. Windows-based, NetWare-aware applications may require files NETWARE.386, NWCALLS.DLL, and NWNET-API.DLL. They are in your SYSTEM32 directory.

Novell supplies a file called NWIPXSPX.DLL that some client-server applications depend upon; Gupta SQLBase and Lotus Notes are two examples. Copy the file to your *systemroot*\\SYSTEM32 directory.

Potential Problems with the Gateway Service

The Gateway Service is terrific, but it still has a few wrinkles. Following are problems you may encounter with the Gateway Service:

Slower than NetWare The gateway overhead of going through NT slows the data transfer process a bit. That's normal, and it's an outgrowth of the

"1.0" nature of the Gateway Service. You can monitor the performance of the IPX/SPX module with the Performance Monitor. You'll see new objects called NWLink NetBIOS, NWLink IPX, and NWLink SPX that contain a number of counters. The Bytes/second counter of NWLink IPX gives some idea of the NetWare traffic being generated.

You may be prompted for a password   When the Gateway is first loading, you may get a message from it asking for a NetWare password. This happens if you've set a different NT password from the Novell password. Just use the Novell *setpass* command to change your password so that the two passwords match.

"This is an invalid device name."   Try to share a part of a Novell volume or set its permissions and you get the following message: "This is an invalid device name." That's perfectly normal, and it reflects the fact that you do *not* control shared Novell volumes through the Network Neighborhood. Instead, you use the GSNW icon in the Control Panel.

Migrating Users from Novell to NT

Migration Tool
for NetWare

The fundamental reason why Microsoft offers the Gateway Service is to make it simple for people to gradually move from being primarily Novell-based to being primarily NT-based. Now, suppose you had a Novell-based network and you wanted to become NT-based. What kinds of things would you have to do? Basically, you would have to

- Rebuild all of your Novell users on your NT server

- Move information from the hard disks of the Novell servers to the hard disks of the NT servers

Using the Migration Tool for NetWare

The first concern, rebuilding all of your Novell users on your NT server, isn't a small one. Running a parallel NetWare/NT network means that every time you create a user on the NetWare side of the network, you have to go and duplicate your efforts on the NT side. It would be nice if there were a simple way to essentially "lock together" the NetWare user administration tools and the User Manager for Domains, so that a change in the roster of NT users would be immediately reflected in the roster of NetWare users.

Unfortunately, there isn't a tool like that, at least not yet. (It's a lucrative third-party opportunity for an enterprising software author, however.) Instead, Microsoft includes a tool with NT called the Migration Tool for NetWare. (Its beta name was "Visine," as in "get the red out." Get it? Yuk. Yuk.) Start up Migration Tool for NetWare by clicking Start ➤ Programs ➤ Administrative Tools ➤ Migration Tool for NetWare or by running \WINNT35\SYSTEM32\ NWCONV.EXE. You see a dialog box that looks like Figure 13.9.

FIGURE 13.9:

Migration Tool for NetWare opening screen

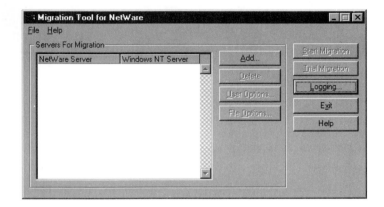

Now, I'm not going to discuss this very much for an important reason: I think it's a niche product with a fairly limited use. If Microsoft had taken the time to create a product that locks together the user accounts of Novell and NT, it would be exciting and worth explaining in detail. But Migration Tool for NetWare is really only of interest to someone *abandoning* Novell for NT.

You start off using this program by selecting which servers you'd like to migrate *from* (the Novell ones) and which servers you'd like migrate *to* (the NT servers). Do that by clicking the Add button. You see a dialog box like the one in Figure 13.10.

FIGURE 13.10:

Specifying source and destination servers for NetWare migration

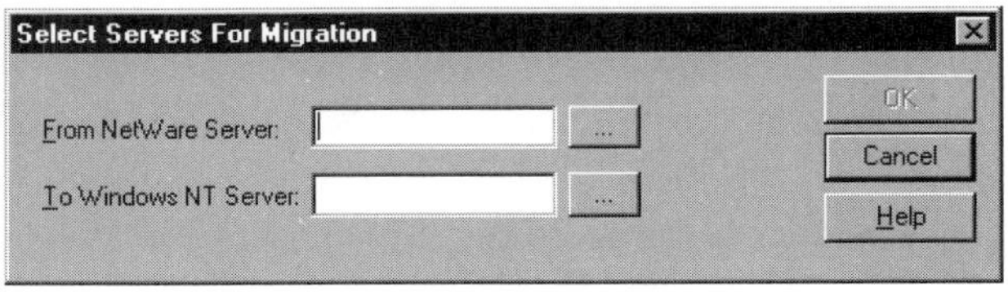

Click the browser buttons (. . .) to the side of From NetWare Server and To Windows NT Server to choose which server will soon be abandoned and which will soon be flush with users. In my case, I've chosen to migrate users from my NetWare 4.01 server MASTER to my NT server MONSTER. The Migration Tool then looks like the Figure 13.11.

FIGURE 13.11:

Migration Tool after selecting servers

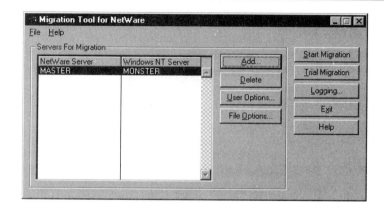

Now that the buttons are enabled, you can see what you can do with this tool. Following is an overview of what each of the buttons does.

Add, Delete, Exit, and Help Buttons The Add button is the one that you press to specify which servers you'll be working with. I clicked it to specify MASTER and MONSTER. Delete would undo that selection. Exit and Help pretty much do what you expect them to do.

User Options Button The User Options button controls how the migration will happen. When you select it, you will see the dialog box in Figure 13.12.

You click the Passwords, Usernames, Group Names, or Defaults tab to bring up "index cards." The aim of Passwords is to ask, "What passwords should I assign to the newly created NT users?" My first thought was, "Well, why not keep their old Novell passwords?" But then I realized (I'm a little slow some days) that *there is no way for the Migration Tool to get the passwords; Novell won't give them up.* So you get the options that you see in Figure 13.12—no password at all, a password that matches the user name, or a fixed password.

FIGURE 13.12:

User and Group options
dialog box

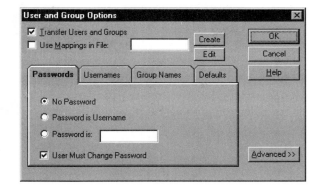

The Usernames and Group Names tabs are concerned with the question, "What should the Migration Tool do if it finds a Novell user named, say, Jack, and it tries to create an NT user named Jack, but there's *already* a user named Jack?" Your options are as follows:

- To not create a user when there's a conflict, and then either log the problem or ignore it.

- To simply create the new user, thereby overwriting the old user.

- To take the user name and prefix it with some fixed text.

You have the same options for group names.

The Defaults tab controls first how to handle account policies (minimum password lengths and the like) and how to treat Novell users with supervisor privileges. You can opt to automatically put any user with supervisor privileges into the Administrators group.

File Options Button   The Migration Tool can blast a whole server's worth of files from a NetWare server to an NT server, kind of like a monster XCOPY command. The File Options button lets you control which files to copy. When you select this button, you see a dialog box for restricting which files or directories get copied to the NT server.

Logging Button   The Logging button brings up the dialog box that you see in Figure 13.13.

FIGURE 13.13:

Logging dialog box

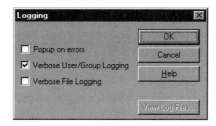

The Popup on errors check box makes the Migration Tool stop and notify you about every single error—*and* warning. I recommend against it. Verbose User/Group Logging is essential, as it produces a record of any problems that arose when converting users from Novell to NT. Verbose File Logging just gives you an exhaustive list of all the files transferred from one server to another.

Trial Migration Button   A server migration is a pretty drastic step, so Microsoft included a "dry run" option: Trial Migration. Click this and you get to see what the results of the migration process will be *before* you commit yourself. This can take *quite* a while, so don't expect immediate results.

The big advantage that I found to a trial migration was that it identified my potential user name and group name conflicts nice and early. I was then able to change the NT names or delete the redundant users, and in so doing prepare for a smoother migration.

Following is an example of the output from the migration process:

```
[ALEX]                          (Added)
Original Account Info:
 Name:
 Account disabled: No
 Account expires: (Never)
 Password expires: (Never)
 Grace Logins: (Unlimited)
 Initial Grace Logins: (Unlimited)
 Minimum Password Length: 0
 # days to Password Expiration: (Never)
 Maximum Number of Connections: (Unlimited)
 Restrictions:
   Anyone who knows password can change it
   Unique passwords required: No
```

```
Number of login failures: 0
Max Disk Blocks: (Unlimited)

Login Times:
Midnight        AM          Noon        PM
   12 1 2 3 4 5 6 7 8 9 10 11 12 1 2 3 4 5 6 7 8 9 10 11
   +------------------------------------+
Sun ** ** ** ** ** ** ** ** ** ** ** ** ** ** ** ** ** ** ** ** ** **
Mon ** ** ** ** ** ** ** ** ** ** ** ** ** ** ** ** ** ** ** ** ** **
Tue ** ** ** ** ** ** ** ** ** ** ** ** ** ** ** ** ** ** ** ** ** **
Wed ** ** ** ** ** ** ** ** ** ** ** ** ** ** ** ** ** ** ** ** ** **
Thu ** ** ** ** ** ** ** ** ** ** ** ** ** ** ** ** ** ** ** ** ** **
Fri ** ** ** ** ** ** ** ** ** ** ** ** ** ** ** ** ** ** ** ** ** **
Sat ** ** ** ** ** ** ** ** ** ** ** ** ** ** ** ** ** ** ** ** ** **
```

The bottom line on the Migration Tool is, again, that it can help you if you're abandoning Novell or you want to set up an NT system with users whose NT accounts mirror their Novell accounts. The Migration Tool only creates NT users and groups that mirror the status of the Novell users and groups *at that moment*, and that's the problem with it. What we need is a *dynamic* Migration Tool.

Between the Client Service, the Gateway Service, and the Migration Tool, Microsoft has assembled a nice set of capabilities for those contemplating a dual Novell/NT network. Get to know them and you can simplify your life as a schizophrenic network administrator.

File and Print Services for NetWare

You may be a "Novell-ean" at heart. You may have spent years of your life remembering the correct syntax to get around in the Novell environment. You might know what the slist, userlist, and map command do. And now someone is putting an NT server in your environment and messing up your grand design. If this is a worry for you, then you want to look at File and Print Services for NetWare (FPNW), an add-on utility available from both Microsoft and Novell. In fact, Microsoft now sells FPNW and DSMS together as "Services for NetWare" for $99. FPNW allows the administrator the ease of installation and administration that NT affords, while at the same time giving clients the ability to

- Load a Novell redirector on the client machine

- Access the NT server as if it were a NetWare server

Pre-Installation Notes

In order for the FPNW to function, you need to install the NWLINK IPX/SPX protocol stack on the system that will run the service. The NT server has to appear as a Novell server to your clients. In order to do this, it must run the protocol that NetWare supports.

When you install FPNW, it creates a folder called SYSVOL on your NT server. This folder becomes the "volume" that is advertised to the NetWare environment. You want to put this folder on an NTFS partition in order to be able to secure the data on this "volume" correctly. If you recall, in NT you can only set directory-level and file-level permissions on NTFS partitions. If you forget, NT reminds you during the installation of FPNW with a message box like the one in Figure 13.14.

FIGURE 13.14:

Reminder to set file permissions

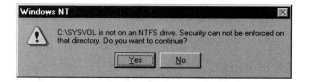

Installing File and Print Services for NetWare

To install FPNW:

1. Open My Computer.

2. Open Control Panel.

3. Double-click on the Network icon.

4. Open Services property page.

5. Click the Add button.

6. Choose File and Print Services for NetWare to install the service. The dialog box in Figure 13.15 appears.

FIGURE 13.15:

Install File and Print Services
for NetWare dialog box

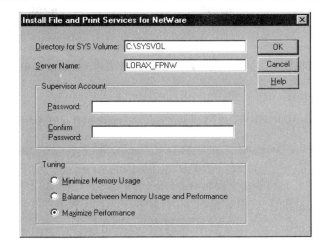

Here is how to fill out this dialog box:

Directory for SYS Volume   Enter the path for the folder known as SYSVOL.
This folder appears as SYSVOL on the NT server, but will be known as SYS to
the NT server that is masquerading as a NetWare server.

Server Name   Enter the name of the server as you wish it to appear to
Novell clients.

Supervisor Account   FPNW will create a new user on the NT server
known as Supervisor. The Supervisor account automatically has access to
the NT server via FPNW. Enter the password for the Supervisor account.
This password can be changed at any time.

Tuning Options   Like many network operating systems, NT would like
to store a lot of the logon information in the memory of the server. Additionally, NT wants to store software that is needed to run the FPNW service itself on the server. If you opt not to do this, then logon information as
well as the FPNW service will be stored on the hard disk, the result being
that logons may take longer and the entire service may run more slowly.
The tuning options give you a chance to determine how you would like to
handle the service. You can choose to store it all in memory for the fastest

performance by clicking on the Maximize Performance radio button. Of course, this leaves less memory for the other services on your NT server to use. You could, in contrast, choose to keep all of the information on the hard disk by clicking the Minimize Memory Usage option button. This option takes up no memory on the server, but logons take a little longer. Or you can choose to balance the information between the hard disk and memory by choosing the mid-range solution. To choose the mid-range solution, click the Balance between Memory Usage and Performance option button.

After you finish entering the information, click OK and NT creates a service account. This is the account your NT server logs in as. The name of the user will be FPNW Service Account. You will need to specify a password for this account in the dialog box shown in Figure 13.16. Please take note of the account password.

FIGURE 13.16:

Creating a password

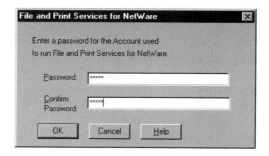

I hear you asking yourself, "When will this password be relevant?" Look at the services running on your system via Control Panel ➤ Services and look at the Start-up option for any of those services. Often there is a password associated with the service when it logs in. If you change the password under services and neglect to change the password for the actual account in User Manager (in our case the FPNW Service Account password), the service will not load. After you specify the password for the system account, you have to reboot your system in order for the changes to take effect.

When your system restarts, the FPNW service automatically starts. You are now ready to grant users access to the NT server by using FPNW.

In User Manager, which is shown in Figure 13.17, you will see that three new accounts have been created:

1. FPNW Service Account (user account)

2. Supervisor (user account)

3. Console Operators (group account)

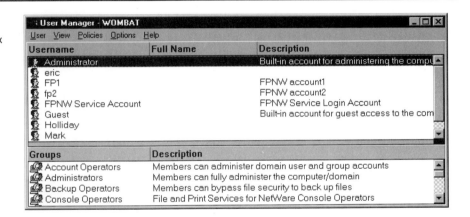

The first two accounts we have already discussed. The Console Operators group is a list of users who can perform administrative functions on the FPNW account both locally and remotely. In essence, this is a list of administrators of the FPNW service.

To grant users access to the NT server via FPNW, you need to edit their user accounts through User Manager. Because the FPNW service is active in the NT server, two new options appear on the New User property page: the Maintain NetWare Compatible Logon check box and the NW Compat button. You can see these new options in Figure 13.18. The NW Compat button is grayed out until you check the Maintain NetWare Compatible Login box.

FIGURE 13.18:

New User dialog box

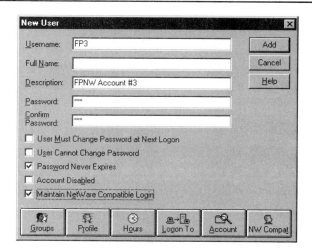

You can now click on the NW Compat button. When you do, you see the dialog box shown in Figure 13.19. This dialog box is for configuring the user's account to support FPNW.

FIGURE 13.19:

NetWare Compatible Properties dialog box

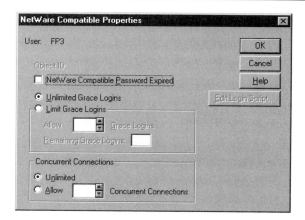

Notice the NetWare Compatible Password Expired check box. This option informs users when their passwords on NT Server are about to expire. The power of this feature is that users are being notified that their passwords are expiring on NT, even though they are logging on to NT using Novell client software. They can use the Setpass command to change their password on the NT server just as if it were a Novell server.

FPNW: A Client Machine's Perspective

In order for a client machine to access the NT Server running the FPNW service, all the client machine has to be running is the normal Novell redirector software. In Figure 13.20, you can see the server list you get by using the Novell command SLIST. FPNWSERVER is the NT server running FPNW.

FIGURE 13.20:

Server list provided by Novell

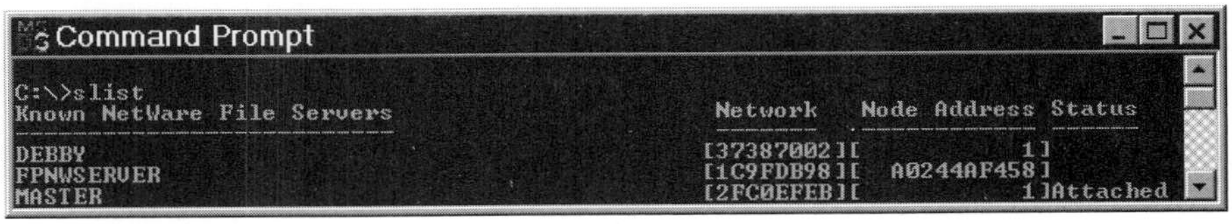

To log on to the NT server from a client, log on as you normally would a Novell server. The password that is provided is the password that was created through User Manager on the NT Server, as shown in Figure 13.21. The user has access to any resource shared in the SYSVOL folder that the user has permission to use.

FIGURE 13.21:

Novell password

Directory Service Manager for NetWare

One of the biggest headaches with managing a multiple-network environment is keeping track of all the user accounts that need to be administered. It is time-consuming to go through the process of adding new users to your environment and remembering all the different locations in which their accounts need to be built. Dealing with users who change their passwords in separate locations is even more time-consuming.

To assist you with this rather daunting administrative task, Microsoft provides the *Directory Service Manager for NetWare* (DSMN). This service allows you to synchronize your accounts on NetWare bindery with accounts on your NT server. DSMN does require you to load the Gateway Service for NetWare in order to function. If you haven't loaded it, you get the error message shown in Figure 13.22. (Installing the Gateway Service is discussed earlier in this chapter.)

FIGURE 13.22:

You get a message forcing you to install GSNW.

Pre-Installation Notes

DSMN requires that the Gateway Service for NetWare be running.

DSMN synchronizes NT accounts with bindery accounts on NetWare. As of this writing, it does not support NDS.

Installing DSMN

To install DSMN:

1. Open My Computer.

2. Open Control Panel.

3. Click on the Network icon.

4. Open the Services Property tab.

5. Click on the Add button.

6. Choose Directory Service Manager for NetWare to install the service. A screen similar to the one in Figure 13.23 appears.

FIGURE 13.23:

Install Directory Service
Manager for NetWare
dialog box

NT will create a new user account called SyncAgentAccount. This is the account that the DSMN service will use to log on to the NT server. You will be prompted to assign a password to this account, just as you were with the FPNW service account. If you change the password for this account, go into Control Panel ➤ Services and specify the new password in the startup property page of the service.

If you load FPNW ahead of DSMN, the warning message shown in Figure 13.24 appears. It informs you that any user accounts that you enabled with NetWare compatibility will not be transported automatically to the NetWare server. This is not a major concern as long as you are aware of this fact. You will be given an opportunity to transport users to NetWare as you continue the installation process of this service.

FIGURE 13.24:

DSMN warning message

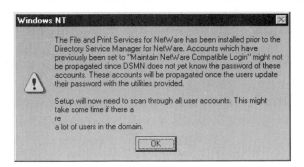

The next step in installing DSMN is to specify the NetWare server that you would like to synchronize accounts with. In Figure 13.25, the name of the NetWare server is Debby. A list of NetWare file servers should appear. Simply select the NetWare server with which you would like to synchronize.

FIGURE 13.25:

Select NetWare Server
dialog box

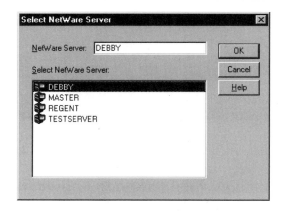

After selecting the NetWare server, you need to log on to the server with the supervisor account or with an account with supervisor authority. In Figure 13.26, I am logging in as Supervisor and have provided the password for the supervisor account on the NetWare server Debby.

FIGURE 13.26:

Logging on as Supervisor

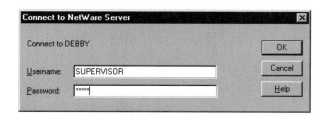

The next dialog box, shown in Figure 13.27, asks you for information about synchronizing your current NT and NetWare accounts. Here are the options:

User Must Change Password   You are beginning the process of moving NetWare users to NT. In the process, the one item that will not transfer is the password, because NetWare uses a proprietary encryption scheme. You can, however, force users to change their password the first time they log onto NT by selecting this option.

Add Supervisors to Administrators Group   By selecting this option, you can make all of the NetWare supervisors NT administrators.

Add File Server Console Operators to Console Operators Group   Along the same lines as the previous option, the NetWare File Console Operators will become part of the NT Console Operators Group that can administrate the server locally.

Synchronize Options   The bottom portion of the screen lets you explicitly state which NetWare accounts you would like to synchronize with NT (called here *propagate*). Every time one of the users changes a password on NT, NT automatically changes the password on NetWare. On the right-hand side of the screen you are given an opportunity to specify how you would like to transfer the passwords. I think that the option you choose is less relevant than forcing users to change their passwords the first time they log on to NT. With the DSMN service running, they will change their NT password and their NetWare password simultaneously.

FIGURE 13.27:

Propagate NetWare Accounts dialog box

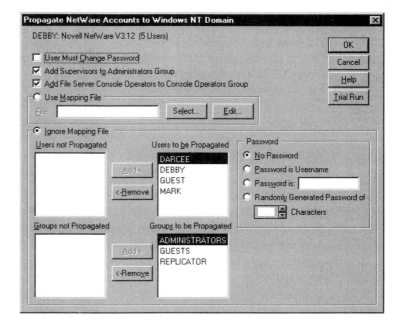

ASCII Text Files for Mapping

Some find the synchronization process easier if they put all of the information in an ASCII text file and have DSMN read that. DSMN refers to this ASCII file as a *mapping file,* and it is a valid method of specifying the NetWare account that you would like to synchronize. The format of the file is quite simple. There are three straightforward parameters separated by commas:

```
Current NetWare UserName, New NT Username, Password
```

Listing 13.1 shows an example of a map file.

Listing 13.1:   **Map File Example**

```
;SyncAgentV1.0
;From NetWare Server: DEBBY

[USERS]
;
; Format of each line:
;
; UserName [, New UserName] [, Password]
;    UserName - The user that is to be migrated from the NetWare server.
;    New UserName - The corresponding user name on Windows NT.
;           If this is blank, then the user name remains the same.
;    Password - The password of the user.
;
DARCEE, , DARCEE
DEBBY, , DEBBY
GUEST, , GUEST
MARK, , MARK

[GROUPS]
; Format of each line:
; GroupName
;    GroupName - The group that is to be migrated from the NetWare
server

ADMINISTRATORS
GUESTS
REPLICATOR
```

After you specify the users to be transferred (called here "propagated"), you need to perform a trial run. The trial run goes through the propagation process without actually creating or synchronizing accounts on NT. It just checks to see if you will encounter any problems when you perform the actual synchronization.

Listing 13.2 shows an example of a trial-run log file.

Listing 13.2:   **A Trial-Run Log File**

```
Directory Service Manager for NetWare: Account Propagation Log File
  From NetWare server: DEBBY
  To Windows NT server: \\TESTSERVER
  Summary:
    4 users were propagated.
    0 users failed to be propagated.
    1 existing Windows NT users' properties were changed.
    3 Windows NT users were added.
    0 users on the NetWare server were renamed.
    0 users were chosen not to be propagated.
    0 users' password were padded to the minimum password length.
    3 groups were propagated.
    0 groups failed to be propagated.
    0 groups added.
    0 groups were chosen not to be propagated.
  [USERS]
  DARCEE
    Added.
    New Password:
  DEBBY
    Added.
    New Password:
  GUEST
    Already exists.
    New Password:
  MARK
    Added.
    New Password:
  [GROUPS]
  ADMINISTRATORS
    Already exists.
```

```
GUESTS
    Already exists.
REPLICATOR
    Already exists.
```

NT will prompt you to back up the bindery on the NetWare server before conducting the actual propagation, as shown in Figure 13.28. Any time an external process accesses and makes changes to the bindery, there is a risk that the bindery will become corrupt and prevent people from logging onto the NetWare server. The risk is small, but why take the chance?

FIGURE 13.28:

Backup warning message

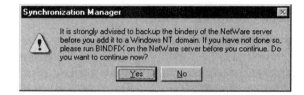

One Final Note...

Before we conclude our discussion on NT and NetWare compatibility, there is one issue that you should be aware of: NT clients accessing the NetWare servers. If you install the Client software for NetWare that comes with NT, you are given the option of processing the NetWare login script. The login scripts usually contain map statements like the following:

```
map z:=den02\sys:public
```

This command makes Z drive the public directory on a NetWare server known as DEN02. This would occur on most DOS client machines, but NT clients only map to the root directory, regardless of the actual map statements. That is to say, if you processed this same statement from an NT client, Z drive would be DEN02\SYS and not the public directory.

The fix for this is straightforward. Instead of using the MAP command, use the MAP ROOT command:

```
Map root z:=den02\sys:public
```

Now the public directory becomes the root directory of Z. If you want to get something from the public directory, simply go to the Z:\—the "root directory" of Z—and you will be in the public directory.

TCP/IP on Windows NT

- Understanding IP addressing

- Setting up and testing TCP/IP

- Using DHCP Servers

- Printing to network printers using IP

- Making your NT Server a mail relay agent using EMWACS

In the last few years, the term *TCP/IP* has moved from obscurity to a "must-know" concept. TCP/IP has become the *lingua franca* of networks, a network language (*transport protocol* is a more accurate term) like NetBEUI, SNA, IPX/SPX, or X.25, with one very important difference: most of these transport protocols are designed to work well either in a LAN environment *or* in a WAN environment, but not both. In contrast, TCP/IP can fill both needs, and that's one of its greatest strengths, as you'll see in this chapter.

This is a *big* chapter, so here is what to expect. In this chapter, I want to do several things:

- Explain what TCP/IP and the Internet are. You will also learn some of the mechanics of putting together networks to form intranets.

- Explore the options you have for setting up IP addresses and computer names: an older method that's a bit more work but is more compatible with other computers doing TCP/IP, and a newer method that incorporates two relatively new protocols called the Dynamic Host Configuration Protocol (DHCP) and the Windows Internet Naming System (WINS). I'll go over how to build an NT-based intranet both ways. I'll also show you how to set up an old standby, DNS (the Domain Naming Service).

- Introduce you to the "big three" of TCP/IP applications—Telnet, FTP, and Internet mail.

When you're done, you'll be at least *dangerous* in TCP/IP administration. As Microsoft says, "On the Internet, no one knows you're running NT."

A Brief History of TCP/IP

Let's start off by asking, "What *is* TCP/IP?" TCP/IP is a collection of software created over the years, much of it with the help of large infusions of government research money. Originally, TCP/IP was intended for the Department of Defense (DoD). You see, DoD tends to buy a *lot* of equipment, and much of that equipment is incompatible with other equipment. For example, back in the late '70s when the work that led to TCP/IP was first begun, it was nearly impossible to get an IBM mainframe to talk to a Burroughs mainframe. That was because the two computers were designed with entirely different *protocols*—something like Figure 14.1.

FIGURE 14.1:

Compatible hardware,
incompatible protocols

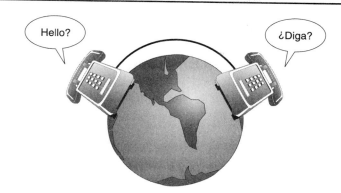

To get some idea of what the DoD was facing, imagine picking up the phone in the U.S. and calling someone in Spain. You have a perfectly good hardware connection, as the Spanish phone system is compatible with the American phone system. But despite the *hardware* compatibility, you face a *software* incompatibility. The person on the other end of the phone is expecting a different protocol, a different language. It's not that one language is better or worse than the other, but the English speaker cannot understand the Spanish speaker, and vice versa. Rather than force the Spanish speaker to learn English or the English speaker to learn Spanish, we can teach them both a "universal language" such as Esperanto, the "universal language" designed in 1888. If Esperanto were used in my telephone example, neither speaker would use it at home, but they would use it to communicate with each other.

That was how TCP/IP began—as a simple *alternative* communications language. As time went on, however, TCP/IP evolved into a mature, well-understood, robust set of protocols, and many sites adopted it as their *main* communication language.

Origins of TCP/IP: From the ARPANET to the Internet

The original DoD network wouldn't just hook up military sites, although that was an important goal of the first defense intranetwork. Much of the basic research in the U.S. was funded by an arm of the Defense Department called the Advanced Research Projects Agency, or ARPA. ARPA gave, and still gives, a lot of money to university researchers to study all kinds of things. ARPA thought it would be useful for these researchers to be able to communicate with one another, as well as with the Pentagon. Figures 14.2 and 14.3 demonstrate networking both before and after ARPANET implementation.

FIGURE 14.2:

Researchers before ARPANET

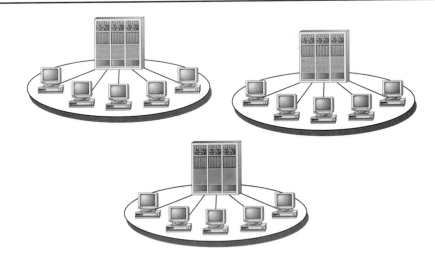

FIGURE 14.3:

Researchers after ARPANET

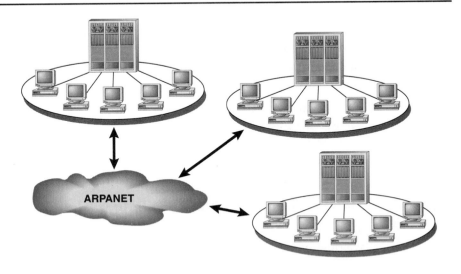

The new network, dubbed ARPANET, was designed and put in place by a private contractor called Bolt, Barenek and Newman. For the first time, it linked university professors both to themselves and to their military and civilian project leaders around the country. Because ARPANET was a network that linked separate private university networks and the separate military networks, it was a "network of networks."

ARPANET ran atop a protocol called the Network Control Protocol (NCP). NCP was later refined into two components, the Internet Protocol (IP) and the Transmission Control Protocol (TCP). The change from NCP to TCP/IP is the technical difference between ARPANET and the Internet. On 1 January 1983, ARPANET packet-switching devices stopped accepting NCP packets and only passed TCP/IP packets, so, in a sense, 1 January 1983 is the "official" birthday of the Internet.

ARPANET became the Internet after a few evolutions. Probably the first major development step occurred in 1974, when Vinton Cerf and Robert Kahn proposed the protocols that would become TCP and IP. (I say "probably" because the Internet didn't grow through a centralized effort, but rather through the largely disconnected efforts of a number of researchers, university professors, and graduate students, most of whom are still alive—and almost *all* of whom have a different perspective on what the "defining" aspects of Internet development were.) Over its more than 20-year history, the Internet and its predecessors have gone through several stages of growth and adjustment. Ten years ago, the Internet could only claim a few thousand users. When last I heard, five *million* computers and 100 million users were on the Internet. The Internet appears to double in size about every year. It can't do that indefinitely, but it's certainly a time of change for this huge network of networks.

Internet growth is fueled not by an esoteric interest in seeing how large a network the world can build, but rather by just a few applications that require the Internet to run. Perhaps most important is Internet e-mail, followed closely by the World Wide Web, and then the File Transfer Protocol (FTP)… but more on those later in this chapter.

Originally, the Internet protocols were intended to support connections between mainframe-based networks, which were basically the only ones that existed through most of the 1970s. But the 1980s saw the growth of Unix workstations, microcomputers, and minicomputers. The Berkeley version of Unix was built largely with government money, and the government said, "Put the TCP/IP protocol in that thing." There was some resistance at first, but adding IP as a built-in part of Berkeley Unix has helped both Unix and intranet working grow. The IP protocol was used on many of the Unix-based Ethernet networks that appeared in the 1980s and still exist to this day. As a matter of fact, you probably have to learn at least a smidgen of Unix to get around the Internet—but don't let that put you off. In this chapter, I'll teach you all the Unix you need and show you how much of the old Unix stuff can be fulfilled by NT.

In the mid-1980s, the National Science Foundation created five supercomputing centers and put them on the Internet. This served two purposes: it made supercomputers available to NSF grantees around the country, and it provided a major "backbone" for the Internet. The National Science Foundation portion of the network, called NSFNET, was for a long time the largest part of the Internet. It is now being superseded by the National Research and Education Network (NREN). For many years, commercial users were pretty much kept off the Internet, as most of the funding was governmental; you had to be invited to join the Net. But those restrictions have been relaxed and now the majority of Internet traffic is routed over commercially-run lines rather than government-run lines.

People now and then predict that the Internet will fall into decline "once the government privatizes it." That's a lot of wind and little substance. First of all, the Internet is *already* privatized for the most part. As time has passed, the concern about the Internet's death due to a lack of government funds has essentially become moot. As more commercial providers hook up with one another, more traffic goes over completely commercial routes than goes over government routes, at least in the continental U.S.

It's customary to refer to the Internet as the "Information Superhighway." I can understand why people say that; after all, it's a long-haul trucking service for data. But I think of it more as "Information Main Street." The Internet is growing because businesses are using it to get things done and to sell their wares. Much of this book was shipped back and forth on the Internet as it was being written. Heck, that sounds more like Main Street than it does like a highway.

If your company isn't on the Internet now, it will be… and soon. Remember when fax machines became popular in the early 1980s? Overnight people stopped saying, "Do you have a fax?" and just started saying, "What's your fax number?" It's getting so that if you don't have an Internet address, you're just not a person. For example, my Internet mail address is help@minasi.com.

Goals of TCP/IP's Design

But let's delve into some of the techie aspects of the Internet's main protocols. When DoD started building this set of network protocols, they had a few design goals. Understanding those design goals helps understand why it's worth making the effort to use TCP/IP in the first place. Its intended characteristics include

- Good failure recovery
- Ability to plug in new networks without disrupting services
- Ability to handle high error rates
- Independence from a particular vendor or type of network
- Very little data overhead

I'm sure no one had any idea how central those design goals would be to the amazing success of TCP/IP both in private intranets and in *the* Internet. Let's take a look at those design goals in more detail.

Good Failure Recovery   Remember, this was to be a *defense* network, so it had to work even if portions of the network hardware suddenly and without warning went off-line. That's kind of a nice way of saying the network had to work even if big pieces got nuked.

Can Plug In New Subnetworks "on the Fly"   This second goal is related to the first one. It says that it should be possible to bring entire new networks into an intranet—and here, again, *intranet* can mean your company's private intranet, or *the* Internet—without interrupting existing network service.

Can Handle High Error Rates   The next goal was that an intranet should be able to tolerate high or unpredictable error rates, and yet still provide a 100-percent reliable end-to-end service. If you're transferring data from Washington, DC, to Portland, Oregon, and the links that you're currently using through Oklahoma get destroyed by a tornado, then any data lost in the storm will be re-sent and rerouted via some other lines.

Host Independence   As I mentioned before, the new network architecture should work with any kind of network, and not be dedicated or tied to any one vendor.

This is essential in the '90s. The days of "We're just an IBM shop" or "We only buy Novell stuff" are gone for many and going fast for others. (Let's hope that it doesn't give way to "We only buy Microsoft software.") Companies must be able to live in a multivendor world.

Very Little Data Overhead The last goal was for the network protocols to have as little overhead as possible. To understand this, let's compare TCP/IP to other protocols. While no one knows what protocol will end up being *the* world protocol 20 years from now—if any protocol *ever* gets that much acceptance—one of TCP/IP's rivals is a set of protocols built by the International Standards Organization, or ISO. ISO has some standards that are very similar to the kinds of things that TCP/IP does, standards named X.25 and TP4. But every protocol packages its data with an extra set of bytes, kind of like an envelope. The vast majority of data packets using the IP protocol (and I promise, I *will* explain soon how it is that TCP and IP are actually two very different protocols, and a bit of what those protocols are) have a simple, fixed-size 20-byte header. The maximum size that the header can be is 60 bytes, if all possible options are enabled. The fixed 20 bytes always appears as the first 20 bytes of the packet. In contrast, X.25 uses dozens of possible headers, with no appreciable fixed portion to it. But why should *you* be concerned about overhead bytes? Really for one reason only: performance. Simpler protocols mean faster transmission and packet switching— and we'll take up packet switching a little later.

But enough about the Internet for now. Let's stop and define something that I've been talking about—namely, just what *are* TCP and IP?

Originally, TCP/IP was just a set of protocols that could hook up dissimilar computers and transfer information between them. But it grew into a large number of protocols that have become collectively known as the *TCP/IP suite*.

The Internet Protocol (IP)

The most basic part of the Internet is the Internet Protocol, or IP. If you want to send data over an intranet, then that data must be packaged in an IP packet. That packet is then *routed* from one part of the intranet to another.

A Simple Internet

IP is supposed to allow messages to travel from one part of a network to another. How does it do this?

An intranet is made of at least two *sub*-nets. The notion of a subnet is built upon the fact that most popular LAN architectures (Ethernet, Token Ring, and ARCNet) are based on something very much like a radio broadcast. Everyone on the same Ethernet segment hears all of the traffic on their segment, just as each device on a given ring in a Token Ring network must examine every message that goes through the network. The trick that makes an Ethernet or a Token Ring work is that while each station *hears* everything, each station knows how to ignore all messages save for the ones intended for it.

You may have never realized it, but that means that in a single Ethernet segment or a single Token Ring ring there is *no routing*. If you've ever sat through one of those interminable explanations of the ISO seven-layer network model, then you know that in network discussions much is made of the *network layer*, which in ISO terms is merely the routing layer. And yet a simple Ethernet or Token Ring never has to route. There are no routing decisions to make; everything is heard by everybody. (Your network adapter filters out any traffic not destined for you, in case you're wondering.)

But now suppose you have *two* separate Ethernets connected to each other, as you see in Figure 14.4.

FIGURE 14.4:

Multisegment intranet

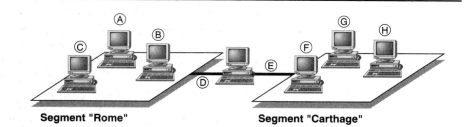

Segment "Rome"   Segment "Carthage"

In Figure 14.4, you see two Ethernet segments, named Rome and Carthage. (I was getting tired of the "shipping" and "finance" examples that everyone uses.) There are three computers that reside solely in Rome that I've labeled A, B, and C. Three more computers reside in Carthage, labeled F, G, and H.

Subnets and Routers

Much of intranet architecture is built around the observation that PCs A, B, and C can communicate directly with each other, and PCs F, G, and H can communicate directly with each other, but A, B, and C *cannot* communicate with F, G, and H without some help from the machine containing Ethernet cards D and E. That

D/E machine will function as a *router*, a machine that allows communication between different network segments. A, B, C, and D could be described as being in each others' "broadcast range," as could E, F, G, and H. What I've just called a broadcast range is called more correctly in intranet terminology a *subnet*, which is a collection of machines that can communicate with each other without the need for routing.

For example, F and H can communicate directly without having to ask the router (E, in their case) to forward the message, and so they're on the same subnet. A and C can communicate directly without having to ask the router (D, in their case) to forward the message, and so they're on the same subnet. But if B wanted to talk to G, it would have to first send the message to D, asking, "D, please get this to G," so they're not on the same subnet.

IP Addresses and Ethernet Addresses

Before continuing, let's briefly discuss the labels A, B, C, and so on, and how those labels actually are manifested in an intranet. Each computer on this net is attached to the net via an Ethernet board, and each Ethernet board on an intranet has two addresses: an *IP address* and an *Ethernet address*. (There are, of course, other ways to get onto an intranet than via Ethernet, but let's stay with the Ethernet example, as it's the most common one on TCP/IP intranets.)

Ethernet Addresses

Each Ethernet board's Ethernet address is a unique 48-bit identification code. If it sounds unlikely that every Ethernet board in the world has a unique address, then consider that 48 bits offers 280,000,000,000,000 possibilities. Ethernet itself only uses about one quarter of those possibilities (two bits are set aside for administrative functions), but that's still a lot of possible addresses. In any case, the important thing to get here is that a board's Ethernet address is predetermined and hard-coded into the board. Ethernet addresses, which are also called Media Access Control (MAC) addresses (it's got nothing to do with Macintoshes) are expressed in twelve hex digits. (*MAC address* is synonymous with *Token Ring address* or *Ethernet address*.) For example, the Ethernet card on the computer I'm working at now has MAC (Ethernet) address 0020AFF8E771 or, as it's sometimes written, 00-20-AF-F8-E7-71. The addresses are centrally administered, and Ethernet chip vendors must purchase blocks of addresses. In the example of my workstation, you know that it's got a 3Com Ethernet card because the Ethernet (MAC) address is 00-20-AF; that prefix is owned by 3Com.

NOTE   You can see an NT machine's MAC address in a number of ways. You can type **net config workstation** or **net config server** (it's the string of hex in parentheses), or run Windows NT Diagnostics and click Network ➤ Transports.

IP Addresses and Quad Format

In contrast to the 48 bits in a MAC address, an IP address is a 32-bit value. IP addresses are numbers set at a workstation (or server) by a network administrator—they're not a hard-coded hardware kind of address, unlike the Ethernet address. That means that there are four billion distinct Internet addresses.

It's nice that there's room for lots of machines, but having to remember—or having to tell someone else—a 32-bit address is no fun. Imagine having to say to a network support person "just set up the machines on the subnet to use a default router address of 10101110100-10101010101100010111." Hmmm… doesn't sound like much fun—we need a more human-friendly way to express 32-bit numbers. That's where *dotted quad* notation comes from.

For simplicity's sake, IP addresses are usually represented as *w.x.y.z*, where *w*, *x*, *y*, and *z* are all decimal values between 0 and 255. For example, the IP address of the machine that I'm currently writing this at is 199.34.57.53. Each of the four numbers is called a *quad*; as they're connected by dots, it's called *dotted quad* notation.

Each of the numbers in the dotted quad corresponds to eight bits of an Internet address. (*IP address* and *Internet address* are synonymous.) As the value for eight bits can range from 0 to 255, each value in a dotted quad can be from 0 to 255. For example, to convert an IP address of 11001010000011111010101000000001 into dotted quad format, it would first be broken up into eight-bit groups:

    11001010   00001111   10101010   00000001

And each of those eight-bit numbers would be converted to their decimal equivalent. (If you're not comfortable with binary-to-decimal conversion, don't worry about it: just load the NT Calculator, click View, then Scientific, and then press the F8 key to put the Calculator in binary mode. Enter the binary number, press F6, and the number will be converted to decimal for you.) Our number converts as follows:

11001010   00001111   10101010   00000001
202   15   170   1

which results in a dotted quad address of 202.15.170.1.

So, to re-cap: each of these computers has at least one Ethernet card in it, and that Ethernet card has a predefined address. The network administrator of this network has gone around and installed IP software on these PCs, and, in the process, has assigned IP addresses to each of them. (Note, by the way, that the phrase "has assigned IP addresses to each of them" may not be true if you are using the Dynamic Host Configuration Protocol, or DHCP. For the first part of this chapter, however, I'm going to assume that you're not using DHCP and that someone must hand-assign an IP address to each Ethernet card.)

Let me redraw our intranet, adding totally arbitrary IP addresses and Ethernet addresses, as shown in Figure 14.5.

FIGURE 14.5:

Two-subnet intranet with Ethernet and IP addresses

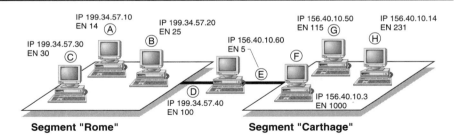

Segment "Rome"   Segment "Carthage"

IP Routers

Now let's return to the computer in the middle. It is part of *both* segments. How do I get one computer to be part of two networks? By putting two Ethernet cards in the computer in the middle. (A computer with more than one network card in it is called a *multihomed* computer.) One of the Ethernet cards is on the Rome subnet, and the other is on the Carthage subnet. (By the way, each computer on an intranet is called a *host* in TCP-ese.)

Now, each Ethernet card must get a separate IP address, so, as a result, the computer in the middle has *two* IP addresses, D and E. If a message is transmitted in Rome, then adapter D hears it, and E doesn't. Then, if a message is transmitted in Carthage, then adapter E hears it, but D doesn't.

How would we build an intranet from these two subnets? How could station A, for example, send a message to station G? Obviously, the only way that message will get from A to G is if the message is received on the Ethernet adapter with address D, and then re-sent out over the Ethernet adapter with address E. Once E re-sends the message, G will hear it, as it is on the same network as E.

In order for this to work, the machine containing boards D and E must be smart enough to perform this function whereby it re-sends data between D and E when necessary. Such a machine is, by definition, an *IP router*. It is possible with Windows NT to use an NT computer—any NT computer, not just an NT Server computer—to act as an IP router, as you'll learn later.

Under IP, the sending station (A, in this case) examines the address of the destination (G, in this case) and realizes that it does not know how to get to G. (I'll explain exactly *how* it knows that in a minute.) Now, if A has to send something to an address that it doesn't understand, then it uses a kind of "catchall" address called the *default router* or, for historical reasons, the *default gateway* address. A's network administrator has already configured A's default router as D, so A sends the message to D. Once D gets the message, it then sees that the message is not destined for itself, but rather for G, and so it resends the message from board E.

Routing in More Detail

Now let's look a little closer at how that message gets from A to G. Each computer, as you've already seen, has one *or more* IP addresses. It's important to understand that there is no relationship whatsoever between an Ethernet card's address and the IP address associated with it: the Ethernet MAC address is hardwired into the card by the card's manufacturer, and the IP addresses are assigned by a network administrator.

But now examine the IP addresses, and you'll see a pattern to them. Rome's addresses all look like 199.34.57.x, where x is some number, and Carthage's addresses all look like 156.40.10.x, where, again, x can be any number. The Ethernet addresses follow no rhyme or reason and are grouped by the board's manufacturer. That similarity of addresses within Rome and Carthage will be important in understanding routing.

Now, let's re-examine how the message gets from A to G.

1. The IP software in A first says, "How do I get this message to G—can I just broadcast it, or must it be routed?" The way that it makes that decision is by finding out whether or not G is on the same *subnet* as A is. A subnet is simply a broadcast area. Host A then, is asking, "Is G part of Rome, like me?"

2. Station A determines that it is on a different subnet from station G by examining their addresses. A knows that it has address 199.34.57.10, and it must send its message to 156.40.10.50. A has a simple rule for this: if the destination address looks like 199.34.57.*x*, where, again, *x* can be any value, then the destination is in the same subnet, and so requires no routing. On the other hand, 156.40.10.50 is clearly *not* in the same subnet.

    If, on the other hand, G *had* been on the same subnet, then A would have "shouted" the IP packet straight to G, referring specifically to its IP and Ethernet address.

3. So station A can't directly send its IP packets to G. A then looks for another way. When A's network administrator set up A's IP software, she told A the IP address of A's *default router*. The default router is basically the address that says, "If you don't know where to send something, send it to me, and I'll try to get it there." A's default router is D.

    A then sends an Ethernet frame from itself to D. The Ethernet frame contains this information:

    - Source Ethernet address: 14
    - Destination Ethernet address: 100
    - Source IP address: 199.34.57.10
    - Destination IP address: 156.40.10.50

4. Ethernet card D receives the frame and hands it to the IP software running in its PC. The PC sees that the IP destination address is not *its* IP address, so the PC knows that it must route this IP packet. Examining the subnet, the PC sees that the destination lies on the subnet that Ethernet adapter E is on, so it sends out a frame from Ethernet adapter E, with this information:

    - Source Ethernet address: 5
    - Destination Ethernet address: 115

- Source IP address: 199.34.57.10

- Destination IP address: 156.40.10.50

5. G then gets the packet. By looking at the Ethernet and IP addresses, G can see that it got this frame from E, but the original message really came from another machine, the 199.34.57.10 machine.

That's a simple example of how IP routes, but its algorithms are powerful enough to serve as the backbone for a network as large as the Internet.

TIP   There are different kinds of routing algorithms in TCP/IP. Windows NT only supports the simplest routing approaches: *static routes* and the Routing Internet Protocol (RIP). NT does not support the more robust protocols, like the Open Shortest Path First (OSPF) or External Gateway Protocol (EGP). You either need third-party software, or a dedicated hardware router to build large, complex intranets with NT. But NT can route adequately in a small to medium-sized intranet.

A, B, and C Networks, CIDR Blocks, and Subnetting

Before leaving IP routing, let's take a more specific look at subnets and IP addresses.

The whole idea behind the 32-bit IP addresses is to make it relatively simple to segment the task of managing the Internet or, for that matter, *any* intranet.

To become part of the Internet, contact the Network Information Center, or NIC; its e-mail address is hostmaster@rs.internic.net, or you can get them at (703) 742-4777 from 7 A.M. through 7 P.M. Eastern time, or point your Web browser to www.internic.net.

A-, B-, and C-Class Networks

The NIC assigns a company a block of IP addresses according to that company's size. Big companies get A-class networks (there are none left; they've all been given out), medium-sized companies get B-class networks (we're out of those, too), and others get C-class networks (they're still available). Although there are three network classes, there are five kinds of IP addresses, as you'll see in Figure 14.6.

FIGURE 14.6:

Internet network classes and reserved addresses

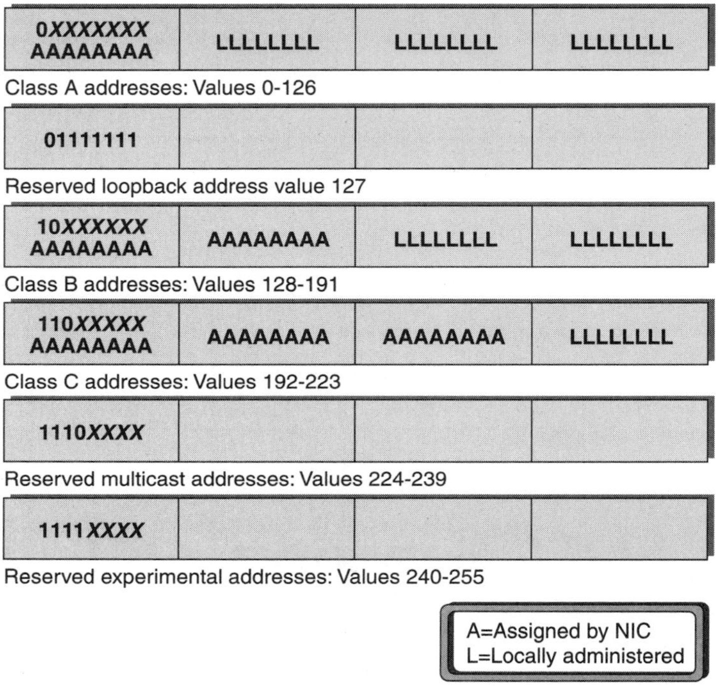

0XXXXXXX AAAAAAAA	LLLLLLLL	LLLLLLLL	LLLLLLLL

Class A addresses: Values 0-126

01111111			

Reserved loopback address value 127

10XXXXXX AAAAAAAA	AAAAAAAA	LLLLLLLL	LLLLLLLL

Class B addresses: Values 128-191

110XXXXX AAAAAAAA	AAAAAAAA	AAAAAAAA	LLLLLLLL

Class C addresses: Values 192-223

1110XXXX			

Reserved multicast addresses: Values 224-239

1111XXXX			

Reserved experimental addresses: Values 240-255

A=Assigned by NIC
L=Locally administered

Because it seemed, in the early days of the Internet, that four billion addresses left plenty of space for growth, the original designers were a bit sloppy. They defined three classes of networks of the Internet: large networks, medium-sized networks, and small networks. The creators of the Internet used 8-bit sections of the 32-bit addresses to delineate the difference between different classes of networks.

A-class networks   A large network would have its first eight bits set by the NIC, and the network's internal administrators could set the remaining 24 bits. The left-most eight bits could have values between 0 and 126, allowing for 127 class A networks. Companies like IBM get these, and there are only 127 of these addresses. As only eight bits have been taken, 24 remain; that means that class A networks can contain up to 2 to the 24th power, or 16 million hosts. Examples of A-class nets are BBN (1.0.0.0), General

Electric (3.0.0.0), Hewlett-Packard (16.0.0.0), Apple (17), Columbia University (15), Xerox (13), IBM (9), DEC (16), and M.I.T. (18).

B-class networks   Medium-sized networks have the left-most *16* bits preassigned to them, leaving 16 bits for local use. Class B addresses always have the values 128 through 191 in their first quad, then a value between 0 and 255 in their second quad. There are then 16,384 possible class B networks. Each of them can have up to 65,535 hosts. Microsoft and Exxon are examples of companies with B-class networks.

C-class networks   Small networks have the left-most *24* bits preassigned to them, leaving only 8 bits for local administration (which is bad, as it means that class C networks can't have more than 254 hosts), but, as the NIC has 24 bits to work with, it can easily give out class C network addresses (which is good). Class C addresses start off with a value between 192 and 223. As the second and third quads can be any value between 0 and 255, that means that there can potentially be 2,097,152 class C networks. (That's what our network, mmco.com, is.) The last C network, when it's assigned, will be 223.255.255.*x*; remember that the owner of that network will be able to control only *x*.

Reserved addresses   A number of addresses are reserved for multicast purposes and for experimental purposes, so they can't be assigned for networks. In particular, address 224.0.0.0 is set aside for *multicasts*, network transmissions to groups of computers.

More and more people have two kinds of IP addresses: addresses used in their company's *internal* Internet (or "intranet," as many say nowadays) and a range of "official" Internet addresses obtained from the central authority that hands out Internet addresses, the InterNIC. How to choose addresses for one's intranet?

You could, of course, just make up any old IP addresses that you feel like; as long as your intranet-to-Internet connection devices are configured properly, there shouldn't be any problem. But if you want your intranet to conform to Internet standards, then you should use numbers from a set of IP addresses set aside for "non-routed" applications—that is, intranets. Specified in RFC 1918, this range of addresses is:

- 10.0.0.0–10.255.255.255

- 172.16.0.0–172.31.255.255

- 192.168.0.0–192.168.255.255

So, for example, suppose your firm had obtained a C-class address range from the InterNIC: 256 addresses. Although you have thousands of computers, the fact that there are only 256 addresses is no problem, as the vast majority of your computers don't need direct Internet access. But for the others, you assign values in the 10.0.0.0 network. Packets from them won't be routed over the Internet—they'll be rejected if they manage to get to an Internet router—but assigning values in the 10.0.0.0 network will make configuring your intranet-to-Internet devices easier, as they usually assume that you'll be using an RFC 1918–compliant set of addresses.

You Can't Use *All* of the Numbers

There are some special rules to intranet names, however. There's a whole bunch of numbers that you can never give to a machine. They're called the loopback address, the network number, the broadcast address, and the default router address.

The Loopback Address   The address 127.0.0.1 is reserved as a loopback. If you send a message to 127.0.0.1, then it should be returned to you, unless there's something wrong on the network. And so no network has an address 127.xxxxxxxx .xxxxxxxx.xxxxxxxx, an unfortunate waste of 24 million addresses.

The Network Number   Sometimes you need to refer to an entire subnet with a single number. Thus far, I've said things like "My C network is 199.34.57.x, and I can make x range from 0 to 255." I was being a bit lazy; I didn't want to write "199.34.57.0 through 199.34.57.255," so I said "199.34.57.x."

It's not proper IP-ese to refer to a range of network addresses that way. And it's necessary to have an official way to refer to a range of addresses.

For example, to tell a router, "To get this message to the subnet that ranges from 100.100.100.0 through 100.100.100.255, first route to the router at 99.98.97.103," you've got to have some way to designate the range of addresses 100.100.100.0–100.100.100.255. We could have just used two addresses with a hyphen between them, but that's a bit cumbersome. Instead, the address that ends in all binary zeros is reserved as the *network number*, the TCP/IP name for the range of addresses in a subnet. In my 100.100.100.x example, the shorthand way to refer to 100.100.100.0 through 100.100.100.255 is "100.100.100.0."

Notice that this means you would never use the address 100.100.100.0—you never give that IP address to a machine under TCP/IP.

For example, to tell that router, "To get this message to the subnet that ranges from 100.100.100.0 through 100.100.100.255, first route to the router at 99.98.97.103," you would type something like **route add 100.100.100.0 99.98.97.103**. (Actually, you'd type a bit more information, and I'll get to that in the upcoming section on using your NT machine as a router, but this example gives you the idea.)

IP Broadcast Address

There's another reserved address, as well—the TCP/IP broadcast address. It looks like the address of one machine, but it isn't; it's the address you'd use to broadcast to each machine on a subnet. That address is all binary ones.

For example, on a simple C-class subnet, the broadcast address would be *x.y.z*.255. When would you need to know this? Some IP software needs this when you configure it; most routers require the broadcast address (as well as the network number). So if I just use my C-class network 199.34.57.0 (see how convenient that .0 thing is?) as a single subnet, then the broadcast address for my network would be 199.34.57.255.

Default Router Address

Every subnet has at least one router; after all, if it didn't have a router, then the subnet couldn't talk to any other networks, and it wouldn't be an intranet.

By convention, the first address after the network number is the default gateway (router) address. For example, on a simple C-class network, the address of the router should be *x.y.z*.1. This is not, by the way, a hard-and-fast rule like the network number and the IP broadcast address—it is, instead, a convention.

Suppose you have just been made the proud owner of a C-class net, 222.210.34.0. You can put 253 computers on your network, as you must not use 222.210.34.0, which describes the entire network; 222.210.34.255, which will be your broadcast address; and 222.210.34.1, which will be used either by you or your Internet service provider for a router address between your network and the rest of the Internet.

Now, once you get a range of addresses from the NIC, then you are said to have an *IP domain*. (*Domain* in Internet lingo has nothing to do with domain in the NT security sense.) For example, my IP domain (which is named mmco.com, but we'll cover names in a minute) uses addresses in the 199.34.57.0 network, and I can have as many NT domains in there as I like. However, from the point of view of the outside Internet, all of my NT domains are just one Internet domain: mmco.com.

Subnet Masks

If you had a trivially small intranet, one with just one subnet, then all the devices in your network can simply transmit directly to each other, and no routing is required. (If you actually had a network like this, then TCP/IP is overkill, and you probably should use NetBEUI instead.) On the other hand, you may have a domain so large that using broadcasting to communicate within it would be unworkable, requiring you to subnet your domain further. Consider IBM's situation, with an A-class network that can theoretically support 16 million hosts. Managing *that* network cries out for routers. For this reason, it may be necessary for your IP software on your PC to route data over a router even if it's staying within your company. Let's ask again, and in more detail this time, "How does a machine know whether to route or not?"

That's where subnets are important. Subnets make it possible, as you've seen, for a host (a PC) to determine whether it can just lob a message straight over to another host, or if it must go through routers. You can tell a host's IP software how to distinguish whether or not another host is in the same subnet through the *subnet mask*.

Recall that all of the IP addresses in Rome looked like 199.34.57.*x*, where *x* was a number between 1 and 255. You could then say that all co-members of the Rome subnet are defined as the hosts whose first three quads match. Now, on some subnets, it might be possible that the only requirement for membership in the same subnet would be that the first *two* quads be the same—a company that decided for some reason to make its entire B-class network a single subnet would be one example of that. (Yes, they *do* exist: I've seen firms that make a single subnet out of a B-class, with the help of some bizarre smart bridges. And no, I don't recommend it.)

When a computer is trying to figure out whether the IP address that it owns is on the same subnet as the place that it's trying to communicate with, then a subnet mask answers the question, "Which bits must match for us to be on the same subnet?"

IP does that with a *mask*, a combination of ones and zeros like so:

```
11111111 11111111 11111111 00000000
```

Here's how a host would use this mask. The host with IP address 199.34.57.10 (station A in the earlier figure) wants to know if it is on the same subnet as the host with IP address 199.34.57.20 (station B in the earlier figure). 199.34.57.10, expressed in binary, is 11000111 00100010 00111001 00001010. The IP address for B is, in binary, 11000111 00100010 00111001 00010100. The IP software in A then compares its own IP address to B's IP address. Look at them right next to each other:

```
11000111 00100010 00111001 00001010 A's address
11000111 00100010 00111001 00010100 B's address
```

The left-most 27 bits match, as does the right-most bit. Does that mean they're in the same subnet? Again, for the two addresses to be in the same subnet, certain bits must match—the ones with "1s" in the subnet mask. Let's stack up the subnet mask, A's address, and B's address to make this clearer.

```
11111111 11111111 11111111 00000000 the subnet mask
11000111 00100010 00111001 00001010 A's address
11000111 00100010 00111001 00010100 B's address
```

Look down from each of the 1s on the subnet mask, and you see that A and B match at each of those positions. Under the 0s in the subnet mask A and B match up sometimes, but not all the time. In fact, it doesn't matter whether or not A and B match in the positions under the 0s in the subnet mask—the fact that there are 0s there means that whether or not they match is irrelevant.

How do you know what value to use for a subnet mask? Well, if you have a class C number, and all of your workstations are on a single subnet, then you have a case like the one we just saw: a subnet mask of 11111111 11111111 11111111 00000000 which, in dotted quad terminology, is 255.255.255.0. Remember that by definition the fact that I have a C network means that the InterNIC has "nailed down" the left-most or top three quads (24 bits), leaving me only the right-most quad (8 bits). Since all of my addresses must match in the left-most 24 bits and I can do anything I like with the bottom 8 bits, my subnet mask must be 11111111111111111111111100000000 or 255.255.255.0.

That, however, assumes that I'll use my entire C network as one big subnet. Instead, I might decide to break one C-class network into two subnets. I could decide that all the numbers from 1 to 127—00000001 to 01111111—are subnet 1, and the numbers from 128 to 255—10000000 to 11111111—are subnet 2. In that case, the values inside my subnets will only vary in the last seven bits, rather than (as in the previous example) varying in the last *eight* bits. The subnet mask would be, then, 11111111 11111111 11111111 10000000, or 255.255.255.128.

The first subnet is a range of addresses from *x.y.z*.0 through *x.y.z*.127, where "x.y.z" are the quads that the NIC assigned me. The second subnet is the range from *x.y.z*.128 through *x.y.z*.255.

Now let's find the network number, default router address, and broadcast address. The network number is the first number in each range, so the first subnet's network number is *x.y.z*.0 and the second's is *x.y.z*.128. The default router address is just the second address in the range, which is *x.y.z*.1 and *x.y.z*.129 for the two subnets. The broadcast address is then the *last* address in both cases, *x.y.z*.127 and *x.y.z*.255 respectively.

Subnetting a C-Class Network

If you're going to break down your subnets smaller than C-class, then having to figure out the subnet mask, network number, broadcast address, and router address can get kind of confusing. Table 14.1 summarizes how you can break a C-class network down into one, two, four, or eight smaller subnets, with the attendant subnet masks, network numbers, broadcast addresses, and router addresses. I've assumed that you are starting from a C-class address, so you'll only be working with the fourth quad. The first three quads I have simply designated *x.y.z*.

TABLE 14.1: Breaking a C-Class Network into Subnets

Number of Desired Subnets	Subnet Mask	Network Number	Router Address	Broadcast Address	Remaining Number of IP Addresses
1	255.255.255.0	*x.y.z*.0	*x.y.z*.1	*x.y.z*.255	253
2	255.255.255.128	*x.y.z*.0	*x.y.z*.1	*x.y.z*.127	125
	255.255.255.	*x.y.z*.128	*x.y.z*.129	*x.y.z*.255	125
4	255.255.255.192	*x.y.z*.0	*x.y.z*.1	*x.y.z*.63	61
	255.255.255.	*x.y.z*.64	*x.y.z*.65	*x.y.z*.127	61

Continued on next page

TABLE 14.1 CONTINUED: Breaking a C-Class Network into Subnets

Number of Desired Subnets	Subnet Mask	Network Number	Router Address	Broadcast Address	Remaining Number of IP Addresses
	255.255.255.	x.y.z.128	x.y.z.129	x.y.z.191	61
	255.255.255.	x.y.z.192	x.y.z.193	x.y.z.255	61
8	255.255.255.224	x.y.z.0	x.y.z.1	x.y.z.31	29
	255.255.255.	x.y.z.32	x.y.z.33	x.y.z.63	29
	255.255.255.	x.y.z.64	x.y.z.65	x.y.z.95	29
	255.255.255.	x.y.z.96	x.y.z.97	x.y.z.127	29
	255.255.255.	x.y.z.128	x.y.z.129	x.y.z.159	29
	255.255.255.	x.y.z.160	x.y.z.161	x.y.z.191	29
	255.255.255.	x.y.z.192	x.y.z.193	x.y.z.223	29
	255.255.255.	x.y.z.224	x.y.z.225	x.y.z.255	29

For example, suppose you want to chop up a C-class network, 200.211.192.*x*, into two subnets. As you see in the table, you'd use a subnet mask of 255.255.255.128 for each subnet. The first subnet would have network number 200.211.192.0, router address 200.211.192.1, and broadcast address 200.211.192.127. You could assign IP addresses 200.211.192.2 through 200.211.192.126, 125 different IP addresses. (Notice that heavily subnetting a network results in the loss of a greater and greater percentage of addresses to the network number, broadcast address, and router address.) The second subnet would have network number 200.211.192.128, router address 200.211.192.129, and broadcast address 200.211.192.255.

In case you're wondering, it is entirely possible to subnet further, into 16 subnets of 13 hosts apiece (remember you always lose three numbers for the network number, router address, and broadcast address) or 32 subnets of 5 hosts apiece, but at that point, you're losing an awful lot of addresses to IP overhead.

I should note that in some cases, subnetting won't work the way I've said that it does. Suppose I chop up my C network using the 255.255.255.192 subnet mask. I've said that this gives me four subnets: 199.34.57.0, 199.34.57.64, 199.34.57.128, and 199.34.57.192. You can set up the network like that, and in every case I've ever encountered, things will work fine. But there may be cases where you'll run into trouble, so it's fair to warn you that RFC 950, the RFC that defines how to subnet an IP network, says this:

> In certain contexts, it is useful to have fixed addresses with functional significance rather than as identifiers of specific hosts. When such usage is called for, the address zero is to be interpreted as meaning "this," as in "this network." The address of all ones are to be interpreted as meaning "all," as in "all hosts." For example, the address 128.9.255.255 could be interpreted as meaning "all hosts on the network 128.9." Or, the address 0.0.0.37 could be interpreted as meaning "host 37 on this network." It is useful to preserve and extend the interpretation of these special addresses in subnetted networks. This means the values of all zeros and all ones in the subnet field should not be assigned to actual (physical) subnets. In the example above, the 6-bit wide subnet field may have any value except 0 and 63.

What this means in English is this: RFC 950 says to use neither the first subnet nor the last subnet. Thus, if you're going to be completely RFC-compliant (which is never a bad idea), you would *not* be able to use subnets 199.34.57.0 and 199.34.57 .192. And my earlier example of dividing 199.34.57.0 into two subnets by using subnet mask 255.255.255.128 would not work at all.

Should you care? If you're using modern routers or NT machines for routers, you won't run into trouble using all possible subnets. But if you've got some routers that are sticklers for the rules (or if you're taking a certification test on IP routing), you might cause trouble by using those other subnets. It's kind of a shame, as the 255.255.255.192 subnet for a C network yields four 62-address subnets, and staying strictly RFC compliant means you only get *two* 62-address subnets.

Classless Internetwork Domain Routing (CIDR)

Now that we've gotten past some of the fine points of subnet masks, let me elaborate on what you see if you ever go to the InterNIC looking for a domain of your own.

The shortage of IP addresses has led the InterNIC to curtail giving out A-, B-, or C-class addresses. Many small companies need an Internet domain, but giving them a C network is overkill, as a C network contains 256 addresses and many small firms only have a dozen or so computers that they want on the Internet. Large companies may also want a similarly small presence on the Internet: for reasons of security, they may not want to put all of the PCs (or other computers) on the Internet, but rather on an internal network not attached to the Internet. These companies *do* need a presence on the Internet, however—for their e-mail servers, FTP servers, Web servers, and the like—so they need a dozen or so addresses. But, again, giving them an entire 256-address C network is awfully wasteful. But, until 1994, it was the smallest block that the NIC could hand out.

Similarly, some companies need a few hundred addresses—more than 256, but not very many more. Such a firm is too big for a C network, but a bit small for the 65,536 addresses of a B network. More flexibility here would be useful.

For that reason, the InterNIC now gives out addresses without the old A-, B-, or C-class restrictions. This newer method that the InterNIC uses is called Classless Internet Domain Routing, or CIDR, pronounced "cider." CIDR networks are described as "slash *x*" networks, where the *x* is a number representing the number of bits in the IP address range that the InterNIC controls.

If you had an A-class network, then the InterNIC controlled the top 8 bits, and you controlled the bottom 24. If you decided somehow to take your A-class network and make it one big subnet, then what would be your subnet mask? Since all of your A network would be one subnet, you'd only have to look at the top quad to see if the source and destination addresses were on the same subnet. For example, if you had network 4.0.0.0, then addresses 4.55.22.81 and 4.99.63.88 would be on the same subnet. (Please note that I can't actually imagine anyone doing this with an A-class net; I'm just trying to make CIDR clearer.) Your subnet mask would be, then, 11111111 00000000 00000000 00000000 or 255.0.0.0. Reading from the left, you have eight ones in the subnet mask before the zeros start. In CIDR terminology, you wouldn't have an *A-class* network; rather, you would have a *slash 8* network.

With a B-class, the InterNIC controlled the top 16 bits, and you controlled the bottom 16. If you decided to take that B-class network and make it a one-subnet network, then your subnet mask would be 11111111 11111111 00000000 00000000 or 255.255.0.0. Reading from the left, the subnet mask would have 16 ones. In CIDR terms, a B network is a *slash 16* network.

With a C-class, the InterNIC controlled the top 24 bits, and you controlled the bottom 8. By now, you've seen that the subnet mask for a C network if you treated it as one subnet is 11111111 11111111 11111111 00000000. Reading from the left, the subnet mask would have 24 ones. In CIDR terms, a C network is a *slash 24* network.

Where the new flexibility of CIDR comes in is that the InterNIC can in theory now not only define the A-, B-, and C-type networks, it can offer networks with subnet masks in between the A, B, and C networks. For example, suppose I wanted a network for 50 PCs. Before, the InterNIC would have to give me a C network, with 256 addresses. But now they can offer me a network with subnet mask 11111111 11111111 11111111 11000000 (255.255.255.192), giving me only six bits to play with. Two to the sixth power is 64, so I'd have 64 addresses to do with as I liked. This would be a *slash 26* network.

In summary, Table 14.2 shows how large each possible network type would be.

TABLE 14.2: CIDR Network Types

InterNIC Network Type	"Subnet Mask" for Entire Network	Approximate Number of IP Addresses
slash 0	0.0.0.0	4 billion
slash 1	128.0.0.0	2 billion
slash 2	192.0.0.0	1 billion
slash 3	224.0.0.0	500 million
slash 4	240.0.0.0	25 million
slash 5	248.0.0.0	128 million
slash 6	252.0.0.0	64 million
slash 7	254.0.0.0	32 million
slash 8	255.0.0.0	16 million
slash 9	255.128.0.0	8 million
slash 10	255.192.0.0	4 million
slash 11	255.224.0.0	2 million
slash 12	255.240.0.0	1 million
slash 13	255.248.0.0	524,288

Continued on next page

TABLE 14.2 CONTINUED: CIDR Network Types

InterNIC Network Type	"Subnet Mask" for Entire Network	Approximate Number of IP Addresses
slash 14	255.252.0.0	262,144
slash 15	255.254.0.0	131,072
slash 16	255.255.0.0	65,536
slash 17	255.255.128.0	32,768
slash 18	255.255.192.0	16,384
slash 19	255.255.224.0	8192
slash 20	255.255.240.0	4096
slash 21	255.255.248.0	2048
slash 22	255.255.252.0	1024
slash 23	255.255.254.0	512
slash 24	255.255.255.0	256
slash 25	255.255.255.128	128
slash 26	255.255.255.192	64
slash 27	255.255.255.224	32
slash 28	255.255.255.240	16
slash 29	255.255.255.248	8
slash 30	255.255.255.252	4
slash 31	255.255.255.254	2
slash 32	255.255.255.255	1

I hope it's obvious that I included all of those networks just for the sake of completeness, as some of them simply aren't available, like the slash 0, and some just don't make sense, like the slash 31—it only gives you two addresses, which would be immediately required for network number and broadcast address, leaving none behind for you to actually use.

CIDR is a fact of life if you're registering networks with the InterNIC nowadays. With the information in this section, you'll more easily be able to understand what an Internet Service Provider (ISP) is talking about when it says it can get you a "slash 26" network.

What IP *Doesn't* Do: Error Checking

Whether you're on *an* intranet or *the* Internet, it looks like your data gets bounced around quite a bit. How can you prevent it from becoming damaged? Let's look briefly at that, and that'll segue me to a short talk on TCP.

An IP packet contains a bit of data called a *checksum header*, which checks whether the header information was damaged on the way from sender to receiver.

Many data communications protocols use checksums that operate like this: I send you some data. You use the checksum to make sure that the data wasn't damaged in transit, perhaps by line noise. Once you're satisfied that the data was not damaged, you send me a message that says, "OK—I got it." If the checksum indicates that it did *not* get to me undamaged, then I send you a message that says, "That data was damaged—please resend it," and you resend it. Such messages are called ACKs and NAKs—positive or negative acknowledgments of data. Protocols that use this check-and-acknowledge approach are said to provide *reliable* service.

But IP does not provide reliable service. If an IP receiver gets a damaged packet, it just discards the packet and says nothing to the receiver. Surprised? I won't keep you in suspense: it's TCP that provides the reliability. The IP header checksum is used to see if a header is valid; if it isn't, then the datagram is discarded.

This underscores IP's job. IP is not built to provide end-to-end guaranteed transmission of data. IP exists mainly for one reason: routing. We'll revisit routing a bit later, when I describe the specifics of how to accomplish IP routing on an NT machine.

But whose job *is* end-to-end integrity, if not IP's? The answer: its buddy's, TCP.

TCP (Transmission Control Protocol)

I said earlier that IP handled routing and really didn't concern itself that much with whether the message got to its final destination or not. If there are seven IP hops from one point to the next, then each hop is an independent action—there's no coordination, no notion of whether a particular hop is hop number three out of seven. Each IP hop is totally unaware of the others. How, then, could we use IP to provide reliable service?

IP packets are like messages in a bottle. Drop the bottle in the ocean, and you have no guarantee that the message got to whomever you want to receive it. But suppose you hired a "message-in-the-bottle end-to-end manager." Such a person (let's call her Gloria) would take your message, put it in a bottle, and toss it in the ocean. That person would also have a partner on the other side of the ocean (let's call him Gaston) and, when Gaston received a message in a bottle from Gloria, Gaston would then pen a short message saying "Gloria, I got your message," put *that* message in a bottle, and drop that bottle into the ocean.

If Gloria didn't get an acknowledgment from Gaston within, say, three months, then she'd drop *another* bottle into the ocean with the original message in it. In data communications terms, we'd say that Gloria "timed out" on the transmission path, and was *resending*.

Yeah, I know, this is a somewhat goofy analogy, but understand the main point: we hired Gloria and Gaston to ensure that our inherently unreliable message-in-a-bottle network became reliable. Gloria will keep sending and resending until she gets a response from Gaston. Notice that she doesn't create a whole new transmission medium, like radio or telephone; she merely adds a layer of her own watchfulness to the existing transmission protocol.

Now think of IP as the message in the bottle. TCP, the Transmission Control Protocol, is just the Gloria/Gaston team. TCP provides reliable end-to-end service.

By the way, TCP provides some other services, most noticeably something called *sockets* which I will discuss in a moment. As TCP has value besides its reliability feature, TCP also has a "cousin" protocol that acts very much like it but does *not* guarantee end-to-end integrity. That protocol is called UDP, or the User Datagram Protocol.

That's basically the idea behind TCP. Its main job is the orderly transmission of data from one intranet host to another. Its main features include:

- Handshake
- Packet sequencing
- Flow control
- Error handling

Whereas IP has no manners—it just shoves data at a computer whether that computer is ready for it or not—TCP makes sure that each side is properly introduced before attempting to transfer. TCP sets up the connection.

Sequencing

As IP does not use a virtual circuit, different data packets may end up arriving at different times, and in fact, in a different order. Imagine a simple intranet transferring four segments of data across a network with multiple possible pathways. The first segment takes the high road, so to speak, and is delayed. The second through the fourth do not, and so get to the destination more quickly. TCP's job on the receiving side is then to reassemble things in order.

Flow Control

Along with sequencing is flow control. What if 50 segments of data had been sent, and they all arrived out of order? The receiver would have to hold them all in memory before sorting them out and writing them to disk. Part of what TCP worries about is *pacing* the data—not sending it to the receiver until the receiver is ready for it.

Error Detection/Correction

And finally, TCP handles error detection and correction, as I've already said. Beyond that, TCP is very efficient in the way that it does error handling. Some protocols acknowledge each and every block, generating a large overhead of blocks. TCP, in contrast, does not do that. It tells the other side, "I am capable of accepting and buffering some number of blocks. Don't expect an acknowledgment until I've gotten that number of blocks. And if a block is received incorrectly, I will not acknowledge it, so if I don't acknowledge as quickly as you expect me to do, then just go ahead and resend the block."

Sockets and the WinSock Interface

Just about anything that you want to do with the Internet or your company's intranet involves two programs talking to each other. When you browse someone's Web site, you have a program (your Web browser, a *client* program) communicating with their Web server (obviously, a *server* program). Using the File

Transfer Protocol, or FTP, which I'll discuss later in this chapter, requires that one machine be running a program called an *FTP server* and that another computer be running an *FTP client*. Internet mail requires that a mail client program talk to a mail server program—and those are just a few examples.

Connecting a program in one machine to another program in another machine is kind of like placing a telephone call. The sender must know the phone number of the receiver, and the receiver must be around his or her phone, waiting to pick it up. In the TCP world, a phone number is called a *socket*. A socket is composed of three parts: the IP address of the receiver, which we've already discussed, the receiving program's *port number*, which we *haven't* yet discussed, and whether it's a TCP port or a UDP port—each protocol has its own set.

Suppose the PC on your desk running Windows NT wants to get a file from the FTP site which is really the PC on *my* desk running Windows NT. Obviously, for this to happen, we've got to know each other's IP addresses. But that's not all; after all, in my PC I have a whole bunch of programs running (my network connection, my word processor, my operating system, my personal organizer, the FTP server, and so on). So if TCP says, "Hey, Mark's machine, I want to talk to you," then my machine would reply, "Which *one* of us—the word processor, the e-mail program, or what?" So the TCP/IP world assigns a 16-bit number to each program that wants to send or receive TCP information, a number called the *port* of that program. The most popular Internet applications have had particular port numbers assigned to them, and those port numbers are known as "well-known ports." Some well-known port numbers include FTP (TCP ports 20 and 21), the common mail protocol SMTP (TCP port 25), Web servers (TCP port 80), Network News Transfer Protocol (NNTP, TCP port 119), and the Post Office Protocol version 3 (POP3, TCP port 110).

How Sockets Work

So, for instance, suppose I've written a TCP/IP-based *chat* program that allows me to type messages to you and receive typed messages from you. This fictitious chat program might get port number 1500. Anyone running chat, then, would install it on port 1500. Then, to chat my computer with an imaginary IP address of 123.124.55.67, your chat program would essentially "place a phone call"—that is, set up a TCP session—with port 1500 at address 123.124.55.67. The combination of port 1500 with IP address 123.124.55.67 is a *socket address*. It's often written 123.124.55.67:1500.

In order for your computer to chat with my computer, my computer must be *ready* to chat. So I have to run my chat program. It would probably say something like, "Do you want to chat with anyone, or do you just want to wait to be called?" I tell it that I just want to wait to be called, so it sits quietly in my PC's memory, but first it tells the PC, "If anyone calls for me, wake me up—I'm willing to take calls at port 1500." That's called a *passive open* on TCP.

Then, when your computer wants to chat with my computer, it sends an *active open* request to my computer, saying, "Want to talk?" It also says, "I can accept up to *x* bytes of data in my buffers." My computer responds by saying, "Sure, I'll talk, and I can accept up to *y* bytes of data in my buffers."

The two computers then blast data back and forth, being careful not to overflow the other computer's buffers. When a buffer's worth of information is sent by your computer, then your computer doesn't send my computer any more data until my computer acknowledges that it received the data.

Once the chat is over, both sides politely say "good-bye," and hang up. My computer can choose to continue to wait for incoming calls, as before.

WinSock Sockets

The value of sockets is that they provide a uniform way to write programs that exploit the underlying Internet communications structure. If, for example, I want to write a networked version of the game Battleship, then I might want to be able to quickly turn out versions for Windows, OS/2, the Mac, and Unix machines. But maybe I don't know much about communications, and don't *want* to know much. (I'm probably supposed to note here that Battleship is a registered trademark of Milton-Bradley or someone like that; consider it done.) I could just sit down with my C compiler and bang out a Battleship that runs on Unix machines. Just a few code changes, and *presto*! I have my PC version.

But the PC market requires some customization, and so a particular version of the sockets interface, called WinSock, was born. It's essentially the sockets interface, but modified a bit to work better in a PC environment.

The benefit of WinSock is that all vendors of TCP/IP software support an identical WinSock programming interface (well, identical in theory, anyway) and so TCP/IP-based programs should run as well atop FTP software's TCP/IP stack as it would atop the TCP/IP stack that ships with NT. That's why you can plop your Netscape Web browser on just about any PC with TCP/IP and it should work without any trouble.

Internet Host Names

Thus far, I've referred to a lot of numbers; hooking up to my Web server, then, seems to require that you point your Web browser to IP address 199.34.57.52, TCP port number 80.

Of course, you don't actually do that. When you send e-mail to your friends, you don't send it to 199.45.23.17; you send it to something like robbie@somefirm .com. What's IP got to do with it?

IP addresses are useful because they're precise and because they're easy to subnet. But they're tough to remember, and people generally prefer more English-sounding names. So TCP/IP allows us to group one or more TCP/IP networks into groups called *domains*, groups that will share a common name like microsoft .com, senate.gov, army.mil, or mit.edu.

Machines within a domain will have names that include the domain name; for example, within my mmco.com domain I have machines named micron133.mmco .com, narn.mmco.com, minbar.mmco.com, zhahadum.mmco.com, and serverted .mmco.com. Those specific machine names are called *host names*.

How does TCP/IP connect the English names—the *host* names—to the IP addresses? And how can I sit at my PC in mmco.com and get the information I need to be able to find another host called archie.au, when archie's all the way on the other side of the world in Australia?

Simple—with HOSTS, DNS, and, later in this chapter, WINS. The process of converting a name to its corresponding IP address is called *name resolution*. Again, how's it work? Read on.

Simple Naming Systems (HOSTS)

When you set up your subnet, you don't want to explicitly use IP addresses every time you want to run some TCP/IP utility and hook up with another computer in your subnet. So, instead, you create a file called HOSTS that looks like this:

```
199.34.57.50  keydata.mmco.com
199.34.57.129 serverted.mmco.com
```

This is just a simple ASCII text file. Each host goes on one line, and the line starts off with the host's IP address. Enter at least one space and the host's English name. Do this for each host. You can even give multiple names in the HOSTS file:

```
199.34.57.50   keydata.mmco.com markspc
199.34.57.129  serverted.mmco.com serverpc bigsv
```

Ah, but now comes the really rotten part:

You have to put one of these HOSTS files on *every single workstation*. That means that every single time you change anyone's HOSTS file, you have to go around and change *everybody's* HOSTS file. Every workstation must contain a copy of this file, which is basically a telephone directory of every machine in your subnet. It's a pain, yes, but it's simple. If you're thinking, "Why can't I just put a central HOSTS file on a server and do all my administration with *that* file?"—what you're really asking for is a *name server*, and I'll show you two of them, the Domain Naming Service (DNS) and the Windows Internet Naming Service (WINS), in this chapter.

You must place the HOSTS file in \WINNT35\SYSTEM32\DRIVERS\ETC on an NT system, in the Windows directory on a Windows for Workgroups or Windows 95 machine, and wherever the network software is installed in other kinds of machines (DOS or OS/2).

HOSTS is re-read every time your system does a name resolution; you needn't reboot to see a change in HOSTS take effect.

Domain Naming System (DNS)

HOSTS is a pain, but it's a necessary pain if you want to communicate within your subnet. How does IP find a name outside of your subnet or outside of your domain?

Suppose someone at exxon.com wanted to send a file to mmco.com. Surely the exxon.com HOSTS files don't contain the IP address of my company, and vice versa?

To take a fictitious example, how would TCP/IP find a machine at some software company named "Macrosoft?" How would IP figure out that a host named, say, database.macrosoft.com really has an IP address of, say, 181.50.47.22?

Within an organization, name resolution can clearly be accomplished by the HOSTS file. Between domains, however, name resolution is handled by the Domain Naming Service, or DNS. There is a central naming clearinghouse for *the* Internet called the InterNIC Registration Services. (Obviously, if you're only running a private intranet, then *you* perform the function of name manager.) There is a hierarchy of names, a hierarchy created specifically to make it simple to add names to the network quickly. After all, with 20 million Internet users, can you imagine having to call the NIC every single time you put a new user on one of your networks? It would take months to get the paperwork done. Instead, the NIC created the Domain Naming System, of which you see only a small portion. The NIC started off with six initial naming domains: EDU was for educational institutions, NET was for network providers, COM for commercial users, MIL was for military users (remember who built this?), ORG was for organizations, and GOV was for civilian government. For example, there is a domain on the Internet called whitehouse.gov; you can send Internet mail to the President that way, at president@whitehouse.gov. There are more root domains these days, like .fi for sites in Finland, .uk for sites in the United Kingdom, and so on.

Anyway, back to the Macrosoft story. Now, in order to get onto the Internet, Macrosoft registers its entire company with the name macrosoft.com, placing itself in the COM—commercial—domain. There are sometimes some gray areas about whether someone is, say, educational or commercial, or perhaps a network provider or a commercial firm, but it's not really that important. From there, Macrosoft dubs someone in their organization the name administrator. That person can then create subsets of the Macrosoft domain; in Figure 14.7, you see a possible arrangement.

FIGURE 14.7:

Name hierarchy in the Internet

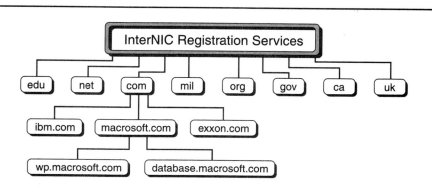

The Macrosoft name administrator has subdivided the macrosoft.com domain into two subdomains: wp.macrosoft.com and database.macrosoft.com. He's entirely within his rights to do this, as the rest of the Internet doesn't care what goes on inside macrosoft.com; his naming control only extends from macrosoft .com *down* in the naming hierarchy.

The Macrosoft name administrator maintains a database of host names within macrosoft.com by running a *name server* program on one of the Macrosoft computers. Name servers are computers whose main job is simply to answer the question, "What's the IP address of the machine somefirm.com?" They're also called *DNS servers*. Sending data from one host (machine) in database.macrosoft .com to another host in database.macrosoft.com would only involve asking the local name server about the receiver's machine's name. In contrast, if someone were to transfer data from some host in database.macrosoft.com to some host in exxon.com, then the request would get bumped up even further, to one of the main Internet name servers. There are nine of these servers in the world, and they reload their massive name databases from the NIC at regular intervals.

NT ships with a DNS server, so you can use an NT server to act as your name resolver. You'll see how later in this chapter.

E-Mail Names: A Note

If you've previously messed around with e-mail under TCP/IP, then you may be wondering something about these addresses. After all, you don't send mail to mmco.com, you'd send it to a name like markm@mmco.com. markm@mmco.com is an e-mail address. The way it works is this: a group of users in a TCP/IP domain decide to implement mail.

In order to receive mail, a machine must be up and running, ready to accept mail from the outside world (that is, some other subnet or domain). Now, mail can arrive at any time of day, so this machine must be up and running all of the time. That seems to indicate that it would be a dumb idea to get mail delivered straight to your desktop. So, instead, TCP mail dedicates a machine to the mail router task of receiving mail from the outside world, holding that mail until you want to read it, taking mail that you wish to send somewhere else, and routing that mail to some other mail router. The name of the most common TCP/IP mail router program is *sendmail*. The name of the protocol used most commonly for routing e-mail on the Internet, by the way, is the *Simple Mail Transfer Protocol*, or SMTP.

Unfortunately, Microsoft did not include an SMTP router program in either the workstation or the server version of NT, so you either have to connect up to a existing mail router in order to get Internet mail, or you have to buy a third-party mail product to work under NT.

You can see how mail works in Figure 14.8.

FIGURE 14.8:

The interrelationship of host names, e-mail names, and the Internet

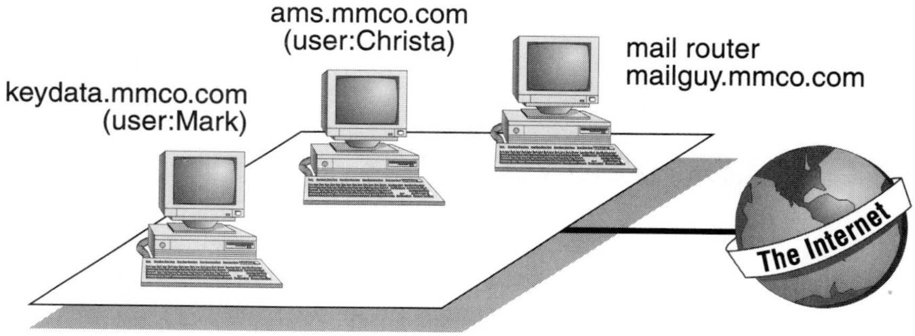

In this small domain, we've got two users: Mark and Christa. (One of the great things about the Internet is that you don't need that pesky Shift key on your keyboard.) Mark works on keydata.mmco.com, and Christa works on ams.mmco .com. Now, suppose Christa wants to send some mail to her friend Corky, executive director of Surfers of America; Corky's address is corky@surferdudes.org. She fires up a program on her workstation, which is called a *mail client*. The mail client allows her to create and send new messages, as well as receive incoming messages. She sends the message and closes her mail client. Notice that her mail client software doesn't do routing—it just lets her create, send, and receive messages.

The mail client has been configured to send messages to the program *sendmail*, which is running in this subnet on mailguy.mmco.com. mailguy is kind of the post office (in Internet lingo, a *mail router*) for this group of users. Sendmail on mailguy.mmco.com stores the message, and it then sends the message off to the machine with the DNS name surferdudes.org, trusting IP to route the message correctly to surferdudes.

Additionally, sendmail knows the names Christa and Mark. It is the workstation that is the interface to the outside world *vis-à-vis* mail. Note, by the way, that *DNS* has no idea who Mark or Christa is; DNS is concerned with *host* names, not *e-mail* names. It's DNS that worries about how to find mailguy.mmco.com.

A bit later, Corky gets the message and sends a reply to Christa. The reply does *not* go to Christa's machine ams.mmco.com; instead, it goes to mailguy.mmco .com, because Corky sent mail to christa@mmco.com. The mail system sends the messages to mmco.com, but what machine has the address mmco.com? Simple: we give mailguy.mmco.com an alias, and mail goes to it.

Eventually, Christa starts up the mail client program once again. The mail program sends a query to the local mail router mailguy.mmco.com, saying, "Any new mail for Christa?" There *is* mail, and Christa reads it.

Getting onto an Intranet

So far, I've talked quite a bit about how an intranet works and what kinds of things there are that you can do with an intranet. But I haven't told you enough yet to actually get *on* an Internet, whether it's your company's private intranet or *the* Internet.

- You can connect to a multi-user system and appear to the Internet as a dumb terminal.

- You can connect to an Internet provider via a serial port and a protocol called either the Serial Line Interface Protocol (SLIP) or the Point to Point Protocol (PPP), and appear to the Internet as a host.

- You can be part of a local area network that is an Internet subnet, and then load TCP/IP software on your system, and appear to the Internet as a host.

Each of these options has pros and cons, as you'll see. The general rule is that in order to access an intranet, all you basically have to do is to connect up to a computer that is already on an intranet.

The essence of an intranet is in *packet switching*, a kind of network game of hot potato whereby computers act communally to transfer each other's data around. Packet switching is what makes it possible to add subnetworks on the fly.

Dumb Terminal Connection

This is a common way for someone to get an account that allows access to *the* Internet. For example, you can get an account with Performance Systems Inc. (PSI), Delphi or Digital Express, to name a few Internet access providers.

Delphi, for example, has computers all around the U.S., so to get onto the Internet all you need to do is simply run a terminal emulation package on your system and dial up to their terminal servers. This kind of access is often quite cheap, at least in the U.S.: $25/month is common. If you wanted to do this with NT, then you needn't even run TCP/IP on your NT machine. Instead, you'd merely need to put a modem on your system and use Terminal to dial up to your Internet access provider.

Now, understand: this is just a *terminal* access capability that I've gotten, so it's kind of limited. Suppose, for example, that I live in Virginia (which is true) and I connect to the Internet via a host in Maine (which is not true). From the Internet's point of view, I'm not in an office in Virginia; instead, I'm wherever the host that I'm connected to is. I work in Virginia, but if I were dialing a host in Maine, then from the Internet's point of view I'd be in Maine. Any requests that I make for file transfers, for example, wouldn't go to Virginia—they'd go to my host in Maine.

Now, that can be a bit of a hassle. Say I'm at my Virginia location logged on to the Internet via the Maine host. I get onto Microsoft's FTP site—I'll cover FTP later in this chapter, but basically FTP is just a means to provide a library of files to the outside world—and I grab a few files, perhaps an updated video driver. The FTP program says, "I got the file," but the file is now on the host in Maine. That means that I'm only half done, as I now have to run some other kind of file transfer program to move the file from the host in Maine to my computer in Virginia.

SLIP/PPP Serial Connection

A somewhat better way to connect to a TCP/IP-based network—that is, an intranet—is by a direct serial connection to an existing intranet host. If you use PCs, then you may know of a program called LapLink that allows two PCs to share each other's hard disks via their RS232 serial ports; SLIP/PPP are similar ideas. An intranet may have a similar type of connection called a SLIP or PPP connection. The connection needn't be a serial port, but it often is. SLIP is the *Serial Line Interface Protocol*, an older protocol that I sometimes think of as the *simple* line interface protocol. There's really nothing to SLIP—no error checking, no security, no flow control. It's the simplest protocol imaginable: just send the data, then send a special byte that means, "This is the end of the data." PPP, in contrast, was designed to retain the low overhead of SLIP, and yet to include some extra information required so that more intelligent parts of an intranet—items like routers—could use it effectively. The *Point to Point Protocol* works by establishing an explicit link between one side and another, then uses a simple error checking system called a *checksum* to monitor noise on the line.

Which protocol should you use? The basic rule that I use is that SLIP doesn't provide error checking but uses less overhead, and PPP provides error checking and uses more overhead. Therefore, when I'm using error-correcting modems, I use SLIP. On noisy lines and without error-correcting modems, I use PPP.

NT supports both PPP and SLIP via Remote Access Services.

LAN Connection

The most common way to connect to an intranet is simply by being a LAN work-station on a local area network that is an intranet subnetwork. Again, this needn't be *the* Internet—almost any LAN can use the TCP/IP protocol suite.

This is the connection that most NT servers will use to provide TCP/IP ser-vices. Microsoft's main reason for implementing TCP/IP on NT is to provide an alternative to NetBEUI, as NetBEUI is quick and applicable to small networks, but inappropriate for large corporate networks. In contrast, TCP/IP has always been good for intranetworking, but one suffered tremendously in speed. That's not true anymore, however; for example, a quick test of TCP/IP versus NetBEUI on one of my workstations showed network read rates of 1250K/sec for NetBEUI and 833K/sec for TCP/IP, and write rates of 312K/sec for NetBEUI and 250K/sec for TCP/IP. Again, TCP's slower, but not by a lot. And NetBEUI doesn't go over routers.

Terminal Connections versus Other Connections

Before moving on to the next topic, I'd like to return to the difference between a terminal connection and a SLIP, PPP, or LAN connection. In Figure 14.9, you see three PCs on an Ethernet attached to two minicomputers, which in turn serve four dumb terminals.

FIGURE 14.9:

When Internet connections involve IP numbers and when they don't

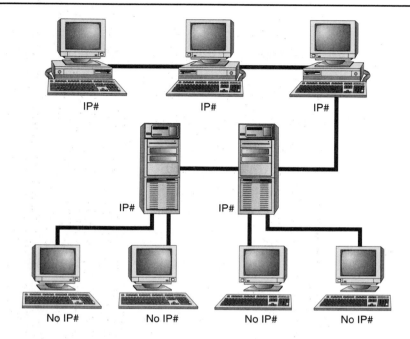

The minicomputer-to-minicomputer link might be SLIP or PPP, or then again they might be LANed together. Notice that only the *computers* in this scenario have intranetwork protocol (IP) addresses. Whenever you send mail to one of the people on the PCs at the top of the picture, it goes to that person's PC. If you were to scrutinize the IP addresses—and most of the time, you will not—then you'd see that everyone had the same IP address. In contrast, the people at the *bottom* of the picture get their mail sent to one of the minicomputers, and so, in this example, each pair of terminals shares an IP address. If Shelly and George in your office access your company's intranet through terminals connected to the same computer, then a close look at mail from them would show that they have the same IP address. But, if you think about it, you already knew that; if you send mail to george@mailbox.acme.com and to shelly@mailbox.acme.com, then the machine name to which the mail goes is the same; it's just the usernames that varies.

So, in summary: if you want to get onto *the* Internet from a remote location, then your best bet is to sign up with a service that will bill you monthly for connect charges, like Delphi. To attach to a private intranet, you need to dial up to a multiuser computer on that intranet, or you need a SLIP or PPP connection, or you have to be on a workstation on a LAN that's part of that intranet. You then need to talk to your local network guru about getting the software installed on your system that will allow your computer to speak TCP/IP so that it can be part of your intranet.

Setting Up TCP/IP on NT with Fixed IP Addresses

Enough talking about intranetting; let's do it, and do it with NT.

Traditionally, one of the burdens of an IP administrator has been that she must assign separate IP numbers to each machine, a bit of a bookkeeping hassle. You can adopt this fixed IP address approach, and in fact there are some good reasons to do it, as it's compatible with more TCP/IP software and systems. It is also possible, however, to have a server assign IP addresses "on the fly" with the DHCP system that I've mentioned earlier.

Some of you will set up your intranet with fixed IP addresses, and some will use dynamic addresses. *Everyone* will use static IP addresses for at least some of your PCs. For that reason, I first want to start the discussion of setting up TCP/IP with just fixed addresses. Then I'll take on dynamic addressing.

Here's basically how to set up TCP/IP on an NT system:

1. Load the TCP/IP protocol.

2. Set the IP address and subnet, default gateway, and DNS server.

3. Prepare the HOSTS file, if you're going to use one.

4. Test the connection with PING.

Let's take a look at those steps, one by one.

Installing TCP/IP Software with Static IP Addresses

You install the TCP/IP protocol (if you didn't choose it when you first installed NT) by opening up the Control Panel, and then choosing the Network icon. You see a dialog box like Figure 14.10.

FIGURE 14.10:

Initial Control Panel dialog
box for installing network
software

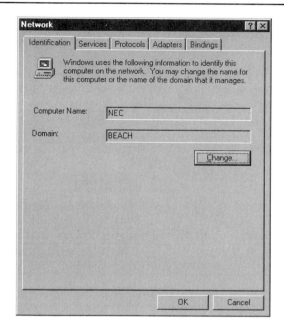

Click the Protocols tab, and your system will look something like Figure 14.11.

FIGURE 14.11:

Protocols tab of Network
property sheet

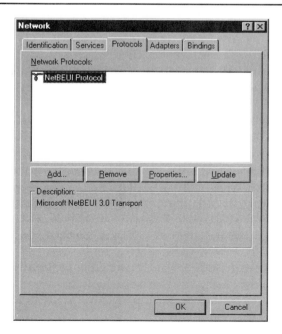

Click Add and you get a list of protocols that you can add. Select TCP/IP, as shown in Figure 14.12.

FIGURE 14.12:

Choosing to add TCP/IP protocol

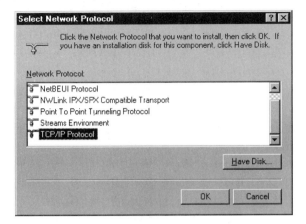

Click OK. The setup routine will then offer you the chance to take the easy way out and have the system automatically set up the TCP/IP protocol using DHCP, which we'll cover later in this chapter. The dialog box is shown in Figure 14.13.

FIGURE 14.13:

Choose not to use DHCP

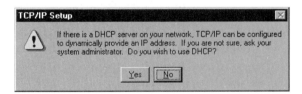

Click No, and NT will prompt you for the location of the installation files; point it wherever you keep them. NT will install a bunch of files, and you'll see that the Protocols window now contains TCP/IP. You need to configure it. Click Close, and NT will rebind all of the protocols, boards, and services, ending up with the following TCP/IP configuration property sheet, as shown in Figure 14.14.

I've already filled in the basic values in that figure—IP address, subnet mask, and default gateway.

First, you put your IP address into the IP Address field. Using the first quad of your address, NT will guess a subnet mask based on your network class—255.0.0.0

for class A, 255.255.0.0 for class B, and 255.255.255.0 for class C. As I indicated in my discussion earlier in this chapter about subnetting, if your network is subnetted *within* its Internet domain, then you have to change the subnet mask.

FIGURE 14.14:

TCP/IP configuration property sheet

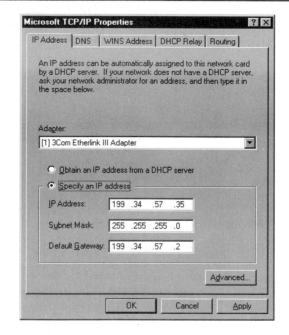

Once you have the subnet mask in place, you should enter the IP address of your default gateway, the machine on your Ethernet segment that connects to the outside world either via a router, a SLIP, or a PPP connection. To clarify that, Figure 14.15 shows a sample intranet connection.

Suppose you're configuring the machine in the upper left-hand corner of the diagram. You type its IP address into the dialog box that you saw earlier, entering the value **199.34.57.35**. Presuming that your class C network—since the first quad is 199, it must be a class C network—is not further subnetted, then the subnet mask would be 255.255.255.0, and the default gateway would be the machine with the SLIP connection to the Internet, so you'd enter 199.34.57.2 for the address of the default gateway. (Why didn't I make that gateway machine .1? Just to underscore that it's not necessary to make the gateway .1; it's just a convention.) Notice the DNS server is at 164.109.1.3. You haven't had a chance to incorporate that information into the TCP/IP setup yet, but you will soon.

FIGURE 14.15:

An example of a connection to the Internet

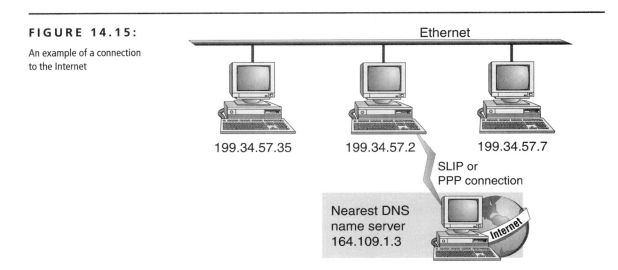

Next, click the DNS tab. You'll see a dialog box like the one in Figure 14.16.

FIGURE 14.16:

The DNS configuration screen

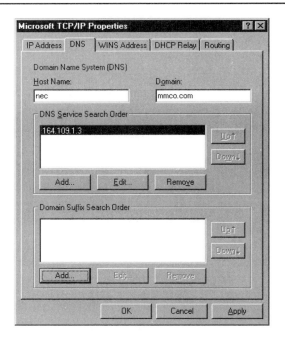

The important parts of this screen are the host name, the TCP domain name, name resolution, and DNS search order. Again, I've already filled them in here.

The TCP domain name is your company's domain name, such as exxon.com, or, if your company is further divided beyond the domain level, perhaps refining.exxon.com. The host name is your computer's name, such as marks-computer, printserver, or the like.

NOTE   Don't use underscores in the name, as it can cause some Internet software to fail. Only a–z, A–Z, 0–9, and the hyphen are accepted characters for Internet host names according to RFC 1034. That's not to say that *some* software won't work fine with other characters, but you may run into trouble later if you don't stay within the Internet rules.

Next, you tell NT where to find a DNS server. You can use a HOSTS file, DNS name servers, or a combination. If you use a DNS name server or servers, however, then you have to tell NT where the nearest DNS name server is. You can specify one, two, or three DNS servers, and the order in which to search them, in the DNS Name Service Search Order field. In general, you only include the name of one or two DNS name servers, a primary and a secondary for use in case the primary name server is down.

When that sheet is arranged as you want it, you next want to configure the name resolution system that you use within your enterprise network, a system called the Windows Internet Naming Systems, or WINS. Click WINS Address and you'll see a page like the one shown in Figure 14.17.

I'll cover WINS in detail later in this chapter, but for now all you need to understand is that you have one or two NT servers acting as name resolvers or WINS servers. This dialog box lets you fill in the names of a primary and secondary WINS server.

I know I've already said that most of the Internet uses something called *DNS* to convert network names to network addresses, but now I'm saying that we'll *also* use something else called *WINS* to do what sounds like the same thing. What's going on? In truth, you shouldn't really have to set up WINS at all; NT and Microsoft enterprise networking in general should use DNS for all of its name resolution, but it doesn't. The reason is that Microsoft wanted NT's networking modules to work like the already-existing LAN Manager system, and LAN Manager used a naming system based on its NetBIOS application program interface. A computer's NetBIOS name is the computer name that you gave it when you installed it. When you type **net view \\ajax**, something must resolve \\ajax into an IP address—a NetBIOS-to-IP resolution. WINS does that. In contrast, the rest of the Internet would see a machine called "ajax" as having a longer name, like "ajax.acme.com." If there were a Web server on ajax, then someone outside the company would have to point her Web browser to http://ajax.acme.com, and some piece of software would have to resolve ajax.acme.com into an IP address. That piece of software is the socket or WinSock interface, and in either case it will rely upon not WINS but *DNS* to resolve the name. In a few words, then, programs written to employ NetBIOS will use WINS for name resolution, and programs written to employ WinSock use DNS for name resolution.

FIGURE 14.17:

Configuring a WINS client

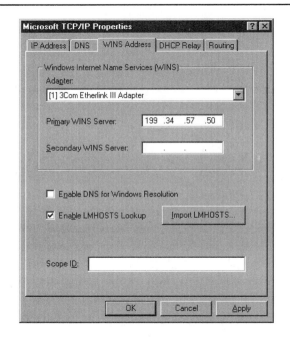

I can probably guess what you're thinking now, and, yes, DNS and WINS should be integrated, and they will be—but not until Windows 2000 Server, the next version of NT. For now, we'll just have to maintain two different name resolvers. (There is, I promise, much more on the subject of WINS versus DNS name resolution later on in the chapter, but that's a quick overview.)

Anyway, there's a check box: Enable DNS for Windows name resolution. I wrote the previous two paragraphs so that I could explain this check box. As you've read, WinSock-based applications use DNS for name resolution, and NetBIOS applications use WINS. But suppose a NetBIOS-based application cannot resolve a name with WINS—WINS comes back and says, "I don't know who this computer is!" If you check this check box, then you are telling your machine, "If WINS fails me on name resolution, let NetBIOS look to DNS to resolve names." If you check it, then some operations may get pretty slow on your system. Consider what happens when you accidentally try an operation on a nonexistent server. Suppose you type **net view \\bigserver** when its real name is \\bigserve. WINS will come back with a failure on the name resolution attempt, but if you have this box checked, then your system will waste even more time asking DNS to resolve the name. On the other hand, some installations have servers with NetBIOS names and use TCP/IP, but do not participate in WINS name resolution. For example, an old LAN Manager/Unix (LM/X) server will have a NetBIOS name, but it doesn't know to register that name with WINS, as its software was written before Microsoft introduced WINS. Ask a WINS server for the LM/X server's IP address, then, and WINS will come up blank. But *DNS* would know how to find the server. So if you have older Microsoft enterprise networking products that run the TCP/IP protocol, then you may want to check the Enable DNS for Windows name resolution box.

You'll enable LMHOSTS if you need the LMHOSTS file; LMHOSTS is a static ASCII file like HOSTS, except that where HOSTS assists in WinSock name resolution, LMHOSTS assists in NetBIOS name resolution. You will almost never use an LMHOSTS file on a modern network. I discuss LMHOSTS later in this chapter. The NetBIOS scope ID should be left blank for most networks. If you've partitioned your network into NetBIOS scopes, then talk to whoever did it and they can tell you what scope names to use. Otherwise, do not fill anything in here.

Click OK to return to the Protocols screen, then Close to close the Network applet. You have to reboot for the changes to take effect.

Just to get started, create your HOSTS file; remember that it goes in WINNT\ SYSTEM32\DRIVERS\ETC. The file is reread every time a name needs to be resolved, so you needn't reboot every time you change the contents of HOSTS.

Testing Your TCP/IP Installation

Your TCP/IP software should now be ready to go, so let's test it.

TCP/IP has a very handy little tool for finding out whether or not your TCP/IP software is up and running, and whether or not you have a connection to another point—*ping*.

Ping is a program that lets you send a short message to another TCP/IP node, asking, "Are you there?" If it is there, then it says yes to the ping, and ping relays this information back to you. You can see an example of ping in Figure 14.18.

FIGURE 14.18:

A sample ping output

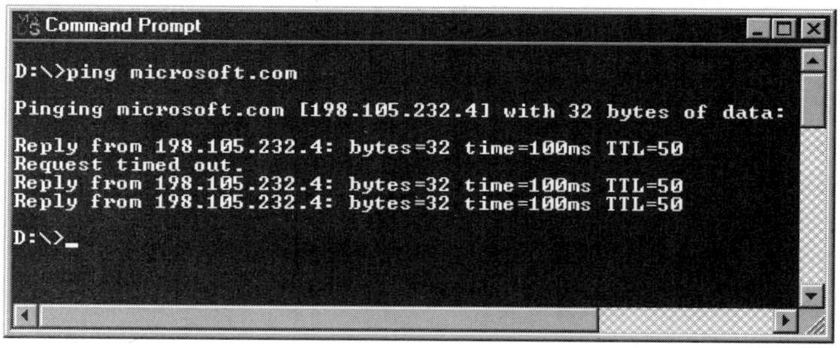

```
Command Prompt                                              _ □ ✕

D:\>ping microsoft.com

Pinging microsoft.com [198.105.232.4] with 32 bytes of data:

Reply from 198.105.232.4: bytes=32 time=100ms TTL=50
Request timed out.
Reply from 198.105.232.4: bytes=32 time=100ms TTL=50
Reply from 198.105.232.4: bytes=32 time=100ms TTL=50

D:\>_
```

In the above figure, I pinged Microsoft or, rather, whatever network Microsoft exposes to the outside world. (Notice it's a B-class network—those Microsoft folks really rate.) The ping was successful, which is all that matters. But *don't* ping Microsoft for your first test; I did that screen shot a while back, before they put their firewall in. (Before they put the firewall in, it was actually possible to browse Microsoft's servers from the comfort of your own home, right over the Internet. I can just hear the "Oops!" that someone exclaimed over *that* one.) So don't bother trying to ping Microsoft, as their system no longer responds to ping requests, anyway. (I guess they couldn't figure out a way to charge for them.) Instead, use ping to gradually test first your IP software, then your connection to the network, your name resolution, and finally your gateway to the rest of your intranet.

How Do I Make Sure That TCP/IP Is Set Up Properly?

First, test that you've installed the IP software by pinging the built-in IP loopback address. Type **ping 127.0.0.1**, and if that fails, then you know that you've done something wrong in the initial installation, so recheck that the software is installed on your system. This does not put any messages out on the network, it just checks that the software is installed. By the way, that's also what happens if you ping your IP address: for example, in the machine I just installed, pinging 127.0.0.1 does exactly the same thing as pinging 199.34.57.35.

If that fails, then your TCP/IP stack probably isn't installed correctly, or perhaps you mistyped the IP number (if it failed on your specific IP address but not on the loopback), or perhaps you gave the *same* IP number to another workstation.

Continued on next page

Ping your gateway to see that you can get to the gateway, which should be on your subnet. In my case, my gateway is at 206.246.253.1, so I type **ping 206.246.253.1**, and all should be well.

If you can't get to the gateway, then check that the gateway is up, and that your network connection is all right. There's nothing more embarrassing than calling in outside network support, only to find that your LAN cable fell out of the back of your computer.

Ping something on the other side of your gateway, like an external DNS server. (Ping me, if you like; 206.246.253.1 ought to be up just about all the time.) If you can't get there, then it's likely that your gateway isn't working properly.

Next, test the name resolution on your system. Ping yourself *by name*. Instead of typing **ping 206.246.253.1**, I'd type **ping nec.mmco.com** (the machine I'm on at the moment). That tests HOSTS and/or DNS.

Then, ping someone else on your subnet. Again, try using a DNS name, like mizar.ursamajor .edu, rather than an IP address, but if that doesn't work, then use the IP address. If the IP address works, but the host name doesn't, then double-check the HOSTS file or DNS.

Finally, ping someone outside of your domain, like house.gov (the U.S. House of Representatives) or ftp.microsoft.com or mmco.com. If that doesn't work, but all the pings inside your network work, then you've probably got a problem with your Internet provider.

If you're successful on all of these tests, it should be set up properly.

Setting Up Routing on NT and Windows Machines

Up to now, I've assumed that all of your Windows NT, Workgroups, and 95 machines had a single default gateway that acted as "router to the world" for your machines. That's not always true, as real-life intranets often have multiple routers that lead a machine to different networks. I've also assumed that your NT network is connected to the Internet, or to your enterprise intranet, via some third-party (Compatible Systems, Bay Networks, Cisco Systems, or whomever) router. That's also not always true, as NT machines can act as IP routers.

Routing problems aren't just *server* problems; they're often workstation problems, as well. So, in this section, I'll take on two topics:

- How to set up routing tables on your Windows workstations
- How to use your NT servers as IP routers

An Example Multi-Router Internet

Suppose you had a workstation (whether it's Windows for Workgroups, Windows NT, or Windows 95) on a network with two gateways, as shown in Figure 14.19.

FIGURE 14.19:

A workstation on a network with two gateways

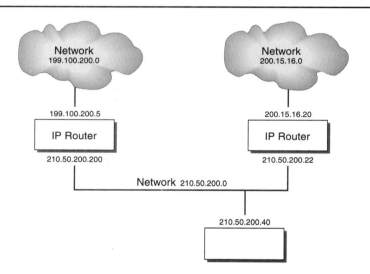

As is the case for most of these diagrams, a multi-network picture can be cryptic, so here's an explanation of what you are looking at.

First, there are three separate Ethernet segments, three separate subnets. They are all C-class networks, just to keep things clean. Two of the networks are only represented by clouds; thus, the cloud on the left containing 199.100.200.0 is just shorthand for an Ethernet with up to 254 computers hanging off it, with addresses ranging from 199.100.200.1 through 199.100.200.254. Notice that I said 254, not 253, because *there is no default gateway for these subnets*. As there are only three subnets, this is an "intranet," not part of the "Internet." One side effect of not being on the Net is that you can use the ".1" address for regular old machines. I left the Internet out of this first example because I found that it confused me when I was first trying to get this routing stuff down. I'll add it later, I promise.

There is also another cloud, to the right, representing a network whose addresses range from 200.15.16.1 through 200.15.16.254—network number 200.15.16.0.

In between is a third subnet with address 210.50.200.0. You see a rectangle representing a PC in the middle which has only one Ethernet card in it, and its IP address is 210.50.200.40. The rectangles on the right and left sides of the picture are routers, computers with two Ethernet cards in them and thus two IP addresses apiece. Each has an address on the 210.50.200.0 network, and each has an address either on the 200.15.16.0 network or on the 199.100.200.0 network.

Adding Entries to Routing Tables: Route Add

Having said that, let's now figure out how to tell the machine at 210.50.200.40 how to route anywhere on this network. Some of the facts that it needs to know are

- To get a message to the 199.100.200.0 network, send it to the machine at 210.50.200.200.

- To get a message to the 200.15.16.0 network, send it to the machine at 210.50.200.22.

- To get a message to the 210.50.200.0 network, just use your own Ethernet card; send it out on the segment, and it'll be heard.

You tell a workstation how to send packets with the *ROUTE ADD* command. Simplified, it looks like this:

```
route add destination mask netmask gatewayaddress
```

Here, *destination* is the address or set of addresses that you want to be able to get to. *Netmask* defines how *many* addresses are there—is it a C network with 250+ addresses, something subnetted smaller, or perhaps a "supernet" of several C networks? *Gatewayaddress* is just the IP address of the machine that will route your packets to their destination.

The ROUTE ADD command for the 199.100.200.0 network would look like this:

```
route add 199.100.200.0 mask 255.255.255.0 210.50.200.200
```

This means, "Send a message anywhere on the 199.100.200.0 network, send it to the machine at 210.50.200.200, and it'll take care of it."

Just a reminder on subnetting, for clarity's sake: suppose the network on the upper left wasn't a full C network, but rather a subnetted part of it. Suppose it was just the range of addresses from 199.100.200.64 through 199.100.200.127. The network number would be, as always, the first address (199.100.200.64), and the subnet mask would be 255.255.255.192. The ROUTE ADD command would then look like

```
route add 199.100.200.64 mask 255.255.255.192 210.50.200.200
```

Anyway, back to the example in the picture. Add a command for the right-hand-side network; it looks like

```
route add 200.15.16.0 mask 255.255.255.0 210.50.200.22
```

That much will get an NT system up and running.

Understanding the Default Routes

Even if you don't ever type a ROUTE ADD command at a Windows workstation, you'll find that there are routing statements that are automatically generated. Let's look at them. First, we'd need an explicit routing command to tell the 210.50.200.40 machine to get to its own subnet:

```
route add 210.50.200.0 mask 255.255.255.0 210.50.200.40
```

Or, in other words, "To get to your local subnet, route to yourself."

Then, recall that the entire 127.*x.y.z* range of network addresses is the loopback. Implement that like so:

```
route add 127.0.0.0 mask 255.0.0.0 127.0.0.1
```

This says, "Take any address from 127.0.0.0 through 127.255.255.255 and route it to 127.0.0.1." The IP software has already had 127.0.0.1 defined for it, so it knows what to do with that. Notice the mask, 255.0.0.0, is a simple class A network mask.

Some NT Internet software uses intranet multicast groups, so the multicast address must be defined. It is 224.0.0.0. It looks like the loopback route command:

```
route add 224.0.0.0 mask 255.0.0.0 210.50.200.40
```

The system knows to multicast by "shouting," which means communicating over its local subnet.

Viewing the Routing Table

Let's find out exactly what routing information this computer has. How? Well, on Windows NT, Workgroups, and 95 workstations there are two commands that will show you what the workstation knows about how to route IP packets. Type either **netstat -rn** or **route print** at a command line—the output is identical, so use either command—and you see something like Figure 14.20.

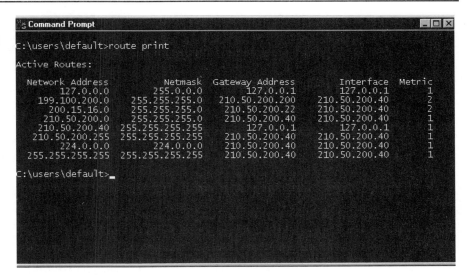

```
 Command Prompt                                                    _ □ ×
C:\users\default>route print

Active Routes:

Network Address        Netmask   Gateway Address        Interface  Metric
      127.0.0.0        255.0.0.0        127.0.0.1        127.0.0.1      1
  199.100.200.0  255.255.255.0    210.50.200.200    210.50.200.40      2
    200.15.16.0  255.255.255.0     210.50.200.22    210.50.200.40      2
   210.50.200.0  255.255.255.0     210.50.200.40    210.50.200.40      1
  210.50.200.40 255.255.255.255        127.0.0.1        127.0.0.1      1
 210.50.200.255 255.255.255.255    210.50.200.40    210.50.200.40      1
      224.0.0.0        224.0.0.0    210.50.200.40    210.50.200.40      1
255.255.255.255 255.255.255.255    210.50.200.40    210.50.200.40      1

C:\users\default>_
```

Notice that the output of ROUTE PRINT is similar to the way you format data in ROUTE ADD. Each line shows a network address, which is the desired destination, the netmask, which indicates how many addresses exist at the desired destination, and the gateway, which is the IP address that the workstation should send its packets to in order to reach the destination. But note two more columns: Interface and Metric.

The Interface Column

Interface asks itself, "Which of my local IP addresses—the ones physically located inside me, like my loopback and all the IP addresses attached to all of my network cards—should I use to get to that gateway?" On this computer, it's a moot point, because it only has one network card in it.

What might this look like on a multihomed machine, like the router on the left-hand side? It has two IP addresses, 199.100.200.5 and 210.50.200.200. A fragment of its ROUTE PRINT output might then look like

```
Network Address Netmask      Gateway Address    Interface      Metric
199.100.200.0   255.255.255.0 199.100.200.5     199.100.200.5     1
210.50.200.0    255.255.255.0 210.50.200.200    210.50.200.200    1
```

There are two networks that the router machine can get to (obviously, or it wouldn't be much use as a router), and each one has a gateway address, which happens to be the local IP address that the router maintains on each network. But now notice the Interface column: rather than staying at the same IP address all the way through, this tells the computer, "I've already told you which gateway to direct this traffic to; now I'll tell you which of your local IP addresses to employ in order to get to that gateway in the first place."

The Metric Column

The metric column (what, no English option?) tells IP how many routers it will have to pass through in order to get to its destination. "1" means "your destination is on the same subnet." A metric value of 2 would mean "you have to go through one router to get to your destination," and so on. Since the .40 workstation must go through a router to get to either the 199.100.200.0 or the 200.15.16.0 network, both of those networks get a metric of 2.

TIP

Just think of it this way: metric = the number of routers you must travel through plus 1.

Ah, but how did the computer know that it would take a router jump to get to those networks? Well, you see, *I* told it.

I have to confess here that I left off a parameter on the ROUTE ADD command, simply to make the explanation palatable. As I knew that the metric was 2 for both routes, I just added the parameter metric 2 to the end of both ROUTE ADD statements. The revised, complete commands look like

```
route add 200.15.16.0 mask 255.255.255.0 210.50.200.22 metric 2
route add 199.100.200.0 mask 255.255.255.0 210.50.200.200 metric 2
```

You'll learn a bit later that a protocol called *RIP* will make this process automatic, but for now I want to stick to this manually constructed set of routing tables. (Using hand-constructed routing tables is called *static routing*; the automatic methods like RIP are called *dynamic routing*, and I'll get to them later.)

ROUTE PRINT Output Explained

Now that you can decipher each column in the ROUTE PRINT output, I'll finish up explaining the output.

The first line is the loopback information, as you've seen before. It's automatically generated on every NT/Workgroups/9*x* machine running the Microsoft TCP/IP stack. The second and third lines are the manually entered routes that tell your machine how to address the 200.15.16.0 and 199.100.200.0 networks. The fourth line is another automatically generated line, and it explains how to address the 210.50.200.0 subnet, which is the local one. The fifth line refers to 210.50.200.40 itself. The mask, 255.255.255.255, means that these aren't routing instructions to get to an entire network, but rather routing instructions to get to a particular computer. It basically says, "If you need to get data to 210.50.200.40, send it to the loopback address." The result: if you ping 210.50.200.40, then no actual communication happens over the network. The sixth line defines how to do a local subnet broadcast. Again, it doesn't point to an entire network, but rather to the particular subnet broadcast address. The seventh line serves Internet multicasting, as you saw before. And the final address is for something called the "limited broadcast address," a kind of generic subnet broadcast address.

Adding the Default Gateway

Suppose you wanted to set up my 210.50.200.40 machine. How would you do it? More specifically, you'd ask me: "Which is the default gateway?"

Well, in the TCP/IP configuration screen that you've seen before, you'd obviously be able to supply the information that the IP address should be 210.50 .200.40 and the subnet mask should be 255.255.255.0. But what should you use to fill in the Default Gateway field? I mean, there are *two* gateways, 210.50.100.22 and 210.50.200.200. Which should you use?

The answer? *Neither.* A *default gateway* is just another entry in the routing table, but it's not specific like the ones you've met so far; it's a catch-all entry. This network doesn't get to the Internet, and it can only see two other subnets, each with their own routers (gateways), so I left the Default Gateway field blank. And there's an advantage to that.

"Destination Host Unreachable"

If I were to try to ping some address not on the three subnets, like 25.44.92.4, then I wouldn't get the message that the ping had timed out, or experienced an error, or anything of the sort; rather, I'd get a "destination host unreachable" message. That's important: "destination host unreachable" doesn't necessarily mean that you can't get to the destination host, but it *does* mean that your workstation doesn't know *how* to get to that host—it lacks any routing information about how to get there at all. Do a ROUTE PRINT and you'll probably be able to see what's keeping you from getting to your destination.

Building a Default Gateway by Hand

When *would* a default gateway make sense in our network? Well, let's add a connection to the Internet to the network, as shown in Figure 14.21.

FIGURE 14.21:

Network with an intranet connection

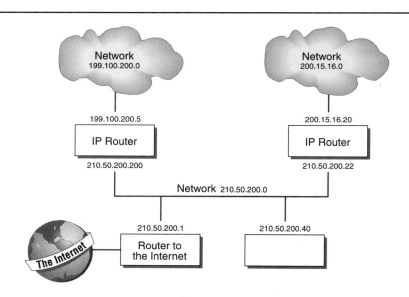

Now we need another ROUTE ADD command—but what should it look like? I mean, what's the generic IP address of the whole Internet?

Believe it or not, there *is* such an address: 0.0.0.0. Think of it as "the network number to end all network numbers." And the network mask? Well, since it doesn't matter *what* address bits match which other address bits—after all, no matter what your address is, you're still on the particular "subnet" which is the entire Internet—the subnet mask is also 0.0.0.0. So the command looks like

```
route add 0.0.0.0 mask 0.0.0.0 210.50.200.1
```

Handling Conflicts in Routing Information

However, it appears that there are some conflicts here. Look at some of the instructions that you've given the IP software about how to route:

- There's a rule about handling the specific address 210.50.200.40: just keep the message local at 127.0.0.1, no routing.

- There's a rule about how to handle the range from 210.50.200.0 through 210.50.200.255: shout it out on the subnet, no routing.

- There's a rule about how to handle the range from 199.100.200.0 through 199.100.200.255: send it to 210.50.200.200.

- There's a rule about how to handle the range from 200.15.16.0 through 200.15.16.255: send it to 210.50.200.22.

- There's a rule about how to handle *all* Internet addresses: send the messages to 210.50.200.1.

Here's what I mean about a conflict: suppose you want to send an IP packet to 200.15.16.33. You have one rule that says, "Send it to 210.50.200.22" and another that says, "Send it to 210.50.200.1." Which rule does the software on your workstation (or server) follow?

Answer: when in doubt, first look for the route with the smallest metric. If there is more than one candidate, then take the *most specific* one—in other words, choose the one with the most specific subnet mask.

In this case, there are two entries in the routing table that point to the destination, 200.15.16.33. I haven't shown you their metrics, but both of them require hopping over one router, so each route has metric 2. As their metrics are tied, you look next to the subnet mask. As the 210.50.200.1 route has a very generic subnet mask (0.0.0.0), your machine would ignore it in comparison to the more specific 210.50.200.22's subnet mask of 255.255.255.0.

Suppose workstation 210.50.200.40 wanted to get a message to another machine on the subnet; let's say that its address is 210.50.200.162. Again, there's a routing conflict, as one route entry just says to send it to 210.50.200.40—in other words, don't route, shout! There's another routing entry—the 0.0.0.0 one again—that says it can also get the IP packet to 210.50.200.162, as it claims it can get any packet *anywhere*. Which to choose? Well, if constructed correctly, an excerpt of the routing table will look something like this:

Destination	Netmask	Gateway	Interface	Metric
0.0.0.0	0.0.0.0	210.50.200.1	210.50.200.40	2
210.50.200.0	255.255.255.0	210.50.200.40	210.50.200.40	1

The first entry is the default gateway. It's got metric 2 because you've got to hop over at least one router to get to the Internet. (In actual fact, it's probably not a bad idea to set this value a bit higher, just to be sure internal IP packets *never* try to get sent over the Internet.) The second entry basically says, "To send data to your local subnet, just say it out loud on your Ethernet card"—again, don't route, shout. As the Internet metric is higher, your machine will know not to try to send a local message by sending it to the default gateway.

One more thing: You wouldn't, of course, want to have to type in those ROUTE ADD commands every time you start up your computer. So you'd use a variation on the ROUTE ADD command. Just type **route -p add...**. When you add the **-p** that entry becomes permanent in your system's routing table.

All Routers Must Know All Subnets

I've talked about how I'd set up my sample network from the point of view of a workstation. It would work, but you can see that it's a real pain to punch in all of those ROUTE ADD statements for each workstation. The answer is to make the routers smarter; *then* you can just pick one router to be the default gateway for the .40 workstation, and the workstation needn't worry about anything. So let's take a minute and see how each of the three routers in this system would be set up.

The first router is the one on the left, that routes between 199.100.200.0 and 210.50.200.0. It must know

- It can get to 199.100.200.0 through its 199.100.200.5 interface.

- It can get to 210.50.200.0 through its 210.50.200.200 interface.

- It can get to the Internet through 210.50.200.1, which it gets to through its 210.50.200.200 interface.

In fact, you would not have to type in routing commands telling it how to get to 199.100.200.0 or 210.50.200.0; assuming it's an NT machine, the NT routing software figures that out automatically. But you can tell it to get to the Internet by setting a default gateway:

```
route add 0.0.0.0 mask 0.0.0.0 210.50.200.1 metric 2
```

The routing software is then smart enough to realize that it should get to 210.50.200.1 via its 210.50.200.200 interface.

The second router, the one on the right, routes between 200.15.16.0 and 210.50 .200.0. It can get to both of those networks directly, and, as with the first router, we don't have to tell it about them. But to get to the Internet, it must route packets to 210.50.200.1, and so, like the first router, it should have a default gateway of 210.50.200.1.

Now let's tackle the third router, the machine at 210.50.200.1, which is the Internet gateway. It must know that it should use the Internet as its default gateway. For example, on my Compatible Systems routers, there is a magic address WAN which just means the modem connection to the Internet. I essentially tell it, "Route add 0.0.0.0 mask 0.0.0.0 WAN," and packets travel to and from the Internet over the modem. The router must then be told of each of the three subnets, like so:

```
route add 210.50.200.0 mask 255.255.255.0 210.50.200.1 metric 1
route add 199.100.200.0 mask 255.255.255.0 210.50.200.200 metric 2
route add 200.15.16.0 mask 255.255.255.0 210.50.200.22 metric 2
```

Using RIP to Simplify Workstation Management

Thus far, I've shown you how to tell your workstations how to exploit routers on the network. In most cases, you won't need to build such large, complex routing tables by hand, and in almost no case will you *want* to build those tables.

Ideally, you shouldn't have to type in static tables; instead, your workstations could just suck up routing information automatically from the nearby routers, using some kind of browser-type protocol. You *can* do such a thing with the *Routing Internet Protocol*, or RIP.

RIP is an incredibly simple protocol. Routers running RIP broadcast their routing tables about twice a minute. Any workstation running RIP software hears the routing tables and incorporates them into its *own* routing tables. Result: you put a new router on the system, and you needn't punch in any static routes.

RIP is part of the Multivendor Protocol Router package for NT 3.51 users, and ships as part of NT 4. The Microsoft implementation supports both IP and IPX. Routes detected by RIP show up in ROUTE PRINT statements just as if they were static routes.

Using an NT Machine as a LAN/LAN Router

In the process of expanding your company's intranet, you need routers. For a network of any size, the best bet is probably to buy dedicated routers, boxes from companies like Cisco Systems, Bay Networks, or Compatible Systems.

Dedicated routers are fast and come with some impressive management tools: neat GUI programs that let you control and monitor your network from your workstation. But routers have one disadvantage: they're expensive. I haven't seen an Ethernet-to-Ethernet IP router available for less than $3,000. Again, don't misunderstand me: these routers are probably worth what they cost in terms of the ease that they bring to network management and the speed with which they route data. But you might not have the three grand, so you're looking for an alternative.

Your NT machine can actually provide you with an alternative. Any NT workstation or server can act as a simple IP router— all you need is a multihomed PC (one with two or more network cards installed in it) and NT.

Just open up the Control Panel, open the Networks applet, then the Protocols tab, and the TCP/IP protocol. Click the Routing tab, and you see an option called Enable IP Routing. That's how you turn on NT's routing capability.

Let's see how to set up this router. Imagine you have an intranet that looks like Figure 14.22.

FIGURE 14.22:

A sample intranet

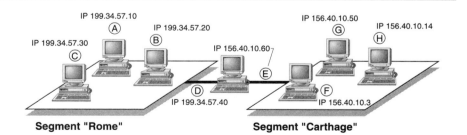

We're going to use the machine that's on both Rome and Carthage as the router. (Actually, there's no choice here, as it's the *only* machine in both TCP/IP domains, and any router between two domains must be a member of both domains.) All you have to do is go to the machine with two Ethernet cards and set up both cards with an IP address. The Enable IP Routing box will no longer be grayed out, and you can then check the box.

For cookbook style directions, see the "How Do I" sidebar.

How Do I Build an IP Router with NT?

Install two network cards (let's use Ethernet for this example) in an NT machine. The NT machine *need not be* an NT Server machine, and, given the cost of NT Server, you're probably better off using a copy of NT Workstation.

1. Configure the Ethernet card on the Rome subnet with an IP address for the Rome subnet. When you are working in the TCP/IP configuration dialog box, you notice a single-selection drop-down list box labeled Adapter: you can use that to control which Ethernet card you are assigning to what IP address.

2. Click the Routing button.

3. Check Enable IP Routing. Notice that the Enable IP Routing box is grayed out unless there are two network cards in your system.

4. Click OK until you get out of the Control Panel.

The system will reboot, and your router will be active.

This will allow an IP router to move traffic from one subnet to another. It will *not*, however, route traffic between three or more subnets.

What do I mean by that last line? Well, the default router software isn't very smart. Look at Figure 14.23, and you'll see what I mean.

Here, you see an intranet with just three subnets: 200.200.1.0, 200.200.2.0, and 200.200.3.0. For ease of discussion, let's call network 200.200.1.0 "network 1," 200.200.2.0 "network 2," and 200.200.3.0 "network 3." The network 1 to network 2 router, machine A, has addresses 200.200.1.1 and 200.200.2.40, and the network 2 to network 3 router, machine B, has addresses 200.200.2.75 and 200.200.3.50.

FIGURE 14.23:

Internet with three subnets

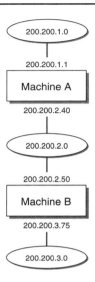

Once you turn on IP routing in machine A, it's smart enough to be able to route packets from network 1 to network 2, and packets from network 2 to network 1. But if it receives a packet from network 1 intended for network 3, it has no idea what to do about it.

Machine B has the same problem, basically. It knows how to go from network 2 to network 3 and from network 3 to network 2, but it has no idea how to find network 1.

How do you solve this problem? Either with static routes or with RIP. The best answer is probably to put the RIP router on both machine A and machine B, and they will end up discovering each other's routes through the RIP broadcasts. But how would you tell machine A how to find network 3 and how would you tell machine B to find network 1? With static ROUTE ADD commands.

On machine A, tell it about network 3 like so:

```
route add 200.200.3.0 mask 255.255.255.0 200.200.2.50
```

You're saying to this machine, "In order to find network 200.200.3.0, use the IP address 200.200.2.50; it's attached to a machine that can get the packets to that network." For the sake of completeness, you might add the "metric 2" parameter to the end.

On machine B, tell it about network 1 in a similar way:

```
route add 200.200.1.0 mask 255.255.255.0 200.200.2.40
```

Remember that in both cases the "mask" information says, "I'm giving you information about a subnet, but the mask says how useful the information is."

Using an NT Server Machine as an Internet Gateway

Consider this. Your company has purchased a full-time PPP account from some Internet provider. You have your LAN all running TCP/IP with NIC-approved IP numbers. All you need is a machine that will route your local traffic over the Internet when you want to FTP, use e-mail, or whatever.

From a hardware point of view, it's pretty easy: you just need a PC containing both an Ethernet card and a serial port, with a dial-up PPP connection. That machine was essentially doing the job of TCP/IP routing. How do you do that in NT?

The Overview

There are a number of "what if's" that you have to consider if you want to use your NT machine as a LAN-to-WAN Internet gateway.

The first piece of advice is: don't, if you can avoid it. In my company, I use the Compatible Systems mr900i, a terrific box that I picked up for $850. It's very easy to manage, does RIP, is much cheaper than buying a Pentium and a copy of NT, and is as fast as the wind. I'd recommend it as the way to go if you want to hook up your net to *the* Net.

But there are times that I don't have access to a dedicated router, and perhaps I'd like to use my NT machine as my Internet router. How do I do it?

Basically, the steps are the following:

1. Put a network card and a modem in an NT system.

2. Put a static IP address on the network card, but leave off the default gateway.

3. Install RAS and tell it how to dial up to your Internet Service Provider (ISP). In setting up the connection, disable Use Remote Gateway.

4. Make a change to the Registry (explained below).

5. Dial up to the ISP and log in.

6. Use a ROUTE ADD command to tell the system how to route to the Internet.

7. Then tell all the computers on your network to use the IP address of the network card as their default gateway.

The Obstacles

Those steps aren't hard, and we'll do a step-by-step "cookbook recipe" in just a minute. But there *are* two things, however, that will make it a bit difficult to explain how to do this, as it varies from ISP to ISP. They are

- How you log on to the ISP: simple character-oriented terminal login, the Password Authentication Protocol (PAP), or the Challenge Handshake Authentication Protocol (CHAP)

- How you set the IP address on your dial-up or frame relay connection

Those are both topics discussed in the Remote Access Services chapter, so I won't go into them in any detail here. I *did* want to point out, however, that there are differences in how you accomplish those two things.

Login Options

When you attach to an ISP network, you must identify yourself and prove who you are, usually with a password. Most ISPs require that when you dial up to them you work with a character-based login screen where you type in the account number and password for your network, and that's how I'll describe my example here. You've probably seen something like this before: "Welcome to XYZ Corporation, your on-ramp to the Information Superhighway; please enter your account number and password…" If your ISP works that way, then you can set up a Dial-Up Networking phone book entry that will create a terminal screen for you that will appear once you're connected to the ISP. In your Dial-Up Networking phone book, click Script and you see a dialog box like Figure 14.24.

FIGURE 14.24:

Telling Dial-Up Networking to
pop up a terminal screen so
you can enter the ID and
password

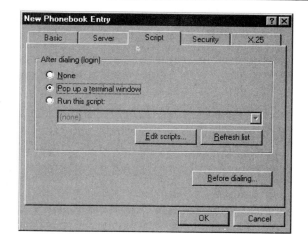

If you have an ISP like this, then you're probably logging in to some old Unix-based portmaster system of some kind. It can be a pain to have to punch in the user ID and password every time you connect to your ISP, so you may want to look into writing a logon script to automate the process; you can read about that in Chapter 18 on Remote Access Service.

Some ISPs, however, offer more modern, automated ways to log in to their networks. Assuming that you link up to the ISPs with PPP (Point to Point Protocol), then the ISP may choose to exploit a couple of extensions to PPP that have become popular: the *Password Authentication* Protocol (PAP) and the *Challenge-Handshake Authentication Protocol* (CHAP). Both are protocols allowing your computer to dial up to another computer and pass user ID and password information back and forth automatically, without you having to type that information in. If you have an ISP that supports PAP or CHAP, then click the None radio button in the Script page and click the Security page. It looks like Figure 14.25.

Why this doesn't just have radio buttons labeled PAP, CHAP, and the like is beyond me, but basically here's what to click. If you are dialing in to your ISP and authenticating with the Password Authentication Protocol, choose Accept Any Authentication. If you are using the generic CHAP protocol to authenticate with an ISP, choose Accept Only Encrypted Authentication. If you are dialing up an NT server, then choose Accept Only Encrypted Microsoft Authentication. Not surprisingly, Microsoft has created their own variation of the standard CHAP protocol that they call Microsoft-CHAP; clicking this last button requires it. Again, the value of using PAP or CHAP is that it absolves you of having to write a logon script.

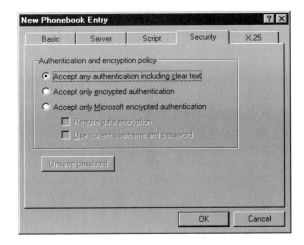

If your ISP is using NT machines, then you're probably in luck; you won't have to do a terminal logon. In most cases, however, terminal logons are still the order of the day. My advice is that you sit at the NT machine that will be the gateway and just try to get *it* attached to your ISP before going any further; figure out how to get to your ISP as a single dial-up machine before trying to share the connection with your LAN.

Obtaining an IP Address from Your ISP

Then there's the problem of IP addresses over your WAN link. Your dial-up connection has an IP address different from the address on the network card—but *what* address?

Most ISPs that I've arranged PPP connections with have a system whereby they tell your PPP connection what IP address to use automatically, as part of the logon sequence. Even if you have to type in your username and password by hand, your workstation will get the IP address automatically from the ISP. In my experience, most of the time ISPs just send you a piece of paper telling you to set up your software to use a certain IP address. Dial-Up Networking can accommodate both, as shown in Figure 14.26.

FIGURE 14.26:

Dial-Up Networking TCP/IP settings

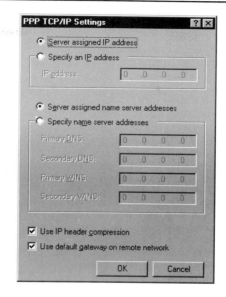

You get this dialog box by editing a Dial-Up Networking phone book entry. Open up the Dial-Up Networking application in My Computer, choose the entry for dialing to your ISP, click More, and click Edit Entry and Modem Properties. Then click Server and TCP/IP settings. Note the radio buttons in the group at the top: either Server assigned IP address (that's the more common automatic option) or Specify an IP address. And while I'm showing this dialog box to you, let me point out that the check box at the bottom of the dialog box, which says "Use default gateway on remote network," is checked by default, as you see in the example screen. In my experience, it's *very* important that you uncheck this box.

Anyway, this how-do-I-get-my-IP-address question is another ISP-specific issue, and another reason why you should dial up and log in to your ISP before going any further. The way that most ISPs seem to work, and, again, the way I'll write this example, is that you just tell your PPP software to get an IP address from the ISP and to require a terminal login.

The Recipe

Here are the steps that you use to make an NT workstation or server into a router that will connect your company's network to the Internet. I'll call that computer the gateway machine (when I say that, I'm *not* referring to computers from South Dakota; I'm just describing that one computer).

In this example, I'll connect my C-class network, 199.34.57.0, to the Internet through my Internet Service Provider, Digital Express, or, as its customers know it, "Digex." I'll need to know the phone number of Digex, which I'll make (301) 555-1212 in this example; my account number, which I'll make "xyzabc123" for this example; and a password, which I'll make "xyzzy."

My gateway machine is running NT Workstation 4 and contains an Ethernet card as well as a 28.8Kbps modem. If you're setting up NT 3.51, then the procedure will be identical save for one thing: go to Microsoft's FTP site and get the Multivendor Protocol Router (MPR).

1. On the gateway machine, install IP with static addressing for the network card. Set the network card's IP address (I'll use 199.34.57.1 in this example) with whatever subnet mask makes sense for your network (255.255.255.0 for basic C-class networks).

2. When you're setting up the IP address on the network card, leave the Default gateway address *blank.*

3. Install Dial-Up Networking. Look in the Dial-Up Networking chapter for details, but basically you open up the Dial-Up Networking icon in the My Computer folder. If it's the first time you've done that, then it'll automatically install Dial-Up Networking. You must tell it what kind of modem you have and what port it's on. Configure it to dial out only—you won't be receiving calls on this machine, not if it's your constant connection to the Internet. Reboot the system to complete installing Dial-Up Networking.

4. In the Registry, go to the key HKEY_LOCAL_MACHINE\System\ CurrentControlSet\Services\RasArp\Parameters and create a new value entry DisableOtherSrcPackets of type DWORD, and set the value to 0. You will have to create a new value entry, as DisableOtherSrcPackets isn't in that key by default.

The reason you do this is that this machine will be a router. This command says, "When you forward an IP packet, don't change the 'source' IP address." Otherwise, if machine B forwards a packet to machine C for machine A, then machine B changes the From: part of the IP packet to B's own IP address, with the result that C thinks the message originated with B, not A. Setting this Registry entry to 0 keeps that from happening.

5. Start up Dial-Up Networking, and it'll observe that there are no phone book entries and will prompt you for a first entry; let's make that the dial-up instructions for your ISP. If you already have Dial-Up Networking entries, then just click New to create another phone book entry. Use the Dial-Up Networking Setup Wizard if you like, or just enter the values directly.

6. Enter a descriptive name and phone number. For my example, I used Digex as the name. The initial screen will look something like Figure 14.27.

FIGURE 14.27:

The Basic tab for setting up an Internet connection

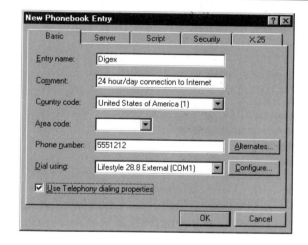

7. Next, I'll tell it that I want a terminal login screen so I can punch in the username and password whenever I need to reconnect my network to the Internet. I click Security and choose Accept any authentication including clear text. Then I choose Script and choose Pop up a terminal window. Then I have to tell Dial-Up Networking what to expect from the ISP that it's about to dial in to, so I choose Server, and I see a screen like Figure 14.28.

8. Be sure to tell it that you're dialing in to a PPP or NT Server server, as that's almost certainly what your ISP is using; PPP is the most common way to set up dial-in Unix servers. Your ISP *may* use SLIP instead, in which case you choose "SLIP: Internet" in the Server field. Check TCP/IP because that's the Internet protocol. Click TCP/IP Settings and you'll be able to configure whether to get the IP address from the ISP or whether to hard-code it, as mentioned earlier.

FIGURE 14.28:

Setting up the Server tab

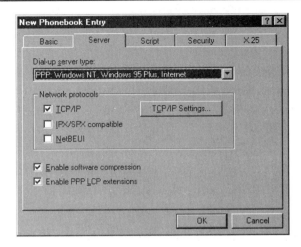

9. In the case of my ISP, I chose Server assigned IP address. Again, this is something that may be different for your ISP, so if things aren't working, then ask them. In the same way, Use IP header compression may work best checked or not checked. It's an option that *you* can enable or disable at your leisure. Which is better for you? In general, for connections slower than 28.8Kbps, turn on IP compression. For a faster system, turn IP compression off. One way to find out is to find a few big files on an FTP site and download them; try it with and without the header compression, and then you'll know which setting is better.

10. Uncheck Use default gateway on remote network.

11. Now you have to get your system to forward IP packets. Open up the Control Panel, then open Network ➢ Protocols ➢ TCP/IP ➢ Routing, and check Enable IP Forwarding. You have to reboot.

12. For those of you using NT 3.51, however, you have some more work to do. In NT 3.51, there is still a check box labeled Enable IP Routing, but it may be grayed out unless there are two or more network cards present in the Control Panel. That presents a problem, because NT only sees one Ethernet card, so it grays out the routing option. This kind of makes sense because you have to have at least two IP addresses in order to route, but it makes no sense that the IP addresses must be on network cards. NT *ought* to be smart enough to enable forwarding when one IP address is a network card and the other is a RAS/PPP-derived IP address, but it isn't: it *must* see two network cards before it'll enable IP routing.

Or mustn't it? There *is* one sneaky trick that you can do to get the Enable IP Routing box enabled. Just click Control Panel ➤ Networks ➤ TCP/IP Protocol ➤ Configure ➤ Advanced. You get the Advanced TCP/IP Configuration screen that you've seen earlier in this chapter. You can actually attach more than one IP address to a network card. So here's the trick to turn on IP routing: go to your one network card and add a bogus IP address. The Enable IP Routing box will become enabled. Check it. Then remove the bogus IP address, and the Enable IP Routing box will gray out, *but it will stay checked!* Again, NT 4 users needn't worry about this, as you don't have to go through all of this rigmarole to make forwarding work.

13. Once you've rebooted, start up Dial-Up Networking and dial up your ISP. When the terminal screen appears, punch in your username and password. When you get a message indicating that your session has started, click Done.

14. Find out what IP address your DUN connection is using. Type **IPCONFIG** and look for the line that looks like "Ethernet adapter NdisWan6:" or something like that, and the IP address below it is the IP address connected to the outside world. Suppose I find that on my example computer it's 199.34.57.2.

15. Your system now must know how to find the outside world. Open a command prompt and type **route add 0.0.0.0 mask 0.0.0.0** *x.y.z.a* metric 2, where *x.y.z.a* is the IP address that you just found for your DUN connection. In my case, I'd type **route add 0.0.0.0 mask 0.0.0.0 199.34.57.2 metric 2**. Now, if you're an RAS expert type, then you're no doubt wondering something like this: I told you to uncheck Use Default Gateway on Remote System. But the only thing that command does is automatically insert the line "route add 0.0.0.0 mask 0.0.0.0 199.34.57.2" in the routing table. Why then do all the extra work? My answer is, try it both ways. I have no idea why, but a Dial-Up Networking box won't route with Use Default Gateway on Remote System. It *will* route if you uncheck the Use Default Gateway box and enter the **route add 0.0.0.0...** by hand. How do I know? It's how my entire company has been connected to the Internet from time to time—we use an NT machine as a backup router.

16. Finally, make sure that all of the PCs on your subnet point to the static IP address attached to the network card, not the RAS connection. In my example, all of my machines point to the default gateway 199.34.57.1.

The machines on your subnet should now be able to ping the outside world.

But If It Doesn't Work...

There are enough pieces to this that you may find you can't get the gateway up first thing. Before you e-mail me asking if I'll troubleshoot your gateway—which is something that's pretty time consuming and is the sort of thing that will lead us to start talking about hourly rates, if you know what I mean—take the same steps that I would take in troubleshooting your gateway. It has been my experience time and time again that people who can't get the gateway to work have skipped a step or two, causing major frustration on their part. Just take it step by step: first, get the gateway machine talking to the local network, and then get it talking to the Internet, and, finally, get it routing right. Do that, and you'll be surfing in no time.

1. You've got to have honest-to-God approved InterNIC addresses. It's not sufficient to have an approved address for the gateway, and then make up random addresses for your local network. All machines on your network must have IP addresses that you got from your ISP or the InterNIC.

2. Make sure the ISP is prepared to route your new addresses. If their routers aren't ready to accept your packets, those packets never get anywhere.

3. Load IP on your local area network and make sure it works. Make sure everyone can ping everyone else. Then you know that the first part is functioning perfectly.

4. If you are using NT 3.51, download Service Pack 4 and the Multivendor Protocol Router (MPR). It's on Microsoft's Web and FTP sites. Install these modules on the gateway machine.

5. Set up the NT machine to dial into your ISP. You'll have to play around with the TCP/IP parameter settings in RAS, depending on how your ISP wants you dial in: Do you preset an IP address? Do you use Van Jacobsen header compression? What's their DNS address? and so on. You'll know you're done when the gateway can ping places in the outside world, FTP to an outside site, and access an outside Web location. Do not try to ping your local network from the gateway yet.

6. Make any necessary changes to the Registry for RAS. The DisableOtherSrc-Packets that I mentioned earlier may be the only setting you'll have to worry about, but there are two others that you should know:

    -   The Registry setting to turn on IP routing is in HKEY_LOCAL_MACHINE\system\CurrentControlSet\Services\TCP/IP\Parameters, and is called IPEnableRouter. It is of type REG_DWORD, and it should be set to 1 to enable IP routing.

- You will sometimes have to modify the value in another Registry parameter named PriorityBasedOnSubNet. It is in HKEY_LOCAL_ MACHINE \SYSTEM\CURRENT.

  ControlSet\Services\RasMan\IPCP is of type REG_DWORD. Its value is either 1 or 0. What it does is this: Since your gateway will have a static route to the outside world—a ROUTE ADD 0.0.0.0—as well as a static route to your local subnet, the gateway machine could get confused. It could get confused because if it wants to route packets to your local subnet, should it use the 0.0.0.0 route (that is, send it over the modem to the Internet), or should it use the Ethernet connection to your local subnet? I discussed this earlier in the chapter, saying that the IP stack on the gateway will use the most specific route. That's not entirely true. Yes, the NT gateway machine thinks it has two routes to the local subnet, and yes, it will ordinarily take the more specific one. But if RAS sets PriorityBased-OnSubnet to 0, then NT will override its normally good judgment, and send traffic destined for the local subnet out the modem. Result: data never gets to the local subnet. You can troubleshoot that problem like this: if the PCs on your local subnet can ping the gateway machine fine at first, but then after the gateway dials up the Internet, the PCs can no longer ping the gateway, change the PriorityBasedOnSubnet value to 1.

7. Remember to do the IPCONFIG statement and get the IP address assigned to you by the ISP. Then add the static route to the Internet.

TIP   Some people have reported to me that they needn't do that at all—they just check the Use Default Gateway on Remote System, and it works fine. (It *hasn't* worked for me, but there may be some quirkiness to my system that makes it not work.)

Make sure that the PCs on the local subnet all refer to the gateway PC as their default gateway, and at this point all your systems should be on the Internet.

Even Better Routing: Steelhead

Realistically, I know that most people will not use their NT boxes as IP routers (although it periodically serves as my LAN-to-WAN router); I've just covered it in the preceding pages (1) to help folks understand IP routing in general—I got tired of reading explanations written in Unix-ese and thought an NT-centric discussion would be useful, and (2) because hey, it *does* work and after struggling to figure it out, I thought I'd share the information.

Clearly Microsoft is unaware that no one's using NT as a router, because they've released an update to their routing software that both adds speed and a GUI interface. Originally code-named "Steelhead" (no doubt because it *scales* so well... sorry, that punning stuff is gonna get me killed one of these days), its latest name is *Routing and Remote Access Services*. I'll cover the Remote Access Services part in Chapter 18, but I wanted to take a few pages and demonstrate how it can make the job described in the previous pages—making your NT machine into a LAN-to-WAN router—easier. As a matter of fact, Microsoft describes my situation pretty well, calling it the "home office LAN" scenario in the Steelhead documentation. I got a copy of Steelhead and reimplemented the LAN-to-WAN router—here's what I did and how it went.

Setting Up the Router

As before, let's start with the ingredients:

- A C network or CIDR block of addresses from my ISP.

- The equipment I needed to set up a router with NT: a machine with 32+MB of RAM, NT Server 4, Service Pack 3 or newer, the RRAS, a modem, ISDN, or other RAS-capable connection, and a network card.

- Other PCs on my local network have network cards, and I must configure them with IP addresses from the block provided by the ISP.

You'll need to get Steelhead/RRAS from Microsoft's Web site, and I'm afraid I can't give you a specific URL, as Microsoft's Web site is Active Server Page–driven. The best you can do is to go to the Downloads section and look in the Windows NT downloads. You'll find RRAS in there, as well as a patch file released about a year later. RRAS downloads as a big executable named MPRI386.EXE; run it and it unpacks both code and documentation into a folder on your computer.

As I said a few pages back, I start with official IP addresses; you must first set up all of the PCs on the LAN with the ISP-provided IP addresses, or your packets won't route. I hate to sound like a broken record, but if you don't put IP addresses *that you got from your ISP* on your computers, this is never gonna work.

Then, I set up the NIC on the router PC, and, again, give it one of the ISP-supplied addresses. The router PC will eventually end up with *two* IP addresses, one for the NIC and another for the RAS connection to the ISP, but for now I just install an ISP-supplied IP address to the NIC. Next I install a fresh copy of NT Server 4 on the router machine from the distribution CD-ROM. Then I point all the PCs' default gateways to the IP address on the NIC of the router PC, and check that every machine can ping every other machine; now I know the LAN works properly.

I install Service Pack 3 or 4 on the system and fire up the RRAS installation program: MPRSETUP. It'll ask what I want to do with this, I'll reply that I'll use it for routing and demand-dial connections. Reboot.

Next, I log on at the server and open up Dial-Up Networking, and figure out what I'll have to do to connect to my ISP. I'm not worried about routing yet; I just want to get the NT server to successfully dial up to the ISP and establish a PPP connection so that I can ping, run Internet Explorer, and the like from the NT Server—I'll handle the routing to the other PCs a bit later. Using DUN to dial in to an ISP under RRAS is exactly identical to the way it worked a few pages back, so I won't repeat how to do it here.

WARNING But if you *do* intend to try this, then know that it's been my experience that you'll have to do some noodling around with the IP parameters to make a PPP connection with your ISP work well. And when I say, "It'll take some noodling," I mean it—my ISP had a specific FAQ on how to connect with RAS/DUN, and some of the recommended settings were wrong. If tech support from your ISP is like tech support from most ISPs—that is, practically nonexistent—then plan to spend a day or two messing with the Dial-Up Networking parameters. If you're using a full-time connection, like a Frame Relay Access Device (FRAD), then look to tech support for that particular device—here's a case where I wouldn't buy the FRAD until I'd spoken to both my ISP and the FRAD maker to be sure that someone would be around to help get me up and running.

You'll also need to experiment to find out how to automate your dial-in. With normal DUN, you can just tell NT to pop up a terminal window allowing you to type in your username and password, but you'll find that RRAS won't allow you to do that. Your ISP will have to support PAP (Password Authentication Protocol) or CHAP (Challenge-Handshake Authentication Protocol), or you'll have to write a login script. *Now* is the time to get the bugs out of this procedure, before you start worrying about routing. In my case, the ISP that I tried this on has fortunately started supporting PAP, so authentication wasn't a problem.

And once I've figured all that ISP configuration stuff out, I write it down and keep the information in a safe place; now I'm ready to route.

If you ever tried to make an NT server act as a LAN/WAN IP router, then you know that at this point I'd normally have to make a handful of Registry changes and reboot. But with Steelhead, it's easy downstream swimming.

RRAS has an administrative tool called RAS and Routing Administrator; it's in the Administrative Tools group, logically. RRAS doesn't yet know about the dial-in connection, so I see a screen like Figure 14.29, where only the Ethernet connection appears.

FIGURE 14.29:

Opening RRAS Administrator screen

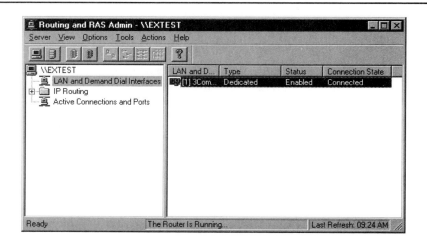

RRAS doesn't know about the modem, so I've next got to build the WAN link. Here's the cool part: I right-click on the Ethernet interface and get an option called Add Interface. That kicks off the Demand Dial Interface Wizard, which looks a lot like the normal Wizard that helps create new phonebook entries. A couple of clicks in, I find the screen that you see in Figure 14.30.

This basically tells RRAS that I'm using this as a dial-up IP router. The next few screens will be familiar to you (so I didn't reproduce them), as they're very similar to normal New Phonebook Entry Wizard screens. The last screen lets me set filters, but we'll just skip it for the moment. RAS and Router Admin then looks like Figure 14.31.

FIGURE 14.30:

Setting up a demand-dial
connection

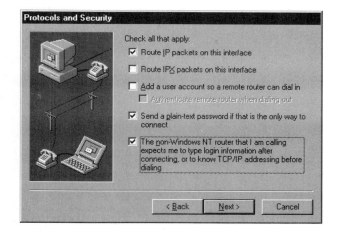

FIGURE 14.31:

RRAS with demand-dial
connection added

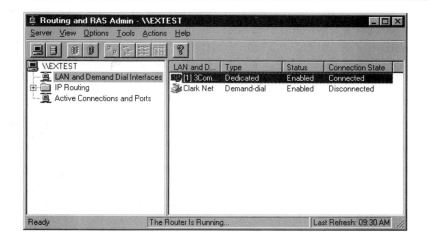

Note the new interface Clark Net. The Clark Net line type is *demand-dial*, meaning that it senses when it's needed. As I haven't tried to route through it yet, it's disconnected.

One more step, and I'll be routing. The router knows that there's an Ethernet interface and a demand-dial interface, but it really doesn't know anything about the demand-dial interface—what IP addresses can the router access through this dial-up interface? RRAS needs a static route to get to the Internet. I add a static route by clicking the plus sign next to IP Routing, then right-clicking the line that appears, labeled Static Routes. That gives me an option, Add Static Route, and I see the dialog box like Figure 14.32.

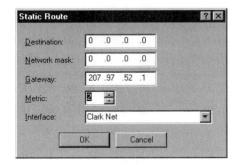

I fill in the values; the first two are trivial, as this is to be a gateway to the Internet, and the Internet's network address is 0.0.0.0 and subnet mask is 0.0.0.0. Note that I have to fill in a Gateway address. That's the address that my ISP assigns to me when I dial in. *Your router must always have the same dial-in IP address*, as near as I can tell. When you get a CIDR block or C network from your ISP, make sure you're always assigned the same address when you dial in. I fill in the metric of 2, as there's a "hop" across the router to get to the Internet; set the metric to 1, and you may no longer be able to route within your local network. The Interface allows me to associate this with my dial-up connection, the Clark Net interface.

Now to wake up the demand-dial connection; I just go over to one of the PCs on my network and try to ping some location, like www.microsoft.com. Here's where the cool stuff happens. From across the Ethernet, my NT server router got the clue that it needed to dial up, and it did. It takes a couple of minutes for the connection to get set up, so your first few pings may fail—I usually set a big timeout, like "ping www.microsoft.com –w 10000." At that point, I'm live on the Net using an NT Server as a router!

How It Worked

Other than the two pitfalls I've mentioned so far—you've got to end up with the same IP address all the time on the demand-dial interface and you've got to either use PAP/CHAP or an authentication script—how well does the rest of RRAS work?

For the application I've explored here, it rates about a B; Steelhead seemed more like a "croaker" sometimes. I found that the modem connection would sometimes drop for no apparent reason while in the middle of transferring data, which could be RRAS's fault, the fault of my ISP, or perhaps line noise. Other times, the connection would stay up, but the RRAS router would stop responding to external pings. I attempted to send the four screen-shot bitmaps that you see in this section over the connection as attachments to a mail message, but the connection would never stay up long enough to perform the operation, and I was forced to SneakerNet the files over in the end. The router was sometimes smart enough to reconnect, but not always. Sometimes the connection would drop—the "off hook" light on the modem was extinguished—but the Routing and RAS Admin program would show the connection as being still up. Other times, I'd have to drop the connection by hand and force it to reset before I could get packets to route correctly. All in all, it wasn't as hands-off as I'd have liked, which is troublesome, but it was a *big* improvement over messing around with Registry parameters. And my old method of making NT act as a LAN/WAN router wasn't kosher in the eyes of Microsoft tech support, meaning that if you couldn't make it work you were high and dry; presumably that won't be true when RRAS is released.

It also would have been nice to see a throughput measure built into the tool, although of course the Performance Monitor lets you watch that via the RAS counters. And the user interface can be a bit clumsy; for example, it takes a bit of fumbling around just to dump the IP routing table from the GUI, although the familiar old ROUTE PRINT command works just as well as it ever did. And best of all for us stodgy old command-line types, there's a command, ROUTEMON, that lets you do everything from the command line that you can do from the GUI.

To separate out the question "Was the problem the router or the ISP?" I reimplemented the C network connection to the ISP with a dedicated router from Compatible Systems (www.compatible.com): the mr900i. The mr900i is a reasonably priced (about $850 discounted) box that comes with an Ethernet connection and a serial port: a nice, basic LAN-to-WAN router. It does *not* do OSPF or port filtering (or at least the one *I* own doesn't; it looks on their Web site like their later models do), but you can do single-seat management of multiple Compatible routers through a Windows program shipped free with the router.

Rebuilding the network with the Compatible router was a snap—no hitches— and the PCs on the network were able to access the Internet without trouble for big and small jobs, suggesting that the instability lay in the RRAS software rather than anywhere else.

What Else Does It Offer?

Well, suppose I were concerned about security in my intranet; in that case, Steelhead is quite a catch. One approach to Internet security is through *virtual private networks* (VPNs), which essentially let you use the Internet as your own big private LAN. The Point to Point Tunneling Protocol (PPTP) lets you do that, but for the best PPTP security it's best if the router machine is also the PPTP server. RRAS's higher performance means that it might even make sense to use an NT machine as your LAN/WAN router even on a T1 connection, and that machine can also of course act as a PPTP server.

Or you might choose to open your network to the Internet but protect yourself from people using NetBIOS over TCP (NBT) to penetrate your network. In that case, you'd want to filter TCP and UDP ports 135–139. Under IP Routing ≻ Summary, right-click the WAN link and choose IP Configuration, and you'll get a dialog box allowing you to filter particular ports from particular locations. With precise control like that, you could, for example, filter out port 25 from a particular IP address—denying that address the ability to send Internet mail to any mail servers inside your network!

As the network got bigger, you'd find having to walk around to all the NT Server machines to do administration on the ones acting as routers tiresome, but the Routing and RAS Admin tool can control any RRAS router from a single location. Larger networks also find the chatty nature of the Routing Internet Protocol (RIP) unacceptable, so RRAS's support of the Open Shortest Path First (OSPF) protocol will be welcome. Both RIP and OSPF are dynamic routing algorithms that "discover" routes through your network rather than requiring static routing.

RRAS takes NT's routing capabilities and moves them forward considerably. First, it runs faster than the built-in IP routing software, and that's important, as it may now be good enough to replace dedicated routers. Second, single-seat management makes it more practical to take care of. Third, taking NT's LAN/WAN routing capabilities "out of the closet" and making them officially supported tools is incredibly significant not only for Internet users, but for ISPs as well: it's a boon for those ISPs that want to move more and more from a Unix-based network to an NT-based network. Add to this the PPTP and packet filtering capabilities, and it's a neat tool, if it turns out to be reasonably priced.

That said, the prospective RRAS user will have to experiment with her own IP environment to see if Steelhead does what she needs. My experience with my ISP and the test C network would not have been sufficiently trustworthy to leave my intranet in the hands (fins?) of RRAS; I'd stay with the Compatible router if I used the network constantly. In fairness, however, I did those tests with a piece of beta software. But it's precisely during the beta period that Microsoft listens best—so try it out on your network and see if it's a good catch or if you should just throw it back.

Interior and Exterior Routing Protocols

In the Internet world, there are two kinds of routing going on. RIP, OSPF, or your network's static routing tables route IP packets within your company's intranet domain (or perhaps those sleek, shiny Cisco routers do), and the routers in your Internet service provider do another kind of routing. Your routers mainly route data from one side of your company to another, and your ISP's routers mainly route data from one company's network to another company's network. Over the years, these routing processes have become refined into two categories of routers: *interior routers*, like RIP or OSPF, and *exterior routers*.

Exterior routers essentially route from the "border" of one Internet domain to the "border" of another, leading some people to dub them Exterior Border Protocols, or EBPs. The most widely used is probably the Exterior Gateway Protocol, or EGP.

Where would you see something like this? Well, suppose I go to the NIC and get myself another C-class network; suppose it's 223.150.100.0. I put it on my 199.34.57.0 network using my NT machines as RIP routers, and the two networks are just pinging one another like mad.

But then I try to ping the outside world from 223.150.100.0. And nothing happens. Why? Because my 199.34.57.0 network only knows about the 223.150.100.0 network because RIP told it. But to get to the outside world would require the complicity of my Internet Service Provider, and *it* doesn't listen to my RIP routers. If the router in my system that talked to my ISP spoke EGP, then perhaps we'd be OK. But, even then, my ISP *might* not even do EGP; perhaps they do only static routing between customer networks. NT doesn't support EGP.

Well, by now, you're on an intranet in the traditional way. Microsoft adds two possible options to this setup: the *Dynamic Host Configuration Protocol* (DHCP) and the *Windows Internet Naming Service* (WINS).

Installing TCP/IP with DHCP

Everything that you've learned so far is just about all you would need to set up an intranet. But you can see that this business of assigning IP addresses can be something of a pain. In particular, consider these problems:

- Wouldn't it be nice not to have to keep track of which IP addresses you've used and which ones remain?

- How do you assign a temporary IP address to a visiting computer, like a laptop?

Looking at these problems—and a possible solution—leads toward an understanding of DHCP and how to install it. Note, by the way, that this discussion assumes that you've already read this chapter up to this point; don't think that if you decided from the start to go with DHCP that you could jump in here without reading the first part of the chapter.

Simplifying TCP/IP Administration: BOOTP

I have a little list...

I keep this list of PCs and IP addresses. It's basically a kind of master directory of which IP addresses have been used so far. Obviously, I have to consult it when I put TCP/IP on each new computer.

That's obvious, but what's unfortunate is that I never seem to have the notebook with me when I need it. So I started keeping this list of computers and IP addresses on one of my servers, in a kind of common HOSTS file. It served two purposes: first, it told me what IP addresses were already used, and second, it gave me a HOSTS file to copy to the local computer's hard disk.

When it comes right down to it, however, this whole thing seems kind of stupid. Why am I doing what is clearly a rote, mechanical job—you know, the kind of job that computers are good at?

The Internet world agreed and invented a TCP/IP protocol called BOOTP, which became DHCP, as you will see. With BOOTP, a network administrator would first collect a list of MAC addresses for each LAN card. MAC, or Media Access Control, addresses are unique 48-bit identifiers for each network card. I've already mentioned the 48-bit identifiers on each Ethernet card, which are good examples of MAC addresses.

Next, the administrator would assign an IP address to each MAC address. A server on the company's intranet would then hold this table of MAC address/IP address pairs. Then, when a BOOTP-enabled workstation would start up for the day, it would broadcast a request for an IP address. The BOOTP server would recognize the MAC address from the broadcaster, and would supply the IP address to the workstation.

This was a great improvement over the static IP addressing system that I've described so far. The administrator didn't have to physically travel to each workstation to give them their own IP addresses; she needed only to modify a file on the BOOTP server when a new machine arrived or if it was necessary to change IP addresses for a particular set of machines.

Another great benefit of BOOTP was that it provided protection from the "helpful user." Suppose you have user Tom, who sits next to user Dick. Dick's machine isn't accessing the network correctly, so helpful user Tom says, "Well, *I'm* getting on the net fine, so let's just copy all of this confusing network stuff from my machine to yours." The result was that both machines ended up with identical configurations—including identical IP addresses, so now neither Tom *nor* Dick can access the network without errors! In contrast, if Tom's machine is only set up to go get its IP address from its local BOOTP server, then setting up Dick's machine identically will cause no harm, as it will just tell Dick's machine to get *its* address from the BOOTP server. Dick will get a different address (provided that the network administrator has typed in an IP address for Dick's MAC address), and all will be well.

DHCP: BOOTP Plus

BOOTP's ability to hand out IP addresses from a central location is terrific, but it's not dynamic. The network administrator must know beforehand what all of the MAC addresses of the Ethernet cards on her network are. This isn't *impossible* information to obtain, but it's a bit of a pain (usually typing **ipconfig /all** from a command line yields the data). Furthermore, there's no provision for handing out temporary IP addresses, like an IP address for a laptop used by a visiting executive.

DHCP improves upon BOOTP in that you just give it a range of IP addresses that it's allowed to hand out, and it just gives them out first-come first-served to whatever computers request them. If, on the other hand, you want to maintain full BOOTP-like behavior, then you can; it's possible with DHCP to preassign IP addresses to particular MAC addresses (it's called *DHCP reservation*), as with BOOTP.

With DHCP, you only have to hard-wire the IP addresses of a few machines, like your BOOTP/DHCP server and your default gateway.

WARNING   Both DHCP and BOOTP use UDP ports 67 and 68, so you won't be able to install both a BOOTP server and a DHCP server on the same computer. Now, Microsoft does not supply a BOOTP server; this note would mostly be only relevant if you tried to install a third-party BOOTP server. But NT also allows you to make a computer a "BOOTP Forwarding Agent." If you enable that software on a DHCP server, the server stops giving out IP addresses.

Let's see how to get a DHCP server up on your network, so the IP addresses will start getting handed out, and then we'll take a look at how DHCP works.

Death to Static IP: Use DHCP Everywhere!

In a minute, I'll get into the nitty-gritty of setting up DHCP servers and handing out IP addresses. But before I do, let's take up a big, overall network configuration question: which machines should have static IP addresses, and which machines should get their addresses from DHCP servers?

In general, the answer is that the only machines that should have static IP addresses should be your WINS servers, DNS servers, and DHCP servers. In actual fact, you'll probably put the WINS, DNS, and DHCP server functions on the same machines.

"But wait!" I hear you cry, "Are you suggesting that I let my domain controllers, mail servers, Web servers, and the like all have floating, random IP addresses assigned by DHCP willy-nilly?" No, not at all. Recall that you can assign a particular IP address to a particular MAC address using a DHCP reservation. My suggestion, then, is that you sit down and figure out which machines need fixed IP addresses, get the MAC addresses of the NICs in those machines, and then create reservations in DHCP for those machines. (From the DHCP Manager, a program you'll soon meet, you just click Scope ➤ Assign Reservation and fill in the blanks.)

What's the value of doing this; how are reserved DHCP addresses superior to static IP addresses? Well, for one thing, controlling IP addresses with DHCP means that you can control those addresses from a central location—a support plus. For another, machines with static IP addresses are sometimes "lost" by the network, and machines with DHCP reservations don't generally suffer from that problem. I know that sounds cryptic, but I'll explain more in the upcoming sections on WINS.

Installing and Configuring DHCP Servers

DHCP servers are the machines that provide IP addresses to machines that request access to the LAN. DHCP only works if the TCP/IP software on the workstations is *built* to work with DHCP—if the TCP/IP software includes a *DHCP client*. NT includes TCP/IP software with DHCP clients for Windows for Workgroups and DOS. NT workstations and Windows 95 workstations are already DHCP-aware.

To get ready for DHCP configuration:

- Have an IP address ready for your DHCP server—this is one computer on your network that *must* have a hard-wired IP address.

- Know which IP addresses are free to assign. You use these available IP addresses to create a pool of IP addresses.

To start up DHCP configuration, open the Control Panel and the Network applet, and click the Services tab. Click Add. Select Microsoft DHCP Server, and click OK. You are prompted, as always, for the location of the files. An information dialog box appears and instructs you to change any IP addresses on your network card(s) to static addresses. Click OK. The DHCP software will install. Click the Close button, and the binding operations will begin. After a while the hard drive activity stops. You see a screen like Figure 14.33. Here you specify a static IP address.

Once the system has rebooted, you find a new icon in the Administrative Tools group, the DHCP Manager. Start it up, and you will see a screen like Figure 14.34.

Not much to look at now, as there are no scopes set up yet. Scopes? What's a scope?

FIGURE 14.33:

Windows TCP/IP Installation
Options dialog box

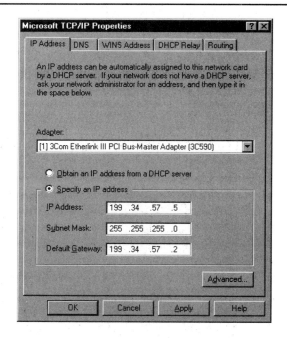

FIGURE 14.34:

DHCP opening screen

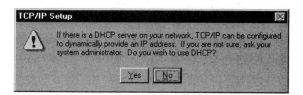

DHCP Scopes

In order for DHCP to give out IP addresses, it must know the range of IP addresses that it can give out. You tell it with a *scope*. You have to create a scope for your DHCP server. Do that by clicking on Scope, and Create. You will see a screen like the one shown in Figure 14.35.

A scope is simply a range of IP addresses—a pool from which they can be drawn. In the example above, I've created a scope that ranges from my .60

address to my .126 address. I don't want to get too sidetracked on the issue of scopes, but let me mention another use for scopes: you can assign a scope to each subnet serviced by your DHCP servers and, yes, it *is* possible for one DHCP server to handle multiple subnets.

FIGURE 14.35:

Create Scope dialog box

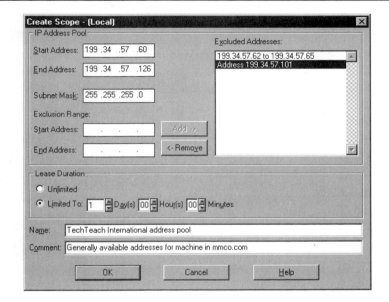

You cannot create multiple scopes for a single subnet on a single server; I'll show you how to get more than one server to act as a DHCP server (for the sake of fault tolerance) in a minute.

Getting back to setting up a scope, note that the dialog box's title is Create Scope (Local). That's because you can control a DHCP server from another NT machine, as is the case with so many NT network functions.

You should also note that I've filled in the Start Address, End Address, Lease Duration, Name, and Comment fields. Let's see what I did.

Start Address and End Address specifies a range of possible IP addresses to give out. Here, I've offered the addresses from my .60 address through my .126 address for the IP pool. That's 67 addresses, which are sufficient for my network.

I *could* have offered all 250-odd addresses and then excluded particular addresses with the Exclusion Range field; that's just as valid an option.

The Name and Comment fields are used mainly for administering scopes later. The Lease Duration field has Unlimited checked by default, but don't *you* use that; instead, set a fixed length of time for DHCP leases. I use seven days in general (although the figure you see here has only one day specified). Click OK, and you see a dialog box like Figure 14.36.

FIGURE 14.36:

Activating a new scope

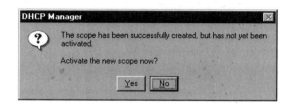

Click Yes, and it will be immediately available. The DHCP manager will then look something like Figure 14.37.

FIGURE 14.37:

DHCP Manager with an active scope

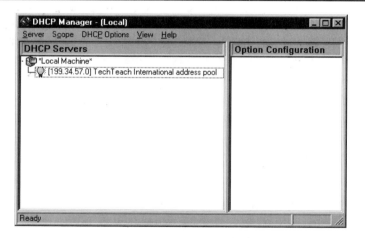

Note the lighted light bulb: that indicates an *active* scope. But you're not done yet. DHCP can provide default values for a whole host of TCP/IP parameters, including these basic items:

- Default gateway
- Domain name

- DNS server

- WINS server (DHCP calls it a WINS/NBNS server)

Remember that you had to type all that stuff in when you assigned fixed IP addresses? Well, DHCP lets you specify some defaults, making it an even more attractive addressing alternative. Just click DHCP Options, and you see options called Global, Scope, and Default.

Click Global to modify options that don't change from subnet to subnet, like the domain name or the DNS and WINS server addresses. Click Local to modify options that are relevant to particular subnets, like the address of the default gateway (which DHCP, for some perverse reason, calls the Router).

TIP

If you set an option like domain name, or WINS server via DHCP, but also specify a value for that option in the client PC in the Control Panel ➤ Network Protocol ➤ TCP/IP ➤ Properties, then the value you set in the Control Panel overrides the DHCP settings.

Most of the settings are global, so click Global, and you see a dialog box like the one shown in Figure 14.38.

FIGURE 14.38:

Setting DHCP global options

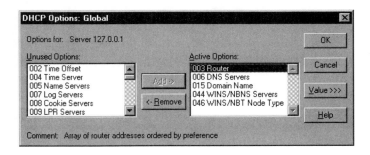

Now, despite the fact that there seem to be bushels of sadly unused parameters, mutely begging to be used, *don't*. Even though they exist, the Microsoft DHCP *client*—the part of Windows, DOS, Windows 95/98, and NT that knows how to get IP addresses from a DHCP server—does not know how to use any options save the ones I just mentioned. Microsoft included the other things just to remain compatible with BOOTP. Again, the five that I adjusted were

- DNS Servers; here I named our two DNS servers.

- Domain name, which is mmco.com for us.

- WINS/NBNS Servers, with the addresses of my WINS servers (which I'll cover soon). Setting this requires that you also set...

- WINS/NBT Node Type, a cryptic-looking setting that you needn't worry about, except to set it to 0x8; that makes WINS run best. I will explain node types in the upcoming discussion on WINS.

- Router (in Local Settings), which is, again, the DHCP equivalent of the Default Gateway option in the TCP/IP setup screen.

I set these by highlighting the option that I want to use, then clicking Add. Then I can click Value and Edit Array. For example, say I want to make my default gateway 199.34.57.2. I click on Router, then Edit Array. I then get a dialog box that looks like Figure 14.39.

FIGURE 14.39:

Setting the default router address

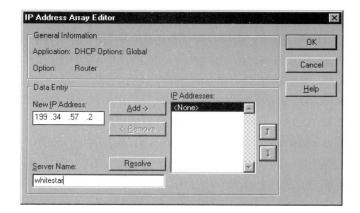

Notice that the original default value is 0.0.0.0, which is a meaningless address in this context. I enter 199.34.57.2 and click Add, but I don't stop there; next, I click on 0.0.0.0 and click on Remove. *Then* I click OK.

I do the same thing with the domain name and the DNS router, and I'm set. The DHCP Manager now looks like Figure 14.40.

Note the different icons for the global settings and the local settings. Close up the DHCP Manager, and your server is set up. You don't even need to reboot.

FIGURE 14.40:

The DHCP Manager

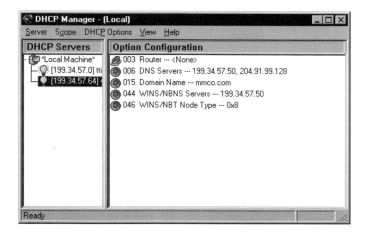

DHCP on the Client Side

Now that you've set up DHCP on a server, how do you tell clients to use that DHCP? Simple. The Windows for Workgroups TCP/IP 32-bit software has DHCP configuration as an installation option, as does the latest Microsoft Client software for DOS and Windows. If you want to find out what IP address a client machine has, go to that machine, open up a command line, and type **ipconfig /all**. On a Windows 95 workstation, click Start and Run, and then type **WINIPCFG** and press Enter. Windows 98 supports both IPCONFIG *and* WINIPCFG. Windows NT only supports IPCONFIG. And if you're running Windows 95 in its original version or its first patched release (OSR 1), then look in the Windows NT 4 CD-ROM for a file called DHCP.VXD. It fixes some problems with Windows 95's DHCP client. Just overwrite the DHCP.VXD file currently on the Windows 95 machine with the one from the NT CD-ROM.

DHCP in Detail

That's setting up DHCP. But, how does it work and, unfortunately, how does it sometimes *not* work?

DHCP supplies IP addresses based on the idea of *client leases*. When a machine (a DHCP client) needs an IP address, it asks a DHCP server for that address. (*How* it does that is important, and I'll get to it in a minute.) A DHCP server then gives an IP address to the client, *but only for a temporary period of time*—hence the term *IP lease*. You might have noticed that you can set the term of an IP lease from DHCP; it's one of the settings in Scope ➤ Properties.

The client then knows how long it's got the lease. Even if you reboot or reset your computer, it'll remember what lease is active for it and how much longer it's got to go on the lease.

TIP   On a Windows 3.*x* machine, that information is kept in DHCP.BIN in the Windows directory. On a Windows 95 machine, it's in HKEY_LOCAL_MACHINE\System\CurrentControlSet\Services\VxD\DHCP\Dhcp-info*xx*, where *xx* is two digits. And if you wish to enable or disable the error messages from the DHCP client on a Windows 95 machine, it's the value PopupFlag in the key HKEY_LOCAL_MACHINE\System\CurrentControlSet\Services\VxD\DHCP; use "00 00 00 00" for false, or "01 00 00 00" for true. Alternatively, opening a command line and typing **IPCONFIG/Release** will erase this information. To find the place in the Registry holding DHCP lease information on an NT machine, run REGEDIT and search for "DHCPIPAddress" in HKEY_LOCAL_MACHINE\System\CurrentControlSet. The key or keys that turn up are the location of the DHCP lease info.

So, if your PC had a four-day lease on some address, and you rebooted two days into its lease, then the PC wouldn't just blindly ask for an IP address; instead, it would go back to the DHCP server that it got its IP address from and request the particular IP address that it had before. If the DHCP server were still up, then it would acknowledge the request, letting the workstation use the IP address. If, on the other hand, the DHCP server has had its lease information wiped out through some disaster, then it will either give the IP address to the machine (if no one else is using the address), or it will send a *negative acknowledgment*, or *NACK* to the machine, and the DHCP server will make a note of that NACK in the Event Log. Your workstation should then be smart enough to start searching around for a new DHCP server. In my experience, sometimes it isn't.

Like BOOTP, DHCP remembers which IP addresses go with what machine by matching up an IP address with a MAC (Media Access Control, that is, Ethernet address).

Normally a DHCP server can send new lease information to a client only at lease renewal intervals. But DHCP clients also "check in" at reboot, so rebooting a workstation will allow DHCP to reset any lease changes such as subnet masks and DNS services.

Getting an IP Address from DHCP: The Nuts and Bolts

A DHCP client gets an IP address from a DHCP server in four steps:

- A *DHCPDISCOVER* broadcasts a request to all DHCP servers in earshot, requesting an IP address.

- The servers respond with *DHCPOFFER* of IP addresses and lease times.

- The client chooses the offer that sounds most appealing and broadcasts back a *DHCPREQUEST* to confirm the IP address.

- The server handing out the IP address finishes the procedure by returning with a *DHCPACK*, an acknowledgment of the request.

Initial DHCP Request: DHCPOFFER

First, a DHCP client sends out a message called a DHCPDISCOVER saying, in effect, "Are there any DHCP servers out there? If so, I want an IP address." This message is shown in Figure 14.41.

FIGURE 14.41:

DHCP step 1: DHCPDISCOVER

DHCP
client

DHCP
server

Enet addr: 00CC00000000
IP addr: 0.0.0.0

Enet addr: 00BB00000000
IP addr: 210.22.31.100

"Is there a DHCP server around?"

IP address used: 255.255.255.255 (broadcast)
Ethernet address used: FFFFFFFFFFFF (broadcast)
Transaction ID: 14321

You might ask, "How can a machine communicate if it doesn't have an address?" Through a different protocol than TCP—UDP, or the *User Datagram Protocol*. It's not a NetBIOS or NetBEUI creature; it's all TCP/IP-suite stuff.

Now, to follow all of these DHCP messages, there are a couple of things to watch. First of all, I'm showing you both the Ethernet addresses (Token Ring addresses for those of you using Token Ring) and the IP addresses because you see that they tell somewhat different stories. Also, there is a "transaction ID" attached to each DHCP packet that's quite useful. The transaction ID makes it possible for a client to know when it receives a response from a server exactly *what* the response is responding to.

In this case, notice that the IP address the message is sent to is 255.255.255.255. That's the generic address for "anybody on this subnet." Now, 210.22.31.255 would also work, assuming that this is a C-class network that hasn't been subnetted, but 255.255.255.255 pretty much always means "anyone who can hear me." If you set up your routers to forward broadcasts, then 255.255.255.255 will be propagated all over the network; 210.22.31.255 would not. Notice also the destination Ethernet address, FFFFFFFFFFFF. That's the Ethernet way of saying, "Everybody—a broadcast."

DHCP Offers Addresses from Near and Far

Any DHCP servers within earshot—that is, any that receive the UDP datagram—respond to the client with an offer, a proposed IP address, like the one shown in Figure 14.42. Again, this is an offer, not the final IP address.

FIGURE 14.42:

DHCP step 2: DHCPOFFER

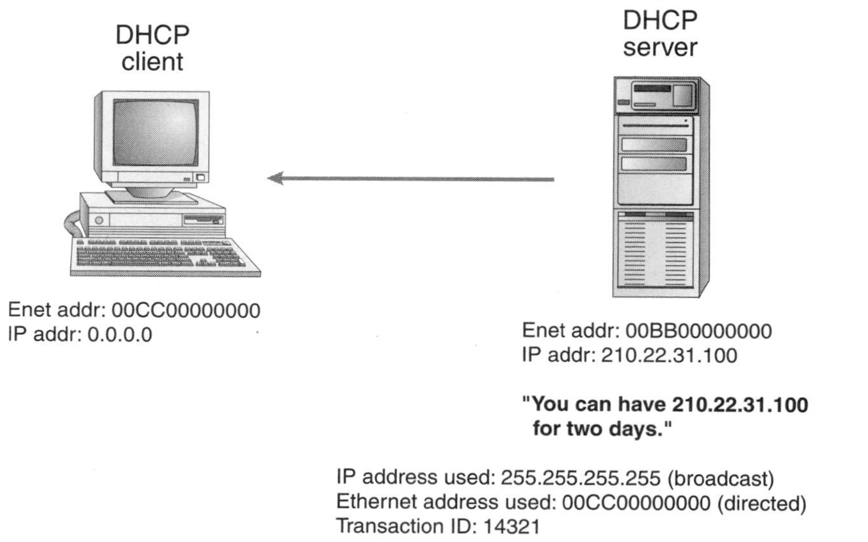

DHCP client

DHCP server

Enet addr: 00CC00000000
IP addr: 0.0.0.0

Enet addr: 00BB00000000
IP addr: 210.22.31.100

"You can have 210.22.31.100 for two days."

IP address used: 255.255.255.255 (broadcast)
Ethernet address used: 00CC00000000 (directed)
Transaction ID: 14321

This offering part of the DHCP process is essential because, as I just hinted, it's possible for more than one DHCP server to hear the original client request. If every DHCP server just thrust an IP address at the hapless client, then it would end up with multiple IP addresses, addresses wasted in the sense that the DHCP servers would consider them all taken, and so they couldn't give those addresses out to other machines.

Side Note: Leapfrogging Routers

Before going further, let's consider a side issue that may be nagging at the back of your mind. As a DHCP client uses *broadcasts* to find a DHCP server, where do routers fit into this? The original UDP message, "Are there any DHCP servers out there?" is a broadcast, recall. Most routers, as you know, do not forward broadcasts—which reduces network traffic congestion and is a positive side effect of routers. But if DHCP requests don't go over routers, then that would imply that you have to have a DHCP server on every subnet—a rather expensive proposition.

The BOOTP standard got around this by defining an RFC 1542, a specification whereby routers following RFC 1542 would recognize BOOTP broadcasts and would forward them to other subnets. The feature must be implemented in your routers' software, and it's commonly known as *BOOTP forwarding*. Even if you live in a one-subnet world, by the way, that's worth remembering, as it's invariably a question on the Microsoft NT exams: "What do you need for client A to communicate with DHCP server B on a different subnet?" Answer: The router between A and B either must be "RFC 1542–compliant" or "must support BOOTP forwarding."

OK, so where do you *get* an RFC 1542–compliant router? Well, most of the IP router manufacturers, like Compatible Systems, Cisco, and Bay Networks, now support 1542. New routers probably already support it, older routers may require a software upgrade. Another approach is to use an NT system as a router, as NT's routing software includes 1542 compliance. But what if you've got dumb routers, or router administrators that refuse to turn on the BOOTP forwarding? Then you can designate an NT machine as a *DHCP Relay Agent*.

A DHCP Relay Agent is just an NT machine that spends a bit of its CPU power listening for DHCP client broadcasts. The DHCP Relay Agent knows that there's no DHCP server on the subnet (because you told it), but the DHCP Relay Agent knows where there *is* a DHCP server on another subnet (because you told it). The DHCP Relay Agent then takes the DHCP client broadcast and converts it into a directed, point-to-point communication straight to the DHCP server. Directed IP communications can cross routers, of course, and so the message gets to the DHCP server.

You can make any NT machine into a DHCP Relay Agent. Just open up the Control Panel, then the Network applet. Click the Protocols tab and double-click on the TCP/IP protocol. In the resulting dialog box, you'll see a tab labeled DHCP Relay. Click it, and you'll see a dialog box like the one shown in Figure 14.43.

FIGURE 14.43:

Configuring a computer to be a DHCP Relay Agent

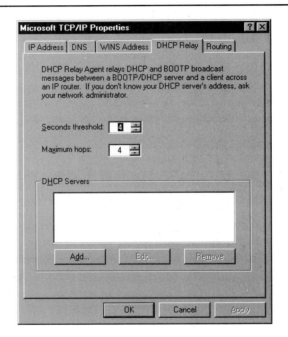

To make this work, just click the Add button and fill in the IP address of a DHCP server or servers. The dialog box is simple, but there are two things that confuse people about making a computer into a DHCP Relay Agent, so let me note them here.

TIP   The DHCP Relay Agent runs on a computer on the subnet, *not* a computer acting as a router on a subnet. You should only have one DHCP Relay Agent on each subnet.

WARNING   Under no circumstances should you make a DHCP server into a DHCP Relay Agent. The net effect will be for the DHCP server to essentially "forget" that it's a DHCP server, and instead to just forward every request that it hears to some other DHCP server. This prompts me to wonder why the silly DHCP Relay Agent function isn't grayed out altogether on a DHCP server—certainly the "Obtain an IP address from a DHCP server" option is. All fixed in Windows 2000, I suppose.

That all leads me to yet another question. What if a DHCP server from another subnet gave an IP address to our client? Wouldn't that put the client in the wrong subnet? If a DHCP server serves a bunch of different subnets, how does it know which subnet an incoming request came from? DHCP keeps that from happening via BOOTP forwarding.

Assuming that you have routers that implement BOOTP forwarding, then a client's original DHCP request gets out to all of them. But how do we keep a DHCP server in an imaginary subnet 200.1.2.*x* from giving an address in 200.1.2.*x* to a PC sitting in another imaginary subnet, 200.1.1.*x*? Simple. When the router forwards the BOOTP request, it attaches a little note to it that says, "This came from 200.1.1.*x*." The DHCP server then sees that information, and so it only responds if it has a scope within 200.1.1.*x*.

Anyway, notice that although to the higher-layer protocol (UDP) this is a broadcast, the lower-layer Ethernet protocol behaves as though it is not, and the Ethernet address embedded in the message is the address of the client, not the FFFFFFFFFFFF broadcast address. Notice also that the transaction ID on the response matches the transaction ID on the original request. End of side trip, let's return to watching that client get its address from DHCP...

Picking from the Offers

The DHCP client then looks through the offers that it has and picks the one that's best for it. If there are multiple offers that look equally good, it picks the one that arrived first. Then it sends another UDP datagram, another broadcast, shown in Figure 14.44.

It's a broadcast because this message serves two purposes. First, the broadcast *will* get back to the original offering server if the first broadcast got to that server, which it obviously did. Second, this broadcast is a way of saying to any *other* DHCP servers who made offers, "Sorry, folks, but I'm taking this other offer."

FIGURE 14.44:

DHCP step 3: DHCPREQUEST

DHCP
client

DHCP
server

Enet addr: 00CC00000000
IP addr: 0.0.0.0

Enet addr: 00BB00000000
IP addr: 210.22.31.100

**"Can I have the 210.22.31.100 IP address,
and thanks for the other offers, but no thanks."**

IP address used: 255.255.255.255 (broadcast)
Ethernet address used: FFFFFFFFFFFF (broadcast)
Transaction ID: 18923

Notice that both the Ethernet and the IP addresses are broadcasts, and there is a new transaction ID.

The Lease Is Signed

Finally, the DHCP server responds with the shiny brand-new IP address, which will look something like Figure 14.45.

It also tells the client its new subnet mask, lease period, and whatever else you specified (gateway, WINS server, DNS server, and the like). Again, notice it's a UDP broadcast, but the Ethernet address is directed, and the transaction ID matches the previous request's ID.

You can find out what your IP configuration looks like after DHCP by typing **IPCONFIG /ALL**. It may run off the screen, so you may need to add **| more** to the line. This works on DOS, Windows for Workgroups, and NT machines. You can see a sample run of IPCONFIG / ALL in Figure 14.46.

Windows 95 machines have a graphical version of IPCONFIG called Winipcfg.

FIGURE 14.45:

DHPC step 4: DHCPACK

DHCP client

DHCP server

Enet addr: 00CC00000000
IP addr: 0.0.0.0

Enet addr: 00BB00000000
IP addr: 210.22.31.100

"Sure; also take this subnet mask, DNS server address, WINS server, node type, and domain name."

IP address used: 255.255.255.255 (broadcast)
Ethernet address used: 00CC00000000 (directed)
Transaction ID: 18923

FIGURE 14.46:

Run of IPCONFIG

```
Command Prompt                                                    _ □ X
G:\USERS\DEFAULT>ipconfig /all

Windows NT IP Configuration

        Host Name . . . . . . . . . : aldebaran.mmco.com
        DNS Servers . . . . . . . . : 199.34.57.50
                                      164.109.1.3
                                      204.91.99.128
        Node Type . . . . . . . . . : Hybrid
        NetBIOS Scope ID. . . . . . :
        IP Routing Enabled. . . . . : No
        WINS Proxy Enabled. . . . . : No
        NetBIOS Resolution Uses DNS : No

Ethernet adapter E159x1:

        Description . . . . . . . . : Fast Ethernet Adapter
        Physical Address. . . . . . : 00-A0-24-A3-EE-DB
        DHCP Enabled. . . . . . . . : No
        IP Address. . . . . . . . . : 199.34.57.47
        Subnet Mask . . . . . . . . : 255.255.255.192
        Default Gateway . . . . . . : 199.34.57.1
        Primary WINS Server . . . . : 199.34.57.50

G:\USERS\DEFAULT>
```

Lost Our Lease! Must Sell!

What happens when the lease runs out? Well, when that happens, you're supposed to stop using the IP address. But that's not likely to happen.

When the lease is half over, the DHCP client begins renegotiating the IP lease by sending a DHCP Request to the server that originally gave it its IP address. The IP and Ethernet addresses are both specific to the server.

The DHCP server then responds with a DHCPACK. The benefit of this is that the DHCPACK contains all of the information that the original DHCPACK had—domain name, DNS server, and so on. That means you can change the DNS server, WINS server, subnet mask, and the like, and the new information will be updated at the clients periodically, but no more than 50 percent of the lease time.

Now, if the DHCPACK doesn't appear, then the DHCP client keeps resending the DHCP Request out every two minutes until the IP lease is 87.5 percent expired. (Don't you wonder where they get these numbers from?) At that point, the client just goes back to the drawing board, broadcasting DHCPDISCOVER messages until someone responds. If the lease expires without a new one, the client will stop using the IP address, effectively disabling the TCP/IP protocol on that workstation.

But if you've messed with the DHCP servers, then the renewal process seems to get bogged down a bit. It's a good idea in that case to force a workstation to restart the whole DHCP process by typing **ipconfig /renew**; that will often clear up a DHCP problem.

Even with an infinite lease, however, a DHCP client checks back with its server whenever it boots. Therefore, you can often change from infinite to fixed leases by just changing the lease value at the server. Then stop and restart the DHCP service.

Designing Multi-DHCP Networks

Clearly the function of the DHCP server is one that shouldn't rest solely on the shoulders of one server (well, OK, servers don't have shoulders, but you know what I mean). So, how can you put two or more DHCP servers online to accomplish some fault tolerance?

Microsoft seems, however, a bit confused about how to go about providing multiple DHCP servers for a given subnet.

In one document, "Windows NT 3.5 Family Upgrade Course," they say several things. First, "There is NO mechanism in DHCP that allows two or more DHCP Servers to coordinate the assignment of IP addresses from overlapping IP address pools."

No argument there. If you had two different DHCP servers on the same subnet, and they both thought that they could give out addresses 202.11.39.10 through 202.11.39.40, then there would be nothing keeping the first server from giving address 202.11.39.29 to one machine, while simultaneously the other server was giving out that same 202.11.39.29 address to another machine. (It's almost as if helpful Tom has returned!)

Then, they go on (pages 147 and 148) to demonstrate two different machines running DHCP server, and each machine has a different scope. Both scopes are, however, taken from a single subnet.

In contrast, the NT *Resource Kit* (version 3.5, but 3.51 has no updates on the matter) takes issue with the idea of more than one scope referring to a subnet like so: "Each subnet can have only one scope with a single continuous range of IP addresses…"

What this boils down to is this: I don't know what the official Microsoft approach to DHCP fault tolerance *is*. I *do*, however, know what works, and what has worked for me. Like many people, I came up with an approach like the one in the NT training guide. I just run DHCP on multiple machines and create multiple scopes which refer to the same subnet. I make absolutely sure that the ranges of addresses in the scopes do not overlap at all, and everything seems to work fine.

DHCP Problems and Service Pack 4 Solutions

While DHCP does a lot of neat stuff, there are still bugs. Service Pack 4 greatly revised DHCP in a few ways; here's an overview of those problems and the SP4 solutions.

DHCP Handles Hundreds of Scopes Now

Some firms put a *lot* of scopes on a single DHCP server—in fact, one large firm put 1,200 scopes on a single machine. The result was kind of interesting: 1,200 scopes mean 1,200 subnets (and presumably a *lot* of DHCP Relay Agents), which means that when a DHCP Discover message came into this server, it first had to find the scope for that particular subnet, *then* it had to figure out which—if any—

IP addresses were available for that subnet. As DHCP wasn't really built to handle that many scopes, the DHCP server's strategy when a DHCP query came in was to lock the DHCP database while searching for the scope, and to *ignore* any incoming DHCP requests during the scope search. While this sounds a bit goofy, it's really not, as Microsoft expected customers to put no more than a dozen or so scopes on any given DHCP server. With 1,200 scopes, however, the lock-and-search process can be quite time consuming, an effect worsened by the fact that the DHCP database is searched on disk each time.

Service Pack 4 fixes that problem in two ways:

- It stores the DHCP database in RAM, making DHCP a little more RAM-thirsty, but not by much.

- It has been redesigned to be multi-threaded, meaning that it can essentially "walk and chew gum at the same time"; that is, it can both search the database and listen for new DHCP queries.

DHCP Handles More Than 570 Reservations

More good news for big-network DHCP administrators. While it's not exactly been a problem I've run across in my network, it seems that if you give a DHCP server more than 570 DHCP reservations, it can only show 570 in the DHCP Manager. That means that while DHCP is handing out all of the reservations, you can't examine anything beyond the last 570, making managing lots of reservations impossible. Service Pack 4 fixes that, presumably making the sky the limit. (Excuse me, I've gotta go punch in 10,000 reservations to see what happens...)

DHCP Server Now Rechecks Bad Addresses

When DHCP gives an IP address to a DHCP client, the client checks to see if some other machine is already using that IP address before getting "comfortable" with its newly leased IP address. Once a DHCP client has received an IP address, say 200.200.100.200, it checks to see that no one else is using the address by broadcasting on the local subnet, "Hey, is anyone out there using 200.200.100.200?" It does this with an ARP (Address Resolution Protocol) request. If no one responds, that means that it's OK for the DHCP client to use the address. If, on the other hand, another machine does respond, then we've got a problem: DHCP has given the client a bad address. The client tells DHCP that by sending a message called DHCP_DECLINE, which basically says, "Keep your IP address, I don't want it!" and the DHCP server wants to remember not to offer that address again. So the

DHCP server stores that particular IP address in its "reserved addresses" database, giving it the machine name BAD_ADDRESS.

So far, so good: DHCP keeping track of which IP addresses are *traif* makes good sense. But the no-good addresses may not *stay* no-good, and that's where the problem arises. Once DHCP thinks an address is bad, it *always* thinks the address is bad. Some large organizations have bazillions of IP addresses locked up unused in their DHCP databases because they once caused an IP address conflict.

Service Pack 4 changes that by treating BAD_ADDRESS records as if they were any other DHCP lease, expiring them after the normal lease period. When you apply SP4, it immediately notices a bunch of BAD_ADDRESS records that have been around *way* longer than the lease period, and as a result one of the side effects you'll see of installing SP4 will be that all of a sudden you'll have a *lot* of new IP addresses available in your DHCP scopes!

The DHCP Client Is More Tenacious

If a DHCP server offers a bad address to a DHCP client and the client discovers that the address is bad through an ARP, it declines the address and asks for another. If the *next* address that the DHCP server offers also turns out to be bad, the DHCP client just gives up.

Under Service Pack 4, it doesn't give up after two tries. Now, Microsoft hasn't said how *many* tries an SP4 client will make, but it's more than two. Notice that this is *client* behavior, not server behavior, and so this problem will still happen on Windows 9x clients.

DHCP Offers More Logs

Open the DHCP Manager, click on a server, and choose Server ➤ Properties, and you'll get the option to log all of DHCP's actions. It's pretty cool and I've found it useful in the past. But you end up with one huge log, which can be a bit cumbersome to look at. Under Service Pack 4, you get seven logs: DHCPSrvLog.Mon, DHCPSrvLog.Tue, and so on. Not a *huge* improvement, but much more manageable.

Expand the Scope, and the Excluded Addresses Are Excluded

A while back, I was playing around with a DHCP scope on my network. When I originally set up the scope on my C network, I created a DHCP scope that handed out addresses between .12 and .100 in the C network, excluding .33 and .50, the addresses of a PDC and a mail server. I extended the scope to offer addresses from .5 to .200.

Some time after, the PDC reported a duplicate IP address. Sure enough, DHCP had given out .33 to a client machine! I scratched my head, gave up trying to figure out what caused it, and just moved the PDC over to .240, outside of the DHCP scope. I later moved the mail server.

This, as it turns out, is a known problem with a DHCP server. Extend the scope, and it *forgets* about the addresses that you told it to exclude. But not any more: SP4 fixes it. And so far, it seems to be working…

A good bit of fixes, and it's free! There are some other, somewhat more obscure DHCP fixes in SP4, but you can read about them in Knowledge Base article Q181774.

Recovering from a DHCP Server Disaster

Suppose one of your servers crashed, and suppose it was your only DHCP server. Suppose also that the server gave out leases for three days.

Once you determine that the server can't be saved, you decide to zap the disk and start over. In a few hours, you rebuild the server, re-create a scope, and activate the scope, so client machines can get IP addresses. You see a fair number of error messages for a few days, because all of those clients still think that they have leases on IP addresses for up to three days—but the DHCP server doesn't know anything about that. The clients start requesting that their DHCP licenses be renewed, and the new DHCP server sends them NACK (negative acknowledgment) messages, saying, in effect, "No! Do *not* use the IP address that you just requested an extension for!"

At that point, the DHCP client is supposed to initiate the DHCP Discover process all over again. In my experience, however, sometimes that doesn't work, and you have to go to the workstation and type the **ipconfig /release** command, followed by **ipconfig /renew**.

How to Back Up a DHCP Database

The way to avoid all of this is to simply back up the DHCP database now and then, enabling you to restore the DHCP database to another computer if the original DHCP server dies. By restoring a DHCP backup from one machine to a different DHCP server, you make that latter DHCP server act exactly like the former

DHCP server, accomplishing disaster recovery. But how to initiate the backups? Fortunately, DHCP does that automatically. Every hour, DHCP makes a backup of its database.

TIP

You can make DHCP back up the database less often or more often with a Registry parameter. In HKEY_LOCAL_MACHINE\System\CurrentControlSet\services\DHCPServer\Parameters, look for (or create) a value entry called BackupInterval of type REG_DWORD. Enter the value (in hexadecimal, of course) in minutes. The smallest value you can enter is five minutes, and the largest is 60 minutes, which (at least on my machines) appears to be the default, despite the fact that the *Resource Kit* claims it's 15 minutes.

Backing Up a 3.51 DHCP Database   The database (in WINNT\SYSTEM32\DHCP) consists of three files. The files differ depending on whether you're running NT 3.51 or NT 4. In NT 3.51 installations, the three files are as follows:

- DHCP.MDB, which is the actual DHCP database.

- SYSTEM.MDB, which every Microsoft document describes as "used by DHCP for holding information about the structure of the database." (Must be a secret, huh?)

- JET.LOG is a transaction log. The value of logs is that the database using them (DHCP, in this case, but lots of other database systems use them) can use log information to find out what changes have been made recently; this allows the database to repair itself in some cases.

NT stores these three files in a directory called \winnt\system32\dhcp\backup\jet. You'll also need another file called DHCPCFG, but I'll explain that next while I'm explaining how to back up a version 4 DHCP database.

Backing Up a Version 4 DHCP Database   If you're running NT 4, the three files are

- DHCP.MDB, same as with NT 3.51

- DHCP.PAT, a smaller file serving a purpose like SYSTEM.MDB's in 3.51

- A LOG file with a name like "j5001F47.log," again a transaction log

---

NOTE   Back these files up and have them handy; they are essential to restoring a DHCP server configuration.

But wait a minute—which LOG file should you use? Simple. Under NT 4, there's a directory named \winnt\system32\dhcp\backup\jet\new containing the three essential files. Those files get backed up automatically every 60 minutes, as noted above.

But that's not all you'll need. Your DHCP server, whether 3.51 or 4, knows the scopes and configuration options that you chose, but none of that information is sitting in DHCP.MDB, DHCP.PAT, or the transaction log. NT stores that information in HKEY_LOCAL_MACHINE\System\currentcontrolset\services\ dhcpserver\Configuration. Conveniently, DHCP backs that information up to a file called DHCPCFG. Both NT 3.51 and 4 store the DHCPCFG backup file in \winnt\system32\dhcp\backup.

So, summarizing, if you need to do a disaster recovery on a DHCP server, you'll grab the three files you'll find in \winnt\system32\dhcp\backup\jet on an NT 3.51 server, or the three files you'll find in \winnt\system32\dhcp\backup\ jet\new on an NT 4 server. You'll also need DHCPCFG, found in \winnt\ system32\dhcp\backup.

Restoring a DHCP Database

OK, the Bad Thing happened. Your DHCP server is toast, but you grab your backups, find the three files and DHCPCFG, and now want some other server to pick up where the dearly departed server left off. Or perhaps DHCP is just acting flaky on a server that *didn't* die, and you'd like to zap DHCP, reinstall it, and restore the database. Here's how.

1. The first step is, of course, to get the Microsoft DHCP Server service running on the new machine. If the machine has never been a DHCP server, it's no sweat; as you've done many times before, just fire up Control Panel, then Network, then click Services, Add, and choose Microsoft DHCP Server.

2. If, on the other hand, you've *already* got DHCP Server running and you just want to reinstall it, go ahead, but be aware of one thing: the first time that

you install DHCP Server, it creates the \winnt\system32\dhcp and \winnt\ system32\dhcp\backup directories. Apparently, even if you wipe DHCP Server off of a system, root out its entries in the Registry, reboot, and then reinstall DHCP Server, somehow NT *remembers* (it's probably some Registry key I didn't find) that DHCP Server was once installed, *and it doesn't re-create the two directories*. When you reboot, DHCP causes a Dr. Watson error in TCPSVCS.EXE and you can't get DHCP Server to start. So a word to the wise: if you're going to wipe and reinstall DHCP Server, then go erase the files in \winnt\system32\dhcp and \winnt\system32\dhcp\backup—but keep those two directories around!

3. Anyway, install the Microsoft DHCP Server service through the Control Panel Network applet, then don't reboot right away: reapply Service Pack 4 (or whatever service pack you use), *then* reboot—it saves having to wait around for yet another reboot. When the server restarts, go to the Control Panel Services applet, locate Microsoft DHCP Server, and stop the service.

4. Next, restore your database. Take the three files—either DHCP.MDB, SYSTEM .MDC, and JET.LOG or DHCP.MDB, DHCP.PAT, and the LOG file—and copy them into \winnt\system32\dhcp. Yes, you'll be overwriting some files that DHCP has just created; don't worry about it, and confirm this when NT asks if it's all right to copy over existing files.

5. After that, restore the Registry key. Open REGEDT32 (REGEDIT won't do here) and navigate to HKEY_LOCAL_MACHINE\System\currentcontrolset\ services\dhcpserver\Configuration, highlighting that key. Make sure you've got the "Configuration" key highlighted, and click the Registry menu, and then choose Restore. You'll be prompted for a filename; point REGEDT32 to wherever you've got the backed-up copy of DHCPCFG. It'll ask if you really want to overwrite the existing Registry keys; tell it OK.

6. Start up the DHCP Server service. Open up the DHCP Manager, and you'll see that your old scopes have been restored. But you're not quite done yet. Click Scope ➤ Active Leases to display the leases that the DHCP Manager knows about; the window will be empty. Click Reconcile, and you'll see a dialog box like the one shown in Figure 14.47.

7. Click OK, and DHCP will reintroduce those addresses into its database— and your DHCP server is recovered!

FIGURE 14.47:

Dialog box showing which IP addresses to reenter into the DHCP database

DHCP's Downside

DHCP has accomplished the task of giving out unique IP addresses, and that's an important task. But it doesn't handle the problem of relating host names to IP addresses. For that, we need a name service of some type. That service is the *Windows Internet Naming Service*, or *WINS*.

Installing TCP/IP with WINS

DHCP made IP addressing simpler but ignored the newly created problem of keeping track of the newly assigned IP numbers and the hosts attached to them. If you sat at a TCP/IP-connected workstation with a host name like, for example, t1000.skynet.com, which received its IP address from a DHCP server, and someone on another subnet were to type **ping t1000.skynet.com**, then she'd get a timed out message. Other systems wouldn't know your computer's name because DHCP didn't tell any DNS server about the IP address that it gave your machine, and presumably no one's updated a HOSTS file. What we need is a kind of dynamic name resolver—recall that *name resolution* is the term for looking up t1000 .skynet.com and finding that it is really 122.44.23.3—sort of a dynamic DNS.

That's the Windows Internet Naming Service, or WINS. Now, while *DHCP* is part of a wider group of BOOTP-related protocols, *WINS* is mainly Microsoft's (although, as you'll see, WINS was inspired by a couple of RFCs), and that's a problem. WINS is a name resolution service that's pretty much only recognized by Microsoft client software (NT, Windows for Workgroups, DOS, Windows machines, and presumably OS/2 clients eventually). WINS will communicate its name information with DNS, but only in a limited way.

What this basically means is that the name resolution task can be handled just fine *inside* your network/intranet by WINS, but name resolution *outside* your network—both someone inside your network trying to resolve "whitehouse.gov" or someone outside the network trying to resolve a name inside your network—requires a DNS server, which is a whole different story (but one we'll get to).

WINS is, therefore, only half of the answer to the name resolution problem, albeit an important half. I'll take that up in this section and show you how to set up DNS in the following part.

Put technically, WINS's job is to provide name resolution for *NetBIOS* names in a routed environment, and DNS's job is to provide name resolution for *WinSock* names in a routed environment. Ah, but what does that mean in English? To find out, let's look more closely into names on an NT network using TCP/IP.

Names in NT: NetBIOS and WinSock

Here is one of the most common questions we get asked about NT and TCP/IP:

> *"I've got an NT server on one subnet, and some Windows for Workgroups machines on another subnet. There is a router between them. I can ping the NT server from the Windows for Workgroups machine, but I can't see the NT machine on my browse list, and I can't NET USE to it. How can this be?"*

The short answer: "Ping relies upon the WinSock programming interface, and the browse list and NET USE rely on the NetBIOS interface. As WinSock and NetBIOS work differently, it's entirely possible that there are situations where one would work and the other would fail—this happens to be one of them. What you have to do is to help out NetBIOS a bit with either a file called LMHOSTS or a service called WINS."

The specifics take a little longer to explain; that's the purpose of this upcoming section.

Consider the two following commands, both issued to the same server:

```
ping server01.bigfirm.com
```

and

```
net use * \\server01\mainshr
```

In the PING command, the server is referred to as "server01.bigfirm.com." In the NET USE command, that same server is called "server01." The difference is important.

Why Two Different Names?

The PING command is clearly a TCP/IP/Internet kind of command. You can't run it unless you're running TCP/IP, and, as a matter of fact, it's a valid command on a Unix, VMS, Macintosh, or MVS machine, so long as that machine is running a TCP/IP protocol stack.

In contrast, NET USE is a Microsoft networking command. You can do a NET USE on an NT network no matter what protocol you're running, but the command usually wouldn't be valid on a Unix, VMS, Macintosh, or whatever kind of machine; in general, Microsoft networking is pretty much built to work on PCs. (Yes, I know, NT is architecture-independent, so you could find an Alpha, a MIPS, or a PowerPC machine using NET USE commands, but on the whole, NT is an Intel *x*86 operating system at this writing—and I haven't seen announcements of an NT/390 for the IBM mainframe world, NT VAX for the Digital world, or NT SPARC for the Sun world.)

The difference is in the network application program interface (API) that the application is built atop. (Look back to the last part of Chapter 2 if you don't recall network APIs.) Ping was built on top of the TCP/IP sockets interface or, actually, the common PC implementation of TCP/IP Sockets, the *WinSock* interface. Building ping atop sockets was a good idea, because then it's simple to create a *ping* for any operating system, as long as there's a Sockets interface on the computer. In fact, people use basically the same source code to create "ping" for the PC, Unix machines, VMS machines, or Macs. The "server01.mmco.com" is a DNS name, so for ping to recognize "server01.mmco.com", you'd need either a HOSTS file or a DNS name resolver—a client code that knows how to talk to DNS servers—on your network. (I'll talk about how to do that in an upcoming section.)

In contrast, NET USE was built on top of the NetBIOS API. You may recall from Chapter 2 that NetBIOS was once a protocol and a very simple one at that. As Microsoft has been selling the software to do NET USE commands since 1985, the NET command has been built—and is still built—to sit atop NetBIOS. The \\server01 name is a NetBIOS name, rather than a DNS name. That seems to imply that to make NET USE work, you'd need a NetBIOS name resolver or a

NetBIOS name server. That's exactly what WINS is, as you'll see in the next few pages.

If the "server01.mmco.com" versus "\\server01" distinction still isn't clear, then think of the APIs as communications devices. Telephones and the mail service are communications devices, also, so I'll use them in an analogy. Ping's job is to communicate with some other PC, and NET USE also wants to communicate with some PC. But ping uses WinSock (the telephone) and NET USE uses NetBIOS (the mail). If you use the telephone to call a friend, then that friend's "name" as far as the phone is concerned may be something like "(707) 555-2121." As far as the mail is concerned, however, the friend's "name" might be "Paul Jones, 124 Main Street, Anytown, VA, zip code 32102." Both are perfectly valid "names" for your friend Paul, but they're different because different communications systems need different name types.

NetBIOS atop TCP/IP (NBT)

The NetBIOS API is implemented on the NetBEUI, IPX/SPX and on the TCP/IP protocols that Microsoft distributes. That makes Microsoft's TCP/IP a bit different from the TCP/IP you find on Unix (for example), because the Unix TCP/IP almost certainly won't have a NetBIOS API on it; it'll probably only have the TCP/IP Sockets API on it. (As with all PC implementations of TCP/IP, Microsoft's TCP/IP form of Sockets is called the "WinSock API.")

NetBIOS on the Microsoft implementation of TCP/IP is essential, because if the TCP/IP *didn't* have a NetBIOS API on it, then you couldn't use the net use, net view, net logon, and similar commands to allow your PC-based workstation to talk to an NT server. (Instead, the closest thing you would be able to find that would do the job of NET would be something called *NFS*, the *Network File System*. But it wouldn't replace all of the functions of NET.) Microsoft's NetBIOS on TCP/IP even has a name—NBT or NetBT.

So the server's name so far as NetBIOS or NBT is concerned is server01, and its name so far as WinSock is concerned is server01.bigfirm.com. (That kind of name is called, by the way, a *Fully Qualified Domain Name*, or *FQDN*.) You can run programs that either call upon NBT or WinSock, but you have to be sure to use the correct name.

Name Resolution Issues: Why DNS Isn't Always the Best Answer

Once NBT has a NetBIOS name or WinSock has a FQDN, they have the same job: resolve that name into an IP address. So computers on a Microsoft-based network that uses TCP/IP need some kind of name resolution.

How about the obvious one—DNS? DNS clearly *could* do the job, so Microsoft could have designed NBT to do its name resolution via DNS. But it didn't, for several reasons.

- As you'll see soon, NetBIOS names use nonprintable characters. DNS names are restricted by RFC 1034 to A–Z, a–z, 0–9, and hyphens—all stuff whose ASCII codes print nicely on printers and show up as recognizable characters rather than playing card symbols on a screen, and whose ASCII values live between 32 (space) and 126.

- Second, DNS is nifty in many ways, but it's not dynamic. What that means in English is that every time you put a new computer on your network, you'd have to trot on over to the machine that was running the DNS server, type in the new computer's name and IP address, and then you'd have to stop the DNS server and restart it to get DNS to recognize the new name. Something more automatic would be more desirable.

- Third, Microsoft didn't even ship a DNS server with NT as of NT version 3.51, and the beta DNS server was absolutely terrible. So they couldn't really *require* people to set up a DNS server, could they?

NetBIOS name resolution over TCP/IP is, then, not a simple nut to crack. Many people realized this, and so there are two Internet RFCs (Requests For Comment) on this topic, RFC 1001 and 1002, published in 1986.

B Nodes, P Nodes, and M Nodes

The RFCs attacked the problem by offering options.

- The first option was sort of simplistic: just do broadcasts. A computer that used broadcasts to resolve NetBIOS names to IP addresses is referred to in the RFCs as a *B node*. To find out who server01 is, then, a PC running B node software would just shout out, "Hey! Anybody here named server01? "

Simple, yes, but fatally flawed: remember what happens to broadcasts when they hit routers? As routers don't re-broadcast the messages to other subnets, this kind of name resolution would only be satisfactory on single-subnet networks.

- The second option was to create a name server of some kind and to use that. Then, when a computer needed to resolve a name of another computer, all it needed to do was send a point-to-point message to the computer running the name server software. As point-to-point messages *do* get retransmitted over routers, this second approach would work fine even on networks with routers. A computer using a name server to resolve NetBIOS names into IP addresses is said to be a *P node*.

Again, a good idea, but it runs afoul of all of the problems that DNS had. *What* name server should be used? Will it be dynamic? The name server for NetBIOS name resolution is, by the way, referred to as a NetBIOS Name Server, or NBNS.

- The most complex approach to NetBIOS name resolution over TCP/IP as described in the RFCs is the *M node*, or *mixed* node. It uses a combination of broadcasts and point-to-point communications to an NBNS.

When Microsoft started out with TCP/IP, they implemented a kind of M node software. It was "point-to-point" in that you could look up addresses in the HOSTS file, or a file called LMHOSTS, and if you had a DNS server, then you could always reference that; other than those options, Microsoft TCP/IP was mainly B node-ish, which limited you to single-subnet networks. (Or required that you repeat broadcasts over the network, clogging up your network.) Clearly, some kind of NBNS was needed, and the simpler it was to work with, the better. As the RFCs were silent on the particulars of a NBNS, vendors had license to go out and invent something proprietary and so they did—several of them, in fact, with the result that you'd expect: none of them talk to each other.

That's where WINS comes in.

WINS is simply Microsoft's proprietary NBNS service. What makes it stand out from the rest of the pack is Microsoft's importance in the industry. They've got the clout to create a proprietary system and make it accepted widely enough so that it becomes a *de facto* standard.

Microsoft's NetBIOS-over-TCP client software not only implements B, P, and M nodes, it also includes a fourth, non-RFC node type. Microsoft calls it an H, or Hybrid node.

But wait a minute; isn't *M node* a hybrid? Yes. Both M nodes and H nodes (and note well that at this writing, M nodes are RFCed and H nodes aren't) use both B node and P node, but the implementation is different.

- In M node, do a name resolution by first broadcasting (B node) and then, if that fails, communicate directly with the NBNS (P node).

- In H node, try the NBNS first. If it can't help you, then try a broadcast.

"Hmmm…" you may be saying, "Why would anyone want to first broadcast, *then* look up the answer in the name server? Why clutter up the network cable with useless broadcasts when we could instead go right to the source, and reduce network chatter?"

The answer is that it's a matter of economics. Recall that the RFCs on NetBIOS over TCP were written back in the mid '80s, when a typical PC had perhaps an 8MHz clock rate and a 5MHz internal bus. An Ethernet full of XTs would have had a lot of trouble loading the network enough for anyone to even notice. The bottleneck in networks in those days was the CPU or disk speed of the network server. But if the network includes routers—and if it doesn't, then broadcasting is all you need—then consider what the routers are connected to: wide area network links, probably expensive 9600, 14,400, or 19,200bps leased lines. In a network like this, the LAN was a seemingly infinite resource, and wasting it with tons of broadcasts was of no consequence. In contrast, creating more traffic over the WAN by having every machine ask for NetBIOS names (presuming the NetBIOS Name Server was across the WAN link) could greatly reduce the effectiveness of that expensive WAN. Besides, the reasoning went, the vast majority of the time a PC only wanted to talk to another PC on the same LAN, so broadcasts would suffice for name resolution most of the time. The result? M nodes.

The economic picture in 1994, when Microsoft was inventing WINS, was another story entirely: LANs are clogged and WAN links are far cheaper—so H nodes made more sense.

You can force any DHCP client to be a B, P, M, or H node. One of the options that you can configure via DHCP is the WINS/NBNS Node Type. You give it a numeric value to set the client's NetBIOS name resolution technique. A value of one creates a B node, two is used for a P node, four for an M node, and eight for an H node, the recommended node type.

Understanding the NBT Names on Your System

A major part of the NetBIOS architecture is its lavish use of names. A workstation attaches up to 16 names to itself. Names in NetBIOS are either group names, which can be shared—workgroups and domains are two examples—or normal names, which can't be shared, like a machine name. As you'll soon see that WINS keeps track of all of these names, you may be curious about what all of them *are*—so let's take a minute and look more closely into your system's NetBIOS names.

You can see the names attached to your workstation by opening a command line from a Windows for Workgroups, Windows 95, or NT machine, and typing **nbtstat -n**. You get an output like this:

```
Node IpAddress: [199.34.57.53] Scope Id: []

    NetBIOS Local Name Table

  Name       Type      Status
  ---------------------------------------------
  MICRON133  <00> UNIQUE   Registered
  ORION      <00> GROUP    Registered
  MICRON133  <03> UNIQUE   Registered
  MICRON133  <20> UNIQUE   Registered
  ORION      <1E> GROUP    Registered
  MARK       <03> UNIQUE   Registered
```

In this example, the ORION group names are my workgroup and domain. MICRON133 is my machine's name, and MARK is my name—notice that NetBIOS registers not only the machine name, but the person's name as well. You can see the list of registered names on any computer in your network by typing **nbtstat -A <ip address>**, where the -A *must* be a capital letter.

But why is there more than one MICRON133? Because different parts of the Microsoft network client software each require names of their own, so they take your machine name and append a pair of hex digits to it. That's what the <00>, <20>, and the like are—suffixes controlled by particular programs. For example, if some other user on the network wanted to connect to a share named STUFF on this computer, she could type **net use * \\micron133\stuff**, and the redirector software on her computer would then do a NetBIOS name resolution on the name MICRON133<00>, as the <00> suffix is used by the redirector. Table 14.3 summarizes suffixes and the programs that use them.

TABLE 14.3: Examples of Machine Names

Unique Names	Where Used
<computername>[00h]	Workstation service. This is the "basic" name that every player in a Microsoft network would have, no matter how little power it has in the network.
<computername>[03h]	Messenger service.
<computername>[06h]	RAS Server service.
<computername>[1Fh]	NetDDE service; will only appear if NetDDE is active, or if you're running a NetDDE application. (You can see this by starting up Network Hearts, for example.)
<computername>[20h]	Server service; name will only appear on machines with file/printer sharing enabled.
<computername>[21h]	RAS Client service.
<computername>[BEh]	Network Monitor agent.
<computername>[BFh]	Network Monitor utility.
<username>[03h]	Messenger service; any computer running the Messenger service (which is just about any MS networking client) would have this so that NET SEND commands to a user could be received.
<domain name>[1Bh]	Primary Domain controller.
<domain name>[1Dh]	Master Browser.
Group Names	
<domain name>[00h] or *<workgroup name>*[00]	Domain name; indicates that the computer is a member of the domain and/or workgroup. If a client is a member of a workgroup whose name is different from a domain, then no domain name will be registered on the client.
<domain name>[1Ch]	PDCs and BDCs would share this; if a machine has this name registered, then it is a domain controller.
<domain name>[1Eh] or *<workgroup name>*[1Eh]	Used in browser elections, indicates that this computer would agree to be a browser. Will only show up on servers. (Potential browser.)
MSBrowse	Domain Master Browser.

No matter what kind of computer you have on a Microsoft enterprise network, it will have at least one name registered—the *<computer name>*[00] name. Most computers also register *<workgroup>*[00] which proclaims them as a member of a workgroup. Those are the only two names you would see if you had a DOS workstation running the old LAN Manager network client without the Messenger service, or a Windows for Workgroups 3.1 (not 3.11) workstation that had file and printer sharing disabled.

Most modern client software would also have the Messenger service enabled and so would have the *<computer name>*[03] and *<username>*[03] names registered, as well.

Adding file and/or printer sharing capabilities to a computer would add the *<computer name>*[20] name. Servers all agree to be candidates for browse master by default, so unless you configure a machine to *not* be a candidate for browse mastering, then the *<workgroup name>*[1E] name will appear on any machine offering file or printer sharing. If the machine happens to be the browse master, it'll also have *<workgroup name>*[1D] as well. Workstations use the [1D] name to initially get a list of browse servers when they first start up: they broadcast a message looking to see if the [1D] machine exists, and, if it does, then the [1D] machine presents the workstation with a list of potential browsers.

Browse masters also get the network name [01][02]__MSBROWSE__[02][01] as well—it's a group name, and only the *master* browsers are members. Master browsers use that name to discover that each other exists.

Master Browsers versus Domain Master Browsers: A Note

This topic is a little out of order, but it's a topic that is relevant both to TCP/IP, network names, and browsing, so this seemed the least "out of order" place for this note.

Let's consider for a moment browse lists under NT. Most of the messages that drive the browsing services in Microsoft enterprise networking are broadcasts. As routers don't generally pass broadcasts, what does that imply for an intranet made up of multiple segments—but only one NT domain?

Before WINS (and in modern NT networks that don't use WINS), each subnet ends up having its own browser elections, and each subnet has its own master browsers as a result. NT centralizes the browse information by dubbing one of these master browsers the Domain Master Browser (DMB). Again, this isn't "domain" in the TCP/IP sense, it's "domain" in the NT sense. The reason DMBs exist is to support browsing of an NT domain that's split up over two or more subnets. Even if your NT domain is only situated on a single subnet, it'll still end up with a DMB. DMBs register the name *<domain>*[1B], and there will, again, be one per NT domain. There can be many DMBs within a single TCP/IP domain, because there can be as many NT domains in a TCP/IP domain as you like.

Name Resolution before WINS: LMHOSTS

Clients written prior to WINS, or clients without a specified WINS server, try to resolve a NetBIOS name to an IP address with a number of methods. The tools they'll use, if they exist are

- A HOSTS file, if present

- Broadcasts

- An LMHOSTS file, if present

- A DNS server, if present

You met HOSTS before—it's just a simple ASCII file. Each line contains an IP address, at least one space, and a name. LMHOSTS works in a similar way to HOSTS.

Introducing LMHOSTS

Recall that HOSTS is an ASCII file that lists IP addresses and Internet names, like the following:

```
100.100.210.13      ducky.mallard.com
211.39.82.15        jabberwock.carroll.com
```

Microsoft reasoned that if a simple ASCII file could supplement or replace DNS to resolve WinSock names, why not create an ASCII file to hold NetBIOS names? The result is the LMHOSTS file. LMHOSTS consists of pairs of IP addresses and names, like HOSTS, but the names are 15-character *NetBIOS* names, not Internet-type names:

```
100.100.210.13      ducky
211.39.82.15        jabberwock
```

I assumed in the above example that the NetBIOS name is identical to the left-most part of the Internet name, although that's not necessary, as you may recall from the earlier discussion in this chapter about setting up TCP/IP on a system.

Representing Hex Suffixes in LMHOSTS

But how to handle the nonprinting characters in a NetBIOS name, the <1B> used by the primary domain controller, the <1C> used by all domain controllers? Recall that the hex suffixes are always the sixteenth character in a NetBIOS name, so write out a suffixed NetBIOS name like so:

- Enclose the name in quotes.

- Add enough spaces to the end of the name so that you've got 15 characters in the name.

- After the spaces, add **\0x** followed by the hex code.

For example, suppose I had a domain named CLOUDS and a domain controller named \\CUMULONIMBUS at address 210.10.20.3. I'm creating an LMHOSTS file that I can put on systems around the network so that they can find \\CUMULO-NIMBUS and recognize it as the primary domain controller for CLOUDS. The LMHOSTS file would look like this:

```
210.10.20.3  cumulonimbus
210.10.20.3    "clouds          \0x1B"
```

This indicates that the machine at IP address 210.10.20.3 has two names (or at *least* two names). As CLOUDS is a six-letter word, I added nine spaces to the end of it.

A Special Suffix for Domain Controllers: #DOM

In most cases, the only hex suffix you'll care about is <1C>, the suffix indicating a domain controller. You can create an entry for it as above, with a \0x1C suffix, or you can use a special metacommand that Microsoft included in LMHOSTS: #DOM.

To indicate that a given entry is a domain controller, enter a normal LMHOSTS entry for it, but add to the end of the line #DOM: and the name of the domain controller. In the CUMULONIMBUS example above, you could register CUMULO-NIMBUS's name and the fact that it was a domain controller for CLOUDS like so:

```
210.10.20.3  cumulonimbus #DOM:clouds
```

But \x01C and #DOM behave a bit differently, in my experience, as I've related in Chapter 12 and will discuss again in Chapter 17. If you enter a \x01C entry in an LMHOSTS, then NT will use it and only it, ignoring WINS or any other information—so if you're going to use an \0x1C entry, make sure it's right! Furthermore, if you try to tell NT about more than one domain controller in a given domain using the \0x1C suffix, it will only pay attention to the *last* one mentioned in the LMHOSTS file.

"Listen to Me!": The #PRE Command

This is a bit out of order, as I haven't taken up WINS in detail yet, but as long as I'm discussing LMHOSTS, it kind of fits. As you'll learn later, a normal H-node type of client will first send a name resolution question to a WINS server before consulting its local LMHOSTS file, if one exists. Only if the WINS server returns a failure, saying, "I'm sorry, I can't resolve that name," does the client look in its LMHOSTS file. But sometimes you want to tell a PC, "I have a particular entry here in LMHOSTS that is more important than anything that WINS tells you. If you need to look up this particular NetBIOS name, use the LMHOSTS entry rather than looking at WINS." For those entries, you can use the #PRE metacommand. In the case of CUMULONIMBUS, the line above would look like

```
cumulonimbus  #DOM:clouds #PRE
```

#PRE's job is this: if WINS and LMHOSTS offer conflicting answers to the question, "What's the IP address of CUMULONIMBUS," then in general the client listens to WINS rather than LMHOSTS—in other words, by default WINS, uh, wins. But #PRE gives an LMHOSTS entry precendence over anything that WINS has to say.

Centralized LMHOSTS: #INCLUDE, #ALTERNATE

LMHOSTS is powerful, but could include a fair amount of running around, because for a user's PC to benefit from LMHOSTS, *the LMHOSTS file must be on the user's PC.* Yuck. That means you'd have to go out Amongst The Users, a happy time for some but a… ummm… mixed blessing for others. Every time you changed LMHOSTS, you'd have to walk around replacing the old LMHOSTS file with a new one on every single machine—ugh, double yuck. Is there a better way?

Sure. You can put a small LMHOSTS file on a user's machine with just one simple command: "Go to this server to read the 'main' LMHOSTS file." Even better, you can specify as many backups for this server as you like. You do it with the #INCLUDE and #ALTERNATE metacommands. Here's a sample LMHOSTS:

```
#BEGIN_ALTERNATE
#INCLUDE      \\shadows\stuff\lmhosts
#INCLUDE      \\vorlons\stuff\lmhosts
#INCLUDE      \\centauri\stuff2\mrhosts
#END_ALTERNATE
```

You can use #INCLUDE without the #ALTERNATEs, but it seems to me that if you're going to go to all the trouble of having a central LMHOSTS, you might as well add some fault tolerance, right? And I would hope that it would go without saying that \\SHADOWS, \\VORLONS, and \\CENTAURI would either have to be on the same subnet as the client PC, or you should add a few lines above the #BEGIN ALTERNATE to tell the PC where to find those three servers.

#INCLUDE also takes local filenames:

```
#INCLUDE D:\MORENAME
```

LMHOSTS is a pretty powerful tool, and it still makes sense in today's networks because, as you'll see, WINS is not without its flaws.

How WINS Works

You've seen that the world before WINS was a rather grim place, where everyone shouts and many questions (well, resolution requests) go unanswered. Now let's look at what happens with WINS.

WINS Needs NT Server

To make WINS work, you must set up an NT Server machine (it won't run on anything else, including NT Workstation) to act as the WINS server. The WINS server then acts as the NBNS server, keeping track of who's on the network and handing out name resolution information as needed.

WINS Holds Name Registrations

Basically, when a WINS client (the shorthand term for "any PC running a Microsoft enterprise TCP/IP network client software designed to use WINS for NBT name resolution") first boots up, it goes to the WINS server and introduces itself, or, in WINS-speak, it does a name registration. (In fact, as you recall, most machines have several NetBIOS names, so clients register each of those names with WINS.) The client knows the IP address of the WINS server either because you hard-coded it right into the TCP/IP settings for the workstation or because the workstation got a WINS address from DHCP when it obtained an IP lease.

You may recall that the client actually gets *two* IP addresses, one for a "primary" and one for a "secondary" WINS server. The client tries to get the attention of the primary and register itself on that machine. But if the machine designated as a primary WINS server doesn't respond within a certain amount of time, the client next tries to register with the secondary WINS server. If the secondary will talk to the client and the primary won't, the client registers with the secondary. You can tell that this has happened by doing an IPCONFIG /ALL at the client. Among other things, this reports the address of the primary WINS server. If that address is the *secondary's* address, then you know that the primary was too busy to talk—and that turns out to be an important diagnostic clue, as you'll see later when I discuss how to design multiserver WINS systems.

In the process of registering its name with a WINS server, the workstation gets the benefit of ensuring that it has a unique name. If the WINS server sees that there's another computer out there with the same name, it will tell the workstation, "You can't use that name." The name registration request and the acknowledgment are both directed IP messages, so they'll cross routers. And when a workstation shuts down, it sends a "name release" request to the WINS server telling it that the workstation will no longer need the NetBIOS name, enabling the WINS server to register it for some other machine.

WINS Client Failure Modes

But what if something goes wrong? What if you try to register a name that some other workstation already has, or if a workstation finds that the WINS server is unavailable?

Duplicate names are simple—instead of sending a "success" response to the workstation, the WINS server sends a "fail" message in response to the workstation's name request. In response, the workstation does not consider the name registered and doesn't include it in its NetBIOS name table; an nbstat -n will not show the name.

But if a workstation can't find the WINS server when it boots up, then the workstation simply stops acting as a hybrid NBT node and reverts to its old ways as a Microsoft modified B node, meaning that it depends largely on broadcasts, but will also consult LMHOSTS (and perhaps HOSTS, if configured to do so) if they're present.

It's My Name, but for How Long?

Like DHCP, WINS only registers names for a fixed period of time called the *renewal interval*. By default, it's six days (144 hours), and there will probably never be a reason for you to change that. Forty minutes seems to be the shortest time that WINS will accept.

In much the same way that DHCP clients attempt to renew their leases early, WINS clients send "name *refresh* requests" to the WINS client before their names expire—*long* before. According to Microsoft documentation, a WINS client attempts a name refresh very early after it gets its names registered—after one-eighth of the renewal interval. (My tests show that it's actually *three*-eighths, but that's not terribly important.) The WINS server will usually reset the length of time left before the name must be renewed again (this time is sometimes called the "time to live" or TTL). Once the client has renewed its name *once*, however, it doesn't renew it again and again every one-eighth of its TTL; instead, it only renews its names every one-half of the TTL. (My tests agree with that.)

We will see later that WINS has historically had some troubles with handling reregistrations. So why not set a really *big* TTL? Well, for one thing, long-lived records mean that dead records stay around a *long* time. For another thing, it's irrelevant for most systems. The reason is this: every time you reboot the system, you reregister with WINS. It's really only the computers that are constantly up and running that ever even get a *chance* to worry about reregistering with WINS. A bit later, I'll have a suggestion about how to avoid problems with reregistrations.

Installing WINS

Installing WINS is much like installing all the other software that we've installed elsewhere in this chapter and in the book.

When you're planning how many WINS servers you need and where to put them, bear in mind that you need not put a WINS server on each subnet (which is one of the great features of WINS). It *is* a good idea to have a second machine running as a secondary WINS server, however, just for fault tolerance's sake. Remember that if a workstation comes up and can't find a WINS server, it reverts to broadcasting, which will limit its name resolution capabilities to just its local subnet and will cause it to do a lot of shouting, which adds traffic to the subnet. Why would a WINS client not find a WINS server if there's a working WINS server?

Well, normally, the client would find the server just fine, but in some small percentage of the cases, the WINS server might be too busy to respond to the client in a timely fashion, causing the client to just give up on the server. That will probably only happen very rarely, unless you're overloading the WINS server. Unfortunately, a very common way to overload a WINS server is to put the WINS server function on the same machine that's also acting as a domain controller. Think about it: when is a WINS server busiest? First thing in the morning, when everyone's booting up and registering names. When's a domain controller busiest? First thing in the morning, when everyone's logging in. That leads to a tip.

TIP   If possible, don't put the WINS server function on a domain controller.

That's where a secondary is useful. If you have a backup domain controller, then put a WINS server on that machine, as well. The WINS software actually does not use a lot of CPU time, so it probably won't affect your server's performance unless you have thousands of users all hammering on one WINS server. If *that's* the case, I'd dedicate a computer solely to WINS-ing.

To get a WINS server set up, follow these directions:

1. Open the Control Panel.

2. Within the Control Panel, open the Networks applet.

3. Click the Services tab.

4. Click the Add button.

5. Choose the Windows Internet Name Service.

6. Tell the program where to find the files on your CD-ROM or whatever drive you used to install NT.

7. Click the Close button.

The system will want to restart; let it. Once your server has rebooted, you find a new icon in the Administrative Tools group, the WINS Manager. Start it up, and it will look like Figure 14.48.

FIGURE 14.48:

The initial WINS Manager screen

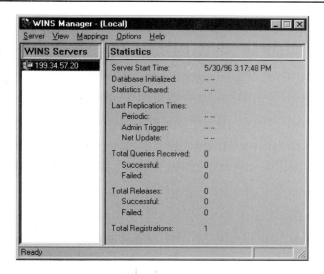

The first thing you should do on your WINS server is inform it of the machines on your subnet that are not WINS clients but use NetBIOS on TCP/IP. There won't be many of them, but they may exist; for example, you may have some old pre-1995 Microsoft Windows machines around. Machines with hard-coded IP addresses don't need to be entered, so long as they use WINS: if they know the address of a primary or secondary WINS server, they will register their names with that server. If you *do* have an old system requiring a static mapping, click Mappings, then Static Mappings; you then see a dialog box like the one shown in Figure 14.49.

In the figure, you see that I've added the IP addresses for two devices with pre-defined IP addresses. Just click Add Mappings, and you get a dialog box that lets you add IP addresses and host names as static values. If you have an existing HOSTS file, you can click Import Mappings and the program will take that information to build a static-mapping database.

FIGURE 14.49:

The Static Mappings table

Backing Up a WINS Database

The second thing to do is to tell the WINS server where to back up its database. If you supply a location to keep WINS database backups, then your WINS server will automatically back itself up once every three hours. You can configure this and a few other things by clicking on a server in the WINS Manager, then clicking Server ➤ Configuration. You'll see a dialog box like the one shown in Figure 14.50.

Actually, if you're following along and your screen looks a bit different, it's because I cheated and clicked the Advanced button to show you all of the options. Note the text field Database Backup Path; fill in a local location there—a name like C:\WINSBACK or the like, not a UNC like \\CENTRAL\BACKUPS\WINSBACK—and WINS will automatically back itself up.

A number of the things in this dialog box are important, and I'll return to them. But before I do, let's finish protecting the WINS database. The database files themselves are called WINS.MDB, WINS.PAT, and J5xxxxxx.LOG, a transaction log. (Actually, if you look in the \winnt\system32\wins directory, you'll see a number of files whose names start with "J5" and have the extension .LOG. Those are the transaction logs that WINS has used since you first installed it—WINS does not erase old logs until it periodically "scavenges" the database. It's only the highest-numbered one that's active at the moment, however, which is why you may see a lot of LOG files in your \winnt\system32\wins directory and only one in the WINS backup directory.)

FIGURE 14.50:

WINS Server Configuration screen

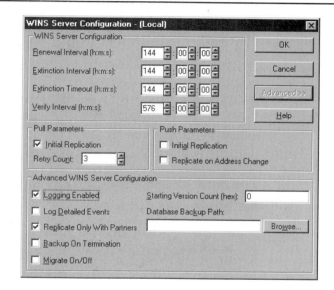

To complete the backup of a WINS server, you should back up a Registry key, \HKEY_LOCAL_MACHINE\System\CurrentControlSet\Services\Wins. You *really* only need to do this if you've modified a setting in the WINS Manager.

Here are the specifics on saving the key:

1. Start the Registry Editor, REGEDT32.

2. Open the HKEY_LOCAL_MACHINE subtree.

3. Click on the SYSTEM\CurrentControlSet\Services\WINS key.

4. Click Registry and Save Key.

5. Point the dialog box by entering the location where you want to save the WINS Registry settings and fill in a filename, then click OK.

Restoring a WINS Database

Now, you'd restore a WINS database in the reverse order. Assuming you've got a dead WINS server, add the WINS service to some other server. Add whatever service packs you're using, and reboot.

You can't make changes to the service while it's running, so stop WINS in the Control Panel (open Control Panel, double-click on Services, click "Windows Internet Naming Service," then click the Stop button, and click Yes to confirm that you want to stop the service).

Next, copy the three files from your backup location to \WINNT\SYSTEM32\ WINS. After that, restore the Registry key, like so:

1. Start the Registry Editor, REGEDT32.

2. Open the HKEY_LOCAL_MACHINE subtree.

3. Click on the SYSTEM\CurrentControlSet\Services\WINS key.

4. Click Registry, and Restore.

5. Point the dialog box by entering the location where you stored the backups, and fill in the name of the backup file; then click OK.

6. Click Yes to confirm that you want to overwrite the old key.

7. Exit the Registry Editor.

8. Restart the WINS service by going to the same place in the Control Panel where you stopped the service and clicking the Start button. You do not need to reboot for these changes to take effect.

So, to summarize what you should do in order to be able to rebuild a WINS server: tell the WINS server where to do backups, and it will do them automatically every day. And, when you make changes to WINS settings, save the part of the Registry that holds the settings. Most importantly, be sure to run a secondary WINS server—then you don't really have to worry about backing up your WINS database at all, as you have two machines working in parallel.

Configuring a WINS Server

Let's return to that dialog box from a page or two back (Figure 14.50) and see if there are any parts worth configuring.

First is the Renewal Interval. This is the amount of time that WINS should allow a computer to use a name without having to reregister it. What's a good value? Well, smaller values mean less trash in the database, but larger values mean that your systems needn't create more WINS traffic by reregistering all the time. Under NT 3.51, the default was four days, but NT 4 upped the default to six, suggesting that perhaps more is better. Remember that, as I've observed earlier, this is mainly only of importance with systems that are up all the time, rather than most user workstations, which tend to be booted daily.

Leave logging enabled, but think twice about Log Detailed Events. Basically, if you enable this then (1) WINS adds a lot of chatter to the Event Viewer, and (2) WINS gets *really* slow. It's not a bad idea if you're trying to get some insight into what WINS does on a small network, but I've had it freeze a WINS server right up on me.

"Replicate Only With Partners" sort of sounds like an anti-adultery message, but it's just a security setting. By default it's checked, and you should probably leave it that way. The idea is this: suppose I'm an evildoer and for some reason getting ahold of your WINS database will assist me in my fell plans for world domination. All I need do is to connect my WINS server to your WINS server and then replicate your database, as there's not much security on WINS. But if the box is checked, then I don't get any data until both you and I agree to be *replication partners*, an upcoming topic.

Backup On Termination tells WINS whether or not to back up a WINS database when you stop the WINS service. WINS always backs up when you shut the server down—this controls whether or not to back up the database when you stop the service. Of course, this is irrelevant if you haven't filled in a location for a WINS backup. The other settings in the dialog box probably won't affect you all that much.

Designing a Multi-WINS Network

Thus far, I've discussed a situation wherein you've got one WINS server and a bunch of clients. I've *also* mentioned the notion of a secondary WINS server, suggesting that at least a second WINS server would be in order. How should you set up this second WINS server? And how about the third, fourth, and so on? And while we're at it, how many WINS servers should you have?

From Many Servers, One Database

The theory with multiple WINS servers is that you might have one in Europe, one in Africa, and one in North America. Europeans do their registrations with the European server, Africans with the African server, and Americans with the North American server. Then, on a regular basis, the three WINS servers get together and create a master worldwide list of WINS records, sort of a sort/merge amalgamating three different databases. But how to do it? We certainly don't want to have to transmit—*replicate* is the WINS term—the entire African name-server database over WAN links to Europe and America, particularly since the database probably hasn't changed all that much since yesterday.

As a result, WINS time-stamps and sequence-numbers name records, so that it can take up less WAN bandwidth. That's great in theory, but in practice it means that WINS servers which are being asked to *do* all that sorting and merging will be pretty occupied CPU-wise, which will of course mean that they're falling down on the job as name resolvers. It also means that it might be a good idea to designate a relatively small number of servers—say, perhaps *one*—to essentially do nothing but the sort/merges.

Minimize the Number of WINS Servers

People assume that as with domain controllers, it's a great idea to have a local WINS server, and lots of them. But it's not, and in fact you should strive to keep the WINS servers to an absolute minimum. Having a local BDC is a great idea because it means that a local machine can authenticate you; why not do the same with WINS?

The database that a BDC relies upon is the SAM database. The copy that the BDC has is a read-only copy and the BDC cannot modify that database. An administrator wanting to modify the SAM database—that is, wanting to change someone's password or create a new account—must be connected in real-time to the one and only one PDC in the domain. In a situation like this, there *is* no worry about time stamping database changes, replicating, sorting and merging as *there's only one writeable copy of the database.*

A local WINS server would be great because it could quickly perform NetBIOS name resolutions for nearby machines. And in fact it would be great if you could install a WINS server in every location that only did name resolutions—but remember that every WINS server does *two* things: name resolutions and name registrations. This, in my opinion, is the crux of why multiple WINS networks can be a pain. If you could simply say, "Go to local machine X for name resolutions, but for those infrequent occasions when you need to do a name *registration*, go across the WAN to the central WINS server named Y," then WINS would be more trouble-free. Sure, a morning logon would get a bit slower, as the registration would happen over the WAN, but you'd not get the corrupted WINS databases that are sadly so common in big WINS installations.

People want a local WINS server for name resolution, but in actual fact they're not getting much for it. If your WINS server were across the WAN from you, how much time will a name resolution take? Well, an entire name-resolution request and response is only 214 bytes. Let's see, at 56Kbps that would be... hmmm, three-hundredths of a second. Here's a case where the wide area network will *not* be the bottleneck! WINS may have its drawbacks, but one thing that it was designed to do, and designed well, is to respond to name-resolution requests quickly. Even a 66MHz 486 can handle 750 resolution requests per minute! So when it comes to WINS servers, remember: less is more.

Adding the Second WINS Server

Of course, having said that, a *second* WINS server isn't a bad idea.

When setting up a Microsoft TCP/IP client, you're prompted for both a primary and a secondary WINS server address. When your PC boots up, the PC goes to the primary WINS server and tries to register the PC's NetBIOS name with that WINS server. If it's successful, it never even tries to contact the secondary WINS server unless a subsequent name-resolution attempt fails.

What's that mean? Well, suppose you've been a good network administrator and created a backup WINS server, and then you've pointed all of your workstation's "Secondary WINS Server" fields to that backup. The primary goes down. Where are you?

Nowhere very interesting, actually. You see, that secondary WINS server doesn't know much, as no one has ever registered with it. If a WINS client successfully registers with its primary server, it does not try to register with the secondary server.

So if the primary goes down and everyone starts asking the secondary to resolve names, the secondary will end up just saying, "Sorry, I can't answer that question." So you've got to convince the primary to replicate to the secondary. Fortunately, there's an easy way—*push/pull partners*.

Keeping the Second Server Up to Date

In general, you've got to configure two WINS servers to be push/pull partners, but it's possible to have them discover each other with (you guessed it) a Registry entry. In HKEY_LOCAL_MACHINE\System\CurrentControlSet\Services\WINS\Parameters, add a new value UseSelfFndPnrs of type REG_DWORD, and set it to 1 to cause the WINS server to periodically broadcast (well, actually it will *multicast*) to find other WINS servers and from there to automatically replicate. This will, however, usually only work for WINS servers on the same subnet, as most routers don't pass IP multicasts.

Alternatively, you've got to introduce the two. WINS database replications transfer data from a *push* partner to a *pull* partner. Those terms "push" and "pull" aren't *bad* terms description-wise, but they need a bit of illumination. Suppose for the purposes of the example that you've got two machines named Primary and Secondary. Suppose also that Primary is the machine that gets the latest information, as it is the *primary* WINS server, and that all we really want to do with Secondary (the name of the machine that is the secondary WINS server) is have it act as a kind of backup to Primary's information. Thus, Secondary never really has any information to offer Primary. In that case, we'd have to set up Primary to *push* its database changes to Secondary.

In a push/pull relationship, data gets from Primary to Secondary in one of two ways. First, Secondary (the pull partner) can request that Primary (the push partner) update Secondary, telling Secondary only what has changed in the database. Alternatively, Primary can say to Secondary, "There's been a fair amount of changes since the last time I updated you. *You really should request an update.*" I italicized the last sentence to underscore that it's really the pull partner that does most of the work in initiating the database replication updates. All the push partner really "pushes" is a suggestion that the pull partner get to work and start requesting updates.

Having said that, could I just tell Secondary to be a pull partner with Primary, without telling Primary to be a push partner for Secondary? Wouldn't it be sufficient to just tell Secondary, "Initiate a replication conversation with Primary every eight hours?" It would seem so, as there wouldn't any longer be a need for Primary to do any pushing—but there's a catch. If Secondary starts pulling from Primary, Primary will refuse to respond to Secondary's pull request unless Primary has been configured as a push partner with Secondary, because WINS servers are configured by default to refuse replication requests from all machines but partners, remember?

TIP

WINS services are totally independent of NT domain security, as is DHCP. A WINS server can serve workstations throughout your network. In fact, if your network is connected to the Internet and doesn't have a firewall, you could actually *publish* your WINS server address, and other networks across the Internet could share browsing capabilities! (Whether or not you'd *want* to do that is another issue.)

Controlling Replication

So now we see that the right thing to do is to make Secondary a pull partner with Primary, and make Primary a push partner with Secondary. What triggers the replication? What kicks off the process of WINS database replication? Well, recall that either the push partner or the pull partner can start the conversation. In the case of a push partner, you configure a push partner to tap its partner on the shoulder and suggest a replication session based on the number of database changes. You can tell Primary, "Notify Secondary whenever 50 changes have occurred to the WINS database on Primary," or whatever number you like, so long as you like numbers above 19; 20 is the minimum number of changes that NT will allow you to use to trigger replication. (You can alternatively trigger replication from the WINS Manager.) You control pushing and pulling, by the way, from the WINS Manager—just click on a server, then click Server ➤ Replication Partners and you'll see a dialog that controls with whom a server pushes and pulls.

A pull partner, in contrast, can't possibly know how many changes have occurred, and so needs another way to know when to request updates. So pull partners request updates based on time—you configure a pull partner to contact its partner every so many minutes, hours, or days.

Replication Design

Now that Microsoft has had four years' experience supporting big clients using WINS, some Microsofties have recommended to me a push/pull partner architecture something like a hub-and-spoke design. You see it pictured in Figure 14.51.

FIGURE 14.51:

Suggested primary/secondary WINS server configuration

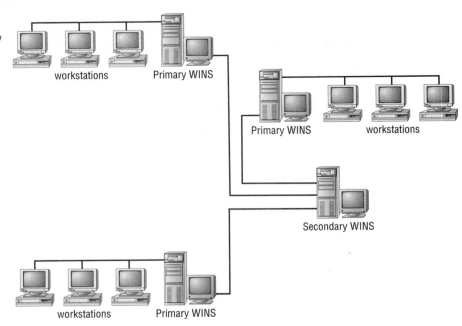

The goal of this design is to keep WINS servers responsive while still handling replication. In the picture, you see three different networks, each served by a WINS server labeled "Primary WINS." In each network, each workstation points to the local WINS server as its primary server and the central machine labeled "Secondary WINS" as their secondary. In other words, then, every machine in the enterprise designates that one central machine as their secondary WINS server, and a more close-by machine as their primary WINS server.

The main job of the central WINS server is to gather the three primary WINS servers' databases, aggregate them into one enterprise-wide WINS database, and replicate that database out to the local primaries. Each primary WINS server, then, designates the central WINS server as their sole push/pull partner.

Many firms implement a mesh-type structure, where every WINS server designates every other WINS server as a push/pull partner. The result is a nightmare of corrupted WINS databases and lost records. To add another WINS server, just make sure that it has some kind of connectivity to the central WINS server and make it a push/pull partner of that machine. If you end up with too many WINS servers for one central machine, just put hubs and spokes on the ends of the hubs and spokes, building a hierarchy.

WARNING   No matter what kind of WINS replication architecture you create, ensure that there are no loops in your replication. For example, if WINS server replicated to B, which replicated to C, which replicated to A, then records can be replicated and re-replicated, causing WINS problems.

Notes on Avoiding WINS Problems

Sources inside Microsoft tell me that WINS generates more support calls than any other of NT's "core" network technologies. That won't be surprising to anyone who's ever tried to track down a WINS problem. Here are a few tips to save you some time and avoid having to pay Microsoft more money to keep the product that you bought from them working.

WINS Servers Should Point to Themselves as a Primary WINS Server Only

When you're configuring the TCP/IP stack on a WINS server, do not fill in a value for a secondary WINS server, and in the "Primary" field fill in the server's own value. This avoids a situation wherein the WINS server is busy, but needs to reregister its own address. As it is busy, however, it cannot—believe it or not—respond quickly enough to *itself*. As a result, the WINS client software on the WINS server seeks out another WINS server, and so WINS server A's name registrations end up on WINS server B. The result is WINS instability, as the WINS server software is built assuming that each WINS server's name is registered on its own database.

Be Careful Replicating to "Test" WINS Servers

Don't set up a "test" WINS server, register a few names on it, have a "production" WINS server pull the names from the test server, and then shut off the test

WINS server for good. WINS will refuse to delete names that it got from another server, no matter how old and expired they are, until it can do a final double-check with the WINS server that it got the names from originally; shut off the test and never turn it back on, and those records will never go away without a bit of operator intervention!

To remove all of the records created by a defunct WINS server, go to one of its replication partners and start WINS Manager. Click Mappings ➤ Show Database. In the resulting window, you'll see in the upper left-hand quadrant of the window a field showing WINS servers and the text label "Select Owner." Click on the IP address of the now-defunct WINS server, then look over to the right and click Delete Owner. That allows WINS to finally purge the old owner's records.

Don't Make a Multihomed PC a WINS Server

A PC with more than one NIC can hear communications from several subnets. That's gotten WINS in trouble when a WINS server is multihomed, as WINS sometimes gets confused about where a name registration came in from. Several service packs have claimed to fix it, but each service pack brings more trouble reports. My suggestion: don't make a multihomed machine a WINS server.

By the way, the same advice goes for PDCs. Multihomed PCs shouldn't be PDCs. The reason is that the PDC ends up being the master browser in a domain and, again, having workgroup announcements coming in from several different network segments causes problems for the browser software.

Don't Make a DC a WINS Server

As explained earlier, both the domain controller and WINS functions are at their busiest at the same time. Mixing DC and WINS responsibilities on a single machine will make a mediocre DC and a mediocre WINS server. (Of course, on a small network this isn't the case; if you have 25 users, feel free to make one machine your domain controller, WINS, DHCP, DNS, and file server—but be sure you know how to do disaster recovery on it!)

WINS Problems and Service Pack 4 Fixes

Service Pack 4 doesn't offer the sheer number of WINS fixes that it does for DNS and DHCP, but the three that it offers are gems.

You Can Re-Register a Server without Rebooting

Machines with static IP addresses tend to be machines that are up and running all of the time. Machines that don't get turned off or rebooted a lot fall prey to a name reregistration problem in WINS. WINS name registrations have a particular lifespan, six days by default. Some time in the first six days that a machine with a static IP address is up, then, it must renew, or, in WINS-ish, *refresh*, its name registration.

The Microsoft literature isn't clear on why this happens, but apparently the code that does the initial WINS registration when a machine is first booted up is more reliable than the code that refreshes the name registration. The result is that after a week or so, the WINS name records for a server may not be available or damaged, and the server essentially "disappears" from the network. I've seen this behavior, and it's quite odd: all of a sudden you can't get to a server from across the network, and so you think, "Hmmm… must have blue screened for some reason," and so you walk down to the server room—only to find that the server seems quite happy, lets you log on interactively, no Event Viewer entries. Rebooting the server solves the problem, but why? According to a person that I spoke with at Microsoft, problems like this come from name-resolution troubles, and the answer is to refresh the name registration.

But how to do it? There's a couple of ways. If the server's IP address is not a static IP address, but instead a DHCP reservation, then DHCP must renew the address to the client periodically. Every time DHCP renews a lease, that causes a WINS registration as a side effect. That's why one way to avoid the problem is to avoid static IP addresses, instead using DHCP reservations. And IPCONFIG /RELEASE followed by IPCONFIG /RENEW can force a WINS re-registration, again as a side effect of renewing a DHCP lease.

SP4 offers another answer: NBTSTAT –RR. This new option on NBTSTAT forces a machine to re-register with WINS. The option RR (which stands, of course, for "re-register"), is *case sensitive*, so use two capital *R*s. How could you use this? Take every computer with a static IP address and use the AT command scheduler to automatically force a re-registration every day or so.

You Can Delete and Tombstone from the GUI

Anyone who's ever been a WINS administrator has at some point looked at the WINS name database and noticed an outdated or otherwise extraneous record.

The logical next thought is "Hey, it's there in front of me, I should be able to delete it!"—but just *try* to figure out how.

The closest thing to a "delete record" button is a button labeled "Delete Owner," but you'll only click that one *once*: it deletes every single record in a given server's WINS database ! (Actually, Delete Owner can be useful if you've decommissioned a WINS server but its records keep getting replicated around the network, most likely if you've created a loop of replicating WINS servers—server A replicates to server B, which replicates to server C, which in turn replicates to server A. In that case, just click on the IP address of the now-defunct WINS server and click Delete Owner; the records that were originally created by that WINS server go away.)

Service Pack 4 changes the WINS Manager so that you can delete any single record. Just click Mapping ➢ Show Database, choose the record that you want dead, and click Delete Mapping. Previously, you could only do this with a *Resource Kit* utility named WINSCL.

But let's return to that idea of a loop of replicating WINS servers. Replicating loops can lead to WINS records with seemingly eternal life, and that's a problem. Server A creates a record about a PC named MAPLE, which it replicates to B. B tells C that it knows about this *great* new PC that C should add to *its* database, and so on. The odd part happens when the original record expires on A. C doesn't know about it yet, and the next time that C replicates with A, it says, "Hey, I see you don't have a record about this MAPLE machine—you ought to add it!" And so MAPLE goes round and round.

Now, WINS *has* a mechanism to prevent this, called *tombstoning*. The idea is that when A zaps MAPLE's record, it doesn't delete the record. Instead, it modifies it to a *tombstone state*. (You can see this in the WINS Manager's list of WINS records, as the record is marked with a cross.)

The purpose of the tombstone is this: A has already written MAPLE off, but it knows that the rest of the enterprise doesn't know that MAPLE is history. So the next time a replicated record boomerangs from B to C back to A about MAPLE, then A may be tempted to insert a new record in its database for a machine named MAPLE—but then it sees the tombstone record with MAPLE's name and so A can say, "Ah, I should just ignore the MAPLE record; I have more up-to-date information than C does. C will eventually figure out that MAPLE's dead." When A next replicates to B, then B will learn via the MAPLE tombstone to ignore any

MAPLE records. B will replicate to C eventually, and MAPLE will be marked as tombstoned in the entire WINS enterprise.

By the way, tombstoned entries don't get purged from a WINS database until WINS runs a *scavenging operation*. That happens every three days by default, or you can initiate a scavenging operation from the WINS Manager by clicking Mappings ➤ Initiate Scavenging.

TIP   If for some reason you stop the WINS service more often than every three days, your WINS database will never be scavenged. If that's the case, manually initiate scavenging from the WINS Manager.

A badly designed WINS replication structure may need a bit of tombstoning help, however, and that's where SP4 comes in. When you click on Delete Mapping, you get an option—delete or tombstone? You'd use tombstone *always* if you want to delete a record on server X, but you're working from server Y. You'd typically delete rather than tombstone if you're sitting right at the server that owns the record that you're about to delete. And if you found that you'd been trying to get rid of a record but it keeps coming back, you'd tombstone it.

WINS Can Handle More Name Registrations

The WINS server under SP4 includes what Microsoft calls *burst mode handling*. Its goal is to help WINS deal with the "bursty" nature of its work. WINS servers don't have a steady workload throughout the day; instead, as you know, they're busiest first thing in the morning, when everyone's logging on, requiring both name registrations and name resolutions. The basic idea is that WINS has a queue where it temporarily stores incoming requests. During a very busy period, WINS may have more requests than make sense to keep in the queue—it's got the memory to store them, but handling them will take too much time, and by the time the WINS server can work its way down that queue, the clients will have timed out. What to do then—just drop the requests, ignoring the clients?

It appears from the Knowledge Base article describing the SP4 fixes to WINS (Q184693) that when WINS gets too busy, it simply responds to name registration requests by saying, "Sure, go ahead, that's a *fine* name, take it. But come back in *x* minutes to re-register it, OK?" The notion seems that WINS approves *all* name registration requests without checking to see if they create duplicate names on the network (which is a very bad thing), but only lets the workstation have those names for a very brief period of time, five or ten minutes. (WINS deliberately varies this amount of time from client to client so that all of the clients don't simultaneously return five minutes later, creating another overflowing queue.)

If that sounds odd, here's what the KB article says:

> *For burst handling, additional client requests beyond the amount specified by the burst queue size are* immediately answered with a positive success response *by the WINS server. (My italics.)*

By telling the workstation to come back in a few minutes and reregister, it ensures that the workstation won't go wandering off bothering the secondary WINS server to register it, but also forces the workstation to return in a short while and go through a complete name-registration process. Under SP4, WINS goes into this "approve everything" mode when there are more than 500 registration requests in its incoming queue. You can adjust that value with a Registry entry located in HKEY_LOCAL_MACHINE\SYSTEM\CurrentControlSet\Services\Wins\Parameters, a REG_DWORD value entry called BurstQueSize. Alternatively, you can tell WINS not to ever enter burst mode with another value entry in the same key, BurstHandling. It's another REG_DWORD; set it to 0 to prevent burst handling.

WINS Proxy Agents

Using an NBNS (NetBIOS Naming Service) like WINS can greatly cut down on the broadcasts on your network, reducing traffic and improving throughput. But, as you've seen, this requires the clients to understand WINS; the older network client software just shouts away as a B node.

WINS can help those older non-WINS-aware clients with a *WINS proxy agent*. A WINS proxy agent is a regular old network workstation that listens for older B node systems helplessly broadcasting, trying to reach NetBIOS names that (unknown to the B node computers) are on another subnet.

To see how this would work, let's take a look at a very simple two-subnet intranet, as shown in Figure 14.52.

FIGURE 14.52:

An example of a two-subnet intranet

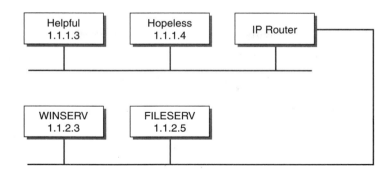

Here, you see two C-class subnets, 1.1.1.0 and 1.1.2.0. There's a router between them. On 1.1.1.0, there are two workstations. One is a WINS-aware client named HELPFUL which is also running a WINS proxy agent. The other is an old B node client named HOPELESS which is not WINS-aware. On 1.1.2.0, there are a couple of servers, a machine acting as a WINS server and a regular old file server.

When HOPELESS first comes up, it'll do a broadcast of its names to ensure that no one else has them. The machine that it really should be talking to, of course, is WINSERV, but WINSERV can't hear it. HELPFUL, however, hears the B node broadcasts coming from HOPELESS and sends a directed message to WINSERV, telling it that there's a workstation named HOPELESS trying to register some names.

WINSERV looks up those names to ensure that they don't already exist. If they *do* exist, then WINSERV sends a message back to HELPFUL, saying, "Don't let that guy register those names!" HELPFUL then sends a message to HOPELESS, saying, "I'm sorry, but *I* already use the name HOPELESS." That keeps HOPE-LESS from registering a name that exists on another subnet.

Assuming that HOPELESS names do *not* currently exist in the WINSERV data-base, however, WINSERV does *not* register the names; putting a WINS proxy agent on 1.1.1.0 doesn't mean that the non-WINS clients will have their names registered with WINS. That means that it's OK to have the same NetBIOS name on two different computers, so long as they are both B node clients and are on dif-ferent subnets.

Suppose then that HOPELESS does a "Net Use d: \\fileserv\files"—in that case, the name "\\fileserv" must be resolved. Assuming that HOPELESS does not have a HOSTS or LMHOSTS file, HOPELESS will start broadcasting, saying, "Is there anyone here named FILESERV? And if so, what's your IP address?" HELPFUL will intercede by sending a directed IP message to WINSERV, saying, "Is there a name registered as FILESERV, and what is its IP address?"

WINSERV will respond with the IP address of FILESERV, and HELPFUL will then send a directed message back to HOPELESS, saying, "Sure, I'm FILESERV, and you can find me at 1.1.2.5." Now HOPELESS can complete its request.

TIP Make sure there is only *one* WINS proxy agent per subnet! Otherwise, two PCs will respond to HOPELESS, causing—how do the manuals put it? Ah yes—"unpredictable results."

DNS in the NT World

You've seen that WINS can effectively resolve NetBIOS names into IP addresses, making it possible for NetBIOS-based applications like NET USE or NT logins to happen. NetBIOS name resolution was top priority for NT's designers simply because Microsoft's logon, browsing, and file and printer sharing services had been written since 1985 to sit atop NetBIOS.

But as time goes on, more and more common networked applications *don't* sit atop NetBIOS; they sit atop WinSock, the API that more closely matches the Sockets interface found throughout the Internet world. Examples of programs that rely on WinSock rather than NetBIOS are Web browsers (like Netscape) and servers (like Microsoft's Internet Information Server), Internet e-mail clients like Eudora, and Telnet client programs, to name just a few.

Since WinSock apps need DNS name resolution, rather than NetBIOS name resolution, that implies that you've probably got to find some kind of DNS server software. As of NT 4, there is finally a DNS server "in the box."

DNS Pros and Cons

DNS is, in general, a bit of a pain to administer. Most DNS servers require that you sit down and type in the names and IP addresses of any machines that you want the outside world to be able to resolve. That simplifies things a bit because you've only got to include the hard-coded IP addresses of the few machines that you wanted the outside world to see, such as:

- Your gateway

- Your mail router

- Any FTP or Telnet servers

DNS is a static protocol in general; for example, DNS knows that "ftp.microsoft .com" is "198.105.232.1" because somebody at Microsoft sat down and typed a list into Microsoft's DNS server, a list detailing what TCP/IP host names correspond to which IP addresses. DNS also does *reverse DNS lookups*, which allow you not only to find out that aardvark.orchard.com is 219.111.29.55, but also to find out that 219.111.29.55 is aardvark.orchard.com, sort of like a reverse phone book that lets you look up (871) 555-5204 and find out that Phineas Jones lives there.

There are a number of DNS servers for NT on the market, but do you really want a traditional DNS server? It's something of a pain to have to type in new entries every time you put a computer on your TCP/IP network, and that's just what DNS requires. Think about it—every time somebody fires up a computer with a DHCP network client, you'd have a new computer on the network, and one more potential name resolution problem.

I suppose you could start up the DHCP manager a few times a day, note the new leases, and type them into your DNS server. But what we really need is a WINS server that can double as a DNS server, offering the information that it has to anyone looking for DNS information. If my domain name is mmco.com, my Net-BIOS name is BIGPC, and my IP address is 199.34.57.88, then this WINS/ DNS combination would know that name resolution requests for bigpc.mmco.com would return 199.34.57.88, and reverse name resolution requests for 199.34.57.88 would return bigpc.mmco.com.

There isn't anything that can do that at the moment, but there *is* something that does some of what we need. Microsoft has written a DNS which runs as a service on an NT machine. It implements a normal DNS service with static name lists but adds a bonus: it includes a dynamic linkage to WINS, so that whenever the DNS server can't find a name in its static lists, it consults WINS. Another bonus is its GUI-based administration tool.

Microsoft's implementation of DNS is not terribly CPU-intensive, so here's an application for an older, slower computer. That computer might need memory, however: a DNS server with 10,000 records will need to dedicate about three megabytes of RAM to DNS, one with 100,000 records would require 10MB for DNS, and a server with two million records would need about 90MB RAM for DNS.

Almost *Everyone* Should Have a DNS Server

Even if you're a network administrator for a small part of a much larger organization, it's still a good idea to set up NT's DNS server and then point your local machines to that server. This makes sense even if you don't have to worry about any name-to-IP-address-translation management, even if you don't "own" any of the naming jobs in your network.

The reason for this is simple: *DNS caches data.* Suppose you've got a small branch office in Louisville, a branch with 40 PCs in it. They all need DNS services, but the "official" company DNS servers are in corporate headquarters in Memphis. You set up a local NT server to be a DNS server, and set up all of the 40 PCs to refer DNS queries to that server. Here's why it makes sense: presumably everyone in the building tends to go to the same places—the corporate intranet, Altavista, CNN, or whatever. The first person in the morning who looks something up on Microsoft's Web site causes that local DNS server to ask Microsoft what the IP address (or addresses, in the case of Microsoft) their Web server resides at. Now, that request generates WAN traffic, and might be a bit slow. But for the rest of the day, anyone needing to get to Microsoft's Web site will find that the first part of surfing microsoft.com—the actual name resolution—happens quite quickly, as their *local* DNS server already knows where Microsoft is.

Such a server is called a *caching* DNS server. To set such a thing up, just

1. Install the Microsoft DNS service.
2. Reboot the server.
3. Point all of the local machines to that server.

That's it—there's nothing else to do.

Setting Up a Small Domain with DNS Manager: An Example

There is a lot to know about running a DNS server. But many small domains will be able to get away with just a few basics, so I'll start the "how-to" part of the DNS story with a look at how to set up a DNS server under NT 4 for a small imaginary domain. I'll follow that up with the nuts and bolts of using the beta DNS Manager for those of you still using 3.51, and some thoughts about making the DNS Manager work better under 4. In the process, I'll also introduce a couple more DNS topics—zones and secondary DNS servers.

Introducing Bowsers.com

Suppose for the sake of argument that I'd like to set up a domain named bowsers .com. It's C-class network number 210.10.20.0. There are just a few machines that are important enough that they must have entries in DNS:

- The mail server for bowsers.com is a machine named retriever.bowsers.com, at 210.10.20.40.

- The Web server for bowsers.com is a machine named www.bowsers.com, at 210.10.20.20.

- That same 210.10.20.20 machine is also the FTP server, and we want it to respond to the name FTP.BOWSERS.COM.

- There is a machine that acts both as a major file server for the organization and as the primary domain controller; it's named BIGDOG.BOWSERS.COM, at 210.10.20.100.

- The DNS server runs on collie.bowsers.com, and it has IP address 210.10.20.55.

Installing the DNS Service

The first thing to do is to load the DNS service. I go to the actual collie.bowsers.com machine and install the DNS service there. Open the Control Panel, start the Network applet, and click Services. Then click the Add button, and choose the Microsoft DNS Server, as you see in Figure 14.53.

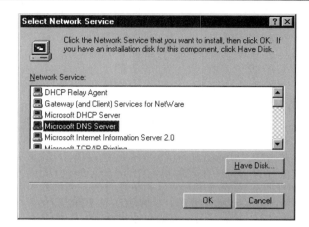

The system will reboot. Look in Administrative Tools, and you'll find the DNS Manager. Start it up, select DNS ➤ New Server, and fill in the address of the local machine; of course, 127.0.0.1 works just as well. You'll see a mostly blank screen, as you see in Figure 14.54.

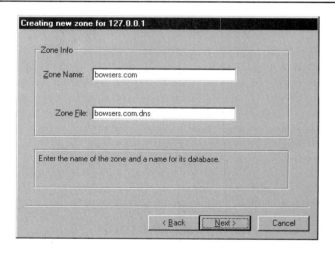

DNS next enables us to create a whole new "zone," but maybe that needs explanation.

Digression: What's a "Zone?"

We're about to create names for the entire bowsers.com domain. But DNS doesn't really talk about domains all that much; it's more interested in *zones*. What, then, is a zone? It's a DNS-specific term that basically means "the range of Internet addresses that this DNS server will be concerned about."

In the DNS world, every part of the Internet has one particular DNS server that keeps track of the host names and similar information for that part of the Internet. For example, a mythical firm named Acme Industries might have an Internet domain named acmeindustry.com and 100 machines in that domain. Someone at Acme has the job of keeping the names and IP addresses of those 100 machines typed into some machine running DNS server software, whether it's an NT machine, a Unix box, or whatever. Call this machine ACMEDNS. In DNS parlance, the DNS server software running on ACMEDNS is *authoritative* for acmeindustry.com.

OK, that makes sense, but where do zones come in? Well, suppose Acme Industries opens up a West Coast office with another 100 machines. They decide to name the machines on the East Coast "*somename*.east.acmeindustry.com," and machines on the West Coast "*somename*.west.acmeindustry.com." The beauty of this approach is that I can then put one DNS server on the West Coast and keep the names of the West Coast machines in it, and have a different server on the East Coast and keep the names of the *East* Coast machines in it. So, if I'm in the West Coast office and am building a new server, I needn't call the East Coast to register the name of my new server; instead I just talk to my local DNS administrator.

If this is still unclear, then think back to Chapter 12. Why have more than one NT domain? Sometimes it's because there are simply so many machines around that it doesn't make sense to dump them all into one big "acmeindustry.com" DNS server. Sometimes it's because of politics—it irritates the West Coast guys that the East Coast guys have already left work when the West Coasters are working late. Sometimes it's geography, as the West Coast folks do most of their name resolution on West Coast machines and East Coast folks mostly resolve East Coast names.

If we break Acme up into East Coast and West Coast areas—heck, let's call them East and West Coast *zones*—then that implies that where we once had *one* authoritative DNS server for all of acmeindustry.com, we now have *two*: one for east.acmeindustry.com and one for west.acmeindustry.com. Now it's easier to define a zone: a zone is the range of Internet names that a given DNS server is authoritative for. If Acme has arranged their network into just acmeindustry .com, then the whole acmeindustry.com is one zone. If they divide it into east.acmeindustry.com and west.acmeindustry.com with two different DNS servers, then east.acmeindustry.com is one zone with some machine acting as its authoritative DNS server, and west.acmeindustry.com is a different zone with some other machine acting as *its* authoritative DNS server.

Creating the Bowsers.com Zone

Anyway, back to setting up the bowsers.com DNS server. All of bowsers.com is one zone, and this server will be authoritative for that zone, so let's tell the DNS server to create a new zone. You do that by choosing DNS ➤ New Zone. Click Primary and the Next button, and then fill in the name of the zone, and you'll see a screen like the one in Figure 14.55.

FIGURE 14.55:

Creating a new zone bowsers.com

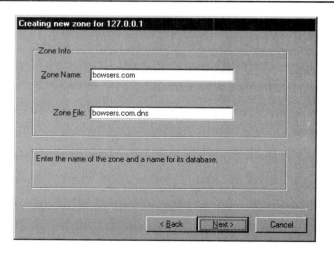

Note that I didn't type in **bowsers.com.dns**—the Wizard created that field. (I had to tab down to the Zone File field for my machine to create it.) When you click Next, the Wizard will say that it has all the information it needs and to click Finish. Do that. It will then set up the DNS Manager, as you see in Figure 14.56.

FIGURE 14.56:

The initial Bowsers screen

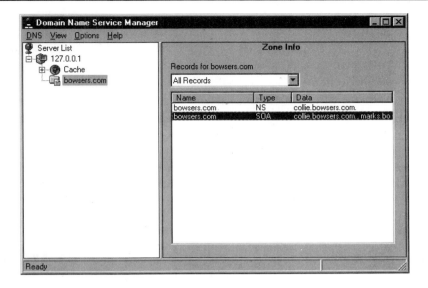

The Wizard has automatically done a few things:

- First, it created an NS record, which identifies this machine—collies .bowsers.com—as the name server, the DNS server for this domain.

- Second, it created something called a *Start of Authority* or SOA record. The SOA record is essential, because it defines some basic parameters about the zone.

Creating the Reverse Lookup Zone

Before going any further, we'll need to create a zone for the *reverse* DNS lookups. As the bowsers.com zone lives in the C-network 210.10.20.0, you must create another zone for reverse lookups; it must be named 20.10.210.in-addr.arpa. (Note the *reverse* numbering of the quads—that *is* correct.) Click the server (127.0.0.1, in my example), and choose DNS ➢ New Zone; again, make it a primary zone, click Next, and in the Zone Name field, type **20.10.210.in-addr.arpa** (I had to tab down to the Zone File field for my machine to create it), and click Next and Finish. Your DNS server will then look like the screen shown in Figure 14.57.

FIGURE 14.57:

DNS server with both forward and reverse lookup zones

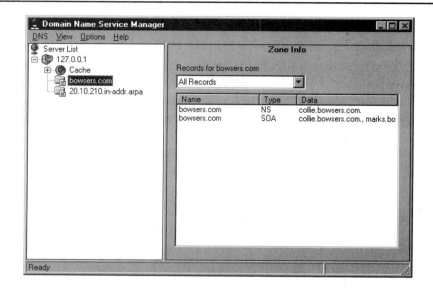

Creating Name Records

Now let's insert a record each for retriever, www, bigdog, and collie. Right-click on bowsers.com, and choose New Record. Fill in the name and IP address, and you'll see a dialog box like the one in Figure 14.58.

FIGURE 14.58:

Creating a name record for Collie

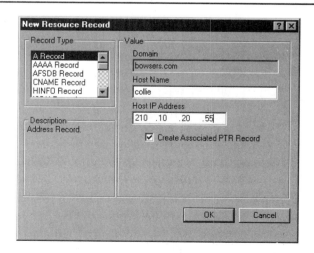

Note that I didn't enter **collie.bowsers.com**, just **collie**. The check box makes sure there is a reverse entry created at the same time. Notice that the dialog box indicates that you are creating an A record—that's the correct name for a name record. There are other types as well—you've already met the NS and SOA records. The DNS Manager screen now looks like the one in Figure 14.59.

FIGURE 14.59:

DNS Manager showing new COLLIE entry

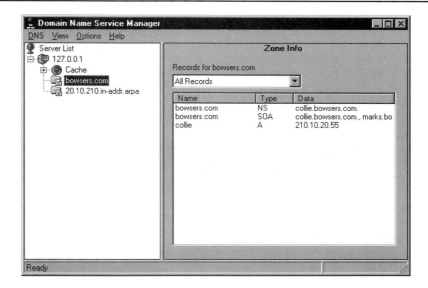

Click on the reverse lookup domain 20.10.210.in-addr.arpa, and you'll see an entry there also (you may have to press F5 to update the display), as you see in Figure 14.60.

Enabling Bowsers.com for E-Mail Delivery: MX Records

Note that a reverse lookup record is yet another record type—a PTR type. I'll enter the records for retriever, www, and bigdog in the same way.

Next, we need an MX (*Mail Exchange*) record. This tells our DNS server where to send mail addressed to bowsers.com. As I've said, the actual mail server in bowsers.com is at retriever.bowsers.com. That means if you have a usernamed Jack on the network you could e-mail him at jack@retriever.bowsers.com. You'd have to use the whole name of the mail server so that the Internet mail system could figure out which machine is the "post office."

FIGURE 14.60:

DNS Manager showing
reverse lookup entry for
COLLIE

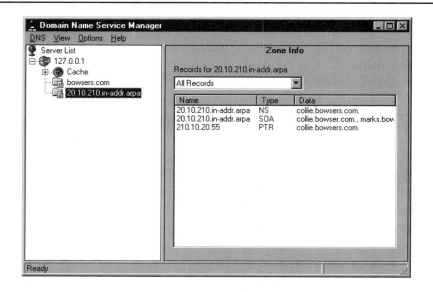

But you'd prefer to be able to send mail to jack@bowsers.com; however, there
is no one machine named bowsers.com. So how do you get mail addressed to
jack@bowsers.com automatically redirected to a machine named retriever.bowsers
.com? With an MX-type DNS record. Right-click the bowsers.com zone and choose
New Record and then choose MX. I've filled in the dialog box, as you can see in
Figure 14.61.

FIGURE 14.61:

Setting up RETRIEVER as the
mail exchange agent

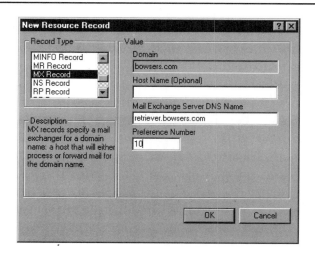

Notice that the Domain field is grayed out—you can't change it. Under Host Name (Optional) I have *not* filled in a name. That's because the Host Name field says, "What computer should this computer be the mail exchange agent *for*?"

You see, if you wanted to, you could create one mail exchange agent for one specific computer; for example, if I filled in **bigdog** here, that would mean whenever someone sent mail to *somename*@bigdog.bowsers.com, it would be redirected to retriever.bowsers.com. By leaving this blank, I'm saying that whenever someone sends mail to *somename*@bowsers.com, *that* goes to retriever. I fill in retriever's name as the mail agent, and set the Preference Number to 10.

A preference number allows you to specify a number of machines to act as mail exchange agents. I could set up mail software on bigdog and have its server as a kind of "emergency" mail server. If I set its preference number value higher than that of retriever, then DNS would know to send mail to retriever unless retriever were down, in which case the mail would go to bigdog.

Giving Multiple Names to One Machine: CNAME Records

Next, I need WWW.BOWSERS.COM to respond to a second name, FTP.BOWSERS .COM. I can do that with a CNAME type record. Create the record as usual by right-clicking the BOWSERS.COM zone and selecting New Record, and then choose CNAME type. I've filled in the dialog box, as you see in Figure 14.62.

FIGURE 14.62:

Creating a CNAME for
FTP.BOWSERS.COM

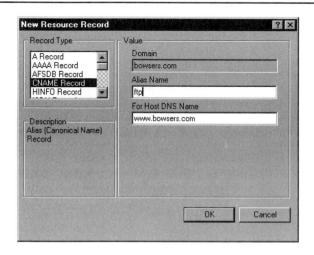

From now on, WWW.BOWSERS.COM will respond to requests for FTP.BOWSERS
.COM. Notice that you don't enter the whole name for the alias, just the leftmost
part. Your DNS screen should look something like the one in Figure 14.63.

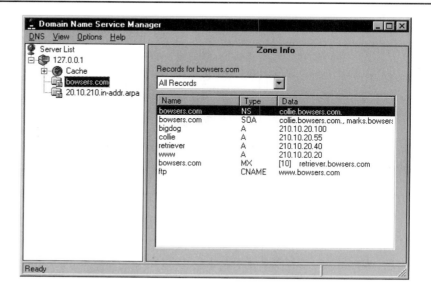

Testing the Configuration

Well, by now, your DNS server should be up. But how to check it? With a diagnostic tool called NSLOOKUP. It's a command-line utility, one of those old cryptic Unix utilities. If DNS is a server, think of NSLOOKUP as a simple diagnostic
client. It'll talk to any DNS server and let you make simple queries, queries that
mimic an outside computer trying to resolve a name. When you type **nslookup**, it
responds with a > prompt. These are the commands I'll use:

- *server 210.10.20.55* tells NSLOOKUP which DNS server to read its data from.
  Since I'm testing COLLIE at 210.10.20.55, I'll point the server there.

- *ls -d BOWSERS.COM* says, "List everything you know about
  BOWSERS.COM."

- *set type mx* and *bowsers.com* says to show the mail exchange records for BOWSERS.COM.

- *exit* exits NSLOOKUP.

You can see the session in Figure 14.64.

FIGURE 14.64:

Running NSLOOKUP to test the DNS server

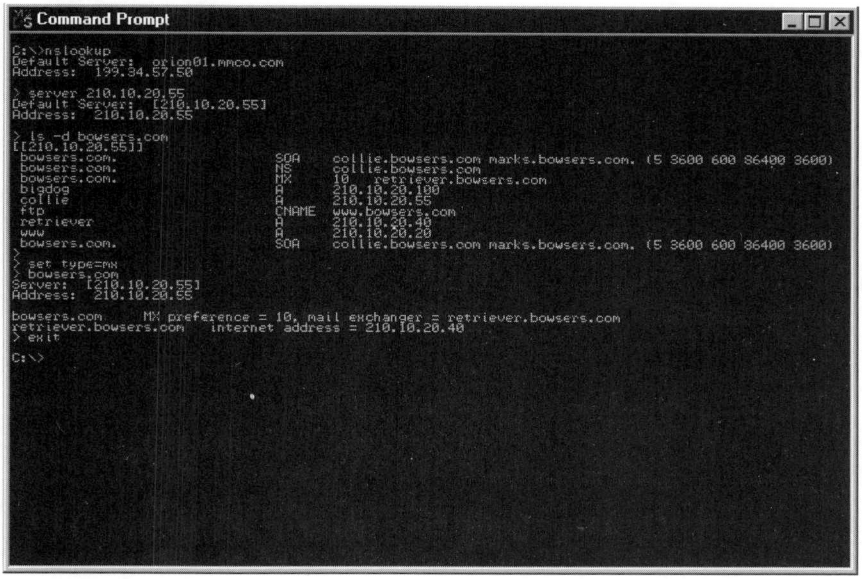

A complete success! There's just one more thing to do, and you're finished. Let's enable the dynamic WINS/DNS link. From the main DNS Manager screen, right-click BOWSERS.COM and choose properties. You'll see a property sheet like the one in Figure 14.65.

I have clicked the WINS Lookup tab, checked Use WINS Resolution, and filled in the address of a WINS server. Click OK, and the connection is made. You should do the same thing for the reverse lookup domain as well. Now just get your ISP to refer to your DNS server, and you're running your own name service.

I had mentioned earlier that we don't use this WINS/DNS link. That's because our ISP's DNS servers could no longer understand our DNS server once we turned it on. This is probably some DNS quirk, but it's annoying in any case— Microsoft can hardly claim that the Unix world should change their software to match Microsoft's.

FIGURE 14.65:

Enabling WINS linkage

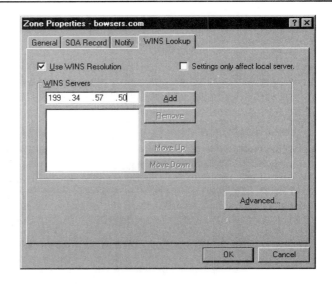

DNS Fault Tolerance: Secondary DNS Servers

Of course, one DNS server may not be enough for a given zone. Breaking that zone up into smaller zones is one answer, but the more common one is to create a *secondary* DNS server for a zone. (In fact, if you want to be authoritative for your domain—rather than having your ISP keep your DNS names—you must have a primary and secondary DNS server running, or the InterNIC won't let you become authoritative.) Setting up a secondary DNS server is easy under NT.

Suppose bowsers.com sets up a new machine named REX (rex.bowsers.com) that will act as a secondary DNS server. First, as before, install Microsoft DNS Server. Start up DNS Manager, also as before. Right-click Server List, choose New Server, and add 127.0.0.1, as before. Under that server, you'd see the bowsers.com zone and the reverse address zone. But *now* add *another* server, filling in the IP address of collies.bowsers.com.

Click back to the local server, 127.0.0.1, and create a new zone as before. But instead of clicking the Primary radio button, click the Secondary radio button. A white hand will appear in the dialog box. Click and drag the white hand over to the bowsers.com domain, releasing the mouse button when the hand is over bowsers.com. Back in the dialog box, click Next twice.

The dialog box will then ask for the IP address of an "IP Master." This is just an obtuse name for the primary DNS. So type in the IP address of the primary DNS server—again, collie.bowser.com's IP address—and click Add, then Next and Finish. Rex is now a secondary DNS server for bowsers! Take a peek in the Event Viewer, and you'll see that Rex has requested (and gotten) a copy of the bowsers .com.dns file. Look in Rex's \winnt\system32\dns directory, and you'll see the bowsers.com.dns file.

Backups, Restores, and Disaster Recovery on NT 4 DNS

After doing all that hard work on a couple of name servers—you pretty much always need a primary and a secondary—you'll want to be sure that you can easily back up and restore your DNS zones. As it turns out, DNS backups and restores are a little quirky, or at least backups and restores on *Microsoft's* DNS are a bit quirky.

What to Back Up

When you create a zone, Microsoft's DNS server creates a zone file whose name is the zone's name with .dns suffixed. For example, if I create a domain named bowsers.com, DNS will store all of the DNS records in a file named bowsers.com .dns. DNS stores this file (and any other zone files) in \winnt\system32\dns. In fact, you'll always find a cache.dns file in that directory, as it contains the names of the root servers. There's also a file called DNS.LOG. (The .dns files are ASCII files, by the way, making them simple to look at in case you need to do some hand-fixing.)

To back up a DNS server, the first thing to save are all the files in the \winnt\ system32\dns directory.

But that's not all. NT's DNS server keeps a bit of configuration-specific information in (surprise) the Registry, in HKEY_LOCAL_MACHINE\System\Current-ControlSet\Services\DNS\Zones. Save that key. (Open REGEDT32, navigate down and highlight the key named above, then click Registry ➤ Save Key and fill in a file name.) You'll only need to back up the Registry key when you create or delete a zone, which probably won't be too often.

Not too difficult, eh? It's the *restoration* that's odd.

How to Restore an NT 4 DNS Server

OK, your NT DNS server has gone on permanent leave. You, however, are always prepared for just such an occasion, and have regularly backed up the \winnt\system32\dns directory, and the HKEY_LOCAL_MACHINE\System\Current-ControlSet\Services\DNS\Zones key.

Choose some other NT server on your network that'll take over the DNS function and do these steps:

1. As described above, install the Microsoft DNS Server. The system will ask if you want to reboot; tell it no, and reinstall whatever service pack you're using, to save yourself a reboot. Once that service pack is in place, reboot.

2. Once the server has rebooted, you are going to restore the old DNS zone data, as you no doubt guessed—but *first* you've got to get the DNS server ready to *use* that data. (This is the quirky part.) Start the DNS Manager program. Create a zone, any old zone. I just right-click on the server, choose New Zone, and create a zone named "banana." You needn't even bother with .COM or the like.

3. Now go back and delete that zone. DNS is now ready for the backup.

4. Stop the DNS service. (Control Panel ➤ Services ➤ Microsoft DNS Server, click Stop.)

5. Copy the backed-up files into \winnt\system32\dns.

6. Use REGEDT32 to replace the HKEY_LOCAL_MACHINE\System\Current-ControlSet\Services\DNS\Zones key: start REGEDT32, highlight that key, and click Registry ➤ Restore and point to wherever you saved the old zone information. It'll ask if you're sure; tell it you are. When done, exit REGEDT32.

7. Go back to the Services applet in the Control Panel and start the Microsoft DNS Server service. (Same as stopping it but instead of clicking Stop, click Start.)

8. Open up the DNS Manager and you'll see that your zones are restored.

An Alternative Backup/Restore Method: BOOT Instead of Registry

There's another way to configure an NT DNS server so that it's both just a bit easier to recover *and* more compatible with a standard BIND-type DNS server: store the zones in a file rather than in the Registry.

You've seen that NT stores zone information in ASCII files: bowsers.com information is stored in a file named bowsers.com.dns by default, mmco.com info goes in mmco.com.dns, and so on. The contents of these zone files on an NT DNS server are identical to zone files on a Unix DNS server. But Unix DNS servers have yet another ASCII file in their configuration—a file naming the zones, a file called simply BOOT. NT doesn't need such a file, as it stores the names of the zones in DNS's Registry key.

But NT can alternatively be configured to store its list of zones in a regular old BOOT file, rather than the Registry. (Well, actually, it *always* stores the names of the zones in the Registry as well, but the BOOT file is the "master" information.)

By default, NT stores the names of the zones in the Registry, and refers to this as *booting from the Registry*. Open up DNS Manager, open a server, right-click on the server and choose Properties. Then click the Boot Method tab and it'll either tell you that DNS is "booting from the Registry" or "booting from the data files." "Booting from the Registry" really means that it looks to the Registry for its list of zones. "Booting from the data files" means that it looks to the BOOT file for its list of zones.

By default, NT uses the Registry. But you can convince it to use BOOT instead; here's how. (By the way, you need Service Pack 4 for this to work reliably.)

1. Stop the DNS service (Control Panel ➤ Services ➤ Microsoft DNS Manager, click Stop).

2. In \winnt\system32\dns, create an ASCII file named BOOT. List the zones that this DNS server is authoritative for. Each line should describe a zone, whether primary or secondary. If describing a zone for which the server is

primary, the line should start out with the word **primary**, then the name of the zone, and then the name of the zone file. If the line describes a secondary zone, then it should start with the word **secondary**, then the name of the zone, then the IP address of the primary DNS server for that zone, and finally the name of the zone file. And you've got to always include a line for the DNS cache, like so:

```
cache                     cache.dns
primary      bowsers.com  bowsers.com.dns
primary      pets.com     pets.com.dns
secondary    mmco.com     199.34.57.50 mmco.com.dns
```

The above example's first line is just the standard "this machine has a DNS cache" line; you'll find it in all BOOT files. The second and third lines show that this machine is the primary DNS server for both the bowsers.com and pets.com domains. The fourth line shows that this server is a secondary DNS server for the mmco.com domain, and the mmco.com domain's primary DNS server is at 199.34.57.50.

3. Open any Registry editor and navigate to HKEY_LOCAL_MACHINE\ System\CurrentControlSet\Services\DNS\Parameters. In that key, you'll see two value entries: BootMethod and EnableRegistryBoot. Delete the EnableRegistryBoot value entry. You'll see that BootMethod will be set to a value of 2, which means, "Keep the zones in the Registry and ignore BOOT." Change that to a value of 1, which tells DNS server to use BOOT. Exit the Registry Editor.

4. Turn the Microsoft DNS Server service back on in the Services applet. Run DNS Manager and you'll see that the "Boot Method" is now set to "The DNS Server is currently configured to boot from data files."

Now let's see how to back up and restore a DNS server that uses the BOOT files; it's much simpler.

To back up a DNS server using boot files: just back up the files in \winnt\ system32\dns.

To restore a DNS server using boot files: install the DNS service and reinstall whatever service packs you're using. Restart the server. Stop the DNS service. Restore the files that you backed up to \winnt\system32\dns. Restart the DNS server service. DNS will see that there's a BOOT file and will gather zone information from it.

DNS Problems and Service Pack 4 Solutions

As with DHCP and WINS, Service Pack 4 brought fixes to a whole bunch (or, in DNS, I suppose you'd call it a whole "zone") of problems—some common, some a bit obscure. I've done my best to try these things out, but some were just plain impossible for me to experiment with.

DNS Servers Using BOOT Update Zones Properly

By default, NT DNS servers keep a list of the zones for which they are primary or secondary in the Registry. But, as you saw in the previous section, you can opt to be more BIND-compliant and instead list the zones in an ASCII file named BOOT.

Prior to Service Pack 4, such a DNS server would start up just fine. But if you added a zone to it—made it a primary or secondary server for some other zone not named in the original BOOT file—the DNS server wouldn't update the BOOT file to name that new zone. It *would* update the Registry's list of zones, but not BOOT. Under Service Pack 4, that's fixed.

DNS Server Now Handles Names with Many Addresses

When asked to resolve a name like www.minasi.com, a DNS server usually gets one or perhaps two IP addresses in response. But some sites respond with a *lot* of IP addresses. If that's not clear, fire up an NT workstation attached to the Internet, open up a command prompt and type **NSLOOKUP**. When you get NSLOOKUP's > prompt, type in **www.microsoft.com**. I get 11 responses. Why 11 responses? Because Microsoft runs a number—well, 11, at the moment that I did the query— of Web servers with identical information on them. Why do they do that? To handle the immense traffic that they get. But some locations return considerably more than 11 responses, and that's where DNS's problem occurred.

When queried for an IP address or addresses associated with a particular name, DNS responds in 512-byte packets. If the IP addresses fit into the 512-byte packet, great, no problem. But if there are too many addresses to fit into a 512-byte packet, DNS notes in the first packet, "These are as many responses as I could fit, but I'm not done yet—ask me for the rest." That "there is more, come get it" message is called the *truncation flag* in DNS argot.

When faced with a truncation flag, NT's DNS server prior to SP4 didn't even *look* at the partial list of addresses, nor did it ask for the remaining addresses. Instead, it said, "Hmmm... too difficult," and just went looking for another DNS server in the hopes of finding one that didn't respond with a truncation bit. Clearly, that meant that some DNS names with many, many IP addresses associated with them could not be resolved by Microsoft's DNS; Service Pack 4 fixes that.

Secondary/Primary Role Transfer Works

You set up a Microsoft DNS server to be a secondary DNS server for some zone, and all works fine. But you decide to take the primary DNS server for that zone off-line, and so you want to change the role of the secondary DNS server to become the primary DNS server for that zone. Sounds simple, but it didn't always work before SP4, as the former secondary might refuse to see itself as the primary, and would continue to search in vain for the "true" primary—but it works better under SP4, although a bit of experimenting shows that swapping the primary and secondary roles in DNS is still a little bumpy.

Responses for Nonexistent Records Are Faster

If you try to look up an IP address for a name that doesn't exist, there is of course a bit of a delay while DNS figures out that there's nobody by that name. But a quirk in NT's DNS added 30 seconds' delay to that wait unnecessarily, until SP4.

Caching DNS Servers Needn't Use Port 53

Part of what makes DNS standard is its port number: 53. If you query Windows NT Magazine's DNS server to find www.winntmag.com, you are querying some IP address at port 53.

Unfortunately, DNS has been the target of a number of attacks by computer lowlife types, and so some firms have closed down port 53 on their firewall. That's no big deal if you only have a few publicly advertised DNS addresses; just stick the company DNS server outside the firewall. But folks inside the firewall need DNS resolution as well, and (as you've read earlier in this chapter) a common way to handle that is to just install a DNS server that's not authoritative for anything; all it does is resolve DNS requests, making use of the value of DNS name caching. But putting such a server inside the firewall means opening port 53.

Now, if your DNS server never *responds* to requests—as is the case with a caching-only server—then you don't particularly care what port it uses, so it would be nice to be able to change the port number. You can with SP4. In HKEY_LOCAL_MACHINE\System\CurrentControlSet\Services\DNS\Parameters, create a new value entry named SendOnNonDnsPort of type REG_DWORD and specify the new port value. Stop and restart the DNS server and then ask the firewall guys to open the new port up, and the caching DNS servers can sit inside the firewall.

Now, for an NT Server 4-based network, this is mostly what you'll need to know. But if you're still running 3.51, then you'll first have to download some software from Microsoft, and you'll have to learn about *bind files,* the Unix approach to DNS servers.

Setting Up DNS on NT 3.51

You can find the DNS beta on the CD-ROM that comes with the NT *Resource Kit.* Failing that, you can FTP to rhino.microsoft.com, logging on with the username **dnsbeta** and the password **dnsbeta**. "Anonymous" won't work here, so don't use your Web browser; just use the FTP client that comes with NT.

Once you're on the FTP site, you see a file at the root named contents.txt, and directories named "63" and "files." Apparently, the last one to appear, "63" contains build 63 of the DNS beta. If there *is* a newer version then you won't see 63, you'll see a higher number. Files contains the things that won't change much from version to version. Within the 63 directory will be subdirectories for each of the four processor platforms. As always, you only need the files that are specific to your particular server, whether it's a PowerPC, Alpha, MIPS, or Intel *x*86 machine.

Get all of the files in the appropriate subdirectory of 63 and all of the files in files, and disconnect from the FTP server.

In the directory that you put all of the files into, there's a file called INSTALL.BAT; run it. It will copy the DLLs into their proper places. Look in the Control Panel under Services, and you'll see that you have a new entry, the Domain Naming Server Service. Do not start the DNS server yet, as you have some files to set up.

The Setup Files

The 3.51 DNS service relies upon a number of ASCII text files:

- BOOT contains basic information about where the other files reside. It *must* go in the \WINNT35\SYSTEM32\DRIVERS\ETC directory.

- ARPA-127.REV contains information required to allow DNS to be able to resolve the name "localhost" into 127.0.0.1 and to allow DNS to be able to resolve 127.*x.y.z* to "localhost," for any values of *x*, *y*, and *z*. In general, you won't touch it.

- CACHE tells DNS where to find the Internet "root servers," the top of the DNS hierarchy.

- You need at least one file with the names of your computers along with their specified IP addresses. You can call it anything that you like, because you direct DNS to find it with a line in BOOT that I'll introduce you to later. For example, I chose to put the list of names for my domain, mmco.com, into a file called MMCO.NMS. (I could have called it MMCO.COM, but I didn't want NT mistaking it for an executable file.)

- You have at least one file with a name like ARPA-202.REV which contains the *reverse* DNS references. The name is built up out of ARPA-*x*.REV, where *x* is the left-most quad of your network. In my case, my network is 199.34.57.0, so I called the file ARPA-199.REV. DNS knows to go looking for this file because, again, you point DNS to the REV file in the BOOT file, as I'll show you soon.

Let's take a look at the files.

The BOOT File

Like the other configuration files, BOOT is an ASCII text file. It must be placed in the WINNT35\SYSTEM32\DRIVERS\ETC directory. In the BOOT file, you specify these things:

- What directory would you like to place the other DNS data files in?

- What is the name of the file that contains the names of the Internet root servers?

- What domain, like mmco.com, will this DNS server resolve names for?

- What IP address range, like 199.34.57.0, will this DNS server do reverse name resolution for?

Let me show you an example of a DNS file, which I will explain in just a moment.

```
directory  C:\dns
cache .  cache
primary mmco.com.  mmco.nms
primary 127.in-addr.arpa arpa-127.rev
primary 57.34.199.in-addr.arpa arpa-199.rev
```

I have removed the comments to keep the file short, but you can add a comment to any DNS file by prefixing it with a semicolon.

The first command, DIRECTORY, tells DNS that I put the other files into the directory C:\DNS. There's got to be a space between "directory" and "C:\DNS."

The second command points to the file containing the names of the Internet root servers. Microsoft provides a file that works just fine, and they call it CACHE. I saw no reason to change its name, so the command CACHE . CACHE means, "You find the Internet root name servers's names in a file called 'cache' (that's the second 'cache'), in the C:\DNS directory."

Next, the *primary* statements define what this DNS server is good for. Its job will mainly be to convert mmco.com names to 199.34.57.x names, convert 199.34.57.x IP addresses into mmco.com names, and also it'll reverse-resolve any local host address references. The `primary mmco.com. mmco.nms` line says, "If someone needs information about any computer in the mmco.com domain, then you can find that information in the file mmco.nms, which is in the C:\DNS directory." Note the extra period on "mmco.com.;" do not leave it off your domain name. The `primary 127.in-addr.arpa arpa-127.rev` means, "If you're ever asked to reverse-resolve any number from 127.0.0.0 through 127.255.255.255, then look in the file arpa-127.rev, which is in the C:\DNS directory." (While my network doesn't include those addresses, they're the range of loopback addresses.) The `primary 57.34.199.in-addr.arpa arpa-199.rev` line means, "If you ever have to do a reverse name resolution for 199.34.57.0 through 199.34.57.255, then look in the file named arpa-199.rev, which is in C:\DNS."

Hey—what's that last primary statement mean? What's 57.34.199? After looking at a time or two, you've probably noticed that it is 199.34.57 backwards. Since the last two primary commands are for *reverse* DNS resolution, the names go in backwards. (I know, it's strange, but blame the Unix folks who invented DNS...) You should specify the level that the DNS server will be authoritative for here. For example, `Primary 199.in-addr.arpa x.rev` would mean, "Any reverse DNS request starting with '199' can be resolved with 'x.rev,'" and that's definitely *not* what I want to do—I've only got 199.34.57.0, not 199.132.22.0 or 199.99.55.0, or whatever. Just to provide another example, `Primary 22.140.in-addr.arpa revs.rev` would mean, "DNS server, you're responsible for addresses 140.22.0.0 through 140.22.255.255, and you'll find the reverse DNS information for that range in the file revs.rev, which is in C:\DNS."

Now that I have the BOOT file in place, let's move to the files in C:\DNS. Do not touch the arpa-127.rev file or the CACHE files that ship with the DNS service; just use them as provided.

The DNS Name Resolver File

Next, I have to create the file that tells my DNS server how to convert my PC's names to IP addresses. Now, as I mentioned before, I don't have to do that for every computer on my network; but I *should* do it for the ones with the static IP addresses—my servers, in particular. Suppose on my network I have an Internet mail server named mailserve.mmco.com, at 199.34.57.20, and a time server named timeserve.mmco.com at 199.34.57.55; those will be the machines whose addresses I must worry about. I'll put my DNS service on a machine named eisa-server.mmco.com, at 199.34.57.50. You may recall that I chose to call the file with my names MMCO.NMS. Let's start off with a look at it, with the comments removed.

```
@    in   soa   eisa-server.mmco.com. mark.mailserve.mmco.com. (
              1996021501    ; serial [ yyyyMMddNN]
              10800     ; refresh [ 3h]
               3600     ; retry  [ 1h]
             691200     ; expire [ 8d]
              86400 )   ; minimum [ 1d]

$WINS 199.34.57.32
@ in ns eisa-server.mmco.com.
@ in mx 10 mailserve
localhost in a 127.0.0.1
mailserve in a 199.34.57.20
timeserve in a 199.34.57.55
```

The first part is the "Start of Authority" record, a bit of boilerplate that you can just type right in. The only things I inserted were the name of the machine running the DNS server (eisa-server.mmco.com.) and where to find me (mark@mailserve .mmco.com). Notice two syntactic oddities that you'd better follow, or DNS won't work. First, add an extra period to the end of the full name of the name server, or DNS will automatically append "mmco.com" to the name. If I'd entered **eisa-server .mmco.com** instead of **eisa-server.mmco.com.**, then DNS would think that the name server was running on a machine named "eisa-server.mmco.com.mmco .com." The second oddity is the format for my e-mail address; DNS wants you to replace the "@" with a period, hence my e-mail name "mark.mailserve .mmco.com."

Notice also the first indented line, the one that looks like "19960215…"—it's the *DNS serial number*. Since my Internet service provider gets name information about my company from my name server, and because my ISP doesn't want to have to read what could be a monstrous DNS list every time it's asked to resolve a name, this serial number tells the outside ISP whether or not things have changed since the last time the ISP looked at my domain's DNS server. The number can be anything at all; just make sure that you change it every time you change the file.

Let me say that again: be sure to change the serial number line in your SOA record every time you change any of the data in the DNS database. I didn't, and it took me two weeks to figure out why my updated name information was being ignored by my ISP.

Next is a command that you won't find in any other DNS server: the $*WINS* command. That tells Microsoft's DNS server, "If you're asked to resolve a name, but cannot find it in the static listing, then ask the WINS server at 199.34.57.32 to resolve it." You can specify multiple WINS servers by listing them on the $WINS line, separated by semicolons.

Following that line is the line that names the name server or DNS server for this domain. It seems a bit redundant—after all, you wouldn't be reading this file if you didn't know who was the name server for this domain—but it's required. The format is just "@ in *ns* 'name of your DNS server.' " The *ns* stands for "*name server.*" The in means "this is information used by an intranet."

After that goes an MX or *mail exchange* record. An MX record makes it possible for someone to send mail to joeblow@bigfirm.com when in actual fact there is no single machine called "bigfirm.com"; rather, bigfirm's got a machine named "mail.bigfirm.com." The MX record translates mail addresses from a generic domain name to a specific machine name. An MX record looks like "@ in mx 10 'name of your mail server.' " You can add particular MX records for particular machines, but it's not necessary. For example, what happens if someone sends mail not to "mark@mmco.com," but to "mark@timeserve.mmco.com?" Well, nothing happens, basically; timeserve isn't prepared to receive mail, and so the message will just be lost. But I *could* idiot-proof the system a bit by adding MX records to every single DNS entry, so no matter what machine an outsider tried to send mail to, the mail would end up at mailserve.

Next is the listing of machines and IP addresses. Each record looks like *"machinename* in a *IP address,"* where *machinename* is just the left-most part of the name, rather than the fully qualified domain name. For example, a machine on my network called "mwm66.mmco.com" would have a record that looked like "mwm66 in a 199.34.57.66" if its IP address were 199.34.57.66. The *in* part is, recall, for *intranet.* The *a* part means that this is an *address* record. You also need a localhost reference, as you see in my example. Microsoft provides a sample name file in a file called PLACE.DOM; in it, they also show you how to create an alias for an FTP and a WWW site. But it's just as easy to type in a file like the one above.

The Reverse Name Resolution Files

As I mentioned earlier, DNS isn't too terribly bright about using the information that you give it; although it knows that mypc.mmco.com is 199.34.57.43, it still can't seem to figure out that given the IP address 199.34.57.43 it should reverse-resolve the DNS name, "mypc.mmco.com." So you have to help it out with the reverse DNS files.

In my example, I told my DNS server in the BOOT file that it could reverse-resolve addresses in the 199.34.57.0 network, and that information was in a file called ARPA-199.REV. It looks like the following, again with the comments removed:

```
@  IN SOA eisa-server.mmco.com. mark.smtphost.mmco.com. (
                1    ; serial number
                10800  ; refresh [3h]
                3600  ; retry  [1h]
                691200 ; expire [8d]
                86400 ) ; minimum [1d]
@ in ns eisa-server.mmco.com.
32 IN PTR eisa-server.mmco.com.
50 IN PTR mailserve.mmco.com.
55 IN PTR timeserve.mmco.com.
35 IN PTR sdg90.mmco.com.
```

It looks a lot like the MMCO.NMS file that we just created, with a few differences. It starts off with a "start of authority" record just like the MMCO.NMS file. There is, again, a pointer to the local name server, eisa-server.mmco.com. Then there are references to the IP addresses of machines in the mmco.com domain. Notice that since the DNS server only looks in here to resolve names looking like "199.34.57.something," you need only specify the last quad on the IN PTR lines.

Notice also that there's no $WINS statement; that's important. For some reason, this WINS-to-DNS dynamic link can do DNS name resolution, but not reverse resolution. That's why I have an extra entry, for a machine named sdg90.mmco.com; it attaches to an FTP site that double-checks who I am before letting me on by requesting a reverse DNS resolution. It sees that I'm attaching from 199.34.57.35, but it needs to be sure that my DNS name is also sdg90.mmco.com. As sdg90 gets its IP address from my DHCP server, I needed to put a specific address into this file so that my DNS server could reverse-resolve the address for that particular PC. (How can I be so sure that sdg90 gets 199.34.57.35? I reserved the address for it in DHCP.)

As your DNS server must also be able to reverse-resolve loopback addresses, you have an ARPA-127.REV, but, as I've already said, don't touch it; it's fine as it comes from Microsoft.

Now all you have to do is to start up the service, point all of your workstations to that machine for DNS resolution, and you have your very own dynamic DNS server. It's still a bit flaky, but it's often useful, and no doubt the final version will be cleaner.

Once the DNS service is up and running, you can point workstations to it: when they need the name of a DNS server, just fill in the IP address of your NT machine running the DNS server. And ask your ISP to tell its DNS server to pull its address resolution information off your DNS server. One warning: the DNS server beta ran well until I installed NT 3.51 Service Pack 3; if you can avoid that Service Pack, then you might want to do that.

Migrating from an NT 3.51 DNS Server to a 4 DNS Server

You just read that NT 3.51 DNS servers store their data in a set of ASCII files called *bind* files. What I haven't told you is that the NT 4 DNS server stores its data in the Registry. How can you get a 4 DNS Server to read a set of *bind* files from a 3.51 installation, so that you can forgo having to retype piles of names?

Here's my recipe.

1. Take all of the *bind* files and put them into \winnt\system32\dns; they *must* be there, or the 4 DNS server can't find them.

2. Install the DNS service.

3. Before creating any zones, right-click the server and choose Properties. Click the Boot Method tab, and choose Boot from BootFile.

4. Click OK.

5. Stop the DNS Service

6. Restart it.

It should now see your *bind* files. At this point, I'd switch it back to Boot from Registry and start and stop the service.

Name Resolution Sequence under WinSock

Now that you know how to configure DNS and WINS, you may be faced with a troubleshooting problem in reference to name resolution. Perhaps you try to FTP to a site inside your organization, but you can't hook up. Even though you know that ftp.goodstuff.acme.com is at one IP address, your FTP client keeps trying to attach somewhere else. You've checked your DNS server, of course, and its information is right. Where else to look?

Review: WinSock versus NBT

Remember first that there are two kinds of name resolution in Microsoft TCP/IP networking, WinSock name resolution and NetBIOS name resolution. A NET VIEW *somename* needs NetBIOS over TCP name resolution, or NBT name resolution. In contrast, as FTP is, like ping, an Internet application, it uses WinSock name resolution. So, to troubleshoot a name resolution problem, you have to follow what your client software does, step by step.

Examining Network Traces

When faced with a problem like this, I turned to the Microsoft documentation for help, but there wasn't much detail. So I ran a network monitor and issued ping commands to computers that didn't exist, to see the sequence of actions that the network client software tried in order to resolve a name. The HOSTS and LMHOSTS files do not, of course, show up in a network trace, so I inserted information into those files that didn't exist on the DNS or WINS servers, and then tried pinging again, to demonstrate where the HOSTS and LMHOSTS files sit in the name resolution hierarchy. Pinging for a nonexistent "apple," I found that the name resolution order proceeds as shown in Figure 14.66.

Step by step, it looks like this.

- First, consult the HOSTS file, if it exists. If you find the name you're looking for, stop.

- Next, if there's a specified DNS server or servers, then query them. First, query "apple." NT machines then query "apple.mmco.com," tacking on the domain name; Windows 95 workstations don't do the second query.

This happens whether or not the box "Enable DNS for Windows Name Resolution" (found in the Advanced Microsoft TCP/IP Configuration dialog boxes of NT 3.51 and Windows for Workgroups), is checked. If DNS has the name, then stop.

- After that, the client looks to see if the name is 16 or more characters. If it is, then the process stops, a failed name resolution attempt. Notice that this means that *LMHOSTS cannot resolve FQDNs longer than 15 characters*—quite a scary bug if you depend on LMHOSTS!

- Next, if there's a specified WINS server or servers, then query the WINS server(s). The name WINS looks for is "apple <00>," the name that *would* be registered by the Workstation service, if the "apple" machine existed.

- If that fails, then do three broadcasts looking for a machine with NetBIOS name "apple <00>," requesting that it identify itself and send back its IP address. Again, this would succeed with a workstation running some NetBIOS-over-TCP/IP client, even a relatively old one, as it would have registered the "apple <00>" name already, if only on its own name table. Unfortunately, this only works if the machine is on the same subnet.

FIGURE 14.66:

The name resolution order

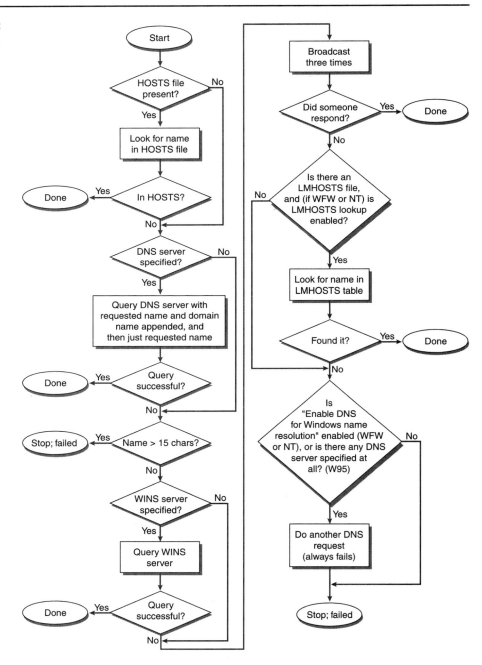

- If the name still hasn't been resolved, read the LMHOSTS file. (Under NT 3.51 and Windows for Workgroups, do not do this if the box labeled "Enable LMHOSTS Lookup" is unchecked; skip this step.) As with the earlier steps, stop if you find a match, or keep going.

- If you're running an NT or Windows for Workgroups machine with the box "Enable DNS for Windows Name Resolution" checked, then you've instructed your system to do a DNS lookup every time a WINS lookup fails. If that box is checked, then a second and last DNS lookup will happen. If, on the other hand, you *don't* have the "Enable DNS" box checked, then there's nothing left to do.

Look at that sequence: HOSTS, DNS, WINS, broadcast, LMHOSTS, and DNS again. This surprised me for a couple of reasons. First, it seems that every unsuccessful name resolution results in broadcasts, the *bête noire* of those of us trying to keep the network traffic to a minimum. My guess is that the broadcasts aren't part of an according-to-Hoyle IP stack, but Microsoft just threw them in for good measure and the WINS query as well. Then, if you've checked "Enable DNS for Windows Name Resolution," the client software performs a DNS lookup as a matter of course after any failed WINS lookup; unfortunately, that leads to a redundant DNS lookup here. In short, if your Windows 95 workstation knows of a DNS server, it will use that DNS server when doing both DNS and NetBIOS name resolutions.

The broadcasts are a pain, but they *would* be of benefit when you tried to execute a TCP/IP command on a computer in your network, but wanted to use the shorter NetBIOS name rather than the longer DNS name, such as "apple" instead of "apple.mmco.com."

What happened on that workstation that could not access the FTP site? There was an old HOSTS file sitting in the Windows directory that pointed to a different IP address, an older IP address for the FTP server. HOSTS is read before anything else, so the accurate information on the DNS or WINS servers never got a chance to be read.

There is an explicit Enable DNS for Windows Name Resolution check box in Windows for Workgroups and NT 3.51 clients, but how do you control whether or not DNS gets into the act on a Windows 95 client? You can't, at least not entirely; where Workgroups and NT 3.51 separate the options about whether to specify a DNS server and whether or not to use that DNS server as a helper when resolving NetBIOS names (that's what "Enable DNS for Windows Name Resolution" means); Windows 95 seems not to do that.

Controlling WINS versus DNS Order in WinSock

Now, what I just showed you is the order of events by default in NT or Windows 95 clients. But if you feel like messing around with the way that WinSock resolves names, you can. As usual, let me take this moment to remind you that it's not a great idea to mess with the Registry unless you know what you're doing.

Look in the Registry under HKEY_LOCAL_MACHINE\System\CurrentControl-Set\Services\TCPIP\ServiceProvider, and you see a HostsPriority, DNSPriority, and NBTPriority value sets. They are followed by hexadecimal values. The lower the value, the earlier that HOSTS, DNS (and LMHOSTS), and WINS (and broadcasts) get done. For example, by default DNS's priority is 7D0 and WINS's is 7D1, so DNS goes before WINS. But change DNS's priority to 7D2, and WINS does its lookup and broadcast *before* the client interrogates the DNS server.

Again, I'm not sure *why* you'd want to do this, but I include it for the sake of completeness and for the enjoyment of those who delight in undocumented features.

Name Resolution Sequence under NetBIOS

Having looked at the steps that the system goes through to resolve a DNS name, what happens when the system attempts to resolve a NetBIOS name? Again, it's an involved process, but in general the factors that affect how NBT resolves names are

- Is the workstation an NT 3.51 or Windows 95 workstation?
- Is LMHOSTS enabled?
- Is DNS enabled to assist in Windows (NetBIOS) name resolution?
- Is the network client software WINS-aware?

Summarized, the name resolution sequence appears in Figure 14.67.

FIGURE 14.67:

Name resolution sequence
under NetBIOS

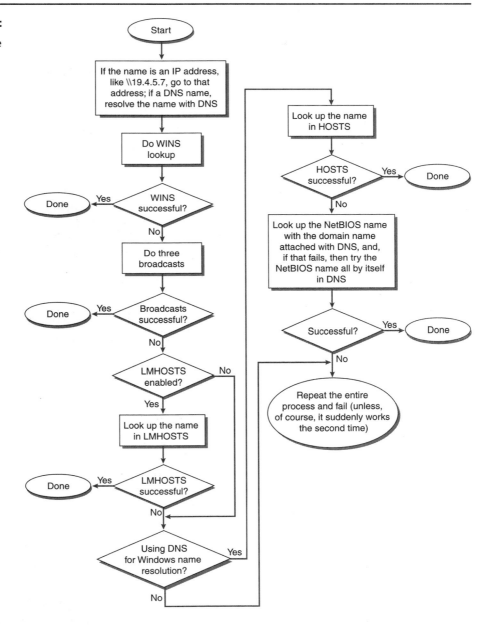

The same components that went into WinSock name resolutions contribute to NBT resolutions, but in a slightly different order. The NBT name resolver uses the following steps; if any succeed, then it stops looking.

- The first part is the WINS client, if the client software is WINS-aware. If WINS is disabled under Windows 95, or if there is no WINS server specified in Workgroups or NT 3.51, then the client skips this step.

- If WINS isn't being used, then the client does three broadcasts. For example, NET VIEW \\APPLE causes three broadcasts looking for a workstation with the name *apple* registered, rather than *apple.mmco.com* or the like.

- Next, if LMHOSTS is enabled—and it appears that LMHOSTS is *always* enabled on Windows 95 clients, but must be enabled with the Enable LMHOSTS check box for NT 3.51 and Workgroups—then the client looks up the name in LMHOSTS. Surprised? When doing NBT name resolutions, LMHOSTS gets consulted *before* HOSTS, a reversal over WinSock name resolutions.

For LMHOSTS to be of help here, it must specify NetBIOS names, not fully qualified domain names. For example, if you have a workstation named rusty .acme.com at 212.11.41.4, but you want to do a "net view \\rusty," then the line in lmhosts should look like this:

```
212.11.41.4 rusty
```

Not "rusty.acme.com," just "rusty".

- If you've checked "Enable DNS for Windows Name Resolution" in Workgroups or NT 3.51, or if you have specified a DNS server in Windows 95, then the workstation's client software will look at HOSTS and, if HOSTS can't help, it will interrogate the DNS server (or servers, as you can specify up to four DNS servers).

The NT/Workgroups clients and the 95 clients use DNS differently. The NT/Workgroups clients do a DNS query for the name with the domain name appended to it, and then a DNS query of just the name. For example, if your domain is "acme.com" and you're doing a "net view \\myserver," then an NT workstation will ask DNS first to resolve the name "myserver.acme.com"—it automatically adds the domain name for the first resolution. Then, if the DNS server can't resolve the name with the domain name attached, then the client will request that the DNS server just resolve "myserver."

In contrast, the Windows 95 client software only asks the DNS server to resolve the name with the domain name appended; in my example, a Windows 95 workstation would ask DNS to resolve "myserver.acme.com," but would not ask about "myserver."

- The last part is *really* strange. If the client software is the NT client (not the Workgroups or Win95 clients), and if it's been unsuccessful so far, then it goes back and does it all over again, I suppose in the hope that it'll work the second time.

You've seen how WinSock and NBT resolve names; now you're ready to look at the "battle of the network names"…

What If DNS and WINS Conflict?

Here's a question that I get in class sometimes. I present it here mainly as a review of what you've read so far.

WINS will generally have accurate name information for your local domain, at least among the WINS-aware machines, as it gets its naming information from the horse's mouth, so to speak; you can't *use* a WINS name server unless you *contribute* a bit of information—that is, address information about yourself. DNS, in contrast, gets its information from people typing data into ASCII files, so the data could be wrong. That leads students to the following question.

What if you have a Microsoft networking client that is not only WINS-aware, but also uses a DNS server: in that case, which name service does the workstation query first? Suppose you have a machine named ollie.acme.com whose IP address is 207.88.52.99. Not only does WINS know of ollie, DNS does too—but suppose DNS incorrectly thinks that ollie's IP address is 207.88.52.100. Type **ping ollie .acme.com**, and what will happen? Will the system look to the .99 address, or the .100 address?

Do you see how to answer this question? First, ask yourself: "Is this a WinSock or a NBT name resolution request?" As the application is ping, the answer is "WinSock." Go to the WinSock name resolution flowchart, and you see that the DNS server gets first crack at answering the name resolution request.

Now, that was the answer for a WinSock resolution, but what about an NBT resolution? For example, suppose I open up a command line and type **nbtstat -a xyz.nyoffice.mmco.com**. What will happen?

This is a bit of a trick question. First of all, understand that NBTSTAT takes a *NetBIOS* name as a parameter, and I've specified a WinSock name. An NBT resolution will choke on that "xyz.nyoffice.mmco.com" name, as it's way over 15 characters. So it truncates it after the 15th character, and does an NBT name resolution on "xyz.nyoffice.mm."

There's a lot more to network name resolution on NT networks than I guessed when I first looked into this, as you can see, but now you're equipped with all the information that you need to tackle a mystery along the lines of "machine X says it can't see machine Y."

Printing to Network Printers Using IP

At my company, we need to put shared printers all over the place, but we haven't got room to put a PC acting as a print server right next to those printers. That's why we like direct network interfaces for printers, like the JetDirect cards that you can buy for Hewlett-Packard printers. With NT 3.1 we had to use the DLC protocol to communicate with those printers. DLC's not bad, but I wanted to minimize the number of protocols on the network. As it turns out, it's not too hard to use IP to communicate directly with network-attached printing devices.

The only difference between setting up a network printer with IP and setting one up with DLC is that first you've got to load a new service on your server, the Microsoft TCP/IP Printing service. You install it in the usual way—Control Panel ➤ Network ➤ Services ➤ Add—and then choose Microsoft TCP/IP Printing. As usual, NT Setup will ask you what the paths to the files are; click Continue to copy the files and then choose Close and then Yes to reboot.

After rebooting the server, you create a new printer. Just double-click the Add Printer icon in the Printers folder. The install is exactly the same as a normal printer install, except for one thing: in the dialog box where you show the printer what interface to attach to, you'll need to add a new port. Click Add Port, and you'll see a dialog like the one in Figure 14.68.

Choose LPR Port and click OK. You'll then be prompted for information on the printer, as you see in the dialog box shown in Figure 14.69.

FIGURE 14.68:

Adding a port for an IP-attached printer

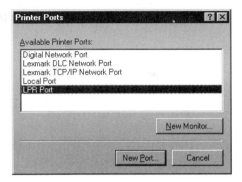

FIGURE 14.69:

Defining the IP-attached printer

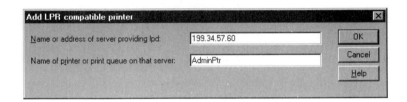

The titles for the fields aren't as obvious as they might be. Put the IP address of the printer in the top field and just fill in any name you like in the bottom field. Now, this driver is assuming that the printer is attached to a Unix machine somewhere, so you'll get an error message similar to the one you see in Figure 14.70.

FIGURE 14.70:

Normal warning message when configuring IP-attached printers

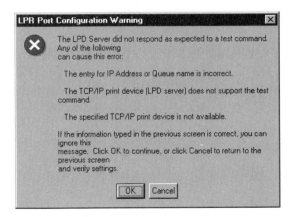

As there's no computer attached to the printer, you get this error message. Just ignore it and click OK. The page in the Wizard will now look like the one in Figure 14.71.

FIGURE 14.71:

New IP-attached port

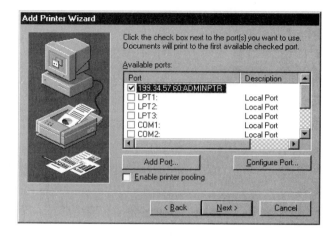

Just check that port and continue as always, and you'll be able to use your IP-attached printer.

Now you know the ins and outs of installing and configuring TCP/IP. It's time to learn how to use the oldest TCP/IP tool—the Telnet remote login program.

Using Telnet for Remote Login

In the early days of TCP/IP and intranetting, people's first concern was getting onto other people's computers. For instance, suppose I worked at the John Von Neumann Supercomputing Center, and I had written a fantastic celestial motion simulator—a program that could compute the location of thousands of planets, planetoids, and comets in the Solar System. Suppose also that I had developed this with government money, and so the Feds wanted to offer this simulator to everyone. Well, how does one get to this simulator?

In all likelihood, in order to get to this program, you'd have to come to the Von Neumann center. That's true for two reasons. First, I developed it on a supercomputer for a good reason—it's too darn big to fit anywhere else. Stick it on a normal computer, and it'll take weeks to get an answer to a simple question like,

"When will Jupiter and Mars next be near to each other and high in the night sky?" The second reason is that we're back in the early days of intranetting, recall, and in those days programs were generally specific to the machines that they were built on. Moving this program to another computer would be a pain in the neck, even *if* I were willing to put up with the slower speed. So it seems that the most likely way to offer this service to everyone is to put some modems on the Von Neumann system and allow anyone to dial into the system in order to access this program. And, in fact, things like that have been done—but they end up generating awfully large phone bills for the people on the other side of the country.

Telnet solves this problem. It lets me work on the terminal or computer on my desk and access other hosts just as if I were there on-site—in the case of the Von Neumann center, just as if I were right at Princeton, New Jersey, where the center is located. Now, there *is* no publicly-available astronomical simulator at Von Neumann, not at least as far as I know, so I can't show you anything like that. What I *can* show you is Archie, an essential Internet tool.

Seeing What's Out There: Using Archie

As we'll discuss later, *the* Internet is a very big source of information, from recipes to rutabaga farming tips to religion, which leads to the question, "How do I know what's available on the Internet?" There are three main ways to find out what's on the Internet, and one is Archie. There are a large number of computers—*hosts*, they're called—on the Internet that hold files that are available for public downloading and use; for example, something called Project Gutenberg puts the text of some well-known books on servers, available for anyone to download. But, again, how would you find out about the existence of these things? Ask Archie.

Site	Location
archie.rutgers.edu	NE US
archie.sura.net	SE US
archie.unl.edu	Western US
archie.ans.net	The Internet backbone
archie.mcgill.ca	Canada
archie.funet.fi	Europe
archie.doc.ic.ac.uk	United Kingdom
archie.au	Australia and Pacific Rim

Archie is available on several servers around the world. It's best to hook up to the Archie server closest to you so as to minimize network traffic. For example, there is quite limited data transfer capability to England, so, although using the UK Archie server might seem cosmopolitan, it's a fairly inconsiderate thing to do if you're intranetting from the U.S. I'll hook up to Archie at Rutgers.

I'll do the Telnet login from the command line. Once the session is active, however, I'll automatically be shifted to the NT Terminal program. I remotely log on to Archie in New Jersey by typing **telnet archie.rutgers.edu**.

After some introductory things, I get a prompt that says, "Login?" I respond by typing **archie**. Now, not every Telnet site will require a login. Some just drop you right into the middle of the application. Others may require that you get an account for their service, and they may charge you money for using whatever service they're purveying over the Net—that's fair game. Expect to see more and more services on the Internet that are for-pay—the Net is slowly going commercial. Anyway, I get a prompt that says "archie>", indicating that when I type something now, when I make a request for information, then that request is not being processed by the computer in Connecticut, but rather by the computer running Archie at Rutgers University in New Jersey. Usually the help command works, and it does in this case, as well. Next, I'll tell Archie that, when I ask it for a file's name, it shouldn't show me only the files whose names match exactly—it should show me *anything* that contains what I'll type. I do this by typing **set sub**. Now, if you do this, then be very careful about what you ask for—search for "e" and you get every file that's got an "e" in its name! I'm going to look for a server that's got the text of *Alice's Adventures in Wonderland* on it, so I'll look for files that contain the word "alice." I do that by typing the command **prog**, which asks for a search of programs, and **alice**. The search shows me...

```
login: archie
Last login: Thu Oct 7 06:06:29 from bix.com
SunOS Release 4.1.3 (TDSERVER-SUN4C) #2: Mon Jul 19 18:37:02 EDT 1993

# Bunyip Information Systems, 1993

# Terminal type set to `vt100 24 80'.
# `erase' character is `^?'.
# `search' (type string) has the value `sub'.
archie> prog alice
# Search type: sub.
# Your queue position: 1
working...
```

```
Host cair.kaist.ac.kr  (143.248.11.170)
Last updated 10:29 4 Oct 1993

Host uceng.uc.edu  (129.137.189.1)
Last updated 20:43 3 Oct 1993

  Location: /pub/wuarchive/doc/misc/if-archive/games/source/gags
    FILE  -r-r-r-  16681 bytes 01:00 18 Mar 1993 alice.zip


Host ftp.sunet.se  (130.238.127.3)
Last updated 11:48 6 Oct 1993

  Location: /pub/etext/gutenberg/etext91
    FILE  -r-r-r- 162153 bytes 22:00 17 Sep 2000 alice29.txt


Host roxette.mty.itesm.mx  (131.178.17.100)
Last updated 21:26 2 Oct 1993

  Location: /pub/next/Literature/Gutenberg/etext91
    FILE  -r-r-r-  64809 bytes 00:00 1 May 1992 alice29.zip


Host ftp.wustl.edu  (128.252.135.4)
Last updated 20:43 2 Oct 1993

  Location: /mirrors/misc/books
    FILE  -rw-r-r-  64809 bytes 00:00 15 Jun 1992 alice29.zip

Host ftp.wustl.edu  (128.252.135.4)
Last updated 20:43 2 Oct 1993

  Location: /systems/amiga/aminet/text/tex
    FILE  -rw-rw-r-  5593 bytes 05:13 27 Sep 1993 decalice.lha
    FILE  -rw-rw-r-   254 bytes 05:13 27 Sep 1993 decalice.readme

  Location: /systems/amiga/boing/video/pics/gif
    FILE  -rw-rw-r- 109870 bytes 01:00 8 Feb 1993 palice.jpg
archie> bye
# Bye.
Connection closed by foreign host.
```

Notice that every group of information starts off with host; that's important, as that's the name of the place that we'd have to go in order to get Alice. Then there's a filename. The parts in front of it are exactly *where* the file is. If you're a PC user, then you may, at first glance, think that you recognize the subdirectory usage, but look again! Instead of backslashes, which DOS uses to separate subdirectory levels, Unix uses *forward* slashes!

Anyway, now we've found Alice. We'll quit Archie by typing **quit**. The message, "Connection closed by foreign host," is a message from my computer to me. It says that the Archie computer at Rutgers—which it calls the *foreign host*, has stopped talking to me.

Non-Standardization Problems

In general, Telnet works fine with computers of all kinds. But some host computers just plain won't talk to you unless you're an IBM 3270-type dumb terminal, so there is another program, tn3270. Tn3270 is a variation of Telnet that emulates an IBM 3270 full-screen type terminal. The main things to know about tn3270 are that 3270-type terminals have a *lot* of functions about them. Not all implementations of tn3270 are equal, so don't be totally shocked if you Telnet to an IBM site using tn3270, work for awhile, and get a message: "Unexpected command sequence— program terminated." It means that your tn3270 couldn't handle some command that the IBM host sent it. And IBM terminal emulation can be a real pain in the neck when it comes to key mapping. On the IBM terminal are a set of function keys labeled PF1, PF2, and so on. As there are no keys labeled like that on a PC or a Mac, what key should you press to get PF4, for instance? Well, it's Esc-4 on some implementations of tn3270, F4 on some others, and there doesn't seem to be any real agreement either on what the key is, or what the key should be. Make sure that you have the documentation for your tn3270 somewhere around before you start telnetting to an IBM host.

NOTE There is no tn3270 shipped with NT.

Why Use Telnet?

Summing up this section, what is Telnet good for, anyway? Several things. First, it is the way to access a number of specialized basic information services. For instance, many large libraries put their entire card catalog on Telnet servers. University researchers can then look for an item, and request it through interlibrary loan. Another example can be found in the University of Michigan's geographic server, a service offering geographic information—just type **telnet martini.eecs .umich.edu 3000**, and you're in.

```
access% telnet martini.eecs.umich.edu 3000
Trying 141.212.99.9...
Connected to martini.eecs.umich.edu.
Escape character is '^]'.
# Geographic Name Server, Copyright 1992 Regents of the University of
Michigan.
# Version 8/19/92. Use "help" or "?" for assistance, "info" for hints.
.
arlington, va 22205
0 Arlington
1 51013 Arlington
2 VA Virginia
3 US United States
R county seat
F 45 Populated place
L 38 52 15 N 77 06 05 W
E 250
Z 22200 22201 22202 22203 22204 22205 22206 22207 22209 22210
Z 22212 22213 22214 22215 22216 22217 22222 22223 22225 22226
```

Or ask U of M for information about the weather by typing **telnet madlab .sprl.umich.edu 3000**, and find out whether or not it's raining in Dallas. Second, a commercial firm might want to offer an online ordering service: you just log on, browse the descriptions of the items available, and place an order electronically. A third, somewhat technical, reason for using Telnet is that Telnet can be used as a debugging tool. Using Telnet, I can essentially impersonate different applications, like FTP and mail (you'll meet them soon). That's a bit beyond the scope of this book, but I mention it in passing.

Then, the final reason for Telnet is simply its original reason for existence—remote login to a service on a distant host. That has become a feature of much less value than it was when it first appeared, largely because of the way that we now use computers. Twenty years ago, you would have had a dumb terminal on your desk. Today, you are likely to have a computer on your desk, a computer with more computing power than a mainframe of 20 years ago. We are less interested today in borrowing someone else's computing power than we are in borrowing their information—with their permission, of course. Specifically, we often seek to transfer files to and from other computers over an intranet. For that reason, we'll consider another TCP/IP application—FTP, the File Transfer Protocol—next.

Using FTP for File Transfer

If you have a PC or Macintosh on your desk, think for a moment about how you use that computer in a network situation. You may have a computer elsewhere in your building that acts as a *file server*, a computer that holds the files shared in your facility or your department. How do you ask that server to transfer a file from itself to your computer? You may say, "I don't do that"—but you *do*. Whenever you attach to a shared network resource, you are asking that system to provide your computer with shared files. Now, how you actually *ask* for them is very simple: you just connect to a server, which looks like an extra folder on your desktop if you're a Mac user, or an extra drive letter, like X: or E: if you are a PC user. The intranet world has a facility like that, a facility that lets you attach distant computers to your computer as if that distant computer were a local drive: it is called NFS, the Network File System. But NFS is relatively recent in the TCP/IP world. It's much more common to attach to a host, browse the files that it contains, and selectively transfer them to your local host. You do that with FTP, the *File Transfer Protocol*.

There are three essentials of FTP: how to start it up, how to navigate around the directories of the FTP server, and how to actually get a file from an FTP server. After that, we'll look at a special kind of FTP called *anonymous FTP*. So let's get started by looking at how the files on an FTP server are organized.

FTP Organization

The first time that you get on an FTP server, you'll probably want to get right off. FTP, like much of the TCP/IP world, was built from the perspective that software's got to be *functional* and not necessarily pretty or, to use an overused phrase, user-friendly. If you're a PC user, the Unix file structure will be somewhat familiar, as the DOS file structure was stolen—uhh, I mean, *borrowed*—from Unix. Mac users will have a bit more trouble.

Now, I just referred to the Unix file structure. That's because FTP servers *usually* use Unix. But some don't, so you may come across FTP servers that don't seem to make any sense. For the purposes of this discussion, I'll assume that the FTP servers here are Unix, but, again, be aware that you may run into non-Unix FTP servers. The occasional FTP server runs on a DEC VAX, and so probably runs the VMS operating system; some others may run on an IBM mainframe, and so may be running either MVS or VM. Very rarely, an FTP server may run under DOS, OS/2, NT, or some other PC operating system. But let's get back to our look at a Unix FTP server.

FTP uses a tree-structured directory represented in the Unix fashion. The top of the directory is called ourfiles, and it has two directories below it—*sub*-directories—called ourfiles/bin and ourfiles/text, as shown in Figure 14.72. In the Unix world, .bin refers to executable files, files we might call program files in other operating systems, or, more specifically, EXE or COM files in the PC world or load modules in the IBM mainframe world. The text directory contains two directories below *it*; one's called contracts and one's called announcements.

FIGURE 14.72:

An example of how files on an FTP server are organized

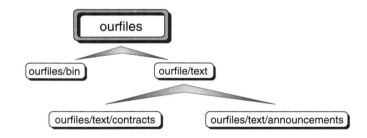

A couple of notes here. PC users may think that things look a bit familiar, but there *are* a couple of differences. First, notice the subdirectory named announcements. That name is more than eight characters long—that's quite acceptable, even though it *isn't acceptable* in the PC world. Unix accepts filenames of hundreds of characters. Second, notice that there are not *backslashes* between the different levels, but instead *forward* slashes; that's also a Unix feature. Now, what complicates matters for users of non-Unix systems is that FTP pretty much assumes that *your* system uses the Unix file system, as well. That means that you have to be comfortable with traversing *two* directory structures—the one on the remote FTP server, and the one on your local hard disk.

File Navigation

You get an FTP command line—I'll demonstrate it in a minute—that expects you to tell it where to get files *from*, *and* where to send files *to*, using these two commands:

- remote—cd
- local—lcd

That's because there's a tree structure on both the remote system—the one that you're getting the files from—and the local system. Let's look at a few examples to nail down exactly how all this cd-ing works.

Moving in FTP

When I enter an FTP site, I start out at the top of the directory structure. This top is called the *root* of the directory. In my example, the root is called ourfiles. To move down one level, to ourfiles/text, I could type **cd files**. That says to FTP, "Move down one level relative to the current location." Alternatively, you could skip the relative reference and say absolutely, "Go to ourfiles/text"—the way that you do that is by typing **cd /ourfiles/text**. The fact that the entry *starts* with a slash tells cd that your command is not a relative one, but an absolute one.

Now let's try moving back up a level. At any point, you can back up one level either by typing the command **cdup**, or by typing **cd ..** The two periods (..) mean one level upward to both DOS and Unix. Or you can do an absolute reference, as in **cd /ourfiles**.

Now suppose I'm all the way at the bottom of this structure. It's a simple three-level directory, and you often see directory structures that are a good bit more complex than this one. To move back up from ourfiles/text/announcements to ourfiles/text, you can do as before, and either type **cdup** or **cd ..** .Or you could do an absolute reference, as in cd /ourfiles/text. To go back *two* levels, you can either issue two separate **cdup** or **cd ..** commands, or use an absolute reference, as in **cd /ourfiles**. To type two **cdup** or **cd ..** commands, you type the command, then press Enter, then type the second command. Do not try to issue two commands on the same line.

An Example of Navigation: Go Get Alice

Now that you can navigate the twisty passages of FTP directories, it's a good time to get Alice.

We found earlier that we could get the *Alice's Adventures in Wonderland* text at a number of sites. One of those sites was roxette.mty.itesm.mx, in the directory pub/next/Literature/Gutenberg/etext91. Let me FTP to that site and get the file. I type **ftp roxette.mty.itesm.mx**, and then I get a Name? prompt. This site doesn't know me, so I can't log on with a local name and password. That's where the idea of *anonymous* FTP becomes useful. You see, you can often log on to an FTP site and download data that's been put there specifically for public use. Anonymous FTP is just the same as regular FTP, except that you log in with the name anonymous. It responds that a guest login is OK but wants my e-mail address for a password. I put in my e-mail address, and I'm in. Now, it might be that there are places on this server that I *cannot* get to because I signed on as anonymous, but that doesn't matter—Alice is in the public area. Next, I can do a dir command and see what's on this directory.

```
ftp> dir
200 PORT command successful.
150 Opening ASCII mode data connection for /bin/ls.
total 2009
drwxr-xr-x 2 root     wheel     1024 Jun 2 02:48 .NeXT
drwxr-xr-x 3 ftpadmin daemon    1024 Apr 5 1993 .NextTrash
drwx--- 2 ftpadmin other     1024 May 20 22:46 .elm
-rw---- 1 ftpadmin other     1706 Sep 21 08:04 .history
-rwxr-x-- 1 ftpadmin wheel      186 Jul 21 1992 .login
-rwxr-x-- 1 ftpadmin wheel      238 Feb 25 1991 .profile
-rw-r-r- 1 ftpadmin wheel       27 May 20 22:53 .rhosts
-rw-r--- 1 ftpadmin wheel      589 Jun 9 1992 .tcshrc
-rw-r-r- 1 ftpadmin wheel  2027520 Oct 2 22:17 IRC.tar
drwx--- 2 ftpadmin other     1024 May 20 22:46 Mail
drwxr-xr-x 2 ftpadmin wheel     1024 May 29 1992 bin
drwxr-xr-x 3 ftpadmin wheel     1024 Nov 11 1992 etc
drwxr-x-- 2 ftpadmin wheel     1024 May 19 01:31 mirror
drwxr-xr-x 6 root     wheel     4096 Jul 15 00:36 pub
226 Transfer complete.
863 bytes received in 0.6 seconds (1.4 Kbytes/s)
ftp> cd pub
```

```
250 CWD command successful.
ftp> dir
200 PORT command successful.
150 Opening ASCII mode data connection for /bin/ls.
total 20
drwxrwxrwt 6 root     daemon    4096 Jun 10 15:58 .NextTrash
-rw-r--- 1 jleon    wheel      205 May 29 02:42 .dir3_0.wmd
drwxr-xr-x 5 ftpadmin other     4096 May 19 01:47 X11R5
drwxrwxrwt 3 ftpadmin other     4096 Sep 26 03:04 incoming
drwxr-xr-x 20 ftpadmin other    4096 Oct 6 02:29 next
```

It's not a very pretty sight, but let's see what we can see. Notice all the *r*'s, *x*'s, *w*'s, and *d*'s to the left of each entry? That represents the privilege levels of access to this file. One of the important things is whether or not the left-most letter is *d*—if it is, then that's not a file, it's a directory. Notice that entry pub; it's a directory, but we already knew that, because Archie told us that we'd find Alice in the directory pub/next/Literature/Gutenberg/etext91. I have to move to that directory to FTP it, so I type **cd pub/next/Literature/Gutenberg/etext91**.

Notice that there are no spaces except between the cd and the directory name, and notice also that, in general, you must be careful about capitalization—if the directory's name is Literature with a capital *L*, then trying to change to a directory whose name is literature with a lowercase *l* will probably fail. Why *probably*? It's another Unix thing; the Unix file system is case-sensitive. In contrast, if you found yourself talking to an OS/2-based TCP/IP host, then case would be irrelevant. How do you know what your host runs? Well, it is sometimes announced in the sign-on message, but not always. The best bet is to always assume that case is important.

Anyway, once I get to the directory, another dir command shows me what's in this directory.

```
ftp> dir
200 PORT command successful.
150 Opening ASCII mode data connection for /bin/ls.
total 7940
-r-r-r- 1 ftpadmin wheel      885 May 1 1992 AAINDEX.NEW.Z
-r-r-r- 1 ftpadmin wheel      885 May 1 1992 INDEX.NEW.Z
-r-r-r- 1 ftpadmin wheel      876 May 1 1992 INDEX91.Z
-r-r-r- 1 ftpadmin wheel     1170 Oct 2 07:01 Index
-r-r-r- 1 ftpadmin wheel     8575 May 1 1992 LIST.COM.Z
-r-r-r- 1 ftpadmin wheel     8917 May 1 1992 README.Z
-r-r-r- 1 ftpadmin wheel    98605 May 1 1992 aesop10.txt.Z
```

```
-r-r-r- 1 ftpadmin wheel    101607 May 1 1992 aesop10.zip
-r-r-r- 1 ftpadmin wheel    67597 May 1 1992 alice29.txt.Z
-r-r-r- 1 ftpadmin wheel    64809 May 1 1992 alice29.zip
-r-r-r- 1 ftpadmin wheel    435039 May 1 1992 feder11.txt.Z
-r-r-r- 1 ftpadmin wheel    463269 May 1 1992 feder11.zip
-r-r-r- 1 ftpadmin wheel    14841 May 1 1992 highways.apl.Z
-r-r-r- 1 ftpadmin wheel    79801 May 1 1992 hisong10.txt.Z
-r-r-r- 1 ftpadmin wheel    75310 May 1 1992 hisong10.zip
-r-r-r- 1 ftpadmin wheel    75541 May 1 1992 lglass16.txt.Z
-r-r-r- 1 ftpadmin wheel    73128 May 1 1992 lglass16.zip
-r-r-r- 1 ftpadmin wheel    606033 May 1 1992 moby.zip
-r-r-r- 1 ftpadmin wheel    530686 May 1 1992 mormon12.txt.Z
-r-r-r- 1 ftpadmin wheel    529476 May 1 1992 mormon12.zip
-r-r-r- 1 ftpadmin wheel    129601 May 1 1992 opion10.txt.Z
-r-r-r- 1 ftpadmin wheel    138296 May 1 1992 opion10.zip
-r-r-r- 1 ftpadmin wheel    203785 May 1 1992 plboss10.txt.Z
-r-r-r- 1 ftpadmin wheel    219257 May 1 1992 plboss10.zip
-r-r-r- 1 ftpadmin wheel    206661 May 1 1992 plrabn10.txt.Z
-r-r-r- 1 ftpadmin wheel    221387 May 1 1992 plrabn10.zip
-r-r-r- 1 ftpadmin wheel    621855 May 1 1992 roget11.txt.Z
-r-r-r- 1 ftpadmin wheel    592247 May 1 1992 roget11.zip
-r-r-r- 1 ftpadmin wheel    657390 May 1 1992 roget12.zip
-r-r-r- 1 ftpadmin wheel    19790 May 1 1992 snark12.txt.Z
-r-r-r- 1 ftpadmin wheel    17184 May 1 1992 snark12.zip
-r-r-r- 1 ftpadmin wheel    789836 May 1 1992 world11.txt.Z
-r-r-r- 1 ftpadmin wheel    825269 May 1 1992 world11.zip
226 Transfer complete.
2214 bytes received in 1.4 seconds (1.5 Kbytes/s)
```

There are the files from Project Gutenberg, including *Moby Dick*, *Alice's Adventures in Wonderland*, *The Book of Mormon*, *The Hunting of the Snark*, *Roget's Thesaurus*, and more. Now, notice the Alice file is offered two ways—alice29.zip and alice29 .txt.z. An extension of ZIP on a file usually means that it has been compressed using the PKZIP algorithm and probably on an MS-DOS system. The Unix counterpart to that is a file ending simply in Z, like the second file. It can be uncompressed with the gzip program that you can find on many libraries. More specifically, suppose you download alice29.zip to a PC. If you tried to look at the file, it would look like gibberish. That's because the file is compressed and must be uncompressed before it can be viewed. It was compressed so that there would be fewer bytes to transfer around the network; after all, this *is* a book, and you don't want to clog up the network with millions of bytes when thousands can do the job. You'd transfer this to your PC, and then you'd use an un-zipper program to un-compress the file. But the file that ends off with .Z, the one done with gzip, can be unzipped *while transferring*! Suppose you don't have a copy of either pkunzip or gzip, and don't want to have to mess around with finding an un-zipper. All you need do is to just request the file not as alice29.txt.z, but instead as alice29.txt. The FTP program is smart enough to know that it should uncompress the file as it transfers it to your machine! A pretty neat feature, I'd say.

Before we get the file, there's one more thing that I should point out. Years ago, most files that were transferred were simple plain text ASCII files. Nowadays, many files are *not* ASCII—even data files created by spreadsheets and word processors contain data other than simple text. Such files are, as you probably know, called *binary* files. FTP must be alerted that it will transfer binary files. You do that by typing **binary** at the ftp> prompt. FTP responds by saying, "Type set to I." That is FTP's inimitable way of saying that it's now ready to do a binary file transfer, or, as FTP calls it, an *image* file transfer.

Transferring a File

Now let's get the file...

```
access% ftp roxette.mty.itesm.mx
Connected to roxette.mty.itesm.mx.
220 roxette FTP server (Version 5.20 (NeXT 1.0) Sun Nov 11, 1990)
ready.
Name (roxette.mty.itesm.mx:mminasi): anonymous
331 Guest login ok, send ident as password.
Password:
230 Guest login ok, access restrictions apply.
ftp> cd pub/next/Literature/Gutenberg/etext91
250 CWD command successful.
ftp> binary
200 Type set to I.
ftp> get alice29.zip
200 PORT command successful.
150 Opening BINARY mode data connection for alice29.zip (64809 bytes).
226 Transfer complete.
local: alice29.zip remote: alice29.zip
64809 bytes received in 16 seconds (4 Kbytes/s)
ftp> bye
221 Goodbye.
access%
```

Notice that once I got the file, the system reported some throughput statistics.

Now, when we get the file, it'll take some time to transfer. There's no nice bar graphic or anything like that to clue us about how far the transfer has proceeded. There *is* a command, however, that will give you *some* idea about how the transfer is progressing—*hash*. Type **hash**, and from that point on, the system will print an octothorpe (#) for each 2K of file transferred. For example, say I'm on a Gutenberg system and I want to download the Bible, bible10.zip. (Is it sacrilegious to compress the Bible? Interesting theological question.) The file is about 1600K in size, so I'll see 800 octothorpes.

Each line shows me 80 characters, so each line of # characters means 160K of file were transferred. It'll take 10 lines of # characters (*10 lines!*) before the file is completely transferred. (Why does this take so long on my system? Well, the Internet is pretty fast, but my connection to it is just a simple v.32 bis modem. My company's part of the information superhighway, but we're kind of an unimproved country road.)

FTP versus Telnet

Now let's review what we've seen so far. First, you use the FTP program to log on to a remote system, in a manner similar to telnetting onto a remote system. In fact, some people have trouble understanding why there's a difference between Telnet and FTP. Telnet is for terminal emulation into another facility's computing power; FTP is for transferring files to and from another facility's computers. Once you FTP to another site, you find that the site usually has its files organized into a set of directories arranged in a tree structure. You move FTP's attention from one directory to another with the CD command. *You*, also, may have a tree-structured directory on your system; if you wish to tell FTP to transfer to or from a particular directory, then you use the local CD command, or lcd. You use the binary command to tell FTP that you're going to transfer files that aren't simple ASCII. The GET command requests that the remote system give you a file, and, although I haven't mentioned it yet, the PUT command requests that the remote system *accept* a file from you. And those are the basics of FTP, the File Transfer Protocol.

Downloading to the Screen

But let's go to *another* Gutenberg site to illustrate another helpful tip. I noticed earlier when I was using Archie that there was a location that had Alice called ftp.wustl.edu. Let's see what *they've* got—maybe a newer version, perhaps? Now,

I know that you're thinking, "A newer version of *Alice's Adventures in Wonderland*? Isn't Lewis Carroll dead?" Well, yes, Mr. Dodgson is long gone, but the text is typed in by volunteers, and mistakes creep in. First, we'll get off this current FTP site by typing **BYE**. That command may vary, but it seems pretty standard for most of the FTP and Telnet world. Again, it informs me that I'm disconnected from the roxette site. I'll FTP to ftp.wustl.edu now… again, I'm doing *anonymous* FTP, so I type in a username **anonymous**—lowercase, remember—and use my e-mail address mminasi@access.digex.net as the password. You don't see that because the password doesn't echo. I get the usual chatter, and then I'm in. Now, Archie told me that Alice was in mirrors/misc/books, so I'll cd over to there—**cd mirrors/misc/books**—and do a dir to see what's there.

```
ftp> dir
200 PORT command successful.
150 Opening ASCII mode data connection for /bin/ls.
total 12060
-rw-r-r-  1 root    archive    3110 May  1 18:00 00-index.txt
-rw-r-r-  1 root    archive  552711 Apr 16 18:00 2sqrt10.zip
-rw-r-r-  1 root    archive  102164 Jun 15 1992  aesop11.zip
-rw-r-r-  1 root    archive   32091 Jun 18 1992  aesopa10.zip
-rw-r-r-  1 root    archive   15768 Apr 16 18:00 alad10.zip
-rw-r-r-  1 root    archive   64809 Jun 15 1992  alice29.zip
-rw-r-r-  1 root    archive  244863 Dec  2 1992  anne10.zip
-rw-r-r-  1 root    archive 1636512 Jun 18 1992  bible10.zip
-rw-r-r-  1 root    archive  358371 Jun 18 1992  crowd13.zip
-rw-r-r-  1 root    archive   50736 Apr 16 18:00 dcart10.zip
-rw-r-r-  1 root    archive  102460 Jun 18 1992  duglas11.zip
-rw-r-r-  1 root    archive  467260 Jun 15 1992  feder15.zip
-rw-r-r-  1 root    archive   78337 Jun 15 1992  hisong12.zip
-rw-r-r-  1 root    archive  136293 Jun 18 1992  hrlnd10.zip
-rw-r-r-  1 root    archive   70714 Oct 23 1992  hyde10.zip
-rw-r-r-  1 root    archive   69860 Oct 23 1992  hyde10a.zip
-rw-r-r-  1 root    archive  176408 Apr 16 18:00 iland10.zip
-rw-r-r-  1 root    archive   73128 Jun 15 1992  lglass16.zip
-rw-r-r-  1 root    archive  149481 Apr 16 18:00 locet10.zip
-rw-r-r-  1 root    archive  606033 Jun 15 1992  moby.zip
-rw-r-r-  1 root    archive  513720 Jun 15 1992  mormon13.zip
-rw-r-r-  1 root    archive   11579 Apr 16 18:00 nren210.zip
-rw-r-r-  1 root    archive  103284 Jun 18 1992  oedip10.zip
-rw-r-r-  1 root    archive   95167 Apr 16 18:00 ozland10.zip
```

```
-rw-r--r--  1 root    archive  692080 Apr 16 18:00 pimil10.zip
-rw-r--r--  1 root    archive  217770 Jun 15 1992  plboss11.zip
-rw-r--r--  1 root    archive  214541 Jun 18 1992  plrabn11.zip
-rw-r--r--  1 root    archive   44204 Apr 16 18:00 rgain10.zip
-rw-r--r--  1 root    archive  580335 Jun 15 1992  roget13.zip
-rw-r--r--  1 root    archive  643011 Jun 15 1992  roget13a.zip
-rw-r--r--  1 root    archive  222695 Jun 30 1992  scrlt10.zip
-rw-r--r--  1 root    archive   35695 Oct 23 1992  sleep10.zip
-rw-r--r--  1 root    archive   17184 Jun 15 1992  snark12.zip
-rw-r--r--  1 root    archive   26009 Apr 16 18:00 surf10.zip
-rw-r--r--  1 root    archive   84641 Jul 31 1992  timem10.zip
-rw-r--r--  1 root    archive   38665 Jun 18 1992  uscen90.zip
-rw-r--r--  1 root    archive   63270 Aug 24 1992  uscen902.zip
-rw-r--r--  1 root    archive  161767 Jul 31 1992  warw10.zip
-rw-r--r--  1 root    archive   79409 Apr 16 18:00 wizoz10.zip
-rw-r--r--  1 root    archive  798086 Jun 15 1992  world12.zip
-rw-r--r--  1 root    archive  724062 Apr 16 18:00 world192.zip
-rw-r--r--  1 root    archive  912325 Jun 18 1992  world91a.zip
-rw-r--r--  1 root    archive  712389 Apr 16 18:00 world92.zip
-rw-r--r--  1 root    archive   71459 Jun 30 1992  zen10.zip
226 Transfer complete.
3008 bytes received in 0.34 seconds (8.6 Kbytes/s)
```

A whole bunch of things! Now, there's a file up top, called 00-index.txt, that looks like it could tell me what's going on. Now, I *could* just get the file. But think about what a pain that would be. First, I get the file. Then I disconnect from ftp .wustl.edu. Then I examine the file with a text editor. A lot of work just to find out what's in a README file. So there's a trick that you can use to see a file—just "get" it, but get it to your screen! You do that by typing **get** *filename* **-**, as I'll do here. I type **get 00-index.txt -** and press Enter. The file zips by, so it's a good thing that I have the ability to scroll text back. But what if I *didn't* have the ability to scroll text back? Then I could make the remote FTP program *pause* by adding **" |more"**—you need quotes around the vertical bar and the more. In this case, I'd type **get 00-index.txt - " |more"**. You can usually temporarily freeze a screen by pressing Ctrl+S for stop; you start it up again with Ctrl+Q.

Now, this depends on the system that you're working with, but it may only be possible to do this "get" and "more" if your FTP session is set for ASCII transfers rather than binary transfers. You can change that by just typing **ascii** at the command line. You see the response type set to A.

That's about all that we'll say here about FTP. There is lots and lots more that FTP can do, but I've given you the basics that you can use to get started and get some work done in the TCP/IP world. If this all looks ugly, user-unfriendly, and hard to remember then, well, it *is*, at least to someone used to a Macintosh or Windows. But there's no reason why a graphical FTP program couldn't exist, and indeed some are appearing. FTP is two things—the FTP protocol, which is the set of rules that the computers on an intranet use to communicate, and the program *called* FTP that you start up in order to do file transfers. The FTP *protocol* doesn't change and probably won't change. But the FTP *program*, which is usually known as the FTP *client*, can be as easy-to-use as its designer can make it. So go on out, learn to spell anonymous, and have some fun on those FTP sites! To set up your own FTP site (as well as your own Web site), read about the Internet Information Server (IIS) in Chapter 15. Right now we're going to look at electronic mail.

E-Mail on TCP/IP

Computers all by themselves are of little value for anything more than acting as a glorified calculator. Hooking up computers via networks has been the thing that's really made computers useful, and of course networks are a big part of communications. But networks are of no value unless people use them—and people won't use them without a reason. This brings me to electronic mail. E-mail is often the "gateway" application for people, the application that is the first network application that they'll use; for some people, it's the *only* application that they'll ever use. And e-mail is probably the most important thing running on the Internet.

Using EMWACS Mail Software to Make Your NT Server a Mail Relay Agent

Most offices have some kind of internal e-mail, such as Microsoft Exchange, Lotus cc:Mail, or the like. But connecting that e-mail to the outside world—that is, the Internet—is an expensive proposition; when we bought our cc:Mail/Internet gateway at TechTeach International, it had a list price of $4,000. That's a shame, as the protocols for Internet mail are well-documented and there's lots of free code around to support them. In this section, I'll tell you about my favorite, a piece of software from the European Microsoft Windows Academic Centre (EMWACS).

Internet E-Mail Protocols

There are two main Internet e-mail protocols that most of us care about: the Simple Mail Transfer Protocol (SMTP) and the Post Office Protocol (POP3).

SMTP is the "mail" Internet e-mail protocol. SMTP grew up at a time when most users on the Internet were running Unix machines, each with their own IP address. Each Unix machine ran two mail programs. The first was a program that could package up a mail message and send it to its destination; the most common one was one named *sendmail*. The second program was a so-called *daemon*, a program that always runs in the background, kind of like a DOS Terminate and Stay Resident (TSR) program. The daemon would constantly listen for incoming mail in the form of TCP/IP packets sent from another system running sendmail.

The SMTP/sendmail approach worked fine as long as every system on the Internet could run some kind of mail daemon, *and* so long as every system was up and running 24 hours a day, seven days a week. But primitive PC operating systems don't handle daemons well, and most people don't leave their workstations up and running all of the time, even if they *are* running an operating system that handles daemons well. Additionally, while many systems may run all of the time and while they may have an operating system that likes daemons just fine, they aren't connected to the Internet all of the time.

In any case, it'd be nice to enhance SMTP with some kind of mail storage system, allowing one computer to act as a kind of "post office." Suppose you've got 500 people on your network with varying operating systems and uptimes. So you set up one computer that *is* up 24 hours a day, seven days a week. This computer runs the mail daemon, the program that listens. You tell that computer, "Accept mail for everyone in the company, and hold onto it." That's the computer I'll call a *post office*. Then, when a user wants her mail, she just connects to that post office and pulls down her mail. In the Internet world, we let a client computer like the one on her desktop communicate with a post office computer with a protocol called POP3, the Post Office Protocol. Such a program is a small program referred to as a *POP3 client*. Actually, every POP3 client that I know of might be better referred to as a *POP3 Message Receiver/SMTP Message Sender*. The program only uses POP3 to get your mail; when you create a new message, it just sends it to a computer running the SMTP receiver service (the daemon), which then hands it to the SMTP delivery service (sendmail or one of sendmail's cousins).

In order for *your* office to send and receive Internet mail, you'll need a computer to act as a post office. The computer uses SMTP to talk to other post offices, and those post offices may choose to communicate with you at any hour of the day, so the computer must be attached to the Internet 24 hours a day, seven days a week. So that your users can retrieve their mail, they'll need programs that act as POP3 clients. Finally, that post office computer will need to run a POP3 *server* so that it can respond to mail requests.

EMWACS's Internet Mail Service (IMS) software can take you a good ways toward that goal. It consists of three services that'll run on any NT Server machine:

- The SMTP receiver service, the listening "daemon" program. The program that does this is called SMTPRS.EXE. When another post office gets mail for you, it will communicate with SMTPRS.EXE. Similarly, if you create a new mail message and tell your mail client to mail it out, the mail client will send the message to SMTPRS.EXE.

- The SMTP delivery service, which sends messages to other post offices. The delivery service is called SMTPDS.EXE. SMTPDS only has to listen to SMT-PRS. When the receiver service gets a new piece of mail, it gives it to SMT-PDS, the delivery service. If the mail is destined for another post office, SMTPDS establishes a connection with that other post office and shoots the mail over there. If the mail is destined for *this* post office, then SMTPDS just drops the mail into the proper user's mail box.

- The POP3 server. Called POP3S.EXE, this program responds to requests from POP3 client programs, delivering mail to those clients when requested.

Where can you find a POP3 client? Right in NT or Windows 95—the program attached to the Inbox tool can act as a POP3 client. I'll show you how to set that up later, but first let's get the server software set up. Or, if you find the Microsoft tool not to your liking, surf on over to http://www.eudora.com/eudoralight, where you'll find Eudora Light, an excellent mail client written by the Qualcomm people. They write terrific software, and, even better, they have a 32-bit version of their Eudora mail client that they give away absolutely free.

Setting Up Your Mail Server: IMS Limitations

Before you install IMS, you should be aware of some of its limitations. There are a few things you must do to an NT machine before it can serve well as a post office. Because you might find some of the constraints unduly confining, let's take a look at them before you go further.

The Mail Server Must Have a Static IP Address

Each service must be able to find the IP address of the computer that it is running on. You can check this by typing the name of each service, followed by the -ipaddress parameter; for example, once you have IMS installed on an NT machine, you can type **smtprs -ipaddress**, and you should see the IP address and DNS name of that machine.

In my experience, the IMS components can't find a machine's IP address if that machine gets its IP address from DHCP; just being in a DNS table doesn't seem to do the trick. So you've got to run IMS on a machine with a static IP address.

DNS Must Be Able to Find the Mail Server

This ought to be kind of obvious, but I thought I'd mention it anyway. If you send mail to bob@fin.shark.com, and DNS can't find fin.shark.com, then the mail isn't going very far. The IMS services actually try to resolve the name of the computer they're sitting on when they first start. If the IMS services *can't* resolve the name, then they will refuse to run.

The Mail Server Only Serves Users in Its Users Group

If the mail server receives mail for a user it doesn't recognize, it just refuses the mail. How, then, does it distinguish the users that it recognizes? They must be in the mail server's Users group. If the mail server has joined a domain, then that domain's Domain Users group will be sitting in the server's local Users group.

The POP3S Server Doesn't Accept Blank Passwords

There may be a way to do this, but I haven't figured it out. If you try to get your mail, then of course you'll be asked for your username and password. If your password is empty, then POP3S will refuse your connection, and you won't be able to retrieve your mail.

The Software Doesn't Have Performance Monitor Counters

Unlike a lot of NT software, the EMWACS mail software won't install Performance Monitor counters. Yes, yes, I know, I'm getting a bit nitpicky about a piece of *free* software, but it'd be nice to use the power of Perfmon with IMS.

How the IMS Software Works

You install the three services on an NT server. Once they're up and running, any-one can send mail to *somename@servername*, where *somename* is a valid NT user on that server, and *servername* is the Internet host name of the server. So, for example, if my local server were named altair.mmco.com and my username were markm, you could send mail to markm@altair.mmco.com.

Downloading the EMWACS Software

As I write this, the EMWACS folks have progressed to version 0.8*x* of their mail software. Always get the most up-to-date version, because they're always work-ing on the program. At this writing, you'll find it at http://emwac.ed.ac.uk/html/internet_toolchest/ims/ims.htm. Just point your Web browser to that loca-tion and you'll see instructions on how to download the software. They also have documentation on the product in HTML format—be sure to get that, because it'll have more detailed installation instructions than you can read here.

Unzipping the EMWACS Software

As I'm using an Intel-based server for my mail system, the file I downloaded was named IMSi386.ZIP. Since it's a zipped file, you'll need PKUNZIP or a similar program to decompress the files.

Create a directory that you'll unzip the files into. (I called mine C:\EMWACS.) Copy the IMSi386.ZIP file there, open up a command line, and type **PKUNZIP -d IMSi386**; that will unzip the file and create any necessary directories. Do the same with the ZIP file containing the documentation; that will create a directory called HTML which will contain the documentation.

Then copy these files to the \WINNT\SYSTEM32 directory:

- SMTPRS.EXE (the receiver daemon)
- SMTPDS.EXE (the sendmail delivery agent)
- POP3S.EXE (the POP3 server)
- IMS.CPL (the Control Panel applet to control the mail server)
- IMSCMN.DLL (a DLL to support the programs)

You can put most of them in different directories, but I find it easiest to just stick them in the SYSTEM32 directory. The IMS.CPL file *must* go in \WINNT\SYSTEM32.

Installing the Services

Next, register the services with NT. Open up a command line, change the drive and directory to the \WINNT\SYSTEM32 DIRECTORY, AND TYPE THE NAME OF EACH SERVICE, FOLLOWED BY **-install**:

```
smtprs -install
smtpds -install
pop3s -install
```

Each module should acknowledge that it has installed correctly. Next, tell NT to automatically start these services whenever your start the computer. Go to the Control Panel and open the Services applet. You'll see three new services named

- IMS POP3 Server

- IMS SMTP Delivery Agent

- IMS SMTP Receiver

One at a time, click each service, and then click the Startup button. Choose Automatic, and the service will start when the computer does. Do this for each of the three services. Because they hasn't been started yet, be sure to also click the Start button for each service.

Set Users to Log On as Batch Jobs

IMS requires that any user who tries to access his mailbox be able to log on to the server running IMS as a *batch job*. Odd as it sounds, it's necessary. Just start up the User Manager and point it at the particular machine that is going to run the IMS services. For example, if you are going to run IMS on a server named MAILSRV, then start up the User Manager or the User Manager for Domains and choose User ➤ Select Domain, and then type in **MAILSRV** where it asks for a domain. You'll just be editing the Security Accounts Manager (SAM) of the mail server machine, rather than the domain.

Click Policies ➤ User Rights, and check Show Advanced User Rights. Then find the right Log on as a batch job, and add in the Users group from this computer. That users group (MAILSRV\Users, in this example) should contain the Domain Users groups of all of the NT domains that this machine will serve as a mail server.

NOTE   Remember that you can only add a Domain Users group from another domain if your domain *trusts* the other domain.

If users aren't able to log on as batch jobs, they'll be denied login to the NT mail server from their client software (Inbox, Eudora, or whatever). And, once again, don't forget that the mail server will *refuse* to receive mail from users who aren't in its local Users directory. So, suppose you want to set up a mail server M1 in domain RED, but you want it to accept mail for people in domain BLUE as well. First, make sure that RED trusts BLUE. Then go to User Manager on server M1 and make sure that the group M1\Users contains both RED\Domain Users and BLUE\Domain Users.

Configuring the Services

Next, you'll see an applet labeled EMWAC IMS in the Control Panel. Double-click on that, and you'll see a screen like in Figure 14.73.

FIGURE 14.73:

Configuring directories for IMS mail

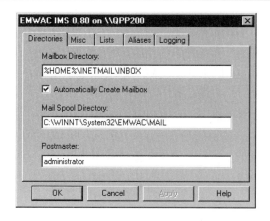

First, tell IMS where to put the mailboxes. Each user gets her own subdirectory in which IMS keeps her mail. If you check the Automatically Create Mailbox check box, then IMS will, as the label suggests, create a user's mailbox automatically. That way, IMS only creates a directory when necessary.

IMS lets you specify a couple of ways to organize user mailboxes—with the %home% and %username% variables. If you use %home% in the mailbox name, IMS will substitute the user's home directory, the one specified in the Profiles button on the User Manager. If you use %username% in the mailbox name, then IMS will substitute the user's NT username.

For example, suppose I've got users named Sue and John as accounts on an NT server. Their home directories are on the server at D:\Users*username*. I could put their mailboxes in a directory E:\MAIL by telling IMS to set Mailbox Directory to E:\MAIL\%username%. As mail came in for Sue and John, IMS would end up creating directories E:\MAIL\JOHN and E:\MAIL\SUE. Mail messages would then accumulate in each directory as each user received mail. Note two things: first, E:\MAIL need not be shared and, second, neither John nor Sue need have File and Directory permissions on E:\MAIL or on either subdirectory.

Does that sound like it violates NT security? It doesn't. You see, neither John nor Sue ever tries to access E:\MAIL; rather, John and Sue run programs—POP3 mail clients—that communicate in client-server fashion with the POP3S service, which in turn provides them with their mail messages. Now, it *is* a fact that POP3S must have access to that mailbox directory or nothing will happen.

If you set up the mailbox directories as I've just suggested, then they are very secure from user tampering. If, on the other hand, you don't care whether users can directly access their mailboxes, then use the %home% variable. For example, if you were to tell IMS to put mail in %home%\mail, John's mail would sit in D:\USERS\JOHN\MAIL, and Sue's would sit in D:\USERS\SUE\MAIL. In general I avoid the %home% variable because, first, it confuses the mail server if a user does not have a home directory, and second, it puts the mail directories under direct user control, which isn't always the best idea.

The Mail Spool Directory is just a temporary holding directory for the mail server, and I just use the default. "Postmaster" is the e-mail name of the person who gets the error messages. (It's a good idea, by the way, to log into the mail server with the postmaster's name.)

Next, click the Misc tab and you'll see Figure 14.74.

FIGURE 14.74:

Misc configuration in IMS

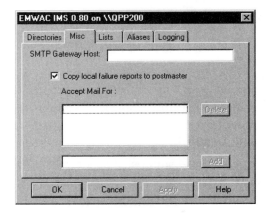

You can use this tab to tell the mail system to accept mail for other Internet domains; however, you *can't* use this to tell it to accept mail for other NT domains—remember, you do that by putting global groups from other domains into the mail server's local Users group. The only thing I'd do here is to check "Copy local failure reports to postmaster." That way, you can keep track of systemic problems. Finally, click the Logging tab and enable logging for each of the three services.

Once you've got IMS configured as you like it, close the Control Panel applet and start and stop each service so your configuration changes take effect. Or, if you don't want to wait around for the services to stop and start, write a batch file to do it:

```
net stop "IMS POP3 Server"
net start "IMS POP3 Server"
net stop "IMS SMTP Delivery Agent"
net start "IMS SMTP Delivery Agent"
net stop "IMS SMTP Receiver"
net start "IMS SMTP Receiver"
```

By now, you should be ready to set up your mail client.

Configuring the Microsoft "Inbox" Exchange Client for Internet Mail

If you've installed Windows 95 or Windows NT, then you've noticed that Microsoft has included a mail client application labeled Inbox or, to some people, the Exchange Client. (The name is misleading, as it's *not* the program that you use to pick up Exchange mail.) This program is actually two programs in one. First, it's a client for someone running Microsoft Mail, and, second, it can act as a POP3 client. Unfortunately, people who aren't using Microsoft Mail, but who need a simple POP3 client, tend to overlook the Inbox. In this section, I'll show you how to configure the Inbox to receive your Internet mail. Double-click on the Inbox icon for the first time, and you'll see the dialog box in Figure 14.75.

FIGURE 14.75:

Initial Inbox setup dialog

Click Yes, and you'll be prompted to insert the NT Setup CD (unless you set up from the hard disk). It'll copy a few files and return you to the desktop. Double-click the Inbox tool again, and you'll see the dialog box in Figure 14.76.

FIGURE 14.76:

Choosing services to configure

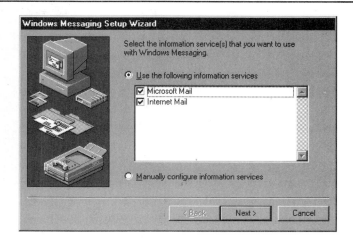

Uncheck Microsoft Mail (unless you *do* use Exchange or Microsoft Mail, of course) and click Next. You'll see a dialog box like Figure 14.77.

FIGURE 14.77:

Connecting via the network

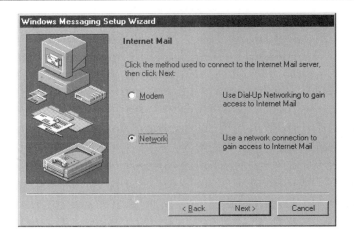

Since you're locally connected to your IMS mail server, choose the Network radio button and then click Next. You'll then see a dialog box like in Figure 14.78.

FIGURE 14.78:

Mail server address

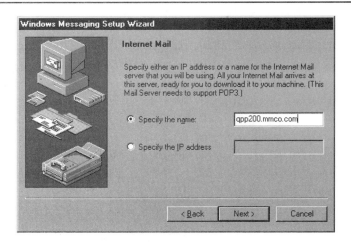

As you can see, there's a radio button that you can use to choose whether to point at the server with its name or its IP address. The machine to specify here is the machine on which you've just installed IMS. Click Next, and you'll see the dialog box in Figure 14.79.

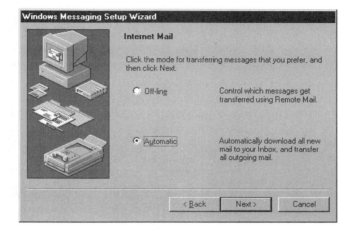

This controls whether you receive your messages as they come in, or if you must request them with the Tools ➢ Deliver Now option. I prefer to control when I retrieve and send my messages, so I choose Off-line; use whichever option works best (you can change it later if you don't like what you first selected.) Click Next, and you'll fill in some information about your mail account, as you see in Figure 14.80.

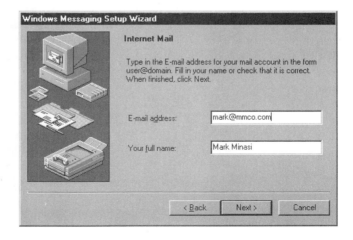

This may seem redundant—you already specified a server, right?—but it's not. Note that I didn't enter **mark@qpp200.mmco.com**; I entered **mark@mmco.com**. I did that because mark@mmco.com is the e-mail address that I give to the outside world; my network then internally figures out that mark@mmco.com really means mark@qpp200.mmco.com.

How it does it is the business of your DNS server. Read the section on setting up the DNS server, and you'll see that you can insert records called MX or Mail Exchange records into the DNS server. In the case of my network, I would insert a record that would tell DNS that whenever someone wants to send mail to me at mark@mmco.com, the mail should go to mark@qpp200.mmco.com. The Your full name field is used to identify you in the header of a message; you can actually put anything in there. Click Next, and you'll see Figure 14.81.

FIGURE 14.81:

NT security logon information

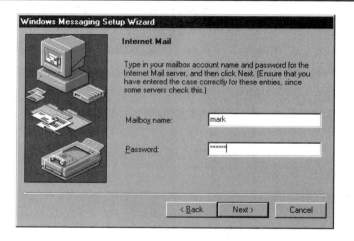

The Inbox mail tool will allow you to log on to a POP3 server running on any kind of operating system. Most will require that you log in with a username and password; you enter that here. Here, you must enter the username and password that the mail server knows you as. In my case, I'm a recognized member of the Users group on QPP200 by virtue of the fact that QPP200\Users contains my domain's Domain Users account, so I fill in my domain username (Mark) and my domain password. Click Next, and you'll have an opportunity to point the Inbox tool to two more files, your personal address book and your personal folders.

I'm not going to reproduce the screens here, as they're straightforward ("Please enter the name of the directory… "); what I *do* want to stress is that you've got to be careful where you put the address book and folders. By default, the Inbox will sometimes want to put them in \WINNT; instead, I'd put them in a personal location.

Be careful about *what* personal area you use, however. Your NT profile contains an area named \WINNT\profiles*username*\personal, and many Microsoft products use that as the place to keep your personal information. But if you reinstall NT as a fresh install (rather than an upgrade), then the NT Setup program *deletes* the old personal folders. My advice: create a directory that's yours—perhaps a home directory on some server—and put the folders and address book there. That way, if you must reinstall NT and the Inbox tool, you can just point the newly installed Inbox at your folders and address book, and you won't lose any old messages or addresses. (The address book is actually not bad; it lets you store snail mail addresses and phone numbers as well as Internet mail addresses.)

The mail client will then be installed. The initial screen looks like Figure 14.82.

FIGURE 14.82:

Initial mail client screen

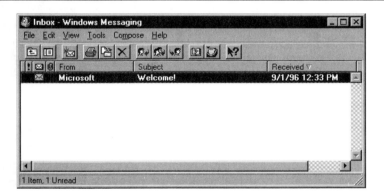

That first "message" is bogus, just an advertisement from Microsoft. To retrieve your mail, click Tools then Deliver now, and you'll get your mail.

By the way, since I first wrote this, Microsoft has improved its free Internet/POP3 mail services. If you've got Internet Explorer 4 on your system, then you also have a neat little POP3 client named *Outlook Express*. If you've got it, I recommend that you use it, it's quite good for the price.

To tell Outlook Express to use your EMWACS mail server, open up Outlook Express and click Tools ➤ Accounts. In the Internet Accounts dialog box, click Add, then Mail. A Wizard will walk you through the configuration information. It basically asks the same information as the older Inbox program did.

If you load up the EMWACS mail service, set it up right and use the built-in Inbox. You can wire your company to the Internet in no time at all—and except for the cost of connecting your network to the Internet, for no cost!

MailSite: "EMWACS Pro"

As you've read, I've been a fan of the free Internet Mail Service (IMS) software for NT from EMWACS for a long time. EMWACS mail doesn't do everything that I'd like; in particular, I wish that it did IMAP4, a protocol that lets you check your mail by only retrieving the *headers* of the mail messages rather than the entire message. That's important because I travel a lot, and it's usually just my luck to dial into the mail server at home at 31Kbps (the actual speed of most of my "56Kbps" sessions) only to find that some idiot has put me on his "joke distribution list" and today's yuk includes a five-megabyte bitmap. (Imagine how much laughing I do after waiting 20 minutes for this laff riot to download.) Additionally, many clients like EMWACS when I show it to them, but are leery of installing software that's not supported; they're looking for something commercial, with support.

I was pleased, then, to hear that Rockliffe Systems (http://www.rockliffe .com/) has taken the EMWACS IMS software, extended it tremendously, and is selling it as a product called *MailSite*. The core is still EMWACS, but there's a lot more, including my much desired IMAP4. (I know, you're asking yourself, "Why doesn't he just use Exchange?" I know Exchange, have run it on client systems and even on my network for a while, but for some reason I just don't *like* it. All I really need is POP3/SMTP/IMAP4, and Exchange seems a bit of overkill. Basically, what I'm saying is that there's nothing *wrong* with Exchange—I just don't like it.)

You can go to their Web site and download MailSite and try it out for 30 days, as is the case with much software nowadays. (The program files are over 5MB in size, so pick a time of Internet quiet for the download.) The good news is that they've added a lot of nice GUI administrative support to IMS, as well as removed the need for any user-rights fiddling. The system's quite fast and of course does IMAP4 as well as all the mailing list stuff you could want. And if you're a current EMWACS IMS administrator, you won't have any trouble—it took me less than five minutes to install the software and get it running. The bad news is the price, about $700. Is it worth it? As always, it depends. If you're managing multiple mail servers, MailSite offers remote mail server administration, a big plus. The MailSite folks seemed helpful when I called their tech support line and asked a few dumb questions. And if your shop is a mixed NT/Unix shop and you don't really want to be assimilated into the Exchange collective, then MailSite's something to check out. (*I'm* certainly enjoying it, although having to bring down the mail server every 30 days so I can go get another 30-day trial license is cumbersome... just kidding.)

E-Mail Security Concerns

As the Internet grows, more and more gateways will be built to other e-mail systems. You can't get everywhere, but, in time, you'll be able to reach anyone from the Internet. Now, that's a good thing, but as e-mail becomes more important, it's also essential to keep your mind on the fact that e-mail is *not secure*. Your mail packets get bounced all around the Internet, as you know—but think about what that means. Suppose you send a message to someone on the Internet, and my computer is part of the Internet—a piece, as it happens, that sits between you and the person to whom you're sending mail. Mail can sit in intermediate computers like mine, *on the hard disk*, for seconds, minutes, or hours at a time. It's a simple matter to use any number of utility programs to peek into the mail queue on the mail that's "just passing through." *Never* say anything on mail that you wouldn't want as public knowledge. Even if someone doesn't peek at your mail, that someone probably backs up his or her disk regularly, meaning that the message may sit on magnetic media for years in some archive. I sometimes imagine that in the middle of the 21st century, we'll see "the unpublished letters of Douglas Adams"—e-mail notes that someone stumbled across while picking through some 70-year-old backups; you know, it'll be the latter-day equivalent of going through some dead celebrity's trash. Anyway, the bottom line is this: don't write anything that you wouldn't want your boss, your spouse, your parents, or your kids to read.

NT Internet Security: Some Thoughts

Now that you know how to put your NT-based network on the Internet, *should* you? Some companies have and they've been quite dismayed to find "open season" declared on their network as computer-wielding slime of all kinds invaded their systems and their data.

Putting your local LAN on the Internet *can* leave you open to attacks from criminals, because the Internet wasn't really designed with security in mind. But remember that you're running NT, one of the more security-conscious networks.

I'm not a security expert, so please don't take this section as guaranteed advice on how to secure your network from outside attack. But follow along with me and let's see if a little common sense can help you shore up your computers and data.

First, where do the security holes exist in an NT network? Again, not speaking as a network expert, here are the main problems that I see, whether on an Internet or not.

Internal Users Can Easily Get a List of User IDs

In Chapter 7, you learned how to configure a set of home directories. First, you create a share called USERS on an NTFS volume, giving the Everyone group or, better, the Domain Users group, Full Control. Then you set the top-level directory permissions to Read and Execute and assign Domain Users no file permissions at all. Users need Read and Execute to navigate from the top-level directory to their individual home directories. Then you set the file and directory permissions for each directory to Full Control for each particular user.

The problem is that there's no way to keep a user from moving up to the top-level directory and seeing the names of all of the users' home directories. Result: now he's got a list of all of the user's IDs, making hacking a bit easier.

Additionally, any user on an NT workstation can type **net user/domain** and get a list of users in the workstation's domain. Again, these are mainly things you're concerned about for internal users, but inside hacking is probably more prevalent than outside hacking.

Internal Users Can Easily Crash Shared Volumes

Since there are no disk quotas, any user with Write access to a volume can, either accidentally or purposefully, write as much data to a shared volume as the volume can hold. The result is that now there's no space left for other users. Worse yet, if that's the volume that held the page file, then the page file can't grow in size, which might crash NT altogether.

Passwords Can Be Sniffed When Changed

In general, NT has a nifty system for exchanging password information that's encrypted and essentially uncrackable. But when you change your password, your workstation must send the new password in clear text over the network. If someone happened to be running a program like Network Monitor at that moment, she would be able to capture that new password.

Microsoft File and Print Services Will Operate across the Internet

There's no surprise here—heck, it's a feature, and I don't mean that facetiously. But it's also a security hole if you don't look closely into it.

First of all, what is it that you want to secure? I'll assume it is your data. Because you don't want an outside intruder to be able to destroy data on your servers or lock you out of your own network, let's consider this question: how could someone get access to your data?

For the moment, I'll assume you are not running any Internet services like ftp, Gopher, or Web servers; I'll get to them in a minute, but let's consider a network consisting of standard file servers.

Attacks could come in the following forms:

- Someone with Read access to your files could steal company information.

- Someone with Write access to your files could modify or delete them.

- Someone with Write access could use your file servers to store her own personal data, data she might not want to keep on her own computers—perhaps because the data is unlawful to have, like someone else's credit card numbers.

- Someone with Write access could cripple your servers by filling up their free space with nonsense files, crashing the servers.

- Presumably someone could crash your mail servers by sending thousands of automatically-generated pieces of mail to the servers. Enough mail messages will fill the hard disks of those servers as well.

- Access to your print servers could, again, let intruders fill up the print servers' hard disks with spooled files, as well as causing your printers to run out of paper.

There are, however, several types of actions you can take to detect and/or deter an outside attack.

Detecting Outside Attacks

NT comes with some built-in tools to make detecting attacks easier.

- Audit failed logons.

- Use the Performance Monitor to alert you when logon failures exceed some reasonable value.

- Periodically log network activity levels. If all of a sudden your network gets really busy at 3 A.M. for no good reason, then look closely into exactly *what's* going on at 3 A.M.

Deterring Attacks

The main steps to take to deter attacks include the following:

- Don't use obvious passwords.

- Don't enable the Guest account.

- Rename the built-in Administrator account.

- Don't let the built-in Administrator account access the servers over the network.

- Lock out users after a certain number of failed attempts.

- Make passwords expire after a certain length of time.

- Install a firewall to filter out UDP ports 136 and 137.

- Put the Web, FTP, and Gopher servers on a separate machine in its own domain, with no trust links to other domains.

- Don't put any services on your DNS servers except DNS.

It seems to me that the only by directly accessing your file servers through the normal NET USE interface, via an NFS interface or through an FTP service, would someone be able to read or write data on your computers over the Internet. I'll assume that you're not going to run NFS, that you'll put the FTP server where compromising it won't matter, and that you'll focus on the file server interface.

In a nutshell, here's the scenario that you should worry about. Suppose I know that you've got a server named S01 whose IP address is 253.12.12.9 and that it has a share on it named SECRET. I just create an LMHOSTS file with one line in it, like so:

```
253.12.12.9 S01
```

Now I can type **net use X: \\s01\secret**, and my Internet-connected PC sends a request to 253.12.12.9 for access to the share. Assuming the Guest account isn't enabled on S01, then S01 will first ask my PC, "Who are you?" I'll see that as a request for a username and password. When I respond with a valid username and password from the server's domain, I'm in. Actually, this is how I access my network's resources from across the Internet when I'm on a client site—two second's work with an LMHOSTS file, a NET USE, and I'm accessing my home directory from thousands of miles away.

To do that, I needed to know

- A valid username on my network

- The password for that account

- The IP address of a server on the domain

- The name of a share on the domain

All right, suppose I want to hack some company with the name bigfirm.com. Where do I start? Step one is to find out what its range of IP addresses is. That's easy. Just telnet to internic.net and type **whois** bigfirm.com, and you'll get the network number and responsible person for that network. You'll also get the IP address of their DNS name servers. The other way to find this information would be to type:

```
nslookup
set type=all
bigfirm.com
```

Bigfirm will dump the names and addresses of their DNS servers and their mail servers. Because there has to be a secondary DNS server to make the InterNIC happy, there will be at least two name servers. Now, if bigfirm is thinking—the way most of us do— "It doesn't take much CPU power to run a DNS server. Let's put some shared directories there, too."

As Joe Slimeball Hacker, I'm thinking, "Cool—fresh meat."

You see, you've got no choice but to publish two of your IP addresses, the addresses of your DNS server and its backup. *So don't put anything else on it*. You know those 25MHz 486es that you can't figure out what to do with? Use them for your DNS servers.

Now suppose you're smart, and there's nothing else on the DNS servers. So I've got to fish a bit, but that's not hard, as whois told me your range of IP addresses. I'm a slimeball, but I'm a *thorough* slimeball (after all, I don't have a life, so I've got lots of time), and I'm willing to try all of your IP addresses to find out which ones have servers. It's a simple matter to create an LMHOSTS file that includes a NetBIOS name for every possible IP address; for example, if I know that you have C-class network 200.200.200.0, then I can create an LMHOSTS file with NetBIOS named N1 which equals 200.200.200.1, N2 equals 200.200.200.2, and so on. Then I need only do a net view *servername* for each name from N1 through N254. The IP addresses that have a computer attached to them running the server service will be the ones that challenge me for a name and password. The ones that *don't* won't respond at all.

What can you do? Well, you could decide not to worry about it, since the bad guys can't get in without a username and password. But if you won't sleep nights until you plug this hole, just go to the servers in question and disable the Browser service.

Next, I'm looking for a user account name or two. How can I get this? I don't think you can do a NET USER remotely without contacting the domain controller, which means you'll have to have a domain ID and password to get NET USER to work from the outside—whew, that's one less thing to worry about!

But there *is* a way to find at least some usernames. When a user logs on to an NT machine, it registers not only its own machine name on the network, but the user's name as well. It does that so alerts with that name on them can get to the proper user. For example, suppose you've asked the Performance Monitor to alert you in your username of JILL02 if a server gets low on free space. How does the network know where you are?

It's quite simple. When you log on, the Messenger Service —assuming that it's running—registers your username as one of the NetBIOS names attached to your workstation. Assuming you are logged on to a server whose IP address is 200.200.200.200, anyone doing an nbtstat -A 200.200.200.200 would not only see the computer's name, they'd see your name as well.

So, supposing that someone named *paulad* was logged in at the 200.200.200.200 machine (that's physically logged in, not connected over the network), a look at the nbtstat output would show me that there's a username *paulad* who's logged on.

So now I've got a username, and probably the username of an administrative account, since paulad is logged on to a server; good news for Joe Hacker. What can you do about that? Disable the Messenger service, and the name never gets registered. And, by the way, speaking of nbtstat, if you run an nbtstat -A and the name MSBROWSE shows up, you've found a browse master. There's a good chance that a browse master is a domain controller, right? So maybe it's a good idea to set MaintainServerList=No for the domain controllers; let the other servers handle the browse master part; you'll remove a clue that a hacker could use. Unfortunately, however, all domain controllers have other names registered to them that pretty much identifies them as domain controllers.

Now that I've got a username, I need a password. Now *that's* a problem. Even if I could physically attach my computer to your network, I wouldn't get a password with a network sniffer—NT uses a challenge/response approach to password verification. When you try to log on to an NT domain, the domain controller sends your workstation a random number that your workstation then applies to your password using some kind of *hashing* function, a mathematical function that produces a number when supplied with two inputs. The result is what gets sent over the network, not the password. (As I said earlier, there is one exception to this rule; when you change your password, the new password *does* go over the network to the server, but that's pretty rare.)

Where do I get the password? I can do one of two things. First, taking what I know about the user, I can try to guess a password. Second, I can run a program that tries to log on repeatedly, using as passwords every word in the dictionary—this is sometimes known as a *dictionary hack.*

The defense against this should be obvious. First, don't use easy-to-guess passwords. Use more than one word with a character between it, like *fungus#polygon.* Second, don't make it easy for people to try a lot of random passwords: lock them out after five bad tries.

That leads me to a caution about the Administrator account. If you don't have the *Resource Kit, you can't lock it out.* Windows NT 4 *Resource Kit* now contains a utility for locking out the Administrator account. It is called Passprop.exe. When enabled, the Administrator account can only be used to log on at the domain controllers, not remotely or over the network.

If you don't have the new *Resource Kit,* then no matter how many times you try a faulty password, the Administrator account doesn't lock. So if you don't do something about it, all the slimeballs on the Internet can spend all of their free time trying to figure out your Administrator password. What can you do about that?

There are two possibilities. First, rename the account. Don't leave it as *Administrator.* Second, limit its powers. You cannot delete the Administrator account, nor can you disable it. But you can remove its right to access the server over the network. By removing this right, you force someone with the Administrator password to physically sit down at the server in order to control that server. Unfortunately, that won't be easy, because the ability to log on to a server locally is granted to the Administrators group, and the Administrator account is a member of that group. You aren't allowed to remove the Administrator account from the Administrators group, so all you can do, I suppose, is to remove the entire Administrators group's right. Then just grant the individual administrative accounts the Log on over the Network right. (You'll also have to remove the Everyone group and add user accounts back in one at a time— unfortunately, the Administrator is built into the Domain Users group and can't be removed.)

Now, these measures—disabling Guest, renaming Administrator, removing Administrator's right to log on over the network, locking out repeated penetration attempts, setting Performance Monitor to alert you to excessive failed logon attempts, using well-chosen passwords—may be sufficient, and you've no doubt noticed that they're all options that don't cost a dime. But if you want greater security, then look into a firewall. The firewall doesn't have to do much, but it's got one really important job: to filter out two ports on UDP.

UDP is the sister protocol to TCP; just as there is a TCP/IP, there is also a UDP/IP. TCP is connection-oriented, whereas UDP is not connection-oriented; it just drops messages on the network like messages in a bottle, hoping that they'll get where they would like to go. Whenever you execute a Microsoft networking command, such as NET USE or NET VIEW, you are running an application that sends commands to a server using UDP and UDP port numbers 136 and 137. *Ports* are software interfaces that are used to identify particular servers; for example, when you send mail from your desktop you usually use TCP port number 25 and when you receive mail from your desktop you usually do it on TCP port 110. Web browsers listen on tcp port 80, in another example.

Firewalls are powerful and sometimes complex devices. Once you install them they have a million setup options and you're likely to wonder if you've caught all the ones you need. Running NetBIOS over IP services happens on UDP ports 136 and 137; tell your firewall to filter those, and it's impossible for someone to access normal file server services.

Application Security Holes

One way that Internet hackers have gotten into Internet domains is through bugs in common Unix Internet programs. Those things happen in NT, as well, which leads me to this final piece of advice: Put the Internet services, such as FTP, Web servers, finger servers, and the like, on a machine all by themselves. Make sure the machine is in a domain all by itself without any trust relationships.

Is this because I know of any security holes in NT implementations of common Internet programs? No, this advice is just common sense—put simply, I don't know that they *can't* be compromised, so I counsel caution.

Many security consultants seem to be approaching Internet security in the same way that they handled virus consulting ten years ago: they're shouting, "The sky is falling!" and spinning frightening worst-case scenarios in the hopes of drawing droves of frantic customers to them. In the end, however, just a few common-sense steps protected most of us from viruses. With a bit of knowledge, we can also move out of the "bogeyman" stage of Internet security and into the "rational planning" stage.

A Brief Summary of a Very Long Chapter

In this chapter, you've been introduced to intranets and *the* Internet, the underlying whys and wherefores, and hopefully you have a little insight into why using the TCP/IP protocol suite in your business is an efficient, intelligent, money-saving thing to do. You should also now be equipped to go out and Telnet to foreign lands, to FTP megabytes of data treasures, and to talk to friends and associates far and near via e-mail. Internet vets call Internet exploration *surfing the net*—the surf's never been up like this, even if your company's intranet doesn't connect to *the* Internet.

CHAPTER
FIFTEEN

15

Internet Information Server

- Setting up your Web site

- Setting up your FTP site

- Managing day-to-day operations

- Using Web-to-database connectivity tools

- Monitoring your Web server's performance

- Troubleshooting your Web server

- Optimizing IIS performance

Microsoft Internet Information Server (IIS) is a Web server designed to deliver a wide range of Internet and intranet services and is the only Web server that is tightly integrated with the NT Server operating system. IIS delivers high performance, good security, and an excellent set of management and administration tools, and you can have it up and running on your server in just a matter of minutes.

In the first part of this chapter, I will concentrate on how to keep your Web site running smoothly from the point of view of the administration tasks you or the site administrator will perform. I'll look at how to control and configure IIS using Microsoft's Internet Service Manager, and I'll discuss how you can take advantage of virtual directories and virtual servers on your Web site.

We'll look at setting up and configuring Web, FTP, and news services on your server, and we'll examine some of the benefits and the drawbacks of using these services. We will also quickly revisit several system security topics relating to the day-to-day operation of a Web site, and we will look at how you can get the most out of Site Server Express.

In the second part of this chapter, I'll take a look at the day-to-day operations on your Web site and at some of the tasks you will be performing. I'll show you how to use the Posting Acceptor and the Web Publishing Wizard to manage your Web and where to find Web server-to-database connectivity tools you can use to link legacy databases to your Web server.

We'll examine the NT Server system tools you can use to monitor Web-server performance, including the Performance Monitor and the Network Monitor. I'll close this chapter with a discussion of IIS troubleshooting and optimization, and I will give you a set of guidelines to help decide when it is time to upgrade your Web server hardware. Let's start by installing IIS on your Windows NT Server.

Installing Internet Information Server

Installing IIS is a very easy and straightforward process, but there are a couple of steps you must take before you start the installation:

- If you are already running other versions of an FTP, Web, or news server, you must disable these services or uninstall them from your system before you start the installation of IIS. Check the documentation provided by the original vendor for information on how to do this.

- You must be logged on to the server with administrator permissions before you can make the IIS installation.

- Make sure that the Internet Explorer is not running on your server.

- Close any applications that use ODBC until after the installation is complete.

Hardware Requirements for Your Web Server

Before we start the installation process, let's take a look at the hardware requirements of a Windows NT Server running as a Web server. As usual, you should plan on spending as much as your budget will allow, especially on the critical areas of processor, memory, hard-disk space, and the communications link to your ISP (Internet Service Provider).

In the Intel world, you should use a Pentium processor running at 100MHz or faster, with 32MB of memory; more if you have it. The amount of hard-disk space you will need depends on how large your Web content files turn out to be. On a busy Internet site, you may find that you are managing a large number of HTML files, graphical images, scripts, and audio and video files. You will need a VGA video card to load NT Server, but you certainly don't need the latest, all-turbo video accelerator board installed on the server. A CD-ROM and a fast tape drive are also essential elements, along with a UPS system and appropriate modems for RAS users.

You will also need the appropriate communications equipment to support your link to the Internet. This can be as small and compact as the terminal adapter needed to hook into an ISDN (Integrated Services Digital Network) link, or it can be a whole room full of equipment for some of the larger data communications connections; in some instances, most of the communications equipment may be located at the phone company's facility rather than at yours. The larger the communications requirement, the more equipment you will need and the more crucial proper air conditioning becomes, even in northern climes and in Europe—areas that don't normally use air conditioners at any time. And depending on the final configuration you choose for your Web server, you may well find yourself looking for a location for a firewall computer, as well as a router or two.

Adding IIS to a Busy Network Server

The hardware we looked at in the last section describes the main components for your Web server, but what should you do if you are adding a Web service to your existing NT Server network, which already has certain hardware installed and an existing population of users?

Do not underestimate the impact that the additional Web traffic will have on the performance of your server, and be ready to upgrade your hardware if the existing installation proves inadequate. Later in this chapter, we'll be looking at some of the tools you can use for performance monitoring, and we'll look at some of the tricks you can use to optimize IIS performance.

If you have to run with your existing systems, you may not only alienate new visitors to your Web site as they wait for an overburdened server to respond but also existing corporate users as they watch their previously speedy applications grind to a halt.

Installing IIS on NT Server 4

Installing IIS is straightforward: all you have to do is run the Setup program from the CD. If you already have your connection to the Internet via your ISP, or if you are publishing content on an intranet, you can simply accept many of the default values during installation, and your Web site will be up and running in no time at all. Your ISP will tell you the IP address to use with your Web server, as well as the subnet mask and the IP address of the default gateway system through which your server will route all traffic to the Internet.

In the IIS Setup program, Microsoft has provided three default installation options to help you complete your installation as quickly as possible: Minimum Install, Typical Install, and Custom Install. The dialog boxes presented to you during the installation of IIS will depend on which of the components described in the next three sections you choose to install. Let's take a look.

Minimum Install

The Minimum Install option offers the following limited IIS components:

Component	Description
Internet Information Server	The Web server.
Microsoft Transaction Server	A transaction-processing server for distributed server applications.

Component	Description
Active Server Pages	A server mechanism that provides dynamic content accessible by all browsers.
Data Access Components	A set of database-access components.
Posting Acceptor	An application used when posting Web site content to your own server or to an ISP's server.
FrontPage and FrontPage extensions	An HTML authoring tool and a set of server extensions.
Microsoft Management Console (MMC)	A new administrative tool that provides a basic set of tools; additional functions are provided by specific snap-ins.
Internet Service Manager Snap-in for MMC	An MMC snap-in application used to configure all aspects of your Web and FTP services.
Index Server	A search engine capable of indexing a wide variety of different document types.

Typical Install

A Typical Install includes all the options provided in the Minimum Install, and adds the following components:

Component	Description
FTP	The FTP server.
Internet Service Manager	An HTML-based version of Internet Service Manager used to administer IIS using a browser.
Scrip Debugger	A tool used to debug server and client scripts.
Java Virtual Machine	A Java environment used to run Java applications on the server.
Documentation	A set of online documentation in HTML format accessible with a browser.

Custom Install

Finally, the Custom Install offers a choice of all the components available in the IIS package. In addition to the elements listed under the Minimum Install and Typical Install, you can choose:

Component	Description
Usage Analyst	A tool used to provide Web site statistical information derived from IIS log files.
Site Analyst	A Web management tool used to look at and explore your Web site.
Web Publishing Wizard	An application used to publish Web content to a server.
News Server	A news server you can use to host local discussion groups.
Certificate Server	A server capable of issuing client and server digital certificates.

Adding IIS Options Later

You can always add (or remove) IIS components once your initial installation is complete by following these steps:

1. Select Start ➤ Programs ➤ Microsoft Internet Information Server ➤ Internet Information Server Setup.

2. In the Options dialog box, click on the Add ➤ Remove button.

3. Select the check boxes for the options you want to install, and clear the boxes for any components you want to remove.

4. Follow the directions given on the screen; these directions will depend on the options you chose to install or remove.

Once your installation is complete, you are ready to use the Internet Service Manager to configure your system. But first, let's look at a new addition from Microsoft to the world of system administration—the Microsoft Management Console.

Introducing the Microsoft Management Console

New in IIS version 4, the *Microsoft Management Console* (MMC) replaces the previous Internet Service Manager (ISM) and brings a new set of concepts to the tasks of Windows NT Server system management. You don't actually use MMC to manage your network. Instead, MMC provides the basic feature set, and then a series of MMC *snap-ins* provide customized features for specific administrative applications. In concept, MMC and these snap-ins work in the same way that a plug-in works with a Web browser; snap-ins provide additional specific features not found in MMC.

MMC also provides a common user interface for a whole range of network-administration tasks and allows you to customize your own management console. You can load specific snap-ins to create a new console that contains only the administrative tools you use on your network. In IIS 4, the Internet Service Manager is implemented as an MMC snap-in, rather than as a separate stand-alone application as in previous releases. Let's take a look.

NOTE   Microsoft has announced that future releases of Windows NT, as well as all the BackOffice products and certain third-party networking products, will provide MMC snap-ins as their administrative programs.

MMC Windows Explained

Before you can understand MMC and how to use it, you need to understand some new jargon; so here goes: every MMC console contains one or more windows, each with two panes. The left pane (known as the *scope pane*) shows a tree view of the *namespace,* the hierarchy of all the objects that MMC can manage. Each item, or *node,* is one of a variety of objects, containers, or tasks. The tree view of the namespace is quite similar to the Windows Explorer view of files and directories.

When you select a node in the namespace, the right pane (known as the *results pane*) displays the results of that selection. What you see depends on the node you selected, of course, and may include a list of the items in that node or another management view such as a properties page or a Performance Monitor graphical display. You administer the network or control IIS using menus, commands, and toolbars found in this results pane.

TIP MMC does not restrict the way you work or limit you to using certain protocols. As long as a snap-in supports either the Component Object Model (COM) or the Distributed Component Object Model (DCOM) standard, MMC can host it.

When you load an MMC snap-in, you add nodes to the namespace, and you can also add elements such as ActiveX controls, folders, and links to Web pages, which let your console link to Web pages or other network-administration products. You can create multiple windows inside the MMC console, and each can display a different view of the current namespace.

Loading and Unloading Snap-Ins

When you load or unload an MMC snap-in, you add or remove its items from the namespace; nothing happens to the snap-in on your hard disk. The procedure for loading snap-ins depends on whether any other snap-ins are already loaded.

To load a snap-in when no other snap-ins are loaded or, in other words, to load the first snap-in, start MMC and then follow these steps:

1. From the Console menu, choose Add/Remove Snap-in.

2. In the Snap-in Manager dialog box, which lists the currently available snap-ins, choose the snap-in you want to load, and click on the Add button at the top right of the dialog box.

3. Click on the OK button to close the dialog box and load the snap-in.

You will see the toolbar on the top right of the MMC window change to reflect the features of the snap-in you just loaded.

Loading an additional snap-in involves a similar process:

1. From the Console menu, choose Add/Remove Snap-in.

2. Click on the node under which you want the new snap-in to load and then click on the Add button on the dialog box toolbar.

3. Click on the snap-in you want to load and then click on the OK button.

To unload or remove a snap-in, follow these steps:

1. From the Console menu, choose Add/Remove Snap-in.

2. In the Snap-in Manager dialog box, which lists the currently loaded snap-ins, choose the snap-in you want to delete and click on the Add button at the top right of the dialog box.

3. Click on the OK button to close the dialog box.

You can add a node to the namespace directly by following these steps:

1. In the scope (or leftmost) pane of the MMC window, select the node under which you want to add the new item.

2. In a child window, select Action ➤ Create New and click on the object you want to add. The options presented here will depend on the character of the node you selected in the scope pane in the previous step. For example, if you click on a Web site object in the scope pane, you will be given the opportunity to create a new Web site or a new FTP site.

3. Further dialog boxes appear, depending on the type of item you selected; configure the new object using these dialog boxes.

Saving and Restoring the MMC Console

Once you create an MMC console that you like, by loading different snap-ins and arranging windows, you can save it to a file (with the filename extension of .MSC). Reloading the file at some later time re-creates all the saved console settings, saving you time and helping to prevent errors. Here are the steps to follow when saving a console to a file:

1. Configure the console to your satisfaction and then choose File ➤ Save Console As.

2. Enter a filename in the File Name box and then click on Save.

To load and run a previously-saved console without first starting MMC, you can either:

• Open the Windows NT Explorer and double-click on the file.

• Choose Start ➤ Run and then specify the saved console filename in the Open box.

If you are already running MMC, you can load a previously-saved console with these steps:

1. Choose File ➤ Open Console.

2. Enter the filename for the saved console and click on Open.

You can also choose Add/Remove Snap-in from the Console menu, as I described in the previous section.

Saved MMC console files are relatively small and are not tied to large amounts of management data, all of which allows you to send them to other administrators as e-mail. You can send them as read-only files so that the recipients can use them but cannot change them.

TIP   Another way to take advantage of the customization features in MMC is to prepare consoles that perform only one task and use them to delegate responsibility to other, perhaps less experienced administrators. With a customized MMC console, they will not be faced with a large number of choices they will never use; you can tailor the console to present only the menu choices they need to get the job done.

Using the Internet Service Manager

When you start the IIS 4 Internet Service Manager (ISM), an MMC console begins running and automatically loads the Internet Service Manager snap-in. In this section, we'll look at all the options you can use to tailor IIS services to your needs with the Property sheets. We'll look at the Property sheets global to IIS operation first; then in two following sections, we'll look at the Property sheets that specifically relate to configuring a Web server and then at the Property sheets you can use to configure your FTP server. Let's begin with an overall look at ISM.

The normal way to start ISM is to choose Start ➤Programs ➤Microsoft Internet Information Server ➤Internet Service Manager, but you can also use the alternative ways of loading an MMC snap-in that we looked at in the last section. Either way, you will see the ISM main window as shown in Figure 15.1.

In addition to the usual menus, ISM has three toolbars, one containing a set of MMC console options immediately below the main menu bar, and then two others a little lower down the screen. The three icons close together are used to open the Property sheets for a specific service (as we'll see in a moment), to navigate around the main screen, and to show or hide the scope pane. The next icon is used to connect to a specific computer; the three VCR-like controls are used to start, stop, or pause the selected IIS service; and the remaining icons are used to load other Windows NT Server system-administration tools, such as the NT Performance Monitor (more on how you can get the most out of Performance Monitor later in this chapter) and the Service Manager.

FIGURE 15.1:

The Internet Service Manager opening screen

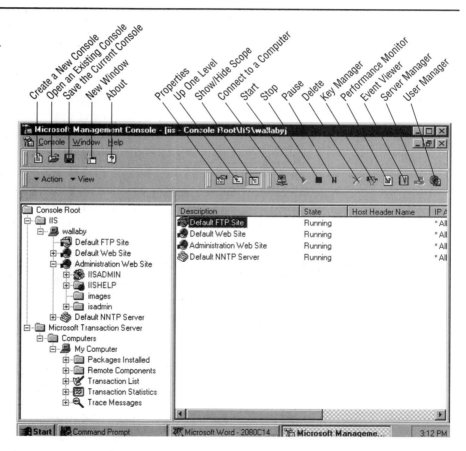

What you see displayed in the ISM windows on your system will not be the same as Figure 15.1, which shows the setup on my system, but it should be similar. The scope pane on the left side displays all the items or nodes in the current name-space, and the results pane on the right side shows the IIS services and their current status. In Figure 15.1, you will see the names of the computers running IIS services on the left side, the name and current status of the service in the center, and additional configuration information on the right side in the results pane.

The IIS services, including the Web and FTP services, are controlled by means of Property sheets or tablike dialog boxes. There are three main sets of Properties in IIS. In the next section, we'll look at those that control computerwide settings. In later sections, we'll look at those used to control your Web site and those used to control your FTP site.

WARNING   Although the HTML version of the ISM has many of the same functions as the ISM snap-in for MMC, there are several things that you cannot do using the HTML version. The HTML version is designed as a Web page, and so right-clicking is not supported. Also, some of the more important IIS configuration options, such as changes to certificate mapping and starting other NT Server utilities, can only be performed using the ISM snap-in.

Setting IIS Computer Properties

To look at or change a Property sheet in ISM, select a computer, Web site, directory, or file, and click on the Property button on the toolbar, or right-click on the item and select the Property option from the pop-up menu. Figure 15.2 shows the IIS Property sheet that is used to configure and control computerwide settings for all IIS operations.

The IIS Property sheet contains the following options:

Global Bandwidth Throttling   Bandwidth throttling can be useful on a server that has to manage other network or corporate functions in addition to running the Web site. If you use a dedicated server, you don't need to allocate bandwidth to other services, and the entire available bandwidth should be made available to IIS. Check the box to enable bandwidth throttling, and then specify the bandwidth you want to use with IIS services in the Maximum Network Use box.

FIGURE 15.2:

The IIS Property sheet

Master Properties   Select the type of service, Web or FTP, from the list box and then click on the Edit button to set the default values used by all current or new sites on this computer. If you have changed a value for a specific Web site, you will be prompted to confirm that the new setting should replace and override the original setting. If you make any changes to a list-based property on your Web site, such as custom error messages or filters (more on both these topics in a moment), these changes will not be merged with the existing settings; they will simply replace the originals.

Computer MIME Map   Select the File Types button to configure MIME (Multipurpose Internet Mail Extension) mappings, used by the server to determine the file type to return to a browser as a result of a specific request. The default file types registered with IIS are listed in the File Types dialog box. To add a new mapping, click on the New Type button in the File Types dialog box. Enter the filename extension associated with the file you are working with in the Associated Extension box; and in the Content Type (MIME) box, enter the MIME type followed by the filename extension in the form <MIME type>/<filename extension>.

To remove a MIME mapping, select the file type in the Registered File Types box and click on the Remove button.

Settings made at this global level cascade downward to the lower levels; in IIS terms, they are *inherited*, and they can be inherited by Web sites, FTP sites directories, virtual directories, and even individual files.

TIP

If the original default values in this property sheet are simply inappropriate for your situation and if you know that you will be creating a number of different sites, go ahead and set the properties to the values you need. They will then be automatically inherited by all the lower IIS elements of Web site, FTP site, directories, and files; this can save you an awful lot or work later, as you won't have to configure each site manually.

Once you have looked at these global IIS properties, you can go on to look at or change these settings in the individual property sheets for Web and FTP services, directories, or files. We'll look at the Web service Property sheets next.

Setting Up Your Web Site

Setting up your Web site is really a two-part process. First, you prepare the content you want to load onto your Web server. Then, you configure the Web service itself, and that's what we are going to look at next.

The Web service Property sheets are as follows:

Web Site configures identification information, logging, and connections.

Security Accounts configures operator privileges.

Performance is used for performance tuning.

ISAPI Filters configures ISAPI filters.

Home Directory specifies the home directory and certain Web site permissions.

Documents specifies default documents and document footers.

Directory Security configures authentication schemes.

HTTP Headers specifies content ratings, MIME mappings, and HTTP information.

Custom Errors specifies custom error messages.

In the next few sections, we'll go through all these Property sheets in detail, starting with the Web Site Property sheet.

Web Site Property Sheet

Click on the Web Site tab to open the Web Site Property sheet shown in Figure 15.3.

FIGURE 15.3:

The Web Site Property sheet

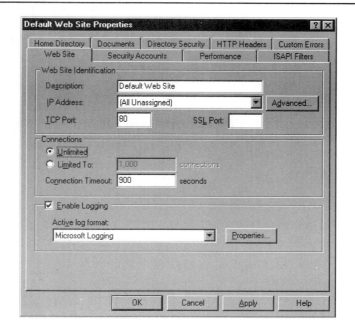

This Property sheet contains the following options:

Web Site Identification   Lets you specify certain identification parameters for your Web site, including:

Description   Enter the name that you want to use in the ISM tree view to identify this Web site; you can use any name you like.

IP address   You must have previously assigned an IP address using the Network applet in the Control Panel to see an address here. If you do not assign a specific IP address, this becomes the default Web address.

Advanced   Click on this button to open the Advanced Web Site Identification dialog box, where you can map multiple domain names or host header names to a single IP address using the Host Header Name box.

TCP Port   The default TCP port for the Web service is port 80, and if you change this, your clients must know in advance to request a different port number. Otherwise, their attempts to connect will fail.

SSL Port   Specifies the port used for SSL access; the default is port 443. Again, you can change this port number, but your clients must know in advance to request a different port number; otherwise, their attempts to connect will fail.

Connections   Lets you control how your Web site is accessed and the number of simultaneous connections:

Unlimited   Allows an unlimited number of simultaneous connections.

Limited To   Limits the number of simultaneous connections to the number you enter in the Connections box.

Connection Timeout   This value ensures that all connections are closed eventually, even if HTTP fails to close a connection for some reason. A typical value might be 300 seconds (equivalent to 5 minutes), after which the connection is closed.

Enable Logging   Allows you to turn on IIS logging. Choose one format from the following:

Microsoft Logging   A fixed ASCII IIS log format.

NCSA Logging   The National Center for Supercomputing Applications fixed ASCII format.

W3C Extended Log File Format   The default; a configurable ASCII format consisting of time, client IP address, method, HTTP, and URL information.

ODBC Logging   A fixed format logged to a database such as Microsoft Access or SQL Server. You must first create the database files before you can use this option. Selecting this format allows you to use database analysis tools on the logged data.

Once you have turned IIS logging on, click on the Properties button to determine how and when log files are created and saved.

How Do I Select Which Fields to Log?

If you select the W3C Extended Log File Format as your IIS logging option, you can select which of the following fields to log. This means that you can collect only the specific information you need, while minimizing the log file size by excluding information you don't need. Select from the following:

Date   Date the event occurred

Time   Time the event occurred

Client IP Address   IP address of the client accessing your server

User Name   Name of the user accessing your server

Service Name   The Internet service running on the client computer

Server Name   The name of the server generating the log entry

Server IP   The IP address of the server generating the log entry

Method   The HTTP method used by the client

URI Stem   The resource accessed by the client—an HTML page, a script, or an ISAPI application

URI Query   The query the client was making

HTTP Status   The status of the request

Win32 Status   The status of the request

Bytes Sent   The number of bytes sent by the server

Bytes Received   The number of bytes received by the server from the client

Time Taken   The length of time the request took

User Agent   Name of the client browser

Cookie   The content of any cookie, sent or received

Referrer   The URL of the Web site the user last visited

Security Accounts Property Sheet

Click on the Security Accounts tab to open the Security Accounts Property sheet shown in Figure 15.4.

FIGURE 15.4:

The Security Accounts Property sheet

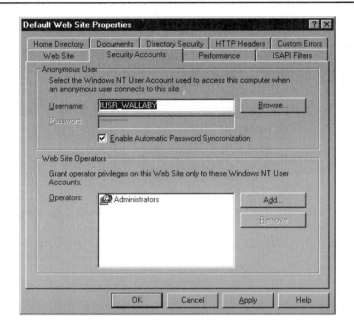

This Property sheet lets you specify which Windows NT users have access to your server:

> **Anonymous User**   By default, the server creates and uses the IUSER_ *computername* account for all anonymous access; in Figure 15.4, this account appears as IUSER_WALLABY because WALLABY is the name of the computer IIS runs on. This account is assigned a random password for both ISM and User Manager for Domains; if you change the password in ISM, you must also change it in User Manager for Domains. If you check the Enable Automatic Password Synchronization box, ISM does this for you. This account must have a password; you cannot leave the field blank or empty.

> **Web Site Operators**   Use this part of the dialog box to designate which NT Server user accounts you want to be able to administer your Web site.

Click on the Add button to add a user account to the current list of accounts shown in the Operators box. To remove a user account select the account in the Operators box and click on the Remove button.

Web site operator accounts do not have to be members of the Windows NT Server Administrators group. An operator can perform certain administrative functions on a specific Web site, including

- Managing Web content expiration dates and times
- Changing default Web documents
- Setting Web server access permissions

An operator cannot do any of the following:

- Change the bandwidth throttling settings
- Create virtual directories or virtual directory paths
- Change the Anonymous Username and password
- Alter the configuration of your Web site

To change these settings, you must be a member of the NT Server Administrators group.

TIP   Operators can work only with the properties that affect the Web site (or FTP site) for which they were created; they cannot access the properties that control overall IIS setup, the NT Server operating system that hosts IIS, or the network on which the system runs.

Performance Property Sheet

The Performance Property sheet, shown in Figure 15.5, lets you adjust several important performance-related functions, including:

Performance Tuning   Adjust the slider to reflect the number of connections, or hits, you expect your Web site to receive each day. If you set it slightly higher than the actual number of connections you receive, connections will be made more quickly, server performance will improve, and your clients will be happier. If you use a setting too far above the actual number of connections you receive, however, you will waste server memory, and server performance will decline substantially.

Enable Bandwidth Throttling   Check this box to limit the bandwidth available to this *specific* Web site and enter the bandwidth you want in the Maximum Network Use box. If you enter a value here that is different from the number you entered in the IIS Property sheet we looked at earlier in this chapter, it will override that number and will be used instead.

Connection Configuration   Check the HTTP Keep-Alives Enabled box to allow a client to maintain an open connection to your server, rather than reopening the connection with each request; enabled by default.

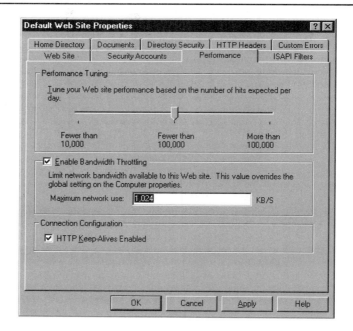

FIGURE 15.5:

The Performance Property sheet

ISAPI Filters Property Sheet

The ISAPI Filters Property sheet, shown in Figure 15.6, lets you set options for ISAPI filters.

FIGURE 15.6:

The ISAPI Filters Property
sheet

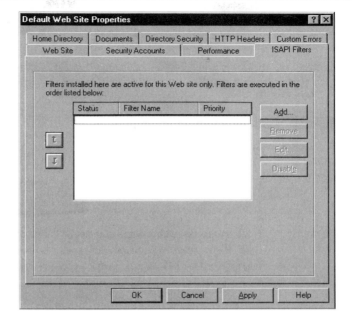

The table lists each ISAPI filter, giving its status (loaded, unloaded, or disabled), the name of the filter, and the priority level established within the DLL (low, medium, or high). Use the Add, Edit, and Remove buttons to modify filter mappings, and click the Enable/Disable button to change the status of a filter.

The ISAPI filters execute in the order shown in the table. To change this sequence, simply highlight a filter in the table and use the two arrow buttons to move the filter up or down within the table.

Home Directory Property Sheet

The Home Directory Property sheet, shown in Figure 15.7, lets you look at and change settings that control Web content delivery, access permissions, and Active Server Page configuration and debugging.

FIGURE 15.7:

The Home Directory Property
sheet

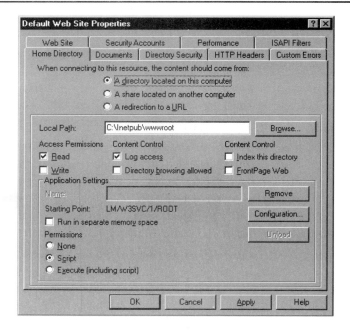

The first step in working with this property sheet is to define where Web content
originates. This is a dynamic Property sheet whose content depends on which
option you choose. The content can come from the following:

A Directory Located on This Computer   When you choose this option,
enter the path information for the directory in the Local Path box. You
can also use the Browse button to help you select the directory. The
default directory /wwwroot was created for you automatically when
you installed IIS.

A Share Located on Another Computer   You can use a network share
and, when prompted, enter the name and password needed to access that
computer. Use a Universal Naming Convention (UNC) server and share
name, for example \\myserver\myfiles\htmlfiles. Click on the Connect
As button to change the username and password.

A Redirection to a URL   To map requests to another Web site, use a fully
qualified URL, as in http://myserver. You can use wildcards and redirection variables in the destination URL to control which parts of the original

URL are maintained and mapped to the new URL. To map requests to a virtual directory, use a virtual path, as in /htmlfiles.

The Access Permissions properties appear when you are working with a local directory or with a network share, but not when you are using a URL:

Read   Allows clients to read or download files from a home directory or virtual directory. You can grant Read access to directories containing Web content files such as HTML pages, but you should not give Read access to directories containing CGI scripts or ISAPI DLLs unless you want clients to be able to download them from your server.

Write   Allows clients using browsers that support the PUT feature of the HTTP 1.1 protocol standard to upload files to the server or to change the content in a write-enabled file.

WARNING   When using NTFS, the settings you make here must match those of the file system; if they don't match, the most stringent or restrictive settings will be applied.

Likewise, the Content Control check boxes appear only when you are working with a local directory or with a network share:

Log Access   Check this box to ensure that visits to this directory are logged into the log file. This option is enabled by default, and there is no good reason to turn it off.

Directory Browsing Allowed   When turned on, directory browsing lets visitors to your site look at a hypertext listing of the directories and files on your system and thus know how to navigate your system. Most administrators do not allow directory browsing because it exposes more of the underlying site structure than they want to show to a casual visitor. A hypertext directory listing is generated automatically and sent to the browser if directory browsing is enabled and no default document is available; virtual directories do not appear in this listing.

Index This Directory   Check this box to tell Index server to include this directory in a full-text index of your Web site.

FrontPage Web   Check this box to create a FrontPage web for this directory.

In this setting, an *application* is defined as the directories and files contained within a directory marked as an application starting point. You can make your Web site's home page an application starting point and, by so doing, allow every virtual and physical directory on your site to participate in the application. Applications are controlled by the Application Setting box, which includes

Name   Type the name of the application in the Name box. This name is used in the Property sheets for all directories within the boundaries of the application.

Run in Separate Memory Space   Check this box to *isolate* the application and run it in a memory area that is separate from the Web server software. See the description of the Pool ODBC Connections property later in this chapter for more information on when you might benefit from using this setting.

Permissions   These permission settings control whether applications can be run in this directory and include

None   Prevents any programs or scripts from running.

Script   Restricts execution to scripts.

Execute   Allows any application to run, including scripts and NT binaries such as .EXE and .DLL files.

To configure an application in more detail, click on the Configure button on this Property sheet to open the Application Configuration dialog box which we'll be looking at in the next section.

First, we need to look at what happens when you select A Redirection to a URL at the top of the Home Directory Property sheet. You will see the following properties:

Redirect To   Enter the destination URL you want to use, based on which choice you make from the following three options:

The Exact URL Entered Above   Check this box to use the redirection URL without adding any information from the original URL.

A Directory Below This One   Check this box to redirect the client to a subdirectory below this one.

A Permanent Redirection for This Resource   Check this box to make a permanent redirection and provide the client with the message "301: Permanent Redirect."

How Do I Use Redirection Variables?

You can use redirection variables to pass portions of the original URL to the destination URL if you type them in the Redirect To text box. These substitutions are performed automatically by the server and include the following:

$S passes the matched suffix of the requested URL. For example, if the original request is for /programs/program.exe and /programs is now redirected to /newprograms, program.exe is the matched suffix and is passed to the new URL.

$P passes any parameters specified in the original URL.

$Q passes any parameters specified in the original URL as well as the delineating question mark character used to separate them.

$V strips the server name from the URL and passes the remaining information specified in the original URL.

$0 to **$9** passes the portion of the requested URL that matches the wildcard.

! prevents redirection.

You can also use the wildcard character * to match any number of characters in the original URL. Separate wildcards with colons and remember to select The Exact URL Entered Above option when you use wildcards.

Application Configuration Property Sheet

Click on the Configuration button in the Home Directory Property sheet to open the Application Configuration Property sheet, which contains four more property sheets, as follows:

Application Mappings lets you map filename extensions to the applications that process those files.

Active Server Pages allows you to configure your ASP scripts.

ASP Debugging lets you set several ASP debugging parameters.

Other lets you look at or change a CGI timeout.

Let's take a look at each of these tabs in turn, starting with the Application Mappings tab.

NOTE   You can set Application Configuration properties at the Web site, directory, or virtual directory level.

Application Mappings Property Sheet

This Property sheet controls which applications process which files by mapping applications to the appropriate filename extensions; it also controls ISAPI caching. You will see the following properties:

Cache ISAPI Applications   Check this box (it is checked by default) to make sure that any ISAPI DLLs that you want to use are loaded and cached. Doing so allows additional requests to be processed without forcing the DLL to reload each time it is called.

Applications Mappings   This table lists the filename extensions, the executable path for the application used to process the file, and any exclusions you might want. Use the Add, Edit, or Remove buttons to modify these application mappings.

TIP   For an excellent description of what Active Server Pages are and how you can use them, see Peter Dyson's *Mastering Microsoft Internet Information Server 4*, available from Sybex. This book covers IIS in much more detail than I can do in this single chapter, and it contains essential information to help you in planning, designing, and building both Internet and intranet Web sites.

Active Server Pages Property Sheet

The Active Server Pages Property sheet, shown in Figure 15.8, lets you look at and change a large number of ASP parameters, including:

Enable Session State   When this option is checked, Active Server Pages creates a new session for each user who accesses an ASP application. This lets you identify the user across several ASP pages in your application. The session ends automatically if the user does not request or refresh a page within the session timeout. To change this timeout, enter a new number (in minutes) in the Session Timeout box.

Enable Buffering   Check this option to buffer all ASP output before it is sent to the browser.

Enable Parent Paths   Check this box to allow ASP scripts to use relative directory paths.

Write Unsuccessful Client Requests to Event Log   Check this box if you want IIS to enter all unsuccessful browser requests in the NT Server Event Log.

Pool ODBC Connections   Pooling is automatically enabled for applications running in the same memory space as the server, but if you run your applications as isolated applications, you can still make IIS pool the connections by checking this box.

FIGURE 15.8:

The Active Server Pages Property sheet

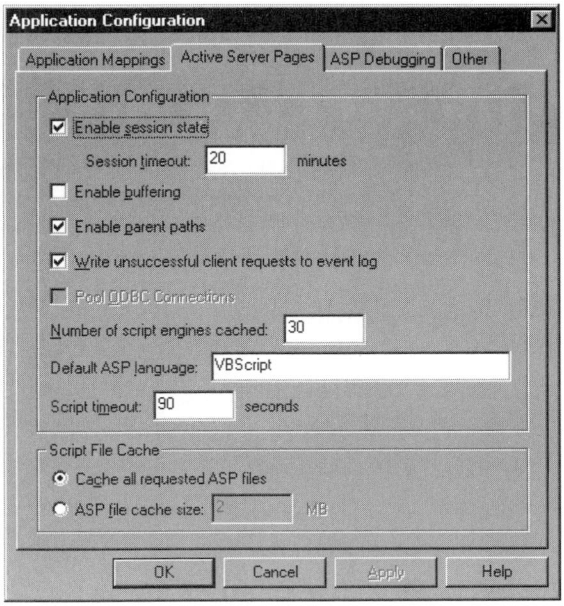

Number of Script Engines Cached   Specifies the number of script engines that ASP will keep cached in memory.

Default ASP Language   Specifies the primary script language used to process ASP commands. The default value is VBScript, but you can specify the name of any ActiveX script engine installed on your server. And you can always override this setting and specify the script language in the ASP page itself by using the <%language%> directive.

Script Timeout   Specifies the length of time ASP allows a script to run; if the script does not complete within this timeout, ASP stops the script and writes an entry into the NT Server Event Log. You can disable the timeout by entering a value of -1.

Cache All Requested ASP Files   Check this box to cache all ASP files. This will increase memory requirements for IIS but will certainly improve overall ASP performance.

ASP File Cache Size   Specifies the size of the cache, in MB. The bigger you make the cache, the more you improve ASP performance.

ASP Debugging Property Sheet

Click on ASP Debugging to open the Property sheet shown in Figure 15.9, which contains these ASP debugging properties:

Enable ASP Server-Side Script Debugging   Check this box to allow the Web server to use the Microsoft Script Debugger while processing ASP scripts.

Enable ASP Client-Side Script Debugging   This option will be added in future versions of ASP.

Send Detailed ASP Error Messages to Client   Check this box if you want ASP to send detailed error messages—including the filename, an error message, and a line number—to the client.

Send Text Error Message to Client   Check this box if you want to send your own error message to the browser whenever an error prevents the

Web server from completing an ASP script. Enter the text of your default message in the text box below.

FIGURE 15.9:

The ASP Debugging Property sheet

Other Property Sheet

At present, the Other Property sheet contains just one property, the CGI Script Timeout, or the length of time a CGI script is given to complete execution and return a value before the script is stopped.

Documents Property Sheet

Compared with the complexity of the Application Configuration Property sheet, the Documents Property sheet, shown in Figure 15.10, is straightforward. It contains a couple properties worth noting.

Enable Default Document   Check this box to display a default document when a browser request fails to specify an HTML filename. This default document can be a home page, or an index page providing links to other pages in the directory. By enabling this option, you make sure that a visitor to your site will always see something. Use the Add and Remove buttons to select the default document you want to use. If you specify more than one document here (use the arrow buttons to change the order in which they are listed and processed), the Web server will display the first one it finds.

Enable Document Footer   Check this box if you want IIS to automatically add the contents of the HTML file you specify as a footer to all your Web pages. You can use this to display copyright information, contact names and telephone numbers, or any other unchanging information you want to add to the end of all your Web pages. The HTML file you specify here should not be a complete HTML page but should just contain the HTML tags needed to display and format the information.

Directory Security Property Sheet

The prefix used with the Security Property sheet depends on the element you are working with; you can set Security properties at the Web site, directory, virtual directory, or file level. Figure 15.11 shows the Directory Security Property sheet, but they all work in much the same way.

FIGURE 15.11:

The Directory Security Property sheet

The Directory Security Property sheet contains the following groups of properties:

Password Authentication Method specifies how password security will be managed.

Secure Communications specifies the secure communications method to use.

TCP/IP Access Restrictions specifies which users can and cannot access this resource.

Because these sets of properties are so important, we'll look at each one in some detail in the next three sections.

Password Authentication Method

Before a user can log on to your Web server and gain access to restricted material, the server must be sure of that user's identity. The authentication process ensures that the user has a valid user account and that the account has all the appropriate permissions for accessing a specific Web site, directory, or file. Click on the Edit button to open the Authentication Methods dialog box, which contains the following options:

Allow Anonymous   When this box is checked, anonymous connections are processed and the anonymous username and password are used. This is the method most often used when accessing a Web server. By default, IIS creates the account IUSR_computername, which is granted local logon user rights. If this box is left unchecked, all anonymous requests are rejected, and one of the two following authentication types must be selected.

Basic Authentication   When this box is checked, basic authentication is used. Remember, this level of authentication sends NT unencrypted usernames and passwords over the network unless used with SSL.

Windows NT Challenge/Response   When this box is checked, a proprietary system is used. Windows NT Challenge/Response authentication is currently available only with the Internet Explorer Web browser.

NOTE   If you leave the Basic Authentication and Windows NT Challenge/Response check boxes unchecked and if you check the Allow Anonymous checkbox, all client requests are processed as anonymous requests. If a client does provide a username and password, he or she will be ignored, and the anonymous account will be used instead, with all the security restrictions that may apply to that account.

Enable SSL Client Authentication   When this box is checked, users with a client SSL certificate can access Web server information that requires SSL authentication. Before you can use these Web server SSL features, you must first install a digital certificate; we'll be looking at Microsoft's Certificate Server in more detail later in this chapter.

Require SSL Client Authentication   Check this box if you want to use a digital certificate with the requesting client browser.

Enable Client Certificate Mapping to Windows NT User Accounts Check this box to map the information in a client's digital certificate to a specific NT Server user account. Click on the Client Mappings button to open the Account Mapping dialog box, in which you can set up the appropriate mappings.

Secure Communications

In the Secure Communications section, click on the Edit button to open the Secure Communications dialog box, which you can use to look at or change the SSL features available on your Web server. Once you set up a secure connection, visitors to your Web site must use a browser capable of supporting such secure communications; all the information passed between client and Web server is encrypted. You can use these secure connections to transfer confidential information such as financial or medical records and credit-card information.

WARNING   Before you can use the Web server's SSL features, you must install a digital certificate. You'll find more on certificates later in this chapter.

Once you click on the Edit button in the Secure Communications dialog box, you can access the following properties:

Require Secure Channel   Check this box to specify that an encrypted channel is used to connect client browser and Web server. The default encryption strength (the number of bits used) is 40 bit.

Require 128-bit Encryption   Within the United States and Canada, you can use a more potent form of encryption that uses 128 bits. Check this box to require that the browser be capable of 128-bit encryption to connect to your Web site.

TIP   For information about upgrading to 128-bit encryption, available with the Windows NT Server North American Service Pack 2, check out www.microsoft.com/NTServerSupport.

Key Manager   Click on this button to use the Key Manager to collect all the relevant information and request a digital certificate from a trusted, third-party organization, known as a certificate authority. Once you receive your certificate, use Key Manager to install the certificate and attach it to your authentication key pair.

TCP/IP Access Restrictions

You can use the settings in the TCP/IP Access Restrictions section to control which users have access to your server. Two check boxes control overall default access:

Granted Access   Check this box to allow all computers access to your server except those specified by IP address in the box below.

Denied Access   Check this box to deny all computers access to your server except those specified by IP address in the box below.

You can then use the list box to enter exceptions to the default access policy. You can block access to specific individuals or to whole networks based on their IP addresses. Use the Add, Edit, and Remove buttons to change these restrictions.

WARNING   Take a moment to think about how this works. If you chose to grant access to all users by default, you will be specifying here that certain computers be *denied* access; if you chose to deny access to all users by default, you will be specifying that certain computers be *granted* access. Simple, really.

In the Grant Access On or Deny Access On dialog box (the name depends on which option you chose), you can specify computers as

Single Computer   Check this button to specify a single computer. Type the IP address of the computer in the IP Address box or click on the DNS Lookup button if your computer uses DNS. In the Enter the DNS Name dialog box, type the computer's domain name.

Group of Computers   Check this button to specify a group of computers. Type the network identification and subnet mask in the Network ID and Subnet Mask boxes.

Domain Name Select this button to specify a Windows NT domain name; type the name in the Domain Name text box.

HTTP Headers Property Sheet

The HTTP Headers Property sheet, shown in Figure 15.12, lets you set values returned to the browser in the header of an HTML page and establish HTML content-expiration dates.

FIGURE 15.12:

The HTTP Headers Property sheet

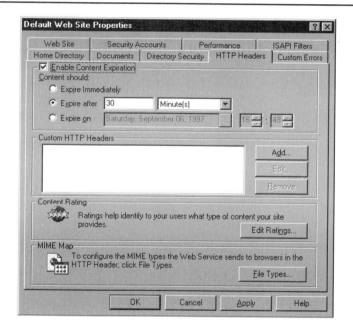

In this Property sheet, you can look at or change the following groups of properties:

Enable Content Expiration Use the settings in this box to specify when you want time-sensitive content, such as special sales promotions or seasonal information, to expire. The browser compares the current date against the expiration date to decide whether to display a cached page or to request an updated page from the server. You can control content expiration in three ways:

Expire Immediately   Content is displayed once and then expires.

Expire After   Select a time period during which the material will be displayed before expiring.

Expire On   Specify a date and time on which you want the content to expire.

Custom HTTP Headers   You can use this box to specify a custom HTTP header for Web server to browser communications. Click on the Add button to open the Add Custom HTTP Header dialog box, where you can enter the name and value of your custom header. To change a header, click on the Edit button; to stop using a custom header, click on the Remove button.

Content Rating   Certain browsers, including Internet Explorer 3 and later, can detect content rating information and help shield users from material they may find offensive. IIS uses the Platform for Internet Content Selection (PICS) rating system developed by the Recreational Software Advisory Council (RSAC), which rates content according to the level of violence, nudity, sexual content, and offensive language it contains. Click on Edit Ratings to open the Rating Service Property sheet; then choose More Information to learn more about the RSAC rating service or select Get Rated and then Rating Questionnaire to complete an RSAC questionnaire to obtain the recommended rating for your own Web content. Once you are clear on the concept, check the Enable Ratings for This Resource box and select a ratings type from the Categories list box using the slider bar. Under Rating Information, enter the name of the person who rated the content and, if you wish, click on Date to select an expiration date for the rating settings.

MIME Map   Use the settings in this box to specify MIME types for your Web server. Click on the File Types button to open the File Types dialog box, which lists the current file type extensions and associated MIME types in the Registered File Types box. To add a new mapping, click on the New Type button to open the File Types dialog box. Here you can enter the filename extension for the file in the Associated Extension box, and you can enter the MIME type in the Content Type (MIME) box using the form *mime type/filename extension.*

Custom Errors Property Sheet

The Custom Errors Property sheet, shown in Figure 15.13, lets you specify your own custom error messages when an HTTP error message is returned to the client browser.

FIGURE 15.13:

The Custom Errors Property sheet

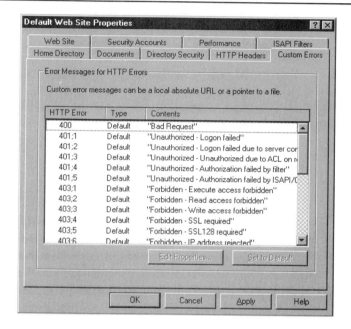

By default, the HTTP 1.1 error messages are listed in this Property sheet, but you can use the Edit Properties button to enter your own custom messages. This opens the Error Mapping Properties dialog box, where you can map the error to a file or to a URL, or you can reinstate the HTTP 1.1 default error message. You can define an ASP script to handle an error or a whole category of errors, and that script is invoked as a URL. Here are the steps to follow when mapping the error to a URL:

1. Create a file that contains your custom error message and place it in a virtual directory.

2. Open ISM and right-click on the Web site, directory, virtual directory, or file in which you want to customize HTTP errors and select Property from the pop-up menu.

3. Find the Custom Errors Property sheet and select the HTTP error you want to customize.

4. Click on the Edit Properties button and select URL from the Message Type box. Type the URL that points to the customized error message and click on the OK button.

See Table 15.10 later in this chapter for a list of the standard HTTP error messages.

Using Virtual Directories

During the discussion in the last few sections, I mentioned virtual directories a couple of times. In this section, let's take a look at how you can use virtual directories to gain some flexible storage options for your Web site. In the next section, we'll look at a related IIS element, the virtual server.

Virtual directories in IIS give you the opportunity to use directories that are not located on your server to hold HTML content, script files, and other files associated with your site; thus, you can locate files where they are more easily updated or maintained rather than on the main server. Using virtual directories gives you a great deal of flexibility when it comes to deciding where to store files for your site and effectively lets you expand your site's storage capacity without adding hardware to or shutting down the server. As far as the visitor's view of your site is concerned, these virtual directories are subdirectories branching from the main \wwwroot directory.

TIP

Virtual directories can be located on the main server or on another computer on the network. The only restriction is that the network drives must be in the same Windows NT Server domain as the IIS system.

There are two kinds of virtual directories:

- A local virtual directory is located on the same system as IIS. Use an alias to identify a local virtual directory.

- A remote virtual directory is located on a networked computer. Use a UNC (Universal Naming Convention) name as an alias to identify a remote virtual directory.

How Do I Refer to Shared Resources?

Universal Naming Convention (UNC) names provide a way to refer to shared resources on other computers without a formal connection to the server. The general form of the UNC is as follows:

```
\\servername\sharename
```

The *servername* parameter specifies the name of the server on which the information is located, and *sharename* specifies the name of the shared file resource under which the information has been shared. You can also add a path and filename to a UNC.

The following advantages are associated with using virtual directories:

- The processing load is distributed. By distributing the contents of your Web site over several hard disks, you can share the associated processing load over several computers. The downside to this approach is that network traffic increases somewhat.

- Security is enhanced. Using a virtual directory structure adds another level of abstraction to your site, altering the way in which Internet users access your information.

- Content management is distributed. Rather than load up the IIS system with content from several departments or organizations, you can let each be in charge of and be responsible for its own content on its own computer systems.

To configure a virtual directory, you must first create the directory with the appropriate permissions so that anonymous users and others can access the directory. After you do so, open ISM and follow these steps:

1. Select the appropriate service in the main Internet Service Manager window.

2. Right-click and, from the pop-up menu, select Create New ➤ Virtual Directory.

3. When the New Virtual Directory Wizard appears, follow the instructions on the screen, using the Next, Back, and Cancel buttons in the usual way.

4. Enter an alias for the directory in the Alias text field if you are creating a local virtual directory. If you are creating a remote virtual directory, enter the UNC in the Alias field. If you entered a UNC name in the Alias field, use the User Name and Password fields to specify the account on the remote system that will host the Web users.

5. In the next screen, enter the physical path of the directory or use the Browse button to locate the directory.

6. Select the appropriate access permissions that users will get in the virtual directory from the choices in the next screen. Choose from

   - Allow Read Access

   - Allow Script Access

   - Allow Execute Access

   - Allow Write Access

   - Allow Directory Browsing

WARNING   Check to make absolutely sure that a directory with Execute access does not also have Read access specified. If both types of access are specified, users may be able to look at the information contained in your scripts, some of which may be confidential. It is much safer to simply isolate the two types of files in different directories.

7. Click on the Finish button to close the Wizard, create the new virtual directory, and return to the ISM main windows, where you will now see your new virtual directory listed.

When you open the Property sheets for a virtual directory, you will see that the Directory Property sheet is now headed Virtual Directory rather than simply Directory; the properties it contains are the same.

Establishing Virtual Servers

You can use a special IIS feature to create what are called *virtual servers* so that a single computer running IIS can appear to support several domain names, perhaps one for each of the major departments within your company. These domain names might appear to the outside world as marketing.dyson.com or technical.dyson.com, even though they both exist on the same IIS system at the same time. This is a particularly significant feature for ISPs that host sites for local businesses.

WARNING   You can set up virtual servers only on a World Wide Web site; virtual servers are not available for FTP servers.

To set up a virtual server, you will need IP addresses for the primary server and for each of the virtual servers that you want to create. This makes your installation look like several computers when viewed from the Internet, when in reality only one copy of IIS is running.

Here are the steps to follow to create a virtual server:

1. From your ISP, get an IP address for each of the separate domains that you want the server to support.

2. Use the Network object in the NT Server Control Panel to specify the additional IP addresses for your network adapter card or cards.

3. Create a different drive or directory for each of the virtual servers, assign appropriate users and permissions, and then create or copy the HTML content into these directories.

4. Open the ISM, right-click on the computer on which you want to create this virtual server, and select Create New to open the New Site Wizard.

5. When the New Web Site Wizard appears, follow the instructions on the screen, using the Next, Back, and Cancel buttons in the usual way.

6. Enter the physical path for the home directory for this server or use the Browse button to locate the directory. Check the box to allow anonymous users to access this Web server.

7.   Select the access permissions from

- Allow Read Access

- Allow Script Access

- Allow Execute Access

- Allow Write Access

- Allow Directory Browsing

8.   Click on the Finish button to close the Wizard, create the new virtual server, and return to the ISM main windows, where you will now see your new virtual server listed.

Now that we have looked at all the Web site Property sheets and covered virtual directories and virtual servers, let's change the pace a little and take a look at setting up your FTP service.

Setting Up Your FTP Site

FTP is the abbreviation for *File Transfer Protocol*, the member of the TCP/IP suite of protocols designed to allow a remote logon, to list files and directories, and to move files from one computer to another. FTP supports a range of file types and formats, including the following:

- ASCII

- EBCDIC (Extended Binary Coded Decimal Interchange Code, an 8-bit character code used on certain IBM mainframe systems)

- Binary files

FTP allows FTP clients to transfer, or upload, files *to* FTP servers, as well as to transfer, or download, files *from* FTP servers. Most common Web browsers also support FTP file transfers.

The FTP Property sheets include the following:

FTP Site configures FTP site identification information, the maximum number of connections, and logging.

Security Accounts configures anonymous access and FTP site operators.

Messages specifies custom FTP messages.

Home Directory defines home directory and directory listing style.

Directory Security configures FTP access restrictions.

In the next few sections, we'll go through all these Property sheets in detail, starting with the FTP Site Property sheet. Then we'll look at some of the other aspects of setting up and populating your FTP server.

How Do I Use an FTP Client?

Just as Web browsers are available for almost all operating systems, so are FTP clients. NT Server, NT Workstation, and Windows 95 contain character-based FTP clients. Type **FTP** at a command prompt and the FTP interpreter starts. Type **?** followed by return to see a list of commands you can use in an FTP session. The normal prompt is ftp>. Although a whole range of commands is available for FTP clients, you can become quite an FTP expert with only a few:

open establishes a connection to a remote computer.

ascii sets the file transfer type to ASCII.

binary sets the file transfer mode to binary.

get transfers a specified file from the server to the client system.

put transfers a specified file from the client to the server system.

quit closes the connection to the remote computer and terminates the FTP session.

You can also use Internet Explorer to access FTP sites; simply remember to preface the URL with ftp rather than http. For example, use ftp://ftp.company.com/.

FTP Site Property Sheet

The FTP Site Property sheet contains the same properties as the Web Site Property sheet we looked at earlier in this chapter, but with the important difference that the properties in this sheet all apply specifically to your FTP service. You can set the FTP site identification information, control the number of connections, and set a connection timeout, as well as enable logging and select the logging format you want to use.

Security Accounts Property Sheet

The FTP Security Accounts Property sheet is also similar to the Web service Security Accounts Property sheet we looked at earlier, but with a couple of important additions.

Check the Allow Anonymous Users box to allow users with the username anonymous to log on to your FTP service. Typically, FTP users log on using the username anonymous and their e-mail address as their password. The FTP server then uses the IUSR_*computername* account as the login account for permissions.

Check the Allow Only Anonymous Connections box to restrict access to only anonymous connections; when this box is checked, users cannot log on with real usernames and passwords. This is a security option you should take advantage of; it prevents access by accounts with administrator permissions. We'll look at the implications of using anonymous connections in more detail later in this chapter.

In the lower part of the Property sheet, you can grant operator privileges to FTP site operators. To add an account, use the Add button as I described in the section "Security Accounts Property Sheet" earlier in this chapter.

Messages Property Sheet

The Messages Property sheet, shown in Figure 15.14, lets you set up your own messages that will be displayed when a browser connects to your FTP site.

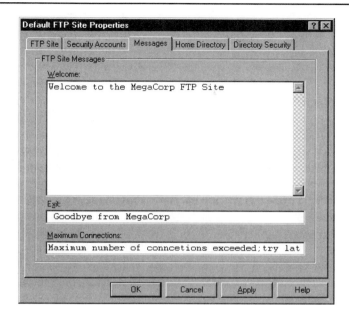

You can use the text boxes to enter various messages specifically for users of your FTP service, including the following:

Welcome   This long message is displayed to FTP clients when they connect to your FTP server, and you can use it to display the rules of your FTP site. You can also use this welcome message to display any legal or copyright text that your company requires.

Exit   This short message is displayed as clients disconnect from your FTP server.

Maximum Connections   This text is displayed if a client attempts to connect to your FTP service when the maximum number of connections allowed has already been reached; you can use it to display a message saying that your FTP server is at its maximum number of connections and that visitors should try again later.

All three of these messages are blank by default.

Home Directory Property Sheet

The FTP Home Directory Property sheet, shown in Figure 15.15, is similar to the Web Home Directory Property sheet we looked at earlier, but with some important differences.

FIGURE 15.15:

The Home Directory Property sheet

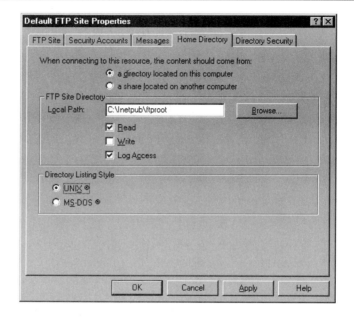

As with the Web service, you can specify that the content come either from a directory located on this computer or from a network share located on another computer; you cannot specify that the content come from a redirection to a URL as you can with the Web service.

In the FTP Site Directory box, you specify the local path where your content is located, and you can specify access permissions using the Read, Write, or Log Access check boxes. The default directory \Ftproot was created for you automatically when you installed the FTP service.

Finally, you can specify the style of the directory listings that IIS sends to an FTP client as either a Unix or an MS-DOS style directory listing. If you are hosting an Internet FTP site, check the UNIX checkbox, as that is the format most familiar to Internet FTP users and is understood by most browsers. On the other hand, if you are running an intranet or internal FTP site, you can choose either format.

Directory Security Property Sheet

And finally, the Directory Security Property sheet, shown in Figure 15.16, lets you control who can access your FTP service based on their IP address.

FIGURE 15.16:

The Directory Security Property sheet

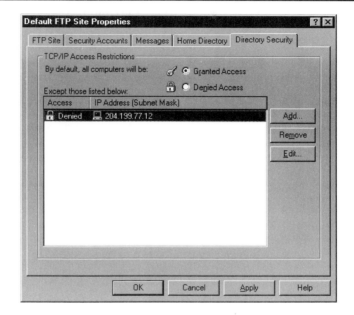

Once again, two check boxes control overall default access:

Granted Access   Check this box to allow all computers access to your server except those specified by IP address in the box below.

Denied Access   Check this box to deny all computers access to your server except those specified by IP address in the box below.

You can then use the list box to enter exceptions to the default access policy. You can block access to specific individuals or to whole networks based on their IP addresses. Use the Add, Edit, and Remove buttons to change these restrictions as circumstances change.

FTP and Internet File Types

Because many files on FTP archive sites were originally created using one of the variations of the Unix operating system, you may encounter files with unusual or unfamiliar filename extensions. Table 15.1 lists some of the file types you may come across when using an FTP client.

TABLE 15.1: Common Internet File Types

File Extension	Description
tar	A tape archive file created by the Unix tar utility.
Z	A file created by the Unix compress utility. You must use the uncompress utility to restore the file before you can use it.
tar.Z	A compressed tape archive file.
z	A compressed file created using pack. You must use unpack to restore the file before you can use it.
ZIP	A compressed file created using PKZIP that must be uncompressed with PKUNZIP before you can use it.
gz	A Unix file compressed by the GNU gzip utility. This file must be decompressed before you can use it.
HQX	A compressed Macintosh file.
SIT	A Macintosh file compressed by StuffIt.
TIF or TIFF	A graphics file in TIFF format.
GIF	A graphics file in GIF format.
JPG or JPEG	A graphics file in JPEG format.
MPG or MPEG	A video file in MPEG format.
TXT	A text file.
1	An nroff source file.
ps	A PostScript file ready for printing on a PostScript printer.
uue	A uuencoded file. You must use uudecode or a program such as XferPro before you can use the file. The Windows NT Server Resource Kit also includes a UUEncoder/UUDecoder.
uue.z	Compressed uuencoded file.
shar	A Usenet newsgroup archive file created by the shar program.
shar.Z	A compressed shar file.

Populating Your FTP Archive

When you start adding files to your FTP archive, separate them in some meaningful way so that they appear as organized as possible. If your company has 10 products, place material for each product in its own directory. If your company is using the FTP site to make new device drivers available, group them by operating system. Create directories named after these operating systems: put the NT files in a directory called \NT4, and put the Macintosh files in a directory called \MACINTOSH.

NOTE   Don't worry if you end up with only a few files in each directory; your users will thank you for making the organization obvious and easy to navigate.

Here are some other features you can include to make it easier for visitors to navigate your FTP site:

- Each directory can contain an annotation file that the visitor's browser will automatically display. Create the file with the name ~FTPSVC~.CKM, and make it a hidden file so that it does not appear in directory listings. Keep this file up to date.

- Include an INDEX.TXT file in each directory to tell visitors exactly what they can expect to find. An index usually contains both the name of the file and a short description of its function. Keep this file up to date.

- Add a terms-and-conditions statement. Your legal department may require you to add this material as a reminder to users about copyright and trademark restrictions on the material on the FTP site.

Internet Information Server also adds some additional useful features. You can create directories with the same name as a user (called a *username directory*); when that user logs on to your FTP server, that directory is used as the root. You can also create a directory called ANONYMOUS. When a visitor logs on using the password "anonymous," this directory is used as that visitor's home directory. This kind of configuration detail can be helpful if users are company employees, but restrict permissions even in a directory such as this so that unauthorized users cannot gain access where you don't want them.

A major benefit of FTP is that almost anyone with an Internet connection can use it; everything is text-based, and there is no place for fancy graphics here. FTP transfers are fairly fast, and they are efficient. The two most common kinds of FTP access are *anonymous FTP* and *user FTP*.

Anonymous FTP

This is the most popular FTP Internet service and is the one you will most probably provide from your IIS server. Anonymous FTP lets anyone access your server, regardless of whether that person has an account on the system. Visitors can simply log on with the username anonymous and then use their e-mail address as a password. These visitors are restricted to that part of your server known as the *anonymous FTP area*. Because this kind of FTP access is relatively safe and can support almost any file type, as Table 15.1 shows, it is a popular way to provide access to large numbers of files of different types; indeed, many large FTP sites are known as FTP archives because of this.

Configuration is a piece of cake with an anonymous FTP service: all you have to do is put the file into the correct directory, and you are done. There is no HTML to worry about, there are no Active Server Pages or scripts, and there are no links to other files or sites. All you have is a directory structure containing the files you want to make available for users to download.

User FTP

This version of FTP is only for users who already have an account on your system. They must log on with a username and password. They can download any file they would be permitted to read if they logged on locally, and they can upload to any directory for which they have Write access.

The FTP service provides for only certain functions, such as listing and changing directories and sending and receiving files; so users do not have full and complete access to your system from within the FTP interpreter.

WARNING   FTP can certainly present a security risk. When a user logs on to the FTP service from the Internet, his or her password is sent as clear text. Anyone with a sniffer program on an intermediate system somewhere can determine the username and password and use them to log on to your system. Also, most FTP client interpreters contain a command that can create an operating system command-line prompt from within the FTP interpreter; so think carefully before allowing too much of the wrong kind of access.

Allowing FTP Uploads

Whether you allow anonymous FTP users to upload files to your site is a decision you will have to make on a server-by-server basis. Uploading a file from a
Web browser to a server is one of the few things that a Web client still cannot do
very well.

WARNING   Allowing users to upload files poses a definite security risk. In many documented
cases, unscrupulous users have exploited FTP archive sites to store their own personal files, including copies of bootlegged software, pornography, and other
material of questionable legality. They don't want this stuff on their own systems,
but they will quite happily use yours for temporary storage, and many administrators are just too busy to notice. Upper management at your company would not
be impressed to find out that your newly established FTP site is known all over the
world as one of the premiere sources of pornographic material or bootlegged
software.

If you have to permit anonymous FTP users to upload files, create a special
directory called \INCOMING to receive the files. Set the permissions so that
users can write and execute only in this directory. This will be slightly inconve-
nient because users will not be able to look at files uploaded by others, but it will
prevent them from altering or deleting those files.

NOTE   The default TCP/IP port number for FTP data services is port 20, and the default for
control services is port 21.

Testing Your FTP Site and Going Online

Before you announce your FTP site to the world at large, spend a little time ensuring that your site works as you think it should. Use an FTP client to access the site,
list a few files, and change to a few directories. Also download at least one ASCII
file and one binary file, and upload a set of test files if you plan to offer uploading
services to your users. Even if you don't plan to allow users to upload files to your
FTP site, you should try to do so to ensure that users can't.

You must also ensure that users can't do any other things that you don't want them to do, such as access files or directories outside the limits you have set or overwrite important files.

Archie is an FTP search utility that maintains a database of FTP servers and the files available on each one. To include your new FTP site in the Archie search indexes, send e-mail to this address:

```
archie-admin@bunyip.com
```

Include the fully qualified domain name of your FTP server and the root directory from which you will be making information available.

Using Services

To round out this section on controlling IIS and related services, I want to remind you that the NT Server Control Panel has several applets that you can use with IIS, including the following:

- The Network applet, which you can use to set up and configure the TCP/IP networking protocol

- The ODBC applet, which you can use to establish ODBC connectivity

- The Services applet

You use the Services applet to start, pause, or stop any NT Server service, including IIS services. Select the Services icon in the Control Panel, and you will see the Services dialog box, as shown in Figure 15.17.

FIGURE 15.17:

Services dialog box

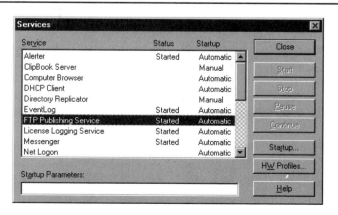

The three columns in the list box in this dialog box are Service, Status, and Startup. On the left side in the Services column, you will see a list of all the Windows NT Server services listed in alphabetic order. In the Status column, you can see whether a specific service is started or is waiting to start, and in the Startup column, you can see an indication of whether the selected service is run automatically when NT Server starts or is started manually.

Select a service and then click on the Startup button (or double-click on the service you want to work with in the list box) to open the Service dialog box. Here you can select the Startup Type from Automatic, Manual, or Disabled, as well as set other logon parameters for the service.

NOTE   Changing the status of the Web server service in this dialog box will override ISM.

Setting Up a News Server

A *news server* is simply a server that collects and distributes short news articles to all users who subscribe to the news service. Most ISPs provide news services, and many companies are using news servers as a part of their corporate intranet to distribute information to their employees, customers, and suppliers.

News servers gather and distribute news articles, submitted by users, via *Network News Transfer Protocol* (NNTP), a set of standards developed to manage the distribution, inquiry, retrieval, and posting of articles over a network running TCP/IP.

In times past, most news servers were Unix-based and were difficult to set up; some even required that the source code be configured and recompiled. All that has now changed; IIS 4 includes the Microsoft News Server that loads as an extension to IIS.

Users can write and post articles to News Server using a News client such as Microsoft Internet News or Free Agent. Once the post is written, the user initiates a connection to News Server and requests that News Server post the article in one or more newsgroups. The client connects to the server through port number 119 by default (or through port 563 if you are using SSL for encrypted posts); however, any available port can be used. News Server receives the request, verifies authentication of the user account, and determines whether the user can post to the newsgroup. Once the user is authenticated, News Server receives the article and puts it into News Server storage, where other users can access it.

TIP   See RFC 977 "Network News Transfer Protocol" and 1036 "Standard for Interchange of Usenet Messages" for more information on NNTP and newsgroups in general.

You can manage the News Server using the ISM; there is also an HTML-based administrator you can use if you wish, but I'll concentrate on the MCC-based ISM in this section. As we saw with the HTML-based ISM for Web and FTP services, there are some minor differences in terminology and labeling between the MMC-based ISM News Server Property sheets and the HTML pages. For example, the Security page in the HTML administrator contains the fields Maximum Post Size and Maximum Connection Size; these same fields in the ISM Security Property sheet are called Limit Post Size and Limit Connection Size, although they do the same thing in the end.

Right-click on the News Server in the ISM and select Properties, or click on the Property button on the toolbar to open the News Server Property sheets. If you have followed the discussion on setting your Web and FTP servers above, you will see that three of the News Server Property sheets—Home Directory, Security Accounts, and Directory Security—are similar to the corresponding Property sheets in the Web or FTP server, and so I won't discuss them again here. Three of the Property sheets are specific to the News Server, and we'll look at them next.

News Site Property Sheet

The News Site Property sheet, shown in Figure 15.18, lets you set up basic information for your news server, using several useful options.

FIGURE 15.18:

The News Site Property sheet

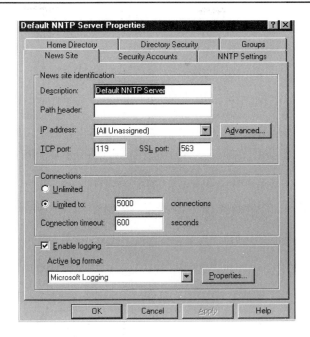

News Site Identification   Use the settings in this box to identify your news site, including

Description   Specify a name for the news server; this name will be used in the ISM window.

Path Header   Specify the path that each news posting must take to reach its destination; see RFC 1036 for detailed information on how path information is generated.

IP Address   Enter the IP address of the news server computer.

TCP Port   Specify the TCP port number to use; the default is port number 119.

SSL Port   Specify the port number to use with SSL encrypted posts; the default is port number 563.

Connections   Use the settings in this box to specify the maximum number of simultaneous users you will allow to access the news server, including

Unlimited   Check this box to allow an unlimited number of simultaneous connections.

Limited To   Check this box to specify a maximum number of simultaneous connections; the default is 5,000, and the maximum is 15,000.

Connection Timeout   Specify the time limit that you will allow inactive connections to stay connected to the news server; the default is 600 seconds, or 10 minutes.

Enable Logging   Check this box to turn logging on for your news server, and then select a log format from the selections in the Active Log Format list box.

NOTE   The News Server is designed for individual newsgroup use and so does not support news feeds from Usenet or other newsgroup agencies. If you feel you need news feeds such as Usenet, you will have to use the Internet News Server, part of the recently announced Microsoft Commercial Internet System.

Groups Property Sheet

The next Property sheet you will want to work with is the Groups Property sheet, shown in Figure 15.19. This Property sheet lets you look at the list of newsgroups already in use on your news server and create new newsgroups as they are required.

In this Property sheet, you will find the following:

Newsgroup Name   Enter the name of the newsgroup you want to work with, or if you have a large number of newsgroups on your news server, type the first few letters and then click on the Find button. You can also use wildcards in this box to narrow the choices.

Limit Results To   Specify the maximum number of newsgroup names to be displayed as a result of using the Find button.

Matching Newsgroups   This box lists the names of the newsgroups that match the search on your news server.

FIGURE 15.19:

The Groups Property sheet

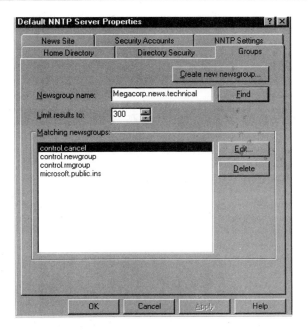

You can now use the Edit and Delete buttons to change or remove one of these existing newsgroups.

To start a brand-new newsgroup, follow these steps:

1. Click on the Create New Newsgroup button in the Groups property sheet.

2. In the Newsgroup box, enter the name you want to use for this newsgroup.

3. In the Description box, type a short description of the function of this newsgroup.

4. Select Read Only if you want to restrict Write access to this newsgroup. This can sometimes be useful when you want to control exactly what information is displayed in the newsgroup.

5. Select Moderated and type an SMTP address or directory location for moderator messages. When a newsgroup is moderated, posts are sent to the moderator before they are posted on the news server. This allows the moderator an opportunity to do exactly that, to moderate the content or tone of

the posts before they are published. In the future, you may have occasion to wish you had specified this option.

6. Click on the OK button to return to the Groups property sheet, where you will now see your newly created newsgroup listed along with all the others on the server.

NNTP Settings Property Sheet

The third News Server Property sheet we need to look at is the NNTP Settings Property sheet, shown in Figure 15.20, where you establish controls for the newsgroups run on the server, including:

Allow Client Posting   Check this box to allow readers to post their own articles; with this box cleared, they cannot.

Limit Post Size   Check this box if you want to limit the size of article that clients can post, and then specify a limit in the text box, a value between 1 and 1,000KB.

Limit Connection Size   Check this box if you want to limit the connection size; use a value between 1 and 4,000MB.

Allow Servers to Pull News Articles from This Server   Check this box to allow other news servers to pull news articles from this server.

Allow Control Messages   Check this box to process control messages automatically and log them into the log file.

SMTP Server for Moderated Groups   If you elected to set up a moderated newsgroup in the Groups Property sheet, this is where you specify a destination for moderated newsgroup messages. News Server automatically sends messages for the newsgroup moderator to the specified SMTP server. Postings to a moderated newsgroup are sent with an empty Mail From entry, which means that if the message cannot be processed normally, a nondelivery report cannot be returned to the original sender. You can either enter a valid DNS computer name and IP address or enter a directory name. For such messages to be processed by SMTP, an appropriate account must exist on the SMTP server.

Default Moderator Domain   Specifies the default fully qualified domain name for all moderated posts; the posts generate messages to the address newsgroup_name@default_moderator_name.

FIGURE 15.20:

The NNTP Settings Property sheet

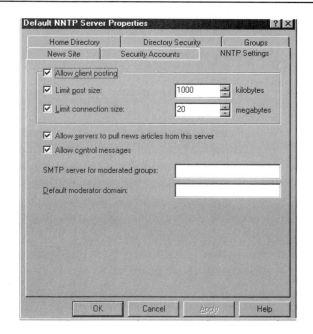

Setting Up Certificate Server

In this section, we'll extend our discussion of system security in NT Server to cover some of the other security elements now available in IIS, including Certificate Server. The need for privacy and authentication over networks that connect to the Internet requires some form of data encryption and decryption as a portion of the software system security.

An *encryption key* is used to encrypt or encode a message, and a corresponding *decryption key* is needed to decrypt the message once it reaches its destination. Once the message (which can be e-mail, a database file, or any data that requires secure transmission) is in encrypted form, it can be stored or transmitted over nonsecure systems and still stay secret.

The Certificate Server package includes the following:

- Certificate Server
- A set of support modules for certificate enrollment, setting policies, and administering Certificate Server
- A Certificate Server API that ISP's development staff and other programmers can use to create custom applications to work in conjunction with Certificate Server
- An Application Programmer's guide that explains how to write custom modules

In this section, we'll concentrate on using and administering Certificate Server; describing how to use the API and create custom applications is, I'm afraid, beyond the scope of this book.

How Do I Configure the Microsoft Internet News Reader?

You can download the Microsoft Internet News Reader from Microsoft's Web site. When you complete the installation on a client, it adds an Internet News item to your Start menu.

Before the newsreader can display any newsgroups, you must first provide the address of the News Server. From the main Internet News Reader window, select News ➢ Options, choose the Server Property sheet, click on the Add button, and enter the name of your News Server. Click on the OK button when you are done, and you will see the name of the server you just added in the News Servers box at the bottom of the Properties sheet. You can add multiple servers in the same way, and the client will be able to read and subscribe to newsgroups from multiple news servers.

Security Elements Explained

System security elements can take several forms, including

Digital signature   A digital signature is attached to a message distributed in text (sometimes called *plain text*) form to ensure that the contents of the message have not been altered by an unauthorized person.

Digital envelope   A digital envelope is used to send a private message that can only be decoded and understood by a single person.

Digital certificate   A digital certificate (often called simply a *certificate*) is a form of identification used in secure communications to prove the identity of users on nonsecure networks, to conduct private conversations, and to confirm the origin of these communications. A digital certificate is short, only a few hundred bytes, and is created by a special algorithm that combines a private key with a message. The recipient then verifies the digital certificate using the sender's public key and the message. The digital certificate is secure in the sense that it is virtually impossible to find another message (other than the message transmitted) that will produce an identical certificate.

Digital certificates are created by trusted third-party organizations known as a Certificate Authorities (CA) and contain information that completely describes an individual, a company, or some other entity. See the section "Using Key Manager" later in this chapter for more information on what is needed to generate a third-party digital certificate.

Certificate Server can generate its own digital certificates in the standard X.509 format, which you can then use for client and server authentication under the *Secure Sockets Layer* (SSL) or *Private Communications Technology* (PCT) protocols.

How SSL Works

Internet Information Server gives users access to a secure communications channel based on support for Secure Sockets Layer (SSL) and RSA encryption. IIS can send and receive communications across the Internet from Microsoft Internet Explorer or from one of the other SSL-enabled Web browsers.

Secure Sockets Layer provides server authentication, encryption and decryption, and data integrity services:

- Authentication assures the Web client that the data is actually being sent to the right server and that the server is secure.

- Encryption/decryption transforms the data so that it cannot be read by anyone other than the secure target server.

- Data integrity ensures that the data stream has not been altered or tampered with in any way.

Instead of replacing HTTP, SSL creates an intermediate layer between the high-level HTTP protocol and the low-level TCP/IP. Rather than calling TCP/IP library routines to open and close connections and to send and receive data, Web browsers and servers call to SSL routines, which manage the task of setting up a secure communications channel. Secure Sockets Layer uses public key encryption to encrypt inbound and outbound messages, as well as to create verifiable digital signatures for user authentication.

The IIS setup program installs the Certificate Server files into the C:\WINNT\System32 directory, and the Web-based administration tools are located in C:\WINNT\System32\CertSrv and the subdirectories \CertAdmin, \CertControl, \CertEnroll, and \CertQue.

Certificate Server runs, like IIS, as a Windows NT Server service and is configured by default to run automatically under the System account when the NT Server system first boots.

Using the Certificate Server Enrollment Page

To qualify your server to perform client authentication and allow clients to perform server authentication, you must first certify the server and then provide an enrollment service for the clients. The process of becoming certified is known as *server certification* and takes place between the server and a certifying authority.

The process of a client submitting a certificate request to the server and then installing the certificate in the client application is known as *client certificate enrollment*, which is managed by the Certificate Server Enrollment Page, shown in Figure 15.21. The Certificate Server Enrollment Page is a Web-based enrollment control used for the following tasks:

- Installing a certificate using the Certificate Authority Certificate List Web page

- Requesting a certificate through the Web Server Enrollment Page

- Requesting a certificate for an Internet Explorer client

- Requesting a certificate for a Netscape Navigator client

To start the Certificate Server Enrollment page, open the Internet Explorer on

```
C:\WINNT\System32\CertSrv\CertEnroll\default.htm
```

FIGURE 15.21:

The Certificate Server Enrollment Page

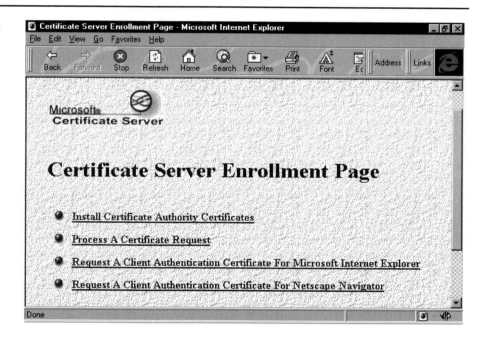

Using Certificate Server Administration Tools

The Certificate Server maintains a two-part database containing the *server queue,* which is a list of all the certificate requests received by the Certificate Server, and server log, which maintains copies of all the issued certificates. To access the information maintained in this database, you can use the Certificate Server Administration Tools, a Web-based package accessed from C:\WINNT\System32\CertSrv\default.htm. Figure 15.22 shows the opening screen. Before you can use this tool, you must be logged on as Administrator, and the Certificate Server must also be running.

FIGURE 15.22:

The Certificate Server Administration Tools

The opening Certificate Server Administration Tools screen contains four options:

Certificate Log Utility lets you look at the Certificate Log Administration page. Each row contains a database record for each certificate, and the rows are displayed in the order in which the certificates were created.

Certificate Queue Utility allows you to look at the Certificate Queue Administration page, where each row contains information on a request for a certificate, and the rows are displayed in the order in which the requests were received.

Certificate Enrollment opens the Certificate Server Enrollment Page we looked at in the last section.

Certificate Server Documentation opens the extensive documentation package that accompanies Certificate Server; this documentation also includes information for application programmers working to create custom modules to use with Certificate Server.

Internet Security and New Products

In recent months, a disturbing number of potential security breaches have been reported in a number of products from several vendors, including Microsoft.

Internet Information Server, Internet Explorer, Netscape Navigator, and Front-Page have all featured in this news. Some of the possible breaches were the result of careless coding; others were program features that allowed the curious user to exploit a particular situation in ways that the original designers did not anticipate. So what does this mean for you and your Web site?

On the one hand, it is an encouragement to hurry up slightly more slowly and not rush into adopting the latest version of each new product just as soon as it is released. And on the other hand, several reputable industry- and university-based groups now try to outdo one another and be the first to report these problem areas. Some software development companies are now offering considerable cash rewards to testers who are the first to report a brand-new bug.

And while all this may give you cause to reflect on the quality of software testing done by the development companies, there is now a much better chance that if a serious error does exist, it will be discovered by someone who is interested in getting it fixed (and fixed quickly), rather than exploiting it for their own malicious gain.

Working with SSL

Once the SSL security is in place and enabled with ISM, you must remember several points:

- Once SSL is enabled and configured, only SSL-enabled Web browsers will be able to access your SSL-protected directories.

- URLs that point to an SSL-protected directory must use https:// instead of http://.

- You can enable SSL security on the root directory (\wwwroot by default) or on one or more virtual directories.

- If your site offers both secure and public content, consider setting up two sets of directories, one for each kind of content; call them C:\Inetpub\ wwwroot\Secure and C:\Inetpub\wwwroot\Public, for example. And do not configure an unsecured directory not protected by SSL as a parent for a secure directory.

WARNING   Do not leave decrypted copies of documents on your system where they may be found by others; if it isn't encrypted, don't keep it.

In addition to the digital certificates created by Certificate Server, you may sometimes need a digital certificate created by a trusted third-party authority, and you use Key Manager for that task.

Using Key Manager

The IIS Key Manager helps you with the background information needed to apply for a digital certificate from an external certificate authority by preparing this information and then creating the files you will need. This process includes the following:

- Generating a key pair file and a request file

- Requesting a digital certificate from a Certification Authority

- Installing the digital certificate on your server

- Activating the SSL security on your server using ISM

- Activating SSL for the directories that require security, usually \wwwroot

Acquiring an SSL digital certificate requires several steps, including contacting a qualified certifying organization such as the Internet security company VeriSign or GTE CyberTrust. See VeriSign's Web site at digitalid.verisign.com for more information on applying for a digital certificate. It makes most sense to complete all these steps long before you want or need to implement SSL security on your Web site. VeriSign has issued more than 500,000 certificates for servers and browsers and more than 1,000 for other purposes, such as secure mail.

VeriSign, a spin-off from RSA Data Security, was established in 1995 to act as a trusted third-party certificate authority, providing digital certificates and certificate management services. It issues several classes of certificates, depending on the types of applications they are used with and the level of assurance required regarding the user's identity:

Class 1 is used for casual Web access and receiving secure e-mail.

Class 2 is used with intracompany e-mail systems and subscription-based on-line services.

Class 3 is used with intercompany e-mail, electronic banking, the purchase of high-value items, and membership-based on-line services.

Class 4 is used for high-level financial transactions.

VeriSign has announced plans to extend digital certificates into secure containers suitable for storing and transmitting almost any kind of data, such as demographic information, including age, gender, address, and phone number, as well as other personal data.

To create a key pair, follow these steps:

1. Choose Programs ➤ Microsoft Internet Information Server ➤ Internet Service Manager and click on the Key Manager button on the ISM toolbar.

2. When the Key Manager opens, choose Key ➤ Create New Key to start the Create New Key and Certificate Request Wizard. Navigate through the Wizard using the Back, Next, and Cancel buttons as normal.

3. Fill in the information for all the fields. Table 15.2 lists this information.

WARNING   Do not enter commas into any field; if you do, they will be interpreted as field separators and will generate an invalid request without any warning.

4. When you are done, click on the Finish button.

Your key will appear in the Key Manager window under the appropriate computer name.

T A B L E 15.2: Information Needed to Create a New Key and Certificate Request File

Option	Description
Key Name	Name of the key file you are creating.
Password	Password used to encrypt the private key.
Bits	Number of bits for the key pair; default is 1024 bits.
Organization	Company name.
Organizational Unit	Name of your division within the company.
Common Name	Domain name of your server.
Country	Two-letter country abbreviation—US, UK, and so on.
State/Province	Complete name of your state or province; Iowa, for example.
Locality	Complete name of your city.
Request File	Name of the request file you are creating; the default filename is NewKeyRq.txt, created in the root directory.

The key created by the Key Manager is not valid for use on the Internet until you obtain a valid key certificate for it from a certifying authority. You can use an IIS command-line utility to submit the certificate requests to Certificate Server if you type

```
certreq newkeyrq.txt newcert.crt
```

from a command prompt. Alternatively, you can send the certificate request file to a third-party authority according to its procedures, and it will send you a digitally signed certificate, containing the following:

- Identification information, including certificate version, serial number, and signature algorithm

- Certificate holder's RSA public key information

- Certificate holder's name, organization, address

- Certificate expiration date

- Name and digital signature of the Certificate Authority

- X.509 version 3 certificate extensions

Once you have that certificate, choose Key ➤ Install Key Certificate in the Key Manager to install it on your server. Once it is installed, you must activate the SSL feature for your Web service using the Directories Property sheet in the Internet Service Manager. To back up the key file, follow these steps:

1. In Key Manager, choose Key ➤ Export Key ➤ Backup File.

2. Read the warning about downloading sensitive information to your hard disk, and click on OK.

3. Type the key name in the File Name box, and click on Save.

The file is given a .REQ filename extension and is saved to your hard disk drive. You can copy it or move it to a floppy disk or magnetic tape once you have completed all the key setup steps; just don't forget the password you gave the key file.

Using Site Server Express

New in IIS 4 is the Site Server Express package, which consists of two main elements:

Usage Analyst imports Web server logs for one server and provides a variety of reporting capabilities.

Site Analyst lets you look at your Web site using a variety of views, manages links, and identify repetitive content.

TIP   A new BackOffice family member also called Site Server makes it easy for organizations using NT Server and IIS to organize, deploy, and manage sophisticated Web sites. It is available in two editions, Site Server Standard Edition and Site Server Enterprise Edition (which contains additional features that let you manage commerce and large sites more easily). See the Microsoft Web site for details on pricing and licensing information at www.microsoft.com/backoffice/siteserver.

Getting the Most Out of Usage Analyst

As you saw earlier in this chapter, you establish the criteria for saving log files using the Internet Service Manager. Open the Web Site or FTP Site Property sheet for the service you are interested in and use the settings to do the following:

- Specify the frequency with which the log information is collected.
- Configure the directory you want to use for the log files.
- Choose the form in which the data will be collected.

Now that you are collecting information into a log file, you can look at that information with Usage Analyst.

Usage Analyst consists of two main components:

> **Usage Analyst Import** reads a log file and determines the visitors, users, and organizations that accessed your Web site. This information is stored in a database for easy access.

> **Usage Analyst Report** creates reports based on the information stored in the database. This version of Usage Analyst includes nine preformatted reports.

When you choose Start ➤ Programs ➤ Microsoft Internet Information Server ➤ Microsoft Site Server Express, you will see these two components listed, along with an additional element, Usage Analyst Start Page. This is an HTML information package you can open with Internet Explorer. It contains links to a Readme file, product support information, upgrade information, documentation for Usage Analyst Standard Edition and Usage Analyst Enterprise Edition in both HTML and Word formats, and Microsoft's BackOffice Web site at backoffice .microsoft.com.

Importing a Log File

The first step in looking at the information contained in the log files your Web server is now creating is to import the log file into the Usage Analyst database format. Here are the steps to follow:

1. Choose Start ➤ Programs ➤ Microsoft Internet Information Server ➤ Microsoft Site Server Express ➤ Usage Analyst Import to run the application.

2. The first time you run Usage Analyst Import, the program walks you through the process; it's not exactly a Wizard, but it certainly automates the process.

3. The Server Manager window opens. In the Log Data Source dialog box, select which of the three log-file formats you use.

4. In the Server Properties dialog box, choose the service type (Web or FTP), specify the names of the directory index filenames, the IP address, and the TCP port number in use. Then configure the time zone you are in and the local domain name, and click on the OK button.

5. In the Site Properties dialog box, enter the home page URL for your site.

6. Once you have configured a server and a site, Usage Analyst Import opens the Log File Manager window. Enter the complete path to your log file or click on the Browse button to locate the file.

7. Click on the green Start Import button on the toolbar to begin the import.

The Usage Analyst Import processes the import and tells you when it is complete; now it's time to create a report from this data.

Creating an Analysis Report

Here are the steps to follow when using Usage Analyst Report:

1. Choose Start ➤ Programs ➤ Microsoft Internet Information Server ➤ Microsoft Site Server Express ➤ Usage Analyst Report.

2. In the Create an Analysis Report box in the Analysis Module dialog box, check the From Analysis Catalog box to select one of the preformatted reports. Usage Analyst Report contains both detail and summary reports:

   Hits Detail Report shows server hits on an hourly, daily, and weekly basis and is used to derive trends. Useful for planning future upgrades.

   Request Detail Report shows the most- and least-frequently requested documents on your Web site so that you can see where users are spending their time.

   User Detail Report displays information about user visits, including frequency and numbers of registered and unregistered users. A high number of repeat users indicates that your Web site is providing a compelling reason for visitors to return, and it can be a good indicator of the quality of your content.

Visits Detail Report displays information on when your users visit your site—hourly, daily, and weekly. Good for seeing trends over time.

Bandwidth Summary Report shows the amount of information transferred, in terms of bytes, on an hourly, daily, and weekly basis. Good for demonstrating the need for additional capacity.

Browser and Operating System Summary Report details information on the browsers used by your visitors and their browser security features, as well as details of the underlying operating system.

Executive Summary Report shows top-level information for an at-a-glance summary of activity. For a more detailed analysis, zoom in on one of the other reports.

Path Summary Report shows the sequence of requests that users make at your site.

3. Choose the report you want to use, and click on the Finish button to run the report, or click on Next to see the full range of options available to refine the report to your exact specifications.

4. From the graphical representation of your report, click on the green Create Analysis Report button on the toolbar. You will be prompted for a filename and a format; the default report type is an HTML document, which will be opened automatically with your browser.

The combinations of reporting options in Usage Analyst Report allow you to get a look at the fine detail of the inner workings of your Web site quickly and easily; the other Site Server Express component, Site Analyst, is also easy to use, as you'll see in this next section.

Working with Site Analyst

Site Server Express Site Analyst lets you look at the structure of your Web site in a variety of ways. A Tree view provides a linear hierarchical representation of your site, and the Cyberbolic view shows all the elements that make up your Web site as a sort of spider web that serves to emphasize the interconnected nature of these elements.

Site Analyst also analyzes the structure of your site, finds broken links for you, lets you manage local and remote sites, and performs a variety of other Web-management tasks.

WARNING   When Site Analyst maps and analyzes the structure of your site, every URL is accessed, which is the equivalent of a user clicking on that link. If you have links that point to a script that performs a specific action, such as manipulating a record in a database, this script is executed. Because such an operation might change data outside the HTML content of your site, think carefully before running Site Analyst on your Web site.

When you choose Start ➤ Programs ➤ Microsoft Internet Information Server ➤ Microsoft Site Server Express, you will see the Usage Analyst components listed, along with an additional element, Site Analyst Start Page. This is an HTML information package you can open with Internet Explorer. It contains links to a Readme file, product support information, upgrade information, documentation for Site Analyst Standard Edition and Site Analyst Enterprise Edition, and a link to Microsoft's Back-Office Web site at backoffice.microsoft.com.

To start the program, select Site Analyst from the Microsoft Site Server Express menu; a dialog box with three buttons appears. Select View User's Guide to open the Site Analyst documentation, click on New WebMap to create a new Site Analyst map of your Web site, or choose Open WebMap to load a map you have previously created. You can also check the Don't Show This Dialog Box at Startup Any More box to go straight into the application the next time you run Site Analyst. Figure 15.23 shows Site Analyst open on the Sample WebMap.

The left pane of the main Site Analyst window in Figure 15.23 contains the Tree view for the Sample WebMap, and the right pane shows the Cyberbolic view for the same WebMap. In the Tree view, the different kinds of files on this Web site are indicated by different icons and colors; GIF files have a Mona Lisa icon, while Java applets show a small cup of coffee. Black indicates the main navigation routes, red indicates a broken link, and green indicates that an alternative route exists to this object. As you would expect, you can click on the plus and minus signs to expand or contract the information displayed in this window.

FIGURE 15.23:

Site Analyst open on the
Sample WebMap

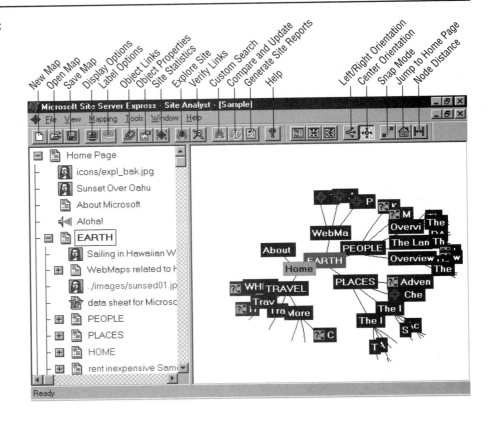

In the Cyberbolic view, you can use the Node Distance button on the toolbar to alter the spacing between objects, and you can use the Left/Right Orientation, Center Orientation, and Jump to Home Page buttons to change the way information is displayed. You can switch between views using the Maximize Tree View, Maximize Cyberbolic View, and Show Tree and Cyberbolic Views buttons. Double-click on an object, and it appears full size in your browser; alternatively, right-click on object in the Cyberbolic view and choose Launch Browser.

Checking Links

Managing a large, complex, and constantly changing Web site can drive you to distraction, with its hundreds of HTML pages, scripts, graphics, video samples, and links to other pages and to other sites. Links can be broken by simple typographical errors in an HTML <HREF> tag, they may refer to a previous version of your Web site content, or they can be broken by other sites going offline. Site Analyst goes a long way toward simplifying the process of checking links for you. Here's how to use it:

1. Choose Verify Links from the Mapping menu or click on the Verify Links button on the toolbar.

2. In the Verify Links dialog box, check the Onsite Links box to evaluate links within your own Web site. Then choose either the All Links or the Broken Links Only check box.

3. Check the Offsite Links box to evaluate links to and between other Web sites. Then, as in the last step, choose either the All Links or the Broken Links Only check box.

4. Click on the Verify button to start the process, and you will see a couple of progress bars that indicate that the links are being checked.

5. All broken links are displayed in red in both the Tree view and the Cyberbolic view. If an object is unavailable, all links to it in the WebMap are shown in red.

You should also verify links to other sites on the Internet, those that point to sites external to your own. These links are not easy to test automatically, and you have to look for two things:

- That the URL still works and that the site is still in use

- That the original content you wanted to include in your site is still there and is still timely and appropriate

You will have to check these links manually.

Using the Link Info Window

To see a list of the links associated with a specific object, right-click on the object and then select Links. You can also choose View ➤ Object Links or click on the Object Links button on the toolbar. Either way, the Link Info window opens, as Figure 15.24 shows.

FIGURE 15.24:

The Link Info window

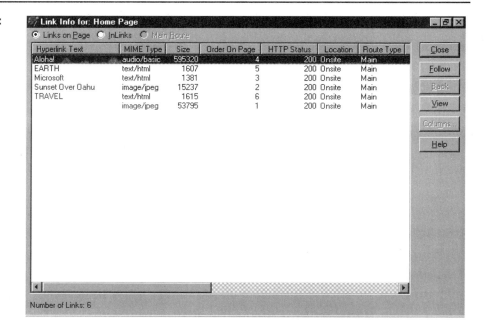

With the Links on Page button checked at the top of this window, you will see a list of all the other Web site elements linked to the chosen object, in this case, the Home Page of this site. The columns in the Link Info window show you lots of detail for each of the linked objects, including the MIME type and size of the object, its HTTP status code and location on the page, even the number of hits on the page, the linking URL, and the actual URL of the object itself. To change the size of a column, simply click and drag the column boundary.

You can use the buttons along the right edge of the Link Info window for a variety of purposes. Click on an object in the main window, and then click Follow to follow the links into and out of the object you selected; then use the Back button to return to your starting point. You can also click on the View button to load your browser and display the selected object or play it if the object is an audio file.

Searching Your Web Site

Site Analyst offers several useful search options you can use when analyzing your Web site. Choose Tools ➢ Quick Search, and you will see the following search options:

Broken Links looks for broken links.

Home Site Objects searches for objects in the same domain as the site's home page.

Images without ALT looks for images without the HTML <ALT> attribute text string. If this string is missing, users browsing in text-only mode will find it exceedingly difficult to navigate your site.

Load Size over 32K looks for pages, plus any inline graphical or audio components, whose size is larger than 32K. Smaller images load more quickly.

Non-Home Site Objects searches for pages and other resources in a domain that is different from that of the site's home page.

Not Found Objects (404) looks for pages and other objects that did not exist at the time Site Analyst mapped the site.

Unavailable Objects looks for pages and other objects that could not be reached at the time Site Analyst mapped the site.

Unverified Objects searches for pages and other resources for which one or more links have been found, but which have not been verified as accessible.

The results of your search are presented in a Search Results window, which looks a lot like the Links Info window I talked about in the last section. Some of the columns will change depending on which search you used.

Looking at Site Statistics

Another useful application of Site Analyst is to collect statistics for your site. Choose View ➣ Site Statistics or click on the Site Statistics button on the toolbar to open the Statistics dialog box shown in Figure 15.25.

FIGURE 15.25:

Statistics dialog box

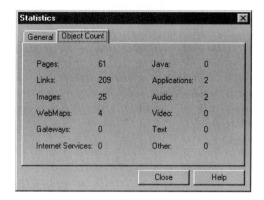

This display gives you an easy-to-use summary of the number of pages and graphical images on your site, the number of links, Java scripts, and applications, and even the number of audio and video files.

Select the General tab of the Statistics dialog box to look at other information, including the domain name, root path, the name of the home page file, and the name of the CGI Bin directory.

Managing Day-to-Day Operations

If you thought that you were done when you finally went on-line to the Internet, I have a surprise for you: the real work is just beginning. You will want to add new material to your Web site to keep it looking fresh and to keep those visitors coming back time after time; you will have to design a strategy you can use to manage the installation of new HTML content from both the client's point of view and also, if you are an ISP, from the server's point of view. As we do this, let's look at the duties and responsibilities of the Web site administrator, or Webmaster, in a little more detail.

Your site may be small enough that one person can perform all the duties needed to keep it in tip-top condition, but if you run a large corporate intranet, you may find that you need a department of people to keep everything ticking along nicely. But no matter how many people it takes to do the job, the duties are essentially the same and include the following:

- Preparing and adding new HTML content

- Inspecting system logs

- Testing active links and locating new links

- Writing and testing new scripts

- Responding to feedback from users

- Keeping up with the latest developments in Web technology

- Backing up the server

- Installing software upgrades and system patches

- Troubleshooting server problems

- Upgrading system hardware

Planning Your Content Directories

If your Web pages are all contained under a single directory tree, all you have to do to install them on the IIS server is to copy them into the default World Wide Web directory called \wwwroot.

But if your content files are in several directories or even on several computers, you will have to create virtual directories to make those files available. If your Web site is very complex, use the Internet Service Manager to specify the directories from which you want to publish.

Note that Web services cannot publish content from redirected network drives or, in other words, from drive letters assigned to network shares. To use network drives, you must specify the server and UNC name (as in \\computername\sharename\wwwfiles). If you specify a username and a password to connect to a network drive, all remote users requesting access to that drive must use the appropriate username and password, rather than the anonymous ISUR_ computername account or any other account you may have specified.

Adding New HTML Material

Keeping your Web site up to date is one of the primary duties of the Webmaster. Your content should be as fresh as possible and should also be as free of errors as possible.

You need not halt or restart IIS when it is time to update the HTML documents; you can simply write the new documents over the top of the existing tree of files.

Some Webmasters like to develop content files off-line from the Web server machine and only transfer them when they are complete and have been thoroughly tested. Others edit files while the server is on-line to the Internet by keeping two parallel Web structures—one for on-line Internet access and the other for off-line editing and content preparation.

I prefer to use the first approach and develop material off-line; there is less potential for damage to the running server by accidentally deleting files or copying the wrong file on top of a good working file.

One thing to watch for is that new Web site content might be provided to you in two different forms:

- As an update to an existing HTML file
- As a new HTML file

In the first case, all you have to do is lay the new version of the file over the top of the old version, but the second case is more complex. You may have to support both the original file and the new file, and so you may have to retrace your steps and create links to the new file; otherwise, visitors to your site will never find it.

From time to time you may have to move large sections of your Web site's content, perhaps when your site undergoes a major reorganization or to deal with disk-space constraints. Many things can go wrong during this sort of operation, so plan the steps carefully and be sure you have a recent backup.

Testing Your Web Site

You have heard this from me before, but I can't emphasize it enough: when you make changes to the content on your site, particularly if you add or change links, be sure you test and test again. If you start to use an addition or extension to the standard HTML you have used in the past, test and test again. Use one of the HTML syntax checkers or validators that are becoming more popular. If you are running on the Internet, test the effects of your changes by looking at them with various browsers so that you will see them as visitors to your site will see them. If you are running an intranet, you can, of course, simply use the company's browser of choice.

Dial in to your site over the Internet to gauge the speed of downloads and the effects that a full load of visitors have on the response time of your site.

In the next section, we'll take a look at one of the most important duties of the Webmaster, that of publishing new Web or intranet content.

Using the Web Publishing Wizard

The Web Publishing Wizard is intended to make the process of posting new Web content to a Web site maintained by an external ISP or to an intranet Web site as easy and straightforward as possible. You simply enter the Web site configuration information once, the first time you use the Wizard, and it remembers this information and uses it in subsequent sessions.

To use the Web Publishing Wizard you must have

- A connection to the Web server. This can be a LAN connection to your internal corporate intranet or an external connection to the ISP who hosts your Web site for you.

- The name of the communications protocol to use, either FTP, HTTP POST, or Microsoft's Content Replication System (CRS). You'll learn more about CRS in the next section.

- The URL for the Web server you use to publish your files.

- The name of the folder or directory on the server where you publish your files.

Once you have collected all this information, choose Start ➤ Programs ➤ Microsoft Web Publishing ➤ Web Publishing Wizard to get things going for the first time. The Web Publishing Wizard will look familiar to anyone who has used similar Wizards in FrontPage or Microsoft Word, with its Back, Next, Cancel, and Help buttons. Figure 15.26 shows the opening Welcome screen.

FIGURE 15.26:

The Web Publishing Wizard Welcome screen

Configuring the Web Publishing Wizard

Before you can use the Web Publishing Wizard to post Web content, you will have to provide some basic information. Let's take a look:

1. Start the Wizard. When the Welcome dialog box opens, click on the Next button.

2. In the Select a File or Folder dialog box, select the file or directory that you want to publish; use the Browse Folders or Browse Files buttons to zero in on your Web content if necessary. Once you have made your selection, click on the Next button.

3. In the Name the Web server dialog box, enter a name in the Descriptive Name field. This name can be anything you like. In the future, the Wizard will use it as a shortcut, and it will appear in the drop-down list box. You might use "Our Intranet" or "My Web Server," for example. Click on the Next button.

4. In the Specify the URL and Directory dialog box, enter the Internet address you use to access your Web server in the URL or Internet Address field; and in the Local Directory box, enter the path to the files on your own local computer that you want to link with this URL. Click on the Next button.

5. In the Select a Service Provider dialog box, make a selection from the drop-down list box. Choose Automatically Select Service Provider to have the Web Publishing Wizard try to locate this information automatically. If the Web Publishing Wizard fails to locate information on your service provider, the Specify a Service Provider dialog box opens so that you can enter the information manually. In either case, click on the Next button when you are done.

6. The next dialog box to open depends on the choices you made in the Select a Service Provider dialog box, and you may have to contact your ISP for more details. For example, if you chose HTTP Post in the Select a Service Provider dialog box, you will have to enter the server name and the posting command used on that server. You may also specify that SSL is used and that post processing of your content is required. In this case, you can also enter the URL of the post-processing command to use after you have published your files. When you are done, click on the Next button.

The Web Publishing Wizard now publishes your files to the Web server you chose, and your job is done. A confirmation dialog box opens to tell you when the task is complete.

If any of the information you just entered changes in the future, simply restart the Wizard, click on the Next button to get to the dialog box containing the information you want to change, enter the new information, and then click on the Finish button. The next time you use the Web Publishing Wizard, it will automatically use this new information.

Publishing a Single File or Folder

Sometimes you want to publish only a single file or folder to your Web server, and you can do this in three ways:

*   Start the Web Publishing Wizard and make your selection using the Select Files or Select Folders buttons when prompted by the Wizard.

- Right-click on a file in the Windows Explorer, select Send To, and click on the Web Publishing Wizard.

- Create a Desktop shortcut to the Wizard and drag files to the Web Publishing Wizard icon.

Publishing Multiple Files

The Web Publishing Wizard will not let you select multiple files; you must use Windows Explorer for this task. Here are the steps:

1. Open Windows Explorer and select the files you want to post. As always, you can select files in several ways:

   - To select multiple files in the folder window, hold down the Ctrl key and click on the items you want to select.

   - Choose Edit ➤ Select All to select all the files and folders in the window.

   - To select a group of contiguous files, click in the blank area of the window and then drag the box around the files you want to select.

2. Right-click on the files you have chosen, select Send To, and then click on Web Publishing Wizard.

3. In the Web Server dialog box, click on the drop-down arrow and select the name of the Web server where you want to publish your files.

4. Click on the Next button and then on the Finish button.

You can use the Web Publishing Wizard to send your Web content, HTML files, and graphics to the Web server that runs your Web site, but what if you are an ISP and you want to receive Web content from your users? In this case, you can use another new addition to the IIS family of programs, the *Posting Acceptor*, and we'll look at it next.

Working with the Posting Acceptor

The Posting Acceptor is an add-on to IIS that ISPs and other Web content providers can use to publish content according to the HTTP Post RFC 1867. Posting Acceptor is the intermediary that allows IIS, Microsoft Peer Web Services, or Microsoft Personal Web Server to accept Web content and HTML pages from the Web Publishing Wizard or from Netscape Navigator, using any standard HTTP connection.

NOTE Posting Acceptor runs on Windows NT Server, Windows NT Workstation, and Windows 9x.

Posting Acceptor allows IIS to receive files from clients using the HTTP multi-part/form-data method to post their Web content. Posting Acceptor can also provide this same function simultaneously to a series of servers by means of the Microsoft Content Replication System (CRS). Posting Acceptor provides the following functions:

Authentication of content publishers Authentication can be performed by any method supported by both the server and the client browser. You can also control which directories users can post into by applying ACLs to the possible destination directories, and you can control who is allowed to post to your Web site by creating user accounts for those users.

WARNING Posting Acceptor does not allow anonymous connections.

Processing a content post once it is received If you want to perform any additional processing after receiving the post, you can call a second URL with all the form data except the contents of the uploaded files forming the post. In place of these contents is a list of locations and sizes of the uploaded files.

Managing content reposting failures In the event of a repost failure, a warning (rather than an error) message is sent back to the user.

Creating mapping modules Posting Acceptor queries each of the installed mapping modules until one of them returns a physical location. If no module returns a location, Posting Acceptor defaults to querying IIS for the physical location of the URL. You can configure Posting Acceptor to use one or several mapping modules when routing incoming files to the right location. When more than one module is available, you can control the routing based on user permissions and configuration information in the mapping modules.

Looking Inside Posting Acceptor

Posting Acceptor is an ISAPI application that accepts HTTP-based "POST" requests that contain a target URL for the associated content material. Posting Acceptor processes the URL to identify and locate a hosted site, and the rest of the URL is assumed to be the appropriate subdirectory. The content material is automatically saved in this subdirectory. An HTTP connection typically has four stages:

1. *Open the connection.* The client contacts the server at the address and port number specified in the URL.

2. *Make a request.* The client sends a message to the server, requesting service. The request consists of HTTP *request headers* defining the method requested for the transaction and providing information about the capabilities of the client. Typical HTTP methods include GET, for getting an object from a server, and POST, for sending data to the server.

3. *Make a response.* The server sends the appropriate response back to the client. The response consists of *response headers* describing the state of the transaction and its status and the type of data being sent.

4. *Close the connection.* The connection is closed. HTTP is a stateless protocol, which means that a client can make a series of requests to the server but that each request is treated independently and the server has no record of the previous connections.

ISPs and Posting Acceptor

As an ISP, you are often required to support and host Web pages for your customers; now Posting Acceptor makes this process even easier. You simply install Posting Acceptor on your Web server and create a virtual directory with an appropriate name, perhaps "users". Your customers can then post their content to the

Web server and look at it with a browser by using a URL such as http:// yourservername/users/username. Two sample pages are provided along with Posting Acceptor. One can accept multi-part/form-data method posts from Netscape Navigator (version 2.02 or later), and the other provides the ActiveX Upload control for Internet Explorer users. The Active Server Pages (ASP) file upload.asp automatically detects the type of the requesting browser and routes the user to the appropriate sample page. If the browser supports ASP, the user is routed to the page containing the ActiveX Upload control; if the control is not yet installed in the browser, the user's system is automatically updated with the control. Let's take a closer look at these files and all the other parts of Posting Acceptor:

Posting Acceptor   An ISAPI called cpshost.dll forms the central core of the Posting Acceptor application.

Content Replication System (CRS)   The module called crsmapr.dll takes care of mapping target URLs into physical locations on the hard disk.

File System Mapping Module   The module called csphost.dll queries IIS for a mapping between the target URL and a physical location on the hard disk.

ActiveX Upload control   This is an ActiveX control called flupl.cab that, when embedded in a Web page, can be used to post content files to the server. Users can drag and drop files and folders or double-click the control to select the files and folders they want to upload to the server.

ASP file   This file, upload.asp, determines the type of browser in use and then directs the browser to the appropriate content uploading form.

Sample page for Netscape Navigator users   This ASP file, uploadN.asp, contains a form with HTTP POST–specific fields in which to post files.

Sample page for Internet Explorer users   This ASP file, uploadX.asp, contains the ActiveX Upload control.

PostInfo files   There are two important PostInfo files:

- *postinfo.asp*, which is retrieved automatically by the Posting Acceptor and is used to automatically configure the client software.

- *postinfo.eg*, which is an example file located in the wwwroot directory. It contains a line that needs to be added to default.htm so that Posting Acceptor can locate the postinfo.asp file and load the information that it contains.

You can use the two sample pages described above as they are, or you can modify them to meet your own specific needs.

To prevent the system from being overpowered by a massive number of uploads, Posting Acceptor limits the total number of outstanding posts as well as the maximum post duration. You can look at or change either of these values using your favorite Registry editor:

MaximumOpenTransactions controls the number of outstanding posts; the default setting is 200.

OpenTransactionTimeout specifies the maximum length of time for each post duration; the default is 5 minutes (often written as 300 seconds).

Installing Scripts on IIS

You can create scripts to run on IIS using several programming languages. Once you have created a script, you should place it in the \scripts directory, a virtual directory for applications that has execute access. This directory is designated an application directory, and only an administrator can add programs to such a directory. Thus, an intruder cannot copy a malicious application into this directory and then execute it—at least not without securing administrator privileges first.

You must also ensure that every process that your script starts uses an account with the appropriate permissions; and if your application uses other files, the account you use with the program must have the right permissions to use those files. The default anonymous account is the IUSR_*computername* account, and this account cannot change or delete files in the NTFS without specific permission from an administrator.

> **NOTE**   Even if an intruder were able to copy a malicious application onto your system, he or she would not be able to do any damage from within the IUSR_*computername* account with its limited permissions.

If your application does not ask a visitor to enter information, you can create a link to your application in an HTML file. If it does require data from a visitor, you will probably use an HTML form or an ASP to collect that information. You can also use a URL, containing data variables, to invoke a program.

Because you can use one of many programming languages to prepare your scripts, IIS uses filename extensions to decide which command interpreter to invoke to process the script. The default interpreter associations are shown in Table 15.3.

TABLE 15.3: Default Script Interpreter Associations

File Extension	Default Interpreter
BAT, CMD, COM, EXE	CMD.EXE
IDC	HTTPODBC.DLL\

You can use the NT Server Registry Editor to create additional associations, as you'll see in the next section.

How Do I Prevent a Single Application from Crashing the Server?

By *isolating* server applications, or running them in a separate memory space, you can prevent a failing application from bringing down the whole server. It is usually a good idea to isolate applications, although you may find that they use slightly more memory. Note that server-side includes and IDC applications cannot be isolated; they must run in the Web server's memory space.

To isolate an application, follow these steps:

1. In the Internet Service Manager, select the directory that is the application starting point.

2. Open the Directory Property sheets and click on the Home Directory or Directory tab.

3. Be sure that the application name is filled in and that the Run in Separate Memory Space box is checked. Click on OK.

IIS will finish processing any current requests for this application and then create a separate process so that when the next request for the application is received, the application will be run in its own memory space.

Using Web-to-Database Connectivity Tools

In line with software developers in other fields, the database vendors are all hurrying to develop usable and convenient connections to the Internet and the corporate intranet. If in the past, you have struggled with the front-end development tools that some of these vendors provide, no doubt the idea of using a Web browser as your user interface has put a gleam into your eye.

No matter which commercial database you use, the fundamental mechanisms are the same, and reduce to three essential processes:

- Using data-entry statements to build the database

- Forming and submitting a Structured Query Language (SQL, pronounced *sequel*) query to the database

- Receiving and processing the results of the query

SQL contains about 60 commands used to create, modify, query, and access data in a database. Originally developed by IBM, SQL has been implemented by all the major database vendors. SQL is implemented in one of two ways:

- *Static SQL statements* are coded into application programs, and as a result, they do not change. These statements are usually processed by a precompiler before being bound into the application.

- *Dynamic SQL statements* are much more interactive, and they can be changed as necessary. If you normally access SQL from a command-line environment, you are using the dynamic version, which may be slower than static SQL, but is obviously much more flexible.

Whether you use an on-screen query or enter the SQL by hand is not important; the objective is the same—to pass the query to the database in a form it can understand. And when the database answers the query, the data must be formatted into a report or a screen so that it can be read by the users. Figure 15.27 summarizes the transactions that take place when accessing database content using a Web browser.

FIGURE 15.27:

Accessing a database using a
Web browser and SQL

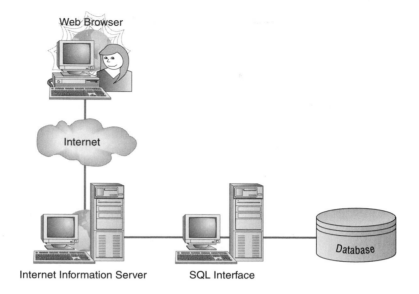

When you use a Web browser to access the database, there are some important differences:

- Your users (or customers if you are connected to the Internet) perform queries by completing HTML data-entry forms with fill-in-the-blank fields.

- CGI scripts or ISAPI programs take the information entered into the form, process it into a SQL query, and then pass it to the database.

- The same set of scripts receive the data back from the database, format the results using dynamic HTML pages, and send the results off for display by the customer's Web browser.

The HTML data-entry screens take the place of the user interface provided by the database vendor, and the scripts replace the custom programming done using the software development tools also provided by the vendor.

Each piece of data entered by the user into the HTML screen can be passed back to the database for processing, but much more data is available in any typical session, including the customer's Web browser type, the TCP/IP address and host-name of the user's computer, the visitor's user ID and access authentication, and the MIME types and subtypes supported by the browser. All this information can be passed back to the database if it is of interest to your company; for example, you can tailor your HTML pages based on the type of browser your visitor is using today.

Looking at ODBC

ODBC (Open Database Connectivity) is a Microsoft API that allows a single application to access many types of database and file formats. Before ODBC was defined, applications programmers had to write specific code to access every database to which they wanted to connect.

ODBC frees programmers from this restriction and uses the same set of function calls to talk to any database from any vendor. Drivers are available for almost all the popular database systems, and you can even access simple text files or Microsoft Excel spreadsheets.

NT Server uses the Registry information to decide which ODBC drivers are needed to talk to a specific data source, and these drivers are loaded automatically.

NOTE   The only disadvantage to using ODBC that programmers have voiced is that using ODBC is a little slower than accessing the database directly; this is the price we have to pay for the convenience of writing code for a single interface, and most people agree that it is a small price to pay.

Using the Internet Database Connector

Windows NT Server 4 includes the Internet Database Connector (IDC), an ISAPI application that lets the Internet Information Server access ODBC-compliant databases (such as Microsoft's own SQL Server) directly.

The Internet Database Connector is an ISAPI DLL called httpodbd.dll that uses ODBC to give access to a database. Figure 15.28 shows how this works.

FIGURE 15.28:

Components connecting IIS
to an ODBC database

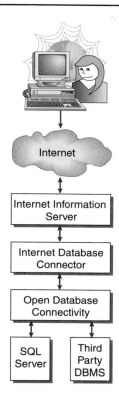

The process is much as I described in the section above but with some subtle differences:

1. A user makes a request using a Web browser.

2. This request is passed through IIS to the ISAPI DLL, which turns the request into a form that ODBC can understand.

3. ODBC passes the processed results to the appropriate driver, which in turn passes the query to the database.

4. The data extracted from the database travels in the reverse direction, going from the database to ODBC to the ISAPI DLL to the IIS and eventually back to the user's Web browser.

The IDC used two types of files to manage database access and Web page construction:

- IDC files (with the filename extension of .IDC) contain the information needed to connect to the right ODBC source and execute the SQL statement. This file also contains the name and location of the HTML extension file.

- An HTML extension file (with the filename extension of .HTX) is the template for the HTML document that will be returned to the Web browser once all the database information has been filled in by IDC.

When you first installed IIS, version 2.5 ODBC components were installed as IIS requires. Version 2.5 supports System Data Source Names (DSN), introduced so that Windows NT can use ODBC.

Using dbWeb from Microsoft

The dbWeb product is designed for people who don't want anything to do with their database other than to create Web pages that incorporate some of the data that it contains.

By using a graphical user interface, you can select data source, tables, and the columns for your query and results pages, and dbWeb then builds the queries and the HTML pages for you automatically.

You can display the results from a single record in the database, or you can display results from several records in a rows-and-columns format. dbWeb can mix and match Access data with data in Microsoft Visual FoxPro, Oracle, SQL Server, and other databases with ODBC drivers.

Unfortunately dbWeb is not a supported Microsoft product; all the help comes from an unmoderated newsgroup. You can download dbWeb free from Microsoft's Web site. For more information, use the Search facility on the home page of Microsoft's Web site to search for "dbWeb" or check the following URL:

```
www.microsoft.com/indev/dbweb/dbweb.htm
```

Creating System Data Sources

You configure ODBC on Windows NT Server using the ODBC icon in the Control Panel. Here are the steps to follow:

1. Choose Start ➤ Settings ➤ Control Panel to open the Control Panel, and then select the ODBC icon.

2. When the Data Sources dialog box opens, you may see several data sources displayed in the list box if you have already installed ODBC drivers.

3. Click on the System DSN button to open the System Data Sources dialog box. Be sure that you use the System DSN button; this is an IDC requirement.

4. Click on the Add button.

5. In the Add Data Sources dialog box, select SQL Server from the list box and click on OK.

6. In the ODBC SQL Server Setup dialog box, as shown in Figure 15.29, enter a description of the data source in the Data Source Name field. For example, for a customer service database, you might enter **Customer Data**.

FIGURE 15.29:

ODBC SQL Server Setup dialog box

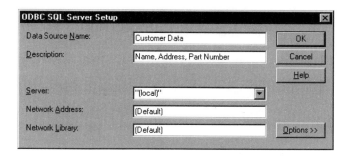

7. Enter a description of the data in the data source in the Description field.

8. In the Server field, enter the name of the SQL Server on your network; you can select a server from the list or type the name yourself. To use a local copy of SQL Server, enter **"(local)"**, including the quotes and the parentheses.

9. Enter the address of the SQL Server from which the ODBC will retrieve data. For Microsoft SQL Server, you can usually leave this set to the default.

10. Enter the name of the SQL Server Net Library DLL that the SQL Server uses to communicate with the network software in the Network Library field. Again, you can usually leave this set to the default.

The server name, network address, and network library are all specific to your NT Server installation. To access the remaining fields in the ODBC SQL Server Setup dialog box, click on the Options button, and follow these steps:

1. In the Database Name field, enter the name of the SQL Server database.

2. Choose the national language you want to use with SQL Server from the Language Name list box.

3. When the Generate Stored Procedures for Prepared Statements option check box is checked (the default setting), the SQL Server driver prepares a statement by placing it in a procedure and compiling it. When this check box is cleared, stored procedures for prepared statements are not created.

4. If a translator has been selected, you will see its name in the Translator box; if this box is blank, a translator has not been chosen. To add or change a translator, click on the Select button and make your choice from the Select Translator dialog box.

NOTE   A *translator* is a DLL that converts the data passing between an application and a data source. The most common use of a translator is to convert data from one character set to another, but a translator can also encrypt and decrypt data or apply and remove data compression.

---

5. When the Convert OEM to ANSI Characters check box is clear and the SQL Server client and server machines are using different characters sets, you must specify a translator. If both are using the same character set, check this box.

6. Click on OK, and the System Data Sources dialog box will reappear, but this time with the name of the data source displayed in the list box.

7. Click on the Close button to close the System Data Sources dialog box; then click on the Close button again to close the Data Sources dialog box.

After ODBC: OLE DB

OLE DB is being hailed as the successor to Microsoft's popular ODBC standard. OLE DB promises to surpass ODBC by providing much broader and more flexible access to both relational and nonrelational data sources for intranet and Internet users. By using OLE DB, companies can attach database functions to data sources, or *providers*, rather than requiring that the data be stored in a traditional database structure before it can be accessed. Users requesting data, or *consumers*, can request information directly from the OLE DB source or can use the services of query optimizers or transaction managers.

This approach allows a more even access method for nontraditional data such as images or 3-D objects. Microsoft is hoping that the simple approach and low cost of entry will encourage application developers to create OLE DB–based data providers for their applications, even if they have considered and rejected using ODBC in the past.

The basic OLE DB–based object is known as a *rowset* and is a collection of rows and columns of data. This data can be the traditional SQL data, such as numbers or strings, or it can be objects bound to ActiveX servers offering custom storage and retrieval mechanisms, designed specifically for the data they contain. A rowset is managed by the OLE DB–based provider, or data source, which may or may not have a traditional database structure. Other traditional database components such as indexers, optimizers, and locking mechanisms can also be included as a part of the provider, but they are not required elements.

Microsoft Advanced Data Connector

The Microsoft Advanced Data Connector (ADC) is the first database connectivity product to allow developers to use Visual Basic or Visual C++ to access remote databases over the Internet.

ADC is based on Microsoft's new OLE DB database connectivity standard and offers a collection of ActiveX components that connect standard ActiveX controls with OLE DB–based providers. Client-side JScript or VBScript applets can also access OLE DB data providers through ADC. An additional benefit is that ADC also allows caching of data from non-SQL sources.

You use ADC by programming its objects into your Active Server Pages or HTML pages for client data. ADC doesn't have a graphical user interface of its own, at least not in the usual visual programming sense. You can use HTML authoring and page-editing tools that allow you to insert nonstandard HTML tags. Working with ADC requires a rather high level of technical understanding of database interaction and Internet and intranet concepts.

ADC works with Microsoft Internet Explorer 3 and IIS 3 or later and provides updatable views only with Microsoft SQL Server, making it of interest mostly to companies using these products. The package includes a tutorial, but there is no manual available yet.

ADC is available as a free download from Microsoft's Web site at

www.microsoft.com/adc

Monitoring Your Web Server Performance

Windows NT Server performance is typically excellent, even right out of the box, and NT Server includes several powerful tools you can use to look at your Web server's system performance:

Task Manager gives you a quick overview of how each application or thread running on your system is using system resources, as well as total CPU and memory use.

Performance Monitor lets you look at how your server is doing and then decide if any tuning steps are needed. You can use the Performance Monitor to do the following:

- Collect maximum, minimum, and average values for critical system values.

- Display a view of your server's performance.

- Dispatch alerts to you (or any other user) when a specific event occurs on the server.

Network Monitor can track and display network frames for troubleshooting and monitoring network applications.

Server Manager tracks session and user activity information, as well as managing server resources.

In the next few sections, we'll look at how to use all these performance-monitoring tools, and we'll look at the sort of evaluation tasks for which each is best suited.

Using Task Manager

To start Task Manager, right-click on the NT Server toolbar, and then select Task Manager from the menu. You can also start Task Manager from the NT Security dialog box. Press Ctrl+Alt+Del (go on, try it), and when the dialog box opens, click on the Task Manager button.

TIP	The name of the Task Manager program is TASKMGR.EXE, and you can choose Start ➤ Run to open the program if you wish.

The Task Manager opens, displaying the main Task Manager window. From the menu bar, you can access the following menus:

File menu   To select a new task or close the Task Manager

Options menu   Which contains selections you can use to customize the Task Manager display

View menu   Which contains selections you can use to change the display update speeds, force the graphics to be refreshed, and display kernel usage times

And, as you would expect, a Help menu is also available.

The main Task Manager display contains three tabs or pages:

Applications   This tab lists all the tasks running on your server and shows the current status of each. You can use the information in this window to find out which of your applications is in trouble (described in the window as Not Responding instead of Running).

Processes   This tab lists all the processes running on your system by name, along with process ID (PID) number, CPU times, and memory usage.

Performance   This tab is the most impressive of the three, with its constantly updating displays of current and historical CPU and memory use. This display also includes useful totals for file handles, processes, and threads and for virtual-memory, physical-memory, and kernel-memory usage.

Even if you think that your server is sitting there doing nothing, when you look at the Performance display, you will see that your server is running somewhere between 20 and 30 processes and that you have a CPU utilization of between 3 to 5 percent, with occasional peaks to 100 percent. Figure 15.30 shows the information displayed by the Performance tab.

FIGURE 15.30:

The Task Manager
Performance tab

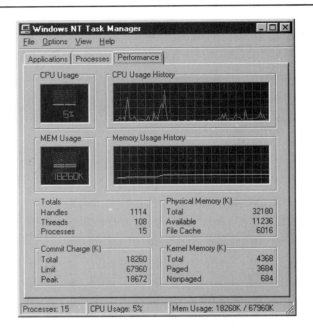

At the top of the Performance tab you will see graphical displays of CPU utilization, with current usage on the left and a display of historical usage on the right. Immediately below you will see similar displays for current and historical memory usage.

The four boxes in the lower part of the Performance tab show you how your system is using memory. The first box lists the total number of handles, processes, and threads running on your system now. The Physical Memory box describes how the memory in your system is currently being used. The Commit Charge box shows how much memory is allocated to system and application programs, and the Kernel Memory box shows the memory in use by the NT Server operating system itself.

The status bar at the bottom of the screen gives a short summary, including the number of active processes, the CPU use percentage, and the memory usage.

The NT Server Task Manager gives you a useful snapshot of the current activity on your server, but if you want more detail on specific aspects of server operation, turn to the NT Server Performance Monitor.

Using Performance Monitor

The Performance Monitor offers more extensive capabilities than the Task Manager and lets you look at resource use for specific NT system-level components. You can even use it to troubleshoot performance problems and to assess hardware upgrade requirements.

Choose Start ➤ Programs ➤ Administrative Tools ➤ Performance Monitor to open the Performance Monitor in chart mode. Time is shown along the horizontal axis of this chart, and the performance item that you are interested in examining is shown on the vertical axis. When you first start Performance Monitor, all you see is a blank screen; you have to select the objects, instances, and counters that you want to monitor. Objects, instances, and counters are defined as follows:

Object   An object is any NT Server system component that possesses a set of measurable properties. An object can be a physical part of the system (such as memory or the processor), a logical component (such as a disk volume), or a software element (such as a process or a thread).

Instance   An instance shows how many occurrences of an object are available in the system.

Counter   A counter represents one measurable characteristic of an object. For example, the Processor object has several counters, including the percentage of processor time in use and the percentage of time the processor spends in Privileged and in User modes.

To look at all the system areas you can monitor, choose Edit ➤ Add to Chart to open the Add to Chart dialog box. The first item, Processor, includes information on several counters listed in the Counter box; for example, the variable that reports how many interrupts per second the system processes is called the Interrupts/sec counter.

Windows NT Server contains hundreds of counters to track system data, such as the number of network packets transmitted per second or the number of pages swapped in and out per second. You can use them to create charts and reports that help you assess and tune system performance.

TIP

You can even use the Performance Monitor to look at activity on several servers at the same time so that you can make accurate comparisons.

Tracking disk space is always a concern for the network administrator, and you can use the Performance Monitor to show you current hard-disk usage. But what is even more useful is that you can configure the Performance Monitor to tell you when the amount of free disk space drops below a certain level. Here are the steps:

1. In the Performance Monitor, choose View ➤ Alerts to open the Add to Alert dialog box.

2. Select Free Megabytes from the list of counters.

3. In the Alert If box, check the Under radio button and enter the number of megabytes of free disk space you want to use as your minimum threshold.

Now you have to decide what you want the Performance Monitor to do when the amount of free space falls below this threshold value.

4. Choose Options ➤ Alerts. You can then choose between adding an entry to the system log or sending a message to a specific computer (such as MARKETING) or to a specific username (such as Duncan).

You can also log the counters that you are interested in to a disk file and then read them back into the Performance Monitor for later review and analysis. Choose View ➤ Log to select the counters you want to store, and then choose Options ➤ Log to name the file and to set the update rate. To play the log back later, choose Options ➤ Data From.

Windows NT Server is usually shipped with the disk-performance counters turned off. You can turn them on by typing this command at a command prompt:

```
diskperf -y
```

followed by Enter. Now restart your server, and you will be able to monitor disk usage. To turn this option off, type

```
diskperf -n
```

from a command prompt, and then shut down and restart your system.

When you install IIS on NT Server, a large number of additional counters are added, as you can see from the following tables. Some counters refer to specific services such as the Web service or the FTP service, and others are global to the whole IIS operation, such as the counters that relate to cache usage and band-width usage for all IIS services. You can use these counters for a real-time evaluation of your Web server. Let's take a look at them by category, starting with those counters associated with the IIS cache.

Cache Counters

Table 15.4 lists the counters associated with the IIS cache. To look at these counters with Performance Monitor, select the Internet Information Services Global object.

TABLE 15.4: Performance Monitor Counters Associated with the IIS Cache

Counter	Description
Cache Flushes	Number of times the cache has been flushed since the service started
Cache Hits	Number of times that a file-open, directory-listing, or service-specific object request has been found in the cache since the service started
Cache Hits %	Ratio of cache hits to all cache requests
Cache Misses	Number of times that a file-open, directory-listing, or service-specific object request was not found in the cache since the service started

Continued on next page

TABLE 15.4 CONTINUED: Performance Monitor Counters Associated with the IIS Cache

Counter	Description
Cache Size	Size of the shared HTTP and FTP cache
Cache Used	Amount of cached data, including directory listings, file-handle tracking, and service-specific objects
Cached File Handles	Number of open file handles cached for all IIS services
Directory Listings	Number of directory listings cached for all IIS services
Objects	Number of directory listings, file-handle tracking, and service-specific objects cached for all IIS services

Bandwidth Counters

Table 15.5 lists the counters associated with bandwidth usage. To look at these counters with Performance Monitor, select the Internet Information Services Global object.

TABLE 15.5: Performance Monitor Counters Associated with Bandwidth Usage

Counter	Description
Current Blocked Async I/O Requests	Number of requests currently blocked by the bandwidth throttle. Blocked requests are held in a buffer until they can be processed or until a timeout occurs.
Measured Async I/O Bandwidth Usage	Total number of bytes sent and received by your Web server, averaged over one minute; an excellent measure of the total amount of traffic on the server.
Total Allowed Async I/O Requests	Number of Web and FTP service requests received since the service started.
Total Blocked Async I/O Requests	Number of requests blocked by the bandwidth throttle since the service started.
Total Rejected Async I/O Requests	Number of requests rejected by bandwidth controls since the service started; rejected requests are not held for later processing.

Throughput Counters

Table 15.6 lists the counters associated with IIS throughput, the number of files sent and received per second, and the rate at which these files are transferred. To look at these counters with Performance Monitor, select the Web Service object.

TABLE 15.6: Performance Monitor Counters Associated with IIS Throughput

Counter	Description
Bytes Received per second	Rate at which bytes are received
Bytes Sent per second	Rate at which bytes are sent
Bytes Total per second	Rate at which bytes are sent and received; the sum of Bytes Received per second and Bytes Sent per second
Files per second	Rate at which files are transferred by the server since the service started
Files Received per second	Rate at which files are uploaded to the server from a client
Files Sent per second	Rate at which files are downloaded from the server to a client
Total Files Received	Number of files received by the Web server since the service started
Total Files Sent	Number of files sent by the Web server since the service started
Total Files Transferred	Number of files sent and received by the Web server since the service started; sum of Total Files Received and Total Files Sent

Request and Error Counters

Table 15.7 lists the counters related to specific requests and to errors. To look at these counters with Performance Monitor, select the Web Service object.

TABLE 15.7: Performance Monitor Counters Associated with Specific Requests and Errors

Counter	Description
CGI Requests per second	Rate at which CGI requests are being processed.
Current CGI Requests	Number of CGI requests being processed simultaneously.
Current ISAPI Extension Requests	Number of ISAPI extension requests being processed simultaneously.

Continued on next page

TABLE 15.7 CONTINUED: Performance Monitor Counters Associated with Specific Requests and Errors

Counter	Description
Delete Requests per second	Rate at which HTTP requests using the DELETE method are being made.
Get Requests per second	Rate at which HTTP requests using the GET method are being made; GET requests are usually made for file retrieval and image maps, though they can also be used in HTML forms.
Head Requests per second	Rate at which HTTP requests using the HEAD method are being made; such requests usually indicate that the client is asking if the current document has changed and needs refreshing.
ISAPI Extension Requests per second	Rate at which ISAPI extension requests are being processed.
Maximum CGI Requests	Maximum number of CGI requests processed since the service started.
Not Found Errors per second	Rate at which Not Found errors are occurring; a Not Found error is reported back to the client by the error code 404.
Other Request Methods per second	Rate at which other request methods occur (not including DELETE, GET, HEAD, POST, PUT, or TRACE requests that are already handled by other counters).
Post Requests per second	Rate at which HTTP requests using the POST method are being made; POST is often used in HTML forms.
Put Requests per second	Rate at which HTTP requests using the PUT method are being made.
Total CGI Requests	Number of CGI requests made since the service started.
Total Delete Requests	Number of DELETE requests made since the service started.
Total Get Requests	Number of GET requests made since the service started.
Total Head Requests	Number of HEAD requests made since the service started.
Total ISAPI Extension Requests	Number of ISAPI extension requests.
Total Method Requests	Number of HTTP DELETE, GET, HEAD, POST, PUT, and TRACE requests.

Continued on next page

TABLE 15.7 CONTINUED: Performance Monitor Counters Associated with Specific Requests and Errors

Counter	Description
Total Method Requests per second	Rate at which HTTP DELETE, GET, HEAD, POST, PUT, and TRACE requests are received.
Total Not Found Errors	Number of Not Found errors.
Total Other Request Methods	Total request methods (not including DELETE, GET, HEAD, POST, PUT, or TRACE requests, which are already handled by other counters).
Total Post Requests	Number of requests using the POST method.
Total Put Requests	Number of requests using the PUT method.
Total Trace Requests	Number of requests using the TRACE method.
Trace Requests per second	Rate at which TRACE method requests are received.

Connection and User Counters

Table 15.8 lists the counters associated with Web connections, logons, and users. To look at these counters with Performance Monitor, select the Web Service object.

WARNING   For all the counters that monitor connection activity, the counts are always shown as the total for all Web sites, regardless of the Instance selection you make in the Performance Monitor.

TABLE 15.8: Performance Monitor Counters Associated with Web Connections and Users

Counter	Description
Anonymous Users per second	Rate at which anonymous user logons are received.
Connection Attempts per second	Rate at which connections to the Web service are being attempted, shown as an average for all Web sites.

Continued on next page

TABLE 15.8 CONTINUED: Performance Monitor Counters Associated with Web Connections and Users

Counter	Description
Current Anonymous Users	Number of users with an anonymous connection to the Web service. If a client requests an anonymous connection and is rejected, but then provides valid authentication information, that connection is not counted as an anonymous connection.
Current Connections	Number of connections to the Web service, shown as the current total for all Web sites and all users, both anonymous and nonanonymous.
Current Non-Anonymous Users	Number of users with a nonanonymous connection to the Web service.
Logon Attempts per second	Rate at which logon attempts are being made to the Web service.
Maximum Anonymous Users	Maximum number of concurrent anonymous user connections.
Maximum Connections	Maximum number of concurrent user connections.
Maximum Non-Anonymous Users	Maximum number of concurrent nonanonymous user connections.
Non-Anonymous Users per second	Rate at which nonanonymous user logons are received.
Total Anonymous Users	Number of users who established an anonymous connection since the Web service started.
Total Connection Attempts	Number of attempts to connect to the Web server since the service started as a total for all Web sites. This count does not include TCP and IP connection attempts; to see these connection attempts, you must use the Connection counters provided by the TCP Performance object. See the Windows NT Server Resource Kit for further information.
Total Logon Attempts	Number of successful logons to the Web server since the service started; this total does not include failed attempts during which a client was able to connect but was unable to log on to the system.
Total Non-Anonymous Users	Number of users who established a nonanonymous connection since the Web service started.

TIP

In addition to the Performance Monitor counters described in this section, you can also look at the counters relating to the TCP, IP, and Network Interface performance objects. You must first install Simple Network Management Protocol (SNMP) to activate these counters. See the Windows NT Server *Resource Kit* documentation for further information.

You can also load previously saved Performance Monitor charts so that you don't have to re-create your favorite displays each time you want to look at a particular counter or at the relationship between two counters. Performance Monitor chart files are saved with the filename extension .PMC, and you will find a particularly useful set of counters in the file msiis.pmc in the windows\system32\inetsrv\wwwroot\samples\tour directory.

Looking at the most important Performance Monitor counters can give you a head start on planning your future hardware acquisitions, and Table 15.9 lists the counters you can use to track specific system resources.

TABLE 15.9: Performance Monitor Counters Used in Resource Planning

System resource	Counter
Logical disk	% Free Space
Memory	Pages/sec, Available Bytes
Physical disk	% Disk Time, Avg Disk sec/Transfer
Processor	% Processor Time, Interrupts/sec
Server Bytes	Total/sec
System	File Read/Write operations/sec

Start by logging this information to a log file at 15-minute intervals every day for a week. Once you identify the peak network usage times, collect this same data at 5-minute intervals. Remember, occasional values of 100 percent on some of these counters are not necessarily bad (unless the processor queue length is too long), but sustained values of 100 percent are unacceptable and certainly call for remedial action.

How Do I Monitor Posting Acceptor Performance?

For performance monitoring on Windows NT Server, Posting Acceptor adds one object called RFC 1867 Posting Acceptor to the list of objects available within the Performance Monitor. This object contains the following counters:

Bytes received per second

Current posts

ForFailed posts per second

Files received per second

Maximum posts

Posts received per second

Re-posts per second

Successful posts per second

Total bytes received

Total failed posts

Total files received

Total posts received

Total reposts

Total successful posts

Unresolved posts

WARNING   Many of the counters available in the Performance Monitor are cumulative, and so you may have to reset them as you make changes to tune your Web server. The only way to reset an IIS-related counter is to use the Internet Service Manager (ISM) to stop and then restart the appropriate service. This obviously has a few drawbacks, so proceed with care.

Using Network Monitor

Network administrators can monitor and troubleshoot network-related problems using the NT Server Network Monitor to capture and display network frames, or *packets*. To make the most of Network Monitor, you have to know a great deal about networking protocols and their data formats, and those topics are well beyond the scope of this book. All I can do is tell you where to find the Network Monitor and what you can use it for; after that, you are on your own.

Network Monitor is not part of the default NT Server installation. To install Network Monitor, follow these steps:

1. Select the Control Panel and open the Network object.

2. Choose the Services tab and then click on the Add button.

3. In the Select Network Services dialog box, choose Network Monitor Tools and Agent from the selections in the Network Services list box.

4. Click on OK, and NT Setup copies the appropriate files from your original NT Server CD-ROM onto your hard disk.

Once installation is complete, you can start the Network Monitor by choosing Programs ➤ Network Administration.

Network Monitor looks at the data stream on your network, which includes all the data being transmitted at any given time—control information as well as data. Because this can be an inordinate amount of data, Network Monitor lets you design a *capture filter* so that you can select a subset of the data frames on your network. You can design this filter on the basis of source or destination address, for a specific protocol property, or by several other methods. That done, you create a *capture trigger* that takes a specific action when a predefined network event occurs.

Once you capture the data, you can use the Network Monitor to display the results, and in fact, one of the best features of this program is that it performs much of the data analysis for you by translating the raw data into its logical frame structure automatically.

The version of Network Monitor that ships with NT Server captures only frames sent to or from the local computer; for a more capable product, use the version of Network Monitor shipped as a part of the Systems Management Services (SMS) package, which can capture packets from any computer on the network upon which the Network Monitor Agent software is installed. Network Monitor also provides password protection and the ability to detect other instances of itself operating on the same network segment.

How Do I Get the Most Out of *netstat*?

You can use the TCP/IP show network status command netstat to look at a snapshot of your network's performance; you will find the program in the WINNT\System32 directory.

Start netstat from a command prompt, or invoke it using the ! command from within the FTP interpreter; you can see a single screen of help information if you type **netstat /?** at a command prompt. Common command-prompt options for netstat include the following:

netstat displays the name of the protocol in use, addresses using friendly names, the port number in use on the local computer, and the state of the connection.

netstat -n displays the name of the protocol in use, socket addresses, and the state of the connection.

netstat -s -p tcp displays TCP/IP statistics, including current connections, failed connection attempts, reset connections, segments received, segments sent, and segments retransmitted.

These netstat command-prompt options are slightly different from the netstat options under Unix.

Because Gopher sessions tend to be short, it is difficult to get the timing exactly right with netstat, and you may not invoke netstat fast enough to collect any meaningful data. Performance Monitor is much better under these circumstances because it can display data over time rather than at a single instant. As you use both these tools, you will find that netstat is the best bet for looking at the status of connections and Performance Monitor is best for checking the status of your users.

Using Server Manager

The NT Server Manager plays two roles:

- It manages server resources.

- It displays up-to-the-minute information on shared resources and relationships between servers.

In this section, I'll concentrate on its monitoring and reporting functions.

Using Server Manager you can look at and track the following:

- Information on the number of printers in use and the number of open file locks
- The resources open during a session
- How long a resource has been open
- How long a session has been idle
- Information on all users with currently active sessions on the selected computer

Server Manager presents a snapshot of system usage. To see the server's usage statistics since startup, from a command prompt type

```
net statistics server
```

and then press Enter.

The best way to start looking at your system is to use the Server Manager's Properties dialog box, which you can open in several ways. Select Programs ➤ Administrative Tools ➤ Server Manager to open the main Server Manager window. Now, do one of the following:

- Select a computer from the list in the main window and choose Properties from the Computer menu.
- Select a computer and press Enter.
- Double-click on the computer's name.

TIP   You can also open this dialog box by clicking on the Server icon in the Control Panel on the computer about which you want to collect statistics.

The Properties dialog box opens, displaying the Usage Summary box and below this a row of five buttons. The Usage Summary box shows the following:

- The total number of user sessions
- The total number of shared resources currently open on the server

- The total number of named pipes currently open on the server

- The total number of file locks held by open resources on the server

The buttons below this box include the following:

> **Users** lets you look at all the users connected to the server and the resources opened by each user. You can disconnect one or all of the currently connected users.
>
> **Shares** displays the server's shared resources and which users are connected to which resource. You can also disconnect one or all of the currently connected users here.
>
> **In Use** displays all the open shared resources on the server and lets you close one or all of the resources.
>
> **Replication** allows you to manage directory replication for the server, as well as the path for logon scripts.
>
> **Alerts** lets you look at and manage the list of computers and users that will be notified when an alert occurs on the server.

Before you disconnect any users, you should send them a message to tell them of your intentions. To do so, choose Computer ➤ Send Message.

Once you become familiar with the information available in all these NT Server monitoring tools under normal operating conditions, you will be much better equipped to detect abnormal conditions when they do occur.

Troubleshooting Your Web Server

One of the main duties of the Webmaster is to troubleshoot server problems. Trained staff should be available on a 24-hour basis to keep your Web site running smoothly, and your ISP should also have staff available at all hours. Server problems invariably fall into one of two areas:

- Configuration problems

- Access problems

Let's look at configuration problems first.

Fixing Configuration Problems

Finding and fixing configuration problems can be a real challenge. Configuration problems can be subtle and hard to pin down, but there is one thing going for the Webmaster: a configuration problem is most likely to occur immediately *after* someone has made some sort of change on the Web server. "It was working OK yesterday" and "I didn't change anything" are two frequently heard cries in Web serverland. Here are some things that can and do go wrong.

Errors in Filenames

Many configuration problems you are likely to encounter will be wrong or misspelled filenames. When HTML files are prepared on a system not connected to the Web server, a simple typo in a filename can prevent all sorts of operations from working properly. Image maps that once performed flawlessly now refuse to work at all, and links that once led to other files on other systems now generate error messages. Nothing is more frustrating than clicking on a link and then seeing the message "ERROR: The requested document is not available."

TIP   Always double-check your typing.

Finding HTML Errors

If you are preparing your HTML content files without the benefit of an HTML publishing application, check your HTML syntax very carefully. Check for missing quotation marks in your HTML code; certain browsers can produce some funny looking output if you forget to close a set of quotation marks.

Look for nesting errors in your HTML code. Almost all HTML elements can be nested, but the rules concerning which element can be nested inside another can be complex. And remember that elements can never overlap; you must always end one element before you start the next one. Certain browsers will apparently let you get away with nesting errors, making them very difficult to spot, which emphasizes the need to test your HTML code with several browsers.

The HTML specification states that when a browser encounters HTML code that it does not understand, the browser should ignore the tag or the attribute. This in itself may lead to unexpected results that have nothing to do with your coding but with the capabilities programmed into the browser.

If you encounter problems with your image maps, be sure that the HTML code contains ISMAP in the <IMG> tag and that the configuration files that map the portions of the image map are still correctly named.

Locating Script Problems

The results of script errors can be obvious and easy to see but the scripts themselves can be very difficult to troubleshoot and fix because several elements are at work:

- IIS itself
- The script
- The file or databases with which the script interacts

It might be as simple as a missing file, or it might be a complex programming problem. If you have a previous version to fall back to, do so as you trace the problem.

Be sure that the permissions are all set appropriately and that the directories containing any executables are all accessible. And don't forget to check the NT Server error logs to see if there is another reason for the script not executing properly. One of the most obvious causes of script failure is that something is wrong with one of the files on which the script itself operates.

Because the main tool used to access the results of a CGI script is the Web browser itself, troubleshooting scripts can be a tedious job indeed. And the browsers can even mask problems with its inconsistent error-message reporting.

If your script manages information that a visitor has entered into a form, don't make assumptions about any data you receive. Even though you have asked a visitor to enter his or her ZIP code in the form, don't assume that the field will actually contain numbers—you never can tell what a visitor will enter.

Isolating Access Problems

The second common kind of error you will encounter is that a visitor can get only limited access to your Web site or, in some cases, no access at all.

Assuming that the visitor has the basic components in place to access any Web site on the Internet—including a browser, a fairly fast modem, and an Internet account—what might prevent someone from accessing your Web site? Let's take a look at what can go wrong on your Web server.

Server Access Problems

If your visitors cannot get through to your Web site, there may be a problem with the communications link between your Web server and your ISP or between your ISP and the rest of the Internet. When you first contact the ISP with a view to using its services, ask about the monitoring equipment it uses and its service guarantees. You can also ask to see its performance statistics.

If the problem is in the communications link between your site and that of your ISP, it is probably time to call the phone company. This kind of problem, unfortunately, can lead to a great deal of fingerpointing as each player blames the problem on someone else.

You can help isolate the problem yourself by using your favorite browser, first on the server itself and then, if that works, by moving farther and farther from your server until the connection ceases to work. This does not have to be physical distance. You might try first to access the server from a computer on your local area network; if that works, try dialing out to the Internet using another computer, and then try connecting to your site as any visitor would.

Errors on Connection

If you can connect to the server, the problem is not in the various communications links between your server and the Internet; it is probably on the server itself.

A visitor may be trying to access a password-protected area of the server using the wrong password, or a visitor may be trying to access the server from a new and unusual location with an IP address that you have decided to screen out.

If the visitor can actually access your site but his or her browser displays an error message when attempting an operation, the error number associated with the message should give some clue as to the nature of the problem. Table 15.10 lists some of the most common HTTP error codes, along with the reasons they might occur.

TABLE 15.10: HTTP Error Numbers and Descriptions

Error Number	Description
400	The request syntax was wrong.
401	The request requires an `Authorization:` field, but none was provided.
402	The requested operation costs money, but the browser did not specify a valid `Chargeto` field in the request header.
403	You have requested a resource that you do not have the permissions to request.
404	The server cannot find the URL you requested.
500	The server has encountered an internal error of some unspecified kind and cannot continue with your request.
501	The request you made is a legal request, but is not supported by this server.

If you are using the latest additions and extensions to HTML, a certain number of visitors to your Web site will not have browsers that support these new features, and they will not be able to see some or all of your content.

And if you have loaded your site with image maps and other complicated graphics, users with slow modems will either go to another site rather than wait for the image to load or will access your site in text mode to avoid the problem altogether and speed their access. Either way, they will not see what you intended them to see.

How Do I Troubleshoot IIS Error Messages?

Here is a short selection of some of the messages that you may receive from IIS:

```
A home directory already exists for this service. Creating a new
home directory will cause the existing directory to no longer be
a home directory. An alias will be created for the existing home
directory.
```

This warning message (which does not appear in the NT Server Event Log) indicates that you are trying to create a home directory when one already exists; you can only have one home directory for each virtual root.

```
No administerable services found.
```

Continued on next page

When trying to connect to a server, no installed services were found. In other words, the Web, FTP, or NetShow servers are not installed on the computer to which you are attempting to connect.

`The alias you have given is invalid for a non-home directory.`

You have tried to assign the alias "/" to a directory which is not a home directory; you can only use the alias "/" with a home directory.

`Invalid server name.`

When attempting to connect to a server, you typed an invalid server name; just keep trying, and check your typing.

`More than 1 home directory was found. An automatic alias will be`
`generated instead.`

IIS has found a duplicate home directory. For more on how to manage IIS error messages, see the section "Custom Errors Property Sheet" earlier in this chapter.

Optimizing IIS Performance

As soon as your Web site goes on-line, someone will tell you that it is too slow. This is going to happen; so you might as well get ready for it now. A visitor's perception of the performance of your Web site is influenced by the following:

- The speed of the visitor's communications link

- The speed of the visitor's computer and the nature of his or her Web browser

- The speed of the Internet connections between the visitor's access point and your server

- The level of traffic on the Internet when the visitor tries to access your site

- The number of simultaneous visitors your Web site is currently managing

- The number of non-Web-related tasks that your Web server is currently handling

- The speed and capacity of your Web server hardware

Notice that I said a visitor's perception of the performance of your Web site; the problem may not be on your server, and it may not be within your control. You should do some checking before you assume that you need more powerful hardware. You should also review the design of your Web pages. Eliminating design faults can help your Web site to be more efficient.

TIP

When running IIS, don't run a screen saver program on the server. Screen savers often perform some quite intense calculations to decide what to do next, which can impose a completely unnecessary load on your server. If you don't want people to see what's displayed on the monitor, just turn it off.

Having said all that, of course, a time comes when you will need to upgrade your Web server hardware. How will you know when? You can either wait for the complaints to start arriving from visitors, or you can keep your finger on the pulse of your Web site by becoming a frequent visitor to the site yourself.

Monitoring Your Server

The main areas that you should monitor when considering system performance are these:

Processor performance   You can upgrade to a faster CPU, or you can add another CPU in a multiprocessor system. Think seriously about using SMP systems for large Web servers. In the Intel world, use a fast Pentium-based system with a PCI bus. If you simultaneously see very high CPU percent utilization numbers and very low network utilization numbers, the CPU is the bottleneck. You can upgrade the existing processor, or you can move to a multiprocessor system, or you can even spread your site over several servers.

Main system memory use   NT Server and NT applications are memory hungry; NT often uses as much as half your hard-disk space as a disk cache. You can't do much to speed up memory, but you can add a faster hard disk so that virtual memory operations are optimized.

Hard disk space and use   Buy big disks with fast seek times, and be sure you don't choke performance by using slow disk controllers. Use 32-bit SCSI-II or SCSI-III host adapters. If the CPU utilization on your site is low, the network card is not saturated; but if the hard-disk measurements are high, you definitely have a hard-disk bottleneck. This can often happen on Web servers where the amount of RAM is small, and either a large number of file requests are made or the files themselves are large, as is the case with audio and video files. Either way, IIS cannot retrieve the requested material from the cache and so must go directly to the hard disk every time. Remember that hard-disk space can be consumed in two ways:

- It can be occupied by your Web-site content—HTML files, CGI scripts, FTP archives, and the like.

- It can be used as virtual memory swap space.

Network interface cards   Use 32-bit network interface cards if your server hardware can support them; PCI and EISA certainly can. In some high-traffic cases, 16-bit network cards can perform poorly. Choose cards with drivers that support interrupt moderation, a feature that prevents the processor from being overwhelmed by large bursts of interrupts.

Improving IIS Performance

IIS running on an Intel Pentium-based system should be capable of handling more than a thousand simultaneous connections, but you may find that specific areas, rather than overall server performance, are causing you problems. Once you start evaluating the performance of your server, you can attack many areas with a view toward improving performance. Here are some areas in which to start:

Improve network performance   If you use several protocols on your network, you may find that TCP/IP drops more messages than you might anticipate. This is because the high-traffic IPX protocol can grab more processor time. Limit your network to supporting only the TCP/IP protocol if you can possibly do so. Use Network Monitor to look at the traffic levels on the different network segments.

Restrict bandwidth   By monitoring and controlling the amount of bandwidth made available for IIS, you can reserve some portion for other essential services, such as e-mail. Look at how demand varies during the day and night and according to the day of the week. If you consistently use more than 50 percent of the bandwidth available, consider upgrading to a faster Internet communications connection.

Limit connections   You can also limit the number of simultaneous connections to your Web server as a way of conserving resources for other services using the server. Keep in mind that a browser typically makes a whole series of connections to the server to download a page of text or text and graphics; once you exceed the limit, any subsequent requests may be refused.

Limiting services   You can also improve overall system performance by removing unnecessary NT services; if you don't have a printer on your Web server, you don't need the Spooler service. Remember that NT starts a large number of services by default; look at the list carefully, and run only the ones you really need.

Redistribute the load   If your server processors are at capacity, consider distributing the load over additional server resources or consider redistributing tasks between existing servers.

Adding processors   Evaluate processor load on your system during periods when you see an average number of connections, and then add sufficient processing power to handle at least twice that average load.

Upgrade the L2 cache   When adding or upgrading processors, be sure to use processors with a large secondary (L2) cache; 2MB or more is ideal.

Redesign your Web site   Look at the number of CGI scripts, ASP files, audio and video, and ODBC applications you run on the server; such applications are all extremely CPU-intensive and require much more power than static HTML pages. Examine each one carefully to ensure that it is absolutely necessary, and if it isn't, get rid of it. And if you use a lot of large bitmapped images, think about getting rid of some of them, too. Try different formats for different kinds of graphics (the JPEG format usually creates the smallest file for a photograph, while GIF usually creates the smallest file for a computer-generated graphic) and choose the format that produces the smallest size.

Reexamine security   SSL, encryption schemes, and complex authentication methods all require significant levels of processing and will impose a heavy load on the processor. Larger encryption keys will demand more physical memory, and all complex security systems create a large network traffic burden. A server using SSL can be tend to be 100 times slower when downloading a file than a server without SSL. Look at your security requirements carefully in light of this additional load.

Balance memory use against response time   In the end, this is what it all comes down to: a trade-off between memory use and response time. If you increase memory use, you will normally increase response time, but as you do so, fewer system resources are available for other NT services.

You can use the NT Server Performance Monitor described earlier in this chapter to track the level of resource utilization on your server and to look at the number and frequency of pages swapped from memory to your hard disk as part of NT Server's virtual memory management system.

Combine this with memory and other system information from the Windows NT Diagnostics displays, and you will quickly build a complete picture of your server's performance. When the server consistently maintains high utilization levels, it is time to upgrade your hardware. If Network Monitor tells you that either the client or the server network connection is close to 100 percent utilized, the network itself is the most likely culprit. Once again, there is no silver bullet, no single right answer for all Web sites; you will have to evaluate the needs and resources on your system using the tools and methods I have described in this chapter and then act accordingly.

CHAPTER

SIXTEEN

16

Tuning and Monitoring Your NT Server Network

■ Using Performance Monitor

■ How to tune your system

■ Working with browsers

■ Using Event Viewer

■ Working with Task Manager

■ Using Network Monitor

Even without any tuning, NT Server usually offers better performance than many other operating systems. It's a good thing that NT tunes itself well, because Microsoft didn't leave us many "levers" with which to tune an NT Server. But there *are* a few such levers, and a little adjustment can increase the responsiveness of your network. All networks are built out of components from many vendors. Only with a systematic approach (and a few tools) can you hope to track down network failures. This chapter offers a simple, down-to-earth approach to network troubleshooting that will get you the fewest network problems for the least money.

Using the Performance Monitor

If you can't measure it, you can't tune it.

NT comes with a number of measurement and monitoring tools, but the two best are the Performance Monitor, or *Perfmon*, and the Network Monitor, or *Netmon*. Of the two, Perfmon is by far the more powerful. Learning to use the Performance Monitor correctly is useful if you want to reduce the amount of work you have to do to maintain the network. (You learn about Network Monitor in Chapter 15.)

The Performance Monitor can

- Log minima, maxima, and averages of critical system values

- Send alerts to you (or any other network member) when important things occur on the network

- Provide a simple, visual view of your network's "vital signs"

- Log network data over a period of time and then export that data to a comma- or tab-delimited file

Start up the Performance Monitor, and you see a screen like the one in Figure 16.1. The Performance Monitor comes up by default in Chart mode. There is also a Report mode, an Alert mode, and a Log mode.

FIGURE 16.1:

Performance Monitor dialog box

FIGURE 16.1:

Performance Monitor dialog box

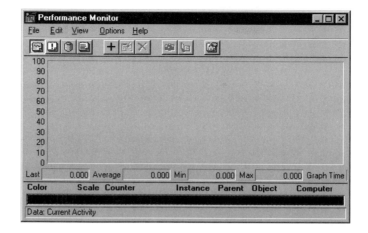

Charting with the Performance Monitor

Start out in the Performance Monitor with the Chart mode. Click Edit and then Add To Chart, and you get a multitude of things that you can monitor. Let's pick an easy one to start. How many bytes per second is the server processing? Once you've clicked Edit and Add To Chart, you see a dialog box like Figure 16.2.

FIGURE 16.2:

Add to Chart dialog box

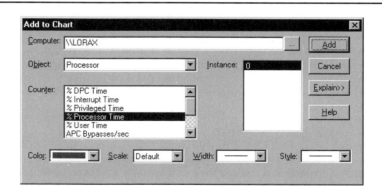

The Object drop-down list box lets you select the general area of items to monitor. The first one, which you can see in the dialog box, is the object Processor, a collection of information about your server's processor. Information is categorized as % Privileged Time, %Processor Time, % User Time, or Interrupts/sec. Each of these particular pieces of information is called a *counter* and is listed in the Counter box. For example, the piece of information that reports how many interrupts per second the system experiences (Interrupts/sec.) is a counter.

Notice also the Computer field. That's important; it means that you can use Perfmon on one computer to monitor another computer across a network.

Pull down the Object list box and choose the Server object. Now the Counter box shows the Bytes Total/sec counter. Click on the Add button. The Cancel button is renamed Done. Click the Done button and you see a screen like the one in Figure 16.3. This gives you some idea of how busy your server is.

FIGURE 16.3:

Adding to the Performance Monitor

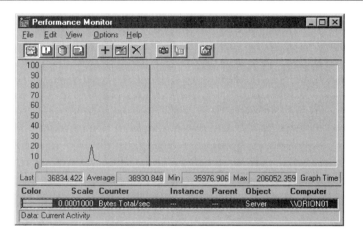

Notice that this server isn't terribly busy. But minimize the Performance Monitor, do some things, and come back to it later—after all, NT *is* a multitasking system, and it can do several things at once. Return to it after a while and you see Last (most recent bytes/second value), Average, Min (minimum value over the sampling period), and Max.

Server bytes/second is one of the basic counters that tells you how busy your server is. Other counters include

- Percentage of processor utilization (object Processor, counter % Processor Time) tells you how CPU-bound the server is.

- Pages swapped in and out (object Memory, counter Pages/sec) shows you how frequently the server is swapping information from memory to disk. If this happens a lot, you know that you're running short of RAM and might want to add more to your server.

Additionally, you can monitor *several* servers at the same time. In Figure 16.4, I'm monitoring processor utilization on both LYDIA and ORION01, two servers on our network.

FIGURE 16.4:

Monitoring several servers at once

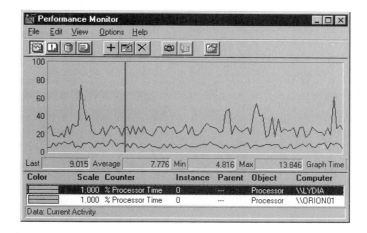

A quick look at this shows that one of the servers, ORION01, is doing a lot more work than is LYDIA, at least at the moment. But keep this running for a while, and you can get the averages and extremes that you need to be able to say that with certainty. And, by the way, that leads me to an important note.

NOTE   Running the Performance Monitor itself can significantly affect the performance of an NT machine. If you want to monitor a machine or machines, then do not run Perfmon on the machines; instead, run Perfmon on another computer—it can be an NT workstation rather than a server—and have that machine collect the data from the other machine or machines. Of course, this strategy isn't without a price, because all of the Perfmon messages generate network traffic, but that overhead usually affects things less than would running Perfmon on the measured machine(s).

What if LYDIA is a relative layabout compared to ORION01? Then you might improve performance for ORION01 users by moving a few of them over to LYDIA, if possible. ("Move a few of them" means move the directories that they use. As their data moves, they follow it.)

Tracking CPU Hogs with a Histogram

But suppose ORION01 *does* have a very high CPU utilization rate, and you'd like to find out *why*. Wouldn't it be nice to find out *what program* on the CPU was doing all the CPU hogging? You can do that with the Performance Monitor.

First, switch the Chart mode to a histogram. Click Options, then Chart. You see a dialog box like the one in Figure 16.5.

FIGURE 16.5:

Chart Options dialog box

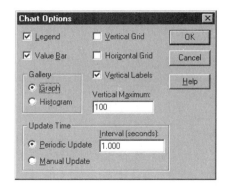

Under Gallery, click the Histogram radio button, then OK to return to the main Performance Monitor window. Next, insert the counters for each process in the system. Just click Edit and then Add to Chart and choose the Process object. You see the Add to Chart dialog box again (see Figure 16.2).

Notice that the Instance list box now names all of the processes active on your computer. One by one, you can click on a process's name in the Instance list box, then click Add to add that process to the list of things being monitored. You can easily select *all* of the processes by clicking one process, then pressing Ctrl+/. You don't want to select the _Total instance, as it's just a redundant sum of all processes, so Ctrl+click it to remove it from the list.

For example, my server shows the screen in Figure 16.6 when I monitor the processes running on it.

FIGURE 16.6:

Performance Monitor histogram

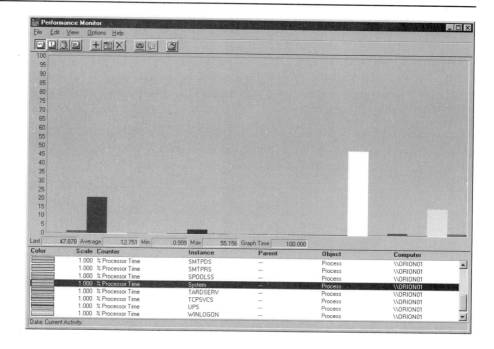

In this particular case, the process named System (whatever that is) grabs a fair amount of the CPU. Where could you use this? Suppose you used an NT server in a client-server network, and the network bogged down. The machine acting as an application server might have more than one application server program running on it, and you could use this tool to find out which of the server programs was grabbing most of the CPU.

Some servers are CPU-blocked; others are memory-constrained and, in fact, it's more likely in the NT world for servers to be constrained by the amount of memory that they have than by their CPU power. To find out which processes are using what memory, just choose the Process object, choose the Working Set counter, and choose the processes with Ctrl+/, just like you did in the last example.

Building Alerts with the Performance Monitor

Another neat thing to be able to keep track of on a server is the amount of free space left on it; if it gets too low, a LAN disaster may follow. (The counter for free space on the server is part of the object LogicalDisk, with counter Free Megabytes.)

You probably don't want to have to *watch* the Performance Monitor to keep an eye on free server space. It would be nice if the server just came and tapped you on the shoulder when the free disk space dropped below some critical value. You control that with Alerts. Click View, then Alert, and the screen will change. Again, you have to add Free Megabytes to the list of observed counters, just as you did for the Chart view. The dialog box that you see when you try to add Free Megabytes to the Alert view, however, looks a bit different, as you see in Figure 16.7.

FIGURE 16.7:

Add to Alert dialog box

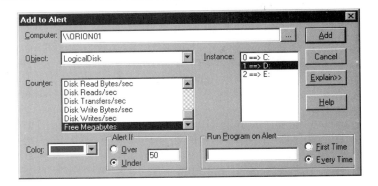

Now there are two new fields—Alert If and Run Program on Alert. I can tell the program to alert me if the disk shows fewer than, say, 50MB free by putting 50 in the Alert If field and clicking on Under. Notice that there are multiple instances in the dialog box because there are multiple drives on the server.

What does the system do when it sees fewer than 50MB free? You control that by clicking Options and then Alert. You see a dialog box giving you the option to either put an entry in the system log or send a message to either a machine name (like MICRON133) or a user name (like Mark). Unfortunately, you can specify only one recipient.

Note that the alerts are NetBIOS messages, and remember that the Messenger service and the NetBIOS interface must be active on both the alerting machine and the receiving machine.

Logging Data for Statistical Reports

Few things that a network administrator can do impress quite as much as those nifty utilization graphs. (Well, better network performance *is* more impressive, but that's why you're reading this book.) By logging statistical information you can later export that data to a graphing program or spreadsheet for reporting purposes. You can log your counters to disk with the Log View command. The log can then be read into the Performance Viewer later (Options, Data From) and examined.

First, choose the Log from the View menu. You see that you can add items to the log, as with the other views, but you can only specify entire objects to add. That means that if you wanted to monitor the number of interrupts per minute, for example, you couldn't tell the log to just keep that counter—you'd have to log the entire Processor object.

Then you click Log on the Options menu and give your log file a name. You also tell the Performance Monitor how often to update the log. Finally, you click the Start Log button. (It then becomes a Stop Log button so you can stop the logging process whenever you want. After all, there are lots of spotted owls in the Northwest… Sorry, couldn't resist that logging joke.)

To play back the log, click Options, then Data From. You can then chart data, but the data in the chart will be the logged data, rather than real-time data. To revert to real-time data, go back to Options ➤ Data From and you see the option to return to displaying real-time data.

Exporting Logged Data to CSV Files

Perfmon has some rudimentary charting and table-preparation capabilities, but if you want to be able to do some really heavy-duty statistical analysis or reporting, then you have to turn to some other tool, like Excel. But a search of the menu options for Perfmon doesn't turn up a feature called anything like "export to Excel," and the lack of a cut-and-paste option means that Perfmon won't let you OLE its data, either.

How, then, do I get Perfmon data to another program? With this multistep procedure: first, you must log the objects that you want to export. Then, you tell NT to use that log file as data. You change over to Chart mode, and finally you "Export chart" to a comma-delimited file. Here's a more specific example: suppose I wanted to log the % processor utilization over some period of time, then graph it in Excel. The counter % processor utilization is in the Processor object.

First, log the object:

1. Choose Log from the View menu to go to logging mode.

2. Click Edit and then click Add to Log to add the Processor object.

3. In the Computer field, type in the name of the computer to monitor; for example, I want to monitor ORION01, so I type in **ORION01**.

4. The counter is, again, Processor, so I click that, Add, and Done.

That doesn't start up the actual logging. To do that:

1. Click Options and Log.

2. In the dialog box that appears, type in the name of the file to log the data to (I used **TEST.LOG**), and click Start Log.

3. You can also set the logging interval, how often to get and save the data. Because I want to log this for a good long time, the default interval of 15 seconds is probably too frequent; I increase it to 120 seconds.

Then, once you have enough data, tell Perfmon to chart from that data:

1. Click Options, then click Log, and then click Stop Log.

2. Go to Chart from the View menu, and click Options and then Data From.

3. Choose the Log File radio button and enter the name of your log file.

4. Click OK to return to the main Perfmon screen.

Note, by the way, that this is a *log* file; it already exists and has data in it; therefore, the data will still be in there.

5. Click Edit and click Add to Chart, and you see that the Add to Chart dialog box has had its options reduced; you can only chart counters from the Processor object.

6. Choose % Processor Time, click Add, and Done.

Finally, to send that data out to a CSV file:

1. Click File and then Export Chart. You see a dialog box that controls how to export the data.

2. Choose a filename.

3. In List files of type, choose Comma Separated Variable (CSV).

4. Under Column Delimiter, choose Comma, and click OK.

The resulting file will be in CSV format, ready for import into many applications.

Tuning Your System: The Big Four

Well, now that you have a new weapon—Perfmon—you need something to point it to. A quick perusal of the Performance Monitor shows that there are *lots* of things to monitor, and I mean *lots* of things. Watching them all would take more time than you have and logging it would require staggering amounts of disk space.

What I want to do next is to (1) introduce you to the art of tuning, (2) point out the most likely causes of problems for file servers and applications servers, and (3) recommend a few Perfmon counters that you can monitor to keep an eye on your network with minimum trouble.

Let me set the following scenario: you have a network up and running. But with time, the network seems to be slowing down. The Powers That Be start applying pressure on you to find out what's wrong and to find it out *now*.

What can you do? Well, the obvious thing to do is to throw money at it, right? Go buy more memory, an extra processor if it's an SMP (Symmetric Multiprocessor) PC; get a faster network card; get a faster disk; give the network administrator a big raise. (*Oops*—how *did* that proposal get in there?)

Doing those things *will* probably get you a faster server. But it's also a good way to throw money down a rat hole, save, of course, for the suggestion about the raise for you. If your server is spending all of its time waiting for the disk drive, then getting a faster CPU may indeed speed it up—but by a tiny percentage. Your money's better spent (logically) on a faster disk controller in this case.

In a few words, you tune a troubled server by locating and removing its bottlenecks. The big four sources of performance bottlenecks are

- The disk subsystem

- The network card and software

- The CPU

- The memory, which includes the RAM and the disk

"Remove the bottlenecks" isn't, strictly speaking, a meaningful phrase; it's kind of like saying, "Measure the top of the sky." That's because bottlenecks never go away; they just move. For example, suppose your goal is to get to work as fast as possible, and you're a law-abiding citizen. It's a 40-minute drive right now. The 30 MPH speed limits on local roads are, you feel, the thing keeping you from getting to work as quickly as you'd like. So you convince the local, state, and federal authorities to remove all the speed limits. The result: you now get to work in 26 minutes. But after a while you notice another limit: the other drivers. They get in your way, forcing you to slow down. So you decide to go to work at 2 A.M., when virtually no one's on the road. That's better: you're down to 18 minutes now. Ah, but that's when you realize that the *real* problem is your Ford Escort, with its maximum speed of 85 MPH. So you pick up a Porsche, reducing your commute to 14 minutes—*when* you make it in to work, that is; at 120 MPH, it's easy to wrap that Porsche around a lamp post. The final bottleneck, then, is a combination of the road (too many twists and turns) and you (reaction time's too slow).

Notice in my example, however, that removing each bottleneck saved time, but less and less time with each improvement. You often find that in networking, too. There is no way to remove all bottlenecks, but you can probably easily get rid of the *big* ones to get the most out of the time you devoted to tuning.

NT servers tend to either act as file servers or application servers. That's important information for tuning, because they tend to bottleneck in different places. File servers tend to respond well to increased memory, as well as speedups in disk and network boards. Application servers tend to respond well to speedups in CPU and memory speed.

Solving Disk Bottlenecks

The disk drive has the dubious honor of being a source of bottlenecks both for file servers and for application servers. For file servers, the bottleneck is obvious;

grabbing data and slapping it on the network is what file servers do. For application servers, the problem with the disk subsystem typically stems from the tremendous amount of memory needed to run application server programs. For example, Microsoft recommends 64MB of RAM for a computer running their Server Management System (SMS). It's simple with SQL Server or Exchange to start banging hard up against the amount of memory that your system has—and when that happens, the system goes after your disk drive for virtual memory. If that's the case, however, then the root bottleneck really isn't the drive, it's the memory. In fact, that's worth a note.

> **NOTE**   The single best thing you can do for an NT server is (usually) to add more memory to it.

You can recognize a disk bottleneck in a few ways. Look in the Performance Monitor and watch the object Physical Disk, and the counters Percent Disk Time and Disk Queue Length. If the percent of disk time is over 90 percent, there's a problem. Similarly, if the disk queue length exceeds the value 2, then the disk is a bottleneck.

You will not be able to record *any* disk-performance counters, however, until you run a program. On each server that you want to monitor, open up a command prompt and type

```
diskperf -y
```

This enables logging of disk counters; they're disabled by default because they slowed down low-speed 386 computers, so Microsoft thought it would be best to leave them disabled unless you decide to enable them. On a 486 or higher processor, you won't see any difference.

What can you do about slow disk performance? First, you can buy some new hardware. Let's see what to buy.

Fast Seek Times

There are two main measures of disk performance: seek time and data-transfer rate. *Seek times* are a characteristic of the particular drive you buy. *Data-transfer rate* is mainly determined by the type of disk host adapter you buy.

The faster the disk can find data, the less time we spend waiting for it. Drives nowadays have seek times in the single digits; buy them.

Better Data-Transfer Rate

Data-transfer rate is the province of the disk controller or host adapter. Here are a few features to keep in mind when purchasing a new disk controller:

- Buy 32-bit SCSI host adapters. Putting a 16-bit host adapter on your server chokes the server's ability to zap data out to the network.

- Use bus mastering host adapters. There are three methods to get the data from the host adapter to the computer's memory: programmed input/output (PIO), direct memory access (DMA), and bus mastering. Bus mastering is the fastest of the three. You can only bus master on MCA, EISA, or PCI buses.

- Get host adapters that support *asynchronous input/output*. Many SCSI-II or SCSI-III host adapters allow multiple drives to work independently. That means that you can buy a bunch of drives, hang them off a host adapter, and have all of the drives seeking at the same time. Note that most host adapters *don't* support this, meaning that you could have a host adapter with five hard disks on it—but only one of the drives operates at a time, so getting multiple drives doesn't do anything for your system's speed.

- I've been saying to "buy SCSI," and here's another reason: ATDISK and ATAPI, the built-in drivers for IDE and EIDE drives, *do not support asynchronous disk I/O*. That means that if you have a computer with two EIDE hard disks, they do not run at the same time. For example, suppose one of the drives is labeled C: and the other D:, and you copy a file from one to the other. If you could watch this copy on a millisecond-by-millisecond basis, you'd see that both C: and D: never run at the same time—they alternate. This wastes a lot of time, which is, again, why you want asynchronous drivers.

- Create stripe sets with multiple drives. Because a stripe set distributes a disk's data over several drives, reading the data can be quite fast, because all of the physical drives on the stripe set can work in parallel—assuming, of course, that you have an asynchronous host adapter.

If All Else Fails...

If you can't buy faster hardware, then try spreading the disk-intensive processes around. If you have several servers, then try moving applications from one server to another to balance the load. (Unfortunately, no Perfmon counter lets you find out which processes are running the disk the hardest.)

Tuning Network Boards and Drivers

Making your network boards work better is partly accomplished by making the software run better as well. Network I/O is a common bottleneck for file servers.

Network Counters: The Ones to Watch

In the Performance Monitor, look in the object Server to ferret out bottlenecks. Look at Sessions errored out, work item shortages, errors system, pool non-paged failures, pool paged failures, and blocking requests rejected. Another counter to watch is Network Segment/% network utilization. If you go looking for it, you probably won't find it; you must first load the Network Monitor Agent, which ships with NT (load it through the Control Panel's Network applet).

There is, however, one "gotcha" to running the Network Monitor Agent. As you know, most of the messages that run past your computer's network connection are ignored by the computer: a message from machine A to machine C passes machine B, but B's hardware will see that the message isn't for B, so it'll ignore the message. If, on the other hand, you load the Network Monitor Agent, that Agent will put your network card in so-called "promiscuous mode," where it takes note of *all* network traffic. While this is nice for logging general levels of network activity—and is essential if you want to monitor the Network Segment object—it *can* slow down your system a trifle.

The % network utilization value should remain below 30 percent on an Ethernet network, and below 90 percent on a token-ring network.

Simplify Protocols

One of the best pieces of network-tuning advice I can give you is to remove unnecessary protocols and services. Protocols and services steal memory and CPU time. Multiple protocols require multiple browse lists, which in turn steal CPU time from the machine that is the master browser, and NT Server machines are often elected as master browsers. One of the most common reasons why an NT system fails to recognize a workstation, leading to a "no domain controller was available to..." error message is that the server simply has too many protocols that it must listen to. Try to pick *one* protocol and work with that one.

If you're using the TCP/IP stack, then you find that it sometimes receives short shrift from the network because the more frenetic IPX and NetBEUI protocols grab more processor attention. As a result, the TCP/IP stack may end up dropping more messages than it would if the other protocols didn't exist; one other symptom is an incomplete browse list. If you can, remove extraneous protocols. If possible, just trim down to TCP/IP.

You can also click on the Bindings button, select NetBIOS, and choose the order in which the transport protocols are bound to NetBIOS. Basically, you're saying to NetBIOS (which is, recall, a network API, not a protocol), "When you have a message to send, send it with TCP/IP first; if that doesn't work, use IPX, and then NetBEUI." That's just one example; you can arrange them in any way that you like. If you are using TCP/IP and WINS, then binding NetBIOS to TCP/IP first will greatly reduce broadcasts in your system.

One Remedy: Segment the Network

If the network utilization is getting excessively high, you have to reduce the network traffic on that network segment. You can do that either by removing network applications—put the company Web server on a segment of its own—or by breaking up existing segments. Instead of three segments of 100 PCs, break it up into six segments of 50 PCs apiece.

But then you have to be sure to get good, fast routers to connect the network segments. NT servers can do the job fairly well on low-volume networks, but look to dedicated routers from companies like Compatible Systems, Bay Networks, or Cisco Systems for more heavy-traffic network segments.

Rearrange Your Redirectors

If you're running the NetWare redirector in combination with the Microsoft redirector, then you see a button in the Network dialog box of the Control Panel. (Actually, it's always there, but it's grayed out unless you have more than one redirector.) Click it and you will see both redirectors. You can then use buttons with up or down arrows on them to highlight a redirector and make it less or more relatively important.

Raise Server Priority

By default, the file server actually has a lower priority than does the print server, causing printing to slow down the server. Printing priority is set by default to 2, and file server priority is set to 1; larger numbers are better. You can change the

priority by modifying the Registry. In the current control set, in Services\
Lanman\Server\Parameters, add a value entry ThreadPriority, type DWORD,
and set it to 2.

Adjust PDC-BDC Traffic

All of the chatter between the PDC and the BDCs takes up processor time and
network bandwidth. In NT 3.5 and later, you can alter how often the PDC asks
the BDCs to schedule SAM updates with the PDC. By default, that time period is
300 seconds (five minutes), but you can change that in the current control set in
HKEY_LOCAL_MACHINE\System\CurrentControlSet\Services\Netlogon\
Pulse. It's of type DWORD, and you can set the value from 60 to 3,600 seconds.
You'd make that change on the PDC.

The BDCs have an important parameter to help control how SAM updates
work, as well—ReplicationGovernor. It's documented in Chapter 11. Basically,
it's a value between 1 and 100 that throttles how quickly the PDC tries to shove
updates at the BDC. At 100—the default—the PDC just sends one block after
another to the BDC until the BDC is up to date. If the PDC and BDC are on the
same network, that's fine, but over a slow WAN link it can seriously affect other
users of that WAN link. Experiment with values below 100 and use Network
Monitor to see how heavily the PDC loads the WAN link as a result.

Use Interrupt 10

IRQ 10 has a slightly higher system priority than does the more commonly
used IRQ 5, so employ it for your boards when possible.

Enable Shared RAM with TCP/IP

While there is no generally accepted benchmark for network performance that is
both generic (runs on all networks) and nontrivial, my tests with TCP/IP drivers on
Ethernet and token-ring cards show that if an option to enable shared RAM is on
your network cards, then you should do it, and use as much as possible.

This does not apply for bus master EISA, PCI, and Micro Channel cards; shared
RAM doesn't seem to improve upon their performance.

Get 32-Bit Bus Master Network Cards

Get 32-bit bus master network cards if you can afford them. You should be *sure* to
afford them for your servers. But be sure that NT drivers exist for them.

Ensure That NT Can Continue to Autotune

NT's file server module includes almost two dozen tuning and control parameters. Most of them control exactly how much memory NT devotes to different parts of the server module. For example, what's the maximum number of sessions that the server will have to keep track of at any moment in time? NT must know that so that it can pre-allocate some RAM as working space, a place in memory to track each session. That's set by an "autotuning" parameter every time you start up a server. Similarly, what's the maximum amount of memory that the server service can use at any time, both in pageable (able to be swapped out to disk) and non-pageable flavors? More autotuned parameters.

Could you choose to control these parameters yourself? If you wanted to, you certainly could, but I wouldn't recommend it. But doing some basic administrative tasks could well inadvertently make it impossible for NT to tune its own parameters.

Elsewhere in this book you'll see commands that start with NET CONFIG SERVER; for example, as you'll read in the upcoming section on the Browser, typing **net config server /hidden:yes** puts a server in "Romulan cloaking device" mode, wherein the server never appears in the Network Neighborhood. Alternatively, you might want to add a comment to the Network Neighborhood's display of your server by typing **net config server /srvcomment:***whatever comment you like*. In either case, using the NET CONFIG SERVER command (lower- or uppercase doesn't matter, by the way, save for whatever case you desire within the message itself) has a nasty side effect.

For some reason, when you set *one* parameter with NET CONFIG SERVER, NT writes out the current values of *all* of the autotuning parameters. (All these parameters are in HKEY_LOCAL_MACHINE\System\CurrentControlSet\Services\ LANManServer\Parameters.) The nasty side effect is this: when NT starts up the Server service, the Server service looks in the Registry to see if these autotunable parameters are written in the Registry. If they are, then NT does *not* attempt to re-tune them.

Why would you care? Mainly you'd care if you have changed the amount of RAM in your system. Add more RAM, reboot, and NT will adjust all of the autotunable parameters. But if they've been inadvertently cast in concrete by the simple act of hiding a server, that autotuning doesn't happen.

How, then, to restore autotuning? Look in HKEY_LOCAL_MACHINE\ System\CurrentControlSet\Services\LANManServer\Parameters; you'll see a whole bunch of entries, *if* you've done a NET CONFIG SERVER at some point. Then start deleting those value entries. Don't get *too* nuts—if you've made your server a time source, don't delete TimeSource, or if you've hidden the server, don't delete Hidden, Srvcomment, ThreadPriority, or any other entry that you have entered in the past for some reason. In particular, you'll probably need to remove entries named *anndelta, enableforcedlogoff, enablesoftcompat, maxnonpaged-memoryusage, maxpagedmemoryusage, maxrawbuflen, maxworkitems, opensearch, sessconns, sessopens, sessusers, sessvcs, userpath, users, Leave NullSessionPipes, Null-SessionShares, Size* (does it matter?), *LMAnnounce,* and *EnableSharedNetDrives.* (And please don't ask me what they do, the documentation on most of them is pretty spotty. If you want, search the Knowledge Base for any of the keywords and you probably will either get nothing or a fairly useless definition. One of the odder parameters has to be anndelta, a holdover from LAN Man; the Knowledge Base says, "This parameter is ignored." Great, guys, so why bother?)

Watching the CPU

I've already shown you how to build a histogram of the processes running on your server. That will help pinpoint any CPU hogs. Two counters can help you watch the overall CPU climate: Processor/% processor time and Processor/Interrupts/second.

Critical CPU Counters

If Processor/% processor time rises above 75 percent on average, then that CPU is working pretty hard. Also, you might keep an eye on Interrupts/second. If it exceeds 1000 on a 486 system or 3500 on a Pentium or RISC system, then more than likely something's going wrong, either a buggy program or a board spewing out spurious interrupts.

Handling Excessive Interrupts

One common cause of excessive interrupts is badly designed device drivers. Are you running any beta device drivers? I've seen beta video drivers that spew out thousands of interrupts per second. You can test this by running the standard VGA driver and comparing the interrupts before and after.

Another source of excessive interrupts are timer-driver programs. One network manager I know was seeing 4000 interrupts/second on a fairly quiet 486-based file server. After some playing around with the system, he realized that he was opening Schedule+ in his Startup group. He shut it down, and his interrupts/ second dropped to a normal rate.

I'd like to tell you that there's a Perfmon counter that lets you track interrupts/ second on a program-by-program basis, but there isn't because much of this is just trial and error. Now and then, I see a board that sends out a blizzard of interrupts if it's failing or, sometimes, even just when it's cold. You might see this when you turn a workstation on Monday morning and it acts strangely for half an hour, then settles down.

Move Programs Around

As I've recommended with other bottlenecks, one way to stop straining a resource is to stop asking so much of it. If you're running SQL Server 6.5 on a 25MHz 486SX with 24MB of RAM, there's not much I can do to help you, except tell you to move SQL elsewhere.

Buying More Silicon

The ultimate (and least desirable) answer is to buy more horsepower. But don't just throw away your money. Remember that there are two ways to make your system faster with CPUs: either buy a faster CPU or add another CPU to an existing multiprocessor computer. (If you don't have them yet, think seriously about buying SMP systems for your big servers.)

You'll find that a second processor does not increase performance by 100 percent, unfortunately. And, sadly, for some programs a second processor offers no improvement at all. That's because not all NT programs are designed to be multithreaded, and so don't take advantage of extra processors. You can pinpoint single-threaded applications by watching Process/% processor utilization, and log activity on all of the processors. If you have a dual-processor system and one processor is working hard (up over 50 percent utilization) and the other processor isn't doing anything at all, that pretty much proves that the application is single-threaded and that you need to start yelling at the application developer!

NOTE   By the way, don't run one of those heavily graphics-intensive screen savers on a server. Something like 3Dpipes could suck up 90 percent of the CPU under NT 3.x. Microsoft says that changes in the NT architecture have removed the problem under version 4, but my experiments show that running 3Dpipes still slows down a file server.

Monitoring Memory

NT and NT apps are memory-hungry. Microsoft suggests 32MB of RAM for a SQL Server machine and 64MB for an SMS machine. Even a lowly file server does well with 16-plus megabytes. You can literally throw memory at your system for as long as you like and it will probably find some way to use it. How?

Checking Memory Status

Well, for one thing, NT uses an enormous amount of its memory—up to one-half of it, in some cases—as a disk cache. The counters to watch are

- Memory/available bytes should be 4MB or more.

- Memory/pages/sec should be less than 20.

- Memory/committed bytes should be less than the physical memory on your system.

"Available bytes" is an attempt on Perfmon's part to answer the question, "How much memory could NT lay its hands on if it needed it?" If it's below 4MB, then it means that most of the memory in your system is not only spoken for, it can't be paged out to disk. That doesn't leave your machine much breathing room.

"Pages/sec" is a measure of virtual memory activity. Lots of paging means lots of juggling between the system's RAM and the disk, and the virtual memory system only does lots of juggling if it's running out of memory.

"Committed bytes" is the sum of memory that every application is using *and actually needs at the moment*. Applications start up and "reserve" memory, but they don't actually try to put data into a memory space without first "committing" the memory. If the applications in your system have collectively reserved 100MB of memory, that's no problem—it just means that there had better be 100MB of page file space on disk. But if all of the system's programs had *committed* 100MB of memory, that would imply that all of the applications running and active *right now* need 100MB—and if you don't have 100MB of RAM, your system will be constantly running the hard disk paging data in and out of the disk. Such a condition, called *thrashing*, means your NT Server will exhibit geologically slow performance.

Take a look at memory status in the Performance Monitor by looking at the Memory object, committed bytes, and pages/second. And make sure that the Available bytes is at least at a megabyte.

Controlling Virtual Memory

Why am I talking about disk usage in a section on memory? Because NT relies so heavily on virtual memory. If you supported Windows 3.*x*, then you probably learned about the paging capability of Windows, a method whereby Windows solves an "out of memory" problem on a computer by using extra *disk* space as if it were RAM space.

If you were a real Windows expert, then you knew that Windows had a particularly inefficient virtual memory algorithm, and that your best bet for Windows performance was to just increase your workstation's memory to 16MB and disable Windows virtual memory altogether.

If you tried to use that logic under Windows NT, then you found that Windows NT is quite different: it seems to require at least *some* virtual memory, no matter how much RAM you have. Oddly enough, that's because of the way that NT does disk caching—NT often allocates half of the system's RAM to a disk cache. As a result, NT is often in need of physical memory to allow it to run some program. So it starts paging.

You can adjust memory needs a bit under NT; open the Control Panel and go to the Network icon, and then click on the Services tab. Click Server and Properties, and you see a dialog box like the one shown in Figure 16.8. The important message of this dialog box is that the file server module takes up a *lot* of memory, this dialog box lets you adjust it as appropriate.

FIGURE 16.8:

Configuring Server memory usage

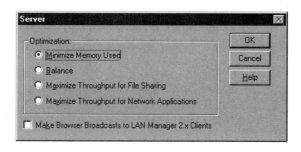

Use these guidelines to set this dialog box:

Optimization Option	When to Choose It
Minimize Memory Used	If the number of users will be under 10.
Balance	If the number of users will between 10 and 64.
Maximize Throughput for File Sharing	For more than 64 users. It allocates the lion's share of the RAM to the file server module.
Maximize Throughput for Network Application	On a client-server application server machine or a computer that will only serve as a domain controller.

The most time-consuming part about the paging process is going out and finding a place to put the data on the disk. So NT allocates a large block of disk into an area that it gives a filename: pagefile.sys. This is a contiguous area of disk. You see, having a contiguous area of disk to work with allows NT to bypass the file system and do direct hardware disk reads and writes. (Remember, this is the kernel—ring 0 on an Intel system, "kernel mode" in general—so it can do direct hardware access.)

You control the amount of allocated space on disk via the Control Panel; just click System ➤ Performance ➤ Change, and you see a dialog box like Figure 16.9.

The pagefile.sys file starts out on a 16MB machine at 27MB. NT knows that it can get to up to 27MB of disk space with direct hardware reads and writes.

How much memory does an NT system require? I'd recommend at least 32MB on an NT server. A workstation that I regularly use runs NT Server as its operating system. Despite the fact that I've got 64MB of RAM on it, it periodically starts running the disk for no apparent reason, meaning that it's juggling disk and RAM.

TIP   You can find out how much memory on an application can't be paged with an application called PMON, which ships with the *Resource Kit*.

Getting back to the virtual memory example, suppose I have a machine with 11MB of free RAM after the operating system. Add the 11 to the 27MB of pagefile.sys space, and NT has 38MB of working room, or, as the Performance Monitor would refer to it, NT on my machine has a 37MB "commit limit." If the sum of the programs that NT is running (called the *working set*) remains at about 37MB or less, then NT need not enlarge the paging file.

FIGURE 16.9:

Establishing page file size

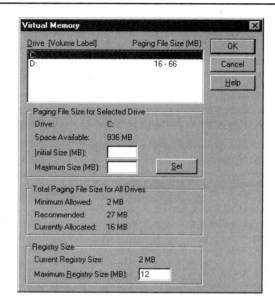

If, on the other hand, NT must get to more memory, it can expand the paging file, albeit at a cost of time. The paging file can grow up to 77MB on my system, meaning that NT can run up to 77 plus 11, or 88MB, of programs on this system before it runs out of memory.

Once NT starts enlarging the paging file, it may not enlarge it *enough*. That leads to a kind of "sawtooth" size of the paging file, as NT continues to "go back to the well" for more space until it finally runs out of space.

You can avoid this by keeping an eye on the commit limit on your machine. Add the counters Commit Limit and Committed Bytes to the Performance Monitor, and watch the difference between them. When the committed bytes exceed the commit limit, then NT must increase the page file size. If you're interested in seeing the size of the things that won't be paged, add the counter Pool Nonpaged Bytes.

One suggestion would be to log the committed bytes over a period of a few weeks with the Performance Monitor, then note the maximum value that the Performance Monitor reports. Increase that by a small amount—10 or 20 percent—and make your NT system's minimum page file that size.

Reducing Paging

NT has a virtual memory algorithm that's a bit disk-happy. It was designed to run reliably in a system with a fairly low amount of memory and lots of disk space, and it does that rather well.

On the other hand, if all that you are doing is running Word under NT Workstation on a laptop with 144MB of RAM, you might find the constantly running hard disk both worrisome and battery-draining. So there's a Registry entry that basically tells NT to chill out a bit and make more use of the RAM—and less of the page file. Located in HKEY_LOCAL_MACHINE\SYSTEM\CurrentControlSet\Control\Session Manager\Memory Management, the key's name is LargeSystemCache. It is of type REG_DWORD; set it to 0 and the disk will run a bit less.

Speeding Up Memory

You can't speed up RAM, but you can speed up the disks that virtual memory sits on. As with disks, just get fast drives and drive controllers. Get multiple drives and spread the pagefile out across drives—but *don't* put the pagefile on a stripe set; you won't get any performance improvement like that.

Defragment the drive that the pagefile sits on, run NTFS, and you squeeze the maximum out of your virtual memory.

You can't speed up RAM...or can you? Adding lots of RAM to your system won't speed it up all that much if the CPU is spending a lot of time waiting around for the RAM, as standard main memory is slower than a CPU. Modern systems use at least three levels of RAM—main memory, a small bit of very fast memory called *L1 cache*, and an intermediate-speed memory called *L2 cache*. Buying more RAM without more L2 cache may be pointless.

Back in the old days (before 1995), you could just add L2 cache to your system by buying some cache chips and popping them on the motherboard. But the Pentium II and Xeon processors only let you use cache that's built right into them, right inside the processor housing. That's a shame, as the Pentium II only includes 512K of L2 cache even though the older Pentium Pro was available with up to 1024K of L2 cache. That's why a 200MHz Pentium Pro can sometimes outperform a 300MHz Pentium II on an NT system with more than 128MB of memory—the L2 cache becomes the system bottleneck on the Pentium II. Fortunately, the Intel Xeon processor (which is still vaporware as I write this in late 1998) has 1024K of L2 cache.

That still seems insufficient, however. 1024K cache on a circa-1995 Pentium Pro was respectable—but on Intel's *flagship* processor in 1999? I don't think so—big mistake, Intel. Now, if you want lots of L2 cache, look to the new Alphas—*eight megabytes* of L2 cache on the processor.

Wondering if L2 cache is a bottleneck? The *Resource Kit* has a few Performance Monitor counters grouped into an object called "Pentium" which, if installed, will tell you how often your system had to sit around waiting for the L2 cache. Run it on the boss's machine for a week, and you just might get her to spring for Xeons—or Alphas—for the next upgrade.

Reducing Memory Requirements

Unfortunately, the best way to improve NT's memory hunger is to cut down on the features that you use, or, again, move the applications. Optional memory-hungry features include

- RAS
- TCP/IP support
- RAID

The other things that really chew up memory are the applications that you may run on your NT Server as applications servers, like SQL Server: it has a recommended memory amount of 32MB of RAM on the server.

One thing to look at, however, is the list of services. NT starts up a lot of services that you may not need. If your server doesn't have a printer, then the Spooler service is unnecessary. If all of your storage devices are SCSI, check to see if the ATDISK—the IDE interface—is active. In both cases, you can shut down a service or device. Even better, get rid of any protocols you're not using any more; they can be memory-hungry.

Locating Memory Leaks

Sometimes you see the free memory in a system just go down and down and down, even though you're not doing anything with it. Or you leave a server on Friday afternoon, go home for the weekend, and come back on Monday to find it crashed, with a message on the screen about being out of memory. You didn't do anything all weekend and hardly anybody is in the office on Saturday and Sunday. What happened?

A memory leak, that's what happened.

Memory leaks are caused by applications that have bugs in them that just make them ask for more and more and more memory from the operating system. They don't *do* anything with the memory, or perhaps they use the memory but don't manage it well. In any case, give them enough time and the memory leakers will kill your machine. Over the years, I've heard rumors of memory leaks in SQL Server, Access 95, and Visual Basic; I can't confirm them, but I've seen behavior that indicates that it's a possibility. In any case, you can locate memory leakers by logging the Process object. Recall that one of the counters for Process is *working set*; that's a measure of the amount of memory an application uses. Log the amount of memory that each process uses over time, and the leakers will stand out. Then talk to the company that wrote the application—with the Perfmon output in hand—and get the vendor to fix the leak.

Tuning Multitasking

Go to the Control Panel and open the System icon. Click on the Performance tab and you see the dialog box shown in Figure 16.10.

FIGURE 16.10:

Performance dialog box

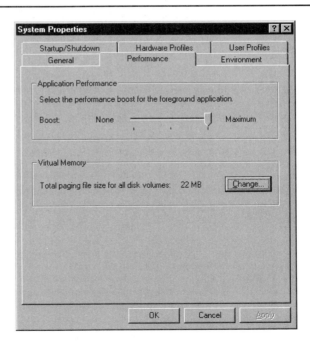

On an NT server, you definitely do *not* want the Maximum Application Response Time option. No one's going to run applications on your NT server anyway (unless it's an application server), and if they do, then it's probably just the administrator fooling around with the network. No need to slow everybody else down. Slide the arrow to None. Essentially, it says, "Don't give any special treatment to the foreground applications." Between Maximum and None, there is really only one middle setting even though it looks like you can set the slide bar to any number of positions.

A Note on Tuning NT for Multiple Applications

Sometimes your tuning problem stems from multiple applications on a single NT Server machine. In that case, I've got some bad news. People will often ask me how best to tune an NT box to run, for example, both SQL Server and Exchange. There *isn't* a best way.

NT is, as I mentioned earlier in this chapter, a "self-tuning" operating system. Perhaps the better word for it would be a "non-tunable" operating system. Think of NT as resembling in some ways a modern automobile. Older automobiles required the driver to adjust the choke (the fuel/air mixture), the spark advance (the rhythm of the spark plugs firing versus the pistons rising and falling), and the transmission gear (the ratio of engine rotation speed to wheel rotation speed). Modern cars don't require any of that. In some cases, automakers accomplished the "automatic adjustment" of car parts by simply fixing settings at a reasonable value for most drivers and leaving them that way. Such a system isn't really auto-tuned; it's pre-tuned and doesn't leave the user any ability to tweak it.

That's largely how NT is designed.

Even though you and I can't tune NT, there are things that applications can do to modify NT's performance, like allocating memory buffers and setting process priorities. These are things that a well-designed NT application like SQL Server or Exchange will do to exploit the full power of the NT box upon which they work. In essence, when you install Exchange on an NT system, Exchange tunes NT to run Exchange well; ditto for SQL Server.

But what happens if you run SQL Server *and* Exchange on the same machine? The answer is that neither application is well taken care of; instead, the NT platform ends up being pulled in different directions, resulting in a suboptimal system. So, while it's not good news, the upshot is clear: if you've got a major heavy-duty application that runs atop NT, dedicate a machine to that application.

A Tuning Summary

Before I leave this topic, let me summarize what I've said about which counters to watch, what their values should be, and what to do if they fall into the "danger" zone. My summary can be found in Table 16.1.

TABLE 16.1: Counters to Watch

Counter to Monitor	Good Values	If Not, Indicates Bottleneck In	Actions
memory/available bytes	>= 4MB	memory	Buy more memory or move big processes to another server.
memory/committed bytes	<= physical memory	memory	Buy more memory or move big processes to another server.
memory/pages/sec	<=20	memory	Buy more memory or move big processes to another server.
processor/% processor time	<= 75 percent	processor	Move processes, buy a faster processor, buy another processor if the app is multithreaded or if you're running many apps.
processor/Interrupts/sec	<=1000 (on a 486), <=3500 (Pentium or RISC)	processor	Sometimes caused by badly written drivers, beta drivers; video drivers can be particularly obvious. Or failing hardware generates interrupt blizzards. Excessive queue lengths on network cards or disk controllers cause extra interrupts.
physical disk/disk queue length	<= 2	disk	Faster disk interface, RAID, asynchronous disk drivers.
physical disk/% disk time	<=90	disk	Move processes.
network segment/% network utilization	<=30 on Ethernet	network	Segment network.

Growth Counters

Before I leave Perfmon, let me suggest a few counters that you may want to log simply because they indicate how large your network is:

- Server/Bytes total/second

- Server/Logons/second

- Server/Logons total

If any of these indicators grows quickly, the network in general is probably growing quickly, so you should zero in on bottlenecks or start planning to buy more hardware.

Understanding and Troubleshooting Browsers

Back in Chapter 2, I introduced the concept of browsers and browsing. Browsing is significant in that it can slow down a workstation's response time and clog a network with unnecessary traffic.

In case you've forgotten, browsing is a method whereby servers on the network tell a computer called the master browser who they are and what they offer to the users of the network. The browsing service in Microsoft enterprise networks makes it possible for a workstation to see what the network has to offer. A few specifics about browsing:

- The master browser designates one backup browser for about every 15 computers.

- If you run multiple transport protocols, then each transport protocol needs its own set of browsers.

- Backup browsers verify their database with the master browser every 15 minutes.

- Servers first announce their existence to the master browser, then they re-announce their existence periodically. Eventually they settle down to announcing themselves only once every 12 minutes.

- If you are running a network on TCP/IP with routers, then there is one master browser for each subnet, and one overall Domain Master Browser. They communicate with each other every 12 minutes.

Electing a Master Browser

The first browsing concept you should understand is the browser election. The first time a server (in the loose Microsoft sense of *server*, any computer that can share data, including a Windows for Workgroups, Windows 95, or NT workstation) starts up, it calls out for the master browser, so the server can advertise itself with that master browser. If no master browser responds, then the server "calls an election," suggesting the network's servers hold an election to find who would best be master browser. Elections are also held when

- A master browser is powered down gracefully.

- A server powers up only to find that a master browser exists, but the master browser computer is of a lower station, so to speak, than the server. For example, if an NT workstation powers up and finds that its master browser is a Windows for Workgroups machine, the NT workstation calls for an election.

- A server powers up and has its MaintainServerList variable (I'll cover it in a bit) set to Yes.

If you're not a master browser, then you're either a backup, a potential browser, or you've opted out of the whole election process. (I'll show you how to do that in a minute.) Backup browse servers also help remove some of the load from the master browser, as they can respond to browse requests. TCP/IP-based networks add yet another layer with a *domain master browser*, but I'll get to that later.

As explained earlier, browsers select themselves via an automatic "election" process. The outcome of that election, and whether or not there is an election at all, is determined by the type of computers on the network (NT servers get priority over NT workstations, which get priority over Windows 95 and Windows for Workgroups machines) and by two Registry settings.

Both Registry settings are in HKEY_LOCAL_MACHINE\System\Current-ControlSet\Services\Browser\Parameters, and they're of type REG_SZ. The first is called MaintainServerList, and it can have three possible settings:

- No, which means it cannot act as a browser

- Auto, which means that it will act as a browser if asked by the Master Browser

- Yes, which means that (1) it will act as a browser if asked by the Master Browser, (2) if it can't find a Master Browser, then it will call an election, and (3) this computer gets a slight advantage in an election—more details on that in a minute

NT workstations by default have this value set to Auto, NT servers have it set by default to Yes. A machine that has set its value to Yes is called a *potential browser*.

The other Registry setting, IsDomainMasterBrowser has two possible values: Yes and No; the default is No for all computers. There are two effects to setting IsDomainMasterBrowser to Yes: first, that machine now gets a fairly significant advantage in an election—again, the specifics in a minute—and, second, that machine will *always* force an election when it boots up. A machine with IsDomainMasterBrowser=Yes is called a *preferred master browser*.

Reviewing, then, you become a *preferred master browser* if your Registry has IsDomainMasterBrowser=Yes, and you become a *potential browser* if MaintainServerList equals either Auto or Yes.

A computer calls an election by issuing a broadcast called an *election datagram* to all potential browsers. The election datagram contains several parts, but the most important is the *election version*, which is essentially the version number of the browser software. The potential browser with the highest election version always wins. Essentially, that means if you had a network with a bunch of NT 4 servers on it, and one NT workstation running some imaginary version 6.5, then the workstation would win, as it's the only member of the latest version of NT.

The election packet also contains the *election criteria*, a set of information about the computer. Some criteria are more important; for example, the most important criterion is *operating system;* NT servers always beat NT workstations, which always beat Windows 95 and Windows for Workgroups machines ("always," that is, assuming the election versions are constant). In order, the criteria are

- Operating system: NT servers always beat NT workstations, which always beat Windows 95 and Windows for Workgroups machines.

- Primary domain controller: Values Yes or No, the PDC wins if it's a tie between two NT server machines.

- WINS client: Believe it or not, this is the next most important criterion. If two machines are tied (for example, suppose the PDC had MaintainServerList=No, and two regular NT Server machines were duking it out to be the master browser), and one uses WINS and the other doesn't, the one that uses WINS, well, *wins.*

- Preferred master browser: If the tie has gotten this far and one machine has IsDomainMasterBrowser set to Yes, then it wins.

- Current master browser: If the tie has gotten this far—equal values or election version, same operating system, neither one is a primary domain controller, both use WINS (or both don't use WINS), both have the same IsDomainMasterBrowser value, but one of them is currently the master browser, then the incumbent wins.

- MaintainServerList=Yes: I told you this was pretty insignificant. You've got to get pretty far down the list for this to matter, but if everything else is equal by the time you've examined all the other possibilities, and one machine has MaintainServerList=Yes and the other is set to Auto, the Yes machine wins.

- Running Backup Browser: Last criterion, only used if all other criteria are equal.

Clearly, by now we've probably got a winner. But what if we don't? Then we look at the amount of time that the computer has been up. The one that's been up longest wins. And, finally, if even *that* is equal, just take the server whose name comes first numerically and alphabetically: server Charlie would win over server Willy, for example.

It may sound as if an election is a blizzard of election broadcasts, but it isn't really. The server starting the election sends out its election packet, and every candidate examines that packet before deciding what to do. If a candidate can't beat the election packet, it just shuts up and doesn't offer an election packet.

If you want to find out which computer is the master browser on your NT Server–based network, you can use the BROWMON.EXE program that comes with the Windows NT *Resource Kit*. When I start it up, I get an opening screen like the partial screen shot in Figure 16.11.

FIGURE 16.11:

Browser Monitor dialog box

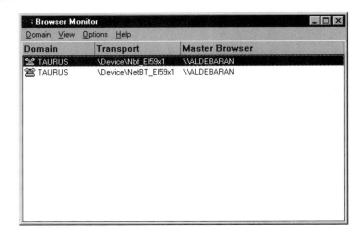

This screen shows that the master browser is \\ALDEBARAN. Transport refers to the transport layer used—NetBEUI, TCP/IP, or IPX/SPX. (DLC can't be used for anything other than printing services, and it doesn't work peer-to-peer, so there is no DLC browse master.) Essentially, this says, "\\ALDEBARAN is the browser for everyone speaking English on the network." This network could simultaneously support people speaking Greek or Spanish or Urdu, but the people speaking Urdu wouldn't be able to understand the browser broadcasts of the English speakers. For that reason, NT supports browsers for each network protocol, each language.

If I double-click on the highlighted line, I get a screen like the one in Figure 16.12. This shows me that two machines (Elnath and Aldebaran) act as browsers on this network, and six machines (Aldebaran, Artemis, Astro, Daffy, Elnath, Jim, and Levendis) act as servers of some type. I can find out more details about Elnath's browsing by double-clicking on its line in the Browsers list box. I then see a dialog box like the one in Figure 16.13.

FIGURE 16.12:

Browser status on TAURUS dialog box

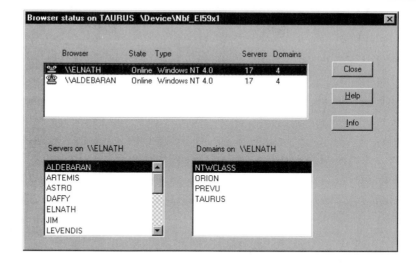

FIGURE 16.13:

Browser Info dialog box

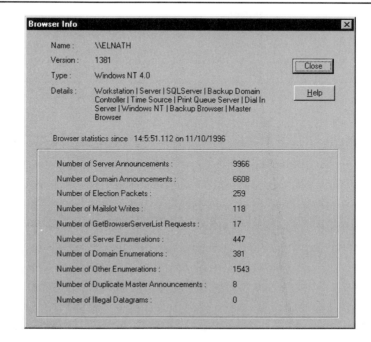

The Browser Info dialog box shows a number of things that we, frankly, aren't interested in, but a few interesting statistics are worth noting. First, look at the Details line. It says that this machine acts as both a workstation and a server, is the domain controller, and, among other things, is a backup browser and a master browser. Confusing as that may sound, it's normal: the master browser is *always* on the backup browser list.

The Browser Info dialog box says that these are the statistics for the browser since 11/10/96, when I last rebooted the server. I ran BROWMON at about 11/20/96, so these are statistics for about 10 days' worth of network browse mastering.

For example, Server Announcements, the first item in the box, are messages received by the browser master from machines on the network that are available to be servers. There are so many of those announcements because each server—that is, every Windows for Workgroups workstation, every NT workstation, and every NT Server machine—broadcasts its presence regularly.

Preventing Computers from Being Browser Masters

Elections can take a lot of time on a network. You can simplify the election process and cut down on the number of elections by forcing a Windows for Workgroups computer to never be the master browser. Do this by adding the following line to the [network] section of SYSTEM.INI:

```
MaintainServerList=No
```

You might do that if you didn't want to accept the performance hit that being master browser entails or if you're running a mixed NT/Windows network. You see, it's possible to end up with an NT master browser and a Windows for Workgroups browse backup. The problem arises in that the Windows workstation must talk to the NT machine to exchange services information. The NT machine isn't allowed to talk to the Windows machine *for any reason at all* unless either the Windows machine has an account on that machine and is logged in or the NT machine has a Guest account that is enabled. If neither of those things is the case, the newly elected backup browser finds itself without any information, and the master browser essentially "keeps it in the dark." If the master browser goes down, then the browser can end up taking its place in a fairly ignorant state, leading to empty browse lists.

You can make Windows 95 machines ineligible for being browse masters either from the Control Panel (easiest) or, if you're feeling arcane, from the Registry. From the Control Panel, click Networks, then select "File and Printer Sharing for Microsoft Networks" from the list of installed network components. Click the

Properties button to move to the next screen, and set the value of the Browse Master property to Disabled. To change the setting from the Registry, run REGEDIT.EXE, and find the entry MaintainServerList. (It's in HKEY_LOCAL_ MACHINE\System\CurrentControlSet\ Services\VxD\VNetSeup, but it's probably easier to press F3 to use the Find utility.) Set the value of Maintain-ServerList to 0 if it isn't already, and the Windows 95 machine will not serve as a master browser.

The default value of MaintainServerList is Auto, which means, "Make me a master browser if needed." You can alternately use a value of Yes, which means two things. First, "If there's a tie when electing browse masters, make me master browser." Second, "When I start up, always force an election." For NT work-stations and servers, there is a corresponding Registry entry, MaintainServer-List, which goes in HKEY_LOCAL_MACHINE\System\CurrentControlSet\ Services\Browser\Parameters. It is of type REG_SZ, and its value can be TRUE, FALSE, or Auto.

Browse Masters on a TCP/IP Network

On a TCP/IP network, things get a little more complicated when the factor of routers enters the picture.

Each segment of the network elects a master browser, as before. But one of the master browsers becomes the *domain master browser* (DMB). The DMB's job is to periodically ask the master browser on each segment (Microsoft doesn't have a name for them really, so let's call them Segment Master Browsers, or SMBs) for its local segment browse list. The DMB then compiles that into an enterprise-wide browse list and replicates it out to the SMBs. In general, you needn't worry about that at all, except for the fact that there are two Registry settings that you can use to tweak the browsing process.

Working in the Registry, you can give a particular machine an edge in becom-ing the DMB by adding a new value, IsDomainMasterBrowser, of type REG_SZ and setting it equal to TRUE. The value is in the key HKEY_LOCAL_MACHINE\ SYSTEM \CurrentControlSet\Services\Browser\Parameters. The other possible value is, of course, FALSE, and it's the default.

If your network segments are connected over low-speed lines, then you might not want all of the chatter between the DMB and the SMBs. You control that with two parameters in the key HKEY_LOCAL_MACHINE\SYSTEM \CurrentControlSet\ Services\Browser\Parameters.

By default, the DMB gathers browse lists from the SMBs and then replicates its consolidated browse lists to the SMBs every 12 minutes. You control how often this conversation goes on with a parameter called MasterPeriodicity. It's a value of type DWORD and is expressed in seconds. The minimum value is 300 seconds (five minutes), and the default is 720 seconds (12 minutes). To make this Registry change, you must at least be running NT Server 3.51 with Service Pack 2 or higher; obviously, NT 4 doesn't need the Service Pack.

Refreshing a Browse List

In general, browse requests are resolved by either the master browser or a backup browser, so you never know who's provided your browse list. But you can force the system to browse via the Browse Master with the command-line command:

```
net view
```

Browsing with LAN Manager

Browse problems can also appear if you have LAN Manager 2.2 servers on the network. LAN Manager used a SAP-like approach, broadcasting data within network segments, making browsing across routers impossible.

Because NT and NT Server don't broadcast, they don't produce browser information that LAN Manager can understand. You can change that by enabling LAN Manager broadcasts in your NT machines, both server and workstation. Read the "How Do I" sidebar to find out how.

How Do I Enable LAN Manager to Understand Broadcasts?

To make LAN Manager understand broadcasts:

1. Open the Control Panel, and double-click on the Network applet.

2. Under Installed Network Software, choose Server, and then click Configure.

3. In the Server configuration window, select the Make Browser Broadcasts to LAN Manager 2.x Clients check box.

Continued on next page

In a similar vein, if you have a LAN Manager domain that is on the same LAN segment as an NT domain but does not contain any NT workstations, then the LAN Manager servers will not show up on the browse lists unless you go into the Control Panel and, in the Computer Browser, set the LAN Manager domains to be "other domains."

And if you're using Windows for Workgroups workstations with LAN Manager servers but the Windows for Workgroups machines don't see the LAN Manager servers, add the following line to the [network] section of SYSTEM.INI:

```
LMAnnounce=yes
```

Why Isn't My Resource on the Browse List?

You can experience browsing trouble (i.e., the browse list isn't available or the list is incorrect) if computers do not exit Windows gracefully—that is, if they just get shut off without first exiting Windows. Such a computer may appear on the master browser's list for up to 45 minutes. Even worse, if a *browser* terminates unexpectedly, it may become impossible to browse for over an hour.

Remember if you can't see something on the browser, that's no big deal. If you know the universal naming convention for the resource—the name like \\MARKSPC\C—then you can always just punch that value in or click Tools ➤ Map Network Drive from the Explorer and get connected with no trouble, even if the browsers are all confused.

The Browsing Trail

Let's look in a bit more detail at how the browse service works. It may take up to 60 minutes for the browser to notice that a resource has disappeared, and in that time the browser may erroneously report that something is available when it is not. Why does that happen? Here are the relevant numbers:

- Once a server has been up for a while, it reannounces itself every 12 minutes.

- A server must announce itself to stay on the browse list, but a master browser gives the server a "grace period" where the server can miss three announcements before the master browser drops the server from the list. In the worst case, that would be 36 minutes.

- If the network uses TCP/IP and is segmented, then there is a domain master browser, which is updated by the segment master browsers every 12 minutes. (Recall that this is the default value and can be changed.) Thus, in the worst case, the domain master browser might not see that a server is off the list until 36 plus 12, or 48, minutes go by.

- If your workstation is getting its browse list from a backup browser, rather than a master browser, then the master browser only updates the backup browser every 12 minutes; this *was* 15 minutes up to 3.51, but it was reduced to 12 minutes with NT 3.51. (Servers reannounce themselves to their local master browser every 12 minutes; master browsers and the domain master browser update each other every 12 minutes, and *that* gets sent to the backup browsers every 12 minutes. Seems like 12 is a mystical number at Microsoft, doesn't it?)

- Since, in the worst case, the master browser needs 36 minutes to figure out the server's gone, 12 more minutes pass before the domain master browser knows, and then 12 more minutes pass before the domain master browser tells a backup browser. Notice that in this analysis I even left out the small slice of time required for the domain master browser to replicate its browse list to the local segment master browsers, so in theory it could take even *longer* for the world to know that a server's dead!

New services, in contrast, are announced to the master browser immediately, and, again, the backup browsers may hear of them as long as 12 minutes later, so the longest that it should take for a new service to appear on the browse list is 12 minutes. But that 12 minutes can be a *long* time.

Adjusting the 12-Minute Interval

You have already learned that you can control how often the domain master browser and the local segment master browsers communicate. But you can also adjust how often a local master browser updates its backup browsers. Again, you've got to have NT version 3.51 with Service Pack 2 or a later version of NT in order to do this.

The value is in HKEY_LOCAL_MACHINE\SYSTEM \Current-ControlSet\ Services\Browser\Parameters. It is called BackupPeriodicity, it's of type REG_ DWORD, and it's measured in seconds.

Server Announcement Intervals

By the way, when I said that servers reannounced themselves to the master browser every 12 minutes, I simplified the truth a bit. The whole truth is that when a service first starts up, it announces itself more frequently. New services announce at intervals of 1, 4, 8, and 12 minutes after they start, and after they reach 12 minutes, they announce at 12-minute intervals.

Each Protocol and Segment Has Its Own Browser

Another reason why you may not see a resource is that its server may be using a different protocol from your workstation. You see, the services offered by the NetBEUI-using machines are maintained on a different browse list than the services offered by the TCP/IP-using machines. There is a different master browser for each transport protocol except DLC.

By the way, how does the network know to hold an election if someone just pulls the plug on the master browser, and the master browser doesn't get a chance to force an election? The next time another computer asks for browse information and doesn't get a response, that computer forces an election.

If you are running TCP/IP, then resources may not appear on the TCP/IP browse list because the IPX and/or NetBEUI protocols are hogging the network's attention. If you can, remove the other protocols, and the TCP/IP browser will work more smoothly. (If you take the other protocols off the PDC, then be sure to re-enable MaintainServerList on some other machine, or NetBEUI and IPX will be without browsers.)

Why Is My Browser So Slow?

Set up Windows for Workgroups, accept all the defaults, and try to connect to a network drive with the File Manager (Disk ➤ Connect Network Drive), and you wait for a couple of minutes. Why?

By default, Windows for Workgroups loads two protocols: NetBEUI and IPX/SPX with NetBIOS. Recall that the way a network-aware program communicates with the network is via the Application Program Interface (API). The API used by NetBEUI is NetBIOS, and the typical API for IPX/SPX is Novell Sockets. But Microsoft has implemented a version of IPX/SPX that has a NetBIOS API on it. (Novell did the same thing long ago.)

Now, the Browser is just a network-aware application that depends on NetBIOS. So the Browser sees *two* NetBIOSes, the one atop NetBEUI and the one atop IPX/SPX. For some reason, that confuses it. Result: the long wait.

You can solve this problem simply. Just go to the Network Setup program in Windows for Workgroups and remove the IPX/SPX with NetBIOS item, replacing it with just IPX/SPX. The system will browse almost instantaneously. In general, getting rid of superfluous protocols will almost always improve performance.

Hiding a Server from the Browser

Now and then, you may want to put a server on your network that doesn't show up on the browse list. You already know that you can keep a share from showing up on the browse list by ending its name with a dollar sign ($), but can you do something like that for servers? Yes, with a little Registry or command-line fiddling.

To hide a server from the browse list, open up a command prompt at that server and type

```
net config server /hidden:yes
```

Alternatively, if you're a Registry nut, you can open up REGEDT32 and look in the HKEY_LOCAL_MACHINE subtree, in System\CurrentControlSet. (I know, you already guessed that, as it seems that everything interesting is in there.) Then look in the key Services\LanmanServer\Parameters, and add a new value entry named Hidden of type REG_DWORD. The value 1 tells the Browser to hide this server; the value 0 says not to hide the server. Of course, the default is 0.

Monitoring the Network with the Event Viewer

NT Server defines an *event* as any significant occurrence in the system or in an application that users should be aware of and perhaps notified about. If the event is critical, such as an interrupted power supply or a full disk on a server, messages are sent to the screens of all of the workstations. Noncritical event information, however, can be fed into a log file once event auditing has been configured. Both successful and unsuccessful events can be audited.

In order to record, retrieve, and store logs of events on an NT server, the administrator must activate and configure event auditing. File and directory access, printer access, and security events can all be audited. File and directory auditing is activated within the Explorer, printer auditing is set within Printers folder, and security auditing is configured in User Manager for Domains.

NT Server maintains three types of logs: the *System log*, the *Security log*, and the *Application log*. Here is what they do:

Log	What It Records
System	Events logged by the Windows NT system components, such as the failure of a driver or other system component to load during startup. As shown in Figure 16.14, this log is displayed the first time you start up the Event Viewer.
Security	Security events (changes in security policy, attempts to log on or access a file or directory, and so on) based on the security auditing policy options specified by the administrator under Auditing in User Manager for Domains. Incidentally, this log can only be accessed by members of the Administrators group. It is shown in Figure 16.15.
Application	Events logged by application on the system. For example, it records a file error that occurred in a database program. The Application log is shown in Figure 16.16.

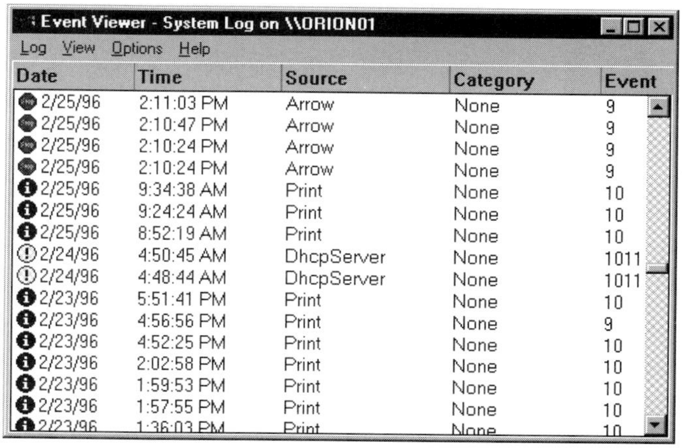

FIGURE 16.14:

The System log

Date	Time	Source	Category	Event
2/25/96	2:11:03 PM	Arrow	None	9
2/25/96	2:10:47 PM	Arrow	None	9
2/25/96	2:10:24 PM	Arrow	None	9
2/25/96	2:10:24 PM	Arrow	None	9
2/25/96	9:34:38 AM	Print	None	10
2/25/96	9:24:24 AM	Print	None	10
2/25/96	8:52:19 AM	Print	None	10
2/24/96	4:50:45 AM	DhcpServer	None	1011
2/24/96	4:48:44 AM	DhcpServer	None	1011
2/23/96	5:51:41 PM	Print	None	10
2/23/96	4:56:56 PM	Print	None	9
2/23/96	4:52:25 PM	Print	None	10
2/23/96	2:02:58 PM	Print	None	10
2/23/96	1:59:53 PM	Print	None	10
2/23/96	1:57:55 PM	Print	None	10
2/23/96	1:36:03 PM	Print	None	10

Event Viewer - System Log on \\ORION01
Log   View   Options   Help

FIGURE 16.15:

The Security log

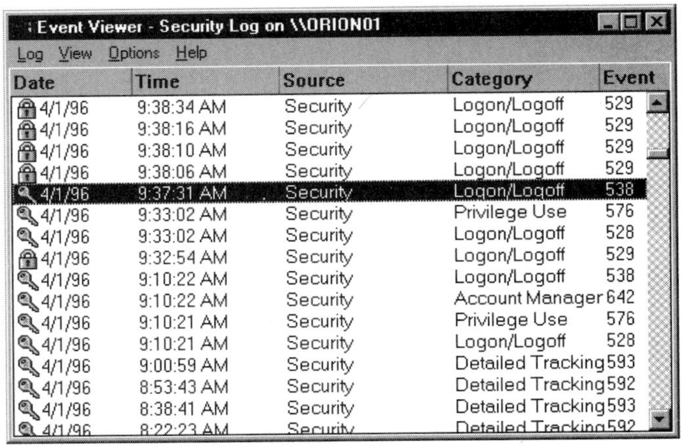

FIGURE 16.16:

The Application log

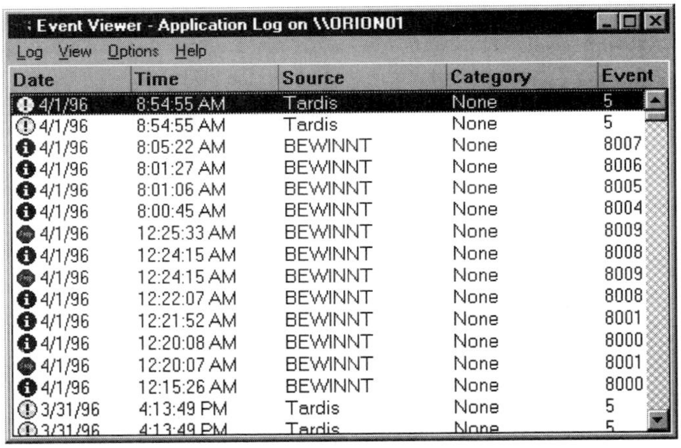

To view any of the logs, open the Event Viewer. Under the Log menu, choose either System, Security, or Application, depending on which log you want to see. Events in the log are listed in sequence by date and time of occurrence, with the default being newest first; you can change this to oldest first in the View menu. Note that the event logs are not automatically updated during the time they are in view. To see any new events that may have been logged after opening the Event Viewer, choose the Refresh command under the View menu (or simply hit the F5 key).

When the Event Viewer is opened, it displays the logs for the local computer by default. To view logs for another computer, choose Select Computer from the Log menu. NT Server allows you to view logs for NT workstations, NT Server servers and domain controllers, and servers using LAN Manager 2.*x*. Select the Low Speed Connection box if the computer you want is across a link with slow transmission rates; when this is checked, NT Server doesn't list all of the computers in the default domain, thereby minimizing network traffic across the link.

Reading Log Information

Log entries are classified into one of five categories. These categories are marked by an icon at the beginning of the entry:

- The Information icon indicates an event that describes the successful operation of a major server service.

- The Warning icon indicates that the event wasn't necessarily significant but might point to possible future problems.

- The Error icon indicates that the event resulted in a loss of data or a loss of functions.

- The Success Audit icon indicates an audited security access event was successful.

- The Failure Audit icon indicates an audited security access event failed.

Following the event type icon is a list of data pertinent to the event:

- The date and time the event occurred.

- The source of the event (typically the software that logged the event, which can be either an application name or a component of the system or of a large application, such as a driver name).

- A categorization of the event by the event source. Not all events are categorized (these events fall in the None category). Application events can be listed as System Events or Administrative. Security events fall into a number of categories, which include Logon/Logoff, Privilege Use, System Event, Policy Change, Account Management, Object Access, and Detailed Tracking.

- The username for the user who was logged on and working when the event occurred is recorded in the event log (the entry N/A indicates that the log entry didn't specify a user).

- The computer name for the computer where the event occurred.

An event number unique to each kind of event can be used to identify the event. For example, in the Security log, events in the Logon/Logoff categories can have one of the event numbers shown in Table 16.2. The numbers are used primarily by product support representatives to track precisely which event occurred within the system. You can check what a specific event ID number indicates by looking at the Event Details (more on that shortly) for any log entry having that particular event ID.

TABLE 16.2: Event ID Numbers for Selected Logon/Logoff Events

Logon/Logoff Event ID number	Meaning
528	Successful logon.
529	Unknown user name or bad password.
531	Account currently disabled.
535	The specified user's password has expired.
537	An unexpected error occurred during logon.
538	User logoff.

Event Display

The default display layout for all of the event logs is to show every entry, with the most recent entries at the top. However, you can filter these details to see only what you need to by selecting the Filter Events option. Filtering merely affects the view and has no effect on the Event Log as a whole; all events specified in the auditing policies are logged all the time, whether or not the filter is active. If you select Save Settings On Exit from the Options menu, then the choices for filtering remain in effect every time you start the Event Viewer.

To filter the log events, choose Filter Events in the View menu. You see the Filter dialog box, as in Figure 16.17. The options available in the Filter dialog box are explained in Table 16.3.

FIGURE 16.17:

Filter dialog box

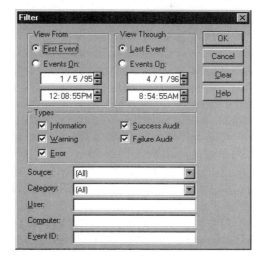

TABLE 16.3: Filter Options

Option	Filters Log For
Category	All events of a particular classification (for example, security event categories include Logon and Logoff, Policy Change, Privilege Use, System Event, Object Access, Detailed Tracking, and Account Management). This option is not available for error logs on LAN Manager 2.x servers.
Computer	Events that occurred for a particular computer by the specified name. This field is not case-sensitive. It is not available for error logs on LAN Manager 2.x servers.
Error*	Error events.
Event ID	Events of a particular type in a category, identified by a specific event ID number. It is not available for audit logs on LAN Manager 2.x servers.
Failure Audit	Audited security access attempts which failed.
Information	Information events.

Continued on next page

TABLE 16.3 CONTINUED: Filter Options

Option	Filters Log For
Source	Events logged by a specific source, such as an application, a system component or a device driver. Not available for audit logs on LAN Manager 2.*x* servers.
Success Audit	Audited security access attempts which were successful.
User	Events that occurred while a specified user was logged on and working; note that not all events have a user associated with them. This field is not case-sensitive. It is not available for error logs on LAN Manager 2.*x* servers.
View From	Events after a specific date and time; default is the date of the first event in the log.
View Through	Events up to (and including) a specific date and time; default is the date of the last event in the log.
Warning*	Warning events.

* Not available for LAN Manager 2.*x* servers.

If you need to, you can also use the Find option to locate a particular type of entry in any of the logs. Under the View menu, choose Find (or hit the F3 key). You are asked for the same type of information as required by the Filter option. Use the Up or Down buttons in the Direction box to determine which direction to make the search.

Interpreting Event Details for Log Entries

By double-clicking on any event within any of the three logs (or by choosing Detail in the View menu), you can call up a more detailed record of that event. Event details contain additional information about the event in question. For example, the details of a System log entry might look like Figure 16.18.

Here, the details confirm that the entry was a rather straightforward information event—printing a document. An Application log entry might look like Figure 16.19.

Security log event details can be relatively straightforward as well, but usually contain a greater amount of information, as shown in Figure 16.20.

Understanding the meaning of these details requires some basic knowledge of how NT Server handles system security.

FIGURE 16.18:

Event details for a System
log entry

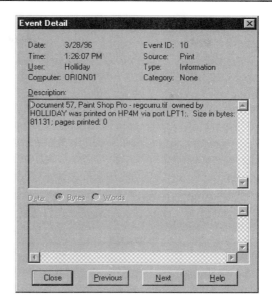

FIGURE 16.19:

Event details for an Application log entry

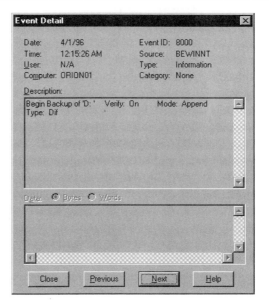

FIGURE 16.20:

Event details from a Security log entry

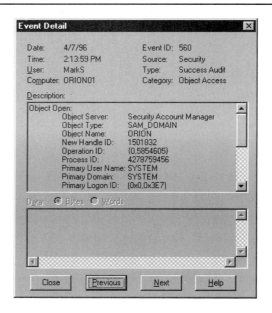

System Security in NT Server

In NT Server, all named objects (as well as some unnamed objects) can be secured. The security attributes for an object are described by a *security descriptor*. The security descriptor is made of the following four parts:

- An owner security ID, which indicates the user or group who owns the object (the owner of the object, you may recall, can change all access permissions for that object).

- A group security ID, which is used only by the POSIX subsystem and is ignored by the rest of NT.

- A discretionary *access control list* (ACL), which identifies which users and groups are granted or denied which access permissions (discretionary ACLs are controlled by the owner of the object).

- A system ACL, which controls which auditing messages the system will generate. System ACLs are controlled by the security administrators.

Whenever an owner of an object assigns permissions to other users and groups, he or she is building the discretionary ACL for that object. Likewise, an administrator's choices as to which events to audit determine the system ACL for the object.

Each of the ACLs in turn is made up of *access control entries* (ACEs). The ACEs for an object specify access or auditing permissions to that object for one user or group. ACEs contain a security ID and a set of access rights for each group or user that can access (or be denied access to) the object. Any process with a matching security ID is either allowed access rights, denied rights, or allowed rights with auditing, depending on the contents of the ACE. There are three ACE types. Two of them, AccessAllowed and AccessDenied, are discretionary ACEs that explicitly grant or deny access to a user or group. The other, SystemAudit, is the system security ACE. It is used to keep a log of security events involving object access and to create and record security audit messages.

By the way, the NT Permissions Editor places any AccessDenied ACEs first in the list of ACEs to check and, once it finds one, disregards any other Access-Allowed ACEs that follow. This way, if someone is a member of two groups, one that has access to a file and another to which access has been denied, that person will not be able to access the file despite his or her multiple group membership.

Included in each object's ACEs is an *access mask*, which is basically a menu from which granted and denied permissions are chosen. The access mask defines all possible actions for a particular directory, file, device, or other object. Access masks contain *access types*, of which there are standard types and specific types.

Standard access types apply to all objects and consist of the access permissions listed in Table 16.4. Specific types vary, depending on the type of object. For example, the specific access types for NT files are ReadData, WriteData, AppendData, ReadEA (Extended Attribute), WriteEA (Extended Attribute), Execute, ReadAttributes, and WriteAttributes.

Specific and standard access types appear in the event details for entries in the Security log. Each type of object (that is, file, file and directory, device, and so on) can have up to 16 specific access types. If you've enabled auditing of process tracking, you can follow a user's (or the system's) activity as it accesses an object by examining the specific and standard accesses shown in the event details.

Let's take a closer look at the example event detail for the Security log entry shown back in Figure 16.20. This particular event is a successful object access event involving a file for which security auditing has been activated. If we read through the entire event detail's description, we'll see the information as shown in Figure 16.21.

TABLE 16.4: Standard Access Types

Standard Access Type	Function
DELETE	Used to grant or deny Delete access.
READ_CONTROL	Used to grant or deny Read access to the security descriptor and owner.
SYNCHRONIZE	Used to synchronize access and to allow a process to wait for an object to enter the signaled state.
WRITE_DAC	Used to grant or deny Write access to the discretionary ACL.
WRITE_OWNER	Used to assign write owner.

FIGURE 16.21:

Event detail description for Security log entry

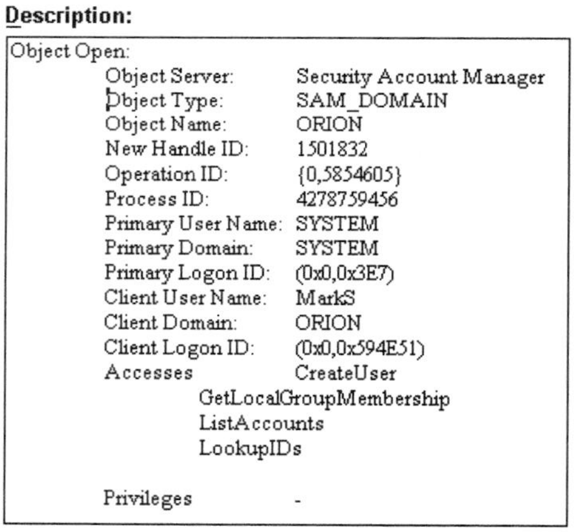

```
Description:
Object Open:
        Object Server:        Security Account Manager
        Object Type:          SAM_DOMAIN
        Object Name:          ORION
        New Handle ID:        1501832
        Operation ID:         {0,5854605}
        Process ID:           4278759456
        Primary User Name:    SYSTEM
        Primary Domain:       SYSTEM
        Primary Logon ID:     (0x0,0x3E7)
        Client User Name:     MarkS
        Client Domain:        ORION
        Client Logon ID:      (0x0,0x594E51)
        Accesses              CreateUser
                     GetLocalGroupMembership
                 ListAccounts
                 LookupIDs

        Privileges            -
```

The first thing we note in the description is that an object was opened, that the object server, in this case, was Security Account Manager, and that the object is SAM_DOMAIN.

We see that there is no new Handle ID associated with this particular event. Handle IDs are assigned (and an audit event generated) when a file is first opened; when the file is closed, another audit event with the same Handle ID is created. This information can be used to see how long a file remained open, but bear in mind that many applications open a file only long enough to read its contents into memory; a handle may be open only for a very short time.

The Operation ID and Process ID numbers are unique numbers assigned to any particular operations within a process and to the process as a whole, respectively. For example, when an application is started, it is assigned a Process ID, and all events involving that application have that same ID. Individual operations within the application, such as opening a particular file, are assigned an Operation ID.

Continuing through the list, we now note the Primary User Name, Primary Domain, and Primary Logon ID, as well as the Client User Name, Client Domain, and Client Logon ID. To ensure that the programs that a user runs have no more access to objects than the user does, NT allows processes to take on the security attributes of another process or user through a technique called *impersonation*. Impersonation allows a program or process to run on the user's behalf with the same accesses that the user has been granted, or to put it another way, to run in the user's *security context*. We can see in our example that the primary user for this event was the system, but the client user, whose security context the process is running under, is also identified. The Client Logon ID is a number assigned to a logon session whenever a user logs on, and, if Logon/Logoff events are being audited, it can be used to search the logon entries to find out when the particular user logged on prior to the event in question.

The last collection of information in the description are lists of Accesses and Privileges that have been used (and thus audited). Since this particular event was a successful one, the Accesses list indicates which actions actually took place. The four accesses are standard accesses for creating a user, assigning membership to a local group, listing domain accounts, and looking up IDs. Since nothing is indicated under Privileges, we can tell that no particular user rights were invoked for this event.

From this particular list of accesses, you can deduce what this actually was: a new user named MarkS was created. In the case of a failure audit entry, the list of accesses displayed usually represents those which were attempted but failed due to lack of access.

Changing the Size and Overwrite Options for an Event Log

The default size for all three of the event logs is 512K, and events older than seven days are overwritten as needed when the log becomes full. To change this, open the Event Viewer, and select Log Settings under the Log menu. You see the Event Log Settings dialog box shown in Figure 16.22.

FIGURE 16.22:

Event Log Settings dialog box

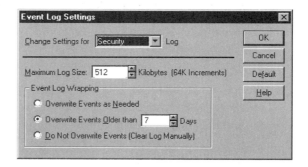

In addition to changing the log size, you can specify how the event log is overwritten by choosing one of three options in this dialog box:

Overwrite Events as Needed   New events will continue to be written into the log. When the log is full, each additional new event will replace the oldest event in the log.

Overwrite Events Older than [ ] Days   Logged events will be retained for the number of days specified (the default is seven) before being overwritten. This is a handy choice if you are archiving logs on a weekly basis.

Do Not Overwrite Events (Clear Log Manually)   With this option, the log is never overwritten. When full, events are no longer logged. When that situation occurs, a message appears on the screen saying that the log is full. Select this particular option only if it is important not to miss any events, and make sure that someone is able to manually clear the log when needed. (You might select this option for Security logs where all of the log info is vital.)

As mentioned earlier, choose carefully the events to be audited and consider the amount of disk space you are willing to devote to the logs when you set up auditing. You cannot make the system add more entries to a full log by simply increasing the log size under Log Settings.

Archiving Event Logs

The event logs displayed in NT Server's Event Viewer can be archived for future inspection and use. The log information can be stored three ways:

- As evt files, a format that allows the data (and all of its details) to be viewed in the Event Viewer whenever desired

- As text files (TXT)

- As comma-delimited text files

The latter two formats allow the log information to be used in other applications.

Archiving the event log saves the entire log, regardless of what the currently selected filtering options are. Event logs saved as text or comma-delimited text, however, are saved in the current sort order. The data is stored in the following sequence: date, time, source, type, category, event, user, computer, and description. Any binary data in the event records is dropped.

Event logs can be archived in two ways, but no matter which method is used, the log that is currently displayed in the Event Viewer is the one that gets archived. To choose the desired log, open the Log menu and select System, Security, or Application.

The first method merely saves the event log as a file without clearing the log. With the desired log displayed, open the Log menu and choose Save As. By writing in a name for the file and picking a file format in the Save As dialog box, you can save the current log information to disk.

If you need to archive the current log and clear it from the Event Viewer too, then select the Clear All Events option under the Log menu. The Clear Event Log dialog box appears, as in Figure 16.23. It gives you the option to save before clearing.

FIGURE 16.23:

Save before clearing
dialog box

Selecting Yes triggers the Save As dialog box. Choose the file format option desired, and enter a file name for the archived log. Upon selecting OK, you get the message shown in Figure 16.24 (in this case, for the System log).

FIGURE 16.24:

Clearing an event log

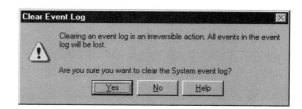

Since you've just saved the current information to a file, those events won't be lost (contrary to what this message implies). Selecting Yes will clear the log of the just-archived information. New event information will be added to the log according to the criteria set under Log Settings. If, in the Log Settings option, you've specified "Overwrite Events Older than 7 Days" (see Figure 16.22), you can archive weekly without necessarily clearing the event log, since the older events are overwritten in the week after archiving the log.

It is important to check, archive, and clear event logs regularly if you select the "Do Not Overwrite Events (Clear Log Manually)" option in the Event Log Settings dialog box (see Figure 16.22). If an event log is full, no more information can be stored, and what might be vital information will not get recorded. When a log is full, the administrator is notified by a message on the screen. If the option Restart, Shutdown, and System has been selected for auditing under the Audit policy in User Manager for Domains, then a log entry, indicating that a log is full, will be recorded.

Viewing Previously Archived Logs

To view a previously archived log, select the Open option in the Log menu of the Event Viewer, and choose which previously archived log you wish to see. After selecting a file, you will be prompted as to which type of log it is, as shown in Figure 16.25. Make sure you make the correct choice when it comes to choosing the log type, because if you don't the event description shown in the log details will be incorrect.

FIGURE 16.25:

Selecting a previously
archived file to view

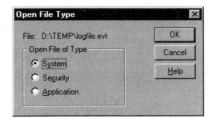

If you need a printed copy of the log, then use the Save As option to save the log as a comma-delimited text file. As mentioned earlier, all information will be saved in the current sort order, and any binary data associated with a log entry will be discarded. You can print a comma-delimited text file for future reference or scrutiny. The example below shows part of the security log stored as a comma-delimited text file:

```
3/10/97,9:27:31 AM,Security,Success Audit,Logon/Logoff ,528,Administra-
tor,EISA SERVER,Successful Logon:
        User Name:      Administrator
        Domain:         US
        Logon ID:               (0x0,0x50D65)
        Logon Type:     2
        Logon Process: User32
        Authentication Package:         MICROSOFT_AUTHENTICATION_PACKAGE_V1_0
3/10/97,9:27:19 AM,Security,Success Audit,Logon/Logoff ,538,Maeve, EISA
SERVER,User Logoff:
        User Name:      Maeve
        Domain:         US
        Logon ID:               (0x0,0x501BC)
        Logon Type:     2

3/10/97,9:27:03 AM,Security,Failure Audit,Object Access ,560,Maeve,EISA
SERVER,Object Open:
        Object Server: Security
        Object Type:    File
        Object Name:    C:\Main\NTCLASS\MVTEXT\prjdata1.txt
        New Handle ID: -
        Operation ID: {0,330786}
        Process ID:     4285798960
```

```
Primary User Name:      Maeve
Primary Domain:         US
Primary Logon ID:       (0x0,0x501BC)
Client User Name:       -
Client Domain: -
Client Logon ID:        -
Accesses                SYNCHRONIZE
ReadAttributes

Privileges              -
```

The first two entries reveal a successful logon by the Administrator and a user logoff. The third entry is a failure audit for a user's attempt to change a file (in this example, PRJDATA1.TXT) for which he or she only has read access.

Using the NT Task Manager

New to NT with version 4 is an interesting version of the Task Manager. It does what the old Task Manager did—lists what programs are running and allows you to stop any of those programs—but it also adds a bunch of utilities useful to a system manager. In short, the Task Manager can

- List running programs

- Let you stop any of those programs

- List running *processes*, which aren't visible otherwise, and stop any of those

- Monitor CPU and memory usage

- Adjust priorities of running processes

- Start programs

You won't find the Task Manager on any of the program menus; you activate it from the NT Desktop by pressing Ctrl+Alt+Del, and then choosing Task Manager. Choose the Performance tab if it is not already chosen. You'll see a screen like the one in Figure 16.26.

At first glance, this may look overly complex, and perhaps to an extent it *is*—you probably don't need to know *all* of this information. But it's a pretty useful snapshot when you understand it, which is what I'll give you now.

FIGURE 16.26:

Opening Task Manager screen

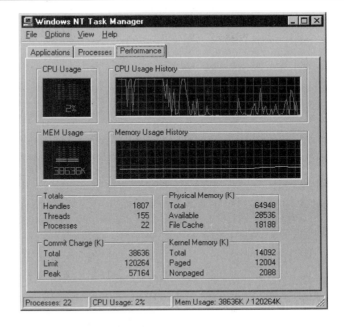

Understanding the Graphics

There are two graphs that appear in the Task Manager, a *CPU utilization graph* and a *memory utilization graph*. The CPU utilization graph is exactly the same thing that you'd get if you ran the Performance Monitor, chose the Processor object and the Percent Utilization counter. (Of course, the nifty oscilloscope-like look to Task Manager is much more impressive.) You can augment this by clicking View ➤ Show Kernel Times to get an additional line on the graph, a line that shows the amount of time that the CPU spends in kernel mode. CPUs using NT run in either kernel mode or user mode. In general, any kernel mode activity is *operating system activity*—CPU time spent on operating system overhead, drivers, or the user interface. It's not an amazingly useful number, but it's fun to know how much of your 200MHz Pentium's CPU time is being burned up running NT.

The other graph, labeled Memory Usage History, is a great snapshot of system memory. As I hinted in the section on optimizing memory, there really *is* no one "memory used" value in NT; NT's memory model is complex enough that it's hard to tie down an answer to the question, "How much free memory do I have at this moment?"

Look first at the Physical Memory (K) section. Available really means if NT moved a bunch of things around to disk and minimized the file cache, it could come up with this much memory. File Cache describes how much of the memory is used for disk caching; you may recall that you can't control that value. Commit Charge (K) looks at both physical and virtual memory. This computer has 64MB of physical RAM and a pagefile with an initial size of 64MB, so it's got a total of 128MB (131,072K) of memory space to work with. The 120264 value is the part of that 128K that NT can move around—some of it can't be paged out. (Where do you see this exact value reported? You don't; this is an example of how annoying NT can be when you try to track down the system memory usage.) Commit Charge (K) reports that I'm only using 38MB of RAM now, but that the peak of today's usage was 57MB. Run the Task Manager for a few days and note the Peak value and the Limit value. The Limit value will change if your page file has been forced to ratchet up a bit, so make sure the initial page file size can cover the Limit value.

If you click the Processes tab, you'll see a screen like the one in Figure 16.27.

FIGURE 16.27:

Task Manager view of running processes

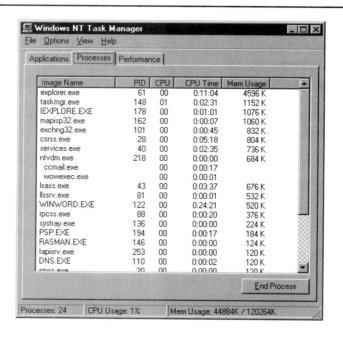

Processes are different from programs. While all programs are processes, not all processes are visible programs. For example, csrss.exe is the process which runs the user interface. You never loaded it, and it doesn't show up on the Taskbar, but it's there.

You can get a number of things done with this screen. First, of course, you can terminate a process. I've found this useful in the following situation: I run a program (Freelance 96 is one that comes to mind) which crashes, but when I try to restart it, the program tells me that it is *already* running. This is curious, because it's obvious that the program isn't running. What's going on? What's happening here is that Freelance left a piece of itself in memory, some process that is still running, and that's confusing Freelance. I look for a process name that suggests it might be Freelance, like FLWMN.EXE, and end the process with the Task Manager. Result: now I can run Freelance.

You can also click on a column heading and sort by memory usage (an easy way to find the memory hogs) or the total amount of CPU that the process has used—that's the column labeled CPU Time. Or you can add other information with View ➢ Select Columns; again, it's another source of Performance Monitor-like information. Finally, you can right-click the process and change its priority. I'm not sure that's a good idea, however, because raising a process's priority too much might give it more priority than the user interface itself. If that happened, and if the process crashed, then the operating system wouldn't recognize your keystrokes and mouse clicks to stop the process.

As a sort of "Perfmon junior," Task Manager can help you keep track of how your system is running, and it lets you do some minor system tweaking. It's worth a look.

The Network Monitor (Netmon)

Sometimes you've done all you can to solve a network problem. You've reinstalled the software, loaded the latest drivers, tweaked the Registry, and still that machine isn't getting an IP address from DHCP. If you could just get down into the network wires and see the data zipping around, perhaps you could figure out what's wrong.

That's when you'll like having the Network Monitor—Netmon to its friends. Netmon is an application that essentially makes your network cables transparent, revealing everything going by. Netmon's been around for a long time, but for years you only got it if you owned the Server Management System (SMS) or the entire BackOffice package. With NT Server 4, Microsoft decided to include Netmon.

There's a bit of bad news about NT Server 4's Netmon, however—Microsoft crippled it. The full-blown version of Netmon that comes with SMS can record all packets on the network; the cut-down version that ships with NT Server will only record broadcast packets, and packets originating at or directed to the particular server that's running Netmon. For example, if there are three servers on the network named A, B, and C, and you run Netmon on system A, then the Netmon on system A will only record packets between A and B or A and C. Conversations between B and C will not be recorded by the Netmon running on machine A. Personally, I find the full-blown SMS version of Netmon more useful because it *can* track all network activity, so for purposes of this discussion, I'll use both the full version and the cut-down version that comes with NT Server.

What Can You Do with Netmon?

You can watch your network and see how things really work. I guess Netmon's almost more of a tutorial tool than a troubleshooting tool, but I think you'll like it any way you use it.

Network Monitor can

- Let you watch network processes occur
- Look into network protocols and identify where they fail
- Capture network names
- Troubleshoot routing and name resolution

In this section, I'll show you Netmon at work.

Installing Netmon

Network Monitor installs as a network service does. Open the Control Panel and then the Network applet. Select the Services tab and click Add, then choose

Network Monitor Agent and Tools. That will load both the Network Monitor program itself *and* a driver called the Network Monitor Agent.

The Network Monitor Agent is essential for capturing network traffic; without it, Network Monitor can only show you previously taken captures.

Running Netmon

Once you've installed it and rebooted your computer, Network Monitor will show up under Administrative Tools. Start it, and you'll see a screen like Figure 16.28.

FIGURE 16.28:

Netmon initial screen

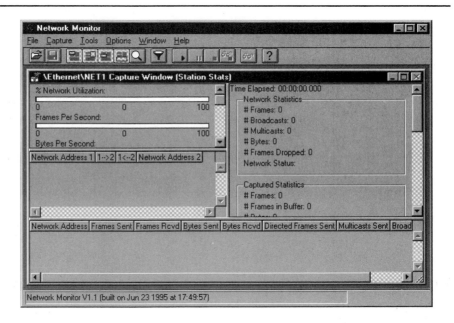

Click the Start Capture button and Netmon will start recording every packet that it hears on your network.

Click the Stop and View Capture button, and Netmon will show you what it's found. For instance, in my network, I see the screen shown in Figure 16.29 after just a few seconds of capturing.

Yikes! *This* is supposed to be useful? Well, it'll get better; trust me. But what's on this screen? First, you see that each frame has a number, and you see at what time the frame was taken.

FIGURE 16.29:

A brief network capture

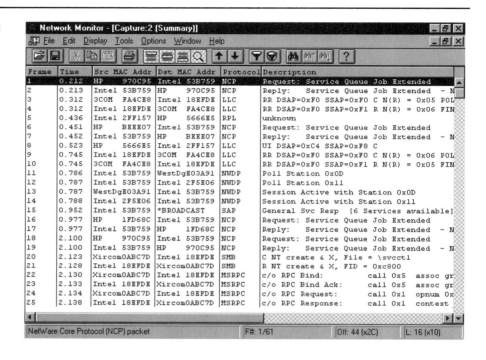

These times are just the number of seconds that have elapsed since the capture started. In the case of this capture, the first frame appeared two tenths of a second after the capture started. Alternatively, you can click Display, then Options, and you'll see an option to display the time of day when the frame appeared rather than "seconds since start." Src MAC Addr and Dst MAC Addr are the addresses of the machine where the frame originated (*src,* short for *source,* and *dst,* short for *destination*). Notice that the names in the columns look like HP 970C95, Intel 56B759, 3COM FA4CE8, and the like. These are the unique 48-bit Ethernet addresses of the network cards that originated the traffic, the Media Access Control (MAC) addresses.

Now, that's not very useful, as most of us don't know offhand the MAC addresses of the servers. You'd rather see Netmon report more human-friendly names, such as MYSERVER or the like.

Well, remember that Netmon is just *listening* on the network; it's kind of an eavesdropper. It just sees frames going by—it doesn't go over to a server and say, "Hey, I see you've got an Intel Ethernet card. What NetBIOS name do you go by?"

There *are*, however, a goodly number of network communications that end up mentioning a NetBIOS name; for example, if a machine does a name registration with WINS, then it must say something to WINS like "I'm IP address such-and-such, Ethernet address such-and-such, and my NetBIOS name is AMBERJACK." If asked, Netmon will sniff its way through the capture file, remembering whatever names it unearths. You can ask it to do this at any time by selecting Display ➤ Find All Names.

Now, in the case of my network capture, which ran for less than three seconds, it should come as no surprise that there *weren't* any frames that gave away name information, and so Netmon didn't find anything. But if I run Netmon for a while, then I'll end up netting most of my segment's names, and I might end up with a partial window like the one shown in Figure 16.30.

FIGURE 16.30:

Netmon run after a few hours

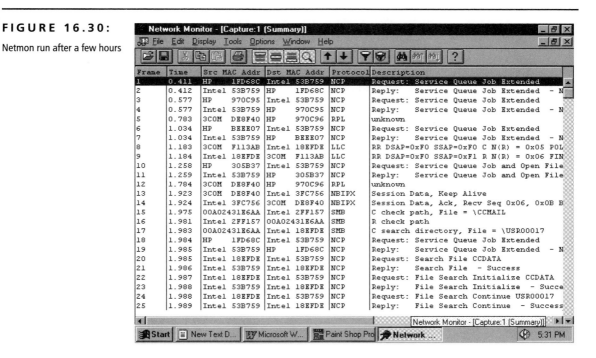

TIP

As a matter of fact, it's not a bad idea to just run Netmon for a while the first day you install it, to provide some grist for its naming mill.

Notice that it doesn't look all that different from the earlier figure. To see what Netmon can find for names, I click Capture ➤ Find All Names to get a dialog box like the one in Figure 16.31.

FIGURE 16.31:

Netmon has found some names

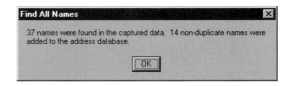

Find All Names

37 names were found in the captured data. 14 non-duplicate names were added to the address database.

OK

So Netmon found 37 names, and all but 14 were duplicates. When I click OK, Netmon will fill in the names it knows, and the capture screen will look like Figure 16.32.

FIGURE 16.32:

Netmon capture after filling in names

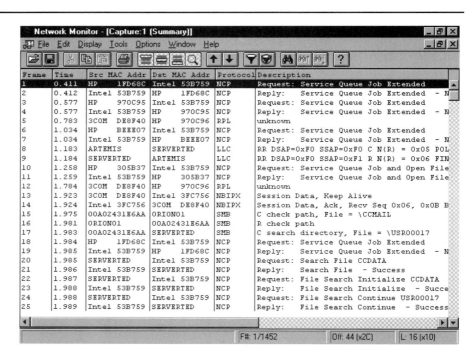

A few frames have names now; in particular, notice that frames 8 and 9 refer to a communication between machines ARTEMIS and SERVERTED (an NT workstation and a Primary Domain Controller). I didn't get a lot of names, but that's just because I wasn't lucky in picking up names.

How else can I help Netmon? Well, there are a number of printers on my network that are directly attached with JetDirect cards. They don't have NetBIOS names, so Netmon has no choice but to refer to them by their MAC names. I know that the printer down the hall from me, ORIONHP1, has MAC address 0800095666E5. Another network-attached printer is connected to our Novell network, and it's called DN_QUEUE; its MAC address is 080009BEEE07—that's HP BEEE07 (row 7). Because you can't see any communication from the other printer in this screen, you don't see HP 5666E5 in the small part of the capture that's visible in the figure. Two of the other HP cards refer to printers named HP01 and HP02 (some days, we're less creative than other days). One of our NetWare 4.*x* servers has the Intel 53B759 Ethernet card; the server's name is MASTER. I can inform Netmon of those names by clicking Display and then Addresses; I'll then see a dialog box like the one in Figure 16.33.

FIGURE 16.33:

Address database

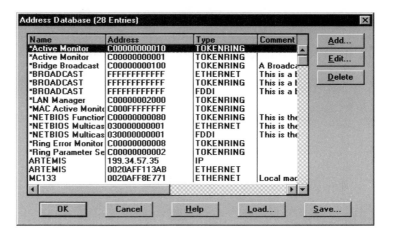

This displays the addresses that Netmon already knows. Click Add, and you can hand-enter a name into the database; you'll see a dialog box like the one in Figure 16.34.

All I've got to do is to fill in the MAC address and name for each Ethernet card, and then the capture screen gets a bit more interesting, as you see in Figure 16.35.

FIGURE 16.34:

Adding a name to the address database

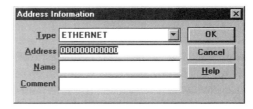

FIGURE 16.35:

Capture data with more name information

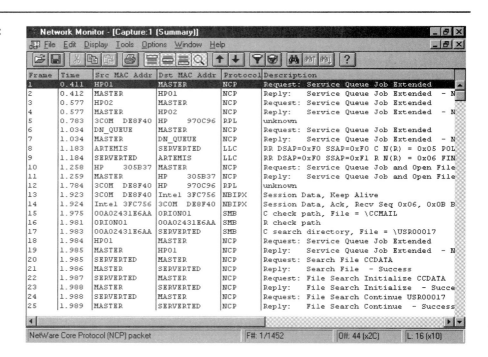

Much better—Netmon's getting downright chatty. Let's see what we can quickly see from this capture. First, notice how often MASTER and DN_QUEUE, HP01, and HP02 communicate. That's how Novell servers keep in touch with network-attached printers: they constantly (well, every 1.5 seconds, which is close enough to constant for me) check that they're still in contact. In contrast, ORIONHP1, which you *can't* see in this capture, only checks with its associated NT server once every 60 seconds.

Hey, there's the first thing that Netmon has helped us discover—there's a significant difference between the way Novell and Microsoft handle directly attached printers! And for sightseeing, there are some other interesting things going on here, as well. Look at the bottom seven frames between SERVERTED and MASTER—that's the Gateway Services for NetWare in action. We put our shared cc:Mail database on a NetWare server, but the folks without NetWare client software just attach to the cc:Mail database via a connection to a SERVERTED share which is actually GSNW.

NOTE The version of Network Monitor that comes with NT Server wouldn't have provided this much information; it can only report on network traffic between the NT Server machine that Network Monitor is running on and any other machine. The version of Network Monitor that ships with SMS can, in contrast, report on network traffic between all machines on the network.

Before going any further, it's a good idea to tell Netmon to save that address database. Just click Display and then Addresses, click the Save button, and save the database as DEFAULT.ADR. You'll be overwriting the original DEFAULT .ADR file.

There are other columns in the Netmon output, as well. The Protocol column indicates Netmon's best guess about what the frame is all about. For example, in that last figure you can see NCP (NetWare Core Protocol), LLC (Logical Link Control), SMB (Server Message Block), and NBIPX (NetBIOS over IPX). That's useful because you can zero in on just the blocks that you want to see, *filtering* the blocks using protocols.

You can filter by a number of methods, but the two I find most useful are to filter by name and by protocol. You can filter the frames you see by clicking Display, then Filter. A dialog box like the one in Figure 16.36 will appear.

Notice that it says to display all names and all protocols. Suppose I wanted to find out what the printer ORIONHP1 had done in the capture. Just double-click the "*ANY <-> *ANY" line, and you'll see the dialog box in Figure 16.37.

I select ORIONHP1, as you see in the figure, and click OK. The entire capture then looks like Figure 16.38.

This way, I can separate the wheat from the chaff when I want to zero in on what a particular PC is doing on the network. Be careful, however, about running

Netmon overnight in the hopes of getting amazing insights into your network; Netmon has a limited buffer for storing frames, and it just drops frames off the front when it runs out of space. To make a larger buffer, click Capture, then Buffer Settings, and you can set any size you like—but the buffer must stay in RAM, so don't get *too* generous!

FIGURE 16.36:

Display Filter dialog box

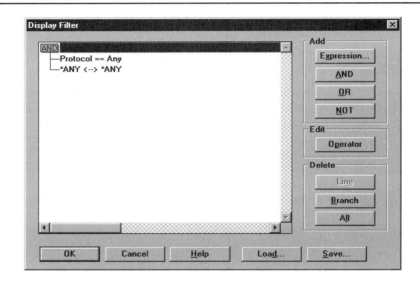

FIGURE 16.37:

Choosing names to filter

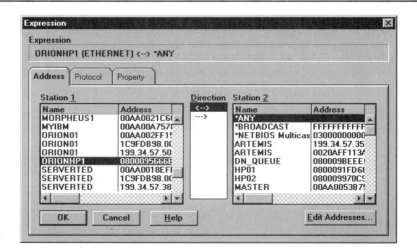

FIGURE 16.38:

Capture after filtering only
ORIONHP1

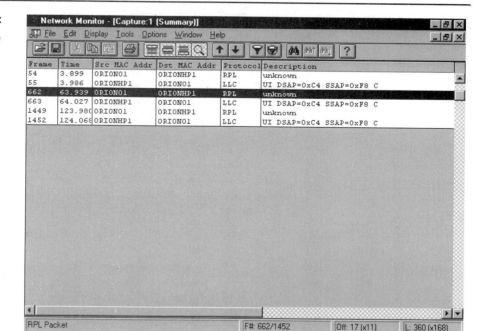

You can also filter protocols. Again, click Display and then Filter; only this time double-click the PROTOCOL line. In a dialog box similar to the one you used to filter names, you can choose which protocols to monitor. I want to see only the DHCP activity, so I click Disable All, and then add DHCP back. The result is Figure 16.39.

Here, you can see that one machine, SWEETIE, renewed its DHCP lease. But let's look at the insides of that DHCP acknowledgment; double-click the second frame (the acknowledgment) and you'll see a screen like Figure 16.40.

What this shows is the different layers of this message: it's a DHCP message, but that was transported via a UDP block. UDP, like TCP, sits atop IP, and IP on my network actually moves around the network on Ethernet's back, hence the Ethernet frame. I'll open up the DHCP part, and, drilling down a bit, I'll get a screen like Figure 16.41.

FIGURE 16.39:

Capture showing only DHCP activity

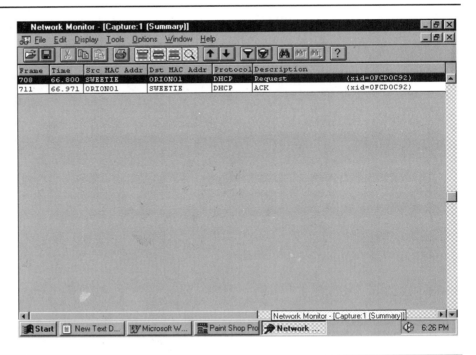

FIGURE 16.40:

Opening up the DHCP acknowledgment

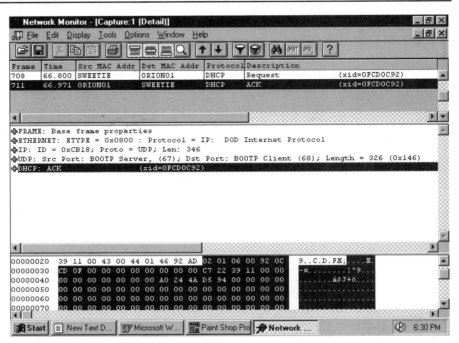

FIGURE 16.41:

DHCP ACK packet

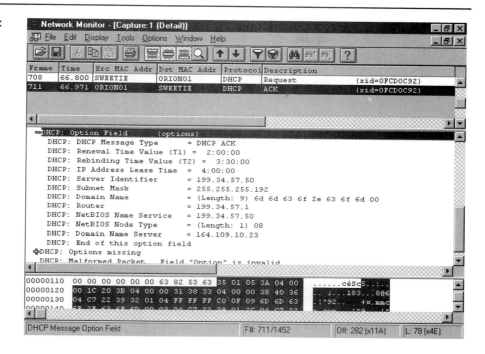

Notice that this shows you exactly what SWEETIE received in the way of configuration information from the DHCP server. Notice *also* that the DHCP packet is "malformed," according to the last line that's partially obscured. This shows up on every DHCP monitor I've ever seen. I often wonder if it means that there's a bug in the NT DHCP software, or in the Netmon software that analyzes DHCP? In any case, it's certainly an interesting item to print out and show to a software vendor.

Netmon Example: Following a PING

Let's take a machine and try a PING to the outside world, perhaps to Microsoft's FTP site: ftp.microsoft.com. If I start a network capture, type **ping ftp.microsoft .com**, and then stop the capture, I'll see something like Figure 16.42.

There were seven frames and a summary frame. The first two frames illustrate an ARP, which stands for *Address Resolution Protocol.* This computer needed to send data out of its local subnet, which meant that it needed to route that data through the default gateway. Its default gateway is a machine with IP address

199.34.57.1. But at a lower level of software, the machine must answer the question: What Ethernet address is associated with 199.34.57.1? That question is answered with ARP. The workstation (named QP200) broadcasts the question, "199.34.57.1, where are you?" In the second frame, 199.34.57.1 responds, saying, "I'm here at Cisco 3F240E." (That's the Ethernet card in one of our routers, which you will have guessed by now is made by Cisco.)

FIGURE 16.42:

Network capture after PING

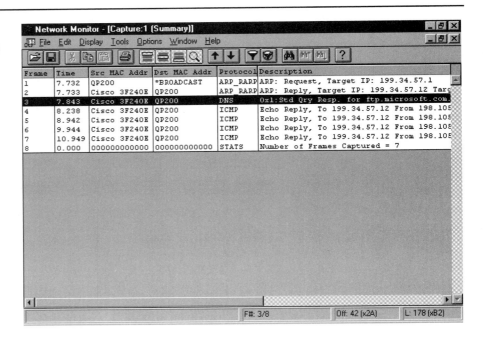

Next, QP200 must find out the IP address of ftp.microsoft.com. It does that by sending a request to a DNS server. But where's that request? You can't see it. This seems to be one of the shortcomings of the Network Monitor version that ships with NT Server: it is more capable of tracking packets *received* than packets *sent* from a station. But you can see the response in the third frame. Expanding that frame with a double-click, you see something like Figure 16.43.

Notice that it shows that ftp.microsoft.com is at 198.105.232.1. The next frame then shows the response from the PING that the system then gives to 198.105.232.1. The following three frames just repeat the PING.

FIGURE 16.43:

DNS response opened in Network Monitor

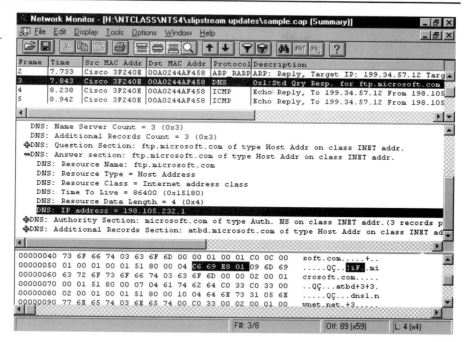

Network Monitor is a nice tool for looking into the network and seeing what it's doing and how it does it. The version that comes with NT Server is pretty lame, but if you have BackOffice around, load the Network Monitor that ships with SMS, and I think you'll find it useful now and then.

It's no good to throw money at a server in the hope that it will get faster. With a good tuning approach, you can decide where best to put your upgrade dollars. But sometimes a network is sluggish or non-responsive in a way that tuning can help—that's when it's time to read the next chapter.

CHAPTER

SEVENTEEN

17

Troubleshooting and Disaster Recovery

■ Protecting your network from physical harm

■ Backing up your data

■ Running NT recovery even without a CD-ROM

■ Recovering from disasters

■ Understanding server boot failures

■ Following the load sequence

■ Debugging NT 4

■ Diagnosing problems

■ Troubleshooting "No Domain Controller Found" problems

No matter how fault-tolerant your system is, there's always *some* fault it can't tolerate. It could be something as simple as an incorrectly configured NT server, or something as dramatic as your server falling down a crack in an earthquake. RAID's nice, but disk mirroring or disk striping is not going to help you here. What you need now is a way to rebuild your server's operating system and data, from the bottom up if need be. And once we've covered that, I'll take up some other annoying troubleshooting problems, including the "no domain controller was found to validate your login" error.

Defeating Disasters: An Overview

I'll get to the particular tools that you can use to examine and recover from disasters in a bit. But first let's look at how to avoid the disasters in the first place. You do that with several approaches:

- Create and maintain physical security on your network. If the bad guys (and the good guys who just happen to be careless) can't get to your network hardware, it's a lot harder for them to damage it.

- Protect your data with a good backup strategy. You have to back up both user data and system areas. There are two different tools for that, named NTBACKUP and RDISK. Now, RDISK requires an undocumented option to make it really useful, but I'll explain that later in this chapter.

- When the worst happens, you must be ready for it with a specific, written-down disaster recovery plan. Everybody must know what they're expected to do in the case of a massive network failure.

- When things go wrong, it's useful to have some knowledge about how the system starts up, when it crashes, and *why* it crashes. Two NT tools called the Kernel Debugger and DUMPEXAM can give you some insight into that.

Network Physical Security

An ounce of prevention is worth a pound of cure, right? One of the main concerns in computer security, and the one that this chapter addresses, is *physical security.* Physical security is a blanket term for the ways in which you *physically* protect your server and network from harm—from stupid accidents, environmental incidents, espionage, and theft.

Preventing Environmental Problems

It would be terrible if you went to all the trouble of protecting your server from theft or tampering and then lost it to a cup of coffee spilled into its air intake vents.

Electrical Protection

The first source of environmental problems that should never be ignored is the wall socket.

- Use a UPS/power conditioner on your servers to protect them from dirty power and power surges. If you don't want to buy a UPS for every workstation (and I don't blame you if you don't—that can get expensive), buy a *power conditioner.* This (roughly) $150 device cleans up noisy power and compensates for low voltage.

- While nothing will guarantee 100 percent protection from lightning damage, you can reduce lightning damage with an odd trick: tie five knots in each workstation's power cord, as close to the wall as you can get them. That way, if lightning strikes the wiring, it will kill the cord rather than travel through the cord and kill the computer.

Does this really work? Well, Washington, DC, where I live, was hit by a terrible lightning storm in 1990. I tied knots in the cords of all the computers in my house beforehand, but hadn't thought to do it to the television. During the storm one of my neighbors took a direct lightning hit and a huge power surge hit my wiring. The cords of all the computers were warmed up a bit, but the power surge never touched the computers themselves. The television was another matter—the surge traveled straight through the cord to the TV's innards and rendered the television DOA. I couldn't have asked for a better test, though at the time I wasn't in a mood to appreciate the benefits of having had an unknotted control group to compare the knotted cords with.

- Don't plug any computer into the same plug as a power hog like a refrigerator, copier, or laser printer. Laser printers periodically draw as much power as an entire kitchen full of appliances.

- If your computers are all in one room and you want to ground the room, don't just ground that room; ground the entire office. Otherwise, it's kind of like putting a giant "KICK ME" sign on your computers, as they will be the easiest thing around for lightning to reach.

If you're looking for a one-stop-shopping answer to your server's power needs, I like the American Power Conversion Smart-UPS series quite a bit. These UPSes are a combination of a power conditioner and a standby power supply.

There is more to know about power and PCs, but so ends the quick overview.

Know Your Building

When you're positioning servers and workstations, know what's in the building that could affect them. For example, are there old (or new) leaks in the building? Putting a server or workstation underneath a suspicious brown stain in the ceiling is a bad idea, even if the leak was "fixed" years ago and the building manager claims that "it can't possibly be a problem."

Excessive heat and moisture is bad for equipment. Is heat-producing equipment mounted in the ceiling? How about equipment that produces water condensation? One company moved into a new building and discovered that the air-conditioning equipment was mounted in the ceiling over the server room. Not only did the AC generate copious amounts of heat in exactly the place where it was least wanted, but the water condensation that the units generated began raining down onto the servers one morning. Luckily, the servers recovered nicely, but it could have been an ugly scene.

If the servers are locked in their own room, is that room staying cool enough for safety? The regular air conditioning that the rest of the office uses might not be enough, due to the restricted ventilation in a closed room and all the heat that computers generate.

Obviously, you shouldn't position *any* computer, whether it's a workstation or a server, in direct sunlight.

Keep Contaminants Away from the Servers

It is hard to keep people from eating or drinking near their workstations, but this should not be true in the server room. A strict no-food-or-beverage policy is necessary in that room to keep someone from pouring a Coke into the file server. The proliferation of nonsmoking offices makes the next comment almost unnecessary, but even if employees can smoke in the office, the one place they should *not* smoke is around the servers or workstations. Smoke particles on the hard disk are a *very* bad idea.

Preventing Theft and Tampering

Although the lion's share of physical security problems stems from accidents, theft and tampering are also things to watch out for if the information on your system might be valuable to someone else. To keep unauthorized people from gaining access to the network's information, do the following.

Keep the Server Room Locked   Most people who use the network don't have a valid reason for going into the server room, so you can keep it locked. If people can't get into the server room, they can't

- Reboot the server. If you are using the FAT file system, an intruder could reboot the server from a floppy (assuming that there are floppy drives on your server) and copy or delete valuable data. This, by the way, is one of the main reasons for using the NTFS file system—NTFS files and directories are invisible to users of the FAT file system.

- Steal the hard drive(s). This might sound improbable, but someone who has the tools and experience can simply remove the hard drive and take it elsewhere to crack into it at their leisure, rather than try to work with it on site. Stealing a hard drive is less awkward than stealing an entire server, but locking the file server room can also prevent server theft.

- Reinstall NT Server. While this sounds like a lot of trouble to go through, it's perfectly possible. Reinstalling the operating system doesn't harm the data already on the drive (unless you repartition it), so someone with the knowledge and the time could reinstall NT Server and change all the passwords, giving themselves access to your data.

Limit Access to the Server

Even if you can't lock up the server for space or administrative reasons, you can still limit people's physical access to it with the following tactics:

- Disable the server's A: drive. Without an A: drive, no one can reboot the system from a floppy unless they reconnect the A: drive first. Admittedly, this means you can't reboot either, but this could buy you some time if someone broke in intending to reboot the server. Use the floplock service that comes with the Windows NT *Resource Kit*. When the floplock service is running, only members of the Administrators group can access the floppy drives.

- Disable the reset button and on/off switch. Most of the time, if you need to reboot the server, you do it with the Shutdown option on the Start menu. Without a Big Red Switch or reset button, no one can boot the server unless they use the Shutdown option.

These are somewhat extreme measures, and truthfully I don't have enough need for security to use them on my network. Some of my clients, however (hint: I live in Washington DC, remember?) have found these suggestions quite implementable.

Using Passwords Well

Well chosen passwords are an important part of the security process. When selecting them, strike a balance between passwords that are too easy to guess and in service too long, and passwords that are so complicated and changed so frequently that users must write them down to remember them. An eight-letter minimum and a 30-day change policy (with the user unable to use the same password more than once every three changes) are probably about right. Experimentation and experience will help you choose a combination that fits your needs.

NT Server passwords are case-sensitive, so you can make them more difficult to guess by capitalizing them in unexpected places (like pAssword). Don't get too creative with this, however, or your users will never be able to type them in right.

There are programs that can guess passwords. These programs feed a dictionary to the system until the system accepts a word. To eliminate this path into your system, use words not found in the dictionary: names (picard), misspelled words (phantum), foreign words (*chamaca*), or made-up words (aooga). At password-changing time in one government installation, the users are presented with a two-column list of four-letter words (not obscenities, just words with four letters in them). The users pick one word from column A and one from column B, and then they combine them to form a new password, leading to such combinations as PINKFEET or BOATHEAD. These passwords are easy to remember and can't be found in the dictionary. Better yet, take the two words and string them together with a punctuation mark, like "stars.geronimo."

Most names are not found in the dictionary, but don't let your users use names of their spouses, children, pets, or anything else as passwords. One branch security manager at the Pentagon tells me that he had to go in and change all of his users' passwords when he discovered that a number of them had chosen the names of Japanese WWII battleships—a subject related to their mission and therefore not impossible to guess.

While the password-generating programs that randomly select a number-letter combination create nearly invulnerable passwords, these passwords may not be the most effective protection. They're too hard for most people to remember and often end up being written down.

Remove old user accounts from the system if the person using the account no longer needs it. If the user may need the account again (a summer intern, for example, could return the following summer), disable it rather than wipe it out altogether, but don't keep accounts active on the system unless someone is using them.

Finally, even if someone figures out a password and breaks into the system, you can reduce the possible damage by giving users only the minimum access to the system and to files that they need. There's more about this in Chapter 6.

Controlling Access to the Printer

The printer might seem like a harmless part of your network, but think again: if you have company secrets, those secrets could leave your network via your printer even if you've adopted diskless workstations. To try to avoid this, take these steps:

- Restrict printer access to those who need it. (You can also restrict access to keep people from playing with an expensive color printer.)

- Audit printer use in the Printers folder so that you know who is printing what. If you discover someone who prints more output to the printer than his work would justify, he may not be stealing company secrets—but he might be wasting company time and resources on personal projects. Be aware, however, that auditing server activity slows down the server.

- Restrict printer access time to normal working hours.

- Don't give out Power User rights to just anyone. Power users can create and connect to network devices, thereby negating all that you've done to control access to the devices.

Preventing Portable Penetration

Say that you have an Ethernet bus network. What happens if someone comes in with a portable and plugs in? What rights does this person have on the network?

Potentially disastrous as this may sound, if you've set up the network as a domain and the person with the portable does not know the administrator's password, plugging the portable into the network won't get that person anywhere. This is because the administrator is the only one who can add a computer to the domain, and a non-member is shut out of the domain.

If, however, your network is set up on a peer-to-peer basis, a plugged-in portable can do a lot more damage, due to the Guest Account on all the machines. Many people never bother to change the Guest account password from the default, and one of the easiest ways of accessing a network is through the guest account. While Guest access is not as powerful as that of the Administrator, a Guest can still view, copy, and delete files to which they have not been expressly refused access.

Therefore, to protect your network best, institute a domain controller so that no one can log on to the system from a new computer. If you *must* have a peer-to-peer setup, eliminate the Guest account on all the network's workstations or, at the very least, change the password on a regular basis.

How Much Protection Is Too Much?

Protecting your system is a never-ending process; for every safeguard you use, there is always a means to get past it. Therefore, when protecting your network, come up with a balance between how much the data is worth and how much the protection costs. If protecting your data costs more than the data is worth, it's time to relax a little. The cost of perfect protection is infinite amounts of money and eternal vigilance. If you hope to ever get anything done or to have money to spend on anything else, weigh your protection costs against what you're protecting and plan accordingly. There's little point in spending the money for more drives so that you can have RAID fault-tolerance, for example, if all that you're protecting are applications for which you have the original disks and backups.

When something goes wrong with your system, think *non-invasive*. Three of your most valuable troubleshooting implements are:

- An NT-bootable disk

- The Emergency Repair Disk for the machine in trouble (don't forget, they're specific to the machine on which they were made)

- Your notebook, in which you record every change you make to the servers and workstations, so that when something goes wrong, you can figure out what changed since the last time it worked

Backup Strategies

Physical security keeps people and the outside environment from getting to your equipment. Now let's consider how to protect your data. The first line of defense against data loss is backups. Backups are like exercise—they're necessary but they often don't get done unless they're easy to do. NT Server does a lot toward making sure that backups get done by providing a tape backup program that is fast and easy to use.

Performing Backups

You can find the Backup icon in the Start menu under the Administrative Tools program group. When you highlight the icon, you see a screen that looks like Figure 17.1.

When you want to back up a drive, you first need to select the drive, even if you only have one on your server. To do so, click in the check box next to the drive until it has an X in it. If for some reason you open the Backup screen and the drives window is only an icon similar to the Tapes icon at the bottom of Figure 17.1, just double-click on it to open it.

Once you've selected the drive that you want to back up and a tape is in the drive, you're ready to go. Click on the Backup button in the upper-left corner or select the Backup option from the Operations drop-down menu. You see a screen that looks like Figure 17.2.

FIGURE 17.1:

Opening screen for Backup

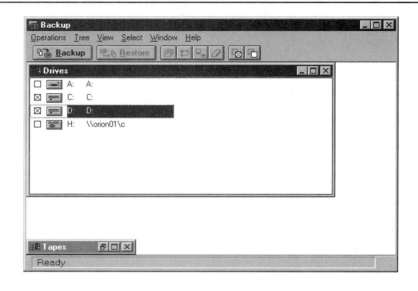

FIGURE 17.2:

Backup Information
dialog box

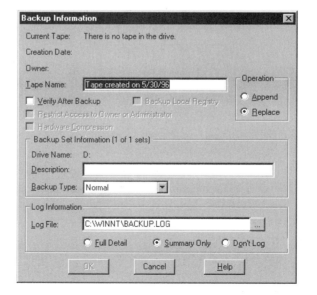

The Backup Information Dialog Box

The Backup Information dialog box gives you information about the tape in the drive and lets you make decisions about how you want the backup to be conducted. Let's look at each part of this dialog box in order:

Option	What It Does
Current Tape	As you might guess, this is the tape that you have in the drive. I'm reusing an old backup, so the Backup program reads and gives me the tape name, which is the tape's creation date. This is good, because if I use this tape for my backup, I'll lose the data from the 5/30 backup, and this reminder of when the tape was made could save me from mistakenly overwriting my data.
Creation Date	If you named the tape something other than the date it was created, this tells you when the current tape was created.
Owner	This is the domain and user name of the person who made the backup.
Tape Name	This is the name that you give the new information on this tape. You can use the default name of "Tape created on [*date*]" if you like, or you can call it something like "Backup before installing OS/2 do not erase" to give your memory a little extra jog. The tape name can be up to 50 characters long, including spaces, but if it's longer than 32 characters you won't be able to see the entire name without scrolling down the line.
Verify After Backup	If you select this option, the Backup program checks to make sure that, after it's done, the backup matches the original data on the disk. Verification takes a little longer, but it's a good way to double-check that your backups are actually complete and accurate when you need them.
Backup Local Registry	Check this box to include a copy of the local Registry files in the backup set. The local Registry files are your disk configuration information, and in the case of disaster, having this information might not be a bad idea.
Operation	Selecting Append or Replace makes a decision about what happens to the data already on the tape, if there is any. Select Append to add the new backup to the backup already on the tape and not lose anything. Make sure that you have enough room on the tape for both the old data and the new. Select Replace to have the new backup overwrite the old one. Be sure that you no longer need an old backup before selecting Replace, because you can't get back the data once you overwrite it.
Restrict Access to Owner or Administrator	Restricting access is probably a good idea for a number of reasons. First, no one but the owner or administrator should have any need to access backed-up files. If someone else needs an old copy of a file, they can ask the people authorized to give it to them. Second, making everyone responsible for their own backups helps avoid recrimination when a backup is missing or corrupted. If no one can use a backup other than its owner, then, if something happens to it, it's clear who did it.

Option	What It Does
Drive Name	The drive name is the name of the drive you selected for the backup before you got to this dialog box. You can't change it here, so if you selected the wrong drive, cancel out of this box and change your selection.
Description	You can fill in a description of the backup in addition to its name. Therefore, if you wanted to record both the date and the contents of the drive, you could name the tape "Backup from 03/09/97" and *describe* it as "Pre-OS/2 installation backup—keep," or some such thing.
Backup Type	If you click on the down-arrow on the right side of this box, you see a number of different backup types to choose from:
Normal	A full backup—everything selected gets backed up, whether or not the archive bit is set. (The archive bit is attached to a file when it's changed and removed during backup, allowing selective backups of the files that have changed since the last backup.) This is the default option. Even if you normally do incremental backups (described below), periodically doing a normal backup to make sure that everything on the disk is backed up is a good idea.
Copy	A full backup of all the selected files on the disk. In this case, however, the archive bit is not reset after the files have been backed up—from looking at Explorer, you can't tell that anything was backed up.
Differential	Backs up only those files with the archive bit set, but doesn't reset it afterwards. This is useful for interim backups between full backups, because restoring the data only requires restoring the last full backup and the most recent differential.
Incremental	Like a differential backup, this option backs up only those files with the archive bit set, but the incremental backup then resets the bit.
Daily	Backs up only those files that have been modified *that day* (as opposed to since the last backup), and does not reset the archive bit. If you want to take home the files that you've worked on during a given day, this can be a good way of getting them all.
Log Information	Backup log records how the backup went: how many files were backed up, how many skipped (if any), how many errors there were (if any), and how long the backup took. You might as well keep the backup logs in the default directory unless you have a good reason to move them elsewhere just so you don't forget where they are.
Full Detail, Summary Only	On the bottom of the dialog box you can see that you have a choice of two kinds of backup log records: Full Detail and Summary Only (or no log). A full log records the name of every file backed up in addition to the other information about major events that are described above. A summary merely records major events. For most purposes a summary log is fine. The only time that you might need a full log is if you were doing a differential backup and wanted to have some record of what files you backed up.

Now that you've filled out the Backup Information dialog box, you're ready to do the backup. Click OK, and, if you're using an old backup tape and you selected the Replace option, you see a screen that looks like Figure 17.3. Once again, if you're sure that you want to overwrite the data, click on Yes. You move now to the dialog box in Figure 17.4, which keeps you informed of the backup's progress.

FIGURE 17.3:

Warning that data will be overwritten

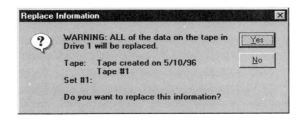

FIGURE 17.4:

Backup Status screen

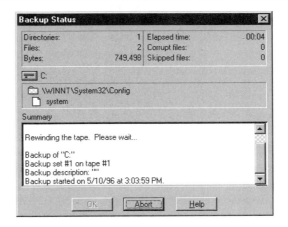

Normally when you see this screen, Abort will not be grayed out unless you had to abort the backup, and OK won't be a viable choice from the time you begin the backup until it's finished. As the backup progresses, you can keep track of it by looking at this screen.

Performing Automatic Backups

To be safe, you should back up your drive every day, since that way you never lose more than one day's worth of work. Unfortunately, running even an easy-to-use backup program like NT Server's takes time away from your day—the task-switching involved causes you to take time from your real work, and you might forget altogether if you get caught up in something else.

How Do I Back Up Data?

With a tape in the drive, start the Backup program, which can be found in the Start menu under the Administrative Tools program group. Select the drive that you want to back up, and then click on the Backup button in the upper-left area of the screen. Fill in the Backup Information dialog box as appropriate, and click OK.

The backup should proceed normally.

Important note: You cannot read or restore tapes backed up in NT Server 4 on a server running a previous version of NT Server.

Fortunately, you don't have to depend on your memory or your schedule to run daily backups. NT Server provides two ways to run backups on a regular schedule: the command prompt and the WINAT.EXE GUI program.

Backing Up from the Command Prompt

Elsewhere in this book, we talked about how to use the net schedule and at commands to schedule batch commands to run at a certain time. Among the other programs that you can run with the AT command is the DOS version of NT Server's Backup program, called ntbackup. The parameters this command uses provide you with almost the same flexibility that the GUI backup program does—it's just a little trickier to use.

To run ntbackup, type the following:

```
ntbackup backup path options
```

where *path* is the drive (and directory, if you're only backing up part of a drive) that you want to back up and *options* is one of the switches shown in Table 17.1. You can select more than one drive at a time—just type the drive letters with colons after them. In the path, you can also specify individual files to back up, or specify all the files of a certain type with the asterisk wildcard (*).

TABLE 17.1: Switches for Use with NT Backup

Switch	Description
/a	Makes the mode of backup append, so that the backed up files will be added to those already on the tape. If this switch is omitted, the new files will overwrite any files now on the tape.
/b	Backs up the local registry.
/d	Lets you describe the backup. Enclose your text in quotation marks after the /d switch.
/l	Writes a log of the backup. You must specify a location for the log to be written, like this: /l "c:\log\log.txt." As shown, you enclose the log's destination in quotation marks.
/r	Restricts access to the tape's owner and the network administrator.
/t	Lets you select the backup type. You can choose to do a Normal, Copy, Incremental, Differential, or Daily backup; /t incremental gives you an incremental backup. If you don't use this switch, you perform a normal backup.
/v	Verifies that the backup was done correctly by comparing the data on the tape with the original data on the drive after the backup is done. Backups take a little longer with verification, but they let you know that the data was written correctly.
/hc:on or /hc:off	Turns on/off your tape drive's hardware compression feature.

Let's start with a simple example. To obtain a full backup of all the files on a C:\wpfiles directory that end with the extension DOC, you would type this:

```
ntbackup backup c:\wpfiles\*.doc
```

Finally, to perform a differential backup of all the files in both drives C: and D:, verify the backup, describe the backup as the monster drives on the server, perform a backup of the local Registry, restrict access to the owner and network administrator, and record a backup log under the name C:\LOG\LOG.TXT, you would type the following on one line:

```
ntbackup backup c: d: /v/r/b/d "The monster drives on the server" /l
"c:\log\log.txt"
```

Now that you're familiar with the DOS parameters for the Backup program, you can use it to do timed backups. Start the scheduler service by typing **net start schedule,** and then use the AT command to set up the automatic backup. For instance, to do an incremental backup every day at 3 A.M. of the \wpfiles directory on drive C, verify the backup, append the files to the ones already on the disk, describe the backup as "My word-processing files," and record the log in c:\log\log.txt, you would type this on one line:

```
at 3:00 /every:M,T,W,Th,F,Sa,Su ntbackup backup c:\wpfiles /t incremen-
tal /v/a/d "My wordprocessing files" /l "c:\log\log.txt"
```

For another example, to back up your C: drive at 11:00 every Wednesday, start the scheduling service by typing **net start schedule**, and then type

```
at 11:00 /every:wednesday ntbackup backup c:
```

These commands would then be entered on the jobs list, which you can view by typing **at** from the command prompt. You don't have to set up the command as you see it in the example; you can use the switches to configure your backup procedure as you see fit. No matter what combination of switches you use to customize your automatic backups, however, using the /a switch to append the new backups to the ones already on your tape is probably a good idea. You're using this daily incremental backup to keep your backups current between weekly full backups, so you want to keep a complete record of all changes made between those full backups.

Using the Scheduler (WINAT) PROGRAM

Unless you're really fond of working from the command prompt, the WINAT GUI program is probably easier to use, even though you still need to know the MS-DOS syntax. WINAT is one of a number of handy applications that come with the Windows NT *Resource Kit*. Once you load the *Resource Kit,* you need to use the Program Manager's New option to add it manually to one of the program groups. You can put the program item wherever you like; I put mine in the Administrative Tools program group.

When you've added WINAT to a program group, you're ready to go. Double-click on the program icon, pull down the File menu, choose Select Computer, type in your computer name if it is not already there, click OK, and then choose the Add button. You see a screen that looks like Figure 17.5.

In the Command text box, type in the command syntax, following the rules in the previous section on using the command prompt. Once you've typed in the command, use the radio buttons to select how often you want the event to occur (since we're configuring a daily incremental backup, choose Every). Next,

Ctrl+click on all the days of the week on which you want the backup to run. For our installation, we selected every day, for those times when someone's working over the weekend, but you may want to choose different days. Finally, choose the time when you want the backup to run. It's best to choose a time very late at night or early in the morning when there is little network activity. Once you've set up the command and the times, click OK to return to the original screen. It should look like Figure 17.6.

FIGURE 17.5:

Add Command dialog box

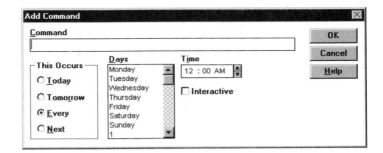

FIGURE 17.6:

Command Scheduler dialog box

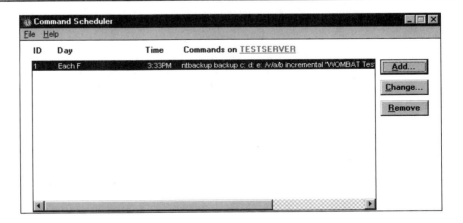

If you need to adjust the settings of your job, click the Change button. You see the Change Command dialog box, which looks much like the Add Command dialog box shown in Figure 17.5. From this screen, you can adjust your backup (or any other scheduled service) as necessary by using the same procedures that you used to add it.

If you need to remove your backup command, select it in the Command Scheduler screen and click Remove. When you do, the system prompts you for confirmation. Click Yes and the command is removed. Don't remove an event unless you're sure that you want to, however, because no Cancel function is on that screen. Every time you add a job to this list, it will be assigned a job identification number. When you remove a job, the numbers assigned to the other jobs in the list do not change, and future jobs take the next highest number available. If you erase job 0, leaving job 1 intact, and then add job 0 back, it will become job 2.

What about the Scheduler service? Yes, it still needs to be running for WINAT to work, just as it does for the at command in the command prompt. You can start it from the Services icon in the Control Panel, or you can just go ahead and start WINAT. A message box will tell you that the Scheduler is not running and ask you if you want to start running it. When you say Yes, the service will begin.

Special Backup Operations

We've just discussed how to do a normal, vanilla-flavored backup that hits every file on your hard disk, only requires one tape, backs up a local disk, and doesn't need to be aborted. However, special circumstances may require you to do the job a bit differently, and that's what this section covers.

Backing Up Only Selected Files

At some point, you may want to back up only certain directories or files on your hard disk; not necessarily the ones with the archive bit set, but an assortment. To do this, you must select the directories or files to be copied, and deselect everything else.

The process begins as though you were backing up the entire disk. Go to the initial Backup screen and select the drive that you want to back up. Rather than clicking on the Backup button, however, double-click on the gray drive icon. You see a screen that looks like Figure 17.7.

When I opened this screen, every directory had a filled check box next to it. Since I only wanted to back up files from some of the directories, I clicked the check box next to the C: drive to deselect it so that I could select the individual directory that I wanted. From here, I chose as many directories as I liked. When I double-clicked on NTCLASS, I got a list of its files and subdirectories, as shown in Figure 17.8.

FIGURE 17.7:

Selection of directories to
back up

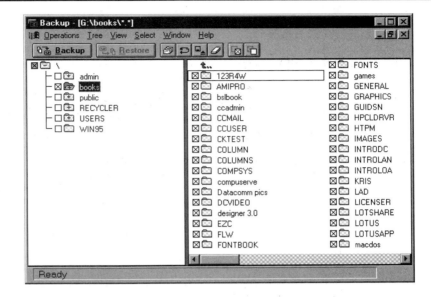

FIGURE 17.8:

Selection of files and
subdirectories to back up

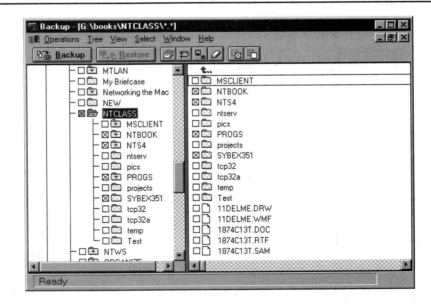

Once again, to keep from selecting every file and subdirectory in the NTCLASS directory, I clicked on the check box for that directory to deselect it. Now, only the files that I selected would be backed up. As you can see in the figure, I chose four files to back up.

Now we're ready to complete the backup. From here, click on the Backup button, as you did earlier to back up the entire drive. You are returned to the initial Backup Information dialog box. The rest of the operation is exactly like backing up an entire directory.

By the way, please note that, although I only selected one directory to draw files from for this example, you can choose files from as many directories and subdirectories as you like. Just make sure that you deselect everything before you select anything, or else you end up backing up more files than you intended.

Using More Than One Tape

Using more than one tape isn't difficult to do. If you choose Append from the Backup Information dialog box or have an absolutely huge hard drive, you may run out of space on your tape before the backup is done. If this happens, the Backup program prompts for a new tape. Just insert the new tape, and press OK.

Aborting a Backup

If you realize that you don't want to back up your data once you've started, you can click on the Abort button to make the process stop. If the program was in the middle of backing up a file and there was less than 1MB to go, the file will be completed; otherwise a message box appears and asks if you really want to stop now and have the file be corrupted on the tape.

Clicking on Abort does not cancel the backup; it only stops it at the point at which you aborted. Whatever files were backed up before you aborted the process will be on the tape.

Backing Up to Floppy Disks

If you don't have a tape drive, you can still back up your most important files to floppy disks. To do so, go to the command prompt and use either the xcopy or the backup command. The backup command is perhaps a little simpler.

When using the BACKUP command, you can specify drives (although that's not likely if you're backing up to floppies), directories, or individual files. The syntax looks like this:

backup *source destination drive: options*

where *source* specifies the source files, directories, or drive. You can use wildcards to specify all the files of a certain type, or you can spell out all the filenames. For example, to back up all of directory C:\WPFILES, you would type **c:\wpfiles**. To back up all the files in that directory with the doc suffix, you would type **c:\wpfiles*.doc**. For *destination drive,* substitute the name of the drive (such as A) where you want the backups to be stored. For *options,* include one or more of the switches shown in Table 17.2.

TABLE 17.2: Switches for Use in Backing Up to Floppy Disks

Switch	Description
/a	Appends the current backup to the files already on the destination disk. Omitting this switch causes the destination disk to be overwritten.
/d:[*date*]	Backs up only the files that have changed after the date you place after the colon, whether or not they have the archive bit set.
/f:[*size*]	Specifies the size of the disk to be formatted, if you want the destination disk to be formatted before you write to it. Put the size of the disk (1.44MB, for example) after the colon.
/l[*drive:path*]	Creates a log file in the drive and path you specify.
/m	Backs up only the files with the archive bit set—the ones that have changed since the last backup.
/s	Tells the backup program to search all subdirectories for files. If you don't select this option, the backup program only backs up the files in the directory that you're actually in—if you specify C:*.DOC for the source directory and don't use the /s switch, only DOC files in the root directory will be backed up.
/t:[*time*]	Backs up only those files that have changed after the time you specify, whether or not they have the archive bit set.

Alternatively, you can use xcopy to back up your files or put files on disk to take them on a trip. Use xcopy rather than copy, because COPY doesn't use the archive bit and is not as easy to customize. While XCOPY has many switches, these are the most relevant to backing up NTFS files:

Switch	What It Does
/a	Copies files with the archive attribute set, but doesn't change the attribute (good for when you're copying the files that you've worked with on a given day but don't want them to get skipped by the daily incremental backup).
/d:*date*	Copies only the files changed on or after the date you specify.
/h	Copies hidden and system files, as well as normal ones.
/m	Copies with the archive bit set and then removes the bit.
/n	Copies NTFS files, using shorter names created for use with FAT file system. Only works on NTFS files.
/u	Updates the files in the destination.

If you want more help with XCOPY, type the following command from the command prompt (there's more than one screen of options):

```
xcopy /? |more
```

Backing Up Removable Media

If you want to back up the data in a removable media drive (such as a Bernoulli or a Floptical), it may seem impossible at first because NT Server's Backup program doesn't recognize removable drives as available for backup. You can, however, get around this fairly easily. To see how, read the "How Do I" sidebar.

How Do I Back Up a Removable Drive?

To back up a removable drive:

1. Go to the File Manager or the command prompt and share the drive that you want to back up.

2. Connect to the shared drive from the File Manager or command prompt.

The Backup program will now be able to see the drive under the letter assigned to it, so long as you have a disk in the drive.

You're now set. Back it up as you would any other drive.

Backing Up a Network Drive

Even if you're using an internal tape drive on your server, you can still use that drive to back up other hard disks on your system. The process is quite straight-forward:

1. Go to the computer that you want to back up and share the drive or directory for backup with the network.

2. From the server's Explorer, map a network drive to the shared directory.

Now, when you start the backup program, you notice a new icon for a network drive in the list of available drives for backup. From here, the backup process is identical to that of backing up a local drive.

Backing Up Open Files

NT's Backup program has one distinct failure: it can't back up open files. If you normally schedule backups for 2 A.M. when no one's working, this wouldn't seem to be a problem. However, if you're connecting to the Internet or just running TCP/IP protocol with DHCP with or without WINS-DNS, some files will be open at 2 A.M. and *must* stay open: the files that control the internal naming services, and, if you're using DHCP, the files that allocate IP addresses.

Luckily, there's an easy way around this. To make sure that the WINS and DHCP files get backed up, make this simple batch file part of your regularly scheduled backup:

```
C:
CD \USERS
CACLS DHCP /T /E /G EVERYONE:F
CACLS WINS /T /E /G EVERYONE:F
net stop "Microsoft DHCP Server"
net stop "Windows internet name service"
xcopy c:\winnt35\system32\dhcp c:\users\sysjunk\dhcp
>>C:\USERS\DBAK.LOG
xcopy c:\winnt35\system32\wins c:\users\sysjunk\wins
>>C:\USERS\DBAK.LOG
net start "Windows internet name service"
net start "Microsoft DHCP Server"
```

It's not hard to tell what's going on here: the files that run the DHCP server and WINS are getting copied from the \SYSTEM32 directory to an (unopened) log file in the \USERS directory so that they can be backed up. This batch file stops the

DHCP Server and the Windows Internet Service before it copies the files and restarts the services after the files are copied. However, because the whole batch file takes only a few seconds to execute, the services are not shut down long enough to present a problem.

If you don't recognize the CACLS command, that's because it's not documented except in Microsoft's TechNet. CACLS is a useful NT command that allows you to change the ownership and control of a file or directory from the command line. In our version of the batch file, we had to include a command giving the Everyone group full control of the WINS and DHCP directories because these directories were owned by the System and thus even Administrators could not copy them. You could give only Administrators or Backup Operators full control if you liked; in our case, it didn't matter if Everyone could control the directories.

If you're using the AT command to schedule backups, you can make this batch file part of your weekly backup: just add it to the scheduler to run a few minutes before the backup job.

Protecting Backups

Backing up your system is a vital part of any decent security program. However, it's quite easy for an intruder to access your confidential files on the tapes that you back up to. If you don't keep an eye on the tapes, they can be rendered useless when you need to restore them. Any user can back up files that he or she has access to, and any Administrator or Backup Operator can back up the entire drive (even if, for example, your Backup Operator cannot normally access the files that she's backing up). Be very careful about who you assign backup rights to.

Once you have your backup tapes, you need to protect them from damage, as well as protect them from theft. To this end, here are some things to consider when storing tapes:

- Tapes are comfortable under approximately the same conditions that you are. Excessive heat and dampness do your backups no good. *Never* store tapes on a windowsill.

- While you want your backups to be fairly convenient, so that you can restore information if you blast your hard drive, it doesn't do you any good to have backups if your office burns down and takes the originals and the backups of all your data with it. For best protection, store all of your backups but the most recent at a safe location (locked, fireproof, waterproof) off-site.

- Enable the Restrict Access to Owner or Administrator option when backing up files. For extra protection, keep server backups locked up and only allow the network administrator or the security manager access to them. If workstations get backed up, the tapes and their usability should be the responsibility of the workstation's user.

- Label your tapes clearly and completely (on both their paper labels and their electronic volume labels), so that you don't erase a vital tape by thinking that it's something else. In NT Server, you can be very explicit about the volume label on a tape, so use this capability to identify tapes that you don't want to reuse.

Restoring Files

Your backups are useless unless you can restore them to your machine in good order. Restoring files is much like backing them up. First, click open the Backup item in the Administrative Tools program group. You see the Backup screen that you saw when you backed up originally. But this time, select the Tapes window instead of a drive. You see a screen that looks like Figure 17.9.

FIGURE 17.9:

Opening Restore screen

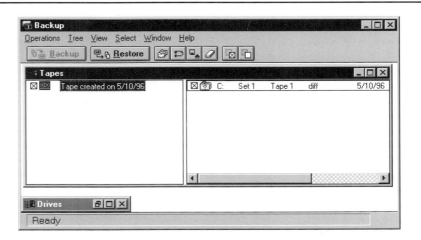

To begin the restoration process, select the tape by clicking in the check box next to it. If you want to restore an entire tape, the selection process is done. However, you probably want to restore only selected files from a tape, not the whole thing, so we'll go through the selection process now.

Double-click on the tape icon and the restore program loads the tape's catalog, so that it can find files on the tape. This process takes a couple of minutes, and while it's doing this, you see a screen that looks like Figure 17.10.

FIGURE 17.10:

Catalog Status message

When the cataloging process is finished, you can click on the yellow files icon on the other side of the initial screen. When you do, you see a screen like the one in Figure 17.11 that shows all the available directories on the tape. Any corrupt files (that is, files that contain errors) and their corresponding directories are marked by an icon with a red X.

FIGURE 17.11:

Available directories for restoration

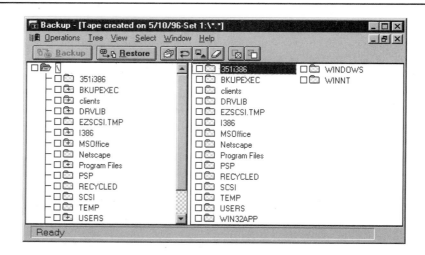

As you can see, everything is currently deselected. I didn't want to restore every file, so I unchecked the drive's check box. Subdirectories can then be selected by double-clicking on their yellow file icons. You don't have to check the check boxes to select a drive or a directory before expanding it, and it's safer not to if you're doing a selective restore as I am in this example. If you select a drive or directory, everything in it will be restored.

Once you've progressed to the directory that you want, click on the file or files that you want to restore, just as you did when you were backing up. Your screen should look something like Figure 17.12.

FIGURE 17.12:

Files selected for restoration

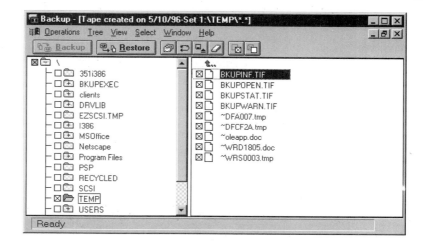

Now you're ready to restore. Go ahead and click on the Restore button. A dialog box similar to the Backup Information box opens, as in Figure 17.13.

FIGURE 17.13:

Restore Information
dialog box

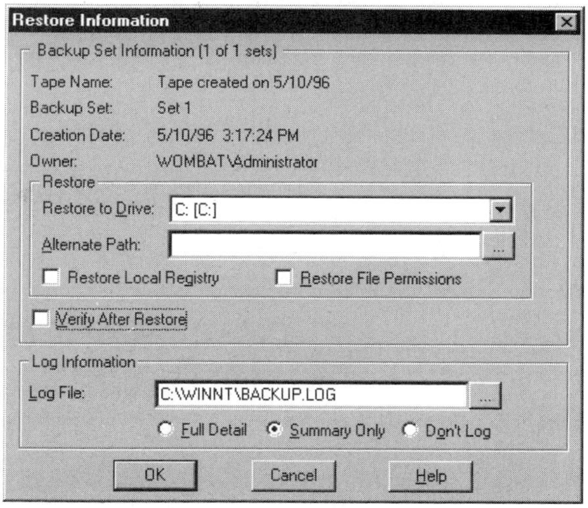

The Restore Information dialog box is much simpler than the Backup Information dialog box. Essentially, all that you must do here is decide whether or not to verify that the information was written correctly (a good idea, even though it adds time to the restoration process), restore the local Registry if you backed it up, and restore the file permissions that were in place for the file when you backed it up. If you like, you can choose to restore the data to a different drive than the one you backed it up from, although you cannot restore Registry information to a drive other than the one from which you backed it up. You can also choose what kind of log file you want and where you would like to store it.

When you're done, click OK, and the restoration progress begins. You can watch the process on the screen, as in Figure 17.14.

FIGURE 17.14:

File restoration progress
screen

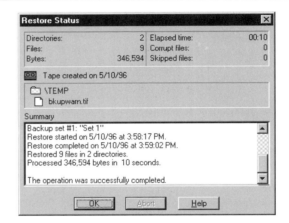

If you're restoring individual files to your drive because the originals were corrupted somehow, the Restore program asks you if you're sure that you want to replace the file on disk with the file on the tape. You see a dialog box like the one in Figure 17.15. Your files are now restored to your hard disk.

FIGURE 17.15:

Confirm File Replace
dialog box

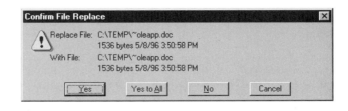

Side Note: Restoring Data After Reinstalling NT Server

When writing this book, there were some things that I could not experiment with unless I reinstalled NT Server. Given that the operating system really isn't too difficult to install (just time-consuming), this wasn't much of a problem, but one instance of reinstalling the operating system and trying to restore my data nearly gave me heart failure.

I was experimenting with the Disk Administrator and needed to re-partition the drive with the NT Server installation on it, so I prepared to back up my data and reinstall the server. I did everything by the book: backed up the hard disk to tape, verified the backup, and restored a couple of files from the backup (just to make sure that the files could be read). Now I was ready to go. I installed NT Server, blowing away my old disk partition in the process so that *none* of the data was left, and then, two hours later when the installation was done, prepared to restore the data.

When I tried to catalog the tape, all I got was a cryptic Dr. Watson message advising me that the system had generated an application error, and then the Backup program closed. When I reopened it, I could see the icon for the tape catalog tantalizingly sitting there, but when I tried to double-click on it to open it, I got the same Dr. Watson message.

In desperation, I selected the catalog and attempted to restore without being able to access it, but all that got me was the data thrown back on the hard disk any which way, not in its original directories but in strange directories with names that the system seemed to have made up from truncated file names. I checked a couple of the files after this strange restoration and they seemed okay, but I knew that I couldn't count on the data's integrity, and I'd never be able to find anything anyway. Restoring the data without the catalog was useless.

If the situation I was in isn't quite clear, let me just explain that the tape that I couldn't read contained all the data on the hard drive: all my books, all the company's manuals, all of *everything* except the mailing list. I had the backup—I was clutching it, white-knuckled, in my hand—but I couldn't read it.

I reinstalled NT Server, just to see if there was a problem with the installation that prevented me from reading my tape. Then I did it again. And again. I scoured the documentation, looking for clues. Finally, I got desperate (well, more desperate), decided that it was time to call in the Marines, and called Microsoft's $150-per-question Tech Support line with my problem. Even at $150 per question, however, they didn't know the answer. (That didn't keep them from charging me, however, and now the price has risen to $195.)

Finally, many hours and several installations later, I decided to try installing all the system software and *then* restoring the data. I reinstalled everything that I had on the system before, including the Service Pack 2 patches (this was under NT 3.1) that had been on the system before, on the theory that it might affect how the backup worked. *This* time, I could restore the data.

The moral of this story? Before trying to restore data after a complete reinstallation of NT Server, install all your system software first. It seems obvious now, but it wasn't at the time, and that mistake nearly killed me. (End of digression.)

How Do I Restore Data from Backups?

With the tape from which you wish to restore in the drive, begin the Backup program in the Administrative Tools program group. Double-click on the tape icon to catalog it. Once it's cataloged, select the item(s) that you wish to restore or select the entire catalog, and then click on the Restore button. A dialog box appears; fill it in as appropriate. The restoration process should take place normally. If you don't have a tape drive, the programs REGBACK and REGREST, available with the NT *Resource Kit,* will save and restore registries to and from floppies.

Special Restoration Operations

Sometimes, you can't restore files in the traditional way described above because a backup set is spread over more than one tape or you've blasted the disk Registry and you need to restore it. In cases like these, you need special restoration techniques.

Restoring from a Tape Set with a Missing Tape

To restore data from a backup set that extends over more than one tape, you need to insert the last tape in the set and load the backup catalog from there.

If that tape has been lost or destroyed, you can still load the backup catalogs from the tapes that you have, but it's a more arduous process. In this case, you must build a partial tape catalog by inserting the available tapes and loading their individual catalogs. Once you've done that, you can restore the data. If you're restoring the data from the command prompt, run NTBACKUP with the /MISSINGTAPE switch.

Restoring Data to a Networked Drive

The process of restoring data to a networked drive is pretty much what you expect. Connect to the drive or directory through the Explorer, and then choose to restore to that drive letter when you're setting up the Restore Options. From here, the process is identical to restoring locally.

NTBACKUP Test Trivia

In general, I find that most people don't use NTBACKUP because its tape library facilities are limited, it can't handle tape auto-loaders, and it doesn't do software compression. Don't misunderstand me, it's great that Microsoft included NTBACKUP for free in the box, and for many small businesses (like mine), it'll be an adequate backup solution.

But when taking the NT 4 core technologies test (exam number 70-67), I was startled by the number of questions about the NTBACKUP program: *four* out of about 54 questions! I *use* the program, as I said, and so I knew about its idiosyncrasies, but it occurred to me that anyone working in a medium-sized or large firm might not know these things. Here's a brief compendium of factoids that you might need to know if you take the NT 4 Server test.

Backing Up the Registry

In order to back up the Registry, you must do two things. Remember that the Registry lives in the \WINNT\SYSTEM32\CONFIGS directory on some drive; Microsoft calls the drive that you've got the \WINNT directory on the "system drive." So, first, you've got to be backing up at least one file on the system drive in order to back up the Registry. Second, either use the /B option from the command line, or check the Backup Registry box from the GUI.

Restoring the Registry

Again, you must be restoring at least one file, or you can't raise the Restore Files dialog box. You must be restoring a file to the same volume that the Registry resides on: the system drive. Then, just check the Restore Local Registry box, and you'll get your old Registry back. You must be running NTBACKUP physically on the machine that you want to do the Registry backup or restore on in order for this to work.

You Can't Restore to Another Name

If you have a file named MYSTUFF.TXT that you want to restore, but you want it restored under the name (for example) MYSTUFF2.TXT, you can't. You can restore a file to a different directory or drive from the one that it came from (that capability first appeared in NT 3.51), but you can't rename it. There *is* a workaround, of course—just restore it under its original name and then rename it.

Restoring a Configuration

Sometimes, no matter how vigilant you've been, mistakes happen or something just goes wrong, and you need to fix your system. These fixes range from easy to horrific.

We'll start with a relatively easy one. What happens if you successfully install NT Server, try to adjust your system configuration, and render your server unusable—or even unbootable? Something as simple as changing the video driver to something that your system can't handle will do that, and it's hard to restore the original driver if you can't read what's on your screen. If you've messed up your system's configuration, what do you do?

One approach to fixing a diseased server would be to simply reinstall it from scratch—wipe the system drive and reinstall. That sounds like a lot of work, and it can be—reconfiguring all those services and reinstalling apps can be time consuming and error prone if you don't have a good disaster-recovery document—but you can make it simpler if you take the time to build an automated install script for each important server. It's my experience that once you've got an installation script working, a complete reinstall, complete with all settings and such, can take as little as 15 minutes. The servers are expensive, yes, but their cost is nothing compared to downtime's cost (and your labor's cost), so a fresh install may well be the strategy that gets a server back up and running. Another great approach is to use a disk-copier program like *Ghost*. Get the system the way you want it and then Ghost the entire system drive to a Jaz drive or some other safe place. Rebuilding the server then takes the 20 or so minutes that Ghost will take to copy back a gigabyte or so.

Of course, many problems don't require anything that drastic, and sometimes you just plain don't have an install script or a Ghost image lying around. In that case, you need to dig in and do some kind of system repair. The remainder of this chapter talks about some tools you can use to accomplish that.

The Last Known Good Menu

If you've changed your system so that it can't boot NT Server, one of the better solutions to this problem can be seen while you're rebooting. If you watch while your machine's booting up, you see a message on a black screen that says

```
Press spacebar NOW to use the Last Known Good Configuration.
```

If you press the spacebar, you see a menu asking you whether you want to

- Use the current configuration

- Use the *Last Known Good Configuration*—the configuration that was used the last time the machine booted successfully

- Restart the computer

- Use another hardware configuration, if you have more than one

The idea with Last Known Good is that NT's Registry contains a key, HKEY_LOCAL_MACHINE\System\CurrentControlSet, which is basically a "CONFIG.SYS" for your NT system. A control set's main job is to list all possible drivers and services that NT knows of, to list the exact filenames and options for those drivers, and to tell NT whether or not to *load* those drivers. For example, if you poke around in a control set you'll see a key called Services, and inside that you'll see a key named Spock. That's the driver for an old PS/2 SCSI host adapter. Now, the chances are *extremely good* that you're not running NT on a PS/2 with a Micro Channel Architecture SCSI host adapter, but NT knows

- There is at least a possibility, however incredibly small, that you *do* have such a thing, and so NT should be ready in case that happens

- What the filename of the driver is, provided that you tell NT to actually use this driver

- Most important, whether or not to actually load the driver

So, for example, if you buy a brand-new SCSI host adapter or video card and load the drivers for it, NT may end up learning about an altogether new piece of hardware. There would be a new key in the control set with information about using that driver. If you wanted NT to *forget* that information, reverting to an old control set (Last Known Good) would be helpful.

If, on the other hand, you haven't changed your hardware, but have updated a driver, then invoking Last Known Good may do nothing for you at all. If you've got an Adaptec 2940 SCSI host adapter in your system, then all the control set knows is that you should load a driver called AIC78XX.SYS. That's important because when you update your Adaptec driver, the name doesn't change (usually); you just use a new AIC78XX.SYS that overrides the old one. The control set *used* to say, "Load AIC78XX.SYS," before you installed the new driver, and now it *still* says, "Load AIC78XX.SYS." The control set would not know about different versions of AIC78XX.SYS, and so if you updated a driver and then decided that you didn't like the driver, Last Known Good couldn't help you.

Where *is* Last Known Good useful? Well, if your machine won't boot, you probably don't want to use the current configuration, so instead go to the Last Known Good Configuration. It should make your machine bootable.

How did Last Known Good get to be considered "good" by the system? To qualify, a configuration must not have produced any system critical errors involving a driver or a system file, and a user must have been able to log on to the system at least once.

A change in drivers isn't the only time that a Last Known Good Configuration can't help you. (Consider how often restoring an old CONFIG.SYS under DOS solves problems—sometimes, but not always—and you'll have an idea about roughly how often Last Known Good is helpful.) If any of the following things is true, you have to use another solution to restore things as you want them:

- You made a change more than one successful boot ago and want to restore things as they were before the change.

- The information that you want to change is not related to control set information—user profiles and file permissions fall into the category of information that can't be changed with the Last Known Good menu.

- The system boots, a user logs on, and then the system hangs.

- You change your video driver to an incompatible driver, restart the system, and log on with the bad driver (you can still type, even if you can't see).

Running an NT Repair

If you've screwed up your operating system setup such that using the Last Known Good Configuration can't help you, you still have another option before (groan) reinstalling the operating system. Every time you make a successful change to your system's configuration, you should back it up with a combination of Disk Administrator, a program called RDISK (you'll see how to do that in just a minute), and whatever your favorite NT backup program is. The information from RDISK and Disk Administrator will often fit on a single floppy, a floppy whose name you may recognize from Setup—the Emergency Repair Disk (ERD). As a matter of fact, you can use NT Repair for a number of useful tasks even if you *don't* have an ERD; I'll get to those tasks in a minute.

Starting NT Repair   You kick off an NT repair in a way that you probably wouldn't expect—by running Setup. Either boot from the three setup floppies, run WINNT, or run WINNT32 just as though you planned to reinstall NT entirely. When you see the "Welcome to Setup" screen, however, you'll notice that you have a number of options besides the one you probably normally choose, pressing Enter to commence NT Setup.

One of those options is

```
To repair a damaged Windows NT 4.0 installation, press R.
```

Press R, and you'll see a screen that says:

```
As part of the repair process, Setup will perform each optional task
shown below with an 'X' in its check box.
To perform the selected tasks, press ENTER to indicate "Continue." If
you want to select or deselect any item in the list, press the UP or
DOWN ARROW key to move the highlight to the item you want to change.
Then press ENTER.
[   ]  Inspect registry files
[   ]  Inspect startup environment
[   ]  Verify Windows NT system files
[   ]  Inspect boot sector
          Continue (perform selected tasks)
```

By default, all of these options are checked.

Understanding Repair Options   Before continuing with Repair, however, let's take a short side trip to see what each option does.

Inspect Registry files   Doesn't actually inspect the files. Instead, it lets you restore a Registry hive file from a backup.

Inspect startup environment   Tells NT to rebuild an erased or damaged BOOT.INI. Repair will search your computer's disks attempting to find any NT installations on the disk. Its performance is, in my experience, not great, but it can't hurt to try, right?

Verify Windows NT system files Checks that all of the hundreds of files that NT installs are still there and that they're in the same shape as they were when first installed. Unfortunately, if you've installed a service pack, this option is pretty useless: Repair's not bright enough to understand that the reason that all of those files are "corrupt" is because they're new-and-improved versions. Give this option a miss.

Inspect boot sector Fixes the boot sector on drive C: so that it starts up NT, loading and executing the NTLDR file. This is useful if NT no longer boots, either because of inadvertent damage to C:'s boot sector—power surges or viruses—or because someone installed DOS or Windows on top of NT. (Even Windows 98 isn't smart enough to understand that when it's installed on top of an NT installation, it should respect the NT boot loader and just insert itself in BOOT.INI.) This happens most often when some dodo sees there's a problem booting an NT machine and decides that the best answer is to boot the server with a bootable DOS disk and then type SYS C:.

Running NT Repair Anyway, back to Repair. Choose the option or options that you want, then highlight "Continue (perform selected tasks)" and press Enter. Just as it did with the initial Setup, NT must figure out what kind of hard disk host adapter you've got. (If you've started Repair with the NT floppies, you'll then have to insert disk 3.) As with Setup, NT Repair auto-detects mass storage devices, and, again as with Setup, if you've got an oddball disk controller you'll have to tell Repair about it here. The process is exactly the same as with Setup, so I'll assume you have already figured this part of Repair out.

Emergency Repair Disk Options The next screen asks for the Emergency Repair Disk:

```
Setup needs to know if you have the Emergency Repair Disk for the Win-
dows NT version 4.0 installation which you want to repair. NOTE: Setup
can only repair Windows NT 4.0 installations.
If you have the Emergency Repair Disk, press ENTER.
If you do not have the Emergency Repair Disk, press ESC. Setup will
attempt to locate Windows NT version 4.0 for you.
```

Now here's some good news. If you were lazy and didn't create an Emergency Repair Disk, NT made one anyway, creating a backup of your ERD information in a directory named \REPAIR inside your NT system root. So, for example, if you installed NT in a directory named D:\WINNTS, then you'll find a directory named D:\WINNTS\REPAIR on your disk. Either choose Enter or Esc, and NT will search the disk to find as many NT installations as it can. It then reports any installed copies of NT. The screen looks a bit different when it finds one copy than when it finds multiple copies; with multiple copies the screen looks like this:

```
The list below shows the Windows NT installation on your computer that
may be repaired.
Use the UP and DOWN ARROW keys to move the highlight to an item in the
list.
To repair the highlighted Windows NT installation, press ENTER.
To return to the previous screen, press ESC.
To exit Setup, press F3.
```

You'll then see a list of the locations for the installations that Repair found. On the system I'm looking at now, it looks like this:

```
E:\WINNT.O "Windows NT Server Version 4.00"
C:\WTSRV "Windows NT Terminal Server Version 4.00"
```

The one problem with this tool is that sometimes NT *can't* find an installation. In that case, it would be nice to see a browse window or to just plain be able to punch in a drive letter and subdirectory name—but you can't, unfortunately.

Following that screen, you see the "Setup will now examine your drive(s) for corruption" message, same as in regular Setup. As with regular Setup, press Esc to skip it or Enter to let Repair do the disk test. What happens next depends on what you asked Repair to do.

"Inspect Registry Files" Actions If you choose Inspect Registry Files, you'll next see a screen that says:

```
Setup will restore each registry file shown below with an 'X' in its
check box.
To restore the selected files, press ENTER to indicate "Continue." If
you want to select or deselect any item in the list, press the UP or
DOWN arrow to move the highlight to the item you want to change. Then
press ENTER.
WARNING: Restore a registry file only as a last resort. Existing con-
figuration may be lost. Press F1 for more information.
```

Repair then offers to restore five Registry files:

- SYSTEM

- SOFTWARE

- DEFAULT (the default user profile, the one that runs when no one's logged on)

- NTUSER.DAT (the profile that new users get)

- A combination of SAM and SECURITY, the two files that contain user accounts, whether a server is a member server, BDC, or PDC, and other domain and local security information

You can't restore SECURITY without SAM or vice versa—they're a matched set. You get a check box for each one, and once you've checked the ones that you want to restore, you choose "Continue (perform selected tasks)." That tells Repair to copy the selected Registry hive files from either an Emergency Repair Disk or the \WINNT\REPAIR directory. Repair then copies the files and reports:

```
Setup has completed repairs.
If there is a floppy disk inserted in drive A:, remove it.
Also remove any compact disks from your CD-ROM drive(s).
Press ENTER to restart your computer.
```

"Inspect Startup Environment" Actions   Choose this if there's an NT installation on your system but the installation is not in your BOOT.INI. As noted earlier, Repair's not that great at finding those old installations, but it has a better chance if the installations are in system roots with names of WINNT or WINNT with a period and digit, as in WINNT.0, WINNT.1, and so on.

If you choose Inspect Startup Environment, then Repair will work as described above, except it will *not* run through the Registry questions. It just runs the disk for a few seconds and ends with this message:

```
Setup has completed repairs.
If there is a floppy disk inserted in drive A:, remove it.
Also remove any compact disks from your CD-ROM drive(s).
Press ENTER to restart your computer.
```

"Inspect Boot Sector" Actions   This option doesn't produce much interaction, either. You use it, again, if there's a copy of NT on your system but you never even see the "OS Loader" message. It'll run for a second or two after you tell it which instance of NT to repair, then you'll see the "Setup has completed repairs" message and have the opportunity to reboot. The only other way in which this option is different is that for some reason Repair does not offer to test the drive.

Running a System Repair without a CD-ROM Drive

For a couple of years, my main laptop was a Digital Ultra Hinote II, a pretty good, light, power-stretching laptop for its time. (96MB of RAM, a 133MHz processor, and an 800×600 screen were pretty sexy not too long ago.) It had one fatal flaw, however: its CD-ROM. The drive wasn't a standard EIDE interface, but instead an oddball PCMCIA interface that, needless to say, required a few oddball drivers to make it work.

Running a system repair caused me trouble, therefore, as NT Setup ➤ Repair could not see the CD-ROM. How to run a repair without a CD-ROM? Well, there wasn't a way until Service Pack 2 came around. Got a server or a laptop that doesn't always have a CD-ROM available? Then use this technique.

First, you'll need at least one drive formatted as FAT so that you can get to the drive from a bootable DOS floppy—DOS doesn't read NTFS very well, as you know. (Yes, I know about the drivers that let DOS read NTFS, but in a repair situation I'm not exactly thrilled about the idea of relying on even more third-party software.) On that drive, place a copy of the I386 directory with your version of NT: Workstation, Server, Enterprise Edition, or Terminal Server. You are then going to make four modifications in order to make this system able to do a repair from the I386 on the disk, rather than insisting on accessing an I386 on a CD-ROM.

1. Create a file inside I386 called CDROM_S.40 if it's Server, Enterprise Edition, or Terminal Server code, or CDROM_W.40 if it's Workstation code. Give the file the appropriate name *exactly*. The file can be empty and this'll work fine. (Right-click the I386 folder, click New ➤ Text Document, then rename it to CDROM_W.40 or CDROM_S.40.)

2. Edit a file named TXTSETUP.SIF, a big text file in I386. (Perhaps it's a good idea to back it up first.) Search for the string ;SetupSourceDevice=. Remove the semicolon from the beginning of the line—this converts the line from a comment to be ignored to a command to be followed. Then indicate which hard disk the I386 directory is on. Of course, you can't use simple labels like C:, E:, or whatever. Instead, use **\device\harddisk***N***\partition***M*, where *N* is the physical drive number (starting with 0 for the first) and *M* is the partition number (starting with 1 for the first). If I386 is on drive C:, then, as C: is usually the first partition on the first hard disk, the line would look like this:

```
SetupSourceDevice=\device\harddisk0\partition1
```

If you've got I386 on drive D:, E:, or some other drive letter, then I can't tell you exactly what values to use because I don't know how your disks are set up. Sometimes people have two hard disks on their system; the first partition of the first drive is C: and the first partition of the second drive is D:. In that case, the device name would be

```
\device\harddisk1\partition1
```

In other cases, the computer has only one hard disk that's been chopped up and D: is the second partition; in that case, the device name would be

```
device\harddisk0\partition2
```

Look in the Disk Administrator to see exactly which hard disk and partition number your drive is.

3. Just a line or two below where you found SetupSourceDevice, you'll find a line saying SetupSourcePath=\. Change the \ to the name of the directory where you put the files. I've been using the example I386, as that's what I name the directory where I keep my NT distribution files, so in my case the revised line would look like this: SetupSourcePath=\I386. Notice that you don't include a drive letter, as you already indicated that with Setup-SourceDevice.

4. In I386 you'll find a file named SETUPDD.SYS. The one that shipped with the original version of NT 4 isn't smart enough to look elsewhere than a CD-ROM, so you need a newer one.

   But where to find one? That turned out to be a fairly interesting story. The SETUPDD.SYS from Service Pack 2, 3, or 4 will do. Service Pack 2 shipped as a whole bunch of files, so if you've got SP2 then go ahead and steal the SETUPDD.SYS from that and copy it into your I386. Service Packs 3 and 4 were available in two formats. Most people who pulled the service packs off the Web got a single, large executable file with a name like NT4SP3_I.EXE or SP4I386.EXE—you ran it and it unpacked all of its files to a temporary directory, installed the service pack, and then erased the temporary files. Alternatively, you could order the entire service pack on a CD-ROM. On the CD-ROM, the files were already extracted. If you have the CD-ROM, you'll find SETUPDD.SYS right there with the other files. If you have the executable, then the story's a bit different.

   First, you've got to get the service pack executable to unpack all of the files and *keep* them unpacked. That's easy; just run the executable with the –X option, either NT4SP3_I –X or SP4I386 –X. The executable will ask you where to put the files, and it'll unpack them to that directory.

Here's the weird part, however: Service Pack 3's unpacked directory includes SETUPDD.SYS. Service Pack 4's unpacked directory *does not*. As a result, if you need a copy of SETUPDD.SYS so that you can do a no-CD repair, you either need Service Pack 2, Service Pack 3 (in either CD or executable format), or Service Pack 4 in a CD format.

5. Once you've done your four changes—created the CDROM_S.40 file, modified SetupSourceDevice, modified SetupSourcePath, and copied over the revised SETUPDD.SYS—then you're ready to do a repair. Again, you need not even use floppies, as you can start a repair with WINNT /B or WINNT32 /B. So you brave souls running NT on a Toshiba Libretto without a CD or a floppy—the floppy is PCMCIA and you might need to put another card in the one slot—can still do NT repairs!

Updating the Repair Disk and/or Directory

It's a good idea now and then to tuck away an updated backup of the Registry. All that repair stuff is of no value if you've never updated the Emergency Repair Disk or the \WINNT\REPAIR directory, as they only contain a Registry based on your initial setup. For example, there are no users save for the Administrator and the Guest unless you've updated the repair files. Additionally, none of the permissions that you've established is on the Repair Disk.

How to update this information? You can update your Repair Disk (or create a completely new disk) with a program called RDISK in the SYSTEM32 directory. Just run it (Start ➤ Run ➤ RDISK) and follow the instructions.

Unfortunately, however, RDISK doesn't back up *all* of the Registry: it overlooks SAM and SECURITY. You can overcome that oversight with the undocumented /S option—click Start, then Run, then type **RDISK/S** and press Enter.

Backing Up Your Disk Configuration

In addition to the Emergency Repair Disk, you can save your partition information so that you can replace it if you do something that you regret doing. Here's how:

1. Go to the Disk Administrator.

2. From the Partition Menu, choose Configuration, and then Save. You see a screen that looks like Figure 17.16.

FIGURE 17.16:

Insert Disk dialog box

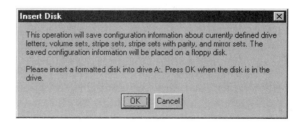

3. Insert the disk and press OK. The system saves the information, and shows the message in Figure 17.17. This message confirms that the configuration was saved.

FIGURE 17.17:

Disk Administrator confirmation of your configuration change

4. Click OK and you're done. Remove the disk from the drive, label it with the date, and put it somewhere safe. You now have a backup of your disk configuration on your Emergency Repair Disk.

WARNING   If you blast a partition and your data, restoring the partition won't restore the data.

Recovering from Bad Video Drivers

You may recall from the earlier discussion of the Last Known Good Configuration that if you change the video drivers to something that your system can't handle and you reboot and log on with the bad drivers (you can still type a password even if the screen is messed up), the Last Known Good solution can no longer help you. You have, after all, successfully rebooted and logged onto the system; the fact that you can't *see* anything is immaterial.

Under NT version 3.1, this was something of a rigmarole. But NT 4 builds into BOOT.INI the option NT Server 4 (VGA drivers). All you have to do then is to shut down the server, restart it, and choose the setup with VGA drivers. Then, once the system is back up, just select Display from the Control Panel and take a second shot at choosing a video driver. Even better, there is a Test button in the display screen that NT forces you to use to find out *before* you commit yourself whether or not the video drivers work.

Backing Up the Registry (and the SAM)

You'll recall that backing up open files is a bit of a pain, impossible sometimes. Few files on an NT machine are more important than the Registry hives. Registry hives are the files named Sam, Security, software, and system, all of which live in \WINNT\SYSTEM32\CONFIG.

Alternatives for Backing Up the Registry

Unfortunately, Registry hives are constantly open. You can't use a simple COPY or XCOPY command. But there are several tools that you can use to back them up.

First, there's NTBACKUP. You'll recall that there is a check box or a command line option (/B) that instructs NTBACKUP, to back up the Registry. You can restore it by using NTBACKUP, as well.

The *Resource Kit* includes two programs named REGBACK and REGREST that back up and restore the Registry to a floppy.

You may recall that the Emergency Repair Disk contains a copy of the Registry as it looked when you first installed your server. If you run NT Setup and choose the Repair option, then one of the things that you can do is restore the Registry to the state found on the Emergency Repair Disk.

Now, that may not sound like an especially attractive option, since a lot of water has no doubt gone under the bridge between the time that you installed the server and now, but it *is* one way to restore a damaged Registry to a "known good" state. Of course, it would be more desirable to simply keep the copy of the Registry on the Emergency Repair Disk up to date—and you can do that.

As you read a page or two back, NT includes a program called RDISK. RDISK will not only write a brand-new Emergency Repair Disk, it will update \WINNT\ REPAIR. But why doesn't RDISK back up SAM and SECURITY without the extra /S option? The problem with putting the Registry on the Emergency Repair Disk is that part of the Registry—the SAM—may be too big. Remember from Chapter 11 that the SAM may be megabytes and megabytes on a domain controller. *That's* why RDISK doesn't back up SAM or SECURITY unless asked. It makes sense; I just wish Microsoft had documented how to do it.

It's a good idea to put RDISK on the Administrative Tools menu to remind you to keep it constantly updated over time as your machine's configuration changes.

Restoring a Registry

If you backed up the Registry with RDISK, restore it by starting up NT Setup and choosing Repair rather than Install NT. If you backed up the Registry with REG-BACK, then use REGREST to restore it.

But what if you can't run an NT system repair? How do you restore the RDISK-created Registry files? You'll need to do two operations:

1. Uncompress the files.

2. Copy them to \WINNT\SYSTEM32\CONFIGS.

Take a look in your \WINNT\REPAIR directory or on your Emergency Repair Disk and you'll see files with names like SAM_, SECURITY._, SYSTEM._, and so on. These are compressed versions of the original Registry hive files SAM, SECURITY, SYSTEM, and the others. You can uncompress them with the Expand program that comes with NT. Just open up a command prompt, CD over to \WINNT\ REPAIR, and type **expand** *compressedname expandedname*. For example, if you uncompress SAM, you'll see something like the next few lines:

```
E:\WINNT\repair>expand sam._ sam
Microsoft (R) File Expansion Utility Version 2.50
Copyright (C) Microsoft Corp 1990-1994. All rights reserved.
Expanding sam._ to sam.
sam._: 6289 bytes expanded to 20480 bytes, 225% increase.
```

The next thing to do is copy it over to \WINNT\SYSTEM32\CONFIGS, but you can't just do that—the current SAM file is locked, and you can't overwrite it. You've got two options here: either you put your system files (\WINNT and the bunch) on a FAT partition, in which case all you need to do is boot to DOS and copy the files; or, if the system's on an NTFS partition, then you'll have to put a *second* copy of NT in a different directory, *then* boot from the second copy of NT (cumbersome, but it works); as the first copy is not active, the files in \WINNT\SYSTEM32\CONFIGS on the first configuration aren't locked, and you can copy SAM to your heart's content.

If your Registry backup is on NTBACKUP, you must restore it from the NTBACKUP program. To restore it from the GUI interface, click on the Restore Registry check box.

You cannot restore a disk Registry to any disk except the one from which you backed it up. In other words, you can't apply the disk Registry from drive C: to drive E:. That way, you can't sneak around NT's security system.

Planning for Disaster Recovery

Sometimes using the Last Known Good Configuration or the Emergency Repair Disk doesn't fix your problems. Hard disk failures or natural disasters require a bit more in the way of hard-core disaster recovery.

What does *disaster recovery* mean? Essentially, it's exactly what it sounds like: a way of recovering from disaster—at best, turning a potential disaster into a minor inconvenience. Disaster can mean anything: theft, flood, an earthquake, a virus, or anything else that keeps you from being able to access your data. After all, it's not really the server that's important. While a server may be expensive, it is replaceable. Your data, on the other hand, is either difficult or impossible to recover. Could you reproduce your client mailing list from memory? What about the corporate accounts?

Creating a Disaster Recovery Plan

The most important part of a disaster recovery plan lies in identifying what "disaster" means to you and your company. Obviously, permanently losing all of your company's data would be a disaster, but what else would? How about your installation becoming inaccessible for a week or longer? When planning for disaster, think about all the conditions that could render your data or your workplace unreachable and plan accordingly.

Implementing Disaster Recovery

Okay, it's 2:00 P.M. on Thursday, and you get a report that the network has died. What do you do?

Write Things Down Immediately write down everything that everyone tells you: what happened, when it happened, who gave you the information, and anything else that happened at the same time that might possibly be related.

Check the Event Logs If you can get to them, look at the security and event logs on the server to see if you can tell what happened right before the server crashed. If you're using directory replication to maintain a physically identical file server (also known as a *hot start* server because it's ready to go whenever you need it), the log information may be on the replicated server even if you can't get to the original.

Ascertain the Cause of the Failure and Fix It "Easy for you to say," I hear someone muttering. It can be done, however. Once you know what events happened, it becomes easier to find out what they happened to.

Find Out If It's a Software Problem Is it a software problem? If it is, have you changed the configuration? If you've changed something, rebooted, and been unable to boot, it's time to use the Last Known Good Configuration discussed earlier. If you can boot but the operating system won't function properly, use the Emergency Repair Disk to restore the hardware configuration.

If you have another server with NT Server already installed identically to the server that failed, switch servers and see if the backup server works before you reinstall the operating system. If the hot start server doesn't work, you could be facing a network problem.

Find Out If It's a Hardware Problem Is it a hardware problem? If you have a hot start server around the office, put it in place of the failed server and see if you can bring the network back up. If so, the problem lies with the dead server and you can fix or replace it while you have the other one in place. If not, check the network's cabling.

If one drive from a stripe set or mirror set has died, the system should still be fine (if the drive that died is not the one with the system partition on it), but you should still fix the set anyway. Striping and mirroring gives you access to your data while the missing data is being regenerated, but if something else happens to the set before you regenerate the missing data, you're sunk because the set can only deal with one error at a time.

If necessary, reload the backups.

Make a Recovery "Coloring Book"

No matter how much you know about re-formatting SCSI drives or rebuilding boot sectors byte by byte, I guarantee you that the fastest way to recover from a disaster will often turn out to be a three-step process: replace the bad hard disk and attendant hardware, install a fresh copy of NT Server on the new hard disk, and restore the data on the disk.

That sounds simple, but it's amazing how complex it can be in the heat of battle. Let's see, I'm reinstalling NT server, but what was the name of the domain? What IP address does the domain controller get? What's the WINS server address? Which services went on this server? What was the administrator's password set to?

At my shop, we decided to sit down and write a step-by-step, click-by-click instruction manual. It tells a future network administrator which buttons to click and what text to type in the unlikely event that he's ever got to take a brand-new machine and rebuild our PDC on it.

Just for an example, we have a primary domain controller on one of our domains that (as the logon traffic is relatively light) is also our DHCP, WINS, and DNS server. So, suppose the machine goes up in smoke, leaving us nothing but backup tapes—how do we rebuild that machine? We sat down and wrote out exactly what to do in order to

- Install NT Server on a new machine
- Restore the SAM and SECURITY databases
- Install DHCP on the machine
- Restore the old DHCP database to the machine
- Install WINS on the machine
- Restore the WINS database
- Install the DNS server on the machine
- Restore our DNS zones and records

Assume that the person who'll be doing this knows nothing more than how to click a mouse and shove CDs into drives, someone with oatmeal for brains. Sound insulting? It's not; I like to think of myself as of at least basic intelligence, but under pressure I sometimes just don't think as well as I need to. If you're good under pressure, then great—but making the disaster recovery guide an easy read is also a big help to your coworkers.

Don't underestimate how long this will take: putting the whole document together took two research assistants a couple of weeks, and it ended up as a 100+ page Word document! (Part of the reason why it was so large is that it made lavish use of screen shots wherever possible, and yours should, too. Just click on the window you want to include in your document, press Alt+Prtsc, choose Edit ➢ Paste Special in Word, choose Bitmap, and uncheck "Float over text.")

NOTE   Once you finish the document, be careful of where you keep it. The document will contain the keys to your network: user names of domain administrator accounts, the passwords of those accounts, and the like.

Making Sure the Plan Works

The first casualty of war isn't always the truth—it's often the battle plan itself.

The most crucial part of any disaster recovery plan lies in making sure that it works down to the last detail. Don't just check the hardware; check everything. When a server crashes, backups do no good at all if they are locked in a cabinet to which only the business manager has the keys and the business manager is on vacation in Tahiti.

In the interest of having your plan actually work, make sure you know the answers to the following questions.

Who Has the Keys? Who has the keys to the backups and/or the file server case? The example mentioned above of the business manager having the only set of keys is not an acceptable situation, for reasons that should be painfully obvious. At any given time, someone *must* have access to the backups.

You could set up a rotating schedule of duty, wherein one person who has the keys is always on call, and the keys are passed on to the next person when a shift is up. However, that solution is not foolproof. If there's an emergency, the person on call could forget to hand the keys off to the next person, or the person on call could be rendered inaccessible through a dead beeper battery or downed telephone line. Better to trust two people with the keys to the backups and server, so that if the person on call can't be reached, you have a backup key person.

Is Special Software Required for the Backups? Must any special software be loaded for the backups to work? I nearly gave myself heart failure when, after repartitioning a hard disk and reinstalling the operating system, I attempted to restore the backups that I'd made before wiping out all the data on the file server's hard disk. The backups wouldn't work. After much frustration, I figured out that Service Pack 2 was installed on the server before. I reinstalled the Service Pack from my copy on another computer and the backups worked. I just wish I had figured that out several hours earlier…

Do the Backups Work and Can You Restore Them? Do the backups work and do you know how to restore them? Verifying backups takes a little longer than just backing them up, but if you verify, you know that what's on the tape matches what's on the drive. So, as far as restoring goes, practice restoring files *before* you have a problem. Learning to do it right is a lot easier if you don't have to learn under pressure, and if you restore files periodically, you know that the files backed up okay.

Have Users Backed Up Their Own Work? In the interest of preventing your operation from coming to a complete halt while you're fixing the downed network, it might not be a bad idea to have people store a copy of whatever they're working on, and the application needed to run it, on their workstation. People who only work on one or two things at a time could still work while you're getting the server back online.

Diagnosing Server Boot Failures

Last Known Good restores are of no value if you can't get to the "Press a key now to restore Last Known Good…" message. In this section, I'll explain the steps that the server goes through in order to boot and I'll tell you what outward signs those steps display so that you can figure out what went wrong when your server won't boot.

Before the Boot: The Hardware Must Work

Before anything else can happen, your server must be free of hardware problems. You may not be able to boot if

- Your boot drive or boot drive's controller is malfunctioning or is not set up correctly.

- You have an interrupt conflict.

- The CPU or some other vital circuitry is failing.

Too often, the fan on the server's power supply has stopped working. As a result, the temperature inside of the server can rise to over 130°F (55°C) and slowly roast your components.

A company in Bonsall, California, by the name of PC Power and Cooling Systems makes a temperature sensor that fits inside a PC's case and squawks when the PC's internal temperature rises above 100 degrees. It's not cheap (it cost $100 the last time I looked), but it's cheaper than replacing the server.

Another problem that I've run into that can make a machine not boot is an EISA misconfiguration. The fact that EISA allows for software configuration of machines is wonderful. EISA is a real dream for those of us who've spent too much of our lives flipping DIP switches and wrestling jumpers out of hard-to-get-to spaces. But the EISA setup routines on some EISA machines have a quirk: if they don't understand *something,* then they respond by knowing *nothing.*

To show what I mean, suppose you have an EISA disk controller in your server. You shut down the server and replace your old ISA LAN board with an EISA LAN board. You put the cover on your system, try to boot, but only get the message "EISA CMOS failure" and a stopped computer. What happened? The system knew to expect the EISA disk controller, but it *didn't* know to expect the EISA LAN board. Just to play it safe, the computer refused to use the EISA disk controller. Result: you can't boot your system from the hard disk. The system will continue to do this until you run the EISA configuration program.

To make matters worse, most people's floppy disk controllers are on the hard disk controller card, which makes it impossible to boot from the floppy. If you can't run the EISA configuration program from either the hard disk *or* the floppy disk, what can you do?

I've found that the best bet in this case is to run the EISA configuration program *before* you install the board. Load the EISA configuration file for the new board and configure the board even before it's in your system. The configuration program will complain a bit about the fact that the board is not actually *in* the system, but all will work in the end. Then shut down the computer and install the new board.

Boot Step One: NTLDR and BOOT.INI

The first thing that your NT server loads is the NTLDR file, a small program in the root directory. NTLDR announces itself by clearing the screen and displaying

```
OS Loader V4.00
```

Now, if you *don't* get that message, it means the boot sector on the boot drive no longer automatically loads NTLDR. What would cause that? Probably somebody booting the server from a DOS floppy and typing **SYS C:**. You can easily fix this with the Emergency Repair Disk. Just run NT Setup until you get to the Welcome to Setup screen. Press **R** to tell Setup to repair rather than install. You'll get several options that Setup can repair; choose Inspect Boot Sector. That will change the boot sector back so that it points to NTLDR.

NTLDR looks for these files:

File	What It Is
BOOT.INI	A text file that tells the NT multi-boot loader which operating systems are available.
NTDETECT.COM	A program that detects the hardware on your NT system.
BOOTSECT.DOS	The file that is present on your root directory if you dual boot with DOS, something unlikely on an NT Server machine.
NTBOOTDD.SYS	This file is present if you boot from a SCSI drive that does not support the INT 13 BIOS interface. (Most SCSI host adapters don't need this unless you're booting from a second controller.) It is just a renamed copy of the SCSI driver for your SCSI host adapter.

At this point, I've seen messages like "Unable to open NTDETECT.COM," followed by an error code. That means something has damaged data in your root directory and made it impossible for NTDETECT.COM to load. The answer in this case is to use the NT Emergency Repair Disk; I've found that it can reconstruct most root structures.

NTLDR then does these things:

1. Shifts your processor to 386 mode (*x*86 systems).

2. Starts the very simple file system based either on a standard disk interface (known as INT13 for non-SCSI systems) or else uses NTBOOTDD.SYS to boot from the SCSI drive.

3. Reads BOOT.INI to find out if there are other operating systems to offer, and shows those options on the screen.

4. Accepts the user's decision on which OS to load.

NTLDR must read and parse BOOT.INI. A typical BOOT.INI might look like the following:

```
[boot loader]
timeout=30
default=multi(0)disk(0)rdisk(0)partition(4)\WINNT
[operating systems]
multi(0)disk(0)rdisk(0)partition(4)\WINNT="NT Server V4"
multi(0)disk(0)rdisk(0)partition(4)\WINNT="NTSV4 [VGA]" /basevideo /sos
C:\="Microsoft Windows"
```

The file is divided into sections: [boot loader] describes which operating system to load by default and how long it should wait for you to choose between operating systems; [operating systems] tells BOOT.INI where it can find the operating systems that you've loaded on your system.

But what *is* all that "multi(0)disk(0)rdisk(0)partition(4)" stuff, anyway? It's intended to be a kind of architecture-independent way of describing disks; after all, RISC machines don't have drives named C:, D:, and so on. Let's take it one piece at a time.

The first part is either multi(0) or scsi(*n*), where *n* is a number. Whether multi or scsi, this first part identifies which disk controller the boot drive is on. You use multi(0) only on *x*86 computers. Multi(0) really means the disk that the BIOS knows how to boot from. Whether you've got an EIDE or SCSI host adapter on your x86 machine, chances are good that your system can boot from that host adapter. If so, go ahead and use multi(0).

If, on the other hand, you've got multiple SCSI host adapters on your system, then you may want to use scsi(*n*), where *n* is a number describing which disk adapter to use. For example, if you had two Adaptec 2940 host adapters in your system, and NT booted from the second one, you'd use scsi(1) in this location.

If you choose to use scsi() rather than multi(), then NT will assume that it can find a device driver named NTBOOTDD.SYS in the root directory. NTBOOTDD.SYS is just a copy of the normal NT driver for that SCSI host adapter. For example, if you've got an Adaptec 2940, which uses a driver named 7800AIC.SYS, then your system will have a copy of 7800AIC.SYS in the root directory, renamed NTBOOTDD.SYS.

There are two peculiarities about multi() and scsi() that you should know. First, you can't use multi(1). Logically, multi(1) would refer to a second EIDE host adapter, but the multi() syntax doesn't support that. Second, the scsi() parameter only refers to one kind of SCSI adapter, the kind of SCSI adapter specified by NTBOOTDD.SYS. If your system had other SCSI adapters that required different drivers, then they wouldn't count in determining which SCSI controller you booted from. For example, if your system contained two Adaptec SCSI adapters and two Future Domain SCSI adapters, but you booted from the Adaptec adapters, then your NTBOOTDD.SYS would be a copy of an Adaptec driver, not a Future Domain driver. Even though there were four SCSI host adapters on your system, the only possible values for scsi() would be scsi(0) and scsi(1), because NTBOOTDD could not "see" the two Future Domain adapters.

Next, consider the disk() parameter. With the scsi() notation, it is the SCSI ID of the disk drive. You'll usually configure SCSI systems so that the boot drive is SCSI ID 0, but a drive can have any SCSI ID from 0 to 6. If you're using the multi() notation, this value is always disk(0); you indicate which drive to choose with multi() by using the rdisk() parameter, covered next.

The rdisk() parameter supports the idea of a SCSI *Logical Unit Number* or LUN. In virtually all cases I've seen in the PC world, there will only be one LUN on a given SCSI ID, so this value will normally be rdisk(0). If you are using the multi() notation, this indicates which drive on the controller has the NT files.

Finally, the partition() value identifies the number of the disk partition where NT is stored. The numbers start from one, not zero, and you count logical drives. As NT is stored on my F: drive, mine is in partition(4).

Knowing how the BOOT.INI file is organized will enable you to fix it if it becomes damaged. There *is* another way to fix BOOT.INI, however: just run NT Setup and choose Repair, and then pick the option labeled Inspect Startup Environment, which checks out BOOT.INI and tries to fix any problems with it.

Useful BOOT.INI Switches

While on the subject of BOOT.INI, I should mention some other useful switches. If you look in a standard machine-written BOOT.INI, you'll notice two switches on the VGA mode line:

- /SOS

- /BASEVIDEO

They're useful, but they're not the only things you may find of value in BOOT.INI.

/SOS tells NT to name the drivers that it's loading, one by one. That can give a clue about which, if any, of your NT drivers is causing a system failure. /BASEVIDEO tells NT to just load the VGA video driver—useful if you've got a flaky or just plain incorrect video driver.

Another one I've found great use for is /MAXMEM. It tells NT to load, but to only use a certain number of megabytes of RAM. This can be useful for testing to see if a particular feature will work with limited RAM, but it can also help track down RAM errors. If, for example, your system is blue-screening as it boots, then it may be that NT's just stumbling over some bad RAM. You can isolate this by modifying BOOT.INI. Just find or create a line in BOOT.INI and add the parameter /MAXMEM:*nnn*, where *nnn* is the number of megabytes of RAM that you want NT to use.

For example, suppose I wanted to add a line to the BOOT.INI displayed above to give me a boot option to run NT in just 16MB of RAM. I'd add a line so that BOOT.INI looked like this:

```
[boot loader]
timeout=30
default=multi(0)disk(0)rdisk(0)partition(4)\WINNT
[operating systems]
multi(0)disk(0)rdisk(0)partition(4)\WINNT="NT Server V4"
multi(0)disk(0)rdisk(0)partition(4)\WINNT="NTSV4 [VGA]" /basevideo /sos
multi(0)disk(0)rdisk(0)partition(4)\WINNT="NT Server V4" /maxmem:16
C:\="Microsoft Windows"
```

You may also find the /crashdebug option useful. You'll read later in this chapter about using the NT kernel debugger, a powerful (but difficult-to-use) tool that'll help you track down significant NT failures. But you've got to activate the debugger—and once the system's crashed, it may be too late. By adding the /crashdebug switch to your BOOT.INI entry, you tell NT that if it ever blue screens, it should immediately activate the kernel debugger.

Boot Step Two: NTDETECT

Next, NTDETECT.COM runs to figure out what kind of hardware you have. It announces itself as

```
NTDETECT V1.0 Checking Hardware...
```

That's the same message it's used since 3.1, so presumably this part of NT hasn't changed at all through the versions. NTDETECT finds

- Your PC's machine ID byte

- Its bus type

- Its video board

- Its keyboard type

- The serial ports attached to your computer

- Any parallel ports on the PC

- Floppy drives on the computer

- A mouse, if present

Using the Debug Version of NTDETECT

If you can't get past the NTDETECT stage, there is likely some kind of hardware conflict on your system. Fortunately, there is a "verbose" version of NTDETECT that shows in excruciating detail exactly what NTDETECT sees as it examines your system.

The "verbose" version of NTDETECT.COM is called NTDETECT.CHK and it's on the NT CD-ROM in SUPPORT\DEBUG\I386\NTDETECT.CHK. Of course, you have to rename the file once you copy it from the CD-ROM, and you should copy the file into the root directory of your C: drive—that's the C: drive, even if NT is not installed on drive C.

Two caveats are worth mentioning here. First, I hope it's obvious, but back up the old NTDETECT.COM before overwriting it. Second, you may not be able to get to the C: drive to install NTDETECT.COM in the first place; if that's true, just DISKCOPY the NT Setup floppy (the first floppy you use to install NT), copy the debug version of NTDETECT.COM onto that floppy, and try to boot from the floppy. That copy of NTDETECT will run and give you a clue about what's going wrong.

Boot Step Three: Load the Kernel

Next, NTLDR loads three files:

- NTOSKRNL.EXE, the NT kernel

- HAL.DLL, the HAL

- %Systemroot%\\WINNT\SYSTEM32\CONFIG\SYSTEM, the "System" hive in the Registry

If it can't find those files, again the best thing to do is to start NT Setup and choose Repair. This time, select Inspect Registry files and Inspect System files, because that will probably restore those three. If all is well, you will see this message:

```
Press spacebar NOW to invoke Hardware Profile/Last Known Good menu
```

Once NTLDR reads the System hive, it can look for drivers to see which ones to load. You can see this information in HKEY_LOCAL_MACHINE\System\CurrentControlSet\Services. (If you told it to use LastKnownGood, then NTLDR will look in a different control set.) For example, Figure 17.18 shows driver information in HKEY_LOCAL_MACHINE\System\CurrentControlSet\Services\Atdisk (Atdisk is the standard IDE disk driver).

FIGURE 17.18:

Disk driver information found in the Registry Editor

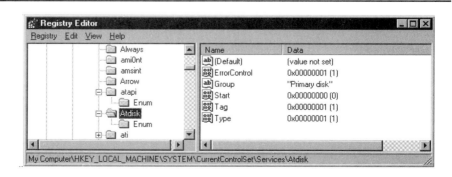

All services have values Start, Type, and Error Control, all useful in figuring out what a driver does and what'll happen if it fails. The Start entry can take one of five values:

- 0 = *boot* load during the boot phase (now)

- 1 = *system* load in load phase (coming up)

- 2 = *autoload,* which happens in the end of the load phase when the Services Manager loads these drivers

- 3 = *on demand,* meaning a user or program can load it (things like DNS, which you can stop from the Control Panel)

- 4 = never load

Services also have the value Type, which can take five values:

- 1 (no, it doesn't start from 0) = kernel device driver

- 2 = file system driver

- 4 = set of arguments for an adapter

- 10 = a Win32 program started by the Service Controller and that runs in a process all by itself

- 20 = a Win32 service that can share a process with other Win32 services

Finally, each service has an Error Control, which basically says, "When this service fails, how severe should it be considered?" There are four values:

- 0 = just ignore any errors.

- 1 = normal error level. Don't interrupt boot process.

- 2 = severe error level. Automatically boot using the LastKnownGood control set.

- 3 = critical error level. Fail the system startup. Automatically boot using the LastKnownGood control set. Run a bug checking routine.

Once NTLDR scans the System hive, it locates the services whose Start value equal zero, and NTLDR then loads them into memory. Each time it loads a driver, it puts a period on the screen. Finally, NTLDR passes control to NTOSKRNL, the NT kernel. The boot sequence is over, and the load sequence has begun.

The Load Sequence

As the NT kernel starts, it clears the screen and colors it blue. That's how you know NT has passed from the boot sequence to the load sequence. The load sequence has three parts:

- The kernel initialization phase
- The services load phase
- The Windows subsystem start phase

Kernel Initialization Phase

As part of the kernel initialization phase, you see a message like

```
Microsoft  Windows NT  Version 4.00 (Build 1381) 1 System Processor
[64 MB Memory]
```

The kernel copies the current control set to a Registry key named CLONE. It then initializes the drivers that NTLDR loaded, and uses the information from NTDETECT to build the information to create HKEY_LOCAL_MACHINE\ Hardware. The kernel then scans the System hive for drivers with Start values equal to 1. They are loaded, and, again, as the kernel loads each driver, a period appears on the screen.

The Services Load Phase

Next, the Services Manager, SMSS.EXE, loads. It then looks in HKEY_LOCAL_ MACHINE\System\CurrentControlSet\Control\Session Manager, where there is a value entry BootExecute. (By default, it's just AUTOCHK.) SMSS then sets up the page file and loads the *required subsystems,* which are in a value entry Required. Required is found in HKEY_LOCAL_MACHINE\System\CurrentControlSet\ Control\Session Manager\subsystems. By default, it just says *debug* and *windows.* Debug doesn't do anything, and Windows starts up the Win32 subsystem.

Windows Subsystem Load

By now, Win32's up. The Win32 subsystem starts WINLOGON.EXE, which kicks off the Local Security Authority, LSASS.EXE. WINLOGON.EXE also puts up the name/password/domain box.

A program named SCREG.EXE (Scan Registry) looks back through the Registry to find the autoload drivers. One of the autoload drivers is SERVICES.EXE, which loads the workstation and server services.

User Login

After the user logs in, Clone is copied to LastKnownGood, and your system is up!

Debugging Windows NT 4

This section defines some terminology and provides an overview of debugging NT 4. I also explain how to set up computers for a debugging session. The rest of this chapter will deal with creating a memory dump file, using utilities to process the dump file, and analyzing the information in the memory dump file.

> **NOTE** For Windows NT version 3.51, WINDBG, the utility used for reading memory dump files in earlier Windows NT releases, was replaced with a set of utilities that automatically read and interpret memory dump files.

Debugging Terminology

You should familiarize yourself with the following terms before debugging your workstation:

Kernel STOP Error   This refers to NT's display of a blue screen containing error information and then stops. Sometimes this error is called a *blue screen*.

Symbols *and* symbol trees   Two types of executable files can be created when compiling programs: debug and nondebug. Debug code contains extra code that enables a developer to debug problems. The nondebug code runs faster and takes up less memory, but can't be debugged.

NT combines the debugging ability of debug code with the speed and smaller size of nondebug code. All driver, executable, dynamic-link libraries, and the like are nondebug versions. However, each program has a corresponding symbol file that contains the debug code. These files are on the NT Workstation CD in the \SUPPORT\DEBUG*platform*\SYMBOLS directory where *platform* is ALPHA, I386, MIPS, or PPC. Each type of file has its own subdirectory within the SYMBOLS directory. This structure is also called a *symbol tree*. Table 17.3 lists the subdirectories in a standard symbol tree.

TABLE 17.3: Symbol Tree Subdirectories

Directory	File Type
ACM	MSACM files
COM	COM files
CPL	Control Panel applets
DLL	DLL files
DRV	DRV files
EXE	EXE files
SCR	Screen Saver files
SYS	SYS driver files

Target computer   Refers to the computer in which a Kernel Stop Error occurs. This is the computer that needs to be debugged.

Host computer   Refers to the computer on which you run the debugger. This computer should have a running version that is at least as current as the version on the target computer.

Finding Kernel STOP Errors

You can find the source of Kernel STOP Errors in either of two ways:

- Configure the target computer to dump the contents of its memory into a file when the Kernel STOP Error occurs. You can then use dump analysis utilities to analyze the file.

- Use a kernel debugger to troubleshoot the error. To do this you must connect a computer with a working version of NT to the computer on which the Kernel STOP Error occurred and enter the debugging commands from the working machine. Debugging the error this way allows you to look at the memory contents of the machine for the source of the Kernel STOP Error.

Memory Dump Files

If you don't have time to do debugging, you can set up a target computer so that it writes a memory dump file each time a Kernel STOP Error occurs. The dumpexam utility uses this file to analyze the error, allowing a host computer to act as if it is actually hooked up to the target, even though it isn't. While creating this file has the advantage of allowing you to analyze the data at any time without having to tie up a couple of computers, it can be cumbersome. The drawback to this debugging method is that a large amount of space must be available on you hard disk in order to write the file, as the file can be as large as the RAM memory of the computer with the stop error. For example, a computer with 32MB of RAM will create a 32MB memory dump file.

You also have to have a page file on your system's root directory that is just as large as your RAM memory. If you don't have enough disk space or you're not sure if you do, you should consider local or remote debugging instead.

Creating the Memory Dump File

Before you can use the dump analysis utilities, you need to configure your NT machine to create a memory dump file when a Kernel STOP Error occurs. You use the Recovery dialog box in the System applet to create the memory file. The contents of your computer's memory at the time of the error are written to this dump file so that you can analyze the problem. Using this option allows you to run the dump analysis utilities on any NT Workstation computer after you load the memory dump file, including the computer on which the error occurred. For a summary, see the "How Do I" sidebar.

Creating a memory dump file is a good option if you want to minimize the time that the host and target computers are unavailable. By running the dump analysis utilities, you can get the information you need for debugging and send it to your technical support staff for analysis. If your computer still runs other applications, you can then go back to a somewhat normal routine.

How Do I Create a Memory Dump File?

To set up the target computer to create a memory dump file, you must do the following:

1. Click on the Recovery button in the System dialog box.

2. Click on the Write Debugging Information To check box.

3. If you want the file to be overwritten every time a Kernel STOP Error occurs, click on the Overwrite Any Existing File check box.

4. Click OK.

Using the Dump Analysis Utilities

You will find three command-line utilities for analyzing memory dump files on NT Server and NT Workstation 4 CDs: dumpflop, dumpchk, and dumpexam. These files can be found in the SUPPORT\DEBUG*platform* directories of the CD, where *platform* is I386, ALPHA, MIPS, or PPC. The utilities create floppy disks or text files that you can send to technical support for analysis.

dumpflop   You can use the dumpflop command to write a memory dump file on floppy disks in order to send it to technical support. Sending floppies away to tech support isn't necessarily a very efficient method of debugging. The information is compressed as it is written to the floppies, so you don't have to worry about writing the 20-something disks for a 32MB dump file, but it still takes time. Fortunately, dumpflop doesn't access the symbol files to write the floppies, so there's at least one good thing about debugging this way.

To write the file to floppies, type the following:

```
dumpflop [options] <MemoryDumpFile> [Drive:]
```

To obtain the dump file after writing it to the floppies, type

```
dumpflop [options] <Drive>: [MemoryDumpFile]
```

The parameters for both writing and reading the file are as follows:

-?   Shows the command syntax.

-p   Prints only the header when assembling.

-v	Displays compression statistics.
-q	Formats the floppy before writing to the disks. When reading the disks, it overwrites the existing dump file.

If the command is executed with no options, it attempts to locate a dump file in the system root directory and writes it to floppies.

dumpchk The dumpchk utility allows you to verify that the dump file was created. It does not require access to the symbol files. To execute the command, type the following:

```
dumpchk [options] MemoryDumpFile
```

where the parameters are as follows:

-?	Shows the command syntax
-p	Prints only the header (no validation)
-v	Verbose mode
-q	Performs a quick test

Dumpchk provides basic information and then verifies all of the addresses in the file. It also reports any errors that are found in the file. This information can be used to determine what Kernel STOP Error occurred and what version of Windows NT was in use.

dumpexam The dumpexam command takes information from the dump file and writes it to a text file. You can then use the text file to find out what caused the Kernel STOP Error. Dumpexam requires three files in order to run. These files are located on the Windows NT Server and Windows NT Workstation 4 CDs in the directory SUPPORT/DEBUG/*platform*. You need the following files:

- DUMPEXAM.EXE

- IMAGEHLP.DLL

- The third file needs to be one of the following, depending on what type of target computer the error occurred on:

    - KDEXTX86.DLL

    - KDEXTALP.DLL

- KDEXTMIP.DLL

- KDEXTPPC.DLL

The command creates a file called MEMORY.TXT (located in the same directory as MEMORY.DMP) that contains information taken from the dump file. In order to run the command, type the following:

```
dumpexam [options] [MemoryDumpFile]
```

where the options are as follows:

-?	Shows the command syntax
-v	Verbose mode
-p	Prints only the header
-f *filename*	Specifies the output file name
-y *path*	Sets the symbol search path

The dumpexam output file displays the same information as the information given in each of the kernel debugger commands given below. You need some knowledge of assembly language and NT kernel processes in order to analyze the data. However, the guidelines given below should give you an idea of what some of the output means.

NOTE   You can also use dumpexam to examine memory dump files created on computers that run earlier versions of Windows NT. However, dumpexam only executes on a system running Windows NT version 3.51 *or higher*, so you need to move the memory dump file or access it over the network. Additionally, you need to replace the KDEXT*.DLL files listed above with copies from the version of Windows NT that was running on the computer on which the dump occurred. These files contain debug information specific to that version of Windows NT. You must also specify the path to the symbols for the operating system version that was running on that computer.

Kernel Debuggers

Kernel debuggers are used on the host computer to debug the Kernel STOP Error on the target computer. Each platform type has its own set of utilities, which are located in the \SUPPORT\DEBUG directory on the NT CD. The debuggers are used for both remote and local debugging. With remote debugging, the host computer can be located anywhere because communication takes place through modems. Local debugging takes place with the target and host computers a few feet away from each other and communicating through a null-modem serial cable. The computers send information to each other through communication ports that must be running at the same baud rate.

Setting Up Your Machine for Kernel Debugging

If you favor using the kernel debugger over the dump analysis utilities, you need to set up two computers, the one on which the error occurred and another with a working version of NT. The only other equipment you need is either a modem or a null-modem cable. Before you start debugging, you need to do several things:

- Set up the modem connection for either local or remote debugging.
- Set up the target computer (the one with the error) for debugging.
- Set up a symbol tree on the host computer.
- Set up the debugger program on the host computer.
- Start the debugger program on the host computer.

The Modem Connection

You need a connection between the host and the target computer if you want to do either remote or local debugging.

Remote Debugging You need to use a modem for remote debugging. Which communications port that you use (COM1 or COM2) depends on how the two computers are configured. The default configuration for the target computer depends on what platform the computer uses. The COM port on the host computer is set up as an environment variable. Your modem's documentation should provide information on the signals.

Connect the modem on the host first. When you are ready to connect to the modem on the target computer, see "Setting Up the Debugger on the Host Computer" later in this chapter. To set the modem on the target computer, you need to

- Connect the modem to one of the target computer's communication ports

- Turn on auto-answer

- Turn off flow-control, hardware compression, and error detection

Local Debugging In order to connect the target and the host computers, you need to have a null-modem serial cable. The procedure for setting up the cable is the same on both computers. However, there's one caveat: the host computer must be started before you can restart the target computer. Don't worry. Nothing bad will happen if you don't do this—you just have to restart the debugger on the host computer.

The cable can be plugged into different ports on either computer. For example, the cable can be connected to COM1 on the host computer and COM2 on the target computer. Just be sure to make note of which ports the cable is connected to.

Setting Up the Target Computer for Debugging

Usually, your computer is run in normal mode, which is the default when you install NT. When a Kernel STOP Error occurs, the debugger is not enabled. In order to enable debug mode, you have to edit the startup file and set some debugging variables.

The startup file for *x86*-based systems is BOOT.INI. You need to edit the file with a text editor and include either of two switches: /debug or /crashdebug. On a RISC-based computer, you edit the firmware environment variable OSLOAD options to include debug or crashdebug.

When you use crashdebug on either system, the debugger remains inactive until a Kernel STOP Error occurs. This mode is useful if errors occur randomly. If you're using debug, the debugger can be activated at any time by a host computer connected to the target computer. This method is usually used when experiencing errors that keep recurring.

Other options that can be added to the startup file are the communications port and baud rate. The defaults for these options vary from computer to computer, so you may want to add these, just in case.

Of course, you should always create a backup of your startup file just to be safe. Once you've finished debugging, you should then return the startup file to its original state.

Setting Up an *x*86-Based Computer for Debugging The default communications port for each computer varies. Some are set to COM1, others to COM2. The default baud rate is 9600 if you're using a modem and 19200 if you're using a null-modem serial cable. You shouldn't normally have to worry about setting these rates—they're set at the fastest reliable speeds already.

Once your modem or serial cable is connected, perform the following steps:

1. If a Kernel STOP Error occurs every time you boot the target computer, you can boot MS-DOS from a boot floppy and use the EDIT command to edit BOOT.INI.

   If the boot partition is NTFS, you have to install NT onto a different partition and boot from that partition because the host computer will not be able to access files on an NTFS partition from MS-DOS.

2. Turn off the read-only attribute of BOOT.INI by clicking on the Properties dialog box in the File menu on the NT Explorer. The file is usually located in the root directory on the partition from which NTLDR is loaded, usually the C: drive.

3. Use a text editor such as Notepad to edit BOOT.INI. The file will look something like the following:

   ```
   [boot loader]
   timeout=30
   default=mult(0)disk(0)rdisk(0)partition(1)\winnt
   [operating systems]
   mult(0)disk(0)rdisk(0)partition(1)\winnt="Windows NT Workstation
   (or Server) Version 4.0"
   mult(0)disk(0)rdisk(0)partition(1)\winnt="Windows NT Workstation
   (or Server) Version 4.0 [VGA mode]" /basevideo /sos
   C:\="MS-DOS"
   ```

4. Add either **/debug** or **/crashdebug** to the end of the line that contains the startup option that you normally use.

5. To specify the communications port, add the switch **/debugport=com*x***, where *x* is the communications port that you want to use.

6. To specify the baud rate, add the switch **/baudrate=<*baudrate*>.**

Here is an example of a line setting the communications port and baud rate:

```
mult(0)disk(0)rdisk(0)partition(1)\winnt="Windows NT Workstation
(or Server) Version 4.0" /debugport=com1 /baudrate=19200
```

7. Save the file and quit the text editor or the MS-DOS editor. If you're using a text editor, make sure to select the Save As option and specifically name the file BOOT.INI. Otherwise, the file automatically becomes a TXT file.

8. Restart the computer and run NT.

Setting Up a RISC-Based Computer for Debugging Setting up a RISC-based computer is similar to setting up an *x*86-based computer, except that accessing the startup file is done differently. Once your modem or serial cable is connected, perform the following steps:

1. Restart the computer and select an action from the main menu.

2. On a MIPS system, choose Run setup to display the Setup menu and then choose Manage startup to display a menu of boot options.

   On an Alpha or PowerPC system, select options listed in Table 17.4 to get the Boot selections menu.

TABLE 17.4: Boot Selections Menu Options for Alpha and PowerPC Systems

Menu	Option
System Boot	Supplementary menu
Supplementary	Setup the system
Setup	Manage boot selections

3. Choose Change a Boot Selection to display a list of the operating systems that are installed on the computer.

4. Choose the NT operating system. If you have more than one version installed, select the one that you want to debug.

5. Select the OSLOADOPTIONS variable from the list and press Enter.

6. Type **debug** or **crashdebug** and press Enter to save it and turn on debug mode.

   You can also set the communications port, as in this example:

```
OSLOADOPTIONS debug debugport=com2
```

If you don't specify a port, the default port is set to COM1. You do not need to specify a baud rate because RISC-based computers are always set to 19200.

7. Press Esc to stop editing.

8. On a MIPS-based system, choose Return to Main Menu and then Exit to return to the ARC System screen.

    On an Alpha-based system, choose Supplementary Menu, save your changes, and then choose Boot Menu to return to the ARC System screen.

9. If this is the first time that you have debugged an Alpha-based system, you must do the following after connecting to the host computer:

    *   Shut down both computers.

    *   Restart the host computer and run ALPHAKD.EXE.

    *   Restart the target computer while ALPHAKD.EXE is running on the host to set up the configuration on the target computer.

10. Restart the computer to run the NT operating system.

Setting Up the Symbol Tree on the Host Computer

The symbol tree that you set up on the host computer must match the version of Windows NT that is running on the target computer. On the NT CD, a symbol tree has already been created for each platform. The trees are located in the path SUPPORT\DEBUG*platform*\SYMBOLS, where *platform* is I386, ALPHA, MIPS, or PPC. The platform must match the target computer.

To construct a symbol tree, do the following:

1. Copy the proper tree from the SUPPORT directory on the CD to the hard drive on the host computer.

2. If you are debugging a multiprocessor, you need to rename NTKRNLMP.DBG to NTOSKRNL.DBG. These files are in the EXE subdirectory of the symbol tree.

At this point, your symbol tree should be all set up unless you are debugging a multiprocessor or if the target computer uses a special HAL. If this is the case, you need to rename some of the symbol files.

If you're debugging a multiprocessor, you only have to rename NTKRNLMP .DBG (located in the EXE subdirectory of the symbol tree) to NTOSKRNL.DBG.

However, if your computer uses a special HAL, you have a wider range of files to choose from. Table 17.5 shows the different HAL files for each platform. Determine which HAL the target computer uses and rename the corresponding DBG file (located in the DLL subdirectory of the symbol tree) to HAL.DBG (located in *\systemroot*\SYSTEM32).

Some of you may have a HAL file that was supplied by your computer's manufacturer. If this is the case, you need to get the symbols from the manufacturer, rename the symbol file HAL.DBG, and place it in the DLL subdirectory of the symbol tree.

TABLE 17.5: HAL Files by Platform

File Name	Type of System
Files for I386-Based Computers	
HAL.DBG	Standard HAL for Intel Systems
HAL486C.DBG	486 c Step processor
HALAPIC.DBG	Uniprocessor version of HALMPS.DBG
HALAST.DBG	AST SMP systems
HALCBUS.DBG	Cbus systems
HALMCA.DBG	MCA-based systems (PS/2 and others)
HALMPS.DBG	Most Intel multiprocessor systems
HALNCR.DBG	NCR SMP computers
HALOLI.DBG	Olivetti SMP computers
HALSP.DBG	Compaq Systempro
HALWYSE7.DBG	Wyse7 systems
Files for Alpha-Based Computers	
HAL0JENS.DBG	Digital DECpc AXP 150
HALALCOR.DBG	Digital AlphaStation 600
HALAVANT.DBG	Digital Alphastation 200/400

Continued on next page

TABLE 17.5 CONTINUED: HAL Files by Platform

File Name	Type of System
Files for Alpha-Based Computers	
HALEB64P.DBG	Digital AlphaPC64
HALGAMMP.DBG	Digital AlphaServer 2x00 5/xxx
HALMIKAS.DBG	Digital AlphaServer 1000 Uniprocessor
HALNONME.DBG	Digital AXPpci33
HALQS.DBG	Digital Multia MultiClient Desktop
HALSABMP.DBG	Digital AlphaServer 2x00 4/xxx
Files for MIPS-Based Computers	
HALACR.DBG	ACER
HALDTI.DBG	DESKStation Evolution
HALDUOMP.DBG	Microsoft-designed dual multiprocessor
HALFXS.DBG	MTI with an r4000 or r4400
HALFXSPC.DBG	MTI with an r4600
HALNECMP.DBG	NEC dual multiprocessor
HALNTP.DBG	NeTpower FASTseries
HALR98MP.DBG	NEC 4 processor multiprocessor
HALSNI4X.DBG	Siemens Nixdorf uniprocessor and multiprocessor
HALTYBE.DBG	DESKStation Tyne
Files for PPC-Based Computers	
HALCARO.DBG	IBM-6070
HALEAGLE.DBG	Motorola PowerStack and Big Bend
HALFIRE.DBG	Powerized_ES, Powerized_MX (uniprocessor and multiprocessor)
HALPOLO.DBG	IBM-6030
HALPPC.DBG	IBM-6015
HALWOOD.DBG	IBM-6020

Setting Up the Debugger on the Host Computer

In order to set up the debugger on the host computer, you first copy some files from the SUPPORT\DEBUG*platform* directory to a debug directory on the hard drive, where *platform* is the platform of the host computer: I386, PPC, Alpha or MIPS.

Some files that you copy must match the platform of the target computer:

- *platform*KD.EXE, where *platform* is the platform of the target computer
  - ALPHAKD.EXE
  - I386KD.EXE
  - MIPSKD.EXE
  - PPCKD.EXE
- IMAGEHLP.DLL
- KDEXT*platform*.DLL, where platform is the platform of the target computer
  - KDEXTALP.DLL
  - KDEXTX86.DLL
  - KDEXTMIP.DLL
  - KDEXTPPC.DLL

Starting the Debugger

After you have constructed the symbol tree and copied the symbol files to it, you need to create a batch file to set the environment variables listed in Table 17.6 on the host computer.

TABLE 17.6: Environment Variables for the Host Computer

Variable	Description
_NT_DEBUG_PORT	COM port used on the host computer for debugging.
_NT_DEBUG_BAUD_RATE	Maximum baud rate for the debug port. This number is either 9600 or 19200 if you're using a modem. If you're using a null-modem cable or a RISC-based computer, the baud rate should be set to 19200.

Continued on next page

TABLE 17.6 CONTINUED: Environment Variables for the Host Computer

Variable	Description
_NT_SYMBOL_PATH	The path containing the symbol files.
_NT_LOG_FILE_OPEN	Creates a log file for the debug session (optional). The log file creates a copy of everything (input and output) that happens during the debugging session.

A sample batch file for local debugging looks similar to the following:

```
set _NT_DEBUG_PORT=com1
set _NT_DEBUG_BAUD_RATE=19200
set _NT_SYMBOL_PATH=c:\support\debug\i386\symbols
set _NT_LOG_FILE_OPEN=c:\temp\debug.log
i386kd -v debug
```

I haven't discussed the last line yet. It is the command to run the debugger program. This line of the batch file (or any other, for that matter) can be run from the command line as well. The parameters for the debugger are as follows:

Parameter	What It Does
-b	Causes the debugger to stop running on the target computer by causing a debug breakpoint (INT 3).
-c	Forces the computer to resynchronize upon connecting to the target computer. This guarantees that the target and host computer are communicating properly.
-m	If you're using a modem, this causes the debugger to monitor control lines. The debugger is only active when the carrier detect line is active. If the line isn't active, all commands are sent to the modem.
-n	Loads symbols immediately instead of in a delayed mode.
-v	Verbose mode. Displays more information than normal mode.
-x	Induces the debugger to break in when an error occurs.

Usually, the easiest way to start the debugger is to set up a batch file by setting up the proper variables followed by the command to run the debugger. That way, you don't have to remember which variables to set and which debugger program to use.

In a local debugging session, you see something similar to the following:

```
Microsoft(R) Windows NT Kernel Debugger
Version 4.0
(C) 1991-1995 Microsoft Corp.
Symbol search path is:
KD: waiting to connect...
```

At this point, the debugger waits for you to press Ctrl+C to connect to the target computer. If this doesn't work, try pressing Ctrl+R to resynchronize the communication between the host and the target computers.

If you're debugging the target computer remotely, the same screen appears but this line is added:

```
KD: No carrier detect - in terminal mode
```

When this happens, you can send any of the AT commands to your modem. Issue commands to disable hardware compression, error detection, and flow control. You need to consult your modem's documentation, as these commands vary from modem to modem. Once you get a carrier detect signal, you can use the debugger.

Starting the Debugger with the Remote Utility

If the host and target computers are on a network and are not easily accessible to one another, you may want to use the remote utility. The command line for starting the debugger from the host is as follows:

```
remote /s "command" Unique_ID
```

For instance, if you were debugging an *x*86-based computer and you wanted the results to be displayed in verbose mode, you would type

```
remote /s "i386kd -v" debug
```

I used the word *debug* as my unique ID, but you can use anything you like. When you're ready to end your session, type **@K** to return to the command prompt.

You can also interact with the host computer from a workstation that is not connected to the session. To connect to the session, you would type

```
remote /c ComputerName Unique_ID
```

where *ComputerName* is the name of the host computer. For example, if a debugging session was started on the host computer WS1 by using the remote /s command, you could connect to it by typing

```
remote /c WS1 debug
```

NOTE   You can't access a debugging session started on another computer unless the host computer started the session with the remote /s command.

Debugger Commands

A number of debugger commands are available. These commands allow you to

- Load symbols from the symbol tree
- Create a log file
- View device drivers on your system
- Display all locks held on resources
- Obtain a description of memory usage
- Display virtual memory usage
- View the kernel error log
- Display a list of pending Interrupt Request Packets (IRPs)
- List all processes and threads
- List currently active processes and threads

Table 17.7 lists the commands that are available.

TABLE 17.7: Kernel Debugger Commands

Command	Description
!bugdump	Display bug check dump data
!calldata *<table name>*	Dump call data hash table
!db *<physical address>*	Display physical memory

Continued on next page

TABLE 17.7 CONTINUED: Kernel Debugger Commands

Command	Description
!dd *<physical address>*	Display physical memory
!devobj *<device address>*	Dump the device object and Irp queue
!drvobj *<driver address>*	Dump the driver object and related information
!drivers	Display information about all loaded system modules
!eb *<physical address> <byte, byte,...>*	Modify physical memory
!ed *<physical address> <dword,dword,...>*	Modify physical memory
!errlog	Dump the error log contents
!exr *<address>*	Dump exception record at specified address
!filecache	Dump information about the file system cache
!frag *[flags]*	Kernel mode pool fragmentation

		flags:	1	List all fragment information
			2	List allocation information
			3	Do both

!handle *<addr> <flags> <process> <TypeName>*	Dump handle for a process

		flags:	2	Dump non-paged object

!heap *<addr> [flags]*	Dump heap for a process

		flags:	-v	Verbose
			-f	Free List entries
			-a	All entries
			-s	Summary
			-x	Force a dump even if the data is bad
		address:		Desired heap to dump or 0 for all

Continued on next page

TABLE 17.7 CONTINUED: Kernel Debugger Commands

Command	Description
!help	Display this table
!ib *<port>*	Read a byte from an I/O port
!id *<port>*	Read a double-word from an I/O port
!iw *<port>*	Read a word from an I/O port
!irp *<address>*	Dump Irp at specified address
!irpzone	Walk the Irp zones looking for active Irps
!locks [-v] *<address>*	Dump kernel mode resource locks
!lpc	Dump lpc ports and messages
!memusage	Dumps the page frame database table
!ob *<port>*	Write a byte to an I/O port
!obja *<TypeName>*	Dump an object manager object's attributes
!object *<TypeName>*	Dump an object manager object
!od *<port>*	Write a double-word to an I/O port
!ow *<port>*	Write a word to an I/O port
!pfn	Dump the page frame database entry for the physical page
!pool *<address> [detail]*	Dump kernel mode heap

address:	0 *or* blank	Only the process heap
	1	All heaps in the process

Otherwise for the heap address listed

detail:	0	Summary Information
	1	Above + location/size of regions
	3	Above + allocated/free blocks in committed regions
	4	Above + free lists

Continued on next page

TABLE 17.7 CONTINUED: Kernel Debugger Commands

Command	Description
!poolfind Tag *[pooltype]*	Find occurrences of the specified Tag
	Tag is 4-character tag, * and ? are wild cards
	Pooltype is 0 for nonpaged (default), and 1 for paged
	NOTE: This can take a long time!
!poolused *[flags]*	Dump usage by pool tag

	flags:	1	Verbose
		2	Sort by NonPagedPool Usage
		4	Sort by PagedPool Usage

Command	Description
!process *[flags]*	Dump process at specified address
!processfields	Show offsets to all fields in a process
!ptov *PhysicalPageNumber*	Dump all valid physical and virtual mappings for the given page directory
!ready	Dump state of all READY system threads
!regkcb	Dump registry key-control-blocks
!regpool *[slr]*	Dump registry allocated paged pool

		s	Save list of registry pages to temporary file
		r	Restore list of registry pages from temp. file

Command	Description
!reload	Load the symbol files
!srb *<address>*	Dump Srb at specified address
!sympath	Display the current symbol path
!sysptes	Dump the system PTEs
!thread *[flags]*	Dump thread at specified address
!threadfields	Show offsets to all fields in a thread
!time	Report PerformanceCounterRate and TimerDifference

Continued on next page

TABLE 17.7 CONTINUED: Kernel Debugger Commands

Command	Description
!timer	Dump timer tree
!token [*flags*]	Dump token at specified address
!tokenfields	Show offsets to all fields in a token
!trap <*address*>	Dump a trap frame
!vad	Dump VADs
!version	Version of extension dll
!vm	Dump virtual management values
***x86*-Specific Commands**	
!apic [*base*]	Dump local apic
!cxr	Dump context record at specified address
!ioapic [*base*]	Dump io apic
!mtrr	Dump MTTR
!npx [*base*]	Dump NPX save area
!pcr	Dump the PCR
!pte	Dump the corresponding PDE and PTE for the entered address
!sel [*selector*]	Examine selector values
!trap [*base*]	Dump trap frame
!tss [*register*]	Dump TSS

!reload

The !reload command loads the symbols from the symbol tree. Output from the command looks like this:

```
kd> !reload
Loading symbols for 0x80100000   ntoskrnl.exe ->
d:\support\debug\i386\symbols\exe\ntoskrnl.dbg
```

```
KD ModLoad: 80100000 801ca740  ntoskrnl.exe
KD ModLoad: 80400000 8040b000  hal.dll
KD ModLoad: 80010000 80013320  atapi.sys
KD ModLoad: 80014000 8001ba80  SCSIPORT.SYS
```

You need to execute this command before any other because the symbols are needed to execute other commands.

Log Files

You will also want to create a log file to review. To create a log file, all you have to do is type

```
.logopen
```

This creates a text file named KD.LOG that can be found in the same directory as the debugger program you are using. With a log file, you can compare output from commands such as !vm and !memusage.

If you already have a log file and just want to append to it, type

```
.logappend
```

This adds any additional output to the end of the log file. When you're ready to close the file, type

```
.logclose
```

!drivers

The !drivers command lists all of the device drivers located on your system. The information from the device drivers looks something like the following (I cleaned it up a bit for the sake of clarity):

```
kd> !drivers
Loaded System Driver Summary
Base       Code   Size     Data   Size    Driver Name    Creation Time
80100000   b31c0  (716kb)  17200  (92kb)  ntoskrnl.exe   Thu Jan 25 19:14:08 1996
80400000   92c0   ( 36kb)  20c0   ( 8kb)  hal.dll        Thu Jan 18 15:28:52 1996
80010000   2940   ( 10kb)  760    ( 1kb)  atapi.sys      Sun Jan 21 19:40:48 1996
80014000   6400   ( 25kb)  13c0   ( 4kb)  SCSIPORT.SYS   Fri Jan 19 12:19:37 1996
```

The following items can be determined from this output:

Base   The starting address (in hex) of the device driver. When the code that causes the Kernel STOP Error falls between the base address for the driver and the base address for the next driver on the list, that driver is likely the cause of the error. As you can see from the output, the base for atapi.sys is 0x8001000. Any address that falls between that and 0x80014000 (the base address for SCSIPORT.SYS) belongs to atapi.sys. If the target computer displays a blue screen, often the first address listed is that of a driver.

Code Size   The size of the driver code in both hex and decimal.

Data Size   The amount of allocated space given to the driver for data in both hex and decimal.

Driver Name   The file name of the driver.

Creation Time   The link date of the driver—in simpler terms, the date when a driver or executable file is compiled.

!locks

The !locks command displays all locks held on resources by threads. Locks can be either shared or exclusive. The information provided by this command is useful, especially when deadlocks occur on the target computer. A deadlock occurs when a non-executing thread has an exclusive lock on a resource that is needed by another executing thread.

The output for the !locks command looks similar to the following:

```
kd> !locks -v -d
**** DUMP OF ALL RESOURCE OBJECTS ****
Resource @ ntoskrnl!MmSystemWsLock (0x80148b90)  Available
  Contention Count = 4
Resource @ ntoskrnl!MmSectionExtendResource (0x80148990)  Available
Resource @ 0xff7143a0 Shared 2 owning threads
  Threads: ffb3ba61-01
0013ffa31: Unable to read ThreadCount for resource
```

!memusage

This command briefly describes the system's current memory usage, after which it gives a more detailed list of memory usage. The output for !memusage looks like this:

```
kd> !memusage
 loading PFN database.................................................
        Zeroed:    0 (    0 kb)
          Free:    2 (    8 kb)
       Standby:  786 ( 3144 kb)
      Modified:   95 (  380 kb)
 ModifiedNoWrite:   0 (    0 kb)
  Active/Valid: 3211 ( 12844 kb)
    Transition:    0 (    0 kb)
       Unknown:    0 (    0 kb)
         TOTAL: 4094 ( 16376 kb)
 Usage Summary in KiloBytes (Kb):
 Control Valid Standby Dirty Shared Locked PageTables name
 ff6ab5c8   0    36    0    0    0     0 mapped_file( GNLI____.TTF )
 ff6aa548   0    40    0    0    0     0 mapped_file( KF_____.TTF )
 ff6ab428   0    32    0    0    0     0 mapped_file( GNM_____.TTF )
 ff6afc68   0    40    0    0    0     0 mapped_file( Latinwd.ttf )
```

TIP   Even though the !memusage command gives some information about memory leaks, it is still better to look at the !vm command for memory information on the most common Kernel STOP Errors.

!vm

The !vm command provides a list of the target system's virtual memory usage. Output from the command looks similar to the following:

```
kd> !vm
*** Virtual Memory Usage ***
Physical Memory:   3950   ( 15800 Kb)
Available Pages:    788   ( 3152 Kb)
Modified Pages:      95   (  380 Kb)
NonPagedPool Usage:  83   (  332 Kb)
PagedPool 0 Usage:  763   ( 3052 Kb)
```

```
PagedPool 1 Usage:    69    (   276 Kb)
PagedPool 2 Usage:    85    (   340 Kb)
PagedPool Usage:     917    (  3668 Kb)
Shared Commit:        88    (   352 Kb)
Process Commit:      285    (  1140 Kb)
Per Process:         787    (  3148 KB)
PagedPool Commit:    917    (  3668 Kb)
Driver Commit:       495    (  1980 Kb)
Committed pages:    2710    ( 10840 Kb)
Commit limit:       9077    ( 36308 Kb)
```

The memory usage you see in the above list is given in both pages and kilobytes. The most useful information for analyzing problems follows:

Physical Memory   The total physical memory on the target computer.

Available Pages   The total number of pages of physical and virtual memory available. If this number is low, the cause might be a problem with a process that allocates too much virtual memory.

NonPagedPool Usage   The number of pages allocated to the non-paged pool. A pool is memory that can't be swapped to the pagefile, so it always occupies physical memory. This number should not be larger than 10 percent of the total physical memory. If it is larger, the target computer may have a memory leak.

!errlog

Sometimes the debugger maintains a log of kernel errors that occur on the target computer. The !errlog command allows you to view this log. Most of the time, however, this log is empty. If an event has been logged, however, you may be able to find out from it which process caused the Kernel STOP Error.

!irpzone full

The !irpzone full command provides a list of all pending *Interrupt Request Packets* (IRP) on the target computer. An IRP is a data structure used by device drivers and other processes to communicate with each other. Output for this program looks like this:

```
kd> !irpzone full
Small Irp region
```

```
Could not allocate 3952 bytes for region
Large Irp region
Irp is from zone and active with 2 stacks 2 is current
 No Mdl System buffer = ff6b8b88 Thread ff6b8020: Irp stack trace.
 cmd flg cl Device  File   Completion-Context
  0  0 0 ff6b8b88 00000000 00000000-00000000
  ff6b8b88: is not a device object
  Args: 00000000 00000000 ff6e6808 00000104
> 3  0 1 ff6d0e70 ff6b8e08 00000000-00000000  pending
  \FileSystem\Npfs
  Args: 00000104 00000000 00000000 00000000
```

This information may be useful if the trap analysis (which you can find in the MEMORY.TXT file) indicates a problem with an IRP that has gone bad. Usually, the IRP listing has a number of entries in both of the large and small IRP lists.

!process 0 0

By using the !process 0 0 command, you can view all of the active processes and their headers. Its output looks like the following:

```
kd> !process 0 0
**** NT ACTIVE PROCESS DUMP ****
PROCESS ff6ef7a0 Cid: 0002  Peb: 00000000 ParentCid: 0000
  DirBase: 00030000 ObjectTable: ff714488 TableSize: 62.
  Image: System
PROCESS ff6d5de0 Cid: 0011  Peb: 7ffdf000 ParentCid: 0002
  DirBase: 007bd000 ObjectTable: ff6d6248 TableSize: 46.
  Image: smss.exe
```

The information that is helpful to know here is

> **Process ID**   The 8-digit hex number following the word PROCESS. The system uses this number to track the process.

> **Image**   The name of the program that owns the process.

!process 0 7

This command is similar to the !process 0 0 command, but instead of a brief summary, it lists all of the information about the process. This is usually a large listing because each system is running a large number of processes and each process usually has one or more threads. Also, if the stack from a thread resides in kernel memory, it is also listed. Output usually looks like this:

```
kd> !process 0 7
**** NT ACTIVE PROCESS DUMP ****
PROCESS ff6ef7a0 Cid: 0002  Peb: 00000000 ParentCid: 0000
  DirBase: 00030000 ObjectTable: ff714488 TableSize: 62.
  Image: System
  VadRoot ff6eed68 Clone 0 Private 5. Modified 338. Locked 0.
  FF6EF95C MutantState Signalled OwningThread 0
  Token                e1000730
  ElapsedTime              13:43:40.0594
  UserTime             0:00:00.0000
  KernelTime           0:00:39.0236
  QuotaPoolUsage[PagedPool]     0
  QuotaPoolUsage[NonPagedPool]  0
  Working Set Sizes (now,min,max) (53, 30, 145)
  PeakWorkingSetSize        125
  VirtualSize             0MB
  PeakVirtualSize         0MB
  PageFaultCount          630
  MemoryPriority          BACKGROUND
  BasePriority            8
  CommitCharge            9
      THREAD ff6ef520 Cid 2.1 Teb: 00000000 Win32Thread: 80148260 WAIT:
(WrFreePage) KernelMode Non-Alertable
        80148980 SynchronizationEvent
    Not impersonating
    Owning Process ff6ef7a0
    WaitTime (seconds)   9123
    Context Switch Count  192
    UserTime          0:00:00.0000
    KernelTime        0:00:32.0707
    Start Address ntoskrnl!Phase1Initialization (0x801b9016)
    Stack Init fdc14000 Current fdc13cfc Base fdc14000 Limit fdc11000
Call 0
    Priority 0 BasePriority 0 PriorityDecrement 0 DecrementCount 0
    ChildEBP RetAddr Args to Child
    fdc13d14 8011500c c0502000 0000053d 00000000
ntoskrnl!KiSwapThread+0xc5
    fdc13d38 801274b2 80148980 00000008 00000000
ntoskrnl!KeWaitForSingleObject+0x1b8
```

You may find the following information important:

UserTime   The length of time the process has been running in user mode.

KernelTime   The length of time the process has been running in kernel mode. If either the UserTime or KernelTime value seems very high, the process may be taking up an exceptional amount of system resources.

Working Set Sizes   Gives the working set size in pages. A very large value for this entry may indicate that a process is leaking memory or taking up a large amount of system resources.

QuotaPoolUsage   Provides the paged and non-paged pool used by the process. If you find that the non-paged pool used by a process is excessive, you may have found your memory leak.

Not only that, you'll find that the thread information also has a list of threads that have locks on resources. This is given right after the thread header. In the output above, the thread has a lock on one resource (a SynchronizationEvent at address 80148260). When comparing this address against the list of locks shown in the !locks output, you should be able to find which threads have exclusive locks on resources.

!process

The !process command displays information on the process currently running on the target computer. The output looks exactly like that of the !process 0 7 command, except it is for only one process and no thread information is given.

!thread

The !thread command behaves in much the same way as !process, except that thread information is given instead.

NOTE   Even though the !process 0 7 command gives information on both processes and threads, the result can be 10–15 pages of output. This can make things a bit difficult when it comes to finding the currently running process and threads. Use !process and !thread instead.

Examining Crash Dumps with DUMPEXAM

What should you do about a blue screen? If you can manage to get a blue screen while the debugger is attached, then you're golden—you can log the output. But the whole debugger system may not be set up, and that's where a crash dump file can be useful.

You can tell an NT machine that if it ever experiences a blue screen, it should dump the entire contents of memory to a file called MEMORY.DMP. You enable that function in the Control Panel. In the System applet, you see a tab labeled Startup/Shutdown, with a group on its page labeled "Recovery." Click the check box that directs the system to create MEMORY.DMP.

If you ever *do* see a blue screen, reboot and you'll see a huge MEMORY.DMP file in your \WINNT directory. You examine that with DUMPEXAM, but you need a few ingredients to use DUMPEXAM.

First, you need the program itself. It's on the CD-ROM in \SUPPORT\ DEBUG\ I386\dumpexam.exe. If you copy it somewhere else, you should also copy kdextx86.dll, because it is needed, too. You also need the folder in \SUPPORT\ DEBUG\i386\symbols because DUMPEXAM needs it to understand what it's seeing in the memory dump. Invoke DUMPEXAM like so:

```
dumpexam -v -f outfile -y x:\support\debug\i386\symbols memory.dmp
```

The -v says, "Be verbose"; the more information we can get, the better. *Outfile* is just the name of an ASCII text file that will contain the output of the dump analysis. For drive *x:*, insert the drive letter of your CD-ROM. MEMORY.DMP is, of course, the name of the original crash dump file. The output file is an expanded-upon blue screen.

Well, now that you have it, what do you do with it? Let's look at the information a blue screen provides.

The first lines are a stop code. They may look like this:

```
** STOP: address1 address2 address3 address4
```

The four numbers are addresses; one of them is the address of the actual program that caused the blue screen.

You next see a line like this:

```
INACCESSIBLE_BOOT_DEVICE or IRQL_NOT_LESS_OR_EQUAL
```

Following that is a list of kernel mode drivers in memory at the time of the blue screen. It is a two-column listing. An excerpt might look like this:

```
DLL Base DateStmp - Name
80100000 2e53fe55 - ntoskrnl.exe
80010000 2e41884b - Aha154x.sys
```

The "Base" is the start address of the DLL. All addresses are above 80000000 hex because the system area starts there. The date-stamp (it's seconds since 1980) can be useful because if you see a system driver with a different date from other system drivers, it could be a newer, corrupted driver.

Below the driver list is a list of modules that are near the area that caused the blue screen; one of them is the culprit.

The Bottom Line: What They're Good For

Blue screens and the Kernel Debugger can be insightful tools, but remember that in the end they can do only a few things:

- Point the finger at a bad driver. Calling a vendor and saying, "Your SCSI driver doesn't work on my system" is much more likely to produce a shrug and a "Says you, pal" from the SCSI vendor. Being able to send the vendor a blue screen output is a bit more damning and *may* motivate the vendor to fix their buggy drivers.

- Give an indication of what's going wrong. Maybe the vendor is blameless and you've just got a corrupted driver. Once you know what file may have caused the trouble, you can try reloading it or checking the vendor's Web site for an updated driver.

- Sometimes give you the ammunition to say to Microsoft, "Look, there's a bug in the [fill in the blank] subsystem, and here's the proof!" There's no guarantee that anyone will *do* anything about it, but at least you have the smoking gun.

The Windows NT Diagnostics Tool

If you want nuts-and-bolts information about the hardware on your NT Server, you *could* go to the documentation for all your hardware and read all the notes you made about changes to the default configurations. Even the most dedicated record keeper doesn't have information about everything, however, so Windows NT keeps information about your system that you might never have known you had. To get a more complete idea of the picture, then, you can check with WinMSD, the Windows NT diagnostics tool.

WinMSD is in the Administrative Tools group under the name Windows NT Diagnostics.

Before getting into the details of WinMSD, let me make clear that it is not a terribly powerful tool. It won't solve a *lot* of problems. Its main value is in allowing you to take a quick "bird's-eye" view of a system, something of considerable use if you've been called in to look at a problem on a server that you've not looked at before.

But wait, that's not all. Windows NT Diagnostic also allows you to view the diagnostic information for all the other Windows NT computers in the domain without having to physically go to those computers. Let's take a look at this new and interesting feature in more detail.

Remote Diagnostic Viewing

Being able to save shoe leather by sitting at your own desk as you ferret out a problem on a machine six flights away sounds like a great improvement. Indeed, it is. However, beware of some restrictions before you kick off your shoes entirely.

The first restriction, of course, is that diagnostic information can only be read from a machine that is running NT. If we assume all machines on a network are running NT, then

- A workstation can read diagnostic information from any server on the network.

- A workstation can read diagnostic information from another workstation as long as both computers are members of the same domain.

- A server can read diagnostic information from any workstation or server on the network.

To view a remote diagnostic window, see the next "How Do I" sidebar.

How Do I Find the Diagnostics Information of a Remote Workstation or Server?

1. In the Start menu, click on Programs and choose Administrative Tools.

2. Open Windows NT Diagnostics.

3. Click on the File menu and choose Select Computer.

4. Type in the name of the computer or, more easily, double-click on the computer you want to see. You see a screen like this one:

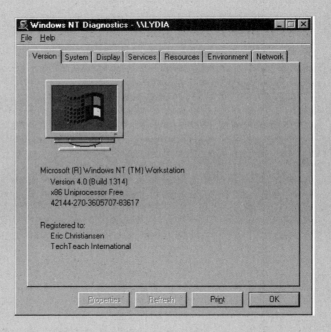

Viewing Diagnostic Information

To view diagnostic information, begin at the Start menu, click on Programs, then on Administrative Tools, and finally on Windows NT Diagnostics. You see a screen that looks like the one in Figure 17.19.

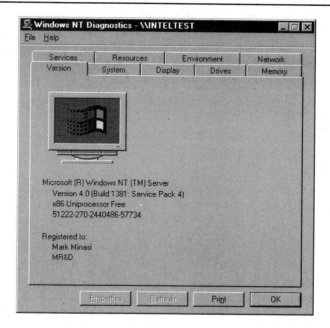

FIGURE 17.19:

Opening Diagnostics screen

There are two main things that I get out of Diagnostics. First, the first screen tells you what Service Pack level you've installed. The second is the listing of IRQs, which can be extremely useful when I'm trying to shoehorn *just one more board* into a machine.

Anyway, the NT Diagnostics program is presented as a single window with nine tabs. Each tab shows different aspects of the computer's components and their present state. The Version tab appears first and acts like a cover page. The other eight tabs are discussed in order of appearance.

Meanwhile, if you have used the Diagnostics in NT Server 3.51 or before, you may notice that the tabs have been renamed and some of the information has been moved around. Here is a brief overview of the main changes:

- The OS Version button is now the Version tab.

- The install date and system root is omitted in version 4.

- The Hardware button is now the System tab.

- The Video resolution is now listed in the Display tab.

- The CPU stepping button is no longer a separate button. A more complete description is now in the System tab itself.

- The Memory button is still the Memory tab, although the Memory load index has been omitted. This oversight represents a loss to the Diagnostics function. Knowing how much memory is being used can be very helpful. Perhaps they will put it back in the next version.

- The Drivers button is now incorporated in the Devices portion of the Services tab.

- The Devices button, IRQ/Port Status button, and DMA/Memory button are all incorporated into the Resources tab.

- The Environment button is still the Environment tab, although the Process Environment section is gone. That information can be found in the Drives tab now.

- The Drives button is the Drives tab and now you can see the drive letter and icon as well as the drive type.

- The new Display tab shows the settings of the monitor and display card.

Now, let's look more closely at the contents of some of the tab sections in Windows NT Diagnostics 4.

Memory Tab

As the title implies, the Memory tab gives you information about your system's memory. It tells how much memory it has and how much is still available. As you can see in Figure 17.20, this server has 16MB of RAM, of which only 1MB is unused. The same information is listed for the Page File space. Here, there are 5.6MB, of which 2.8MB are available.

The *paging file* is the amount of data that can be passed back and forth when NT Workstation is using virtual memory—in this case, 5.6MB. What is virtual memory? In order to get more work out of the system RAM than it could provide on its own, NT Workstation uses a special file on the hard disk called a virtual memory *paging file*, or *swap file*. When Windows NT is demanding more of the system memory than the system can really give, it keeps some of the program code and other information in RAM and puts some of it in the paging file on the hard disk. When that information is required, NT Workstation pulls it out of virtual memory (swapping other information into the paging file, if necessary). The end result is more bang for your RAM buck.

FIGURE 17.20:

Diagnostics Memory tab

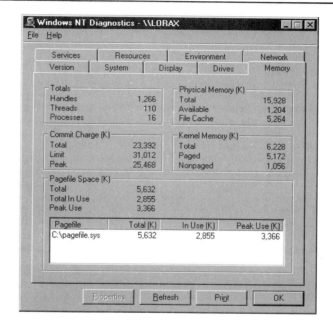

Services Tab

The Services tab contains two buttons. Click on Services and you can see the services that are available on the system, as shown in Figure 17.21. Click on Devices to see all of the devices on the system, as shown in Figure 17.22. Both lists show whether each device or service is stopped or running at the time.

For the details of individual servers or devices, highlight the one in question and click on Properties. Or, more easily, just double-click on the service or device in question. The properties screen that appears includes two tabs, General and Dependencies, as you can see in Figure 17.23.

FIGURE 17.21:

Diagnostics Services screen

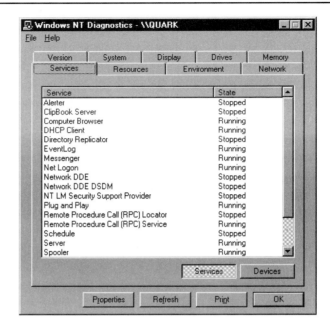

FIGURE 17.22:

Diagnostics Devices screen

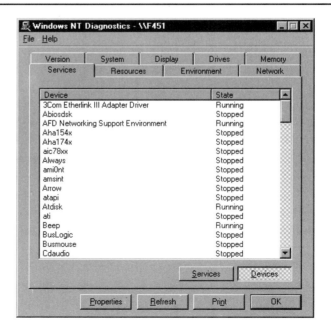

FIGURE 17.23:

Diagnostics Service screen
showing general properties

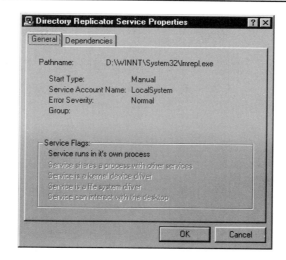

General Service and Device Information

The general properties of services and devices includes the following information:

- The path where the driver is found.

- The Start Type, which can be one of several things:

Boot	Begin at computer bootup. Applies to drivers for hardware without which the computer cannot function, such as disk drives.
System	Begin when the operating system starts up. Applies to devices that are critical to the operation of the operating system, such as display drivers like ET4000.
Automatic	Begin when the operating system has begun, like the system drivers, but are not crucial to the operation of the operating system. The NetBIOS interface is one example of such a driver.
Manual	Begin when started by the user or a dependent device.
Disabled	These drivers cannot be started by a user, but the system can start them. This is why you may see drivers that are running but are listed as being disabled—that threw me for

a loop the first time that I noticed it. The FastFAT is one example of such a driver.

- What kind of error control they have. The level of error control determines what happens to the system startup if a given driver fails:

Critical	Don't start up the system.
Severe	Switch to the Last Known Good setup, or, if already using that setup, continue on.
Normal	Continue startup, but display an error message stating that the driver did not load.
Ignore	Don't halt the system or display an error message: just skip that driver.

- The group that they are associated with (SCSI miniport, video, and so on) determines their load order, as, for example, the boot file system loads before video, and SCSI miniports load before each of these.

Users with administrative privileges can add device drivers to the system from the Drivers icon in the Control Panel, or adjust their startup time or error control from the Devices icon. Be careful about adjusting these things, however, because if you change a Boot or System driver to a different time, you could keep your system from working.

- Service Flags that tell how the service interacts with the rest of the machine by indicating if the service
  - Runs in its own process
  - Shares a process with other services
  - Is a kernel device driver
  - Is a file system driver
  - Can interact with the desktop

Dependencies of Services and Devices

Click on the Dependencies tab and you can see what services and groups are dependent on this service, as shown in Figure 17.24. This is helpful for tracking an error and better understanding the flow of information through the computer.

FIGURE 17.24:

Dependencies tab in Services screen

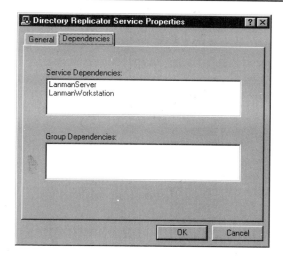

Resources Tab

The Resources tab lists the hardware resources that are attached to the computer and how they are attached. Click on any of the five buttons (IRQ, I/O Port, DMA, Memory, or Devices) to see what you have.

The IRQ and I/O Port windows give you information about what interrupts, memory accesses, and ports your system is using. For an example of each, see Figures 17.25 and 17.26. You can't change anything with these dialog boxes, but they *can* help resolve interrupt conflicts or memory port conflicts.

> **NOTE**   What would you use a hex address for? It can serve as a partial guide to current port addresses on your computer and keep you from installing a new device that causes a port conflict. This is invaluable information for adding components to your computer.

The DMA and Memory windows show you the location and size of fixed blocks of memory. They also report which devices are using Direct Memory Access (DMA) ports. The report for each looks like Figures 17.27 and 17.28.

FIGURE 17.25:

IRQ portion of the Resources
tab in the Diagnostics
dialog box

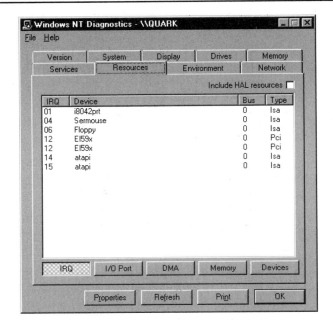

FIGURE 17.26:

IO Port screen of the
Resources tab

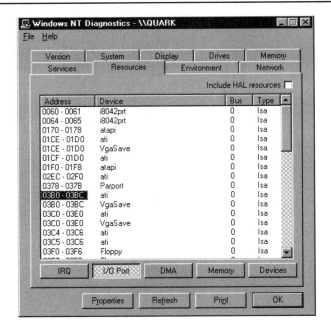

FIGURE 17.27:

DMA screen of the
Resources tab

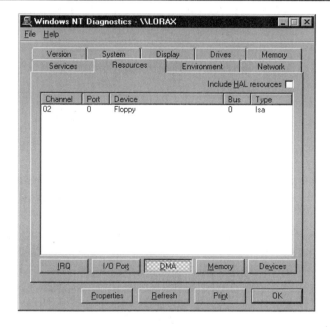

FIGURE 17.28:

Memory screen of the
Resources tab

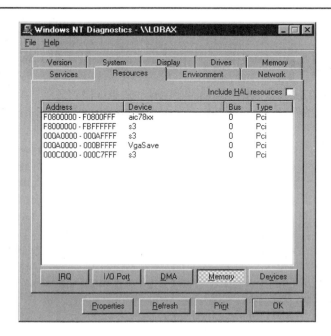

Only one device uses a DMA channel on this machine: the floppy uses channel 2. The Memory section displays fixed blocks of memory, the areas of physical memory that must not be moved by the operating system. Those areas are rare and are typically buffers for peripherals. The areas displayed by WINMSD here are the video memory buffer, the video BIOS, and the SCSI BIOS on this system.

The Devices window shows you all the devices that are present on the computer that you are looking at. If you double-click on one of the items in the list, you see a screen that looks like Figure 17.29. This screen recaps, by device, the IRQ, I/O port, and DMA.

FIGURE 17.29:

Properties of the Device dialog box

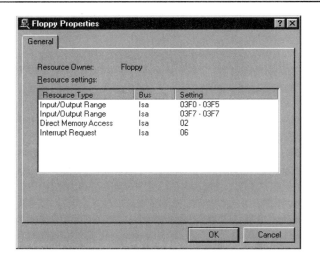

The information on this screen is useful if you plan to set up more hardware on your system and want to make sure that two devices don't conflict. You could adjust these settings by reinstalling your hardware and adjusting the IRQ and DMA settings, but in most cases that isn't necessary. This dialog box (like the ones that show the IRQs and DMA channels in use) is really for information purposes only.

Environment Tab

Every computer has information that is specific only to itself: the command interpreter it is using, its home drive, and the like. That information is stored in NT in the *environment*, an area of memory that stores configuration-specific information. Figure 17.30 shows an example.

FIGURE 17.30:

Environment tab in Diagnostics dialog box

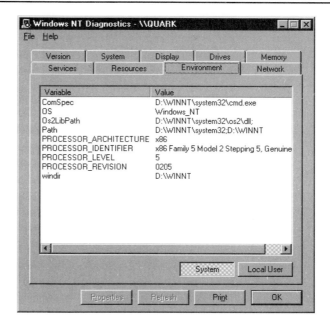

Users with Administrative privileges can change this information from the System icon in the Control Panel.

This dialog box lists the processor architecture, operating system type, and so on, for that particular machine's system.

Network Tab

The Network tab shows the relationship between the current user, his or her computer, and the network. There are four sections to the Network tab:

Section	What It Is
General	A nice summary of your machine's name, your username, logon information, and the like.
Transports	A convenient way to find out which transport layers you're running. In theory, if you were running a TCP/IP stack, this would be a quick way to find out what IP address you were using.

Settings	Dozens of settings that you can use to tune an NT Server installation. This window shows you their current values. The interesting part is that the window can give you ideas about what kinds of things you can control with NT Server—things that you might not have known you could do. (The important ones are covered in the book, by the way, so you don't have to do any digging.)
Statistics	As the network works, statistical monitors in each computer keep track of how many bytes have been transmitted or received, how many errors occurred, and the like. This section reports those values.

Printing the Results

Seeing this information is good, but being able to print it and have it at your fingertips when someone says, "My computer won't... " is even better.

The Print button at the bottom of each tab allows you to create and print a report of the information on the tab as well as print the whole diagnostics file. See the following "How Do I" sidebar for specifics on creating a printed report.

TIP Tape an envelope to the computer with a recent report of the Diagnostic information in case of emergencies.

How Do I Print a Report of a Single Tab Section of the Diagnostics File?

To create a printed report of what is on a Diagnostics tab:

1. Open the Windows NT Diagnostics screen.

2. Click on the tab containing the information you wish to print in a report.

3. Click on the Print option at the bottom right of the window. You see the Create Report dialog box.

Continued on next page

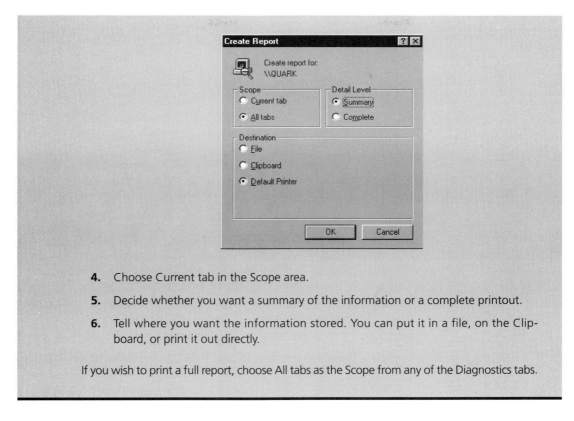

4. Choose Current tab in the Scope area.

5. Decide whether you want a summary of the information or a complete printout.

6. Tell where you want the information stored. You can put it in a file, on the Clipboard, or print it out directly.

If you wish to print a full report, choose All tabs as the Scope from any of the Diagnostics tabs.

NT version 4 provides a diagnostics tool that can help you keep track of the components of your computer. Knowing what you have and what it is attached to can help you plan ahead. It also gives you another place to look when diagnosing a problem.

Troubleshooting Login Failures: "No Domain Controller Found..."

One of the most confusing and common NT mysteries is the one that occurs when you sit down at a computer and try to log in to your domain, only to be told that no domain controller could be found to validate your login.

It can happen from any client type, whether DOS, Mac, Windows 9*x*, or NT, and the same things tend to make it happen. But be ready for some bad news: you can't always fix it.

When you tell your workstation to try to log you in to a domain, your workstation must first find one of the machines that contain a copy of the database of domain users in passwords—in other words, a domain controller, whether primary or backup. You may recall from the discussion of NetBIOS names in Chapter 14 that all domain controllers announce themselves to the world by registering a NetBIOS name of *domainname*<1C>; for example, if a domain named URSAMA-JOR had a domain controller named MIZAR, then MIZAR would register not only its personal NetBIOS name MIZAR<00> but also URSAMAJOR<1C>.

NOTE   Recall that the "<1C>" is just an easily written way of saying "the hexadecimal value 1C." As all NetBIOS names are 16 characters in length and URSAMAJOR is only nine characters long, the full NetBIOS name would look like "URSAMAJOR" followed by seven blanks, nine bytes of value hexadecimal 20—hex 20 is the ASCII code for blank—finally ending with a hex 1C. It's just easier to write "URSA-MAJOR<1C>," which is why I represent it that way here.

The URSAMAJOR<1C> name is different from the MIZAR<00> name, however, as only one machine has the MIZAR<00> name, but many machines can claim the URSAMAJOR<1C> name; it's a "group" name, and each and every other domain controller in URSAMAJOR registers the name.

But how does your workstation find one of these domain controllers? Step One is a broadcast, a simple shout of "Is there a machine named URSAMAJOR<1C> here?" This is the first step no matter what protocol you're using. (There is *one* way to keep this broadcast from happening—only one—and I'll cover it in a minute.) The idea is that it's always best to find a local domain controller, if one exists, and a broadcast will find that. If you're using NetBEUI, IPX, or TCP/IP in broadcast-only mode, that's as far as the workstation goes to find a domain controller. If there's not one within "earshot," so to speak, then the logon will fail.

If you're using TCP/IP with LMHOSTS, then the client will look in its LMHOSTS file for an entry with a #DOM symbol, like so:

```
200.116.73.18 MIZAR #DOM:URSAMAJOR #PRE
```

Sometimes that won't work, however, due to quirks in the TCP client software. An alternative form of the LMHOSTS line sometimes works better:

```
200.116.73.18 "MIZAR      \0x1C" #PRE
```

I discussed this back in Chapter 14, but let's re-examine it from the point of view of troubleshooting. In this formulation, you directly enter the hex 1C rather than relying on the #DOM metacommand. It leads to some interesting behavior. First, entering one of these 0x1C entries *completely short circuits the domain controller–discovery process*. The machine doesn't broadcast, it doesn't talk to WINS, and it doesn't even do all that much looking around in LMHOSTS, either. In fact, if you enter several domain controller names, all using the 0x1C formulation, the NT machine will only look at the *last* one. Furthermore, if the domain controller named in LMHOSTS isn't up and available, then the NT machine simply cannot log on, because again it doesn't even think to look in WINS or to broadcast.

Using the 0x1C formulation, then, can be quite powerful because it guarantees that an NT server or workstation can find a domain controller, but it has two drawbacks: it's labor intensive, as you'll have to put an LMHOSTS file on every NT machine, and it's not at all fault-tolerant, as you end up creating a life-and-death relationship between a particular NT machine and its assigned domain controller.

A TCP/IP-using system that has been pointed to a WINS server will look in the WINS server's database of machine names for a machine with the URSA-MAJOR<1C> name. (Look back to Chapter 14 for more details on how NetBIOS names are resolved on TCP/IP systems if you've forgotten.) WINS maintains a list of up to 25 domain controllers, and it sends that list to the workstation. The workstation then sends messages to all of those domain controllers asking them if they'll log it on. The first one to respond to your workstation is the one that the workstation uses to log on.

Assuming that the workstation has located a domain controller, it then asks the domain controller to verify the requested user's credentials. The domain controller does that, and all is well; that's basically all there is to a login.

Check the Basics

So what can go wrong? There are a few basic, obvious things that can go wrong and, while it may seem that I'm insulting you by asking you to check them, I can only say that I've done every one of these at least once.

- Check that the domain name is spelled correctly. It's not possible to misspell a domain name on an NT workstation, as you couldn't join a domain in the first place if you'd misspelled it, but it's quite easy to do so on a DOS, Windows, or Mac system.

- Check that there's network connectivity. It may just be that the Ethernet hub had its power cord kicked out, or that the network cable fell off the back of the card.

- Check that you typed your name and password correctly.

If You're Dialing In

Many login failures occur because you're dialing in to an NT network. How you attack them depends on whether you're running NT or Windows.

If you're running Windows NT Workstation, then the usual reason that your system can't find a domain controller is that it's not hooked up to a WINS server or an LMHOSTS file. I strongly recommend that when you set up a Dial-Up Networking phone book entry for dial-in to a RAS server, you pre-specify the address of your WINS server or servers right in the phone book entry. (You'll see more about this in the next chapter.) Consider building a simple LMHOSTS file with entries pointing to the domain controllers in your organization.

If you're trying to get Windows 95 or 98 to dial in to an NT domain and for some reason can't always make it work, don't feel bad—Dial-Up Networking for 9x has some problems. Fortunately, there is a solution—patch files from Microsoft. Microsoft rearranges their Web site too often for me to tell you exactly where to find it, but there is a file called MSDUN13.EXE which completely updates the Windows 95 Dial-Up Networking code; there's a similar one for Windows 98, I'm told.

If You're Local

Local systems can also benefit from a double-check that you've got a proper WINS server nearby or an LMHOSTS file. In some cases, it makes sense to have LMHOSTS even *if* you've got WINS servers—here's why.

Suppose you have a geographically scattered domain with many domain controllers, many systems whose names are registered as URSAMAJOR<1C>. WINS should know of all of them, shouldn't it? Sadly, it doesn't: WINS only remembers the last 25 domain controllers that it's heard of. If a domain controller local to you has fallen off the edge, then WINS won't tell you about it, with the result that you'll end up trying to log in over a presumably slower WAN link. Even if WINS knows of all of your domain controllers, however, how will it know which one is geographically closest to you? It doesn't.

How, then, to ensure that you find a local domain controller? Two thoughts.

First, there's always LMHOSTS. Sorry if I sound like a broken record, but it's a very useful tool.

Second, you might modify the order in which NetBIOS name resolution takes place. By default, when your system goes looking for URSAMAJOR<1C>, it first looks in its name cache in RAM. If it can't find the domain controller there, it looks to WINS. If WINS doesn't have the answer, then the PC broadcasts to find the answer, and so on.

All logins start with a single broadcast. But perhaps your local DC is busy and doesn't respond quickly enough. Can you bias things a bit more in its favor? Yes, by modifying how NetBIOS names are resolved over TCP/IP. If you told Net-BIOS to always first broadcast, *then* ask WINS, you'd be more likely to find local domain controllers if they were within shouting distance. The downside would be, of course, that every single time your workstation tried to resolve *any* name it would broadcast first, so be aware of that. But if this sounds like a good answer to you, then change the NetBIOS node type (it's in DHCP) from hex 0x8, a "hybrid node," to hex 0x4, a "mixed node."

One more thing to try is a utility that comes with Service Pack 4 called SET-PRFDC, or *set preferred domain controller*. It lets you bias your workstation in favor of a particular domain controller. The program is, again, only available in Service Pack 4 or later.

Tell the Workstation to Be More Patient

Sometimes you do everything and you still can't find a domain controller, particularly if you're logging in from an NT machine. Here's why: you may recall that NT machines also log in to the domain, just as users do. If you try to log in the very first second that the login screen appears, your system may simply be too busy to get the login done quickly—and it times out.

The fix? Well, there are a couple of possibilities. The first one's not pretty, but it'll work: when you turn your workstation on, wait a bit and let the hard disk settle down before trying to log on.

That's about the best you can do on a Windows 9*x* or 3.*x* workstation. But if your workstations are NT, we can do a bit better.

The problem is that the Netlogon service is the part of an NT workstation that goes out and finds a domain controller. But it's impatient and only waits about 15 seconds for a response. How to tell it to be more patient? Why, with a Registry entry, of course. Remember, you're trying to make the *client* more patient, not the server, so this Registry change goes on your workstations, although it could benefit the servers as well: recall that trust relationships can be broken if domain-controller-to-domain-controller logins across trusts don't happen quickly enough.

Anyway, the modification goes in HKEY_LOCAL_MACHINE\System\CurrentControlSet\Services\Netlogon\Parameters. It's a REG_DWORD entry named ExpectedDialupDelay. Set it to the number of seconds that you'd like your workstation to wait before deciding to give up on finding a domain controller. Minimum acceptable value is 0, maximum 600.

> **TIP**   If you've got a particularly busy network, or some very overloaded domain controllers, you might consider adding this to all of your workstations via a system policy.

Troubleshooting Startup Mysteries: How Do I Get Rid of That Program?

Here's a short problem-and-solution, but I promise you it'll be useful one day.

You install some piece of software and the install crashes, so you decide to just forget it and throw the software away. But the next time you boot the system, you see an error message because NT's trying to start the software but can't find it, or perhaps it *does* load some piece of it, leading to more error messages. What's causing the program to run?

The obvious place to look is in Start ➣ Programs ➣ Startup; any icons in there will run automatically when you log on. Many people do not know that NT has a file named WIN.INI which contains a RUN= and a LOAD= command, both of which can start programs. But the *really* sneaky one is a Registry key: HKEY_LOCAL_MACHINE\Software\Microsoft\Windows\CurrentVersion\Run. In it, you'll see value entries of type REG_SZ where the value entry is some descriptive name and the data are a program's filename and any startup options. If you've got a mysteriously starting program, chances are good it's in that Registry key.

Disasters shouldn't happen, but they sometimes do. With the proper preventive planning beforehand, they can become entertaining war stories, rather than sources of battle fatigue.

CHAPTER
EIGHTEEN

Remote Access Service

18

Less and less of our "office work" actually takes place *in* the office. Some people telecommute, others travel as part of their job, and some need to access the office network after hours simply because they're network administrators who've been called to fix some network problem at 10:30 P.M., but who don't want to have to drive to the office—call them "late-night telecommuters."

Wide area networking used to come in two varieties: the expensive mainframe-to-mainframe kind that was solely the province of large companies, and the guy with the PC and the modem dialing up to CompuServe, the bulletin board run by somebody in the next town, or the like. The horrifically slow nature of modems prior to the '90s—most of us had 2400bps modems back in 1989—meant that there just wasn't much that most of us could do over a dial-up connection.

The greatly improved speed of modems and the wider availability of Integrated Services Digital Network (ISDN) connections have made wide area networking both affordable and desirable. NT's technology for enabling connections is called *Remote Access Service*, or RAS. With NT 4, Microsoft renamed the *client* side of RAS to Dial-Up Networking, or DUN; this, however, appears to have confused Microsoft's technical editors, so you'll see references to RAS and DUN appear interchangeably in NT dialog boxes. (It's confused *me*, too, so I'll use both RAS and DUN to refer to the client-side software.) Basically, RAS's job is to turn your modem, serial, X.25, or ISDN connection into a slow, long-distance Ethernet card, making it simple to dial up one server and get instant access to your company's Microsoft enterprise servers, your NetWare servers, and even the Internet itself. Along the way, it also provides excellent remote access security and auditing of dial-up clients and is built, unlike most other Microsoft products, atop well-understood communications standards—in particular, RAS is built mainly to work with the popular Internet protocol called the Point to Point Protocol, or PPP, described in RFC 1660. (*Requests For Comments* are proposed and accepted TCP/IP protocol standards available freely to all from InterNIC on the Internet).

NT 4 brought to RAS a convenient technology called TAPI, the *Telephony Application Program Interface*. Prior to NT 4, every NT application controlled the modem on its own, with little help from the operating system. Microsoft operating systems released since 1995 centralize the control of modems with the single programming interface, TAPI. TAPI-aware applications don't have to worry about what kind of modem you've got—they just let TAPI worry about it. This puts a layer of software between the communications program and the communications hardware, which makes writing communications programs easier. Just as writers of graphics programs under Windows don't worry about what graphics board you're using since the Windows graphics driver handles the video board-specific details, TAPI also means that communications program designers can finally enjoy the benefits of hardware independence that graphics programmers have enjoyed for over 12 years.

TAPI's disconnection of the hardware from the software is just the right idea, and at just the right time. ISDN will eat away more and more of the modems' market share. (Of course, that won't happen until ISDN gets a bit cheaper.) ISDN *looks* like a modem technology, but it's not; it is a dial-up communications system that is completely digital and can communicate at up to 144,000 bits per second. But getting software that supports ISDN has been difficult, since it's a relatively new technology in the eyes of most software designers. NT, in contrast, has ISDN support built right in, which relies on the TAPI component's abstraction of communications from specific modem hardware.

NT 4 also brings a couple of new technologies for Internetters: multilink PPP (RFC 1990) and PPTP, the Point to Point Tunneling Protocol. You'll meet both of them in this chapter.

The idea of accessing a local area network remotely is by no means a new one. People quite commonly use a program like Carbon Copy or pcANYWHERE to accomplish remote LAN access. These programs work by allowing you to take remote control of a PC that is physically on the office premises, a PC that's a workstation on your network's LAN. By taking control of a workstation PC remotely, you can access the LAN, since it is connected to the remotely controlled PC. This sounds like a perfectly reasonable approach, and it is, except that you end up transferring lots of screenfuls of data back and forth over the phone line; every mouse click can potentially change the whole screen, which could result in having to transfer a megabyte of information. At the common modem speeds of roughly 20,000–30,000bps (bits per second) with compression, transferring that megabyte could take six minutes. Waiting six minutes for each mouse click requires a bit more patience than *I* have, which is why I prefer the NT approach.

An Overview of Remote Access Service

The whole idea of the Remote Access Service (RAS) is that it runs basically any of the NT protocol stacks over the phone line, essentially converting your serial ports into Ethernet cards, so to speak. Furthermore, RAS will *tunnel* NetBEUI,

IPX/SPX, or TCP/IP through a protocol called PPP (Point to Point Protocol), making it possible to gain access to servers *not* running NT or Remote Access Service. For example, you could set up a Windows 95 computer with the IPX/SPX protocol and a NetWare client, then dial in to an NT Server machine running Remote Access Service. The Windows 95 machine would dial an NT machine running the Remote Access Service server software and log in to it. The Remote Access Service server would receive the IPX/SPX packets, which it would probably have no way of interpreting. Its job is just to get the packets off the WAN and drop them on the LAN. Once it did that, the NetWare server would receive the packets and allow the remote Windows 95 workstation to log in to the NetWare server.

Additionally, RAS supports an old but popular protocol named SLIP (Serial Line Internet Protocol, described in RFC 1055), which allows you to connect an NT machine to many Internet hosts. More and more Internet hosts don't use SLIP, however, using instead the newer PPP protocol. Microsoft's choice to use PPP for Remote Access Service was a good one because PPP is so widespread in its use and provides better connectivity.

NOTE   RAS will only allow your NT machine to act as a SLIP client—that is, it will allow you to dial in to a SLIP server. The RAS software does not allow your PC to act as a SLIP server.

RAS won't just be interesting to network *users*; network administrators can use RAS, too. You can do any administrative work over the remote connection that doesn't require you actually touch the remote workstation. Anything you can do across the LAN to control a server will work equally well on a RAS-connected machine.

Why use RAS rather than another remote-access package? Well, for starters, you've already paid for it—you get it with NT Server.

Remote clients can access files and network devices just as though they were using the network from inside the office, and administering their accounts is just like administering any other user account. Another advantage to using RAS over using other remote-access software is that RAS has the same built-in security measures that other NT Server user accounts have, with a few more for good measure (like encrypted data streams). A RAS link does not provide the same access to your network that other kinds of remote access connections provide.

Finally, RAS is flexible. Running from an NT Server machine, it can support up to 256 simultaneous connections. Simple NT workstations, however, can only support one RAS connection.

In this chapter, you'll see how to operate Remote Access Service both from the server and the client side.

Sample RAS Applications

Here are a few ideas of what you can do with Remote Access Service.

Dialing In to Company NT Servers Remotely

The obvious application is simple remote access to an NT network. A remote DOS, Windows for Workgroups, Windows 95, or Windows NT workstation can dial in to a server on the company premises that's hooked up to a modem and a phone line (or 256 modems and phone lines, for that matter). Once on, the workstation can access network resources just as if that workstation were connected to the company network, albeit more slowly.

The DOS and Windows for Workgroups machines will be a bit limited in what they can do, as they will only be able to dial in using the NetBEUI protocol. I don't think they're ever going to fix that, although there are a few third-party PPP solutions for DOS and Windows for Workgroups; any of those would allow you to dial into a RAS server using TCP/IP.

Dialing In to NetWare and Unix Servers Remotely

There's no need to install a separate set of modems and software in order to get to your NetWare servers from afar. As long as you're running Windows 95 or NT on your remote machine, you can dial in to a RAS server and get to NetWare with no sweat.

The way it works is this: you just dial in to a RAS server. All the RAS server does is pick up the packets your system sends out and copies them onto the LAN. If you're *also* running protocol and client software that let you talk to a NetWare or Unix server, that server will see your logon packets and respond. With no more work than just getting connected to your RAS server, you'll get hooked up to other servers on the LAN.

Dialing In to Internet Service Providers

As I suggested a few paragraphs back, one of the benefits of the Remote Access Service architecture is that it's built atop a protocol called PPP, which acts as a kind of packaging service for other protocols. If you want to route data on IPX/SPX or TCP/IP over a wide area network (WAN) link like a modem, ISDN connection, or X.25, then Remote Access Service can do it. The Remote Access Service server doesn't interpret the packets it receives; it just puts them onto the network, so that the packets reach their destinations. Most Internet Service Providers (ISPs) support dial-in via PPP, so RAS can act as the perfect client for hooking up to a PPP (or SLIP) account on an ISP.

Remote Access Service as an Internet Gateway

As you learned in Chapter 14, you can use Remote Access Service to connect your company's network to the Internet. An NT machine (running either Server *or* Workstation—NT Workstation is allowed 10 connections according to its license) can act as a router, routing packets between an Internet Service Provider and your company's intranet.

However, Remote Access Service can't act as a firewall or a proxy server for the connection between your company's network and the Internet. For that, you need Microsoft Proxy Server.

Remote Access Service as an Internet Service Provider

Remote Access Service will even allow *you* to act as the ISP. You can set up a bunch of modems on an NT server running Remote Access Service and people can call in to your network, and from there they can surf the Internet (assuming, of course, that you're connected to the Internet). Now, don't get me wrong—if you're thinking of setting up shop as an ISP, you're probably better off doing your routing and other TCP/IP "plumbing" with some flavor of Unix. But, if you're a dyed-in-the-wool NT lover, it *is* probably possible to build an ISP's network with nothing but NT machines. One large communications network, CompuServe, relies heavily on NT machines but uses them more as servers than as communications controllers.

Remote Access Service as a LAN/WAN Gateway

Got a network uptown that needs to talk to your network downtown? Remote Access Service can accomplish that. A machine on one network runs Remote Access Service and calls into a machine on the other network, which is also running Remote Access Service. With the right setup, these two networks then become one network.

This is still a rudimentary feature that requires some fiddling around to make it work. *Furthermore, it isn't supported by Microsoft.* It's also not too bright; in particular, you can't set up this LAN-to-LAN connection so it only dials up when data must go from one network to another; this pretty much only works if you dial up and don't hang up. But, again, it's free—you already paid for the RAS software.

Virtual Private Networking with PPTP

Remote Access Service with NT Server 4 introduces support for the *Point to Point Tunneling Protocol*, a system that allows you to connect to your local network via the Internet through firewalls.

RAS Hardware Connection Options

That's the overview. Now let's get to the particulars. First, what kinds of connections does RAS support? Basically, you can connect via anything you can find a RAS for or, more likely, a TAPI driver for. But the most common connection types will be

- Modems
- ISDN
- Direct serial connections
- X.25
- Frame Relay

Modem Support

Most DUN servers will connect to their clients through a modem (modulator/demodulator). On the sending end, modems convert digital computer signals into analog signals that can be transferred over ordinary telephone lines. On the receiving end, another modem takes the analog signals and reverts them to the original digital signal. For this modulation/demodulation process to work, the modems must be compatible.

Modem Compatibility Issues

Not all modems will work with DUN. In the NT Server Hardware Compatibility List, Microsoft has provided a list of the modems with which it has successfully tested DUN. If you're buying a modem specifically for DUN, make sure that you choose one from this list. Alternatively, you can venture into the depths of a file called MODEMS.INF, and you can program NT to support your modem. (I'm not going to cover that in this book, but it's explained in the NT DUN documentation.)

Even if you choose modems from the approved list, they may not be able to work together in all modes. It's best if you use the same model of modem on both the sending and receiving end of the DUN connection. It's not vital that you do this if both modems conform to industry standards, like V.32 *bis* or V.34 (the 14,400 and 28,800bps standards). But getting the same modem model can avoid compatibility problems that can arise even in machines conforming to the same standard. The higher the speed, the more likely compatibility problems will arise, since modems use different methods to achieve high speeds. Another answer is to use Hayes modems, as modem designers seem to use Hayes modems to test *their* modem's compatibility. Everything seems to talk to a Hayes.

Hardware Requirements for Using DUN

In addition to the software, you need the following hardware to use DUN over a modem connection:

- Two compatible modems, one for the server and one for the client
- A telephone line

Pooling Modems

Just as you can connect more than one physical printer to a logical printer name (see Chapter 8 for details on how to do this), you can pool identical modems so that more than one modem is connected to the same number. The modems must be of the same manufacturer and model. If you pool modems, you can avoid some traffic problems that occur when a number of DUN clients are trying to connect to the same server simultaneously.

ISDN Support

Running DUN over a modem is inexpensive, but it's also slow; a good modem connection runs over an analog voice channel at about 28,800bps. If you want a faster remote connection, you need a point-to-point service like ISDN. Basic Rate Interface (BRI) ISDN runs over a digital line at either 64 or 128 kilobits (*thousands* of bits) per second. Given the startup costs (not huge but more than buying a modem and getting another digital telephone line), this connection may not be worth it if your transmission needs are small and mostly text-based, but if a good deal of data will be traveling between the DUN server and client, ISDN could save you transmittal time for nonmobile clients.

If BRI ISDN doesn't provide as much throughput as you need, you can subscribe to its faster sibling, Primary Rate Interface (PRI) ISDN. Rather than the copper wire that BRI uses, PRI uses T-1 cable (with 23 64-kilobit data-carrying channels plus one 64-kilobit control channel that can handle data transfer at a maximum of 1.544mbps (*millions* of bits per second).

Hardware Requirements

To use DUN over an ISDN connection, you need the following hardware:

- Two ISDN cards, one card in each computer at either end of the connection.

- A digital-grade cable connecting the cards (either copper or fiber).

- A network termination (NT1) device usually built in to the newer ISDN equipment and that connects the cards to the cable. Inside the U.S., the telephone company owns the NT1; outside, the customer owns it. This NT device can have up to eight ports for multiple ISDN connections.

Basically, if you're thinking of going to ISDN, contact your local telephone company to see if they offer ISDN (not all locations have it yet) and then look to either Digiboard or Intel for ISDN interface hardware. Check the latest NT compatibility list as always.

Differences in Transmission Speed

As noted above, BRI ISDN transmits at either 64 or 128 Kbps. Where does the difference in transmittal speed come from? A BRI ISDN line comes with three channels: two bearer (B) channels for data, which transmit at 64Kbps, and one D channel for signaling to the other ISDN card, which transmits at 16Kbps. When you're setting up the connection, you can either configure each B channel to be its own port, or logically combine the two into a single port, and get twice the bandwidth, thus doubling your transmission speed.

What merits does each approach have? Two channels are better for DUN servers that have a number of clients, as more clients will be able to get through at one time. For most people, this will be the most efficient use of bandwidth. If, however, your DUN configuration has only one client, you don't need more than one port and you can combine the bandwidth.

X.25 Connection

X.25 is a protocol that coordinates communication between your machine and another one, routing information through a packet-switched public data network. Operating at the two lowest levels of the OSI protocol model (physical and data link), X.25 operates at a top speed of 64Kbps. Although this isn't terribly fast by modern standards, it is still faster than most modem connections. X.25 can also run more slowly if the type of line that it's using requires it.

If you're familiar with some of the new WAN technologies for connecting point A to point B, X.25 may seem slow to you. Truthfully, it is; X.25 was developed at a time when telephone lines were not as reliable as they are now, so it includes extensive error-checking at every node in its path to ensure that the data arrives at its destination in the same condition in which it left. Error-checking takes time, so X.25 is slower than other WAN protocols that don't use it, like Frame Relay.

If it's slower than other protocols in use, why use X.25? First of all, it's available. No matter where in the world you go, it's almost certain that that country will offer X.25 service. Even countries with unreliable telephone systems can use it because of its error-checking capabilities. For international applications, X.25 may be the only way for one country to connect to another.

Even within the U.S., X.25 has the advantage of being offered by most carriers. You could even build a private X.25 network with on-site switching equipment and lease lines connecting the sites.

You can set up DUN to work with X.25 lines without too much difficulty. Like setting up the system for ISDN, it's mostly a matter of making sure that things are coordinated with the telephone company and that your connections are made properly. We'll discuss the process of configuring your system for X.25 shortly.

There are two main ways in which you can arrange DUN to work with X.25: either as a dial-up asynchronous packet assembler-disassembler (PAD) or via a direct connection to the X.25 service provider.

A Packet Assembler-Disassembler A PAD is in charge of taking non-packet data streams, such as the start and stop bits that begin and end a transmission, and converting them to packets that can be transported over the X.25 network. Once the converted packets reach their destinations, another PAD reverts the packets to their original form.

With a PAD hookup, a dial-up connection connects the remote workstation and the server through PAD services offered by a public network, such as Sprintnet. The client's software has a "conversation" with the PAD, and then the PAD has a "conversation" with the server that gets the data to the server.

PAD configurations include the client external PAD and the server external PAD layouts. In the client external PAD configuration, an RS-232 cable attached to the client's serial port connects the client and the PAD. In the PAD.INF file, you must have a script telling the client how to connect to the server. The server external PAD configuration specifies how to receive incoming calls. (Given that you're using the server to connect your LAN to remote clients, this is probably what you want to do anyway.)

Direct Connection The other approach to an X.25 connection is a direct connection. Connecting directly from the remote workstation to the server requires a device called a *smart card*, which acts like a modem, in both the server and the client. (Clients not using the direct X.25 connection don't need smart cards.) A smart card is a piece of hardware with a PAD embedded in it. It fools the computer into thinking that its communication ports are already attached to PADs.

Hardware Requirements for Using DUN with X.25

To use DUN with X.25, you need the following:

- A modem (for dial-up connections)
- A "smart" X.25 direct interface card (for direct connections)
- A leased line (for direct connections)

We'll discuss the mechanics of how to set up DUN to work with X.25 in the section on installation and configuration.

Direct Serial Connection

The final way that you can use DUN is to avoid having to get a network card. Using a null-modem cable, you can connect the server and client directly through the serial port. Although this setup eliminates the need for a network card in either machine (assuming the server is not connected to any other clients), serial connections are much slower than networks, and performance will suffer.

To use DUN through a serial connection, you need the following:

- One client and one server machine

- A 9-pin or 25-pin (depending on your serial connector) null-modem cable

Now, there are null-modem cables, and there are null-modem cables. Many computer null-modem applications work fine with simple null-modem cables, but DUN is pretty exacting in its requirements. Table 18.1 summarizes the requirements for constructing a DUN-ready null-modem cable. The table covers both 25-pin connectors and 9-pin connectors.

TABLE 18.1: Requirements for Constructing DUN-Ready Null-Modem Cable

Host[1]	Pin No.\ 9-pin	Pin No.\ 25-pin	Workstation[2]	Pin No.\ 9-pin	Pin No.\ 25-pin
Transmit data	3	2	Receive data	2	3
Receive data	2	3	Transmit data	3	2
Request to send	7	4	Clear to send	8	5
Clear to send	8	5	Request to send	7	4
Data set ready and data carrier detect	6,1	6,8	Data terminal ready	4	20
Data terminal ready	4	20	Data set ready and data carrier detect	6,1	6,8
Signal ground	5	7	Signal ground	5	7

(1) This column lists the NT Server machine serial port signal name.
(2) This column lists the workstation serial port signal name.

NOTE   Having said all that, I feel I should also mention that it seems impossible to get null-modem cables to work under NT 4. They worked fine with 3.*x*, but I've never gotten a direct connection to work with 4.

Frame Relay

People used X.25 for a long time to solve a particular set of problems. But the market niche inhabited by X.25 is quickly being taken over by a technology called *Frame Relay*. You typically attach to a Frame Relay network with a synchronous interface card, which in turn connects to a Frame Relay device of some kind. The interface card needs a RAS driver, and there aren't any in the NT box, but there are a growing number of vendors offering those driver types.

Authentication Options

Once you're wired, you'll need to get authenticated. RAS/DUN was built late enough in computer history that it's got a pretty tough job—it must offer 21st century features and also be able to dial in to an old PDP-8 with a modem on it. That's why RAS offers so many authentication options.

There are two main factors motivating authentication options: first, security, and second, simplicity for you when you log on.

On the one hand, you obviously want logging in to your distant host to be as simple as possible. On the other hand, wide area communications lines can be tapped, and so your username and password can potentially be stolen from a long-distance communications link. If security is your concern, you'll like that Microsoft supports security protocols like CHAP, SPAP, and MD5.

On the other hand, you may not worry all that much about security, but you *may* be tired of having to punch in a user ID and password every time you log on. If that's the case, you'll find the built-in scripting capabilities and PAP support useful.

Entering Clear Text with Terminal

Most people with Internet accounts dial in using the Point to Point Protocol (PPP), and most Internet Service Providers (ISPs) use Unix machines as front ends to their dial-in PPP accounts. Unix grew up in an age of teletypes, character-by-character interfaces well suited to dumb terminals. You'd turn on the dumb terminal, which was connected to a phone/modem combination. Then you'd dial the phone number of the Unix host, wait for the familiar modem squeal, and push the Modem button on the phone. Then you'd tap the Enter key a few times to get the attention of the distant Unix host, which would reply, "Please enter your login ID" or something like that. You'd specify your login, and then you'd be prompted for a password, which you'd enter.

Now, I used to do that 20 years ago, and unfortunately most ISPs still work like that. So, assuming that you get an Internet access account that requires you dial up and enter a username and password by hand, then you'll have to tell RAS/DUN to dial you up as clear text with a pop-up terminal. If you want to see an example, look ahead to Figure 18.36. Notice that one option is "Accept any authentication including clear text;" that's the setting you'd use to dial in to one of these older systems.

Using Clear Text with Scripts

Of course, just because your ISP wants you to sit there like a robot and supply a username and password when it tells you to doesn't mean you've got to *do* it. That's why NT offers not one, but two ways to automatically respond to login information requests: a SWITCH.INF script or a Windows 95 script. You control scripting with the Script tab of the Dial-Up Networking Phone Book. I'll discuss that a bit later, so forgive me if I don't include a screen shot just yet—right now I want to explain the scripting languages.

Understanding SWITCH.INF Logon Scripts

One of my ISP accounts involves a logon that looks like Figure 18.1.

Basically, I log on and wait for the ISP to prompt me with Username:, and I reply with **mminasi**. Then I wait for a response of Password:, and I reply with **opensesame**. Then it puts a menu up on the screen, and when it says (1-8):, I reply **4**, and at that point I'm connected.

I need a script that will mimic those functions.

FIGURE 18.1:

Logging on to an ISP

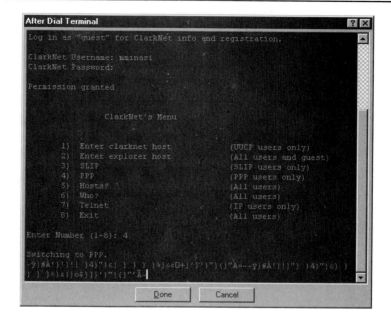

Ever since NT 3.5, NT has had a simple command language to allow that. Here's how it worked:

You can write as many scripts as you like, but they're all contained in a single file called SWITCH.INF, located in \WINNT\SYSTEM32\RAS. You separate scripts from one another with sections, as in an old Windows 3.*x* INI file. For example, I'm going to create a script to dial in to my ISP, so I'll call the script dial-ISP. Lines that start with semicolons are comments. I then start the script by opening up SWITCH.INF and adding the following lines:

```
[dialISP]
;Script to dial my ISP
```

The first command you'll use in the SWITCH.INF language looks like this:

```
command=string
```

where *string* is a string to send to the distant machine. You've *got* to start a script with a COMMAND= even if you have nothing to say.

After a command= statement comes any number of other commands. The most common are OK=, LOOP=, and NoResponse.

The OK= command basically says, "Wait until a condition is satisfied." The most common condition is OK=<match>*string*, which says, "Wait until you see *string* come from the distant computer." Sometimes you'll use OK=<ignore>, which means just throw away whatever appears from the distant computer. So, for example, a script might start out like so:

```
command=
ok=<match>"Username: "
```

The command= is just required. The OK=<match>"Username: " just says to wait for the string "Username:" to be transmitted from the distant computer. Actually, one trick to making these scripts work is to make the match string as short as possible. For example, the shortest unique set of characters that specifically identifies the Username: prompt is actually just a colon ":", so I could tell the script to just keep looking until it sees a colon. On the other hand, if my system received some line noise, that could show up as a colon—so I'll play it a bit safe and have it look for "e:", the last two characters.

Okay so far, but you must understand that there is one trick to the OK= command: *it won't wait forever*. In fact, it'll only wait two seconds for a match to appear. After that, it gives up—which is why the LOOP=<ignore> command is useful.

The LOOP=<ignore> command says, "If the previous OK= command failed, go back and try it again." So suppose I'm waiting for that initial "Username:," but, like my ISP, your ISP is a bit slow—more than the two seconds that each script command will wait—when you're logging on. The LOOP=<ignore> solves that problem by making the script return to the OK= command directly above the LOOP= command. So, for example, if I want the script to wait around for however long it takes to get a "Username:" out of the ISP, I'd code it so:

```
OK=<match>"Username: "
LOOP=<ignore>
```

Actually, that's all you need in order to build the ISP logon script. It looks like this:

```
[DialISP]
;Dials my ISP
; start things off
command=
; wait for "Username:"; just loop until it shows up
```

```
ok=<match>"e:"
loop=<ignore>
; now have the prompt; shoot my user ID out to the ISP
command=mminasi<cr>
; note the "<cr>" is just a carriage return. Note also no quotes are
needed around the string. Now wait for "Password:"
ok=<match>"d:"
loop=<ignore>
; enter the password
command=opensesame<cr>
; wait around for the menu to finish, then choose 4 for "PPP"
ok=<match>"8):"
loop=<ignore>
command=4<cr>
; now we're in, but I need one final line, so I can use either OK= or
NoResponse; they do the same thing
OK=
```

You've probably noticed one major problem here: my username and password are written in the script. I could instead use the built-in variables *<username>* and *<password>*, which just take the values that you enter when you start the dial-in process.

Writing Windows 95–Type Scripts

NT 4 introduced a new scripting language, one that actually appeared first in Windows 95. It will be a bit more familiar to folks used to a standard procedural language. You use it a bit differently than SWITCH.INF scripts.

Each script is stored in a different file. Script files must have the extension SCP, and they must be located in the \WINNT\SYSTEM32\RAS directory. This directory also contains a file called SCRIPTS.DOC, which has some information on writing the scripts.

Debugging a Script: DEVICE.LOG

What if you try to write a script and find that it just isn't working? What do you do? There is a Registry setting that can help. In HKEY_LOCAL_MACHINE\System\CurrentControlSet\Services\RASMAN\Parameters, you can add a parameter of REG_DWORD type called Logging, and set it to 1. You'll then get a log of what happens when you try to run your script. The file is called

DEVICE.LOG, and it's kept in \WINNT\SYSTEM32\RAS. For example, after I used my script to log on to my ISP, the DEVICE.LOG looked like the following:

```
Remote Access Service Device Log  10/16/1996  15:34:36
------------------------------------
Port: Command to Device:
Port: Response from Device:
Annex Command Line Interpreter   *   Copyright 1991 Xylogics, Inc.
Checking authorization, Please wait...
Connecting to port 55 on
Port: Response from Device:annex10.clark.net.
   Welcome to ClarkNet!
Log in as "guest" for ClarkNet info and registration.
ClarkNet Use
Port: Response from Device:rname:
Port: Command to Device:mminasi

Port: Echo from Device :mminasi

Port: Response from Device:ClarkNet Password:
Port: Command to Device:opensesame
Port: Echo from Device :
Permi
Port: Response from Device:ssion granted
                ClarkNet's Menu


         1)  Enter clarknet host        (UUCP users only)
         2)  Enter explorer host        (All users and guest)
         3)  SLIP                       (SLIP users only)

Port: Response from Device:   4)  PPP
Port: Response from Device:                          (PPP usersonly)
         5)  Hosts?                  (All users)
         6)  Who?                    (All users)
         7)  Telnet                  (IP users only)
         8)  Exit
Port: Response from Device:
Port: Response from Device:(All users)
Enter Number (1-8):
Port: Command to Device:4

Port: Echo from Device :4

Port: Response from Device:
Switching to PPP.
```

The Port: lines precede logging information. Look it over, and you can see how the script logon worked. Remember that DEVICE.LOG is a log file, so it'll contain all of the results of *previous* logons as well, so it's a good idea to clean it out now and then.

Using Clear Text PAP

If your ISP is a bit more up to date, then they may have PPP software smart enough to automatically ask your computer for your username and password. Such a thing is called the *Password Authentication Protocol* (PAP), discussed in RFC 1334.

There's not really anything you need to do in order to have RAS use PAP when logging you on. If the distant host can process PAP, then RAS/DUN will figure that out automatically.

Writing Standard Encrypted Logons

PAP's nice, but of course the whole idea that your passwords zip around the Net unprotected can be a bit scary. That's why RFC 1334 also defines CHAP, the *Challenge-Handshake Authentication Protocol*; RFC 1334 was later revised by RFC 1994, and the changes only affect CHAP. With a challenge protocol, the login server sends a key to the workstation. The workstation then uses that key to encrypt the password, and sends the encrypted key. The server then encrypts the password that it knows for the user, and the result should match the value sent over the wire. It's secure because the same key is never used twice.

Here's a much simplified example. Suppose all passwords were numbers. You say you want to log in, your username is Larry, and your password is 121. I say, "Okay, Larry, encrypt your password with 5." You encrypt your password 121 with the key 5 by dividing 121 by 5 and sending the remainder, 1. I know that your password is 121, and I divide by 5, leaving 1. You sent me a 1, and I computed a 1, so you're validated. Perhaps next time I'll send the key 33, and so you'll end up with a different remainder.

That's not the only kind of data encryption. RAS/DUN also supports Shiva PAP (SPAP) and MD5, two methods used for encrypting dial-up logon data. NT uses SPAP when dialing as a client into a Shiva LAN Rover, and the RAS server can accept SPAP data streams when a Shiva client dials in to it. RAS supports MD5 only as a client—it can dial in to PPP servers using MD5, but it does not support it on RAS server.

Creating Microsoft Encrypted Logons

There are good standards out there for encryption, but Microsoft seems to like building their own "standards," and this area is no exception: Microsoft includes something they call MSCHAP, their CHAP-like encryption. What's particularly nice about it is that if you use the Microsoft encryption then you can encrypt the entire dial-up session.

RAS Server Setup

Although the Remote Access Service comes with NT Server, it is not automatically installed when you install the operating system. Therefore, don't look for it on the hard disk—you'll need to go to the Control Panel to install it. Once it's installed, you can customize it for your needs from the DUN Administrator program, which you'll find in a newly created Remote Access Service program group.

In the following pages, I'll explain how to install and configure a Remote Access Service server. The remote client workstations will also need to install Remote Access Services using essentially the same procedure before they can access your server, but I'll explain the dial-in and connection process between the two in a later section.

Installing the Remote Access Service Module

Go to the Control Panel and open the Network applet. As when you've installed other components, you'll see the Services tab; click it and the Add button. One option you'll see is Remote Access Service. Choose that and click OK. You'll be prompted for the location of the original NT setup files; point it to wherever you've got those files. (I'm being terse here because this installation is essentially identical to all the other installs that you've done if you've been following this book.) NT will copy some files.

Installing a Modem for Remote Access Service

If you haven't yet installed a modem, ISDN, or X.25 driver on your system, Remote Access Service will note that, saying that there are no drivers that it can use. It then asks if it should invoke the Modem Installer. Tell it yes, and you'll see Figure 18.2.

FIGURE 18.2:

Modem installation Wizard
opening screen

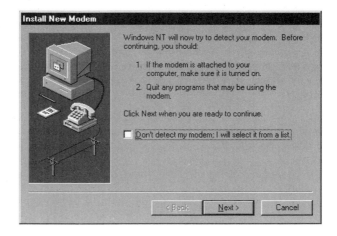

Click Next, and Remote Access Service will attempt to detect your modem.
It's often wrong, and when it's not sure it just detects Standard Modem. That's
probably fine, because most modems work pretty similarly these days. Or, if
you like, you can click Change, and you'll see a screen similar to that displayed
in Figure 18.3.

FIGURE 18.3:

Choosing a modem type
by hand

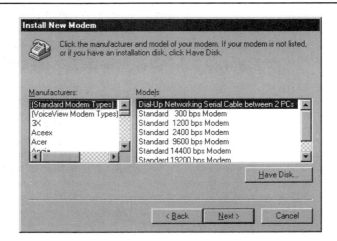

If you choose a modem, then Remote Access Service will want to know what
port it's attached to, as you see in Figure 18.4.

FIGURE 18.4:

Selecting modem port

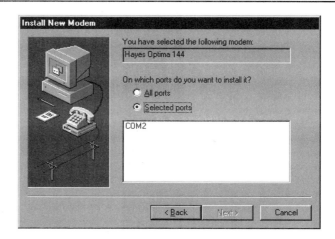

Whether you do an automatic installation or a manual installation, the Modem Installer finishes up at this point and prompts you to click Finish. This returns you to the main Remote Access Service installation routine, which double-checks what you've done with Figure 18.5.

FIGURE 18.5:

Remote Access Service checks that this is the modem you want to use.

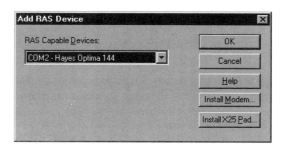

It's a bit of overkill on Remote Access Service's part, but just click OK and it'll be happy.

RAS Server or Client?

Once you've chosen a modem, Remote Access Service Setup leads to Figure 18.6, which is a fairly important one.

FIGURE 18.6:

Remote Access Setup
dialog box

This is an important dialog box because you do three main things with it. First, you use it to put more modems under Remote Access Service's control with the Add button. Along those lines, you remove modems with the Remove button, and add new modems that are identical to existing modems with the Clone button. (By the way, when I say *modem* here, what I really mean is modem, ISDN connection, X.25 connection, or any other Remote Access Service–compatible wide area networking interface—but *modem* doesn't take as long to write, so I'll stick with that.)

Second, this is the dialog box where you control whether this machine will dial out via Remote Access Service (a Remote Access Service client), accept other machines dialing in to it (a Remote Access Service server), or both. You control that by clicking Configure. If you do, then you'll see Figure 18.7.

FIGURE 18.7:

Controlling whether this
machine is a Remote Access
Service client, server, or both

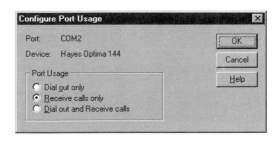

Since we're setting up a RAS server here, click Receive calls only. If you choose to just be a client or just be a server, Remote Access Service will create only one "phantom" network card. You'll see that phantom network card if you type

IPCONFIG with TCP/IP—it's a board with a name like Ndiswan4, or the like. Note that this is the *only* place where you can control whether this machine is a server, client, or both. If you change your mind later and want to change its role, you access this dialog box by opening Control Panel ➢ Network ➢ Services ➢ Remote Access Services ➢ Properties, and then click Configure on the resulting dialog box. And yes, you'll have to reboot when you do that.

Choosing Protocols for Remote Access Service

The third thing that you do with the Remote Access Setup dialog box is to control exactly what protocols will be used over the Remote Access Service connection. Click Network, and you'll see a dialog box like the one in Figure 18.8.

FIGURE 18.8:

Configuring Remote Access Service protocols and login requirements

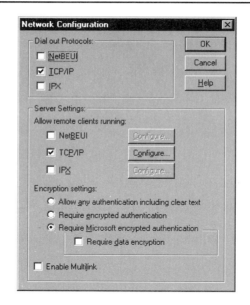

Note that that dialog box mainly affects the *server* portion of Remote Access Service; you configure most of the client parts from the Remote Access Service phone book, which we'll see later. Notice the check box labeled Enable Multilink. It enables multilink PPP, a system that lets you add a bunch of separate connections into a single connection. To see how this works, suppose you had two 28.8Kbps modems on your remote PC. You'd like to somehow make this into one big 57.6Kbps connection to the office. All you've got to do is to check Enable Multilink on this dialog box on the server side *and* check Enable Multilink on the client side, and Remote Access Service will use two or more connections like one connection. Just imagine the applications for this! For example, suppose you're using RAS to connect two networks on opposite sides of town. You've got a single ISDN connection, but you want some better speed without having to move up to the expense of the next step in wide-area connections, a T1 line. With multilink PPP, you can just put in another ISDN line and double the throughput of your connection. And there's even more beauty to this answer, if you think about it. If you've already got *one* ISDN line in place, then you've already struggled with getting lines installed, connecting ISDN devices, configuring the connection, and so on. Putting in a second line will be a breeze—much easier than having to learn about a new network technology like T1. Granted, the day will come when you'll want faster service, but this lets you put that off for a while. Note that at this writing you can only make multilink PPP work between Windows NT machines; I don't know of any way to do it with Windows 95 machines.

NOTE   Most people will be interested in multilink PPP as a way to get a faster connection to the Internet. Unfortunately, you will only be able to do that if your Internet Service Provider (ISP) supports multilink PPP; I don't know of any that do, but I'm sure that some will as time goes on. But be prepared to pay extra for the extra speed!

You choose which protocols can dial in with the check boxes under "Allow remote clients running" and, not surprisingly, the options are NetBEUI, TCP/IP, and IPX. The NetBEUI and IPX configuration boxes ask whether a dial-in client should be able to access just the Remote Access Service server's resources, or if the Remote Access Service server should act as a bridge to the network, duplicating all of the client's packets onto the LAN. Click the Configure button on TCP/IP, and you'll see the dialog box shown in Figure 18.9.

Like the other protocols, TCP/IP lets you control whether to let callers access this server only, or the entire network. The dialog box also lets you control how they get their IP addresses.

There is, in general, no way for you to assign an IP address to a particular person. Instead, you hand out IP addresses to ports. The best answer is to let DHCP hand out addresses, as it probably does on your LAN. Alternatively, you can create a pool of IP addresses that Remote Access Service will hand out, sort of like a mini-DHCP. Click OK to clear this dialog box.

FIGURE 18.9:

Controlling TCP/IP connections on a Remote Access Service server

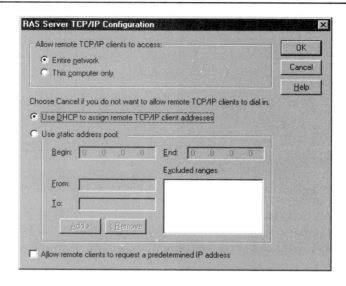

NOTE

There is a quirk about the way that RAS sets aside IP addresses. For some reason, it always takes at least two addresses. For example, on my RAS server, there's only one modem port, but DHCP always reserves *two* addresses for RAS. Trying to create a static IP address pool has the same result—always two addresses. I can't explain it, but that's the behavior I see.

Controlling Login Security

Back to the Network Configuration dialog box (Figure 18.8), where you also tell your system what kind of dial-in authentication to require. The options are

Allow Any Authentication Including Clear Text   Means that a client using PAP can connect. You may need to use this if you are running an Internet Service Provider network, as it's the least demanding logon requirement.

Require Encrypted Authentication   An extended way of saying "require CHAP."

Require Microsoft Encrypted Authentication   Means use Microsoft's own brand of CHAP, MSCHAP. If you do this, only Microsoft clients will be able to attach.

If you choose to require MSCHAP, and if you are using only NT machines on your network, then you can check Require Data Encryption; NT will encrypt not only passwords but data with this check box. Click OK to clear the Network Configuration dialog box.

Because you're installing Remote Access Service, the system thrashes around for a bit during the installation process and then you'll get a message that Remote Access Service installed properly. Close the Control Panel, and your system will reboot. You're almost ready to start receiving calls with a Remote Access Service server.

TIP

Once you've attached a modem to a Remote Access Service server, you cannot use it for anything else; the port that the modem is on is now committed to Remote Access Service only. If you're using Remote Access Service for dialing *out*, in contrast, then you can use the port and the attached modem whenever Remote Access Service isn't activated. If you ever *do* need to use the port on a RAS server, you can temporarily stop the RAS service.

Setup Considerations When Using ISDN

If you're using an ISDN connection rather than a modem on your server, you need to do just a little additional tweaking to make sure that it's set up properly. If you're making an ISDN connection from an old modem connection, you don't need to trash the old one and start over. Just select the entry in the phone book and edit it to use ISDN. If you're using BRI ISDN, tell the system that you'll be using two channels. In addition to the tweaking that you do, you need to arrange some tweaking with the telephone company. When setting up your ISDN connection, be sure to have the connection set up in the following way:

Switch protocols

- AT&T 5ESS switch: proprietary, or NI-1 protocol (if it is available)

- Northern Telecom DMS100 switch: Functional or NI-1 protocol

- National ISDN-1 compatible switch: NI-1

Terminal type   The terminal type is A, or D if A is not available or is already being used by other equipment on the box.

TEL assignment   The TEL assignment should be Auto.

Multipoint   Multipoint should be set to Yes, meaning that each B channel (remember those are the ones the data travels on) can be used for separate purposes by the machine. One B channel could be used for inbound traffic, and one could be used for outbound traffic. You might have to explain this one to the telephone company, since *multipoint* may mean something different to them, depending on what part of the country you live in.

SPIDs   If you want to be able to use the channels independently, you *must* make sure the telephone company sets the number of SPIDs (*logical terminals*) to 2. This will give you two telephone numbers on the same ISDN line. If you don't have two logical terminals, you won't be able to use the channels independently, as the SPID controlling the transmission will be unavailable once the channel is in use.

EKTS   Set EKTS to No.

TIP   ISDN is a new technology and, as such, can be a bit finicky at times. If you're having connection problems, try switching the ISDN interface off and back on again. If the problems persist, check with the telephone company or the company who installed ISDN for you. There could be problems with the telephone company's connection, or you may have configured the ISDN setup incorrectly.

Setup Considerations for X.25

Setting up DUN to work with X.25 isn't much different from setting it up to work with ISDN:

1. Go to the DUN Phone Book and click the Add, Edit, or Clone button, depending on whether you're making a new entry, changing an existing one, or copying an existing one.

2. In the Phone Book entry dialog box, click the Advanced button.

3. Choose Any X.25 port from the list of available ports and then click on the X.25 button. You'll see a box that looks like Figure 18.10.

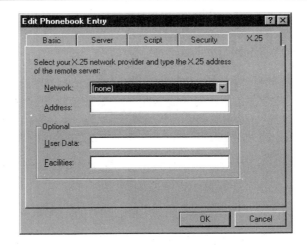

The settings in this dialog box are as follows:

Address   The address is the X.25 equivalent of a telephone number. Enter the one associated with the machine that you want to call.

User Data   Any additional information that the X.25 host computer needs to make the connection is placed in the User Data box. Typically, there won't be anything.

Facilities   In the Facilities box, put any additional parameters that your X.25 provider supplies, such as reverse charging. If you're not sure what options you have, check with your provider or your documentation.

Once you've filled in the boxes here, you should be ready to use DUN over X.25. The connection process, which is discussed below, doesn't change with the kind of connection that's in place.

TIP   X.25 has one drawback. You can't use the Callback security feature with it. (You'll meet the Callback feature in the next section.)

Using Remote Access Service Administrator

In the Administrative Tools group, you'll find a new program called Remote Access Admin. Start it up and you'll see a screen like Figure 18.11.

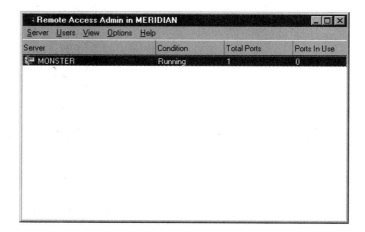

I ran this program on the server MONSTER, and so by default it shows me only the Remote Access Service server MONSTER; if there are other RAS servers on the domain, then they would also show up.

Note that if your RAS server is not a domain controller, you won't see your domain members on the list of users. Choose Server ➢ Select Domain or Server, and type the name of your domain—then the names of your domain users will appear.

Figure 18.11 shows that there's one Remote Access Service server named MONSTER, with one port—one modem, ISDN connection, or whatever—on it. Furthermore, no one is dialing into that port at the moment. Now, if *you* try to dial in to a Remote Access Service server on your domain, you'll be in for a surprise. You've got to use the DUN Admin program to allow particular users to call in to the server—merely being a user on this network is not sufficient to be able to call in on a DUN server.

Now, you want domain users to be able to dial in to this Remote Access Service server so as to access the domain. But right now the Remote Access Service

Administrator program is focused on just this one server, rather than the domain as a whole. As a result, the only user accounts that it is aware of are the local Administrator and Guest accounts. To move its focus to the domain as a whole, click Server ➤ Select Domain or Server, and look for the icon next to the name of your *domain*—do not click on a particular server, but rather the name of the entire domain. As the servers appear indented in a nice, neat column under the domain's name, I'm always tempted to assume that I must click on a particular server. If I do, however, I will not be able to grant dial-in permissions to domain accounts as a whole. Click the domain name and then OK. You may see in the Remote Access Admin window the message, "No Remote Access Service servers were found in the selected domain," which *seems* to mean that no primary or backup domain controllers are running RAS. Ignore the message.

Click Users and then Permissions, and you'll see the dialog box displayed in Figure 18.12.

FIGURE 18.12:

Setting user permissions on Remote Access Service

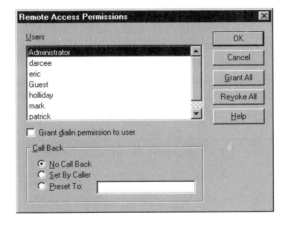

By default, *no one* can connect to the network via Remote Access Service. You must click on a user's name and then check "Grant dialin permission to user" or click the Grant All button. Alternatively, you can open up the User Manager for Domains; you'll notice that it has an extra button on it labeled Dialin, which you use to grant dial-in permissions.

The Remote Access Permissions dialog box is also where you control software-based callback modems. Callback modems are a way to provide security for your system and, perhaps, to save money for your users. The way it works is this: you, the user, call and are authenticated by the system. The system then hangs up on you and calls you back. This can save your users money because your company is paying the phone charges for most of the connection. It can also make your network more secure because you can preset a phone number for each user. Suppose my username is MARKM and I have a preset callback number of 555-5555. Someone steals my user ID and logon password, and tries to attach to the system. The system says, in effect, "I accept you as Mark; now I'll call you back at Mark's house," hangs up on the intruder, and calls my computer at my house. I hear the ringing, but *I* didn't try to log on! The intruder doesn't get very far and, in fact, trumpets the fact that he's working with a stolen ID by the callback feature.

For every account that has permission to dial in, you must choose how it is to be done with the Call Back options listed at the bottom of the dialog box.

> **No Call Back**   This option offers no extra system security. With it checked, users dial in directly from wherever they are. This is the default option.

> **Set By Caller**   Although it doesn't offer any system security either, this option allows on-the-road users to avoid big telephone bills. With this option checked, the DUN server calls the user back at the number the user indicates once the user's account has been validated.

> **Preset To**   This is the most secure option. For users who routinely call in from the same location, you can preset a telephone number from which they must always call. After the user dials in and is validated, the DUN server severs the connection and then calls the user back at the preset telephone number. If the user is calling from a different number than the one in the DUN database, she won't be able to make the connection.

If you mess up when establishing who can dial in and how, you can always start over by clicking the Revoke All button and eliminating all dial-in permissions.

Allowing Users from Other Domains to Log In to a Remote Access Service Server

This is a problem that stumped me for a year. Our network has two major domains, named ORION and TAURUS. Our main Remote Access Service server is on a machine in the TAURUS domain. ORION people want to be able to dial in to our enterprise network via the Remote Access Service server, so my TAURUS administrator tried to grant dial-in access to the ORION users by using the Remote Access Admin.

The problem was that the Remote Access Admin would only display the names of TAURUS users, and we couldn't get it to display the names of the ORION users for love or money. But eventually we found the answer.

In the Remote Access Admin, click Server ➤ Select Domain or Server; this part we'd figured out a long time ago. But when we selected the ORION domain, the Remote Access Admin said something like "No Remote Access Service servers were found in the selected domain," an apparent error message. The trick was that it wasn't an error message at all. I just clicked Users ➤ Permissions like before, and all the ORION users appeared on the list. I granted them access, and all was well.

Now that the server is set up, let's take a look at dialing in with different kinds of RAS clients.

RAS Client Setup

Once you've set up the service and have it running on both the server and the workstation from which you want to access the server, you're ready to make the remote connection. The process for doing this is somewhat different, depending on whether you're running NT's DUN or the special version used with Windows 95 or Windows for Workgroups. There is supposed to be a way to run Remote Access Service using a DOS workstation, but I've never been able to make it work.

Connecting from an NT Machine

First, you've got to have Remote Access Service running on the NT machine, either NT Workstation or NT Server. The installation is the same for Remote Access Service client as it was for Remote Access Service workstation, save for the dialog box that asked whether you will dial out, dial in, or do both.

To dial out, however, you must use the Remote Access Service icon in the My Computer folder. It maintains a "phone book" of places that you can call.

To make the remote connection from an NT or NT Server machine:

First, go to the DUN icon and open it. When you first open up the Remote Access Service folder, it will complain that there are no dialing directory entries, as you see in Figure 18.13.

FIGURE 18.13:

No entries in Remote Access
Service dialing directory

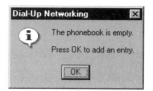

Click OK, and you'll get the chance to create a new phone book entry. (You
can also use a Wizard to automatically set up the new phone entry). Phone book
entries have several tabs: Basic, Server, Script, Security, and X.25. I clearly won't
have need of X.25 here, but we'll take a look at each of the other tabs.

The first tab, Basic, looks like Figure18.14.

FIGURE 18.14:

Basic phone directory tab

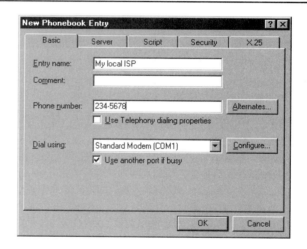

Much of this is self-explanatory—Phone number, Comment, Dial using, and
Entry name. The Alternates button is new to NT 4, and it's a welcome addition. If
you have a service that you dial in to, but whose phone lines are often busy, then
it's convenient to be able to store some secondary phone numbers; this lets you
do that. The Configure button is also useful; click it, and you'll see the dialog box
in Figure 18.15.

FIGURE 18.15:

Controlling modem
configuration

The options on this screen are as follows:

Enable Hardware Flow Control   Checking this option enables hand-shaking between the modem and the computer, so that, if the modem falls behind in receiving, it can halt the flow of data rather than just registering an overflow error. In short, keeping this enabled allows the modem to slow its eating speed rather than choke.

Enable Modem Error Control   Checking this option enables error checking through cyclical redundancy checks (CRCs). Enabling this option increases modem efficiency, because it eliminates the need for start and stop bits (bits that signal the beginning and end of data transmission).

Enable Modem Compression   This option is not checked by default, but I recommend checking it. This allows your modem to compress the data stream using the V.42 *bis* compression algorithm. Not all modems support compression, which is probably why this is disabled by default. Most high-speed modems *do* support compression nowadays, however, so it's probably a safe bet to enable compression. Just as data compression programs like Stacker work better on some kinds of files than others, the amount of compression that takes place depends on how much redundancy is in the data transmission. This will vary with the type of transmission.

Disable Modem Speaker   This is pretty self-explanatory: without a check in the box, every squeal and grunt from the modem is broadcast through its speaker; checked, the modem works silently.

If you realize after you've finished that you didn't set up the modem correctly, click on the Configure button and you'll be able to change the settings and configurations that you assigned.

Click OK to return to the Basic tab, and then click Server to tell your system about the server you'll be dialing in to. You'll see a dialog box like in Figure 18.16.

FIGURE 18.16:

Configuring Remote Access Service to dial in to a server type

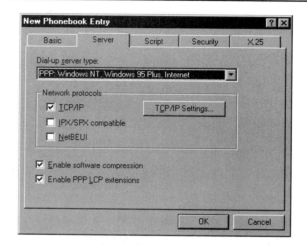

As on the server side, you tell it which protocols you expect to be able to communicate with. The Dial-Up Server Type drop-down list box lists three kinds of servers:

- *Windows NT 3.1, Windows for Workgroups 3.11* gets its own setting because Dial-Up Networking—or Remote Access Service, as it was called—used to be built not atop PPP, but instead, on a home-grown Microsoft protocol known as AsyBEUI, basically NetBEUI with a wide area network flavor. It could only transport NetBEUI data and was worthless for Internet access. (If you choose this option, you'll even notice that all protocol options gray out except for NetBEUI.) As the name suggests, only use this if you're dialing in to an old NT 3.1 RAS server or a Windows for Workgroups machine set up to receive calls.

- *Internet SLIP* is the older of the two most popular Internet dial-up protocols, PPP being the other one. SLIP has a lot of positive features, most particularly that it's simple and imposes little overhead on an already slow dial-up line. But the flexibility and ever-growing functionality of PPP (recall that PPP has PAP and CHAP, as well as multilink PPP) is causing SLIP to wither away slowly.

- *PPP: Windows NT, Windows 95 Plus, Internet* is the option that you'll choose most often. You can use this to either dial in to a Remote Access Service server, as I'm about to do, or to dial in to an Internet Service Provider (ISP), as most ISPs offer PPP dial-in.

Here, I've chosen PPP. For network protocols, I use TCP/IP, so I've checked that. It requires some configuration, so I'll click TCP/IP Configuration and see a dialog like Figure 18.17. By the way, if your intention in using RAS client is to dial in to an Internet Service Provider, then look ahead to the section entitled "Dialing to the Internet with DUN/RAS" later in this chapter.

FIGURE 18.17:

Configuring TCP/IP for dial-in

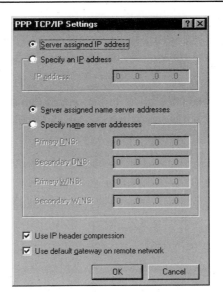

If you're going to be part of someone else's TCP/IP network, then of course you'll need an IP address. In most cases, the network that you dial in to will want to assign that address, rather than letting you set your own IP address, which could potentially cause all kinds of havoc. I should note in passing, however, that if you're dialing in to some ISPs with particularly primitive dial-in capabilities, then they may require that you set your IP address from your workstation, only because their server software can't set your workstation's IP address. If that's the case, then the ISP will supply you with an IP address, and you'd better be sure to use it. If you're dialing in to an NT server, then you'll usually want the Remote Access Service server to set your IP address. Again, however, the installation that you're dialing in to may have set things up differently, so check with them if you're unsure.

You'll also need the address of a DNS server and, if it's an NT network, a WINS server, as well. A Remote Access Service server can, of course, supply those addresses automatically, but there may be a reason why you'd want to set them yourself. Alternatively, if you are dialing in to an ISP, the ISP may not be able to supply that information automatically. Again, sorry to be vague about this, but the fact is that it's possible for different installations to handle things differently. If you're dialing into a Remote Access Service server like the one we set up earlier in this chapter, just let it do everything—set IP address, name server, and (coming up), default gateway.

VJ header compression is an option created to speed data transfer on slow dial-up links. Above 28.8Kbps, it's irrelevant, but it may speed you up a bit at 28.8 or slower rates. The only way to know if it's a good idea to do VJ header compression is to try it both ways—hook up to an FTP site and try transferring data with and without the compression—and see which is faster.

Use Default Gateway on Remote Network just means that any IP addresses that your system doesn't know how to route to should just go over the Remote Access Service connection. Look back to Chapter 14 for the discussion on TCP/IP routing for more information. Remember that in the end, it really doesn't matter whether you do this or not, because you can always just add a ROUTE ADD statement to make *any* IP address your default gateway.

Click OK to return to the Server tab, and click Script to look at the Script tab. It will look like Figure 18.18.

This tab won't do anything for us when connecting to a Remote Access Service server, but as long as I'm explaining how to set up a Remote Access Service client, let's take a look at it.

FIGURE 18.18:

Script tab

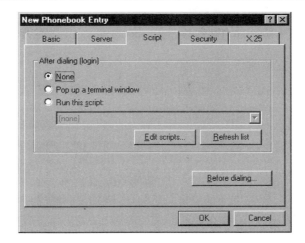

As I've said before, you will sometimes use Remote Access Service to establish a connection to the Internet through an ISP, and many ISPs use Unix machines. Those Unix machines need, of course, to verify that you are a valid user on the network, so they've got to get a name and password from you. The ways that they can do that are

- With a standard terminal screen asking you to type in a name and password, requiring you to be present when Remote Access Service connects to the ISP.

- Some systems can exchange name and password automatically without the need for user intervention. The name and password are transmitted across the line in an unencrypted fashion, and the protocol that does it is called the *Password Authentication Protocol,* or PAP.

- Other systems use something that's like PAP but that encrypts the data; that protocol is called the *Challenge-Handshake Authentication Protocol,* or CHAP.

- Finally, Microsoft has its own nonstandard version of CHAP that it uses, called MSCHAP. Obviously, you'll only use this to connect to Remote Access Service servers, which most ISPs aren't using (or at least aren't using *currently;* I'd wager that the market share of ISPs using NT is growing pretty fast).

If you are connecting to an ISP that uses the first approach—pop up a terminal screen and punch in a name and password by hand—then you should choose either Pop Up a Terminal Window or Run This Script. For the other approaches, simply choose None. Because I'm dialing in to a Remote Access Service server, I choose None.

Pop Up a Terminal Window allows you to respond to the ISP's request for a name and password. Running this script tells Remote Access Service to automatically run a script that mimics you typing in a name and password; look in the file SWITCH.INF for some guidance on how to write one of those for yourself if your ISP doesn't use PAP or CHAP. Click the Security tab, and you'll see the next tab, which meshes pretty closely with this one. The screen will look something like Figure 18.19.

FIGURE 18.19:

Security tab

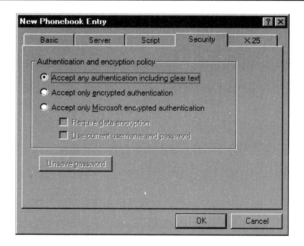

If you chose either the pop-up terminal or script in the previous tab, choose Accept any authentication. For a system using PAP, also choose this. For a system running standard CHAP, choose Accept only encrypted authentication. For an MSCHAP system, like the Remote Access Service server I'm dialing in to, choose Accept only Microsoft encrypted authentication. That server may even require that you encrypt the data; if so, check the Require data encryption box.

Click OK, and the dialing screen appears, as you see in Figure 18.20.

FIGURE 18.20:

Ready to dial the server

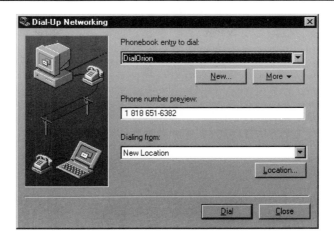

You can, if you like, override the phone number here. And, by the way, if you ever want to change any of the phone book settings that you just created, just return to this screen, choose the particular phone book entry that you want to change, click More, and click Edit entry configuration.

Remote Access Service needs to know how it should identify your client, so it displays a dialog box before dialing, as you see in Figure 18.21. If you're using a script, you can leave the fields blank.

FIGURE 18.21:

Username, password, and domain to present to Remote Access Service server

When you're connected, you'll see a dialog box like in Figure 18.22.

FIGURE 18.22:

Confirmation of a successful connection

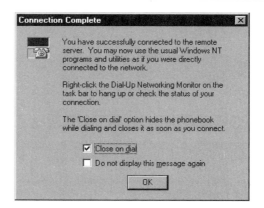

Now just access the network in the usual way, with net use and net view commands, or with the Network Neighborhood.

Connecting from a Windows 95 Client

Hooking up Windows 95 clients to a Remote Access Service server is fairly easy because Windows 95 comes with a Remote Access Service module built right in. Installing Remote Access Service in Windows 95 is a three-step process:

1.   Install the Remote Access Service software.

2.   Install the dial-up adapter.

3.   Create and configure the Remote Access Service connection.

Got your Windows 95 CD-ROM disc handy? Then let's have at it…

Installing the Remote Access Service Software

You install Remote Access Service as a built-in application under Windows 95. Follow these steps to put it on your computer:

1.   Click on Control Panel.

2.   Select Add ➤ Remove Programs.

3.   Select the Setup tab.

4. Click the Communications option and then select Details.

5. Select Remote Access Service from the list.

6. You will be returned to the Add ➤ Remove Programs Screen. To continue with the setup, click the OK button.

Next, you'll install the networking part. Click on Control Panel, and then open the Network applet and select the Configuration tab (it should be at this location by default). Click the Add button, select Adapter, and click Add; you will be presented with a list of network adapter manufacturers. If you select Microsoft from this list, you'll see Figure 18.23.

FIGURE 18.23:

Selecting the Dial-Up Adapter

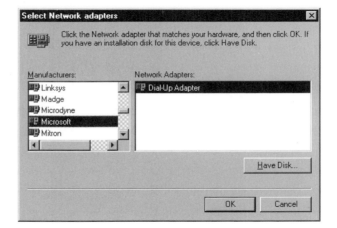

The only adapter in the right-hand side of this screen should be the Dial-Up Adapter. Select it and click OK. That will return you to the main Network screen, shown in Figure 18.24.

In the box where the currently installed network components are listed, Dial-Up Adapter should now be on the list. As far as Windows 95 is concerned, the Dial-Up Adapter is a network interface card. The Dial-Up Adapter does require that a modem be installed on your system. If, during the time that you are installing the Dial-Up Adapter, you have not configured your modem in Windows 95, the Hardware Wizard will launch to walk you through its configuration.

FIGURE 18.24:

Main Network Control Panel applet

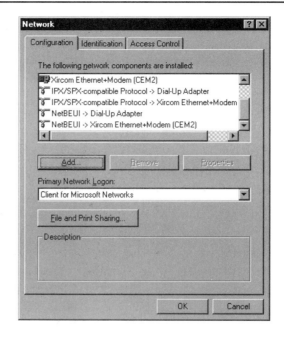

You may notice several protocols on the list and an arrow pointing to the Dial-Up Adapter. That is Windows 95's way of showing bindings. Networking components always bind "up"; network boards bind to protocols, and protocols bind to Services.

At this point you can click OK on the main Network screen to have Windows 95 copy the appropriate software—and yes, you will have to restart your system to have the changes take effect.

Creating and Configuring the DUN Connection

Now that you've got the underlying pieces in place, the next step is to create a new Remote Access Service (DUN) connection. Look in My Computer, and you'll see the Remote Access Service icon, just as in Windows NT. Open it up, and its folder will resemble the one in Figure 18.25.

FIGURE 18.25:

Windows 95 Remote Access
Service folder

Choose the Make New Connection option.

> **NOTE**
> If this is your first time clicking on the Remote Access Service icon, Windows 95 will automatically launch the Make New Connection Wizard to assist you with creating your first connection. Every subsequent connection you create will require you to click on Make New Connection.

The Wizard looks like Figure 18.26.

FIGURE 18.26:

Make New Connection
Wizard's initial screen

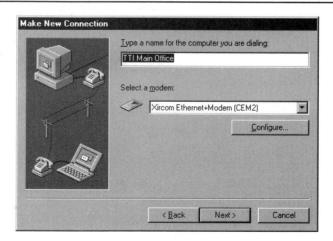

Give your connection a name and verify the modem selected. On the next screen you will be asked for the phone number you want to dial. This creates a Connection icon in the Remote Access Service folder.

To configure a DUN client connection, simply right-click the Connection icon created in the preceding section and select Properties. The opening screen should just confirm the information you typed in when you created the connection.

To connect to the NT Server, click the Server Type button. You'll see Figure 18.27.

FIGURE 18.27:

Configuring the server type under Windows 95 Remote Access Service

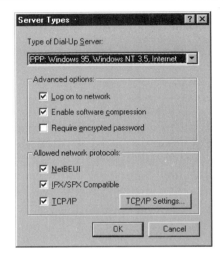

Make sure that the Server type is PPP: Windows 95, Windows NT 3.5, Internet. (Yes, I realize that it says NT 3.5 and you are connecting to NT Server 4, but it works—trust me…) Under Allowed Network Protocols, select the protocols that you would like to use over the DUN connection.

NOTE   TCP/IP alert: If you want to use TCP/IP over the DUN connection, you must configure TCP/IP by clicking the TCP/IP Settings on the above screen. Any TCP/IP settings that you have created in Control Panel ➤ Network are discarded as soon as you start the DUN connection.

You'll see other settings, as well. Here's a brief synopsis of them:

Log On to Network   This option, which is enabled by default, will dial up and log you in to the network using the username and password you typed in when you logged in to Windows 95. If this option is deselected, it will ask you for a logon name and password every time you attempt a new connection.

Enable Software Compression   This option will compress the data before it is sent to the modem (or the like) for transmission.

Require Encrypted Password   This option enables the use of the Challenge-Handshake Authentication protocol (CHAP).

Once you have configured your DUN connection, just double-click and the connection will be made immediately. You should see the lights of your modem flashing, and, if you have enabled the modem speaker, you should hear the distinctive squelching noise that indicates that Windows 95 is negotiating a connection.

Using Microsoft's Universal Naming Conventions (UNCs), you should now be able to access any network resource for which you have permission.

Once you have established a connection for the first time, any of the following actions will activate Remote Access Service:

- When you select a network resource that is not part of your network
- When a UNC directs you toward a network resource (\\server\public_)
- When an application calls for a network resource
- Shortcuts to Popular Network Information

Once you have created the DUN connection, double-click the Connection icon at any time to dial up the network. It may ask for the name of the sever or domain that you want to log on to, as well as a password. DUN will then dial the location, verify the username and the password, and if everything checks out, allow you access to the server. At this point, the user can now do anything that the user normally could if he or she were local to the network (only more slowly).

One final note: if you are using DUN on a machine that is also connected to a network via a network interface card, you can access a network via the DUN connection, or you can access a network via your NIC; you cannot do both simultaneously. It is my guess that if you could do this, your Windows 95 machine could become a WAN router allowing people from the outside to access resources throughout their network, and this is a feature reserved for the NT operating system.

Connecting from a Windows for Workgroups PC

Setting up a Windows for Workgroups machine is pretty straightforward; open up the Network group in the Program Manager, double-click Remote Access, and follow the prompts. There is just one thing to remember when setting up a Windows for Workgroups connection: it can only use AsyBEUI. You must tell the NT Server machine that is running the Remote Access Service server that it can accept authentication of any type, and that it can accept NetBEUI protocol packets.

How Do I Connect a Non-NT Workstation to a DUN Server?

If you are running DOS and LAN Manager Enhanced on a dual-role computer, start at step 1. If you are running DOS and any other configuration (except Windows for Workgroups), start at step 2. If you are running OS/2, start at step 3.

1. From the command prompt, type **unload protocol**.

2. Type **rasload** to load the DUN drivers.

3. Type **rasphone** to open the DUN Phone Book.

4. Create and save a Phone Book entry. To do so, click on the File menu and choose Create. Fill in the blanks for the connection name (this is up to you—the name is for your identification purposes only), the domain and the telephone number.

5. Press Alt+D to reach the Dial menu and choose Connect. You will be prompted for your password, but, if you've selected an entry, the other information should be filled in. Type in your password and press Enter.

6. You will see a dialog box telling you that the system is trying to make the connection, and asking you to wait. If you need to stop before the connection is made, press Enter to cancel.

Once the connection is complete, you will see a message telling you that you can now access the network as though you were connected to the LAN.

Connecting from Other Operating Systems

The process of connecting to a DUN server from an operating system other than NT varies, depending on which system you're using. The basic steps are the same, but you don't need to include all of them when you're working with certain systems.

Connecting to a NetWare Server

Due to the large market share that Novell has, it's not unlikely that you might need to connect an NT client to a NetWare server through DUN. One approach is to run the Client Service for NetWare on the client machine, call the DUN server for the initial connection to the network, and then let CSNW do the rest. Another approach is to install the Gateway Services for NetWare on the NT network; the NetWare drives then look like normal NT shared drives to any user of the network.

As long as the drive connection between the servers is maintained, the NT server will make the shared NetWare drive connection accessible to all Microsoft clients that are linked to it, either locally or remotely.

Monitoring and Troubleshooting RAS

Just as with any other network connection, there are times when DUN won't work. If you happen across one of those times, here are some ways in which you can see what's wrong.

Watching RAS/DUN Users

Remote users are a bigger potential security problem than others; that's why you'll find the RAS Administrator useful. Open up the RAS Administrator, shown in the Figure 18.28, and you'll get a report on how many ports are active.

Double-click on the server, and you'll see the dialog box, shown in Figure 18.29, offering the information that MarkS is connected.

You can see how long he's been on, disconnect him, or send him a message. Click Port Status, and you'll see the dialog box in Figure 18.30.

FIGURE 18.28:

One active port on a Remote Access Service server

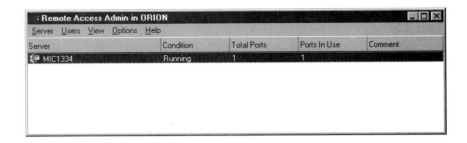

FIGURE 18.29:

Viewing port usage on a Remote Access Service server

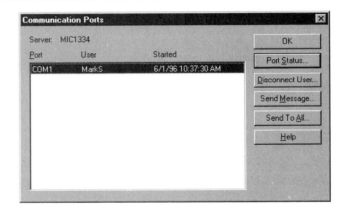

The information on this screen will change during the connection, depending on the level of compression, the amount of data traveling between the server and client, any errors that take place, and so forth. If things go well, the values in the Errors section should remain at 0. Errors aren't the end of the world, however; a few of them won't hurt anything.

Click the Reset button if you want to reset all the values back to 0. This doesn't break the connection—the counting just starts over. This could be useful if you're trying to determine, for example, the number of line errors that take place in a 10-minute period.

You can disconnect a user with the Disconnect User button, shown in Figure 18.31 (of course, a message beforehand would be nice, unless she's an intruder).

FIGURE 18.30:

Port Status dialog box

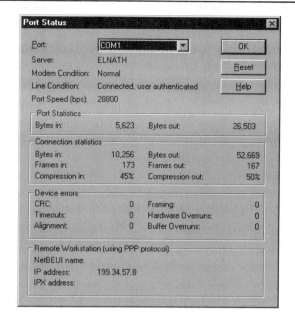

FIGURE 18.31:

Disconnecting a user forcibly from Remote Access Service server

Notice how convenient this is; you can not only kick someone off, but you can revoke their permissions to access the network, as well. That way, you can identify and bar miscreants with just a few mouse clicks.

Checking the Audit Records

You don't have to rely merely on intuition and your problem-solving ability when it comes to troubleshooting and monitoring RAS. You can either monitor connection attempts as they occur, using the RAS Administrator, or you can check the record of all audits and error messages stored in the Event Viewer.

Using the Event Viewer to Monitor Problems

To monitor past problems, you can check the Event Viewer to see what it has to say about a situation. Make sure auditing is enabled (it is by default). There are three kinds of events recorded in the Event Viewer: audits, warnings, and errors:

Audit   A normal event recorded for administrative reasons. A normal connection would be recorded as an audit. You can choose to audit only successful events, failed events, or both.

Warning   An irregular event that doesn't affect how the system functions.

Error   A failed event or network error.

Examining Logged Information

You can create a log of modem activity by going to the Control Panel, choosing Modem ➤ Properties ➤ Connection ➤ Advanced, and checking Record a log file. This creates a file called MODEMLOG.TXT, which keeps track of the modem commands sent and received.

If you are doing PPP-type connections, you can tell RAS to create a file called PPP.LOG, which, as you'd suspect, logs PPP transactions. Start it by going to the Registry and modifying the REG_DWORD parameter Logging=1. You'll find the parameter in HKEY_LOCAL_MACHINE\System\CurrentControlSet\Services\RasMan\PPP.

PPP.LOG is written to \WINNT\SYSTEM32\RAS. It will only be of help to you if you're familiar with the nuts and bolts of the PPP protocol.

You read earlier about the DEVICE.LOG file and how it can help you to troubleshoot modem scripts. Under NT 3.51, an ASCII file named SERIAL.INI allowed you to control settings for modem ports, but it apparently no longer functions under NT 4, probably due to the changes in device control brought on by TAPI.

Troubleshooting: If the Connection Has Never Worked Before

If you're trying to use DUN for the first time after you've set it up and it won't work, these are some potential gremlins in the system:

Incorrect configuration   Have you used the DUN Administrator to give all the users proper dial-in permission? Have you configured the server so that it is able to receive calls? Is the preset number at which the server is trying to call a user the correct one?

Modem problems   If you're using a new modem, the problem could lie with it. It could be a compatibility problem, or the modem simply might not work. Use the Hyperterminal program, which comes with NT, to try out the modem. Just start up Hyperterminal and tell it that you want to establish a direct connection. Turn the modem on and off, and then type **ATT** and press Enter. If your modem is working right, then you'll get the response OK or 0. Try reducing the modem's connection speed; running your modem at 57,600bps may not be the best idea, particularly if your system is doing software compression and/or encryption.

> **NOTE**   What if your terminal test was successful and the modem still doesn't seem to work? Modems from different manufacturers, or even different models from the same manufacturer, are not always fully compatible with each other. In addition, compatibility problems are exacerbated at high speeds, so modems that run at 9600bps or faster may not always be able to talk to each other and may fall back to 2400—sort of negating the reason why you got the fast modems in the first place. Even modems that claim to follow the Hayes AT standard may not be able to communicate with each other under every circumstance.

ISDN problems   If you're running DUN over ISDN, is the ISDN connection set up properly?

If the Connection Has Worked Before

If the connection *used* to run and now doesn't, pinpointing the problem is generally a matter of establishing what's different: what has changed between the last time the service worked and now? Sometimes the problem is an internal one you can control, and sometimes it's something that you can't do much about, like a downed telephone line.

If the problem is an internal one, ask yourself these questions:

- Is the service running on both the server and client machines?

- Has a user with a preset callback number changed his or her telephone number?

- Have you reinstalled the operating system and forgotten to reinstall DUN?

- Is the modem running?

If the problem is external, ask yourself if the telephone lines between the DUN server and client working. If you're using an ISDN connection, is the telephone company's hub working?

Troubleshooting: If Your Network Neighborhood Is Empty

A user sits at home or in a hotel room at a Windows 95 workstation and uses Dial-Up Networking to dial in to her company's NT network. She gets connected fine, and we know that because she can PING locations inside the company's network. But when she opens up Network Neighborhood, there are no computers in it, save her own.

Over the past couple of years, people have asked me about this problem. I don't like using RAS all that much, as the flaky nature of dial-up connections irritates me. But recently I've had to use it more and more, so I've run across the problem, as well. Working at a remote site, I needed to access some files on my server. Using a Windows 95 workstation, I dialed in to my domain, connected without trouble and PINGed everywhere in my network. The network at home is a domain named ORION, so I'd set the Windows 95 machine's workgroup name equal to ORION before dialing up. I opened up the Windows 95 machine's Network Neighborhood…and sure enough, the only machine in ORION seemed to be a machine named PRESARIO: the machine at the beach with me. Rebooting under NT Workstation, I got a similar result.

As I could PING but not view machine names, it seemed pretty obvious that this was a NetBIOS naming problem. (As it turned out, I was only half right.)

First I tried creating an LMHOSTS file containing the names of the domain controllers in ORION, using the #PRE metacommand explained earlier in Chapters 12 and 14.

That didn't fix Windows 95, but it helped NT Workstation, although NT Workstation still needed a "nudge," as I had to press F5 to refresh Network Neighborhood before all of the ORION machines appeared. I then erased the LMHOSTS file and forced the TCP/IP stack to look to the WINS server back home for NetBIOS name resolutions; the screen to do that is in the Dial-Up Networking phone book. For some reason, a RAS server sometimes doesn't properly assign a WINS server address to a client, with the result that if you do an IPCONFIG from a DUN client running either Windows 98 or NT, or a WINIPCFG from a DUN client running Windows 95/98, you'll see no specified WINS server address. If that's the case—if your workstation dials in to a RAS server but has no WINS address—then you can directly punch one into the DUN phone book under TCP/IP Settings; Figure 18.34 shows that dialog box in a few pages. (In the TCP/IP Settings dialog, just click the "Specify name server addresses" radio button, then enter the IP address for a primary WINS server on the network you're dialing in to and, if one is available, the address for any secondary WINS servers.)

The first "fix" for this problem, then, is either to build an LMHOSTS file for dialing-in workstations, or to make sure that they can find a WINS server. And by the way, if you're running NT 3.51 Workstation, you'll need one more thing: NetBEUI. You won't be able to browse a network you've dialed in to under NT 3.51 unless one of your protocols is NetBEUI.

That fixed the problem for the NT workstation—but not for the Windows 95 one. As I said, when I guessed NetBIOS was the culprit, I was half right—LMHOSTS/WINS fixed NT Workstation, but not Win 95. Next I tried helping out the 95 machine by using Find Computer. That worked, but even after BETELGEUSE was "found," it didn't show up in the Network Neighborhood.

What causes this? According to several Microsoft Knowledge Base articles, a bug in the interface between NetBIOS and TCP. The computer resolves NetBIOS names all right, but it can't pass the results on to TCP afterward. Here's how it happens.

You connect your laptop to your corporate intranet locally with a high-speed direct connection like an Ethernet PCMCIA card. More than likely, you get an IP address from a DHCP server. The DHCP configuration information for the IP address bound to the PCMCIA card gets stored in your Registry. That's the key here: *the workstation that you're using to dial in to a network has or has had in the past a NIC that's received an IP address from a DHCP server.* The browsing problem doesn't occur otherwise.

When you're about to go off on a trip, you disconnect the computer from the network *but do not remove the PCMCIA board.* Arriving at your destination, you hook up a modem and dial in to your corporate RAS server. As the PCMCIA network card is powered up, Windows thinks that the network card may weigh in with some useful information now and then, remembering that it once had an IP address from DHCP. Windows has been unable to renew the DHCP lease on the PCMCIA card, but that doesn't make Windows deactivate the card, unfortunately. Then, when you dial in to your corporate intranet, you probably get also an IP address for your RAS/DUN connection from DHCP via your RAS server. Here's where the weird part starts. Even though it's obvious that the IP address that your system got from DHCP over the modem is up and running, and even though it's obvious that the IP address which your system's PCMCIA card got days ago is no longer functional, browsing traffic ends up trying to run out that currently dormant card. The result is, of course, that browsing—the Network Neighborhood—doesn't work.

What can you do about it? There're several options. First, you could just pop the PCMCIA card out of the laptop. Reboot, redial, and your problems may have gone away. But this can actually happen in *any* case wherein the workstation has one TCP/IP stack running on a network card and another on a dial-in connection. If you have a computer at home connected to a small home network but the computer also dials in to work, you can see the same behavior; people dialing in to a central office from a branch office can fall prey to the problem, as well. For those folks, Microsoft recommends building an alternative hardware profile that does not include the network card. Not a bad answer, but there's an even better one.

There are two patches to Windows 95 that you should put on your client systems. One replaces Dial-Up Networking altogether, with the side benefit of giving Windows 95 the ability to do PPTP dialups. The other is a patch that works with the first one to fix the browse problem. You can get both on Microsoft's Web site.

The update to Dial-Up Networking is called MSDUN13.EXE, last updated in September 1998. I'd intended to give you a specific URL where you can find MSDUN13.EXE, but Microsoft's Web site is so ASP-ized that the URL comes out looking like http://www.microsoft.com/windows/downloads/default.asp? CustArea=pers&Site=95&Product=Windows+95&Category=Service+Packs+%26

+Updates&x=14&y=6 or worse. The best that I can offer is to recommend that you go to http://www.microsoft.com/msdownload/ and look in the section labeled "Support Drivers, Patches and Service Packs" for the link labeled "Windows 95 Shareware and Utilities." Click that and you'll be sent to another page listing a couple dozen patches and fixes for Windows 95. On the page that follows, click "Windows Dial-Up Networking 1.3 Performance and Security Update for Windows 95" and follow the rest of the links to download the file, which is about 2.2MB in size.

The other file that you'll need is smaller, only about a tenth the size of MSDUN13.EXE. If you're running Windows 95 in its original August 1995 version or Windows 95 OSR 1, then you'll need a patch file called RASUPD.EXE; for OSR 2 or OSR 2.1 you instead use RAS2UPD.EXE. As far as I can tell, the only way to get these files is by looking up an article in the Knowledge Base, but only on the Web itself—the version on TechNet won't work. Again, get to Microsoft's Web site. This time, click the Support hotlink and then choose "Support Online." You'll be stepped through a form asking for personal information about yourself, information that Microsoft requires before they'll give you the update files. (Let me get this straight; I paid for a product that doesn't work and they make me give them my name for junk mail lists before they'll hand over the fix; hmmm…) Once you get to the Search page on Support Online, search for Knowledge Base article Q154434. Inside that article are hotlinks to download RAS2UPD.EXE and RASUPD.EXE. Download the appropriate one and apply it, and your Network Neighborhood will be populated.

By the way, MSDUN13.EXE also extends Windows 95's capabilities in that it includes client software to enable Windows 95 to dial in to a PPTP server. If you use DUN on Windows 95, it's a very good idea to get this patch. Windows 98 seems not to have the problem, in case you're wondering.

If You *Still* Can't See a Computer in Network Neighborhood Over RAS

Sometimes, despite all of the new patches that you apply, the distant server *still* doesn't appear in Network Neighborhood. Sometimes you can use Find Computer, but that's not reliable either.

In that case, there's a fairly foolproof way to make a connection to another machine over an RAS link. The only catch is that although it always works if you're running NT on your desktop and *may* work if you're running Windows 98, it isn't any help for Windows 95 users.

Windows 98 and NT 4 allow you to refer to a server using its IP address as a UNC. Thus, for example, if I had a share named PICTURES on a server whose IP address was 204.193.88.4, I could do a NET USE like the following:

```
Net use * \\204.193.88.4\pictures
```

That will work from either Windows 98 or NT 4. But it'll only work if the server already recognizes your user name and password. NT lets us take things a step further, recall, by allowing you to specify both a user name and password that the server will recognize. Thus, if that server recognizes users in a domain named BLUE and if I've got a user account in BLUE by the name of *administrator* with a password of *chief* then I could log onto the server over the WAN link with this command:

```
Net use * \\204.193.88.4\pictures chief /user:blue\administrator
```

That's all one line, even if it's broken on the page that you're reading. And the sequence of information *is* non-intuitive, in case you're wondering—why punch in the password before the account name?—but it's correct, that's what Net Use wants to see.

Running Applications Remotely

This is a short topic: I don't recommend it. Accessing files over a DUN connection is one thing, but using a remote *application* is something else again. Assuming that you have permissions that permit you to, there is nothing stopping you from putting an icon in your Program Manager for a remote executable file, but loading that program will take forever, and doing anything with that program will take just as long. The problem is that every time that you access the program file, all of it must travel to you, because the program stays stored on the computer where it resides. Most programs aren't set up to be client-server packages in which the client only takes the parts of the programs that it needs.

RAS Connectivity via the Internet

You've seen that you use RAS to dial in to your company's RAS servers from distant places. But you can also use RAS to access your company from *over the Internet*! (Well, that's true if your company doesn't have a firewall; read on to see.)

Suppose your company has an IP-based network. It is on the Internet. The company's on the east coast, and you're temporarily in a hotel or at a client site on the west coast, with Windows NT or 95 on your laptop. How can you connect to your firm's intranet from across the country?

Of course, there's the obvious way: just set up a RAS server on the east coast, put a modem on it, buy a modem for your laptop, and just dial in to the company. It's not a bad approach, although it *does* mean that you'll have to deal with all the standard pain and suffering of getting a modem on a laptop in a hotel room to successfully dial long distance. It's not impossible, but it ain't fun either, and if you *don't* have this problem—that is, if you can afford to dial long distance from a *hotel* phone—then heck, you shouldn't be reading this book; you should hire me to come teach it to you. (Just kidding.) Not only must you deal with in-hotel modem-ing, you'll also have to set up modems and phone lines on the receiving end, and some companies are kind of skittish about attaching modems to their network.

Making the Internet into Your Private Network

Often, I'll find it easier to get to the Internet than to dial long distance back home. There's a bit of a trick that, if performed correctly, will let you take any Internet-attached PC and make it think that it's locally connected to your corporate intranet. The trick is this: just get on to the Internet, then point your WINS server to the WINS server at the office, and *voilà*! If your company doesn't have a firewall or some other filtering device between your company's LAN and the Internet, you'll be able to log in to your NT-based network right over the Internet.

The Overview

If that's all a bit fast, let me slow down and consider this in some detail. Step One is to get on to the Internet. As usual, you can either connect directly to a LAN that's connected to the Internet, or you can dial up to an Internet Service Provider (ISP).

If you're at another firm and they allow you to connect your laptop to their corporate network, you'll need a local IP address, subnet mask, and default gateway; talk to someone on that site to get those numbers, or perhaps they support DHCP.

On the other hand, it's quite possible that you've got an account with some national ISP like AOL or CompuServe, and there's probably an access number local to your hotel, no matter how remote the city you're in. In this case, you can dial out to the Internet via the access provider from the hotel without a lot of complex dialing and also without breaking the bank.

No matter how you connect to the Internet, make sure your IP configuration includes a WINS server entry that points to the WINS server on your network back at your company. If you're directly connected to the Internet via a LAN connection, just set the Primary WINS Server address equal to the address back home. But before going on, let me take a short side-trip and show you exactly how to use Dial-Up Networking to get on to the Internet.

Dialing to the Internet with DUN/RAS

Whether you're trying to access your corporate network or you're just trying to dial up to your ISP to surf the Web, getting connected to the Internet is the first step to using the Net to get your work done. It's fairly simple to do that with DUN; here's how.

First, open up the Dial-Up Networking phone book in My Computer. Click the New button to bring up the New Phone Book Entry Wizard. Forget the dumb Wizard; just check the box labeled I Know All about Phone Book Entries and Would Rather Edit the Properties Directly, and then Next; that'll finish the process and you'll see a screen like Figure 18.32.

As you expected, I've filled in the name of the phone book entry and a phone number. Where you end up doing the tweaking is in the Server, Script, and Security tabs. Click Server, shown in Figure 18.33, and let's get started.

All I did here was to check the TCP/IP box and uncheck the other protocols. Also, check Enable software compression; you won't see amazing compression, but anything's a help in squeezing a bit more speed out of that slow phone line. The PPP LCP extensions will, in general, be irrelevant, I uncheck them, because ISPs running older software may not be able to connect if you're using these extensions.

FIGURE 18.32:

Basic phone book tab

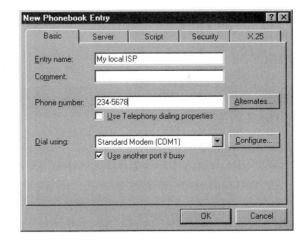

FIGURE 18.33:

Server tab

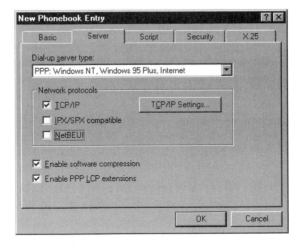

Next, let's configure the TCP/IP stack by pressing the TCP/IP Settings button. The dialog box looks like Figure 18.34.

FIGURE 18.34:

Configuring DUN TCP/IP settings

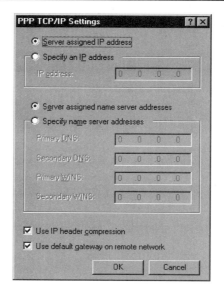

This is a tough dialog box to help you configure, but it's absolutely essential that you get it right. I say it's difficult for me to guide you through the dialog box simply because different ISPs require different settings—what is "right" solely depends on how your ISP is configured. On *most* ISPs that I've worked with, you'll choose Server assigned IP address. But if your ISP tells you to set up your software to use a given IP address, then click Specify an IP address, and punch in that address.

The next setting is, however, easy. Assuming that you want ultimately to connect with your company's network (and assuming, again, that your company is on the Internet and doesn't have a fierce firewall of some kind), then you will *not* want to use your ISP's DNS name servers, and, of course, most ISPs do not have WINS servers. So click Specify name server addresses, and fill in the IP addresses of the DNS and WINS servers at your firm.

NOTE   If you're just reading this to get your NT machine to dial in to the Internet and have no interest in connecting to a corporate network, then check with your ISP to find out whether their machine will automatically give your PC a DNS address (again, I've not met an ISP that uses WINS, although there may be a few that do). Or, if you need to, punch in the DNS address directly. In my experience, most ISPs require that you manually specify the DNS address.

The Use IP Header Compression option is a matter of choice. It's a method of getting slightly faster throughput, but truthfully it's usually a toss-up at 28.8Kbps or faster; it usually doesn't matter what you pick.

Finally, you'll choose Use default gateway on remote network. That just tells the IP stack on your computer that it shouldn't try to route any packets locally—since, after all, you're connected via a *modem*, and there really *isn't* a local network to try to route packets over. If you didn't do that, then the system would have no idea how to route packets, and you'd be unable to get anything done. Alternatively, you could *not* check the box, and type in a ROUTE ADD statement by hand every time you dialed up—but I can't see how that'll make things easier. Click OK when you're done, and then click the Script tab; it'll look like Figure 18.35.

FIGURE 18.35:

Script tab

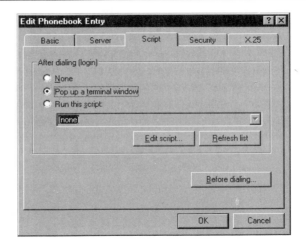

If you have written a logon script to automatically log you on to your ISP, then specify it here. Alternatively, click the button labeled Pop Up a Terminal Window. Then click the Security tab. It'll look like Figure 18.36.

FIGURE 18.36:

Security tab

Edit Phonebook Entry
Basic
Server
Script
Security
X.25
Authentication and encryption policy
Accept any authentication including clear text
Accept only encrypted authentication
Accept only Microsoft encrypted authentication
Require data encryption
Use current username and password
Unsave password
OK
Cancel

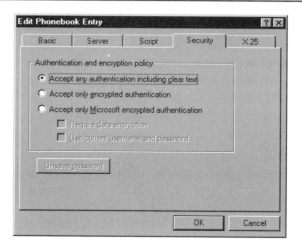

For most ISPs, you'll have to choose Accept Any Authentication Including Clear Text to get connected. Click OK, and you'll be back to the main screen of the Phone Book. Before dialing, open up a command window and type **route print** to dump your current IP routing table, and then **ipconfig** to show the current IP configuration information. It'll look something like Figure 18.37.

FIGURE 18.37:

IP routing and configuration information before connecting

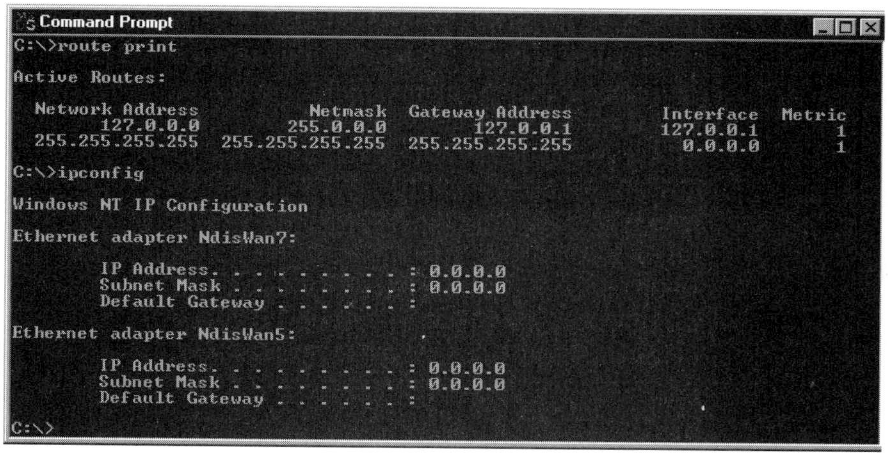

Command Prompt
C:\>route print
Active Routes:
Network Address Netmask Gateway Address Interface Metric
127.0.0.0 255.0.0.0 127.0.0.1 127.0.0.1 1
255.255.255.255 255.255.255.255 255.255.255.255 0.0.0.0 1
C:\>ipconfig
Windows NT IP Configuration
Ethernet adapter NdisWan7:
IP Address. . . . . : 0.0.0.0
Subnet Mask . . . . : 0.0.0.0
Default Gateway . . . . . . :
Ethernet adapter NdisWan5:
IP Address. . . . . : 0.0.0.0
Subnet Mask . . . . : 0.0.0.0
Default Gateway . . . . . . :
C:\>

The sparse routing table indicates that all your IP stack knows how to do is to route to itself (the 127.0.0.1 entry); it also contains the generic IP broadcast address 255.255.255.255. Notice that there is not yet a 0.0.0.0 route, so your system doesn't yet know how to get out to the Internet. As a matter of fact, the IPCONFIG shows that you don't have an IP address yet; there are two NDISWAN adapters because I've loaded a RAS driver for both a modem and for PPTP, and RAS keeps separate information on each of them. After connecting, we'll see that the ROUTE PRINT and the IPCONFIG change quite a bit. Click Dial, and you'll see a dialog box from RAS/DUN asking for your name, password, and domain. *This dialog box is irrelevant for most ISPs.* This is the dialog box that DUN uses to collect your name and password so that it has that data in the event you're using PAP, CHAP, or a similar protocol to automatically log in. If your ISP is like most ISPs, however, it won't support anything but a regular old terminal-based login where you've got to punch in your username and password. As this dialog box is probably irrelevant, I just click OK to dismiss it. The modem will then dial up and connect to your ISP. If you chose to display a terminal window, then you'll see something that looks like Figure 18.38.

FIGURE 18.38:

Entering username and password for ISP

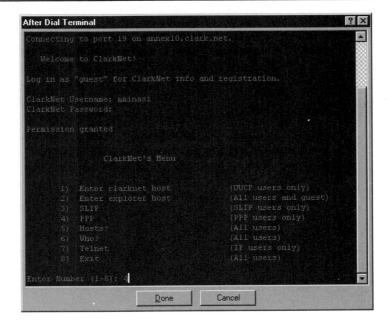

Here, my ISP requires that I enter my username and password, and then enter **4** to choose PPP. Once that happens, some garbage appears on the screen, but that doesn't matter—I just click Done, and the dialog box disappears. I'm now on the Internet. If I open up a command line and type **IPCONFIG /ALL**, I get a lot more information this time, as you see in Figure 18.39.

FIGURE 18.39:

IPCONFIG /ALL after connecting

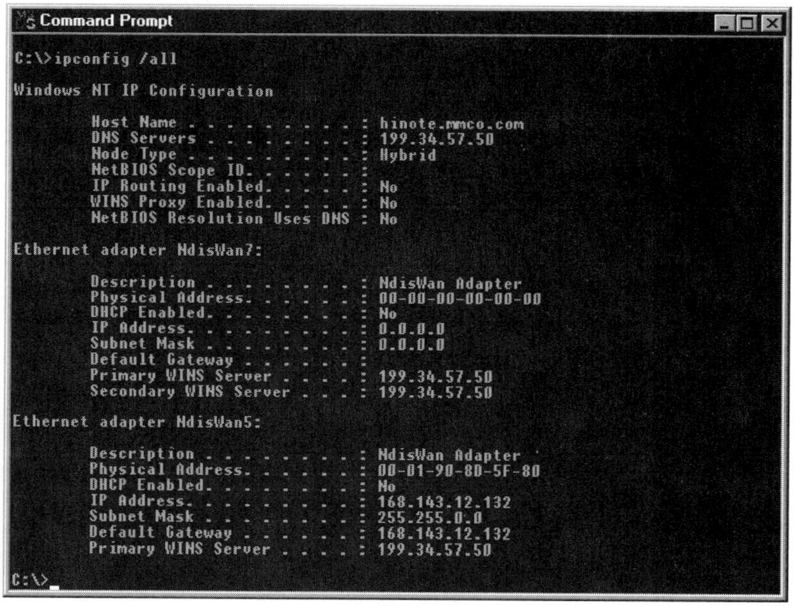

```
Command Prompt                                                    _ □ X

C:\>ipconfig /all

Windows NT IP Configuration

        Host Name . . . . . . . . . . : hinote.mmco.com
        DNS Servers . . . . . . . . . : 199.34.57.50
        Node Type . . . . . . . . . . : Hybrid
        NetBIOS Scope ID. . . . . . . :
        IP Routing Enabled. . . . . . : No
        WINS Proxy Enabled. . . . . . : No
        NetBIOS Resolution Uses DNS : No

Ethernet adapter NdisWan7:

        Description . . . . . . . . . : NdisWan Adapter
        Physical Address. . . . . . . : 00-00-00-00-00-00
        DHCP Enabled. . . . . . . . . : No
        IP Address. . . . . . . . . . : 0.0.0.0
        Subnet Mask . . . . . . . . . : 0.0.0.0
        Default Gateway . . . . . . . :
        Primary WINS Server . . . . . : 199.34.57.50
        Secondary WINS Server . . . : 199.34.57.50

Ethernet adapter NdisWan5:

        Description . . . . . . . . . : NdisWan Adapter
        Physical Address. . . . . . . : 00-01-90-80-5F-80
        DHCP Enabled. . . . . . . . . : No
        IP Address. . . . . . . . . . : 168.143.12.132
        Subnet Mask . . . . . . . . . : 255.255.0.0
        Default Gateway . . . . . . . : 168.143.12.132
        Primary WINS Server . . . . . : 199.34.57.50

C:\>
```

I entered the host name in the Control Panel when I installed TCP/IP and specified the DNS server when I set up the DUN Phone Book entry. There's no information on the Ndiswan7 adapter because, again, that's the placeholder for any information that will appear if I connect with PPTP, which I haven't done yet. The information on Ndiswan5 is the IP configuration information on my connection—my ISP supplied an IP address, subnet mask, and default gateway. I specified the WINS address in the DUN Phone Book entry. Next, try a ROUTE PRINT and see how it's different; mine looks like Figure 18.40.

There are now a number of new routes. The first 0.0.0.0 route is the one that results from Use Default Gateway on Remote System; it says to send packets out over DUN. The 168.143.0.0 route is pretty redundant; it just describes the local subnet. The 168.143.12.132 and 168.143.255.255 routes describe the local address and the subnet broadcast address. The 224.0.0.0 is an *Internet Multicast Address*, which Microsoft uses for some intra-domain chatter and will actually be irrelevant here; it just gets added automatically.

FIGURE 18.40:

ROUTE PRINT after connecting

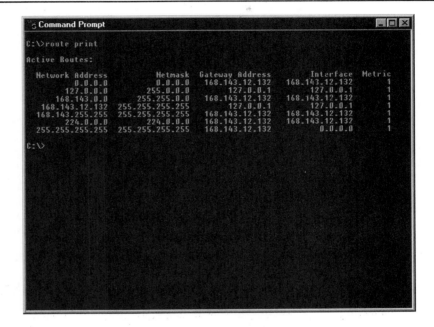

If you set up your system the same way I set mine up, you should now be able to do things like ping www.mmco.com, or run a Web browser and surf the Web. Any NT-compatible, WinSock-compliant application should run without trouble now.

NOTE By the way, when RAS messes with your IP routing tables it can cause some *real* trouble on a system that is already connected to a LAN. See the next section "Digression: Default Gateways on RAS May Cause TCP/IP Problems!" if you're already connected to a LAN, but you plan to dial out with RAS to the Internet.

Digression: Default Gateways on RAS May Cause TCP/IP Problems!

This is a bit out of place, but it didn't fit anywhere else. Suppose you do what I just showed you how to do—dial an ISP to hook up to the Internet—but you're *already* connected to the Internet? Well, you just might find that once you get connected to the Internet, you can no longer access your *intranet*! To see why, suppose I'm locally connected to my company's Ethernet, with network addresses in the 199.34.57.0 network. First, take a look at my ROUTE PRINT, as you see in Figure 18.41.

FIGURE 18.41:

ROUTE PRINT before connecting to the Internet with RAS/DUN

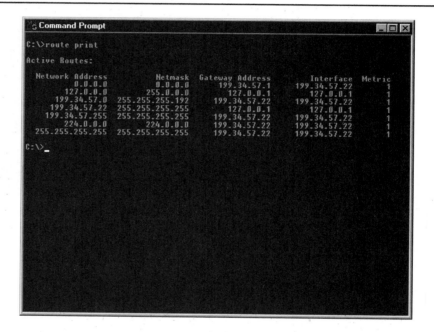

The routes that I want you to notice are the first and the third. The first, the "0.0.0.0" route, tells my PC how to access the Internet. It says to use the IP address 199.34.57.1, which is our router out to the Internet. It accesses it via 199.34.57.22 because that is the IP address of the Ethernet card in the PC. Notice also the third route, the "199.34.57.0" route. That tells my PC how to route to *its own local subnet*. Basically, it says, "To get to 199.34.57.0, just send the message via 199.34.57.22," or, in other words, to talk to the local subnet, just *talk*—no routing is necessary.

Now let me dial up to my ISP with RAS/DUN. The routing table is a bit larger here, as you see in Figure 18.42.

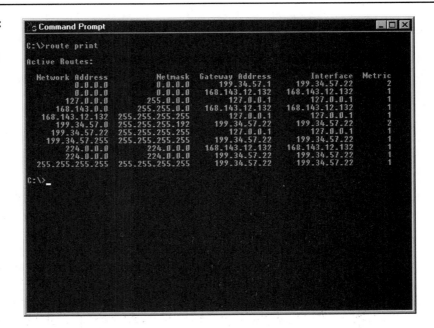

```
Command Prompt                                                    _ □ ×

C:\>route print

Active Routes:

  Network Address          Netmask  Gateway Address       Interface  Metric
          0.0.0.0          0.0.0.0      199.34.57.1    199.34.57.22       2
          0.0.0.0          0.0.0.0   168.143.12.132  168.143.12.132       1
        127.0.0.0        255.0.0.0        127.0.0.1       127.0.0.1       1
      168.143.0.0      255.255.0.0   168.143.12.132  168.143.12.132       1
   168.143.12.132  255.255.255.255        127.0.0.1       127.0.0.1       1
      199.34.57.0  255.255.255.192     199.34.57.22    199.34.57.22       2
     199.34.57.22  255.255.255.255        127.0.0.1       127.0.0.1       1
    199.34.57.255  255.255.255.255     199.34.57.22    199.34.57.22       1
        224.0.0.0        224.0.0.0   168.143.12.132  168.143.12.132       1
        224.0.0.0        224.0.0.0     199.34.57.22    199.34.57.22       1
  255.255.255.255  255.255.255.255     199.34.57.22    199.34.57.22       1

C:\>_
```

There are now a number of new entries, inasmuch as my computer now has *two* IP addresses—the 199.34.57.22 address attached to the Ethernet card and the 168.143.12.132 address attached to the dial-up session on the modem. Notice also that there are now *two* 0.0.0.0 entries. In other words, my PC now has *two* possible routes to the Internet—either via 199.34.57.1 or via 168.143.12.132. Sounds like things are better all around, right? Nope.

RAS cheated.

It's true. Look in the Metric column of the output. That rascally RAS has *changed the Metric value* for two entries! There is now a Metric value of 2 for the 199.34.57.0 route and the 0.0.0.0 route attached to 199.34.57.1! In case you don't recall what that means, it says to my PC, "Well, you *could* get to 199.34.57.0 through 199.34.57.22, and you *could* get to the Internet through 199.34.57.1, but it would take much longer—a Metric of 2—than if you go through 168.143.12.132." In other words, RAS has now fixed the game so that I'll never use my Ethernet for IP communications—my system will always think that talking over a 28.8K modem to my own network is faster than using an Ethernet card.

What caused this? Setting the check box in TCP/IP Settings labeled "Use default gateway on remote network." Now, adding the Registry parameter PriorityBasedOnSubNetwork (discussed in Chapter 14) is *supposed* to fix this— but in my experience it doesn't.

What would you do in a case like this? Simple—modify the routing table. Just type

```
route delete 0.0.0.0
route delete 199.34.57.0
route add 0.0.0.0 mask 0.0.0.0 199.34.57.1
route add 199.34.57.0 mask 255.255.255.192 199.34.57.22
```

The first statement would wipe out any default gateway references, the second deletes the command showing how to get to the local subnet, and the last two install correct routing entries for those destinations.

In a situation like this, probably the best thing to do is to just omit checking the "Use default gateway on remote network" box.

Attaching to Your Company's NT Network

Assuming that you're reading this because you want to access your company's network over the Internet, what's the next step to getting onto your firm's LAN? Surprisingly, you may already *be* attached to your company's LAN!

Once you're connected to the Internet, try opening up the Network Neighborhood folder. You will probably see the flashlight wave around a few times, and after a few minutes you'll probably get the list of servers in your workgroup. Remember when you specified that the primary WINS server as the server on your company's LAN? This is the payoff: despite being thousands of miles away from your firm's network, the fact that you're using its WINS server means that your system will act just as if you were hooked up to the company LAN, except, of course, for the speed. Presuming that you set your workgroup name on your stand-alone computer to be the same as your workgroup or domain back at the office, you'll naturally get the browse list for your systems back in the office.

But wait—what about NT security? Can just *anybody* look at your browse list? Recall that NT doesn't really secure browse lists. In order to get a browse list, of course, you'd have to know the IP address of the WINS server in a company, but that's not impossible to get. People being able to see your browse lists isn't much of a security hole (in my opinion), but if you're worried about it then you can always install a firewall. Where NT gets picky is when you want to drill down into that browse list, to see a list of the available shares on a computer. For example, in my case, if I try to see the list of shares on my server named ALDEBARAN by double-clicking on that server, then it'll hesitate for a few seconds, and show me a dialog box like in Figure 18.43.

FIGURE 18.43:

Requesting a username and password

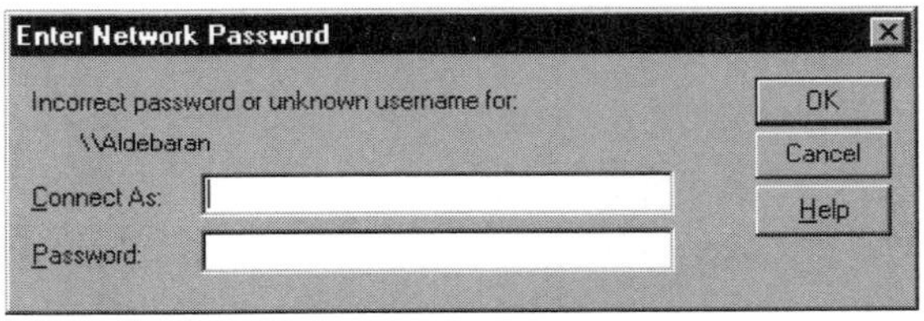

What was going on during that pause? The distant NT server named Aldebaran was trying to see if it could gather enough information to log me on automatically. When I logged on to my NT laptop in my hotel room, I had to punch in a username and password. Since I wasn't connected to a network when I logged in, I had to enter a username and password recognized by the SAM on the local NT machine. (Of course, if you're running Windows 95, then you needn't use a username and password.) I logged on as user **MarkM** with a blank password. The MarkM account existed on the SAM of the laptop running NT, not on my domain back home.

When my laptop tried to get a list of shares from distant Aldebaran, it said to my machine, "Who are *you*?" My machine, named HINOTE, said, "This is HINOTE\MarkM, password blank." Aldebaran is a member of a domain named TAURUS. If that distant NT Server machine had a usernamed MarkM in its SAM—that is, if there were a usernamed ALDEBARAN\MarkM, or if the domain that the distant NT server belongs to had a usernamed MarkM in its SAM—that is, if there were a usernamed TAURUS\MarkM, then the Aldebaran machine or the TAURUS domain would compare the password that it had for *its* usernamed MarkM to the MarkM dialing in via DUN. If the passwords matched, then I'd automatically get logged on to Aldebaran, invisibly. If there were a MarkM account but the account had a different password, then I'd see a message indicating that the password was wrong. And if both Aldebaran and TAURUS couldn't find a MarkM, they'd ask every domain that they trusted whether *that* domain contained a MarkM!

There's no usernamed MarkM anywhere in my network, however, so Aldebaran says to my laptop, "I never heard of you. Give me a name and password I'll recognize." So my workstation popped up the dialog box in Figure 18.43. As I'm a member of a domain that TAURUS trusts, a domain named ORION, I punch in my domain account name, **ORION\MarkJ**, and password, and I'm in! From this point on, my workstation acts just the same as if I were locally connected.

> **NOTE**
>
> In my experience, your workstation remembers this username and password for the entire session. Even if you disconnect from the Internet and re-connect, you'll be able to get back into your home network the second time without having to offer a username and password.

And remember that if your system challenges you for a username and password, it's always a good idea to enter the username as *domain name\username*, for example **SALES\Patricia**, so that the network knows which domain to look in for your account. After one successful security challenge, the network will treat you like a local user.

Going Further: PPTP (Point to Point Tunneling Protocol)

What I've just described is extremely convenient, and I use it all the time to get to my home network from the road. But most firms won't let just anyone connect to their corporate network via the Internet. Instead, they use some kind of device in between the Internet and their intranet—a *firewall*—that may make a logon impossible. How can you allow people to log on to your network from the Internet, and still have security? One answer might be PPTP, the Point to Point Tunneling Protocol.

PPTP is one of NT 4's few all-new features, and, like most new things, it's often misunderstood. The first misconception that people have about PPTP is that it's somehow a connectivity tool. It is not; it's a security tool, plain and simple. But to explain that, let me work from an example.

PPTP is a relatively recent Internet protocol. The concept is pretty simple: just as the common dial-up Internet protocol PPP acts as a kind of "wrapping paper" for delivering protocol blocks of all kinds, so also does PPTP act as a kind of wrapping paper for PPP. Put simply, you want your laptop in San Francisco to be able to deliver some file server-oriented requests ("please log me on," "please print this on the print servers," "please get me this data from the file servers") straight to your company's servers in New York. As you read in Chapter 11, it's not a simple matter for a network's security officer to kick someone off an NT network—not impossible, but not simple, either. Now add the wide-open nature of the Internet, and you can see why IS managers might be a bit worried about over-the-Internet logons.

The whole problem of throwing off-site people off the network is really *not* a problem if they access the company network via a dial-in or ISDN RAS server. With dial-in users, it's always been simple to deny them access to the network—just go to the RAS Administrator program and disconnect them. So it would be nice if (1) people could access the company network via the Internet, and (2) you could disconnect people who attach to your company network via the Internet just as easily—and with PPTP, you can.

With PPTP, your PC sends its PPP packets to a RAS server. The RAS server then unpacks these packets and puts them on the company network, allowing you to use the company's servers. But anytime an administrator wants to cut you off from the network, all he needs to do is to just run RAS Administrator and disconnect you; it's as simple as that. Of course, for maximum protection, a company would have to set up the RAS PPTP server so that it *was* the gateway to the Internet—a PC with a WAN link to the Internet as well as a LAN link to the company LAN.

Getting onto a network via PPTP, then, involves three steps. First, you've got to have an NT machine back at the office running the RAS server with the PPTP protocol enabled. That machine will validate PPTP logins. It could even act as a kind of firewall if it stands between the Internet and the company's intranet. (Another way to make your intranet more secure is to use non-InterNIC addresses for most of your machines, and let the RAS server act as a go-between between the Internet and your intranet.)

Next, on the client side, you'll first have to install the PPTP protocol. You install it in the Control Panel in the Networking applet under Protocols; click Add and you'll see an option, Point to Point Tunneling Protocol.

In the process of installing PPTP, NT will add a new "modem" to your Dial-Up Networking installation, a modem called RASPPTPM. NT will also modify your Dial-Up Networking setup so you'll have an extra modem listed, as you see in Figure 18.44.

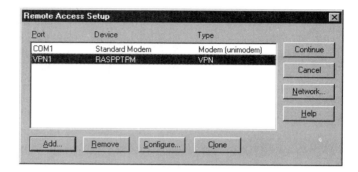

Once installed, PPTP will run *on top of* an existing IP connection. That's important to understand: you do *not* use PPTP to dial in to the Internet; you must first be connected to the Internet, and *then* you run PPTP.

Once your connection to the Internet is in place, open DUN and create a phone book entry. This new entry will *not* dial out on the modem. Instead, it'll dial out on the new device called RASPPTPM, a sort of "logical modem" that activates PPTP and establishes a connection with the RAS server running PPTP. It looks very much like a normal phone book entry, save for a few things:

- First, and most important, when creating the phone book entry to dial the PPTP server, fill in the Phone number field with the *IP address of the PPTP server*. And, as I just said, tell it to dial with the RASPPTPM modem.

- Second, if you're going to all the trouble to use PPTP, you may as well use Microsoft encryption and encrypt the data stream as well.

Suppose I have a PPTP server on my network (say its IP address is 199.34.57.42) and I want to dial in to it from on the road. First, I call an ISP somewhere and get on the Internet, as you've seen in the previous section. Then, I create a DUN phone book entry and instead of entering a phone number, I enter 199.34.57.33. I tell DUN to dial, and I get connected. *Now* let's look at my IPCONFIG /ALL; there's one in Figure 18.45.

FIGURE 18.45:

IPCONFIG /ALL after PPTP connection

```
Command Prompt                                              _ □ ×

C:\>ipconfig /all

Windows NT IP Configuration

        Host Name . . . . . . . . . : hinote.mmco.com
        DNS Servers . . . . . . . . : 199.34.57.50
        Node Type . . . . . . . . . : Hybrid
        NetBIOS Scope ID. . . . . . :
        IP Routing Enabled. . . . . : No
        WINS Proxy Enabled. . . . . : No
        NetBIOS Resolution Uses DNS : No

Ethernet adapter NdisWan7:

        Description . . . . . . . . : NdisWan Adapter
        Physical Address. . . . . . : 00-02-50-59-5F-80
        DHCP Enabled. . . . . . . . : No
        IP Address. . . . . . . . . : 199.34.57.8
        Subnet Mask . . . . . . . . : 255.255.255.0
        Default Gateway . . . . . . : 199.34.57.8
        Primary WINS Server . . . . : 199.34.57.50
        Secondary WINS Server . . . : 199.34.57.50

Ethernet adapter NdisWan5:

        Description . . . . . . . . : NdisWan Adapter
        Physical Address. . . . . . : 00-01-50-2D-5F-80
        DHCP Enabled. . . . . . . . : No
        IP Address. . . . . . . . . : 168.143.12.132
        Subnet Mask . . . . . . . . : 255.255.0.0
        Default Gateway . . . . . . : 168.143.12.132
        Primary WINS Server . . . . : 199.34.57.50

C:\>
```

Notice that now Ndiswan7 is activated and has a totally different IP address. The ISP that I dialed into gave me an IP address on my company's LAN. But how does IP traffic get routed now? After all, I've got an IP address on my ISP at 168.143.12.132 *and* an IP address that the PPTP server gave me at 199.34.57.8. Which is used for routing Internet traffic? To find out, I'll use the tracert command, which tracks IP packets. You see the tracert results in Figure 18.46.

The interesting thing to see here is that this output is incomplete; the tracert is completely silent on the question of how the data got to the 199.34.57.0 network from over the Internet in the first place. Apparently running PPTP on Dial-Up Networking completely "hypnotizes" the computer into thinking it's situated on the local company subnet. For comparison's sake, suppose I disconnect from the PPTP connection and just keep my connection to my ISP, *then* run the tracert to Microsoft; notice Figure 18.47; it looks quite different.

You see here that tracert reports a completely different route. In actuality, however, all of the packets in the *previous* report had to make this trip, as well; after all, the IP packets still needed to get from my ISP to my RAS PPTP server. But for some reason that information gets left out of data reported once a PPTP connection is up. Let's also look at DUN's report for the session, as you see in Figure 18.48.

FIGURE 18.46:

Tracing an IP packet to
Microsoft.com

```
 Command Prompt                                                          _ □ X

C:\>tracert microsoft.com

Tracing route to microsoft.com [207.68.137.9]
over a maximum of 30 hops:

   1    221 ms    220 ms    220 ms  199.34.57.21
   2    250 ms    250 ms    231 ms  199.34.57.1
   3    240 ms    220 ms    231 ms  dca1-cpe7-s6.atlas.DIGEX.NET [206.181.92.65]
   4    230 ms    221 ms    350 ms  dca1-core2-f0-0.atlas.DIGEX.NET [206.205.242.10]
   5    240 ms    230 ms    261 ms  iad1-core1-h1-0.atlas.DIGEX.NET [165.117.50.89]
   6    261 ms    460 ms    391 ms  br1.tco1.alter.NET [192.41.177.248]
   7    240 ms    261 ms    210 ms  331.atm10-0.cr2.tco1.alter.NET [137.39.13.10]
   8    320 ms    341 ms    300 ms  189.Hssi6-0.CR2.SCL1.alter.NET [137.39.69.174]
   9    310 ms    421 ms    430 ms  Fddi3-0.AR1.SCL1.alter.NET [137.39.19.38]
  10    351 ms    300 ms    301 ms  Dist1-SCL.MOSWEST.MSN.NET [137.39.100.58]
  11    311 ms    310 ms    311 ms  msft1-f0.MOSWEST.MSN.NET [207.68.145.46]
  12    330 ms    321 ms    310 ms  microsoft.com [207.68.137.9]

Trace complete.

C:\>_
```

FIGURE 18.47:

Tracing from the ISP

```
 Command Prompt                                                          _ □ X

C:\>tracert microsoft.com

Tracing route to microsoft.com [207.68.137.35]
over a maximum of 30 hops:

   1    171 ms    160 ms    160 ms  annex10.CLARK.NET [168.143.254.252]
   2    210 ms    181 ms    200 ms  router.CLARK.NET [168.143.0.1]
   3    210 ms    230 ms    261 ms  newoffice.CLARK.NET [168.143.15.228]
   4    230 ms    211 ms    260 ms  s0.baltimore.CLARK.NET [207.97.14.2]
   5    210 ms    241 ms    200 ms  e1.mae-east.CLARK.NET [207.97.14.6]
   6    211 ms    220 ms    220 ms  mae-east-1-E02.net99.NET [204.157.228.1]
   7    211 ms    210 ms    200 ms  sl-mae-e-f0/0.SPRINTLINK.NET [192.41.177.241]
   8    200 ms    411 ms    440 ms  sl-dc-8-H1/0-T3.SPRINTLINK.NET [144.228.10.41]
   9    231 ms    320 ms    330 ms  198.67.0.6
  10    270 ms    251 ms    270 ms  sl-stk-5-H1/0-T3.SPRINTLINK.NET [144.228.10.2]
  11    281 ms    270 ms    251 ms  198.67.6.1
  12    491 ms    460 ms    501 ms  sl-sea-1-H2/0-T3.SPRINTLINK.NET [144.228.10.58]
  13    361 ms    361 ms    450 ms  sl-sea-5-F0/0.SPRINTLINK.NET [144.228.90.5]
  14    310 ms    321 ms    280 ms  sl-mic-2-H-T3.SPRINTLINK.NET [144.228.95.10]
  15    290 ms    311 ms    310 ms  msft1-f0.MOSWEST.MSN.NET [207.68.145.46]
  16    300 ms    290 ms    301 ms  microsoft.com [207.68.137.35]

Trace complete.

C:\>
```

For one thing, notice the line speed of 10,000,000bps. Hey, not bad for a $150 modem! Actually, this seems to be reporting the speed of communications within the subnet that the RAS PPTP server is on. Notice that the compression ratios are pretty good, better than you usually get from RAS/DUN. My guess is that there's a lot of empty space in PPTP packets, and *that's* what's getting so compressed. Notice also the name of the modem, RASPPTPM (VPN1).

FIGURE 18.48:

Status of PPTP session

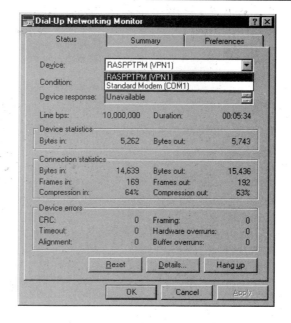

> **NOTE**
>
> Speaking of speed, that's one thing *not* to expect from PPTP. Running PPTP over a dial-up 56K modem can often get you *actual* throughput under 14.4Kbps.

Connecting your enterprise network over the Internet is quite possible so long as you know *how*. You may need PPTP or not, depending on how your company's network security is configured.

Notes on Using "Steelhead": Routing and Remote Access Service

In 1996, Microsoft released a program named *Routing and Remote Access Services*, or RRAS. Often known by its code-name "Steelhead," RRAS's main purposes were to make IP routing under NT faster and more flexible (as you read in

Chapter 14) and to speed up PPTP. It *does* speed up PPTP a bit, but again, don't use PPTP unless you need the security, as you're going to pay in speed.

Microsoft distributes RRAS from its Web site. To install RRAS, you'll need two files: MPRI386.EXE (the original Steelhead files) and RRASFIXI.EXE. (If you've got an Alpha, look for MPRALPHA.EXE and RRASFIXA.EXE.) I cannot give you a specific URL due to the way that Microsoft arranges its Web site, but if you search for "RRAS" or "Routing and Remote Access Service" you'll find the files. (I covered some of this in Chapter 14, as well, but I'm repeating the information here in case you're reading this and haven't yet read Chapter 14.)

The MPRI386.EXE file expands into a bunch of program files and a folder full of documentation on RRAS. (You must be running at least Service Pack 3 in order to get RRAS to work.) Run MPRI386, and you'll see a license agreement which you must accept; MPRI386 then prompts you for a directory in which to save the RRAS files. Once MPRI386 has finished copying files to whatever directory you specified, it reminds you that it can't install on a system with files earlier than Service Pack 3, and asks, "Do you want to continue?" Click Yes, and you'll see the dialog box shown in Figure 18.49.

FIGURE 18.49:

Choosing RRAS functions

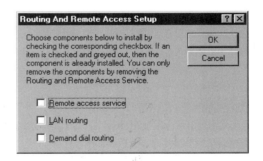

Demand Dial Routing only applies if you're using RRAS as a LAN-to-WAN router, not if your system will just be a simple RAS server. LAN routing enables OSPF, RIP v2, and RRAS's faster routing capabilities. As you've guessed, you'd check Remote Access Server if you need this machine to accept RAS/DUN dial-ins.

WARNING Before going on, I should mention that if all you're going to use the server for *is* normal RAS/DUN dial-ins, then there's probably not a strong reason to get RRAS. It won't *hurt* to use it for simple RAS, but it doesn't particularly help, either.

MPRI386 will then install in pretty much the same way that old RAS does, invoking the modem installer and prompting you to tell the computer what kind of "modem" you have. (Remember "modem" here is a code word for "any old WAN connection doodad.") One way that it *is* different is in the Network Configuration dialog, as you can see in Figure 18.50.

FIGURE 18.50:

Revised Network Configuration dialog box

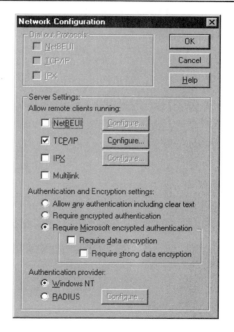

You can see the new items toward the bottom of the dialog box. First, notice that there's a new option for data encryption: *strong* data encryption. You can also require users to use a login-authentication approach different from the usual NT authentication, called Remote Authentication Dial-In User Service, or RADIUS—it's a tool used by some ISPs to authenticate dial-in customers, and you probably won't use it if your goal is, again, just simple RAS support.

The TCP/IP, IPX, and NetBEUI configuration dialog boxes that you see buttons for look exactly the same as with earlier RAS. Click OK until MPRI386 is satisfied; as it finishes it'll ask to reboot your computer.

Reboot and look in Administrative Tools, and you'll see that the RAS Administrator is now gone, replaced by the Routing and RAS Admin program. Start it up, and you'll see something like Figure 18.51.

FIGURE 18.51:

Opening RRAS Admin screen

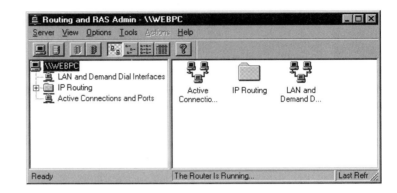

Notice the three parts of the left-hand pane; they're there because I've got this particular machine configured as a router as well as a RAS server. If all you did was set it up as a RAS server, you'd only see Active Connections and Ports. Click on Active Connections and Ports, and you'll see a screen like Figure 18.52.

FIGURE 18.52:

Displaying active RAS sessions

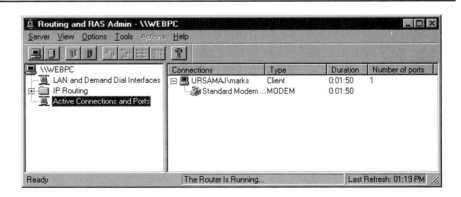

This shows that someone is dialed in as Marks from domain URSAMAJOR. Right-click that and choose Status, and you'll see a screen like the one shown Figure 18.53.

FIGURE 18.53:

Viewing RRAS session statistics

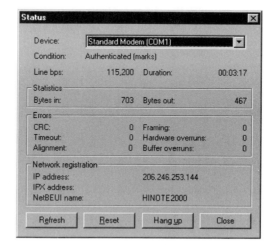

As you can see, it looks very much like a normal RAS dialog box. What's different about using RRAS as a RAS server, then? Not a lot, save for one thing: you cannot use RRAS to grant dial-in privileges to users. If you've loaded RRAS atop RAS, you'll have to use the Dialin button in the User Manager to grant dial-in permission.

Becoming Your Own ISP: A RAS Application

I thought I'd finish the book off by demonstrating how to do something pretty neat, but you've got to understand a lot of NT things in order to be able to accomplish it; it's an application that demonstrates both TCP/IP routing and RAS. Using just the tools in NT, a phone line, and two machines with two modems, I'll set up a network dialing *into* a network that's connected to the Internet, and then I'll set that RAS connection up so that all networks can route to one another. You can see the scenario in Figure 18.54.

I have a C network 199.34.57.0. I put all of the normal production machines into a subnet of that, using addresses .0 through .63. That means that the production machines are in network 199.34.57.0 subnet 255.255.255.192. It leaves me three other subnets to play with, so I decide to open a branch office (well, okay, it's really my house) wired for Ethernet using the second bunch of addresses that range from 199.34.57.64 through 199.34.57.127 or, in network number terminology, 199.34.57.64 subnet mask 255.255.255.192. I have a RAS server in the main office. I want to use an NT workstation in my house to act as an IP router so that I can access the Internet from home on any of my computers. All I want to have to do is to walk over to the NT workstation, tell it to dial up the NT server, and instantly I'll have Internet access.

FIGURE 18.54:

Describing the problem

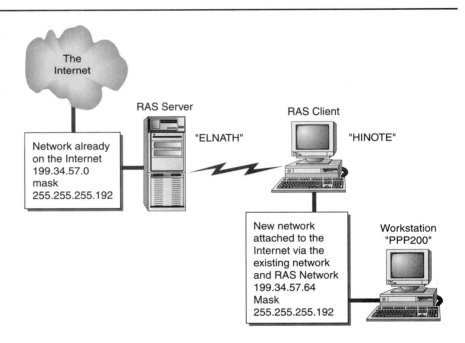

As it turned out, it wasn't that hard. Here's how I did it.

On the RAS server side, I didn't do much other than set up a garden-variety RAS server. I installed RAS Server on a machine named ELNATH. The only parts of the installation that you should be sure to do follow:

- I installed RAS on ELNATH and told it that it would receive calls. I configured it to only accept TCP/IP, and had it hand out IP addresses using DHCP. Of course, I already had IP installed on ELNATH, but I enabled IP routing. (Control Panel ➤ Networking ➤ Protocols ➤ TCP/IP ➤ Properties ➤ Routing, and then check Enable IP Forwarding.) Then I rebooted ELNATH.

- After rebooting ELNATH, a quick look at DHCP showed that DHCP had set aside the address 199.34.57.8 for my dial-in connection. Thus, when the NT workstation called this server, it would get address 199.34.57.8.

- So that ELNATH would be ready to route packets to the 199.34.57.64 subnet once the connection was up, I added a route to its table, like so: "Route add 199.34.57.64 mask 255.255.255.192 199.34.57.8." In other words, I told ELNATH, "If you ever have to route something in the range 199.34.57.64 through 199.34.57.127, send it to 199.34.57.8"—and 199.34.57.8 will be the IP address of the computer on the other side of the modem.

ELNATH, the RAS server, was then ready for the RAS client. But just to be sure, I checked that ELNATH could ping both its local subnet and some location on the Internet.

Once the server was ready, I got the client side—the machine on my home subnet—ready. That machine was running NT Workstation version 4 and was connected to another computer with an Ethernet. Here's what I did on the RAS client machine, HINOTE, exactly:

1. I installed TCP/IP on the Ethernet and established a connection with the other machine. The RAS client got IP address 199.34.57.100 subnet mask 255.255.255.192, with no default gateway. While configuring the TCP/IP stack on HINOTE, I enabled IP routing. The other machine on that subnet, PPP200, had address 199.34.57.101 subnet mask 255.255.255.192, default gateway 199.34.57.100—in other words, PPP200 pointed to HINOTE for a default gateway.

2. I ensured that PPP200 could ping HINOTE, and vice versa.

3. I installed RAS on HINOTE, denoting that it would dial out only. Before rebooting, I added a value to HINOTE's Registry. Located in HKEY_LOCAL_ MACHINE\System\CurrentControlSet\Services\RasArp\Parameters, the new entry is now called DisableOtherSrcPackets, is of type REG_DWORD, and takes a value of 0. Then I rebooted HINOTE.

4. Once HINOTE was back up, I set up the Dial-Up Networking phone book entry to dial the RAS server. I took all of the default values *except* I unchecked

the box in Server ➤ TCP/IP Properties that says Use default gateway on remote network.

5. I dialed up to ELNATH, the RAS server from HINOTE. Once connected, I first pinged 199.34.57.101, the other machine on my subnet. Why bother? Recall that RAS messes with the Metric values on the routing tables when you check the use default gateway on remote system option; sure, I told you *not* to, but just in case... The modem lights should not flash while I'm pinging PPP200, 199.34.57.101. (If they do, then look at your routing table for clues.) Doing a ROUTE PRINT shows that I don't have a 0.0.0.0 route, but I do have routes to both 199.34.57.0 and 199.34.57.64. I checked that I can ping to addresses in both of those networks from HINOTE. Moving over to PPP200, I will not be able to ping the across-the-RAS-link 199.34.57.0 subnet.

    Why not? Suppose QPP200 (199.34.57.101) pings BETELGEUSE (199.34.57.50). The IP packet goes from PPP200 to HINOTE. HINOTE sees that it's for a computer in the 199.34.57.0 subnet rather than the 199.34.57.64 subnet, so it sends the packet over the modem link. The distant RAS server ELNATH then knows how to route the packet to 199.34.57.50. BETELGEUSE and tries to respond to 199.34.57.101. But BETELGEUSE has a pretty simple routing table that says, "If the destination isn't on the local subnet, send it to 199.34.57.1." Now, 199.34.57.1 is our T1-attached router to the Internet. In effect, BETELGEUSE says to the route at 199.34.57.1, "Please get this packet to 199.34.57.101." Now, 199.34.57.1 has no idea where to find 199.34.58.101. As a result, the response to the ping never gets back to PPP200. I see that while watching the modem—the Send Data light flashes when PPP200 pings 199.34.57.50, but there's no corresponding Receive Data light, as the ping never returns. That leads to my next step. Since 199.34.57.1 is set as the default gateway for all of the machines in the 199.34.57.0 subnet, none of those machines will be able to find its way to the 199.34.57.64 subnet except, of course, for the RAS server.

6. As I just explained, the main router for our company knew nothing of the 199.34.57.64 subnet. As it knew no other way to get to the 199.34.57.64 subnet, the router at 199.34.57.1 just sent packets for 199.34.57.64 out to the Internet, where they got lost. So I went next to the routing table of our main router to the Internet and added a route: "Route add 199.34.57.64 mask 255.255.255.192 199.34.57.8;" in other words, if this router gets packets for 199.34.57.64 through 199.34.57.127, route them to 199.34.57.8, the RAS client connection.

7. Once the router restarts, I find that PPP200 can now ping the 199.34.57.0 network. It still can't get to the Internet, but that's no surprise, as the RAS client/router machine HINOTE can't either, since it has no default gateway. I insert a default gateway, "Route add 0.0.0.0 mask 0.0.0.0 199.34.57.1 metric 2," and now both HINOTE and PPP200 can access the entire Internet. Success!

Summarizing, then, here's what I had to do to allow the ELNATH-HINOTE connection to route packets to the Internet:

- The main router to the Internet needed to be told how to find the new subnet; a static route solved that problem.

- The RAS server ELNATH needed a route added (by hand) to tell it how to find the new subnet, and it needed IP routing enabled.

- The RAS client HINOTE needed the DisableOtherSrcPackets Registry entry set to zero, IP routing enabled, and an entry added to its routing table to tell it how to find the Internet. Also, when configuring the IP address on the Ethernet card in HINOTE, do not specify a default gateway.

- From there, just have any machines on HINOTE's subnet use HINOTE as their default gateway.

Now, that only worked because I kept my range of addresses within the range given me by my ISP. Had I tried to just make up a range of addresses out of thin air, then they would have never have work—once they got out to the Internet, the Net would have no way to know how to route them *back*. But if you're subnetting an existing network and want a cheap LAN/WAN/LAN routing system, RAS can do it. But remember the limitations: first, you've got to dial up and stay connected. There isn't any way to tell the RAS server and client to only dial up each other when they've got something to say—even the 4 RAS autodial feature won't do that. And you'll have to enter those route statements by hand. But in a pinch I'm sure you'd rather use a modem and existing phone lines and NT machines than buy a pile of routers!

Well, here we are, hundreds of pages since the Introduction. If you've made it to here, then you've got much of the ammunition that you need to design, install, and build a useful, functioning NT-based enterprise network. If you've gotten this far and haven't actually *done* anything, then now's the time to plug in a few Ethernet cards, run a few Setup programs, and put all this stuff to good use. Best of luck, and, as the Netizens say, "See you in the bitstream!"

CHAPTER
NINETEEN

Using the Best Resource Kit Utilities

- Understand which resource kit tools are most effective for network administrators

- Understand the specific problem each resource kit tool can solve

- Examine clear examples of syntax for each tool

Throughout the book, I've made references to the NT resource kits. If you have the Microsoft Windows NT Server Resource Kit or the Microsoft Windows NT Workstation Resource Kit, you know that they're full of great-sounding utilities. But figuring out some of those utilities can be a problem. In this chapter, I'll take you through some of the ones that I like (and occasionally hate) the most.

One of the biggest problems I've run up against in using the resource kit utilities is their skimpy documentation. Many utilities have zillions of scary-looking options that I'll never have any use for, and in the case of the majority of them, I simply find myself wondering what problem they're trying to solve in the first place. In this chapter, I'll first describe a problem that network admins are likely to come across, and then I'll use that problem to motivate a discussion of the utility that can best solve the problem. I'll walk you through its syntax and a specific example of its use. This material is adapted from a series of columns that I wrote for *Windows NT Magazine,* and I thank them for the opportunity to work from the original columns and include them here.

Background Info on Resource Kits

When Microsoft first started shipping resource kits for Windows 3.*x*, the software that came with the resource kits was something of an afterthought. The Microsoft Windows 3 Resource Kit came with several goofy demonstration programs, such as Windows Fishtank, but few system utilities.

By the time the Microsoft Windows NT 3.1 Resource Kit shipped, the package included three books that were worth the resource kit's price and a CD-ROM that was chock full of applications. Most of the applications were utilities that simplified NT administration or software development, but Microsoft didn't make the utilities as useful as they could have been. Microsoft didn't document many of the applications and poorly documented most of the others. Most of the utilities had extremely basic user interfaces (UIs). And most important, Microsoft didn't support any of the utilities. Some of the utilities didn't work, and Microsoft refused to offer customers advice. Nevertheless, many of the NT 3.1 Resource Kit's utilities were absolutely essential.

When I asked Microsoft representatives why the company didn't support the resource kit applications, they replied that the applications were free—customers paid for the resource kit books but not the software. That statement was defensible because in those days you could download any of the resource kit utilities for free from Microsoft's FTP site. As you'll see, however, that soon changed.

That first NT resource kit set the tone for resource kit utilities: a combination of the valuable and the useless, all with quirky documentation, difficult-to-use interfaces, and no support from Microsoft. When NT 3.5's resource kit arrived, Microsoft continued to refuse to support resource kit applications, but the company didn't offer the new resource kit's utilities for free. Apparently, Microsoft realized that the resource kit utilities were valuable, so the company forced customers to buy the resource kit to get the utilities. If you have a TechNet or Microsoft Developer Network (MSDN) subscription, however, then you get resource kits free.

The most recent supplements to the Microsoft Windows NT Server 4 Resource Kit demonstrate that the company no longer considers books to be the only valuable part of resource kits. Neither Supplement Two nor Supplement Three comes with any books. Of course, Microsoft still doesn't support resource kit software.

TIP   On the plus side, however, Microsoft's license for RK software is quite liberal—you need only buy one copy for each one of your geographical sites.

Supplement Three is a larger-than-22MB file that contains new utilities and all the utilities that previous versions of the NT 4 Resource Kit contained, including updates to some of the older utilities. As far as I can tell, you can buy Supplement Three only by joining Microsoft Press's ResourceLink (http://mspress.microsoft .com/reslink/nt40/toolbox/download/download.htm) and downloading the file. You can join ResourceLink for $70. Alternatively, again if you are an MSDN or TechNet subscriber, then you probably get the resource kits free—just take a look on your pile of CDs and you may find it in there.

However, if you've got to buy it, then it's reasonable to ask, "is Supplement Three worth this price?" Probably. The supplement provides several useful new tools, and I've paid $70 for one utility before.

One of Supplement Three's useful tools is a link-checking Wizard, which verifies that all your file associations make sense. If the Wizard finds a problem with a file association (e.g., if you deleted Microsoft Excel's program files to remove the application and your system incorrectly thinks it can still handle XLS files), the Wizard removes the file association. This functionality might not sound important, but I do so much fiddling with my systems that I carry the link-checking Wizard around on a disk. I run the Wizard as part of my standard preventive maintenance routine on my NT 4 workstations.

Another new Supplement Three tool, Typeperf, is a command-line version of Performance Monitor. Typeperf regularly generates reports containing the values of Performance Monitor counters and reports those values to Stdout. Performance Monitor generates similar reports, but Typeperf is unique because it gives users a wealth of possibilities for output redirection. And speaking of performance, if you're trying to track down a memory leak, you need Supplement Three's Dot-crash. Dotcrash forces NT to perform a memory dump of a running process.

Finally, Supplement Three includes Windows Scripting Host. WSH has been available for downloading for a while, but if you don't already have the software, obtaining a copy of WSH is another benefit of downloading Supplement Three.

WARNING You may wonder why I'm spending so much time describing this latest supplement. Many RK utilities have over the years been pretty unreliable, and as you've already read, Microsoft doesn't really support resource kit utilities. But they update them now and then, and the updates often contain bug fixes. Unfortunately, most of the utilities that I'll discuss in this chapter aren't reliable save the latest version of the resource kit utilities, so I'll assume in this chapter that you are working from Supplement Three of the resource kit utilities.

SU: A Utility for Dual-Personality Users

Let's start our exploration of the resource kit with one of my favorites, SU.EXE. Copied from the Unix world, this useful little tool lets you start a program under the guise of a different user.

When This Utility Is Useful

Suppose you're a network administrator in domain EARTH. You have two accounts on your network: CKENT and KALEL. One afternoon, you're logged on to your CKENT account, your ordinary user account, working on a monthly report in Word. A user calls and says he's forgotten his password and asks you to reset it for him. No problem. You start up the User Manager for Domains. You find his account and double-click on it, only to be told "Access Denied: The User Properties Cannot Be Edited or Viewed at This Time."

Then you remember you're logged on with your user account. You have to shut down Word, log off CKENT, and log back on as KALEL, an account with administrative powers. But, you have a better idea: SU.EXE.

SU lets you start up the User Manager for Domains (or any other application) under the KALEL account, even if you're not currently logged on as KALEL. You can then change the user's password, exit the User Manager, and return to your Word document.

Step-by-Step

In its simplest form, an SU invocation looks like

```
su <name of account you want to use> <name of program>   <domain of
account>
```

In my example then, all you have to do is open up a command line and type

```
su kalel usrmgr earth
```

SU will prompt you for the password for the KALEL account. Once you've entered the password, User Manager for Domains starts.

Suppose I have two user accounts, Mark (ordinary user account) and MarkA (administrative account), in domain ANDROMEDA. I'm logged on to my NT workstation as Mark and want to change my system's time. However, ordinary users can't change system times. To use the TIME command, I need a command line. So, I type

```
su MarkA cmd andromeda
```

I'm prompted for MarkA's password, I supply it, and I get a command-prompt window. Then I can use the TIME command to change the computer's time. Notice also that I used an example wherein you're working at your workstation and need to change identities; you'll also find this useful at a user's workstation. Rather than making the user log off and then you log on, you can simply use SU to open a command-prompt window that has your admin powers in place.

There's no need to log on, and you need only close the window to end your session and avoid accidentally leaving the user's machine set up with a session and potentially dangerous administrative powers.

What Can Go Wrong

SU is a neat utility, but you have to modify a user's rights before SU will work. If you just fire up a command line on a system that's installed with all default rights, the previous examples won't work. The CKENT account (the account running SU) must have two advanced user rights that NT users of all stripes don't have by default: Act as Part of the Operating System and Replace a Process Level Token.

An administrator can easily give those rights to CKENT. Before you try SU the first time, log on to your Windows NT machine with the administrative account—KALEL in this example—and open up the User Manager for Domains.

If you're running User Manager for Domains, you'll need to direct the User Manager to modify the rights granted on the machine you're working at. By default, the User Manager for Domains modifies the rights that domain controllers, not machines in general, grant. For example, suppose you have two domain controllers, D1 and D2, and three member servers, S1, S2, and S3, and you're at a workstation named W1. All are NT machines that are members of a domain. If you're sitting at W1 logged on as CKENT and want to run SU, then CKENT must have the Act as Part of the Operating System and Replace a Process Level Token rights on W1. Once again, before CKENT can run SU, you'll have to log on to W1 with an administrative account to grant CKENT those rights.

If you're using User Manager for Domains, click User/Select Domain and type in **W1**. (Yes, W1 is a machine, not a domain, but that's how you control W1's rights.) Now click OK. (If you're just sitting at W1 and running the simple User Manager, you don't have to click User/Select Domain.) Then click Policies/User Rights, and check the box labeled Show Advanced User Rights. Select Act as Part of the Operating System, and add CKENT's name. Do the same for Replace a Process Level Token. CKENT can now run SU.

Addusers: User Management on a Grand Scale

Next, let's take a look at some tools that duplicate the job of a GUI-based administrative tool but that let you do that administration from the command line—and therefore can be automated with batch files.

Systems administrators who need to create or delete hundreds or thousands of Windows NT user accounts *en masse* must appreciate addusers.exe, a command-line tool that comes in Microsoft Windows NT Server 4 Resource Kit. If you have a database of users whom you want to add or delete accounts for, AddUsers provides an automated alternative to the User Manager. You control AddUsers through simple, comma-delimited ASCII text files.

Creating an Account

To create accounts, you must first create an ASCII text file that lists the users you want to add. The first line of the file must contain the word *user,* in brackets. The file's following lines must each contain information about one user whom you want to create an account for. The user lines need to list the username, user full name, password, description, home drive letter, home drive Uniform Naming Convention (UNC), profile location, and logon batch script, in that order.

For example, suppose I want to create an account for a user whose username is *marty,* full name is *Martin Jones,* password is *opensesame,* and description is *writer.* Further, suppose Marty connects his local H drive to \\server1\users\marty, which he uses as a home directory; he stores his profile in \\server1\users\ marty\profile; and he runs start.bat for his logon. I create an ASCII file for Marty and call it add1.txt. It looks like

```
[user]
marty,Martin Jones,opensesame,
Writer,H:,\\server1\usersmarty,\\server1\users\marty\profile,start.bat
```

In the ASCII file, each user's information must appear on one continuous line; press Enter only to begin entering information about a new user. In addition, make sure that you don't add spaces after the commas. If your file includes a space between a comma and a piece of user information, AddUsers will include the space in the user information.

After I create the necessary ASCII file, I must tell it to execute. AddUsers' /c option creates user accounts, so I open a command prompt and type

```
addusers /c add1.txt
```

AddUsers' Options

You can give a user a local path instead of a home directory; just leave the home drive letter field empty and specify the local path in the home drive UNC field. For example, if I want Marty's default path to be his local C drive, I make his user line

```
marty,Martin Jones,opensesame,Writer,,C:\,
\\server1\users\marty\profile,start.bat
```

You can also create groups with AddUsers. To create a global group, add a section to your ASCII file named *global* and a line for each global group you want to create. Each global group line must contain the global group name, a comment about the global group, and the username for each user you want to include in the group. (The resource kit documentation says you must end each line with a comma, but I've found this comma unnecessary.) I can create a global group called *WriterGuys* that includes accounts for users *mark* and *marty* and the comment Guys Who Write by adding the following lines to my ASCII file:

```
[global]
WriterGuys,Guys Who Write,mark,marty
```

You create local groups the same way you create global groups, except that you name the section *local*, not *global*.

Finally, you can use AddUsers' /e option to delete user accounts. Create an ASCII text file with the word *user* (in brackets) on the first line, and list the usernames of users you want to delete on the following lines. Place one username on each line, and follow each username with seven commas. When you've created your ASCII file (e.g., kill.txt), tell AddUsers to delete the users by opening a command prompt and typing

```
addusers /e kill.txt
```

You can't control every aspect of user accounts through AddUsers: you can't specify logon hours, an account expiration date, or restrictions on which workstations a user can access. You can't use AddUsers to change user information in existing user accounts and groups, either. If you include the username or group name for an existing user or group in an AddUsers ASCII file, you'll get an error message. Nevertheless, AddUsers is a time-saving alternative to NT's User Manager that makes bulk operations easier to perform.

RMTSHARE: Command-Line Share Control

Suppose you're building a disaster-recovery script. You have everything about your Windows NT installation scripted perfectly, except for the creation of shares. Building shares and setting share permissions is simple from Windows NT Explorer, but you want to build shares from a batch file. The Microsoft Windows NT Server 4 Resource Kit's Rmtshare utility lets you create and delete file shares, modify the share's permissions, and display information about the shares. Rmtshare lets you create and modify shares on remote machines, but the tool doesn't work for print shares.

To create a share with Rmtshare, type

```
rmtshare \\<server name>\<share name>=<drive:\directory>
```

The *server name* variable is the name of the machine that the share resides on. *Share name* is the name that you want to give the new share. And *drive:\directory* is the path to the directory you want to share. Suppose you want to share a directory called C:\finance that resides on a machine named *Wally,* and you want to call the share Bucksdata. Log on to any machine with an account that Wally recognizes as administrative, and type

```
rmtshare \\wally\bucksdata=c:finance
```

After you type this command line, you'll see the message "The Command Completed Successfully." At that point, the share is immediately available. Permissions on the share are Full Control for the Everyone group.

You can then use Rmtshare's /grant option to restrict users' permissions on Bucksdata. A /grant command line looks like

```
rmtshare \\<server name>\<share name> /grant <username>:<permission>
```

This command line is simple, but it isn't quite as simple as it looks. The *username* variable obviously refers to a username. But if you're sitting at machine A and instructing machine B to change permissions for a user named *Jennifer,* machine B might not know whether you want to change Jennifer's account in machine A's SAM database, her account in machine B's SAM database, or her domain account. If you're referring to Jennifer's domain account and the domain's name is *Corporate*, I recommend using corporate\jennifer as the /grant command line's username.

The /grant command line's *permission* value can be *fc,* which stands for Full Control; *r,* which specifies Read Only rights; *c,* which gives the user Change access; or *n,* which specifies No Access. Suppose I have two users with accounts in the Corporate domain. The accounts' usernames are *jennifer* and *joe.* I want to change the accounts' permissions on the Bucksdata share on Wally; I want Jennifer to have Change access and Joe to have No Access. I need to type

```
rmtshare \\wally\bucksdata /grant corporate\jennifer:c corporate\joe:n
```

Rmtshare has a couple of other notable options. The /remove option lets you remove all references to a user from the share's permissions list. To remove Joe's No Access designation, type

```
rmtshare \\wally\bucksdata /remove corporate\joe
```

Rmtshare's /delete option lets you stop sharing a directory:

```
rmtshare \\wally\bucksdata /delete
```

And finally, you can use Rmtshare with just a server name and share name to find out information about a particular share. Type

```
rmtshare \\wally\bucksdata
```

to see detailed information about Bucksdata, including the share's path, its permissions, and any comment you've added to the share. Or use the command line without \bucksdata to list all the shares on Wally, including the hidden shares.

For command-line aficionados, Rmtshare fills an important NT gap. If only Rmtshare managed printer shares!

XCACLS: A Tool for Adjusting File and Directory Permissions

You've installed a domain controller with 200 user accounts. Now you have to create home directories for the users. Because you're a well-read Windows NT administrator, you know that User Manager for Domains can do much of that work for you. Your only problem is that User Manager for Domains sets a directory's permissions to full control for its user, which means you won't have access to those directories.

How can you add your user account to each directory's access control list (ACL) without replacing the directory's current owner? You have two options. You can make the change in each directory, one at a time, or you can use Extended Change Access Control List (XCACLS).

XCACLS is an improved version of the NT command-line tool CACLS, which surprisingly few people know about (but you know about it, as we covered it back in Chapter 7). XCACLS lets you change the ACLs of files and directories on NTFS volumes (although it can't modify permissions on file shares). Here's the syntax for XCACLS:

```
<file/directoryname> /g <username>:<desired_file_ACLs>;[<desired_
directory_ACLs>] [/e] [/t] [/y]
```

The first parameter in XCACLS specifies the names of the files and directories whose ACLs you want to change. When you give XCACLS a file or directory name, the tool reports current permissions. For example, if I want to see the permissions on directory F1, I type

```
xcacls f1
```

This query produces the following output:

```
E:\reskit\f1 MYNTWS\fred:(OI)(IO)F
    MYNTWS\fred:(CI)F
    ORION\MarkA:(OI)(IO)F
    ORION\MarkA:(CI)F
```

Two users have permissions on directory F1: Fred, whose account resides on MYNTWS, and MarkA, who has an account on the domain ORION. Each user produces two lines of XCACLS output: one for file permissions and one for directory permissions. The F at the end of each line stands for *full control*. Both Fred and MarkA have full control in file and directory permissions. According to Microsoft, (OI), (IO), and (CI) refer to inheritance information. I can't say I understand what they do, but in my experience, file-permissions lines always begin with (OI) (IO), and directory-permissions lines always begin with (CI).

The /G option in XCACLS lets you specify which permissions you want to grant a user. The /G option has three parts. The first part contains the user's name, such as ORION\MarkA, followed by a colon. The second part specifies the file permissions you want to give the user, followed by a semicolon. The third part specifies the directory permissions you want to give the user. You must always set file permissions, but you can choose not to set directory permissions. The permissions values you can choose from are R (read and execute), C (write and delete), F (full control), P (change permissions), O (take ownership), X (execute), E (read only), W (write), and D (delete). To grant MarkA on domain ORION full control of directory F1, I enter

```
xcacls f1 /g orion\marka:f;f
```

However, this command wipes out all previous permissions on F1.

If you want to add file- or directory-permissions information without eliminating existing permissions, you can use the /E (Edit) switch. If I add /E to the end of the previous command line, XCACLS will give MarkA full control on F1 but will not delete any existing permissions on F1's ACL. If I add the /T option to the end of the command line, XCACLS will ripple the permissions change all the way down the subdirectory tree.

Suppose MarkA is an administrator who wants to add full control for himself to all the home directories located in a directory called E:\Users, without disturbing user access to those directories. He can type

```
xcacls e:\users\*.* /g orion\marka:f;f /e
```

Now, suppose MarkA wants to kick all the users off their directories, because he is decommissioning a server. He could just leave the /E off his command, but then XCACLS would bug him with an *Are you sure?* prompt for every directory. Instead, he can use the /Y switch, which automatically answers all the prompts with Yes. His command line would look like

```
xcacls e:\users\*.* /g orion\marka:f;f /y
```

Get to know XCACLS and it'll come in handy any time you need to create automated backup scripts or perform home directory maintenance. XCACLS is an ACL power tool.

DHCPCMD: A Command-Line DHCP Manager

About once a month, I get a letter from a reader looking for a program that can generate an ASCII text file showing all of a system's existing Dynamic Host Configuration Protocol (DHCP) leases. Fortunately, a tool in Microsoft Windows NT Server 4 Resource Kit offers a solution to this common problem.

The Problem

The DHCP service simplifies assigning IP addresses to computers on a network. After you designate a range of IP addresses (a *scope* in DHCP terminology) on a Windows NT server that acts as a DHCP server, you no longer need to manually enter IP addresses on your NT or other Windows workstations. Like magic, your PCs find the DHCP server, and the DHCP server gives them the next available IP address automatically.

Because DHCP gives the addresses only for a fixed length of time, the PCs *lease* their IP addresses from the server. The DHCP Manager that comes with NT Server lets you see a list of all currently leased IP addresses, or *active leases,* but you can view them only through the DHCP Manager GUI.

You cannot use the DHCP Manager to output a list of active leases to a file. However, you might want to dump lease information to an ASCII file for several reasons: you need to feed information about active leases into your Domain Name System (DNS) servers (the link between the Windows Internet Naming Service—WINS—and DNS can be troublesome); you want to use the information as input into a homegrown network management tool; you want to back up the data; or you are just curious.

Problem Solved

DHCPCMD solves the text-dump problem. DHCPCMD is a command-line tool that lists active leases, creates new scopes, and modifies DHCP server parameters. I'll focus on the active lease listing function, because it's the most useful. The syntax looks like

```
dhcpcmd <serveripaddress> enumclients <scopeaddress> [-v] [-h]
```

Serveripaddress is the IP address of the DHCP server. You must use the server's IP address or a NetBIOS name (such as \\JUBJUB); DHCPCMD cannot resolve DNS names. *Scopeaddress* is the network number of the DHCP scope. Look in the left pane of the DHCP Manager, and you'll see the network number under the server's name. (If you're not clear about what a network number is, see Chapter 14.) The DHCP Manager lets you use labels, such as basic scope, as the scope address, but DHCPCMD takes only the network number. If you use the -v option, DHCPCMD will give you a lot of information through long, descriptive messages. If you use the -h option, DHCPCMD will include hardware information about the machines with active leases.

Suppose you have a DHCP server named Numberman at IP address 200.200.100.7 that hands out leases from 200.200.100.10 through 200.200.100.67, and the network number of this scope is 200.200.100.0. You can ask the server to show you its active leases with either of the following commands:

```
dhcpcmd 200.200.100.7 enumclients 200.200.100.0
```

or

```
dhcpcmd \\numberman enumclients 200.200.100.0
```

DHCP's response might look like

```
1200.200.100.10MYIBM01/30/1998 02:32:41
2200.200.100.11DOODAD01/30/1998 02:47:41
Command successfully completed.
```

In this example, only two computers have IP addresses on Numberman, but DHCPCMD will dump IP addresses for as many computers as you have. You can redirect the output to capture the list of computers for future reference. To save the previous list, I type

```
dhcpcmd \\numberman enumclients 200.200.100.0 >saveit.txt
```

DHCPCMD will save the output to saveit.txt.

DHCPCMD is a cool tool that you're likely to find useful. Just remember that you must refer to DHCP servers by their IP address or NetBIOS name (not their DNS name), and you must refer to scopes by their network number (not their scope name). In addition, I found a limitation of DHCPCMD: I couldn't run the tool on a DHCP server from a workstation in a non-trusted domain, even though

NT had authenticated me on the DHCP server with an account that the DHCP server recognized as an administrative account. Thus, a final rule: Run DHCPCMD from NT machines in trusted domains.

WINSCL: A Command-Line Tool for Controlling WINS Servers

Well, we've tamed DHCP to the command line. How about WINS?

At two recent conferences, I gave a presentation that covered how Windows Internet Naming Service (WINS) and Domain Name System (DNS) work. Attendees of both talks asked me, "How can I delete a specific record from a WINS database?" and "How can I dump a complete list of WINS registrations to an ASCII file?"

The graphical WINS manager that ships with NT can't perform either of these jobs, but a utility called winscl.exe, which comes with Microsoft Windows NT Server 4 Resource Kit and Microsoft Windows NT Server 3.51 Resource Kit, can. WINSCL offers much of the same functionality as the graphical WINS manager, and it provides a few functions the GUI program doesn't offer.

Despite its power, WINSCL can be frustrating. I'm not exaggerating when I say that it makes Debug's user interface (UI) look friendly. To start WINSCL, you type

```
winscl
```

on a command line, and the utility greets you with

```
TCP/IP or named pipe. Enter 1 for TCP/IP —
```

WINSCL is asking you to specify whether you want to enter an IP address or NetBIOS name to identify the WINS server you want to use WINSCL to control. If you enter 1, WINSCL will ask for the server's IP address (such as my WINS server's address, 10.10.10.21). If you enter 0, it'll ask for the machine's Uniform Naming Convention (UNC) name, which is your cue to enter the server's name preceded by two backslashes (e.g., \\WINS01).

After you select a server, WINSCL produces a description of each of its 31 commands. By default, it lists all 31 commands after it completes every job. If you enter the NOME (no menu) command, WINSCL won't display its menu of commands again until you exit and restart the utility. Another WINSCL quirk is that you must capitalize all commands.

WINSCL Commands

WINSCL's two most useful commands are DN (delete name) and GRBV (get records by version numbers). DN helps you clean out a WINS database. GRBV lets you dump all of a WINS server's records to an ASCII file.

Several months ago, someone registered with my WINS server as JOE<03>. I used WINSCL to remove Joe from the WINS database. My dialog with my WINS server follows:

```
Command — DN
Name? JOE
Do you want to input a 16 char (1 for yes) — 1
16th char in hex — 03
Scope — 1 for yes — 0
Status returned is (SUCCESS — 0)
```

Thank heavens that post-SP4 WINS systems can delete records from the GUI, but it's still great to be able to delete records from the command line.

The other useful WINSCL command, GRBV, lets you extract WINS records for storage in an ASCII file based on the records' *version numbers*, the Microsoft term for the order in which they were created. (The first WINS record that a WINS database creates is version number X, the next record's version number is X+1, and so on.) GRBV is convenient, but it doesn't give up the data easily. You get a bit of interrogation along the way, as the following dialogue demonstrates.

```
Command — GRBV
Address of owner WINS? 10.10.10.21
Want to specify range — (input 1) or all (default) — 0
Use filter (1 for yes) — 0
Put records in wins.rec file (1 for yes) — 1
Status returned is (SUCCESS — 0)
```

If this example looks like too much work, you can create an ASCII text file to automatically answer WINSCL's questions. Enter one answer per line for the WINSCL dialog. For example:

```
1
10.10.10.21
```

```
GRBV
10.10.10.21
0
0
1
EX
```

EX is the command to exit WINSCL. Name your ASCII file WINSIN.TXT, and invoke it by typing

```
WINSCL <WINSIN.TXT
```

The text dump process will run automatically.

WARNING   Have fun playing with WINSCL, but don't bother trying to use the CR (count records) command. CR makes WINSCL crash every time.

Command-Line Search-and-Replace with MUNGE

Imagine this scenario. This week, you got a really Good Thing done—you consolidated a bunch of servers. The shares and applications formerly on \\ATLAS, \\REDSTONE, and \\TITAN are now all together on a single monster server with RAID, clustering, and all that jazz—a server named \\SATURN. You're just about done—or so you think—when a chilling thought occurs to you.

The login scripts.

They've got hard-wired references to \\ATLAS, \\REDSTONE, and \\TITAN.

Every *one* of them. All *638* of them.

You pull one up and give it a look. It contains lines like "net use v: \\atlas\pix" or "\\redstone\desktopapp\vscan c: d: e:" or the like. When you moved the shares onto \\SATURN, you retained all of their old names, so the problem is really simple to state. Just edit all 638 login scripts and change all references from \\atlas, \\redstone, or \\titan to \\saturn. Simple to state, but torture to do. This is the kind of repetitive task that computers are good at, so let's automate it—with MUNGE.EXE.

MUNGE is a command-line search-and-replace tool. To use it, you create an ASCII file called a *script file* that lists the changes that you'd like made. Then you feed that script file and the file that you'd like changed to MUNGE. MUNGE makes the changes requested and writes them back to a file with the original file's name. For safety's sake, it keeps the original data file around, changing its extension to .bak.

Here's a simple example of how MUNGE works. Suppose I've got a file called ANIMALS and I want to change every instance of *cat* to *dog*. Using Notepad or some other ASCII text editor, I create a script file—call it CHANGES—with just one line:

```
cat   dog
```

I then invoke MUNGE like so:

```
munge   changes animals
```

MUNGE will then report all of the changes that it made and exit. ANIMALS will now contain those changes, and I'll have a file on my hard disk named ANIMALS.BAK that contains the ANIMALS file from *before* the MUNGE. And in case you're wondering, if you ask MUNGE to do search-and-replace operations on files with the extension .BAK, then MUNGE complies but stumbles over a bug: your modified file now has the extension .MGE, and the original .BAK file has been erased.

Suppose all of my login batch files are in one directory. To accomplish all of those search-and-replaces, I'll use MUNGE in combination with an old batch trick, the FOR…DO command. First, create the script file; call it SRVCHG. We'll need three change commands, so there will be three lines:

```
atlas saturn
redstone saturn
titan saturn
```

You could then use MUNGE on each file like so: MUNGE SRVCHG *filename*. But you can tell NT to do that to a group of files with the FOR…DO command as follows:

```
for %f in (*.bat) do munge srvchg %f
```

This statement finds each file with the extension .bat in the current directory. Then, one file at a time, it constructs a command MUNGE SRVCHG %f, but substitutes the file's name for %f. Once FOR finishes constructing the command, it tells NT to execute the command, and then FOR returns to construct the next command, finally stopping when it runs out of files with the .bat extension.

MUNGE is nice, but it's got a few quirks. If your script file contains non-alphanumeric values, such as if we'd put "\\atlas \\saturn" in the script file above, then MUNGE requires that you surround each item with quotes, so the line would be

```
"\\atlas"   "\\saturn"
```

That's a problem because of case. We'd like this search-and-replace to work whether \\ATLAS is spelled \\atlas, \\ATLAS, or anything in between. When you specify before and after values without quotes, then MUNGE is case-insensitive. But when you surround the before value with quotes, then MUNGE becomes case-sensitive, and only "\\atlas" with all lowercase letters would be changed to "\\saturn."

NLTEST: A Trust Monitor

Trusts can be so hard to keep. Relationships break down. If you have many trusts in your Windows NT enterprise network, you're likely to find that some domains that should trust one another don't. NetLogon, the service that provides secure NT-to-NT communications, has failed. NetLogon communications serve three important relationships: connections between an NT machine and its domain controller (adding a machine to a domain establishes a kind of trust relationship); connections between Primary Domain Controllers (PDCs) and Backup Domain Controllers (BDCs—synchronizing the domain's Security Accounts Manager— SAM—database requires a trust link); and standard, domain-to-domain trust relationships. Any one of these links can dissolve, causing mysterious problems.

Microsoft Windows NT Server Resource Kit and Microsoft Windows NT Workstation Resource Kit include a tool, nltest.exe, which lets you quickly test the status of the NetLogon linkages between machines. This utility usually can't repair trust relationships, but because NLTEST is a command-line tool, you can incorporate it into batch files to automatically monitor machine connections.

To test a machine's link to its domain, you use NLTEST's /query option, which verifies that NetLogon is running. For example, if you have an NT server (or NT workstation) named MINBAR and you want to see if NetLogon is running and functioning properly on that machine, open a command line and type

```
nltest /server:minbar /query
```

You'll see a few messages and finally the "Command completed successfully" message.

Each active domain member should have a functioning secure channel to a domain controller. To check that status, you use the /sc_query option. If MIN-BAR is a member of a domain named B5, you test its domain connection with:

```
nltest /server:minbar /sc_query:B5
```

The command responds with success or failure, and provides the name of the domain controller that MINBAR has a secure channel to. If the command reports a problem, you can replace /sc_query with /sc_reset to try to reset the secure connection. The /sc_reset option might also work to reset a broken trust relationship.

NetLogon also governs PDC-BDC communications. You can find out what machines are domain controllers on a domain with the /dclist option. For the B5 domain example, you can list the domain controllers with

```
nltest /dclist:b5
```

You can get the name of the PDC with /dcname.

You can control PDC-BDC SAM replications with the /repl option or resynchronize the entire SAM database with the /sync option. For example, if you have a BDC named AJAX, you can force that BDC to dump its copy of the domain's SAM and request a new one from the domain's PDC with

```
nltest /server:ajax /sync
```

To tell the BDC to request the changes to the SAM since the last replication, replace /sync with /repl. If that domain has a PDC named XERXES, you can initiate the process from the PDC's side with

```
nltest /server:xerxes /pdc_repl
```

Domain-domain trust relationships get a little tricky. The /trusted_domains option shows you what domains are trusted by the domain that your machine is in. Suppose you have a two-domain enterprise with domains MASTER and RESOURCE. All the user accounts are in MASTER, and all the NT machines are members of domain RESOURCE. You've established a trust relationship so that RESOURCE trusts MASTER. You're logged on to a machine with your user account, which lives in domain MASTER, and the machine you're logged on to is a member of domain RESOURCE. If you run

```
nltest /trusted_domains
```

you'll be told that MASTER is trusted. The fact that you're logged on as a member of MASTER is irrelevant. The message means that RESOURCE, the machine's domain, trusts MASTER. If you logged on to the domain controller at MASTER and ran the same command, you'd get a blank list.

NLTEST lets you determine whether you can establish a NetLogon session with a particular machine. If NetLogon is up, you can use the /sc_query option to test connections to a domain controller and the /sc_reset option to try to repair a link. The remaining options let you examine a machine's link to its domain, PDC-BDC connections, and trust relationships.

Netdom: Command-Line Trust Control

NLTEST is the X-ray tool for domain diagnosticians. But for complete diagnostic *and* therapeutic needs, Netdom's the guy. Anyone who manages a large network knows that although Windows NT provides a broad suite of administrative tools, the tools' GUIs can be a pain. The fact that User Manager for Domains is a GUI tool is wonderful for first-time administrators, because they can leverage skills they learned playing Solitaire when they maintain their network. But User Manager for Domains isn't fit for administering hundreds of user accounts because you can't automate the tool's functions.

One administrative function that has always been difficult to automate is fixing broken trusts. However, the NETDOM utility in Microsoft Windows NT Server 4 Resource Kit can maintain trust relationships. NETDOM lets you build new trust relationships and reset existing trusts from the command line.

Think about how you build trust relationships without NETDOM. Suppose your network contains two domains—TRUSTED and TRUSTING—and you want to create a trust relationship that makes TRUSTING trust TRUSTED. To create this trust, you need an administrative account in the TRUSTING and TRUSTED domains. Log on to a TRUSTING domain controller with your TRUSTING administrative account, and log on to a TRUSTED domain controller with your TRUSTED administrative account. Then, fire up User Manager for Domains, point the tool at the TRUSTED domain, and tell User Manager for Domains that TRUSTING can trust TRUSTED. Refocus User Manager for Domains on the TRUSTING domain, and NT sets TRUSTING to trust TRUSTED. Whew!

Creating Trust Relationships from the Command Line

NETDOM's approach is easier. Like User Manager for Domains, NETDOM requires you to have two administrative accounts, one in TRUSTED and one in TRUSTING. NETDOM sometimes becomes confused if your username in TRUSTED is the same as your username in TRUSTING and the two accounts have different passwords. I recommend using different account names in the two domains or using accounts with identical names and identical passwords.

NETDOM accepts the username and password for your TRUSTING account but not for your TRUSTED account—I'm not sure why NETDOM has this discrepancy. However, you can use the old NET USE ... IPC$ trick to establish your credentials in the TRUSTED domain. Just type

```
net use \\<name_of_PDC_in_TRUSTED_domain>\IPC$
/user:TRUSTED\<your_username>
```

Or you can run NETDOM from a domain administrator account in TRUSTED, in which case you don't need to use NET USE to connect to the IPC$ share.

Suppose the name of your administrative account in TRUSTING is *admin* and the account's password is *swordfish*. If you're logged on as a TRUSTED administrator, you make TRUSTING trust TRUSTED by typing

```
netdom /domain:TRUSTING /user:TRUSTING\admin /password:swordfish master
TRUSTED /trust
```

That's a long command line; it boils down to

```
netdom <info_about_the_trusting_domain> master
<name_of_the_trusted_domain> /trust
```

You might be thinking, "So what? I rarely build trusts." Remember that you can run NETDOM to do more than just build trust relationships; you can use the utility to *rebuild* trust relationships. If you come to work one morning and find domain controllers complaining that they can't establish a link with a trusted domain, what do you do? Until now, your best option was to reboot the domain controller—not a great answer for a production server. Your worst option was to rebuild the trust relationship. Now, NETDOM offers a better solution than either of those: Run NETDOM /trust to rebuild an existing trust relationship in a flash. As a bonus, NETDOM breaks trust relationships, too. For example, type

```
netdom /domain:TRUSTING /user:TRUSTING\admin /password:swordfish master
TRUSTED /delete
```

Adding Accounts to a Domain

One common method for getting a machine to join a domain involves using Server Manager to create a machine account and then sitting down at the machine you want to add and telling it to join the domain. Another method requires you to start the target computer, tell the system's Setup program to join the domain, and enter a domain administrator's username and password. Neither of these processes lets you work remotely, so neither is ideal for adding machine accounts in bulk. To tell machine B to join domain C while you're sitting at machine A, you need Netdom's member option.

Suppose you want a computer named Fido to be a member of a domain named Bowsers. Log on to any NT machine that has the resource kit. Open a command prompt, and type

```
netdom /domain:bowsers member \\fido /joindomain
```

This command line tells your NT machine to find the PDC for Bowsers and create a machine account for Fido, then locate Fido, and instruct Fido to log on to Bowsers the next time Fido powers up. If the machine you're working at is a member of the Bowsers domain, you can leave off the /domain: parameter.

Netdom has one requirement: You must be a domain administrator for Bowsers and a local administrator for Fido. Suppose Fido is a functional NT workstation that hasn't joined a domain and you're trying to issue the Netdom command for Fido from another machine. (I'll call it Mastiff.) The first part of the Netdom command locates the PDC and asks it to create a machine account for Fido. If you logged on to Mastiff with a domain administrator account, the PDC creates a machine account for Fido without a problem. Then, the second part of the Netdom command contacts Fido and instructs Fido to join Bowsers. But before Fido follows your command to join the domain, it must recognize you as a local administrator. You need to establish your administrative credentials with Fido before you use Netdom. If Fido has a local administrative account named *Marco* and that account has the password *polo,* you can establish those credentials by typing

```
net use \\fido\ipc$ /user:marco polo
```

before you type the Netdom command line.

Other Netdom Member Commands

Netdom's member option lets you do some other neat things. Suppose you want to detach Fido from Bowsers. You need to tell Fido to stop logging on to Bowsers and delete Fido's machine account. The command line

```
netdom member \\fido /joinworkgroup bowsers
```

tells Fido that it's no longer a member of a domain; instead, it's a member of a workgroup named Bowsers. (You don't need to give the workgroup the same name as the domain.) The command line

```
netdom member \\fido /delete
```

tells NT to find a PDC and zap Fido's account. In addition, you can use the command line netdom member \\fido /query to find out Fido's domain-membership status. For example

```
netdom member \\fido /add
```

tells NT to create a machine account for Fido in Bowsers but doesn't tell Fido to log on to the domain under that account. Netdom lets you do things from the command line that used to require a lot of walking around.

SETPRFDC: Take Control of Your Domain Authentications

As you read earlier in the book, SP4 contains SETPRFDC, a cool utility that lets you adjust secure connections between Windows NT machines. It's not a resource kit utility, but it's a good one, so we'll cover it here. It doesn't ship with the standard SP4 download (or SP5 or SP6) but only appears on the CD-ROM version.

Because NT is a secure OS, NT machines must perform many authentications each day. On domain-based NT networks, computers must find a domain controller for those authentications. Which domain controller does an NT machine use? The machine logon process involves finding a domain controller; the computer uses that domain controller for subsequent authentications until a user reboots the machine. This link is a secure remote procedure call, or *secure RPC*.

Unfortunately, that machine logon might not be the beginning of a beautiful friendship. Sometimes busy local domain controllers force NT machines to find authentication buddies far away. For example, users at a large firm in Austin might find one day that their computers' domain controllers are in Paris. One long-distance authentication isn't a problem, but if an Austin workstation requires a lot of authentication traffic, that traffic could stress the bandwidth of a slow transatlantic WAN link. The firm's administrators would undoubtedly be happy to hear about SETPRFDC, a utility that lets you specify a new authentication buddy for a running NT machine.

The utility's syntax looks like

```
SETPRFDC <domain_name> <first_domain_controller>,  <second_domain_
controller>, <third_domain_controller>
```

Austin users whose systems are in the TEXAS domain and whose local domain controllers are named *TX1* and *TX2* can open a command line and type

```
SETPRFDC TEXAS TX1,TX2
```

The workstations will attempt to connect to TX1 first; if that connection attempt fails, they'll attempt to connect to TX2. If both connection attempts fail, the machines will maintain their current secure RPC to the Paris domain controller. If SETPRFDC changes the users' connection, it will report which local domain controller each machine is connected to.

Is this utility useful? Absolutely. Links similar to the authentication-buddy connections exist between member servers and domain controllers, PDCs and BDCs, and domain controllers in trusting domains. Under some circumstances—such as Windows Internet Naming Service (WINS) failures—domain controllers in one domain lose track of their authentication buddies in other domains. When such a situation arises, users face network delays at best and an inability to log on to the domain at worst. Suppose you arrive at your network operations center one morning and see an Event Viewer entry that indicates your network has lost its trust link to another domain. Do you start rebooting servers until the problem disappears? No. You just pull out your list of domain controllers in the trusted domain and use SETPRFDC to dial for secure RPCs.

You can avoid this problem by finding each domain controller an authentication buddy on the same network segment; if WINS gets loopy, the domain controller can find its buddy via broadcasts. Or you can use LMHOSTS files to solve this problem, as you've read earlier.

Consider how you can use SETPRFDC. Your domain's member servers, file and print servers, Web servers, and Exchange Server systems constantly need authentication help from a domain controller. If they become disconnected from their authentication buddy, they float around the enterprise looking for a new favorite domain controller. To prevent such a server from connecting to a faraway machine, place a SETPRFDC command in an AT command to force your servers to establish secure RPCs with particular domain controllers.

A Better AT: Three Tools for Controlling NT's Schedule Service

Elsewhere in this book, I describe some features of the Windows NT Schedule service and the service's management tool, at.exe. Three tools in the Microsoft Windows NT Server Resource Kit and Microsoft Windows NT Workstation Resource Kit can make AT even better.

I use the Command Scheduler (winat.exe) more than any other resource kit tool. If you've used the AT command, you know that it can be frustrating to work with. You must type long strings of commands, and if you mistype one character, you have to start over. Worse yet, you have to deal with the quotes-inside-quotes problem. The Command Scheduler lets you use a GUI to implement the Schedule service.

The Command Scheduler lists the jobs in a computer's schedule queue, each job's ID, the day and time each job is scheduled for, and whether the job includes the /interactive option (which lets an AT program display dialog boxes and receive commands via the GUI). Double-click an item in the schedule queue, and the Command Scheduler provides a dialog box that lets you adjust the job's features. Like the Schedule service, the Command Scheduler can control schedules for every NT machine on your network.

I also frequently use the resource kit's SOON tool. If you ever try to do a dry run of some time-sensitive utility, such as a backup program, then you're likely to have run into the "What time *is* it?" problem. Suppose I want to run a program called beep.bat that makes my computer beep. I have to look at my computer's clock and schedule beep.bat for a later time. If the computer thinks the time is 11:43 A.M. and 37 seconds, I might open a command line and type

```
at 11:44 c:\beep.bat
```

If I press Enter before the clock hits 11:44, the computer will beep. However, if I'm not quick enough, the computer will schedule the command for 11:44 A.M. tomorrow.

The SOON tool eliminates this timing problem. It lets you schedule events for a future time, relative to the current time (in seconds). For instance, you can use SOON to schedule a beep for one minute from now, rather than for 11:44. SOON replaces AT, and the syntax is similar to AT's:

```
soon <\\machinename> <delay_in_seconds> [/interactive] <command>
```

SOON's greatest strength is scheduling repetitive commands. For example, suppose I want my computer to beep every hour. I can write the following batch file, which I'll call beepit.bat:

```
@echo off
echo ^G
soon 3600 c:\beepit.bat
```

I created the ^G in the second line of this batch file by holding down the Ctrl key and pressing the G key; I created the file with the old DOS "copy com" approach. Alternatively, you can use EDIT rather than Notepad—there's no way that I know of to stuff control characters like Ctrl+G into Notepad. Because I did not include a machine name, the computer I typed the command on will beep. To start the beeping, I type

```
beepit
```

from a command line. The system will beep once, and SOON will schedule the batch file to run again an hour later.

The third AT-related resource kit tool, sleep.exe, lets you schedule a program to wait for a specified period (also in seconds) before continuing. Suppose you want to schedule a backup of a computer's D drive, and you need to kick all users off the server. First, use the NET PAUSE SERVER command to keep users from attaching to the server. Next, use the NET SEND * command to notify users who are already on the server that their connection will terminate in five minutes. Use the SLEEP command to instruct the computer to wait five minutes before continuing. Finally, use the NET STOP SERVER command to kick everyone off the server. Here's the command sequence:

```
@echo off
net pause server
net send * Please get off this server. It will go down in 5 minutes.
```

```
sleep 300
net stop server
ntbackup d: ... <whatever_options_you_need>
net start server
```

The Command Scheduler, SOON, and SLEEP are three powerful resource kit tools that I use regularly to control the NT Schedule service. Now, if only they could control my daily schedule....

Telnet Server Speeds Up Remote Administration

For the poor souls who remotely administer Windows NT networks, I have a real treat: a Telnet server. Remote NT administration is a great irritant compared with Unix administration. Many of the GUI-based NT administration tools let you remotely administer other servers, but using these tools isn't practical on any line slower than 128Kbps. (The tools are noticeably sluggish even over 128Kbps.)

Consider having the User Manager program on machine A control machine B's user accounts: machine A does a tremendous amount of work to request a hunk of data from machine B; machine A then massages and ships the data back to machine B. This process keeps both machines busy. A better solution is for machine B, the remote system, to do all the computing, shipping of graphical output, and sending of keystrokes back and forth—the same process Windows NT Server 4, Terminal Server Edition uses. Terminal Server, however, is graphical. If you don't want delays and you're using a 28.8Kbps line, you need the simple, text-only interface that a Telnet server provides.

Installing Telnet's Services

When you install the Windows NT Server 4 Resource Kit into a directory, the resource kit's Setup program creates another directory named Telnet. The Telnet directory contains two services called the Remote Session Manager and the Telnet daemon. You install them as you would install any network service: from Control Panel ➢ Network ➢ Services, click Add. When the system prompts you to pick a service, click Have Disk. Then you need to locate and point to the directory in which you installed the resource kit; this directory now has \Telnet appended to it. For example, if you told the resource kit to install to D:\Reskit, point Control Panel to D:\Reskit\Telnet. First, install the Remote Service Manager service, and then, without rebooting, install Telnet Service Beta (Inbound Telnet). Then, reboot.

Put It to the Test

To test the Telnet server, go to any machine on your network, and click Start, Run; then in the text box, type

```
telnet <machine name>
```

where *machine name* is the name of the server on which you installed the Telnet server. The system prompts you for a username, and you must use explicit domains. If Janet is your username, for example, and the domain name is Dorians, specify dorians\janet (i.e., don't just specify *janet*). The system then prompts you for a password; enter the password, and you see a regular command prompt such as D:\Winnt>. Type any command-line command, and notice how quickly you get a response! Network overhead doesn't exist because the remote server does all the hard work and provides you with only a small amount of ASCII output.

The resource kit obviously provides needed relief from graphical tools for remote NT administration. Here are a few suggestions to replace your missing GUI tools. To administer user accounts, use Adduser. To control machine accounts and trust relationships, use Netdom. To create or delete file shares, or to modify their permissions, use Rmtshare. To control Windows Internet Naming Service (WINS), Dynamic Host Configuration Protocol (DHCP), or Domain Name System (DNS) servers, use Winscl, Dhcpcmd, and Dnscmd. To see which processes are running on a system and to stop runaway processes, use Tlist and Kill.

Proceed with Caution

Unfortunately, you'll pay a price for this cool tool: security. Telnet clients pass their text in clear text, so someone could easily sniff your password when you log on. So even though the Telnet daemon is neat, it's not for everyone. Although you could put Point-to-Point Tunneling Protocol (PPTP) on the server with the Telnet daemon and require everyone to PPTP into it, PPTP adds enough overhead to a server that you may end up losing more response time than you gain.

RCMD: Another Simple Remote-Control Tool

How often do you wish you could open up a command-prompt window on another computer, and work at the C: prompt of a machine from across the network?

The resource kit has some great tools that do from the command line what standard NT only lets you do from the GUI. For example, as you've already read, ADDUSERS lets you modify user accounts and group membership, NETDOM lets you change a workstation's domain membership as well as create and destroy trust relationships, DHCPCMD lets you control your DHCP server and scopes, WINSCL administers a WINS server, RMTSHARE creates, destroys, and modifies permissions on file shares, and XCACLS does the same for NTFS permissions, just to name a few.

But most of these tools can only control the machine that they're run on. If you want to use NETDOM to move a workstation's membership from one domain to another, you've got to first walk over to that workstation, sit down, and run NET-DOM from that machine. And you may be doing a *lot* of running NETDOM soon, as it's the primary in-the-box tool for moving NT 4 resource domains into Windows 2000 organizational units. It'd be really nice to be able to run some of these tools remotely.

You've already read about the Telnet service in the resource kit. It's nice, but not secure—as you log onto the Telnet server, someone sniffing network packets could intercept your password. So if Telnet's not your cup of tea, then let me introduce an alternative that uses NT authentication, the RCMD service. There are two parts: the server portion and the client portion. The RCMD service only comes with the server resource kit, not the Workstation one, and I strongly recommend that you have the Supplement Three version of the NT 4 Resource Kit.

The server portion is built as a standard NT service and consists of just two files, RCMDSVC.EXE and OEMNSVRC.INF. You'll find those two files in whatever directory you installed the resource kit to. To install the service, *first* copy those two files to your \WINNT\SYSTEM32 directory. Then start up the Control Panel and open up the Network applet. Click the Services tab to show the network services (Server, DHCP, etc.) Then click the Add... button and wait a moment as NT prepares its list of possible network services. You'll see a new option, Remote Command Server; choose that, and click OK to close that box. The Control Panel will want to rebind the network services, and so (no surprise, right?) you'll have to reboot your system. Before you do, however, configure that service to start automatically. Do that by closing the Network applet in the Control Panel, and then open the Services applet. Look down the list and you'll see that you now have a service called "Remote Command Server." Click that and then the Startup… button. Choose Automatic to have the service start automatically whenever you boot it. *Now* reboot the server.

When it's backed up, look in whatever directory you put the resource kit files for a program called RCMD.EXE. Put it on your workstation—the resource kit license allows you to copy its files to all computers in a single location—and run it. There are several ways.

To run just one command on a remote server, type

```
Rcmd \\servername command
```

For example, rcmd \\IGNATZ dir would open up a window and display the entire SYSTEM32 directory on the remote server named IGNATZ. (Not an exciting example, but an easy one to understand.) As soon as the command is finished, the window closes. Just typing RCMD prompts you to type in the name of a server—do it without the backslashes: IGNATZ rather than \\IGNATZ. That opens up a command window that allows you to type in as many commands as you like, and of course EXIT closes that window; at that point, RCMD prompts you for another server name. A Ctrl+C shuts off RCMD.

Every administrative task in the Windows 2000 world is supposed to be possible from the command line. Learn RCMD now and be all the more ready for Win2K!

AUTOEXNT: Set Up NT Programs to Run Automatically

Five years ago, I ran a company with two locations. Each location had a separate cc:Mail post office. The locations exchanged mail through a Lotus dial-up gateway tool, a simple DOS program that dialed in to one post office from another post office and exchanged mail between the two.

At first, I dedicated a DOS machine to the task of exchanging mail. I later tried running the gateway program on a Windows NT machine, hoping that NT would eliminate my need to run the program on a dedicated computer. The gateway worked wonderfully on NT, and it didn't require a dedicated machine. But every time the NT machine rebooted, someone needed to remember to log on to the computer and start the cc:Mail gateway. This necessity was a pain. I needed an autoexec.bat file for NT.

Now, my company uses an NT-based mail product that runs as a service. Services start automatically, so I don't need to manually start the mail-exchange program every time I reboot. But I still get letters from systems administrators who need to set up non-service programs to start every time NT powers up.

Microsoft Windows NT Server 4 Resource Kit and Microsoft Windows NT Workstation 4 Resource Kit offer the tool that I was looking for back in my cc:Mail days: AUTOEXNT. It lets you create an autoexnt.bat batch file and move commands to that file, just as you could do in DOS. After you create the batch file, the AUTOEXNT service runs autoexnt.bat whenever you power up your NT system.

How to Make It Work

Installing AUTOEXNT is simple. Look in the directory in which you installed the resource kit files. Copy the autoexnt.exe and servmess.dll files from that directory into your NT machine's System32 directory. Build a batch file that contains the commands that you want to run automatically when your system boots, name the file autoexnt.bat, and put it in the System32 directory.

Next, install AUTOEXNT as a service. In the resource kit directory, you'll find a program called instexnt.exe. This program tells the Services database to recognize the AUTOEXNT service. To install the AUTOEXNT service, type either

```
instexnt install
```

or

```
instexnt install /interactive
```

at a command prompt. Which command you choose affects how AUTOEXNT works.

Interactive AUTOEXNT

You must use the /interactive switch to run programs that need to communicate with the user. If you place a program that requires user interaction (for example, User Manager) into autoexnt.bat and don't use the /interactive switch, the program's windows won't appear. If User Manager's windows don't appear, the program is useless. You usually won't have a problem installing programs without the /interactive switch because most of the programs that you'll need to start automatically (such as a mail gateway) don't have an interactive component, just as NT services don't require user interaction.

If you use the /interactive option to install the AUTOEXNT service, you open yourself to interesting logistical and security questions. For example, suppose I put the regedit command into autoexnt.bat. Does the Registry Editor window appear at the initial logon screen, or only after a user logs on? Suppose the first person logging on to the PC isn't an administrator. What kind of rights would that user have from regedit's point of view? And does regedit appear every time someone logs on, or only when the PC first boots?

My recent AUTOEXNT experimentation demonstrated that if a program you invoke through AUTOEXNT is not interactive, the program starts immediately during the machine's startup and does not wait for anyone to log on. However, interactive programs don't seem to do anything until someone logs on. After a user logs on, the interactive program's window appears. I'm sure NT techies have guessed the answer to the second question: Because AUTOEXNT runs as a service, every program AUTOEXNT starts has the authority of the service's account, which by default is the System Account. Placing regedit in an AUTOEXNT batch file starts an instance of regedit that lets any user who logs on to that machine make unlimited changes to the Registry. You need to think twice about running interactive programs under the AUTOEXNT service. Finally, I discovered that programs in the AUTOEXNT batch file run only when a machine boots, not every time a new user logs on.

AUTOEXNT is a cool tool. I wish I'd had it back in 1993.

WinExit: Log Off Those Idle Users!

You adopted Windows NT because it's supposed to be a secure OS. You use access control lists (ACLs) to secure most objects on your NT network, and you prevent users from accessing NT workstations without a password. You implemented Service Pack 3's (SP3's) cool passfilt.dll, which forces users to choose complex, difficult-to-crack passwords. (For more information about passfilt.dll, see R. Franklin Smith, "Protect Your Passwords," *Windows NT Magazine,* October 1998.) Running NT on desktops throughout your enterprise seems like a great way to keep your network secure, right?

Your network might not be as secure as you think it is. Many networks let users stay logged on indefinitely. If you walk around many corporations, you'll see NT desktops that users have logged on to and walked away from. Unattended desktops weren't a problem when networks ran off mainframes because mainframes automatically log off users after a certain period of inactivity. How can you perform an automatic logoff in NT?

You can use WinExit to secure inactive workstations. This screen saver program ships in Microsoft Windows NT Server 4 Resource Kit. WinExit consists of one file, winexit.scr, which you can find in the resource kit directory.

WinExit Options

Right-click winexit.scr and you'll see the options Install, Test, and Configure. Select Install. A Display Properties dialog box will appear. The Display Properties dialog box shows the Screen Saver tab from the standard Control Panel Display applet; the Screen Saver dropdown menu will have the Logoff Screen Saver option selected.

You can change the value in the Wait spin box to select how long you want your network's computers to wait from the time users become inactive until WinExit starts the logoff process. The default Wait value is 15 minutes.

After the Wait period expires, WinExit starts. The utility displays an Auto Logoff in Progress dialog box that warns users that WinExit is going to log them off. Users can click Cancel or press any key to stop the logoff process. The dialog box counts down for a period of time (30 seconds by default). When the period expires, WinExit logs off the user.

To change the length of time the Auto Logoff in Progress dialog box counts down, click Settings on the Screen Saver tab. You can configure three settings in the WinExit Setup Dialog box that appears: Force logoff, Time to logoff, and Logoff Message. You configure the logoff countdown period in the Time to Logoff section's Countdown text box. The text box's value is the length of the logoff countdown in seconds. WinExit accepts values from 0 to 999. If you set the value to 0, the computer will wait for the period you specify in the Wait spin box, then log off users without giving them a chance to avert the logoff.

The Logoff Message text box lets you customize the Auto Logoff in Progress dialog box. Double-click the WinExit icon to see the Auto Logoff in Progress dialog box; the message you enter in the Logoff Message text box replaces the default message "Use Setup to change the text in this line." You can leave the Logoff Message text box empty or enter a message such as "The network is going to log you off because your machine is inactive" or "To maximize network throughput, the network automatically logs off inactive sessions."

The WinExit Setup Dialog box's Force Application Termination check box lets WinExit terminate users' applications without saving their data. When users log off NT workstations, they receive messages from applications that have open, unsaved files. These dialog boxes question whether users want to save unsaved data. The default WinExit logoff process waits for users to respond to applications' dialog boxes before logging the users off. However, users who aren't at their desk can't choose to save or reject changes to documents.

If you don't select the Force Application Termination check box, WinExit won't log off users who have unsaved data. If you select the check box, WinExit won't wait for users to respond to applications' logoff dialog boxes, and users will lose unsaved data. Whether you need to select the Force Application Termination check box depends on your company's policies and whether all your users diligently run their software's automatic save options.

Regardless of whether you choose to terminate programs that have unsaved data, you can use WinExit to make your network more secure. Make WinExit your next system policy.

DELPROF: A Tool That Remotely Deletes User Profiles

User profiles in Windows NT 4 are collections of user-specific data, including desktop settings, the Programs menu, application settings (such as whether Microsoft Word hyphenates words), and the contents of the Send To menu that pops up when you right-click items on the NT desktop. If you store user profiles on a network share, every time users log on to a computer on the network their profile follows them.

Profiles' Problems

These roaming profiles are useful, but they can create clutter on network workstations. Suppose I'm an administrator with a roaming profile and I log onto the network from your workstation to fix a problem. NT downloads my entire profile to your hard disk and leaves my profile on your hard disk after I log off.

This residual profile is troublesome for two reasons. First, it consumes space on your hard disk. Second, it might include sensitive information that I don't want you to access. For example, if I write myself a note in Notepad and leave the note on my desktop, my profile includes a copy of the note. When I log off your workstation, the note remains on your hard disk. If your computer has an NTFS-formatted system disk, NTFS permissions protect access to the profile. But if the disk is FAT-formatted, nothing prevents you from reading my note.

As an administrator, I can change your computer's Registry to tell NT not to keep local copies of roaming profiles on your machine after the profile's owner logs off. If I go to HKEY_LOCAL_MACHINE\SOFTWARE\ Microsoft\Windows NT\ CurrentVersion\Winlogon, add the DeleteRoamingCache value entry (type **REG_DWORD**), and set DeleteRoamingCache to 1; your workstation won't keep my profile after I log off.

But if *you* have a roaming profile, your workstation won't keep *your* profile after you log off either; this Registry change will force you to wait for the profile to download every time to log on to your workstation. You probably won't thank me for making this change.

I need to remove my profile from your machine without affecting the way your workstation treats your profile. In addition, I can't simply go to the User Profiles tab on Control Panel's System applet to remove my profile before I log off your computer because I can't remove the profile I'm logged on under.

Delete Remote Profiles

To remove my profile from your hard disk, I need a remote profile zapper, a program I can run when I get back to my desk that erases the copy of my profile from your hard disk. Microsoft Windows NT Server 4 Resource Kit provides just such a tool, DELPROF.

The syntax for DELPROF is

```
delprof [/p] /c:\\<remotecomputername>
```

The /p option tells DELPROF to prompt me before it deletes any profiles from your machine. If your computer's name is GOLDEN, I type

```
delprof /p /c:\\golden
```

on my computer to remove my profile from your hard disk. NT then shows me all GOLDEN's profiles, one at a time, and asks whether I want to delete each profile. Here's a sample dialog:

```
Delete \\GOLDEN\admin$\Profiles\Administrator? (Yes/No/All) n
Delete \\GOLDEN\admin$\Profiles\NormUser? (Yes/No/All) n
Delete \\GOLDEN\admin$\Profiles\Mark? (Yes/No/All) y
Deleting \\GOLDEN\admin$\Profiles\Mark...  [Ok]
```

Clean Up Your Local Hard Disk

DELPROF can also easily remove multiple profiles from one computer. When I try out new programs on my NT workstation, I create user accounts that I use only once. After a while, my Profiles directory contains a lot of profiles that I haven't used in months.

I could use Control Panel's System applet to delete these accounts one by one, but DELPROF offers a better solution:

```
delprof [/q] /d:<numdays>
```

This command deletes all profiles that no one has touched in *numdays* days. The /q option tells DELPROF to complete the deletions without prompting me for responses. For the easy solution to the tricky problem of removing unneeded roaming profiles, DELPROF earns a spot on the resource kit's Wall of Fame.

INSTMON: Installation Cleanups Get Easier

Remember the good old days when all you needed to do to uninstall an application was delete its directory and remove the directory from the PATH command? Nowadays, application installers don't just create directories and files; they modify the Registry, profiles, and who knows what else.

These invasive installations leave administrators asking, "What exactly did this program do when it installed?" More important, administrators wonder, "What must I do to completely uninstall the application?"

Sure, many programs come with un-installation programs, but these uninstallers are of limited value. They usually don't remove Registry settings, and they often leave directories and files behind. Windows NT administrators need a set of utilities that can spy on a setup program, note every change the program makes, and use that information to undo the installation.

The INSTMON Trio

Microsoft Windows NT Server 4 Resource Kit, Supplement Two comes with a trio of utilities—INSTALER, SHOWINST, and UNDOINST—that work together to completely remove applications from NT. After you install the resource kit, you find the un-installation utilities in the INSTMON subdirectory of the directory you installed the resource kit utilities in.

INSTALER is the trio's spy. Instead of directly running a setup program, you tell INSTALER to run the setup when you want to monitor an application's installation. INSTALER records everything the Setup program does, including obscure operations such as making API calls and debugging output. INSTALER records the Setup program's changes to your system in a non-ASCII file with the extension .iml. The utility saves the .iml file in the INSTMON directory.

SHOWINST is the tattler. It reads the .iml file that INSTALER creates and reports to you the information that INSTALER records.

UNDOINST is the fixer. It uses the information from the .iml file to ruthlessly zap files, directories, and Registry entries.

When UNDOINST finishes, the application is gone, and your system contains almost no trace of it. (The only trace of files that UNDOINST has trouble removing is the application's listing on your Programs menu. Hey, no utility's perfect.)

Putting the Trio to the Test

To try the INSTMON utilities, install a 32-bit program such as winzip95.exe, which you can download from SHAREWARE.COM (http://www.shareware .com). WinZip 6.3 is a good 32-bit file compression and un-compression routine, and winzip95.exe is WinZip's setup routine.

To use INSTALER to install WinZip, type

```
instaler wzip winzip95.exe
```

at a command prompt. (Wzip is the filename I selected for the .iml and log files INSTALER creates during the WinZip installation.) INSTALER displays hundreds of lines of information about what winzip95.exe is doing. You can safely ignore this information as it scrolls by, but if you'd like to look at the information in detail after the installation completes, open the wzip.log file. (You don't need wzip.log to uninstall WinZip.)

After you enter the INSTALER command, winzip95.exe runs, installing WinZip. After WinZip installs, INSTALER terminates, telling you it created a file called wzip.iml.

If you want to find out the names of the files winzip95.exe created and see what other changes the WinZip installation made, type

```
showinst wzip >report.txt
```

at a command prompt. This command will generate a text file, report.txt, that summarizes all the file, directory, Registry, and .ini file changes that winzip95.exe made to your system.

If you want to wipe WinZip off your computer altogether, use the application terminator, UNDOINST. Open a command prompt and type

```
undoinst wzip
```

In my tests, UNDOINST removed all traces of WinZip except for its presence on my Programs menu. I still see a WinZip entry when I click Start ➢ Programs, even though the application is no longer on my machine. The INSTMON programs don't offer the functionality of Zero Administration for Windows (ZAW), but they're pretty neat!

A Resource Kit Gem (BROWMON) and an Enigma (DOMMON)

Windows NT networks contain machines that serve many functions. Two of the most important NT functions are browse master and domain controller. You usually don't need a utility to discover which of your machines are domain controllers because you must explicitly create your domain controllers. But computers become browse masters because the other NT and non-NT machines in their workgroup elect them to that task, and sometimes you need to figure out which computer is acting as browse master. Microsoft Windows NT Server 4 Resource Kit includes a tool for finding your workgroup's browse master and a similar tool for finding domain controllers.

Jewel of a Tool

Imagine that your shop has stayed with NT 3.51 servers and you run Windows 95 on users' desktop systems. People start complaining that the Network Neighborhood is randomly misbehaving. You open Event Viewer and see that your domain controller is refusing to act as browse master. The domain controller claims that another computer has asserted that *it* is the browse master. How can you find out which computer is causing your problems?

Use the resource kit's Browser Monitor to determine which machine is acting as browse master. Invoke the tool from the command line by typing

```
browmon
```

or start it from the Programs menu by selecting Start, Programs, Resource Kit 4, Diagnostics, Browser Monitor.

After you start Browser Monitor, select Domain, Add Domain and enter the name of the workgroup whose browsers you want to find.

In this scenario, you'll probably find that a Win95 workstation has seized browser mastership from your domain controller. If so, the Win95 machine will appear in Browse Monitor. How can you solve this problem? Simple. Either turn off your Win95 machines' file- and print-sharing module or set Maintain-ServerList to No on the Win95 machines. (You can use a system policy to set MaintainServerList to No, or you can make the change through Control Panel by selecting Networking ➤ File and Printer Sharing ➤ Properties ➤ Advanced.)

Monitor Mystery

Domain Monitor, a tool that sniffs out domain controllers, appears near Browser Monitor on your Programs menu, but Domain Monitor doesn't work correctly. If you don't believe me, try the following test: install NT on a server, and make that server the PDC of a new domain. Install the resource kit (or just dommon.exe) on your new PDC. Then, run Domain Monitor and ask it which machine is your new domain's PDC. Domain Monitor will probably give you the message "PDC not found."

Why does Domain Monitor have this quirk? I don't know. Microsoft includes many utilities in the resource kit rather than the shrink-wrapped OS, because resource kit utilities don't require as much quality testing. The resource kit includes some stellar tools, but it also includes tools that just don't work. For example, Microsoft claimed that a basic Internet server tool that used to be in the NT Server 4 Resource Kit offered Simple Mail Transfer Protocol (SMTP) and Post Office Protocol 3 (POP3) services, but I have never been able to make the tool work.

Because Microsoft doesn't support resource kit tools, the tools' users must take the bad with the good. Use Browser Monitor, but leave Domain Monitor alone.

Group-Aware Login Scripts

The basic problem with login scripts is that they're only batch files. As a result, they're no more capable than batch files in general. Folks used to the greater power of login scripts from the Novell or Unix worlds may end up a bit frustrated; fortunately, there are a few RK tools that can help.

For example, suppose you're writing a batch file and want to take *one* kind of action if the person running the batch file is an administrator and another if she's a user. More specifically, let's say that you've got a share with some administrative tools in it called \SX01\ATOOLS, and you want to map that share to drive letter W: *if* the person is an administrator and not to map the drive if the person is just a non-administrative user. How do you make this distinction? How do you tell a batch file whether someone's in a particular group or not? Well, there's no simple tool built into the command interpreter CMD.EXE, but there *are* a couple of useful tools included in the resource kit.

The first tool is called KiXtart 95 and despite the *95* in its name, you can use it to build very flexible batch files on Windows 95/98 *and* Windows NT workstations. KiXtart is a whole programming environment, with a complete programming language with IF/THEN/ELSE, procedures, GOTOs, SELECT statements, and just about all of the program control that you know if you've ever done any BASIC programming. It's also got a rich set of built-in functions, including a function named INGROUP which allows you to write program lines such as

```
IF INGROUP("Domain Admins")  RUN    "net use w: \\sx01\atools"
```

KiXtart's great, but it's not for everyone. For those who are old-time DOS/Windows/NT batch experts, there's IFMEMBER.

IFMEMBER.EXE ships with the Windows NT 4 Resource Kit (both Workstation and Server, as far as I can see). Many resource kit utilities run on a server and so need not be distributed to workstations, but IFMEMBER.EXE is a *client-side* tool, so it needs to be present on or available to each user's workstation in order to work. You *could* just put it on every user's hard disk, but that's way too much work; the easier way is to put IFMEMBER.EXE into the same directory as the logon batch files. (That directory, the NETLOGON directory, is the default directory while the logon batch file is running—ergo, putting a program into NETLOGON essentially "instantly installs" the program, hands-off. Neat, eh?)

IFMEMBER is a simple program; it looks like

```
IFMEMBER group1 group2 group3…
```

where each of those groups are the names of user groups. If the group's name includes a space, such as Domain Admins, just surround them with quotes. If the person running IFMEMBER is a member of one of the groups named, then IFMEMBER ends with return code 1. You can then use ERRORLEVEL to test that, as in the following example:

```
@echo off
ifmember "domain admins"
if not errorlevel 1 goto user
echo you're an admin!
goto quit
user:
echo just a regular user
:quit
```

This batch file looks up your groups and sees if you are a member of the Domain Admins group. (Note that case seems not to matter to IFMEMBER. The next line, "if not errorlevel 1 goto user" says that IFMEMBER's return code wasn't equal to 1, then the batch file should skip ahead to the line "user:." When that happens, the batch file displays the message "just a regular user" and then the batch file ends. On the other hand, if the return code is equal to 1, then the batch file *doesn't* jump to "user:" and instead executes the next line, which is to display "you're an admin!," and then to jump to the end of the batch file. The drive map example described above could be implemented like so:

```
@echo off
ifmember administrators "domain admins"
if not errorlevel 1 goto quit
net use w: \\sx01\atools
:quit
```

There's just one bit of bad news about IFMEMBER—it only works on your Windows NT workstations. For Win 9*x* machines, KiXtart is your only option.

Compress

Many Microsoft products come packaged as a directory of files compressed with some Microsoft compression algorithms. You can tell a compressed file because the final character in its file extension is an underscore: test.txt after compression becomes test.tx_. Why they never just licensed the ZIP or TAR format is beyond me, but in any case there are times that you'll want to replace files in the I386 directory with new and improved files, and that's where it'd be nice to be able to do your own home-grown file compression.

For example, suppose your hardware has a desperate need of a driver XYZ.SYS, and the distribution version XYZ.SY_ is buggy. You do installs from a central, networked I386 and want to make any future installs go smoothly. So you get an improved XYZ.SYS file and want future NT installs to work from *that* driver rather than the original. You should not *have to* compress the file in actual fact. You *should* be able to simply copy the newer XYZ.SYS file to the I386 directory. Then, according to Microsoft documentation, if NT Setup finds both an XYZ.SYS and an XYZ.SY_, Setup will use the uncompressed version, ignoring the compressed version. Now, in general, that works, at least according to my tests. But it doesn't always work—it appears that Setup is in the compressed versions of some device drivers. So just to be sure, I compress revised files before putting them into my distribution I386 directory. COMPRESS.EXE does that for me:

```
Compress -r xyz.sys
```

The -r option tells COMPRESS to create a compressed version of xyz.sys in the same directory asxyz.sys, calling the compressed file xyz.sy_. Alternatively, you can specify a directory for COMPRESS to put the files in, which enables you to tell COMPRESS to crunch up an entire directory:

```
Compress -r *.* c:\crunched
```

Freedisk

This one's useful for us die-hard batch file writers. I'm going to get around to learning Windows Scripting Host one of these days, but for now I know that I can whip together a batch file in no time at all. But of course the batch language isn't exactly the richest tool.

One problem in particular crops up when writing batch files that set up directories, such as perhaps copying I386 from a central distribution point to a local hard disk. I do this fairly regularly when setting up my NT seminars—I bring along a laptop with the NT source files and ask the client to provide a machine for demonstrations that I'll install NT onto. One of the first things I do is copy the I386 directory from the laptop to the demonstration machine's local hard disk. Now, as NT's command interpreter integrates better with the network redirector than DOS's did, copying a set of files from a shared named I386 on a server named SOURCE is simplicity itself: xcopy \\source\i386 c:\i386 /s does the job, no mapping of drive letters needed. As the hour or two before class is usually a busy one, I don't want to have to babysit the copy process.

Once in a while, however, the demo machine doesn't have enough free space on its hard disk. It happens infrequently enough that I don't always remember to check for free space, which is where FREEDISK helps out. FREEDISK looks like

```
Freedisk driveletter required_number_of_bytes
```

FREEDISK then returns either "OK" if the drive has the requested number of bytes (and it *is* in bytes, not kilobytes or megabytes), or "To small!!" (remember, resource kit programs don't get proofread for output). FREEDISK also sets a return code of 0 if there's enough space or 1 if there isn't. The only trouble with

FREEDISK is the unnecessary "OK" or "To small!!," but that can be eliminated with a redirection, as in the following example batch file using FREEDISK.

```
@echo off
freedisk c: 300000000 >NUL:
if errorlevel == 1 goto nogood
xcopy \\source\i386 c:\i386 /s
goto quit
:nogood
echo Not enough space to copy I386 files and do an NT installation
:quit
```

TWEAKUI: A Power Toy You'll Love to Play With

Shortly after Windows 95 first appeared, Microsoft placed a set of cool utilities called PowerToys on its Web site. TWEAKUI was probably the most popular of these utilities. It's a Control Panel applet that lets you tweak the user interface (UI). Basically, TWEAKUI is the result of a Microsoft programmer's efforts to give a bunch of useful Registry settings a nice GUI.

After you install Microsoft Windows NT Server 4 Resource Kit or Microsoft Windows NT Workstation 4 Resource Kit on your machine's hard disk, find the PowerToys folder. Inside PowerToys, find a file named tweakui.inf. Right-click the file, and select Install. TWEAKUI will install, and you'll see a Help file about the utility.

Open Control Panel, and you'll find that you now have the TWEAKUI applet. Open the applet, and you'll see a dialog box with tabs labeled Mouse, Network, General, New, Add/Remove, Explorer, Repair, Desktop, My Computer, and Paranoia. (No, I'm not kidding.)

TWEAKUI Tabs

The Mouse tab controls mouse sensitivity to double-clicks and drags; this functionality is no big deal. But it can also speed up the appearance of your Start menu. You can configure in the Registry the duration of the delay between the time you click Start and the time the menu appears; TWEAKUI provides a nice slider to control the delay, so you can play around with the delay and discover which setting you like best.

The Network tab answers a question I often hear: "How do I get my NT machine to automatically boot and log me on without waiting for me to type a password?" If you tell TWEAKUI your name and password, NT will eliminate your logon sequence and immediately take you to the desktop when the system boots. (Bypassing your password obviously creates a security problem, but you might want to use this TWEAKUI feature on your home computer.)

The General tab provides check boxes that let you turn on and off error beeps, smooth scrolling, and window animation. You can also specify locations for your Desktop, Favorites, My Documents, Recent Documents, and other user-specific folders. This functionality is useful because NT tends to stick all of its files on the drive that you install the operating system (OS) on. If that drive fills up, you might be able to free up necessary space by moving the desktop to another drive.

The Explorer tab lets you control how Explorer identifies an icon as a shortcut rather than an object. You can tell Explorer not to automatically prefix a shortcut's title with *Shortcut to,* and you can suppress the small boxed arrow that appears by default in the lower left corner of shortcut icons. If you turn off your Welcome Screen tips, you can use the Explorer tab to turn them back on.

The Repair tab rebuilds icons, repairs the font folder, and repairs system files. The New tab lets you customize the menu that appears when you right-click a container and select New. For example, on my system, I can right-click my C drive and create a new text file, HTML file, or Word document. The New tab lets you add file types to the menu's list and remove file types from the list.

Paranoia has two subsections: Covering Your Tracks and Things That Happen Behind Your Back. The first section lets you tell your system to automatically erase the queue of recently visited documents when you log on so other people can't easily see which files you've been using.

The second section lets you stop music CDs and Autorun CD-ROMs from automatically playing when you put them in the CD-ROM drive. Removing that functionality is one of the first things I do when I set up a new system; getting a *Do you want to install NT?* message every time I place the NT Server CD-ROM in my CD-ROM drive is incredibly irritating.

TWEAKUI Online

TWEAKUI is a cool tool, no doubt about it. You can take advantage of TWEAKUI even if you don't have the resource kit. Download the utility from the Microsoft Web site at http://www.microsoft.com/windows/downloads/contents/ PowerToys/W95TweakUI/default.asp.

NETDOM 2000: A Domain Consolidation Tool

Let's finish this chapter off with an early look at two tools from the Windows 2000 Resource Kit. Why cover them in an NT 4 book? Because these tools help you get the job done of *migrating* NT 4 domains to Windows 2000.

Windows 2000's ability to support larger domains means that many of us will want to reduce the number of domains in our enterprises. It would be great if Windows 2000 included a generic domain consolidation tool, but there's nothing like that included. There *is*, however, a spiffy new version of NETDOM that can help consolidate an old NT 4 resource domain into a Windows 2000 domain.

Suppose you decided to simplify your domain structure by replacing an existing resource domain with an organizational unit (OU) in what was once a master domain, moving NT accounts from the resource domain to the OU. A separate OU accomplishes much of the goals of an old resource domain, as you can cede control of the OU to a departmental group of administrators who then have local control.

Creating the OU, the group, and delegating the power over the OU to the group are all fairly easy and wouldn't take more than a minute or two. But to make this useful, you must move all of those workstations' and servers' machine accounts to the OU; additionally, if the machines are currently members of another domain, then you'll have to change their domain affiliation as well—requiring a trip to every one of those machines. Yuck.

NETDOM will let you move a machine's domain and OU affiliation without having to visit the machine. The command line's long, though:

```
Netdom move /d:domain_to_join workstation_NetBIOS_name
/uo:local_admin_account_name /po:local_admin_password
```

```
/ud:domain_admin_account_name /pd:domain_admin_password /reboot:seconds
/OU:organization_unit_name /verbose
```

To put a machine in a domain, you need an admin account that the machine recognizes (so the machine will accept being put in a domain) and an admin account that the domain recognizes (so the domain will let you create the machine account). /uo: and /po: are the account name and password for a local machine administrator account, although if the machine's currently a member of some domain, then a domain admin account from that domain will do. /ud: and /pd: are the name and password for an admin account on the domain that you're joining. For either account, you can either use the old domain\name construction, as in BIGDOGS\Joan, or if it's an account on some domain rather than a local SAM account, then you can use the newer e-mail-like construction, as in joan@bigdogs.com. The /reboot: option will then remotely reboot the machine that you've just moved to the domain and OU. Notice also that for some strange reason you must refer to the machine by its NetBIOS name rather than its newer DNS-like name: if you were moving machine lemon.fruit.com to citrus.com, the command would start out netdom move /d:citrus.com lemon rather than netdom move /d:citrus.com lemon.fruit.com.

For example, suppose I want to move machine LEMON to domain fruit.com. LEMON has a local administrator account with a blank password (shame, shame, shame...) and fruit.com has an administrator account named carmen with password ascorbic. There's an OU in fruit.com called Citrus, and I want the LEMON machine account in there, and we want LEMON rebooted five seconds after the command finishes so the changes take effect. The NETDOM command would look like

```
Netdom move /d:fruit.com lemon /uo:lemon\administrator /po:"" /ud:car-
men@fruit.com /pd:ascorbic /ou:citrus /reboot:5 /verbose
```

The /verbose switch helps figure out what's wrong if the command fails. And yes, you must type this for each machine, but that could probably be automated with a bit of VBScript.

NETDOM's syntax basically looks like "NETDOM *command options*," where the possible commands are ADD, JOIN, MOVE, or REMOVE (which add machine accounts, join a machine to a domain, move a machine from one domain to another, or removes a machine from a domain), RESET or VERIFY (which reset a machine's password or verify that its machine account and password are on the domain), TRUST (which creates, destroys, or verifies one-way or two-way domain trusts), QUERY (which retrieves information about trust relationships), or TIME (which synchronizes time within a domain). NETDOM's Help talks more about what those commands do, so I'll refer you to the resource kit help for info—what I want to focus on in the remaining space are the options for TRUST.

In general, joining two things together, whether by creating a trust relationship between two domains or by joining a machine to a domain, requires that you be recognized as an administrator by both of those things. NETDOM arbitrarily calls one of the things the *object* and the other the *domain*. As you've already read, you inform NETDOM of the account name and password of an account recognized as an administrative account by the object with the /uo: and /po: options, and you do the same for the domain with the /ud: and /pd: options. When joining (or disconnecting) a machine to a domain, the machine is the object, and the domain is the domain, which makes a fair amount of sense. But when you're setting up a trust relationship where a trusting domain will trust a trusted domain, then the trusting domain becomes the object and the trusted domain becomes the domain—thus, you'd use the /uo: and /po: options to specify the admin account for the trusting domain, and the /ud: and /pd: options for the trusted domain's administrator.

In the same way, you name the domain with the /d: option and then follow it with the object's name; "netdom trust /d:B A ..." would start off the command to make domain A trust domain B.

You create a trust relationship by adding the /ADD and optionally the /TWOWAY options to NETDOM TRUST. So, suppose you want domain A.com to trust domain B.com, that A.com's administrator is *admina* and B.com's is *adminb* with passwords *pwa* and *pwb* respectively. The NETDOM command would look like

```
Netdom trust /d:B.com A.com /add /uo:admina@a.com /po:pwa
/ud:adminb@b.com /pd:pwb /verbose
```

I always use the /verbose option because as you've seen, building a NETDOM command can be complex and /verbose helps me figure out where I've screwed up if it didn't work. You can build two-way trusts by just adding the /TWOWAY command, and of course, in that case it doesn't matter which domain is the object and which is the domain:

```
Netdom trust /d:B.com A.com /add /uo:admina@a.com /po:pwa
/ud:adminb@b.com /pd:pwb /verbose /twoway
```

You break a trust relationship by replacing the /add option with the /remove option. If you've created a two-way trust, then you need to include the /twoway option when breaking it, as in this example:

```
Netdom trust /d:B.com A.com /remove /uo:admina@a.com /po:pwa
/ud:adminb@b.com /pd:pwb /verbose /twoway
```

In the world of Windows 2000, we hopefully can reduce the number of trust relationships in our enterprise—but as long as we've still got any trusts at all, NETDOM's invaluable.

Movetree: An Active Directory Restructuring Tool

Sometimes it seems that I never design anything right the first time. That's why I like MOVETREE. MOVETREE is a command-line tool that lets you move user accounts, computer accounts, groups or organizational units from one domain in an Active Directory forest to another domain *in the same forest.*

MOVETREE's syntax, abbreviated, looks like

Movetree *operation* /s *source DC* /d *destination DC* /sdn *name and location of object to move* /ddn *destination address and name*

The *operation* field is either /check, /start, or /continue. /Check does a test run to see if your syntax makes sense and if you have the permissions to do whatever it is that you're trying to do. Remember that you're moving an object from one domain to another, so you need to first log in with an account recognized as an administrator in both domains. In my experience, the /check option won't catch all problems; I've run /check and been told that all is well, only to actually run MOVETREE in "do it for real" mode and have MOVETREE fail. The /start option is "do it for real" mode, as you've probably guessed. And /continue restarts MOVETREE if it got partially through an operation and then ran up against a problem. Rather than starting from scratch, running a MOVETREE /continue lets MOVETREE deal with starting from a partially-completed move.

The source DC and destination DC are just the DNS names of a DC from the source and destination domains, as the name suggests. Thus, for example, suppose I'm running the pepsi.com and tacobell.com domains, and the tacobell.com domain has an organizational unit named *gorditas* that does marketing for part of the product line. Now suppose that Pepsi wants to centralize all of the marketing folks in all of the divisions—including Taco Bell—into the pepsi.com domain. The first bits of information we'll need to build a command are the names of one of the pepsi.com DCs and one of the tacobell.com DCs; suppose they are pepsgen .pepsi.com and bigbell.tacobell.com.

Next, we'll need to tell MOVETREE that the thing that it's moving is an OU named *gorditas* in tacobell.com. We want to end up with an OU named *gorditas* inside pepsi.com. /sdn (source *distinguished name*, explained in a minute) is the option that you use to specify the thing that you're moving, and /ddn (destination distinguished name) is the option that you use to say where it should end up. The tricky part is writing an "OU named gorditas in tacobell.com" in a format known as a distinguished name. It looks like this: ou=gorditas,dc=tacobell, dc=com. OU refers to an organizational unit, of course. DC is *device context* and you use as many of them as are necessary to express the parts of the DNS name: downtown.acme.com would look like dc=downtown,dc=acme,dc=com. Things that aren't OUs or parts of the DNS name use CN,common name. User accounts, groups, and non-OU folders (like Users or Computers) use CNs. The ddn for an account named *sue* inside the Users folder of tacobell.com would then be cn=sue,cn=Users,dc=tacobell,dc=com.

To move gorditas from tacobell.com to pepsi.com

```
Movetree /start /d pepsigen.pepsi.com /s bigbell.tacobell.com
/sdn ou=gorditas,dc=tacobell,dc=com /ddn ou=gorditas,dc=pepsi
,dc=com
```

Here's another example. Suppose I want to move Larry's account from an OU named burritos in tacobell.com to the Users folder in pepsi.com:

```
Movetree /start /d pepsigen.pepsi.com /s bigbell.tacobell.com
/sdn cn=larry,ou=burritos,dc=tacobell,dc=com /ddn cn=larry
,cn=users,dc=pepsi,dc=com
```

It's got a few limitations, unfortunately. You can't use MOVETREE to consolidate users, computers, or OUs from one forest to another, unfortunately. You also can't move groups unless you're also moving all of the group's members—if you move a group from domain A to domain B, but that group has members from domain A whose user accounts are not also moving to domain B, then MOVETREE won't be able to move the group. And, while the MOVETREE documentation doesn't warn you, MOVETREE seems to only work on AD domains running in native mode—that is, with no NT 4 domain controllers.

Windows 2000 Server Preview

- Getting ready for 2000

- Microsoft's overall goals for Windows 2000

- Specific new capabilities and features

- Making Windows 2000/NT more enterprising

- Modernizing NT

- Lowering TCO and warming administrators' hearts

- Bad news

Congratulations, you made it through a book this big! Quite an impressive feat. But now I'm afraid I have some bad news: soon, you'll have to start learning how to use NT, all over again. Because it won't *be* NT 4.

You probably know what I'm talking about—the *next* version of NT. I first heard Bill Gates talk about it in April 1992, when he predicted a day not far off (1995 was the original projected ship date that I heard about) when we'd have a version of NT code-named Cairo that had a cool object-oriented GUI, an "object file system" that would let you disconnect the physical location of resources from the names of those resources, the ability to support millions of user accounts, disk space quotas, Plug and Play and more. NT 4 got *some* of that—the GUI Bill was talking about is the Windows 95/98/NT 4 desktop—but the rest arrives with Windows 2000. The "object file system" became the "distributed file system," and disk quotas and Plug and Play as well as lots more all found their way into a product originally called NT 5 but eventually renamed to Windows 2000.

So what took so long? Was it worth the wait? For many, the answer will be "yes." Much of NT's foundation—the internal kernel structure, how drivers are designed, how Windows 2000 multitasks—hasn't changed all that terribly much from NT 4, but network professionals really don't see that part of NT. Instead, we network types will notice that the *above-ground* structures, the tools built atop the foundation, are so different as to render Windows 2000 Server almost unrecognizable as a descendant of NT 3.*x* and 4.*x*. For comparison's sake, and to extend the structural metaphor, think of using 1994's Windows NT 3.1 Advanced Server as renting a room in someone's basement, using NT 4 as renting a 2-bedroom apartment, and using Windows 2000 Server as living in Bill Gates's new mansion on Puget Sound: more rooms than anyone can count all filled with new and wonderful electronic gadgets.

In the mansion, many of the things that you know from the basement room are unchanged—the electricity comes out of sockets in the wall, the pipes are copper or PVC, bathrooms have sinks and commodes in them—but there's so much more of it all, as well as so many new things, both useful ("Hey, cool, a garden, and automatic sprinklers for it!") and of debatable value ("What does this bidet thing do, anyway?"). That's not to say that NT's underpinnings will never change, not at all—the next (and still-unnamed) version of NT will go a step further, digging up NT's 32-bit foundation and replacing it with a 64-bit one.

The main point, however, is this: If you're an NT network administrator, be prepared for culture shock. The difference between NT 4 and Windows 2000 is at least 10 times as great as the difference between NT 3.1 and NT 4. And if you've never worked with NT in any flavor, be prepared to find Windows 2000 both delightful and frustrating—as is the case with most Microsoft software.

   I can't tell you everything that you'll need to know about Windows 2000 in just one chapter, it wouldn't fit. (And besides, it just so happens that I've got this book coming out soon....) What I'd like to do here in our valedictory chapter is to briefly discuss the big picture and what Microsoft's trying to accomplish; then I'll move along to those new features and, finally, take a look at a few of Windows 2000's shortcomings.

Microsoft's Overall Goals for Windows 2000

The changes in Windows 2000 from NT 4 are quite significant, but they were long in coming. What was the wait all about?

Make NT an Enterprise OS

Microsoft wants your company to shut off its mainframes and do your firm's work on big servers running NT. That's why there is a version of Windows 2000 Server called Datacenter Server. Microsoft is also hoping that "enterprise" customers will exploit new Windows 2000 Server facilities such as Active Directory and Microsoft Application Server (nee MTS) and COM+ to write gobs of new and hardware-hungry distributed applications. Before they can accomplish that, however, they need to clear three hurdles: reliability, availability, and scalability.

NT Must Be More Reliable

Since their appearance in the late '70s, microcomputer-based network operating systems have been seen as fundamentally different from "big-system" OSes like IBM's MVS and OS/400, Compaq's Open VMS, and the myriad flavors of Unix. PC-based network operating systems weren't exactly seen as toys, but neither were they seen as something that one would base one's business on, if one's business was truly critical. For example, it's hard to imagine the New York Stock Exchange announcing that they'd decided to get rid of their current trading system and to replace it with a NetWare 4.1 or NT 4-based client-server system. PC-based stuff just wasn't (and largely still isn't) seen as sufficiently reliable yet to take on the big guys.

Nor is that an unfair assessment. Most of us would be a bit uncomfortable about discovering in midflight that the state-of-the-art airliner taking us across the Pacific was run by NT, or that the Social Security Administration had decided to dump their old mainframe-based software in favor of a Lotus Notes–based system running atop NT. Years ago, many firms discovered that NT servers crashed far less often if rebooted weekly; it's hard to imagine running a heart-and-lung machine on something like that.

But Microsoft wants to shed that image. They want very much to build an OS that is sufficiently industrial-strength in reliability so that one day it wouldn't be silly to suggest that AT&T's long distance network could run atop some future version of NT, Windows 2000-something. With Windows 2000, Microsoft believes that they've taken some steps in that direction.

NT Must Be More Available

A server that is being rebooted to change some parameters is just as down as one that is being rebooted after a Blue Screen Of Death, the symptom of a system crash that is all too familiar to NT 4 veterans. Many Windows 2000 parameters can be changed without a reboot where a change to the corresponding parameter in Windows NT 4 would require one. Unfortunately, in my experience many common parameter changes still require a reboot.

NT Must Be Able to "Scale" to Use Big Computers

Reliability's not the only big-network issue that Microsoft faces. The other one is the limit on the raw power that NT can use—to use a word that the PC industry created a few years ago; NT must be more *scalable*.

Being an "enterprise" operating system requires two different kinds of scalability which are somewhat at odds with each other: performance scalability and administrative scalability. The first asks, "If I need to do more work with NT, can I just run it on a bigger computer?" The second asks, "If I need to support more users/computers/gigabytes of hard disk/etc., can I do it without hiring more administrators?"

Performance Scalability CPUs are simply not getting all that much faster in terms of the things they can do. To create faster or higher-capacity computers, then, computer manufacturers have been putting more and more CPUs into a box. And while NT has in theory been designed to use up to 32 processors since its first incarnation, in reality, very few people have been able to get any use out of more than four processors. With Windows 2000, Microsoft claims to have improved the scalability of NT—although I've not yet heard anyone say with a straight face that Windows 2000 will "run like a top" on a 32-processor system.

The three versions of Server support different numbers of CPUs. Windows 2000 Server supports four processors, Windows 2000 Advanced Server supports eight, and Windows 2000 Datacenter Server supports 32 processors.

Besides the ability to use a larger number of CPUs, there were internal restrictions within Windows NT, such as the number of users that a SAM database would allow, that simply had to go. With Active Directory, many restrictions, including this one, have been removed.

NOTE   Oh, and if you're looking in your Webster's for a definition of *scalability,* don't bother; it's not a real word. Microsoft made it up a few years ago. Basically, *scalable* roughly means, "As the job's demands grow, you can meet them by throwing in more hardware—processors and memory—and the system will meet the needs." It's become an issue because, while NT has theoretically supported 32 processors since its inception, much of the basic NT operating system itself can't use many processors—for example, adding a ninth processor to an eight-processor domain controller won't produce any faster logins. That's also true of NT programs; depending on whom you ask, SQL Server maxes out at four or eight processors. Beyond that, adding more processors does nothing more than run up the electric bill.

Administrative Scalability/Manageability Large enterprises do not like to add headcount in their core business areas, much less just to administer Windows NT. Windows 2000 Server contains a number of facilities such as Intellimirror, designed to allow customers to support more users running with more complex desktop environments with fewer support personnel. Microsoft typically refers to this area as "Manageability," though I think "Administrative Scalability" better captures the flavor of the topic.

In this area, one of the most important additions to Windows 2000 is its support for both issuing and honoring digital certificates in place of user IDs and passwords for identification and authentication. The overall system needed to manage the life cycles of digital certificates and verify their authenticity and current validity is called Public Key Infrastructure (PKI). PKI-based security is both more secure and vastly more administratively scalable than user ID + password-based security, but it is also much, much more technically complex.

Modernize NT

Three years can be an awfully long time in the computer business. The years since 1996 have seen the emergence of Universal Serial Bus, IEEE 1394, Fiber Channel, and 3-D video cards, just to name a few areas of technological growth, as well as the introduction of hundreds of new network cards, video boards, sound cards, SCSI host adapters, and so on. A new crop of network-aware PCs has appeared, PCs that understand networking right in their BIOSes and that are designed to be taken straight out of the box without anything on their hard drives, plugged into the network, and started up from the network rather than from any on-disk software. And on a more mundane note, nearly every PC sold in the past five years supports a hardware system called Plug and Play (PnP).

NT supports none of these things right out of the box. Some of these devices can be made to work, but some can't. Hardware support has always been something of an afterthought in NT, and it's amazing that Microsoft shipped NT 4 without any Plug-and-Play support save an undocumented driver that could *sometimes* make a PnP ISA board work but that more commonly simply rendered a system unusable. NT 4's offhand support of PC Card laptops and its near-complete lack of support for Cardbus slots forced many an NT-centric shop to put NT Server on their servers, NT Workstation on their corporate desktops…and Windows 95 on their laptops.

One of Windows 2000's goals, then—and an essential one—is to support the new types of hardware and greatly improve the way that it works on laptops.

Make NT Easier to Support

The past 10 years have seen the rise of the graphical user interface (GUI), which brought a basically uniform "look and feel" to PC applications and made learning a PC application and PCs in general so much easier for users. We've seen programming tools go from some very simple development environments that crashed more often than they worked to today's very stable 32-bit suite of programming tools, making it possible for developers to create large and powerful 32-bit applications. Users and developers are better off—sounds good, doesn't it?

Well, it is, for them. But many of us fall into a third category: support staff. And while some things have gotten better—the graphical nature of many of NT's administrative tools helped get many new admins started on a networking career—the actual job of support hasn't gotten any easier. Consider this: Would you rather rebuild a CONFIG.SYS file to stitch back together a damaged DOS machine from memory, or would you prefer to pick through a broken Registry trying to figure out what's ailing it?

Microsoft's competition knew that support was the Achilles' heel of both Windows and NT, and so in the mid-'90s, Sun and others began extolling the importance of considering the Total Cost of Ownership (TCO) of any desktop system. It wasn't hard to make the argument that the biggest cost of putting Windows on a desktop isn't the hardware or the software—it's the staff hours required to get it up and keep it running.

With Windows 2000, Microsoft starts to reduce desktop TCO. A group of Windows 2000 improvements called Change and Configuration Management tools makes life easier for support folks and network administrators in general. But you'll pay a price for that: most TCO enhancements only work if you've got Windows 2000 running on your workstations as well as your servers.

Specific New Capabilities and Features

So much for the good intentions. What about the new goodies?

Microsoft lists pages and pages of enhancements to Windows 2000—the PR people have, after all, had over three years to cook up those lists. I'm sure they're all of value to someone, but here are the things that I find most valuable in Windows 2000, arranged according to my three earlier categories—making NT more enterprise ready, modernizing NT, and improving its administrative tools/ lowering TCO.

Making Windows 2000/NT More "Enterprising"

Several functions help push NT's latest incarnation to a place in the big leagues. In particular, the most significant "big network" changes to NT include:

- Active Directory
- Improved TCP/IP-based networking infrastructure
- More scalable security infrastructure options
- More powerful file sharing with the Distributed File System and the File Replication Service
- Freedom from drive letters with junction points and mountable drives
- More flexible online storage via the Removable Storage Manager

The biggest and most significant of these changes is Active Directory, so first I'll take that up in a fairly long section, then I'll consider the other new benefits.

Active Directory

The crown jewel of Windows 2000, Active Directory is also the single most pervasive piece of the OS. Many of the compelling features of Windows 2000 simply cannot function without Active Directory. Group policies, domain trees and forests, centralized deployment of applications, and the best features of the Distributed File System (to name a few) will not operate until you've got a system acting as an Active Directory server.

What does Active Directory mean for those of us who've been working with NT domains, trust relationships, and the like since 1993? Are things all that different?

How Active Directory Affects Existing One-Domain Enterprises

Well, let's first get the easy part of the answer out of the way: if your firm currently runs a single-domain NT enterprise, or even just a bunch of NT servers in a workgroup without a domain, then no, Active Directory won't change your life all that much. You'll probably choose to remain as one domain. You'll still create user accounts, albeit with a different tool than User Manager for Domains. There are still user groups, file permissions, and the like. You may have to learn a thing or two about DNS if you've never done anything with it, but even then a small network can get away with a fair amount of DNS ignorance with impunity. You *will* have to learn a lot of new management tools—as I just suggested, the User Manager for Domains is dead and is largely replaced by a thing called Active Directory Users and Groups or "the DSA"—Directory Services Administrator—and you'll likely have to buy new servers, as Windows 2000 requires some horsepower (350MHz Pentium II and 256MB RAM *minimum* for a domain controller), but that's about it.

How Active Directory Affects Multi-Domain Enterprises

For many NT 4 users, even the vaguest outlines of AD's capabilities sound like manna from heaven. Bigger domains and more flexible domain structures—it all sounds great.

But how much new stuff will you have to learn? Is it true that "everything that you know is wrong?" Well, some things are very different, yes. But they're rooted in what you already know.

Windows 2000 Still Has Domains

First of all, Windows 2000 still has domains, and in many ways they still look like NT 4 domains. Where NT 4 stored information about user and machine accounts in a file named SAM, Windows 2000 stores that—and much else—in a file called NTDS.DIT. Under NT 4, a user in a multi-domain environment had to identify both herself and the name of the domain whose SAM contained her user account. That's still true under Windows 2000, but it gets a bit easier, as Windows 2000 has a database called the *global catalog* that knows every user and what domain she's from. The GC knows every user by a name called User Principal Name, or UPN. A UPN looks like an e-mail address—joeblow@acme.com. A user can then either decide to log in as "Joe from domain sales.acme.com," in which case his workstation will contact a domain controller from domain sales.acme.com, or he could log in as joe@acme.com, which would prompt his workstation to ask the GC what domain joe@acme.com belongs to. The GC would respond that he's from sales.acme.com, and the workstation would then contact a domain controller from sales.acme.com to get the information that it needs to log Joe in.

Notice another thing about domains: where NT 4 had domains with 15-character names, Windows 2000 uses DNS-style naming for domains—but more about that in a minute.

Windows 2000 Domains Can Be Bigger

You can fit about 5,000 user accounts comfortably in an NT 4 domain, forcing large enterprises to create multiple domains in order to accommodate all of their user accounts; such a domain design was called a *multi-master* model. In contrast, a Windows 2000 domain can fit 1.5 million users (or more, depending on whom you talk to) into its Active Directory database—which ought to be a sufficient number of user accounts for even the largest companies. Windows 2000 will allow many large companies forced to use multiple domains because of the sheer size of their workforce to consolidate all of their user account domains into a single domain. Such domains can be large enough that many large enterprises can probably get away with one domain—for example, at this writing, a very large oil company is trying to implement their entire worldwide enterprise as a single Windows 2000 domain.

Many More Enterprises Can Be a Single Domain

Not only can domains be bigger, they can be wider—or at least more widely dispersed geographically.

Under NT 4, some relatively small companies decided to implement multi-domain enterprises because of geography. Say a company's got an office uptown and another downtown, with a thousand or so employees in each location and about 3,000 employees in total. Should they be one domain or many? Three hundred user accounts fit comfortably in one domain, but then there would probably have to be a domain controller in each location. Say for example that the PDC's in the uptown office and a BDC is in the downtown office. As there's a DC in each office, everyone can be logged in by a local DC. Those two DCs must, however, be connected with some kind of full-time connection; let's suppose it's a 56K Frame Relay link, so that the PDC can inform the BDC of any changes to user accounts, passwords, and the like.

Password-changing day comes along and all 3,000 employees dutifully change their passwords. The folks in the downtown office will find changing passwords quite slow, unfortunately, because while a BDC can log a downtowner in, it can't help with password changes; logins require only reading the SAM, and a BDC can do that just fine. But changing a password requires modifying the domain's SAM, and only the PDC can do that. Password-changing traffic, then, must go over the Frame Relay link. (The downtowners have no idea that this is why password changing is so slow, by the way.) To add insult to injury, the Frame Relay link will be excessively slow on password-changing day, as the PDC will be using much of the Frame Relay's bandwidth to *tell* the BDC about these new passwords. This becomes so frustrating that the firm eventually decides to create two different domains, one for the uptown office and one for the downtown office.

Windows 2000 lets them get back together for two reasons. First, all DCs can accept changes, so a downtowner can conduct the entire password-changing ritual while talking to the local DC. But when the downtown DC updates the uptown DC about the new passwords, won't that choke the Frame Relay? No, not at all. Where NT 4 used the same chatty, bandwidth-wasting protocol to update BDCs whether they were connected with a fast or slow link, Windows 2000 detects DCs with slow connections and compresses its data before sending, and compresses it well—tests show about a 10:1 compression ratio. This firm can become one domain again.

In general, intra-domain replication is far more efficient than it was under NT 4. That means that where previously under NT 4 you might have wisely chosen to implement a network in two separate cities as two domains so as to reduce replication traffic over a slow WAN link. Under Windows 2000 you might just as wisely choose to build a single domain spread over a wide geographical area.

Domains Can Be Divided into Subdomains

But perhaps there's another concern—*politics*. The woman running the downtown office insists that the people who run the servers uptown not have admin control of "her" servers downtown. Now, in the NT 4 days, she could segregate her servers security-wise by just keeping them in a different domain. But there wasn't a simple way to "protect" a set of servers in domain X from some subset of domain X's domain administrators.

With Windows 2000, however, there is. The domain's architects can just create a subdomain called an organizational unit (call it *downtown servers*) and put the downtown servers in that OU. Next, they create a group called *downtown admins* or something like that and put the downtown administrators' user accounts into the downtown admins group. Finally, they tell Windows 2000 to allow only the downtown admins group to administer the downtown servers OU. This process of assigning control of an OU's contents to a group is called *delegating* and Windows 2000 even has a Wizard to assist in the process.

It's Easier to Build and Maintain Multiple-Domain Networks

If it sounds like I'm a proponent of single-domain networks, I am. The more "moving parts" (read: domains) in your network, the more things there are to break. So Windows 2000's ability to support bigger and more diverse single-domain networks is pretty cool.

If, however, after examining Windows 2000's capabilities you still choose to remain with a multi-domain model, you'll find multi-domain Windows 2000 networks a bit easier to manage than multi-domain NT 4 networks.

If you choose to have more than one domain, Windows 2000 makes it easier to automatically build trust relationships among them by letting you create a "forest" of domains. Forests of domains can be subdivided into "trees"; the main reason you'd do that is, as you'll see, to make it easier to integrate your domain naming scheme with your DNS naming scheme.

Multiple Domains with NT 4   For example, consider the following NT 4 domain structure, pictured in Figure 20.1.

FIGURE 20.1:

NT 4 domain structure

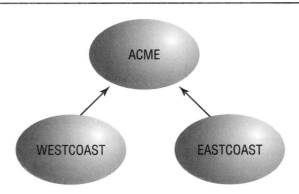

Here, Acme has decided to create three domains—ACME, which probably contains all of the *user* accounts in the entire enterprise, EASTCOAST, which probably contains all of the workstation and server accounts in their east coast office, and WESTCOAST, which probably contains all of the workstation and server accounts in their west coast office. For whatever reason, Acme's divided itself geographically, whether for political or bandwidth reasons.

In order to set this up, the Acme administrators had to do these steps:

1. Create the ACME domain and populate it with user accounts.

2. Create the EASTCOAST domain and populate it with server and workstation accounts.

3. Create the WESTCOAST domain and populate it with server and workstation accounts.

4. Build a trust relationship between EASTCOAST and ACME so that EAST-COAST trusts ACME. (In case you've forgotten what trust relationships are, they are a necessary first step when you intend to do some kind of sharing across domain lines. They're sort of like the initial treaties that formerly enemy countries sign so as to enable trade relations and begin selling things to one another.)

5. Build a trust relationship between WESTCOAST and ACME so that WEST-COAST trusts ACME.

6. Go to every machine in WESTCOAST, log in as a local administrator, and add ACME's Domain Users group to that machine's local Users group. Also, add ACME's Domain Admins group to that machine's local Administrators group.

7. Go to every machine in EASTCOAST, log in as a local administrator, and add ACME's Domain Users group to that machine's local Users group. Also, add ACME's Domain Admins group to that machine's local Administrators group.

Sound like fun? It's not. And the fun's not over. The Acme admins really should do a few other things as well. For one, they should sprinkle backup domain controllers from the ACME domain in both the east coast and west coast offices so that people at both offices can easily log in. Furthermore, those administrators should expect to have to monitor the two trust relationships, as they're prone to "breaking."

And remember—that example was almost the simplest multi-domain example imaginable. Real-world enterprises often incorporate *hundreds* of domains.

Multiple Domains with Windows 2000 Now let's see what's involved with doing this under Windows 2000. Assuming that Acme would stay with three domains (a questionable assumption, recall, but let's use it to illustrate how much easier multi-domain enterprises are under Windows 2000), their domain structure would probably look like Figure 20.2.

FIGURE 20.2:

Corresponding Windows 2000 domain structure

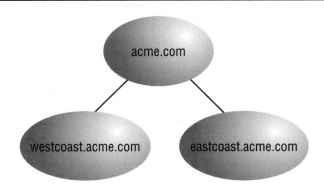

Looks similar at first glance, but a closer look shows differences. First of all, notice the names for the domains. NT 4 domain names had to be 15 characters or fewer in length, and periods in the names were a bad idea. Windows 2000 domain names are hierarchical and can be basically as long as you like. Notice also the .com suffix: Windows 2000 uses a DNS-type naming system, and for good reason—Windows 2000 *uses* DNS to keep track of domain structure. By default, one of the domain controllers in acme.com is a DNS server.

NOTE   Does this mean that you must use Microsoft's DNS as your DNS server? No, it doesn't require that. You *can* run a Unix-based DNS server (or some other DNS server, for that matter), but that DNS server software will have to be pretty modern as it's got to implement some DNS features that only entered the DNS standards in the spring of 1997.

You can extend the hierarchical naming structure as far as you like. For example, if you wanted to subdivide eastcoast.acme.com into engineering, administrative, and research divisions, you could create three more domains named engineering.eastcoast.acme.com, administrative.eastcoast.acme.com, and research.eastcoast.acme.com. The hierarchical naming structure of DNS has always been DNS's strength and Windows 2000 exploits that.

Enough of the high-level stuff—how does this make life easier for administrators? Here are the steps that admins would take in order to create the three-domain system in Figure 20.2.

1. Create the acme.com domain by running a program called DCPROMO. DCPROMO is a Wizard that asks questions of the admin and from there decides how to build the domain. The admin must tell DCPROMO that acme.com is a new domain, that the domain is the first domain in a new tree, and that the new tree is the first tree in a forest.

2. Once DCPROMO finishes its work—about 20 minutes of database creation—the admin creates the user accounts. If he's got an ASCII file listing the desired names, passwords, and the like, then Windows 2000 comes with a built-in VBScript program to do that automatically.

3. Next, locate a different Windows 2000 server machine and create the eastcoast.acme.com domain, again with DCPROMO. This time, the admin tells DCPROMO that eastcoast.acme.com is a *child domain* of acme.com. Join any machines/servers to eastcoast.acme.com.

4. Do the same thing for westcoast.acme.com.

At this point, the admin is *done*. Windows 2000 automatically creates trust relationships between acme.com and eastcoast.acme.com as well as between acme.com and westcoast.acme.com. It also does all of the work necessary so that users in acme.com are recognized as users in the two child domains. Furthermore, there's an already-created group called Enterprise Administrators whose members are automatically recognized as administrators throughout the forest (that is, the three domains). Not bad, eh?

Active Directory Enables Many of Windows 2000's New Features

In addition to making domain building simpler and more flexible, Active Directory makes a bunch of Windows 2000's new features possible.

Basically, AD is a database, as you've already read. But in addition to being a database of users and machines, it's also the place that Windows 2000 stores much of its administrative information. In the following sections, I'll give you some examples.

AD Stores Zero Administration Info Ever had to rebuild a user's workstation from scratch? How long did it take—would you measure it in minutes, hours, days, or weeks? There are commercial tools like Ghost from Symantec that can assist in that task, but Windows 2000 has a Ghost-like tool built right in called the Remote Installation Services. RIS lets you take a new computer right out the box, plug it into the network, and boot a floppy. The floppy gets the computer onto the network and locates an Active Directory server. From there, AD takes over and directs the process of getting a working disk image onto the workstation in 30 to 45 minutes, unattended. The information about where to keep those disk images and who gets which ones is stored in AD.

Anyone who's ever struggled with system policies under NT 4 knows that they're no picnic: you've got to generate an NTCONFIG.POL file, put it on a domain controller, and set up replication for NTCONFIG.POL among domain controllers. With Windows 2000, however, all of the system policy stuff—which is now called *group policies*—is stored and automatically replicated by AD.

Ever tried to "push" out an application with SMS or a similar tool? Again, no fun. But one of AD's functions is to store and decide who gets what applications.

AD Supports Directory-Enabled Networking Windows 2000 allows you to control bandwidth within your intranet using QoS (Quality of Service) control in TCP/IP. You can, then, say that a particular person should get more bandwidth on Tuesday afternoons when she needs it for videoconferencing. And where is that information stored? In Active Directory.

AD Replaces the Browser Over the years, Microsoft has gamely tried to support a simple way of browsing the servers on your local network. First called the Browser, then Network Neighborhood, the whole idea was that you could just open up a window and see what was available on your company's network. You'd first see the servers, and then you could drill down into a particular server to see its file and print shares.

The problem with the Browser has always been that Microsoft's networking model grew out of a peer-to-peer paradigm rather than a client-server model. Rather than letting a central server maintain a list of available servers, Microsoft's Browser depended on servers finding each other and electing one of their number to act temporarily as the keeper of the server list. It was a good try, but it never really worked that well.

The Browser still exists in Windows 2000, but it's supplemented by a central list of servers and shared resources maintained on the Active Directory. That list includes the names of servers, the shares available on the system, and the printers available on the system. As more and more Windows 2000–aware applications appear, we'll see AD act more and more as the place to go to find network services.

While AD's great, it's not the whole Windows 2000 story. Windows 2000 also changes the way that you build your network protocol-wise, as virtually everyone will use TCP/IP. Next, let's look at some of the ways in which TCP/IP works better under Windows 2000.

Network Infrastructure Improvements

Anyone building an NT-based network around the TCP/IP protocol needed three important infrastructure tools:

- The Windows Internet Name Service (WINS) which helped Windows and NT-based servers and workstations locate domain controllers (which handled logins and authentication in general) as well as file and print servers.

- The Dynamic Host Configuration Protocol (DHCP), which simplified and centralized the once-onerous task of configuring TCP/IP on workstations.

- The Domain Name System (DNS), which did the same kind of job as WINS—it keeps track of names and addresses—but instead of helping workstations locate domain controllers and file/print servers, DNS helps programs like Web browsers and e-mail clients to find Web and mail servers. Some firms have avoided moving their networks to TCP/IP, staying instead with IPX (a protocol that owes its popularity to Novell's networking products) or NetBEUI (the main protocol for Microsoft networking prior to 1995). But with Windows 2000, pretty much everyone should be using TCP/IP, making WINS, DNS, and DHCP essential parts of any Windows 2000–based network.

WINS

Why did NT have two services—WINS and DNS—that kept track of names? As you read earlier in this book, it happened because of a questionable choice that Microsoft made back in 1994. Of the two, WINS was the most troublesome and, for some networks, unfortunately the most vital. Thus, it was quite excellent news to many people when Microsoft announced that Windows 2000 would be the end of WINS.

Reports of its death, however, turned out to be greatly exaggerated. The actual story is that if you have a network that is 100 percent Windows 2000, both on the workstation and server, then yes, you can stop using WINS. But most of us won't have that for years, so Windows 2000 still has a WINS service. Thankfully, it's greatly improved; one expert commented to me that it's ironic that Microsoft finally "fixed" WINS, just as they were about to kill it.

DNS

DNS was something of a sidelight under NT 4 as NT didn't really need DNS— DNS's main value was to assist Internet-oriented programs like Web, FTP, and POP3/SMTP mail clients in finding their corresponding servers. Under Windows 2000, however, DNS takes center stage. Without it, Active Directory won't work.

NT 4's DNS server was a pleasure to work with, although that's just my opinion: I've spoken with people who tell me that it couldn't handle high volume loads. *I* didn't have any bad experiences with it, so I can't comment. NT 4's DNS wrapped a well-designed GUI around a standard DNS implementation, making basic DNS tasks simpler than they would be for a Unix DNS implementation at the time. Windows 2000 takes that a step further with improved Wizards. First-time DNS administrators will find that Windows 2000's DNS server almost does all the hand-holding you could need.

Additionally, Windows 2000's DNS supports dynamic updates, a process wherein adding information about new machines to a DNS database can be automated. Based on the Internet-standard document RFC 2136 (the Internet's standards are described in documents called Request for Comments, or RFCs), it combines the best of NT 4's WINS and DNS servers. The DNS server also supports another Internet standard, RFC 2052, which greatly expands the kind of information that DNS servers can hold onto. For example, a pre-2052 DNS server could tell you what machines acted as mail servers for a given Internet domain, but not which machines were Web or FTP servers. 2052-compliant DNS servers can do that, and more: Active Directory now uses RFC 2052 to allow DNS to help workstations find domain controllers and other Active Directory–specific server types.

DHCP

DHCP frees network administrators from having to walk around and visit every single desktop in order to configure the TCP/IP protocol. The basic idea is that a workstation broadcasts over the network, seeking an IP address (every computer on an intranet must have a unique IP address); a DHCP server hears the plea and assigns that computer its own unique IP address.

The End of Rogue DHCP Servers This is in general great, but now and then some dodo would decide to "practice" with DHCP by setting up a DHCP server on some PC. The budding new administrator's new DHCP server would then start handing out completely bogus addresses to unsuspecting workstations. Those workstations would then have IP addresses, but they'd be worthless ones, and as a result those workstations would be unable to function on the company's network.

With Windows 2000, however, not just anyone can create a DHCP server. Now, DHCP servers must be authorized in the Active Directory before they're allowed to start handing out addresses. This is a great advance, the end of what we used to call "rogue" DHCP servers.

DHCP Works with DNS to Register Clients You read before that the new DNS supports dynamic updates, a process standardized in RFC 2136 whereby the DNS server will automatically collect address information about machines on the network. This is an improvement over NT 4's DNS server because that DNS server couldn't automatically collect DNS information about machines— you, the administrator, had to type the names and IP addresses of new machines into the DNS Manager administration tool.

Windows 2000's DNS server collects its information about machines on the network with the help of those machines. When a machine starts up, one of the things it's doing while booting up—one of the reasons that booting modern PCs takes so long—is that it's contacting the DNS server to tell the DNS server that the machine exists. In effect, each workstation and server on the network must know to *register* itself with the DNS server.

Unfortunately, as RFC 2136 is a fairly recent development in the DNS world, most existing operating systems—DOS, Windows for Workgroups, Windows 9*x*, NT 3.*x*, and 4.*x*—do not know to register themselves with a DNS server. That's where Windows 2000's DHCP server helps out. You can optionally tell the DHCP server to handle the DNS registrations for non-2136–aware workstations. This is a very useful new feature because, without it, dynamic updates wouldn't be worth much except for the rare firm that runs solely Windows 2000 on its desktops, laptops, and servers.

Quality of Service

The Internet's underlying protocols, TCP/IP, have something of an egalitarian nature; when the Net's busy, it's first come, first served. But the protocols have always had a built-in capability that would theoretically allow an Internet operator to give greater priority to one user over another, to dial in a better response time for some than for others. That's called Quality of Service, or QoS. It was always there but not really implemented as it sort of ran against the way the Net was run.

The growth of corporate intranets, however, changes that story. Network operators in corporate networks aren't serving a mass public; rather, they're serving a diverse and hierarchical organization whose leaders may well want to be able to say, "We direct that this individual get more bandwidth and faster access to network resources than this other individual." That's possible if you're using expensive Cisco routers—but now you can do it if you use Windows 2000 machines as your IP routers as well.

New Security Infrastructure

As one security expert once said to me, "We knew that NT had 'made it' when hackers started targeting it." Hardly a month goes by without word of a new security hole in NT 4 and the hot fixes that are intended to plug that hole. Patch a plaster wall with Spackle enough and eventually you have to wonder if you've got a plaster wall or a Spackle wall—so Microsoft must have decided early on that one of the things that Windows 2000 couldn't live without was a new security system.

So they built *two*.

Originally, Windows 2000 was supposed to replace NT 4's authentication system, known as NTLM (for NT LAN Manager), with a system popular in the Unix world called Kerberos. Kerberos is well understood and works well in large-scale systems, assisting Microsoft in their "scalability" (there's that nonword again) goal.

Partway through the Windows 2000 development process, Microsoft decided to supplement Kerberos with a *third* security system, a public key system based on the X.509 standard. They did that mainly because a public key system is considered far more scalable than either an NTLM or Kerberos system. Several companies offer hardware readers that allow users to log in by inserting credit card–sized devices called *smart cards* into the readers.

Kerberos and public key provide as a side effect a feature that NT administrators have asked after for a long time—transitive trust relationships.

Distributed File System

NT's first and probably still most prevalent job is as a file server. And as time has gone on and versions have appeared, it's gotten better at it. Some benchmarks have rated it as fast or faster than NetWare, the guys to beat. And where NT 4's file server software was largely unable to deliver throughput faster than 90Mbps, Windows 2000 can transfer data almost 10 times faster.

Disconnecting Physical Locations from Names

But NT's file server system is hampered by the way it addresses shares on servers. A share named DATA on a server named WALLY would be accessed as \\WALLY\DATA. Although that makes sense, it's limiting. Suppose the WALLY server goes up in a puff of smoke? We install a new server, perhaps named SALLY rather than WALLY, restore the data from WALLY, and re-create the DATA share. But now it's \\SALLY\DATA rather than \\WALLY\DATA, and configurations that are hardwired to look for and expect \\WALLY\DATA will fail. In other words, if a share's physical location changes, so must its "logical" location—its name. It'd be nice to be able to give a share a name that it could keep no matter what server it happened to be on.

Windows 2000 takes NT beyond that with the Distributed File System. In combination with Active Directory, Dfs—note the lowercase in the acronym; apparently someone already owned *DFS* when Microsoft started working on the Distributed File System—allows you to give all of your shares names like *domainname**sharename* rather than *servername**sharename*. You needn't know the name of the file server that the share is on.

Fault Tolerance

You probably know that Windows 2000 offers you many ways to add reliability to your network through RAID storage and two-system computer clusters. RAID boxes aren't cheap, and clusters require a lot of hardware (two identical machines, external SCSI storage, extra network cards, and either the Advanced or Datacenter edition of Windows 2000 Server). But there are some very inexpensive fault tolerance options for Windows 2000 networks as well; Dfs provides one.

If you have a file share that you want to be available despite network misfortune and failure, then one way to accomplish that is with a *fault tolerant Dfs share*. To create one, just create two or more file shares that contain the same information, then tell Dfs to treat them like one share. So, for example, in a domain named ROCKS, you might have a share named STUFF on a server named S1 and a share named STUFF on a server named S2. To the outside world, however, only one share would be visible as \\ROCKS\STUFF. Then, when someone tries to access \\ROCKS\STUFF, Dfs will basically flip a coin and either send her to \\S1\STUFF or \\S2\STUFF. It's not full-blown fault tolerance—if S1 goes down, nothing automatically transfers people from \\S1\STUFF to \\S2\STUFF—but it's a low-cost way to increase the chance that a given share will be available, even under network "fire."

File Replication Service

Fault tolerant Dfs requires that you maintain several network shares all containing the same information. That can be a lot of work, but then fault tolerant Dfs sounds like it could be worth it.

For example, as you'll read later, Windows 2000 makes deploying applications from a central location or a few central locations possible. So instead of having to visit hundreds of desktops to install Office 2000, you can instead put Office 2000's distribution files on a server and set up everyone's system to install Office 2000 from that server. Hmmm… hundreds of people all trying to download an application package from one file share, all at the same time, won't be very satisfactory.

It'd be better to have exactly the same application package copied to perhaps 10 other shares. You *could*, of course, create the 10 shares and copy the package to each one—but you needn't. Windows 2000 includes the File Replication Service, or FRS. FRS is a vastly improved version of an old NT feature called Directory Replication. Anyone who's ever tried to use NT 4's Directory Replication knows that it needed work—FRS is the happy result.

Junction Points and Mounted Drives

All of this helpful misdirection in file shares—the ability to disconnect file share names from their physical locations—is pretty useful. In fact, it'd be nice to be able to start doing some of that physical/logical misdirection on *local* drives—and you can.

NT's always been hampered by the fact that it can only support 26 storage volumes, A: through Z:. Tying storage volumes to letters in the alphabet was a great idea when CP/M (an early pre-PC microcomputer operating system) started doing it back in 1978, but nowadays it seems more a bug than a feature.

With NT 4, you created partitions on drives and then assigned drive letters to those partitions. With Windows 2000, in contrast, you can tie any number of drive partitions to a single drive letter. The trick is this: You first create a folder (a sub-directory) in any existing NTFS drive (NTFS is a file format that—not surprisingly—only NT supports, rather than the FAT file system that DOS uses or the FAT32 file system that Windows 95/98 use). You can then associate—*mount* is the Windows 2000 term—any drive partition with that folder.

Thus, for example, suppose you've got a drive D:, which is NTFS. (If you want to follow along with this example—although you needn't in order to understand it—you'll need a drive D: formatted as NTFS and an H: drive formatted in any way, it doesn't matter.) You've got a bunch of partitions on your system and you're up to drive P:. You'd like to free up drive letter H: so you can use it to map to a home directory. Well, under NT 4, you *could* just highlight the partition currently assigned to H: and change its drive letter to Q: or some other still-unused letter.

Under Windows 2000, however, you can both free up the H: drive letter *and* keep access to the partition, *without* having to use another drive letter. First, create an empty directory on D:. (It needn't be D:; any NTFS drive will do.) Just for the sake of example, call it D:\OLDH—again, any directory name will do. Then you'd go into the Disk Manager, Windows 2000's version of the Disk Administrator. You do that by right-clicking My Computer, choosing Manage, opening up Storage in the left pane, and then opening up Disk Management inside *that*. Find the H: partition, right-click it, and choose Change Drive Letter and Path.

Where NT 4 only allowed you to associate *one* drive letter with a partition, Windows 2000 lets you associate a partition with as many drive letters as you like. Now, that won't help us much because we're trying to get *rid* of a drive letter—

but the very same dialog box that allows you to add a new drive letter also lets you associate a partition with "an empty folder that supports drive paths"—in other words, with D:\OLDH. Once you've added D:\OLDH as an acceptable "name" for the partition, you can type either **DIR H:** or **DIR D:\OLDH** and you'll see the same files, because both names refer to the same directory.

But the plan was to free up H:, and we haven't done that yet. Returning to the Disk Manager, again right-click the H: partition and choose Change Drive Letter and Path. This time, you'll see that H: has two acceptable names, H: and D:\OLDH. Highlight H: and choose delete. Once you reboot (yes, you've got to reboot for this change to take effect; some things never change), H: will be free and you'll only be able to access the partition's data through D:\OLDH. And if you didn't want to do all of that with a GUI tool, there's a command-line tool named MOUNTVOL that allows you to mount and unmount drives.

Remote Storage Manager

As you've already read, the Distributed File System and the File Replication Service appeared in Windows 2000. As you'll read later, Windows 2000 includes disk quotas (finally) and there's a better Backup. Clearly, storage was an issue for the Windows 2000 design team. But perhaps the most unusual new storage-related capability is the Remote Storage Manager (RSM), a program whose goal is to allow you to mix tape-drive space and hard-disk space as if they were one thing.

The idea with RSM is this. Suppose you have a 24GB hard disk on your server; perhaps it's a nice amount of storage but not quite enough for your users' needs. Suppose also that you've got a tape backup device of the kind mentioned a few paragraphs back, a carousel device that can automatically mount any one of 16 tapes into the tape drive without the need for human intervention. Perhaps it's a DLT loader and each tape can store 20 gigabytes of data; that works out to about 320GB of tape storage and, again, 24GB of hard disk storage. Here's what RSM lets you do:

It lets you lie about the amount of hard disk space you have.

You essentially advertise that you've got a volume containing 320 plus 24, or 344, gigabytes of online storage space. As people save data to that volume, the RSM first saves the data to the hard disk. But eventually, of course, all of that user data fills up the hard disk; at that point, the RSM shows off its value. The RSM searches the hard disk and finds which files have lain untouched for the longest time. A file could have, for example, been saved eight months ago by some user but not read or modified since. The RSM takes these infrequently accessed files and moves them from the hard disk onto the tape drives, freeing up hard disk space.

Ah, but what happens if someone decides to go looking for that file that was untouched for eight months? The RSM has been claiming that the file is ready and available at any time. If some user tries to access the file, the RSM finds the file on tape and puts it back on the hard disk, where the user can get to it. Yes, it's slow, but the fact is that many files are created and never reexamined, which means there's a good chance that putting the file on tape and off the hard disk will never inconvenience anyone.

I worked with mainframe systems that did things like this years ago and it was quite convenient—files untouched for six months or so would be said to be "migrated" to tape. I could "un-migrate" the tapes, and of course that would take a while, but it wasn't that much of a nuisance and it helped keep the mainframe's disks free.

Modernizing NT

NT is an operating system first introduced in the '90s, so it couldn't have needed all *that* much modernizing. But it was getting awfully embarrassing not to be able to Plug and Play, so Microsoft fixed that. And while they were at it, what's a new release of Windows or NT without a bit of fiddling with the user interface?

Win2K Can Plug and Play

In what may be the feature awaited for the second-longest time (disks are no doubt the longest-awaited feature), Windows 2000 finally offers a version of NT that knows how to do Plug And Play (PnP).

That's good news, but, as when PnP first appeared in Windows 95 and ever since, sometimes the playing doesn't happen right after the plugging. Sometimes it works that way, but inserting a new board into a system often still requires a knowledge of interrupt request levels (IRQs) and other hardware characteristics, as well as a bit of CMOS spelunking. Still, it's nice to be able to finally shut up those Windows 95 guys smirking about how easy it is to add new cards to their systems.

NT Gets a User Inter-Facelift

Windows 95 introduced a brand-new, more Macintosh-like user interface to the Windows world. NT 4 followed that but didn't exactly copy the Windows 95 UI, instead improving upon it. Internet Explorer 4 brought Active Desktop, which brought a more Web-like feel to the Windows/NT desktop, although at an often unacceptable cost in performance. Perhaps Active Desktop's best innovation was the Quick Launch bar, a portion of the Taskbar that can hold any number of tiny icons representing oft-used programs: One click and the program starts. Windows 98's user interface built further upon that, and Windows 2000's desktop offers even more new features, many of which are quite useful.

For example, as time goes on, your Start Programs menu will probably actually get *smaller*. Windows 2000 tracks how often you use programs, and if you don't use a program for a while, the program disappears off the Start Programs menu. It doesn't disappear forever, however—instead, Windows 2000 displays a set of chevrons at the end of the menu. To see the programs (and even groups) that have disappeared because of disuse, just click the chevrons and the entire program menu returns. The Control Panel also uses this frequency-of-use information; as you no doubt know from experience with Windows 9*x* and/or NT 4, the Control Panel's Add/Remove Programs allows you to uninstall programs. That's still true with Windows 2000, but in addition to telling you what programs you can uninstall, Windows 2000 tells you how often you *use* that program. Pretty neat—if you need some more disk space and you're trying to choose which program to remove in order to *get* that space, the Control Panel even gives you useful hints about which programs you won't miss!

The "user inter-facelift" isn't an unalloyed blessing, however. When I first installed beta 2 of Windows 2000, it took me about 10 minutes to find the Network Control Panel. After many years, I was used to just opening up the Control Panel, then opening the Network applet—but here, no go. Instead, I right-click on My Network Places (the name for Network Neighborhood's replacement), choose Properties, then find Local Area Connection in the resulting screen, then right-click *that*, and choose Properties again. Intuitive, no? Well, okay, intuitive NO. In any case, don't be surprised if you have to search a bit to find the new tools to do some old jobs.

Lowering TCO and Warming Administrators' Hearts

Okay, I hear you thinking, "So now Windows 2000 lets us build bigger NT networks than before—heck, maybe there's a couple of bucks in overtime to be made from larger networks—and now there's Plug and Play, great, so long as there are drivers, and by the way, many NT 4 drivers will not work under Windows 2000, so there had *better* be drivers—and now the new user interface has hidden or rearranged all of the tools that I know and lo... well, like."

So you're probably thinking, "Tell me again why I'm going to like this."

You're going to like Windows 2000 because it's got a bunch of new tools. Several tools, like the Remote Installation Service (RIS), Terminal Services, the Group Policy Editor, and the Microsoft Installer Service, will make rollouts easier; they'll simplify getting an operating system on a new computer and then simplify getting applications onto that computer. Some tools, like (again) Terminal Services, Windows 2000's new built-in Telnet server, and Windows Management Instrumentation, will make remote control easier. As you'll see, it's far easier to administer Windows 2000 servers from a distance than it ever was to administer NT 4 servers remotely. And some tools, such as disk quotas, client-side caching, RUNAS, a more powerful command line, and the Internet Connection Sharing feature, are either very effective administrative tools or just plain cool.

Remote Installation Services

Those choosing to put NT not only on their servers but on their workstations as well have never had an easy time of it. Rolling out DOS or Windows 9*x* to hundreds of similarly equipped machines is relatively simple: Set up the operating system on one "model" computer, get it configured the way your firm needs it, and then essentially "clone" that entire configuration byte-by-byte from the model computer's hard disk to the hard disks of all of the similarly equipped computers. From there, all that needs doing is usually a bit of fiddling on each of the new workstations to customize and make each machine unique in some way. Products like Ghost and Drive Image Professional are excellent tools for getting that job done, in effect "Xeroxing" a master disk image from the central model computer to other computers.

Unfortunately, NT has never lent itself to that. Its secure nature has always required that an administrator run NT's Setup program separately on every would-be NT system, making big NT Workstation rollouts a painful process. The Ghost and Drive Image Pro folks have built some tools to try to allow administrators to use those mass-copying programs to get NT onto a computer's hard disk, but those solutions have never been sanctioned by Microsoft, putting anyone who uses them in a kind of support "Twilight Zone."

Windows 2000 solves that problem by providing a new service called the Remote Installation Services. As with Ghost-like programs, RIS directs you to first create a workstation the way that you want it configured, then a Wizard (RIPRep) copies that workstation's disk image to a server—it can be any Windows 2000 server. (Unfortunately, RIS won't help you install Windows 2000 Server, just Windows 2000 Professional.) Just take a new computer out of the box, then attach it to the network, and boot it with a floppy whose image ships with Windows 2000. It asks you to identify the user who will work at that computer, and from that point on, it's a hands-off installation. RIS copies the disk image down to the new computer, runs a hardware detection to ensure that the system gets the correct drivers, the new computer reboots, and Windows 2000 Professional (for some reason, Microsoft chose to name Windows 2000 Workstation "Windows 2000 Professional") is up and running on the new system.

Windows Terminal Server Becomes Standard

Centralized systems like mainframes were great for support people because all of the user data and configuration information resided on a small number of central locations. Solving a user's problem was then easier as most support calls could be handled from one location. Centralized systems also meant easy backup.

On the other hand, centralized systems like mainframes weren't very good at highly interactive "personal productivity" applications such as word processors or spreadsheets or more modern applications like Web browsers. The decentralized nature of desktop PCs solved that problem. Unfortunately, having computers scattered geographically around an enterprise made for a tougher support job.

How, then, to have a system that allows users to run highly interactive PC-type applications and at the same time keep all of the computing and storage in a centrally located, cheaper-to-support place?

Windows Terminal Server, that's how. WTS turns an NT machine into a kind of a mainframe. You attach dumb terminals—or PCs running programs that make them look like dumb terminals—to the Terminal Server over a network or dial-up connection, and to all intents and purposes it looks as if the user's just running a standard Windows 2000 Professional desktop. But all the user's machine is doing is providing keystrokes and mouse clicks and receiving graphic images of the desktop. Everything else—all the data and all of the computation—is going on in the centrally located Windows 2000 servers.

Now, Windows Terminal Server first shipped late in NT 4's life, but it was a separate product. Windows 2000 lets you convert *any* Windows 2000 server into a Terminal Server with just a few mouse clicks. Additionally, users on a Windows 2000 Terminal Server have more options than did users on an NT 4 Windows Terminal Server.

Group Policy Editor Replaces System Policies

One way to reduce TCO in a firm with dozens, hundreds, or thousands of Windows or NT desktops is to standardize those desktops and to control in some way what gets done on those desktops.

Windows NT 4 had a feature called *system policies* that let an administrator lock down a desktop to a certain extent. If applied in full, system policies would allow an administrator to create a user workstation that could run just a few applications—say, Word, Outlook, and Internet Explorer—and nothing else.

But system policies were difficult to work with and some of them just plain never worked. Furthermore, it was impossible to apply system policies to a group of *machines*—only groups of users. So Microsoft went back to the drawing board and redesigned the idea from the ground up. The result is the Group Policy Editor. It creates and assigns "group" policies. The word *group* is in the name to underscore something missing from NT 4's system policies. It was simple to apply some kind of control to one user, but it was more difficult to apply policies to groups of users, which is really the only reasonable way to create and manage a control structure—it's far easier to manage a large enterprise wholesale, with groups, than to manage in a retail fashion, user by user.

NOTE   The odd part about group policies is that they don't *apply* to groups. Instead, they apply to subunits of Windows 2000, the *organizational units* that you read about earlier in this chapter. You can certainly control whether a policy affects a particular individual or machine based on what group or groups they belong to, but you basically can't apply a policy to a group—instead, you apply policies to organizational units.

NT 4–style system policies furthermore required building some files with the desired policy information, placing those files on a domain controller, and having to ensure that those policy files replicated properly amongst the other domain controllers. Group policies live in the Active Directory, meaning that they get replicated automatically without any necessary fussing from the administrator.

But that's not all you'll like about group policies. The list of available system policies was relatively short, and the vast majority of those policies were of no value. In contrast, there's a rich variety of group policies in the Group Policy Editor, and many of them will solve some common administrative nightmares.

Installer Service and Application Deployment

While I commented earlier that support people had gotten the short end of previous NT upgrades, that's not the case in Windows 2000. As part of their Zero Administration Windows initiative, Microsoft has built a tool into the Group Policy Editor that allows an administrator to sit in a central location and place applications on a user's desktop without having to visit that desktop.

Previously, firms wanting to do this needed to buy and deploy the Microsoft's Systems Management Server (SMS) tool to accomplish deployment at a distance; with Windows 2000; it's built right in. But that's only the first part of the story.

We usually install programs by running the Setup program that they come with. But we never know beforehand just what the Setup program's going to do, what messes it may make on the computer. Windows 2000 has an answer for that, as well: the Installer service.

The idea with the Installer service is that you no longer run Setup programs to install applications. Instead, you feed to the Installer a file called a *Microsoft Installer* file; they're recognizable because they have the extension .MSI. But an MSI file isn't a program. Instead, it's a set of commands telling the Installer how to install an application—what Registry entries to create, where to copy files, what icons to place on the program menu, and so on. And you can examine an MSI file before installing it to find out what it's going to tell Installer to do—which means you can head off trouble at the pass.

Better Remote Control and Command Lines

One of my pet peeves with NT has always been that there are very few good remote administration tools. For example, if you want to create a file share on a remote machine, you can do it, but it's cumbersome and involves a different tool—you create a local file share from the Explorer, but you must use NT 4's Server Manager to create remote shares. Even then, Server Manager won't let you control share permissions on remote shares; for that, you've got to look to the Resource Kit and its RMTSHARE.EXE program. And that's just one example: In general, it seems as if NT 4's administrative tools are originally built to only control the local machine; any remote administration abilities either don't exist or have a distinctly "tacked on afterward" feel.

Windows Management Instrumentation

While Windows 2000 doesn't completely solve that problem, you'll find that most administrative tools work as well on remote computers as they do on the local machine. Virtually all hardware functions are now built around something called the Windows Management Instrumentation, or WMI, an eminently "remoteable" software interface. As a result, Device Manager lets you view and modify hardware settings not only for the computer you're sitting at, but any machine on the network that you can see (and on which you have administrative rights); the same is true for storage management. Where Disk Administrator let you format and partition disks, it only operated on locally attached disks—its successor, Disk Manager, lets you do any of those things locally or over the network. (Finally, we network administrators will have the respect we deserve! Just think: "Call *me* a geek, will ya? I'll just attach to your computer across the network and reformat your drive...." Just joking, just joking—we network types would *never* use our powers for Evil....)

Windows 2000 Includes a Telnet Server

Furthermore, every Windows 2000 Server ships with a Telnet server. If you choose to run the Telnet server on a server, you can then connect to that server with any Telnet client.

Odd as it may sound, you may sometimes find yourself Telnetting to your own local machine. Why? Because when you log in with a Telnet session, you identify yourself with a name and password. That means that, if you're currently logged in to a machine as a user and you need to run some administrative-level command, you need to make the machine suddenly recognize you as an administrator. Telnetting is one way—but there's another as well, a new command called RUNAS that you'll meet in a bit.

Better Admin Tools: A More Powerful Command Line

That kind of leads me into my discussion of tools that aren't so much classifiable as rollout tools or as remote control tools; rather, they just fall into a category of "neat new administrative tools." Telnet offers me a segue.

Once connected, the telnet session then gives you a command-line prompt. From there, you can run any *command-line* application remotely. "But," you may be wondering, "what good is the command line? Can I create user accounts, reset passwords, and the like from the command line?" Well, according to Microsoft, one of the "must-do" items on its Windows 2000 things-to-do list was to ensure that you could do all of your administration from the command line, that in theory you would never have to use a GUI tool. I've not found that I can do *everything* from the command line, but there's a whole lot more that you can do from a command line.

Unix's SU Comes to Windows 2000

I often find myself, as mentioned before, needing to change status in the machine's eyes. For example, suppose I'm at a user's workstation trying to figure out a computer problem that's plaguing her. I realize that something's set incorrectly on her workstation and I know how to fix it, but she's currently logged in, and she's only got user-level privilege, so I can't execute whatever administrative command I had in mind. What to do?

As mentioned earlier, I could Telnet to the system as an administrator, but the Telnet server only ships with Windows 2000 Server, not Professional. I *could* ask her to log off, and then I could log on with my administrative account. But I might not want to do that—sometimes I've got a roaming profile set up and I don't want to wait for the profile to download *and* I don't want to have to worry about deleting that profile off the user's machine. The answer? RUNAS.

The scenario described above, where someone's logged on to the system as a user and needs to briefly take on administrative powers, and perhaps doesn't want to have to wait for a logoff/logon sequence, is an old one in the Unix world. That's why most Unix implementations have a so-called Super User (SU) command. It lets you run *just one program* with a different set of credentials. In the Windows 2000 world, the command's name is RUNAS—in other worlds, "*run* this particular application *as* if someone else—presumably an administrator— were running it."

You must run RUNAS either from the command line or from Start/ Run. RUNAS's syntax looks like this:

```
runas /user:username command
```

Username is the administrative username, and *command* is whatever command you want to run as an administrator. If the administrator's account is not in the same domain as the Windows 2000 Professional machine, then you may have to include the name of the administrator's domain as well. For example, if I wanted to modify a user account, I would do it with a tool named Directory Services Administrator, a file named dsa.msc. If my administrative account were named Bigmark from a domain named LANGUYS, I could start up the DSA like so:

```
runas /user:languys\bigmark dsa.msc
```

Under Windows 2000, you have *two* ways of identifying an account—through the old NT 4–flavor domain\username approach, as I used earlier, or through a newer user-specific logon name called the *User Principal Name*. A UPN looks a lot like an e-mail address; for example, Bigmark's UPN might be bigmark@languys .com. I could use that formulation as well in my RUNAS command:

```
runas /user:bigmark@languys.com dsa.msc
```

Oh, and by the way, in case you were wondering, when you do a RUNAS, the system prompts you to enter a password; merely knowing an administrative account name isn't sufficient to become an administrator.

Disk Quotas

Let's get a drum roll on this one.... After years of waiting, it's now possible to control how much space a given user takes up on a given volume. You can only set quotas on NTFS volumes.

The disk quota system is fairly simple—you can only set quotas on entire volumes, not directories, so you could, for example, say that Joe couldn't use more than 400MB of space on E, but you *couldn't* say that he couldn't use more than 200MB in E:\DATA1 and 200MB in E:\DATA2—you can't get directory specific.

Oddly enough, you also cannot set quotas on particular user groups. Instead, you determine a good generic quota value and set that on the volume; that's the disk space limitation for each user. So, for example, suppose you set the quota to 20MB. That means that each user's personal quota is set to 20MB. You can then override that for any particular user. Sound cumbersome? It is; if you have 1,000 users from 10 different groups that access a particular volume and you want to set each user's quota based on its group membership, there's not much to do save to hand-set each user's quota amount, one at a time. But it's free, and at least it's of more value than Proquota, the profile size quota manager available under NT 4.

Backup Continues to Improve

Few things grow as rapidly as the apparent need for storage space. In the late '70s, network file servers were often built around a single shared 10MB hard disk; nowadays, it's not unusual for a desktop *workstation* to have one thousand times that much disk space.

Hard drives have gotten larger, faster, cheaper, and more reliable. But one thing that hasn't changed is the need for backup. NT's always come with a backup program, but it's always been a bit limited. It could only back up to a tape drive, so you couldn't use the NT Backup program to back up to a Jaz drive or network drive; it didn't support robotic tape changers, carousels that could automatically change the tape in a tape drive; and it was very cumbersome to use for a full server recovery.

With Windows 2000, those three objections go away. If you want to save to tape, then of course you can do that, but now you can also save to anything with a drive letter—Jaz, Superdisk, some Web-based backup system, or the like. If you use tapes but your server's disks are larger than the capacity of a single tape, you need no longer baby-sit the server waiting for the chance to swap tapes.

Windows 2000 supports many tape loaders. And if you find yourself with a dead server that you need to revive quickly, you can take the most recent backup tapes from the dead server and a new computer and quickly get the contents of those tapes onto the new computer. The new computer acts in the role of the server, making disaster recovery simpler and quicker than it was under NT 4.

Client-Side Caching/Offline Files

This next aspect of Windows 2000 is not really a server function, it's a workstation (Windows 2000 Professional) function; but it'll gladden the hearts of users and administrators alike. Called either *client-side caching* or *Offline Files* by Microsoft, this function makes the network more reliable and faster and simplifies laptop/server file synchronization for mobile users.

Offline Files acts by automatically caching often-accessed network files, storing the cached copies in a folder on a local hard drive. Your desktop computer then uses those cached copies to speed up network access (or rather, they speed *apparent* network access), as subsequent accesses of a file can be handled out of the local hard disk's cached copy rather than having to go over the network. Offline Files can also use the cached copies of the files to act as a stand-in for the network when that network has failed or isn't present—such as when you're on the road.

You'll like Offline Files for several reasons. As these oft-used cached files will reside on the local hard disk, you'll immediately see what seems to be an increase in network response speed; opening up a file that appears to be on the network but is really in a local disk directory will yield apparently stunning improvements in response time, as little or no actual network activity is actually required. It also produces the side effect of reducing network traffic, as cached files needn't be retransmitted over the LAN. Having frequently used files on a local cache directory also solves the problem of "What do I do when the network's down and I need a file from a server?" If you try to access a file on a server that's not responding (or if you're not physically connected to the network), Offline Files shifts to *offline* mode. When in offline mode, Offline Files looks on your local Offline Files network cache, and if Offline Files finds a copy of that file in the cache, it delivers the file to the user just as if the server were up, running, and attached to the user's workstation.

Anyone who's ever had to get ready for a business trip knows two of the worst things about traveling with a laptop: the agony of getting on the plane only to realize that you've forgotten one or two essential files and the irritation of having to make sure that whatever files you changed while traveling get copied back to the network servers when you return. Offline Files greatly reduces the chance of the first problem because, again, often-used files tend to automatically end up in the local network cache directory. It greatly reduces the work of the second task by automating the laptop-to-server file synchronization process.

Internet Connection Sharing

A very large percentage of us have some kind of connection to the Internet, whether it is a simple dial-up connection, cable modem, or DSL. A substantial portion of us have more than one PC in our house, which leads to one of the most common pieces of e-mail that I get: "How do I share my Internet connection with all of the computers in the house?" Once, the answer to that question was a fairly lengthy discussion of routers and proxy servers.

Now, however, the answer's easy: Just use Internet Connection Sharing (ICS). Anyone who's ever used Windows 9x or NT 4 to dial in to an ISP will be able to use ICS without any trouble—using it involves little more than just checking a box.

Here's how it works. You run ICS on the computer that's dialed in (or cable modem-ed or DSL-ed) to the Internet. That computer can be running either Windows 2000 Professional or Windows 2000 Server. (It can even be running the updated version of Windows 98, Win 98 Second Edition.) You check a box labeled Shared Access in your connection's properties; this activates ICS. At this point, the ICS machine acts as a DHCP server (which provides the other computers at home with their IP addresses) and as a router (which ensures that their packets get from the home LAN to the Internet and back).

Bad News

It's not all wine and roses with Windows 2000, however. While it's a great improvement over NT 4, it still lacks in a number of ways.

DHCP Isn't Fault Tolerant

The Dynamic Host Configuration Protocol (DHCP) is an essential bit of network infrastructure, and when it goes down, the network is at least partially crippled.

Adding some kind of fault tolerance to DHCP made good sense and Microsoft told us it would offer it. Unfortunately, however, to implement fault tolerance on DHCP you must invest tens of thousands of dollars in hardware and software for a server cluster—a great answer for a large corporation, but impractical for the rest of us.

No Fax-Server Software

NT's all-in-one small business version, BackOffice Small Business Edition, shipped with a nice, basic fax server—nothing so fancy that it would put the third-party fax server folks out of business, just a nice basic system that is to fax servers what WordPad is to word processors.

For some reason, Microsoft did not ship a fax server with Windows 2000, however. There *is* fax support, but only on a workstation-by-workstation basis. Thus, you could walk over to a server equipped with a fax modem and fax something from there, but you couldn't fax from your desktop using the server. This seems odd given that Microsoft clearly has NT-ready fax code, but perhaps the fear of Justice has stayed their hand on this matter....

Requires Powerful Hardware

Every new version of NT (or Windows, for that matter) renders entire product lines of formerly useful computers useless: For example, NT 3.1, 3.5, and 3.51 ran relatively well on 486 computers, but running NT 4 on a 486 was a quixotic venture. In the same way, Windows 2000 puts the final nail in the Pentium and the MMX coffins. Yes, you *can* run Windows 2000 on a Pentium—I've done some of my experimental Windows 2000 work with a 266 MHz MMX laptop, and some of my braver (or more patient) colleagues have used 133 MHz machines with Windows 2000—but at a noticeable loss in speed. Anyone wanting to get anything done on Windows 2000 will need at least a 350MHz Pentium II and 128MB of RAM. Domain controllers will run best with two physical SCSI hard disks. Much of the same advice goes for anyone wanting to run the Workstation version of Windows 2000, Professional; at the moment all I'm doing on my Professional workstation is editing this chapter with Word 97, and I'm using 96MB of RAM—so 96MB to 128MB minimum is definitely indicated!

Hardware/DirectX Support Is Still Spotty

One of the great frustrations about NT, whether in its 3.*x* and 4.*x* versions or in its current Windows 2000 incarnation, is its relatively thin hardware support, particularly when compared to its Windows 9*x* little brother. Windows 2000 improves upon this as it supports a wider range of hardware and because Plug and Play now makes it easier to install that hardware—but there are still many boards that plain won't work.

Furthermore, Windows 2000 claims to support the DirectX interface, the interface that most modern games are written to, but in actual fact, DirectX's performance makes the few games that I've tried on Windows 2000 unplayable. "What's that?" you say, "Games are irrelevant on servers?" Well, yes, that's probably true—but if *one* much-touted but easily tested subsystem of Windows 2000 (DirectX) doesn't work, isn't it reasonable to be concerned about the other subsystems, the ones that aren't so easy to test?

AD Is Inferior to Existing Directory Services

Directory services have been around for ages. I recall working with a competing network operating system named Banyan VINES almost 10 years ago, when Banyan introduced a directory service called StreetTalk. StreetTalk was more flexible in 1992 than Active Directory is now. For example, it's inconceivable that you cannot take two existing domains and join them into an Active Directory forest—such "pruning and grafting" has been possible in Novell Directory Services (NDS) for years. Nor are Active Directory's weaknesses the fault of NT somehow; Banyan has been selling an implementation of its StreetTalk directory service for NT for at least three years, and Novell's got a version of NDS for NT as well.

Granted, Active Directory's relative weakness probably stems from the fact that it's a "version 1.0" product. But will it improve? As with all companies, Microsoft isn't primarily motivated to create good products; instead, they're motivated to sell a lot of whatever they make—and making good stuff is usually one good way to sell a lot of stuff. But that's not the only way. Sometimes the battle for market share is won by effective advertising rather than quality. And if Microsoft wins the directory services war with marketing, then there won't *be* any incentive to improve the product.

There Are Still Far Too Many Reboots

Back in 1992, I interviewed one of the higher-ups in the NT project, a fellow named Bob Muglia. Bob is a heckuva nice guy and he provided me with a lot of useful information. But I remember one comment that he made to me, a promise that we're still waiting to see fulfilled.

"NT's going to be stable," he told me. "Once you get it set up with your drivers and applications, you should never have to reboot it. If you do, then we've failed."

I've run into Bob since then on several occasions and I've never had the heart to needle him about his quote. But what he told me in 1992 made eminent sense: At minimum, an enterprise-quality operating system *doesn't need to be rebooted all the time*. And in fact, Microsoft has gone to some pains to advertise that you needn't reboot Windows 2000 as often as you did NT 4. The number of necessary reboots *has* been reduced, but it's still too much.

Having observed the positive and negative aspects, how does Windows 2000 come out in the balance? It depends on your expectations. If you wanted a vastly improved version of NT 4 with a raft of cool new doodads like Internet Connection Sharing, then you'll like Windows 2000 quite a bit. On the other hand, if you were hoping for a rock-solid, enterprise-capable network operating system that could potentially replace your existing MVS, VMS, or Unix systems, then Windows 2000 may disappoint you. While it's good, I wouldn't feel really confident about the Dow Jones running solely on Windows 2000, nor would I be very happy about finding out that the airliner I was sitting in depended on Windows 2000. But it's definitely a positive step, a step in the direction of more power and better reliability.

For that other stuff, the airliner stuff, we'll clearly have to wait for NT 6…

APPENDIX

A

NET-ing Results: Using the Command Prompt

- Using NET commands

- Accessing help

- Working with user accounts

- Getting computer and session information

- Connecting to networked devices

- Working with network services

- Sending messages

Just as you could with LAN Manager, you can control your network's settings from the MS-DOS command prompt in NT Server. In this appendix, we'll discuss these commands, their switches, and how to use them.

This appendix covers how to use the command prompt, but first there are a few things that you should know:

- Those of you who have used LAN Manager will notice that some of the commands look familiar (but not quite as you remember them) and that some are missing altogether. This is because the way that NT Server works affected the way that some commands worked in LAN Manager, and made others totally useless (like NET LOGON, for example, since logging on to the network is inherent to NT Server).

- A single entry from the command prompt is limited to 1,024 characters. This limit will probably not restrict you, but if you are sending a long message with NET SEND (discussed later in this chapter) and you suddenly can't enter any more characters, you've exceeded the 1,024 limit.

- Most of the commands in this chapter work on both NT workstations and NT Server servers, but a few only work under NT Server. When a command applies only to a server, you will see the NT Server margin icon shown here.

What You Can Do with the NET Commands

What can you do with the NET commands? You can adjust your system, manipulating accounts and connections to much the same extent that you can from the graphical interface. There are six categories of things that you can do from the command prompt.

Manipulate User Accounts From the command line, you can add or delete users from user groups, view group memberships, and adjust the configuration of user accounts.

View and Change Domain Memberships As you no doubt remember from elsewhere in this book, users are members of groups, while computers are members of domains. From the command prompt, you can add or delete computers to and from domains, or view the membership of domains.

Connect to Shared Resources and Share Resources The biggest advantage to networking is the ability it gives you to connect to other computers' drives and peripheral devices, such as printers. From the command prompt, you can connect to others' devices and share your own, setting whatever passwords you like.

Start and Stop Services The services that you can begin from the Server Manager or Control Panel can also be reached from the command prompt. From here, you can start, stop, pause, and continue network services.

Send and Receive Messages Although the messaging capabilities of NT Server are no substitute for an e-mail package, you can use it to send messages on the network that alert people to situations. For example, you could send this message: "The server is going down in five minutes—save whatever you're working on."

Set or View Time If you have a time server on your network, you can set workstation clocks to synchronize with it. You can also check the time on workstations and servers.

Getting Help

This section comes first because, if you get completely stuck while trying to use a NET command, the two commands discussed here may be able to help you. NET HELP and NET HELPMSG are not universal panaceas, and sometimes they're downright unhelpful, but they come in handy at times.

NET HELP: Getting Help from the Command Prompt

You probably use the NET HELP command most when you're first learning how to use the rest of the network commands. When you enter this command you see a screen like the one in Figure A.1.

FIGURE A.1:

The NET HELP command

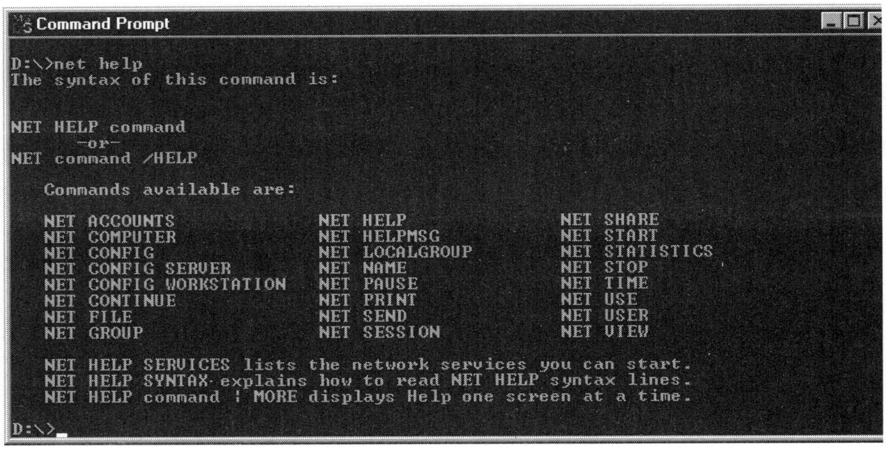

For example, if you need help with the command NET PRINT, you can simply type

    net help net print |more

to get all the help file information attached to that command. The |more switch is necessary for commands that have more than one screen of information.

If you prefer, you can get the same information by typing

    net print /help

instead of NET HELP NET PRINT. Just typing NET PRINT /? to get command information, as you might under MS-DOS, doesn't net you much information (no pun intended) under NT Server—it merely gives you the proper syntax for the command. To view an explanation of all of the command syntax symbols, just type

    net help syntax

By the way, regardless of what the net help services command tells you, no online help is available for the following services from the command prompt:

- Client Service for Netware

- DHCP Client

- File Server for the Macintosh

- Gateway Service for Netware

- LPDSVC

- Microsoft DHCP Server

- Network DDE DSDM

- Network Monitoring Agent

- NT LM Security Support Provider

- OLE

- Print Server for Macintosh

- Remote Procedure Call (RPC) Locator

- Remote Access Connection Manager

- Remote Access Server

- Remote Access ISNSAP Service

- Remote Procedure Call (RPC) Service

- Remoteboot

- Simple TCP/IP Services

- Spooler

- TCP/IP NETBIOS Helper

- Windows Internet Name Service

How Do I Get Help from the Command Prompt?

If you need help with the syntax or other particulars of a command, type

```
net help command
```

where *command* is the command name. The command's help file will be displayed. If the file takes up more than one screen, add the More switch to the end of the help request.

NET HELPMSG: Decoding Error, Warning, and Alert Messages

NET HELPMSG works as a decoder for the NT error, warning, and alert messages. If you see a message, such as "Error 2223," that doesn't tell you much, type NET HELPMSG 2223 and you see a screen like the one in Figure A.2.

FIGURE A.2:

A sample NET HELPMSG screen

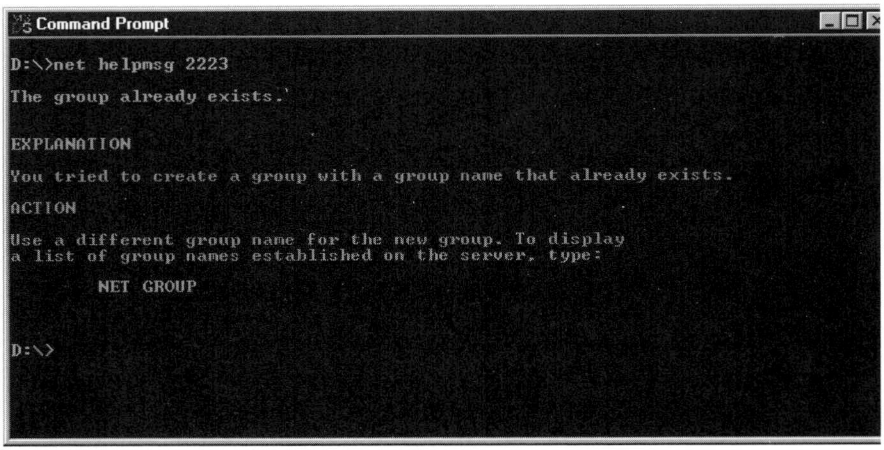

This command is not always terribly helpful. When you're trying out commands and aren't sure of their syntax, you may not always get the command to work. NET HELPMSG may only tell you that you misspelled a user's name and then refer you to the regular help file for that command.

How Do I Decipher the Help Message Numbers?

When you get an error message with a number attached, type

    net helpmsg number

to see the help file attached to that error message.

Manipulating User Accounts

When it comes to user accounts, you can do just about everything from the command prompt that you can from NT Server's GUI programs: adding and deleting accounts, viewing and changing group membership, and configuring user accounts. Here's how.

NET USER: Creating User Accounts

You can use the NET USER command from the server to control user accounts—to add them, delete them, and change them. If you type this command without parameters, you get a list of the user accounts for that server. You can use switches and parameters to manipulate accounts.

To view the existing account of a user on your domain named, for example, Christa, you would type

```
net user christa
```

The case, even of usernames, doesn't matter. You don't need to include any passwords to view the account information. Once you enter the NET USER command, you see a screen that looks like Figure A.3.

Most of the information that you see should be pretty self-explanatory. Essentially, you see a description of the account, its name, its limitations, and when it was last accessed. To actually *change* anything, you need to use the switches and parameters included in the command. For example, to add a user named Frank to your home domain, you could type

```
net user frank /add
```

That was simple enough: Frank now has an account. At this point, however, he can't use it—primarily because no password was specified. If, instead, you type

```
net user frank * /add
```

with an asterisk to create the new account, you are prompted for a password to assign to the account, and once you've assigned it, Frank is able to log on (provided you give him the password).

At this point, Frank's account exists, but all parameters have been given the default values, and the account information doesn't even include his real name, as you can see in the listing from the command NET USER FRANK in Figure A.4. Now you need to configure the account with the options available to this command. Table A.1 shows these options.

FIGURE A.3:

A sample NET USER screen

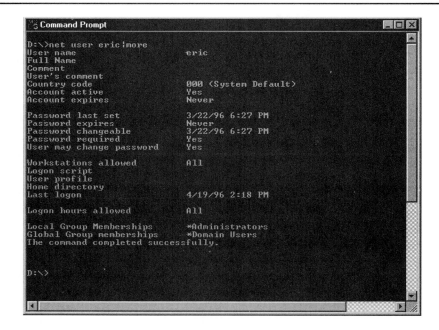

FIGURE A.4:

Frank's new account

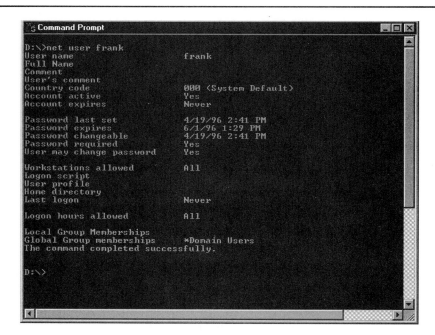

TABLE A.1:   User Account Options Determined with the NET USER Command

Options	Description
asterisk (*)	Placing an asterisk after the user's name prompts you to enter and confirm a new password for the user account.
/ACTIVE:{YES | NO}	This option determines whether the account is active or inactive. If inactive, the user cannot log onto this account. Deactivating an account is not the same thing as deleting it: a deactivated account can be reinstated simply by reactivating it, but a deleted account is dead; its parameters are lost, and even if you create a new account with the same name and password, you need to rebuild the user rights and other account information. The default for this option is YES.
/COMMENT:"*text*"	You don't have to put a comment on an account, but it could be useful if you have a large number of users and you can't recall which account belongs to the Miller account representative. Enclose the text (no more than 48 characters, including spaces) in quotation marks.
/COUNTRYCODE:*nnn*	Selects the operating system's country code so that the operating system knows what language to use for help and error messages. The default for this option is 0.
/EXPIRES:{*date* | NEVER}	If you enter a date after the colon, the account will expire on that date; NEVER sets no time limit on the account. Depending on the country code, type the expiration date as *mm,dd,yy* or *dd,mm,yy*—the format in the US is *mm,dd,yy*. You can enter the year with either four characters or two, and months as a number, spelled out, or abbreviated to two letters. Use commas or front slashes (/) to separate the parts of the date, not spaces.
/FULLNAME:"*name*"	This is the user's full name, as opposed to the username. Enclose this name in quotation marks, as it has a space in it.
/HOMEDIR:*pathname*	If you've set up a home directory for the user, this is where you include the pointers to that directory. You have to set up the home directory before you set up this part of the account.
/HOMEDIRREQ:{YES | NO}	If the user is required to use a home directory, say so here. You must have already created the directory and used the /HOMEDIR switch to specify where it is.
/PASSWORDCHG:{YES | NO}	Here, you specify whether or not users can change their own passwords. The default is YES.
/PASSWORDREQ: {YES | NO}	This determines whether or not a password is required on the user account. The default is YES.

Continued on next page

TABLE A.1 CONTINUED: User Account Options Determined with the NET USER Command

Options	Description
/PROFILEPATH:*path*	This line selects a path for the user's logon profile, if there is one for the account.
/SCRIPTPATH:*pathname*	This tells where the user's logon script is located.
/TIMES:{*times* I ALL}	You determine the user's logon hours here. Unless you specify ALL, you must spell out the permitted logon times for every day of the week. Days can be spelled out or abbreviated to three letters; hours can be indicated with either 12- or 24-hour notation. Separate day and time entries with a comma and days with a semicolon. Don't leave this option blank: if you do, the user will never be able to log on.
/USERCOMMENT:*"text"*	Administrator can add or change the User Comment for the account.
/WORKSTATIONS:{*computername*{,...I*}	Lists up to 8 computers from which a user can log on to the network. If no list exists or the list is *, the user can log on from any computer.

To add an option to a user's account, type

```
net user frank /option
```

substituting whatever option you want to adjust for *option*. The options and their syntax are listed in Table A.1. You can include more than one option when configuring an account.

To delete Frank's account, you would just type

```
net user frank /delete
```

Finally, if you're performing this operation on a workstation that does not have NT Server loaded, add the switch /domain to the end of the command to make the command apply to the domain controller of the domain you're in.

How Do I Set Up a User Account from the Command Prompt?

To create and customize a user account, first create the user account by typing

```
net user name /add
```

where *name* is the user name for the new account. Once you've created the account, customize it with the options in Table A.1 by typing

```
net user name /option
```

where *option* is the option that you want to add to the account.

NET ACCOUNTS: Making Adjustments to the Entire User Database

To make individual adjustments to user accounts, you use the NET USER command. To make adjustments concerning such things as forcible logoffs and password ages to the *entire user account database*, you use the NET ACCOUNTS command. When used without switches, NET ACCOUNTS displays the current account information, showing you a screen that looks something like Figure A.5.

FIGURE A.5:

A sample NET ACCOUNTS screen

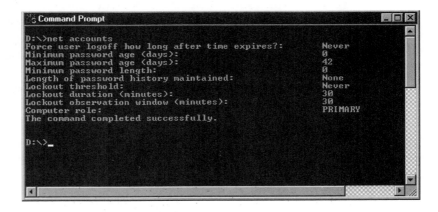

In the screen shown in Figure A.5, you can see that users will never be forcibly logged off after their logon hours expire, that they must change their passwords every 42 days but may do so at any time before that point, and that there is no limit to how long their passwords must be.

So much for looking at the status quo; how do you amend this information? That's where the switches come in. With the switches listed below, you can change all the information that you see on a screen like the one in Figure A.5.

NET ACCOUNTS Switches

Although I've listed the switches here individually for the sake of clarity, you can, of course, include more than one switch in the NET ACCOUNTS command if you want to change more than one part of a user account.

NET ACCOUNTS /SYNC   This switch updates the user account database immediately, rather than waiting for a logoff/logon action.

NET ACCOUNTS /FORCELOGOFF   This switch sets the number of minutes a user has between the time that his account expires or logon period ends and the time that the server forcibly disconnects the user. The default is No, but if you've arranged for a user's account to expire or decided that the user has only certain hours in which to log on, you might want to activate this option so that the user has to log off when he or she is supposed to.

NET ACCOUNTS /MINPWLEN   This switch specifies the minimum number of characters that a user's password account must have, from zero to 14. The default is six. Clearly, the more letters that a password has, the harder it is to guess and the more random combinations a random password-guessing program would have to cycle through, but it's a bit of a tradeoff, however. You must choose between higher security and the possibility that users will forget their passwords all the time because they can't remember all 14 characters.

NET ACCOUNTS /MAXPWAGE *OR* /MINPWAGE   These switches specify the minimum and maximum number of days that must pass before the user modifies his or her password. The possible range for /maxpwage is 0 to 49,710 days (a little more than 136 years, which makes you wonder how Microsoft decided on that maximum value), with a default value of 90 days. You can also set the value to UNLIMITED if you want the password never to expire.

The /minpwage can also be set from 0 to 49,710 days, but its default value is 0 days, meaning that the user can change the password whenever she wants to, even more than once a day.

Setting a maximum password age is a good security measure. It will foil an intruder who gets a user account name and password, because the information will only be useful to the intruder until the next time the user changes the password. There is a tradeoff between changing passwords often enough that they don't become common knowledge and changing them so often that the person using them has to write them down.

NET ACCOUNTS /UNIQUEPW   Determines the number of unique passwords a user must cycle through before repeating one. The highest value that you can assign to this variable is 24. Since people are likely to use old passwords over and over because they're easier to remember, activating this option might not be a bad idea lest an intruder get an old password. The /uniquepw switch doesn't prevent users from reusing passwords, but it puts a longer stretch between repeats than might otherwise be the case.

NET ACCOUNTS /DOMAIN   You use the net accounts /domain switch if you are performing the net accounts command on a domain machine on which NT Server is not loaded. If the machine has NT Server on board, the information automatically passes to the domain controller.

How Do I Make Changes to the Entire User Account Database?

To change settings on the entire user account database concerning such matters as forcible logoff times and password ages, type

```
net accounts /option
```

where *option* is a NET ACCOUNTS switch. These switches are shown in the section above.

NET GROUP: Changing Global Group Membership

The NET GROUP command provides you with information on global groups on a server and gives you the ability to modify this information. Typed without parameters, NET GROUP just gives you a list of the global groups on your server, but you can use the options to modify the membership of global groups, check on their membership, add comments to the group names, or add or delete global groups on the server.

To view the membership of a local group, such as the domain users, type out the following:

```
net group "domain users"
```

(if you're not working right at the domain controller, then type the /domain switch at the end of the command). Notice that, since the group name has a blank space in it, you have to enclose it in quotation marks. If the group name had no blank spaces in it—for example, if the group name was a single word like *administrators*—you wouldn't need the quotation marks. The NET GROUP command gets you a screen like Figure A.6. The names that end with a dollar sign ($) are domain controllers.

FIGURE A.6:

A sample NET GROUP screen

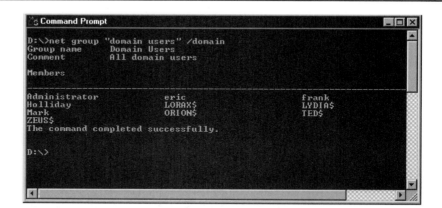

To add a new global group to the domain, list the group's name in quotation marks. For example, if the new global group is "mail administrators," you would type

```
net group "mail administrators" /add
```

To delete a group with this name, you'd substitute the /delete switch for the /add switch. Once again, if the group name has no blank spaces in it, you don't need to enclose it in quotation marks.

To add a descriptive comment to a new or existing group, add the /comment: switch and enclose the comment in quotation marks at the end of the command, like so:

```
/comment:"These are the mail administrators"
```

To add a user to a group, type

```
net group "mail administrators"
```

If you are executing the NET GROUP command from a workstation on which NT Server is not installed, add the /domain switch to the end of the statement to make the command apply to the domain controller. Otherwise, you only perform the action that you requested at the workstation you are working from. If you're working on a server with NT Server installed, the /domain switch isn't necessary.

How Do I Change Global Group Settings?

To change anything about a global group (that is, a group that extends across the domain), type the following from the command prompt:

```
net group /option
```

where *option* is the name of a switch.

NET LOCALGROUP: Changing Local Group Membership

The NET LOCALGROUP command is very similar to net group, which is discussed above. The only difference is that net localgroup refers to local user groups, and net group refers to global, or domain-wide, ones. It would probably have been helpful had net group been called net globalgroup instead, so as to avoid confusion. Unlike net group, this command can be used on NT workstations as well as NT Server servers.

Typed without parameters, net localgroup just gives you a list of the local groups on your server, but you can use the options to modify the membership of local groups, check on their membership, add comments to the group names, or add or delete global groups on the server.

Checking Membership   To view the membership of a local user group, such as one named "backup operators," you type

```
net localgroup "backup operators"
```

Notice that, since the user group name has a blank space in it, you have to enclose it in quotation marks. For a name with no blank spaces in it like *administrators*, you don't need the quotation marks.

Adding Groups   To add a new local group to the server, such as one named "relief administrators," you type

```
net group "relief administrators" /add
```

To delete a group with this name, you'd substitute the /delete for /add switch. Once again, if the group name has no blank spaces in it, you don't need to enclose it in quotation marks.

Describing Groups   To add a descriptive comment to a new or existing group, add the word /comment: and then the text in quotation marks at the end of the command, like so:

```
/comment:"These are the relief administrators"
```

Adding Users to Groups   To add a user named Paul to a group, you would type

```
net group "relief administrators" paul /add
```

If Paul were from another domain, such as Engineering, you would type

```
net group "relief administrators" engineering\paul /add.
```

To remove Paul from the group, you'd substitute the /delete switch for the /add switch.

You can add either local users or global groups to local groups, but you cannot add one entire local group to another one. Just put the name of the group or user that you want to add after the name of the group you want to add to. If you add users or groups to a local group, you must set up an account for them on that server or workstation.

Updating the Domain Controller If you are executing this command from a computer other than the domain controller, add the /domain switch to the end of the statement to make the command apply to the domain controller. Otherwise, you only perform the action that you requested at the workstation you are working from. If you're working at the domain controller, the /domain switch isn't necessary.

How Do I Change Local Group Settings?

To change anything about a local group (a group particular to the computer on which it exists, not to the entire domain), type

```
net localgroup /option
```

where *option* is one of the choices from the section above.

Computer and Session Information

You can get a variety of computer, domain, and session information from the command prompt. Using the commands found in this section, you can

- View computer information
- Add computers to or delete them from a domain
- Get information about sessions between workstations and the server

NET COMPUTER: Adding or Deleting Computers from a Domain

The NET COMPUTER command adds or deletes computers (not users) from a domain. Since domains are administrative units, you might use this command, for example, if a workstation that was used by a person in the Personnel domain began to be used by a person in the Accounting domain. As long as it's attached to the network, the workstation does not need to physically move—it's just logically reassigned.

The syntax for net computer looks like this:

```
net computer \\computername\ /add
```

(or /delete if you want to remove the computer from the domain). *Computername* is the name of the computer to be added to the local domain. This command works only on computers running NT Server, and can only be applied to the local domain—I can't assign a computer to a domain other than the one that I am logged on to. If, however, my domain and another have a trust relationship, I can log on to that domain and add or delete computers on that domain that way.

Note, by the way, that NET COMPUTER applies to computers, not to users. Users are not members of domains, only computers are. (I know, I know, I keep harping on that, but it's important to understand the difference when you're configuring your network, and it's not always an easy distinction to grasp.)

How Do I Change the Domain That a Computer Is In?

To add a computer to the local domain, type

```
net computer \\computername /add
```

To delete it, substitute the /delete for the /add switch. You can only add computers to the domain that you are currently logged on to.

NET CONFIG: Learning about and Changing Configurations

You can use the NET CONFIG command to see how a machine is configured to behave on the network and, to a limited extent, change that configuration.

Viewing Current Server and Workstation Settings

Used without switches, NET CONFIG names the configurable services (namely, the server and the workstation). If you include one of the configurable services in the command, for example, if you type NET CONFIG SERVER, you see a screen something like Figure A.7. This screen tells you the following:

- The name of the computer (LORAX in the case of the figure).

FIGURE A.7:

A sample NET CONFIG
SERVER screen

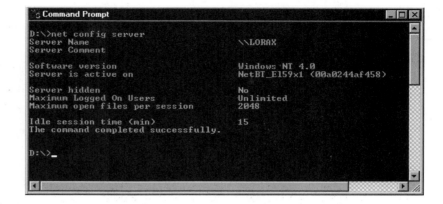

- The software version is Windows NT 4 (yes, it says the same thing whether you run this on an NT Workstation or NT Server machine—it's always Windows NT 4).

- The network card's name and address, which are listed below the software version.

- That the server is visible to the network, there is no limit to the number of users who can log on, and the maximum number of files that can be open per session with another computer is 2048—a restriction that isn't likely to cause most users much grief.

- The idle session time is 15 minutes.

Although you can run this command on any NT workstation or any NT Server (net config means something different in other operating systems, and the command net config server or net config workstation won't work) it doesn't mean that the NT workstations are set up to be servers.

Suppose you type the following command on the machine from Figure A.7:

```
net config workstation
```

You see a screen like the one in Figure A.8. This screen gives you information about how this computer is configured for use as a network workstation. You see the computer and user names, the network card address, the domain, and so forth. Why run net config workstation on a server? Bear in mind that there is no *physical* reason why an NT Server machine can't be a workstation. It's possible, if not likely, that you could be using the NT Server machine for a workstation, especially if you're short of machines and don't have a dedicated server.

FIGURE A.8:

A sample NET CONFIG WORKSTATION screen

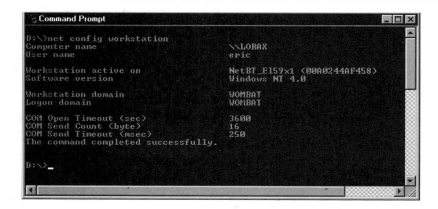

To get basic information about a computer, such as its domain, name, the name of its current user, and so forth, type either of these commands:

```
net config server
net config workstation
```

depending on whether you want information about its setup as a server or a workstation.

Changing Server and Workstation Settings

You can use the NET CONFIG commands for more than just information; within a limited scope, you can use them to adjust the way that a machine works on the network. If you type

```
net help net config server
```

you see that this command has three suboptions that you can adjust:

Suboption	Description
/autodisconnect:*time*	Sets the number of minutes a user's session with that computer can be inactive before it's disconnected. If you specify -1, the session will never disconnect. The upper limit is 65,535 minutes (don't use commas when using the command), a little more than 45 hours. The default is 15 minutes.

Continued on next page

Suboption	Description
/srvcomment:"text"	Adds a comment to a server (here, that means any machine that's sharing resources with the network) that people can see when they view network resources with NET VIEW. Your comment, which can be up to 48 characters long including spaces, should be enclosed in quotation marks.
/hidden:yes *or* no	Allows you the option of not displaying that server on the list of network resources. Hiding a server doesn't change people's ability to access it, but only keeps people who don't need to know about it from accessing it. The default is no.

The workstation settings are a little different, the differences having to do with how the machine collects data from and sends it to communication devices. You probably don't have much need for these commands. If you type

```
net help net config workstation
```

you see that this command also has three options:

Option	Description
/charcount:*bytes*	Sets the amount of data that NT collects before sending the data to a communication device. The range is 0 to 65,535 bytes (don't use commas in the number), and the default is 16.
/charcount:*msec*	Sets the length of time during which the machine collects data for transmittal before forwarding it to the communication device. If the /charcount/*bytes* option is also used, the specification satisfied first will be the one that NT acts on. You can set the *msec* value from 0 to 655,350,000, and the default is 250 milliseconds.
/charwait:*sec*	Sets the number of seconds that NT waits for a communication device to become available. The range is 0 to 65,535 seconds and the default is 3600.

NET SESSION: Accessing Connection Information

Used on servers, this command displays information about sessions between the server and other computers on the network. If you type the command without switches, you get a screen showing all the computers that are logged on to that server.

If you include net session switches, you can get more detailed information about a session with a particular computer, or delete a session (that is, disconnect a computer from the server). For example, to get more information about a session with computer LORAX, you'd type

```
net session \\LORAX.
```

You'd see a screen that looks like Figure A.9. This screen tells you

- The user who logged into computer LORAX is called Eric.

- The user is not logged in as a guest.

- This machine is running Windows NT. If it were working in a DOS environment, this doesn't necessarily mean that the user is using DOS programs (in fact, Eric could have been logged on under Windows for Workgroups), but that DOS is the basic operating system. Don't forget: unlike NT Workstation or NT Server, Windows is not a true operating system, but an operating environment.

- Eric has been logged on for two minutes and one second. His machine has been idle for two minutes and one second.

FIGURE A.9:

A sample NET SESSION screen

How do I get information about current sessions? To view the current sessions open between a computer and the rest of the network, type

```
net session
```

on the computer for which you want the information. To remove the connection between the server and LORAX, type

```
net session \\lorax /delete
```

WARNING   Be *careful* when using the /delete switch! If you neglect to include the computer name in the command, you end all current sessions and everyone has to reconnect to the server.

In case you were wondering, you cannot use this command to initiate sessions between the server and networked computers. Each user does that when he or she logs on.

How Do I Forcibly Break a Connection between Computers?

To end a connection between two networked computers, go to one of the two computers and type

```
net session \\computername /delete
```

where *computername* is the name of the computer you wish to disconnect. If you don't specify a specific computer, you will break all connections between the computer you're typing on and the rest of the network.

NET STATISTICS: Getting a Report on a Computer

The NET STATISTICS command gives you a report on the computer on which you run it. If you just type the following command, you get a list of the services for which statistics are available (server and/or workstation, depending on whether you use the command on an NT or NT Server machine):

```
net statistics
```

But if you type either of the following two commands, you get, respectively, a server report like the one in Figure A.10, and a workstation report like the one in Figure A.11.

```
net statistics server
net statistics workstation
```

FIGURE A.10:

A sample NET STATISTICS SERVER screen

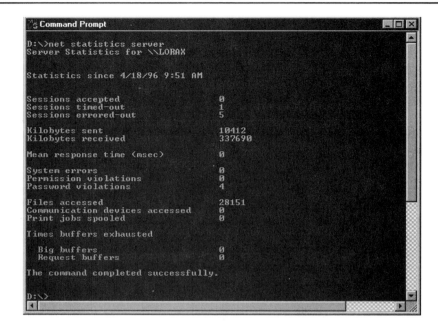

FIGURE A.11:

A sample NET STATISTICS WORKSTATION screen

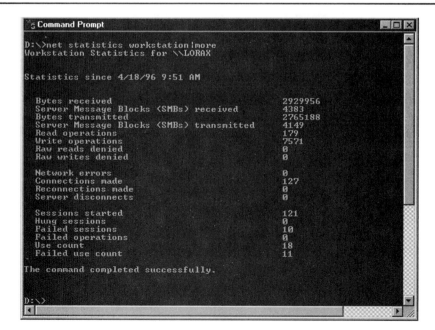

You can use either net statistics server or net statistics workstation from any NT Workstation or NT Server machine, but the command can only give you information about the machine on which you run it. You can't use this command to get information about computer AMS, for example, if you type the command from computer TSC.

What's Out There? Connecting to Networked Devices

Since the main point of a network is to allow networked users to access devices that belong to computers other than their own, you would expect to be able to make these connections from the command prompt, just as you can from the graphical interface. You would be right. With the NET commands, you can connect to drives and printers on the network with the same flexibility that you can when using the icons. In this section, we'll talk about how to see what's available on the network, how to connect to it, and (if you're using this command from a server), who's using what.

If you're working from the command prompt, you must make sure that the workstation service is started before you can use any of the commands listed in this section. To do so from the command prompt, type

```
net start workstation
```

NET VIEW: Seeing the Resources Being Shared

You can't change anything with the NET VIEW command; you can only use it to see the resources being shared on the servers and domains on the network.

- If you type the following command on its own, you get a list of the local servers on the domain—that is, the services shared by the computer upon which you would type

  ```
  net view
  ```

- If you want to see a list of the resources that the server is sharing with the network, you can amend the name of the server that you want to look at to the command. For example, if the server is named TED, you would type

  ```
  net view \\ted
  ```

- You can check this for any server on the network.

- If you want to look at a server in another domain (perhaps server BIGDOG in domain ENGINEERING), type

```
net view \\bigdog /domain:engineering
```

If you omit the domain name from the command, you see a list of all domains on the network.

TIP
Although this takes a pretty specific set of circumstances, if your network has both servers running NT Server *and* servers running Windows for Workgroups, you may see the error message "There are no entries in the list" when you enter the NET VIEW command. This happens when a Windows for Workgroups machine is the backup master browser for the workgroup, and the Guest account is disabled on the NT server that is the usual master browser. This error occurs because a workgroup (unlike a domain) has no centralized account database. The Workgroups server must use the database on the NT server to obtain the list of resources shared with the network, and if the Guest account on the NT server is disabled, the Workgroups server may not be able to access the list of servers. Therefore, to avoid this potential problem, just keep the Guest account on the master browser enabled.

NET USE: Connecting to Other Drives and Printer Ports

Once you've browsed the network with NET VIEW, you can connect to all the available goodies (or disconnect from those you don't want) with the NET USE command. Use this command to connect to drives D through Z and printer ports LPT1 through LPT9. (If you get help on this command, you notice that it claims that you can only use printer ports LPT1 through LPT3. Technically, this isn't true, but the help file probably puts it this way because some MS-DOS applications are not able to access printer ports with numbers higher than 3.)

To get information about the workstation's current connections, type

```
net use
```

without options. To actually *make* connections, use the command's switches. They are described below.

How Do I View the Available Resources on the Network?

To see what servers are available in your domain, type

```
net view
```

To see the resources that a particular server is sharing with the domain, type

```
net view \\servername
```

where *servername* is the name of the server that you want to view (incidentally, if the server name contains spaces, use "*\\servername*" instead).

If you want to see a server in another domain, type

```
net view /domain
```

To see the domains available, type

```
net view /domain:domainname
```

to see the list of available servers on a particular domain. Then type

```
net view \\servername /domain:domainname
```

when you've selected the server that you want.

Connecting to a Resource in the Local Domain

To connect to a shared resource, such as the printer shared as HP4M on server TED, type

```
net use lpt1: \\ted\hp4m
```

In this case, if you wanted to connect to a directory called wpfiles on that server and to make that your E drive, you'd substitute *e:* for *lpt1* and *wpfiles* for *hp4m* in the example above. You get to specify the port name or drive letter that you want to connect a resource to, but you're restricted to drive letters D through Z and ports LPT1 through LPT9. (Remember, although the help file will say that LPT3 is the highest port that you can specify, this is not true.) Also, if the computer that you're getting the resource from has a blank character in its name (that is, has two words in it), you must put the name in quotation marks, as in "\\eisa server".

If there is a password (let's say it's "artuser") attached to the resource that you're trying to connect to, you need to include that in your connection command, like this:

```
net use lpt1: \\ted\hp4m artuser
```

Or, if you want the computer to prompt you for the password so that it isn't displayed on the screen, append an asterisk:

```
net use lpt1: \\ted\hp4m *
```

To connect to your home directory (the directory on the server that has been assigned to you, assuming that there is one), type

```
net use /home
```

with the password on the end as explained above if one is attached.

If you want to make the connection for another user rather than for yourself, add the user's name (Frank) to the end of the line, like this:

```
net use lpt1: \\ted\hp4m user:frank
```

Passwords go before the user's name in the statement. If the user for whom you are making the connection is in another domain, the user part of the statement looks like this:

```
user:domainname/frank
```

where *domainname* is the name of that user's home domain.

How Do I Connect to a Shared Resource?

To access a shared resource on the network, type

```
net use devicename: \\servername\sharename
```

where *devicename* is what you intend to call the connection (such as D: or LPT1), *servername* is the name of the server sharing the resource, and *sharename* is the name by which the server is sharing the resource.

Connecting to a Resource in Another Domain

If you want to connect to a resource in a different domain from your usual one, you must first log on to that domain. If your domain and that one don't have a trust relationship with each other, you need to create a user account for yourself on that domain. Once you've logged on to the proper domain, the process is the same as described above.

Other Switches

No matter what kind of connection you make, you can make it persistent (that is, remake it every time you connect to the network), by adding the **switch /persistent:yes** to the end of the line. If don't want it to be persistent, type **/persistent: no** instead.

If you don't specify one or the other, the default is whatever you chose last. If you want to make all future connections persistent, type

```
net use /persistent:yes
```

(or type **:no** if you want all future connections to be temporary). Typing **/persistent** by itself at the end of the line won't do anything.

To disconnect from a resource, type

```
net use devicename /delete
```

where *devicename* is the connection (such as D: or LPT1). You don't have to provide a password or say anything about persistency to disconnect from a resource.

NET SHARE: Creating and Deleting Shared Resources

If you're administering a server, you probably spend more time making resources available to the resource than you do connecting yourself to resources that belong to other machines. The NET SHARE command applies to resources that the server is sharing with the network. Used alone, it gives you a list of all resources currently being shared with the network. With its switches, you can create and delete shared resources.

The NET SHARE command provides you with information about that particular shared resource:

```
net share sharename
```

For example, if one of the printers on the server is called HP4M (the share-name), you could type NET SHARE hp4m and see a screen like the one in Figure A.12. From this screen, you can tell what that resource's share name and path are, see any descriptive remarks attached to the shared resource, and see how many users may use the device at one time and how many are currently using it.

FIGURE A.12:

A sample NET SHARE screen

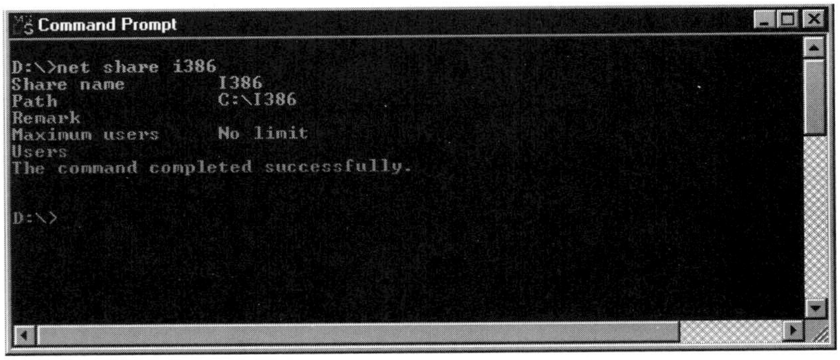

```
D:\>net share i386
Share name          I386
Path                C:\I386
Remark
Maximum users       No limit
Users
The command completed successfully.


D:\>
```

NET SHARE is a useful command not only for viewing the setup of existing shared devices, but for creating new ones and configuring existing shares. You must be using an account with administrative rights to use this command; ordinary user accounts can't use it.

Specifying Absolute Path To share a device or drive, you must tell the system where to find it. Thus, to share the directory C:\MAIN as drive C:, you would type

    net share C=c:\main

Limiting User Access To specify the number of users who can use a particular device at the same time, add the parameter /users:*number*, where *number* is the number of users that you want to be able to use the device at once. To place no limit on the number of users, substitute the parameter /unlimited. From the example above, you would type

    net share C=c:\main /users:5

if you wanted, at any given time, five users to be able to access the \MAIN directory on the server's C drive. If you don't use the /users switch, an unlimited number of users can access the device.

Describing Shared Devices You can add a descriptive comment to a shared device to give the network's users a better idea of exactly what device it is that they are reaching. Do this by adding /remark switch and adding a comment to the end of the NET SHARE statement, like so:

```
/remark:"This is the main data storage directory"
```

Note that there are no spaces between the colon and the text, and that the text must be enclosed in quotation marks.

Stop Sharing To stop sharing a device, type **net share**, the sharename, device name, or drive and path, and then add the /delete switch.

When using the net share command, keep in mind that if the guest account is enabled, any devices that you share with the network are automatically available to the entire network; you can't set individual or group permissions with this command. If you want to restrict access to devices or drives, you must set the permissions on the pertinent device or drive from the Explorer or Printers folder.

How Do I Share a Device with the Network?

To share a device with the network, type

```
net share sharename=directory
```

where *sharename* is the name by which the device will be known on the network, and *directory* is the location where the device is found. For example, to share the directory c:\public on the network as Public, you'd type

```
net share Public=c:\public
```

NET FILE: Finding Out What's Open and Who's Using It

NT SERVER

Without switches, the NET FILE command is used on servers to display the open files. If you type NET FILE from a server, you see a screen something like Figure A.13.

FIGURE A.13:

A sample NET FILE screen

This screen output lets you know what's open and who (users, not computers) is using it. If you add the switches, you can identify that file to the server and shut it down, removing all file locks. For example, in this situation, you might want to shut down PSP.EXE. To do so, you'd type

```
net file 27780 /close
```

as 27780 is that file's ID number. Note that more than one person can access a file at a time, but that each access has its own ID number.

NET PRINT: Controlling Print Jobs

You can use the command prompt not only to connect to networked devices, but, in some cases, to control them. With the NET PRINT command, you can control print jobs, just as you can with the Print Manager.

If you type the following command, you get a list of all the jobs currently printing or waiting on that printer:

```
net print \\computername\sharename
```

where *sharename* is the name by which the printer is shared on the network. You see that each job is assigned a job number. To delete a print job, refer to that number and type

```
net print \\computername job# /delete
```

substituting the job number for *job#*. If you want to hold a print job (keep it in the print queue but let other jobs print ahead of it) or release it (free a held job to print), substitute /hold or /release for /delete.

While it is possible to control print jobs from the command line, it's much easier to do it from the Print Manager. When you try to delete a print job, it might be done printing by the time you type the server name and queue incorrectly, notice the problem, and re-enter the data.

TIP   If you have configured your default printer to print directly to ports, you won't be able to print to a local port from the command prompt. Currently, there isn't anything that you can do about this except go into the Printers folder, remove the Print Directly to Ports option, and resend the job.

How Do I Control a Print Job from the Command Prompt?

To pause, continue, or delete a print job from the command prompt, first type

```
net print \\computername\sharename
```

where \\computername\sharename is the name of the computer and printer with the print job that you wish to control. This command gives you a list of the pending print jobs for that printer and their job numbers. Find the number that corresponds to the print job that you want to control, and, to delete a job, type

```
net print \\computername job# /delete
```

To hold or release the job instead of deleting it, substitute the word "hold" or "release" for "delete." You don't need to specify the sharename with this command.

Using Network Services

The NET START *servicename* command is not capable of starting all the services that are available from the Services icon in the Control Panel, but only the network-related ones. In this section, we'll talk about what those commands are and how to start, pause, continue, and stop them.

NET START: Starting a Service

The NET START command encompasses a long list of network services that can be started. On its own, it doesn't do anything except list the services that have already been started. Be warned: the list that you see when you type **net start** is not a complete list of all the network services available. To view the available services, type either of these commands:

```
net start /help |more
net help net start |more.
```

How Do I Start a Network Service?

To start a network service from the command prompt, type

```
net start servicename
```

where *servicename* is the name of the service to start. This command works only for the network services described in this section.

All two-word commands, such as "clipbook server" and "computer browser" must be enclosed within quotation marks for the NET START commands to work.

The default services in Windows NT Server are described below.

NET START ALERTER The alerter service sends messages about the network to users. You select events which you want to trigger alerts in the Performance Monitor. For these alerts to be sent, both the alerter and messenger services must be running on the computer originating the alerts, and the messenger service must be running on the computer receiving them.

NET START "CLIPBOOK SERVER" The Clipbook Viewer is a temporary or permanent storage place for text or graphics that you want to cut and paste between applications. From the command line, start this service by typing

```
net start "clipbook server"
```

You see either a message that the service has been started, or, if you've already started it from NT Server, you see a message that the service was already started.

NET START "COMPUTER BROWSER"   The computer browser service allows your computer to browse and be browsed on the network. When you start it from the command prompt, however, you get no further information than that the service has started.

NET START "DIRECTORY REPLICATOR"   You can type this command in either of two ways:

```
net start "directory replicator"
net start replicator
```

It begins the service that allows you to dynamically update files between servers. You must have replication rights to use this command, which means you have to set up a user account with replication rights before you start this service. (There is a default user group with those rights that comes with NT Server, so you can just assign an account to that group.)

NET START EVENTLOG   This command begins the event log, which audits selected events on the network, such as file access, user logons and logoffs, and the starting of programs. You can select what events you want to log, and also whether you want the log to consist of both successful and failed attempts, just failures, or just successes (although just recording successes doesn't sound terribly useful if you're trying to monitor the system).

NET START MESSENGER   A command called NET SEND allows you to send brief messages over the network when working from the command prompt. For this command to work, however, the messenger service must first be running on both the machine sending the message and the one(s) receiving it. To begin the messenger service, type

```
net start messenger
```

If you're running the alerter service to keep yourself informed of what's going on at the server, the messenger service must also be running on both the server and the workstation where you want to receive the messages.

NET START "NET LOGON"   This command starts the netlogon service, which verifies logon requests and controls replication of the user accounts database (see NET START "DIRECTORY REPLICATOR"). The netlogon service isn't used for logging on to your computer, but for logging on to the domain that your computer is part of; if you log on just to a computer, you can use anything there that isn't dependent on domain membership (such as directory replication). Even if you don't log on to the domain, you can still access resources shared with the network if you have rights and permissions to use them. The process of logging on to the domain, as opposed to just the workstation, is called *pass-through validation*.

NET START "NETWORK DDE" This service provides a network transport for dynamic data exchange (DDE) conversations and provides security for them.

NET START "NETWORK DDE DSDM" Used by the DDE service described above, the DDE share database manager (DSDM) manages the DDE conversations.

NET START "NT LM SECURITY SUPPORT PROVIDER" This service provides Windows NT security to RPC applications that use transports other than LAN Manager named pipes.

NET START "REMOTE PROCEDURE CALL (RPC) SERVICE" The Remote Procedure Call (RPC) Service is a mechanism that enables programmers to develop distributed applications more easily by providing pointers to direct the applications. Before you can use RPC, you need to configure it by specifying the Name Service Interface (NSI) that it will use. You have to know what NSI provider it will use and, if you are using the DCE Cell Directory Service, the network address of the provider. The default name service is the Windows NT Locator.

NET START "REMOTE PROCEDURE CALL (RPC) LOCATOR" This service allows distributed applications to use the RPC-provided pointer by directing the applications to those pointers. This service manages the RPC NSI database.

NET START SCHEDULE This command starts the scheduling service, which must be running to use the at command. The at command can be used to schedule commands and programs (like the backup program, for instance) to run on a certain computer at a specific time and date. By default, the scheduling service is configured to log on under the system account, but if it logs on under that account, the at command can only be used for programs to which the Guest users have access. Thus, to run a restricted program (like the backup operation), you'd need to configure the scheduling service to log on under an account with rights to the programs you want to run.

To start a program at a certain time, you would specify

- The computer on which you want the program to run. (If you don't specify one, the default is the computer at which you execute the AT command.)

- The time and date when you want the program to begin running. (If you don't specify a date, the program will run on the day that you execute the command, at the appointed time.) You can also schedule an event for the next date (such as a Thursday), or make the event a repeating event scheduled to run on every occasion of a date.

- The command that you want to run (typed in quotation marks).

For example, to change the name of a file from JUNK.SAM to JUNKER.SAM on the local computer at 10:52 today, you would type

```
at 10:52 "rename c:\ntclass\junk.sam junker.sam"
```

If you wanted to perform a similar action on a networked computer named AMS, and set the "alarm clock" for 11:00 next Wednesday, you'd type

```
at \\ams 11:00 /next:wednesday "rename c:\ntclass\junk.sam junker.sam"
```

To make this command happen every Wednesday, you'd substitute every:wednesday for next:wednesday. For every 7th, 14th, and 21st of the month, you'd type **every:7,14,21** (make sure there are no blanks between the colon and the numbers). By the way, you can abbreviate day names like this: M, T, W, Th, F, Sa, Su.

NET START SERVER   To control access to network resources from the command line, you must type

```
net start server
```

This service must be running before you can perform certain actions:

- Directory sharing
- Printer sharing
- Remote procedure call (RPC) access
- Named pipe sharing

When you stop the server service, you disconnect all users attached to your machine, so before doing so, you should follow these steps:

1. From the command line, type

    ```
    net pause server
    ```

    to pause the server service. This keeps any new users from connecting to the server but does not disrupt any current connections.

2. Notify those people who are connected that you're going to shut it down, and that they need to log off before a certain time. You can use the NET SEND command to do this. To see the NET SEND message, NT machines must be running the messenger service; Windows, Windows for Workgroups, and Windows 95 machines must be running WinPopup.

3. After that time has passed, you can type

    ```
    net stop server
    ```

    to end the service without messing anyone up.

When you end the server service, you take the computer browser and netlogon with it, so if you stop the server service and then restart it, you need to restart those programs as well.

NET START SPOOLER   As its name implies, this service provides print spooler capabilities.

NET START UPS   One of the best things about Windows NT is its built-in preparedness to contend with disaster. Like the backup program, disk mirroring, duplexing, and striping, the UPS (uninterrupted power supply) service links your workstation or server with a UPS to protect your computer from dirty power, power surges, and power failures. You still have to buy the UPS, but this service makes the hardware even more useful than it already is.

Before you run the UPS service for the first time from the command prompt (by typing **net start ups**) you must first configure the service. When configuring, you make a number of choices about how the service will function, including

*   The serial port to which the UPS is connected

*   Whether or not the UPS signals you when the following events occur: power supply interruption and low battery power (UPSes run from batteries when normal power fails)

- How the computer will shut down

- How long the battery life is and how long it will take to recharge

- How frequently you will see warning messages

Obviously, you need to check with your UPS's documentation before configuring the UPS service a certain way. Once it's up and running, the UPS service protects your machine from power problems and keeps you as notified of what's going on as you want to be.

NET START WORKSTATION As you'd guess from the name, this command is intended for workstations, to enable them to connect to and use shared network resources. Once you start this service, you can see what's on the network and connect to it.

NT Server also offers a number of special services that can also be started with the NET START command. These include

- Client Server for Netware

- DHCP Client

- File Server for Macintosh

- FTP Server

- Gateway Service for Netware

- LPDSVC

- Microsoft DHCP Server

- Network Monitoring Agent

- OLE

- Print Server for Macintosh

- Remote Access Connection Manager

- Remote Access ISNSAP Service

- Remote Access Server

- Remoteboot

- Simple TCP/IP Services

- SNMP
- TCP/IP NETBIOS Helper
- Windows Internet Name Service

NET PAUSE and NET CONTINUE: Halting a Service Temporarily

If you need to temporarily halt a service, you can use the NET PAUSE command to do it. Just type

```
net pause service
```

and that *service* will be temporarily suspended. To restart the paused service, type

```
net continue service
```

The NET PAUSE and NET CONTINUE commands affect the following default services:

- NET LOGON
- NETWORK DDE
- NETWORK DDE DSDM
- SCHEDULE
- SERVER
- WORKSTATION

NET STOP: Stopping a Service

NET STOP works in the same way that NET START does. On its own, it can't do anything, but when you add the name of a service that you want to stop, it stops it. See the NET START section for details on what each of the services does.

WARNING Be careful when stopping a service! Some services are dependent on others (such as NET START NET LOGON and NET START WORKSTATION), so if you shut down one, you may shut down another without meaning to. If you just need to stop a service temporarily, use NET START PAUSE instead. You need administrative rights to stop a service.

How Do I Stop, Pause, and Continue a Service?

Once you've started a service, you can pause, continue, or stop it in much the same way that you started it in the first place. Just type

```
net action servicename
```

where *action* is what you want to do (pause, continue, or stop) and *servicename* is the name of the service that you want to control.

Sending Messages

You're not dependent on e-mail to send messages across the network. From the command prompt, you can send messages and arrange to have your own forwarded so that they catch up with you wherever you are. As long as your computer and the computer to which you direct the messages are running the message service, you can reach anywhere on the network.

NET NAME: Adding or Deleting a Messaging Name

The NET NAME command adds or deletes a *messaging name* (also known as an *alias*) at a workstation. The messaging name is the name that receives messages at that station; any messages sent over the network will go to where the messaging name is. Although this command comes with two switches, /add and /delete, the /add switch is not necessary to add a messaging name to a workstation; instead, you would only need to type

```
net name username
```

and that would add that messaging name to the appropriate workstation.

To add the messaging name "Eric" to the computer in Figure A.14, I would only have to type

```
net name Eric
```

But if I wanted to remove him, I'd have to type

```
net name Eric /delete.
```

FIGURE A.14:

A sample NET NAME screen

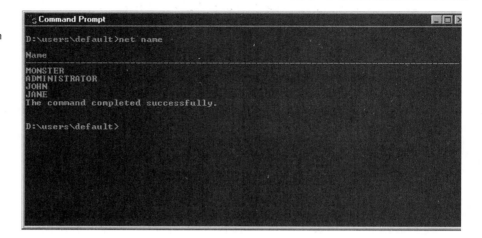

The difference between messaging names and usernames may not be immediately clear. The username is the name of the person who is logged onto a particular machine. It can be deleted from the messaging name list; that is, messages can be re-routed from the machine at which a user is working to another machine, if you use this command to add the name to that machine. While you can delete both the username and any messaging names from a computer, you cannot delete the computer's name from the list. In Figure A.14, the name of the computer is MONSTER, Administrator is the username, and John and Jane are messaging names.

How Do I Forward My Messages to Another Machine?

If you're working at another machine than the one that you're accustomed to using, you can make sure that your messages follow you there. Just type

```
net name username
```

(or *machinename*) on the machine where you are working. All messages addressed to that username or machine name will show up at that location. Messaging names cannot be already in use anywhere else on the network. If you try to add a name that's already in use to a messaging name list, it won't work.

NET SEND: Sending Messages

NET SEND is a messaging service for sending a message to one person, to all the people in your group, to all the people in your domain, to all the people on the network, or to all the users connected to the server. NET SEND does not work without its parameters, as you need to tell it something to send and where to send it. The basic parameters are as follows:

```
net send name message text
```

where

- *name* is the name (username, messaging name, or computername) that you want to send the message to.

TIP   According to the help file, substituting an asterisk (*) in place of a name sends the message to everyone in your user group, but when I used it the Messenger Service sent the message to everyone connected to the domain controller, rather than to the user group of the account that did the sending.

- *message text* is whatever text you wish to include in your message. It doesn't have to be enclosed in quotation marks. Even though NET SEND isn't meant to be a substitute for an e-mail program, you can send fairly hefty messages with it. if you try to send too long a message, the system refuses to let you type any more characters, but in a test message it took 13 full lines to reach that point. If you want to send a message longer than that, it's probably easier to use e-mail.

NET SEND Options

Sometimes you need more than the basic parameters to get your message where it needs to go. In that case, you can use whichever of these options is necessary (only one at a time):

Option	Description
/domain	Sends the message to everyone in your domain. Just substitute your domain's name for the word *domain*. If you include a name of a domain or workgroup like this: `domain:`*`domainname`*

Continued on next page

Option	Description
	where *domainname* is the name of the domain or workgroup that you wish to receive the message, then the message is sent to all users in the domain or workgroup. If you don't include a name with this switch, the message is sent to the local domain.
/broadcast	Sends the message to all users on the network—not the domain, not the user group, but the network.
/users	Sends the message to all users connected to the server.

Using NET SEND

Even with the explanation for the parameters, getting NET SEND to work can be a little confusing. This would probably be a good time for some real-life examples.

To send a message that says "This is a test message" to Paula, who is part of your domain, type

```
net send paula This is a test message.
```

If you want to send a message that says "This is a test message" to Sam, who is part of the Engineering domain, type

```
net send sam \engineering This is a test message.
```

If you want to send a message that says "This is a test message" to everyone in your domain, type

```
net send * This is a test message.
```

Once you've successfully sent a message, everyone who meets these criteria sees a message like the one in Figure A.15:

- The message was directed to them
- They are logged on at the time of transmittal
- They have the messenger service running on their machines

Which is better, e-mail or messaging? Each has its time and place. E-mail works better for messages that have files attached, since it's not limited to text transmittal, but it does have the disadvantage of being ignorable. Even if you've arranged to be notified when mail is waiting, you can ignore the notification or not hear it at all if you've stepped away from your machine.

FIGURE A.15:

A sample Messenger Service pop-up window

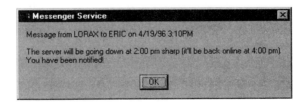

Therefore, if you have a question for someone and you need an answer *right now*, the messenger service is probably the way to go. When you send a message to someone at an NT workstation, the dialog box shown in Figure A.15 appears on their screen and does not disappear until they click the OK button.

How Do I Send Messages?

To send messages from the command prompt, use the NET SEND command. Using the parameters described above, you can send messages to individuals or groups, and within a domain or across domains. Again, NT machines need to be running the messenger service to see NET SEND messages; Windows, Windows for Workgroups, and Windows 95 machines must be running WinPopup.

Getting Synched: Viewing and Setting the Time

Some services, such as directory replication, depend on the server's and the workstations' clocks being set to the same time. To automate this process, you can use the NET TIME command.

NET TIME: Coordinating Server and Workstation Clocks

The NET TIME command works differently when you execute it from a server or a workstation. If you run it from a server, it displays the current time; if you run it from a workstation, you can synchronize your computer's clock with that of the time server, even selecting a server from another domain if there is a trust relationship between your domain and the other one. Ordinary users cannot set the server time from a workstation; only members of the Administrators or Server Manager groups, logged on to the server (logically if not physically) can set the system time.

To coordinate the clocks from a workstation:

1. Check the time on a time server (here named EISA SERVER) by typing

    ```
    net time \\eisa server
    ```

    If you type only **net time**, by default you get the current time on the server that serves as your time server. (If no time server is on your domain, you get a message that says the system could not locate a time server.)

    To check the time on a time server in another domain (called TED, for instance), type

    ```
    net time /domain:ted
    ```

2. Set the time from the time server. In our example, you would type

    ```
    net time \\eisa server /set
    ```

    If no time server is set up for your domain but you want to synchronize a workstation's clock with that of the domain controller for the domain named TED, for example, you would type

    ```
    net time /domain:ted /set
    ```

    Set the time from a time server in another domain (here called OTHERS) by typing

    ```
    net time /domain:others /set
    ```

From a server, you use the same commands to check the time on another server or set the time to correspond with that on another domain, but if you type **net time** without switches, the screen shows the time on the time server for that domain, if one exists.

How Do I Synchronize a Workstation's Time with the Server's?

To coordinate a workstation's time with the server's, type

```
net time \\servername /set
```

where *servername* is the name of the server with which you want to coordinate.

Why Use the Command Prompt?

I hope that most of the time you won't have to use the command prompt. Although you should now have a pretty good idea of how to do just about anything from the command prompt that you can do in a normal session, typing a command correctly is a bit more awkward than pointing and clicking. The only real advantage I can see to using the command prompt over the graphical interface is that you don't have to remember where anything is: if you can remember the command name, you can do everything from the same place.

In general, the people who need to use the command prompt to connect are the network's OS/2 and DOS clients. If you're administering the server, you probably don't have much occasion to use the command prompt, except when making adjustments to DOS and OS/2 workstations.

INDEX

Note to the Reader: Page numbers in **bold** indicate the principal discussion of a topic or the definition of a term. Page numbers in *italic* indicate illustrations.

B

D

E

F

G

H

L

M

N

S

T

U

V

W

X

Y

Z

SYBEX BOOKS ON THE WEB

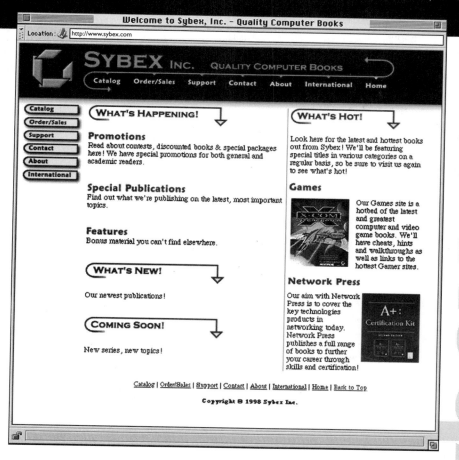

At the dynamic and informative Sybex Web site, you can:

- view our complete online catalog
- preview a book you're interested in
- access special book content

- order books online at special discount prices
- learn about Sybex

www.sybex.com

SYBEX Inc. • 1151 Marina Village Parkway, Alameda, CA 94501 • 510-523-8233

SYBEX

low Do I?

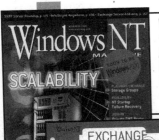